Shon Harris and the "All-in-One CISSP" book have been the secret to my success. While at RSA I engaged Shon in getting 90 percent of the worldwide sales engineers CISSP certified, all with the assistance of this book. I took this same program with me to Symantec, and Shon worked with me to ensure we had the same type of results with both security engineers and security executives at Symantec. Her straightforward approach contained in this book gave each individual the specific information they needed to take the CISSP exam. As a plus, each of them gained a great deal of knowledge and solid base that is required by today's security professionals. I count myself as fortunate to have been introduced to Shon and the "All-in-One CISSP" early in my security career!

Rick Hanson, CISSP
Symantec Security Business Practice

I have no hesitation in recommending Shon Harris' "All-in-One Exam Guide"—the consummate guide to (a) passing the prestigious CISSP examination specifically and (b) more generally—a great insight into the wider world of information security.

Mike Rabbitt, CISSP, CISA
Information Security Officer

A *must-have* for anyone serious about becoming a CISSP.

Clément Dupuis, CD
Owner and Founder of The CCCure Family of Portals
www.cccure.org

This is the best book to prepare for CISSP exam. Period.

Sabyasachi Hazra
CISSP, CISA, CISM, PMP, CCSE, ISO 2700 1LA,
CEH, CCSP, CCSA, CCSE, CCSE+, MCSA, CCNP
Deloitte & Touche

I studied for the CISSP exam with the "All-in-One" and it was a real pleasure (and I mean the word "pleasure").

The explanations are very clear and straightforward.
The touch of humor is exactly what the student needs not to give up.
The tables and schemas are great.
This is exactly what the student needs to succeed.
Thank you for your great work; I feel I owe you for passing the exam. :)

David Broda

Shon Harris is amazing at explaining the most complicated technologies in very simplified terms. This is a great book for studying for the CISSP exam, but also the only reference manual needed for any technical library.

Casey Batz
Network Security Engineer, VMware

Shon's "CISSP All-in-One Guide" has been the go-to study guide for the more than 200 new CISSP holders developed in our region over the last two years. It continues to be a great asset for both the novice and experienced security practitioner.

Alex Humber
Symantec Corporation

This is the absolute gold standard, the one-stop shopping reference for CISSP certification! The price is economical enough to highlight its passages and put notes in its margins. Every IT professional I met who passed the CISSP test the *first* time credits the Shon Harris CISSP manual.

C.W. Thompson

Shon is brilliant when it comes to network security, and even better at conveying network security concepts to others. Her book, *CISSP All-in-One Exam Guide,* single-handedly helped me to achieve the CISSP certification....

Tony Bradley
Freelance Writer, S3KUR3, Inc.

Shon's fluid writing style is enjoyable to read, and communicates effectively, much better than what I've seen from any other CISSP book.

A. Bell

I cannot say enough good things about this book. I used this and Exam Cram as my sole sources to prepare for this exam and I passed on my first try.

D.A. Smith

I used the Shon Harris guide as my main resource to study for the CISSP exam and passed the first time, but I also re-read it several times, took all of the practice exams from the CD and other sources, and skimmed through other authors' texts. Overall, I believe it's the one text that helps you understand the basics and concepts better than the others, especially the cram books, but you still have to put in the time to study and prepare. It's a six-hour exam for a reason—good luck!

D. Wolf

I had some core competencies in a couple of the domains, some knowledge of a few others, and virtually no knowledge of at least two others. That's where I started, but Shon Harris' style is so readable and compelling that I ended up reading the entire volume and learning more, even in those areas where I thought I had it knocked. The result was finishing the six-hour CISSP exam in three and a half hours, taking another hour to review, and finally learning that I passed. I also have the $(ISC)^2$ book, and while it contains much of the same information, Harris' book makes it more accessible and makes reading what might be otherwise dry, mundane topics interesting and even (at times) fun... Highly recommended.

Typeaux

ALL ■ IN ■ ONE

CISSP®

EXAM GUIDE

Seventh Edition

Shon Harris
Fernando Maymí

New York Chicago San Francisco
Athens London Madrid Mexico City
Milan New Delhi Singapore Sydney Toronto

Library of Congress Cataloging-in-Publication Data

Names: Harris, Shon, author. | Maymi, Fernando, author.
Title: CISSP exam guide / Shon Harris, Fernando Maymi.
Other titles: CISSP all-in-one exam guide
Description: Seventh edition. | New York : McGraw-Hill Education, 2016. | Includes index.
Identifiers: LCCN 2016017045 (print) | LCCN 2016017235 (ebook) | ISBN 9780071849272 (set : alk. paper) | ISBN 9780071849616 (book : alk. paper) | ISBN 9780071849258 (CD) | ISBN 0071849270 (set : alk. paper) | ISBN 0071849610 (book : alk. paper) | ISBN 0071849254 (CD) | ISBN 9780071849265 ()
Subjects: LCSH: Computer networks—Examinations—Study guides. | Telecommunications engineers—Certification.
Classification: LCC TK5105.5 .H368 2016 (print) | LCC TK5105.5 (ebook) | DDC 005.8—dc23
LC record available at https://lccn.loc.gov/2016017045

McGraw-Hill Education books are available at special quantity discounts to use as premiums and sales promotions, or for use in corporate training programs. To contact a representative, please visit the Contact Us pages at www.mhprofessional.com.

CISSP® All-in-One Exam Guide, Seventh Edition

1 2 3 4 5 6 7 8 9 DOC 21 20 19 18 17 16

ISBN: Book p/n 978-0-07-184961-6 and CD p/n 978-0-07-184925-8
of set 978-0-07-184927-2

MHID: Book p/n 0-07-184961-0 and CD p/n 0-07-184925-4
of set 0-07-184927-0

Sponsoring Editor
Wendy Rinaldi

Editorial Supervisor
Janet Walden

Project Manager
Yashmita Hota,
Cenveo® Publisher Services

Acquisitions Coordinator
Amy Stonebraker

Technical Editor
Jonathan Ham

Copy Editor
William McManus

Proofreader
Lisa McCoy

Indexer
Karin Arrigoni

Production Supervisor
James Kussow

Composition
Cenveo Publisher Services

Illustration
Cenveo Publisher Services

Art Director, Cover
Jeff Weeks

We dedicate this book to all those who have served selflessly.

ABOUT THE AUTHORS

Shon Harris, CISSP, was the founder and CEO of Shon Harris Security LLC and Logical Security LLC, a security consultant, a former engineer in the Air Force's Information Warfare unit, an instructor, and an author. Shon owned and ran her own training and consulting companies for 13 years prior to her death in 2014. She consulted with Fortune 100 corporations and government agencies on extensive security issues. She authored three best-selling CISSP books, was a contributing author to *Gray Hat Hacking: The Ethical Hacker's Handbook* and *Security Information and Event Management (SIEM) Implementation*, and a technical editor for *Information Security Magazine.*

Fernando Maymí, Ph.D., CISSP, is a security practitioner with over 25 years' experience in the field. He currently leads a multidisciplinary team charged with developing disruptive innovations for cyberspace operations as well as impactful public-private partnerships aimed at better securing cyberspace. Fernando has served as a consultant for both government and private-sector organizations in the United States and abroad. He has authored and taught dozens of courses and workshops in cyber security for academic, government, and professional audiences in the United States and Latin America. Fernando is the author of over a dozen publications and holds three patents. His awards include the U.S. Department of the Army Research and Development Achievement Award and he was recognized as a HENAAC Luminary. He worked closely with Shon Harris, advising her on a multitude of projects, including the sixth edition of the *CISSP All-in-One Exam Guide*. Fernando is also a volunteer puppy raiser for Guiding Eyes for the Blind and has raised two guide dogs, Trinket and Virgo.

About the Contributor

Bobby E. Rogers is an information security engineer working as a contractor for Department of Defense agencies, helping to secure, certify, and accredit their information systems. His duties include information system security engineering, risk management, and certification and accreditation efforts. He retired after 21 years in the U.S. Air Force, serving as a network security engineer and instructor, and has secured networks all over the world. Bobby has a master's degree in information assurance (IA) and is pursuing a doctoral degree in cybersecurity from Capitol Technology University in Maryland. His many certifications include CISSP-ISSEP, CEH, and MCSE: Security, as well as the CompTIA A+, Network+, Security+, and Mobility+ certifications.

About the Technical Editor

Jonathan Ham, CISSP, GSEC, GCIA, GCIH, is an independent consultant who specializes in large-scale enterprise security issues, from policy and procedure, through staffing and training, to scalable prevention, detection, and response technology and techniques. With a keen understanding of ROI and TCO, he has helped his clients achieve greater success for more than 12 years, advising in both the public and private sectors, from small upstarts to the Fortune 500. Jonathan has been commissioned to teach NCIS investigators how to use Snort, has performed packet analysis from a facility more than 2,000 feet underground, and has chartered and trained the CIRT for one of the largest U.S. civilian federal agencies. He is a member of the GIAC Advisory Board and is a SANS instructor teaching their MGT414: SANS Training Program for CISSP Certification course. He is also co-author *of Network Forensics: Tracking Hackers Through Cyberspace*, a textbook published by Prentice-Hall.

CONTENTS AT A GLANCE

Chapter 1	Security and Risk Management	1
Chapter 2	Asset Security	189
Chapter 3	Security Engineering	247
Chapter 4	Communication and Network Security	477
Chapter 5	Identity and Access Management	721
Chapter 6	Security Assessment and Testing	859
Chapter 7	Security Operations	923
Chapter 8	Software Development Security	1077
Appendix A	Comprehensive Questions	1213
Appendix B	About the CD-ROM	1269
	Glossary	1273
	Index	1291

CONTENTS

In Memory of Shon Harris xxi
Foreword xxiii
Acknowledgments xxv
From the Author xxvii
Why Become a CISSP? xxix

Chapter 1 Security and Risk Management 1

Fundamental Principles of Security 3
- Availability 3
- Integrity 4
- Confidentiality 5
- Balanced Security 5

Security Definitions 6
Control Types 8
Security Frameworks 13
- ISO/IEC 27000 Series 16
- Enterprise Architecture Development 19
- Security Controls Development 33
- Process Management Development 37
- Functionality vs. Security 45

The Crux of Computer Crime Laws 45
Complexities in Cybercrime 48
- Electronic Assets 49
- The Evolution of Attacks 50
- International Issues 54
- Types of Legal Systems 58

Intellectual Property Laws 62
- Trade Secret 63
- Copyright 64
- Trademark 65
- Patent 65
- Internal Protection of Intellectual Property 67
- Software Piracy 68

Privacy 70
- The Increasing Need for Privacy Laws 72
- Laws, Directives, and Regulations 73
- Employee Privacy Issues 81

Data Breaches ... 84
U.S. Laws Pertaining to Data Breaches ... 84
Other Nations' Laws Pertaining to Data Breaches ... 85
Policies, Standards, Baselines, Guidelines, and Procedures ... 86
Security Policy ... 87
Standards ... 90
Baselines ... 91
Guidelines ... 92
Procedures ... 93
Implementation ... 93
Risk Management ... 94
Holistic Risk Management ... 95
Information Systems Risk Management Policy ... 95
The Risk Management Team ... 96
The Risk Management Process ... 97
Threat Modeling ... 98
Vulnerabilities ... 98
Threats ... 100
Attacks ... 100
Reduction Analysis ... 101
Risk Assessment and Analysis ... 102
Risk Analysis Team ... 103
The Value of Information and Assets ... 104
Costs That Make Up the Value ... 105
Identifying Vulnerabilities and Threats ... 106
Methodologies for Risk Assessment ... 107
Risk Analysis Approaches ... 112
Qualitative Risk Analysis ... 116
Protection Mechanisms ... 119
Putting It Together ... 123
Total Risk vs. Residual Risk ... 123
Handling Risk ... 124
Outsourcing ... 126
Risk Management Frameworks ... 126
Categorize Information System ... 128
Select Security Controls ... 128
Implement Security Controls ... 129
Assess Security Controls ... 129
Authorize Information System ... 130
Monitor Security Controls ... 130
Business Continuity and Disaster Recovery ... 130
Standards and Best Practices ... 133
Making BCM Part of the Enterprise Security Program ... 136
BCP Project Components ... 139

Personnel Security 154
Hiring Practices 155
Termination 157
Security-Awareness Training 157
Degree or Certification? 159
Security Governance 159
Metrics 160
Ethics 165
The Computer Ethics Institute 166
The Internet Architecture Board 166
Corporate Ethics Programs 168
Summary 168
Quick Tips 170
Questions 175
Answers 184

Chapter 2 Asset Security 189

Information Life Cycle 190
Acquisition 190
Use 191
Archival 191
Disposal 192
Information Classification 193
Classifications Levels 194
Classification Controls 197
Layers of Responsibility 199
Executive Management 199
Data Owner 203
Data Custodian 204
System Owner 204
Security Administrator 205
Supervisor 205
Change Control Analyst 205
Data Analyst 205
User 206
Auditor 206
Why So Many Roles? 206
Retention Policies 206
Developing a Retention Policy 207
Protecting Privacy 210
Data Owners 210
Data Processers 211
Data Remanence 211
Limits on Collection 214

Protecting Assets 215
  Data Security Controls 216
  Media Controls 219
Data Leakage 225
  Data Leak Prevention 226
Protecting Other Assets 234
  Protecting Mobile Devices 234
  Paper Records 235
  Safes 236
Summary 236
Quick Tips 237
  Questions 239
  Answers 243

Chapter 3 Security Engineering 247

System Architecture 248
Computer Architecture 252
  The Central Processing Unit 252
  Multiprocessing 257
  Memory Types 258
Operating Systems 271
  Process Management 271
  Memory Management 280
  Input/Output Device Management 285
  CPU Architecture Integration 287
  Operating System Architectures 291
  Virtual Machines 298
System Security Architecture 301
  Security Policy 301
  Security Architecture Requirements 302
Security Models 307
  Bell-LaPadula Model 307
  Biba Model 308
  Clark-Wilson Model 309
  Noninterference Model 310
  Brewer and Nash Model 311
  Graham-Denning Model 311
  Harrison-Ruzzo-Ullman Model 312
Systems Evaluation 313
  Common Criteria 313
  Why Put a Product Through Evaluation? 317
Certification vs. Accreditation 318
  Certification 318
  Accreditation 319

Open vs. Closed Systems 320
Open Systems 320
Closed Systems 320
Distributed System Security 321
Cloud Computing 322
Parallel Computing 323
Databases 324
Web Applications 326
Mobile Devices 327
Cyber-Physical Systems 328
A Few Threats to Review 332
Maintenance Hooks 333
Time-of-Check/Time-of-Use Attacks 333
Cryptography in Context 335
The History of Cryptography 335
Cryptography Definitions and Concepts 340
Kerckhoffs' Principle 342
The Strength of the Cryptosystem 343
Services of Cryptosystems 344
One-Time Pad 345
Running and Concealment Ciphers 347
Steganography 348
Types of Ciphers 350
Substitution Ciphers 351
Transposition Ciphers 351
Methods of Encryption 353
Symmetric vs. Asymmetric Algorithms 353
Symmetric Cryptography 354
Block and Stream Ciphers 359
Hybrid Encryption Methods 364
Types of Symmetric Systems 369
Data Encryption Standard 370
Triple-DES 377
Advanced Encryption Standard 378
International Data Encryption Algorithm 378
Blowfish 379
RC4 379
RC5 379
RC6 379
Types of Asymmetric Systems 380
Diffie-Hellman Algorithm 380
RSA 383
El Gamal 386
Elliptic Curve Cryptosystems 386
Knapsack 387
Zero Knowledge Proof 387

Message Integrity 388
The One-Way Hash 388
Various Hashing Algorithms 393
MD4 394
MD5 394
SHA 395
Attacks Against One-Way Hash Functions 395
Digital Signatures 396
Digital Signature Standard 398
Public Key Infrastructure 399
Certificate Authorities 399
Certificates 402
The Registration Authority 402
PKI Steps 403
Key Management 404
Key Management Principles 406
Rules for Keys and Key Management 407
Trusted Platform Module 407
TPM Uses 408
Attacks on Cryptography 409
Ciphertext-Only Attacks 410
Known-Plaintext Attacks 410
Chosen-Plaintext Attacks 410
Chosen-Ciphertext Attacks 410
Differential Cryptanalysis 411
Linear Cryptanalysis 412
Side-Channel Attacks 412
Replay Attacks 413
Algebraic Attacks 413
Analytic Attacks 413
Statistical Attacks 413
Social Engineering Attacks 413
Meet-in-the-Middle Attacks 414
Site and Facility Security 414
The Site Planning Process 415
Crime Prevention Through Environmental Design 420
Designing a Physical Security Program 426
Protecting Assets 439
Protecting Mobile Devices 439
Using Safes 440
Internal Support Systems 440
Electric Power 441
Environmental Issues 446
Fire Prevention, Detection, and Suppression 448

Summary 455
Quick Tips 455
Questions 461
Answers 471

Chapter 4 Communication and Network Security 477

Telecommunications 479
Open Systems Interconnection Reference Model 479
Protocol 480
Application Layer 483
Presentation Layer 484
Session Layer 485
Transport Layer 487
Network Layer 489
Data Link Layer 490
Physical Layer 491
Functions and Protocols in the OSI Model 492
Tying the Layers Together 494
Multilayer Protocols 495
TCP/IP Model 497
TCP 498
IP Addressing 503
IPv6 506
Layer 2 Security Standards 509
Converged Protocols 511
Types of Transmission 512
Analog and Digital 512
Asynchronous and Synchronous 514
Broadband and Baseband 516
Cabling 517
Coaxial Cable 517
Twisted-Pair Cable 518
Fiber-Optic Cable 519
Cabling Problems 520
Networking Foundations 522
Network Topology 523
Media Access Technologies 526
Transmission Methods 536
Network Protocols and Services 538
Domain Name Service 547
E-mail Services 555
Network Address Translation 560
Routing Protocols 562
Networking Devices 567
Repeaters 567
Bridges 567

Routers 570
Switches 571
Gateways 576
PBXs 577
Firewalls 581
Proxy Servers 605
Honeypot 607
Unified Threat Management 607
Content Distribution Networks 608
Software Defined Networking 609
Intranets and Extranets 612
Metropolitan Area Networks 614
Metro Ethernet 615
Wide Area Networks 617
Telecommunications Evolution 617
Dedicated Links 620
WAN Technologies 624
Remote Connectivity 644
Dial-up Connections 644
ISDN 645
DSL 647
Cable Modems 648
VPN 649
Authentication Protocols 657
Wireless Networks 659
Wireless Communications Techniques 660
WLAN Components 664
Evolution of WLAN Security 665
Wireless Standards 672
Best Practices for Securing WLANs 677
Satellites 678
Mobile Wireless Communication 678
Network Encryption 685
Link Encryption vs. End-to-End Encryption 685
E-mail Encryption Standards 687
Internet Security 690
Network Attacks 696
Denial of Service 696
Sniffing 698
DNS Hijacking 699
Drive-by Download 700
Summary 700
Quick Tips 701
Questions 706
Answers 715

Chapter 5 Identity and Access Management 721
Security Principles 723
Availability 723
Integrity 723
Confidentiality 724
Identification, Authentication, Authorization, and Accountability ... 724
Identification and Authentication 727
Authentication 739
Authorization 762
Federation 776
Identity as a Service 785
Integrating Identity Services 786
Access Control Models 787
Discretionary Access Control 787
Mandatory Access Control 789
Role-Based Access Control 791
Rule-Based Access Control 794
Access Control Techniques and Technologies 796
Constrained User Interfaces 796
Access Control Matrix 797
Content-Dependent Access Control 798
Context-Dependent Access Control 799
Access Control Administration 799
Centralized Access Control Administration 800
Decentralized Access Control Administration 807
Access Control Methods 807
Access Control Layers 808
Administrative Controls 809
Physical Controls 810
Technical Controls 811
Accountability 814
Review of Audit Information 816
Protecting Audit Data and Log Information 818
Keystroke Monitoring 818
Access Control Practices 819
Unauthorized Disclosure of Information 819
Access Control Monitoring 822
Intrusion Detection Systems 822
Intrusion Prevention Systems 830
Threats to Access Control 834
Dictionary Attack 835
Brute-Force Attacks 835
Spoofing at Logon 836
Phishing and Pharming 836

Summary 840
Quick Tips 840
Questions 845
Answers 854

Chapter 6 Security Assessment and Testing 859

Audit Strategies 860
Internal Audits 862
Third-Party Audits 863
Auditing Technical Controls 865
Vulnerability Testing 866
Penetration Testing 869
War Dialing 874
Other Vulnerability Types 875
Postmortem 876
Log Reviews 878
Synthetic Transactions 881
Misuse Case Testing 882
Code Reviews 884
Interface Testing 886
Auditing Administrative Controls 886
Account Management 886
Backup Verification 889
Disaster Recovery and Business Continuity 892
Security Training and Security Awareness Training 899
Key Performance and Risk Indicators 903
Reporting 905
Technical Reporting 906
Executive Summaries 907
Management Review 908
Before the Management Review 909
Reviewing Inputs 909
Management Actions 911
Summary 911
Quick Tips 911
Questions 914
Answers 919

Chapter 7 Security Operations 923

The Role of the Operations Department 924
Administrative Management 925
Security and Network Personnel 928
Accountability 929
Clipping Levels 930

Assurance Levels 930
Operational Responsibilities 931
    Unusual or Unexplained Occurrences 931
    Deviations from Standards 932
    Unscheduled Initial Program Loads (aka Rebooting) 932
Configuration Management 933
    Trusted Recovery 933
    Input and Output Controls 936
    System Hardening 937
    Remote Access Security 939
Physical Security 940
    Facility Access Control 941
    Personnel Access Controls 949
    External Boundary Protection Mechanisms 950
    Intrusion Detection Systems 960
    Patrol Force and Guards 962
    Dogs 963
    Auditing Physical Access 963
Secure Resource Provisioning 964
    Asset Inventory 964
    Configuration Management 966
    Provisioning Cloud Assets 969
Network and Resource Availability 970
    Mean Time Between Failures 971
    Mean Time to Repair 972
    Single Points of Failure 973
    Backups 981
    Contingency Planning 983
Preventative Measures 984
    Firewalls 985
    Intrusion Detection and Prevention Systems 986
    Antimalware 988
    Patch Management 988
    Honeypots 991
The Incident Management Process 993
    Detection 998
    Response 998
    Mitigation 999
    Reporting 1000
    Recovery 1001
    Remediation 1001
Disaster Recovery 1002
    Business Process Recovery 1006
    Facility Recovery 1006

Supply and Technology Recovery 1013
Choosing a Software Backup Facility 1018
End-User Environment 1021
Data Backup Alternatives 1021
Electronic Backup Solutions 1025
High Availability 1028
Insurance 1030
Recovery and Restoration 1031
Developing Goals for the Plans 1034
Implementing Strategies 1036
Investigations 1038
Computer Forensics and Proper Collection of Evidence 1039
Motive, Opportunity, and Means 1041
Computer Criminal Behavior 1042
Incident Investigators 1042
The Forensic Investigation Process 1043
What Is Admissible in Court? 1049
Surveillance, Search, and Seizure 1051
Interviewing Suspects 1052
Liability and Its Ramifications 1053
Liability Scenarios 1056
Third-Party Risk 1058
Contractual Agreements 1058
Procurement and Vendor Processes 1059
Compliance 1060
Personal Safety Concerns 1063
Summary 1064
Quick Tips 1064
Questions 1067
Answers 1072

Chapter 8 Software Development Security 1077

Building Good Code 1077
Where Do We Place Security? 1078
Different Environments Demand Different Security 1080
Environment vs. Application 1081
Functionality vs. Security 1082
Implementation and Default Issues 1082
Software Development Life Cycle 1084
Project Management 1084
Requirements Gathering Phase 1085
Design Phase 1086
Development Phase 1089
Testing/Validation Phase 1093
Release/Maintenance Phase 1095

Secure Software Development Best Practices 1097
Software Development Models 1098
    Build and Fix Model 1099
    Waterfall Model 1099
    V-Shaped Model (V-Model) 1100
    Prototyping 1101
    Incremental Model 1101
    Spiral Model 1102
    Rapid Application Development 1104
    Agile Models 1105
Integrated Product Team 1109
    DevOps 1109
Capability Maturity Model Integration 1111
Change Control 1113
    Software Configuration Management 1114
    Security of Code Repositories 1116
Programming Languages and Concepts 1116
    Assemblers, Compilers, Interpreters 1119
    Object-Oriented Concepts 1121
    Other Software Development Concepts 1129
    Application Programming Interfaces 1131
Distributed Computing 1132
    Distributed Computing Environment 1132
    CORBA and ORBs 1134
    COM and DCOM 1136
    Java Platform, Enterprise Edition 1138
    Service-Oriented Architecture 1138
Mobile Code 1142
    Java Applets 1142
    ActiveX Controls 1144
Web Security 1146
    Specific Threats for Web Environments 1146
    Web Application Security Principles 1154
Database Management 1155
    Database Management Software 1155
    Database Models 1157
    Database Programming Interfaces 1161
    Relational Database Components 1164
    Integrity 1166
    Database Security Issues 1169
    Data Warehousing and Data Mining 1174
Malicious Software (Malware) 1178
    Viruses 1179
    Worms 1182

Rootkit 1182
Spyware and Adware 1184
Botnets 1184
Logic Bombs 1186
Trojan Horses 1186
Antimalware Software 1187
Spam Detection 1190
Antimalware Programs 1192
Assessing the Security of Acquired Software 1193
Summary 1194
Quick Tips 1194
Questions 1199
Answers 1207

Appendix A Comprehensive Questions 1213
Answers 1249

Appendix B About the CD-ROM 1269
System Requirements 1269
Total Tester Premium Practice Exam Software 1269
Installing and Running Total Tester Premium Practice Exam Software 1270
Hotspot and Drag-and-Drop Questions 1270
PDF Copy of the Book 1270
Technical Support 1271
Total Seminars Technical Support 1271
McGraw-Hill Education Content Support 1271

Glossary 1273

Index 1291

IN MEMORY OF SHON HARRIS

In the summer of 2014, Shon asked me to write a foreword for the new edition of her *CISSP All-in-One Exam Guide*. I was honored to do that, and the following two paragraphs are that original foreword. Following that, I will say more about my friend, the late Shon Harris.

The cyber security field is still relatively new and has been evolving as technology advances. Every decade or so, we have an advance or two that seems to change the game. For example, in the 1990s we were focused primarily on "perimeter defense." Lots of money was spent on perimeter devices like firewalls to keep the bad guys out. Around 2000, recognizing that perimeter defense alone was insufficient, the "defense in depth" approach became popular, and we spent another decade trying to build layers of defense and detect the bad guys who were able to get past our perimeter defenses. Again, lots of money was spent, this time on intrusion detection, intrusion prevention, and end-point solutions. Then, around 2010, following the lead of the U.S. government in particular, we began to focus on "continuous monitoring," the goal being to catch the bad guys inside the network if they get past the perimeter defense and the defense in depth. Security information and event management (SIEM) technology has emerged as the best way to handle this continuous monitoring requirement. The latest buzz phrase is "active defense," which refers to the ability to respond in real time through a dynamic and changing defense that works to contain the attacker and allow the organization to recover quickly and get back to business. We are starting to see the re-emergence of honeypots combined with sandbox technology to bait and trap attackers for further analysis of their activity. One thing is common throughout this brief historical survey: the bad guys keep getting in and we keep responding to try and keep up, if not prevent them in the first place. This cat-and-mouse game will continue for the foreseeable future.

As the cyber security field continuously evolves to meet the latest emerging threats, each new strategy and tactic brings with it a new set of terminology and concepts for the security professional to master. The sheer bulk of the body of knowledge can be overwhelming, particularly to newcomers. As a security practitioner, consultant, and business leader, I am often asked by aspiring security practitioners where to start when trying to get into the field. I often refer them to Shon's *CISSP All-in-One Exam Guide*, not necessarily for the purpose of becoming a CISSP, but so that they may have in one resource the body of knowledge in the field. I am also often asked by experienced security practitioners how to advance in the field. I encourage them to pursue CISSP certification and, once again, I refer them to Shon's book. Some are destined to become leaders in the field, and the CISSP is a solid certificate for managers. Other security professionals I encounter are just looking for more breadth of knowledge, and I recommend Shon's book to them too as a good one-stop reference for that. This book has stood the test of time. It has evolved as the field has evolved and stands as the single most important book in the cyber security field, period. I have personally referred to it several times throughout my career and keep a copy near me at all times on my Kindle. Simply put, if you are in the cyber security field, you need a copy of this book.

On a personal note, little did I know that within months of writing the preceding foreword, Shon would no longer be with us. I counted Shon as a good friend and still admire her for her contribution to the field. I met Shon at a CISSP boot camp in 2002. I had just learned of the CISSP and within weeks found myself in her class. I had no clue that she had already written several books by that time and was a true leader in the field. I must have chattered away during our lunch sessions, because a few months after the class, she reached out to me and said, "Hey, I remember you were interested in writing. I have a new project that I need help on. Would you like to help?" After an awkward pause, as I picked myself up from the floor, I told her that I felt underqualified, but yes! That started a journey that has blessed me many times over. The book was called *Gray Hat Hacking* and is now in the fourth edition. From the book came many consulting, writing, and teaching opportunities, such as Black Hat. Then, as I retired from the Marine Corps, in 2008, there was Shon, right on cue: "Hey, I have an opportunity to provide services to a large company. Would you like to help?" Just like that, I had my first large client, launching my company, which I was able to grow, with Shon's help, and then sell a couple of years ago. During the 12 years I knew her, Shon continued to give me opportunities to become much more than I could have dreamed. She never asked for a thing in return, simply saying, "You take it and run with it, I am too busy doing other things." As I think back over my career after the Marine Corps, I owe most of my success to Shon. I have shared this story with others and found that I am not the only one; Shon blessed so many people with her giving spirit. I am convinced there are many "Shon" stories like this one out there. She touched so many people in the security field and more than lived up to the nickname I had for her, Miss CISSP.

Without a doubt, Shon was the most kindhearted, generous, and humble person in the field. If you knew Shon, I know you would echo that sentiment. If you did not know Shon, I hope that through these few words, you understand why she was so special and why there had to be another edition of this book. I have been asked several times over the last year, "Do you think there will be another edition? The security field and CISSP certification have both changed so much, we need another edition." For this reason, I am excited this new edition came to be. Shon would have wanted the book to go on helping people to be the best they can be. I believe we, as a profession, need this book to continue. So, I am thankful that the team from McGraw-Hill and Fernando are honoring Shon in this way and continuing her legacy. She truly deserves it. Shon, you are missed and loved by so many. Through this book, your generous spirit lives on, helping others.

Allen Harper, CISSP (thanks to Shon)
EVP and Chief Hacker, Tangible Security, Inc.

FOREWORD

I'm excited and honored to introduce the seventh edition of *CISSP All-in-One Exam Guide* to cyber security experts worldwide. This study guide is essential for those pursuing CISSP certification and should be part of every cyber security professional's library.

After 39 years of service in the Profession of Arms, I know well what it means to be a member of a profession and the importance of shared values, common language, and identity. At the same time, expert knowledge gained through training, education, and experience are critical ingredients to a profession, but formal certifications based on clearly articulated standards are the coin of the realm for cyber security professionals.

In every operational assignment, I sought ways to leverage technology and increase digitization, while assuming our freedom to operate was not at risk. Today's threats coupled with our vulnerabilities and the potential consequences create a new operational reality—national security is at risk. When we enter any network, we must fight to ensure we maintain our security, and cyber security experts are the professionals we will call on to out-think and out-maneuver the threats we face from cyberspace.

As our world becomes more interconnected, we can expect cyber threats to continue to grow exponentially. While our cyber workforce enabled by technology must focus on preventing threats and reducing vulnerabilities, we will not eliminate either. This demands professionals who understand risk management and security—experts who are trusted and committed to creating and providing a wide range of security measures tailored to mitigate enterprise risk and assure all missions, public and private.

Current, relevant domain expertise is the key, and the *CISSP All-in-One Exam Guide* is the king of the hill. In this edition, Shon's quality content is present and is being stewarded forward by Fernando Maymí. You're in good hands, and you will grow personally and professionally, from your study. As competent, trusted professionals of character, this book is essential to you, your organization, and our national security.

Rhett Hernandez
Lieutenant General, U.S. Army Retired
Former Commander, U.S. Army Cyber Command
Current West Point Cyber Chair, Army Cyber Institute

ACKNOWLEDGMENTS

We would like to thank all the people who work in the information security industry who are driven by their passion, dedication, and a true sense of doing right. The best security people are the ones who are driven toward an ethical outcome.

In this seventh edition, we would also like to thank the following:

- Ronald Dodge, who brought the two authors of this book together and, in doing so, set off a sequence of events that he couldn't have possibly anticipated.
- David Miller, whose work ethic, loyalty, and friendship have continuously inspired us.
- All the teammates from Logical Security.
- The men and women of our armed forces, who selflessly defend our way of life.
- Kathy Conlon, who, more than anyone else, set the conditions that led to seven editions of this book.
- David Harris.
- Emma Fernandez.

Most especially, we thank you, our readers, for standing on the frontlines of our digital conflicts and for devoting your professional lives to keeping all of us safe in cyberspace.

FROM THE AUTHOR

For the first time in seven editions, the *CISSP All-in-One Exam Guide* bears the names of two authors. For the first time in 15 years, Shon Harris will not be with us as we go to print on a new edition of her seminal work. Still, she remains with us in the pages of the hundreds of thousands of books sold, which have enriched the lives of security professionals worldwide. It is no exaggeration to say that Shon was one of the most influential authors in our field. Her legacy lives on in the pages of this latest edition.

Our goal in this seventh edition of Shon's book was both to address the newly revised CISSP body of knowledge and to allow you to hear Shon's voice as you read the words on its pages. You see, much of the content in this book was actually authored by Shon. We have reorganized, enhanced, augmented, and updated it, but the content is still largely hers. If you have read any of her multitude of other works or had the blessing of having met her, you will recognize her distinctive tone in these pages. We also hope that you will perceive her penchant for excellence in every aspect of professional development.

The goal of this book is not just to get you to pass the CISSP exam, but to provide you the bedrock of knowledge that will allow you to flourish as an information systems security professional before and after you pass the certification exam. If you strive for excellence in your own development, the CISSP certification will follow as a natural byproduct. This approach will demand that you devote time and energy to topics and issues that may seem to have no direct or immediate return on investment. That is OK. We each have our own areas of strength and weakness, and many of us tend to reinforce the former while ignoring the latter. This leads to individuals who have tremendous depth in a very specific topic, but who lack the breadth to understand context or thrive in new and unexpected conditions. What we propose is an inversion of this natural tendency, so that we devote appropriate amounts of effort to those areas in which we are weakest. What we propose is that we balance the urge to be specialists with the need to be well-rounded professionals. This is what our organizations and societies need from us.

The very definition of a profession describes a group of trusted, well-trained individuals that performs a critical service that societies cannot do for themselves. In the case of the CISSP, this professional ensures the confidentiality, integrity, and availability of our information systems. This cannot be done simply by being the best firewall administrator, or the best forensic examiner, or the best reverse engineer. Instead, our service requires a breadth of knowledge that will allow us to choose the right tool for the job. This relevant knowledge, in turn, requires a foundation of (apparently less relevant) knowledge upon which we can build our expertise. This is why, in order to be competent professionals, we all need to devote ourselves to learning topics that may not be immediately useful.

This book provides an encyclopedic treatment of both directly applicable and foundational knowledge. It is designed, as it always was, to be both a study guide and an enduring reference. Our hope is that, long after you obtain your CISSP certification, you will turn to this tome time and again to brush up on your areas of weakness as well as to guide you in a lifelong pursuit of self-learning and excellence.

WHY BECOME A CISSP?

As our world changes, the need for improvements in security and technology continues to grow. Corporations and other organizations are desperate to identify and recruit talented and experienced security professionals to help protect the resources on which they depend to run their businesses and remain competitive. As a Certified Information Systems Security Professional (CISSP), you will be seen as a security professional of proven ability who has successfully met a predefined standard of knowledge and experience that is well understood and respected throughout the industry. By keeping this certification current, you will demonstrate your dedication to staying abreast of security developments.

Consider some of the reasons for attaining a CISSP certification:

- To broaden your current knowledge of security concepts and practices
- To demonstrate your expertise as a seasoned security professional
- To become more marketable in a competitive workforce
- To increase your salary and be eligible for more employment opportunities
- To bring improved security expertise to your current occupation
- To show a dedication to the security discipline

The CISSP certification helps companies identify which individuals have the ability, knowledge, and experience necessary to implement solid security practices; perform risk analysis; identify necessary countermeasures; and help the organization as a whole protect its facility, network, systems, and information. The CISSP certification also shows potential employers you have achieved a level of proficiency and expertise in skill sets and knowledge required by the security industry. The increasing importance placed on security in corporate success will only continue in the future, leading to even greater demands for highly skilled security professionals. The CISSP certification shows that a respected third-party organization has recognized an individual's technical and theoretical knowledge and expertise, and distinguishes that individual from those who lack this level of knowledge.

Understanding and implementing security practices is an essential part of being a good network administrator, programmer, or engineer. Job descriptions that do not specifically target security professionals still often require that a potential candidate have a good understanding of security concepts as well as how to implement them. Due to staff size and budget restraints, many organizations can't afford separate network and security staffs. But they still believe security is vital to their organization. Thus, they often try to combine knowledge of technology and security into a single role. With a CISSP designation, you can put yourself head and shoulders above other individuals in this regard.

The CISSP Exam

Because the CISSP exam covers the eight domains making up the CISSP Common Body of Knowledge (CBK), it is often described as being "an inch deep and a mile wide," a reference to the fact that many questions on the exam are not very detailed and do not require you to be an expert in every subject. However, the questions do require you to be familiar with many *different* security subjects.

The CISSP exam comprises 250 multiple-choice and innovative questions, which must be answered in no more than 6 hours. Innovative questions incorporate drag-and-drop (i.e., take a term or item and drag it to the correct position in the frame) or hotspot (i.e., click the item or term that correctly answers the question) interfaces, but are otherwise weighed and scored just like any other question. The questions are pulled from a much larger question bank to ensure the exam is as unique as possible for each entrant. In addition, the test bank constantly changes and evolves to more accurately reflect the real world of security. The exam questions are continually rotated and replaced in the bank as necessary. Only 225 questions are graded, while 25 are used for research purposes. The 25 research questions are integrated into the exam, so you won't know which go toward your final grade. To pass the exam, you need a scale score of 700 points out of 1,000. Questions are weighted based on their difficulty; not all questions are worth the same number of points. The exam is not product or vendor oriented, meaning no questions will be specific to certain products or vendors (for instance, Windows, Unix, or Cisco). Instead, you will be tested on the security models and methodologies used by these types of systems.

EXAM TIP There is no penalty for guessing. If you can't come up with the right answer in a reasonable amount of time, then you should guess and move on to the next question.

(ISC)^2, which stands for International Information Systems Security Certification Consortium, also includes scenario-based questions in the CISSP exam. These questions present a short scenario to the test taker rather than asking the test taker to identify terms and/or concepts. The goal of the scenario-based questions is to ensure that test takers not only know and understand the concepts within the CBK, but also can apply this knowledge to real-life situations. This is more practical because in the real world, you won't be challenged by having someone asking you "What is the definition of collusion?" You need to know how to detect and prevent collusion from taking place, in addition to knowing the definition of the term.

After passing the exam, you will be asked to supply documentation, supported by a sponsor, proving that you indeed have the type of experience required to obtain this certification. The sponsor must sign a document vouching for the security experience you are submitting. So, make sure you have this sponsor lined up prior to registering for the exam and providing payment. You don't want to pay for and pass the exam, only to find you can't find a sponsor for the final step needed to achieve your certification.

The reason behind the sponsorship requirement is to ensure that those who achieve the certification have real-world experience to offer organizations. Book knowledge is extremely important for understanding theory, concepts, standards, and regulations, but it can never replace hands-on experience. Proving your practical experience supports the relevance of the certification.

A small sample group of individuals selected at random will be audited after passing the exam. The audit consists mainly of individuals from $(ISC)^2$ calling on the candidates' sponsors and contacts to verify the test taker's related experience.

One of the factors that makes the CISSP exam challenging is that most candidates, although they work in the security field, are not necessarily familiar with all eight CBK domains. If a security professional is considered an expert in vulnerability testing or application security, for example, she may not be familiar with physical security, cryptography, or forensics. Thus, studying for this exam will broaden your knowledge of the security field.

The exam questions address the eight CBK security domains, which are described in Table 1.

Domain	Description
Security and Risk Management	This domain covers many of the foundational concepts of information systems security. Some of the topics covered include • The principles of availability, integrity, and confidentiality • Security governance and compliance • Legal and regulatory issues • Professional ethics • Personnel security policies • Risk management • Threat modeling
Asset Security	This domain examines the protection of information assets throughout their life cycle. Some of the topics covered include • Information classification • Maintaining ownership • Privacy • Retention • Data security controls • Handling requirements
Security Engineering	This domain examines the development of information systems that remain secure in the face of a myriad of threats. Some of the topics covered include • Security design principles • Selection of effective controls • Mitigation of vulnerabilities • Cryptography • Secure site and facility design • Physical security

Table 1 Security Domains That Make Up the CISSP CBK (*continued*)

Domain	Description
Communication and Network Security	This domain examines network architectures, communications technologies, and network protocols with a goal of understanding how to secure them. Some of the topics covered include • Secure network architectures • Network components • Secure communications channels • Network attacks
Identity and Access Management	Identity and access management is one of the most important topics in information security. This domain covers the interactions between users and systems as well as between systems and other systems. Some of the topics covered include • Controlling physical and logical access • Identification and authentication • Identity as a Service • Third-party identity services • Authorization methods • Access control attacks
Security Assessment and Testing	This domain examines ways to verify the security of our information systems. Some of the topics covered include • Assessment and testing strategies • Testing security controls • Collecting security process data • Analyzing and reporting results • Conducting and facilitating audits
Security Operations	This domain covers the many activities involved in the daily business of maintaining the security of our networks. Some of the topics covered include • Supporting investigations • Logging and monitoring • Secure provisioning of resources • Incident management • Preventative measures • Change management • Business continuity • Managing physical security
Software Development Security	This domain examines the application of security principles to the acquisition and development of software systems. Some of the topics covered include • Security in the software development life cycle • Security controls in development activities • Assessing software security • Assessing the security implications of acquired software

Table 1 Security Domains That Make Up the CISSP CBK

(ISC)² attempts to keep up with changes in technology and methodologies in the security field by adding numerous new questions to the test question bank each year. These questions are based on current technologies, practices, approaches, and standards. For example, the CISSP exam given in 1998 did not have questions pertaining to wireless security, cross-site scripting attacks, or IPv6.

What Does This Book Cover?

This book covers everything you need to know to become an (ISC)²-certified CISSP. It teaches you the hows and whys behind organizations' development and implementation of policies, procedures, guidelines, and standards. It covers network, application, and system vulnerabilities; what exploits them; and how to counter these threats. The book explains physical security, operational security, and why systems implement the security mechanisms they do. It also reviews the U.S. and international security criteria and evaluations performed on systems for assurance ratings, what these criteria mean, and why they are used. This book also explains the legal and liability issues that surround computer systems and the data they hold, including such subjects as computer crimes, forensics, and what should be done to properly prepare computer evidence associated with these topics for court.

While this book is mainly intended to be used as a study guide for the CISSP exam, it is also a handy reference guide for use after your certification.

Tips for Taking the CISSP Exam

Many people feel as though the exam questions are tricky. Make sure to read each question and its answer choices thoroughly instead of reading a few words and immediately assuming you know what the question is asking. Some of the answer choices may have only subtle differences, so be patient and devote time to reading through the question more than once.

A common complaint heard about the CISSP exam is that some questions seem a bit subjective. For example, whereas it might be easy to answer a technical question that asks for the exact mechanism used in Transport Layer Security (TLS) that protects against man-in-the-middle attacks, it's not quite as easy to answer a question that asks whether an eight-foot perimeter fence provides low, medium, or high security. Many questions ask the test taker to choose the "best" approach, which some people find confusing and subjective. These complaints are mentioned here not to criticize (ISC)² and the exam writers, but to help you better prepare for the exam. This book covers all the necessary material for the exam and contains many questions and self-practice tests. Most of the questions are formatted in such a way as to better prepare you for what you will encounter on the actual exam. So, make sure to read all the material in the book, and pay close attention to the questions and their formats. Even if you know the subject well, you may still get some answers wrong—it is just part of learning how to take tests.

In answering many questions, it is important to keep in mind that some things are inherently more valuable than others. For example, the protection of human lives and welfare will almost always trump all other responses. Similarly, if all other factors are equal and you are given a choice between an expensive and complex solution and a simpler and cheaper one, the second will win most of the time. Expert advice (e.g., from an attorney) is more valuable than that offered by someone with lesser credentials. If one of the possible responses to a question is to seek or obtain advice from an expert, pay close attention to that question. The correct response may very well be to seek out that expert.

Familiarize yourself with industry standards and expand your technical knowledge and methodologies outside the boundaries of what you use today. We cannot stress enough that just because you are the top dog in your particular field, it doesn't mean you are properly prepared for every domain the exam covers.

When you take the CISSP exam at the Pearson VUE test center, other certification exams may be taking place simultaneously in the same room. Don't feel rushed if you see others leaving the room early; they may be taking a shorter exam.

How to Use This Book

Much effort has gone into putting all the necessary information into this book. Now it's up to you to study and understand the material and its various concepts. To best benefit from this book, you might want to use the following study method:

- Study each chapter carefully and make sure you understand each concept presented. Many concepts must be fully understood, and glossing over a couple here and there could be detrimental to you. The CISSP CBK contains hundreds of individual topics, so take the time needed to understand them all.
- Make sure to study and answer all of the questions. If any questions confuse you, go back and study those sections again. Remember, some of the questions on the actual exam are a bit confusing because they do not seem straightforward. Do not ignore the confusing questions, thinking they're not well worded. Instead, pay even closer attention to them because they are there for a reason.
- If you are not familiar with specific topics, such as firewalls, laws, physical security, or protocol functionality, use other sources of information (books, articles, and so on) to attain a more in-depth understanding of those subjects. Don't just rely on what you think you need to know to pass the CISSP exam.
- After reading this book, study the questions and answers, and take the practice tests. Then review the $(ISC)^2$ exam outline and make sure you are comfortable with each bullet item presented. If you are not comfortable with some items, revisit those chapters.
- If you have taken other certification exams—such as Cisco, Novell, or Microsoft—you might be used to having to memorize details and configuration parameters. But remember, the CISSP test is "an inch deep and a mile wide," so make sure you understand the concepts of each subject *before* trying to memorize the small, specific details.
- Remember that the exam is looking for the "best" answer. On some questions test takers do not agree with any or many of the answers. You are being asked to choose the best answer out of the four being offered to you.

CHAPTER 1

Security and Risk Management

This chapter presents the following:

- Security terminology and principles
- Protection control types
- Security frameworks, models, standards, and best practices
- Computer laws and crimes
- Intellectual property
- Data breaches
- Risk management
- Threat modeling
- Business continuity and disaster recovery
- Personnel security
- Security governance

The only truly secure system is one that is powered off, cast in a block of concrete and sealed in a lead-lined room with armed guards—and even then I have my doubts.

—Eugene H. Spafford

In reality, organizations have many other things to do than practice security. Businesses exist to make money. Most nonprofit organizations exist to offer some type of service, as in charities, educational centers, and religious entities. None of them exist specifically to deploy and maintain firewalls, intrusion detection systems, identity management technologies, and encryption devices. No business really wants to develop hundreds of security policies, deploy antimalware products, maintain vulnerability management systems, constantly update its incident response capabilities, and have to comply with the alphabet soup of security laws, regulations, and standards such as SOX (Sarbanes-Oxley), GLBA (Gramm-Leach-Bliley Act), PCI DSS (Payment Card Industry Data Security Standard), HIPAA (Health Insurance Portability and Accountability Act), and FISMA (Federal Information Security Management Act). Business owners would like to be able to make their widgets, sell their widgets, and go home. But those simpler days are long gone. Now organizations are faced with attackers who want to steal businesses' customer data to carry out identity theft and banking fraud. Company secrets are commonly being stolen by internal and external entities for economic espionage purposes. Systems are being hijacked and used within botnets to attack other organizations or to spread spam. Company funds are being secretly siphoned off through complex and hard-to-identify digital methods, commonly by organized criminal rings in different countries. And organizations that find themselves in the crosshairs of attackers may come under constant attack that brings their systems and websites offline for hours or days. Companies are required to practice a wide range of security disciplines today to keep their market share, protect their customers and bottom line, stay out of jail, and still sell their widgets.

In this chapter we will cover many of the disciplines that are necessary for organizations to practice security in a holistic manner. Each organization must develop an enterprise-wide security program that consists of technologies, procedures, and processes covered throughout this book. As you go along in your security career, you will find that most organizations have some pieces to the puzzle of an "enterprise-wide security program" in place, but not all of them. And almost every organization struggles with the best way to assess the risks it faces and how to allocate funds and resources properly to mitigate those risks. Many of the security programs in place today can be thought of as lopsided or lumpy. The security programs excel within the disciplines that the team is most familiar with, and the other disciplines are found lacking. It is your responsibility to become as well rounded in security as possible so that you can identify these deficiencies in security programs and help improve upon them. This is why the CISSP exam covers a wide variety of technologies, methodologies, and processes—you must know and understand them holistically if you are going to help an organization carry out security holistically.

We will begin with the foundational pieces of security and build upon them through the chapter and then throughout the book. Building your knowledge base is similar to building a house: without a solid foundation, it will be weak, unpredictable, and fail in the most critical of moments. Our goal is to make sure you have solid and deep roots of understanding so that you can not only protect yourself against many of the threats we face today, but also protect the commercial and government organizations who depend upon you and your skill set.

The essence of our work as security professionals is our understanding of two key terms: security and risk. Since security is what we are charged with providing to our organizations, it is a good idea to spend some time defining this and related terms. A good way to understand key terms in a broader societal context is to explore the laws and crimes around them, together with the concomitant tradeoffs that we must make lest we sacrifice privacy in the name of crime fighting. Building on this foundation, we next turn our attention to the concept that should underlie every decision made when defending our information systems: risk. Risk is so important that we will cover it in detail in this chapter, but will also return to it time and again in the rest of the book. We start off narrowly, but focusing on the malicious threats to our organizations; we also widen our aperture to include accidental and environmental threats and how to prepare for them by planning for business continuity and disaster recovery. Finally, we will close with discussions on personnel, governance, and ethics and how they apply to all that has preceded them in this chapter.

Fundamental Principles of Security

We need to understand the core goals of security, which are to provide availability, integrity, and confidentiality (AIC triad) protection for critical assets. Each asset will require different levels of these types of protection, as we will see in the following sections. All security controls, mechanisms, and safeguards are implemented to provide one or more of these protection types, and all risks, threats, and vulnerabilities are measured for their potential capability to compromise one or all of the AIC principles.

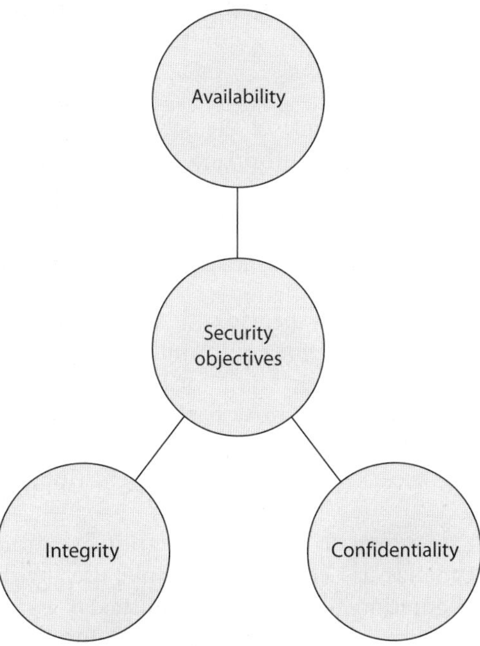

NOTE In some documentation, the "triad" is presented as CIA: confidentiality, integrity, and availability.

Availability

Availability protection ensures reliability and timely access to data and resources to authorized individuals. Network devices, computers, and applications should provide adequate functionality to perform in a predictable manner with an acceptable level of performance. They should be able to recover from disruptions in a secure and quick fashion so productivity is not negatively affected. Necessary protection mechanisms must be in place to protect against inside and outside threats that could affect the availability and productivity of all business-processing components.

Like many things in life, ensuring the availability of the necessary resources within an organization sounds easier to accomplish than it really is. Networks have many pieces that must stay up and running (routers, switches, DNS servers, DHCP servers, proxies, firewalls, and so on). Software has many components that must be executing in a healthy manner (operating system, applications, antimalware software, and so forth). And an organization's operations can potentially be negatively affected by environmental aspects (such as fire, flood, HVAC issues, or electrical problems), natural disasters, and physical theft or attacks. An organization must fully understand its operational environment and its availability weaknesses so that it can put in place the proper countermeasures.

Integrity

Integrity is upheld when the assurance of the accuracy and reliability of information and systems is provided and any unauthorized modification is prevented. Hardware, software, and communication mechanisms must work in concert to maintain and process data correctly and to move data to intended destinations without unexpected alteration. The systems and network should be protected from outside interference and contamination.

Environments that enforce and provide this attribute of security ensure that attackers, or mistakes by users, do not compromise the integrity of systems or data. When an attacker inserts a virus, logic bomb, or back door into a system, the system's integrity is compromised. This can, in turn, harm the integrity of information held on the system by way of corruption, malicious modification, or the replacement of data with incorrect data. Strict access controls, intrusion detection, and hashing can combat these threats.

Users usually affect a system or its data's integrity by mistake (although internal users may also commit malicious deeds). For example, users with a full hard drive may unwittingly delete configuration files under the mistaken assumption that deleting a file must be okay because they don't remember ever using it. Or, for example, a user may insert incorrect values into a data-processing application that ends up charging a customer $3,000 instead of $300. Incorrectly modifying data kept in databases is another common way users may accidentally corrupt data—a mistake that can have lasting effects.

Security should streamline users' capabilities and give them only certain choices and functionality, so errors become less common and less devastating. System-critical files should be restricted from viewing and access by users. Applications should provide mechanisms that check for valid and reasonable input values. Databases should let only authorized individuals modify data, and data in transit should be protected by encryption or other mechanisms.

Confidentiality

Confidentiality ensures that the necessary level of secrecy is enforced at each junction of data processing and prevents unauthorized disclosure. This level of secrecy should prevail while data resides on systems and devices within the network, as it is transmitted, and once it reaches its destination.

Attackers can thwart confidentiality mechanisms by network monitoring, shoulder surfing, stealing password files, breaking encryption schemes, and social engineering. These topics will be addressed in more depth in later chapters, but briefly, *shoulder surfing* is when a person looks over another person's shoulder and watches their keystrokes or views data as it appears on a computer screen. *Social engineering* is when one person tricks another person into sharing confidential information, for example, by posing as someone authorized to have access to that information. Social engineering can take many forms. Any one-to-one communication medium can be used to perform social engineering attacks.

Users can intentionally or accidentally disclose sensitive information by not encrypting it before sending it to another person, by falling prey to a social engineering attack, by sharing a company's trade secrets, or by not using extra care to protect confidential information when processing it.

Confidentiality can be provided by encrypting data as it is stored and transmitted, by enforcing strict access control and data classification, and by training personnel on the proper data protection procedures.

Availability, integrity, and confidentiality are critical principles of security. You should understand their meaning, how they are provided by different mechanisms, and how their absence can negatively affect an organization.

Balanced Security

In reality, when information security is dealt with, it is commonly only through the lens of keeping secrets secret (confidentiality). The integrity and availability threats can be overlooked and only dealt with after they are properly compromised. Some assets have a critical confidentiality requirement (company trade secrets), some have critical integrity requirements (financial transaction values), and some have critical availability requirements (e-commerce web servers). Many people understand the concepts of the AIC triad, but may not fully appreciate the complexity of implementing the necessary controls to provide all the protection these concepts cover. The following provides a *short* list of some of these controls and how they map to the components of the AIC triad.

Availability:

- Redundant array of independent disks (RAID)
- Clustering
- Load balancing
- Redundant data and power lines

- Software and data backups
- Disk shadowing
- Co-location and offsite facilities
- Rollback functions
- Failover configurations

Integrity:

- Hashing (data integrity)
- Configuration management (system integrity)
- Change control (process integrity)
- Access control (physical and technical)
- Software digital signing
- Transmission cyclic redundancy check (CRC) functions

Confidentiality:

- Encryption for data at rest (whole disk, database encryption)
- Encryption for data in transit (IPSec, TLS, PPTP, SSH, described in Chapter 4)
- Access control (physical and technical)

All of these control types will be covered in this book. What is important to realize at this point is that while the concept of the AIC triad may seem simplistic, meeting its requirements is commonly more challenging.

Security Definitions

The words "vulnerability," "threat," "risk," and "exposure" are often interchanged, even though they have different meanings. It is important to understand each word's definition and the relationships between the concepts they represent.

A *vulnerability* is a weakness in a system that allows a threat source to compromise its security. It can be a software, hardware, procedural, or human weakness that can be exploited. A vulnerability may be a service running on a server, unpatched applications or operating systems, an unrestricted wireless access point, an open port on a firewall, lax physical security that allows anyone to enter a server room, or unenforced password management on servers and workstations.

A *threat* is any potential danger that is associated with the exploitation of a vulnerability. If the threat is that someone will identify a specific vulnerability and use it against the company or individual, then the entity that takes advantage of a vulnerability is referred to as a *threat agent*. A threat agent could be an intruder accessing the network through a port on the firewall, a process accessing data in a way that violates the security policy, or an employee circumventing controls in order to copy files to a medium that could expose confidential information.

A *risk* is the likelihood of a threat source exploiting a vulnerability and the corresponding business impact. If a firewall has several ports open, there is a higher likelihood that an intruder will use one to access the network in an unauthorized method. If users are not educated on processes and procedures, there is a higher likelihood that an employee will make an unintentional mistake that may destroy data. If an intrusion detection system (IDS) is not implemented on a network, there is a higher likelihood an attack will go unnoticed until it is too late. Risk ties the vulnerability, threat, and likelihood of exploitation to the resulting business impact.

An *exposure* is an instance of being exposed to losses. A vulnerability exposes an organization to possible damages. If password management is lax and password rules are not enforced, the company is exposed to the possibility of having users' passwords compromised and used in an unauthorized manner. If a company does not have its wiring inspected and does not put proactive fire prevention steps into place, it exposes itself to potentially devastating fires.

A *control*, or countermeasure, is put into place to mitigate (reduce) the potential risk. A countermeasure may be a software configuration, a hardware device, or a procedure that eliminates a vulnerability or that reduces the likelihood a threat agent will be able to exploit a vulnerability. Examples of countermeasures include strong password management, firewalls, a security guard, access control mechanisms, encryption, and security-awareness training.

NOTE The terms "control," "countermeasure," and "safeguard" are interchangeable terms. They are mechanisms put into place to reduce risk.

If a company has antimalware software but does not keep the signatures up to date, this is a vulnerability. The company is vulnerable to malware attacks. The threat is that a virus will show up in the environment and disrupt productivity. The risk is the likelihood of a virus showing up in the environment and causing damage and the resulting potential damage. If a virus infiltrates the company's environment, then a vulnerability has been exploited and the company is exposed to loss. The countermeasures in this situation are to update the signatures and install the antimalware software on all computers. The relationships among risks, vulnerabilities, threats, and countermeasures are shown in Figure 1-1.

Applying the right countermeasure can eliminate the vulnerability and exposure, and thus reduce the risk. The company cannot eliminate the threat agent, but it can protect itself and prevent this threat agent from exploiting vulnerabilities within the environment.

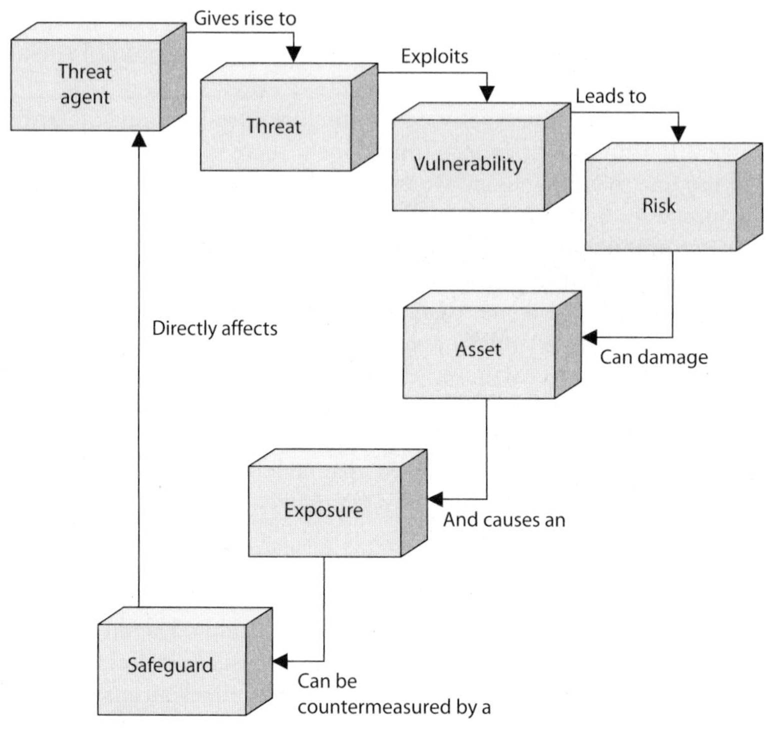

Figure 1-1 The relationships among the different security concepts

Many people gloss over these basic terms with the idea that they are not as important as the sexier things in information security. But you will find that unless a security team has an agreed-upon language in place, confusion will quickly take over. These terms embrace the core concepts of security, and if they are confused in any manner, then the activities that are rolled out to enforce security are commonly confused.

Control Types

Up to this point we have covered the goals of security (availability, integrity, confidentiality) and the terminology used in the security industry (vulnerability, threat, risk, control). These are foundational components that must be understood if security is going to take place in an organized manner. The next foundational issue we are going to tackle is control types that can be implemented and their associated functionality.

Controls are put into place to reduce the risk an organization faces, and they come in three main flavors: administrative, technical, and physical. *Administrative controls* are commonly referred to as "soft controls" because they are more management oriented. Examples of administrative controls are security documentation, risk management, personnel security, and training. *Technical controls* (also called logical controls) are

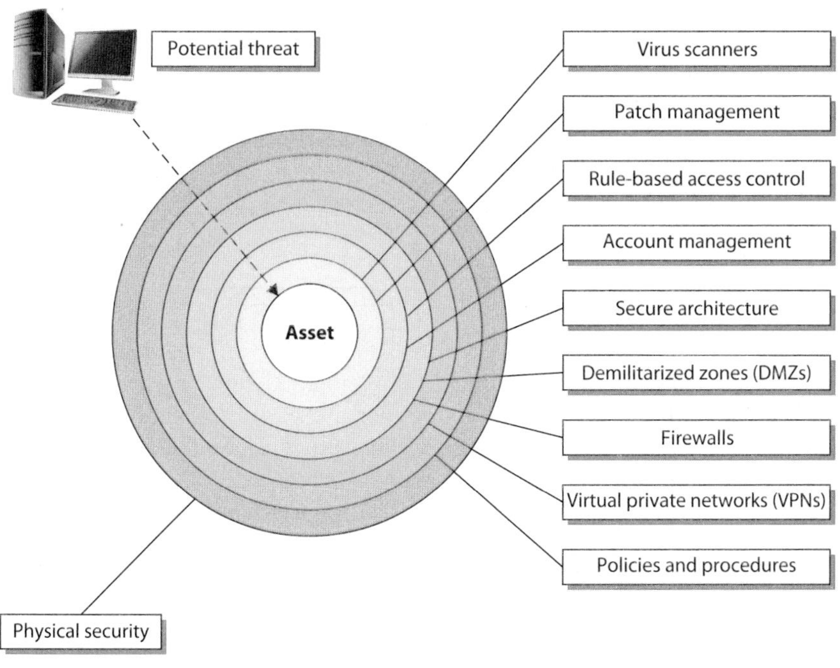

Figure 1-2 Defense-in-depth

software or hardware components, as in firewalls, IDS, encryption, and identification and authentication mechanisms. And *physical controls* are items put into place to protect facility, personnel, and resources. Examples of physical controls are security guards, locks, fencing, and lighting.

These control types need to be put into place to provide *defense-in-depth*, which is the coordinated use of multiple security controls in a layered approach, as shown in Figure 1-2. A multilayered defense system minimizes the probability of successful penetration and compromise because an attacker would have to get through several different types of protection mechanisms before she gained access to the critical assets. For example, Company A can have the following physical controls in place that work in a layered model:

- Fence
- Locked external doors
- Closed-circuit TV
- Security guard
- Locked internal doors
- Locked server room
- Physically secured computers (cable locks)

Technical controls that are commonly put into place to provide this type of layered approach are

- Firewalls
- Intrusion detection system
- Intrusion prevention systems
- Antimalware
- Access control
- Encryption

The types of controls that are actually implemented must map to the threats the company faces, and the number of layers that are put into place must map to the sensitivity of the asset. The rule of thumb is the more sensitive the asset, the more layers of protection that must be put into place.

So the different *categories* of controls that can be used are administrative, technical, and physical. But what do these controls actually *do* for us? We need to understand the different functionality that each control type can provide us in our quest to secure our environments.

The different functionalities of security controls are *preventive*, *detective*, *corrective*, *deterrent*, *recovery*, and *compensating*. By having a better understanding of the different control functionalities, you will be able to make more informed decisions about what controls will be best used in specific situations. The six different control functionalities are as follows:

- **Preventive** Intended to avoid an incident from occurring
- **Detective** Helps identify an incident's activities and potentially an intruder
- **Corrective** Fixes components or systems after an incident has occurred
- **Deterrent** Intended to discourage a potential attacker
- **Recovery** Intended to bring the environment back to regular operations
- **Compensating** Controls that provide an alternative measure of control

Once you understand fully what the different controls do, you can use them in the right locations for specific risks.

When looking at a security structure of an environment, it is most productive to use a preventive model and then use detective, corrective, and recovery mechanisms to help support this model. Basically, you want to stop any trouble before it starts, but you must be able to quickly react and combat trouble if it does find you. It is not feasible to prevent everything; therefore, what you cannot prevent, you should be able to quickly detect. That's why preventive and detective controls should always be implemented together and should complement each other. To take this concept further: what you can't prevent, you should be able to detect, and if you detect something, it means you weren't able to prevent it, and therefore you should take corrective action to make sure it is indeed prevented the next time around. Therefore, all three types work together: preventive, detective, and corrective.

The control types described next (administrative, physical, and technical) are preventive in nature. These are important to understand when developing an enterprise-wide security program.

Preventive: Administrative

- Policies and procedures
- Effective hiring practices
- Pre-employment background checks
- Controlled termination processes
- Data classification and labeling
- Security awareness

Preventive: Physical

- Badges, swipe cards
- Guards, dogs
- Fences, locks, mantraps

Preventive: Technical

- Passwords, biometrics, smart cards
- Encryption, secure protocols, call-back systems, database views, constrained user interfaces
- Antimalware software, access control lists, firewalls, intrusion prevention system

Table 1-1 shows how these types of control mechanisms perform different security functions. Many students get themselves wrapped around the axle when trying to get their mind around which control provides which functionality. This is how this train of thought usually takes place: "A firewall is a preventive control, but if an attacker knew that it was in place it could be a deterrent." Let's stop right here. Do not make this any harder than it has to be. When trying to map the functionality requirement to a control, think of the *main* reason that control would be put into place. A firewall tries to prevent something bad from taking place, so it is a preventative control. Auditing logs is done after an event took place, so it is detective. A data backup system is developed so that data can be recovered; thus, this is a recovery control. Computer images are created so that if software gets corrupted, they can be reloaded; thus, this is a corrective control.

One control functionality that some people struggle with is a compensating control. Let's look at some examples of compensating controls to best explain their function. If your company needed to implement strong physical security, you might suggest to

Functionality:	Preventive	Detective	Corrective	Deterrent	Recovery
Type:					
Physical					
Fences				X	
Locks	X				
Badge system	X				
Security guard	X				
Biometric system	X				
Mantrap doors	X				
Lighting				X	
Motion detectors		X			
Closed-circuit TVs		X			
Offsite facility					X
Administrative					
Security policy	X				
Monitoring and supervising		X			
Separation of duties	X				
Job rotation		X			
Information classification	X				
Personnel procedures	X				
Investigations		X			
Testing	X				
Security-awareness training	X				
Technical					
ACLs	X				
Encryption	X				
Audit logs		X			
IDS		X			
Antivirus software	X				
Server images			X		
Smart cards	X				
Dial-up call-back systems	X				
Data backup					X

Table 1-1 Control Types and Functionality

management that they employ security guards. But after calculating all the costs of security guards, your company might decide to use a compensating (alternative) control that provides similar protection but is more affordable—as in a fence. In another example, let's say you are a security administrator and you are in charge of maintaining the company's firewalls. Management tells you that a certain protocol that you know is vulnerable to exploitation has to be allowed through the firewall for business reasons. The network needs to be protected by a compensating (alternative) control pertaining to this protocol, which may be setting up a proxy server for that specific traffic type to ensure that it is properly inspected and controlled. So a compensating control is just an alternative control that provides similar protection as the original control, but has to be used because it is more affordable or allows specifically required business functionality.

Several types of security controls exist, and they all need to work together. The complexity of the controls and of the environment they are in can cause the controls to contradict each other or leave gaps in security. This can introduce unforeseen holes in the company's protection that are not fully understood by the implementers. A company may have very strict technical access controls in place and all the necessary administrative controls up to snuff, but if any person is allowed to physically access any system in the facility, then clear security dangers are present within the environment. Together, these controls should work in harmony to provide a healthy, safe, and productive environment.

Security Frameworks

With each section we are getting closer to some of the overarching topics of this chapter. Up to this point we know what we need to accomplish (availability, integrity, confidentiality) and we know the tools we can use (administrative, technical, and physical controls) and we know how to talk about this issue (vulnerability, threat, risk, control). Before we move into how to develop an organization-wide security program, let's first explore what *not* to do, which is referred to as security through obscurity. The concept of *security through obscurity* is assuming that your enemies are not as smart as you are and that they cannot figure out something that you feel is very tricky. A nontechnical example of security through obscurity is the old practice of putting a spare key under a doormat in case you are locked out of the house. You assume that no one knows about the spare key, and as long as they don't, it can be considered secure. The vulnerability here is that anyone could gain easy access to the house if they have access to that hidden spare key, and the experienced attacker (in this example, a burglar) knows that these kinds of vulnerabilities exist and takes the appropriate steps to seek them out.

In the technical realm, some vendors work on the premise that compiling their product's code provides more protection than exists in products based upon open-source code, because no one can view their original programming instructions. But attackers have a wide range of reverse-engineering tools available to them to reconstruct the product's original code, and there are other ways to figure out how to exploit software without reverse-engineering it, as in fuzzing, data validation inputs, etc. The proper approach to security is to ensure that the original software does not contain flaws—not to assume that putting the code into a compiled format provides the necessary level of protection.

Another common example of practicing security through obscurity is to develop cryptographic algorithms in-house instead of using algorithms that are commonly used within the industry. Some organizations assume that if attackers are not familiar with the logic functions and mathematics of their homegrown algorithms, this lack of understanding by the attacker will serve as a necessary level of security. But attackers are smart, clever, and motivated. If there are flaws within these algorithms, attackers will most likely identify and exploit them. The better approach is to use industry-recognized algorithms that have proven themselves to be strong.

Some network administrators will remap protocols on their firewalls so that HTTP is not coming into the environment over the well-known port 80, but instead over port 8080. The administrator assumes that an attacker will not figure out this remapping, but in reality a basic port scanner and protocol analyzer will easily detect this port remapping. So don't try to outsmart the bad guy with trickery; instead, practice security in a mature, solid approach. Don't try to hide the flaws that can be exploited; get rid of those flaws altogether by following proven security practices.

Reliance on confusion to provide security is obviously dangerous. Though everyone wants to believe in the innate goodness of their fellow man, no security professional would have a job if this were actually true. In security, a good practice is illustrated by the old saying, "There are only two people in the world I trust: you and me—and I'm not so sure about you." This is a better attitude to take, because security really can be compromised by anyone, at any time.

So we do not want our organization's security program to be built upon smoke and mirrors, and we understand that we most likely cannot out-trick our enemies—what do we do? Build a fortress, aka security program. Hundreds of years ago your enemies would not be attacking you with packets through a network; they would be attacking you with big sticks while they rode horses. When one faction of people needed to protect themselves from another, they did not just stack some rocks on top of each other in a haphazard manner and call that protection. (Well, maybe some groups did, but they died right away and do not really count.) Groups of people built castles based upon architectures that could withstand attacks. The walls and ceilings were made of solid material that was hard to penetrate. The structure of the buildings provided layers of protection. The buildings were outfitted with both defensive and offensive tools, and some were surround by moats. That is our goal, minus the moat.

A security program is a framework made up of many entities: logical, administrative, and physical protection mechanisms; procedures; business processes; and people that all work together to provide a protection level for an environment. Each has an important place in the framework, and if one is missing or incomplete, the whole framework may be affected. The program should work in layers: each layer provides support for the layer above it and protection for the layer below it. Because a security program is a *framework*, organizations are free to plug in different types of technologies, methods, and procedures to accomplish the necessary protection level for their environment.

A security program based upon a flexible framework sounds great, but how do we build one? Before a fortress was built, the structure was laid out in blueprints by an architect. We need a detailed plan to follow to properly build our security program. Thank goodness industry standards were developed just for this purpose.

Many Standards, Best Practices, and Frameworks

As you will see in the following sections, various for-profit and nonprofit organizations have developed their own approaches to security management, security control objectives, process management, and enterprise development. We will examine their similarities and differences and illustrate where each is used within the industry.

The following is a basic breakdown.

Security Program Development:

- **ISO/IEC 27000 series** International standards on how to develop and maintain an ISMS developed by ISO and IEC

Enterprise Architecture Development:

- **Zachman Framework** Model for the development of enterprise architectures developed by John Zachman
- **TOGAF** Model and methodology for the development of enterprise architectures developed by The Open Group
- **DoDAF** U.S. Department of Defense architecture framework that ensures interoperability of systems to meet military mission goals
- **MODAF** Architecture framework used mainly in military support missions developed by the British Ministry of Defence
- **SABSA model** Model and methodology for the development of information security enterprise architectures

Security Controls Development:

- **COBIT 5** A business framework to allow for IT enterprise management and governance that was developed by Information Systems Audit and Control Association (ISACA)
- **NIST SP 800-53** Set of controls to protect U.S. federal systems developed by the National Institute of Standards and Technology
- **COSO Internal Control—Integrated Framework** Set of internal corporate controls to help reduce the risk of financial fraud developed by the Committee of Sponsoring Organizations (COSO) of the Treadway Commission

(*Continued*)

Process Management Development:

- **ITIL** Processes to allow for IT service management developed by the United Kingdom's Office of Government Commerce
- **Six Sigma** Business management strategy that can be used to carry out process improvement
- **Capability Maturity Model Integration (CMMI)** Organizational development for process improvement developed by Carnegie Mellon University

ISO/IEC 27000 Series

British Standard 7799 (BS7799) was developed in 1995 by the United Kingdom government's Department of Trade and Industry and published by the British Standards Institution. The standard outlined how an information security management system (ISMS) (aka security program) should be built and maintained. The goal in developing the standard was to provide guidance to organizations on how to design, implement, and maintain policies, processes, and technologies to manage risks to its sensitive information assets.

The reason that this type of standard was even needed was to try and centrally manage the various security controls deployed throughout an organization. Without a security management system, the controls would be implemented and managed in an ad hoc manner. The IT department would take care of technology security solutions, personnel security would be within the human relations department, physical security in the facilities department, and business continuity in the operations department. We needed a way to oversee all of these items and knit them together in a holistic manner. This British Standard met this need.

The British Standard actually had two parts: BS7799 Part 1, which outlined control objectives and a range of controls that can be used to meet those objectives, and BS7799 Part 2, which outlined how a security program (ISMS) can be set up and maintained. BS7799 Part 2 also served as a baseline that organizations could be certified against.

BS7799 was considered a de facto standard, which means that no specific standards body was demanding that everyone follow it—but the standard seemed to be a really good idea and fit an industry need, so everyone decided to follow it. When organizations around the world needed to develop an internal security program, there were no guidelines or direction to follow except BS7799. However, as BS7799 was being updated, it went through a long range of confusing titles, including different version numbers. So you could see this referenced as BS7799, BS7799v1, BS7799v2, ISO 17799, BS7799-3:2005, and so on.

The need to expand and globally standardize BS7799 was identified, and this task was taken on by the International Organization for Standardization (ISO) and the International Electrotechnical Commission (IEC). ISO is the world's largest developer and publisher of international standards. The standards this group works on range from meteorology, food technology, and agriculture to space vehicle engineering, mining, and information technology. ISO is a network of the national standards institutes of 162 countries. So these are the really smart people who come up with really good ways of doing stuff, one being how to set up information security programs within organizations. The IEC develops and publishes international standards for all electrical, electronic, and related technologies. These two organizations worked together to build on top of what was provided by BS7799 and launch the new version as a global standard, known as the *ISO/IEC 27000 series.*

NOTE Though IEC is an acronym (for International Electrotechnical Commission), ISO is not. The name ISO is simply a derivation of the Greek word for equal (isos).

The industry has moved from the more ambiguous BS7799 standard to the ISO/IEC 27000 series, an ever-evolving list of ISO/IEC standards that attempt to compartmentalize and modularize the necessary components of an ISMS. The currently published standards (with a few omitted) include the following:

- **ISO/IEC 27000** Overview and vocabulary
- **ISO/IEC 27001** ISMS requirements
- **ISO/IEC 27002** Code of practice for information security management
- **ISO/IEC 27003** ISMS implementation
- **ISO/IEC 27004** ISMS measurement
- **ISO/IEC 27005** Risk management
- **ISO/IEC 27006** Certification body requirements
- **ISO/IEC 27007** ISMS auditing
- **ISO/IEC 27008** Guidance for auditors
- **ISO/IEC 27011** Telecommunications organizations
- **ISO/IEC 27014** Information security governance
- **ISO/IEC 27015** Financial sector
- **ISO/IEC 27031** Business continuity
- **ISO/IEC 27032** Cybersecurity
- **ISO/IEC 27033** Network security
- **ISO/IEC 27034** Application security
- **ISO/IEC 27035** Incident management
- **ISO/IEC 27037** Digital evidence collection and preservation
- **ISO/IEC 27799** Health organizations

The ISO/IEC 27000 series serves as industry best practices for the management of security controls in a holistic manner within organizations around the world. The list of standards that makes up this series grows each year. Each standard has a specific focus (such as metrics, governance, auditing, and so on).

It is common for organizations to seek an ISO/IEC 27001 certification by an accredited third party. The third party assesses the organization against the ISMS requirements laid out in ISO/IEC 27001 and attests to the organization's compliance level. Just as (ISC)² attests to a person's security knowledge once he passes the CISSP exam, the third party attests to the security practices within the boundaries of the company it evaluates.

It is useful to understand the differences between the ISO/IEC 27000 series of standards and how they relate to each other. Figure 1-3 illustrates the differences between general requirements, general guidelines, and sector-specific guidelines.

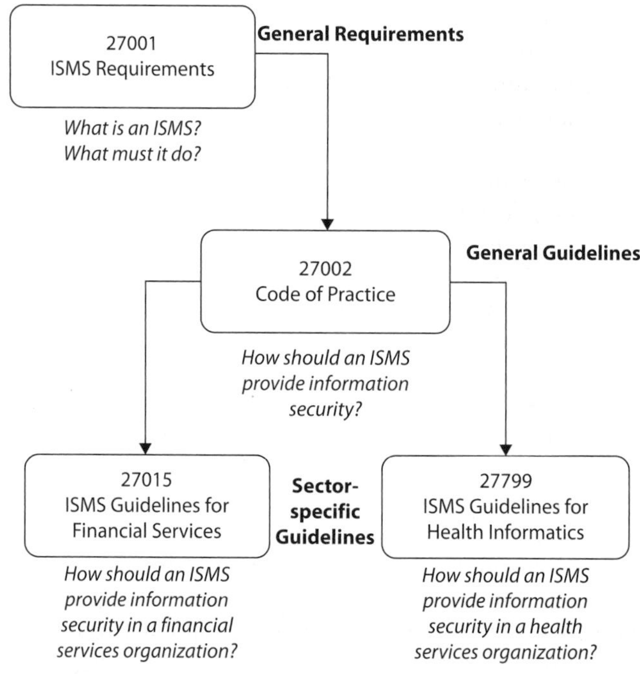

Figure 1-3 ISO/IEC 27000 standards

NOTE The CISSP common body of knowledge places *all* architectures (enterprise and system) within the domain Security Engineering. Enterprise architectures are covered in this chapter because they directly relate to the organizational security program components covered throughout the chapter. Chapter 3 deals specifically with system architectures that are used in software engineering and design.

Enterprise Architecture Development

Organizations have a choice when attempting to secure their environment as a whole. They can just toss in products here and there, which are referred to as point solutions or stovepipe solutions, and hope the ad hoc approach magically works in a manner that secures the environment evenly and covers all of the organization's vulnerabilities. Or the organization can take the time to understand the environment, understand the security requirements of the business and environment, and lay out an overarching framework and strategy that maps the two together. Most organizations choose option one, which is the "constantly putting out fires" approach. This is a lovely way to keep stress levels elevated and security requirements unmet, and to let confusion and chaos be the norm.

The second approach would be to define an enterprise security architecture, allow it to be the guide when implementing solutions to ensure business needs are met, provide standard protection across the environment, and reduce the amount of security surprises the organization will run into. Although implementing an enterprise security architecture will not necessarily promise pure utopia, it does tame the chaos and gets the security staff, and organization into a more proactive and mature mindset when dealing with security as a whole.

Developing an architecture from scratch is not an easy task. Sure, it is easy to draw a big box with smaller boxes inside of it, but what do the boxes represent? What are the relationships between the boxes? How does information flow between the boxes? Who needs to view these boxes, and what aspects of the boxes do they need for decision making? An architecture is a conceptual construct. It is a tool to help individuals understand a complex item (such as an enterprise) in digestible chunks. If you are familiar with the OSI networking model, this is an abstract model used to illustrate the architecture of a networking stack. A networking stack within a computer is very complex because it has so many protocols, interfaces, services, and hardware specifications. But when we think about it in a modular framework (seven layers), we can better understand the network stack as a whole and the relationships between the individual components that make it up.

NOTE The OSI network stack will be covered extensively in Chapter 4.

An enterprise architecture encompasses the essential and unifying components of an organization. It expresses the enterprise structure (form) and behavior (function). It embodies the enterprise's components, their relationships to each other, and their relationships to the environment.

In this section we will be covering several different enterprise architecture frameworks. Each framework has its own specific focus, but they all provide guidance on how to build individual architectures so that they are useful tools to a diverse set of individuals. Notice the difference between an architecture *framework* and an actual architecture. You use the framework as a guideline on how to build an architecture that best fits your company's needs. Each company's architecture will be different because companies have different business drivers, security and regulatory requirements, cultures, and organizational structures—but if each starts with the same architecture *framework*, then their architectures will have similar structures and goals. It is similar to three people starting with a ranch-style house blueprint. One person chooses to have four bedrooms built because they have three children, one person chooses to have a larger living room and three bedrooms, and the other person chooses two bedrooms and two living rooms. Each person started with the same blueprint (framework) and modified it to meet their needs (architecture).

When developing an architecture, first the *stakeholders* need to be identified, the people who will be looking at and using the architecture. Next, the *views* need to be developed, which is how the information that is most important to the different stakeholders will be illustrated in the most useful manner. The U.S. National Institute of Standards and Technology (NIST) developed a framework, illustrated in Figure 1-4, which shows that companies have several different viewpoints. Executives need to understand the company from a business point of view, business process developers need to understand what type of information needs to be collected to support business activities, application developers need to understand system requirements that maintain and process the information, data modelers need to know how to structure data elements, and the technology group needs to understand the network components required to support the layers above it. They are all looking at an architecture of the same company; it is just being presented in views that they understand and that directly relate to their responsibilities within the organization.

An enterprise architecture allows you to not only understand the company from several different views, but also understand how a change that takes place at one level will affect items at other levels. For example, if there is a new business requirement, how is it going to be supported at each level of the enterprise? What type of new information must be collected and processed? Do new applications need to be purchased or current ones modified? Are new data elements required? Will new networking devices be required? An architecture allows you to understand all the things that will need to change just to support one new business function. The architecture can be used in the opposite direction also. If a company is looking to do a technology refresh, will the new systems still support all of the necessary functions in the layers above the technology level? An architecture allows you to understand an organization as one complete organism and illustrate how changes to one internal component can directly affect another one.

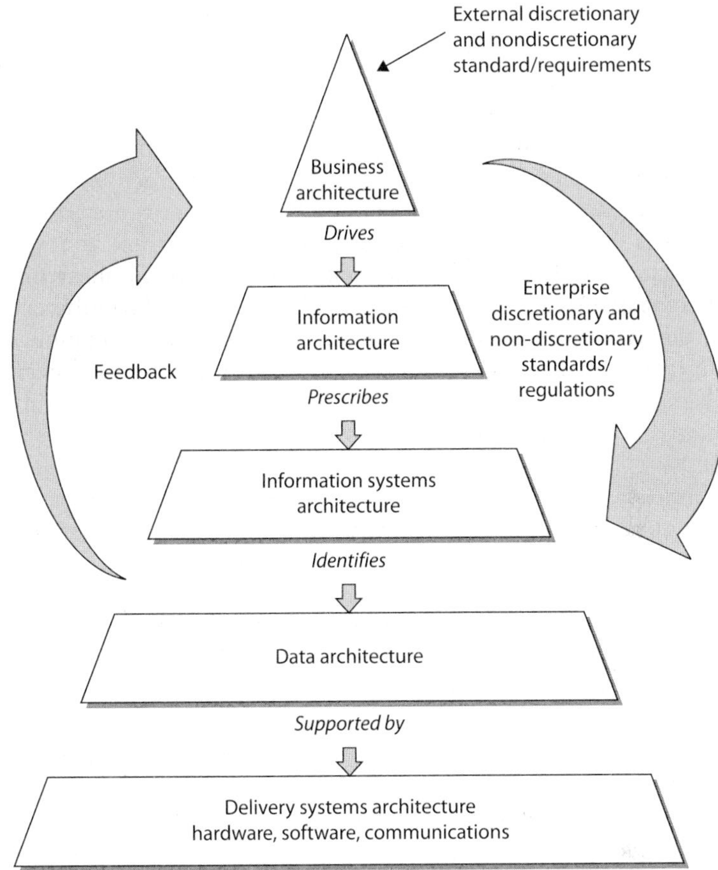

Figure 1-4 NIST enterprise architecture framework

Why Do We Need Enterprise Architecture Frameworks?

As you have probably experienced, business people and technology people sometimes seem like totally different species. Business people use terms like "net profits," "risk universes," "portfolio strategy," "hedging," "commodities," etc. Technology people use terms like "deep packet inspection," "level three devices," "cross-site scripting," "load balancing," etc. Think about the acronyms techies like us throw around—TCP, APT, ICMP, RAID, UDP, L2TP, PPTP, IPSec, AES, and DES. We can have complete conversations between ourselves without using any real words. And even though business people and technology people use some of the same words, they have totally different meanings to the individual groups. To business people, a protocol is a set of approved processes that must be followed to accomplish a task. To technical people, a protocol is a standardized manner of communication between computers or applications. Business and technical people use the term "risk," but each group is focusing on very different risks a company can face—market share versus security breaches. And even though each group uses the term "data" the same, business people look at data only from a functional point of view and security people look at data from a risk point of view.

This divide between business perspectives and technology perspectives can not only cause confusion and frustration—it commonly costs money. If the business side of the house wants to offer customers a new service, as in paying bills online, there may have to be extensive changes to the current network infrastructure, applications, web servers, software logic, cryptographic functions, authentication methods, database structures, etc. What seems to be a small change in a business offering can cost a lot of money when it comes to adding up the new technology that needs to be purchased and implemented, programming that needs to be carried out, re-architecting of networks, etc. It is common for business people to feel as though the IT department is more of an impediment when it comes to business evolution and growth, and in turn the IT department feels as though the business people are constantly coming up with outlandish and unrealistic demands with no supporting budgets.

Because of this type of confusion between business and technology people, organizations around the world have implemented incorrect solutions because the business functionality to technical specifications was not understood. This results in having to repurchase new solutions, carry out rework, and waste an amazing amount of time. Not only does this cost the organization more money than it should have in the first place, business opportunities may be lost, which can reduce market share. This type of waste has happened so much that the U.S. Congress passed the Clinger-Cohen Act, which requires federal agencies to improve their IT expenditures. So we need a tool that both business people and technology people can use to reduce confusion, optimize business functionality, and not waste time and money. This is where business enterprise architectures come into play. It allows both groups (business and technology) to view the same organization in ways that make sense to them.

When you go to the doctor's office, there is a poster of a skeleton system on one wall, a poster of a circulatory system on the other wall, and another poster of the organs that make up a human body. These are all different views of the same thing, the human body. This is the same functionality that enterprise architecture frameworks provide: different views of the same thing. In the medical field we have specialists (podiatrists, brain surgeons, dermatologists, oncologists, ophthalmologists, etc.). Each organization is also made up of its own specialists (HR, marketing, accounting, IT, R&D, management, etc.). But there also has to be an understanding of the entity (whether it is a human body or company) holistically, which is what an enterprise architecture attempts to accomplish.

Zachman Architecture Framework

One of the first enterprise architecture frameworks that was created is the *Zachman Framework*, created by John Zachman. This model is generic, and is well suited to frame the work we do in information systems security. A sample (though fairly simplified) representation is depicted in Table 1-2.

The Zachman Framework is a two-dimensional model that uses six basic communication interrogatives (What, How, Where, Who, When, and Why) intersecting with different perspectives (Executives, Business Managers, System Architects, Engineers,

Perspective (Audience)		Interrogatives					
		What	**How**	**Where**	**Who**	**When**	**Why**
	Contextual (Executives)	Assets and Liabilities	Business Lines	Business Locales	Partners, Clients, and Employees	Milestones and Major Events	Business Strategy
	Conceptual (Business Mgrs.)	Products	Business Processes	Logistics and Communications	Workflows	Master Calendar	Business Plan
	Architectural (System Architects)	Data Models	Systems Architectures	Distributed Systems Architectures	Use Cases	Project Schedules	Business Rule Models
	Technological (Engineers)	Data Management	Systems Designs	System Interfaces	Human Interfaces	Process Controls	Process Outputs
	Implementation (Technicians)	Data Stores	Programs	Network Nodes and Links	Access Controls	Network & Security Operations	Performance Metrics
	Enterprise	Information	Functions	Networks	Organizations	Schedules	Strategies

Table 1-2 Zachman Framework for Enterprise Architecture

Technicians, and Enterprise-wide) to give a holistic understanding of the enterprise. This framework was developed in the 1980s and is based on the principles of classical business architecture that contain rules that govern an ordered set of relationships. One of these rules is that each row should describe the enterprise completely from that row's perspective. For example, IT personnel's jobs require them to see the organization in terms of data stores, programs, networks, access controls, operations, and metrics. Though they are (or at least should be) aware of other perspectives and items, the performance of their duties in the example organization is focused on these items.

The goal of this framework is to be able to look at the same organization from different viewpoints. Different groups within a company need the same information, but presented in ways that directly relate to their responsibilities. A CEO needs financial statements, scorecards, and balance sheets. A network administrator needs network schematics, a systems engineer needs interface requirements, and the operations department needs configuration requirements. If you have ever carried out a network-based vulnerability test, you know that you cannot tell the CEO that some systems are vulnerable to SYN-based attacks, or that the company software allows for client-side browser injections, or that some Windows-based applications are vulnerable to alternative data stream attacks. The CEO needs to know this information, but in a language she can understand. People at each level of the organization need information in a language and format that is most useful to them.

A business enterprise architecture is used to optimize often fragmented processes (both manual and automated) into an integrated environment that is responsive to change and supportive of the business strategy. The Zachman Framework has been around for many years and has been used by many organizations to build or better define their business environment. This framework is not security oriented, but it is a good template to work with because it offers direction on how to understand an actual enterprise in a modular fashion.

The Open Group Architecture Framework

Another enterprise architecture framework is *The Open Group Architecture Framework (TOGAF)*, which has its origins in the U.S. Department of Defense. It provides an approach to design, implement, and govern an enterprise information architecture.

TOGAF is a framework that can be used to develop the following architecture types:

- Business architecture
- Data architecture
- Applications architecture
- Technology architecture

TOGAF can be used to create these individual architecture types through the use of its *Architecture Development Method (ADM)*. This method is an iterative and cyclic process that allows requirements to be continuously reviewed and the individual architectures updated as needed. These different architectures can allow a technology architect to understand the enterprise from four different views (business, data, application, and technology) so she can ensure her team develops the necessary technology to work within the environment and all the components that make up that environment and meet business requirements. The technology may need to span many different types of networks, interconnect with various software components, and work within different business units. As an analogy, when a new city is being constructed, people do not just start building houses here and there. Civil engineers lay out roads, bridges, waterways, and commercial and housing zoned areas. A large organization that has a distributed and heterogeneous environment that supports many different business functions can be as complex as a city. So before a programmer starts developing code, the architecture of the software needs to be developed in the context of the organization it will work within.

NOTE Many technical people have a negative visceral reaction to models like this. They feel it's too much work, that it's a lot of fluff, is not directly relevant, and so on. If you handed the same group of people a network schematic with firewalls, IDSs, and virtual private networks (VPNs), they would say, "Now we're talking about security!" Security technology works within the construct of an organization, so the organization must be understood also.

Military-Oriented Architecture Frameworks

It is hard enough to construct enterprise-wide solutions and technologies for one organization—think about an architecture that has to span many different complex government agencies to allow for interoperability and proper hierarchical communication channels. This is where the *Department of Defense Architecture Framework (DoDAF)* comes into play. When the U.S. DoD purchases technology products and weapon systems, enterprise architecture documents must be created based upon DoDAF standards to illustrate how they will properly integrate into the current infrastructures. The focus of the architecture framework is on command, control, communications, computers, intelligence, surveillance, and reconnaissance systems and processes. It is not only important that these different devices communicate using the same protocol types and interoperable software components, but also that they use the same data elements. If an image is captured from a spy satellite, downloaded to a centralized data repository, and then loaded into a piece of software to direct an unmanned drone, the military personnel cannot have their operations interrupted because one piece of software cannot read another software's data output. The DoDAF helps ensure that all systems, processes, and personnel work in a concerted effort to accomplish its missions.

The *Ministry of Defence Architecture Framework (MODAF)* developed by the British MOD is another recognized enterprise architecture framework based upon the DoDAF. The crux of the framework is to be able to get data in the right format to the right people as soon as possible. Modern warfare is complex, and activities happen fast, which requires personnel and systems to be more adaptable than ever before. Data needs to be captured and properly presented so that decision makers understand complex issues quickly, which allows for fast and (hopefully) accurate decisions.

NOTE While both DoDAF and MODAF were developed to support mainly military missions, they have been expanded upon and morphed for use in business enterprise environments.

When attempting to figure out which architecture framework is best for your organization, you need to find out who the stakeholders are and what information they need from the architecture. The architecture needs to represent the company in the most useful manner to the people who need to understand it the best. If your company has people (stakeholders) who need to understand the company from a business process perspective, your architecture needs to provide that type of view. If there are people who need to understand the company from an application perspective, your architecture needs a view that illustrates that information. If people need to understand the enterprise from a security point of view, that needs to be illustrated in a specific view. So one main difference between the various enterprise architecture frameworks is what type of information they provide and how they provide it.

Enterprise Security Architecture

An *enterprise security architecture* is a subset of an enterprise architecture and defines the information security strategy that consists of layers of solutions, processes, and procedures and the way they are linked across an enterprise strategically, tactically, and operationally. It is a comprehensive and rigorous method for describing the structure and behavior of all the components that make up a holistic ISMS. The main reason to develop an enterprise security architecture is to ensure that security efforts align with business practices in a standardized and cost-effective manner. The architecture works at an abstraction level and provides a frame of reference. Besides security, this type of architecture allows organizations to better achieve interoperability, integration, ease of use, standardization, and governance.

How do you know if an organization does not have an enterprise security architecture in place? If the answer is "yes" to most of the following questions, this type of architecture is not in place:

- Does security take place in silos throughout the organization?
- Is there a continual disconnect between senior management and the security staff?
- Are redundant products purchased for different departments for overlapping security needs?
- Is the security program made up of mainly policies without actual implementation and enforcement?
- When user access requirements increase because of business needs, does the network administrator just modify the access controls without the user manager's documented approval?

- When a new product is being rolled out, do unexpected interoperability issues pop up that require more time and money to fix?
- Do many "one-off" efforts take place instead of following standardized procedures when security issues arise?
- Are the business unit managers unaware of their security responsibilities and how their responsibilities map to legal and regulatory requirements?
- Is "sensitive data" defined in a policy, but the necessary controls are not fully implemented and monitored?
- Are stovepipe (point) solutions implemented instead of enterprise-wide solutions?
- Are the same expensive mistakes continuing to take place?
- Is security governance currently unavailable because the enterprise is not viewed or monitored in a standardized and holistic manner?
- Are business decisions being made without taking security into account?
- Are security personnel usually putting out fires with no real time to look at and develop strategic approaches?
- Are security efforts taking place in business units that other business units know nothing about?
- Are more and more security personnel seeking out mental health professionals and going on antidepressant or anti-anxiety medication?

If many of these answers are "yes," no useful architecture is in place. Now, the following is something very interesting the authors have seen over several years. Most organizations have multiple problems in the preceding list and yet they focus on each item as if it is unconnected to the other problems. What the CSO, CISO, and/or security administrator does not always understand is that these are just *symptoms* of a treatable disease. The "treatment" is to put one person in charge of a team that develops a phased-approach enterprise security architecture rollout plan. The goals are to integrate technology-oriented and business-centric security processes; link administrative, technical, and physical controls to properly manage risk; and integrate these processes into the IT infrastructure, business processes, and the organization's culture.

The main reason organizations do not develop and roll out an enterprise security architecture is that they do not fully understand what one is and the task seems overwhelming. Fighting fires is more understandable and straightforward, so many companies stay with this familiar approach.

A group developed the *Sherwood Applied Business Security Architecture (SABSA)*, as shown in Table 1-3, which is similar to the Zachman Framework. It is a layered framework, with its first layer defining business requirements from a security perspective. Each layer of the framework decreases in abstraction and increases in detail so it builds upon the others and moves from policy to practical implementation of technology and solutions. The idea is to provide a chain of traceability through the contextual, conceptual, logical, physical, component, and operational levels.

	Assets (What)	Motivation (Why)	Process (How)	People (Who)	Location (Where)	Time (When)
Contextual	The business	Business risk model	Business process model	Business organization and relationships	Business geography	Business time dependencies
Conceptual	Business attributes profile	Control objectives	Security strategies and architectural layering	Security entity model and trust framework	Security domain model	Security-related lifetimes and deadlines
Logical	Business information model	Security policies	Security services	Entity schema and privilege profiles	Security domain definitions and associations	Security processing cycle
Physical	Business data model	Security rules, practices, and procedures	Security mechanisms	Users, applications, and user interface	Platform and network infrastructure	Control structure execution
Component	Detailed data structures	Security standards	Security products and tools	Identities, functions, actions, and ACLs	Processes, nodes, addresses, and protocols	Security step timing and sequencing
Operational	Assurance of operation continuity	Operation risk management	Security service management and support	Application and user management and support	Security of sites, networks, and platforms	Security operations schedule

Table 1-3 SABSA Architecture Framework

The following outlines the questions that are to be asked and answered at each level of the framework:

- ***What* are you trying to do at this layer?** The assets to be protected by your security architecture.
- ***Why* are you doing it?** The motivation for wanting to apply security, expressed in the terms of this layer.
- ***How* are you trying to do it?** The functions needed to achieve security at this layer.
- ***Who* is involved?** The people and organizational aspects of security at this layer.
- ***Where* are you doing it?** The locations where you apply your security, relevant to this layer.
- ***When* are you doing it?** The time-related aspects of security relevant to this layer.

SABSA is a framework and methodology for enterprise security architecture and service management. Since it is a *framework*, this means it provides a structure for individual architectures to be built from. Since it is a *methodology* also, this means it provides the processes to follow to build and maintain this architecture. SABSA provides a life-cycle model so that the architecture can be constantly monitored and improved upon over time.

For an enterprise security architecture to be successful in its development and implementation, the following items must be understood and followed: strategic alignment, business enablement, process enhancement, and security effectiveness.

Strategic Alignment *Strategic alignment* means the business drivers and the regulatory and legal requirements are being met by the security enterprise architecture. Security efforts must provide and support an environment that allows a company to not only survive, but thrive. The security industry has grown up from the technical and engineering world, not the business world. In many organizations, while the IT security personnel and business personnel might be located physically close to each other, they are commonly worlds apart in how they see the same organization they work in. Technology is only a tool that supports a business; it is not the business itself. The IT environment is analogous to the circulatory system within a human body; it is there to support the body—the body does not exist to support the circulatory system. And security is analogous to the immune system of the body—it is there to protect the overall environment. If these critical systems (business, IT, security) do not work together in a concerted effort, there will be deficiencies and imbalances. While deficiencies and imbalances lead to disease in the body, deficiencies and imbalances within an organization can lead to risk and security compromises.

ISMS vs. Security Enterprise Architecture

What is the difference between an ISMS and an enterprise security architecture? An ISMS outlines the controls that need to be put into place (risk management, vulnerability management, business continuity planning, data protection, auditing, configuration management, physical security, etc.) and provides direction on how those controls should be managed throughout their life cycle. The ISMS specifies the pieces and parts that need to be put into place to provide a holistic security program for the organization overall and how to properly take care of those pieces and parts. The enterprise security architecture illustrates how these components are to be integrated into the different layers of the current business environment. The security components of the ISMS have to be interwoven throughout the business environment and not siloed within individual company departments.

For example, the ISMS will dictate that risk management needs to be put in place, and the enterprise architecture will chop up the risk management components and illustrate how risk management needs to take place at the strategic, tactical, and operational levels. As another example, the ISMS could dictate that data protection needs to be put into place. The architecture can show how this happens at the infrastructure, application, component, and business level. At the infrastructure level we can implement data loss protection technology to detect how sensitive data is traversing the network. Applications that maintain sensitive data must have the necessary access controls and cryptographic functionality. The components within the applications can implement the specific cryptographic functions. And protecting sensitive company information can be tied to business drivers, which is illustrated at the business level of the architecture.

The ISO/IEC 27000 series (which outlines the ISMS) is very policy oriented and outlines the necessary components of a security program. This means that the ISO standards are general in nature, which is not a defect—they were created that way so that they could be applied to various types of businesses, companies, and organizations. But since these standards are general, it can be difficult to know how to implement them and map them to your company's infrastructure and business needs. This is where the enterprise security architecture comes into play. The architecture is a tool used to ensure that what is outlined in the security standards is implemented throughout the different layers of an organization.

Business Enablement When looking at the *business enablement* requirement of the security enterprise architecture, we need to remind ourselves that each organization exists for one or more specific business purposes. Publicly traded companies are in the business of increasing shareholder value. Nonprofit organizations are in the business of furthering a specific set of causes. Government organizations are in the business of providing services to their citizens. Companies and organizations do not exist for the sole purpose of being secure. Security cannot stand in the way of business processes, but should be implemented to better enable them.

Business enablement means the core business processes are integrated into the security operating model—they are standards based and follow a risk tolerance criteria. What does this mean in the real world? Let's say a company's accountants have figured out that if they allow the customer service and support staff to work from home, the company would save a lot of money on office rent, utilities, and overhead—plus, the company's insurance would be cheaper. The company could move into this new model with the use of VPNs, firewalls, content filtering, and so on. Security enables the company to move to this different working model by providing the necessary protection mechanisms. If a financial institution wants to enable its customers to view bank account information and carry out money transfers online, it can offer this service if the correct security mechanisms are put in place (access control, authentication, secure connections, etc.). Security should help the organization thrive by providing the mechanisms to do new things safely.

Process Enhancement The *process enhancement* piece can be quite beneficial to an organization if it takes advantage of this capability when it is presented to it. An organization that is serious about securing its environment will have to take a close look at many of the business processes that take place on an ongoing basis. Many times these processes are viewed through the eyeglasses of security, because that's the reason for the activity, but this is a perfect chance to enhance and improve upon the same processes to increase productivity. When you look at many business processes taking place in all types of organizations, you commonly find a duplication of efforts, manual steps that can be easily automated, or ways to streamline and reduce time and effort that are involved in certain tasks. This is commonly referred to as *process reengineering.*

When an organization is developing its security enterprise components, those components must be integrated into the business processes to be effective. This can allow for process management to be refined and calibrated. This allows for security to be integrated in system life cycles and day-to-day operations. So while business enablement means "we can do new stuff," process enhancement means "we can do stuff better."

Security Effectiveness *Security effectiveness* deals with metrics, meeting service level agreement (SLA) requirements, achieving return on investment (ROI), meeting set baselines, and providing management with a dashboard or balanced scorecard system. These are ways to determine how useful the current security solutions and architecture as a whole are performing.

Many organizations are just getting to the security effectiveness point of their architecture, because there is a need to ensure that the controls in place are providing the necessary level of protection and that finite funds are being used properly. Once baselines are set, then metrics can be developed to verify baseline compliancy. These metrics are then rolled up to management in a format they can understand that shows them the health of the organization's security posture and compliance levels. This also allows management to make informed business decisions. Security affects almost everything today in business, so this information should be readily available to senior management in a form they can actually use.

Enterprise vs. System Architectures

There is a difference between enterprise architectures and system architectures, although they do overlap. An enterprise architecture addresses the structure of an organization. A system architecture addresses the structure of software and computing components. While these different architecture types have different focuses (organization versus system), they have a direct relationship because the systems have to be able to support the organization and its security needs. A software architect cannot design an application that will be used within a company without understanding what the company needs the application to do. So the software architect needs to understand the business and technical aspects of the company to ensure that the software is properly developed for the needs of the organization.

It is important to realize that the rules outlined in an organizational security policy have to be supported all the way down to application code, the security kernel of an operating system, and hardware security provided by a computer's CPU. Security has to be integrated at every organizational and technical level if it is going to be successful. This is why some architecture frameworks cover company functionality from the business process level all the way down to how components within an application work. All of this detailed interaction and interdependencies must be understood. Otherwise, the wrong software is developed, the wrong product is purchased, interoperability issues arise, and business functions are only partially supported.

As an analogy, an enterprise and system architecture relationship is similar to the relationship between a solar system and individual planets. A solar system is made up of planets, just like an enterprise is made up of systems. It is very difficult to understand the solar system as a whole while focusing on the specific characteristics of a planet (soil compensation, atmosphere, etc.). It is also difficult to understand the complexities of the individual planets when looking at the solar system as a whole. Each viewpoint (solar system versus planet) has its focus and use. The same is true when viewing an enterprise versus a system architecture. The enterprise view is looking at the whole enchilada, while the system view is looking at the individual pieces that make up that enchilada.

Enterprise Architectures: Scary Beasts

If these enterprise architecture models are new to you and a bit confusing, do not worry; you are not alone. While enterprise architecture frameworks are great tools to understand and help control all the complex pieces within an organization, the security industry is still maturing in its use of these types of architectures. Most companies develop policies and then focus on the technologies to enforce those policies, which skips the whole step of security enterprise development. This is mainly because the information security field is still learning how to grow up and out of the IT department and into established corporate environments. As security and business truly become more intertwined, these enterprise frameworks won't seem as abstract and foreign, but useful tools that are properly leveraged.

Security Controls Development

Up to now we have our ISO/IEC 27000 series, which outlines the necessary components of an organizational security program. We also have our security enterprise architecture, which helps us integrate the requirements outlined in our security program into our existing business structure. Now we are going to get more focused and look at the objectives of the controls we are going to put into place to accomplish the goals outlined in our security program and enterprise architecture.

COBIT

The *Control Objectives for Information and related Technology (COBIT)* is a framework for governance and management developed by ISACA (formerly the Information Systems Audit and Control Association) and the IT Governance Institute (ITGI). It helps organizations optimize the value of their IT by balancing resource utilization, risk levels, and realization of benefits. This is all done by explicitly tying stakeholder drivers to stakeholder needs to organizational goals (to meet those needs) to IT goals (to meet or support the organizational goals). It is a holistic approach based on five key principles:

1. Meeting stakeholder needs
2. Covering the enterprise end to end
3. Applying a single integrated framework
4. Enabling a holistic approach
5. Separating governance from management

Everything in COBIT is ultimately linked to the stakeholders through a series of transforms called cascading goals. The concept is pretty simple. At any point in our IT governance or management processes, we should be able to ask the question "why are we doing this?" and be led to an IT goal that is tied to an enterprise goal, which is in turn tied to a stakeholder need. COBIT specifies 17 enterprise and 17 IT-related goals that take the guesswork out of ensuring we consider all dimensions in our decision-making processes.

These two sets of 17 goals are different but related. They ensure that we meet the second goal of covering the enterprise end to end by explicitly tying enterprise and IT goals in both the governance and management dimensions. They also help us apply a single integrated framework to our organizations, which is the third principle. These 17 goals were identified by looking for commonalities (or perhaps universal features) of a large set of organizations. The purpose of this analysis is to enable a holistic approach, which is our fourth key principle in COBIT.

The COBIT framework includes, but differentiates, enterprise governance and management. The difference between these two is that governance is a set of higher-level processes aimed at balancing the stakeholder value proposition, while management is the set of activities that achieve enterprise objectives. As a simplifying approximation, you can think of governance as the things that the C-suite leaders do and management

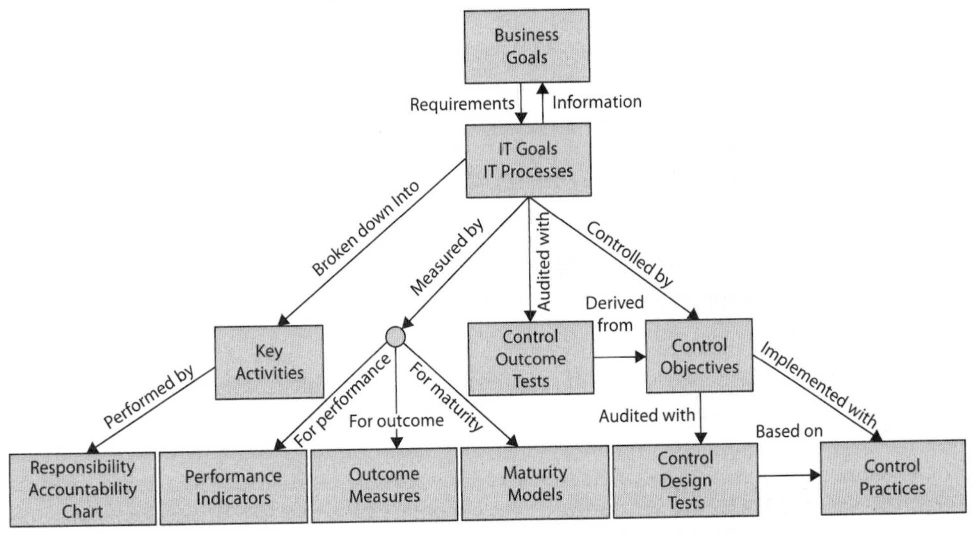

Figure 1-5 COBIT framework

as the things that the other organizational leaders do. Figure 1-5 illustrates how the 37 governance and management processes defined by COBIT are organized.

A majority of the security compliance auditing practices used today in the industry are based off of COBIT. So if you want to make your auditors happy and pass your compliancy evaluations, you should learn, practice, and implement the control objectives outlined in COBIT, which are considered industry best practices.

TIP Many people in the security industry mistakenly assume that COBIT is purely security focused, when in reality it deals with all aspects of information technology, security only being one component. COBIT is a set of practices that can be followed to carry out IT governance, which requires proper security practices.

NIST SP 800-53

COBIT contains control objectives used within the private sector; the U.S. government has its own set of requirements when it comes to controls for federal information systems and organizations.

The National Institute of Standards and Technology (NIST) is a nonregulatory body of the U.S. Department of Commerce and its mission is "...to promote U.S. innovation and industrial competitiveness by advancing measurement science, standards, and technology in ways that enhance economic security and improve quality of life." One of the standards that NIST has been responsible for developing is called Special Publication 800-53, "Security and Privacy Controls for Federal Information Systems and Organizations," which outlines controls that agencies need to put into place to be compliant with the Federal Information Security Management Act of 2002 (FISMA). Table 1-4 outlines the control categories that are addressed in this publication.

Identifier	Family	Class
AC	Access Control	Technical
AT	Awareness and Training	Operational
AU	Audit and Accountability	Technical
CA	Security Assessment and Authorization	Management
CM	Configuration Management	Operational
CP	Contingency Planning	Operational
IA	Identification and Authentication	Technical
IR	Incident Response	Operational
MA	Maintenance	Operational
MP	Media Protection	Operational
PE	Physical and Environmental Protection	Operational
PL	Planning	Management
PM	Program Management	Management
PS	Personnel Security	Operational
RA	Risk Assessment	Management
SA	System and Services Acquisition	Management
SC	System and Communications Protection	Technical
SI	System and Information Integrity	Operational

Table 1-4 NIST SP 800-53 Control Categories

The control categories (families) are the management, operational, and technical controls prescribed for an information system to protect the availability, integrity, and confidentiality of the system and its information.

Just as IS auditors in the commercial sector follow COBIT for their "checklist" approach to evaluating an organization's compliancy with business-oriented regulations, government auditors use SP 800-53 as their "checklist" approach for ensuring that government agencies are compliant with government-oriented regulations. While these control objective checklists are different (COBIT versus SP 800-53), there is extensive overlap because systems and networks need to be protected in similar ways no matter what type of organization they reside in.

EXAM TIP The categorization of controls can be confusing on the CISSP exam. Sometimes it calls out administrative, technical, and physical categories and sometimes it refers to management, technical, and operational control categories. The exam is not contradicting itself. The commercial sector uses the first category set, whereas government-oriented security standards use the second set of categories because historically government agencies and military units have more of an IT operational focus when it comes to securing assets.

COSO Internal Control—Integrated Framework

COBIT was derived from the COSO *Internal Control—Integrated Framework*, developed by the Committee of Sponsoring Organizations (COSO) that sponsored the Treadway Commission in 1985 to deal with fraudulent financial activities and reporting. The COSO IC framework, first released in 1992 and last updated in 2013, identifies 17 internal control principles that are grouped into five internal control components as listed here.

Control Environment:

1. Demonstrates commitment to integrity and ethical values
2. Exercises oversight responsibilities
3. Establishes structure, authority, and responsibility
4. Demonstrates commitment to competence
5. Enforces accountability

Risk Assessment:

6. Specifies suitable objectives
7. Identifies and analyzes risk
8. Assesses fraud risk
9. Identifies and analyzes significant change

Control Activities:

10. Selects and develops control activities
11. Selects and develops general controls over technology
12. Deploys through policies and procedures

Information and Communication:

13. Uses relevant, quality information
14. Communicates internally
15. Communicates externally

Monitoring Activities:

16. Conducts ongoing and/or separate evaluations
17. Evaluates and communicates deficiencies

The COSO IC framework is a model for *corporate* governance, and COBIT is a model for *IT* governance. COSO IC deals more at the strategic level, while COBIT focuses more at the operational level. You can think of COBIT as a way to meet many of the COSO objectives, but only from the IT perspective. COSO IC deals with non-IT items also, as in company culture, financial accounting principles, board of director responsibility, and internal communication structures. COSO IC was formed to provide sponsorship for the National Commission on Fraudulent Financial Reporting, an organization that studied deceptive financial reports and what elements lead to them.

There have been laws in place since the 1970s that basically state that it is illegal for a corporation to "cook its books" (manipulate its revenue and earnings reports), but it took the Sarbanes–Oxley Act (SOX) of 2002 to really put teeth into those existing laws. SOX is a U.S. federal law that, among other things, could send executives to jail if it was discovered that their company was submitting fraudulent accounting findings to the U.S. Securities and Exchange Commission (SEC). SOX is based upon the COSO model, so for a corporation to be compliant with SOX, it has to follow the COSO model. Companies commonly implement ISO/IEC 27000 standards and COBIT to help construct and maintain their internal COSO structure.

EXAM TIP The CISSP exam does not cover specific laws, as in FISMA and SOX, but it does cover the security control model frameworks, as in ISO/IEC 27000 series standards, COBIT, and COSO.

Process Management Development

Along with ensuring that we have the proper controls in place, we also want to have ways to construct and improve our business, IT, and security processes in a structured and controlled manner. The security controls can be considered the "things," and processes are how we use these things. We want to use them properly, effectively, and efficiently.

ITIL

ITIL (formerly the *Information Technology Infrastructure Library*) was developed in the 1980s by the UK's Central Computer and Telecommunications Agency (which was subsumed in the late 1990s by the Office of Government Commerce or OGC). It is now controlled by Axelos, which is a joint venture between the government of the UK and the private firm Capita. ITIL is the de facto standard of best practices for IT service management. ITIL was created because of the increased dependence on information technology to meet business needs. Unfortunately, as previously discussed, a natural divide exists between business people and IT people in most organizations because they use different terminology and have different focuses within the organization. The lack of a common language and understanding of each other's domain (business versus IT) has caused many companies to ineffectively blend their business objectives and IT functions. This improper blending usually generates confusion, miscommunication, missed deadlines, missed opportunities, increased cost in time and labor, and frustration on both the business and technical sides of the house. ITIL is a customizable framework that is provided either in a set of books or in an online format. It provides the goals, the general activities necessary to achieve these goals, and the input and output values for each process required to meet these determined goals. Although ITIL has a component that deals with security, its focus is more toward internal SLAs between the IT department

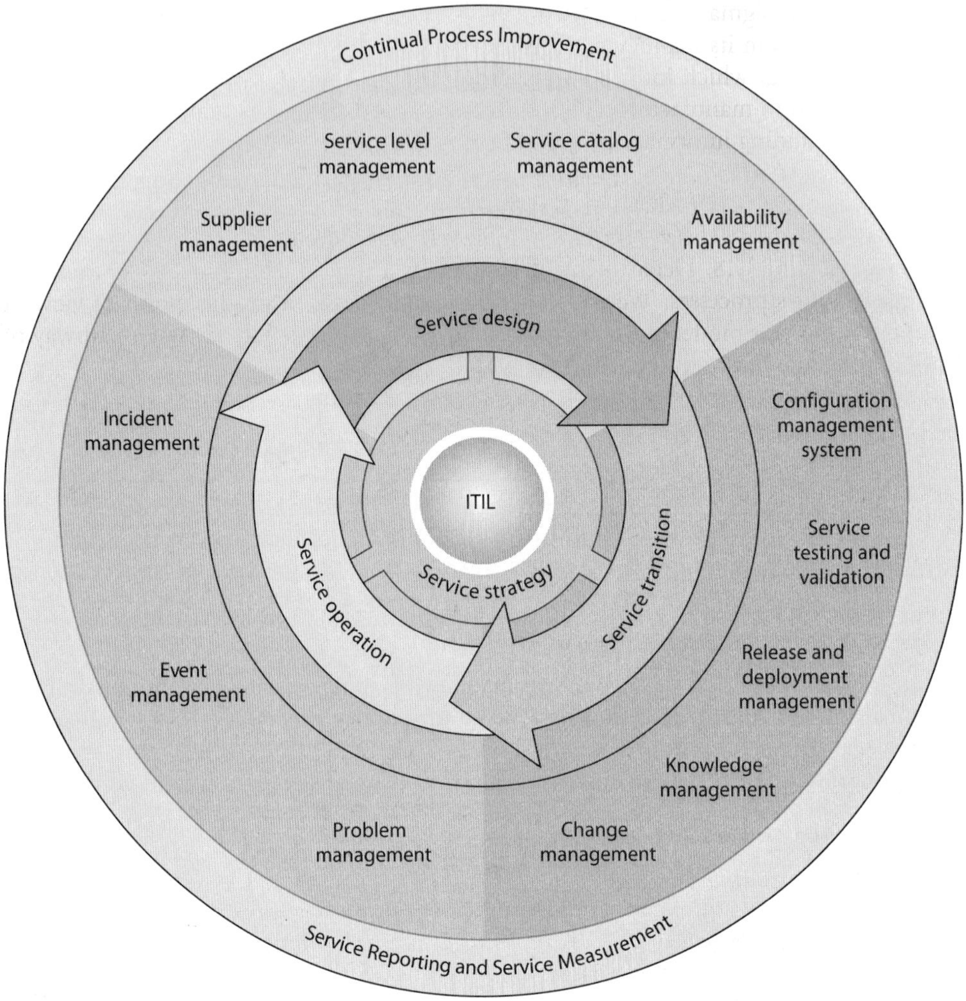

Figure 1-6 ITIL

and the "customers" it serves. The customers are usually internal departments. The main components that make up ITIL are illustrated in Figure 1-6.

Six Sigma

Six Sigma is a process improvement methodology. It is the "new and improved" Total Quality Management (TQM) that hit the business sector in the 1980s. Its goal is to improve process quality by using statistical methods of measuring operation efficiency and reducing variation, defects, and waste. Six Sigma is being used in the security assurance industry in some instances to measure the success factors of different controls and procedures. Six Sigma was developed by Motorola with the goal of identifying and removing defects in its manufacturing processes. The maturity of a process is described by a sigma rating, which indicates the percentage of defects that the process contains. While it started in manufacturing, Six Sigma has been applied to many types of business functions, including information security and assurance.

Capability Maturity Model Integration

Capability Maturity Model Integration (CMMI) was developed by Carnegie Mellon University for the U.S. Department of Defense as a way to determine the maturity of an organization's processes. We will cover it more in depth from that point of view in Chapter 8, but this model is also used within organizations to help lay out a pathway of how incremental improvement can take place.

While we know that we constantly need to make our security program better, it is not always easy to accomplish because "better" is a vague and nonquantifiable concept. The only way we can really improve is to know where we are starting from, where we need to go, and the steps we need to take in between. Every security program has a maturity level, which is illustrated in Figure 1-7. Each maturity level within this CMMI model represents an evolutionary stage. Some security programs are chaotic, ad hoc, unpredictable, and

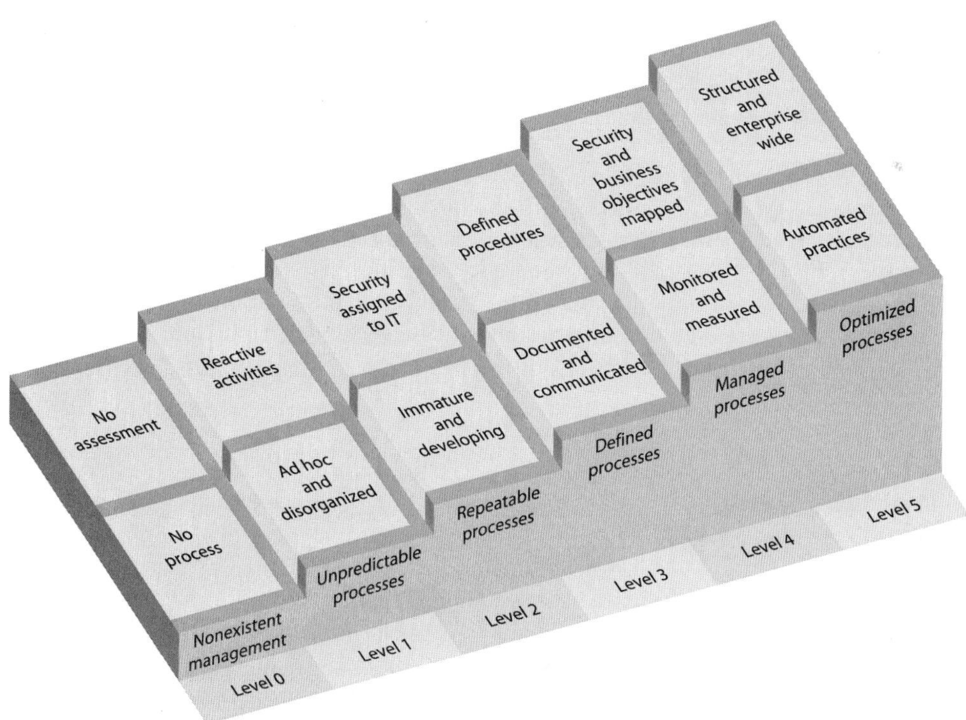

Figure 1-7 Capability Maturity Model for a security program

usually insecure. Some security programs have documentation created, but the actual processes are not taking place. Some security programs are quite evolved, streamlined, efficient, and effective.

EXAM TIP The CISSP exam puts more emphasis on CMMI compared to ITIL and Six Sigma because it is more heavily used in the security industry.

Security Program Development

No organization is going to put all the previously listed items (ISO/IEC 27000, COSO IC, Zachman Framework, SABSA, COBIT, NIST SP 800-53, ITIL, Six Sigma, CMMI) in place. But it is a good toolbox of things you can pull from, and you will find some fit the organization you work in better than others. You will also find that as your organization's security program matures, you will see more clearly where these various standards, frameworks, and management components come into play. While these items are separate and distinct, there are basic things that need to be built in for any security program and its corresponding controls. This is because the basic tenets of security are universal no matter if they are being deployed in a corporation, government agency, business, school, or nonprofit organization. Each entity is made up of people, processes, data, and technology and each of these things needs to be protected.

The crux of CMMI is to develop structured steps that can be followed so an organization can evolve from one level to the next and constantly improve its processes and security posture. A security program contains a lot of elements, and it is not fair to expect them all to be properly implemented within the first year of its existence. And some components, as in forensics capabilities, really cannot be put into place until some rudimentary pieces are established, as in incident management. So if we really want our baby to be able to run, we have to lay out ways that it can first learn to walk.

Top-down Approach

A security program should use a top-down approach, meaning that the initiation, support, and direction come from top management; work their way through middle management; and then reach staff members. In contrast, a bottom-up approach refers to a situation in which staff members (usually IT) try to develop a security program without getting proper management support and direction. A bottom-up approach is commonly less effective, not broad enough to address all security risks, and doomed to fail. A top-down approach makes sure the people actually responsible for protecting the company's assets (senior management) are driving the program. Senior management are not only ultimately responsible for the protection of the organization, but also hold the purse strings for the necessary funding, have the authority to assign needed resources, and are the only ones who can ensure true enforcement of the stated security rules and policies. Management's support is one of the most important pieces of a security program. A simple nod and a wink will not provide the amount of support required.

While the cores of these various security standards and frameworks are similar, it is important to understand that a security program has a life cycle that is always continuing, because it should be constantly evaluated and improved upon. The life cycle of any process can be described in different ways. We will use the following steps:

1. Plan and organize
2. Implement
3. Operate and maintain
4. Monitor and evaluate

Without setting up a life-cycle approach to a security program and the security management that maintains the program, an organization is doomed to treat security as merely another project. Anything treated as a project has a start and stop date, and at the stop date everyone disperses to other projects. Many organizations have had good intentions in their security program kickoffs, but do not implement the proper structure to ensure that security management is an ongoing and continually improving process. The result is a lot of starts and stops over the years and repetitive work that costs more than it should, with diminishing results.

The main components of each phase are provided here.

Plan and Organize:

- Establish management commitment.
- Establish oversight steering committee.
- Assess business drivers.
- Develop a threat profile on the organization.
- Carry out a risk assessment.
- Develop security architectures at business, data, application, and infrastructure levels.
- Identify solutions per architecture level.
- Obtain management approval to move forward.

Implement:

- Assign roles and responsibilities.
- Develop and implement security policies, procedures, standards, baselines, and guidelines.
- Identify sensitive data at rest and in transit.
- Implement the following blueprints:
  - Asset identification and management
  - Risk management
  - Vulnerability management
  - Compliance
  - Identity management and access control
  - Change control
  - Software development life cycle
  - Business continuity planning
  - Awareness and training
  - Physical security
  - Incident response
- Implement solutions (administrative, technical, physical) per blueprint.
- Develop auditing and monitoring solutions per blueprint.
- Establish goals, SLAs, and metrics per blueprint.

Operate and Maintain:

- Follow procedures to ensure all baselines are met in each implemented blueprint.
- Carry out internal and external audits.
- Carry out tasks outlined per blueprint.
- Manage SLAs per blueprint.

Monitor and Evaluate:

- Review logs, audit results, collected metric values, and SLAs per blueprint.
- Assess goal accomplishments per blueprint.
- Carry out quarterly meetings with steering committees.
- Develop improvement steps and integrate into the Plan and Organize phase.

Many of the items mentioned in the previous list are covered throughout this book. This list was provided to show how all of these items can be rolled out in a sequential and controllable manner.

Although the previously covered standards and frameworks are very helpful, they are also very high level. For example, if a standard simply states that an organization must secure its data, a great amount of work will be called for. This is where the security professional really rolls up her sleeves, by developing security blueprints. *Blueprints* are important tools to identify, develop, and design security requirements for specific business needs. These blueprints must be customized to fulfill the organization's security requirements, which are based on its regulatory obligations, business drivers, and legal obligations. For example, let's say Company Y has a data protection policy, and its security team has developed standards and procedures pertaining to the data protection strategy the company should follow. The blueprint will then get more granular and lay out the processes and components necessary to meet requirements outlined in the policy, standards, and requirements. This would include at least a diagram of the company network that illustrates:

- Where the sensitive data resides within the network
- The network segments that the sensitive data transverses
- The different security solutions in place (VPN, TLS, PGP) that protect the sensitive data
- Third-party connections where sensitive data is shared
- Security measures in place for third-party connections
- And more…

The blueprints to be developed and followed depend upon the organization's business needs. If Company Y uses identity management, there must be a blueprint outlining roles, registration management, authoritative source, identity repositories, single sign-on solutions, and so on. If Company Y does not use identity management, there is no need to build a blueprint for this.

So the blueprint will lay out the security solutions, processes, and components the organization uses to match its security and business needs. These blueprints must be applied to the different business units within the organization. For example, the identity management practiced in each of the different departments should follow the crafted blueprint. Following these blueprints throughout the organization allows for standardization, easier metric gathering, and governance. Figure 1-8 illustrates where these blueprints come into play when developing a security program.

To tie these pieces together, you can think of the ISO/IEC 27000 that works mainly at the policy level as a *description* of the type of house you want to build (ranch style, five bedrooms, three baths). The security enterprise framework is the *architecture* layout of the house (foundation, walls, ceilings). The blueprints are the detailed descriptions of specific components of the house (window types, security system, electrical system, plumbing). And the control objectives are the building specifications and codes that need

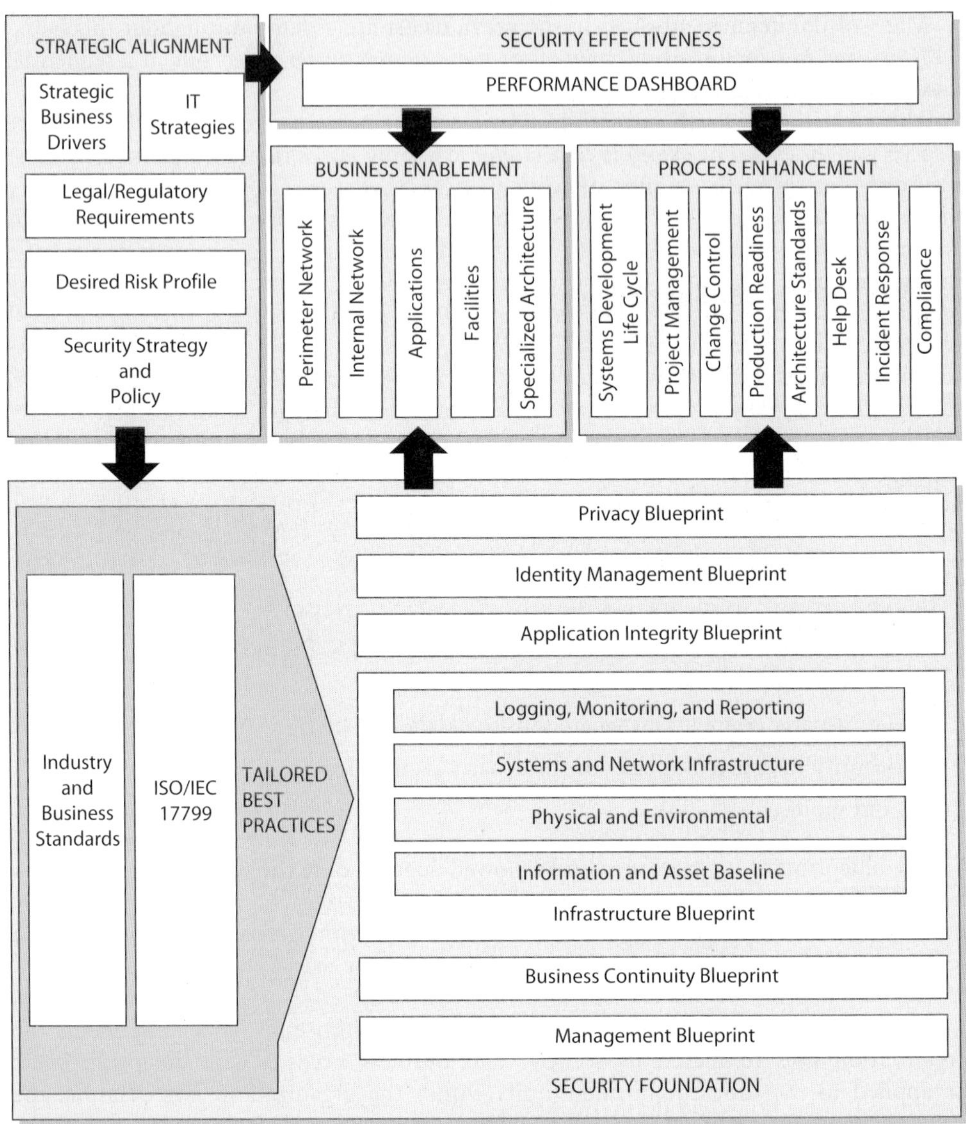

Figure 1-8 Blueprints must map the security and business requirements.

to be met for safety (electrical grounding and wiring, construction material, insulation, and fire protection). A building inspector will use his checklists (building codes) to ensure that you are building your house safely. Which is just like how an auditor will use his checklists (COBIT or NIST SP 800-53) to ensure that you are building and maintaining your security program securely.

Once your house is built and your family moves in, you set up schedules and processes for everyday life to happen in a predictable and efficient manner (dad picks up kids from school, mom cooks dinner, teenager does laundry, dad pays the bills, everyone does yard work). This is analogous to ITIL—process management and improvement. If the family is made up of anal overachievers with the goal of optimizing these daily activities to be as efficient as possible, they could integrate a Six Sigma approach where continual process improvement is a focus.

Functionality vs. Security

Anyone who has been involved with a security initiative understands it involves a balancing act between securing an environment and still allowing the necessary level of functionality so that productivity is not affected. A common scenario that occurs at the start of many security projects is that the individuals in charge of the project know the end result they want to achieve and have lofty ideas of how quick and efficient their security rollout will be, but they fail to consult the users regarding what restrictions will be placed upon them. The users, upon hearing of the restrictions, then inform the project managers that they will not be able to fulfill certain parts of their job if the security rollout actually takes place as planned. This usually causes the project to screech to a halt. The project managers then must initialize the proper assessments, evaluations, and planning to see how the environment can be slowly secured and how to ease users and tasks delicately into new restrictions or ways of doing business. Failing to consult users or to fully understand business processes during the planning phase causes many headaches and wastes time and money. Individuals who are responsible for security management activities must realize they need to understand the environment and plan properly before kicking off the implementation phase of a security program.

The Crux of Computer Crime Laws

The models and frameworks that we have discussed in detail in the preceding sections exist because undesirable things happened and organizations wanted to keep them from happening again. It makes a lot of sense; if you have something in your own house that you don't like, you figure out an effective and repeatable way to correct it. Sometimes, these undesirable things are so bad that they force society at large to enact laws that deter or punish those who would do them. This is where computer crime laws come into play. Sadly, these laws tend to lag years or even decades behind the adoption of the technologies that enable these crimes. Still, significant progress has been made by governments around the globe, as we describe in this section.

Computer crime laws (sometimes referred to as *cyberlaw*) around the world deal with some of the core issues: unauthorized modification or destruction, disclosure of sensitive information, unauthorized access, and the use of malware (malicious software).

Although we usually only think of the victims and their systems that were attacked during a crime, laws have been created to combat three categories of crimes. A *computer-assisted crime* is where a computer was used as a tool to help carry out a crime. A *computer-targeted crime* concerns incidents where a computer was the victim of an attack crafted to harm it (and its owners) specifically. The last type of crime is where a computer is not necessarily the attacker or the attackee, but just happened to be involved when a crime was carried out. This category is referred to as *computer is incidental*.

Some examples of computer-assisted crimes are

- Attacking financial systems to carry out theft of funds and/or sensitive information
- Obtaining military and intelligence material by attacking military systems
- Carrying out industrial spying by attacking competitors and gathering confidential business data
- Carrying out information warfare activities by attacking critical national infrastructure systems
- Carrying out hacktivism, which is protesting a government's or company's activities by attacking its systems and/or defacing its website.

Some examples of computer-targeted crimes include

- Distributed denial-of-service (DDoS) attacks
- Capturing passwords or other sensitive data
- Installing malware with the intent to cause destruction
- Installing rootkits and sniffers for malicious purposes
- Carrying out a buffer overflow to take control of a system

NOTE The main issues addressed in computer crime laws are unauthorized modification, disclosure, destruction, or access and inserting malicious programming code.

Some confusion typically exists between the two categories—computer-assisted crimes and computer-targeted crimes—because intuitively it would seem any attack would fall into both of these categories. One system is carrying out the attacking, while the other system is being attacked. The difference is that in computer-assisted crimes, the computer is only being used as a tool to carry out a traditional type of crime. Without computers, people still steal, cause destruction, protest against companies (for example, companies that carry out experiments upon animals), obtain competitor information, and go to war. So these crimes would take place anyway; it is just that the computer is simply one of the tools available to the evildoer. As such, it helps the evildoer become more efficient at carrying out a crime. Computer-assisted crimes are usually covered by regular criminal laws in that they are not always considered a "computer crime." One way to look at it is that a computer-*targeted* crime could not take place without a computer, whereas a computer-*assisted* crime could. Thus, a computer-targeted crime is one that did not, and could not, exist before computers became of common use. In other words, in the good old days, you could not carry out a buffer overflow on your neighbor or install malware on your enemy's system. These crimes require that computers be involved.

If a crime falls into the "computer is incidental" category, this means a computer just happened to be involved in some secondary manner, but its involvement is still significant. For example, if you had a friend who worked for a company that runs the state lottery and he gives you a printout of the next three winning numbers and you type them into your computer, your computer is just the storage place. You could have just kept the piece of paper and not put the data in a computer. Another example is child pornography. The actual crime is obtaining and sharing child pornography pictures or graphics. The pictures could be stored on a file server or they could be kept in a physical file in someone's desk. So if a crime falls within this category, the computer is not attacking another computer and a computer is not being attacked, but the computer is still used in some significant manner.

You may say, "So what? A crime is a crime. Why break it down into these types of categories?" The reason these types of categories are created is to allow current laws to apply to these types of crimes, even though they are in the digital world. Let's say someone is on your computer just looking around, not causing any damage, but she should not be there. Should the legislation have to create a new law stating, "Thou shall not browse around in someone else's computer," or should we just use the already created trespassing law? What if a hacker got into a system that made all of the traffic lights turn green at the exact same time? Should the government go through the hassle of creating a new law for this type of activity, or should the courts use the already created (and understood) manslaughter and murder laws? Remember, a crime is a crime, and a computer is just a new tool to carry out traditional criminal activities.

Now, this in no way means countries can just depend upon the laws on the books and that every computer crime can be countered by an existing law. Many countries have had to come up with new laws that deal specifically with different types of computer crimes. For example, the following are just *some* of the laws that have been created or modified in the United States to cover the various types of computer crimes:

- 18 USC 1029: Fraud and Related Activity in Connection with Access Devices
- 18 USC 1030: Fraud and Related Activity in Connection with Computers
- 18 USC 2510 et seq.: Wire and Electronic Communications Interception and Interception of Oral Communications
- 18 USC 2701 et seq.: Stored Wire and Electronic Communications and Transactional Records Access
- Digital Millennium Copyright Act
- Cyber Security Enhancement Act of 2002

EXAM TIP You do not need to know these laws for the CISSP exam; they are just examples.

Complexities in Cybercrime

Since we have a bunch of laws to get the digital bad guys, this means we have this whole cybercrime thing under control, right?

Alas, hacking, cracking, and attacking have only increased over the years and will not stop anytime soon. Several issues deal with why these activities have not been properly stopped or even curbed. These include proper identification of the attackers, the necessary level of protection for networks, and successful prosecution once an attacker is captured.

Most attackers are never caught because they spoof their addresses and identities and use methods to cover their footsteps. Many attackers break into networks, take whatever resources they were after, and clean the logs that tracked their movements and activities. Because of this, many companies do not even know they have been violated. Even if an attacker's activities trigger an intrusion detection system (IDS) alert, it does not usually find the true identity of the individual, though it does alert the company that a specific vulnerability was exploited.

Attackers commonly hop through several systems before attacking their victim so that tracking them down will be more difficult. Many of these criminals use innocent people's computers to carry out the crimes for them. The attacker will install malicious software on a computer using many types of methods: e-mail attachments, a user downloading a Trojan horse from a website, exploiting a vulnerability, and so on. Once the software is loaded, it stays dormant until the attacker tells it what systems to attack and when. These compromised systems are called *zombies*, the software installed on them are called *bots*, and when an attacker has several compromised systems, this is known as a *botnet*. The botnet can be used to carry out DDoS attacks, transfer spam or pornography, or do whatever the attacker programs the bot software to do.

Within the United States, local law enforcement departments, the FBI, and the Secret Service are called upon to investigate a range of computer crimes. Although each of these entities works to train its people to identify and track computer criminals, collectively they are very far behind the times in their skills and tools, and are outnumbered by the number of hackers actively attacking networks. Because the attackers use tools that are automated, they can perform several serious attacks in a short timeframe. When law enforcement is called in, its efforts are usually more manual—checking logs, interviewing people, investigating hard drives, scanning for vulnerabilities, and setting up traps in case the attacker comes back. Each agency can spare only a small number of people for computer crimes, and generally they are behind in their expertise compared to many hackers. Because of this, most attackers are never found, much less prosecuted.

Really only a handful of laws deal specifically with computer crimes, making it more challenging to successfully prosecute the attackers who are caught. Many companies that are victims of an attack usually just want to ensure that the vulnerability the attacker exploited is fixed, instead of spending the time and money to go after and prosecute the attacker. (Most common business concerns pertaining to breaches are shown in Figure 1-9.) This is a huge contributing factor as to why cybercriminals get away with their activities. Some regulated organizations—for instance, financial institutions—by law, must report breaches. However, most organizations do not have to report breaches or computer crimes. No company wants its dirty laundry out in

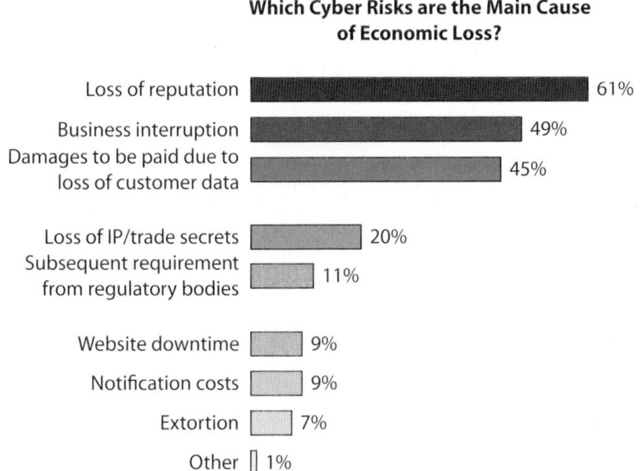

Figure 1-9 Common approaches to security breaches (Source: Allianz Risk Barometer 2015, Allianz Global Corporate & Specialty)

the open for everyone to see. The customer base will lose confidence, as will the shareholders and investors. We do not actually have true computer crime statistics because most are not reported.

Although regulations, laws, and attacks help make senior management more aware of security issues, when their company ends up in the headlines with reports of how they lost control of over 100,000 credit card numbers, security suddenly becomes very important to them.

CAUTION Even though financial institutions must, by law, report security breaches and crimes, that does not mean they all *follow* this law. Some of these institutions, just like many other organizations, often simply fix the vulnerability and sweep the details of the attack under the carpet.

Electronic Assets

Another complexity that the digital world has brought upon society is defining what has to be protected and to what extent. We have gone through a shift in the business world pertaining to assets that need to be protected. Fifteen years ago and more, the assets that most companies concerned themselves with protecting were tangible ones (equipment, building, manufacturing tools, inventory). Now companies must add data to their list of assets, and data is usually at the very top of that list: product blueprints, Social Security numbers, medical information, credit card numbers, personal information, trade secrets, military deployments and strategies, and so on. Although the military has always had to worry about keeping its secrets secret, it has never had so many entry points to the secrets that have to be controlled. Companies are still having a hard time not only protecting their data in digital format, but also defining what constitutes sensitive data and where that data should be kept.

NOTE In many countries, to deal more effectively with computer crime, legislative bodies have broadened the definition of property to include data.

As many companies have discovered, protecting intangible assets (for example, data and reputation) is much more difficult than protecting tangible assets.

The Evolution of Attacks

Perpetrators of cybercrime have evolved from bored teenagers with too much time on their hands to organized crime rings with very defined targets and goals. A few decades ago, hackers were mainly made up of people who just enjoyed the thrill of hacking. It was seen as a challenging game without any real intent of harm. Hackers used to take down large websites (Yahoo!, MSN, Excite) so their activities made the headlines and they won bragging rights among their fellow hackers. Back then, virus writers created viruses that simply replicated or carried out some benign activity, instead of the more malicious actions they could have carried out. Unfortunately, today, these trends have taken on more sinister objectives.

Although we still have script kiddies and people who are just hacking for the fun of it, organized criminals have appeared on the scene and really turned up the heat regarding the amount of damage done. In the past, script kiddies would scan thousands and thousands of systems looking for a specific vulnerability so they could exploit it. It did not matter if the system was on a company network, a government system, or a home user system. The attacker just wanted to exploit the vulnerability and "play" on the system and network from there. Today's attackers are not so noisy, however, and they certainly don't want any attention drawn to themselves. These organized criminals are after specific targets for specific reasons, usually profit oriented. They try and stay under the radar and capture credit card numbers, Social Security numbers, and personal information to carry out fraud and identity theft. Figure 1-10 shows how cybercriminals use compromised computers.

NOTE *Script kiddies* are hackers who do not necessarily have the skill to carry out specific attacks without the tools provided for them on the Internet and through friends. Since these people do not necessarily understand how the attacks are actually carried out, they most likely do not understand the extent of damage they can cause.

Many times hackers are just scanning systems looking for a vulnerable running service or sending out malicious links in e-mails to unsuspecting victims. They are just looking for any way to get into any network. This would be the shotgun approach to network attacks. Another, more dangerous attacker has you in his crosshairs and he is determined to identify your weakest point and do with you what he will.

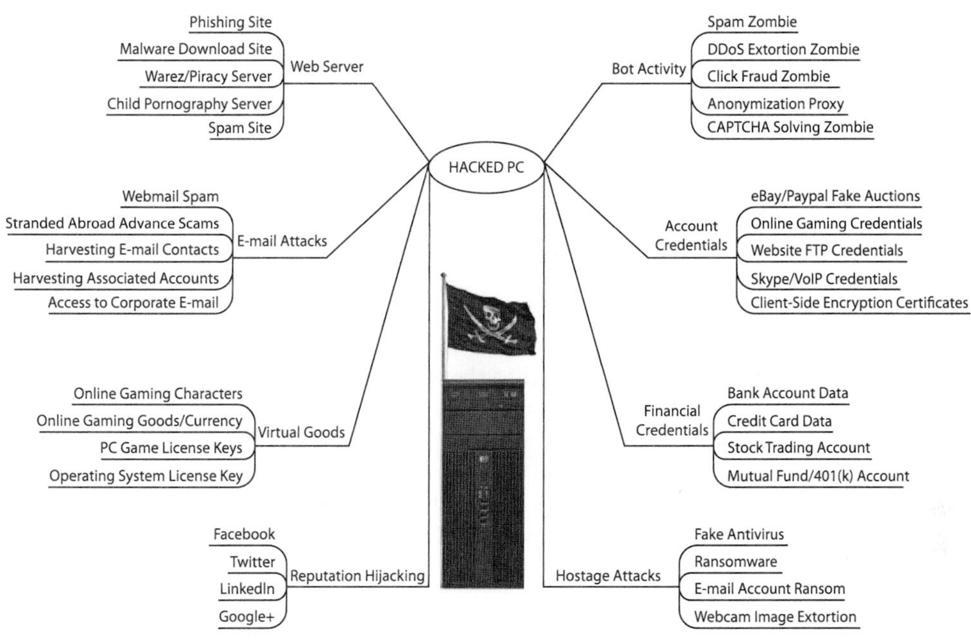

Figure 1-10 Malicious uses for a compromised computer (Source: www.krebsonsecurity.com)

As an analogy, the thief that goes around rattling door knobs to find one that is not locked is not half as dangerous as the one who will watch you day in and day out to learn your activity patterns, where you work, what type of car you drive, and who your family is and patiently wait for your most vulnerable moment to ensure a successful and devastating attack.

In the computing world, we call this second type of attacker an *advanced persistent threat (APT)*. This is a military term that has been around for ages, but since the digital world is becoming more of a battleground, this term is more relevant each and every day. How APTs differ from the regular old vanilla attacker is that it is commonly a group of attackers, not just one hacker, who combines knowledge and abilities to carry out whatever exploit that will get them into the environment they are seeking. The APT is very focused and motivated to aggressively and successfully penetrate a network with variously different attack methods and then clandestinely hide its presence while achieving a well-developed, multilevel foothold in the environment. The "advanced" aspect of this term pertains to the expansive knowledge, capabilities, and skill base of the APT. The "persistent" component has to do with the fact that the group of attackers is not in a hurry to launch an attack quickly, but will wait for the most beneficial moment and attack vector to ensure that its activities go unnoticed. This is what we refer to as a "low-and-slow" attack. This type of attack is coordinated by human involvement, rather than just a virus-type of threat that goes through automated steps to inject its payload. The APT has specific objectives and goals and is commonly highly organized and well funded, which makes it the biggest threat of all.

An APT is commonly custom-developed malicious code that is built specifically for its target, has multiple ways of hiding itself once it infiltrates the environment, may be able to polymorph itself in replication capabilities, and has several different "anchors" so eradicating it is difficult if it is discovered. Once the code is installed, it commonly sets up a covert back channel (as regular bots do) so that it can be remotely controlled by the group of attackers. The remote control functionality allows the attackers to transverse the network with the goal of gaining continuous access to critical assets.

APT infiltrations are usually very hard to detect with host-based solutions because the attackers put the code through a barrage of tests against the most up-to-date detection applications on the market. A common way to detect these types of threats is through network traffic changes. When there is a new Internet Relay Chat (IRC) connection from a host, that is a good indication that the system has a bot communicating to its command center. Since several technologies are used in environments today to detect just that type of traffic, the APT may have multiple control centers to communicate with so that if one connection gets detected and removed, the APT still has an active channel to use. The APT may implement some type of VPN connection so that its data that is in transmission cannot be inspected. Figure 1-11 illustrates the common steps and results of APT activity.

The ways of getting into a network are basically endless (exploit a web service, induce users to open e-mail links and attachments, gain access through remote maintenance accounts, exploit operating systems and application vulnerabilities, compromise connections from home users, etc.). Each of these vulnerabilities has its own fixes (patches, proper configuration, awareness, proper credential practices, encryption, etc.). It is not only these fixes that need to be put in place; we need to move to a more effective

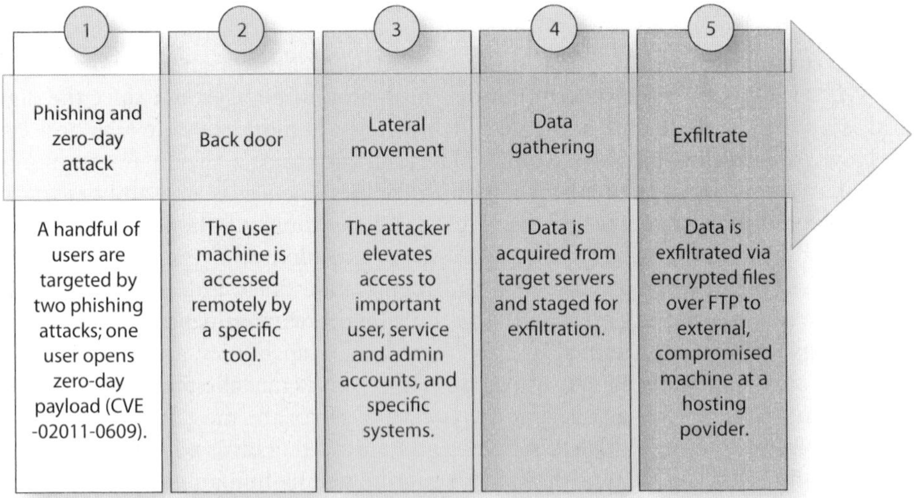

1	2	3	4	5
Phishing and zero-day attack	Back door	Lateral movement	Data gathering	Exfiltrate
A handful of users are targeted by two phishing attacks; one user opens zero-day payload (CVE -02011-0609).	The user machine is accessed remotely by a specific tool.	The attacker elevates access to important user, service and admin accounts, and specific systems.	Data is acquired from target servers and staged for exfiltration.	Data is exfiltrated via encrypted files over FTP to external, compromised machine at a hosting povider.

Figure 1-11 Gaining access into an environment and extracting sensitive data

situational awareness model. We need to have better capabilities of knowing what is happening throughout our network in near to real time so that our defenses can react quickly and precisely.

Our battlefield landscape is changing from "smash-and-grab" attacks to "slow-and-determined" attacks. Just like military offensive practices evolve and morph as the target does the same, so must we as an industry.

We have already seen a decrease in the amount of viruses created just to populate as many systems as possible, and it is predicted that this benign malware activity will continue to decrease, while more dangerous malware increases. This more dangerous malware has more focused targets and more powerful payloads—usually installing back doors, bots, and/or loading rootkits.

Common Internet Crime Schemes

- Auction fraud
- Counterfeit cashier's check
- Debt elimination
- Parcel courier e-mail scheme
- Employment/business opportunities
- Escrow services fraud
- Investment fraud
- Lotteries
- Nigerian letter, or "419"
- Ponzi/pyramid
- Reshipping
- Third-party receiver of funds

Find out how these types of computer crimes are carried out by visiting www.ic3.gov/crimeschemes.aspx.

So while the sophistication of the attacks continues to increase, so does the danger of these attacks. Isn't that just peachy?

Up until now, we have listed some difficulties of fighting cybercrime: the anonymity the Internet provides the attacker; attackers are organizing and carrying out more sophisticated attacks; the legal system is running to catch up with these types of crimes; and companies are just now viewing their data as something that must be protected. All these complexities aid the bad guys, but what if we throw in the complexity of attacks taking place between different countries?

Do You Trust Your Neighbor?

Most organizations do not like to think about the fact that the enemy might be inside and working internally to the company. It is more natural to view threats as the faceless unknowns that reside on the outside of our environment. Employees have direct and privileged access to a company's assets, and they are commonly not as highly monitored compared to traffic that is entering the network from external entities. The combination of too much trust, direct access, and the lack of monitoring allows for a lot of internal fraud and abuse to go unnoticed.

There have been many criminal cases over the years where employees at various companies have carried out embezzlement or have carried out revenge attacks after they were fired or laid off. While it is important to have fortified walls to protect us from the outside forces that want to cause us harm, it is also important to realize that our underbelly is more vulnerable. Employees, contractors, and temporary workers who have direct access to critical resources introduce risks that need to be understood and countermeasured.

International Issues

If a hacker in Ukraine attacked a bank in France, whose legal jurisdiction is that? How do these countries work together to identify the criminal and carry out justice? Which country is required to track down the criminal? And which country should take this person to court? Well, we don't really know exactly. We are still working this stuff out.

When computer crime crosses international boundaries, the complexity of such issues shoots up considerably and the chances of the criminal being brought to any court decreases. This is because different countries have different legal systems, some countries have no laws pertaining to computer crime, jurisdiction disputes may erupt, and some governments may not want to play nice with each other. For example, if someone in Iran attacked a system in Israel, do you think the Iranian government would help Israel track down the attacker? What if someone in North Korea attacked a military system in the United States? Do you think these two countries would work together to find the hacker? Maybe or maybe not—or perhaps the attack was carried out by their specific government.

There have been efforts to standardize the different countries' approaches to computer crimes because they happen so easily over international boundaries. Although it is very easy for an attacker in China to send packets through the Internet to a bank in Saudi Arabia, it is very difficult (because of legal systems, cultures, and politics) to motivate these governments to work together.

The *Council of Europe (CoE) Convention on Cybercrime* is one example of an attempt to create a standard international response to cybercrime. In fact, it is the first international treaty seeking to address computer crimes by coordinating national laws and improving investigative techniques and international cooperation. The convention's objectives include the creation of a framework for establishing jurisdiction and extradition of the accused. For example, extradition can only take place when the event is a crime in both jurisdictions.

Many companies communicate internationally every day through e-mail, telephone lines, satellites, fiber cables, and long-distance wireless transmission. It is important for a company to research the laws of different countries pertaining to information flow and privacy.

Global organizations that move data across other country boundaries must be aware of and follow the Organisation for Economic Co-operation and Development (OECD) *Guidelines on the Protection of Privacy and Transborder Flows of Personal Data*. Since most countries have a different set of laws pertaining to the definition of private data and how it should be protected, international trade and business get more convoluted and can negatively affect the economy of nations. The OECD is an international organization that helps different governments come together and tackle the economic, social, and governance challenges of a globalized economy. Because of this, the OECD came up with guidelines for the various countries to follow so that data is properly protected and everyone follows the same type of rules.

The core principles defined by the OECD are as follows:

- **Collection Limitation Principle** Collection of personal data should be limited, obtained by lawful and fair means, and with the knowledge of the subject.
- **Data Quality Principle** Personal data should be kept complete and current, and be relevant to the purposes for which it is being used.
- **Purpose Specification Principle** Subjects should be notified of the reason for the collection of their personal information at the time that it is collected, and organizations should only use it for that stated purpose.
- **Use Limitation Principle** Only with the consent of the subject or by the authority of law should personal data be disclosed, made available, or used for purposes other than those previously stated.
- **Security Safeguards Principle** Reasonable safeguards should be put in place to protect personal data against risks such as loss, unauthorized access, modification, and disclosure.
- **Openness Principle** Developments, practices, and policies regarding personal data should be openly communicated. In addition, subjects should be able to easily establish the existence and nature of personal data, its use, and the identity and usual residence of the organization in possession of that data.
- **Individual Participation Principle** Subjects should be able to find out whether an organization has their personal information and what that information is, to correct erroneous data, and to challenge denied requests to do so.
- **Accountability Principle** Organizations should be accountable for complying with measures that support the previous principles.

NOTE Information on OECD Guidelines can be found at www.oecd.org/sti/ieconomy/oecdguidelinesontheprotectionofprivacyandtransborderflowsofpersonaldata.htm.

Although the OECD is a great start, we still have a long way to go to standardize how cybercrime is dealt with internationally.

Organizations that are not aware of and/or do not follow these types of rules and guidelines can be fined and found criminally negligent, their business can be disrupted, or they can go out of business. If your company is expecting to expand globally, it would be wise to have legal counsel that understands these types of issues so this type of trouble does not find its way to your company's doorstep.

The European Union (EU) in many cases takes individual privacy much more seriously than most other countries in the world, so the EU has strict laws pertaining to data that is considered private, which are based on the *European Union Principles on Privacy*. This set of principles addresses using and transmitting information considered private in nature. The principles and how they are to be followed are encompassed within the EU's *Data Protection Directive*. All states in Europe must abide by these principles to be in compliance, and any company that wants to do business with an EU company must comply with this directive if the business will include exchanging privacy type of data.

A construct that outlines how U.S.-based companies can comply with the EU privacy principles has been developed, which is called the Safe Harbor Privacy Principles. If a non-European organization wants to do business with a European entity, it will need to adhere to the *Safe Harbor* requirements if certain types of data will be passed back and forth during business processes. Europe has always had tighter control over protecting privacy information than the United States and other parts of the world. So in the past when U.S. and European companies needed to exchange data, confusion erupted and business was interrupted because the lawyers had to get involved to figure out how to work within the structures of the differing laws. To clear up this mess, a "safe harbor" framework was created, which outlines how any entity that is going to move privacy data to and from Europe must go about protecting it. U.S. companies that deal with European entities can become certified against this rule base so data transfer can happen more quickly and easily. The privacy data protection rules that must be met to be considered "Safe Harbor" compliant are listed here:

NOTE The European Union Court of Justice ruled in early October 2015 that the Safe Harbor pact violates privacy because U.S. intelligence services could get their hands on European citizens' data. As of this writing, the EU and United States were renegotiating a pact that would satisfy the courts.

- **Notice** Individuals must be informed that their data is being collected and about how it will be used.
- **Choice** Individuals must have the ability to opt out of the collection and forward transfer of the data to third parties.
- **Onward Transfer** Transfers of data to third parties may only occur to other organizations that follow adequate data protection principles.
- **Security** Reasonable efforts must be made to prevent loss of collected information.

- **Data Integrity** Data must be relevant and reliable for the purpose it was collected for.
- **Access** Individuals must be able to access information held about them and correct or delete it if it is inaccurate.
- **Enforcement** There must be effective means of enforcing these rules.

Import/Export Legal Requirements

Another complexity that comes into play when an organization is attempting to work with organizations in other parts of the world is import and export laws. Each country has its own specifications when it comes to what is allowed in its borders and what is allowed out. For example, the *Wassenaar Arrangement* implements export controls for "Conventional Arms and Dual-Use Goods and Technologies." It is currently made up of 41 countries and lays out rules on how the following items can be exported from country to country:

- **Category 1** Special Materials and Related Equipment
- **Category 2** Materials Processing
- **Category 3** Electronics
- **Category 4** Computers
- **Category 5** Part 1: Telecommunications
- **Category 5** Part 2: Information Security
- **Category 6** Sensors and Lasers
- **Category 7** Navigation and Avionics
- **Category 8** Marine
- **Category 9** Aerospace and Propulsion

The main goal of this arrangement is to prevent the buildup of military capabilities that could threaten regional and international security and stability. So everyone is keeping an eye on each other to make sure no one country's weapons can take everyone else out. The idea is to try and make sure everyone has similar military offense and defense capabilities with the hope that we won't end up blowing each other up.

One item the agreement deals with is cryptography, which is seen as a dual-use good. It can be used for military and civilian uses. It is seen to be dangerous to export products with cryptographic functionality to countries that are in the "offensive" column, meaning that they are thought to have friendly ties with terrorist organizations and/or want to take over the world through the use of weapons of mass destruction. If the "good" countries allow the "bad" countries to use cryptography, then the "good" countries cannot snoop and keep tabs on what the "bad" countries are up to.

The specifications of the Wassenaar Arrangement are complex and always changing. The countries that fall within the "good" and "bad" categories change and what can be exported to who and how changes. In some cases, no products that contain cryptographic functions can be exported to a specific country, a different country could be allowed products with limited cryptographic functions, some countries require certain licenses to be granted, and then other countries (the "good" countries) have no restrictions.

While the Wassenaar Arrangement deals mainly with the exportation of items, some countries (China, Russia, Iran, Iraq, etc.) have cryptographic *import* restrictions that have to be understood and followed. These countries do not allow their citizens to use cryptography because they follow the Big Brother approach to governing people.

This obviously gets very complex for companies who sell products that use integrated cryptographic functionality. One version of the product may be sold to China if it has no cryptographic functionality. Another version may be sold to Russia if a certain international license is in place. A fully functioning product can be sold to Canada, because who are they ever going to hurt?

It is important to understand the import and export requirements your company must meet when interacting with entities in other parts of the world. You could be breaking a country's law or an international treaty if you do not get the right type of lawyers involved in the beginning and follow the approved processes.

Types of Legal Systems

As stated earlier, different countries often have different legal systems. In this section, we will cover the core components of these systems and what differentiates them.

Civil (Code) Law System

- System of law used in continental European countries such as France and Spain.
- Different legal system from the common law system used in the United Kingdom and United States.
- Civil law system is rule-based law not precedence based.
- For the most part, a civil law system is focused on codified law—or written laws.
- The history of the civil law system dates to the sixth century when the Byzantine emperor Justinian codified the laws of Rome.
- Civil *legal systems* should not be confused with the civil (or tort) *laws* found in the United States.
- The civil legal system was established by states or nations for self-regulation; thus, the civil law system can be divided into subdivisions, such as French civil law, German civil law, and so on.
- It is the most widespread legal system in the world and the most common legal system in Europe.
- Under the civil legal system, lower courts are not compelled to follow the decisions made by higher courts.

Common Law System

- Developed in England.
- Based on previous interpretations of laws:
  - In the past, judges would walk throughout the country enforcing laws and settling disputes.
  - They did not have a written set of laws, so they based their laws on custom and precedent.
  - In the 12th century, the king of England (Henry II) imposed a unified legal system that was "common" to the entire country.
  - Reflects the community's morals and expectations.
  - Led to the creation of barristers, or lawyers, who actively participate in the litigation process through the presentation of evidence and arguments.
- Today, the common law system uses judges and juries of peers. If the jury trial is waived, the judge decides the facts.
- Typical systems consist of a higher court, several intermediate appellate courts, and many local trial courts. Precedent flows down through this system. Tradition also allows for "magistrate's courts," which address administrative decisions.
- The common law system is broken down into criminal, civil/tort, and administrative.

Criminal:

- Based on common law, statutory law, or a combination of both.
- Addresses behavior that is considered harmful to society.
- Punishment usually involves a loss of freedom, such as incarceration, or monetary fines.
- Responsibility is on the prosecution to prove guilt beyond a reasonable doubt (innocent until proven guilty).

Civil/tort:

- Offshoot of criminal law.
- Under civil law, the defendant owes a legal duty to the victim. In other words, the defendant is obligated to conform to a particular standard of conduct, usually set by what a "reasonable man of ordinary prudence" would do to prevent foreseeable injury to the victim.
- The defendant's breach of that duty causes injury to the victim; usually physical or financial.

- Categories of civil law:
  - **Intentional** Examples include assault, intentional infliction of emotional distress, or false imprisonment.
  - **Wrongs against property** An example is nuisance against landowner.
  - **Wrongs against a person** Examples include car accidents, dog bites, and a slip and fall.
  - **Negligence** An example is wrongful death.
  - **Nuisance** An example is trespassing.
  - **Dignitary wrongs** Include invasion of privacy and civil rights violations.
  - **Economic wrongs** Examples include patent, copyright, and trademark infringement.
  - **Strict liability** Examples include a failure to warn of risks and defects in product manufacturing or design.

Administrative (regulatory):

- Laws and legal principles created by administrative agencies to address a number of areas, including international trade, manufacturing, environment, and immigration.

Customary Law System

- Deals mainly with personal conduct and patterns of behavior.
- Based on traditions and customs of the region.
- Emerged when cooperation of individuals became necessary as communities merged.
- Not many countries work under a purely customary law system, but instead use a mixed system where customary law is an integrated component. (Codified civil law systems emerged from customary law.)
- Mainly used in regions of the world that have mixed legal systems (for example, China and India).
- Restitution is commonly in the form of a monetary fine or service.

Religious Law System

- Based on religious beliefs of the region.
  - In Islamic countries, the law is based on the rules of the Koran.
  - The law, however, is different in every Islamic country.
  - Jurists and clerics have a high degree of authority.

- Cover all aspects of human life, but commonly divided into:
  - Responsibilities and obligations to others.
  - Religious duties.
- Knowledge and rules as revealed by God, which define and govern human affairs.
- Rather than create laws, lawmakers and scholars attempt to discover the truth of law.
- Law, in the religious sense, also includes codes of ethics and morality, which are upheld and required by God. For example, Hindu law, Sharia (Islamic law), Halakha (Jewish law), and so on.

Mixed Law System

- Two or more legal systems are used together and apply cumulatively or interactively.
- Most often mixed law systems consist of civil and common law.
- A combination of systems is used as a result of more or less clearly defined fields of application.
- Civil law may apply to certain types of crimes, while religious law may apply to other types within the same region.
- Examples of mixed law systems include those in Holland, Canada, and South Africa.

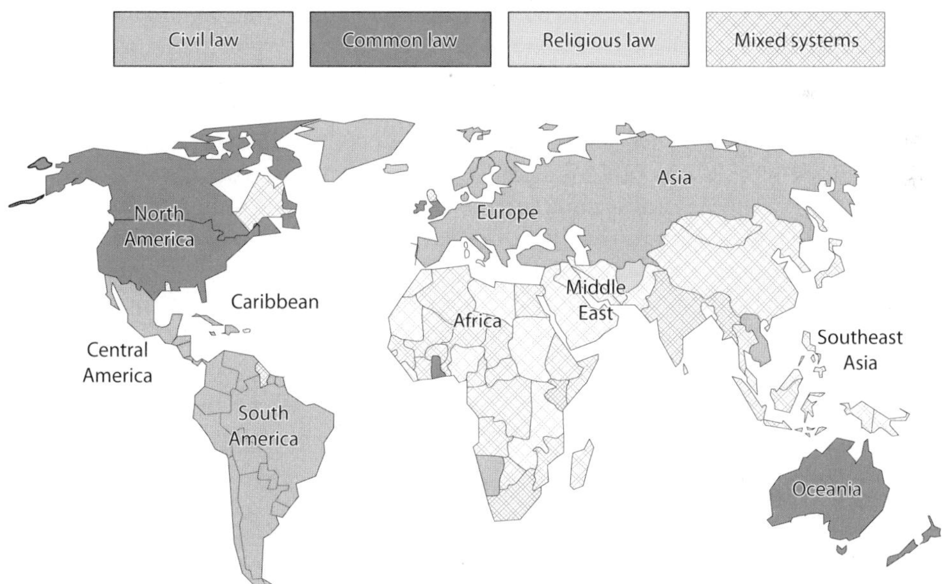

These different legal systems are certainly complex, and while you are not expected to be a lawyer to pass the CISSP exam, having a high-level understanding of the different types (civil, common, customary, religious, mixed) is important. The exam will dig more into the specifics of the common law legal system and its components. Under the common law legal system, *civil law* deals with wrongs against individuals or companies that result in damages or loss. This is referred to as *tort law.* Examples include trespassing, battery, negligence, and product liability. A successful civil lawsuit against a defendant would result in financial restitution and/or community service instead of a jail sentence. When someone sues another person in civil court, the jury decides upon *liability* instead of innocence or guilt. If the jury determines the defendant is liable for the act, then the jury decides upon the compensatory and/or punitive damages of the case.

Criminal law is used when an individual's conduct violates the government laws, which have been developed to protect the public. Jail sentences are commonly the punishment for criminal law cases that result in conviction, whereas in civil law cases the punishment is usually an amount of money that the liable individual must pay the victim. For example, in the O.J. Simpson case, the defendant was first tried and found not guilty in the criminal law case, but then was found liable in the civil law case. This seeming contradiction can happen because the burden of proof is lower in civil cases than in criminal cases.

EXAM TIP Civil law generally is derived from common law (case law), cases are initiated by private parties, and the defendant is found liable or not liable for damages. Criminal law typically is statutory, cases are initiated by government prosecutors, and the defendant is found guilty or not guilty.

Administrative/regulatory law deals with regulatory standards that regulate performance and conduct. Government agencies create these standards, which are usually applied to companies and individuals within those specific industries. Some examples of administrative laws could be that every building used for business must have a fire detection and suppression system, must have clearly visible exit signs, and cannot have blocked doors, in case of a fire. Companies that produce and package food and drug products are regulated by many standards so that the public is protected and aware of their actions. If an administrative law case determines that a company did not abide by specific regulatory standards, high officials in the company could even be held accountable. For example, if a company makes tires that shred after a couple of years of use because the company doesn't comply with manufacturing safety standards, the officers in that company could be liable under administrative, civil, or even criminal law if they were aware of the issue but chose to ignore it to keep profits up.

Intellectual Property Laws

Intellectual property laws do not necessarily look at who is right or wrong, but rather how a company or individual can protect what it rightfully owns from unauthorized duplication or use, and what it can do if these laws are violated.

A major issue in many intellectual property cases is what the company did to protect the resources it claims have been violated in one fashion or another. A company must implement safeguards to protect resources that it claims to be intellectual property and must show that it exercised due care (reasonable acts of protection) in its efforts to protect those resources. For example, if an employee sends a file to a friend and the company terminates the employee based on the activity of illegally sharing intellectual property, then in a wrongful termination case brought by the employee, the company must show the court why this file is so important to the company, what type of damage could be or has been caused as a result of the file being shared, and, most important, what the company had done to protect that file. If the company did not secure the file and tell its employees that they were not allowed to copy and share that file, then the company will most likely lose the case. However, if the company implemented safeguards to protect that file and had an acceptable use policy in its employee manual that explained that copying and sharing the information within the file was prohibited and that the punishment for doing so could be termination, then the company could not be found liable of wrongfully terminating the employee.

Intellectual property can be protected by several different laws, depending upon the type of resource it is. Intellectual property is divided into two categories: industrial property—such as inventions (patents), industrial designs, and trademarks—and copyrighted property, which covers things like literary and artistic works. These topics are addressed in depth in the following sections.

Trade Secret

Trade secret law protects certain types of information or resources from unauthorized use or disclosure. For a company to have its resource qualify as a trade secret, the resource must provide the company with some type of competitive value or advantage. A trade secret can be protected by law if developing it requires special skill, ingenuity, and/or expenditure of money and effort. This means that a company cannot say the sky is blue and call it a trade secret.

A *trade secret* is something that is proprietary to a company and important for its survival and profitability. An example of a trade secret is the formula used for a soft drink, such as Coke or Pepsi. The resource that is claimed to be a trade secret must be confidential and protected with certain security precautions and actions. A trade secret could also be a new form of mathematics, the source code of a program, a method of making the perfect jelly bean, or ingredients for a special secret sauce. A trade secret has no expiration date unless the information is no longer secret or no longer provides economic benefit to the company.

Many companies require their employees to sign a nondisclosure agreement (NDA), confirming that they understand its contents and promise not to share the company's trade secrets with competitors or any unauthorized individuals. Companies require this both to inform the employees of the importance of keeping certain information secret and to deter them from sharing this information. Having them sign the NDA also gives the company the right to fire the employee or bring charges if the employee discloses a trade secret.

A low-level engineer working at Intel took trade secret information that was valued by Intel at $1 billion when he left his position at the company and went to work at his new employer, rival chipmaker Advanced Micro Devices (AMD). It was discovered that this person still had access to Intel's most confidential information even after starting work at AMD. He even used the laptop that Intel provided to him to download 13 critical documents that contained extensive information about the company's new processor developments and product releases. Unfortunately, these stories are not rare, and companies are constantly dealing with challenges of protecting the very data that keeps them in business.

Copyright

In the United States, *copyright law* protects the right of the creator of an original work to control the public distribution, reproduction, display, and adaptation of that original work. The law covers many categories of work: pictorial, graphic, musical, dramatic, literary, pantomime, motion picture, sculptural, sound recording, and architectural. Copyright law does not cover the specific resource, as does trade secret law. It protects the *expression* of the idea of the resource instead of the resource itself. A copyright is usually used to protect an author's writings, an artist's drawings, a programmer's source code, or specific rhythms and structures of a musician's creation. Computer programs and manuals are just two examples of items protected under the Federal Copyright Act. The program or manual is covered under copyright law once it has been written. Although including a warning and the copyright symbol (©) is not required, doing so is encouraged so others cannot claim innocence after copying another's work.

The protection does not extend to any method of operations, process, concept, or procedure, but it does protect against unauthorized copying and distribution of a protected work. It protects the form of expression rather than the subject matter. A patent deals more with the subject matter of an invention; copyright deals with how that invention is represented. In that respect, copyright is weaker than patent protection, but the duration of copyright protection is longer. People are provided copyright protection for life plus 50 years.

Computer programs can be protected under the copyright law as literary works. The law protects both the source and object code, which can be an operating system, application, or database. In some instances, the law can protect not only the code, but also the structure, sequence, and organization. The user interface is part of the definition of a software application structure; therefore, one vendor cannot copy the exact composition of another vendor's user interface.

Copyright infringement cases have exploded in numbers since the rise of "warez" sites that use the common BitTorrent protocol. BitTorrent is a peer-to-peer file sharing protocol and is one of the most common protocols for transferring large files. Warez is a term that refers to copyrighted works distributed or traded without fees or royalties, in general violation of the copyright law. The term generally refers to unauthorized releases by groups, as opposed to file sharing between friends.

Once a warez site posts copyrighted material, it is very difficult to have it removed because law enforcement is commonly overwhelmed with larger criminal cases and does not have the bandwidth to go after these "small fish." Another issue with warez sites is that the actual servers may reside in another country; thus, legal jurisdiction makes things more difficult and the country that the server resides within may not even have a copyright law.

The film and music recording companies have had the most success in going after these types of offenders because they have the funds and vested interest to do so.

Trademark

A *trademark* is slightly different from a copyright in that it is used to protect a word, name, symbol, sound, shape, color, or combination of these. The reason a company would trademark one of these, or a combination, is that it represents the company (brand identity) to a group of people or to the world. Companies have marketing departments that work very hard to create something new that will cause the company to be noticed and stand out in a crowd of competitors, and trademarking the result of this work with a government registrar is a way of properly protecting it and ensuring others cannot copy and use it.

Companies cannot trademark a number or common word. This is why companies create new names—for example, Intel's Pentium and Standard Oil's Exxon. However, unique colors can be trademarked, as well as identifiable packaging, which is referred to as "trade dress." Thus, Novell Red and UPS Brown are trademarked, as are some candy wrappers.

NOTE In 1883, international harmonization of trademark laws began with the Paris Convention, which in turn prompted the Madrid Agreement of 1891. Today, international trademark law efforts and international registration are overseen by the World Intellectual Property Organization (WIPO), an agency of the United Nations.

There have been many interesting trademark legal battles over the years. In one case a person named Paul Specht started a company named "Android Data" and had his company's trademark approved in 2002. Specht's company failed, and although he attempted to sell it and the trademark, he had no buyers. When Google announced that it was going to release a new mobile operating system called the Android, Specht built a new website using his old company's name to try and prove that he was indeed still using this trademark. Specht took Google to court and asked for $94 million in trademark infringement damages. The court ruled in Google's favor and found that Google was not liable for damages.

Patent

Patents are given to individuals or companies to grant them legal ownership of, and enable them to exclude others from using or copying, the invention covered by the patent. The invention must be novel, useful, and not obvious—which means, for example, that a company could not patent air. Thank goodness. If a company figured out how to patent air, we would have to pay for each and every breath we took!

After the inventor completes an application for a patent and it is approved, the patent grants a limited property right to exclude others from making, using, or selling the invention for a specific period of time. For example, when a pharmaceutical company develops a specific drug and acquires a patent for it, that company is the only one that can manufacture and sell this drug until the stated year in which the patent is up (usually 20 years from the date of approval). After that, the information is in the public domain, enabling all companies to manufacture and sell this product, which is why the price of a drug drops substantially after its patent expires.

This also takes place with algorithms. If an inventor of an algorithm acquires a patent, she has full control over who can use it in their products. If the inventor lets a vendor incorporate the algorithm, she will most likely get a fee and possibly a license fee on each instance of the product that is sold.

Patents are ways of providing economical incentives to individuals and organizations to continue research and development efforts that will most likely benefit society in some fashion. Patent infringement is huge within the technology world today. Large and small product vendors seem to be suing each other constantly with claims of patent infringement. The problem is that many patents are written at a very high level and maybe written at a functional level. For example, if Inge developed a technology that accomplishes functionality A, B, and C, you could actually develop your own technology in your own way that also accomplished A, B, and C. You might not even know that Inge's method or patent existed; you just developed this solution on your own. Yet, if Inge did this type of work first and obtained the patent, then she could go after you legally for infringement.

TIP A patent is the strongest form of intellectual property protection.

At the time of this writing, the amount of patent litigation in the technology world is overwhelming. Kodak filed suit against Apple and RIM alleging patent infringement pertaining to resolution previews of videos on on-screen displays. While the U.S. International Trade Commission ruled against Kodak in that case, Kodak had won similar cases against LG and Samsung, which provided it with a licensing deal of $864 million. Soon after the Trade Commission's ruling, RIM sued Kodak for different patent infringements and Apple also sued Kodak for a similar matter.

Apple has also filed multiple patent infringement complaints against the mobile phone company HTC, Cupertino did the same with Nokia, and Microsoft sued Motorola over everything from synchronizing e-mail to handset power control functionality. Microsoft sued a company called TomTom over eight car navigation and file management systems patents. A company called i4i, Inc., sued Microsoft for allegedly using its patented XML-authoring technology within its product Word. And Google lost a Linux-related infringement case that cost it $5 million.

This is just a small list of recent patent litigation. These cases are like watching 100 Ping-Pong matches going on all at the same time, each containing its own characters and dramas, and involving millions and billions of dollars.

While the various vendors are fighting for market share in their respective industries, another reason for the increase in patent litigation is the emergence of nonpracticing entities (NPEs), also known as patent trolls. NPE (or patent troll) is a term used to describe a person or company who obtains patents, not to protect their invention, but to aggressively and opportunistically go after another entity that tries to create something based upon them. A patent troll has no intention of manufacturing an item based upon their patent, but wants to get licensing fees from an entity that does manufacture the item. For example, let's say that Donald has ten new ideas for ten different technologies. He puts them through the patent process and gets them approved, but he has no intention of putting in all the money and risk it takes to actually create these technologies and attempt to bring them to market. He is going to wait until you do this and then he is going to sue you for infringing upon his patent. If he wins the court case, you have to pay him licensing fees for the product you developed and brought to market.

US District Court Patent Litigation Volume

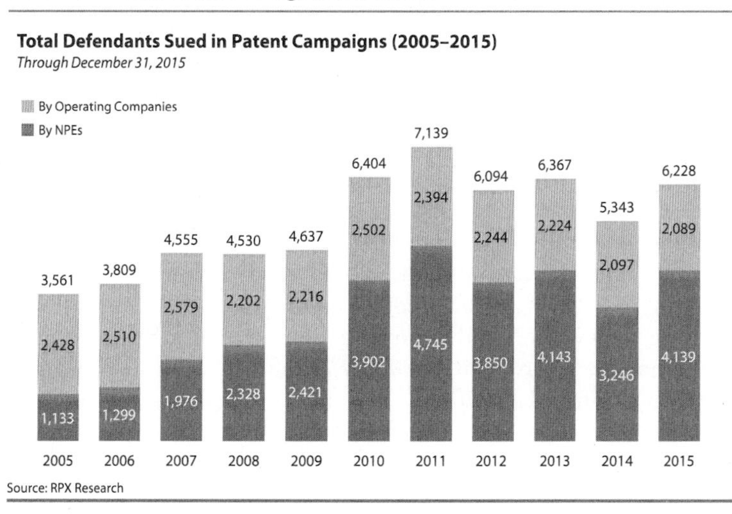

It is important to do a patent search before putting effort into developing a new methodology, technology, or business method.

Internal Protection of Intellectual Property

Ensuring that specific resources are protected by the previously mentioned laws is very important, but other measures must be taken internally to make sure the resources that are confidential in nature are properly identified and protected.

The resources protected by one of the previously mentioned laws need to be identified and integrated into the company's data classification scheme. This should be directed by management and carried out by the IT staff. The identified resources should have the necessary level of access control protection, auditing enabled, and a proper storage environment. If it is deemed secret, then not everyone in the company should be able to access it. Once the individuals who are allowed to have access are identified, their level of access and interaction with the resource should be defined in a granular method. Attempts to access and manipulate the resource should be properly audited, and the resource should be stored on a protected system with the necessary security mechanisms.

Employees must be informed of the level of secrecy or confidentiality of the resource and of their expected behavior pertaining to that resource.

If a company fails in one or all of these steps, it may not be covered by the laws described previously, because it may have failed to practice due care and properly protect the resource that it has claimed to be so important to the survival and competitiveness of the company.

Software Piracy

Software piracy occurs when the intellectual or creative work of an author is used or duplicated without permission or compensation to the author. It is an act of infringement on ownership rights, and if the pirate is caught, he could be sued civilly for damages, be criminally prosecuted, or both.

When a vendor develops an application, it usually licenses the program rather than sell it outright. The license agreement contains provisions relating to the approved use of the software and the corresponding manuals. If an individual or company fails to observe and abide by those requirements, the license may be terminated and, depending on the actions, criminal charges may be leveled. The risk to the vendor that develops and licenses the software is the loss of profits it would have earned.

There are four categories of software licensing. *Freeware* is software that is publicly available free of charge and can be used, copied, studied, modified, and redistributed without restriction. *Shareware*, or *trialware*, is used by vendors to market their software. Users obtain a free, trial version of the software. Once the user tries out the program, the user is asked to purchase a copy of it. *Commercial* software is, quite simply, software that is sold for or serves commercial purposes. And, finally, *academic* software is software that is provided for academic purposes at a reduced cost. It can be open source, freeware, or commercial software.

Some software vendors sell bulk licenses, which enable several users to use the product simultaneously. These master agreements define proper use of the software along with restrictions, such as whether corporate software can also be used by employees on their home machines. One other prevalent form of software licensing is the End User License Agreement (EULA). It specifies more granular conditions and restrictions than a master agreement. Other vendors incorporate third-party license-metering software that keeps track of software usability to ensure that the customer stays within the license limit and otherwise complies with the software licensing agreement. The information security officer should be aware of all these types of contractual commitments required by software companies. This person needs to be educated on the restrictions the company is under and make sure proper enforcement mechanisms are in place. If a company is found guilty of illegally copying software or using more copies than its license permits, the security officer in charge of this task may be primarily responsible.

Thanks to easy access to high-speed Internet, employees' ability—if not the temptation—to download and use pirated software has greatly increased. The June 2014 BSA Global Software Survey, a study conducted by the Business Software Alliance (BSA) and International Data Corporation (IDC), found that 43 percent of the software installed on personal computers globally in 2013 was not properly licensed. This means that for every two dollars' worth of legal software that is purchased, one dollar's worth is pirated. Software developers often use these numbers to calculate losses resulting from pirated copies. The assumption is that if the pirated copy had not been available, then everyone who is using a pirated copy would have instead purchased it legally.

Not every country recognizes software piracy as a crime, but several international organizations have made strides in curbing the practice. The Federation Against Software Theft (FAST) and the Business Software Alliance (author of the Global Software Survey) are organizations that promote the enforcement of proprietary rights of software. This is a huge issue for companies that develop and produce software, because a majority of their revenue comes from licensing fees. Figure 1-12 shows the results of BSA's 2014 Global Software Survey illustrating the breakdown of which world regions are the top software piracy offenders. The study also estimates that the total economic damage experienced by the industry was $62.7 billion in losses in 2013.

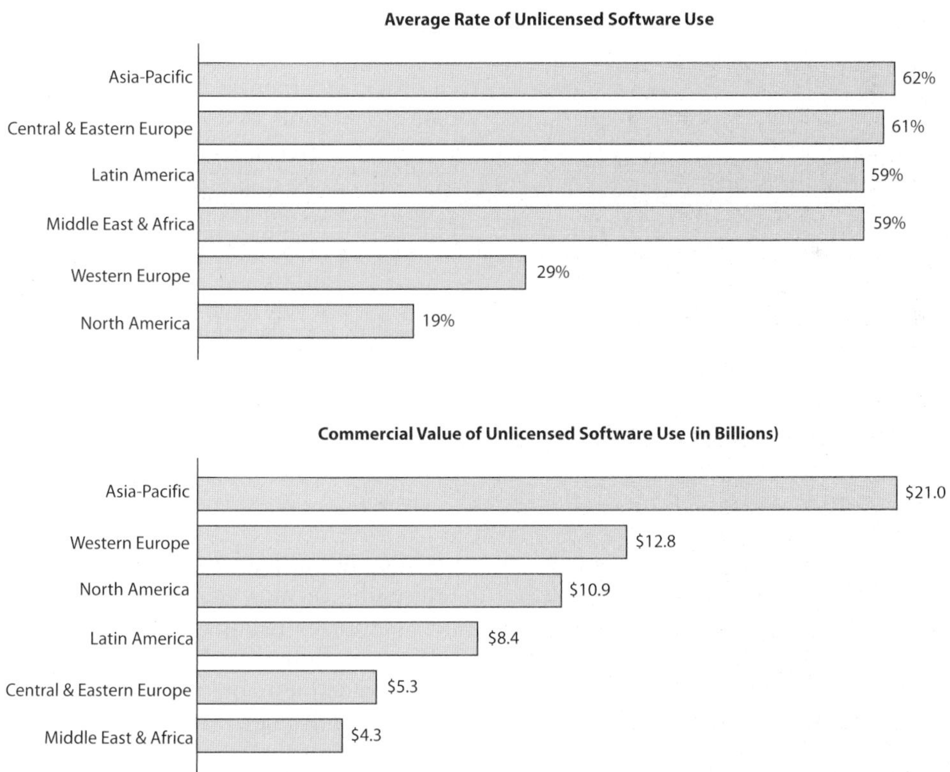

Figure 1-12 Software piracy rates by region (Source: BSA Global Software Survey, June 2014. BSA | The Software Alliance)

One of the offenses an individual or company can commit is to decompile vendor object code. This is usually done to figure out how the application works by obtaining the original source code, which is confidential, and perhaps to reverse-engineer it in the hope of understanding the intricate details of its functionality. Another purpose of reverse-engineering products is to detect security flaws within the code that can later be exploited. This is how some buffer overflow vulnerabilities are discovered.

Many times, an individual decompiles the object code into source code and either finds security holes to exploit or alters the source code to produce some type of functionality that the original vendor did not intend. In one example, an individual decompiled a program that protects and displays e-books and publications. The vendor did not want anyone to be able to copy the e-publications its product displayed and thus inserted an encoder within the object code of its product that enforced this limitation. The individual decompiled the object code and figured out how to create a decoder that would overcome this restriction and enable users to make copies of the e-publications, which infringed upon those authors' and publishers' copyrights.

The individual was arrested and prosecuted under the *Digital Millennium Copyright Act (DMCA)*, which makes it illegal to create products that circumvent copyright protection mechanisms. Interestingly enough, many computer-oriented individuals protested this person's arrest, and the company prosecuting (Adobe) quickly decided to drop all charges.

DMCA is a U.S. copyright law that criminalizes the production and dissemination of technology, devices, or services that circumvent access control measures that are put into place to protect copyright material. So if you figure out a way to "unlock" the proprietary way that Barnes & Noble protects its e-books, you can be charged under this act. Even if you don't share the actual copyright-protected books with someone, you still broke this specific law and can be found guilty.

NOTE The European Union passed a similar law called the Copyright Directive.

Privacy

Privacy is becoming more threatened as the world increasingly relies on computing technology. There are several approaches to addressing privacy, including the generic approach and regulation by industry. The generic approach is horizontal enactment—rules that stretch across all industry boundaries. It affects all industries, including government. Regulation by industry is vertical enactment. It defines requirements for specific verticals, such as the financial sector and health care. In both cases, the overall objective is twofold. First, the initiatives seek to protect citizens' personally identifiable information (PII). Second, the initiatives seek to balance the needs of government and businesses to collect and use PII with consideration of security issues.

Personally Identifiable Information

Personally identifiable information (PII) is data that can be used to uniquely identify, contact, or locate a single person or can be used with other sources to uniquely identify a single individual. PII needs to be highly protected because it is commonly used in identity theft, financial crimes, and various criminal activities.

While it seems as though defining and identifying PII should be easy and straightforward, what different countries, federal governments, and state governments consider to be PII differs.

The U.S. Office of Management and Budget in its memorandum M-10-23, "Guidance for Agency Use of Third-Party Websites and Applications," defines PII as "information that can be used to distinguish or trace an individual's identity, either alone or when combined with other personal or identifying information that is linked or linkable to a specific individual." Determining what constitutes PII, then, depends on a specific risk assessment of the likelihood that the information can be used to uniquely identify an individual. This is all good and well, but doesn't really help us recognize information that might be considered PII. Typical components are listed here:

- Full name (if not common)
- National identification number
- IP address (in some cases)
- Vehicle registration plate number
- Driver's license number
- Face, fingerprints, or handwriting
- Credit card numbers
- Digital identity
- Birthday
- Birthplace
- Genetic information

The following items are less often used because they are commonly shared by so many people, but they can fall into the PII classification and may require protection from improper disclosure:

- First or last name, if common
- Country, state, or city of residence
- Age, especially if nonspecific
- Gender or race
- Name of the school they attend or workplace
- Grades, salary, or job position
- Criminal record

In response, countries have enacted privacy laws. For example, although the United States already had the Federal Privacy Act of 1974, it has enacted new laws, such as the Gramm-Leach-Bliley Act of 1999 and the Health Insurance Portability and Accountability Act (HIPAA), in response to an increased need to protect personal privacy information. These are examples of a vertical approach to addressing privacy, whereas Canada's Personal Information Protection and Electronic Documents Act and New Zealand's Privacy Act of 1993 are horizontal approaches.

Technology is continually advancing in the amount of data that can be kept in data warehouses, data mining and analysis techniques, and distribution of this mined data. Companies that are data aggregators compile in-depth profiles of personal information on millions of people, even though many individuals have never heard of these specific companies, have never had an account with them, and have not given them permission to obtain personal information. These data aggregators compile, store, and sell personal information.

It seems as though putting all of this information together would make sense. It would be easier to obtain, have one centralized source, be extremely robust—and be the delight of identity thieves everywhere. All they have to do is hack into one location and get enough information to steal hundreds of thousands of identities.

The Increasing Need for Privacy Laws

Privacy is different from security, and although the concepts can intertwine, they are distinctively different. Privacy is the ability of an individual or group to control who has certain types of information about them. Privacy is an individual's right to determine what data they would like others to know about themselves, which people are permitted to know that data, and when those people can access it. Security is used to enforce these privacy rights.

The following issues have increased the need for more privacy laws and governance:

- **Data aggregation and retrieval technologies advancement**
  - Large data warehouses are continually being created full of private information.
- **Loss of borders (globalization)**
  - Private data flows from country to country for many different reasons.
  - Business globalization.
- **Convergent technologies advancements**
  - Gathering, mining, and distributing sensitive information.

While people around the world have always felt that privacy is important, the fact that almost everything that there is to know about a person (age, sex, financial data, medical data, friends, purchasing habits, criminal behavior, and even Google searches) is in some digital format in probably over 50 different locations makes people even more concerned about their privacy.

Having data quickly available to whoever needs it makes many things in life easier and less time consuming. But this data can just as easily be available to those you do not want to have access to it. Personal information is commonly used in identity theft, financial crimes take place because an attacker knows enough about a person to impersonate him, and people experience extortion because others find out secrets about them.

While some companies and many marketing companies want as much personal information about people as possible, many other organizations do not want to carry the burden and liability of storing and processing so much sensitive data. This opens the organization up to too much litigation risk. But this type of data is commonly required for various business processes. A new position in many organizations has been created to just deal with privacy issues—chief privacy officer. This person is usually a lawyer and has the responsibility of overseeing how the company deals with sensitive data in a responsible and legal manner. Many companies have had to face legal charges and civil suits for not properly protecting privacy data, so they have hired individuals who are experts in this field.

Privacy laws are popping up like weeds in a lawn. Many countries are creating new legislation, and as of this writing over 45 U.S. states have their own privacy information disclosure laws. While this illustrates the importance that society puts on protecting individuals' privacy, the number of laws and their variance make it very difficult for a company to ensure that it is in compliance with all of them.

As a security professional, you should understand the types of privacy data your organization deals with and help to ensure that it is meeting all of its legal and regulatory requirements pertaining to this type of data.

Laws, Directives, and Regulations

Regulations in computer and information security covers many areas for many different reasons. Some issues that require regulations are data privacy, computer misuse, software copyright, data protection, and controls on cryptography. These regulations can be implemented in various arenas, such as government and private sectors for reasons dealing with environmental protection, intellectual property, national security, personal privacy, public order, health and safety, and prevention of fraudulent activities.

Security professionals have so much to keep up with these days, from understanding how the latest worm attacks work and how to properly protect against them, to how new versions of denial-of-service (DoS) attacks take place and what tools are used to accomplish them. Professionals also need to follow which new security products are released and how they compare to the existing products. This is followed up by keeping track of new technologies, service patches, hotfixes, encryption methods, access control mechanisms, telecommunications security issues, social engineering, and physical security. Laws and regulations have been ascending the list of things that security professionals also need to be aware of. This is because organizations must be compliant with more and more laws and regulations, and noncompliance can result in a fine or a company going out of business, and in some cases certain executive management individuals ending up in jail.

Laws, regulations, and directives developed by governments or appointed agencies do not usually provide detailed instructions to follow to properly protect computers and company assets. Each environment is too diverse in topology, technology, infrastructure, requirements, functionality, and personnel. Because technology changes at such a fast pace, these laws and regulations could never successfully represent reality if they were too detailed. Instead, they state high-level requirements that commonly puzzle companies about how to be compliant with them. This is where the security professional comes to the rescue. In the past, security professionals were expected to know how to carry out penetration tests, configure firewalls, and deal only with the technology issues of security. Today, security professionals are being pulled out of the server rooms and asked to be more involved in business-oriented issues. As a security professional, you need to understand the laws and regulations that your company must comply with and what controls must be put in place to accomplish compliance. This means the security professional now must have a foot in both the technical world and the business world.

If You Are Not a Lawyer, You Are Not a Lawyer

Many times security professionals are looked to by organizations to help them figure out how to be compliant with the necessary laws and regulations. While you might be aware of and have experience with some of these laws and regulations, there is a high likelihood that you are not aware of all the necessary federal and state laws, regulations, and international requirements your company must meet. These laws, regulations, and directives morph over time and new ones are added, and while you think you may be interpreting them correctly, you may be wrong. It is critical that an organization get its legal department involved with compliancy issues. Many security professionals have been in this situation over many years. At many companies, the legal staff does not know enough about all of these issues to ensure the company is properly protected. In this situation, advise the company to contact outside counsel to help them with these issues.

Companies look to security professionals to have all the answers, especially in consulting situations. You will be brought in as the expert. But if you are not a lawyer, you are not a lawyer and should advise your customer properly in obtaining legal help to ensure proper compliance in all matters. The increasing use of cloud computing is adding an incredible amount of legal and regulatory compliance confusion to current situations.

It is a good idea to have a clause in any type of consulting agreement you use that explicitly outlines these issues so that if and when the company gets hauled to court after a computer breach, your involvement will be understood and previously documented.

Over time, the CISSP exam has become more global in nature and less U.S.-centric. Specific questions on U.S. laws and regulations have been taken out of the test, so you do not need to spend a lot of time learning them and their specifics. Be familiar with why laws are developed and put in place and their overall goals, instead of memorizing specific laws and dates.

Thus, the following sections on laws and regulations contain information you do not need to memorize, because you will not be asked questions on these items directly. But remember that the CISSP exam is a *cognitive* exam, so you do need to know the different reasons and motivations for laws and regulations, which is why these sections are provided. This list covers U.S. laws and regulations, but almost every country either has laws similar to these or is in the process of developing them.

Federal Privacy Act of 1974

In the mid-1960s, a proposal was made that the U.S. government compile and collectively hold in a main federal data bank each individual's information pertaining to the Social Security Administration, the Census Bureau, the Internal Revenue Service, the Bureau of Labor Statistics, and other government departments. The committee that made this proposal saw this as an efficient way of gathering and centralizing data. Others saw it as a dangerous move against individual privacy and too "Big Brother." The federal data bank never came to pass because of strong opposition.

To keep the government in check on gathering information on U.S. citizens and other matters, a majority of its files are considered open to the public. Government files are open to the public unless specific issues enacted by the legislature deem certain files unavailable. This is what is explained in the Freedom of Information Act. This is different from what the *Privacy Act of 1974* outlines and protects; it applies to records and documents developed and maintained by specific branches of the federal government, such as executive departments, government organizations, independent regulatory agencies, and government-controlled corporations. It does not apply to congressional, judiciary, or territorial subdivisions.

As specified in the Privacy Act, an actual *record* is information about an individual's education, medical history, financial history, criminal history, employment, and other similar types of information. Government agencies can maintain this type of information only if it is necessary and relevant to accomplishing the agency's purpose. The Privacy Act dictates that an agency cannot disclose this information without written permission from the individual. However, like most government acts, legislation, and creeds, there is a list of exceptions.

So what does all of this dry legal mumbo-jumbo mean? Basically, agencies can gather information about individuals, but it must be relevant and necessary to the agency's official functions. In addition, an agency cannot share people's private information. If it does, private citizens have the right to sue that agency to protect their privacy.

The Privacy Act applies to the computer world because this information is usually held by one type of computer or another. If an agency's computer holds an individual's confidential information, the agency must provide the necessary security mechanisms to ensure that information cannot be compromised or copied in an unauthorized way.

Federal Information Security Management Act of 2002

The *Federal Information Security Management Act (FISMA)* of 2002 is a U.S. law that requires every federal agency to create, document, and implement an agency-wide security program to provide protection for the information and information systems that support the operations and assets of the agency, including those provided or managed by another agency, contractor, or other source. It explicitly emphasizes a "risk-based policy for cost-effective security."

FISMA requires agency program officials, chief information officers, and inspectors general (IGs) to conduct annual reviews of the agency's information security program and report the results to the Office of Management and Budget (OMB). OMB uses these data to assist in its oversight responsibilities and to prepare this annual report to Congress on agency compliance with the act. Requirements of FISMA are as follows:

- Inventory of information systems
- Categorize information and information systems according to risk level
- Security controls
- Risk assessment
- System security plan
- Certification and accreditation
- Continuous monitoring

As described earlier in the chapter, NIST SP 800-53 outlines all of the necessary security controls that need to be in place to protect federal systems (refer back to Table 1-4 for a list of control categories addressed in this publication). This NIST document, among others such as SP 800-37, "Guide for Applying the Risk Management Framework to Federal Information Systems," is used to help ensure compliance with FISMA.

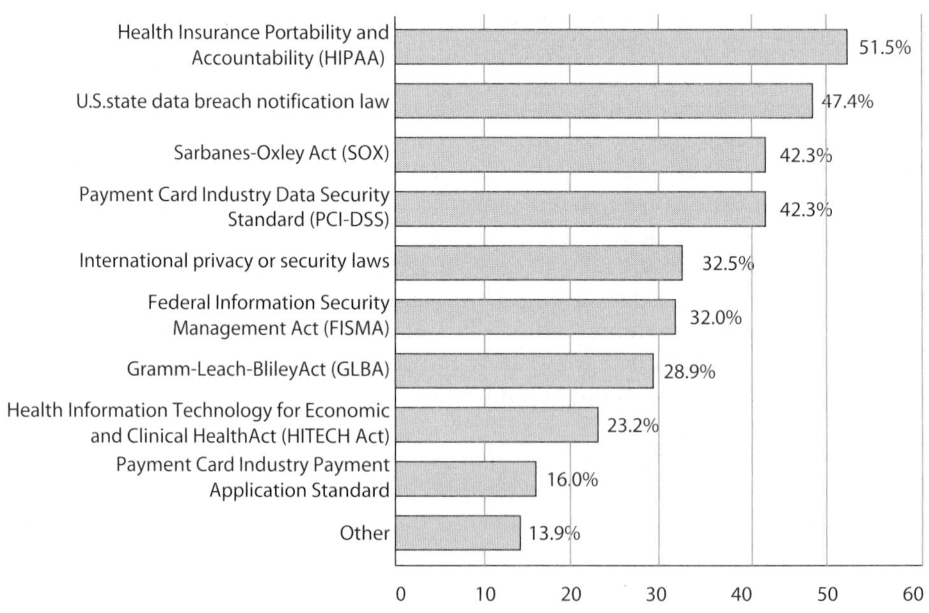

Department of Veterans Affairs Information Security Protection Act

In May 2006, a laptop computer issued to a Department of Veterans Affairs (VA) employee was stolen from his home in Aspen Hill, Maryland. The computer's hard drive contained the names, birth dates, and Social Security numbers of some 26.5 million veterans. Though the laptop was eventually recovered by law enforcement, the breach rippled through the federal government and led to the enactment of the Department of Veterans Affairs Information Security Protection Act.

This law has an extremely narrow scope (it only applies to the VA), but is representative of efforts to bolt on security after a breach. The VA was already required to comply with FISMA, but the fact that it failed to do so received a lot of attention in the wake of the theft of the laptop. Rather than simply enforcing FISMA, the federal government created a new law that requires the VA to implement additional controls and to report its compliance to Congress.

Health Insurance Portability and Accountability Act (HIPAA)

The *Health Insurance Portability and Accountability Act (HIPAA)*, a U.S. federal regulation, has been mandated to provide national standards and procedures for the storage, use, and transmission of personal medical information and healthcare data. This regulation provides a framework and guidelines to ensure security, integrity, and privacy when handling confidential medical information. HIPAA outlines how security should be managed for any facility that creates, accesses, shares, or destroys medical information.

People's health records can be used and misused in different scenarios for many reasons. As health records migrate from a paper-based system to an electronic system, they become easier to maintain, access, and transfer, but they also become easier to manipulate and access in an unauthorized manner. Traditionally, healthcare facilities have lagged behind other businesses in their information and network security mechanisms, architecture, and security enforcement because there was no real business need to expend the energy and money to put these items in place. Now there is.

HIPAA mandates steep federal penalties for noncompliance. If medical information is used in a way that violates the privacy standards dictated by HIPAA, even by mistake, monetary penalties of $100 per violation are enforced, up to $1,500,000 per year, per standard. If protected health information is obtained or disclosed knowingly, the fines can be as much as $50,000 and one year in prison. If the information is obtained or disclosed under false pretenses, the cost can go up to $250,000 with 10 years in prison if there is intent to sell or use the information for commercial advantage, personal gain, or malicious harm. This is serious business.

Health Information Technology for Economic and Clinical Health (HITECH) Act

In 2009 the *Health Information Technology for Economic and Clinical Health (HITECH) Act*, enacted as part of the American Recovery and Reinvestment Act, was signed into law to promote the adoption and meaningful use of health information technology. Subtitle D of the HITECH Act addresses the privacy and security concerns associated with the electronic transmission of health information, in part through several provisions that strengthen the civil and criminal enforcement of the HIPAA rules.

Section 13410(d) of the HITECH Act revised Section 1176(a) of the Social Security Act by establishing

- Four categories of violations that reflect increasing levels of culpability
- Four corresponding tiers of penalty amounts that significantly increase the minimum penalty amount for each violation
- A maximum penalty amount of $1.5 million for all violations of an identical provision

USA PATRIOT Act

The Uniting and Strengthening America by Providing Appropriate Tools Required to Intercept and Obstruct Terrorism Act of 2001 (aka USA PATRIOT Act) deals with many issues within one act:

- Reduces restrictions on law enforcement agencies' ability to search telephone, e-mail, medical, financial, and other records
- Eases restrictions on foreign intelligence gathering within the United States
- Expands the Secretary of the Treasury's authority to regulate financial transactions, particularly those involving foreign individuals and entities
- Broadens the discretion of law enforcement and immigration authorities in detaining and deporting immigrants suspected of terrorism-related acts
- Expands the definition of terrorism to include domestic terrorism, thus enlarging the number of activities to which the USA PATRIOT Act's expanded law enforcement powers can be applied

The law made many changes to already existing laws, which are listed here:

- Foreign Intelligence Surveillance Act of 1978
- Electronic Communications Privacy Act of 1986
- Money Laundering Control Act of 1986
- Bank Secrecy Act (BSA)
- Immigration and Nationality Act

This law has generated more privacy debate than perhaps any other. Particularly troublesome to privacy advocates are many provisions in Title II, which deals with surveillance. While advocates of the Patriot Act point to the significant number of foiled acts of terrorism, its opponents point to a significant number of unwarranted privacy violations.

Gramm-Leach-Bliley Act (GLBA)

The *Gramm-Leach-Bliley Act (GLBA)*, also known as the Financial Services Modernization Act of 1999, requires financial institutions to develop privacy notices and give their customers the option to prohibit financial institutions from sharing their information with nonaffiliated third parties. The act dictates that the board of directors is responsible for many of the security issues within a financial institution, that risk management must be implemented, that all employees need to be trained on information security issues, and that implemented security measures must be fully tested. It also requires these institutions to have a written security policy in place.

Major components put into place to govern the collection, disclosure, and protection of consumers' nonpublic personal information, or PII, include

- **Financial Privacy Rule** Provide each consumer with a privacy notice that explains the data collected about the consumer, where that data is shared, how that data is used, and how that data is protected. The notice must also identify the consumer's right to opt out of the data being shared with unaffiliated parties pursuant to the provisions of the Fair Credit Reporting Act.
- **Safeguards Rule** Develop a written information security plan that describes how the company is prepared to, and plans to continue to, protect clients' nonpublic personal information.
- **Pretexting Protection** Implement safeguards against pretexting (social engineering).

GLBA would be considered a vertical regulation in that it deals mainly with financial institutions.

CAUTION Financial institutions within the world of GLBA are not just banks. They include any organization that provides financial products or services to individuals, like loans, financial or investment advice, or insurance.

Personal Information Protection and Electronic Documents Act

Personal Information Protection and Electronic Documents Act (PIPEDA) is a Canadian law that deals with the protection of personal information. One of its main goals is to oversee how the private sector collects, uses, and discloses personal information in regular business activities. The law was enacted to help and promote consumer trust and facilitate electronic commerce. It was also put into place to reassure other countries that Canadian businesses would protect privacy data so that cross-border transactions and business activities could take place in a more assured manner.

Some of the requirements the law lays out for organizations are as follows:

- Obtain consent when they collect, use, or disclose their personal information
- Collect information by fair and lawful means
- Have personal information policies that are clear, understandable, and readily available

If your organization plans to work with entities in Canada, these types of laws need to be understood and followed.

Payment Card Industry Data Security Standard (PCI DSS)

Identity theft and credit card fraud are increasingly more common. Not that these things did not occur before, but the advent of the Internet and computer technology have combined to create a scenario where attackers can steal millions of identities at a time.

The credit card industry took proactive steps to curb the problem and stabilize customer trust in credit cards as a safe method of conducting transactions. Each of the four major credit card vendors in the United States developed its own program that its customers had to comply with:

- **Visa** Cardholder Information Security Protection (CISP)
- **MasterCard** Site Data Protection (SDP)
- **Discover** Discover Information Security and Compliance (DISC)
- **American Express** Data Security Operating Policy (DSOP)

Eventually, the credit card companies joined forces and devised the *Payment Card Industry Data Security Standard (PCI DSS)*. The PCI Security Standards Council was created as a separate entity to maintain and enforce the PCI DSS.

The PCI DSS applies to any entity that processes, transmits, stores, or accepts credit card data. Varying levels of compliance and penalties exist and depend on the size of the customer and the volume of transactions. However, credit cards are used by tens of millions of people and are accepted almost anywhere, which means just about every business in the world is affected by the PCI DSS.

The PCI DSS is made up of 12 main requirements broken down into six major categories. The six categories of PCI DSS are Build and Maintain a Secure Network and Systems, Protect Cardholder Data, Maintain a Vulnerability Management Program, Implement Strong Access Control Measures, Regularly Monitor and Test Networks, and Maintain an Information Security Policy.

NOTE According to PCI DSS 3.1, Secure Sockets Layer (SSL) and early Transport Layer Security (TLS) are not considered secure. New systems should not use them, and existing systems can only use them until June 2016 provided they incorporate risk mitigations.

The control objectives are implemented via 12 requirements, as stated at https://www.pcisecuritystandards.org/security_standards/pci_dss.shtml:

- Install and maintain a firewall configuration to protect cardholder data.
- Do not use vendor-supplied defaults for system passwords and other security parameters.
- Protect stored cardholder data.
- Encrypt transmission of cardholder data across open, public networks.
- Protect all systems against malware and regularly update antivirus software or programs.

- Develop and maintain secure systems and applications.
- Restrict access to cardholder data by business need to know.
- Identify and authenticate access to system components.
- Restrict physical access to cardholder data.
- Track and monitor all access to network resources and cardholder data.
- Regularly test security systems and processes.
- Maintain a policy that addresses information security for all personnel.

The PCI DSS is a private-sector industry initiative. It is not a law. Noncompliance or violations of the PCI DSS may result in financial penalties or possible revocation of merchant status within the credit card industry, but not jail time. However, Minnesota became the first state to mandate PCI compliance as a law, and other states, as well as the U.S. federal government, are implementing similar measures.

NOTE As mentioned before, privacy is being dealt with through laws, regulations, self-regulations, and individual protection. The PCI DSS is an example of a self-regulation approach. It is not a regulation that came down from a government agency. It is an attempt by the credit card companies to reduce fraud and govern themselves so the government does not have to get involved. While the CISSP exam will not ask you specific questions on specific laws, in reality you should know this list of regulations and laws (at the minimum) if you are serious about being a security professional. Each one of these directly relates to information security. You will find that most of the security efforts going on within companies and organizations today are regulatory driven. You need to understand the laws and regulations to know what controls should be implemented to ensure compliancy.

Many security professionals are not well versed in the necessary laws and regulations. One person may know a lot about HIPAA, another person might know some about GLBA, but most organizations do not have people who understand all the necessary legislation that directly affects them. You can stand head and shoulders above the rest by understanding cyberlaw and how it affects various organizations.

Employee Privacy Issues

Within a corporation, several employee privacy issues must be thought through and addressed if the company wants to be properly protected against employee claims of invasion of privacy. An understanding that each state and country may have different privacy laws should prompt the company to investigate exactly what it can and cannot monitor before it does so.

If a company has a facility located in a state that permits keyboard, e-mail, and surveillance camera monitoring, for example, the company must take the proper steps to ensure that the employees of that facility know that these types of monitoring may be put into place. This is the best way for a company to protect itself legally, if necessary, and to avoid presenting the employees with any surprises.

The monitoring must be work related, meaning that a manager may have the right to listen in on his employees' conversations with customers, but he does not have the right to listen in on personal conversations that are not work related. Monitoring also must happen in a consistent way, such that *all* employees are subjected to monitoring, not just one or two people.

If a company feels it may be necessary to monitor e-mail messages and usage, this must be explained to the employees, first through a security policy and then through a constant reminder such as a computer banner or regular training. It is best to have employees read a document describing what type of monitoring they could be subjected to, what is considered acceptable behavior, and what the consequences of not meeting those expectations are. The employees should be asked to sign this document, which can later be treated as a legally admissible document if necessary. This document is referred to as a waiver of reasonable expectation of privacy (REP). By signing the waiver, employees waive their expectation to privacy.

CAUTION It is important to deal with the issue of *reasonable expectation of privacy (REP)* when it comes to employee monitoring. In the U.S. legal system, the REP standard is used when defining the scope of the privacy protections provided by the Fourth Amendment of the Constitution. If employees are not specifically informed that work-related monitoring is possible and/or probable, when the monitoring takes place, employees could claim that their privacy rights have been violated and launch a civil suit against your company.

Prescreening Personnel

It is important to properly screen individuals before hiring them into a corporation. These steps are necessary to help the company protect itself and to ensure it is getting the type of employee required for the job. This chapter looks at some of the issues from the other side of the table, which deals with that individual's privacy rights.

Limitations exist regarding the type and amount of information that an organization can obtain on a potential employee. The limitations and regulations for background checks vary from jurisdiction to jurisdiction, so the hiring manager needs to consult the legal department. Usually human resources has an outline for hiring managers to follow when it comes to interviews and background checks.

A company that intends to monitor e-mail should address this point in its security policy and standards. The company should outline who can and cannot read employee messages, describe the circumstances under which e-mail monitoring may be acceptable, and specify where the e-mail can be accessed. Some companies indicate that they will only monitor e-mail that resides on the mail server, whereas other companies declare the right to read employee messages if they reside on the mail server or the employee's computer. A company must not promise privacy to employees that it does not then provide, because that could result in a lawsuit. Although IT and security professionals have access to many parts of computer systems and the network, this does not mean it is ethical and right to overstep the bounds in a way that could threaten a user's privacy and put the company at risk of legal action. Only the tasks necessary to enforce the security policy should take place and nothing further that could compromise another's privacy.

Many lawsuits have arisen where an employee was fired for doing something wrong (downloading pornographic material, using the company's e-mail system to send out confidential information to competitors, and so on), and the employee sued the company for improper termination. If the company has not stated in its policy that these types of activities are prohibited and has not made reasonable effort to inform the employee (through security awareness, computer banners, the employee handbook, and so on) of what is considered acceptable and not acceptable and the resulting repercussions for noncompliance, then the employee could win the lawsuit and receive a large chunk of money from the company. So policies, standards, and security-awareness activities need to spell out these issues; otherwise, the employee's lawyer will claim the employee had an assumed right to privacy.

Personal Privacy Protection

End users are also responsible for their own privacy, especially as it relates to protecting the data that is on their own systems. End users should be encouraged to use common sense and best practices. This includes the use of encryption to protect sensitive personal information, as well as firewalls, antivirus software, and patches to protect computers from becoming infected with malware. Documents containing personal information, such as credit card statements, should also be shredded. Also, it's important for end users to understand that when data is given to a third party, it is no longer under their control.

Review of Ways to Deal with Privacy

Current methods of privacy protection and examples are as follows:

- **Laws on government** FPA, VA ISA, USA PATRIOT
- **Laws on corporations** HIPAA, HITECH, GLBA, PIDEDA
- **Self-regulation** PCI DSS
- **Individual user** Passwords, encryption, awareness

Data Breaches

It is a rare month indeed when one doesn't read or hear about a major data breach. Information is the lifeblood of most major corporations nowadays, and threat actors know this. They have been devoting a lot of effort over the past several years to compromising and exploiting the data stores that, in many ways, are more valuable to companies than any vault full of cash. This trend continues unabated, which makes data breaches one of the most important issues in cyber security today.

In a way, data breaches can be thought of as the opposite of privacy: data owners lose control of who has the ability to access their data. When an organization fails to properly protect the privacy of its customers' data, it increases the likelihood of experiencing a data breach. It should not be surprising, therefore, that some of the same legal and regulatory issues that apply to one also apply to the other.

It is important to note that data breaches need not involve a violation of personal privacy. Indeed, some of the most publicized data breaches have had nothing to do with PII but with intellectual property (IP). It is worth pausing to properly define the term *data breach* as a security event that results in the actual or potential compromise of the confidentiality or integrity of protected information by unauthorized actors. Protected information can be PII, IP, personal health information (PHI), classified information, or any other information that can cause damage to an individual or organization.

As a security professional, it is important to understand which legal and regulatory requirements are triggered by data breaches. To further complicate matters, most U.S. states, as well as many other countries, have enacted distinct laws with subtle but important differences in notification stipulations. As always when dealing with legal issues, it is best to consult with your attorney. This section is simply an overview of some of the legal requirements of which you should be aware.

U.S. Laws Pertaining to Data Breaches

The preceding sections introduced various U.S. statutes dealing with privacy protections for an individual's personal information. Despite our best efforts, there will be times when our information systems are compromised and personal information security controls are breached. Let us now revisit some of the laws from our previous discussion of privacy and see what they have to say about data breaches.

Health Insurance Portability and Accountability Act

HIPAA applies to healthcare providers who transmit or store personal health information (PHI). While this law requires the protection of PHI and imposes penalties for failing to do so, it does not require notification of data breaches. This major flaw of the law was not corrected for almost 13 years until the HITECH Act was signed into law.

Health Information Technology for Economic and Clinical Health Act

The 2009 HITECH Act addresses the breach issue in HIPAA. Specifically, it directs the U.S. Secretary of Health and Human Services (HHS) to publish annual guidance to affected corporations on effective technical controls to protect data. If a company complies with these recommendations, it is not required to report a data breach. Otherwise (i.e., the PHI was not properly protected), the breach must be reported to HHS and to the affected individuals generally within 60 days of discovery of the breach.

Gramm-Leach-Bliley Act of 1999

GLBA applies to institutions that provide financial or insurance services. It requires that, upon identification of an incident of unauthorized access to sensitive customer information, the institution determine the likelihood that the information has or will be misused. If the institution determines that misuse occurred or is reasonably likely to occur, GLBA requires notification to federal regulators, law enforcement authorities, and affected customers.

Economic Espionage Act of 1996

Prior to 1996, industry and corporate espionage was taking place with no real guidelines for who could properly investigate the events. The *Economic Espionage Act* of 1996 provides the necessary structure when dealing with these types of cases and further defines trade secrets to be technical, business, engineering, scientific, or financial. This means that an asset does not necessarily need to be tangible to be protected or be stolen. Thus, this act enables the FBI to investigate industrial and corporate espionage cases.

It is worth recalling here that data breaches are not only violations of customer privacy. When a threat actor compromises a target corporation's network and exposes its intellectual property (IP), a breach has occurred. While the other laws we have discussed in this section deal with protecting customer's PII, the Economic Espionage Act protects corporations' IP. When you think of data breaches, it is critical that you consider both PII and IP exposure.

State Laws

Almost every U.S. state has enacted legislation that requires government and private entities to disclose data breaches involving PII. In almost every case, PII is defined by the states as the combination of first and last name with any of the following:

- Social Security number
- Driver's license number
- Credit or debit card number with the security code or PIN

Unfortunately, that is where the commonalities end. The laws are so different that compliance with all of them is a difficult and costly issue for most corporations. In some states, simple access to files containing PII triggers a notification requirement, while in other states the organization must only notify affected parties if the breach is reasonably likely to result in illegal use of the information.

Other Nations' Laws Pertaining to Data Breaches

While it would be infeasible to include a detailed discussion of each country's data breach laws, it is worthwhile to consider an international perspective on the issue.

The European Union (EU) is in a particularly good position to harmonize the laws of many key countries in the global economy, so we discuss what they are doing. Conversely, we also present an overview of the countries that have no data breach notification requirements.

European Union

The EU is standardizing data breach notification requirements as part of the EU Data Protection Regulation, which will have various national laws as its implementation mechanism. Already, the EU has taken other steps, such as EU Regulation 611/2013, which applies to telecoms and Internet service providers operating in Europe. It requires notification to the affected parties to take place within 24 hours of discovery of the data breach. If it is not possible to provide a complete disclosure of the event, a preliminary notification must still go out within 24 hours, with a more complete one being distributed no later than three days after discovery.

Other Countries

As might be expected, the rest of the world is a hodgepodge of laws with varying data breach notification conditions and requirements. Notably, as of this writing, at least 12 countries have no notification requirements whatsoever: Argentina, Brazil, Chile, China, Colombia, Hong Kong, India, Israel, Malaysia, Peru, Russia, and Singapore. This is concerning because unscrupulous organizations have been known to outsource their data-handling operations to countries with no data breach laws in order to circumvent the difficulties in reconciling the different country and state requirements.

Policies, Standards, Baselines, Guidelines, and Procedures

Laws, directives, and government regulations are external to our organizations. They focus on what we can and cannot do, but largely stay away from specifying how these actions are accomplished or prevented. It is up to us to devise the right internal guidance that satisfies external requirements as well as our own internal ones. This is where we turn our attention next.

Computers and the information processed on them usually have a direct relationship with a company's critical missions and objectives. Because of this level of importance, senior management should make protecting these items a high priority and provide the necessary support, funds, time, and resources to ensure that systems, networks, and information are protected in the most logical and cost-effective manner possible. A comprehensive management approach must be developed to accomplish these goals successfully. This is because everyone within an organization may have a different set of personal values and experiences they bring to the environment with regard to security. It is important to make sure everyone is regarding security at a level that meets the needs of the organization as determined by laws, regulations, requirements, and business goals that have been determined by risk assessments of the environment of the organization.

For a company's security plan to be successful, it must start at the top level and be useful and functional at every single level within the organization. Senior management needs to define the scope of security and identify and decide what must be protected and to what extent. Management must understand the regulations, laws, and liability issues it is responsible for complying with regarding security and ensure that the company as a whole fulfills its obligations. Senior management also must determine what is expected from employees and what the consequences of noncompliance will be. These decisions should be made by the individuals who will be held ultimately responsible if something goes wrong. But it is a common practice to bring in the expertise of the security officers to collaborate in ensuring that sufficient policies and controls are being implemented to achieve the goals being set and determined by senior management.

A security program contains all the pieces necessary to provide overall protection to a corporation and lays out a long-term security strategy. A security program's documentation should be made up of security policies, procedures, standards, guidelines, and baselines. The human resources and legal departments must be involved in the development and enforcement of rules and requirements laid out in these documents.

The language, level of detail, formality of the documents, and supporting mechanisms should be examined by the policy developers. Security policies, standards, guidelines, procedures, and baselines must be developed with a realistic view to be most effective. Highly structured organizations usually follow documentation in a more uniform way. Less structured organizations may need more explanation and emphasis to promote compliance. The more detailed the rules are, the easier it is to know when one has been violated. However, overly detailed documentation and rules can prove to be more burdensome than helpful. The business type, its culture, and its goals must be evaluated to make sure the proper language is used when writing security documentation.

There are a lot of legal liability issues surrounding security documentation. If your organization has a policy outlining how it is supposed to be protecting sensitive information and it is found out that your organization is not practicing what it is preaching, criminal charges and civil suits could be filed and successfully executed. It is important that an organization's security does not just look good on paper, but in action also.

Security Policy

A *security policy* is an overall general statement produced by senior management (or a selected policy board or committee) that dictates what role security plays within the organization. A security policy can be an organizational policy, an issue-specific policy, or a system-specific policy. In an *organizational security policy*, management establishes how a security program will be set up, lays out the program's goals, assigns responsibilities, shows the strategic and tactical value of security, and outlines how enforcement should be carried out. This policy must address relative laws, regulations, and liability issues and how they are to be satisfied. The organizational security policy provides scope and direction for all future security activities within the organization. It also describes the amount of risk senior management is willing to accept.

The organizational security policy has several important characteristics that must be understood and implemented:

- Business objectives should drive the policy's creation, implementation, and enforcement. The policy should not dictate business objectives.
- It should be an easily understood document that is used as a reference point for all employees and management.
- It should be developed and used to integrate security into all business functions and processes.
- It should be derived from and support all legislation and regulations applicable to the company.
- It should be reviewed and modified as a company changes, such as through adoption of a new business model, a merger with another company, or change of ownership.
- Each iteration of the policy should be dated and under version control.
- The units and individuals who are governed by the policy must have easy access to it. Policies are commonly posted on portals on an intranet.
- It should be created with the intention of having the policies in place for several years at a time. This will help ensure policies are forward-thinking enough to deal with potential changes that may arise.
- The level of professionalism in the presentation of the policies reinforces their importance as well as the need to adhere to them.
- It should not contain language that isn't readily understood by everyone. Use clear and declarative statements that are easy to understand and adopt.
- It should be reviewed on a regular basis and adapted to correct incidents that have occurred since the last review and revision of the policies.

A process for dealing with those who choose not to comply with the security policies must be developed and enforced so there is a structured method of response to noncompliance. This establishes a process that others can understand and thus recognize not only what is expected of them, but also what they can expect as a response to their noncompliance.

Organizational policies are also referred to as master security policies. An organization will have many policies, and they should be set up in a hierarchical manner. The organizational (master) policy is at the highest level, and then there are policies underneath it that address security issues specifically. These are referred to as issue-specific policies.

An *issue-specific policy*, also called a functional policy, addresses specific security issues that management feels need more detailed explanation and attention to make sure a comprehensive structure is built and all employees understand how they are to comply with these security issues. For example, an organization may choose to have an e-mail security policy that outlines what management can and cannot do with employees' e-mail messages for monitoring purposes, that specifies which e-mail functionality employees can or cannot use, and that addresses specific privacy issues.

As a more specific example, an e-mail policy might state that management can read any employee's e-mail messages that reside on the mail server, but not when they reside on the user's workstation. The e-mail policy might also state that employees cannot use e-mail to share confidential information or pass inappropriate material, and that they may be subject to monitoring of these actions. Before they use their e-mail clients, employees should be asked to confirm that they have read and understand the e-mail policy, either by signing a confirmation document or clicking Yes in a confirmation dialog box. The policy provides direction and structure for the staff by indicating what they can and cannot do. It informs the users of the expectations of their actions, and it provides liability protection in case an employee cries "foul" for any reason dealing with e-mail use.

TIP A policy needs to be technology and solution independent. It must outline the goals and missions, but not tie the organization to specific ways of accomplishing them.

A common hierarchy of security policies is outlined here, which illustrates the relationship between the master policy and the issue-specific policies that support it:

- Organizational policy
    - Acceptable use policy
    - Risk management policy
    - Vulnerability management policy
    - Data protection policy
    - Access control policy
    - Business continuity policy
    - Log aggregation and auditing policy
    - Personnel security policy
    - Physical security policy
    - Secure application development policy
    - Change control policy
    - E-mail policy
    - Incident response policy

A *system-specific policy* presents the management's decisions that are specific to the actual computers, networks, and applications. An organization may have a system-specific policy outlining how a database containing sensitive information should be protected, who can have access, and how auditing should take place. It may also have a system-specific policy outlining how laptops should be locked down and managed. This policy type is directed to one or a group of similar systems and outlines how they should be protected.

Policies are written in broad terms to cover many subjects in a general fashion. Much more granularity is needed to actually support the policy, and this happens with the use of procedures, standards, guidelines, and baselines. The policy provides the foundation. The procedures, standards, guidelines, and baselines provide the security framework. And the necessary security controls (administrative, technical, and physical) are used to fill in the framework to provide a full security program.

Types of Policies

Policies generally fall into one of the following categories:

- **Regulatory** This type of policy ensures that the organization is following standards set by specific industry regulations (HIPAA, GLBA, SOX, PCI DSS, etc.). It is very detailed and specific to a type of industry. It is used in financial institutions, healthcare facilities, public utilities, and other government-regulated industries.
- **Advisory** This type of policy strongly advises employees as to which types of behaviors and activities should and should not take place within the organization. It also outlines possible ramifications if employees do not comply with the established behaviors and activities. This policy type can be used, for example, to describe how to handle medical or financial information.
- **Informative** This type of policy informs employees of certain topics. It is not an enforceable policy, but rather one that teaches individuals about specific issues relevant to the company. It could explain how the company interacts with partners, the company's goals and mission, and a general reporting structure in different situations.

Standards

Standards refer to mandatory activities, actions, or rules. Standards can give a policy its support and reinforcement in direction. Organizational security standards may specify how hardware and software products are to be used. They can also be used to indicate expected user behavior. They provide a means to ensure that specific technologies, applications, parameters, and procedures are implemented in a uniform (standardized) manner across the organization. An organizational standard may require that all employees wear their company identification badges at all times, that they challenge unknown individuals about their identity and purpose for being in a specific area, or that they encrypt confidential information. These rules are compulsory within a company, and if they are going to be effective, they must be enforced.

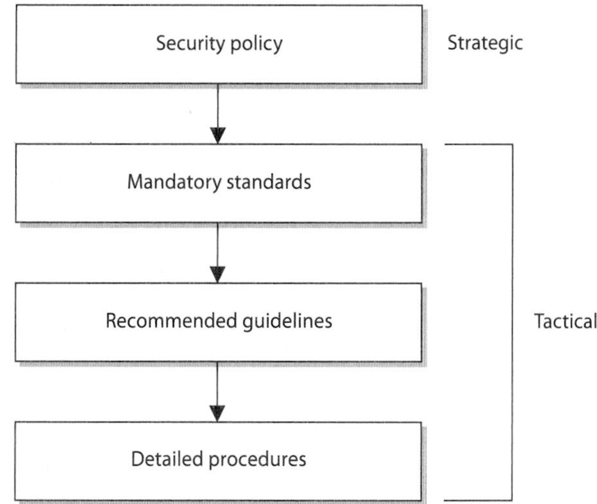

Figure 1-13 Policy establishes the strategic plans, and the lower elements provide the tactical support.

An organization may have an issue-specific data classification policy that states "All confidential data must be properly protected." It would need a supporting data protection standard outlining how this protection should be implemented and followed, as in "Confidential information must be protected with AES256 at rest and in transit."

As stated in an earlier section, tactical and strategic goals are different. A strategic goal can be viewed as the ultimate endpoint, while tactical goals are the steps necessary to achieve it. As shown in Figure 1-13, standards, guidelines, and procedures are the tactical tools used to achieve and support the directives in the security policy, which is considered the strategic goal.

EXAM TIP The term *standard* has more than one meaning in our industry. Internal documentation that lays out rules that must be followed is a standard. But sometimes, best practices, as in the ISO/IEC 27000 series, are referred to as standards because they were developed by a standards body. And as we will see later, we have specific technologic standards, as in IEEE 802.11. You need to understand the context of how this term is used. The CISSP exam will not try and trick you on this word; just know that the industry uses it in several different ways.

Baselines

The term *baseline* refers to a point in time that is used as a comparison for future changes. Once risks have been mitigated and security put in place, a baseline is formally reviewed and agreed upon, after which all further comparisons and development are measured against it. A baseline results in a consistent reference point.

Let's say that your doctor has told you that you weigh 400 pounds due to your diet of donuts, pizza, and soda. (This is very frustrating to you because the TV commercial said you could eat whatever you wanted and just take their very expensive pills every day and lose weight.) The doctor tells you that you need to exercise each day and elevate your heart rate to double its normal rate for 30 minutes twice a day. How do you know when you are at double your heart rate? You find out your baseline (regular heart rate) by using one of those arm thingies with a little ball attached. So you start at your baseline and continue to exercise until you have doubled your heart rate or die, whichever comes first.

Baselines are also used to define the minimum level of protection required. In security, specific baselines can be defined per system type, which indicates the necessary settings and the level of protection being provided. For example, a company may stipulate that all accounting systems must meet an Evaluation Assurance Level (EAL) 4 baseline. This means that only systems that have gone through the Common Criteria process and achieved this rating can be used in this department. Once the systems are properly configured, this is the necessary baseline. When new software is installed, when patches or upgrades are applied to existing software, or when other changes to the system take place, there is a good chance the system may no longer be providing its necessary minimum level of protection (its baseline). Security personnel must assess the systems as changes take place and ensure that the baseline level of security is always being met. If a technician installs a patch on a system and does not ensure the baseline is still being met, there could be new vulnerabilities introduced into the system that will allow attackers easy access to the network.

NOTE Baselines that are not technology oriented should be created and enforced within organizations as well. For example, a company can mandate that while in the facility all employees must have a badge with a picture ID in view at all times. It can also state that visitors must sign in at a front desk and be escorted while in the facility. If these are followed, then this creates a baseline of protection.

Guidelines

Guidelines are recommended actions and operational guides to users, IT staff, operations staff, and others when a specific standard does not apply. They can also be used as a recommended way to achieve specific standards when those do apply. Guidelines can deal with the methodologies of technology, personnel, or physical security. Life is full of gray areas, and guidelines can be used as a reference during those times. Whereas standards are specific mandatory rules, guidelines are general approaches that provide the necessary flexibility for unforeseen circumstances.

A policy might state that access to confidential data must be audited. A supporting guideline could further explain that audits should contain sufficient information to allow for reconciliation with prior reviews. Supporting procedures would outline the necessary steps to configure, implement, and maintain this type of auditing.

Procedures

Procedures are detailed step-by-step tasks that should be performed to achieve a certain goal. The steps can apply to users, IT staff, operations staff, security members, and others who may need to carry out specific tasks. Many organizations have written procedures on how to install operating systems, configure security mechanisms, implement access control lists, set up new user accounts, assign computer privileges, audit activities, destroy material, report incidents, and much more.

Procedures are considered the lowest level in the documentation chain because they are closest to the computers and users (compared to policies) and provide detailed steps for configuration and installation issues.

Procedures spell out how the policy, standards, and guidelines will actually be implemented in an operating environment. If a policy states that all individuals who access confidential information must be properly authenticated, the supporting procedures will explain the steps for this to happen by defining the access criteria for authorization, how access control mechanisms are implemented and configured, and how access activities are audited. If a standard states that backups should be performed, then the procedures will define the detailed steps necessary to perform the backup, the timelines of backups, the storage of backup media, and so on. Procedures should be detailed enough to be both understandable and useful to a diverse group of individuals.

To tie these items together, let's walk through an example. A corporation's security *policy* indicates that confidential information should be properly protected. It states the issue in very broad and general terms. A supporting *standard* mandates that all customer information held in databases must be encrypted with the Advanced Encryption Standard (AES) algorithm while it is stored and that it cannot be transmitted over the Internet unless IPSec encryption technology is used. The standard indicates what type of protection is required and provides another level of granularity and explanation. The supporting *procedures* explain exactly how to implement the AES and IPSec technologies, and the *guidelines* cover how to handle cases when data is accidentally corrupted or compromised during transmission. Once the software and devices are configured as outlined in the procedures, this is considered the *baseline* that must always be maintained. All of these work together to provide a company with a security structure.

Implementation

Unfortunately, security policies, standards, procedures, baselines, and guidelines often are written because an auditor instructed a company to document these items, but then they are placed on a file server and are not shared, explained, or used. To be useful, they must be put into action. No one is going to follow the rules if people don't know the rules exist. Security policies and the items that support them not only must be developed, but must also be implemented and enforced.

To be effective, employees need to know about security issues within these documents; therefore, the policies and their supporting counterparts need visibility. Awareness training, manuals, presentations, newsletters, and screen banners can achieve this visibility. It must be clear that the directives came from senior management and that the full management staff supports these policies. Employees must understand what is expected of them in their actions, behaviors, accountability, and performance.

Implementing security policies and the items that support them shows due care by the company and its management staff. Informing employees of what is expected of them and the consequences of noncompliance can come down to a liability issue. As stated in an earlier example, if a company fires an employee because he was downloading pornographic material to the company's computer, the employee may take the company to court and win if the employee can prove he was not properly informed of what was considered acceptable and unacceptable use of company property and what the consequences were. Security-awareness training is covered in later sections, but understand that companies that do not supply this training to their employees are not practicing due care and can be held negligent and liable in the eyes of the law.

Risk Management

Risk in the context of security is the possibility of damage happening and the ramifications of such damage should it occur. *Risk management (RM)* is the process of identifying and assessing risk, reducing it to an acceptable level, and ensuring it remains at that level. There is no such thing as a 100-percent secure environment. Every environment has vulnerabilities and threats. The skill is in identifying these threats, assessing the probability of them actually occurring and the damage they could cause, and then taking the right steps to reduce the overall level of risk in the environment to what the organization identifies as acceptable.

Risks to an organization come in different forms, and they are not all computer related. When a company purchases another company, it takes on a lot of risk in the hope that this move will increase its market base, productivity, and profitability. If a company increases its product line, this can add overhead, increase the need for personnel and storage facilities, require more funding for different materials, and maybe increase insurance premiums and the expense of marketing campaigns. The risk is that this added overhead might not be matched in sales; thus, profitability will be reduced or not accomplished.

When we look at information security, note that an organization needs to be aware of several types of risk and address them properly. The following items touch on the major categories:

- **Physical damage** Fire, water, vandalism, power loss, and natural disasters
- **Human interaction** Accidental or intentional action or inaction that can disrupt productivity
- **Equipment malfunction** Failure of systems and peripheral devices
- **Inside and outside attacks** Hacking, cracking, and attacking
- **Misuse of data** Sharing trade secrets, fraud, espionage, and theft
- **Loss of data** Intentional or unintentional loss of information to unauthorized receivers
- **Application error** Computation errors, input errors, and buffer overflows

Threats must be identified, classified by category, and evaluated to calculate their damage potential to the organization. Real risk is hard to measure, but prioritizing the potential risks in order of which ones must be addressed first is obtainable.

Holistic Risk Management

Who really understands risk management? Unfortunately, the answer to this question is that not enough people inside or outside of the security profession really understand risk management. Even though information security is big business today, the focus is more on applications, devices, viruses, and hacking. Although these items all must be considered and weighed in risk management processes, they should be considered small pieces of the overall security puzzle, not the main focus of risk management.

Security is a business issue, but businesses operate to make money, not just to be secure. A business is concerned with security only if potential risks threaten its bottom line, which they can in many ways, such as through the loss of reputation and customer base after a database of credit card numbers is compromised; through the loss of thousands of dollars in operational expenses from a new computer worm; through the loss of proprietary information as a result of successful company espionage attempts; through the loss of confidential information from a successful social engineering attack; and so on. It is critical that security professionals understand these individual threats, but it is more important that they understand how to calculate the risk of these threats and map them to business drivers.

In order to properly manage risk within an organization, you have to look at it holistically. Risk, after all, exists within a context. NIST SP 800-39 defines three tiers to risk management:

- **Organizational tier** Concerned with risk to the business as a whole, which means it frames the rest of the conversation and sets important parameters such as the risk tolerance level.
- **Business process tier** Deals with the risk to the major functions of the organization, such as defining the criticality of the information flows between the organization and its partners or customers. The bottom tier.
- **Information systems tier** Addresses risk from an information systems perspective. Though this is where we will focus our discussion, it is important to understand that it exists within the context of (and must be consistent with) other, more encompassing risk management efforts.

Carrying out risk management properly means that you have a holistic understanding of your organization, the threats it faces, the countermeasures that can be put into place to deal with those threats, and continuous monitoring to ensure the acceptable risk level is being met on an ongoing basis.

Information Systems Risk Management Policy

Proper risk management requires a strong commitment from senior management, a documented process that supports the organization's mission, an information systems risk management (ISRM) policy, and a delegated ISRM team.

The ISRM policy should be a subset of the organization's overall risk management policy *(risks to a company include more than just information security issues)* and should be mapped to the organizational security policies. The ISRM policy should address the following items:

- The objectives of the ISRM team
- The level of risk the organization will accept and what is considered an acceptable level of risk
- Formal processes of risk identification
- The connection between the ISRM policy and the organization's strategic planning processes
- Responsibilities that fall under ISRM and the roles to fulfill them
- The mapping of risk to internal controls
- The approach toward changing staff behaviors and resource allocation in response to risk analysis
- The mapping of risks to performance targets and budgets
- Key indicators to monitor the effectiveness of controls

The ISRM policy provides the foundation and direction for the organization's security risk management processes and procedures, and should address all issues of information security. It should provide direction on how the ISRM team communicates information on company risks to senior management and how to properly execute management's decisions on risk mitigation tasks.

The Risk Management Team

Each organization is different in its size, security posture, threat profile, and security budget. One organization may have one individual responsible for ISRM or a team that works in a coordinated manner. The overall goal of the team is to ensure the company is protected in the most cost-effective manner. This goal can be accomplished only if the following components are in place:

- An established risk acceptance level provided by senior management
- Documented risk assessment processes and procedures
- Procedures for identifying and mitigating risks
- Appropriate resource and fund allocation from senior management
- Security-awareness training for all staff members associated with information assets
- The ability to establish improvement (or risk mitigation) teams in specific areas when necessary
- The mapping of legal and regulation compliancy requirements to control and implement requirements

- The development of metrics and performance indicators so as to measure and manage various types of risks
- The ability to identify and assess new risks as the environment and company change
- The integration of ISRM and the organization's change control process to ensure that changes do not introduce new vulnerabilities

Obviously, this list is a lot more than just buying a new shiny firewall and calling the company safe.

The ISRM team, in most cases, is not made up of employees with the dedicated task of risk management. It consists of people who already have a full-time job in the company and are now tasked with something else. Thus, senior management support is necessary so proper resource allocation can take place.

Of course, all teams need a leader, and ISRM is no different. One individual should be singled out to run this rodeo and, in larger organizations, this person should be spending 50 to 70 percent of their time in this role. Management must dedicate funds to making sure this person receives the necessary training and risk analysis tools to ensure it is a successful endeavor.

The Risk Management Process

By now you should believe that risk management is critical to the long-term security (and even success) of your organization. But how do you get this done? NIST SP 800-39 describes four interrelated components that comprise the risk management process. Let's consider each of these components briefly now, since they will nicely frame the remainder of our discussion of risk management.

- **Frame risk** Risk framing defines the context within which all other risk activities take place. What are our assumptions and constraints? What are the organizational priorities? What is the risk tolerance of senior management?
- **Assess risk** Before we can take any action to mitigate risk, we have to assess it. This is perhaps the most critical aspect of the process, and one that we will discuss at length. If your risk assessment is spot-on, then the rest of the process becomes pretty straightforward.
- **Respond to risk** By now, we've done our homework. We know what we should, must, and can't do (from the framing component), and we know what we're up against in terms of threats, vulnerabilities, and attacks (from the assess component). Responding to the risk becomes a matter of matching our limited resources with our prioritized set of controls. Not only are we mitigating significant risk, but, more importantly, we can tell our bosses what risk we can't do anything about because we're out of resources.
- **Monitor risk** No matter how diligent we've been so far, we probably missed something. If not, then the environment likely changed (perhaps a new threat source emerged or a new system brought new vulnerabilities). In order to stay one step ahead of the bad guys, we need to continuously monitor the effectiveness of our controls against the risks for which we designed them.

You will notice that our discussion of risk so far has dealt heavily with the whole framing process. In the preceding sections, we've talked about the organization (top to bottom), the policies, and the team. The next step is to assess the risk, and what better way to start than by modeling the threat.

Threat Modeling

Before we can develop effective defenses, it is imperative to understand the assets that we value, as well as the threats against which we are protecting them. Though multiple definitions exist for the term, for the purposes of our discussion we define *threat modeling* as the process of describing feasible adverse effects on our assets caused by threat sources. That's quite a mouthful, so let's break it down. When we build a model of the threats we face, we want to ground them in reality, so it is important to only consider dangers that are reasonably likely to occur. To do otherwise would dilute our limited resources to the point of making us unable to properly defend ourselves.

You could argue (correctly) that threat modeling is a component task to the risk assessment that we will discuss in the next section. However, many organizations are stepping up threat intelligence efforts at an accelerated pace. Threat intelligence is becoming a resource that is used not only by the risk teams, but also by the security operations, development, and even management teams. We isolate threat modeling from the larger discussion of risk assessment here to highlight the fact that it serves more than just risk assessment efforts and allows an organization to understand what is in the realm of the probable and not just the possible.

To focus our efforts on the likely (and push aside the less likely), we need to consider what it is that we have that someone (or something) else may be able to degrade, disrupt, or destroy. As we will see shortly, inventorying and categorizing our information systems is a critical early step in the process. For the purpose of modeling the threat, we are particularly interested in the vulnerabilities inherent in our systems that could lead to the compromise of their confidentiality, integrity, or availability. We then ask the question, "Who would want to exploit this vulnerability, and why?" This leads us to a deliberate study of our potential adversaries, their motivations, and their capabilities. Finally, we determine whether a given threat source has the means to exploit one or more vulnerabilities in order to attack our assets.

Vulnerabilities

Everything built by humans is vulnerable to something. Our information systems, in particular, are riddled with vulnerabilities even in the best-defended cases. One need only read news accounts of the compromise of the highly protected and classified systems of defense contractors and even governments to see that this universal principle is true. In order to properly analyze vulnerabilities, it is useful to recall that information systems consist of information, processes, and people that are typically, but not always, interacting with computer systems. Since we discuss computer system vulnerabilities in detail in Chapter 3 (which covers domain 3, Security Engineering), we will briefly discuss the other three components here.

Information

In almost every case, the information at the core of our information systems is the most valuable asset to a potential adversary. Information within a computer information system (CIS) is represented as data. This information may be stored (data at rest), transported between parts of our system (data in motion), or actively being used by the system (data in use). In each of its three states, the information exhibits different vulnerabilities, as listed in the following examples:

- **Data at rest** Data is copied to a thumb drive and given to unauthorized parties by an insider, thus compromising its confidentiality.
- **Data in motion** Data is modified by an external actor intercepting it on the network and then relaying the altered version (known as a man-in-the-middle or MitM attack), thus compromising its integrity.
- **Data in use** Data is deleted by a malicious process exploiting a "time of check to time of use" (TOC/TOU) or "race condition" vulnerability, thus compromising its availability. We address this in detail in Chapter 3 (which covers domain 3, Security Engineering).

Processes

Processes are almost always instantiated in software as part of a CIS. Therefore, process vulnerabilities can be thought of as a specific kind of software vulnerability. We will address these in detail in Chapter 8 (which covers domain 8, Software Development Security). As security professionals, however, it is important that we take a broader view of the issue and think about the business processes that are implemented in our software systems.

People

There are many who would consider the human the weakest link in the security chain. Whether or not you agree with this, it is important to consider the specific vulnerabilities that people present in a system. Though there are many ways to exploit the human in the loop, there are three that correspond to the bulk of the attacks, summarized briefly here:

- **Social engineering** This is the process of getting a person to violate a security procedure or policy, and usually involves human interaction or e-mail/text messages.
- **Social networks** The prevalence of social network use provides potential attackers with a wealth of information that can be leveraged directly (e.g., blackmail) or indirectly (e.g., crafting an e-mail with a link that is likely to be clicked) to exploit people.
- **Passwords** Weak passwords can be cracked in milliseconds using rainbow tables (discussed in Chapter 5) and are very susceptible to dictionary or brute-force attacks. Even strong passwords are vulnerable if they are reused across sites and systems.

Threats

As you identify the vulnerabilities that are inherent to your organization and its systems, it is important to also identify the sources that could attack them. The International Organization for Standardization and the International Electrotechnical Commission in their ISO/IEC standard 27000 define a *threat* as a "potential cause of an unwanted incident, which may result in harm to a system or organization." While this may sound somewhat vague, it is important to include the full breadth of possibilities.

Perhaps the most obvious threat source is the malicious attacker who intentionally pokes and prods our systems looking for vulnerabilities to exploit. In the past, this was a sufficient description of this kind of threat source. Increasingly, however, organizations are interested in profiling the threat in great detail. Many organizations are implementing teams to conduct cyberthreat intelligence that allows them to individually label, track, and understand specific cybercrime groups. This capability enables these organizations to more accurately determine which attacks are likely to originate from each group based on their capabilities as well as their tactics, techniques, and procedures (TTP).

Another important threat source is the insider, who may be malicious or simply careless. The malicious insider is motivated by a number of factors, but most frequently by disgruntlement and/or financial gain. In the wake of the massive leak of classified data attributed to Edward Snowden in 2012, there's been increased emphasis on techniques and procedures for identifying and mitigating the insider threat source. While the deliberate insider dominates the news, it is important to note that the accidental insider can be just as dangerous, particularly if they fall into one of the vulnerability classes described in the preceding section.

Finally, the nonhuman threat source can be just as important as the ones we've previously discussed. Hurricane Katrina in 2005 and the Tohoku earthquake and tsunami in 2011 serve as reminders that natural events can be more destructive than any human attack. They also force the information systems security professional to consider threats that fall way outside the norm. Though it is easier and in many cases cheaper to address likelier natural events such as a water main break or a fire in a facility, one should always look for opportunities to leverage countermeasures that protect against both mild and extreme events for small price differentials.

Attacks

If the vulnerability is on one end of a network and the threat source is on the other, it is the attack that ties them together. In other words, if a given threat (e.g., a disgruntled employee) wants to exploit a given vulnerability (e.g., the e-mail inbox of the company's president), but lacks the means to do so, then an attack would likely not be feasible and this scenario would not be part of our threat model. It is not possible to determine the feasibility of an attack if we don't know who would execute it and against which vulnerability. This shows how it is the triads formed by an existent vulnerability, a feasible attack, and a capable threat that constitute the heart of a threat model.

Typically, there are multiple ways to accomplish a given objective. For example, if a disgruntled employee wanted to steal the contents of the president's mailbox, this could be accomplished by either accessing the e-mail server, obtaining the password, or stealing

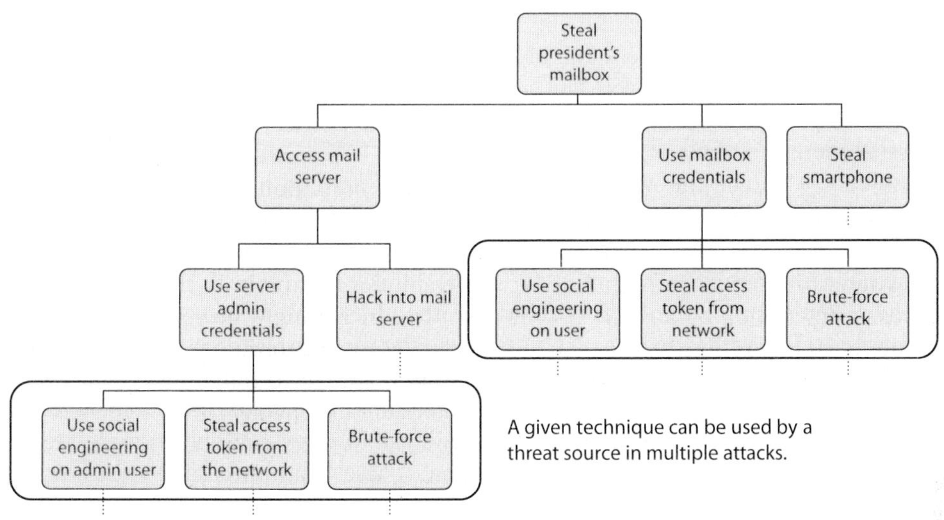

Figure 1-14 A simplified attack tree

the president's laptop. Accessing the e-mail server could be accomplished by using administrative credentials or by hacking in. To get the credentials, one could use brute force or social engineering. The branches created by each decision point create what is known as an *attack tree*, an example of which for this scenario is shown in Figure 1-14. Each of the leaf nodes represents a specific condition that must be met in order for the parent node to be effective. For instance, to effectively obtain the mailbox credentials, the employee could have stolen a network access token. Given that the employee has met the condition of having the credentials, he would then be able to steal the contents of the president's mailbox. A successful attack, then, is one in which the attacker traverses from a leaf node all the way to the root of the tree.

NOTE The terms "attack chain" and "kill chain" are commonly used. They refer to a specific type of attack tree that has no branches and simply proceeds from one stage or action to the next. The attack tree is much more expressive in that it shows many ways in which an attacker can accomplish each objective.

Reduction Analysis

The generation of attack trees for an organization usually requires a large investment of resources. Each vulnerability-threat-attack triad can be described in detail using an attack tree, so you end up with as many trees as you do triads. To defeat each of the attacks you identify, you would typically need a control or countermeasure at each leaf node. Since one attack generates many leaf nodes, this has a multiplicative effect that could make it very difficult to justify the whole exercise. However, attack trees lend themselves to a technique known as *reduction analysis*.

There are two aspects of reduction analysis in the context of threat modeling: one aspect is to reduce the number of attacks we have to consider, and the other is to reduce the threat posed by the attacks. The first aspect is evidenced by the commonalities in the example shown in Figure 1-14. To satisfy the conditions for logging into the mail server or the user's mailbox, an attacker can use the exact same three techniques. This means we can reduce the number of conditions we need to mitigate by finding these commonalities. When you consider that these three sample conditions apply to a variety of other attacks, you realize that we can very quickly cull the number of conditions to a manageable number.

The second aspect of reduction analysis is the identification of ways to mitigate or negate the attacks we've identified. This is where the use of attack trees can really benefit us. Recall that each tree has only one root but many leaves and internal nodes. The closer you are to the root when you implement a mitigation technique, the more leaf conditions you will defeat with that one control. This allows you to easily identify the most effective techniques to protect your entire organization. These techniques are typically called *controls* or *countermeasures*.

Risk Assessment and Analysis

A *risk assessment*, which is really a tool for risk management, is a method of identifying vulnerabilities and threats and assessing the possible impacts to determine where to implement security controls. After a risk assessment is carried out, the results are analyzed. Risk analysis is used to ensure that security is cost effective, relevant, timely, and responsive to threats. Security can be quite complex, even for well-versed security professionals, and it is easy to apply too much security, not enough security, or the wrong security controls and to spend too much money in the process without attaining the necessary objectives. Risk analysis helps companies prioritize their risks and shows management the amount of resources that should be applied to protecting against those risks in a sensible manner.

A risk analysis has four main goals:

- Identify assets and their value to the organization.
- Identify vulnerabilities and threats.
- Quantify the probability and business impact of these potential threats.
- Provide an economic balance between the impact of the threat and the cost of the countermeasure.

Risk analysis provides a *cost/benefit comparison*, which compares the annualized cost of controls to the potential cost of loss. A control, in most cases, should not be implemented unless the annualized cost of loss exceeds the annualized cost of the control itself. This means that if a facility is worth $100,000, it does not make sense to spend $150,000 trying to protect it.

It is important to figure out what you are *supposed* to be doing before you dig right in and start working. Anyone who has worked on a project without a properly defined scope can attest to the truth of this statement. Before an assessment and analysis is started, the team must carry out *project sizing* to understand what assets and threats should be evaluated. Most assessments are focused on physical security, technology security, or personnel security. Trying to assess all of them at the same time can be quite an undertaking.

One of the risk analysis team's tasks is to create a report that details the asset valuations. Senior management should review and accept the list and make them the scope of the risk management project. If management determines at this early stage that some assets are not important, the risk assessment team should not spend additional time or resources evaluating those assets. During discussions with management, everyone involved must have a firm understanding of the value of the security AIC triad—availability, integrity, and confidentiality—and how it directly relates to business needs.

Management should outline the scope of the assessment, which most likely will be dictated by organizational compliance requirements as well as budgetary constraints. Many projects have run out of funds, and consequently stopped, because proper project sizing was not conducted at the onset of the project. Don't let this happen to you.

A risk analysis helps integrate the security program objectives with the company's business objectives and requirements. The more the business and security objectives are in alignment, the more successful the two will be. The analysis also helps the company draft a proper budget for a security program and its constituent security components. Once a company knows how much its assets are worth and the possible threats they are exposed to, it can make intelligent decisions about how much money to spend protecting those assets.

A risk analysis must be supported and directed by senior management if it is to be successful. Management must define the purpose and scope of the analysis, appoint a team to carry out the assessment, and allocate the necessary time and funds to conduct the analysis. It is essential for senior management to review the outcome of the risk assessment and analysis and to act on its findings. After all, what good is it to go through all the trouble of a risk assessment and *not* react to its findings? Unfortunately, this does happen all too often.

Risk Analysis Team

Each organization has different departments, and each department has its own functionality, resources, tasks, and quirks. For the most effective risk analysis, an organization must build a risk analysis team that includes individuals from many or all departments to ensure that all of the threats are identified and addressed. The team members may be part of management, application programmers, IT staff, systems integrators, and operational managers—indeed, any key personnel from key areas of the organization. This mix is necessary because if the risk analysis team comprises only individuals from the IT department, it may not understand, for example, the types of threats the accounting department faces with data integrity issues, or how the company as a whole would be affected if the accounting department's data files were wiped out by an accidental or intentional act. Or, as another example, the IT staff may not understand all the risks the employees in the warehouse would face if a natural disaster were to hit, or what it would mean to their productivity and how it would affect the organization overall. If the risk analysis team is unable to include members from various departments, it should, at the very least, make sure to interview people in each department so it fully understands and can quantify all threats.

The risk analysis team must also include people who understand the processes that are part of their individual departments, meaning individuals who are at the right levels of each department. This is a difficult task, since managers tend to delegate any sort of risk analysis task to lower levels within the department. However, the people who work at these lower levels may not have adequate knowledge and understanding of the processes that the risk analysis team may need to deal with.

Asking the Right Questions

When looking at risk, it's good to keep several questions in mind. Raising these questions helps ensure that the risk analysis team and senior management know what is important. Team members must ask the following:

- What event could occur (threat event)?
- What could be the potential impact (risk)?
- How often could it happen (frequency)?
- What level of confidence do we have in the answers to the first three questions (certainty)?

A lot of this information is gathered through internal surveys, interviews, or workshops. Viewing threats with these questions in mind helps the team focus on the tasks at hand and assists in making the decisions more accurate and relevant.

The Value of Information and Assets

The value placed on information is relative to the parties involved, what work was required to develop it, how much it costs to maintain, what damage would result if it were lost or destroyed, what enemies would pay for it, and what liability penalties could be endured. If a company does not know the value of the information and the other assets it is trying to protect, it does not know how much money and time it should spend on protecting them. If the calculated value of your company's secret formula is *x*, then the total cost of protecting it should be some value less than *x*. The value of the information supports security measure decisions.

The previous examples refer to assessing the value of *information* and protecting it, but this logic applies toward an organization's facilities, systems, and resources. The value of the company's facilities must be assessed, along with all printers, workstations, servers, peripheral devices, supplies, and employees. You do not know how much is in danger of being lost if you don't know what you have and what it is worth in the first place.

Costs That Make Up the Value

An asset can have both quantitative and qualitative measurements assigned to it, but these measurements need to be derived. The actual value of an asset is determined by the importance it has to the organization as a whole. The value of an asset should reflect all identifiable costs that would arise if the asset were actually impaired. If a server cost $4,000 to purchase, this value should not be input as the value of the asset in a risk assessment. Rather, the cost of replacing or repairing it, the loss of productivity, and the value of any data that may be corrupted or lost must be accounted for to properly capture the amount the organization would lose if the server were to fail for one reason or another.

The following issues should be considered when assigning values to assets:

- Cost to acquire or develop the asset
- Cost to maintain and protect the asset
- Value of the asset to owners and users
- Value of the asset to adversaries
- Price others are willing to pay for the asset
- Cost to replace the asset if lost
- Operational and production activities affected if the asset is unavailable
- Liability issues if the asset is compromised
- Usefulness and role of the asset in the organization

Understanding the value of an asset is the first step to understanding what security mechanisms should be put in place and what funds should go toward protecting it. A very important question is how much it could cost the company to *not* protect the asset.

Determining the value of assets may be useful to a company for a variety of reasons, including the following:

- To perform effective cost/benefit analyses
- To select specific countermeasures and safeguards
- To determine the level of insurance coverage to purchase
- To understand what exactly is at risk
- To comply with legal and regulatory requirements

Assets may be tangible (computers, facilities, supplies) or intangible (reputation, data, intellectual property). It is usually harder to quantify the values of intangible assets, which may change over time. How do you put a monetary value on a company's reputation? This is not always an easy question to answer, but it is important to be able to do so.

Identifying Vulnerabilities and Threats

Earlier, it was stated that the definition of a risk is the probability of a threat agent exploiting a vulnerability to cause harm to an asset and the resulting business impact. Many types of threat agents can take advantage of several types of vulnerabilities, resulting in a variety of specific threats, as outlined in Table 1-5, which represents only a sampling of the risks many organizations should address in their risk management programs.

Other types of threats can arise in an environment that are much harder to identify than those listed in Table 1-5. These other threats have to do with application and user errors. If an application uses several complex equations to produce results, the threat can be difficult to discover and isolate if these equations are incorrect or if the application is using inputted data incorrectly. This can result in *illogical processing* and *cascading errors* as invalid results are passed on to another process. These types of problems can lie within applications' code and are very hard to identify.

User errors, whether intentional or accidental, are easier to identify by monitoring and auditing user activities. Audits and reviews must be conducted to discover if employees are inputting values incorrectly into programs, misusing technology, or modifying data in an inappropriate manner.

Once the vulnerabilities and associated threats are identified, the ramifications of these vulnerabilities being exploited must be investigated. Risks have *loss potential*, meaning what the company would lose if a threat agent actually exploited a vulnerability. The loss may be corrupted data, destruction of systems and/or the facility, unauthorized disclosure of confidential information, a reduction in employee productivity, and so on. When performing a risk analysis, the team also must look at *delayed loss* when assessing the damages that can occur. Delayed loss is secondary in nature and takes place well

Threat Agent	Can Exploit This Vulnerability	Resulting in This Threat
Malware	Lack of antivirus software	Virus infection
Hacker	Powerful services running on a server	Unauthorized access to confidential information
Users	Misconfigured parameter in the operating system	System malfunction
Fire	Lack of fire extinguishers	Facility and computer damage, and possibly loss of life
Employee	Lack of training or standards enforcement Lack of auditing	Sharing mission-critical information Altering data inputs and outputs from data-processing applications
Contractor	Lax access control mechanisms	Stealing trade secrets
Attacker	Poorly written application Lack of stringent firewall settings	Conducting a buffer overflow Conducting a denial-of-service attack
Intruder	Lack of security guard	Breaking windows and stealing computers and devices

Table 1-5 Relationship of Threats and Vulnerabilities

after a vulnerability is exploited. Delayed loss may include damage to the company's reputation, loss of market share, accrued late penalties, civil suits, the delayed collection of funds from customers, resources required to reimage other compromised systems, and so forth.

For example, if a company's web servers are attacked and taken offline, the immediate damage (loss potential) could be data corruption, the man-hours necessary to place the servers back online, and the replacement of any code or components required. The company could lose revenue if it usually accepts orders and payments via its website. If it takes a full day to get the web servers fixed and back online, the company could lose a lot more sales and profits. If it takes a full week to get the web servers fixed and back online, the company could lose enough sales and profits to not be able to pay other bills and expenses. This would be a delayed loss. If the company's customers lose confidence in it because of this activity, it could lose business for months or years. This is a more extreme case of delayed loss.

These types of issues make the process of properly quantifying losses that specific threats could cause more complex, but they must be taken into consideration to ensure reality is represented in this type of analysis.

Methodologies for Risk Assessment

The industry has different standardized methodologies when it comes to carrying out risk assessments. Each of the individual methodologies has the same basic core components (identify vulnerabilities, associate threats, calculate risk values), but each has a specific focus. As a security professional it is your responsibility to know which is the best approach for your organization and its needs.

NIST developed a guide for conducting risk assessments, which is published in *SP 800-30, Revision 1*. It is specific to information systems threats and how they relate to information security risks. It lays out the following steps:

1. Prepare for the assessment.
2. Conduct the assessment:
   a. Identify threat sources and events.
   b. Identify vulnerabilities and predisposing conditions.
   c. Determine likelihood of occurrence.
   d. Determine magnitude of impact.
   e. Determine risk.
3. Communicate results.
4. Maintain assessment.

The NIST risk management methodology is mainly focused on computer systems and IT security issues. It does not explicitly cover larger organizational threat types, as in succession planning, environmental issues, or how security risks associate to business risks. It is a methodology that focuses on the operational components of an enterprise, not necessarily the higher strategic level.

A second type of risk assessment methodology is called *FRAP*, which stands for *Facilitated Risk Analysis Process*. The crux of this qualitative methodology is to focus only on the systems that really need assessing, to reduce costs and time obligations. It stresses prescreening activities so that the risk assessment steps are only carried out on the item(s) that needs it the most. FRAP is intended to be used to analyze one system, application, or business process at a time. Data is gathered and threats to business operations are prioritized based upon their criticality. The risk assessment team documents the controls that need to be put into place to reduce the identified risks along with action plans for control implementation efforts.

This methodology does not support the idea of calculating exploitation probability numbers or annual loss expectancy values. The criticalities of the risks are determined by the team members' experience. The author of this methodology (Thomas Peltier) believes that trying to use mathematical formulas for the calculation of risk is too confusing and time consuming. The goal is to keep the scope of the assessment small and the assessment processes simple to allow for efficiency and cost effectiveness.

Another methodology called *OCTAVE* (Operationally Critical Threat, Asset, and Vulnerability Evaluation) was created by Carnegie Mellon University's Software Engineering Institute. It is a methodology that is intended to be used in situations where people manage and direct the risk evaluation for information security within their company. This places the people who work inside the organization in the power positions as being able to make the decisions regarding what is the best approach for evaluating the security of their organization. This relies on the idea that the people working in these environments best understand what is needed and what kind of risks they are facing. The individuals who make up the risk assessment team go through rounds of facilitated workshops. The facilitator helps the team members understand the risk methodology and how to apply it to the vulnerabilities and threats identified within their specific business units. It stresses a self-directed team approach. The scope of an OCTAVE assessment is usually very wide compared to the more focused approach of FRAP. Where FRAP would be used to assess a system or application, OCTAVE would be used to assess all systems, applications, and business processes within the organization.

While NIST, FRAP, and OCTAVE methodologies focus on IT security threats and information security risks, *AS/NZS 4360* takes a much broader approach to risk management. This Australian and New Zealand methodology can be used to understand a company's financial, capital, human safety, and business decisions risks. Although it can be used to analyze security risks, it was not created specifically for this purpose. This risk methodology is more focused on the health of a company from a business point of view, not security.

If we need a risk methodology that is to be integrated into our security program, we can use one that was previously mentioned within the "ISO/IEC 27000 Series" section earlier in the chapter. As a reminder, *ISO/IEC 27005* is an international standard for how risk management should be carried out in the framework of an information security management system (ISMS). So where the NIST risk methodology is mainly focused on IT and operations, this methodology deals with IT *and* the softer security issues (documentation, personnel security, training, etc.). This methodology is to be integrated into an organizational security program that addresses all of the security threats an organization could be faced with.

Failure Modes and Effect Analysis (FMEA) is a method for determining functions, identifying functional failures, and assessing the causes of failure and their failure effects through a structured process. FMEA is commonly used in product development and operational environments. The goal is to identify where something is most likely going to break and either fix the flaws that could cause this issue or implement controls to reduce the impact of the break. For example, you might choose to carry out an FMEA on your organization's network to identify single points of failure. These single points of failure represent vulnerabilities that could directly affect the productivity of the network as a whole. You would use this structured approach to identify these issues (vulnerabilities), assess their criticality (risk), and identify the necessary controls that should be put into place (reduce risk).

The FMEA methodology uses failure modes (how something can break or fail) and effects analysis (impact of that break or failure). The application of this process to a chronic failure enables the determination of where exactly the failure is most likely to occur. Think of it as being able to look into the future and locate areas that have the potential for failure and then applying corrective measures to them before they do become actual liabilities.

By following a specific order of steps, the best results can be maximized for an FMEA:

1. Start with a block diagram of a system or control.
2. Consider what happens if each block of the diagram fails.
3. Draw up a table in which failures are paired with their effects and an evaluation of the effects.
4. Correct the design of the system, and adjust the table until the system is not known to have unacceptable problems.
5. Have several engineers review the Failure Modes and Effect Analysis.

Table 1-6 is an example of how an FMEA can be carried out and documented. Although most companies will not have the resources to do this level of detailed work for every system and control, it can be carried out on critical functions and systems that can drastically affect the company.

FMEA was first developed for systems engineering. Its purpose is to examine the potential failures in products and the processes involved with them. This approach proved to be successful and has been more recently adapted for use in evaluating risk management priorities and mitigating known threat vulnerabilities.

FMEA is used in assurance risk management because of the level of detail, variables, and complexity that continues to rise as corporations understand risk at more granular levels. This methodical way of identifying potential pitfalls is coming into play more as the need for risk awareness—down to the tactical and operational levels—continues to expand.

Prepared by:							
Approved by:							
Date:							
Revision:							
				Failure Effect on . . .			
Item Identification	**Function**	**Failure Mode**	**Failure Cause**	**Component or Functional Assembly**	**Next Higher Assembly**	**System**	**Failure Detection Method**
IPS application content filter	Inline perimeter protection	Fails to close	Traffic overload	Single point of failure Denial of service	IPS blocks ingress traffic stream	IPS is brought down	Health check status sent to console and e-mail to security administrator
Central antivirus signature update engine	Push updated signatures to all servers and workstations	Fails to provide adequate, timely protection against malware	Central server goes down	Individual node's antivirus software is not updated	Network is infected with malware	Central server can be infected and/or infect other systems	Heartbeat status check sent to central console, and e-mail to network administrator
Fire suppression water pipes	Suppress fire in building 1 in 5 zones	Fails to close	Water in pipes freezes	None	Building 1 has no suppression agent available	Fire suppression system pipes break	Suppression sensors tied directly into fire system central console
Etc.							

Table 1-6 How an FMEA Can Be Carried Out and Documented

While FMEA is most useful as a survey method to identify major failure modes in a given system, the method is not as useful in discovering complex failure modes that may be involved in multiple systems or subsystems. A *fault tree analysis* usually proves to be a more useful approach to identifying failures that can take place within more complex environments and systems. Fault trees are similar to the attack trees we discussed earlier and follow this general process. First, an undesired effect is taken as the root or top event of a tree of logic. Then, each situation that has the potential to cause that effect is added to the tree as a series of logic expressions. Fault trees are then labeled with actual numbers pertaining to failure probabilities. This is typically done by using computer programs that can calculate the failure probabilities from a fault tree.

Figure 1-15 shows a simplistic fault tree and the different logic symbols used to represent what must take place for a specific fault event to occur.

When setting up the tree, you must accurately list all the threats or faults that can occur within a system. The branches of the tree can be divided into general categories, such as physical threats, networks threats, software threats, Internet threats, and component failure threats. Then, once all possible general categories are in place, you can trim them and effectively prune the branches from the tree that won't apply to the system in question. In general, if a system is not connected to the Internet by any means, remove that general branch from the tree.

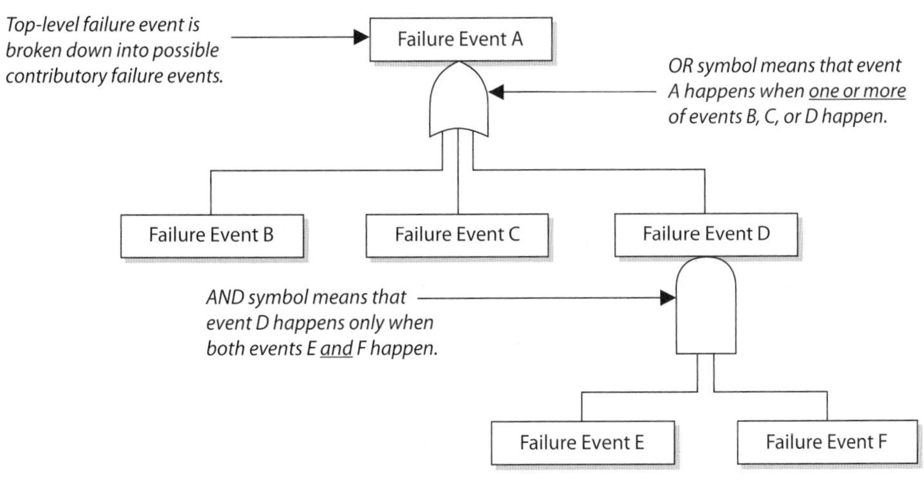

Figure 1-15 Fault tree and logic components

Some of the most common software failure events that can be explored through a fault tree analysis are the following:

- False alarms
- Insufficient error handling
- Sequencing or order
- Incorrect timing outputs
- Valid but not expected outputs

Of course, because of the complexity of software and heterogeneous environments, this is a very small sample list.

Just in case you do not have enough risk assessment methodologies to choose from, you can also look at *CRAMM* (Central Computing and Telecommunications Agency Risk Analysis and Management Method), which was created by the United Kingdom, and its automated tools are sold by Siemens. It works in three distinct stages: define objectives, assess risks, and identify countermeasures. It is really not fair to call it a unique methodology, because it follows the basic structure of any risk methodology. It just has everything (questionnaires, asset dependency modeling, assessment formulas, compliancy reporting) in automated tool format.

Similar to the "Security Frameworks" section that covered things such as ISO/IEC 27000, CMMI, COBIT, COSO IC, Zachman Framework, SABSA, ITIL, NIST SP 800-53, and Six Sigma, this section on risk methodologies could at first take seem like another list of confusing standards and guidelines. Remember that the methodologies have a lot of overlapping similarities because each one has the specific goal of identifying things that could hurt the organization (vulnerabilities and threats) so that those things can be addressed (risk reduced). What make these methodologies different from each other are their unique approaches and focuses. If you need to deploy an organization-wide risk management program and integrate it into your security program, you should follow the ISO/IEC 27005 or OCTAVE methods. If you need to focus just on IT security risks during your assessment, you can follow NIST SP 800-30. If you have a limited budget and need to carry out a focused assessment on an individual system or process, you can follow the Facilitated Risk Analysis Process. If you really want to dig into the details of how a security flaw within a specific system could cause negative ramifications, you could use Failure Modes and Effect Analysis or fault tree analysis. If you need to understand your company's business risks, then you can follow the AS/NZS 4360 approach.

So up to this point, we have accomplished the following items:

- Developed a risk management policy
- Developed a risk management team
- Identified company assets to be assessed
- Calculated the value of each asset
- Identified the vulnerabilities and threats that can affect the identified assets
- Chose a risk assessment methodology that best fits our needs

The next thing we need to figure out is if our risk analysis approach should be quantitative or qualitative in nature, which we will cover in the following section.

EXAM TIP A risk assessment is used to gather data. A risk analysis examines the gathered data to produce results that can be acted upon.

Risk Analysis Approaches

The two approaches to risk analysis are quantitative and qualitative. A *quantitative risk analysis* is used to assign monetary and numeric values to all elements of the risk analysis process. Each element within the analysis (asset value, threat frequency, severity of vulnerability, impact damage, safeguard costs, safeguard effectiveness, uncertainty, and probability items) is quantified and entered into equations to determine total and residual risks. It is more of a scientific or mathematical approach to risk analysis compared to qualitative. A *qualitative risk analysis* uses a "softer" approach to the data elements of a risk analysis. It does not quantify that data, which means that it does not assign numeric values to the data so that it can be used in equations. As an example, the results of a quantitative risk analysis could be that the organization is at risk of losing $100,000 if a buffer overflow were exploited on a web server, $25,000 if a database were compromised, and $10,000 if a file server were compromised. A qualitative risk analysis would not present these findings in monetary values, but would assign ratings to the risks, as in Red, Yellow, and Green.

A quantitative analysis uses risk calculations that attempt to predict the level of monetary losses and the probability for each type of threat. Qualitative analysis does not use calculations. Instead, it is more opinion and scenario based and uses a rating system to relay the risk criticality levels.

Quantitative and qualitative approaches have their own pros and cons, and each applies more appropriately to some situations than others. Company management and the risk analysis team, and the tools they decide to use, will determine which approach is best.

In the following sections we will dig into the depths of quantitative analysis and then revisit the qualitative approach. We will then compare and contrast their attributes.

Automated Risk Analysis Methods

Collecting all the necessary data that needs to be plugged into risk analysis equations and properly interpreting the results can be overwhelming if done manually. Several automated risk analysis tools on the market can make this task much less painful and, hopefully, more accurate. The gathered data can be reused, greatly reducing the time required to perform subsequent analyses. The risk analysis team can also print reports and comprehensive graphs to present to management.

EXAM TIP Remember that vulnerability assessments are different from risk assessments. A vulnerability assessment just finds the vulnerabilities (the holes). A risk assessment calculates the probability of the vulnerabilities being exploited and the associated business impact.

The objective of these tools is to reduce the manual effort of these tasks, perform calculations quickly, estimate future expected losses, and determine the effectiveness and benefits of the security countermeasures chosen. Most automatic risk analysis products port information into a database and run several types of scenarios with different parameters to give a panoramic view of what the outcome will be if different threats come to bear. For example, after such a tool has all the necessary information inputted, it can be rerun several times with different parameters to compute the potential outcome if a large fire were to take place; the potential losses if a virus were to damage 40 percent of the data on the main file server; how much the company would lose if an attacker were to steal all the customer credit card information held in three databases; and so on. Running through the different risk possibilities gives a company a more detailed understanding of which risks are more critical than others, and thus which ones to address first.

Steps of a Quantitative Risk Analysis

Recapping the previous sections in this chapter, we have already carried out our risk assessment, which is the process of gathering data for a risk analysis. We have identified the assets that are to be assessed, associated a value to each asset, and identified the vulnerabilities and threats that could affect these assets. Now we need to carry out the risk analysis portion, which means that we need to figure out how to interpret all the data that was gathered during the assessment.

If we choose to carry out a quantitative analysis, then we are going to use mathematical equations for our data interpretation process. The most common equations used for this purpose are the *single loss expectancy (SLE)* and the *annual loss expectancy (ALE)*.

The SLE is a dollar amount that is assigned to a single event that represents the company's potential loss amount if a specific threat were to take place. The equation is laid out as follows:

Asset Value × Exposure Factor (EF) = SLE

The *exposure factor (EF)* represents the percentage of loss a realized threat could have on a certain asset. For example, if a data warehouse has the asset value of $150,000, it can be estimated that if a fire were to occur, 25 percent of the warehouse would be damaged, in which case the SLE would be $37,500:

Asset Value ($150,000) × Exposure Factor (25%) = $37,500

This tells us that the company could potentially lose $37,500 if a fire were to take place. But we need to know what our annual potential loss is, since we develop and use our security budgets on an annual basis. This is where the ALE equation comes into play. The ALE equation is as follows:

SLE × Annualized Rate of Occurrence (ARO) = ALE

The *annualized rate of occurrence (ARO)* is the value that represents the estimated frequency of a specific threat taking place within a 12-month timeframe. The range can be from 0.0 (never) to 1.0 (once a year) to greater than 1 (several times a year) and anywhere in between. For example, if the probability of a fire taking place and damaging our data warehouse is once every 10 years, the ARO value is 0.1.

So, if a fire taking place within a company's data warehouse facility can cause $37,500 in damages, and the frequency (or ARO) of a fire taking place has an ARO value of 0.1 (indicating once in 10 years), then the ALE value is $3,750 ($37,500 × 0.1 = $3,750).

The ALE value tells the company that if it wants to put in controls to protect the asset (warehouse) from this threat (fire), it can sensibly spend $3,750 or less per year to provide the necessary level of protection. Knowing the real possibility of a threat and how much damage, in monetary terms, the threat can cause is important in determining how much should be spent to try and protect against that threat in the first place. It would not make good business sense for the company to spend more than $3,750 per year to protect itself from this threat.

Now that we have all these numbers, what do we do with them? Let's look at the example in Table 1-7, which shows the outcome of a quantitative risk analysis. With this data, the company can make intelligent decisions on what threats must be addressed first because of the severity of the threat, the likelihood of it happening, and how much could be lost if the threat were realized. The company now also knows how much money it should spend to protect against each threat. This will result in good business decisions, instead of just buying protection here and there without a

Asset	Threat	Single Loss Expectancy (SLE)	Annualized Rate of Occurrence (ARO)	Annualized Loss Expectancy (ALE)
Facility	Fire	$230,000	0.1	$23,000
Trade secret	Stolen	$40,000	0.01	$400
File server	Failed	$11,500	0.1	$1,150
Data	Virus	$6,500	1.0	$6,500
Customer credit card info	Stolen	$300,000	3.0	$900,000

Table 1-7 Breaking Down How SLE and ALE Values Are Used

clear understanding of the big picture. Because the company has a risk of losing up to $6,500 if data is corrupted by virus infiltration, up to this amount of funds can be earmarked toward providing antivirus software and methods to ensure that a virus attack will not happen.

When carrying out a quantitative analysis, some people mistakenly think that the process is purely objective and scientific because data is being presented in numeric values. But a purely quantitative analysis is hard to achieve because there is still some subjectivity when it comes to the data. How do we know that a fire will only take place once every 10 years? How do we know that the damage from a fire will be 25 percent of the value of the asset? We don't know these values exactly, but instead of just pulling them out of thin air, they should be based upon historical data and industry experience. In quantitative risk analysis, we can do our best to provide all the correct information, and by doing so we will come close to the risk values, but we cannot predict the future and how much the future will cost us or the company.

Uncertainty

In risk analysis, uncertainty refers to the degree to which you lack confidence in an estimate. This is expressed as a percentage, from 0 to 100 percent. If you have a 30 percent confidence level in something, then it could be said you have a 70 percent uncertainty level. Capturing the degree of uncertainty when carrying out a risk analysis is important, because it indicates the level of confidence the team and management should have in the resulting figures.

Results of a Quantitative Risk Analysis

The risk analysis team should have clearly defined goals. The following is a short list of what generally is expected from the results of a risk analysis:

- Monetary values assigned to assets
- Comprehensive list of all possible and significant threats

- Probability of the occurrence rate of each threat
- Loss potential the company can endure per threat in a 12-month time span
- Recommended controls

Although this list looks short, there is usually an incredible amount of detail under each bullet item. This report will be presented to senior management, which will be concerned with possible monetary losses and the necessary costs to mitigate these risks. Although the reports should be as detailed as possible, there should be executive abstracts so senior management can quickly understand the overall findings of the analysis.

Qualitative Risk Analysis

Another method of risk analysis is *qualitative*, which does not assign numbers and monetary values to components and losses. Instead, qualitative methods walk through different scenarios of risk possibilities and rank the seriousness of the threats and the validity of the different possible countermeasures based on opinions. (A wide-sweeping analysis can include hundreds of scenarios.) Qualitative analysis techniques include judgment, best practices, intuition, and experience. Examples of qualitative techniques to gather data are Delphi, brainstorming, storyboarding, focus groups, surveys, questionnaires, checklists, one-on-one meetings, and interviews. The risk analysis team will determine the best technique for the threats that need to be assessed, as well as the culture of the company and individuals involved with the analysis.

The team that is performing the risk analysis gathers personnel who have experience and education on the threats being evaluated. When this group is presented with a scenario that describes threats and loss potential, each member responds with their gut feeling and experience on the likelihood of the threat and the extent of damage that may result. This group explores a scenario of each identified vulnerability and how it would be exploited. The "expert" in the group, who is most familiar with this type of threat, should review the scenario to ensure it reflects how an actual threat would be carried out. Safeguards that would diminish the damage of this threat are then evaluated, and the scenario is played out for each safeguard. The exposure possibility and loss possibility can be ranked as high, medium, or low on a scale of 1 to 5 or 1 to 10.

A common qualitative risk matrix is shown in Figure 1-16. Once the selected personnel rank the possibility of a threat happening, the loss potential, and the advantages of each safeguard, this information is compiled into a report and presented to management to help it make better decisions on how best to implement safeguards into the environment. The benefits of this type of analysis are that communication must happen among team members to rank the risks, evaluate the safeguard strengths, and identify weaknesses, and the people who know these subjects the best provide their opinions to management.

Let's look at a *simple* example of a qualitative risk analysis.

The risk analysis team presents a scenario explaining the threat of a hacker accessing confidential information held on the five file servers within the company. The risk analysis team then distributes the scenario in a written format to a team of five people (the IT manager, database administrator, application programmer, system operator,

Likelihood	Consequences				
	Insignificant	Minor	Moderate	Major	Severe
Almost certain	M	H	H	E	E
Likely	M	M	H	H	E
Possible	L	M	M	H	E
Unlikely	L	M	M	M	H
Rare	L	L	M	M	H

Figure 1-16 Qualitative risk matrix: likelihood vs. consequences (impact)

and operational manager), who are also given a sheet to rank the threat's severity, loss potential, and each safeguard's effectiveness, with a rating of 1 to 5, 1 being the least severe, effective, or probable. Table 1-8 shows the results.

This data is compiled and inserted into a report and presented to management. When management is presented with this information, it will see that its staff (or a chosen set) feels that purchasing a firewall will protect the company from this threat more than purchasing an intrusion detection system or setting up a honeypot system.

Threat = Hacker Accessing Confidential Information	Severity of Threat	Probability of Threat Taking Place	Potential Loss to the Company	Effectiveness of Firewall	Effectiveness of Intrusion Detection System	Effectiveness of Honeypot
IT manager	4	2	4	4	3	2
Database administrator	4	4	4	3	4	1
Application programmer	2	3	3	4	2	1
System operator	3	4	3	4	2	1
Operational manager	5	4	4	4	4	2
Results	3.6	3.4	3.6	3.8	3	1.4

Table 1-8 Example of a Qualitative Analysis

This is the result of looking at only one threat, and management will view the severity, probability, and loss potential of each threat so it knows which threats cause the greatest risk and should be addressed first.

The Delphi Technique

The Delphi technique is a group decision method used to ensure that each member gives an honest opinion of what he or she thinks the result of a particular threat will be. This avoids a group of individuals feeling pressured to go along with others' thought processes and enables them to participate in an independent and anonymous way. Each member of the group provides his or her opinion of a certain threat and turns it in to the team that is performing the analysis. The results are compiled and distributed to the group members, who then write down their comments anonymously and return them to the analysis group. The comments are compiled and redistributed for more comments until a consensus is formed. This method is used to obtain an agreement on cost, loss values, and probabilities of occurrence without individuals having to agree verbally.

Quantitative vs. Qualitative

Each method has its advantages and disadvantages, some of which are outlined in Table 1-9 for purposes of comparison.

The risk analysis team, management, risk analysis tools, and culture of the company will dictate which approach—quantitative or qualitative—should be used. The goal of

Attribute	Quantitative	Qualitative
Requires no calculations		X
Requires more complex calculations	X	
Involves high degree of guesswork		X
Provides general areas and indications of risk		X
Is easier to automate and evaluate	X	
Used in risk management performance tracking	X	
Allows for cost/benefit analysis	X	
Uses independently verifiable and objective metrics	X	
Provides the opinions of the individuals who know the processes best		X
Shows clear-cut losses that can be accrued within one year's time	X	

Table 1-9 Quantitative vs. Qualitative Characteristics

either method is to estimate a company's real risk and to rank the severity of the threats so the correct countermeasures can be put into place within a practical budget.

Table 1-9 refers to some of the positive aspects of the quantitative and qualitative approaches. However, not everything is always easy. In deciding to use either a quantitative or qualitative approach, the following points might need to be considered.

Quantitative Cons:

- Calculations can be complex. Can management understand how these values were derived?
- Without automated tools, this process is extremely laborious.
- More preliminary work is needed to gather detailed information about the environment.
- Standards are not available. Each vendor has its own way of interpreting the processes and their results.

Qualitative Cons:

- The assessments and results are subjective and opinion based.
- Eliminates the opportunity to create a dollar value for cost/benefit discussions.
- Hard to develop a security budget from the results because monetary values are not used.
- Standards are not available. Each vendor has its own way of interpreting the processes and their results.

NOTE Since a purely quantitative assessment is close to impossible and a purely qualitative process does not provide enough statistical data for financial decisions, these two risk analysis approaches can be used in a hybrid approach. Quantitative evaluation can be used for tangible assets (monetary values), and a qualitative assessment can be used for intangible assets (priority values).

Protection Mechanisms

The next step is to identify the current security mechanisms and evaluate their effectiveness.

This section addresses identifying and choosing the right countermeasures for computer systems. It gives the best attributes to look for and the different cost scenarios to investigate when comparing different types of countermeasures. The end product of the analysis of choices should demonstrate why the selected control is the most advantageous to the company.

Control Selection

A security control must make good business sense, meaning it is cost effective (its benefit outweighs its cost). This requires another type of analysis: a *cost/benefit analysis*. A commonly used cost/benefit calculation for a given safeguard (control) is

> (ALE before implementing safeguard) – (ALE after implementing safeguard) – (annual cost of safeguard) = value of safeguard to the company

For example, if the ALE of the threat of a hacker bringing down a web server is $12,000 prior to implementing the suggested safeguard, and the ALE is $3,000 after implementing the safeguard, while the annual cost of maintenance and operation of the safeguard is $650, then the value of this safeguard to the company is $8,350 each year.

The cost of a countermeasure is more than just the amount filled out on the purchase order. The following items should be considered and evaluated when deriving the full cost of a countermeasure:

- Product costs
- Design/planning costs
- Implementation costs
- Environment modifications
- Compatibility with other countermeasures
- Maintenance requirements
- Testing requirements
- Repair, replacement, or update costs
- Operating and support costs
- Effects on productivity
- Subscription costs
- Extra man-hours for monitoring and responding to alerts

Many companies have gone through the pain of purchasing new security products without understanding that they will need the staff to maintain those products. Although tools automate tasks, many companies were not even carrying out these tasks before, so they do not save on man-hours, but many times require more hours. For example, Company A decides that to protect many of its resources, purchasing an IDS is warranted. So, the company pays $5,500 for an IDS. Is that the total cost? Nope. This software should be tested in an environment that is segmented from the production environment to uncover any unexpected activity. After this testing is complete and the security group feels it is safe to insert the IDS into its production environment, the security group must install the monitoring management software, install the sensors, and properly direct the communication paths from the sensors to the management console. The security group may also need to reconfigure the routers to redirect traffic flow, and it definitely needs to ensure that users cannot access the IDS management console. Finally, the security group should configure a database to hold all attack signatures and then run simulations.

Costs associated with an IDS alert response should most definitely be considered. Now that Company A has an IDS in place, security administrators may need additional alerting equipment such as smartphones. And then there are the time costs associated with a response to an IDS event.

Anyone who has worked in an IT group knows that some adverse reaction almost always takes place in this type of scenario. Network performance can take an unacceptable hit after installing a product if it is an inline or proactive product. Users may no longer be able to access the Unix server for some mysterious reason. The IDS vendor may not have explained that two more service patches are necessary for the whole thing to work correctly. Staff time will need to be allocated for training and to respond to all of the alerts (true or false) the new IDS sends out.

So, for example, the cost of this countermeasure could be $23,500 for the product and licenses; $2,500 for training; $3,400 for testing; $2,600 for the loss in user productivity once the product is introduced into production; and $4,000 in labor for router reconfiguration, product installation, troubleshooting, and installation of the two service patches. The real cost of this countermeasure is $36,000. If our total potential loss was calculated at $9,000, we went over budget by 300 percent when applying this countermeasure for the identified risk. Some of these costs may be hard or impossible to identify before they are incurred, but an experienced risk analyst would account for many of these possibilities.

Functionality and Effectiveness of Countermeasures The risk analysis team must evaluate the safeguard's functionality and effectiveness. When selecting a safeguard, some attributes are more favorable than others. Table 1-10 lists and describes attributes that should be considered before purchasing and committing to a security protection mechanism.

Characteristic	Description
Modular	It can be installed or removed from an environment without adversely affecting other mechanisms.
Provides uniform protection	A security level is applied to all mechanisms it is designed to protect in a standardized method.
Provides override functionality	An administrator can override the restriction if necessary.
Defaults to least privilege	When installed, it defaults to a lack of permissions and rights instead of installing with everyone having full control.
Independent of safeguards and the asset it is protecting	The safeguard can be used to protect different assets, and different assets can be protected by different safeguards.
Flexibility and security	The more security the safeguard provides, the better. This functionality should come with flexibility, which enables you to choose different functions instead of all or none.

Table 1-10 Characteristics to Seek When Obtaining Safeguards (*continued*)

Characteristic	Description
User interaction	Does not panic users.
Clear distinction between user and administrator	A user should have fewer permissions when it comes to configuring or disabling the protection mechanism.
Minimum human intervention	When humans have to configure or modify controls, this opens the door to errors. The safeguard should require the least possible amount of input from humans.
Asset protection	Asset is still protected even if countermeasure needs to be reset.
Easily upgraded	Software continues to evolve, and updates should be able to happen painlessly.
Auditing functionality	There should be a mechanism that is part of the safeguard that provides minimum and/or verbose auditing.
Minimizes dependence on other components	The safeguard should be flexible and not have strict requirements about the environment into which it will be installed.
Easily usable, acceptable, and tolerated by personnel	If the safeguard introduces barriers to productivity or adds extra steps to simple tasks, users will not tolerate it.
Must produce output in usable and understandable format	Important information should be presented in a format easy for humans to understand and use for trend analysis.
Must be able to reset safeguard	The mechanism should be able to be reset and returned to original configurations and settings without affecting the system or asset it is protecting.
Testable	The safeguard should be able to be tested in different environments under different situations.
Does not introduce other compromises	The safeguard should not provide any covert channels or back doors.
System and user performance	System and user performance should not be greatly affected.
Universal application	The safeguard can be implemented across the environment and does not require many, if any, exceptions.
Proper alerting	Thresholds should be able to be set as to when to alert personnel of a security breach, and this type of alert should be acceptable.
Does not affect assets	The assets in the environment should not be adversely affected by the safeguard.

Table 1-10 Characteristics to Seek When Obtaining Safeguards

Safeguards can provide deterrence attributes if they are highly visible. This tells potential evildoers that adequate protection is in place and that they should move on to an easier target. Although the safeguard may be highly visible, attackers should not be able to discover the way it works, thus enabling them to attempt to modify the safeguard, or know how to get around the protection mechanism. If users know how to disable the antivirus program that is taking up CPU cycles or know how to bypass a proxy server to get to the Internet without restrictions, they will do so.

Putting It Together

To perform a risk analysis, a company first decides what assets must be protected and to what extent. It also indicates the amount of money that can go toward protecting specific assets. Next, it must evaluate the functionality of the available safeguards and determine which ones would be most beneficial for the environment. Finally, the company needs to appraise and compare the costs of the safeguards. These steps and the resulting information enable management to make the most intelligent and informed decisions about selecting and purchasing countermeasures.

Total Risk vs. Residual Risk

The reason a company implements countermeasures is to reduce its overall risk to an acceptable level. As stated earlier, no system or environment is 100 percent secure, which means there is always some risk left over to deal with. This is called *residual risk*.

We Are Never Done

Only by reassessing the risks on a periodic basis can a statement of safeguard performance be trusted. If the risk has not changed and the safeguards implemented are functioning in good order, then it can be said that the risk is being properly mitigated. Regular risk management monitoring will support the information security risk ratings.

Vulnerability analysis and continued asset identification and valuation are also important tasks of risk management monitoring and performance. The cycle of continued risk analysis is a very important part of determining whether the safeguard controls that have been put in place are appropriate and necessary to safeguard the assets and environment.

Residual risk is different from *total risk*, which is the risk a company faces if it chooses not to implement any type of safeguard. A company may choose to take on total risk if the cost/benefit analysis results indicate this is the best course of action. For example, if there is a small likelihood that a company's web servers can be compromised and the necessary safeguards to provide a higher level of protection cost more than the potential loss in the first place, the company will choose not to implement the safeguard, choosing to deal with the total risk.

There is an important difference between total risk and residual risk and which type of risk a company is willing to accept. The following are conceptual formulas:

threats × vulnerability × asset value = total risk
(threats × vulnerability × asset value) × controls gap = residual risk

You may also see these concepts illustrated as the following:

total risk – countermeasures = residual risk

NOTE The previous formulas are not constructs you can actually plug numbers into. They are instead used to illustrate the relation of the different items that make up risk in a conceptual manner. This means no multiplication or mathematical functions actually take place. It is a means of understanding what items are involved when defining either total or residual risk.

During a risk assessment, the threats and vulnerabilities are identified. The possibility of a vulnerability being exploited is multiplied by the value of the assets being assessed, which results in the total risk. Once the controls gap (protection the control cannot provide) is factored in, the result is the residual risk. Implementing countermeasures is a way of mitigating risks. Because no company can remove all threats, there will always be some residual risk. The question is what level of risk the company is willing to accept.

Handling Risk

Once a company knows the amount of total and residual risk it is faced with, it must decide how to handle it. Risk can be dealt with in four basic ways: transfer it, avoid it, reduce it, or accept it.

Many types of insurance are available to companies to protect their assets. If a company decides the total risk is too high to gamble with, it can purchase insurance, which would *transfer the risk* to the insurance company.

If a company decides to terminate the activity that is introducing the risk, this is known as *risk avoidance*. For example, if a company allows employees to use instant messaging (IM), there are many risks surrounding this technology. The company could decide not to allow any IM activity by users because there is not a strong enough business need for its continued use. Discontinuing this service is an example of risk avoidance.

Another approach is *risk mitigation*, where the risk is reduced to a level considered acceptable enough to continue conducting business. The implementation of firewalls, training, and intrusion/detection protection systems or other control types represent types of risk mitigation efforts.

The last approach is to *accept the risk*, which means the company understands the level of risk it is faced with, as well as the potential cost of damage, and decides to just live with it and not implement the countermeasure. Many companies will accept risk when the cost/benefit ratio indicates that the cost of the countermeasure outweighs the potential loss value.

A crucial issue with risk acceptance is understanding why this is the best approach for a specific situation. Unfortunately, today many people in organizations are accepting risk and not understanding fully what they are accepting. This usually has to do with the relative newness of risk management in the security field and the lack of education and experience in those personnel who make risk decisions. When business managers are charged with the responsibility of dealing with risk in their department, most of the time they will accept whatever risk is put in front of them because their real goals pertain to getting a project finished and out the door. They don't want to be bogged down by this silly and irritating security stuff.

Risk acceptance should be based on several factors. For example, is the potential loss lower than the countermeasure? Can the organization deal with the "pain" that will come with accepting this risk? This second consideration is not purely a cost decision, but may entail non cost issues surrounding the decision. For example, if we accept this risk, we must add three more steps in our production process. Does that make sense for us? Or if we accept this risk, more security incidents may arise from it, and are we prepared to handle those?

The individual or group accepting risk must also understand the potential visibility of this decision. Let's say a company has determined that it does not need to protect customers' first names, but it does have to protect other items like Social Security numbers, account numbers, and so on. So these current activities are in compliance with the regulations and laws, but what if your customers find out you are not properly protecting their names and they associate such things with identity fraud because of their lack of education on the matter? The company may not be able to handle this potential reputation hit, even if it is doing all it is supposed to be doing. Perceptions of a company's customer base are not always rooted in fact, but the possibility that customers will move their business to another company is a potential fact your company must comprehend.

Figure 1-17 shows how a risk management program can be set up, which ties together all the concepts covered in this section.

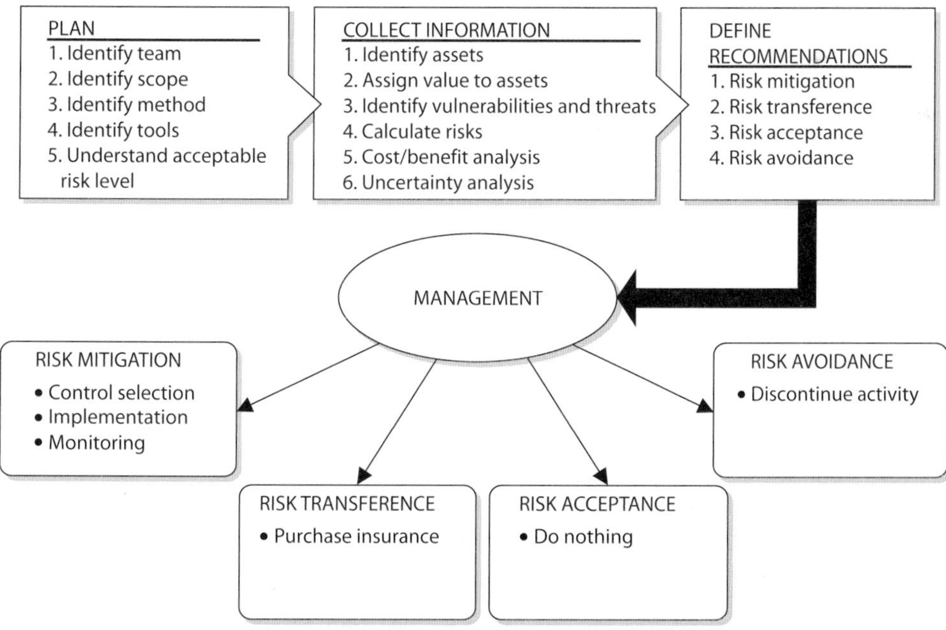

Figure 1-17 How a risk management program can be set up

Outsourcing

More organizations are outsourcing business functions to allow them to focus on their core business functions. Companies use hosting companies to maintain websites and e-mail servers, service providers for various telecommunication connections, disaster recovery companies for co-location capabilities, cloud computing providers for infrastructure or application services, developers for software creation, and security companies to carry out vulnerability management. It is important to realize that while you can outsource functionality, you cannot outsource risk. When your company is using these third-party companies for these various services, your company can still be ultimately responsible if something like a data breach takes place. Let's look at some things an organization should do to reduce its risk when it comes to outsourcing.

- Review the service provider's security program
- Conduct onsite inspection and interviews
- Review contracts to ensure security and protection levels are agreed upon
- Ensure service level agreements are in place
- Review internal and external audit reports and third-party reviews
- Review references and communicate with former and existing customers
- Review Better Business Bureau reports
- Ensure they have a business continuity plan (BCP) in place
- Implement a nondisclosure agreement (NDA)
- Understand provider's legal and regulatory requirements
- Require a Statement on Auditing Standards (SAS) 70 audit report

NOTE SAS 70 is an internal controls audit carried out by a third-party auditing organization.

Outsourcing is prevalent within organizations today but is commonly forgotten about when it comes to security and compliance requirements. It may be economical to outsource certain functionalities, but if this allows security breaches to take place, it can turn out to be a very costly decision.

Risk Management Frameworks

We have covered a lot of material dealing with risk management in general and risk assessments in particular. By now, you may be asking yourself, "How does this all fit together into an actionable process?" This is where frameworks come to the rescue. The *Oxford English Dictionary* defines *framework* as a basic structure underlying a system, concept, or text. By combining this with our earlier definition of risk management, we can define a *risk management framework (RMF)* as a structured process that allows an organization to identify and assess risk, reduce it to an acceptable level, and ensure that it remains at that level. In essence, an RMF is a structured approach to risk management.

As you might imagine, there is no shortage of RMFs out there. What is important to you as a security professional is to ensure your organization has an RMF that works for you. That being said, there are some frameworks that have enjoyed widespread success and acceptance (see sidebar). You should at least be aware of these, and ideally adopt (and perhaps modify) one of them to fit your particular needs.

Commonly Accepted Risk Management Frameworks

- **NIST RMF (SP 800-37r1)** U.S. federal government agencies are required to implement the provisions of this document. It takes a systems life-cycle approach to risk management and focuses on certification and accreditation of information systems. Many public and corporate organizations have adopted it directly, or with some modifications.
- **ISO 31000:2009** This international standard takes a very unique tack on risk management by focusing on uncertainty that leads to unanticipated effects. In essence, this standard acknowledges that there are things outside our control and that these can have negative (e.g., financial loss) or positive (e.g., business opportunity) consequences. Unlike the NIST RMF, this framework is not focused on information systems, but can be applied more broadly to an organization.
- **ISACA Risk IT** This framework, developed by ISACA in collaboration with a working group of academic and corporate risk professionals, aims at bridging the gap between generic frameworks such as ISO 31000 and IT-centric ones such as NIST's. Unsurprisingly, it is very well integrated with COBIT, which was also developed by ISACA, as discussed earlier in this chapter.
- **COSO Enterprise Risk Management—Integrated Framework** Originally published in 2004, this framework is currently undergoing a full review. It is a generic (i.e., not IT-centric) framework used by management and therefore takes a decidedly top-down approach. This framework can be thought of as being a superset of the COSO Internal Control—Integrated Framework we discussed earlier in this chapter.

In this section, we will focus our discussion on the NIST risk management framework, SP 800-37, Revision 1, "Guide for Applying the Risk Management Framework to Federal Information Systems," since it incorporates the most important components that you should know as a security professional. It is important to keep in mind, however, that this framework is geared toward federal government entities and may have to be modified to fit your own needs. The NIST RMF outlines the following six-step process of applying the RMF, each of which will be addressed in turn in the following sections:

1. Categorize information system.
2. Select security controls.
3. Implement security controls.
4. Assess security controls.
5. Authorize information system.
6. Monitor security controls.

Categorize Information System

The first step is to identify and categorize the information system. What does this mean? First, you have to identify what you have in terms of systems, subsystems, and boundaries. For example, if you have a customer relationship management (CRM) information system, you need to inventory its components (e.g., software, hardware), any subsystems it may include (e.g., bulk e-mailer, customer analytics), and its boundaries (e.g., interface with the corporate mail system). You also need to know how this system fits into your organization's business process, how sensitive it is, and who owns it and the data within it. Other questions you may ask are

- How is the information system integrated into the enterprise architecture?
- What types of information are processed, stored, and transmitted by the system?
- Are there regulatory or legal requirements applicable to the information system?
- How is the system interconnected to others?
- What is the criticality of this information system to the business?

Clearly, there are many other questions you would want to ask as you categorize the system, so this list is not meant to be all-inclusive. You could use this as a starting point, but you really should have your own list of questions that you use consistently across all of your organization's information systems. Doing so ensures that you don't forget any important details, or that if you do, it only happens once (presuming you then add it to your list, of course). At the end of this step, you should have all the information you need in order to determine what countermeasures you can apply to manage your risk.

Select Security Controls

Recall that we already defined a security control or countermeasure as a mechanism that is put in place to mitigate (reduce) a potential risk. It then makes sense to assess our risk exposure before we select security controls for our information systems. In this step, there is an inherent assumption that you have already performed a risk assessment and have identified a number of *common controls* across your organization. An example of this are so-called "gold master" images that are applied to all workstations and profiles that are installed on mobile devices. These common controls ensure that the entire enterprise has a common baseline.

As you consider a new system, you have to determine if there are any risks that are specific to it or are introduced into your overall architecture by the introduction of this system. This means that you will likely conduct another risk assessment that looks at both this new system and its effects on the larger ecosystem. Having done this, you compare the results of this assessment with the common controls in your organization and determine if you need to modify any of these (i.e., create *hybrid controls*) or develop brand-new ones (i.e., create *system-specific controls*) in order to maintain the security baseline. Finally, you need to address how these new controls (if any) integrate into your continuous monitoring strategy that tells you whether or not your security is maintained over time.

Implement Security Controls

There are two key tasks in this step: implementation and documentation. The first part is very straightforward. For example, if you determined in the previous step that you need to add a rule to your intrusion prevention system to mitigate a risk, you implement that rule. Simple. The part with which many of us struggle is the documentation of this change.

The documentation is important for two obvious reasons. First, it allows everyone to understand what controls exist, where, and why. Have you ever inherited a system that is configured in a seemingly nonsensical way? You try to understand why certain parameters or rules exist but hesitate to change them because the system might fail. Likely, this was the result of either improper documentation or (even worse) a successful attack. The second reason why documentation is important is that it allows us to fully integrate the controls into the overall assessment and monitoring plan. Failing to do this invites having controls that quietly become obsolete and ineffective over time and result in undocumented risks.

Assess Security Controls

The security controls we implement are useful to our overall risk management effort only insofar as we can assess them. It is absolutely essential to our organizations to have a comprehensive plan that assesses all security controls (common, hybrid, and system-specific) with regard to the risks they are meant to address. This plan must be reviewed and approved by the appropriate official(s), and it must be exercised.

To execute an assessment plan, you will, ideally, identify an assessor who is both competent and independent from the team that implemented the controls. This person must act as an honest broker that not only assesses the effectiveness of the controls, but also ensures the documentation is appropriate for the task. For this reason, it is important to include all necessary assessment materials in the plan.

The assessment will determine whether or not the controls are effective. If they are, then the results are documented in the report so that they are available as references for the next assessment. If the controls are not effective, then the report documents the results, the remediation actions that were taken to address the shortcomings, and the outcome of the reassessment. Finally, the appropriate security plans are updated to include the findings and recommendations of the assessment.

Authorize Information System

As we already discussed, no system is ever 100 percent risk-free. At this stage in the RMF, we present the results of both our risk and controls assessments to the appropriate decision-maker in order to get approval to connect our information system into our broader architecture and operate it. This person (or group) determines whether the risk exposure is acceptable to the organization. This normally requires a review of a plan of action that addresses how the organization will deal with the remaining weaknesses and deficiencies in the information system. In many organizations this authorization is given for a set period of time, which is usually tied to the milestones in the plan of action.

Monitor Security Controls

These milestones we just mentioned are a key component of the monitoring or continuous improvement stage of the RMF. At a minimum, we must periodically look at all our controls and determine whether they are still effective. Has the threat changed its tactics, techniques, and procedures (TTPs)? Have new vulnerabilities been discovered? Has an undocumented/unapproved change to our configuration altered our risk equations? These are only some of the issues that we address through ongoing monitoring and continuous improvement.

Business Continuity and Disaster Recovery

Though we strive to drive down the risks of negative effects in our organizations, we can be sure that sooner or later an event will slip through and cause negative impacts. Ideally, the losses are contained and won't affect the major business efforts. However, as security professionals we need to have plans in place for when the unthinkable happens. Under those extreme (and sometimes unpredictable) conditions, we need to ensure that our organizations continue to operate at some minimum acceptable threshold capacity and quickly bounce back to full productivity.

The goal of *disaster recovery* is to minimize the effects of a disaster or disruption. It means taking the necessary steps to ensure that the resources, personnel, and business processes are able to resume operation in a timely manner. This is different from *continuity planning*, which provides methods and procedures for dealing with longer-term outages and disasters. The goal of a *disaster recovery plan (DRP)* is to handle the disaster and its ramifications right after the disaster hits; the disaster recovery plan is usually very information technology (IT) focused.

A disaster recovery plan is carried out when everything is still in emergency mode and everyone is scrambling to get all critical systems back online. A *business continuity plan (BCP)* takes a broader approach to the problem. It can include getting critical systems to another environment while repair of the original facilities is under way, getting the right people to the right places during this time, and performing business in a different mode until regular conditions are back in place. It also involves dealing with customers, partners, and shareholders through different channels until everything returns to normal. So, disaster recovery deals with, "Oh my goodness, the sky is falling," and continuity planning deals with, "Okay, the sky fell. Now, how do we stay in business until someone can put the sky back where it belongs?"

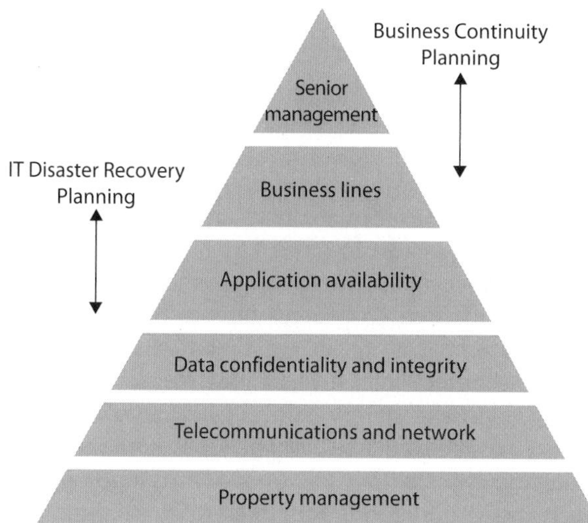

While disaster recovery and business continuity planning are directed at the development of plans, *business continuity management (BCM)* is the holistic management process that should cover both of them. BCM provides a framework for integrating resilience with the capability for effective responses in a manner that protects the interests of an organization's key stakeholders. The main objective of BCM is to allow the organization to continue to perform business operations under various conditions.

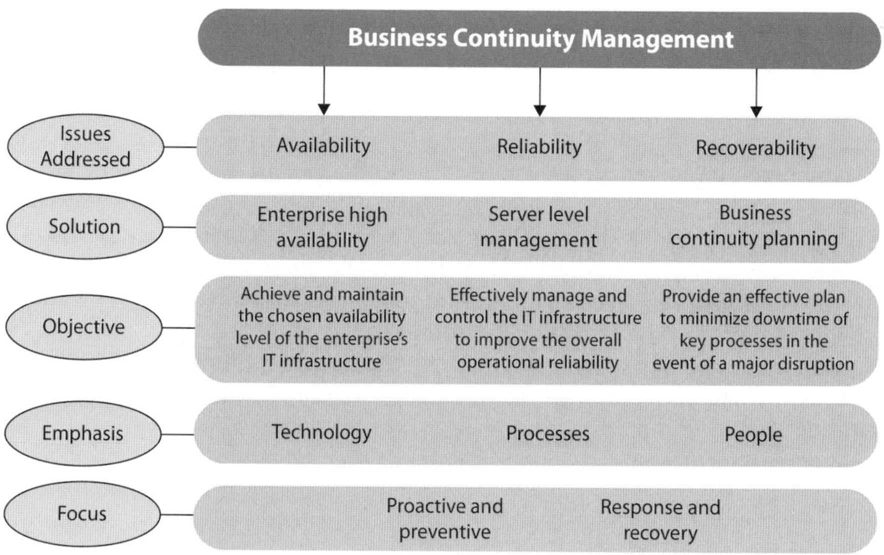

Certain characteristics run through many of the chapters in this book: availability, integrity, and confidentiality. Here, we point out that integrity and confidentiality must be considered not only in everyday procedures, but also in those procedures undertaken immediately after a disaster or disruption. For instance, it may not be appropriate to leave a server that holds confidential information in one building while everyone else moves to another building. Equipment that provides secure VPN connections may be destroyed and the team might respond by focusing on enabling remote access functionality while forgetting about the needs of encryption. In most situations the company is purely focused on getting back up and running, thus focusing on functionality. If security is not integrated and implemented properly, the effects of the physical disaster can be amplified as hackers come in and steal sensitive information. Many times a company is much more vulnerable *after* a disaster hits, because the security services used to protect it may be unavailable or operating at a reduced capacity. Therefore, it is important that if the business has secret stuff, it stays secret.

Availability is one of the main themes behind business continuity planning, in that it ensures that the resources required to keep the business going will continue to be available to the people and systems that rely upon them. This may mean backups need to be done religiously and that redundancy needs to be factored into the architecture of the systems, networks, and operations. If communication lines are disabled or if a service is rendered unusable for any significant period of time, there must be a quick and tested way of establishing alternative communications and services. We will be diving into the many ways organizations can implement availability solutions for continuity and recovery purposes throughout this section.

When looking at business continuity planning, some companies focus mainly on backing up data and providing redundant hardware. Although these items are extremely important, they are just small pieces of the company's overall operations pie. Hardware and computers need people to configure and operate them, and data is usually not useful unless it is accessible by other systems and possibly outside entities. Thus, a larger picture of how the various processes within a business work together needs to be understood. Planning must include getting the right people to the right places, documenting the necessary configurations, establishing alternative communications channels (voice and data), providing power, and making sure all dependencies are properly understood and taken into account.

It is also important to understand how automated tasks can be carried out manually, if necessary, and how business processes can be safely altered to keep the operation of the company going. This may be critical in ensuring the company survives the event with the least impact to its operations. Without this type of vision and planning, when a disaster hits, a company could have its backup data and redundant servers physically available at the alternative facility, but the people responsible for activating them may be standing around in a daze, not knowing where to start or how to perform in such a different environment.

Business Continuity Planning

Preplanned procedures allow an organization to

- Provide an immediate and appropriate response to emergency situations
- Protect lives and ensure safety
- Reduce business impact
- Resume critical business functions
- Work with outside vendors and partners during the recovery period
- Reduce confusion during a crisis
- Ensure survivability of the business
- Get "up and running" quickly after a disaster

Standards and Best Practices

Although no specific scientific equation must be followed to create continuity plans, certain best practices have proven themselves over time. The National Institute of Standards and Technology is responsible for developing best practices and standards as they pertain to U.S. government and military environments. It is common for NIST to document the requirements for these types of environments, and then everyone else in the industry uses NIST's documents as guidelines. So these are "musts" for U.S. government organizations and "good to have" for other, nongovernment entities.

NIST outlines the following steps in SP 800-34, Revision 1, "Continuity Planning Guide for Federal Information Systems":

1. *Develop the continuity planning policy statement.* Write a policy that provides the guidance necessary to develop a BCP and that assigns authority to the necessary roles to carry out these tasks.
2. *Conduct the business impact analysis (BIA).* Identify critical functions and systems and allow the organization to prioritize them based on necessity. Identify vulnerabilities and threats, and calculate risks.
3. *Identify preventive controls.* Once threats are recognized, identify and implement controls and countermeasures to reduce the organization's risk level in an economical manner.
4. *Create contingency strategies.* Formulate methods to ensure systems and critical functions can be brought online quickly.
5. *Develop an information system contingency plan.* Write procedures and guidelines for how the organization can still stay functional in a crippled state.

6. *Ensure plan testing, training, and exercises.* Test the plan to identify deficiencies in the BCP, and conduct training to properly prepare individuals on their expected tasks.
7. *Ensure plan maintenance.* Put in place steps to ensure the BCP is a living document that is updated regularly.

Although the NIST SP 800-34 document deals specifically with IT contingency plans, these steps are similar when creating enterprise-wide BCPs and BCM programs.

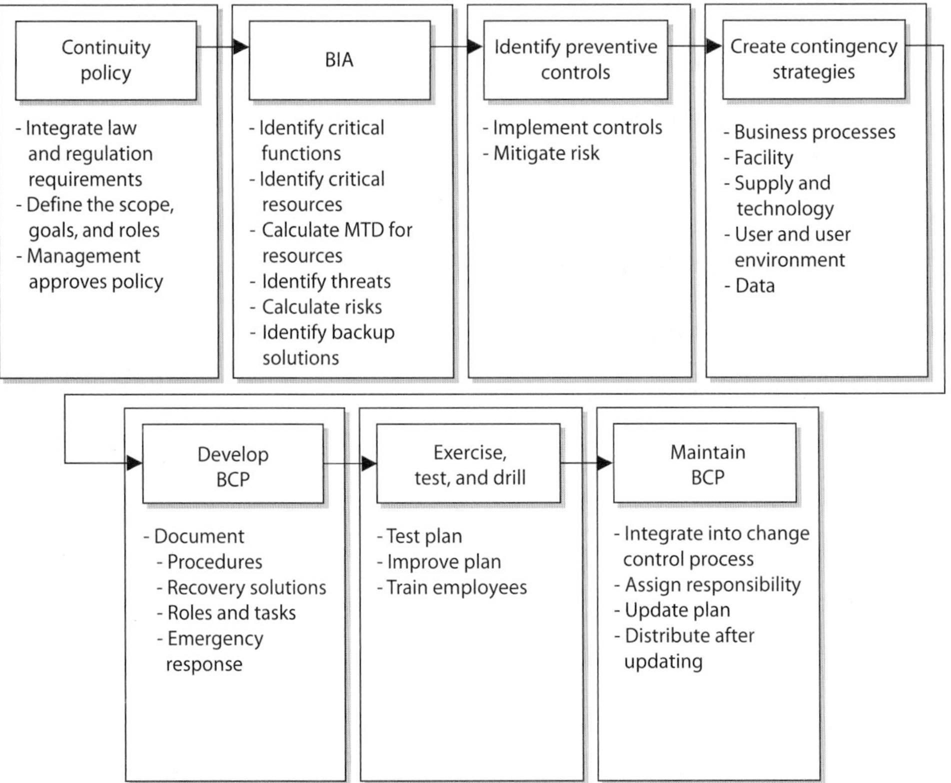

Since BCM is so critical, it is actually addressed by other standards-based organizations, listed here:

ISO/IEC 27031:2011 Guidelines for information and communications technology readiness for business continuity. This ISO/IEC standard is a component of the overall ISO/IEC 27000 series.

ISO 22301:2012 International standard for business continuity management systems. The specification document against which organizations will seek certification. This standard replaced BS 25999-2.

Business Continuity Institute's Good Practice Guidelines (GPG) BCM best practices, which are broken down into the following management and technical practices.

Management Practices:

- Policy and Program Management
- Embedding BCM in the Organization's Culture

Technical Practices:

- Understanding the Organization
- Determining BCM Strategy
- Developing and Implementing a BCM Response
- Exercising, Maintaining, and Reviewing

DRI International Institute's Professional Practices for Business Continuity Planners Best practices and framework to allow for BCM processes, which are broken down into the following sections:

- Program Initiation and Management
- Risk Evaluation and Control
- Business Impact Analysis
- Business Continuity Strategies
- Emergency Response and Operations
- Plan Implementation and Documentation
- Awareness and Training Programs
- Business Continuity Plan Exercise, Audit, and Maintenance
- Crisis Communications
- Coordination with External Agencies

Why are there so many sets of best practices and which is the best for your organization? If your organization is part of the U.S. government or a government contracting company, then you need to comply with the NIST standards. If your organization is in Europe or your company does business with other companies in Europe, then you might need to follow the BSI's list of standard requirements. While we are not listing all of them here, there are other country-based BCM standards that your company might need to comply with if it is residing in or does business in one of those specific countries. If your organization needs to get ISO certified, then ISO/IEC 27031 and ISO 22301 are the standards to follow. While the first of these is focused on IT, the second is broader in scope and addresses the needs of the entire organization.

So some of these best practices/standards have a specific focus (DRP, BCP, government, technology), some are still evolving, and some directly compete against each other because BCM is a big and growing industry. There is a lot of overlap between them all because they all have one main focus of keeping the company in business after something bad happens. Your company's legal and regulatory requirements commonly point toward one of these best practice standards, so find out these specifics before hitching your wagon to one specific set of practices. For example, if your company is a government contracting company that works with the U.S. government, then you follow NIST because that is the "checklist" your auditors will most likely follow and grade you against. If your company does business internationally, then following the ISO list of requirements would probably be the best bet.

Making BCM Part of the Enterprise Security Program

As we already explained, every company should have security policies, procedures, standards, and guidelines. People who are new to information security commonly think that this is one pile of documentation that addresses all issues pertaining to security, but it is more complicated than that—of course.

Understanding the Organization First

A company has no real hope of rebuilding itself and its processes after a disaster if it does not have a good understanding of how its organization works in the first place. This notion might seem absurd at first. You might think, "Well, of course a company knows how it works." But you would be surprised at how difficult it is to fully understand an organization down to the level of detail required to rebuild it. Each individual may know and understand his or her little world within the company, but hardly anyone at any company can fully explain how each and every business process takes place.

The Zachman Business Enterprise Framework, introduced earlier in this chapter, is one of the most comprehensive approaches to understanding a company's architecture and all the pieces and parts that make it up. This framework breaks down the core portions of a corporate enterprise to illustrate the various requirements of every business process. It looks at the data, function, network, people, time, and motivation components of the enterprise's infrastructure and how they are tied to the roles within the company. The beauty of this framework is that it dissects business processes down to the atomic level and shows the necessary interdependencies that exist, all of which must be working correctly for effective and efficient processes to be carried out.

It would be very beneficial for a BCP team to use this type of framework to understand the core components of an organization, because the team's responsibility is to make sure the organization can be rebuilt if need be.

An enterprise security program is made up of many different disciplines. The Common Body of Knowledge (CBK) for the CISSP exam did not just fall out of the sky one day, and it was not just made up by some lonely guys sitting in a room. The CBK is broken down into the eight high-level disciplines of any enterprise security program (Security and Risk Management, Asset Security, Security Engineering, Communication and Network Security, Identity and Access Management, Security Assessment and Testing, Security Operations, and Software Development Security). These top-tier disciplines are then broken down into supporting subcomponents. What this means is that every company actually needs to have *at least* eight sets of policies, standards, guidelines, and procedures—one per top-tier discipline.

We will go more in depth into what should be encapsulated in a BCP policy in a later section, but for now let's understand why it has to be integrated into the security program as a whole. Business continuity should be a part of the security program and business decisions, as opposed to being an entity that stands off in a corner by itself. The BCM team will be responsible for putting Humpty Dumpty back together again, so it better understand all the pieces and parts that make up Humpty Dumpty *before* it goes falling off a wall.

Business continuity planning ought to be fully integrated into the organization as a regular management process, just like auditing or strategic planning or other "normal" processes. Instead of being considered an outsider, BCP should be "part of the team." Further, final responsibility for BCP should belong not to the BCP team or its leader, but to a high-level executive manager, preferably a member of the executive board. This will reinforce the image and reality of continuity planning as a function seen as vital to the organizational chiefs.

By analyzing and planning for potential disruptions to the organization, the BCP team can assist such other business disciplines in their own efforts to effectively plan for and respond effectively and with resilience to emergencies. Given that the ability to respond depends on operations and management personnel throughout the organization, such capability should be developed organization-wide. It should extend throughout every location of the organization and up the employee ranks to top-tier management.

As such, the BCP program needs to be a living entity. As a company goes through changes, so should the program, thereby ensuring it stays current, usable, and effective. When properly integrated with change management processes, the program stands a much better chance of being continually updated and improved upon. Business continuity is a foundational piece of an effective security program and is critical to ensuring relevance in time of need.

A very important question to ask when first developing a BCP is *why* it is being developed. This may seem silly and the answer may at first appear obvious, but that is not always the case. You might think that the reason to have these plans is to deal with an unexpected disaster and to get people back to their tasks as quickly and as safely as possible, but the full story is often a bit different. Why are most companies in business? To make money and be profitable. If these are usually the main goals of businesses, then any BCP needs to be developed to help achieve and, more importantly, maintain these goals. The main reason to develop these plans in the first place is to reduce the risk of financial loss by improving the company's ability to recover and restore operations. This encompasses the goals of mitigating the effects of the disaster.

Not all organizations are businesses that exist to make profits. Government agencies, military units, nonprofit organizations, and the like exist to provide some type of protection or service to a nation or society. While a company must create its BCP to ensure that revenue continues to come in so it can stay in business, other types of organizations must create their BCPs to make sure they can still carry out their critical tasks. Although the focus and business drivers of the organizations and companies may differ, their BCPs often will have similar constructs—which is to get their critical processes up and running.

NOTE Protecting what is most important to a company is rather difficult if what is most important is not first identified. Senior management is usually involved with this step because it has a point of view that extends beyond each functional manager's focus area of responsibility. The company's BCP should define the company's critical mission and business functions. The functions must have priorities set upon them to indicate which is most crucial to a company's survival.

As stated previously, for many companies, financial operations are most critical. As an example, an automotive company would be affected far more seriously if its credit and loan services were unavailable for a day than if, say, an assembly line went down for a day, since credit and loan services are where it generates the biggest revenues. For other organizations, customer service might be the most critical area, to ensure that order processing is not negatively affected. For example, if a company makes heart pacemakers and its physician services department is unavailable at a time when an operating room surgeon needs to contact it because of a complication, the results could be disastrous for the patient. The surgeon and the company would likely be sued, and the company would likely never be able to sell another pacemaker to that surgeon, her colleagues, or perhaps even the patient's health maintenance organization (HMO) ever again. It would be very difficult to rebuild reputation and sales after something like that happened.

Advanced planning for emergencies covers issues that were thought of and foreseen. Many other problems may arise that are not covered in the plan; thus, flexibility in the plan is crucial. The plan is a systematic way of providing a checklist of actions that should take place right after a disaster. These actions have been thought through to help the people involved be more efficient and effective in dealing with traumatic situations.

The most critical part of establishing and maintaining a current BCP is management support. Management must be convinced of the necessity of such a plan. Therefore, a business case must be made to obtain this support. The business case may include current vulnerabilities, regulatory and legal obligations, the current status of recovery plans, and recommendations. Management is mostly concerned with cost/benefit issues, so preliminary numbers need to be gathered and potential losses estimated. A cost/benefit analysis should include shareholder, stakeholder, regulatory, and legislative impacts, as well as those on products, services, and personnel. The decision of how a company should recover is commonly a business decision and should always be treated as such.

BCP Project Components

Before everyone runs off in 2,000 different directions at one time, let's understand what needs to be done in the project initiation phase. This is the phase in which the company really needs to figure out what it is doing and why.

Once management's support is solidified, a *business continuity coordinator* must be identified. This person will be the leader for the BCP team and will oversee the development, implementation, and testing of the business continuity and disaster recovery plans. It is best if this person has good social skills, is somewhat of a politician, and has a cape, because he will need to coordinate a lot of different departments and busy individuals who have their own agendas. This person needs to have direct access to management and have the credibility and authority to carry out leadership tasks.

A leader needs a team, so a *BCP committee* needs to be put together. Management and the coordinator should work together to appoint specific, qualified people to be on this committee. The team must comprise people who are familiar with the different departments within the company, because each department is unique in its functionality and has distinctive risks and threats. The best plan is developed when all issues and threats are brought to the table and discussed. This cannot be done effectively with a few people who are familiar with only a couple of departments. Representatives from each department must be involved with not only the planning stages, but also the testing and implementation stages.

The committee should be made up of representatives from *at least* the following departments:

- Business units
- Senior management
- IT department
- Security department
- Communications department
- Legal department

If the BCP coordinator is a good management leader, she will understand that it is best to make these team members feel a sense of ownership pertaining to their tasks and roles. The people who develop the BCP should also be the ones who execute it. (If you knew that in a time of crisis you would be expected to carry out some critical tasks, you might pay more attention during the planning and testing phases.) This may entail making it very clear what the roles and responsibilities of team members are during a crisis and recovery, so that existing managers do not feel that their decision making is being overridden. The project must have proper authorization from the top.

The team must then work with the management staff to develop the ultimate goals of the plan, identify the critical parts of the business that must be dealt with first during a disaster, and ascertain the priorities of departments and tasks. Management needs to help direct the team on the scope of the project and the specific objectives.

EXAM TIP While the term "BCP" actually applies to a plan and "BCM" applies to the overall management of continuity, these terms are commonly used interchangeably.

The BCP effort has to result in a sustainable, long-term program that serves its purpose—assisting the organization in the event of a disaster. The effort must be well thought out and methodically executed. It must not be perceived as a mere "public relations" effort to make it simply appear that the organization is concerned about disaster response.

The initiation process for the BCP program might include the following:

- Setting up a budget and staff for the program before the BCP process begins. Dedicated personnel and dedicated hours are essential for executing something as labor intensive as a BCP.
- Assigning duties and responsibilities to the BCP coordinator and to representatives from all of the functional units of the organization.
- Senior management kick-off of the BCP program with a formal announcement or, better still, an organization-wide meeting to demonstrate high-level support.
- Awareness-raising activities to let employees know about the BCP program and to build internal support for it.
- Establishment of skills training for the support of the BCP effort.
- The start of data collection from throughout the organization to aid in crafting various continuity options.
- Putting into effect "quick wins" and gathering of "low-hanging fruit" to show tangible evidence of improvement in the organization's readiness, as well as improving readiness.

After the successful execution of a BCP program, the organization should have an adequate level of response to an emergency. A desktop exercise that walks through the incident management steps that have been established should offer a scorecard of where the organization stands.

From that point, the team can hold regular progress reviews to check the accuracy of readiness levels and program costs and to see if program milestones are being met. The BCP management team then can adjust the plan to any changes in meeting cost or schedule. To assist in this, the team should choose a project management tool or method to track progress or its lack.

Scope of the Project

At first glance, it might seem as though the scope and objectives are quite clear—protect the company. But it is not that simple. The high-level organizational requirements that the BCP should address, and the resources allocated for them, must be evaluated. You want to understand the focus and direction of a business before starting on risk assessment or continuity planning. This would include the organization's plans for growth, reorganizing, or downsizing. Other major events in an organization to consider are changes in personnel levels; relocation of facilities; new suppliers; and introduction of new products, technologies, or processes. Obtaining hard numbers or estimates for any of these areas will make things smoother for the BCP team. Of course, due to the sensitivity of some information, some of this data may not be made available to the BCP team. In such cases, the team should realize that the lack of full information may make some of its findings less than fully accurate.

Knowing how the overall organization is going to change will aid in drawing up the right contingency plans in the event of emergencies. Also, if the team identifies organizational requirements at the start and is in accord with top management on the identification and definition of such requirements, then it will be much easier to align the policy to the requirements.

Many questions must be asked. For instance, is the team supposed to develop a BCP for just one facility or for more than one facility? Is the plan supposed to cover just large potential threats (hurricanes, tornadoes, floods) or deal with smaller issues as well (loss of a communications line, power failure, Internet connection failure)? Should the plan address possible terrorist attacks and other manmade threats? What is the threat profile of the company? If the scope of the project is not properly defined, how do you know when you are done? Then there's resources—what personnel, time allocation, and funds is management willing to commit to the BCP program overall?

NOTE Most companies outline the scope of their BCP to encompass only the larger threats. The smaller threats are then covered by independent departmental contingency plans.

A frequent objection to a BCP program is that it is unlimited in its scope when it is applied to all the functions of an organization in one fell swoop. An alternative is to break up the program into manageable pieces and to place some aspects of the organization outside the scope of the BCP. Since the scope fundamentally affects what the plan will cover, the BCP team should consider the scope from the start of the project.

Deciding whether and how to place a component of an organization outside the BCP scope can be tricky. In some cases, a product, service, or organizational component may remain within the scope, but at a reduced level of funding and activity. At other times, executives will have to decide whether to place a component outside the scope after an incident takes place—when the costs of reestablishing the component may outweigh the benefits. Senior executives, not BCP managers and planners, should make these kinds of decisions.

Enterprise-Wide BCP

The agreed-upon scope of the BCP will indicate if one or more facilities will be included in the plan. Most BCPs are developed to cover the enterprise as a whole, instead of dealing with only portions of the organization. In larger organizations, it can be helpful for each department to have its own specific contingency plan that will address its specific needs during recovery. These individual plans need to be compatible with the enterprise-wide BCP.

BCP Policy

The *BCP policy* supplies the framework for and governance of designing and building the BCP effort. The policy helps the organization understand the importance of BCP by outlining the BCP's purpose. It provides an overview of the principles of the organization and those behind BCP, and the context for how the BCP team will proceed.

The contents of a policy include its scope, mission statement, principles, guidelines, and standards. The policy should draw on any existing policies if they are relevant. Note that a policy does not exist in a vacuum, but within a specific organization. Thus, in drawing up a policy, the team should examine the overall objectives and functions, including any business objectives, of the organization. The policy also should draw on standard "good practices" of similar organizations and professional standards bodies.

The BCP team produces and revises the policy, although top-tier management is actually responsible for it. A policy should be revamped as needed when the operating environment in which the organization operates changes significantly, such as a major expansion in operations or a change in location.

The process of drawing up a policy includes these steps:

1. Identify and document the components of the policy.
2. Identify and define policies of the organization that the BCP might affect.
3. Identify pertinent legislation, laws, regulations, and standards.
4. Identify "good industry practice" guidelines by consulting with industry experts.
5. Perform a gap analysis. Find out where the organization currently is in terms of continuity planning, and spell out where it wants to be at the end of the BCP process.
6. Compose a draft of the new policy.
7. Have different departments within the organization review the draft.
8. Incorporate the feedback from the departments into a revised draft.
9. Get the approval of top management on the new policy.
10. Publish a final draft, and distribute and publicize it throughout the organization.

Project Management

Sound project management processes, practices, and procedures are important for any organizational effort, and doubly so for BCP. Following accepted project management principles will help ensure effective management of the BCP process once it gets underway.

BCP projects commonly run out of funds and resources before they are fully completed. This typically occurs for one or more of the following reasons: the scope of the project is much larger than the team estimated; the BCP team members are expected to still carry out their current daily tasks along with new BCP tasks; or some other project shifts in importance and requires the attention of the BCP team members.

When technical people hear "risk management" they commonly think of security threats and technical solutions. Understanding the *risk of a project* must also be understood and properly planned for. If the scope of a project and the individual objectives that make up the scope are not properly defined, a lot of time and money can be easily wasted.

The individual objectives of a project must be analyzed to ensure that each is actually attainable. A part of scope analysis that may prove useful is a SWOT analysis. SWOT stands for *Strengths/Weaknesses/Opportunities/Threats*, and its basic tenants are as follows:

- **Strengths** Characteristics of the project team that give it an advantage over others
- **Weaknesses** Characteristics that place the team at a disadvantage relative to others
- **Opportunities** Elements that could contribute to the project's success
- **Threats** Elements that could contribute to the project's failure

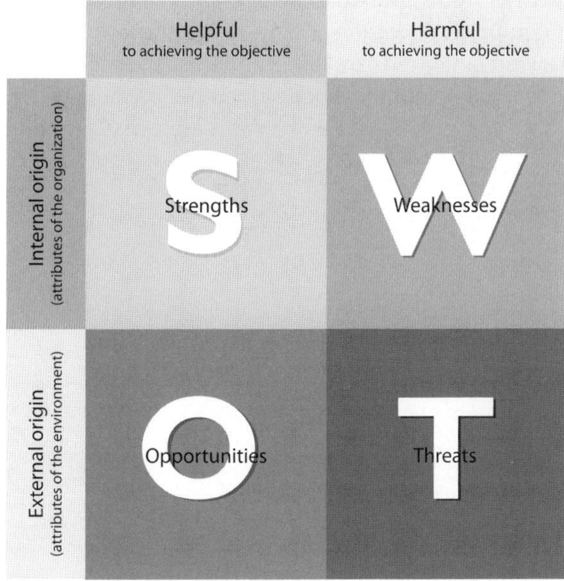

A SWOT analysis can be carried out to ensure that the defined objectives within the scope can be accomplished and issues identified that could impede upon the necessary success and productivity required of the project as a whole.

The BCP coordinator would need to implement some good old-fashioned project management skills, as listed in Table 1-11. A project plan should be developed that has the following components:

- Objective-to-task mapping
- Resource-to-task mapping
- Workflows
- Milestones
- Deliverables
- Budget estimates
- Success factors
- Deadlines

Once the project plan is completed, it should be presented to management for written approval before any further steps are taken. It is important to ensure that no assumptions are included in the plan. It is also important that the coordinator obtain permission to use the necessary resources to move forward.

NOTE Any early planning or policy documents should include a Definition of Terms, or Terms of Reference, namely a document that clearly defines the terminology used in the document. Clearly defining terms will avoid a great deal of confusion down the line by different groups, who might otherwise have varying definitions and assumptions about the common terms used in the continuity planning. Such a document should be treated as a formal deliverable and published early on in the process.

BCP Activity	Start Date	Required Completion Date	Completed? Initials/Date	Approved? Initials/Date
Initiate project				
Assign responsibilities				
Define continuity policy statement				
Perform business impact analysis				
Identify preventive controls				
Create recovery strategies				
Develop BCP and DRP documents				
Test plans				
Maintain plans				

Table 1-11 Steps to Be Documented and Approved in Continuity Planning

Business Continuity Planning Requirements

A major requirement for anything that has such far-reaching ramifications as business continuity planning is management support, as mentioned previously. It is critical that management understand what the real threats are to the company, the consequences of those threats, and the potential loss values for each threat. Without this understanding, management may only give lip service to continuity planning, and in some cases, that is worse than not having any plans at all because of the false sense of security it creates. Without management support, the necessary resources, funds, and time will not be devoted, which could result in bad plans that, again, may instill a false sense of security. Failure of these plans usually means a failure in management understanding, vision, and due-care responsibilities.

Executives may be held responsible and liable under various laws and regulations. They could be sued by stockholders and customers if they do not practice due diligence and due care. *Due diligence* can be defined as doing everything within one's power to prevent a bad thing from happening. Examples of this would be setting appropriate policies, researching the threats and incorporating them into a risk management plan, and ensuring audits happen at the right times. *Due care*, on the other hand, means taking the precautions that a reasonable and competent person would take in the same situation. For example, someone who ignores a security warning and clicks through to a malicious website would fail to exercise due care.

EXAM TIP Due diligence is normally associated with leaders, laws, and regulations. Due care is normally applicable to everyone and could be used to show negligence.

Executives must fulfill all of their responsibilities when it comes to disaster recovery and business continuity items. Organizations that work within specific industries have strict regulatory rules and laws that they must abide by, and these should be researched and integrated into the BCP program from the beginning. For example, banking and investment organizations must ensure that even if a disaster occurs, their customers' confidential information will not be disclosed to unauthorized individuals or be altered or vulnerable in any way.

Disaster recovery, continuity development, and continuity planning work best in a top-down approach, not a bottom-up approach. This means that management, not the staff, should be driving the project.

Many companies are running so fast to try to keep up with a dynamic and changing business world that they may not see the immediate benefit of spending time and resources on disaster recovery issues. Those individuals who *do* see the value in these efforts may have a hard time convincing top management if management does not see a potential profit margin or increase in market share as a result. But if a disaster does hit and they did put in the effort to properly prepare, the result can literally be priceless. Today's business world requires two important characteristics: the drive to produce a great product or service and get it to the market, and the insight and wisdom to know that unexpected trouble can easily find its way to your doorstep.

It is important that management set the overall goals of continuity planning, and it should help set the priorities of what should be dealt with first. Once management sets the goals and priorities, other staff members who are responsible for developing the different components of the BCP program can fill in the rest. However, management's support does not stop there. It needs to make sure the plans and procedures developed are actually implemented. Management must make sure the plans stay updated and represent the real priorities—not simply those perceived—of a company, which change over time.

Business Impact Analysis (BIA)

Business continuity planning deals with uncertainty and chance. What is important to note here is that even though you cannot predict whether or when a disaster will happen, that doesn't mean you can't plan for it. Just because we are not planning for an earthquake to hit us tomorrow morning at 10 A.M. doesn't mean we can't plan the activities required to successfully survive when an earthquake (or a similar disaster) does hit. The point of making these plans is to try to think of all the possible disasters that could take place, estimate the potential damage and loss, categorize and prioritize the potential disasters, and develop viable alternatives in case those events do actually happen.

A *business impact analysis (BIA)* is considered a *functional analysis*, in which a team collects data through interviews and documentary sources; documents business functions, activities, and transactions; develops a hierarchy of business functions; and finally applies a classification scheme to indicate each individual function's criticality level. But how do we determine a classification scheme based on criticality levels?

The BCP committee must identify the threats to the company and map them to the following characteristics:

- Maximum tolerable downtime and disruption for activities
- Operational disruption and productivity
- Financial considerations
- Regulatory responsibilities
- Reputation

The committee will not truly understand all business processes, the steps that must take place, or the resources and supplies these processes require. So the committee must gather this information from the people who do know—department managers and specific employees throughout the organization. The committee starts by identifying the people who will be part of the BIA data-gathering sessions. The committee needs to identify how it will collect the data from the selected employees, be it through surveys, interviews, or workshops. Next, the team needs to collect the information by actually conducting surveys, interviews, and workshops. Data points obtained as part of the information gathering will be used later during analysis. It is important that the team members ask about how different tasks—whether processes, transactions, or services, along with any relevant dependencies—get accomplished within the organization. Process flow diagrams should be built, which will be used throughout the BIA and plan development stages.

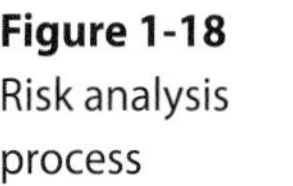

Figure 1-18 Risk analysis process

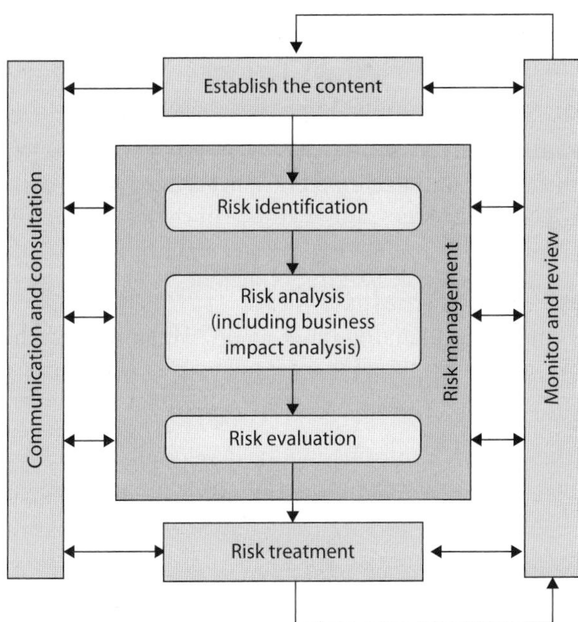

Upon completion of the data collection phase, the BCP committee needs to conduct a BIA to establish which processes, devices, or operational activities are critical. If a system stands on its own, doesn't affect other systems, and is of low criticality, then it can be classified as a tier-two or tier-three recovery step. This means these resources will not be dealt with during the recovery stages until the most critical (tier one) resources are up and running. This analysis can be completed using a standard risk assessment as illustrated in Figure 1-18.

Risk Assessment To achieve success, the organization should systematically plan and execute a formal BCP-related risk assessment. The assessment fully takes into account the organization's tolerance for continuity risks. The risk assessment also makes use of the data in the BIA to supply a consistent estimate of exposure.

As indicators of success, the risk assessment should identify, evaluate, and record all relevant items, which may include

- Vulnerabilities for all of the organization's most time-sensitive resources and activities
- Threats and hazards to the organization's most urgent resources and activities
- Measures that cut the possibility, length, or effect of a disruption on critical services and products
- Single points of failure; that is, concentrations of risk that threaten business continuity
- Continuity risks from concentrations of critical skills or critical shortages of skills

- Continuity risks due to outsourced vendors and suppliers
- Continuity risks that the BCP program has accepted, that are handled elsewhere, or that the BCP program does not address

Risk Assessment Evaluation and Process In a BCP setting, a risk assessment looks at the impact and likelihood of various threats that could trigger a business disruption. The tools, techniques, and methods of risk assessment include determining threats, assessing probabilities, tabulating threats, and analyzing costs and benefits.

The end goals of a risk assessment include

- Identifying and documenting single points of failure
- Making a prioritized list of threats to the particular business processes of the organization
- Putting together information for developing a management strategy for risk control and for developing action plans for addressing risks
- Documenting acceptance of identified risks, or documenting acknowledgment of risks that will not be addressed

The risk assessment is assumed to take the form of the equation: Risk = Threat × Impact × Probability. However, the BIA adds the dimension of time to this equation. In other words, risk mitigation measures should be geared toward those things that might most rapidly disrupt critical business processes and commercial activities.

The main parts of a risk assessment are

- Review the existing strategies for risk management
- Construct a numerical scoring system for probabilities and impacts
- Make use of a numerical score to gauge the effect of the threat
- Estimate the probability of each threat
- Weigh each threat through the scoring system
- Calculate the risk by combining the scores of likelihood and impact of each threat
- Get the organization's sponsor to sign off on these risk priorities
- Weigh appropriate measures
- Make sure that planned measures that alleviate risk do not heighten other risks
- Present the assessment's findings to executive management

Threats can be manmade, natural, or technical. A manmade threat may be an arsonist, a terrorist, or a simple mistake that can have serious outcomes. Natural threats may be tornadoes, floods, hurricanes, or earthquakes. Technical threats may be data corruption, loss of power, device failure, or loss of a data communications line. It is important to identify all possible threats and estimate the probability of them happening. Some issues may not immediately come to mind when developing these plans, such as an employee strike, vandals, disgruntled employees, or hackers, but they do need to be identified. These issues are often best addressed in a group with scenario-based exercises. This ensures that if a threat becomes reality, the plan includes the ramifications on *all* business tasks, departments, and critical operations. The more issues that are thought of and planned for, the better prepared a company will be if and when these events take place.

The BCP committee needs to step through scenarios in which the following problems result:

- Equipment malfunction or unavailable equipment
- Unavailable utilities (HVAC, power, communications lines)
- Facility becomes unavailable
- Critical personnel become unavailable
- Vendor and service providers become unavailable
- Software and/or data corruption

The specific scenarios and damage types can vary from organization to organization.

BIA Steps

The more detailed and granular steps of a BIA are outlined here:

1. Select individuals to interview for data gathering.
2. Create data-gathering techniques (surveys, questionnaires, qualitative and quantitative approaches).
3. Identify the company's critical business functions.
4. Identify the resources these functions depend upon.
5. Calculate how long these functions can survive without these resources.
6. Identify vulnerabilities and threats to these functions.
7. Calculate the risk for each different business function.
8. Document findings and report them to management.

We cover each of these steps in this chapter.

Assigning Values to Assets Qualitative and quantitative impact information should be gathered and then properly analyzed and interpreted. The goal is to see exactly how a business will be affected by different threats. The effects can be economical, operational, or both. Upon completion of the data analysis, it should be reviewed with the most knowledgeable people within the company to ensure that the findings are appropriate and that it describes the real risks and impacts the organization faces. This will help flush out any additional data points not originally obtained and will give a fuller understanding of all the possible business impacts.

Loss criteria must be applied to the individual threats that were identified. The criteria may include the following:

- Loss in reputation and public confidence
- Loss of competitive advantages
- Increase in operational expenses
- Violations of contract agreements
- Violations of legal and regulatory requirements
- Delayed-income costs
- Loss in revenue
- Loss in productivity

These costs can be direct or indirect and must be properly accounted for.

For instance, if the BCP team is looking at the threat of a terrorist bombing, it is important to identify which business function most likely would be targeted, how all business functions could be affected, and how each bulleted item in the loss criteria would be directly or indirectly involved. The timeliness of the recovery can be critical for business processes and the company's survival. For example, it may be acceptable to have the customer-support functionality out of commission for two days, whereas five days may leave the company in financial ruin.

After identifying the critical functions, it is necessary to find out exactly what is required for these individual business processes to take place. The resources that are required for the identified business processes are not necessarily just computer systems, but may include personnel, procedures, tasks, supplies, and vendor support. It must be understood that if one or more of these support mechanisms is not available, the critical function may be doomed. The team must determine what type of effect unavailable resources and systems will have on these critical functions.

The BIA identifies which of the company's critical systems are needed for survival and estimates the outage time that can be tolerated by the company as a result of various unfortunate events. The outage time that can be endured by a company is referred to as the *maximum tolerable downtime (MTD)* or *maximum period time of disruption (MPTD)*, which is illustrated in Figure 1-19.

The following are some MTD estimates that an organization may use. Note that these are sample estimates that will vary from organization to organization and from business unit to business unit:

- **Nonessential** 30 days
- **Normal** 7 days
- **Important** 72 hours

- **Urgent** 24 hours
- **Critical** Minutes to hours

Each business function and asset should be placed in one of these categories, depending upon how long the company can survive without it. These estimates will help the company determine what backup solutions are necessary to ensure the availability of these resources. The shorter the MTD, the higher priority of recovery for the function in question. Thus, the items classified as Urgent should be addressed before those classified as Normal.

For example, if being without a T1 communication line for three hours would cost the company $130,000, the T1 line could be considered Critical and thus the company should put in a backup T1 line from a different carrier. If a server going down and being unavailable for ten days will only cost the company $250 in revenue, this would fall into the Normal category, and thus the company may not need to have a fully redundant server waiting to be swapped out. Instead, the company may choose to count on its vendor's service level agreement (SLA), which may promise to have it back online in eight days.

Sometimes the MTD will depend in large measure on the type of business in question. For instance, a call center—a vital link to current and prospective clients—will have a short MTD, perhaps measured in minutes instead of weeks. A common solution is to split up the calls through multiple call centers placed in differing locales. If one call center is knocked out of service, the other one can temporarily pick up the load. Manufacturing can be handled in various ways. Examples include subcontracting the making of products to an outside vendor, manufacturing at multiple sites, and warehousing an extra supply of products to fill gaps in supply in case of disruptions to normal manufacturing.

The BCP team must try to think of all possible events that might occur that could turn out to be detrimental to a company. The BCP team also must understand it cannot possibly contemplate all events, and thus protection may not be available for every scenario introduced. Being properly prepared specifically for a flood, earthquake,

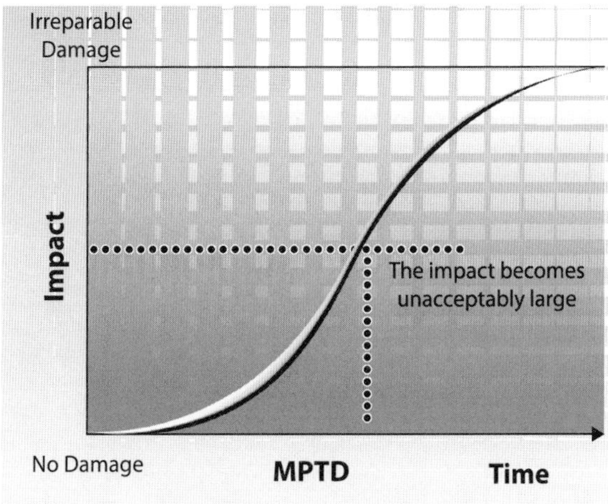

Figure 1-19 Maximum period of disruption

terrorist attack, or lightning strike is not as important as being properly prepared to respond to *anything* that damages or disrupts critical business functions.

All of the previously mentioned disasters could cause these results, but so could a meteor strike, a tornado, or a wing falling off a plane passing overhead. So the moral of the story is to be prepared for the loss of any or all business resources, instead of focusing on the events that could cause the loss.

EXAM TIP A BIA is performed at the beginning of business continuity planning to identify the areas that would suffer the greatest financial or operational loss in the event of a disaster or disruption. It identifies the company's critical systems needed for survival and estimates the outage time that can be tolerated by the company as a result of a disaster or disruption.

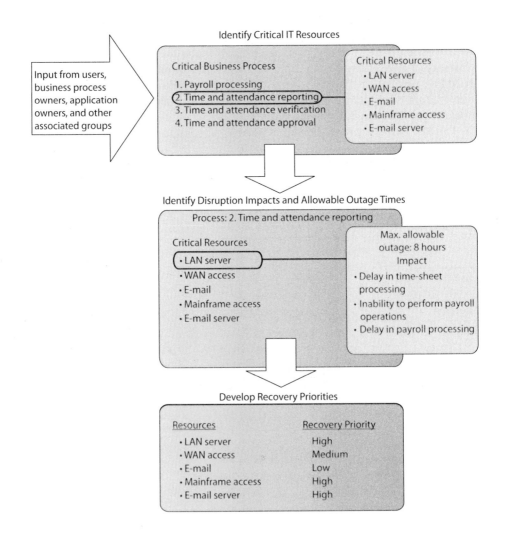

Input from users, business process owners, application owners, and other associated groups

Identify Critical IT Resources

Critical Business Process
1. Payroll processing
2. Time and attendance reporting
3. Time and attendance verification
4. Time and attendance approval

Critical Resources
• LAN server
• WAN access
• E-mail
• Mainframe access
• E-mail server

Identify Disruption Impacts and Allowable Outage Times

Process: 2. Time and attendance reporting

Critical Resources
• LAN server
• WAN access
• E-mail
• Mainframe access
• E-mail server

Max. allowable outage: 8 hours
Impact
• Delay in time-sheet processing
• Inability to perform payroll operations
• Delay in payroll processing

Develop Recovery Priorities

Resources	Recovery Priority
• LAN server	High
• WAN access	Medium
• E-mail	Low
• Mainframe access	High
• E-mail server	High

Interdependencies

It is important to look at a company as a complex animal instead of a static two-dimensional entity. It comprises many types of equipment, people, tasks, departments, communications mechanisms, and interfaces to the outer world. The biggest challenge of true continuity planning is understanding all of these intricacies and their interrelationships. A team may develop plans to back up and restore data, implement redundant data-processing equipment, educate employees on how to carry out automated tasks manually, and obtain redundant power supplies. But if all of these components don't know how to work together in a different, disruptive environment to get the products out the door, it might all be a waste of time.

The BCP team should carry out and address in the resulting plan the following interrelation and interdependency tasks:

- Define essential business functions and supporting departments.
- Identify interdependencies between these functions and departments.
- Discover all possible disruptions that could affect the mechanisms necessary to allow these departments to function together.
- Identify and document potential threats that could disrupt interdepartmental communication.
- Gather quantitative and qualitative information pertaining to those threats.
- Provide alternative methods of restoring functionality and communication.
- Provide a brief statement of rationale for each threat and corresponding information.

The main goal of business continuity is to resume normal business as quickly as possible, spending the least amount of money and resources. The overall business interruption and resumption plan should cover all organizational elements, identify critical services and functions, provide alternatives for emergency operations, and integrate each departmental plan. This can be accomplished by in-house appointed employees, outside consultants, or a combination of both. A combination can bring many benefits to the company, because the consultants are experts in this field and know the necessary steps, questions to ask, and issues to look for and offer general, reasonable advice, whereas in-house employees know their company intimately and have a full understanding of how certain threats can affect operations. It is good to cover all the necessary ground, and many times a combination of consultants and employees provides just the right recipe.

Up until now, we have established management's responsibilities as the following:

- Committing fully to the BCP
- Setting policy and goals
- Making available the necessary funds and resources
- Taking responsibility for the outcome of the development of the BCP
- Appointing a team for the process

The BCP team's responsibilities are as follows:

- Identifying regulatory and legal requirements that must be met
- Identifying all possible vulnerabilities and threats
- Estimating the possibilities of these threats and the loss potential
- Performing a BIA
- Outlining which departments, systems, and processes must be up and running before any others
- Identifying interdependencies among departments and processes
- Developing procedures and steps in resuming business after a disaster

Several software tools are available for developing a BCP that simplify this complex process. Automation of these procedures can quicken the pace of the project and allow easier gathering of the massive amount of information entailed. This information, along with other data explained in previous sections, should be presented to senior management. Management usually wants information stated in monetary, quantitative terms, not in subjective, qualitative terms. It is one thing to know that if a tornado were to hit, the result would be *really bad*, but it is another to know that if a tornado were to hit and affect 65 percent of the facility, the company could be at risk of losing computing capabilities for up to 72 hours, power supply for up to 24 hours, and a full stop of operations for 76 hours, which would equate to a loss of $125,000 each day.

Personnel Security

Many facets of the responsibilities of personnel fall under management's umbrella, and several facets have a direct correlation to the overall security of the environment.

Although society has evolved to be extremely dependent upon technology in the workplace, people are still the key ingredient to a successful company. But in security circles, people are often the weakest link. Either accidentally through mistakes or lack of training, or intentionally through fraud and malicious intent, personnel cause more serious and hard-to-detect security issues than hacker attacks, outside espionage, or equipment failure. Although the future actions of individuals cannot be predicted, it is possible to minimize the risks by implementing preventive measures. These include hiring the most qualified individuals, performing background checks, using detailed job descriptions, providing necessary training, enforcing strict access controls, and terminating individuals in a way that protects all parties involved.

Several items can be put into place to reduce the possibilities of fraud, sabotage, misuse of information, theft, and other security compromises. *Separation of duties* makes sure that one individual cannot complete a critical task by herself. In the movies, when a submarine captain needs to launch a nuclear torpedo to blow up the enemy and save civilization as we know it, the launch usually requires three codes to be entered into the launching mechanism by three different senior crewmembers. This is an example of separation of duties, and it ensures that the captain cannot complete such an important and terrifying task all by himself.

Separation of duties is a preventative administrative control put into place to reduce the potential of fraud. For example, an employee cannot complete a critical financial transaction by herself. She will need to have her supervisor's written approval before the transaction can be completed.

In an organization that practices separation of duties, collusion must take place for fraud to be committed. *Collusion* means that at least two people are working together to cause some type of destruction or fraud. In our example, the employee and her supervisor must be participating in the fraudulent activity to make it happen.

Two variations of separation of duties are *split knowledge* and *dual control*. In both cases, two or more individuals are authorized and required to perform a duty or task. In the case of split knowledge, no one person knows or has all the details to perform a task. For example, two managers might be required to open a bank vault, with each only knowing part of the combination. In the case of dual control, two individuals are again authorized to perform a task, but both must be available and active in their participation to complete the task or mission. For example, two officers must perform an identical key-turn in a nuclear missile submarine, each out of reach of the other, to launch a missile. The control here is that no one person has the capability of launching a missile, because they cannot reach to turn both keys at the same time.

Rotation of duties (rotation of assignments) is an administrative detective control that can be put into place to uncover fraudulent activities. No one person should stay in one position for a long time because they may end up having too much control over a segment of the business. Such total control could result in fraud or the misuse of resources. Employees should be moved into different roles with the idea that they may be able to detect suspicious activity carried out by the previous employee carrying out that position. This type of control is commonly implemented in financial institutions.

Employees in sensitive areas should be forced to take their vacations, which is known as a *mandatory vacation*. While they are on vacation, other individuals fill their positions and thus can usually detect any fraudulent errors or activities. Two of the many ways to detect fraud or inappropriate activities would be the discovery of activity on someone's user account while they're supposed to be away on vacation, or if a specific problem stopped while someone was away and not active on the network. These anomalies are worthy of investigation. Employees who carry out fraudulent activities commonly do not take vacations because they do not want anyone to figure out what they are doing behind the scenes. This is why they must be forced to be away from the organization for a period of time, usually two weeks.

Hiring Practices

Depending on the position to be filled, a level of screening should be done by human resources to ensure the company hires the right individual for the right job. Skills should be tested and evaluated, and the caliber and character of the individual should be examined. Joe might be the best programmer in the state, but if someone looks into his past and finds out he served prison time because he continually flashes old ladies in parks, the hiring manager might not be so eager to bring Joe into the organization.

Nondisclosure agreements (NDAs) must be developed and signed by new employees to protect the company and its sensitive information. Any conflicts of interest must be addressed, and there should be different agreements and precautions taken with temporary and contract employees.

References should be checked, military records reviewed, education verified, and, if necessary, a drug test should be administered. Many times, important personal behaviors can be concealed, and that is why hiring practices now include scenario questions, personality tests, and observations of the individual, instead of just looking at a person's work history. When a person is hired, he is bringing his skills and whatever other baggage he carries. A company can reduce its heartache pertaining to personnel by first conducting useful and careful hiring practices.

The goal is to hire the "right person" and not just hire a person for "right now." Employees represent an investment on the part of the organization, and by taking the time and hiring the right people for the jobs, the organization will be able to maximize their investment and achieve a better return.

A more detailed background check can reveal some interesting information. Things like unexplained gaps in employment history, the validity and actual status of professional certifications, criminal records, driving records, job titles that have been misrepresented, credit histories, unfriendly terminations, appearances on suspected terrorist watch lists, and even real reasons for having left previous jobs can all be determined through the use of background checks. This has real benefit to the employer and the organization because it serves as the first line of defense for the organization against being attacked from within. Any negative information that can be found in these areas could be indicators of potential problems that the potential employee could create for the company at a later date. Take the credit report for instance. On the surface, this may seem to be something the organization doesn't need to know about, but if the report indicates the potential employee has a poor credit standing and a history of financial problems, it could mean you don't want to place them in charge of the organization's accounting, or even the petty cash.

Ultimately, the goal here is to achieve several different things at the same time by using a background check. You're trying to mitigate risk, lower hiring costs, and also lower the turnover rate for employees. All this is being done at the same time you are trying to protect your existing customers and employees from someone gaining employment in your organization who could potentially conduct malicious and dishonest actions that could harm you, your employees, and your customers as well as the general public. In many cases, it is also harder to go back and conduct background checks after the individual has been hired and is working. This is because there will need to be a specific cause or reason for conducting this kind of investigation. If any employee moves to a position of greater security sensitivity or potential risk, a follow-up investigation should be considered.

Possible background check criteria could include

- A Social Security number trace
- A county/state criminal check
- A federal criminal check
- A sexual offender registry check
- Employment verification
- Education verification

- Professional reference verification
- An immigration check
- Professional license/certification verification
- Credit report
- Drug screening

Termination

Because terminations can happen for a variety of reasons, and terminated people have different reactions, companies should have a specific set of procedures to follow with every termination. For example:

- The employee must leave the facility immediately under the supervision of a manager or security guard.
- The employee must surrender any identification badges or keys, be asked to complete an exit interview, and return company supplies.
- That user's accounts and passwords should be disabled or changed immediately.

These actions may seem harsh when they actually take place, but too many companies have been hurt by vengeful employees who have lashed out at the company when their positions were revoked for one reason or another. If an employee is disgruntled in any way or the termination is unfriendly, that employee's accounts should be disabled right away, and all passwords on all systems changed.

Practical Tips on Terminations

Without previous arrangement, an employee cannot be compelled to complete an exit interview, despite the huge value to the company of conducting such interviews. Neither can an employee be compelled to return company property, as a practical matter, if he or she simply chooses not to. The best way to motivate departing employees to comply is to ensure that any severance package they may be eligible for is contingent upon completion of these tasks, and that means having them agree to such conditions up front, as part of their employment agreement.

Security-Awareness Training

For an organization to achieve the desired results of its security program, it must communicate the what, how, and why of security to its employees. Security-awareness training should be comprehensive, tailored for specific groups, and organization-wide. It should repeat the most important messages in different formats; be kept up to date; be entertaining, positive, and humorous; be simple to understand; and—most important—be supported by senior management. Management must allocate the resources for this activity and enforce its attendance within the organization.

The goal is for each employee to understand the importance of security to the company as a whole and to each individual. Expected responsibilities and acceptable behaviors must be clarified, and noncompliance repercussions, which could range from a warning to dismissal, must be explained before being invoked. Security-awareness training is performed to modify employees' behavior and attitude toward security. This can best be achieved through a formalized process of security-awareness training.

Because security is a topic that can span many different aspects of an organization, it can be difficult to communicate the correct information to the right individuals. By using a formalized process for security-awareness training, you can establish a method that will provide you with the best results for making sure security requirements are presented to the right people in an organization. This way you can make sure everyone understands what is outlined in the organization's security program, why it is important, and how it fits into the individual's role in the organization. The higher levels of training typically are more general and deal with broader concepts and goals, and as the training moves down to specific jobs and tasks, it becomes more situation specific as it directly applies to certain positions within the company.

A security-awareness program is typically created for at least three types of audiences: management, staff, and technical employees. Each type of awareness training must be geared toward the individual audience to ensure each group understands its particular responsibilities, liabilities, and expectations. If technical security training were given to senior management, their eyes would glaze over as soon as protocols and firewalls were mentioned. On the flip side, if legal ramifications, company liability issues pertaining to protecting data, and shareholders' expectations were discussed with the IT group, they would quickly turn to their smartphone and start tweeting, browsing the Internet, or texting their friends.

Members of management would benefit the most from a short, focused security-awareness orientation that discusses corporate assets and financial gains and losses pertaining to security. They need to know how stock prices can be negatively affected by compromises, understand possible threats and their outcomes, and know why security must be integrated into the environment the same way as other business processes. Because members of management must lead the rest of the company in support of security, they must gain the right mindset about its importance.

Middle management would benefit from a more detailed explanation of the policies, procedures, standards, and guidelines and how they map to the individual departments for which each middle manager is responsible. Middle managers should be taught why their support for their specific departments is critical and what their level of responsibility is for ensuring that employees practice safe computing activities. They should also be shown how the consequences of noncompliance by individuals who report to them can affect the company as a whole and how they, as managers, may have to answer for such indiscretions.

The technical departments must receive a different presentation that aligns more to their daily tasks. They should receive a more in-depth training to discuss technical configurations, incident handling, and how to recognize different types of security compromises.

	Awareness	Training	Education
Attribute	"What"	"How"	"Why"
Level	Information	Knowledge	Insight
Learning objective	Recognition and retention	Skill	Understanding
Example teaching method	**Media:** Videos Newsletters Posters CBT Social engineering testing	**Practical Instruction:** Lecture and/or demo Case study Hands-on practice	**Theoretical Instruction:** Seminar and discussion Reading and study Research
Test measure	True/False, multiple choice (identify learning)	Problem solving—i.e., recognition and resolution (apply learning)	Essay (interpret learning)
Impact timeframe	Short-term	Intermediate	Long-term

Table 1-12 Aspects of Awareness, Training, and Education

It is usually best to have each employee sign a document indicating they have heard and understand all the security topics discussed, and that they also understand the ramifications of noncompliance. This reinforces the policies' importance to the employee and also provides evidence down the road if the employee claims they were never told of these expectations. Awareness training should happen during the hiring process and at least annually after that. Attendance of training should also be integrated into employment performance reports.

Various methods should be employed to reinforce the concepts of security awareness. Things like screen banners, employee handbooks, and even posters can be used as ways to remind employees about their duties and the necessities of good security practices.

Degree or Certification?

Some roles within the organization need hands-on experience and skill, meaning that the hiring manager should be looking for specific industry certifications. Some positions require more of a holistic and foundational understanding of concepts or a business background, and in those cases a degree may be required. Table 1-12 provides more information on the differences between awareness, training, and education.

Security Governance

An organization may be following many of the items laid out in this chapter: building a security program, integrating it into their business architecture, developing a risk management program, documenting the different aspects of the security program, performing data protection, and training its staff. But how does the organization know that it is doing everything correctly, and doing so on an ongoing basis? This is where security governance comes into play. *Security governance* is a framework that allows for the security goals of an organization to be set and expressed by senior management, communicated throughout the different levels of the organization. It grants power to the entities needed to implement and enforce security, and provides a way to verify the performance of these necessary security activities. Not only does senior management need to set the direction of security; it also needs a way to be able to view and understand how their directives are being met or not being met.

If a board of directors and CEO demand that security be integrated properly at all levels of the organization, how do they know it is really happening? Oversight mechanisms must be developed and integrated so that the people who are ultimately responsible for an organization are constantly and consistently updated on the overall health and security posture of the organization. This happens through properly defined communication channels, standardized reporting methods, and performance-based metrics.

Let's compare two companies. Company A has an effective security governance program in place and Company B does not. Now, to the untrained eye it would seem as though Companies A and B are equal in their security practices because they both have security policies, procedures, and standards in place, the same security technology controls (firewalls, IDSs, identity management, and so on), defined security roles, and security-awareness training. You may think, "Man, these two companies are on the ball and quite evolved in their security programs." But if you look closer, you will see some critical differences (listed in Table 1-13).

Does the organization you work for look like Company A or Company B? Most organizations today have many of the pieces and parts to a security program (policies, standards, firewalls, security team, IDS, and so on), but management may not be truly involved, and security has not permeated throughout the organization. Some organizations rely just on technology and isolate all security responsibilities within the IT group. If security were just a technology issue, then this security team could properly install, configure, and maintain the products, and the company would get a gold star and pass the audit with flying colors. But that is not how the world of information security works today. It is much more than just technological solutions. Security must be utilized throughout the organization, and having several points of responsibility and accountability is critical. Security governance is a coherent system of integrated processes that helps to ensure consistent oversight, accountability, and compliance. It is a structure that we should put in place to make sure that our efforts are streamlined and effective and that nothing is being missed.

Metrics

We really can't just build a security program, call it good, and go home. We need a way to assess the effectiveness of our work, identify deficiencies, and prioritize the things that still need work. We need a way to facilitate decision making, performance improvement, and accountability through collection, analysis, and reporting of the necessary information. As the saying goes, "You can't manage something you can't measure." In security there are many items that need to be measured so that performance is properly

Company A	Company B
Board members understand that information security is critical to the company and demand to be updated quarterly on security performance and breaches.	Board members do not understand that information security is in their realm of responsibility and focus solely on corporate governance and profits.
CEO, CFO, CIO, CSIO, and business unit managers participate in a risk management committee that meets each month, and information security is always one topic on the agenda to review.	CEO, CFO, and business unit managers feel as though information security is the responsibility of the CIO, CISO, and IT department and do not get involved.
Executive management sets an acceptable risk level that is the basis for the company's security policies and all security activities.	The CISO took some boilerplate security policies and inserted his company's name and had the CEO sign them.
Executive management holds business unit managers responsible for carrying out risk management activities for their specific business units.	All security activity takes place within the security department; thus, security works within a silo and is not integrated throughout the organization.
Critical business processes are documented along with the risks that are inherent at the different steps within the business processes.	Business processes are not documented and not analyzed for potential risks that can affect operations, productivity, and profitability.
Employees are held accountable for any security breaches they participate in, either maliciously or accidentally.	Policies and standards are developed, but no enforcement or accountability practices have been envisioned or deployed.
Security products, managed services, and consultants are purchased and deployed in an informed manner. They are also constantly reviewed to ensure they are cost effective.	Security products, managed services, and consultants are purchased and deployed without any real research or performance metrics to determine the return on investment or effectiveness.
The organization is continuing to review its processes, including security, with the goal of continued improvement.	The organization does not analyze its performance for improvement, but continually marches forward and makes similar mistakes over and over again.

Table 1-13 Security Governance Program: A Comparison of Two Companies

understood. We need to know how effective and efficient our security controls are, not only to make sure that assets are properly protected, but also to ensure that we are being financially responsible in our budgetary efforts.

There are different methodologies that can be followed when it comes to developing security metrics, but no matter what model is followed, some things are critical across the board. Strong management support is necessary, because while it might seem that developing ways of counting things is not overly complex, the actual implementation and use of a metric and measuring system can be quite an undertaking. The metrics have to be developed, adopted, integrated into many different existing and new processes, interpreted, and used in decision-making efforts. Management needs to be on board if this effort is going to be successful.

Another requirement is that there has to be established policies, procedures, and standards to measure against. How can you measure policy compliance when there are no policies in place? A full security program needs to be developed and matured before attempting to measure its pieces and parts.

Measurement activities need to provide quantifiable performance-based data that is repeatable, reliable, and produces results that are meaningful. Measurement will need to happen on a continuous basis, so the data collection methods must be repeatable. The same type of data must be continuously gathered and compared so that improvement or a drop in efficacy can be identified. The data collection may come from parsing system logs, incident response reports, audit findings, surveys, or risk assessments. The measurement results must also be meaningful for the intended audience. An executive will want data portrayed in a method that allows him to understand the health of the security program quickly and in terms he is used to. This can be a heat map, graph, pie chart, or scorecard. A balanced scorecard, shown in Figure 1-20, is a traditional strategic tool used for performance measurement in the business world. The goal is to present the most relevant information quickly and easily. Measurements are compared with set target values so that if performance deviates from expectations, that deviation can be conveyed in a simplistic and straightforward manner.

If the audience for the measurement values are not executives, but instead security administrators, then the results are presented in a manner that is easiest for them to understand and use.

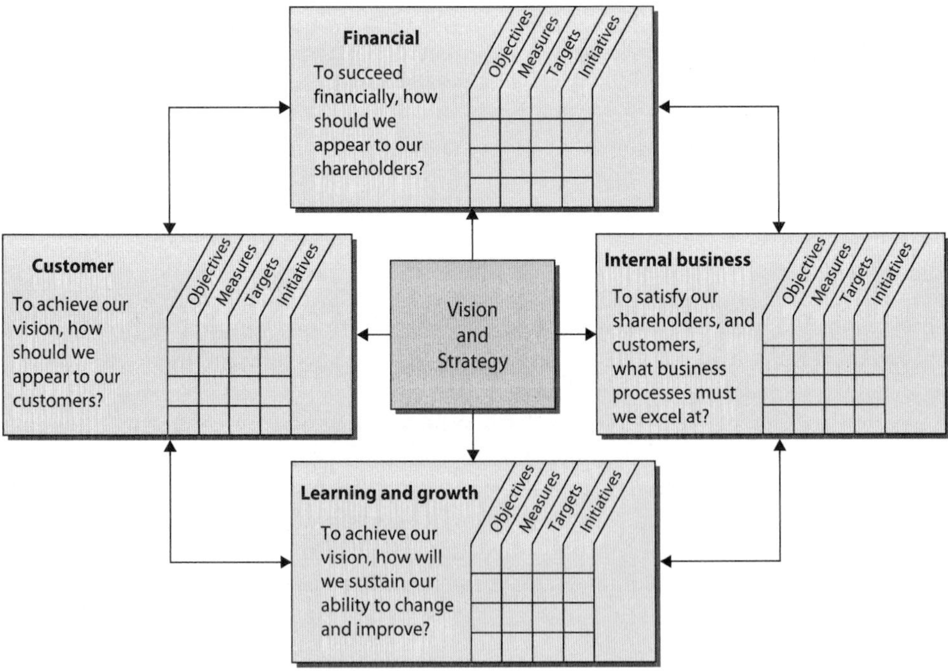

Figure 1-20 Balanced scorecard

CAUTION It is not uncommon to see scorecards, pie charts, graphics, and dashboard results that do not map to what is really going on in the environment. Unless real data is gathered and the *correct* data is gathered, the resulting pie chart can illustrate a totally different story than what is really taking place. Some people spend more time making the colors in the graph look eye-pleasing than perfecting the raw data-gathering techniques. This can lead to a false sense of security and ultimately to breaches.

There are industry best practices that can be used to guide the development of a security metric and measurement system. The international standard is *ISO/IEC 27004:2009*, which is used to assess the effectiveness of an ISMS and the controls that make up the security program as outlined in ISO/IEC 27001. So ISO/IEC 27001 tells you how to build a security program and then ISO/IEC 27004 tells you how to measure it. The *NIST SP 800-55, Revision 1* also covers performance measuring for information security, but has a U.S. government slant. The ISO standard and NIST approaches to metric development are similar, but have some differences. The ISO standard breaks individual metrics down into base measures, derived measures, and then indicator values. The NIST approach is illustrated in Figure 1-21, which breaks metrics down into implementation, effectiveness/efficiency, and impact values.

If your organization has the goal of becoming ISO/IEC 27000 certified, then you should follow ISO/IEC 27004:2009. If your organization is governmental or a

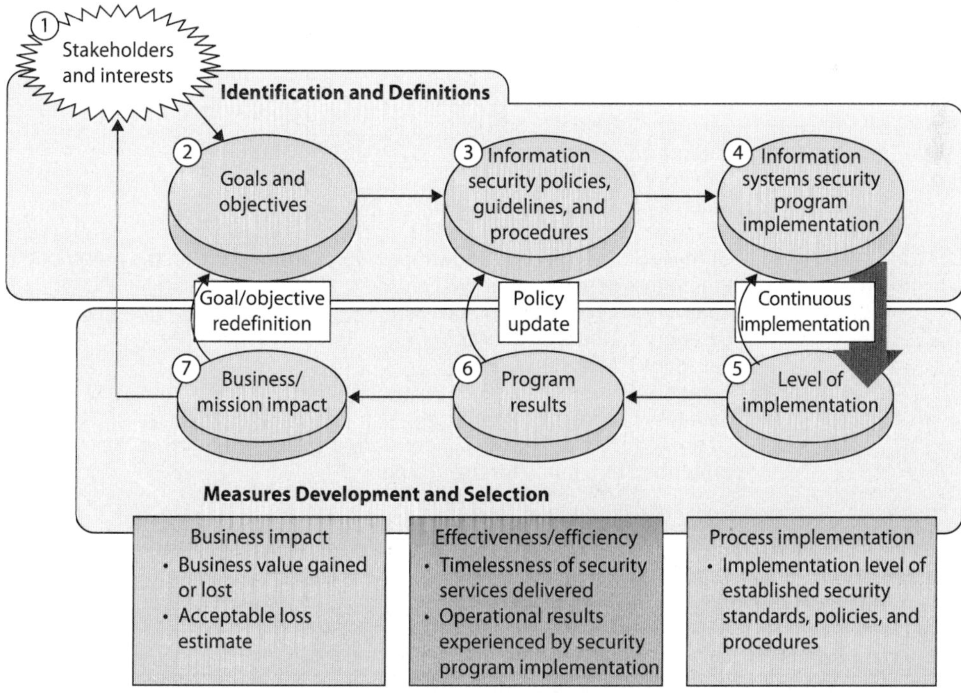

Figure 1-21 Security measurement processes

government contracting company, then following the NIST standard would make more sense. What is important is consistency. For metrics to be used in a successful manner, they have to be standardized and have a direct relationship to each other. For example, if an organization used a rating system of 1–10 to measure incident response processes and a rating system of High, Medium, and Low to measure malware infection protection mechanisms, these metrics could not be integrated easily. An organization needs to establish the metric value types it will use and implement them in a standardized method across the enterprise. Measurement processes need to be thought through at a detailed level before attempting implementation. Table 1-14 illustrates a metric template that can be used to track incident response performance levels.

Field	Data
Measure ID	Incident Response Measure 1
Goal	Strategic Goal: Make accurate, timely information on the organization's programs and services readily available. Information Security Goal: Track, document, and report incidents to appropriate organizational officials and/or authorities.
Measure	Percentage of incidents reported within required timeframe per applicable incident category.
Measure Type	Effectiveness
Formula	For each incident category (number of incidents reported on time/total number of reported incidents) × 100
Target	85%
Implementation Evidence	How many incidents were reported during the period of 12 months? Category 1. Unauthorized Access? ______ Category 2. Denial of Service? ________ Category 3. Malicious Code? _________ Category 4. Improper Usage? _________ Category 5. Access Attempted? ________ How many incidents involved PII? Of the incidents reported, how many were reported within the prescribed timeframe for their category? Category 1. Unauthorized Access? ______ Category 2. Denial of Service? ________ Category 3. Malicious Code? _________ Category 4. Improper Usage? _________ Category 5. Access Attempted? ________ Of the PII incidents reported, how many were reported within the prescribed timeframe for their category?
Frequency	Collection Frequency: Monthly Reporting Frequency: Annually
Responsible Parties	CIO, CISO
Data Source	Incident logs, incident tracking database
Reporting Format	Line chart that illustrates individual categories

Table 1-14 Incident Response Measurement Template

The types of metrics that are developed need to map to the maturity level of the security program. In the beginning, simplistic items are measured (i.e., number of completed policies), and as the program matures the metrics mature and can increase in complexity (i.e., number of vulnerabilities mitigated).

The use of metrics allows an organization to truly understand the health of its security program because each activity and initiative can be measured in a quantifiable manner. The metrics are used in governing activities because this allows for the best strategic decisions to be made. The use of metrics also allows the organization to implement and follow the capability maturity model described earlier. A maturity model is used to carry out incremental improvements, and the metric results indicate what needs to be improved and to what levels. Metrics can also be used in process improvement models, as in Six Sigma and the measurements of service-level targets for ITIL. We need to know not only what to do (implement controls, build a security program), but also how well we did it and how to continuously improve.

Ethics

Ethics are based on many different issues and foundations. They can be relative to different situations and interpreted differently from individual to individual. Therefore, they are often a topic of debate. However, some ethics are less controversial than others, and these types of ethics are easier to expect of all people.

(ISC)^2 requires all certified system security professionals to commit to fully supporting its Code of Ethics. If a CISSP intentionally or knowingly violates this Code of Ethics, he or she may be subject to a peer review panel, which will decide whether the certification should be revoked.

The full set of (ISC)^2 Code of Ethics for the CISSP is listed on the (ISC)^2 site at www.isc2.org. The following list is an overview, but each CISSP candidate should read the full version and understand the Code of Ethics before attempting this exam:

- Protect society, the common good, necessary public trust and confidence, and the infrastructure.
- Act honorably, honestly, justly, responsibly, and legally.
- Provide diligent and competent service to principals.
- Advance and protect the profession.

An interesting relationship exists between law and ethics. Most often, laws are based on ethics and are put in place to ensure that others act in an ethical way. However, laws do not apply to everything—that is when ethics should kick in. Some things may not be illegal, but that does not necessarily mean they are ethical.

Corporations should have a guide developed on computer and business ethics. This can be part of an employee handbook, used in orientation, posted, and made a part of training sessions.

Certain common ethical fallacies are used by many in the computing world to justify unethical acts. They exist because people look at issues differently and interpret (or misinterpret) rules and laws that have been put into place. The following are examples of these ethical fallacies:

- Hackers only want to learn and improve their skills. Many of them are not making a profit off of their deeds; therefore, their activities should not be seen as illegal or unethical.
- The First Amendment protects and provides the right for U.S. citizens to write viruses.
- Information should be shared freely and openly; therefore, sharing confidential information and trade secrets should be legal and ethical.
- Hacking does not actually hurt anyone.

The Computer Ethics Institute

The *Computer Ethics Institute* is a nonprofit organization that works to help advance technology by ethical means.

The Computer Ethics Institute has developed its own Ten Commandments of Computer Ethics:

1. Thou shalt not use a computer to harm other people.
2. Thou shalt not interfere with other people's computer work.
3. Thou shalt not snoop around in other people's computer files.
4. Thou shalt not use a computer to steal.
5. Thou shalt not use a computer to bear false witness.
6. Thou shalt not copy or use proprietary software for which you have not paid.
7. Thou shalt not use other people's computer resources without authorization or proper compensation.
8. Thou shalt not appropriate other people's intellectual output.
9. Thou shalt think about the social consequences of the program you are writing or the system you are designing.
10. Thou shalt always use a computer in ways that ensure consideration and respect for your fellow humans.

The Internet Architecture Board

The *Internet Architecture Board (IAB)* is the coordinating committee for Internet design, engineering, and management. It is responsible for the architectural oversight of the Internet Engineering Task Force (IETF) activities, Internet Standards Process oversight and appeal, and editor of Requests for Comments (RFCs). Figure 1-22 illustrates the IAB's place in the hierarchy of entities that help ensure the structure and standardization of the Internet. Otherwise, the Internet would be an unusable big bowl of spaghetti and we would all still be writing letters and buying stamps.

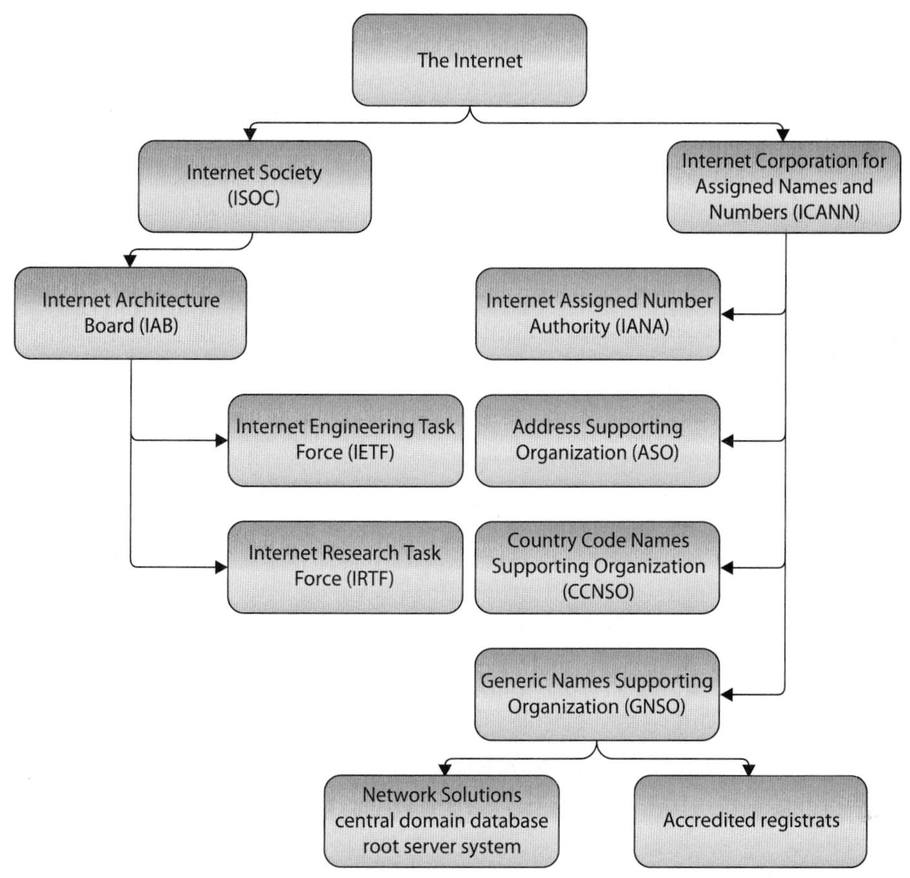

Figure 1-22 Where the Internet Architecture Board (IAB) fits

The IAB issues ethics-related statements concerning the use of the Internet. It considers the Internet to be a resource that depends upon availability and accessibility to be useful to a wide range of people. It is mainly concerned with irresponsible acts on the Internet that could threaten its existence or negatively affect others. It sees the Internet as a great gift and works hard to protect it for all who depend upon it. The IAB sees the use of the Internet as a privilege, which should be treated as such and used with respect.

The IAB considers the following acts unethical and unacceptable behavior:

- Purposely seeking to gain unauthorized access to Internet resources
- Disrupting the intended use of the Internet
- Wasting resources (people, capacity, and computers) through purposeful actions
- Destroying the integrity of computer-based information
- Compromising the privacy of others
- Conducting Internet-wide experiments in a negligent manner

The IAB vows to work with federal agencies to take whatever actions are necessary to protect the Internet. This could be through new technologies, methods, or procedures that are intended to make the Internet more resistant to disruption. A balance exists between enhancing protection and reducing functionality. One of the Internet's main purposes is to enable information to flow freely and not be prohibited; thus, the IAB must be logical and flexible in its approaches and in the restrictions it attempts to implement. The Internet is everyone's tool, so everyone should work together to protect it.

NOTE RFC 1087 is called "Ethics and the Internet." This RFC outlines the concepts pertaining to what the IAB considers unethical and unacceptable behavior.

Corporate Ethics Programs

More regulations are requiring organizations to have an ethical statement and potentially an ethical program in place. The ethical program is to serve as the "tone at the top," which means that the executives need to ensure not only that their employees are acting ethically, but also that they themselves are following their own rules. The main goal is to ensure that the motto "succeed by any means necessary" is not the spoken or unspoken culture of a work environment. Certain structures can be put into place that provide a breeding ground for unethical behavior. If the CEO gets more in salary based on stock prices, then she may find ways to artificially inflate stock prices, which can directly hurt the investors and shareholders of the company. If managers can only be promoted based on the amount of sales they bring in, these numbers may be fudged and not represent reality. If an employee can only get a bonus if a low budget is maintained, he might be willing to take shortcuts that could hurt company customer service or product development. Although ethics seem like things that float around in the ether and make us feel good to talk about, they have to be actually implemented in the real corporate world through proper business processes and management styles.

Summary

This chapter (and its corresponding domain) is one of the longest in the book, and with good reason. It lays down the foundation on which the rest of the CISSP body of knowledge is built. Information systems security boils down to ensuring the availability, integrity, and confidentiality of our information in an environment rich in influencers. These include organizational goals, assets, laws, regulations, privacy, threats, and people. Each of these was discussed in some detail in the preceding sections. Along the way, we also covered tangible ways in which we can link security to each of the influencers. We discussed a variety of frameworks that enable our organizations to provide governance and management of business, IT, and security issues. In many cases, these frameworks are driven by legal or regulatory requirements. In other cases, they represent best practices for security. As CISSPs we must be knowledgeable of all these as we are trusted to be able to apply the right solution to any security problem.

We also took a very detailed look at the way in which we manage risk to our information systems. We know that no system is truly secure, so our job is to find the most likely and the most dangerous threat actions so that we can address them first. The process of quantifying losses and their probabilities of occurring is at the heart of risk assessments. Armed with that information, we are able to make good decisions in terms of controls, processes, and costs. Our approach is not solely focused on the human adversary, but also on any source of loss to our organizations. Most importantly, we use this information to devise ways in which to ensure we can continue business operations in the face of any reasonable threat. Figure 1-23 illustrates many of the elements that go into a complete security program.

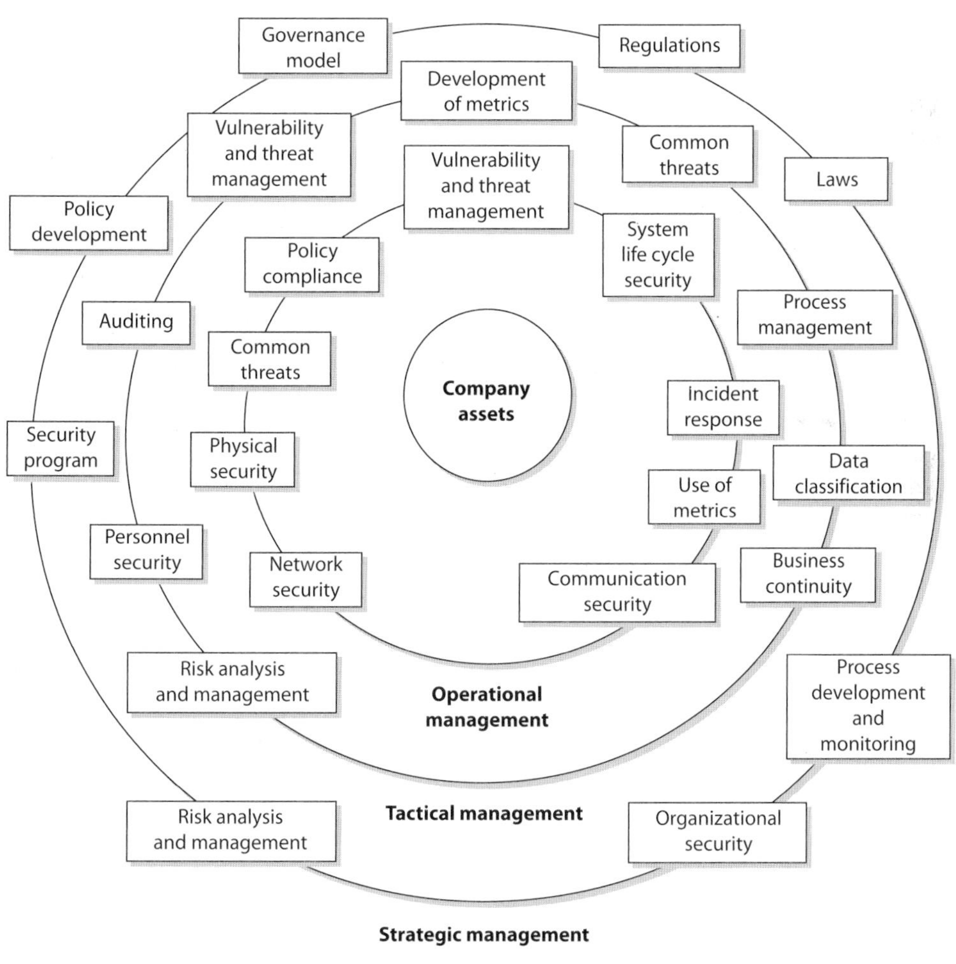

Figure 1-23 A complete security program contains many items.

Quick Tips

- The objectives of security are to provide availability, integrity, and confidentiality protection to data and resources.
- A vulnerability is a weakness in a system that allows a threat source to compromise its security.
- A threat is the possibility that someone or something would exploit a vulnerability, either intentionally or accidentally, and cause harm to an asset.
- A risk is the probability of a threat agent exploiting a vulnerability and the loss potential from that action.
- A countermeasure, also called a safeguard or control, mitigates the risk.
- A control can be administrative, technical, or physical and can provide deterrent, preventive, detective, corrective, or recovery protection.
- A compensating control is an alternative control that is put into place because of financial or business functionality reasons.
- COBIT is a framework of control objectives and allows for IT governance.
- ISO/IEC 27001 is the standard for the establishment, implementation, control, and improvement of the information security management system.
- The ISO/IEC 27000 series were derived from BS 7799 and are international best practices on how to develop and maintain a security program.
- Enterprise architecture frameworks are used to develop architectures for specific stakeholders and present information in views.
- An information security management system (ISMS) is a coherent set of policies, processes, and systems to manage risks to information assets as outlined in ISO\IEC 27001.
- Enterprise security architecture is a subset of business architecture and a way to describe current and future security processes, systems, and subunits to ensure strategic alignment.
- Blueprints are functional definitions for the integration of technology into business processes.
- Enterprise architecture frameworks are used to build individual architectures that best map to individual organizational needs and business drivers.
- Zachman Framework is an enterprise architecture framework, and SABSA is a security enterprise architecture framework.
- COSO Internal Control—Integrated Framework is a governance model used to help prevent fraud within a corporate environment.
- ITIL is a set of best practices for IT service management.

- Six Sigma is used to identify defects in processes so that the processes can be improved upon.
- CMMI is a maturity model that allows for processes to improve in an incremented and standard approach.
- Security enterprise architecture should tie in strategic alignment, business enablement, process enhancement, and security effectiveness.
- NIST SP 800-53 uses the following control categories: technical, management, and operational.
- Civil law system
  - Uses prewritten rules and is not based on precedence.
  - Is different from civil (tort) laws, which work under a common law system.
- Common law system
  - Made up of criminal, civil, and administrative laws.
- Customary law system
  - Addresses mainly personal conduct and uses regional traditions and customs as the foundations of the laws.
  - Is usually mixed with another type of listed legal system rather than being the sole legal system used in a region.
- Religious law system
  - Laws are derived from religious beliefs and address an individual's religious responsibilities; commonly used in Muslim countries or regions.
- Mixed law system
  - Uses two or more legal systems.
- Criminal law deals with an individual's conduct that violates government laws developed to protect the public.
- Civil law deals with wrongs committed against individuals or companies that result in injury or damages. Civil law does not use prison time as a punishment, but usually requires financial restitution.
- Administrative, or regulatory, law covers standards of performance or conduct expected by government agencies from companies, industries, and certain officials.
- A patent grants ownership and enables that owner to legally enforce his rights to exclude others from using the invention covered by the patent.
- Copyright protects the expression of ideas rather than the ideas themselves.
- Trademarks protect words, names, product shapes, symbols, colors, or a combination of these used to identify products or a company. These items are used to distinguish products from the competitors' products.

- Trade secrets are deemed proprietary to a company and often include information that provides a competitive edge. The information is protected as long as the owner takes the necessary protective actions.
- Crime over the Internet has brought about jurisdiction problems for law enforcement and the courts.
- Privacy laws dictate that data collected by government agencies must be collected fairly and lawfully, must be used only for the purpose for which it was collected, must only be held for a reasonable amount of time, and must be accurate and timely.
- When choosing the right safeguard to reduce a specific risk, the cost, functionality, and effectiveness must be evaluated and a cost/benefit analysis performed.
- A security policy is a statement by management dictating the role security plays in the organization.
- Procedures are detailed step-by-step actions that should be followed to achieve a certain task.
- Standards are documents that outline rules that are compulsory in nature and support the organization's security policies.
- A baseline is a minimum level of security.
- Guidelines are recommendations and general approaches that provide advice and flexibility.
- OCTAVE is a team-oriented risk management methodology that employs workshops and is commonly used in the commercial sector.
- Security management should work from the top down (from senior management down to the staff).
- Risk can be transferred, avoided, reduced, or accepted.
- Threats × vulnerability × asset value = total risk
- (Threats × vulnerability × asset value) × controls gap = residual risk
- The main goals of risk analysis are the following: identify assets and assign values to them, identify vulnerabilities and threats, quantify the impact of potential threats, and provide an economic balance between the impact of the risk and the cost of the safeguards.
- Failure Modes and Effect Analysis (FMEA) is a method for determining functions, identifying functional failures, and assessing the causes of failure and their failure effects through a structured process.
- A fault tree analysis is a useful approach to detect failures that can take place within complex environments and systems.
- A quantitative risk analysis attempts to assign monetary values to components within the analysis.

- A purely quantitative risk analysis is not possible because qualitative items cannot be quantified with precision.
- Capturing the degree of uncertainty when carrying out a risk analysis is important, because it indicates the level of confidence the team and management should have in the resulting figures.
- Automated risk analysis tools reduce the amount of manual work involved in the analysis. They can be used to estimate future expected losses and calculate the benefits of different security measures.
- Single loss expectancy × frequency per year = annualized loss expectancy (SLE × ARO = ALE)
- Qualitative risk analysis uses judgment and intuition instead of numbers.
- Qualitative risk analysis involves people with the requisite experience and education evaluating threat scenarios and rating the probability, potential loss, and severity of each threat based on their personal experience.
- The Delphi technique is a group decision method where each group member can communicate anonymously.
- Job rotation is a detective administrative control to detect fraud.
- Mandatory vacations are a detective administrative control type that can help detect fraudulent activities.
- Separation of duties ensures no single person has total control over a critical activity or task. It is a preventative administrative control.
- Split knowledge and dual control are two aspects of separation of duties.
- Management must define the scope and purpose of security management, provide support, appoint a security team, delegate responsibility, and review the team's findings.
- The risk management team should include individuals from different departments within the organization, not just technical personnel.
- Social engineering is a nontechnical attack carried out to manipulate a person into providing sensitive data to an unauthorized individual.
- Personally identifiable information (PII) is a collection of identity-based data that can be used in identity theft and financial fraud, and thus must be highly protected.
- Security governance is a framework that provides oversight, accountability, and compliance.
- ISO/IEC 27004:2009 is an international standard for information security measurement management.
- NIST SP 800-55 is a standard for performance measurement for information security.
- Business continuity management (BCM) is the overarching approach to managing all aspects of BCP and DRP.

- A business continuity plan (BCP) contains strategy documents that provide detailed procedures that ensure critical business functions are maintained and that help minimize losses of life, operations, and systems.
- A BCP provides procedures for emergency responses, extended backup operations, and post-disaster recovery.
- A BCP should have an enterprise-wide reach, with individual organizational units each having its own detailed continuity and contingency plans.
- A BCP needs to prioritize critical applications and provide a sequence for efficient recovery.
- A BCP requires senior executive management support for initiating the plan and final approval.
- BCPs can quickly become outdated due to personnel turnover, reorganizations, and undocumented changes.
- Executives may be held liable if proper BCPs are not developed and used.
- Threats can be natural, manmade, or technical.
- The steps of recovery planning include initiating the project; performing business impact analyses; developing a recovery strategy; developing a recovery plan; and implementing, testing, and maintaining the plan.
- The project initiation phase involves getting management support, developing the scope of the plan, and securing funding and resources.
- The business impact analysis (BIA) is one of the most important first steps in the planning development. Qualitative and quantitative data on the business impact of a disaster need to be gathered, analyzed, interpreted, and presented to management.
- Executive commitment and support are the most critical elements in developing the BCP.
- A business case must be presented to gain executive support. This is done by explaining regulatory and legal requirements, exposing vulnerabilities, and providing solutions.
- Plans should be prepared by the people who will actually carry them out.
- The planning group should comprise representatives from all departments or organizational units.
- The BCP team should identify the individuals who will interact with external players, such as the reporters, shareholders, customers, and civic officials. Response to the disaster should be done quickly and honestly, and should be consistent with any other organizational response.
- ISO/IEC 27031:2011 describes the concepts and principles of information and communication technology (ICT) readiness for business continuity.
- ISO/IEC 22301 is the standard for business continuity management (BCM).

Questions

Please remember that these questions are formatted and asked in a certain way for a reason. Keep in mind that the CISSP exam is asking questions at a conceptual level. Questions may not always have the perfect answer, and the candidate is advised against always looking for the perfect answer. Instead, the candidate should look for the best answer in the list.

1. When can executives be charged with negligence?
   - **A.** If they follow the transborder laws
   - **B.** If they do not properly report and prosecute attackers
   - **C.** If they properly inform users that they may be monitored
   - **D.** If they do not practice due care when protecting resources
2. To better deal with computer crime, several legislative bodies have taken what steps in their strategy?
   - **A.** Expanded several privacy laws
   - **B.** Broadened the definition of property to include data
   - **C.** Required corporations to have computer crime insurance
   - **D.** Redefined transborder issues
3. Which factor is the most important item when it comes to ensuring security is successful in an organization?
   - **A.** Senior management support
   - **B.** Effective controls and implementation methods
   - **C.** Updated and relevant security policies and procedures
   - **D.** Security awareness by all employees
4. Which of the following standards would be most useful to you in ensuring your information security management system follows industry best practices?
   - **A.** NIST SP 800-53
   - **B.** Six Sigma
   - **C.** ISO/IEC 27000 series
   - **D.** COSO IC
5. Which of the following is true about data breaches?
   - **A.** They are exceptionally rare.
   - **B.** They always involve personally identifiable information (PII).
   - **C.** They may trigger legal or regulatory requirements.
   - **D.** The United States has no laws pertaining to data breaches.

6. When is it acceptable to not take action on an identified risk?
    A. Never. Good security addresses and reduces all risks.
    B. When political issues prevent this type of risk from being addressed.
    C. When the necessary countermeasure is complex.
    D. When the cost of the countermeasure outweighs the value of the asset and potential loss.
7. Which is the most valuable technique when determining if a specific security control should be implemented?
    A. Risk analysis
    B. Cost/benefit analysis
    C. ALE results
    D. Identifying the vulnerabilities and threats causing the risk
8. Which best describes the purpose of the ALE calculation?
    A. Quantifies the security level of the environment
    B. Estimates the loss possible for a countermeasure
    C. Quantifies the cost/benefit result
    D. Estimates the loss potential of a threat in a span of a year
9. How do you calculate residual risk?
    A. Threats × risks × asset value
    B. (Threats × asset value × vulnerability) × risks
    C. SLE × frequency = ALE
    D. (Threats × vulnerability × asset value) × controls gap
10. Why should the team that will perform and review the risk analysis information be made up of people in different departments?
    A. To make sure the process is fair and that no one is left out.
    B. It shouldn't. It should be a small group brought in from outside the organization because otherwise the analysis is biased and unusable.
    C. Because people in different departments understand the risks of their department. Thus, it ensures the data going into the analysis is as close to reality as possible.
    D. Because the people in the different departments are the ones causing the risks, so they should be the ones held accountable.
11. Which best describes a quantitative risk analysis?
    A. A scenario-based analysis to research different security threats
    B. A method used to apply severity levels to potential loss, probability of loss, and risks

C. A method that assigns monetary values to components in the risk assessment

D. A method that is based on gut feelings and opinions

12. Why is a truly quantitative risk analysis not possible to achieve?

A. It is possible, which is why it is used.

B. It assigns severity levels. Thus, it is hard to translate into monetary values.

C. It is dealing with purely quantitative elements.

D. Quantitative measures must be applied to qualitative elements.

13. What is COBIT and where does it fit into the development of information security systems and security programs?

A. Lists of standards, procedures, and policies for security program development

B. Current version of ISO 17799

C. A framework that was developed to deter organizational internal fraud

D. Open standards for control objectives

14. What is the ISO/IEC 27799 standard?

A. A standard on how to protect personal health information

B. The new version of BS 17799

C. Definitions for the new ISO 27000 series

D. The new version of NIST SP 800-60

15. OCTAVE, NIST SP 800-30, and AS/NZS 4360 are different approaches to carrying out risk management within companies and organizations. What are the differences between these methods?

A. NIST SP 800-30 and OCTAVE are corporate based, while AS/NZS is international.

B. NIST SP 800-30 is IT based, while OCTAVE and AS/NZS 4360 are corporate based.

C. AS/NZS is IT based, and OCTAVE and NIST SP 800-30 are assurance based.

D. NIST SP 800-30 and AS/NZS are corporate based, while OCTAVE is international.

Use the following scenario to answer Questions 14–16. A server that houses sensitive data has been stored in an unlocked room for the last few years at Company A. The door to the room has a sign on the door that reads "Room 1." This sign was placed on the door with the hope that people would not look for important servers in this room. Realizing this is not optimum security, the company has decided to install a reinforced lock and server cage for the server and remove the sign. The company has also hardened the server's configuration and employed strict operating system access controls.

16. The fact that the server has been in an unlocked room marked "Room 1" for the last few years means the company was practicing which of the following?
    A. Logical security
    B. Risk management
    C. Risk transference
    D. Security through obscurity
17. The new reinforced lock and cage serve as which of the following?
    A. Logical controls
    B. Physical controls
    C. Administrative controls
    D. Compensating controls
18. The operating system access controls comprise which of the following?
    A. Logical controls
    B. Physical controls
    C. Administrative controls
    D. Compensating controls

Use the following scenario to answer Questions 19–21. A company has an e-commerce website that carries out 60 percent of its annual revenue. Under the current circumstances, the annualized loss expectancy for a website against the threat of attack is $92,000. After implementing a new application-layer firewall, the new annualized loss expectancy would be $30,000. The firewall costs $65,000 per year to implement and maintain.

19. How much does the firewall save the company in loss expenses?
    A. $62,000
    B. $3,000
    C. $65,000
    D. $30,000
20. What is the value of the firewall to the company?
    A. $62,000
    B. $3,000
    C. –$62,000
    D. –$3,000
21. Which of the following describes the company's approach to risk management?
    A. Risk transference
    B. Risk avoidance

C. Risk acceptance

D. Risk mitigation

Use the following scenario to answer Questions 22–24. A small remote office for a company is valued at $800,000. It is estimated, based on historical data, that a fire is likely to occur once every ten years at a facility in this area. It is estimated that such a fire would destroy 60 percent of the facility under the current circumstances and with the current detective and preventative controls in place.

22. What is the single loss expectancy (SLE) for the facility suffering from a fire?

A. $80,000

B. $480,000

C. $320,000

D. 60%

23. What is the annualized rate of occurrence (ARO)?

A. 1

B. 10

C. .1

D. .01

24. What is the annualized loss expectancy (ALE)?

A. $480,000

B. $32,000

C. $48,000

D. .6

25. The international standards bodies ISO and IEC developed a series of standards that are used in organizations around the world to implement and maintain information security management systems. The standards were derived from the British Standard 7799, which was broken down into two main pieces. Organizations can use this series of standards as guidelines, but can also be certified against them by accredited third parties. Which of the following are incorrect mappings pertaining to the individual standards that make up the ISO/IEC 27000 series?

i. ISO/IEC 27001 outlines ISMS implementation guidelines, and ISO/IEC 27003 outlines the ISMS program's requirements.

ii. ISO/IEC 27005 outlines the audit and certification guidance, and ISO/IEC 27002 outlines the metrics framework.

iii. ISO/IEC 27006 outlines the program implementation guidelines, and ISO/IEC 27005 outlines risk management guidelines.

iv. ISO/IEC 27001 outlines the code of practice, and ISO/IEC 27004 outlines the implementation framework.

A. i, iii

B. i, ii

C. ii, iii, iv

D. i, ii, iii, iv

26. The information security industry is made up of various best practices, standards, models, and frameworks. Some were not developed first with security in mind, but can be integrated into an organizational security program to help in its effectiveness and efficiency. It is important to know of all of these different approaches so that an organization can choose the ones that best fit its business needs and culture. Which of the following best describes the approach(es) that should be put into place if an organization wants to integrate a way to improve its security processes over a period of time?

i. Information Technology Infrastructure Library should be integrated because it allows for the mapping of IT service process management, business drivers, and security improvement.

ii. Six Sigma should be integrated because it allows for the defects of security processes to be identified and improved upon.

iii. Capability Maturity Model Integration should be integrated because it provides distinct maturity levels.

iv. The Open Group Architecture Framework should be integrated because it provides a structure for process improvement.

A. i, iii

B. ii, iii, iv

C. ii, iii

D. ii, iv

Use the following scenario to answer Questions 27–29. Todd is a new security manager and has the responsibility of implementing personnel security controls within the financial institution where he works. Todd knows that many employees do not fully understand how their actions can put the institution at risk; thus, an awareness program needs to be developed. He has determined that the bank tellers need to get a supervisory override when customers have checks over $3,500 that need to be cashed. He has also uncovered that some employees have stayed in their specific positions within the company for over three years. Todd would like to be able to investigate some of the bank's personnel activities to see if any fraudulent activities have taken place. Todd is already ensuring that two people must use separate keys at the same time to open the bank vault.

27. Todd documents several fraud opportunities that the employees have at the financial institution so that management understands these risks and allocates the funds and resources for his suggested solutions. Which of the following best describes the control Todd should put into place to be able to carry out fraudulent investigation activity?
    A. Separation of duties
    B. Rotation of duties
    C. Mandatory vacations
    D. Split knowledge
28. If the financial institution wants to force collusion to take place for fraud to happen successfully in this situation, what should Todd put into place?
    A. Separation of duties
    B. Rotation of duties
    C. Social engineering
    D. Split knowledge
29. Todd wants to be able to prevent fraud from taking place, but he knows that some people may get around the types of controls he puts into place. In those situations he wants to be able to identify when an employee is doing something suspicious. Which of the following incorrectly describes what Todd is implementing in this scenario and what those specific controls provide?
    A. Separation of duties by ensuring that a supervisor must approve the cashing of a check over $3,500. This is an administrative control that provides preventative protection for Todd's organization.
    B. Rotation of duties by ensuring that one employee only stays in one position for up to three months at a time. This is an administrative control that provides detective capabilities.
    C. Security awareness training, which is a preventive administrative control that can also emphasize enforcement.
    D. Dual control, which is an administrative detective control that can ensure that two employees must carry out a task simultaneously.

Use the following scenario to answer Questions 30–32. Susan has been told by her boss that she will be replacing the current security manager within her company. Her boss explained to her that operational security measures have not been carried out in a standard fashion, so some systems have proper security configurations and some do not. Her boss needs to understand how dangerous it is to have some of the systems misconfigured, along with what to do in this situation.

30. Which of the following best describes what Susan needs to ensure the operations staff creates for proper configuration standardization?
    A. Dual control
    B. Redundancy
    C. Training
    D. Baselines
31. Which of the following is the best way for Susan to illustrate to her boss the dangers of the current configuration issues?
    A. Map the configurations to the compliancy requirements.
    B. Compromise a system to illustrate its vulnerability.
    C. Audit the systems.
    D. Carry out a risk assessment.
32. Which of the following is one of the most likely solutions that Susan will come up with and present to her boss?
    A. Development of standards
    B. Development of training
    C. Development of monitoring
    D. Development of testing
33. What is one of the first steps in developing a business continuity plan?
    A. Identify a backup solution.
    B. Perform a simulation test.
    C. Perform a business impact analysis.
    D. Develop a business resumption plan.
34. The purpose of initiating emergency procedures right after a disaster takes place is to prevent loss of life and injuries, and to ________________.
    A. secure the area to ensure that no looting or fraud takes place
    B. mitigate further damage
    C. protect evidence and clues
    D. investigate the extent of the damages
35. Which of the following would you use to control the public distribution, reproduction, display, and adaptation of an original white paper written by your staff?
    A. Copyright
    B. Trademark
    C. Patent
    D. Trade secret

36. Many privacy laws dictate which of the following rules?
   A. Individuals have a right to remove any data they do not want others to know.
   B. Agencies do not need to ensure that the data is accurate.
   C. Agencies need to allow all government agencies access to the data.
   D. Agencies cannot use collected data for a purpose different from what they were collected for.
37. The term used to denote a potential cause of an unwanted incident, which may result in harm to a system or organization is
   A. Vulnerability
   B. Exploit
   C. Threat
   D. Attacker
38. A CISSP candidate signs an ethics statement prior to taking the CISSP examination. Which of the following would be a violation of the (ISC)^2 Code of Ethics that could cause the candidate to lose his or her certification?
   A. E-mailing information or comments about the exam to other CISSP candidates
   B. Submitting comments on the questions of the exam to (ISC)^2
   C. Submitting comments to the board of directors regarding the test and content of the class
   D. Conducting a presentation about the CISSP certification and what the certification means
39. Which of the following has an incorrect definition mapping?
   i. Civil (code) law: Based on previous interpretations of laws
   ii. Common law: Rule-based law, not precedence-based
   iii. Customary law: Deals mainly with personal conduct and patterns of behavior
   iv. Religious law: Based on religious beliefs of the region
   A. i, iii
   B. i, ii, iii
   C. i, ii
   D. iv

Answers

1. **D.** Executives are held to a certain standard and are expected to act responsibly when running and protecting a company. These standards and expectations equate to the due care concept under the law. Due care means to carry out activities that a reasonable person would be expected to carry out in the same situation. If an executive acts irresponsibly in any way, she can be seen as not practicing due care and be held negligent.
2. **B.** Many times, what is corrupted, compromised, or taken from a computer is data, so current laws have been updated to include the protection of intangible assets, as in data. Over the years, data and information have become many companies' most valuable asset, which must be protected by the laws.
3. **A.** Without senior management's support, a security program will not receive the necessary attention, funds, resources, and enforcement capabilities.
4. **C.** The ISO/IEC 27000 series is the only option that addresses best practices across the breadth of an ISMS. COSO IC and NIST SP 800-53 both deal with controls, which are a critical but not the only component of an ISMS.
5. **C.** Organizations experiencing a data breach may be required by laws or regulations to take certain actions. For instance, many countries have disclosure requirements that require notification to affected parties and/or regulatory bodies within a specific timeframe.
6. **D.** Companies may decide to live with specific risks they are faced with if the cost of trying to protect themselves would be greater than the potential loss if the threat were to become real. Countermeasures are usually complex to a degree, and there are almost always political issues surrounding different risks, but these are not reasons to not implement a countermeasure.
7. **B.** Although the other answers may seem correct, B is the best answer here. This is because a risk analysis is performed to identify risks and come up with suggested countermeasures. The ALE tells the company how much it could lose if a specific threat became real. The ALE value will go into the cost/benefit analysis, but the ALE does not address the cost of the countermeasure and the benefit of a countermeasure. All the data captured in answers A, C, and D is inserted into a cost/benefit analysis.
8. **D.** The ALE calculation estimates the potential loss that can affect one asset from a specific threat within a one-year time span. This value is used to figure out the amount of money that should be earmarked to protect this asset from this threat.
9. **D.** The equation is more conceptual than practical. It is hard to assign a number to an individual vulnerability or threat. This equation enables you to look at the potential loss of a specific asset, as well as the controls gap (what the specific countermeasure cannot protect against). What remains is the residual risk, which is what is left over after a countermeasure is implemented.

10. **C.** An analysis is only as good as the data that goes into it. Data pertaining to risks the company faces should be extracted from the people who understand best the business functions and environment of the company. Each department understands its own threats and resources, and may have possible solutions to specific threats that affect its part of the company.

11. **C.** A quantitative risk analysis assigns monetary values and percentages to the different components within the assessment. A qualitative analysis uses opinions of individuals and a rating system to gauge the severity level of different threats and the benefits of specific countermeasures.

12. **D.** During a risk analysis, the team is trying to properly predict the future and all the risks that future may bring. It is somewhat of a subjective exercise and requires educated guessing. It is very hard to properly predict that a flood will take place once in ten years and cost a company up to $40,000 in damages, but this is what a quantitative analysis tries to accomplish.

13. **D.** The Control Objectives for Information and related Technology (COBIT) is a framework developed by the Information Systems Audit and Control Association (ISACA) and the IT Governance Institute (ITGI). It defines goals for the controls that should be used to properly manage IT and ensure IT maps to business needs.

14. **A.** It is referred to as the *health informatics*, and its purpose is to provide guidance to health organizations and other holders of personal health information on how to protect such information via implementation of ISO/IEC 27002.

15. **B.** NIST SP 800-30, Revision 1, "Guide for Conducting Risk Assessments," is a U.S. federal standard that is focused on IT risks. OCTAVE is a methodology to set up a risk management program within an organizational structure. AS/NZS 4360 takes a much broader approach to risk management. This methodology can be used to understand a company's financial, capital, human safety, and business decisions risks. Although it can be used to analyze security risks, it was not created specifically for this purpose.

16. **D.** Security through obscurity is not implementing true security controls, but rather attempting to hide the fact that an asset is vulnerable in the hope that an attacker will not notice. Security through obscurity is an approach to try and fool a potential attacker, which is a poor way of practicing security. Vulnerabilities should be identified and fixed, not hidden.

17. **B.** Physical controls are security mechanisms in the physical world, as in locks, fences, doors, computer cages, etc. There are three main control types, which are administrative, technical, and physical.

18. **A.** Logical (or technical) controls are security mechanisms, as in firewalls, encryption, software permissions, and authentication devices. They are commonly used in tandem with physical and administrative controls to provide a defense-in-depth approach to security.

19. **A.** $62,000 is the correct answer. The firewall reduced the annualized loss expectancy (ALE) from $92,000 to $30,000 for a savings of $62,000. The formula for ALE is single loss expectancy × annualized rate of occurrence = ALE. Subtracting the ALE value after the firewall is implemented from the value before it was implemented results in the potential loss savings this type of control provides.

20. **D.** –$3,000 is the correct answer. The firewall saves $62,000, but costs $65,000 per year. 62,000 – 65,000 = –3,000. The firewall actually costs the company more than the original expected loss, and thus the value to the company is a negative number. The formula for this calculation is (ALE before the control is implemented) – (ALE after the control is implemented) – (annual cost of control) = value of control.

21. **D.** Risk mitigation involves employing controls in an attempt to reduce the either the likelihood or damage associated with an incident, or both. The four ways of dealing with risk are accept, avoid, transfer, and mitigate (reduce). A firewall is a countermeasure installed to reduce the risk of a threat.

22. **B.** $480,000 is the correct answer. The formula for single loss expectancy (SLE) is asset value × exposure factor (EF) = SLE. In this situation the formula would work out as asset value ($800,000) × exposure factor (60%) = $480,000. This means that the company has a potential loss value of $480,000 pertaining to this one asset (facility) and this one threat type (fire).

23. **C.** The annualized rate occurrence (ARO) is the frequency that a threat will most likely occur within a 12-month period. It is a value used in the ALE formula, which is SLE × ARO = ALE.

24. **C.** $48,000 is the correct answer. The annualized loss expectancy formula (SLE × ARO = ALE) is used to calculate the loss potential for one asset experiencing one threat in a 12-month period. The resulting ALE value helps to determine the amount that can reasonably be spent in the protection of that asset. In this situation, the company should not spend over $48,000 on protecting this asset from the threat of fire. ALE values help organizations rank the severity level of the risks they face so they know which ones to deal with first and how much to spend on each.

25. **D.** Unfortunately, you will run into questions on the CISSP exam that will be this confusing, so you need to be ready for them. The proper mapping for the ISO/IEC standards are as follows:

    - **ISO/IEC 27001** ISMS requirements
    - **ISO/IEC 27002** Code of practice for information security management
    - **ISO/IEC 27003** Guideline for ISMS implementation
    - **ISO/IEC 27004** Guideline for information security management measurement and metrics framework
    - **ISO/IEC 27005** Guideline for information security risk management
    - **ISO/IEC 27006** Guidance for bodies providing audit and certification of information security management systems

26. **C.** The best process improvement approaches provided in this list are Six Sigma and the Capability Maturity Model. The following outlines the definitions for all items in this question:
    - **TOGAF** Model and methodology for the development of enterprise architectures developed by The Open Group
    - **ITIL** Processes to allow for IT service management developed by the United Kingdom's Office of Government Commerce
    - **Six Sigma** Business management strategy that can be used to carry out process improvement
    - **Capability Maturity Model Integration (CMMI)** Organizational development for process improvement developed by Carnegie Mellon
27. **C.** Mandatory vacation is an administrative detective control that allows for an organization to investigate an employee's daily business activities to uncover any potential fraud that may be taking place. The employee should be forced to be away from the organization for a two-week period and another person should be put into that role. The idea is that the person who was rotated into that position may be able to detect suspicious activities.
28. **A.** Separation of duties is an administrative control that is put into place to ensure that one person cannot carry out a critical task by himself. If a person were able to carry out a critical task alone, this could put the organization at risk. Collusion is when two or more people come together to carry out fraud. So if a task was split between two people, they would have to carry out collusion (working together) to complete that one task and carry out fraud.
29. **D.** Dual control is an administrative preventative control. It ensures that two people must carry out a task at the same time, as in two people having separate keys when opening the vault. It is not a detective control. Notice that the question asks what Todd is *not* doing. Remember that on the exam you need to choose the *best* answer. In many situations you will not like the question or the corresponding answers on the CISSP exam, so prepare yourself. The questions can be tricky, which is one reason why the exam itself is so difficult.
30. **D.** The operations staff needs to know what minimum level of security is required per system within the network. This minimum level of security is referred to as a baseline. Once a baseline is set per system, then the staff has something to compare the system against to know if changes have not taken place properly, which could make the system vulnerable.
31. **D.** Susan needs to illustrate these vulnerabilities (misconfigured systems) in the context of risk to her boss. This means she needs to identify the specific vulnerabilities, associate threats to those vulnerabilities, and calculate their risks. This will allow her boss to understand how critical these issues are and what type of action needs to take place.

32. **A.** Standards need to be developed that outline proper configuration management processes and approved baseline configuration settings. Once these standards are developed and put into place, then employees can be trained on these issues and how to implement and maintain what is outlined in the standards. Systems can be tested against what is laid out in the standards, and systems can be monitored to detect if there are configurations that do not meet the requirements outlined in the standards. You will find that some CISSP questions seem subjective and their answers hard to pin down. Questions that ask what is "best" or "more likely" are common.

33. **C.** A business impact analysis includes identifying critical systems and functions of a company and interviewing representatives from each department. Once management's support is solidified, a business impact analysis needs to be performed to identify the threats the company faces and the potential costs of these threats.

34. **B.** The main goal of disaster recovery and business continuity plans is to mitigate all risks that could be experienced by a company. Emergency procedures first need to be carried out to protect human life, and then other procedures need to be executed to reduce the damage from further threats.

35. **B.** A copyright fits the situation precisely. A patent could be used to protect a novel invention described in the paper, but the question did not imply that this was the case. A trade secret cannot be publicly disseminated, so it does not apply. Finally, a trademark protects only a word, symbol, sound, shape, color or combination of these.

36. **D.** The Federal Privacy Act of 1974 and the European Union Principles on Privacy were created to protect citizens from government agencies that collect personal data. These acts have many stipulations, including that the information can only be used for the reason for which it was collected.

37. **C.** The question provides the definition of a threat in ISO/IEC 27000. The term attacker (option D) could be used to describe a threat agent that is, in turn, a threat, but use of this term is much more restrictive. The best answer is a threat.

38. **A.** A CISSP candidate and a CISSP holder should never discuss with others what was on the exam. This degrades the usefulness of the exam to be used as a tool to test someone's true security knowledge. If this type of activity is uncovered, the person could be stripped of their CISSP certification because this would violate the terms of the NDA upon which the candidate enters prior to taking the test. Violating an NDA is a violation of the ethics canon that requires CISSPs to act honorably, honestly, justly, responsibly and legally.

39. **C.** The following has the proper definition mappings:

    i. Civil (code) law: Rule-based law, not precedence-based

    ii. Common law: Based on previous interpretations of laws

    iii. Customary law: Deals mainly with personal conduct and patterns of behavior

    iv. Religious law: Based on religious beliefs of the region

CHAPTER 2

Asset Security

This chapter presents the following:

- Information life cycle
- Information classification and protection
- Information ownership
- Protection of privacy
- Information retention
- Data security controls
- Data handling requirements

Information is the oil of the 21st century.

—Peter Sondergaard

An asset is, by definition, anything of worth to an organization. This includes people, partners, equipment, facilities, reputation, and information. While every asset needs to be protected, as discussed in Chapter 1 in the context of risk management, this chapter's coverage of the second CISSP domain focuses exclusively on protecting information assets. Information is typically the most valuable asset to an organization and lies at the heart of every information system, so precision focus on its protection makes a lot of sense.

Information, of course, exists in context; it is acquired or created at a particular point in time through a specific process and (usually) for a purpose. It moves through an organization's information systems, sometimes adding value to processes and sometimes waiting to be useful. Eventually, the information outlives its utility and must be disposed of appropriately. We start off our discussion of asset security by examining an information life-cycle model that applies to most organizations, as well as specific examples. We will then cover the evaluation, use, maintenance, and destruction of the information in the context of its life cycle. This all sets the stage for a discussion of the various organizational roles that deal with information assets, as well as the need for effective retention policies. Finally, we discuss specific threats to information and what controls can be helpful in mitigating the risks of data loss.

Information Life Cycle

A life-cycle model describes the changes that an entity experiences during its lifetime. Unlike biological systems, information cannot really be said to reproduce, but it can beget other information in a process that is not totally unlike reproduction. Think of entries in a customer relationship management (CRM) information system. A sales lead can be useful in and of itself by being converted into one or more sales, but it can also lead to the acquisition of other leads. These, in turn, can be thought of as having been spawned or descended from the first or parent lead. Eventually, the lead is no longer useful (e.g., the person moves on or the company goes belly up) and becomes a liability that occupies storage space and needlessly increases exposure in the event of a data breach. You would want to properly dispose of that information when its costs and risks exceed any possible benefits.

There are a number of information life-cycle models out there. The one we will use for our discussion of asset security is fairly simple but still effective when considering the changing nature of information and the security implications of those dynamics. At a macro level, we can divide the life of our information into four phases: acquisition, use, archival, and disposal. See Figure 2-1.

Acquisition

Generally speaking, information is acquired by an organization in only one of two ways: copied from elsewhere or created from scratch. Copying is by far the most common approach to acquiring new information. Think about it: unless your organization is heavily involved in research and development, odds are that the information it acquires already exists somewhere else.

After the information is acquired, but before it can be used, there are steps we must take to make the information useful. Typically, we attach both system metadata (e.g., author, date/time of creation, and permissions) and business process metadata (e.g., classification, project, and owner) to it. Finally, the information is indexed to facilitate searching and assigned to one or more data stores. In smaller organizations, much of this

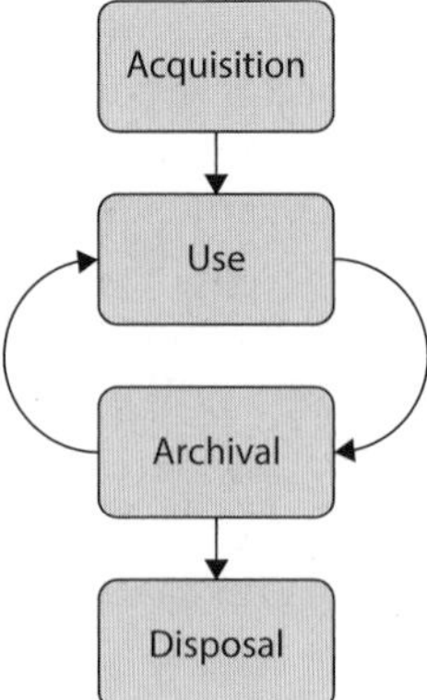

Figure 2-1 The information life cycle

process is invisible to the user. All that person knows is that when they create a contact in the CRM, an order in the purchasing system, or a ticket in the workflow system, the entry is magically available to everyone in the organization who needs to access the information. In larger organizations, the process needs to be carefully architected.

Finally, there are policy controls that we have to apply. For instance, we have to encrypt credit card numbers and certain other personally identifiable information (PII) wherever we store them. We also have to implement strict controls on who gets to access sensitive information. Additionally, we may have to provide some sort of roll-back capability to revert data to a previous state, particularly if users or processes may be able to corrupt it. These and many other important considerations must be deliberately addressed at the point of information acquisition and not as an afterthought.

Use

After the information is prepared and stored, it will spend much of its time being used. That is to say it will be read and modified by a variety of users with the necessary access level. From a security perspective, this stage in the information life cycle presents the most challenges in terms of ensuring confidentiality, integrity, and availability. You want the information available, but only to the right people who should then be able to modify it in authorized ways.

As the information is being used, we have to ensure that it remains internally consistent. For instance, if we have multiple data stores for performance or reliability purposes, we must ensure that modifications to the information are replicated. We also need to have mechanisms for automatically resolving inconsistencies, such as those that would occur from a server having a power outage after information has been modified but before it has been replicated. This is particularly important in very dynamic systems that have roll-back capabilities.

Consistency is also an issue with regard to policy and regulatory compliance. As the information is used and aggregated, it may trigger requirements that must be automatically enforced. For example, a document that refers to a project using a code word or name may be unclassified and freely available, but if that word/name is used in conjunction with other details (a place, purpose, or team members' names), then it would make the entire document classified. Changes in the information as it is in use must be mapped to the appropriate internal policies, and perhaps to regulations or laws.

Archival

The information in our systems will likely stop being used regularly (or at all) at some point. When this happens, but before we get rid of it, we probably want to retain it for a variety of reasons. Maybe we anticipate that it will again be useful at a later time, or maybe we are required to keep it around for a certain period of time, as is the case with certain financial information. Whatever the reason for moving this data off to the side, the fact that it is no longer regularly used could mean that unauthorized or accidental access and changes to it could go undetected for a long time if we don't implement appropriate controls. Of course, the same lack of use could make it easier to detect this threat if we do have the right controls.

Another driver for retention is the need for backups. Whether we're talking about user or back-end backups, it is important to consider our risk assessment when deciding which backups are protected and how. To the extent that end-user backups are performed to removable disk drives, it is difficult to imagine a scenario in which these backups should not be encrypted. Every major operating system provides a means to perform automatic backups as well as encrypt those backups. Let's take advantage of this.

This all leads us to the question of how long we need to retain data. If we discard it too soon, we risk not being able to recover from a failure or an attack. We also risk not being able to comply with e-discovery requests or subpoenas. If we keep the data for too long, we risk excessive costs as well as increased liabilities. The answer, once again, is that this is all part of our risk management process and needs to be codified in policies.

Backup vs. Archive

The terms backup and archive are sometimes used interchangeably. In reality, they have different meanings that are best illustrated using the life-cycle model described in this section. A data *backup* is a copy of a data set currently in use that is made for the purpose of recovering from the loss of the original data. Backup data normally becomes less useful as it gets older.

A data *archive* is a copy of a data set that is no longer in use, but is kept in case it is needed at some future point. When data is archived, it is usually removed from its original location so that the storage space is available for data in use.

Disposal

Sooner or later, every organization will have to dispose of data. This usually, but not always, means data destruction. Old mailboxes, former employee records, and past financial transactions are all examples of data sets that must, at some point, be destroyed. When this time comes, there are two important issues to consider: that the data does in fact get destroyed, and that it is destroyed correctly. When we discuss roles and responsibilities later in this chapter, we'll see who is responsible for ensuring that both of these issues are taken care of.

A twist on the data destruction issue is when we need to transfer the data to another party and then destroy it on our data stores. For instance, organizations hosting services for their clients typically have to deal with requests to do a bulk export of their data when they migrate to another provider. Companies sometimes sell accounts (e.g., home mortgages) to each other, in which case the data is transferred and eventually (after the mandatory retention period) destroyed on the original company's systems.

No matter the reason, we have to ensure the data is properly destroyed. How this is done is, again, tied to our risk management. The bottom line is that it must be rendered sufficiently difficult for an adversary to recover so that the risk of such recovery is acceptable to our organization. This is not hard to do when we are dealing with physical devices such as hard disk drives that can be wiped, degaussed, or shredded (or all the above in particularly risk-adverse organizations such as certain government entities). Data destruction can be a bit more complicated when we deal with individual files (or parts thereof) or database records (such as many e-mail systems use for mailbox storage). Further complicating matters, it is very common for multiple copies of each data item to exist across our information systems. How can you ensure that all versions are gone? The point is that the technical details of how and where the data is stored are critical to ensuring its proper destruction.

Information Classification

An important metadata item that should be attached to all our information is a classification level. This classification tag, which remains attached (and perhaps updated) throughout the life cycle of the information, is important to determining the protective controls we apply to the information.

The rationale behind assigning values to different types of data is that it enables a company to gauge the amount of funds and resources that should go toward protecting each type of data, because not all data has the same value to a company. After identifying all important information, it should be properly classified. A company copies and creates a lot of information that it must maintain, so classification is an ongoing process and not a one-time effort.

Information can be classified by sensitivity, criticality, or both. Either way, the classification aims to quantify how much loss an organization would likely suffer if the information was lost. The *sensitivity* of information is commensurate with the losses to an organization if that information was revealed to unauthorized individuals. This kind of compromise has made headlines in recent years with the losses of information suffered by organizations such as the National Security Agency, the Office of Personnel Management, and even websites like Ashley Madison. In each case, the organizations lost trust and had to undertake expensive responses because sensitive data was compromised.

The *criticality* of information, on the other hand, is an indicator of how the loss of the information would impact the fundamental business processes of the organization. In other words, critical information is that which is essential for the organization to continue operations. For example, Code Spaces, a company that provided code repository services, was forced to shut down in 2014 after an unidentified individual or group deleted its code repositories. This data was critical to the operations of the company and without it, the corporation had no choice but to go out of business.

Once data is segmented according to its sensitivity or criticality level, the company can decide what security controls are necessary to protect different types of data. This ensures that information assets receive the appropriate level of protection, and classifications indicate the priority of that security protection. The primary purpose of data classification is to indicate the level of confidentiality, integrity, and availability protection that is required for each type of data set. Many people mistakenly only consider the confidentiality aspects of data protection, but we need to make sure our data is not modified in an unauthorized manner and that it is available when needed.

Data classification helps ensure that data is protected in the most cost-effective manner. Protecting and maintaining data costs money, but spending money for the information that actually requires protection is important. If you were in charge of making sure Russia does not know the encryption algorithms used when transmitting information to and from U.S. spy satellites, you would use more extreme (and expensive) security measures than you would use to protect your peanut butter and banana sandwich recipe from your next-door neighbor.

Each classification should have separate handling requirements and procedures pertaining to how that data is accessed, used, and destroyed. For example, in a corporation, confidential information may be accessed only by senior management and a select few trusted employees throughout the company. Accessing the information may require two or more people to enter their access codes. Auditing could be very detailed and its results monitored daily, and paper copies of the information may be kept in a vault. To properly erase this data from the media, degaussing or overwriting procedures may be required. Other information in this company may be classified as sensitive, allowing a slightly larger group of people to view it. Access control on the information classified as sensitive may require only one set of credentials. Auditing happens but is only reviewed weekly, paper copies are kept in locked file cabinets, and the data can be deleted using regular measures when it is time to do so. Then, the rest of the information is marked public. All employees can access it, and no special auditing or destruction methods are required.

EXAM TIP Each classification level should have its own handling and destruction requirements.

Classifications Levels

There are no hard and fast rules on the classification levels that an organization should use. An organization could choose to use any of the classification levels presented in Table 2-1. One organization may choose to use only two layers of classifications, while another company may choose to use four. Table 2-1 explains the types of classifications available. Note that some classifications are more commonly used for commercial businesses, whereas others are military classifications.

The following shows the common levels of sensitivity from the highest to the lowest for commercial business:

- Confidential
- Private
- Sensitive
- Public

Classification	Definition	Example	Organizations That Would Use This
Public	• Disclosure is not welcome, but it would not cause an adverse impact to company or personnel.	• How many people are working on a specific project • Upcoming projects	Commercial business
Sensitive	• Requires special precautions to ensure the integrity and confidentiality of the data by protecting it from unauthorized modification or deletion. • Requires higher-than-normal assurance of accuracy and completeness.	• Financial information • Details of projects • Profit earnings and forecasts	Commercial business
Private	• Personal information for use within a company. • Unauthorized disclosure could adversely affect personnel or the company.	• Work history • Human resources information • Medical information	Commercial business
Confidential	• For use within the company only. • Data exempt from disclosure under the Freedom of Information Act or other laws and regulations. • Unauthorized disclosure could seriously affect a company.	• Trade secrets • Healthcare information • Programming code • Information that keeps the company competitive	Commercial business Military
Unclassified	• Data is not sensitive or classified.	• Computer manual and warranty information • Recruiting information	Military
Sensitive but unclassified (SBU)	• Minor secret. • If disclosed, it may not cause serious damage.	• Medical data • Answers to test scores	Military
Secret	• If disclosed, it could cause serious damage to national security.	• Deployment plans for troops • Unit readiness information	Military
Top secret	• If disclosed, it could cause grave damage to national security.	• Blueprints of new weapons • Spy satellite information • Espionage data	Military

Table 2-1 Commercial Business and Military Data Classifications

The following shows the levels of sensitivity from the highest to the lowest for military purposes:

- Top secret
- Secret
- Confidential
- Sensitive but unclassified
- Unclassified

The classifications listed in Table 2-1 are *commonly* used in the industry, but there is a lot of variance. An organization first must decide the number of data classifications that best fit its security needs, then choose the classification naming scheme, and then define what the names in those schemes represent. Company A might use the classification level "confidential," which represents its most sensitive information. Company B might use "top secret," "secret," and "confidential," where confidential represents its least sensitive information. Each organization must develop an information classification scheme that best fits its business and security needs.

EXAM TIP The terms "unclassified," "secret," and "top secret" are usually associated with governmental organizations. The terms "private," "proprietary," and "sensitive" are usually associated with nongovernmental organizations.

It is important to not go overboard and come up with a long list of classifications, which will only cause confusion and frustration for the individuals who will use the system. The classifications should not be too restrictive and detailed oriented either, because many types of data may need to be classified.

Each classification should be unique and separate from the others and not have any overlapping effects. The classification process should also outline how information is controlled and handled through its life cycle (from creation to termination).

NOTE An organization must make sure that whoever is backing up classified data—and whoever has access to backed-up data—has the necessary clearance level. A large security risk can be introduced if low-level technicians with no security clearance have access to this information during their tasks.

Once the scheme is decided upon, the organization must develop the criteria it will use to decide what information goes into which classification. The following list shows some criteria parameters an organization may use to determine the sensitivity of data:

- The usefulness of data
- The value of data

- The age of data
- The level of damage that could be caused if the data were disclosed
- The level of damage that could be caused if the data were modified or corrupted
- Legal, regulatory, or contractual responsibility to protect the data
- Effects the data has on security
- Who should be able to access the data
- Who should maintain the data
- Who should be able to reproduce the data
- Lost opportunity costs that could be incurred if the data were not available or were corrupted

Data is not the only thing that may need to be classified. Applications and sometimes whole systems may need to be classified. The applications that hold and process classified information should be evaluated for the level of protection they provide. You do not want a program filled with security vulnerabilities to process and "protect" your most sensitive information. The application classifications should be based on the assurance (confidence level) the company has in the software and the type of information it can store and process.

CAUTION The classification rules must apply to data no matter what format it is in: digital, paper, video, fax, audio, and so on.

Now that we have chosen a sensitivity scheme, the next step is to specify how each classification should be dealt with. We must specify provisions for access control, identification, and labeling, along with how data in specific classifications is stored, maintained, transmitted, and destroyed. We also must iron out auditing, monitoring, and compliance issues. Each classification requires a different degree of security and, therefore, different requirements from each of the mentioned items.

Classification Controls

As mentioned earlier, which types of controls are implemented per classification depends upon the level of protection that management and the security team have determined is needed. The numerous types of controls available are discussed throughout this book. But some considerations pertaining to sensitive data and applications are common across most organizations:

- Strict and granular access control for all levels of sensitive data and programs
- Encryption of data while stored and while in transmission
- Auditing and monitoring (determine what level of auditing is required and how long logs are to be retained)

- Separation of duties (determine whether two or more people must be involved in accessing sensitive information to protect against fraudulent activities; if so, define and document procedures)
- Periodic reviews (review classification levels, and the data and programs that adhere to them, to ensure they are still in alignment with business needs; data or applications may also need to be reclassified or declassified, depending upon the situation)
- Backup and recovery procedures (define and document)
- Change control procedures (define and document)
- Physical security protection (define and document)
- Information flow channels (where does the sensitive data reside and how does it transverse the network)
- Proper disposal actions, such as shredding, degaussing, and so on (define and document)
- Marking, labeling, and handling procedures

Data Classification Procedures

The following outlines the necessary steps for a proper classification program:

1. Define classification levels.
2. Specify the criteria that will determine how data is classified.
3. Identify data owners who will be responsible for classifying data.
4. Identify the data custodian who will be responsible for maintaining data and its security level.
5. Indicate the security controls, or protection mechanisms, required for each classification level.
6. Document any exceptions to the previous classification issues.
7. Indicate the methods that can be used to transfer custody of the information to a different data owner.
8. Create a procedure to periodically review the classification and ownership. Communicate any changes to the data custodian.
9. Indicate procedures for declassifying the data.
10. Integrate these issues into the security-awareness program so all employees understand how to handle data at different classification levels.

Layers of Responsibility

Senior management and other levels of management understand the vision of the company, the business goals, and the objectives. The next layer down is the functional management, whose members understand how their individual departments work, what roles individuals play within the company, and how security affects their department directly. The next layers are operational managers and staff. These layers are closer to the actual operations of the company. They know detailed information about the technical and procedural requirements, the systems, and how the systems are used. The employees at these layers understand how security mechanisms integrate into systems, how to configure them, and how they affect daily productivity. Every layer offers different insight into what type of role security plays within an organization, and each should have input into the best security practices, procedures, and chosen controls to ensure the agreed-upon security level provides the necessary amount of protection without negatively affecting the company's productivity.

EXAM TIP Senior management always carries the ultimate responsibility for the organization.

Although each layer is important to the overall security of an organization, some specific roles must be clearly defined. Individuals who work in smaller environments (where everyone must wear several hats) may get overwhelmed with the number of roles presented next. Many commercial businesses do not have this level of structure in their security teams, but many government agencies and military units do. What you need to understand are the responsibilities that must be assigned and whether they are assigned to just a few people or to a large security team. These roles are the board of directors, security officer, data owner, data custodian, system owner, security administrator, security analyst, application owner, supervisor (user manager), change control analyst, data analyst, process owner, solution provider, user, product line manager, and the guy who gets everyone coffee.

Executive Management

The individuals designated as executive management typically are those whose titles start with "chief," and collectively they are often referred to as the "C-suite." Executive leaders are ultimately responsible for everything that happens in their organizations, and as such are considered the ultimate business and function owners. This has been evidenced time and again (as we will see shortly) in high-profile cases wherein executives have been fired, sued, or even prosecuted for organizational failures or fraud that occurred under their leadership. Let's start at the top of a corporate entity, the CEO.

Chief Executive Officer

The *chief executive officer (CEO)* has the day-to-day management responsibilities of an organization. This person is often the chairperson of the board of directors and is the highest-ranking officer in the company. This role is for the person who oversees the company's finances, strategic planning, and operations from a high level. The CEO is usually seen as the visionary for the company and is responsible for developing and modifying the company's business plan. The CEO sets budgets, forms partnerships, decides on what markets to enter, what product lines to develop, how the company will differentiate itself, and so on. This role's overall responsibility is to ensure that the company grows and thrives.

NOTE The CEO can delegate tasks, but not necessarily responsibility. More and more regulations dealing with information security are holding the CEO accountable for ensuring the organization practices due care and due diligence with respect to information security, which is why security departments across the land are receiving more funding. Personal liability for the decision makers and purse-string holders has loosened those purse strings, and companies are now able to spend more money on security than before.

Chief Financial Officer

The *chief financial officer (CFO)* is responsible for the corporation's accounting and financial activities and the overall financial structure of the organization. This person is responsible for determining what the company's financial needs will be and how to finance those needs. The CFO must create and maintain the company's capital structure, which is the proper mix of equity, credit, cash, and debt financing. This person oversees forecasting and budgeting and the processes of submitting quarterly and annual financial statements to the Securities and Exchange Commission (SEC) and stakeholders.

Executives Behind Bars

The CFO and CEO are responsible for informing stakeholders (creditors, analysts, employees, management, investors) of the firm's financial condition and health. After the corporate debacles at Enron, Adelphia, Tyco, and WorldCom uncovered in 2001–2002, the U.S. government and the SEC started doling out stiff penalties to people who held these roles and abused them. The following list provides a sampling of some of the cases in the past decade:

- **January 2007** Former Cendant Corporation CEO Walter Forbes is sentenced to over 12 years in prison and ordered to pay over $3 billion in restitution after being found guilty of conspiracy to commit securities fraud.
- **March 2012** The former CEO of the Stanford Financial Group, R. Allen Stanford, was sentenced to 110 years in prison for defrauding investors out of $7 billion.

- **June 2015** Joe White, the former CFO of Shelby Regional Medical Center, was sentenced to 23 months in federal prison after making false claims to receive payments under the Medicare Electronic Health Record Incentive Program.
- **August 2015** Former Chief Financial Officer of the Lawrence Family Jewish Community Center in California, Nancy Johnson was sentenced to over a year in jail for embezzling over $400,000.
- **September 2015** KIT Digital's former CEO Kaleil Isaza Tuzman and his former CFO Robin Smyth were arrested and charged with accounting fraud. They face up to 20 years in jail if convicted.
- **December 2015** Martin Shkreli, a notorious pharmaceutical executive, was charged with securities fraud stemming from his alleged use of funds from new companies to pay down debts previously incurred by financially troubled companies. If convicted, he faces a maximum sentence of 20 years.

These are only some of the big cases that made it into the headlines. Other CEOs and CFOs have also received punishments for "creative accounting" and fraudulent activities.

Chief Information Officer

The *chief information officer (CIO)* may report to either the CEO or CFO, depending upon the corporate structure, and is responsible for the strategic use and management of information systems and technology within the organization. Over time, this position has become more strategic and less operational in many organizations. CIOs oversee and are responsible for the day-in-day-out technology operations of a company, but because organizations are so dependent upon technology, CIOs are being asked to sit at the corporate table more and more.

CIO responsibilities have extended to working with the CEO (and other management) on business-process management, revenue generation, and how business strategy can be accomplished with the company's underlying technology. This person usually should have one foot in techno-land and one foot in business-land to be effective because she is bridging two very different worlds.

The CIO sets the stage for the protection of company assets and is ultimately responsible for the success of the company security program. Direction should be coming down from the CEO, and there should be clear lines of communication between the board of directors, the C-level staff, and mid-management. The Sarbanes–Oxley Act (SOX), introduced in Chapter 1, prescribes to the CEO and CFO financial reporting responsibilities and includes penalties and potential *personal* liability for failure to comply. SOX gave the SEC more authority to create regulations that ensure these officers cannot simply pass along fines to the corporation for personal financial misconduct. Under SOX, they can personally be fined millions of dollars and/or go to jail.

Chief Privacy Officer

The *chief privacy officer (CPO)* is a newer position, created mainly because of the increasing demands on organizations to protect a long laundry list of different types of data. This role is responsible for ensuring that customer, company, and employee data is kept safe, which keeps the company out of criminal and civil courts and hopefully out of the headlines. This person is usually an attorney and is directly involved with setting policies on how data is collected, protected, and given out to third parties. The CPO often reports to the chief security officer.

It is important that the CPO understand the privacy, legal, and regulatory requirements the organization must comply with. With this knowledge, the CPO can then develop the organization's policies, standards, procedures, controls, and contract agreements to ensure that privacy requirements are being properly met. Remember also that organizations are responsible for knowing how their suppliers, partners, and other third parties are protecting this sensitive information. The CPO may be responsible for reviewing the data security and privacy practices of these other parties.

Some companies have carried out risk assessments without including the penalties and ramifications they would be forced to deal with if they do not properly protect the information they are responsible for. Without including these liabilities, risk cannot be properly assessed.

The organization should document how privacy data is collected, used, disclosed, archived, and destroyed. Employees should be held accountable for not following the organization's standards on how to handle this type of information.

Privacy

Privacy is different from security. *Privacy* indicates the amount of control an individual should be able to have and expect to have as it relates to the release of their own sensitive information. *Security* refers to the mechanisms that can be put into place to provide this level of control.

It is becoming more critical (and more difficult) to protect PII because of the increase of identity theft and financial fraud threats. PII is a combination of identification elements (name, address, phone number, account number, etc.). Organizations must have privacy policies and controls in place to protect their employee and customer PII.

Chief Security Officer

The *chief security officer (CSO)* is responsible for understanding the risks that the company faces and for mitigating these risks to an acceptable level. This role is responsible for understanding the organization's business drivers and for creating and maintaining a security program that facilitates these drivers, along with providing security, compliance with a long list of regulations and laws, and any customer expectations or contractual obligations.

The creation of this role is a mark in the "win" column for the security industry because it means security is finally being seen as a business issue. Previously, security was relegated to the IT department and was viewed solely as a technology issue. As organizations began to recognize the need to integrate security requirements and business needs, creating a position for security in the executive management team became more of a necessity. The CSO's job is to ensure that business is not disrupted in any way due to security issues. This extends beyond IT and reaches into business processes, legal issues, operational issues, revenue generation, and reputation protection.

CSO vs. CISO

The CSO and CISO may have similar or very different responsibilities, depending on the individual organization. In fact, an organization may choose to have both, either, or neither of these roles. It is up to an organization that has either or both of these roles to define their responsibilities. By and large, the CSO role usually has a further-reaching list of responsibilities compared to the CISO role. The CISO is usually focused more on technology and has an IT background. The CSO usually is required to understand a wider range of business risks, including physical security, not just technological risks.

The CSO is usually more of a businessperson and typically is present in larger organizations. If a company has both roles, the CISO reports directly to the CSO.

The CSO is commonly responsible for ensuring *convergence*, which is the formal cooperation between previously disjointed security functions. This mainly pertains to physical and IT security working in a more concerted manner instead of working in silos within the organization. Issues such as loss prevention, fraud prevention, business continuity planning, legal/regulatory compliance, and insurance all have physical security and IT security aspects and requirements. So one individual (CSO) overseeing and intertwining these different security disciplines allows for a more holistic and comprehensive security program.

Data Owner

The *data owner* (information owner) is usually a member of management who is in charge of a specific business unit, and who is ultimately responsible for the protection and use of a specific subset of information. The data owner has due care responsibilities and thus will be held responsible for any negligent act that results in the corruption or disclosure of the data. The data owner decides upon the classification of the data she is responsible for and alters that classification if the business need arises. This person is also responsible for ensuring that the necessary security controls are in place, defining security requirements per classification and backup requirements, approving any disclosure activities, ensuring that proper access rights are being used, and defining user access criteria. The data owner approves access requests or may choose to delegate this function to business unit managers. And the data owner will deal with security violations pertaining to the data she is responsible for protecting. The data owner, who obviously has enough on her plate, delegates responsibility of the day-to-day maintenance of the data protection mechanisms to the data custodian.

NOTE Data ownership takes on a different meaning when outsourcing data storage requirements. You may want to ensure that the service contract includes a clause to the effect that all data is and shall remain the sole and exclusive property of your organization.

Data Custodian

The *data custodian* (information custodian) is responsible for maintaining and protecting the data. This role is usually filled by the IT or security department, and the duties include implementing and maintaining security controls; performing regular backups of the data; periodically validating the integrity of the data; restoring data from backup media; retaining records of activity; and fulfilling the requirements specified in the company's security policy, standards, and guidelines that pertain to information security and data protection.

System Owner

The *system owner* is responsible for one or more systems, each of which may hold and process data owned by different data owners. A system owner is responsible for integrating security considerations into application and system purchasing decisions and development projects. The system owner is responsible for ensuring that adequate security is being provided by the necessary controls, password management, remote access controls, operating system configurations, and so on. This role must ensure the systems are properly assessed for vulnerabilities and must report any to the incident response team and data owner.

Data Owner Issues

Each business unit should have a data owner who protects the unit's most critical information. The company's policies must give the data owners the necessary authority to carry out their tasks.

This is not a technical role, but rather a business role that must understand the relationship between the unit's success and the protection of this critical asset. Not all businesspeople understand this role, so they should be given the necessary training.

Security Administrator

The *security administrator* is responsible for implementing and maintaining specific security network devices and software in the enterprise. These controls commonly include firewalls, an intrusion detection systems (IDS), intrusion prevention system (IPS), antimalware, security proxies, data loss prevention, etc. It is common for a delineation to exist between the security administrator's responsibilities and the network administrator's responsibilities. The security administrator has the main focus of keeping the network secure, and the network administrator has the focus of keeping things up and running.

A security administrator's tasks commonly also include creating new system user accounts, implementing new security software, testing security patches and components, and issuing new passwords. The security administrator must make sure access rights given to users support the policies and data owner directives.

Supervisor

The *supervisor* role, also called *user manager*, is ultimately responsible for all user activity and any assets created and owned by these users. For example, suppose Kathy is the supervisor of ten employees. Her responsibilities would include ensuring that these employees understand their responsibilities with respect to security; making sure the employees' account information is up to date; and informing the security administrator when an employee is fired, suspended, or transferred. Any change that pertains to an employee's role within the company usually affects what access rights they should and should not have, so the user manager must inform the security administrator of these changes immediately.

Change Control Analyst

Since the only thing that is constant is change, someone must make sure changes happen securely. The *change control analyst* is responsible for approving or rejecting requests to make changes to the network, systems, or software. This role must make certain that the change will not introduce any vulnerabilities, that it has been properly tested, and that it is properly rolled out. The change control analyst needs to understand how various changes can affect security, interoperability, performance, and productivity.

Data Analyst

Having proper data structures, definitions, and organization is very important to a company. The *data analyst* is responsible for ensuring that data is stored in a way that makes the most sense to the company and the individuals who need to access and work with it. For example, payroll information should not be mixed with inventory information; the purchasing department needs to have a lot of its values in monetary terms; and the inventory system must follow a standardized naming scheme. The data analyst may be responsible for architecting a new system that will hold company information or advise in the purchase of a product that will do so.

The data analyst works with the data owners to help ensure that the structures set up coincide with and support the company's business objectives.

User

The *user* is any individual who routinely uses the data for work-related tasks. The user must have the necessary level of access to the data to perform the duties within their position and is responsible for following operational security procedures to ensure the data's confidentiality, integrity, and availability to others.

Auditor

The function of the *auditor* is to periodically check that everyone is doing what they are supposed to be doing and to ensure the correct controls are in place and are being maintained securely. The goal of the auditor is to make sure the organization complies with its own policies and the applicable laws and regulations. Organizations can have internal auditors and/or external auditors. The external auditors commonly work on behalf of a regulatory body to make sure compliance is being met.

While many security professionals fear and dread auditors, they can be valuable tools in ensuring the overall security of the organization. Their goal is to find the things you have missed and help you understand how to fix the problems.

Why So Many Roles?

Most organizations will not have all the roles previously listed, but what is important is to build an organizational structure that contains the necessary roles and map the correct security responsibilities to them. This structure includes clear definitions of responsibilities, lines of authority and communication, and enforcement capabilities. A clear-cut structure takes the mystery out of who does what and how things are handled in different situations.

Retention Policies

There is no universal agreement on how long an organization should retain data. Legal and regulatory requirements (where they exist) vary among countries and business sectors. What is universal is the need to ensure your organization has and follows a documented data retention policy. Doing otherwise is flirting with disaster, particularly when dealing with pending or ongoing litigation. It is not enough, of course, to simply have a policy; you must ensure it is being followed, and you must document this through regular audits.

NOTE When outsourcing data storage, it is important to specify in the contract language how long the storage provider will retain your data after you stop doing business with them and what process they will use to eradicate your data from their systems.

A very straightforward and perhaps tempting approach would be to look at the lengthiest legal or regulatory retention requirement imposed on your organization and then apply that timeframe to all your data retention. The problem with this approach is that it will probably make your retained data set orders of magnitude greater than it needs to be. Not only does this impose additional storage costs, but it also makes it more difficult to comply with electronic discovery (e-discovery) orders. When you receive an e-discovery order from a court, you are typically required to produce a specific amount of data (usually pretty large) within a given timeframe (usually very short). Obviously, the more data you retain, the more difficult and expensive this process will be.

A better approach is to segregate the specific data sets that have mandated retention requirements and handle those accordingly. Everything else should have a retention period that minimally satisfies the business requirements. You probably will find that different business units within medium and large organizations will have different retention requirements. For instance, a company may want to keep data from its research and development (R&D) division for a much longer period than it keeps data from its customer service division. R&D projects that are not particularly helpful today may be so at a later date, but audio recordings of customer service calls probably don't have to hang around for a few years.

NOTE Be sure to get buy-in from your legal counsel when developing or modifying data retention and privacy policies.

Developing a Retention Policy

At its core, every data retention policy answers three fundamental questions:

- What data do we keep?
- How long do we keep this data?
- Where do we keep this data?

Most security professionals understand the first two questions. After all, many of us are used to keeping tax records for three years in case we get audited. The "what" and the "how long" are easy. The last question, however, surprises more than a few of us. The twist is that the question is not so much about the location per se, but rather the manner in which the data is kept at that location. In order to be useful to us, retained data must be easy to locate and retrieve.

Think about it this way. Suppose your organization had a business transaction with Acme Corporation in which you learned that they were involved in the sale of a particular service to a client in another country. Two years later, you receive a third-party subpoena asking for any information you may have regarding that sale. You know you retain all your data for three years, but you have no idea where the relevant data may be. Was it an e-mail, a recording of a phone conversation, the minutes from a meeting, or something else? Where would you go looking for it? Alternatively, how could you make a case to the court that providing the data would be too costly for your organization?

How We Retain

In order for retained data to be useful, it must be accessible in a timely manner. It really does us no good to have data that takes an inordinate (and perhaps prohibitive) amount of effort to query. To ensure this accessibility, we need to consider various issues, including the ones listed here.

- **Taxonomy** A taxonomy is a scheme for classifying data. This classification can be made using a variety of categories, including functional (e.g., human resources, product development), chronological (e.g., 2015), organizational (e.g., executives, union employees), or any combination of these or other categories.
- **Classification** The sensitivity classification of the data will determine the controls we place on it both while it is in use and when it gets archived. This is particularly important because many organizations protect sensitive information while in use, but not so much after it goes into the archives.
- **Normalization** Retained data will come in a variety of formats, including word processing documents, database records, flat files, images, PDF files, video, and so on. Simply storing the data in its original format will not suffice in any but the most trivial cases. Instead, we need to develop tagging schemas that will make the data searchable.
- **Indexing** Retained data must be searchable if we are to quickly pull out specific items of interest. The most common approach to making data searchable is to build indexes for it. Many archiving systems implement this feature, but others do not. Either way, the indexing approach must support the likely future queries on the archived data.

Ideally, archiving occurs in a centralized, regimented, and homogenous manner. We all know, however, that this is seldom the case. We may have to compromise in order to arrive at solutions that meet our minimum requirements within our resource constraints. Still, as we plan and execute our retention strategies, we must remain focused on how we will efficiently access archived data many months or years later.

How Long We Retain

Once upon a time, there were two main data retention longevity approaches: the "keep nothing" camp and the "keep everything" camp. As the legal processes caught up with modern computer technology, it became clear that (except in very limited cases) these approaches were not acceptable. For starters, whether they retained nothing or everything, organizations following one of these extreme approaches found out it was difficult to defend themselves in lawsuits. The first group had nothing with which to show due diligence, for instance, while those in the second group had too much information that plaintiffs could use against them. So what is the right data retention policy? Ask your legal counsel. Seriously.

There are myriads of statutory and regulatory retention requirements, which vary from jurisdiction to jurisdiction (sometimes even within the same country). There are also best practices and case law to consider, so we won't attempt to get too specific here.

Still, the following are some general guidelines sufficient to start the conversation with your attorneys:

Type of Data	General Period of Retention
Business documents (e.g., meeting minutes)	7 years
Invoices	5 years
Accounts payable and receivable	7 years
Human resource files	7 years (for employees who leave) or 3 years (for candidates who were not hired)
Tax records	4 years after taxes were paid
Legal correspondence	Permanently

What Data We Retain

In addition to the categories listed previously, there are many other records we would want to retain. Again, legal counsel must be involved in this process to ensure all legal obligations are being met. Beyond these obligations, there will be specific information that is important to the business for a variety of reasons. It is also worth considering what data might be valuable in light of business arrangements, partnerships, or third-party dealings.

The decision to retain data must be deliberate, specific, and enforceable. We want to keep only the data that we consciously decide to keep, and then we want to ensure that we can enforce that retention. If this sounds painful, we need only consider the consequences of not getting this process right. Many companies have endured undue hardships because they couldn't develop, implement, and enforce a proper retention policy. Among the biggest challenges in this realm is the balance between business needs and employee or customer privacy.

e-Discovery

Discovery of electronically stored information (ESI), or *e-discovery*, is the process of producing for a court or external attorney all ESI pertinent to a legal proceeding. For example, if your company is being sued for damages resulting from a faulty product, the plaintiff's attorney could get an e-discovery order compelling you to produce all e-mail between the QA team and senior executives in which the product's faults are discussed. If your data retention policy and procedures are adequate, e-discovery should not require excessive efforts. If, on the other hand, you have been slack about retention, such an order could cripple the organization.

The Electronic Discovery Reference Model (EDRM) identifies eight steps, though they are not necessarily all required, nor are they performed in a linear manner:

1. **Identification** of data required under the order.
2. **Preservation** of this data to ensure it is not accidentally or routinely destroyed while complying with the order.

3. **Collection** of the data from the various stores in which it may be.
4. **Processing** to ensure the correct format is used for both the data and its metadata.
5. **Review** of the data to ensure it is relevant.
6. **Analysis** of the data for proper context.
7. **Production** of the final data set to those requesting it.
8. **Presentation** of the data to external audiences to prove or disprove a claim.

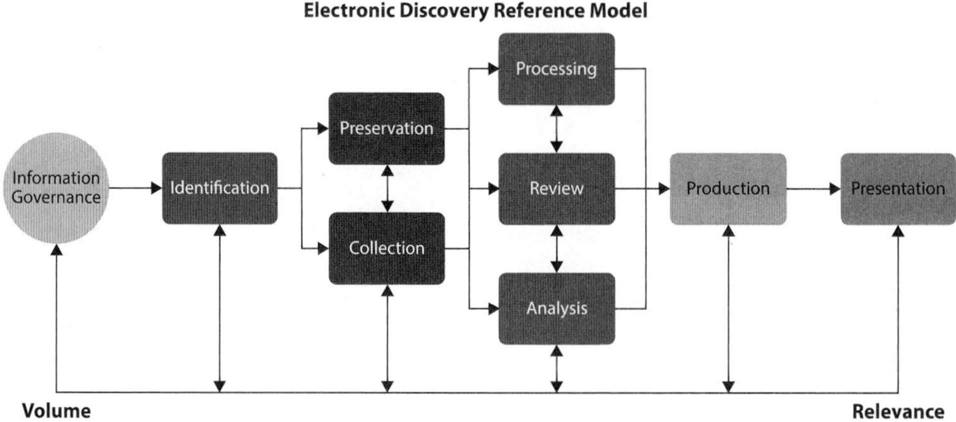

(Source: EDRM; edrm.net)

Protecting Privacy

Privacy protections have long been a major concern of Western democracies, but over the past 15 years, the debate between privacy and security advocates has intensified, perhaps to its highest level ever. The terrorist attacks of September 11, 2001, in New York and Washington, DC led multiple countries to swing the pendulum away from privacy and toward security. In other words, many legislatures decided that a higher degree of protection against terrorist or criminal attacks warranted a lesser degree of privacy. However, in the wake of the security leaks attributed to Edward Snowden in 2013, the pendulum has swung in the opposite direction: toward more privacy protections. Attempting to ride the pendulum as it swings back and forth are the many organizations that have to find practical ways of balancing these requirements within their information systems.

Data Owners

As discussed earlier in this chapter, among the responsibilities of the data owners are data classification and the approval of disclosure requests. These have particular importance in the context of privacy protections. The data owners, therefore, indirectly or directly decide who gets access to specific data. This is particularly important given that these individuals typically are senior managers within the organization. In reality, the majority of these decisions should be codified in formal written policies. Any exceptions to policy should be just that—exceptions—and must be properly documented.

Data Processers

The group of users best positioned to protect (or compromise) data privacy consists of those who deal with that data on a routine basis: *data processers*. These individuals can be found in a variety of places within the organization depending on what particular data is of concern. The critical issue here with respect to privacy is that these individuals understand the boundaries of what is acceptable behavior and (just as importantly) know what to do when data is accidentally or intentionally handled in a manner that does not conform to applicable policies. The key issues in terms of privacy protections for this group are training and auditing. On the one hand, data processers must be properly trained to handle their duties and responsibilities. On the other hand, there must be routine inspections to ensure their behavior complies with all applicable laws, regulations, and policies.

Data Remanence

Even when policies exist (and are enforced and audited) to ensure the protection of privacy, it is possible for technical issues to threaten this privacy. It is a well-known fact that most data deletion operations do not, in fact, erase anything; normally, they simply mark the memory as available for other data without wiping (or even erasing) the original data. This is true not only of file systems, but also of databases. Since it is difficult to imagine a data store that would not fit in either of these two constructs, it should be clear that simply "deleting" data will likely result in data remanence issues.

NOTE NIST Special Publication 800-88, Revision 1, "Guidelines for Media Sanitization" (December 2014), describes the best practices for combating data remanence.

Let's consider what happens when we create a text file using the File Allocation Table (FAT) file system. Though this original form of FAT is antiquated, its core constructs (e.g., disk blocks, free block list/table, file metadata table) are also found at the heart of all other modern file systems. Its simplicity makes it a wonderful training tool for the purpose of explaining file creation and deletion.

Suppose we type up the famous Aesop fable titled "The Lion and the Mouse" in a text editor and save it to disk. The operating system will ask us for a filename, which will be Story2.txt for this example. The system will then check the File Allocation Table for available blocks on which to store the text file. As shown in Figure 2-2, the system creates a directory entry for the file containing the name (Story2.txt), location of the first block (163), and the file size in bytes (714). In our simplistic example, each block is 512 bytes in size, so we'll need two of them. Fortunately, block 164 is right next to the start block and is also free. The system will use the entry for block 163 (the first block of the file)

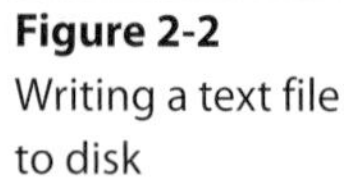

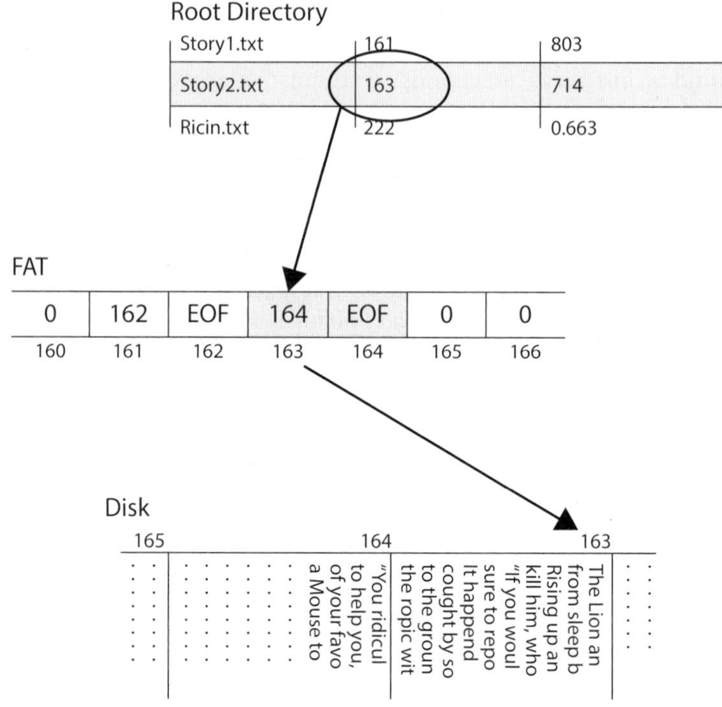

Figure 2-2 Writing a text file to disk

to point to the next block containing it (164). This allows files to occupy discontinuous blocks if the disk is heavily fragmented. That chain of blocks could be quite long if the file was big enough and we didn't run out of disk space first. In our simple example, however, we just need two blocks, so block 164 is the final one in use and gets a special label of EOF to denote the end of the file.

Suppose we decide to delete the file. Instead of cleaning up the table, the FAT file system will simply replace the first character of the filename in the directory table with a reserved character (shown in Figure 2-3 as a question mark) to indicate that the file was deleted. The starting block will be preserved in the directory, but the corresponding entries in the File Allocation Table are zeroed out to show that those blocks are available for other files. As you can see in Figure 2-3, the contents of the file on the disk remain intact. This is why data remanence is such a big problem: because file systems almost never securely wipe data when deleting files.

At some point, however, users will create new files and save them to disk, which could result in our original data being partly or completely overwritten. This is shown in Figure 2-4. In this case, the new file requires only one block of disk space because it only contains the text "Hello World!" Suppose the user calls this file "hello.txt" and the system stores it in block 163, which used to be the start block for the previous Story2 .txt file. That block will be overwritten with the new file's content and almost certainly padded with empty characters to fill out the block. The next block, however, contains

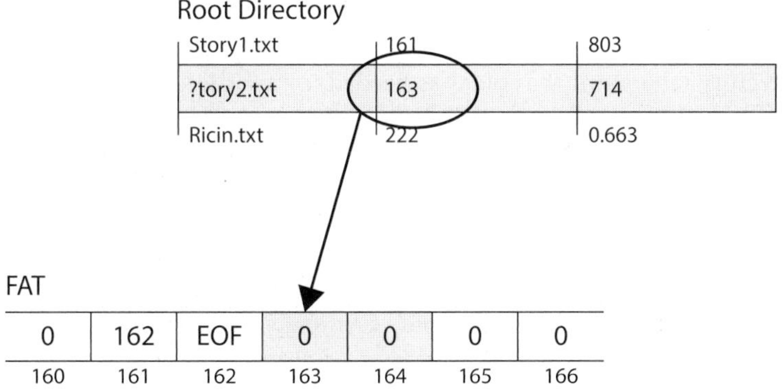

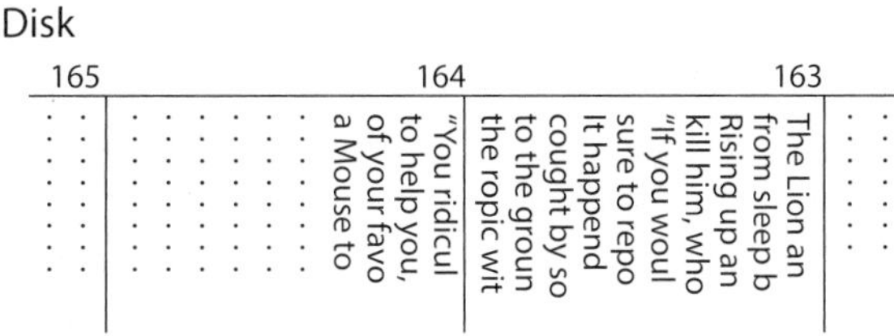

Figure 2-3 Deleting a file

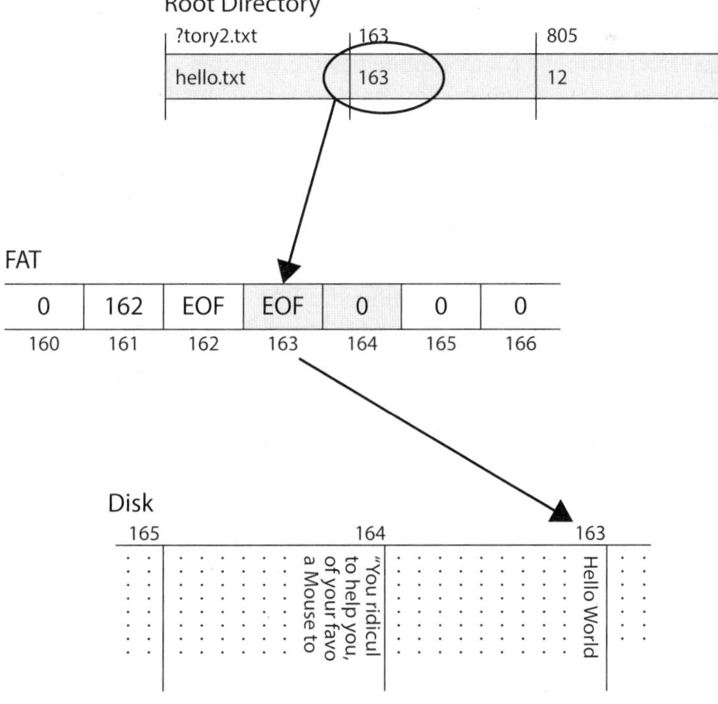

Figure 2-4 Partially overwriting a file

the remainder of the deleted file, so partial contents are still available to anyone with the right recovery tools. Note also that the original file's metadata is preserved in the directory table until that block is needed for another file.

This example, though simplistic, illustrates the process used by almost every file system when creating and deleting files. The data structures may be named differently in modern versions of Windows, Linux, and Mac OS X, but their purpose and behavior remain essentially the same. In fact, many databases use a similar approach to "deleting" entries by simply marking them as deleted without wiping the original data.

To counter data remanence, it is important to identify procedures for ensuring that private data is properly removed. Generally speaking, there are four approaches to eliminating data remanence:

- **Overwriting** Overwriting data entails replacing the 1's and 0's that represent it on storage media with random or fixed patterns of 1's and 0's in order to render the original data unrecoverable. This should be done at least once (e.g., overwriting the medium with 1's, 0's, or a pattern of these), but may have to be done more than that. For many years the U.S. Department of Defense (DoD) standard 5220.22-M required that media be overwritten seven times. This standard has since been superseded. DoD systems with sensitive information must now be degaussed.
- **Degaussing** This is the process of removing or reducing the magnetic field patterns on conventional disk drives or tapes. In essence, a powerful magnetic force is applied to the media, which results in the wiping of the data and sometimes the destruction of the motors that drive the platters. While it may still be possible to recover the data, it is typically cost prohibitive to do so.
- **Encryption** Many mobile devices take this approach to quickly and securely render data unusable. The premise is that the data is stored on the medium in encrypted format using a strong key. To render the data unrecoverable, the system simply needs to securely delete the encryption key, which is many times faster than deleting the encrypted data. Recovering the data in this scenario is typically computationally infeasible.
- **Physical destruction** Perhaps the best way to combat data remanence is to simply destroy the physical media. The two most commonly used approaches to destroying media are to shred it or expose it to caustic or corrosive chemicals that render it unusable. Another approach is incineration.

Limits on Collection

Securely deleting data is necessary, but not enough. We must also ensure that the data we collect in the first place, particularly when it is personal in nature, is necessary for our jobs. Generally speaking, organizations should collect the least amount of private personal data required for the performance of their business functions. In many cases, this is not a matter of choice but of law. As of 2014, over 100 countries have enacted privacy protection laws that affect organizations within their jurisdictions. It is important to note that privacy protections vary widely among countries. Argentina is one of the most restrictive countries with respect to privacy, while China effectively has no restrictions. The United States has very few restrictions on the collection of private data by nongovernmental organizations, and the European Union has yet to coalesce on a common set of standards in this regard. The point is that you have to be aware of the specific privacy laws that pertain to the places in which your organization stores or uses its data. This is particularly important when you outsource services (which may require access to your data) to third parties in a different country.

Apart from applicable laws and regulations, the types of personal data that your organization collects, as well as its life-cycle considerations, must be a matter of explicit written policy. Your privacy policy needs to cover your organization's collection, use, disclosure, and protection of employee and client data. Many organizations break their privacy policy into two documents: one internal document that covers employee data, and a second external document that covers customer information. At a minimum, you want to answer the following questions when writing your policy:

- What personal data is collected (e.g., name, website visits, e-mail messages, etc.)?
- Why do we collect this data and how do we use it (e.g., to provide a service, for security)?
- With whom do we share this data (e.g., third-party providers, law enforcement agencies)?
- Who owns the collected data (e.g., subject, organization)?
- What rights does the subject of this data have with regard to it (e.g., opt out, restrictions)?
- When do we destroy the data (e.g., after five years, never)?
- What specific laws or regulations exist that pertain to this data?

Protecting Assets

The main threats that physical security components combat are theft, interruptions to services, physical damage, compromised system and environment integrity, and unauthorized access. Real loss is determined by the cost to replace the stolen items, the negative effect on productivity, the negative effect on reputation and customer confidence, fees for consultants that may need to be brought in, and the cost to restore lost data and production levels. Many times, companies just perform an inventory of their hardware and provide value estimates that are plugged into risk analysis to determine what the cost to the company would be if the equipment were stolen or destroyed. However, the information held within the equipment may be much more valuable than the equipment itself, and proper recovery mechanisms and procedures also need to be plugged into the risk assessment for a more realistic and fair assessment of cost. Let's take a look at some of the controls we can use in order to mitigate risks to our data and to the media on which it resides.

Data Security Controls

Which controls we choose to use to mitigate risks to our information depend not only on the value we assign to that information, but also on the dynamic state of that information. Generally speaking, data exists in one of three states: at rest, in motion, or in use. These states and their interrelations are shown in Figure 2-5. The risks to each state are different in significant ways, as described next.

Data at Rest

Information in an information system spends most of its time waiting to be used. The term *data at rest* refers to data that resides in external or auxiliary storage devices, such as hard disk drives (HDDs), solid-state drives (SSDs), optical discs (CD/DVD), or even on magnetic tape. A challenge with protecting data in this state is that it is vulnerable, not only to threat actors attempting to reach it over our systems and networks, but also to anyone who can gain physical access to the device. It is not uncommon to hear of data breaches caused by laptops or mobile devices being stolen. In fact, one of the largest personal health information (PHI) breaches occurred in San Antonio, Texas, in September 2009 when an employee left unattended in his car backup tapes containing PHI on some 4.9 million patients. A thief broke into the vehicle and made off with the data. The solution to protecting data in such scenarios is as simple as it is ubiquitous: encryption.

Every major operating system now provides means to encrypt individual files or entire volumes in a way that is almost completely transparent to the user. Third-party software is also available to encrypt compressed files or perform whole-disk encryption. What's more, the current state of processor power means that there is no noticeable decrease in the performance of computers that use encryption to protect their data. Unfortunately, encryption is not yet the default configuration in any major operation system. The process of enabling it, however, is so simple that it borders on the trivial.

Many medium and large organizations now have policies that require certain information to be encrypted whenever it is stored in an information system. While typically this applies to PII, PHI, or other regulated information, some organizations are taking the proactive step of requiring whole-disk encryption to be used on all portable computing devices such as laptops and external hard drives. Beyond what are clearly easily pilfered devices, we should also consider computers we don't normally think of as mobile. Another major breach of PHI was reported by Sutter Health of California in 2011 when a thief broke a window and stole a desktop computer containing the

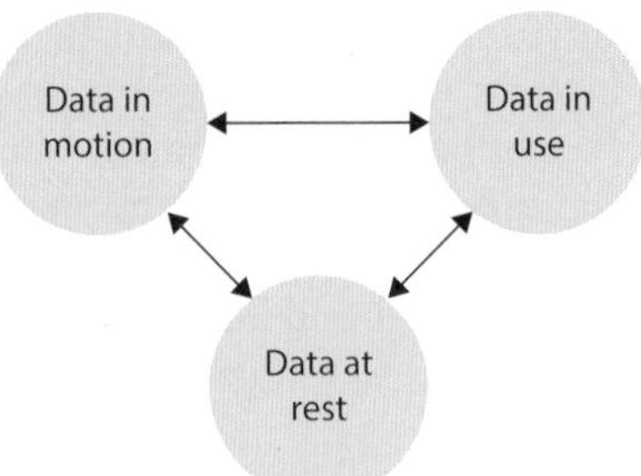

Figure 2-5 The states of data

unencrypted records on more than 4 million patients. We should really try to encrypt all data being stored anywhere, and modern technology makes this easier than ever. This approach to "encrypt everywhere" reduces the risk of users accidentally storing sensitive information in unencrypted volumes.

NOTE NIST Special Publication 800-111, "Guide to Storage Encryption Technologies for End User Devices," provides a good, if somewhat dated (2007), approach to this topic.

Where in the World Is Your Data?

Certain countries require that data within its geographic borders, regardless of country of ownership, be made available to certain government organizations such as law enforcement and intelligence agencies with proper authorization. If the data is encrypted, then the organization hosting the data in that country is responsible for providing the keys or could face criminal charges. For this reason, many organizations require their data to be stored only within specific geographical boundaries. This can pose serious challenges to multinational organizations and to some users of cloud computing services. Additionally, even if properly stored in the right places, the data could find its way to other countries when certain services, such as customer support, are outsourced. When planning your data storage architectures, it is imperative that you understand exactly where in the world your data could end up going.

Data in Motion

Data in motion is data that is moving between computing nodes over a data network such as the Internet. This is perhaps the riskiest time for our data: when it leaves the confines of our protected enclaves and ventures into that Wild West that is the Internet. Fortunately, encryption once again rises to the challenge. The single best protection for our data while it is in motion (whether within or without our protected networks) is strong encryption such as that offered by Transport Layer Security (TLS version 1.1 and later) or IPSec. We will discuss strong (and weak) encryption in Chapter 3, but for now you should be aware that TLS and IPSec support multiple cipher suites and that some of these are not as strong as others. Weaknesses typically are the result of attempts at ensuring backward compatibility, but result in unnecessary (or perhaps unknown) risks.

By and large, TLS relies on digital certificates (more on those in the next chapter) to certify the identity of one or both endpoints. Typically, the server uses a certificate but the client doesn't. This one-way authentication can be problematic because it relies on the user to detect a potential impostor. A common exploit for this vulnerability is known as a man-in-the-middle (MitM) attack. The attacker intercepts the request from the client to the server and impersonates the server, pretending to be, say, Facebook. The attacker presents to the client a fake web page that looks exactly like Facebook and requests the user's credentials. Once the user provides that information, the attacker can forward the log-in request to Facebook and then continue to relay information back and forth between the client and the server over secure connections, intercepting all traffic in the process. A savvy client would detect this by noticing that the web browser reports a problem with the server's certificate. (It is extremely difficult for all but certain nation-states to spoof a legitimate certificate.) Most users, however, simply click through any such warnings without thinking of the consequences. This tendency to ignore the warnings underscores the importance of security awareness in our overall efforts to protect our information and systems.

Another approach to protecting our data in motion is to use trusted channels between critical nodes. Virtual private networks (VPNs) are frequently used to provide secure connections between remote users and corporate resources. VPNs are also used to securely connect campuses or other nodes that are physically distant from each other. The trusted channels we thus create allow secure communications over shared or untrusted network infrastructure.

Data in Use

Data in use is the term for data residing in primary storage devices, such as volatile memory (e.g., RAM), memory caches, or CPU registers. Typically, data remains in primary storage for short periods of time while a process is using it. Note, however, that anything stored in volatile memory could persist there for extended periods (until power is shut down) in some cases. The point is that data in use is being touched by the CPU or ALU in the computer system and will eventually go back to being data at rest, or end up being deleted.

As discussed earlier, data at rest should be encrypted. The challenge is that, in most operating systems today, the data must be decrypted before it is used. In other words, data in use generally cannot be protected by encrypting it. Many people think this is safe, the thought process being, "If I'm encrypting my data at rest and in transit already, why would I worry about protecting it during the brief period in which it is being used by the CPU? After all, if someone can get to my volatile memory, I probably have bigger problems than protecting this little bit of data, right?" Not really.

Various independent researchers have demonstrated effective side-channel attacks against memory shared by multiple processes. A *side-channel attack* exploits information that is being leaked by a cryptosystem. As we will see in our later discussion of cryptology, a cryptosystem can be thought of as connecting two channels: a plaintext channel and an encrypted one. A *side channel* is any information flow that is the electronic byproduct of this process. As an illustration of this, imagine yourself being transported in the windowless back of a van. You have no way of knowing where you are going, but you can infer some aspects of the route by feeling the centrifugal force when the van makes a turn or follows a curve. You could also pay attention to the engine noise or the pressure in your ears as you climb or descend hills. These are all side channels. Similarly, if you are trying to recover the secret keys used to encrypt data, you could pay attention to how much power is being consumed by the CPU or how long it takes for other processes to read and write from memory. Researchers have been able to recover 2,048-bit keys from shared systems in this manner.

But the threats are not limited to cryptosystems alone. The infamous Heartbleed security bug of 2014 demonstrated how failing to check the boundaries of requests to read from memory could expose information from one process to others running on the same system. In that bug, the main issue was that anyone communicating with the server could request an arbitrarily long "heartbeat" message from it. Heartbeat messages are typically short strings that let the other end know that an endpoint is still there and wanting to communicate. The developers of the library being used for this never imagined that someone would ask for a string that was hundreds of characters in length. The attackers, however, did think of this and in fact were able to access crypto keys and other sensitive data belonging to other users.

So, how do we protect our data in use? For now, it boils down to ensuring our software is tested against these types of attacks. Obviously, this is a tricky proposition, since it is very difficult to identify and test for every possible software flaw. Still, secure development practices, as we will see in Chapter 8, have to be a critical component of our security efforts. In the near future, whole-memory encryption will mitigate the risks described in this section, particularly when coupled with the storage of keys in CPU registers instead of in RAM. Until these changes are widely available, however, we must remain vigilant to the threats against our data while it is in use.

Media Controls

As we have seen, data can exist in many types of media. Even data in motion and data in use can be temporarily stored or cached on devices throughout our systems. These media and devices require a variety of controls to ensure data is properly preserved and that its integrity, confidentiality, and availability are not compromised. For the purposes of this discussion, "media" may include both electronic (disk, CD/DVD, tape, Flash devices such as USB "thumb drives," and so on) and nonelectronic (paper) forms of information; and media libraries may come into custody of media before, during, and/or after the information content of the media is entered into, processed on, and/or removed from systems.

The operational controls that pertain to these issues come in many flavors. The first are controls that prevent unauthorized access (protect confidentiality), which, as usual, can be physical, administrative, and technical. If the company's backup tapes are to be properly protected from unauthorized access, they must be stored in a place where only authorized people have access to them, which could be in a locked server room or an offsite facility. If media needs to be protected from environmental issues such as humidity, heat, cold, fire, and natural disasters (to maintain availability), the media should be kept in a fireproof safe in a regulated environment or in an offsite facility that controls the environment so it is hospitable to data processing components.

Companies may have a media library with a librarian in charge of protecting its resources. If so, most or all of the responsibilities described in this chapter for the protection of the confidentiality, integrity, and availability of media fall to the librarian. Users may be required to check out specific types of media and resources from the library, instead of having the resources readily available for anyone to access them. This is common when the media library includes the distribution media for licensed software. It provides an accounting (audit log) of uses of media, which can help in demonstrating due diligence in complying with license agreements and in protecting confidential information (such as PII, financial/credit card information, and PHI) in media libraries containing those types of data.

Media should be clearly marked and logged, its integrity should be verified, and it should be properly erased of data when no longer needed. After large investment is made to secure a network and its components, a common mistake is for old computers along with their hard drives and other magnetic storage media to be replaced, and the obsolete equipment shipped out the back door along with all the data the company just spent so much time and money securing. This puts the information on the obsolete equipment and media at risk of disclosure and violates legal, regulatory, and ethical obligations of the company. Thus, overwriting (see Figure 2-6) and secure overwriting algorithms are required. And if any part of a piece of media containing highly sensitive information cannot be cleared or purged, then physical destruction must take place.

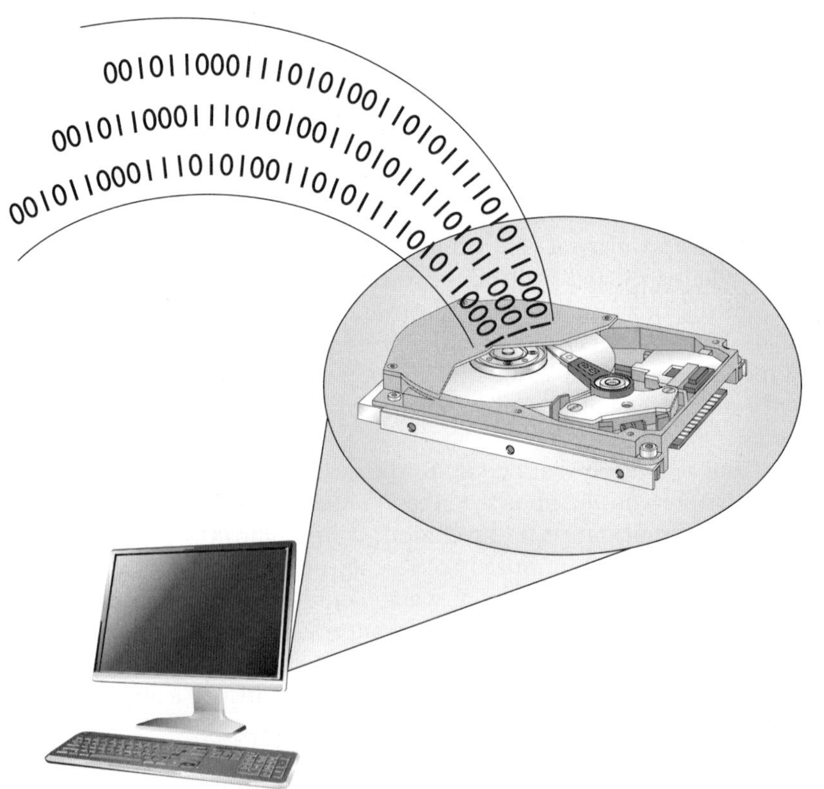

Figure 2-6 Overwriting media to protect sensitive data

When media is erased (*cleared* of its contents), it is said to be *sanitized*. In military/government classified systems terms, this means erasing information so it is not readily retrieved using routine operating system commands or commercially available forensic/data recovery software. Clearing is acceptable when media will be reused in the same physical environment for the same purposes (in the same compartment of compartmentalized information security) by people with the same access levels for that compartment.

Not all clearing/purging methods are applicable to all media—for example, optical media is not susceptible to degaussing, and overwriting may not be effective when dealing with solid-state devices. The degree to which information may be recoverable by a sufficiently motivated and capable adversary must not be underestimated or guessed at in ignorance. For the highest-value commercial data, and for all data regulated by government or military classification rules, read and follow the rules and standards.

The guiding principle for deciding what is the necessary method (and cost) of data erasure is to ensure that the enemies' cost of recovering the data exceeds the value of the data. "Sink the company" (or "sink the country") information has value so high that the destruction of the media, which involves both the cost of the destruction and the total loss of any potential reusable value of the media, is justified. For most other categories of information, multiple or simple overwriting is sufficient. Each company must evaluate the value of its data and then choose the appropriate erasure/disposal method.

Methods were discussed earlier for secure clearing, purging, and destruction of electronic media. Other forms of information, such as paper, microfilm, and microfiche, also require secure disposal. "Dumpster diving" is the practice of searching through trash at homes and businesses to find valuable information that was simply thrown away without being first securely destroyed through shredding or burning.

Atoms and Data

A device that performs degaussing generates a coercive magnetic force that reduces the magnetic flux density of the storage media to zero. This magnetic force is what properly erases data from media. Data is stored on magnetic media by the representation of the polarization of the atoms. Degaussing changes this polarization (magnetic alignment) by using a type of large magnet to bring it back to its original flux (magnetic alignment).

Media management, whether in a library or managed by other systems or individuals, has the following attributes and tasks:

- **Tracking** (audit logging) who has custody of each piece of media at any given moment. This creates the same kind of audit trail as any audit logging activity—to allow an investigation to determine where information was at any given time, who had it, and, for particularly sensitive information, why they accessed it. This enables an investigator to focus efforts on particular people, places, and times if a breach is suspected or known to have happened.

- **Effectively implementing access controls** to restrict who can access each piece of media to only those people defined by the owner of the media/information on the media, and to enforce the appropriate security measures based on the classification of the media/information on the media. Certain media, due to its physical type and/or the nature of the information on it, may require special handling. All personnel who are authorized to access media must have training to ensure they understand what is required of such media. An example of special handling for, say, classified information may be that the media may only be removed from the library or its usual storage place under physical guard, and even then may not be removed from the building. Access controls will include *physical* (locked doors, drawers, cabinets, or safes), *technical* (access and authorization control of any automated system for retrieving contents of information in the library), and *administrative* (the actual rules for who is supposed to do what to each piece of information). Finally, the data may need to change format, as in printing electronic data to paper. The data still needs to be protected at the necessary level, no matter what format it is in. Procedures must include how to continue to provide the appropriate protection. For example, sensitive material that is to be mailed should be sent in a sealable inner envelope and use only courier service.
- **Tracking the number and location of backup versions** (both onsite and offsite). This is necessary to ensure proper disposal of information when the information reaches the end of its lifespan, to account for the location and accessibility of information during audits, and to find a backup copy of information if the primary source of the information is lost or damaged.
- **Documenting the history of changes to media.** For example, when a particular version of a software application kept in the library has been deemed obsolete, this fact must be recorded so the obsolete version of the application is not used unless that particular obsolete version is required. Even once no possible need for the actual media or its content remains, retaining a log of the former existence and the time and method of its deletion may be useful to demonstrate due diligence.
- **Ensuring environmental conditions do not endanger media.** Each media type may be susceptible to damage from one or more environmental influences. For example, all media formats are susceptible to fire, and most are susceptible to liquids, smoke, and dust. Magnetic media formats are susceptible to strong magnetic fields. Magnetic and optical media formats are susceptible to variations in temperature and humidity. A media library and any other space where reference copies of information are stored must be physically built so all types of media will be kept within their environmental parameters, and the environment must be monitored to ensure conditions do not range outside of those parameters. Media libraries are particularly useful when large amounts of information must be stored and physically/environmentally protected so that the high cost of environmental control and media management may be centralized in a small number of physical locations and so that cost is spread out over the large number of items stored in the library.

- **Ensuring media integrity** by verifying on a media-type and environment-appropriate basis that each piece of media remains usable and transferring still-valuable information from pieces of media reaching their obsolescence date to new pieces of media. Every type of media has an expected lifespan under certain conditions, after which it can no longer be expected that the media will reliably retain information. For example, a commercially produced CD or DVD stored in good environmental conditions should be reliable for at least ten years, whereas an inexpensive CD-R or DVD-R sitting on a shelf in a home office may become unreliable after just one year. All types of media in use at a company should have a documented (and conservative) expected lifespan. When the information on a piece of media has more remaining lifespan before its scheduled obsolescence/destruction date than does the piece of media on which the information is recorded, then the information must be transcribed to a newer piece or a newer format of media. Even the availability of hardware to read media in particular formats must be taken into account. A media format that is physically stable for decades, but for which no working device remains available to read, is of no value. Additionally, as part of maintaining the integrity of the specific contents of a piece of media, if the information on that media is highly valuable or mandated to be kept by some regulation or law, a cryptographic signature of the contents of the media may be maintained, and the contents of the piece of media verified against that signature on a regular basis.
- **Inventorying the media on a scheduled basis** to detect if any media has been lost/changed. This can reduce the amount of damage a violation of the other media protection responsibilities could cause by detecting such violations sooner rather than later, and is a necessary part of the media management life cycle by which the controls in place are verified as being sufficient.
- **Carrying out secure disposal activities.** Disposition includes the lifetime after which the information is no longer valuable and the minimum necessary measures for the disposal of the media/information. Secure disposal of media/information can add significant cost to media management. Knowing that only a certain percentage of the information must be securely erased at the end of its life may significantly reduce the long-term operating costs of the company. Similarly, knowing that certain information must be disposed of securely can reduce the possibility of a piece of media being simply thrown in a dumpster and then found by someone who publicly embarrasses or blackmails the company over the data security breach represented by that inappropriate disposal of the information. It is the business that creates the information stored on media, not the person, library, or librarian who has custody of the media, that is responsible for setting the lifetime and disposition of that information. The business must take into account the useful lifetime of the information to the business, legal, and regulatory restrictions, and, conversely, the requirements for retention and archiving when making these decisions. If a law or regulation requires the information to be kept beyond its normally useful lifetime for the business, then disposition may involve archiving—moving the information from the ready (and possibly more expensive) accessibility of a library to a long-term stable and (with some effort) retrievable format that has lower storage costs.

- **Internal and external labeling** of each piece of media in the library should include
  - Date created
  - Retention period
  - Classification level
  - Who created it
  - Date to be destroyed
  - Name and version

Taken together, these tasks implement the full life cycle of the media and represent a necessary part of the full life cycle of the information stored thereon.

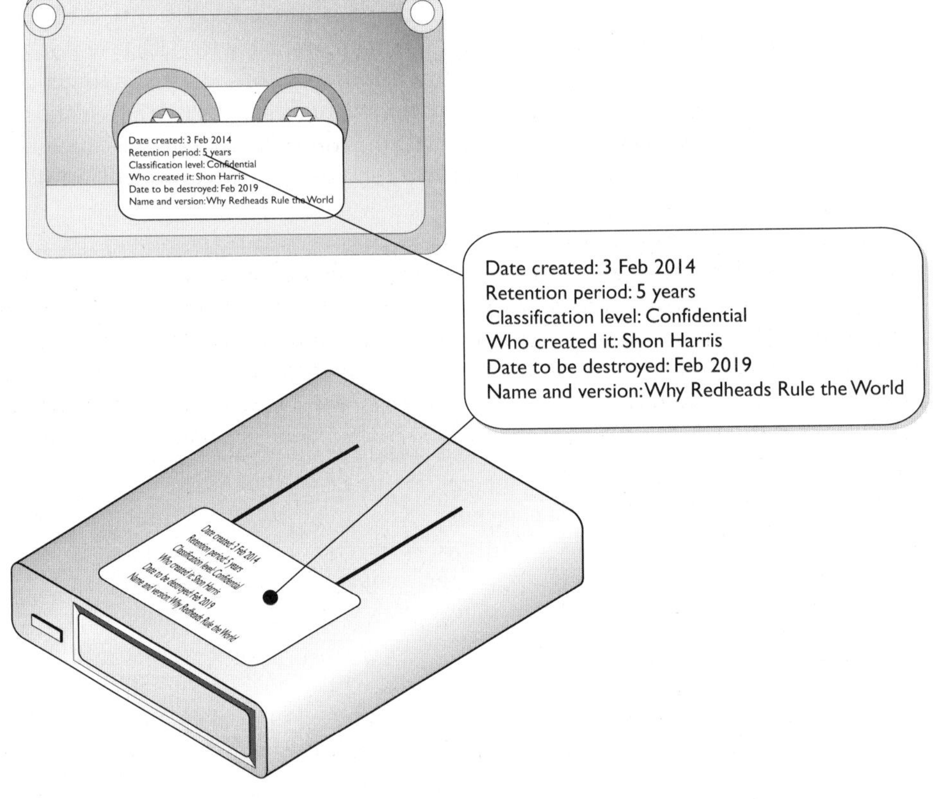

Date created: 3 Feb 2014
Retention period: 5 years
Classification level: Confidential
Who created it: Shon Harris
Date to be destroyed: Feb 2019
Name and version: Why Redheads Rule the World

Data Leakage

Unless we diligently apply the right controls to our data wherever it may be, we should expect that some of it will eventually end up in the wrong hands. In fact, even if we do everything right, the risk of this happening will never be eliminated. Leaks of personal information by an organization can cause large financial losses. The costs commonly include

- Investigating the incident and remediating the problem
- Contacting affected individuals to inform them about the incident
- Penalties and fines to regulatory agencies
- Contractual liabilities
- Mitigating expenses (such as free credit monitoring services for affected individuals)
- Direct damages to affected individuals

In addition to financial losses, a company's reputation may be damaged and individuals' identities may be stolen.

The most common cause of data breach for a business is a lack of awareness and discipline among employees—an overwhelming majority of all leaks are the result of negligence. The most common forms of negligent data breaches occur due to the inappropriate removal of information—for instance, from a secure company system to an insecure home computer so that the employee can work from home—or due to simple theft of an insecure laptop or tape from a taxi cab, airport security checkpoint, or shipping box. However, breaches also occur due to negligent uses of technologies that are inappropriate for a particular use—for example, reassigning some type of medium (say, a page frame, disk sector, or magnetic tape) that contained one or more objects to an unrelated purpose without securely ensuring that the media contained no residual data.

It would be too easy to simply blame employees for any inappropriate use of information that results in the information being put at risk, followed by breaches. Employees have a job to do, and their understanding of that job is almost entirely based on what their employer tells them. What an employer tells an employee about the job is not limited to, and may not even primarily be in, the "job description." Instead, it will be in the feedback the employee receives on a day-to-day and year-to-year basis regarding their work. If the company in its routine communications to employees and its recurring training, performance reviews, and salary/bonus processes does not include security awareness, then employees will not understand security to be a part of their job.

The more complex the environment and types of media used, the more communication and training that are required to ensure that the environment is well protected. Further, except in government and military environments, company policies and even awareness training will not stop the most dedicated employees from making the best use of up-to-date consumer technologies, including those technologies not yet integrated into the corporate environment, and even those technologies not yet reasonably secured for the corporate environment or corporate information. Companies must stay aware of new consumer technologies and how employees (wish to) use them in the corporate environment. Just saying "no" will not stop an employee from using, say, a personal smartphone, a USB thumb drive, or webmail to forward corporate data to their home e-mail address in order to work on the data when out of the office. Companies must include in their technical security controls the ability to detect and/or prevent such actions through, for example, computer lockdowns, which prevent writing sensitive data to non-company-owned storage devices, such as USB thumb drives, and e-mailing sensitive information to non approved e-mail destinations.

Data Leak Prevention

Data leak prevention (DLP) comprises the actions that organizations take to prevent unauthorized external parties from gaining access to sensitive data. That definition has some key terms. First, the data has to be considered *sensitive*, the meaning of which we spent a good chunk of the beginning of this chapter discussing. We can't keep every single datum safely locked away inside our systems, so we focus our attention, efforts, and funds on the truly important data. Second, DLP is concerned with *external parties*. If somebody in the accounting department gains access to internal R&D data, that is a problem, but technically it is not considered a data leak. Finally, the external party gaining access to our sensitive data must be *unauthorized* to do so. If former business partners have some of our sensitive data that they were authorized to get at the time they were employed, then that is not considered a leak either. While this emphasis on semantics may seem excessive, it is necessary to properly approach this tremendous threat to our organizations.

EXAM TIP The terms data loss and data leak are used interchangeably by most security professionals. Technically, however, *data loss* means we do not know where the data is (e.g., after the theft of a laptop), while *data leak* means that the confidentiality of the data has been compromised (e.g., when the laptop thief posts the files on the Internet).

The real challenge to DLP is in taking a holistic view of our organization. This perspective must incorporate our people, our processes, and then our information. A common mistake when it comes to DLP is to treat the problem as a technological one. If all we do is buy or develop the latest technology aimed at stopping leaks, we are very likely to leak data. If, on the other hand, we consider DLP a program and not a project, and we pay due attention to our business processes, policies, culture, and people, then we have a good fighting chance at mitigating many or even most of the potential leaks. Ultimately, like everything else concerning information system security, we have to acknowledge that despite our best efforts, we will have bad days. The best we can do is stick to the program and make our bad days less frequent and less bad.

General Approaches to DLP

There is no one-size-fits-all approach to DLP, but there are tried-and-true principles that can be helpful. One important principle is the integration of DLP with our risk management processes. This allows us to balance out the totality of risks we face and favor controls that mitigate those risks in multiple areas simultaneously. Not only is this helpful in making the most of our resources, but it also keeps us from making decisions in one silo with little or no regard to their impacts on other silos. In the sections that follow, we will look at key elements of any approach to DLP.

Data Inventories It is difficult to defend an unknown target. Similarly, it is difficult to prevent the leaking of data of which we are unaware or whose sensitivity is unknown. Some organizations try to protect all their data from leakage, but this is not a good approach. For starters, acquiring the resources required to protect everything is likely cost prohibitive to most organizations. Even if an organization is able to afford this level of protection, it runs a very high risk of violating the privacy of its employees and/or customers by examining every single piece of data in its systems.

A good approach is to find and characterize all the data in your organization before you even look at DLP solutions. The task can seem overwhelming at first, but it helps to prioritize things a bit. You can start off by determining what is the most important kind of data for your organization. A compromise of these assets could lead to direct financial losses or give your competitors an advantage in your sector. Are these health care records? Financial records? Product designs? Military plans? Once you figure this out, you can start looking for that data across your servers, workstations, mobile devices, cloud computing platforms, and anywhere else it may live. Keep in mind that this data can live in a variety of formats (e.g., DBMS records or files) and media (e.g., hard drives or backup tapes). If your experience doing this for the first time is typical, you will probably be amazed at the places in which you find sensitive data.

Once you get a handle on what is your high-value data and where it resides, you can gradually expand the scope of your search to include less valuable, but still sensitive, data. For instance, if your critical data involves designs for next-generation radios, you would want to look for information that could allow someone to get insights into those designs even if they can't directly get them. So, for example, if you have patent filings, FCC license applications, and contracts with suppliers of electronic components, then an adversary may be able to use all this data to figure out what you're designing even without direct access to your new radio's plans. This is why it is so difficult for Apple to keep secret all the features of a new iPhone ahead of its launch. Often there is very little you can do to mitigate this risk, but some organizations have gone as far as to file patents and applications they don't intend to use in an effort to deceive adversaries as to their true plans. Obviously, and just as in any other security decision, the costs of these countermeasures must be weighted against the value of the information you're trying to protect. As you keep expanding the scope of your search, you will reach a point of diminishing returns in which the data you are inventorying is not worth the time you spend looking for it.

NOTE We cover the threats posed by adversaries compiling public information (aggregation) and using it to derive otherwise private information (inference) in Chapter 8.

Once you are satisfied that you have inventoried your sensitive data, the next step is to characterize it. We already covered the classification of information earlier in this chapter, so you should know all about data labels. Another element of this characterization is ownership. Who owns a particular set of data? Beyond that, who should be authorized to read or modify it? Depending on your organization, your data may have other characteristics of importance to the DLP effort, such as which data is regulated and how long it must be retained.

Data Flows Data that stays put is usually of little use to anyone. Most data will move according to specific business processes through specific network pathways. Understanding data flows at this intersection between business and IT is critical to implementing DLP. Many organizations put their DLP sensors at the perimeter of their networks, thinking that is where the leakages would occur. But if that's the only location these sensors are placed, a large number of leaks may not be detected or stopped. Additionally, as we will discuss in detail when we cover network-based DLP, perimeter sensors can often be bypassed by sophisticated attackers.

A better approach is to use a variety of sensors tuned to specific data flows. Suppose you have a software development team that routinely passes finished code to a quality assurance (QA) team for testing. The code is sensitive, but the QA team is authorized to read (and perhaps modify) it. However, the QA team is not authorized to access code under development or code from projects past. If an adversary compromises the computer used by a member of the QA team and attempts to access the source code for different projects, a DLP solution that is not tuned to that business process will not detect the compromise. The adversary could then repackage the data to avoid your perimeter monitors and successfully extract the data.

Data Protection Strategy The example just described highlights the need for a comprehensive, risk-based data protection strategy. A simple way for an adversary (internal or remote) to extract data from our systems is to encrypt it and/or use steganography to hide it within an innocuous file. *Steganography*, which we discuss in detail in Chapter 3, is the process of hiding data within other data such that it is difficult or impossible to detect the hidden content. The extent to which we attempt to mitigate these exfiltration routes depends on our assessment of the risk of their use. Obviously, as we increase our scrutiny of a growing set of data items, our costs will grow disproportionately. We usually can't watch everything all the time, so what do we do?

Once we have our data inventories and understand our data flows, we have enough information to do a risk assessment. Recall that we described this process in detail in Chapter 1. The trick is to incorporate data loss into that process. Since we can't guarantee that we will successfully defend against all attacks, we have to assume that sometimes our adversaries will gain access to our networks. Not only does our data protection strategy have to cover our approach to keeping attackers out, but it also must describe how we protect our data against a threat agent that is already inside. The following are some key areas to consider when developing data protection strategies:

- **Backup and recovery** Though we have been focusing our attention on data leaks, it is also important to consider the steps to prevent the loss of this data due to electromechanical or human failures. As we take care of this, we need to also consider the risk that, while we focus our attention on preventing leaks of our primary data stores, our adversaries may be focusing their attention on stealing the backups.

- **Data life cycle** Most of us can intuitively grasp the security issues at each of the stages of the data life cycle. However, we tend to disregard securing the data as it transitions from one stage to another. For instance, if we are archiving data at an offsite location, are we ensuring that it is protected as it travels there?
- **Physical security** While IT provides a wealth of tools and resources to help us protect our data, we must also consider what happens when an adversary just steals a hard drive left in an unsecured area, as happened to Sentara Heart Hospital in Norfolk, Virginia, in August 2015.
- **Security culture** Our information systems users can be a tremendous control if properly educated and incentivized. By developing a culture of security within our organizations, we not only reduce the incidence of users clicking on malicious links and opening attachments, but we also turn each of them into a security sensor, able to detect attacks that we may not otherwise be able to.
- **Privacy** Every data protection policy should carefully balance the need to monitor data with the need to protect our users' privacy. If we allow our users to check personal e-mail or visit social media sites during their breaks, would our systems be quietly monitoring their private communications?
- **Organizational change** Many large organizations grow because of mergers and acquisitions. When these changes happen, we must ensure that the data protection approaches of all entities involved are consistent and sufficient. To do otherwise is to ensure that the overall security posture of the new organization is the lesser of its constituents' security postures.

Implementation, Testing, and Tuning All the elements of a DLP process that we have discussed so far (i.e., data inventories, data flows, and data protection strategies) are administrative in nature. We finally get to discuss the part of DLP with which most of us are familiar: deploying and running a toolset. The sequence of our discussion so far has been deliberate in that the technological part needs to be informed by the other elements we've covered. Many organizations have wasted large sums of money on so-called solutions that, though well known and regarded, are just not suitable for their particular environment.

Assuming we've done our administrative homework and have a good understanding of our true DLP requirements, we can evaluate products according to our own criteria, not someone else's. The following are some aspects of a possible solution that most organizations will want to consider when comparing competing products:

- **Sensitive data awareness** Different tools will use different approaches to analyzing the sensitivity of documents' contents and the context in which they are being used. In general terms, the more depth of analysis and breadth of techniques that a product offers, the better. Typical approaches to finding and tracking sensitive data include keywords, regular expressions, tags, and statistical methods.

- **Policy engine** Policies are at the heart of any DLP solution. Unfortunately, not all policy engines are created equal. Some allow extremely granular control but require obscure methods for defining these policies. Other solutions are less expressive but are simple to understand. There is no right answer here, so each organization will weigh this aspect of a set of solutions differently.
- **Interoperability** DLP tools must play nicely with existing infrastructure, which is why most vendors will assure you that their product is interoperable. The trick becomes to determine precisely how this integration takes place. There are products that are technically interoperable but, in practice, require so much effort to integrate that they become infeasible.
- **Accuracy** At the end of the day, DLP solutions keep your data out of the hands of unauthorized entities. Therefore, the right solution is one that is accurate in its identification and prevention of incidents that result in the leakage of sensitive data. The best way to assess this criterion is by testing a candidate solution in an environment that mimics the actual conditions in the organization.

Once we select a DLP solution, the next interrelated tasks are integration, testing, and tuning. Obviously, we want to ensure that bringing the new toolset online won't disrupt any of our existing systems or processes, but testing needs to cover a lot more than that. The most critical elements when testing any DLP solution are to verify that it allows authorized data processing and to ensure that it prevents unauthorized data processing.

Verifying that authorized processes are not hampered by the DLP solution is fairly straightforward if we have already inventoried our data and the authorized flows. The data flows, in particular, will tell us exactly what our tests should look like. For instance, if we have a data flow for source code from the software development team to the QA team, then we should test that it is in fact allowed to occur by the new DLP tool. We probably won't have the resources to exhaustively test all flows, which means we should prioritize them based on their criticality to the organization. As time permits, we can always come back and test the remaining, and arguably less common or critical, processes (before our users do).

Testing the second critical element, that the DLP solution prevents unauthorized flows, requires a bit more work and creativity. Essentially, we are trying to imagine the ways in which threat agents might cause our data to leak. A useful tool in documenting these types of activities is called the misuse case. *Misuse cases* describe threat actors and the tasks they want to perform on the system. They are related to *use cases*, which are used by system analysts to document the tasks that authorized actors want to perform on a system. By compiling a list of misuse cases, we can keep a record of which data leak scenarios are most likely, most dangerous, or both. Just like we did when testing authorized flows, we can then prioritize which misuse cases we test first if we are resource constrained. As we test these potential misuses, it is important to ensure that the DLP system behaves in the manner we expect. That is to say, that it *prevents* a leak and doesn't just alert to it. Some organizations have been shocked to learn that their DLP solution has been alerting them about data leaks but doing nothing to stop them, letting their data leak right into the hands of their adversaries.

NOTE We cover misuse cases in detail in Chapter 6.

Finally, we must remember that everything changes. The solution that is exquisitely implemented, finely tuned, and effective immediately is probably going to be ineffective in the near future if we don't continuously maintain and improve it. Apart from the efficacy of the tool itself, our organizations change as people, products, and services come and go. The ensuing cultural and environmental changes will also change the effectiveness of our DLP solutions. And, obviously, if we fail to realize that users are installing rogue access points, using thumb drives without restriction, or clicking malicious links, then it is just a matter of time before our expensive DLP solution will be circumvented.

DLP Resiliency

Resiliency is the ability to deal with challenges, damage, and crises and bounce back to normal or near-normal condition in short order. It is an important element of security in general and of DLP in particular.

Assume your organization's information systems have been compromised (and it wasn't detected): what does the adversary do next, and how can you detect and deal with *that*? It is a sad reality that virtually all organizations have been attacked and that most have been breached. A key differentiator between those who withstand attacks relatively unscathed and those who suffer tremendous damage is their attitude toward operating in contested environments. If an organization's entire security strategy hinges on keeping the adversaries off its networks, then it will likely fail catastrophically when they manage to break in. If, on the other hand, the strategy builds on the concept of resiliency and accounts for the continuation of critical processes even with adversaries operating inside the perimeter, then the failures will likely be less destructive and restoration may be much quicker.

Network DLP

Network DLP (NDLP) applies data protection policies to data in motion. NDLP products are normally implemented as appliances that are deployed at the perimeter of an organization's networks. They can also be deployed at the boundaries of internal subnetworks and could be deployed as modules within a modular security appliance. Figure 2-7 shows how an NDLP solution might be deployed with a single appliance at the edge of the network and communicating with a DLP policy server.

From a practical perspective, the high cost of NDLP devices leads most organizations to deploy them at traffic choke points rather than throughout the network. Consequently, NDLP devices likely will not detect leaks that don't traverse the network segment on which the devices are installed. For example, suppose that an attacker is able to connect

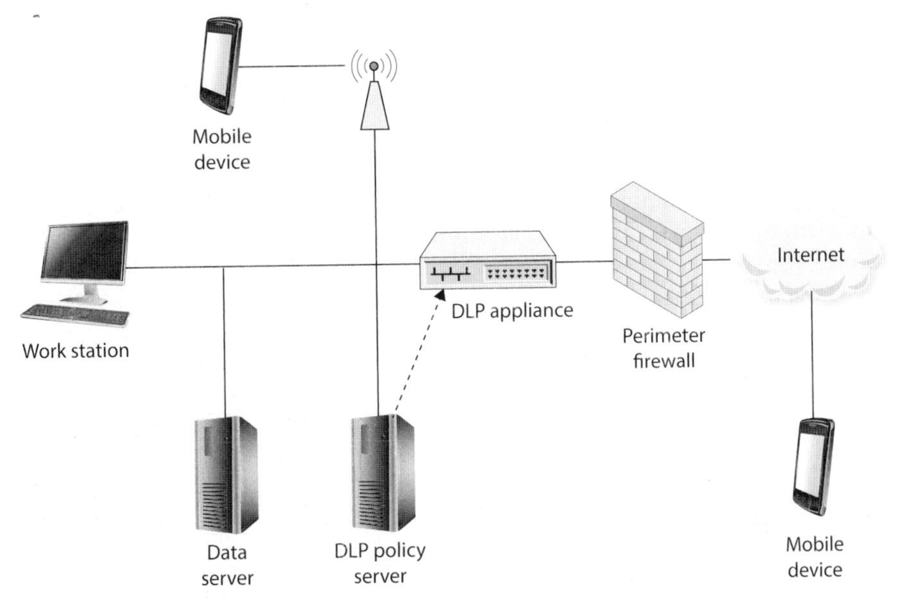

Figure 2-7 Network DLP

to a wireless access point and gain unauthorized access to a subnet that is not protected by an NDLP tool. This can be visualized in Figure 2-7 by supposing the attacker to be using the device connected to the WAP. Though this might seem like an obvious mistake, many organizations fail to consider their wireless subnets when planning for DLP. Alternatively, malicious insiders could connect their workstations directly to a mobile or external storage device, copy sensitive data, and remove it from the premises completely undetected.

The principal drawback of an NDLP solution is that it will not protect data on devices that are not on the organizational network. Mobile device users will be most at risk, since they will be vulnerable whenever they leave the premises. Since we expect the ranks of our mobile users to continue to increase into the future, this will be an enduring challenge for NDLP.

Endpoint DLP

Endpoint DLP (EDLP) applies protection policies to data at rest and data in use. EDLP is implemented in software running on each protected endpoint. This software, usually called a DLP agent, communicates with the DLP policy server to update policies and report events. Figure 2-8 illustrates an EDLP implementation.

EDLP allows a degree of protection that is normally not possible with NDLP. The reason is that the data is observable at the point of creation. When a user enters PII on the device during an interview with a client, the EDLP agent detects the new sensitive

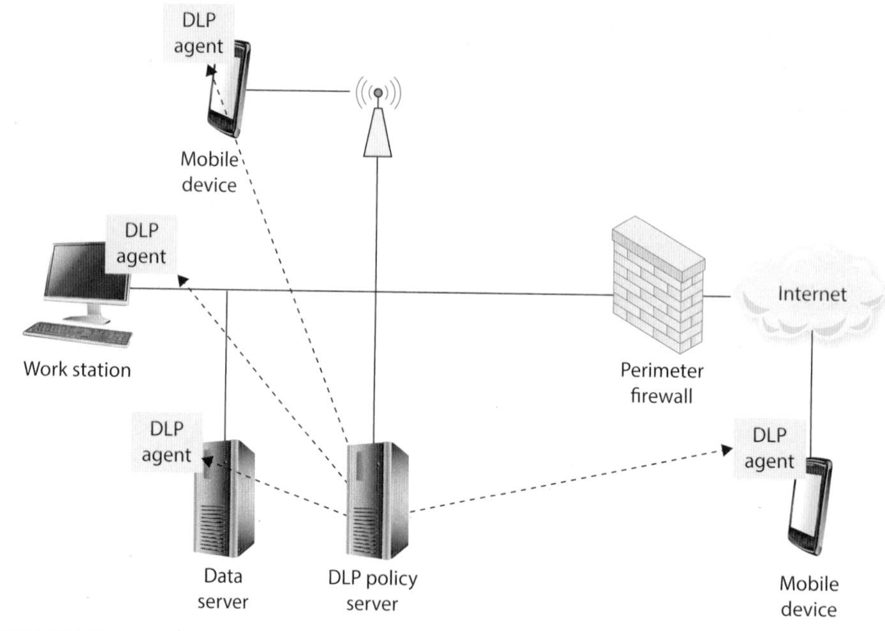

Figure 2-8 Endpoint DLP

data and immediately applies the pertinent protection policies to it. Even if the data is encrypted on the device when it is at rest, it will have to be decrypted whenever it is in use, which allows for EDLP inspection and monitoring. Finally, if the user attempts to copy the data to a non-networked device such as a thumb drive, or if it is improperly deleted, EDLP will pick up on these possible policy violations. None of these examples would be possible using NDLP.

The main drawback of EDLP is complexity. Compared to NDLP, these solutions require a lot more presence points in the organization, and each of these points may have unique configuration, execution, or authentication challenges. Additionally, since the agents must be deployed to every device that could possibly handle sensitive data, the cost could be much higher than that of an NDLP solution. Another challenge is ensuring that all the agents are updated regularly, both for software patches and policy changes. Finally, since a pure EDLP solution is unaware of data-in-motion protection violations, it would be possible for attackers to circumvent the protections (e.g., by disabling the agent through malware) and leave the organization blind to the ongoing leakages. It is typically harder to disable NDLP, because it is normally implemented in an appliance that is difficult for attackers to exploit.

Hybrid DLP

Another approach to DLP is to deploy both NDLP and EDLP across the enterprise. Obviously, this approach is the costliest and most complex. For organizations that can

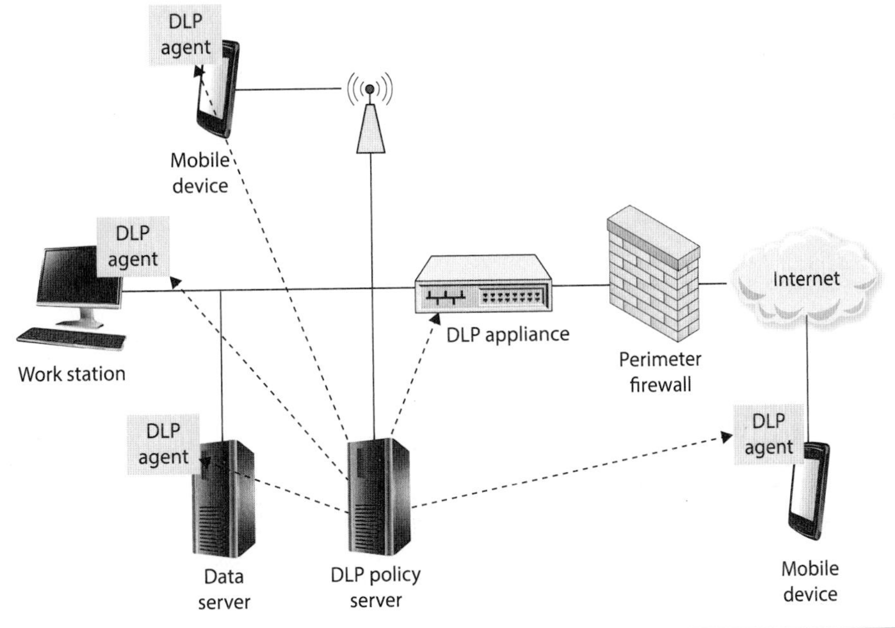

Figure 2-9 Hybrid NDLP/EDLP

afford it, however, it offers the best coverage. Figure 2-9 shows how a hybrid NDLP/ EDLP deployment might look.

Protecting Other Assets

Thus far we have focused our attention on protecting electronic data, but we must also protect all other information assets. The goal of this section is not to provide an inclusive list of all assets that require protection, but rather to highlight some of the most important and pilferable of such assets. After all, if we lock our digital egress points tightly enough, our adversaries may simply resort to old-fashioned burglary.

Protecting Mobile Devices

Mobile device theft is increasing at incredible rates each year. Stealing mobile devices is not a new trend, but in the past they were stolen mainly to sell the hardware. Now mobile devices are increasingly being stolen to gain sensitive data for identity theft crimes. What is important to understand is that this is a rampant, and potentially very dangerous, crime. For many of us, significant chunks of our professional and personal lives are chronicled in our laptops or smartphones. Employees who use these devices as they travel for work may have extremely sensitive company or customer data on their systems that

can easily fall into the wrong hands. The following list provides many of the protection mechanisms that can be used to protect mobile devices and the data they hold:

- Inventory all mobile devices, including serial numbers, so they can be properly identified if they are stolen and then recovered.
- Harden the operating system by applying baseline secure configurations.
- Password-protect the BIOS on laptops.
- Register all devices with their respective vendors, and file a report with the vendor when a device is stolen. If a stolen device is sent in for repairs after it is stolen, it will be flagged by the vendor if you have reported the theft.
- Do not check mobile devices as luggage when flying. Always carry them on with you.
- Never leave a mobile device unattended, and carry it in a nondescript carrying case.
- Engrave the device with a symbol or number for proper identification.
- Use a slot lock with a cable to connect a laptop to a stationary object whenever possible.
- Back up all data on mobile devices to an organizationally controlled repository.
- Encrypt all data on a mobile device.
- Enable remote wiping of data on the device.

Tracing software can be installed so that your device can "phone home" if it is taken from you. Several products offer this tracing capability. Once installed and configured, the software periodically sends in a signal to a tracking center or allows you to track it through a website or application. If you report that your device has been stolen, the vendor of this software may work with service providers and law enforcement to track down and return your laptop.

Paper Records

It is easy to forget that most organizations still process information on paper records. The fact that this is relatively rare compared to the volume of their electronic counterparts is little consolation when a printed e-mail with sensitive information finds its way into the wrong hands and potentially causes just as much damage. Here are some principles to consider when protecting paper records:

- Educate your staff on proper handling of paper records.
- Minimize the use of paper records.
- Ensure workspaces are kept tidy so it is easy to tell when sensitive papers are left exposed, and routinely audit workspaces to ensure sensitive documents are not exposed.
- Lock away all sensitive paperwork as soon as you are done with it.

- Prohibit taking sensitive paperwork home.
- Label all paperwork with its classification level. Ideally, also include its owner's name and disposition (e.g., retention) instructions.
- Conduct random searches of employees' bags as they leave the office to ensure sensitive materials are not being taken home.
- Destroy unneeded sensitive papers using a crosscut shredder. For very sensitive papers, consider burning them instead.

Safes

A company may have need for a safe. Safes are commonly used to store backup data tapes, original contracts, or other types of valuables. The safe should be penetration resistant and provide fire protection. The types of safes an organization can choose from are

- **Wall safe** Embedded into the wall and easily hidden
- **Floor safe** Embedded into the floor and easily hidden
- **Chests** Stand-alone safes
- **Depositories** Safes with slots, which allow the valuables to be easily slipped in
- **Vaults** Safes that are large enough to provide walk-in access

If a safe has a combination lock, it should be changed periodically, and only a small subset of people should have access to the combination or key. The safe should be in a visible location, so anyone who is interacting with the safe can be seen. The goal is to uncover any unauthorized access attempts. Some safes have passive or thermal relocking functionality. If the safe has a *passive relocking* function, it can detect when someone attempts to tamper with it, in which case extra internal bolts will fall into place to ensure it cannot be compromised. If a safe has a *thermal relocking* function, when a certain temperature is met (possibly from drilling), an extra lock is implemented to ensure the valuables are properly protected.

Summary

Protecting assets, particularly information, is critical to any organization and must be incorporated into the comprehensive risk management process described in the previous chapter. This protection will probably require different controls at different phases in the information life cycle, so it is important to consider phase-specific risks when selecting controls. Rather than trying to protect all information equally, our organizations need classification standards that help us identify, handle, and protect data according to its sensitivity and criticality. We must also consider the roles played by various people in the organization. From the senior executives to the newest and most junior member of the team, everyone who interacts with our information has (and should understand) specific responsibilities with regard to protecting our assets.

A key responsibility is the protection of privacy of personal information. For various legal, regulatory, and operational reasons, we want to limit how long we hold on to personal information. There is no one-size-fits-all approach to data retention, so it is incumbent on the organization's leadership to consider a multitude of factors when developing privacy and data retention policies. These policies, in turn, should drive risk-based controls, baselines, and standards applied to the protection of our information. A key element in applying controls needs to be the proper use of strong cryptography.

Quick Tips

- Information goes through a life cycle that starts with its acquisition and ends with its disposal.
- Each phase of the information life cycle requires different considerations when assessing risks and selecting controls.
- New information is prepared for use by adding metadata, including classification labels.
- Ensuring the consistency of data must be a deliberate process in organizations that use data replication.
- Data aggregation may lead to an increase in classification levels.
- Cryptography can be an effective control at all phases of the information life cycle.
- The data retention policy drives the timeframe at which information transitions from the archival phase to the disposal phase of its life cycle.
- Information classification corresponds to the information's value to the organization.
- Each classification should have separate handling requirements and procedures pertaining to how that data is accessed, used, and destroyed.
- Senior executives are ultimately responsible to the shareholders for the successes and failures of their corporations, including security issues.
- The data owner is the manager in charge of a specific business unit and is ultimately responsible for the protection and use of a specific subset of information.
- Data owners specify the classification of data, and data custodians implement and maintain controls to enforce the set classification levels.
- The data retention policy must consider legal, regulatory, and operational requirements.
- The data retention policy should address what data is to be retained, where, how, and for how long.

- Electronic discovery (e-discovery) is the process of producing for a court or external attorney all electronically stored information (ESI) pertinent to a legal proceeding.
- Normal deletion of a file does not permanently remove it from media.
- NIST SP 800-88, Revision 1, "Guidelines for Media Sanitization," describes the best practices for combating data remanence.
- Overwriting data entails replacing the 1's and 0's that represent it on storage media with random or fixed patterns of 1's and 0's to render the original data unrecoverable.
- Degaussing is the process of removing or reducing the magnetic field patterns on conventional disk drives or tapes.
- Privacy pertains to personal information, both from your employees and your customers.
- Generally speaking, organizations should collect the least amount of private personal data required for the performance of their business functions.
- Data at rest refers to data that resides in external or auxiliary storage devices, such as hard drives or optical discs.
- Every major operating system supports whole-disk encryption, which is a good way to protect data at rest.
- Data in motion is data that is moving between computing nodes over a data network such as the Internet.
- TLS, IPSec, and VPNs are typical ways to use cryptography to protect data in motion.
- Data in use is the term for data residing in primary storage devices, such as volatile memory (e.g., RAM), memory caches, or CPU registers.
- A data leak means that the confidentiality of the data has been compromised.
- Data leak prevention (DLP) comprises the actions that organizations take to prevent unauthorized external parties from gaining access to sensitive data.
- Network DLP (NDLP) applies data protection policies to data in motion.
- Endpoint DLP (EDLP) applies data protection policies to data at rest and data in use.
- Mobile devices are easily lost or stolen and should proactively be configured to mitigate the risks of data loss or leakage.
- Paper products oftentimes contain information that deserves controls commensurate to the sensitivity and criticality of that information.

Questions

Please remember that these questions are formatted and asked in a certain way for a reason. Keep in mind that the CISSP exam is asking questions at a conceptual level. Questions may not always have the perfect answer, and the candidate is advised against always looking for the perfect answer. Instead, the candidate should look for the best answer in the list.

1. Which of the following statements is true about the information life cycle?
   - **A.** The information life cycle begins with its archival and ends with its classification.
   - **B.** Most information must be retained indefinitely.
   - **C.** The information life cycle begins with its acquisition/creation and ends with its disposal/destruction.
   - **D.** Preparing information for use does not typically involve adding metadata to it.
2. Ensuring data consistency is important for all the following reasons, *except*
   - **A.** Replicated data sets can become desynchronized.
   - **B.** Multiple data items are commonly needed to perform a transaction.
   - **C.** Data may exist in multiple locations within our information systems.
   - **D.** Multiple users could attempt to modify data simultaneously.
3. Which of the following makes the most sense for a single organization's classification levels for data?
   - **A.** Unclassified, Secret, Top Secret
   - **B.** Public, Releasable, Unclassified
   - **C.** Sensitive, Sensitive But Unclassified (SBU), Proprietary
   - **D.** Proprietary, Trade Secret, Private
4. Which of the following is the most important criterion in determining the classification of data?
   - **A.** The level of damage that could be caused if the data were disclosed
   - **B.** The likelihood that the data will be accidentally or maliciously disclosed
   - **C.** Regulatory requirements in jurisdictions within which the organization is not operating
   - **D.** The cost of implementing controls for the data
5. The effect of data aggregation on classification levels is best described by which of the following?
   - **A.** Data classification standards apply to all the data within an organization.
   - **B.** Aggregation is a disaster recovery technique with no effect on classification.
   - **C.** A low-classification aggregation of data can be deconstructed into higher-classification data items.
   - **D.** Items of low-classification data combine to create a higher-classification set.

6. Who bears ultimate responsibility for the protection of assets within the organization?
   A. Data owners
   B. Cyber insurance providers
   C. Senior management
   D. Security professionals
7. During which phase or phases of the information life cycle can cryptography be an effective control?
   A. Use
   B. Archival
   C. Disposal
   D. All the above
8. A transition into the disposal phase of the information life cycle is most commonly triggered by
   A. Senior management
   B. Insufficient storage
   C. Acceptable use policies
   D. Data retention policies
9. Information classification is most closely related to which of the following?
   A. The source of the information
   B. The information's destination
   C. The information's value
   D. The information's age
10. The data owner is most often described by all of the following *except*
    A. Manager in charge of a business unit
    B. Ultimately responsible for the protection of the data
    C. Financially liable for the loss of the data
    D. Ultimately responsible for the use of the data
11. Data at rest is commonly
    A. Using a RESTful protocol for transmission
    B. Stored in registers
    C. Being transmitted across the network
    D. Stored in external storage devices

12. Data in motion is commonly
    A. Using a RESTful protocol for transmission
    B. Stored in registers
    C. Being transmitted across the network
    D. Stored in external storage devices
13. Data in use is commonly
    A. Using a RESTful protocol for transmission
    B. Stored in registers
    C. Being transmitted across the network
    D. Stored in external storage devices
14. Who has the primary responsibility of determining the classification level for information?
    A. The functional manager
    B. Senior management
    C. The owner
    D. The user
15. If different user groups with different security access levels need to access the same information, which of the following actions should management take?
    A. Decrease the security level on the information to ensure accessibility and usability of the information.
    B. Require specific written approval each time an individual needs to access the information.
    C. Increase the security controls on the information.
    D. Decrease the classification label on the information.
16. What should management consider the most when classifying data?
    A. The type of employees, contractors, and customers who will be accessing the data
    B. Availability, integrity, and confidentiality
    C. Assessing the risk level and disabling countermeasures
    D. The access controls that will be protecting the data
17. Who is ultimately responsible for making sure data is classified and protected?
    A. Data owners
    B. Users
    C. Administrators
    D. Management

18. Which of the following requirements should the data retention policy address?
    A. Legal
    B. Regulatory
    C. Operational
    D. All the above
19. Which of the following is *not* addressed by the data retention policy?
    A. What data to keep
    B. For whom data is kept
    C. How long data is kept
    D. Where data is kept
20. Which of the following best describes an application of cryptography to protect data at rest?
    A. VPN
    B. Degaussing
    C. Whole-disk encryption
    D. Up-to-date antivirus software
21. Which of the following best describes an application of cryptography to protect data in motion?
    A. Testing software against side-channel attacks
    B. TLS
    C. Whole-disk encryption
    D. EDLP
22. Which of the following best describes the mitigation of data remanence by a physical destruction process?
    A. Replacing the 1's and 0's that represent data on storage media with random or fixed patterns of 1's and 0's
    B. Converting the 1's and 0's that represent data with the output of a cryptographic function
    C. Removing or reducing the magnetic field patterns on conventional disk drives or tapes
    D. Exposing storage media to caustic or corrosive chemicals that render it unusable

23. Which of the following best describes the mitigation of data remanence by a degaussing destruction process?
    A. Replacing the 1's and 0's that represent data on storage media with random or fixed patterns of 1's and 0's
    B. Converting the 1's and 0's that represent data with the output of a cryptographic function
    C. Removing or reducing the magnetic field patterns on conventional disk drives or tapes
    D. Exposing storage media to caustic or corrosive chemicals that render it unusable
24. Which of the following best describes the mitigation of data remanence by an overwriting process?
    A. Replacing the 1's and 0's that represent data on storage media with random or fixed patterns of 1's and 0's
    B. Converting the 1's and 0's that represent data with the output of a cryptographic function
    C. Removing or reducing the magnetic field patterns on conventional disk drives or tapes
    D. Exposing storage media to caustic or corrosive chemicals that render it unusable

Answers

1. **C.** Although various information life-cycle models exist, they all begin with the creation or acquisition of the information and end with its ultimate disposal (typically destruction).
2. **B.** Although it is typically true that multiple data items are needed for a transaction, this has much less to do with the need for data consistency than do the other three options. Consistency is important because we oftentimes keep multiple copies of a given data item.
3. **A.** This is a typical set of classification levels for government and military organizations. Each of the other options has at least two terms that are synonymous or nearly synonymous.
4. **A.** There are many criteria for classifying information, but it is most important to focus on the value of the data or the potential loss from its disclosure. The likelihood of disclosure, irrelevant jurisdictions, and cost considerations should not be central to the classification process.

5. **D.** Data aggregation can become a classification issue whenever someone can combine data items and end up with a higher-classification aggregate. For instance, a person's name, address, phone number, or date of birth are normally not PII by themselves. However, when combined, they do become PII under the definition of most jurisdictions with applicable laws.
6. **C.** Senior management always carries the ultimate responsibility for the organization.
7. **D.** Cryptography can be an effective control at every phase in the information life cycle. During information acquisition, a cryptographic hash can certify its integrity. When sensitive information is in use or in archives, encryption can protect it from unauthorized access. Finally, encryption can be an effective means of destroying the data.
8. **D.** Data retention policies should be the primary reason for the disposal of most of our information. Senior management or lack of resources should seldom, if ever, be the reason we dispose of data, while acceptable use policies have little, if anything, to do with it.
9. **C.** Information classification is very strongly related to the information's value and/or risk. For instance, trade secrets that are the key to a business's success are highly valuable, which will lead to a higher classification level. Similarly, information that could severely damage a company's reputation presents a high level of risk and is similarly classified at a higher level.
10. **C.** The data owner is the manager in charge of a specific business unit, and is ultimately responsible for the protection and use of a specific subset of information. In most situations, this person is not financially liable for the loss of his or her data.
11. **D.** Data at rest is characterized by residing in secondary storage devices such as disk drives, DVDs, or magnetic tapes. Registers are temporary storage within the CPU and are used for data storage only when the data is being used.
12. **C.** Data in motion is characterized by network or off-host transmission. The RESTful protocol, while pertaining to a subset of data on a network, is not as good an answer as option C.
13. **B.** Registers are used only while data is being used by the CPU, so when data is resident in registers, it is, by definition, in use.
14. **C.** A company can have one specific data owner or different data owners who have been delegated the responsibility of protecting specific sets of data. One of the responsibilities that goes into protecting this information is properly classifying it.
15. **C.** If data is going to be available to a wide range of people, more granular security should be implemented to ensure that only the necessary people access the data and that the operations they carry out are controlled. The security implemented can come in the form of authentication and authorization technologies, encryption, and specific access control mechanisms.

16. **B.** The best answer to this question is B, because to properly classify data, the data owner must evaluate the availability, integrity, and confidentiality requirements of the data. Once this evaluation is done, it will dictate which employees, contractors, and users can access the data, which is expressed in answer A. This assessment will also help determine the controls that should be put into place.
17. **D.** The key to this question is the use of the word "ultimately." Though management can delegate tasks to others, it is ultimately responsible for everything that takes place within a company. Therefore, it must continually ensure that data and resources are being properly protected.
18. **D.** The data retention policy should follow the laws of any jurisdiction within which the organization's data resides. It must similarly comply with any regulatory requirements. Finally, the policy must address the organization's operational requirements.
19. **B.** The data retention policy should address what data to keep, where to keep it, how to store it, and for how long to keep it. The policy is not concerned with "for whom" the data is kept.
20. **C.** Data at rest is best protected using whole-disk encryption on the user workstations or mobile computers. None of the other options apply to data at rest.
21. **B.** Data in motion is best protected by network encryption solutions such as TLS, VPN, or IPSec. None of the other options apply to data in motion.
22. **D.** Two of the most common approaches to destroying data physically involve shredding the storage media or exposing it to corrosive or caustic chemicals. In certain highly sensitive government organizations, these approaches are used in tandem to make the risk of data remanence negligible.
23. **C.** Degaussing is typically accomplished by exposing magnetic media (such as hard disk drives or magnetic tapes) to powerful magnetic fields in order to change the orientation of the particles that physically represent 1's and 0's.
24. **A.** Data remanence can be mitigated by overwriting every bit on the storage medium. This is normally accomplished by writing all 0's, or all 1's, or a fixed pattern of them, or a random sequence of them. Better results can be obtained by repeating the process with different patterns multiple times.

CHAPTER 3

Security Engineering

This chapter presents the following:

- System architecture
- Trusted computing base and security mechanisms
- Information security software models
- Assurance evaluation criteria and ratings
- Certification and accreditation processes
- Distributed systems security
- Cryptography components and their relationships
- Steganography
- Public key infrastructure (PKI)
- Site and facility design considerations
- Physical security risks, threats, and countermeasures
- Electric power issues and countermeasures
- Fire prevention, detection, and suppression

As an engineer I'm constantly spotting problems and plotting how to solve them.

—James Dyson

Organizations today are concerned with a myriad of potential security issues, including those pertaining to the confidential data stored in their databases, the security of their web farms that are connected directly to the Internet, the integrity of data-entry values going into applications that process business-oriented information, external attackers attempting to bring down servers and affecting productivity, malware spreading, the internal consistency of data warehouses, mobile device security, advanced persistent threats, and much more. These issues have the potential to not only affect productivity and profitability, but also raise legal and liability issues. Companies, and the management that runs them, can be held accountable if a security issue arises in any one of the many areas previously mentioned. So it is, or at least it should be, very important for companies to know what security measures they need to put in place and to establish means to properly assure that the necessary level of protection is actually being provided by the products they develop or purchase.

Many of these security issues must be thought through as we develop or engineer any service or product. Security is best if it is designed and built into the foundation of anything we build and not added as an afterthought. Once security is integrated as an important part of the design, it has to be engineered, implemented, tested, evaluated, and potentially certified and accredited. The security of a product must be evaluated against the availability, integrity, and confidentiality it claims to provide. What gets tricky is that organizations and individuals commonly do not fully understand what it actually takes for software to provide these services in an effective manner. Of course a company wants a piece of software to provide solid confidentiality, but does the person who is actually purchasing this software product know the correct questions to ask and what to look for? Does this person ask the vendor about cryptographic key protection, encryption algorithms, and what software development life-cycle model the vendor followed? Does the purchaser know to ask about hashing algorithms, message authentication codes, fault tolerance, and built-in redundancy options? The answer is "not usually." Not only do most people not fully understand what has to be in place to properly provide availability, integrity, and confidentiality, but it is very difficult to decipher what a piece of software is and is not carrying out properly without the necessary knowledge base.

This chapter covers security engineering from the ground up. It then goes into how systems are evaluated and rated by governments and other agencies, and what these ratings actually mean. We spend a good amount of time discussing cryptology, because it underlies most of our security controls. Finally, after covering how to keep our adversaries from virtually touching our systems, we also cover how to keep them from physically reaching them as well. However, before we dive into these concepts, it is important to understand what we mean by system-based architectures and the components that make them up.

EXAM TIP It is no coincidence that Security Engineering is the second largest domain in the CISSP BOK. The degree to which we properly engineer security into our systems will enable or hinder everything else we do.

System Architecture

In Chapter 1 we covered enterprise architecture frameworks and introduced their direct relationship to system architecture. As explained in that chapter, an *architecture* is a tool used to conceptually understand the structure and behavior of a complex entity through different views. An *architecture description* is a formal description and representation of a system, the components that make it up, the interactions and interdependencies between those components, and the relationship to the environment. An architecture provides different views of the system, based upon the needs of the stakeholders of that system.

CAUTION It is common for people in technology to not take higher-level, somewhat theoretical concepts such as architecture seriously because they see them as fluffy and nonpractical, and they cannot always relate these concepts to what they see in their daily activities. While knowing how to configure a server is important, it is actually more important for more people in the industry to understand how to actually build that server securely in the first place. Make sure to understand security across the spectrum, from a high-level theoretical perspective to a practical hands-on perspective. If no one focuses on how to properly carry out secure system architecture, we will be doomed to always have insecure systems.

Before digging into the meat of system architecture, we need to establish the correct terminology. Although people use terms such as "design," "architecture," and "software development" interchangeably, each of these terms has a distinct meaning that you need to understand to really learn system architecture correctly.

A system *architecture* describes the major components of the system and how they interact with each other, with the users, and with other systems. An architecture is at the highest level when it comes to the overall process of system development. It is at the architectural level that we are answering questions such as "How is it going to be used?," "What environment will it work within?," "What type of security and protection is required?," and "What does it need to be able to communicate with?" The answers to these types of questions outline the main goals the system must achieve, and they help us construct the system at an abstract level. This abstract architecture provides the "big picture" goals, which are used to guide the rest of the development process.

The term *development* refers to the entire life cycle of a system, including the planning, analysis, design, building, testing, deployment, maintenance, and retirement phases. Though many people think of development as simply the part of this process that results in a new system, the reality is that it must consider if not include the entire cradle-to-grave lifetime of the system. Within this development, there is a subset of activities that are involved in deciding how the system will be put together. This *design* phase starts with the architecting effort described previously and progresses through the detailed description of everything needed to build the system.

It is worth pausing briefly here to make sure you understand what "system" means in the context of system architecture. When most people hear this term, they think of an individual computer, but a system can be an individual computer, an application, a select set of subsystems, a set of computers, or a set of networks made up of computers and applications. A system can be simplistic, as in a single-user operating system dedicated to a specific task, or as complex as an enterprise network made up of heterogeneous multiuser systems and applications. So when we look at system architectures, this could apply to very complex and distributed environments or very focused subsystems. We need to make sure we understand the scope of the target system before we can develop or evaluate it or its architecture.

There are evolving standards that outline the specifications of system architectures. First IEEE came up with a standard (Standard 1471) that was called *IEEE Recommended Practice for Architectural Description of Software-Intensive Systems*. This was adopted by ISO and published in 2011 as ISO/IEC/IEEE 42010, *Systems and software engineering—Architecture description*. The standard is evolving and being improved upon. The goal is to internationally standardize how system architecture takes place so that product developers aren't just "winging it" and coming up with their own proprietary approaches. A disciplined approach to system architecture allows for better quality, interoperability, extensibility, portability, and security.

One of the purposes of ISO/IEC 42010:2011 is to establish a shared vocabulary among all the stakeholders. Among these terms are the following:

- **Architecture** Fundamental organization of a system embodied in its components, their relationships to each other and to the environment, and the principles guiding its design and evolution.
- **Architecture description (AD)** Collection of document types to convey an architecture in a formal manner.
- **Stakeholder** Individual, team, or organization (or classes thereof) with interests in, or concerns relative to, a system.
- **View** Representation of a whole system from the perspective of a related set of concerns.
- **Viewpoint** A specification of the conventions for constructing and using a view. A template from which to develop individual views by establishing the purposes and audience for a view and the techniques for its creation and analysis.

As an analogy, if you are going to build your own house, you are first going to have to work with an architect. She will ask you a bunch of questions to understand your overall "goals" for the house, as in four bedrooms, three bathrooms, family room, game room, garage, 3,000 square feet, ranch style, etc. Once she collects your goal statements, she will create the different types of documentation (blueprint, specification documents) that describe the architecture of the house in a formal manner (architecture description). The architect needs to make sure she meets several people's (stakeholders) goals for this house—not just yours. She needs to meet zoning requirements, construction requirements, legal requirements, and your design requirements. Each stakeholder needs to be presented with documentation and information (views) that map to their needs and understanding of the house. One architecture schematic can be created for the plumber, a different schematic can be created for the electrician, another one can be created for the zoning officials, and one can be created for you. Each stakeholder needs to have information about this house in terms that they understand and that map to their specific concerns. If the architect gives you documentation about the electrical current requirements and location of where electrical grounding will take place, that does not help you. You need to see the view of the architecture that directly relates to your needs.

The same is true with a system. An architect needs to capture the goals that the system is supposed to accomplish for each stakeholder. One stakeholder is concerned about the functionality of the system, another one is concerned about the performance, another is concerned about interoperability, and yet another stakeholder is concerned about security. The architect then creates documentation that formally describes the architecture of the system for each of these stakeholders that will best address their concerns from their own viewpoints. Each stakeholder will review the architecture description to ensure that the architect has not missed anything. After the architecture description is approved, the software designers and developers are brought in to start building the system.

The relationship between these terms and concepts is illustrated in Figure 3-1.

The *stakeholders* for a system include (but are not limited to) the users, operators, maintainers, developers, and suppliers. Each stakeholder has his own *concerns* pertaining to the system, which can include performance, functionality, security, maintainability, quality of service, usability, cost, etc. The system's architecture description needs to express the architect's decisions addressing each concern of each stakeholder, which is done through *architecture views*. Each view conforms to a particular viewpoint. Useful viewpoints on a system include logical, physical, structural, behavioral, management, cost, and security, among many others.

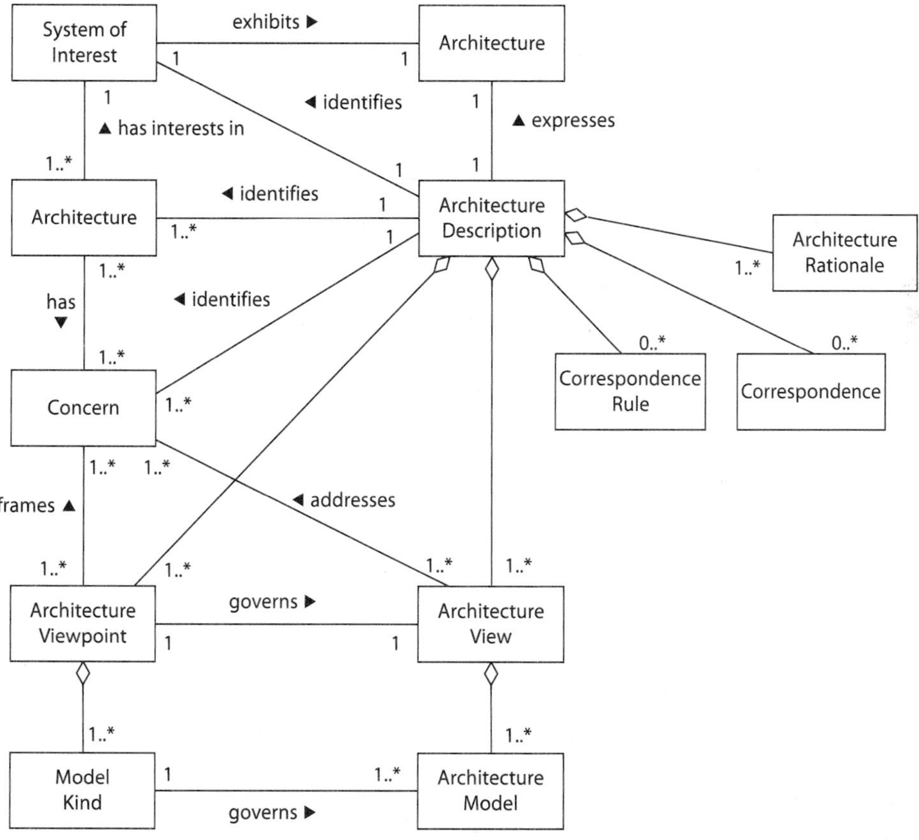

Figure 3-1 Formal architecture terms and relationships (Image from www.iso-architecture.org/42010/cm/)

The creation and use of system architect processes are evolving, becoming more disciplined and standardized. In the past, system architectures were developed to meet the identified stakeholders' concerns (functionality, interoperability, performance), but a new concern has come into the limelight—security. So new systems need to meet not just the old concerns, but also the new concerns the stakeholders have. Security goals have to be defined *before* the architecture of a system is created, and specific security views of the system need to be created to help guide the design and development phases. When we hear about security being "bolted on," that means security concerns are addressed at the development (programming) phase and not the architecture phase. When we state that security needs to be "baked in," this means that security has to be integrated at the architecture phase.

EXAM TIP While a system architecture addresses many stakeholder concerns, we will focus on the concern of security since information security is the crux of the CISSP exam.

Computer Architecture

Computer architecture encompasses all of the parts of a computer system that are necessary for it to function, including the central processing unit, memory chips, logic circuits, storage devices, input and output devices, security components, buses, and networking interfaces. The interrelationships and internal working of all of these parts can be quite complex, and making them work together in a secure fashion consists of complicated methods and mechanisms. Thank goodness for the smart people who figured this stuff out! Now it is up to us to learn how they did it and why.

The more you understand how these different pieces work and process data, the more you will understand how vulnerabilities actually occur and how countermeasures work to impede and hinder vulnerabilities from being introduced, found, and exploited.

NOTE This chapter interweaves the hardware and operating system architectures and their components to show you how they work together.

The Central Processing Unit

The *central processing unit (CPU)* is the brain of a computer. In the most general description possible, it fetches instructions from memory and executes them. Although a CPU is a piece of hardware, it has its own instruction set that is necessary to carry out its tasks. Each CPU type has a specific architecture and set of instructions that it can carry out. The operating system must be designed to work within this CPU architecture. This is why one operating system may work on a Pentium Pro processor but not on an AMD processor. The operating system needs to know how to "speak the language" of the processor, which is the processor's instruction set.

The chips within the CPU cover only a couple of square inches, but contain millions of transistors. All operations within the CPU are performed by electrical signals at different voltages in different combinations, and each transistor holds this voltage, which represents 0's and 1's to the operating system. The CPU contains registers that point to memory locations that contain the next instructions to be executed and that enable the CPU to keep status information of the data that needs to be processed. A *register* is a temporary storage location. Accessing memory to get information on what instructions and data must be executed is a much slower process than accessing a register, which is a component of the CPU itself. So when the CPU is done with one task, it asks the registers, "Okay, what do I have to do now?" And the registers hold the information that tells the CPU what its next job is.

The actual execution of the instructions is done by the *arithmetic logic unit (ALU)*. The ALU performs mathematical functions and logical operations on data. The ALU can be thought of as the brain of the CPU, and the CPU as the brain of the computer.

Software holds its instructions and data in memory. When an action needs to take place on the data, the instructions and data memory addresses are passed to the CPU registers, as shown in Figure 3-2. When the control unit indicates that the CPU can process them, the instructions and data memory addresses are passed to the CPU. The CPU sends out requests to fetch these instructions and data from the provided addresses and then actual processing, number crunching, and data manipulation take place. The results are sent back to the requesting process's memory address.

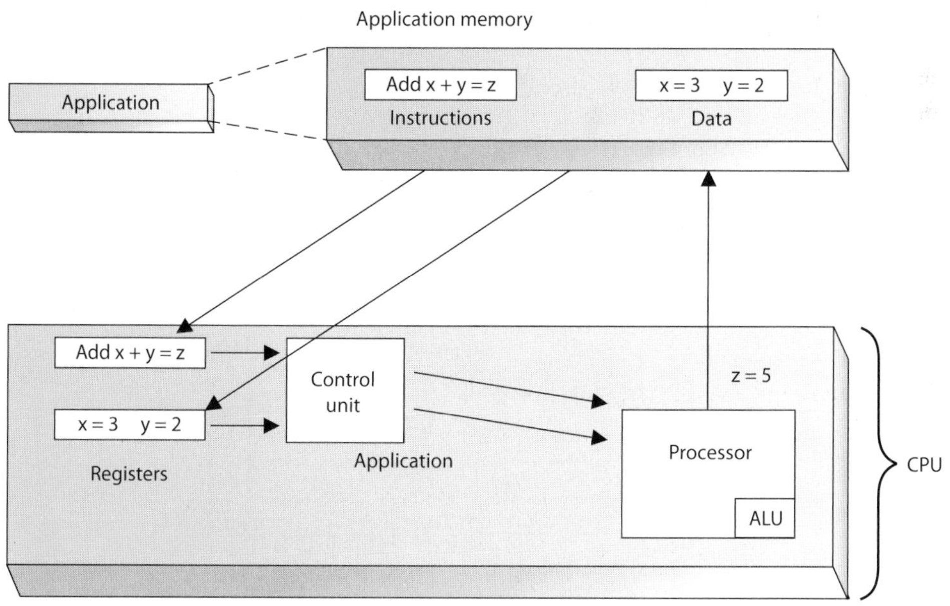

Figure 3-2 Instruction and data addresses are passed to the CPU for processing.

An operating system and applications are really just made up of lines and lines of instructions. These instructions contain empty variables, which are populated at run time. The empty variables hold the actual data. There is a difference between instructions and data. The instructions have been written to carry out some type of functionality on the data. For example, let's say you open a Calculator application. In reality, this program is just lines of instructions that allow you to carry out addition, subtraction, division, and other types of mathematical functions that will be executed on the data you provide. So, you type in 3 + 5. The 3 and the 5 are the data values. Once you click the = button, the Calculator program tells the CPU it needs to take the instructions on how to carry out addition and apply these instructions to the two data values 3 and 5. The ALU carries out this instruction and returns the result of 8 to the requesting program. This is when you see the value 8 in the Calculator's field. To users, it seems as though the Calculator program is doing all of this on its own, but it is incapable of this. It depends upon the CPU and other components of the system to carry out this type of activity.

The *control unit* manages and synchronizes the system while different applications' code and operating system instructions are being executed. The control unit is the component that fetches the code, interprets the code, and oversees the execution of the different instruction sets. It determines what application instructions get processed and in what priority and time slice. It controls when instructions are executed, and this execution enables applications to process data. The control unit does not actually process the data. It is like the traffic cop telling vehicles when to stop and start again, as illustrated in Figure 3-3. The CPU's time has to be sliced up into individual units and assigned to processes. It is this time slicing that fools the applications and users into thinking the system is actually carrying out several different functions at one time. While the operating system can carry out several different functions at one time (multitasking), in reality, the CPU is executing the instructions in a serial fashion (one at a time).

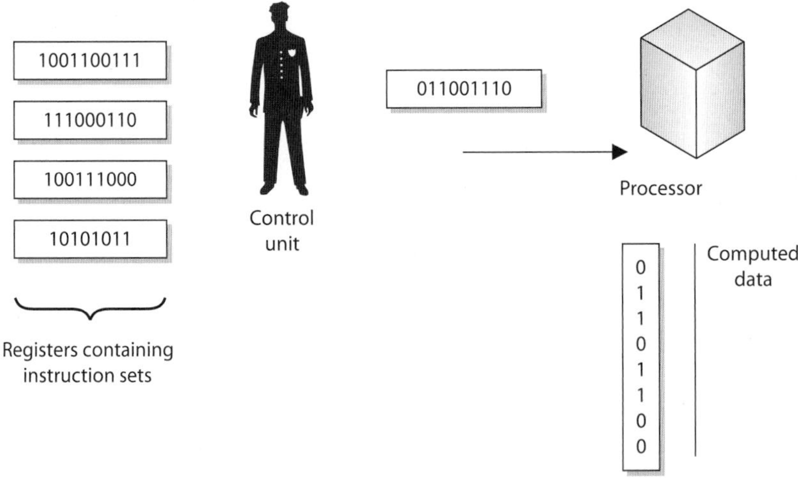

Figure 3-3 The control unit works as a traffic cop, indicating when instructions are sent to the processor.

A CPU has several different types of registers, containing information about the instruction set and data that must be executed. *General registers* are used to hold variables and temporary results as the ALU works through its execution steps. The general registers are like the ALU's scratch pad, which it uses while working. *Special registers* (dedicated registers) hold information such as the program counter, stack pointer, and program status word (PSW). The *program counter* register contains the memory address of the next instruction to be fetched. After that instruction is executed, the program counter is updated with the memory address of the next instruction set to be processed. It is similar to a boss-and-secretary relationship. The secretary keeps the boss on schedule and points her to the necessary tasks she must carry out. This allows the boss to just concentrate on carrying out the tasks instead of having to worry about the "busy work" being done in the background.

The *program status word (PSW)* holds different condition bits. One of the bits indicates whether the CPU should be working in *user mode* (also called *problem state*) or *privileged mode* (also called *kernel* or *supervisor mode*). An important theme of this chapter is to teach you how operating systems protect themselves. They need to protect themselves from applications, software utilities, and user activities if they are going to provide a stable and safe environment. One of these protection mechanisms is implemented through the use of these different execution modes. When an application needs the CPU to carry out its instructions, the CPU works in user mode. This mode has a lower privilege level, and many of the CPU's instructions and functions are not available to the requesting application. The reason for the extra caution is that the developers of the operating system and CPU do not know who developed the application or how it is going to react, so the CPU works in a lower privilege mode when executing these types of instructions. By analogy, if you are expecting visitors who are bringing their two-year-old boy, you move all of the breakables that someone under three feet tall can reach. No one is ever sure what a two-year-old toddler is going to do, but it usually has to do with breaking something. An operating system and CPU are not sure what applications are going to attempt, which is why this code is executed in a lower privilege and critical resources are out of reach of the application's code.

If the PSW has a bit value that indicates the instructions to be executed should be carried out in privileged mode, this means a trusted process (an operating system process) made the request and can have access to the functionality that is not available in user mode. An example would be if the operating system needed to communicate with a peripheral device. This is a privileged activity that applications cannot carry out. When these types of instructions are passed to the CPU, the PSW is basically telling the CPU, "The process that made this request is an all-right guy. We can trust him. Go ahead and carry out this task for him."

Memory addresses of the instructions and data to be processed are held in registers until needed by the CPU. The CPU is connected to an *address bus*, which is a hardwired connection to the RAM chips in the system and the individual input/output (I/O) devices. Memory is cut up into sections that have individual addresses associated with them. I/O devices (optical discs, USB devices, printers, and so on) are also allocated specific unique addresses. If the CPU needs to access some data, either from memory or from an I/O device, it sends a *fetch request* on the address bus. The fetch request contains the address of where the needed data is located. The circuitry associated with the memory or I/O device recognizes the address the CPU sent down the address bus and instructs the memory or device to read the requested data and put it on the *data bus*. So the address bus is used by the CPU to indicate the location of the instructions to be processed, and the memory or I/O device responds by sending the data that resides at that memory location through the data bus. As an analogy, if Sally calls you on the telephone and tells you the book she needs you to mail to her, this would be like a CPU sending a fetch request down the address bus. You locate the book Sally requested and send it to her in the mail, which would be similar to how an I/O device finds the requested data and puts it on the data bus for the CPU to receive.

This process is illustrated in Figure 3-4.

Once the CPU is done with its computation, it needs to return the results to the requesting program's memory. So, the CPU sends the requesting program's address down the address bus and sends the new results down the data bus with the command `write`. This new data is then written to the requesting program's memory space. Following our earlier example, once the CPU adds 3 and 5 and sends the new resulting data to the Calculator program, you see the result as 8.

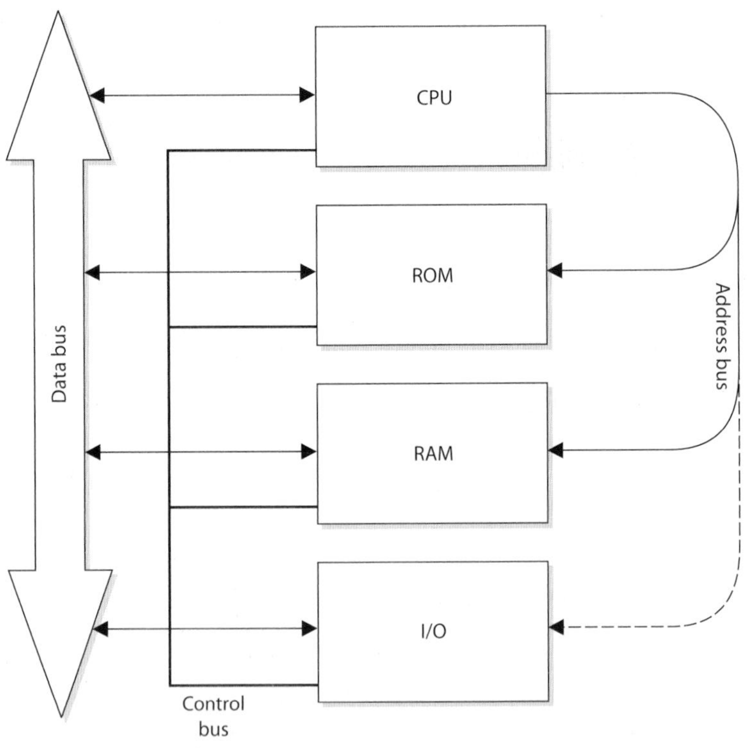

Figure 3-4 Address and data buses are separate and have specific functionality.

The address and data buses can be 8, 16, 32, or 64 bits wide. Most systems today use a 64-bit address bus, which means the system can have a large address space (2^{64}). Systems can also have a 64-bit data bus, which means the system can move data in parallel back and forth between memory, I/O devices, and the CPU of this size. (A 64-bit data bus means the size of the chunks of data a CPU can request at a time is 64 bits.) But what does this really mean and why does it matter? A two-lane highway can be a bottleneck if a lot of vehicles need to travel over it. This is why highways are increased to four, six, and eight lanes. As computers and software get more complex and performance demands increase, we need to get more instructions and data to the CPU faster so it can do its work on these items and get them back to the requesting program as fast as possible. So we need fatter pipes (buses) to move more stuff from one place to another place.

Multiprocessing

Many modern computers have more than one CPU for increased performance. An operating system must be developed specifically to be able to understand and work with more than one processor. If the computer system is configured to work in *symmetric mode*, this means the processors are handed work as needed, as shown with CPU 1 and CPU 2 in Figure 3-5. It is like a load-balancing environment. When a process needs instructions to be executed, a scheduler determines which processor is ready for more work and sends it on. If a processor is going to be dedicated to a specific task or application, all other

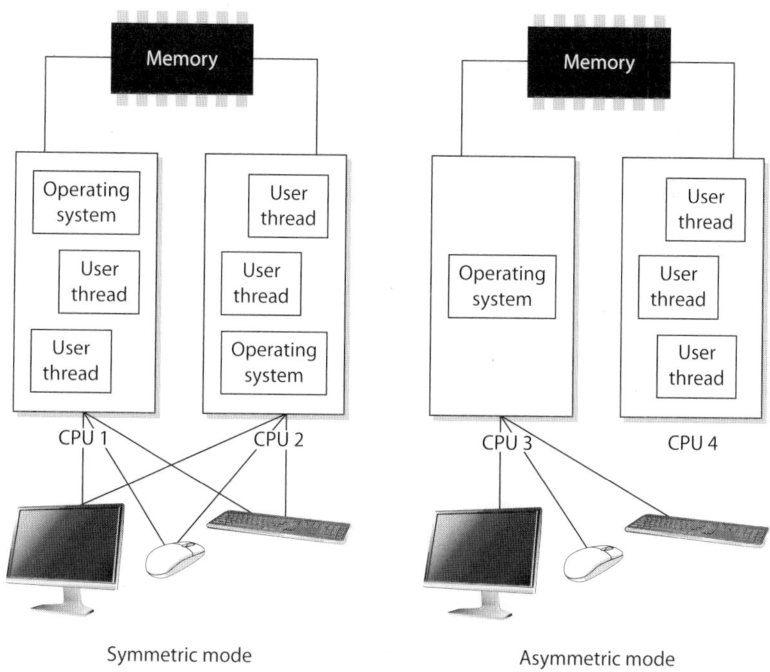

Figure 3-5 Symmetric mode and asymmetric mode of multiprocessing

software would run on a different processor. In Figure 3-5, CPU 4 is dedicated to one application and its threads, while CPU 3 is used by the operating system. When a processor is dedicated, as in this example, the system is working in *asymmetric mode*. This usually means the computer has some type of time-sensitive application that needs its own personal processor. So, the system scheduler will send instructions from the time-sensitive application to CPU 4 and send all the other instructions (from the operating system and other applications) to CPU 3.

Memory Types

Memory management is critical, but what types of memory actually have to be managed? As stated previously, the operating system instructions, applications, and data are held in memory, but so are the basic input/output system (BIOS), device controller instructions, and firmware. They do not all reside in the same memory location or even the same type of memory. The different types of memory, what they are used for, and how each is accessed can get a bit confusing because the CPU deals with several different types for different reasons.

The following sections outline the different types of memory that can be used within computer systems.

Random Access Memory

Random access memory (RAM) is a type of temporary storage facility where data and program instructions can temporarily be held and altered. It is used for read/write activities by the operating system and applications. It is described as volatile because if the computer's power supply is terminated, then all information within this type of memory is lost.

RAM is an integrated circuit made up of millions of transistors and capacitors. The capacitor is where the actual charge is stored, which represents a 1 or 0 to the system. The transistor acts like a gate or a switch. A capacitor that is storing a binary value of 1 has several electrons stored in it, which have a negative charge, whereas a capacitor that is storing a 0 value is empty. When the operating system writes over a 1 bit with a 0 bit, in reality, it is just emptying out the electrons from that specific capacitor.

One problem is that these capacitors cannot keep their charge for long. Therefore, a memory controller has to "recharge" the values in the capacitors, which just means it continually reads and writes the same values to the capacitors. If the memory controller does not "refresh" the value of 1, the capacitor will start losing its electrons and become a 0 or a corrupted value. This explains how *dynamic RAM (DRAM)* works. The data being held in the RAM memory cells must be continually and dynamically refreshed so your bits do not magically disappear. This activity of constantly refreshing takes time, which is why DRAM is slower than static RAM.

TIP When we are dealing with memory activities, we use a time metric of nanoseconds (ns), which is a billionth of a second. So if you look at your RAM chip and it states 70 ns, this means it takes 70 nanoseconds to read and refresh each memory cell.

Static RAM (SRAM) does not require this continuous-refreshing nonsense; it uses a different technology, by holding bits in its memory cells without the use of capacitors, but it *does* require more transistors than DRAM. Since SRAM does not need to be refreshed, it is faster than DRAM, but because SRAM requires more transistors, it takes up more space on the RAM chip. Manufacturers cannot fit as many SRAM memory cells on a memory chip as they can DRAM memory cells, which is why SRAM is more expensive. So, DRAM is cheaper and slower, and SRAM is more expensive and faster. It always seems to go that way. SRAM has been used in cache, and DRAM is commonly used in RAM chips.

Because life is not confusing enough, we have many other types of RAM. The main reason for the continual evolution of RAM types is that it directly affects the speed of the computer itself. Many people mistakenly think that just because you have a fast processor, your computer will be fast. However, memory type and size and bus sizes are also critical components. Think of memory as pieces of paper used by the system to hold instructions. If the system had small pieces of papers (small amount of memory) to read and write from, it would spend most of its time looking for these pieces and lining them up properly. When a computer spends more time moving data from one small portion of memory to another than actually processing the data, it is referred to as *thrashing*. This causes the system to crawl in speed and your frustration level to increase.

The size of the data bus also makes a difference in system speed. You can think of a data bus as a highway that connects different portions of the computer. If a ton of data must go from memory to the CPU and can only travel over a 4-lane highway, compared to a 64-lane highway, there will be delays in processing.

Increased addressing space also increases system performance. A system that uses a 64-bit addressing scheme can put more instructions and data on a data bus at one time compared to a system that uses a 32-bit addressing scheme. So a larger addressing scheme allows more stuff to be moved around and processed, and a larger bus size provides the highway to move this stuff around quickly and efficiently.

So the processor, memory type and amount, memory addressing, and bus speeds are critical components to system performance.

The following are additional types of RAM you should be familiar with:

- **Synchronous DRAM (SDRAM)** Synchronizes itself with the system's CPU and synchronizes signal input and output on the RAM chip. It coordinates its activities with the CPU clock so the timing of the CPU and the timing of the memory activities are synchronized. This increases the speed of transmitting and executing data.
- **Extended data out DRAM (EDO DRAM)** This is faster than DRAM because DRAM can access only one block of data at a time, whereas EDO DRAM can capture the next block of data while the first block is being sent to the CPU for processing. It has a type of "look ahead" feature that speeds up memory access.
- **Burst EDO DRAM (BEDO DRAM)** Works like (and builds upon) EDO DRAM in that it can transmit data to the CPU as it carries out a read option, but it can send more data at once (burst). It reads and sends up to four memory addresses in a small number of clock cycles.

- **Double data rate SDRAM (DDR SDRAM)** Carries out read operations on the rising and falling cycles of a clock pulse. So instead of carrying out one operation per clock cycle, it carries out two and thus can deliver twice the throughput of SDRAM. Basically, it doubles the speed of memory activities, when compared to SDRAM, with a smaller number of clock cycles. Pretty groovy.

TIP These different RAM types require different controller chips to interface with them; therefore, the motherboards that these memory types are used on often are very specific in nature.

Well, that's enough about RAM for now. Let's look at other types of memory that are used in basically every computer in the world.

Hardware Segmentation

Systems of a higher trust level may need to implement *hardware segmentation* of the memory used by different processes. This means memory is separated physically instead of just logically. This adds another layer of protection to ensure that a lower-privileged process does not access and modify a higher-level process's memory space.

Read-Only Memory

Read-only memory (ROM) is a nonvolatile memory type, meaning that when a computer's power is turned off, the data is still held within the memory chips. When data is written into ROM memory chips, the data cannot be altered. Individual ROM chips are manufactured with the stored program or routines designed into it. The software that is stored within ROM is called *firmware.*

Programmable read-only memory (PROM) is a form of ROM that can be modified after it has been manufactured. PROM can be programmed only one time because the voltage that is used to write bits into the memory cells actually burns out the fuses that connect the individual memory cells. The instructions are "burned into" PROM using a specialized PROM programmer device.

Erasable programmable read-only memory (EPROM) can be erased, modified, and upgraded. EPROM holds data that can be electrically erased or written to. To erase the data on the memory chip, you need your handy-dandy ultraviolet (UV) light device that provides just the right level of energy. The EPROM chip has a quartz window, which is where you point the UV light. Although playing with UV light devices can be fun for the whole family, we have moved on to another type of ROM technology that does not require this type of activity.

To erase an EPROM chip, you must remove the chip from the computer and wave your magic UV wand, which erases *all* of the data on the chip—not just portions of it. So someone invented *electrically erasable programmable read-only memory (EEPROM)*, and we all put our UV light wands away for good.

EEPROM is similar to EPROM, but its data storage can be erased and modified electrically by onboard programming circuitry and signals. This activity erases only 1 byte at a time, which is slow. And because we are an impatient society, yet another technology was developed that is very similar, but works more quickly.

Flash memory is a special type of memory that is used in digital cameras, BIOS chips, memory cards, and video game consoles. It is a solid-state technology, meaning it does not have moving parts and is used more as a type of hard drive than memory.

Flash memory basically moves around different levels of voltages to indicate that a 1 or 0 must be held in a specific address. It acts as a ROM technology rather than a RAM technology. (For example, you do not lose pictures stored on your memory stick in your digital camera just because your camera loses power. RAM is volatile, and ROM is non-volatile.) When Flash memory needs to be erased and turned back to its original state, a program initiates the internal circuits to apply an electric field. The erasing function takes place in blocks or on the entire chip instead of erasing 1 byte at a time.

Flash memory is used as a small disk drive in most implementations. Its benefits over a regular hard drive are that it is smaller, faster, and lighter. So let's deploy Flash memory everywhere and replace our hard drives! Maybe one day. Today it is relatively expensive compared to regular hard drives.

Cache Memory

Cache memory is a type of memory used for high-speed writing and reading activities. When the system assumes (through its programmatic logic) that it will need to access specific information many times throughout its processing activities, it will store the information in cache memory so it is easily and quickly accessible. Data in cache can be accessed much more quickly than data stored in other memory types. Therefore, any information needed by the CPU very quickly and very often is usually stored in cache memory, thereby improving the overall speed of the computer system.

An analogy is how the brain stores information it uses often. If one of Marge's primary functions at her job is to order parts, which requires telling vendors the company's address, Marge stores this address information in a portion of her brain from which she can easily and quickly access it. This information is held in a type of cache. If Marge was asked to recall her third-grade teacher's name, this information would not necessarily be held in cache memory, but in a more long-term storage facility within her noggin. The long-term storage within her brain is comparable to a system's hard drive. It takes more time to track down and return information from a hard drive than from specialized cache memory.

TIP Different motherboards have different types of cache. Level 1 (L1) is faster than Level 2 (L2), and L2 is faster than L3. Some processors and device controllers have cache memory built into them. L1 and L2 are usually built into the processors and the controllers themselves.

Memory Mapping

Because there are different types of memory holding different types of data, a computer system does not want to let every user, process, and application access all types of memory anytime they want to. Access to memory needs to be controlled to ensure data does not get corrupted and that sensitive information is not available to unauthorized processes. This type of control takes place through memory mapping and addressing.

The CPU is one of the most trusted components within a system, and can access memory directly. It uses physical addresses instead of pointers (logical addresses) to memory segments. The CPU has physical wires connecting it to the memory chips within the computer. Because physical wires connect the two types of components, physical addresses are used to represent the intersection between the wires and the transistors on a memory chip. Software does not use physical addresses; instead, it employs logical memory addresses. Accessing memory indirectly provides an access control layer between the software and the memory, which is done for protection and efficiency. Figure 3-6 illustrates how the CPU can access memory directly using physical addresses and how software must use memory indirectly through a memory mapper.

Let's look at an analogy. You would like to talk to Mr. Marshall about possibly buying some acreage in Iowa that he has listed for sale on Craigslist. You don't know Mr. Marshall personally, and you do not want to give out your physical address and have him show up at your doorstep. Instead, you would like to use a more abstract and controlled way of communicating, so you give Mr. Marshall your phone number so you can talk to him about the land and determine whether you want to meet him in person. The same type of thing happens in computers. When a computer runs software, it does not want to expose

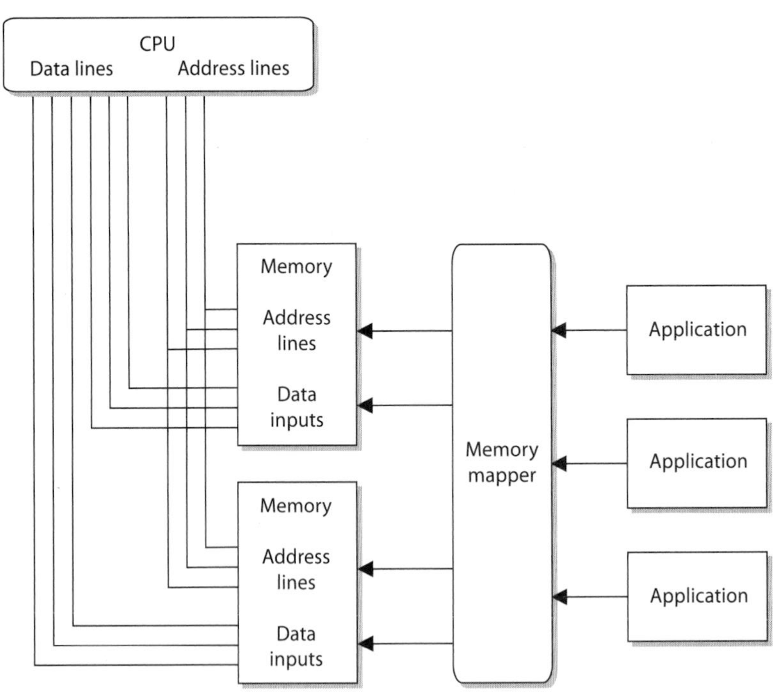

Figure 3-6 The CPU and applications access memory differently.

itself unnecessarily to software written by good and bad programmers alike. Operating systems enable software to access memory indirectly by using index tables and pointers, instead of giving them the right to access the memory directly. This is one way the computer system protects itself. If an operating system has a programming flaw that allows an attacker to directly access memory through physical addresses, there is no memory manager involved to control how memory is being used.

When a program attempts to access memory, its access rights are verified and then instructions and commands are carried out in a way to ensure that badly written code does not affect other programs or the system itself. Applications, and their processes, can only access the memory allocated to them, as shown in Figure 3-7. This type of memory architecture provides protection and efficiency.

The physical memory addresses that the CPU uses are called *absolute addresses*. The indexed memory addresses that software uses are referred to as *logical addresses*. And *relative addresses* are based on a known address with an offset value applied. As explained previously, an application does not "know" it is sharing memory with other applications. When the program needs a memory segment to work with, it tells the memory manager how much memory it needs. The memory manager allocates this much physical memory, which could have the physical addressing of 34000 to 39000, for example. But the application is not written to call upon addresses in this numbering scheme. It is most likely developed to call upon addresses starting with 0 and extending to, let's say, 5000.

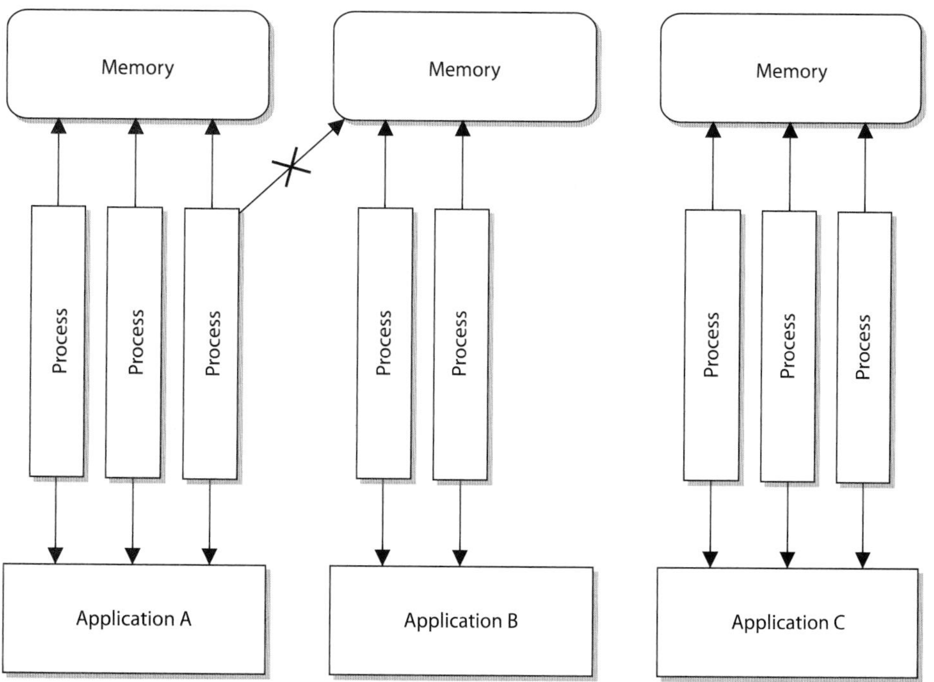

Figure 3-7 Applications, and the processes they use, access their own memory segments only.

So the memory manager allows the application to use its own addressing scheme—the logical addresses. When the application makes a call to one of these "phantom" logical addresses, the memory manager must map this address to the actual physical address. (It's like two people using their own naming scheme. When Bob asks Diane for a ball, Diane knows he really means a stapler. Don't judge Bob and Diane; it works for them.)

The mapping process is illustrated in Figure 3-8. When a thread indicates the instruction needs to be processed, it provides a logical address. The memory manager maps the logical address to the physical address, so the CPU knows where the instruction is located. The thread will actually be using a relative address because the application uses the address space of 0 to 5000. When the thread indicates it needs the instruction at the memory address 3400 to be executed, the memory manager has to work from its mapping of logical address 0 to the actual physical address and then figure out the physical address for the logical address 3400. So the logical address 3400 is relative to the starting address 0.

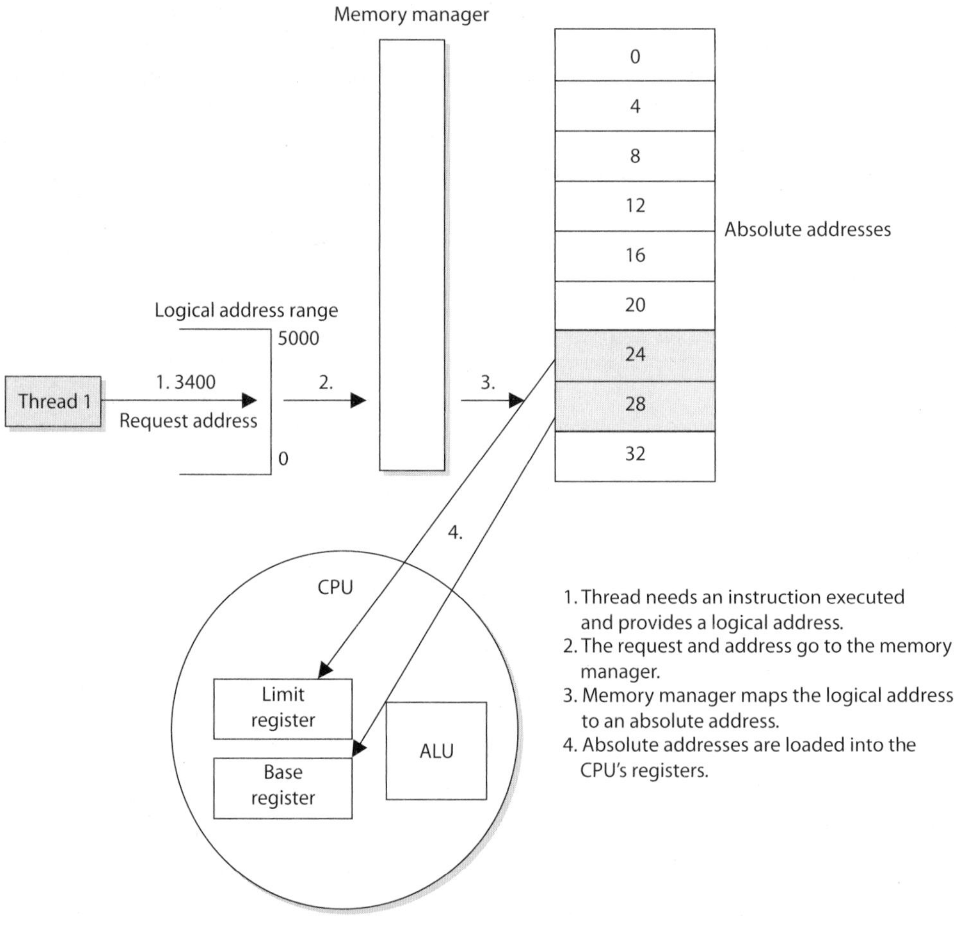
Memory manager
0
4
8
12
16
20
24
28
32
Absolute addresses
Logical address range
5000
0
Thread 1
1. 3400
Request address
2.
3.
4.
CPU
Limit register
Base register
ALU
1. Thread needs an instruction executed and provides a logical address.
2. The request and address go to the memory manager.
3. Memory manager maps the logical address to an absolute address.
4. Absolute addresses are loaded into the CPU's registers.

Figure 3-8 The CPU uses absolute addresses, and software uses logical addresses.

As an analogy, if Jane knows you use a different number system than everyone else in the world, and you tell her that you need 14 cookies, she would need to know where to start in *your* number scheme to figure out how many cookies to really give you. So, if you inform Jane that in "your world" your numbering scheme starts at 5, she would map 5 to 0 and know that the offset is a value of 5. So when you tell her you want 14 cookies (the relative number), she takes the offset value into consideration. She knows that you start at the value 5, so she maps your logical address of 14 to the physical number of 9.

So the application is working in its "own world" using its "own addresses," and the memory manager has to map these values to reality, which means the absolute address values.

Memory management is complex, and whenever there is complexity, there are most likely vulnerabilities that can be exploited by attackers. It is very easy for people to complain about software vendors and how they do not produce software that provides the necessary level of security, but hopefully you are gaining more insight into the actual complexity that is involved with these tasks.

Buffer Overflows

Today, many people know the term "buffer overflow" and the basic definition, but it is important for security professionals to understand what is going on beneath the covers.

A *buffer overflow* takes place when too much data is accepted as input to a specific process. A *buffer* is an allocated segment of memory. A buffer can be overflowed arbitrarily with too much data, but for it to be of any use to an attacker, the code inserted into the buffer must be of a specific length, followed up by commands the attacker wants executed. So, the purpose of a buffer overflow may be either to make a mess, by shoving arbitrary data into various memory segments, or to accomplish a specific task, by pushing into the memory segment a carefully crafted set of data that will accomplish a specific task. This task could be to open a command shell with administrative privilege or execute malicious code.

Let's take a deeper look at how this is accomplished. Software may be written to accept data from a user, website, database, or another application. The accepted data needs something to happen to it because it has been inserted for some type of manipulation or calculation, or to be used as a parameter to be passed to a procedure. A procedure is code that can carry out a specific type of function on the data and return the result to the requesting software, as shown in Figure 3-9.

When a programmer writes a piece of software that will accept data, this data and its associated instructions will be stored in the buffers that make up a stack. The buffers need to be the right size to accept the inputted data. So if the input is supposed to be one character, the buffer should be 1 byte in size. If a programmer does not ensure that only 1 byte of data is being inserted into the software, then someone can input several characters at once and thus overflow that specific buffer.

TIP You can think of a buffer as a small bucket to hold water (data). We have several of these small buckets stacked on top of one another (memory stack), and if too much water is poured into the top bucket, it spills over into the buckets below it (buffer overflow) and overwrites the instructions and data on the memory stack.

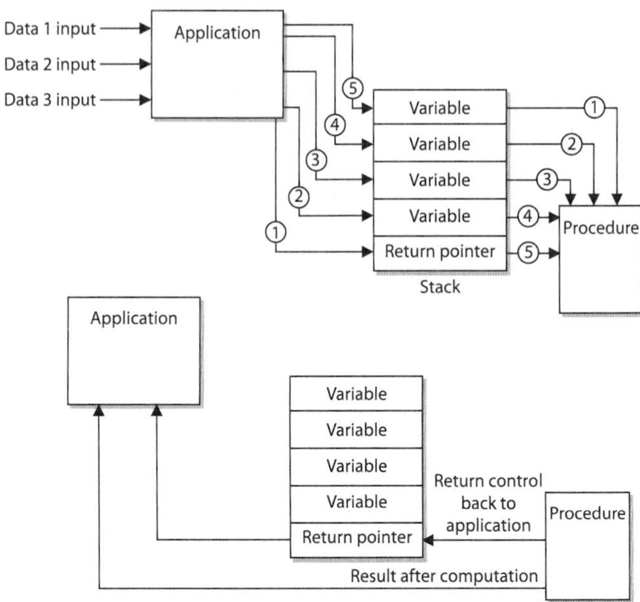

Figure 3-9 A memory stack has individual buffers to hold instructions and data.

If you are interacting with an application that calculates mortgage rates, you have to put in the parameters that need to be calculated—years of loan, percentage of interest rate, and amount of loan. These parameters are passed into empty variables and put in a linear construct (memory stack), which acts like a queue for the procedure to pull from when it carries out this calculation. The first thing your mortgage rate application lays down on the stack is its return pointer (RP). This is a pointer to the requesting application's memory address that tells the procedure to return control to the requesting application after the procedure has worked through all the values on the stack. The mortgage rate application then places on top of the return pointer the rest of the data you have input and sends a request to the procedure to carry out the necessary calculation, as illustrated in Figure 3-9. The procedure takes the data off the stack starting at the top, so they are first in, last out (FILO). The procedure carries out its functions on all the data and returns the result and control back to the requesting mortgage rate application once it hits the return pointer in the stack.

An important aspect of the stack is that, in most modern operating systems, it grows downward. This means that if you have a 32-bit architecture and push a 4-byte value (also known as a word) into the stack at, say, memory address 102, then the next 4-byte value you push will go into address 101. The practical offshoot of this is that if you overflow a variable in the stack (for instance, by writing 8 bytes into a 4-byte variable), you will start overwriting the values of whatever variable was pushed into the stack before the one you're writing. Keep this in mind when we start exploiting the stack in the following paragraphs.

So the stack is just a segment in memory that allows for communication between the requesting application and the procedure or subroutine. The potential for problems comes into play when the requesting application does not carry out proper *bounds checking* to ensure the inputted data is of an acceptable length. Look at the following C code to see how this could happen:

```
#include<stdio.h>
char color[5];
void getColor () {
    char userInput[5];
    printf ("Enter your favorite color: pink or blue ");
    gets (userInput);
    strcpy (userInput, color);
}
int main(int argc, char **argv)
{
    // some program features...
    getColor (userInput);
    // other program features...
    return 0;
}
```

EXAM TIP You do not need to know C programming for the CISSP exam. We are digging deep into this topic because buffer overflows are so common and have caused grave security breaches over the years. For the CISSP exam, you just need to understand the overall concept of a buffer overflow.

Let's focus on the part of this sample vulnerable program that receives as input a user's favorite color (pink or blue) and stores it in an array of characters called `color`. Since the only choice the user should enter is pink or blue, the programmer naively assumed he would only need a five-character array (four for the letters of each word and one for the null character that denotes the end of the string). When the program runs, it eventually calls a function called `getColor` that displays a prompt to the user, receives the user's input in a temporary variable called `userInput`, and copies the user's input from the temporary variable to the `color` array. Execution then returns to the `main` function, and the program does other things and eventually terminates normally.

There are three key elements that make this program vulnerable to a buffer overflow:

- We are not validating the user's input, which violates one of the golden rules of secure programming: never trust any inputs! If the user inadvertently or maliciously chooses a color or string longer than four characters, we will have a crashed program.
- We make a function call, which pushes the return pointer (as well as the address of the `userInput` temporary variable) into the stack. There is nothing wrong with calling functions (in fact, it is almost always necessary), but it is the function call mechanism that makes a stack overflow possible.
- We use an insecure function (`strcpy`) that copies values without ensuring they do not exceed the size of the destination. In fact, this last issue is so critical that the compiler will give you a warning if you try to compile this program.

The first and third elements should be pretty self-evident. But why is the function call a key element to a buffer overflow vulnerability? To understand why this is so, recall that we mentioned that whenever a function is called, we push the return pointer (RP)—the address of the next instruction to be executed when the function returns—into the stack. In other words, we are leaving a value that is critical to the correct behavior of the process in an unprotected place (the stack), wherein user error or malice can compromise it.

So how would this be exploited? In our simple code example, there are probably only two values that get pushed onto the stack when the function is called: `userInput` and the RP. Since the stack grows downward in most operating systems, putting too many characters into the stack will eventually lead to overwriting the RP. Why? Because the RP is written to the stack first whenever a function is called. Depending on how much memory you have between the vulnerable variable and the RP, you could insert malicious code all the way up to the RP and then overwrite the RP to point to the start of the malicious code you just inserted. This allows the malicious instructions to be executed in the security context of the requesting application. If this application is running in a privileged mode, the attacker has more permissions and rights to carry out more damage. This is shown in Figure 3-10.

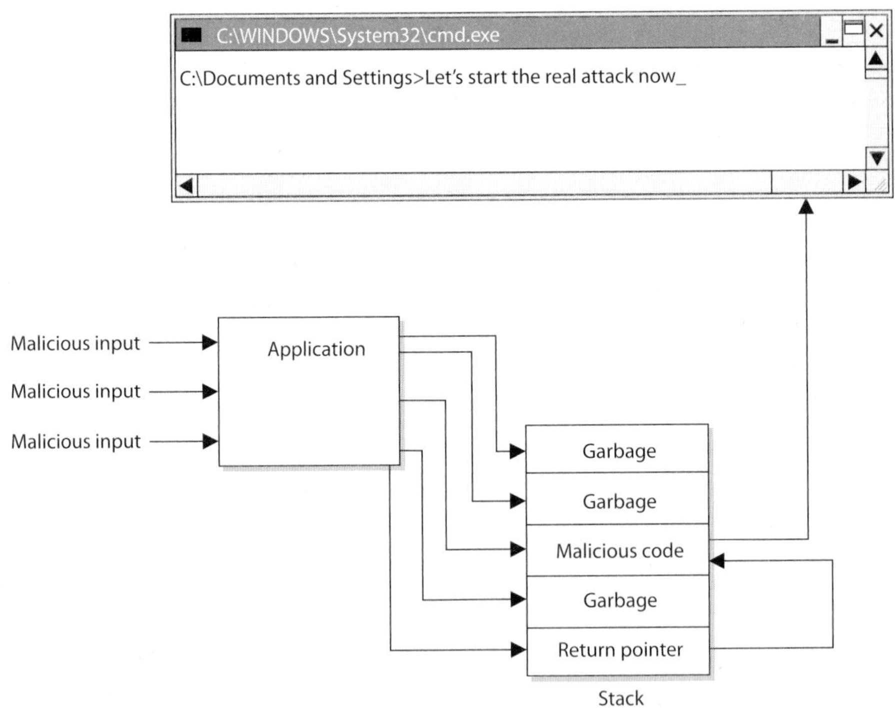

Figure 3-10 A buffer overflow attack

The attacker must know the size of the buffer to overwrite and must know the addresses that have been assigned to the stack. Without knowing these addresses, she could not lay down a new return pointer to her malicious code. The attacker must also write this dangerous payload to be small enough so it can be passed as input from one procedure to the next.

Windows' core is written in the C programming language and has layers and layers of object-oriented code on top of it. When a procedure needs to call upon the operating system to carry out some type of task, it calls upon a system service via an API call. The API works like a doorway to the operating system's functionality.

The C programming language is susceptible to buffer overflow attacks because it allows for direct pointer manipulations to take place. Specific commands can provide access to low-level memory addresses without carrying out bounds checking. The C functions that do perform the necessary boundary checking include `strncpy()`, `strncat()`, `snprintf()`, and `vsnprintf()`.

NOTE An operating system must be written to work with specific CPU architectures. These architectures dictate system memory addressing, protection mechanisms, and modes of execution and work with specific instruction sets. This means a buffer overflow attack that works on an Intel chip will not necessarily work on an AMD or a SPARC processor. These different processors set up the memory address of the stacks differently, so the attacker may have to craft a different buffer overflow code for different platforms.

Buffer overflows are in the source code of various applications and operating systems. They have been around since programmers started developing software. This means it is very difficult for a user to identify and fix them. When a buffer overflow is identified, the vendor usually sends out a patch, so keeping systems current on updates, hotfixes, and patches is usually the best countermeasure. Some products installed on systems can also watch for input values that might result in buffer overflows, but the best countermeasure is proper programming. This means use bounds checking. If an input value is only supposed to be nine characters, then the application should only accept nine characters and no more. Some languages are more susceptible to buffer overflows than others, so programmers should understand these issues, use the right languages for the right purposes, and carry out code review to identify buffer overflow vulnerabilities.

Memory Protection Techniques

Since your whole operating system and all your applications are loaded and run in memory, this is where the attackers can really do their damage. Vendors of different operating systems (Windows, Unix, Linux, OS X, etc.) have implemented various types of protection methods integrated into their memory manager processes. For example, Windows Vista was the first version of Windows to implement *address space layout randomization (ASLR)*, which was first implemented in OpenBSD.

(*Continued*)

If an attacker wants to maliciously interact with a process, he needs to know what memory address to send his attack inputs to. If the operating system changes these addresses continuously, which is what ASLR accomplishes, the potential success of his attack is greatly reduced. You can't mess with something if you don't know where it is.

Many of the main operating systems use some form of *data execution prevention (DEP)*, which can be implemented via hardware (CPU) or software (operating system). The actual implementations of DEP vary, but the main goal is to help ensure that executable code does not function within memory segments that could be dangerous. It is similar to not allowing someone suspicious in your house. You don't know whether this person is really going to try to do something malicious, but just to make sure he can't, you do not unlock the door for him to enter and be in a position where he could bring harm to you or your household. DEP can mark certain memory locations as "off limits" with the goal of reducing the "playing field" for hackers and malware.

Memory Leaks

As stated earlier, when an application makes a request for a memory segment to work within, it is allocated a specific memory amount by the operating system. When the application is done with the memory, it is supposed to tell the operating system to release the memory so it is available to other applications. This is only fair. But some applications are written poorly and do not indicate to the system that this memory is no longer in use. If this happens enough times, the operating system could become "starved" for memory, which would drastically affect the system's performance.

When a memory leak is identified in the hacker world, this opens the door to new DoS attacks. For example, when it was uncovered that a Unix application and a specific version of a Telnet protocol contained memory leaks, hackers amplified the problem. They continuously sent Telnet requests to systems with these vulnerabilities. The systems would allocate resources for these network requests, which in turn would cause more and more memory to be allocated and not returned. Eventually the systems would run out of memory and freeze.

NOTE Memory leaks can take place in operating systems, applications, and software drivers.

Two main countermeasures can protect against memory leaks: developing better code that releases memory properly, and using a *garbage collector*, software that runs an algorithm to identify unused committed memory and then tells the operating system to mark that memory as "available." Different types of garbage collectors work with different operating systems and programming languages.

Operating Systems

An operating system provides an environment for applications and users to work within. Every operating system is a complex beast, made up of various layers and modules of functionality. Its responsibilities include managing processes, memory, input/output (I/O), and the CPU. We next look at each of these responsibilities that every operating system type carries out. However, you must realize that whole books are written on just these individual topics, so the discussion here will only scratch the surface.

Process Management

Operating systems, software utilities, and applications, in reality, are just lines and lines of instructions. They are static lines of code that are brought to life when they are initialized and put into memory. Applications work as individual units, called *processes*, and the operating system also has several different processes carrying out various types of functionality. A process is the set of instructions that is actually running. A program is not considered a process until it is loaded into memory and activated by the operating system. When a process is created, the operating system assigns resources to it, such as a memory segment, CPU time slot (interrupt), access to system application programming interfaces (APIs), and files to interact with. The *collection* of the instructions and the assigned resources is referred to as a *process*. So the operating system gives a process all the tools it needs and then loads the process into memory, at which point it is off and running.

The operating system has many of its own processes, which are used to provide and maintain the environment for applications and users to work within. Some examples of the functionality that individual processes provide include displaying data onscreen, spooling print jobs, and saving data to temporary files. Operating systems provide *multiprogramming*, which means that more than one program (or process) can be loaded into memory at the same time. This is what allows you to run your antivirus software, word processor, personal firewall, and e-mail client all at the same time. Each of these applications runs as individual processes.

EXAM TIP Many resources state that today's operating systems provide multiprogramming and multitasking. This is true, in that multiprogramming just means more than one application can be loaded into memory at the same time. But in reality, multiprogramming was replaced by multitasking, which means more than one application can be in memory at the same time *and* the operating system can deal with requests from these different applications *simultaneously*. Multiprogramming is a legacy term.

Earlier operating systems wasted their most precious resource—CPU time. For example, when a word processor would request to open a file on a floppy drive, the CPU would send the request to the floppy drive and then wait for the floppy drive to initialize, for the head to find the right track and sector, and finally for the floppy drive to send the data via the data bus to the CPU for processing. To avoid this waste of CPU time, multitasking was developed, which enabled the operating system to maintain different processes in their various execution states. Instead of sitting idle waiting for activity from one process, the CPU could execute instructions for other processes, thereby speeding up the system as a whole.

TIP If you are not old enough to remember floppy drives, they were like our USB thumb drives we use today. They were just flatter and slower and could not hold as much data.

As an analogy, if you (CPU) put bread in a toaster (process) and just stand there waiting for the toaster to finish its job, you are wasting time. On the other hand, if you put bread in the toaster and then, while it's toasting, feed the dog, make coffee, and come up with a solution for world peace, you are being more productive and not wasting time. You are multitasking.

Operating systems started out as cooperative and then evolved into preemptive multitasking. *Cooperative multitasking*, used in Windows 3.*x* and early Macintosh systems, required the processes to voluntarily release resources they were using. This was not necessarily a stable environment because if a programmer did not write his code properly to release a resource when his application was done using it, the resource would be committed indefinitely to his application and thus be unavailable to other processes. With *preemptive multitasking*, used in Windows 9*x* and later versions and in Unix systems, the operating system controls how long a process can use a resource. The system can suspend a process that is using the CPU and allow another process access to it through the use of time sharing. So in operating systems that used cooperative multitasking, the processes had too much control over resource release, and when an application hung, it usually affected all the other applications and sometimes the operating system itself. Operating systems that use preemptive multitasking run the show, and one application does not negatively affect another application as easily.

Different operating system types work within different process models. For example, Unix and Linux systems allow their processes to create new children processes, which is referred to as *spawning*. Let's say you are working within a shell of a Linux system. That shell is the command interpreter and an interface that enables the user to interact with the operating system. The shell runs as a process. When you type in a shell the command `cat file1 file2|grep stuff`, you are telling the operating system to concatenate (`cat`) the two files and then search (`grep`) for the lines that have the value of "stuff" in them. When you press the ENTER key, the shell spawns two children processes—one for the `cat` command and one for the `grep` command. Each of these children processes takes on the characteristics of the parent process, but has its own memory space, stack, and program counter values.

A process can be in a *running state* (CPU is executing its instructions and data), *ready state* (waiting to send instructions to the CPU), or *blocked state* (waiting for input data, such as keystrokes, from a user). These different states are illustrated in Figure 3-11. When a process is blocked, it is waiting for some type of data to be sent to it. In the preceding example of typing the command `cat file1 file2|grep stuff`, the

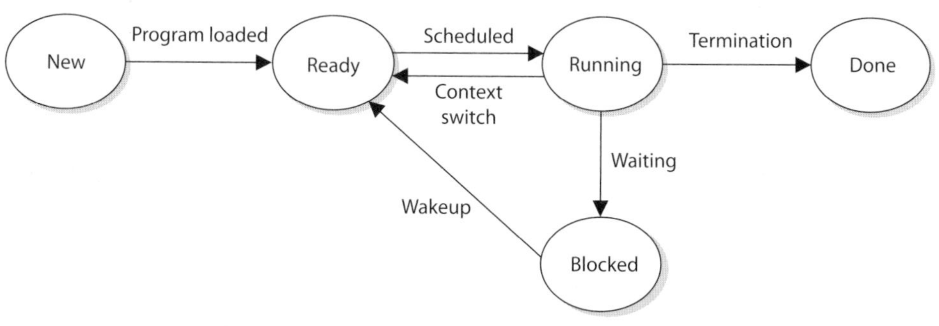

Figure 3-11 Processes enter and exit different states.

grep process cannot actually carry out its functionality of searching until the first process (cat) is done combining the two files. The grep process will put itself to *sleep* and will be in the blocked state until the cat process is done and sends the grep process the input it needs to work with.

NOTE Though the implementation details vary widely, every modern operating system supports the spawning of new child processes by a parent process. They also provide mechanisms for determining the parent-child relationships among processes.

Is it really necessary to understand this stuff all the way down to the process level? Well, this is where everything actually takes place. All software works in "units" of processes. If you do not understand how processes work, you cannot understand how software works. If you do not understand how software works, you cannot know if it is working securely. So yes, you need to know this stuff at this level. Let's keep going.

The operating system is responsible for creating new processes, assigning them resources, synchronizing their communication, and making sure nothing insecure is taking place. The operating system keeps a *process table*, which has one entry per process. The table contains each individual process's state, stack pointer, memory allocation, program counter, and status of open files in use. The reason the operating system documents all of this status information is that the CPU needs all of it loaded into its registers when it needs to interact with, for example, process 1. When process 1's CPU time slice is over, all of the current status information on process 1 is stored in the process table so that when its time slice is open again, all of this status information can be put back into the CPU registers. So, when it is process 2's time with the CPU, its status information is transferred from the process table to the CPU registers and transferred back again when the time slice is over. These steps are shown in Figure 3-12.

How does a process know when it can communicate with the CPU? This is taken care of by using *interrupts*. An operating system fools us, and applications, into thinking it and the CPU are carrying out all tasks (operating system, applications, memory, I/O,

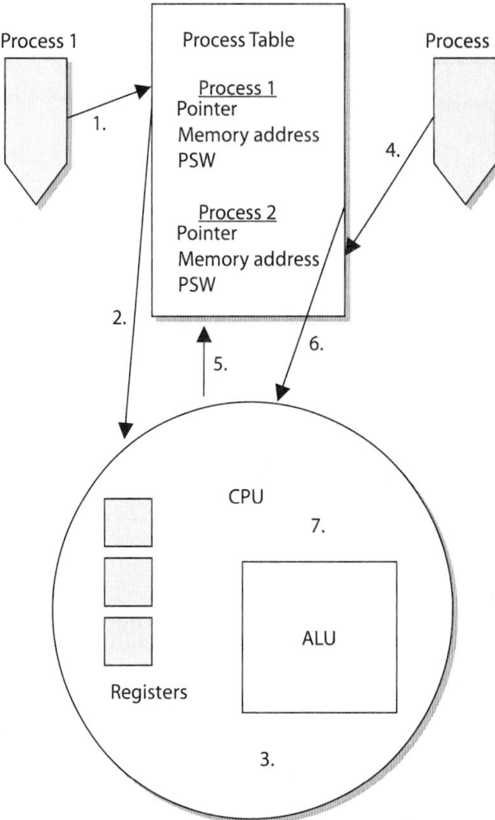

1. Process 1 needs its code executed.
2. OS moves process 1's status data into the CPU registers.
3. CPU works on process l's data.
4. Process 2 needs its code to be executed.
5. OS moves process 1's data back to the process table.
6. OS moves process 2's status data into the CPU registers.
7. CPU works on process 2's data.

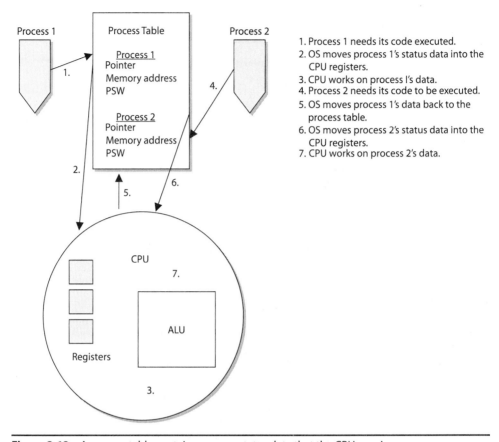

Figure 3-12 A process table contains process status data that the CPU requires.

and user activities) simultaneously. In fact, this is impossible. Most CPUs can do only one thing at a time. So the system has hardware and software interrupts. When a device needs to communicate with the CPU, it has to wait for its interrupt to be called upon. The same thing happens in software. Each process has an interrupt assigned to it. It is like pulling a number at a customer service department in a store. You can't go up to the counter until your number has been called out.

When a process is interacting with the CPU and an interrupt takes place (another process has requested access to the CPU), the current process's information is stored in the process table, and the next process gets its time to interact with the CPU.

NOTE Some critical processes cannot afford to have their functionality interrupted by another process. The operating system is responsible for setting the priorities for the different processes. When one process needs to interrupt another process, the operating system compares the priority levels of the two processes to determine if this interruption should be allowed.

There are two categories of interrupts: maskable and nonmaskable. A *maskable interrupt* is assigned to an event that may not be overly important, and the programmer can indicate that if that interrupt calls, the program does not stop what it is doing. This means the interrupt is ignored. A *nonmaskable interrupt* can never be overridden by an application because the event that has this type of interrupt assigned to it is critical. As an example, the reset button would be assigned a nonmaskable interrupt. This means that when this button is pushed, the CPU carries out its instructions right away.

As an analogy, a boss can tell her administrative assistant she is not going to take any calls unless the Pope or Elvis phones. This means all other people will be ignored or masked (maskable interrupt), but the Pope and Elvis will not be ignored (nonmaskable interrupt).

The *watchdog timer* is an example of a critical process that must always do its thing. This process will reset the system with a warm boot if the operating system hangs and cannot recover itself. For example, if there is a memory management problem and the operating system hangs, the watchdog timer will reset the system. This is one mechanism that ensures the software provides more of a stable environment.

Memory Stacks

Each process has its own *stack*, which is a data structure in memory that the process can read from and write to in a last in, first out (LIFO) fashion. Let's say you and John need to communicate through a stack. What John does is put all of the things he needs to say to you in a stack of papers. The first paper tells you how you can respond to him when you need to, which is called a *return pointer*. The next paper has some instructions he needs you to carry out. The next piece of paper has the data you must use when carrying out these instructions. So, John writes down on individual pieces of paper all that he needs you to do for him and *stacks* them up. When he is done, he tells you to read his stack of papers. You take the first page off the stack and carry out the request. Then you take the second page and carry out that request. You continue to do this until you are at the bottom of the stack, which contains John's return pointer. You look at this return pointer (which is his memory address) to know where to send the results of all the instructions he asked you to carry out. This is how processes communicate to other processes and to the CPU. One process stacks up its information that it needs to communicate to the CPU. The CPU has to keep track of where it is in the stack, which is the purpose of the *stack pointer*. Once the first item on the stack is executed, then the stack pointer moves down to tell the CPU where the next piece of data is located.

Thread Management

As described earlier, a process is a program in memory. More precisely, a process is the program's instructions and all the resources assigned to the process by the operating system. It is just easier to group all of these instructions and resources together and control them as one entity, which is a process. When a process needs to send something to the

CPU for processing, it generates a thread. A *thread* is made up of an individual instruction set and the data that must be worked on by the CPU.

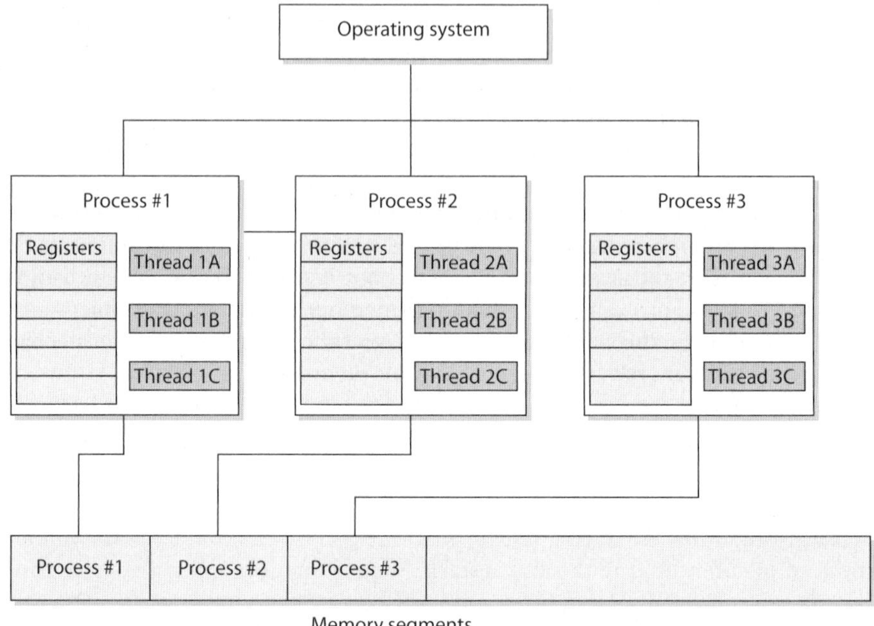

Most applications have several different functions. Word processing applications can open files, save files, open other programs (such as an e-mail client), and print documents. Each one of these functions requires a thread (instruction set) to be dynamically generated. So, for example, if Tom chooses to print his document, the word processing process generates a thread that contains the instructions of how this document should be printed (font, colors, text, margins, and so on). If he chooses to send a document via e-mail through this program, another thread is created that tells the e-mail client to open and what file needs to be sent. Threads are dynamically created and destroyed as needed. Once Tom is done printing his document, the thread that was generated for this functionality is broken down.

A program that has been developed to carry out several different tasks at one time (display, print, interact with other programs) is capable of running several different threads simultaneously. An application with this capability is referred to as a *multithreaded* application.

Each thread shares the same resources of the process that created it. So, all the threads created by a word processing application work in the same memory space and have access to all the same files and system resources. And how is this related to security? Software security ultimately comes down to what threads and processes are doing. If they are behaving properly, things work as planned and there are no issues to be concerned about. But if a thread misbehaves and it is working in a privileged mode, then it can carry out malicious activities that affect critical resources of the system. Attackers commonly inject code into a running process to carry out some type of compromise. Let's think this through. When an operating system is preparing to load a process into memory, it goes through a type of criteria checklist to make sure the process is valid and will not negatively affect the system. Once the process passes this check, the process is loaded into memory and is assigned a specific operation mode (user or privileged). An attacker "injects" instructions into this running process, which means the process is his vehicle for destruction. Since the process has already gone through a security check before it was loaded into memory, it is trusted and has access to system resources. If an attacker can inject malicious instructions into this process, this trusted process carries out the attacker's demands. These demands could be to collect data as the user types it in on her keyboard, steal passwords, send out malware, etc. If the process is running at a privileged mode, the attacker can carry out more damage because more critical system resources are available to him through this running process. When she creates her product, a software developer needs to make sure that running processes will not accept unqualified instructions and allow for these types of compromises. Processes should only accept instructions for an approved entity, and the instructions that it accepts should be validated before execution. It is like "stranger danger" with children. We teach our children to not take candy from a stranger, and in turn we need to make sure our software processes are not accepting improper instructions from an unknown source.

Process Scheduling

Scheduling and synchronizing various processes and their activities is part of process management, which is a responsibility of the operating system. Several components need to be considered during the development of an operating system, which will dictate how process scheduling will take place. A scheduling policy is created to govern how threads will interact with other threads. Different operating systems can use different schedulers, which are basically algorithms that control the timesharing of the CPU. As stated earlier, the different processes are assigned different priority levels (interrupts) that dictate which processes overrule other processes when CPU time allocation is required. The operating system creates and deletes processes as needed and oversees them changing state (ready, blocked, running). The operating system is also responsible for controlling deadlocks between processes attempting to use the same resources.

If a process scheduler is not built properly, an attacker could manipulate it. The attacker could ensure that certain processes do not get access to system resources (creating a denial-of-service attack) or that a malicious process has its privileges escalated (allowing for extensive damage). An operating system needs to be built in a secure manner to ensure that an attacker cannot slip in and take over control of the system's processes.

When a process makes a request for a resource (memory allocation, printer, secondary storage devices, disk space, and so on), the operating system creates certain data structures and dedicates the necessary processes for the activity to be completed. Once the action takes place (a document is printed, a file is saved, or data is retrieved from the drive), the process needs to tear down these built structures and release the resources back to the resource pool so they are available for other processes. If this does not happen properly, the system may run out of critical resources—as in memory. Attackers have identified programming errors in operating systems that allow them to starve the system of its own memory. This means the attackers exploit a software vulnerability that ensures that processes do not properly release their memory resources. Memory is continually committed and not released and the system is depleted of this resource until it can no longer function. This is another example of a denial-of-service (DoS) attack.

Another situation to be concerned about is a *software deadlock*. One example of a deadlock situation is when process A commits resource 1 and needs to use resource 2 to properly complete its task, but process B has committed resource 2 and needs resource 1 to finish its job. Both processes are in deadlock because they do not have the resources they need to finish the function they are trying to carry out. This situation does not take place as often as it used to as a result of better programming. Also, operating systems now have the intelligence to detect this activity and either release committed resources or control the allocation of resources so they are properly shared between processes.

Operating systems have different methods of dealing with resource requests and releases and solving deadlock situations. In some systems, if a requested resource is unavailable for a certain period of time, the operating system kills the process that is "holding on to" that resource. This action releases the resource from the process that had committed it and restarts the process so it is "clean" and available for use by other applications. Other operating systems might require a program to request all the resources it needs *before* it actually starts executing instructions, or require a program to release its currently committed resources before it may acquire more.

Process Activity

Computers can run different applications and processes at the same time. The processes have to share resources and play nice with each other to ensure a stable and safe computing environment that maintains its integrity. Some memory, data files, and variables are actually shared between different processes. It is critical that more than one process does not attempt to read and write to these items at the same time. The operating system is the master program that prevents this type of action from taking place and ensures that programs do not corrupt each other's data held in memory. The operating system works with the CPU to provide time slicing through the use of interrupts to ensure that processes are provided with adequate access to the CPU. This also makes certain that critical system functions are not negatively affected by rogue applications.

To protect processes from each other, operating systems commonly have functionality that implements process isolation. *Process isolation* is necessary to ensure that processes do not "step on each other's toes," communicate in an insecure manner, or negatively affect each other's productivity. Older operating systems did not enforce process isolation as well as systems do today. This is why in earlier operating systems, when one of your programs hung, all other programs, and sometimes the operating system itself, hung. With process isolation, if one process hangs for some reason, it will not affect the other software running. (Process isolation is required for preemptive multitasking.) Different methods can be used to enforce process isolation:

- Encapsulation of objects
- Time multiplexing of shared resources

- Naming distinctions
- Virtual memory mapping

When a process is *encapsulated*, no other process understands or interacts with its internal programming code. When process A needs to communicate with process B, process A just needs to know how to communicate with process B's interface. An interface defines how communication must take place between two processes. As an analogy, think back to how you had to communicate with your third-grade teacher. You had to call her Mrs. So-and-So, say please and thank you, and speak respectfully to get whatever it was you needed. The same thing is true for software components that need to communicate with each other. They must know *how* to communicate properly with each other's interfaces. The interfaces dictate the type of requests a process will accept and the type of output that will be provided. So, two processes can communicate with each other, even if they are written in different programming languages, as long as they know how to communicate with each other's interface. Encapsulation provides *data hiding*, which means that outside software components will not know how a process works and will not be able to manipulate the process's internal code. This is an integrity mechanism and enforces modularity in programming code.

If a process is not isolated properly through encapsulation, this means its interface is accepting potentially malicious instructions. The interface is like a membrane filter that our cells within our bodies use. Our cells filter fluid and molecules that are attempting to enter them. If some type of toxin slips by the filter, we can get sick because the toxin has entered the worker bees of our bodies—cells. Processes are the worker bees of our software. If they accept malicious instructions, our systems can get sick.

Time multiplexing was already discussed, although we did not use this term. *Time multiplexing* is a technology that allows processes to use the same resources. As stated earlier, a CPU must be shared among many processes. Although it seems as though all applications are running (executing their instructions) simultaneously, the operating system is splitting up time shares between each process. Multiplexing means there are several data sources and the individual data pieces are piped into one communication channel. In this instance, the operating system is coordinating the different requests from the different processes and piping them through the one shared CPU. An operating system must provide proper time multiplexing (resource sharing) to ensure a stable working environment exists for software and users.

NOTE Today's CPUs have multiple cores, meaning that they have multiple processors. This basically means that there are several smaller CPUs (processors) integrated into one larger CPU. So in reality the different processors on the CPU can execute instruction code simultaneously, making the computer overall much faster. The operating system has to multiplex process requests and "feed" them into the individual processors for instruction execution.

While time multiplexing and multitasking is a performance requirement of our systems today and is truly better than sliced bread, it introduces a lot of complexity to our systems. We are forcing our operating systems to not only do more things faster, we are forcing them to do all of these things simultaneously. As the complexity of our systems increases, the potential of truly securing them decreases. There is an inverse relationship between complexity and security: as one goes up, the other one usually goes down. But this fact does not necessarily predict doom and gloom; what it means is that software architecture and development has to be done in a more disciplined manner.

Naming distinctions just means that the different processes have their own name or identification value. Processes are usually assigned process identification (PID) values, which the operating system and other processes use to call upon them. If each process is isolated, that means each process has its own unique PID value. This is just another way to enforce process isolation.

Virtual address memory mapping is different from the physical addresses of memory. An application is written such that it basically "thinks" it is the only program running within an operating system. When an application needs memory to work with, it tells the operating system how much memory it needs. The operating system carves out that amount of memory and assigns it to the requesting application. The application uses its own address scheme, which usually starts at 0, but in reality, the application does not work in the *physical* address space it thinks it is working in. Rather, it works in the address space the operating system assigns to it. The physical memory is the RAM chips in the system. The operating system chops up this memory and assigns portions of it to the requesting processes. Once the process is assigned its own memory space, it can address this portion however it is written to do so. Virtual address mapping allows the different processes to have their own memory space; the operating system ensures no processes improperly interact with another process's memory. This provides integrity and confidentiality for the individual processes and their data and an overall stable processing environment for the operating system.

If an operating system has a flaw in the programming code that controls memory mapping, an attacker could manipulate this function. Since everything within an operating system actually has to operate in memory to work, the ability to manipulate memory addressing can be very dangerous.

Memory Management

To provide a safe and stable environment, an operating system must exercise proper memory management—one of its most important tasks. After all, everything happens in memory.

The goals of memory management are to

- Provide an abstraction level for programmers
- Maximize performance with the limited amount of memory available
- Protect the operating system and applications loaded into memory

Abstraction means that the details of something are hidden. Developers of applications do not know the amount or type of memory that will be available in each and every system their code will be loaded on. If a developer had to be concerned with this type of detail, then her application would be able to work only on the one system that maps to all of her specifications. To allow for portability, the memory manager hides all of the memory issues and just provides the application with a memory segment. The application is able to run without having to know all the hairy details of the operating system and hardware it is running on.

Every computer has a memory hierarchy. Certain small amounts of memory are very fast and expensive (registers, cache), while larger amounts are slower and less expensive (RAM, hard drive). The portion of the operating system that keeps track of how these different types of memory are used is lovingly called the *memory manager*. Its jobs are to allocate and deallocate different memory segments, enforce access control to ensure processes are interacting only with their own memory segments, and swap memory contents from RAM to the hard drive.

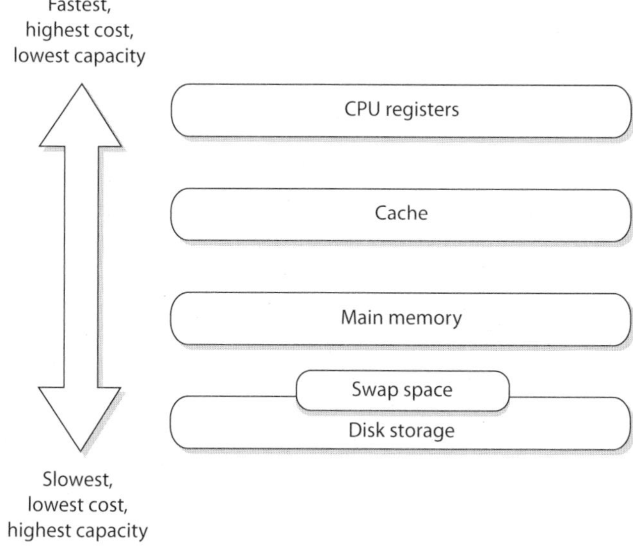

The memory manager has five basic responsibilities:

Relocation:

- Swap contents from RAM to the hard drive as needed (explained later in the "Virtual Memory" section of this chapter)
- Provide pointers for applications if their instructions and memory segment have been moved to a different location in main memory

Protection:

- Limit processes to interact only with the memory segments assigned to them
- Provide access control to memory segments

Sharing:

- Use complex controls to ensure integrity and confidentiality when processes need to use the same shared memory segments
- Allow many users with different levels of access to interact with the same application running in one memory segment

Logical organization:

- Segment all memory types and provide an addressing scheme for each at an abstraction level
- Allow for the sharing of specific software modules, such as dynamic link library (DLL) procedures

Physical organization:

- Segment the physical memory space for application and operating system processes

NOTE A dynamic link library (DLL) is a set of functions that applications can call upon to carry out different types of procedures. For example, the Windows operating system has a crypt32.dll that is used by the operating system and applications for cryptographic functions. Windows has a set of DLLs, which is just a library of functions to be called upon, and crypt32.dll is just one example.

How can an operating system make sure a process only interacts with its memory segment? When a process creates a thread because it needs some instructions and data processed, the CPU uses two registers. A *base register* contains the beginning address that was assigned to the process, and a *limit register* contains the ending address, as illustrated in Figure 3-13. The thread contains an address of where the instruction and data reside that need to be processed. The CPU compares this address to the base and limit registers to make sure the thread is not trying to access a memory segment outside of its bounds. So, the base register makes it impossible for a thread to reference a memory address below its allocated memory segment, and the limit register makes it impossible for a thread to reference a memory address above this segment.

If an operating system has a memory manager that does not enforce the memory limits properly, an attacker can manipulate its functionality and use it against the system. There have been several instances over the years where attackers would do just this and bypass these types of controls. Architects and developers of operating systems have to think through these types of weaknesses and attack types to ensure that the system properly protects itself.

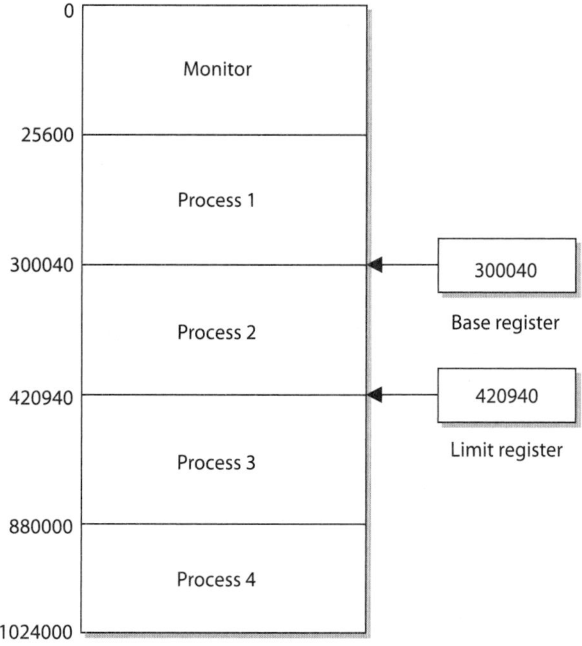

Figure 3-13 Base and limit registers are used to contain a process in its own memory segment.

Memory Protection Issues

- Every address reference is validated for protection.
- Two or more processes can share access to the same segment with potentially different access rights.
- Different instruction and data types can be assigned different levels of protection.
- Processes cannot generate an unpermitted address or gain access to an unpermitted segment.

All of these issues make it more difficult for memory management to be carried out properly in a constantly changing and complex system.

Virtual Memory

Secondary storage is considered nonvolatile storage media and includes such things as the computer's hard drive, USB drives, and optical discs. When RAM and secondary storage are combined, the result is *virtual memory*. The system uses hard drive space to extend its RAM memory space. *Swap space* is the reserved hard drive space used to extend RAM capabilities. Windows systems use the pagefile.sys file to reserve this space. When a system fills up its volatile memory space, it writes data from memory onto the hard drive. When a program requests access to this data, it is brought from the hard drive back into memory in specific units, called *pages*. This process is called *virtual memory paging*. Accessing data kept in pages on the hard drive takes more time than accessing data kept in RAM memory because physical disk read/write access must take place. Internal control blocks, maintained by the operating system, keep track of what page frames are residing in RAM and what is available "offline," ready to be called into RAM for execution or processing, if needed. The payoff is that it seems as though the system can hold an incredible amount of information and program instructions in memory, as shown in Figure 3-14.

A security issue with using virtual swap space is that when the system is shut down or processes that were using the swap space are terminated, the pointers to the pages are reset to "available" even though the actual data written to disk is still physically there. This data could conceivably be compromised and captured. On various operating systems, there are routines to wipe the swap spaces after a process is done with it before it is used again. The routines should also erase this data before a system shutdown, at which time the operating system would no longer be able to maintain any control over what happens on the hard drive surface.

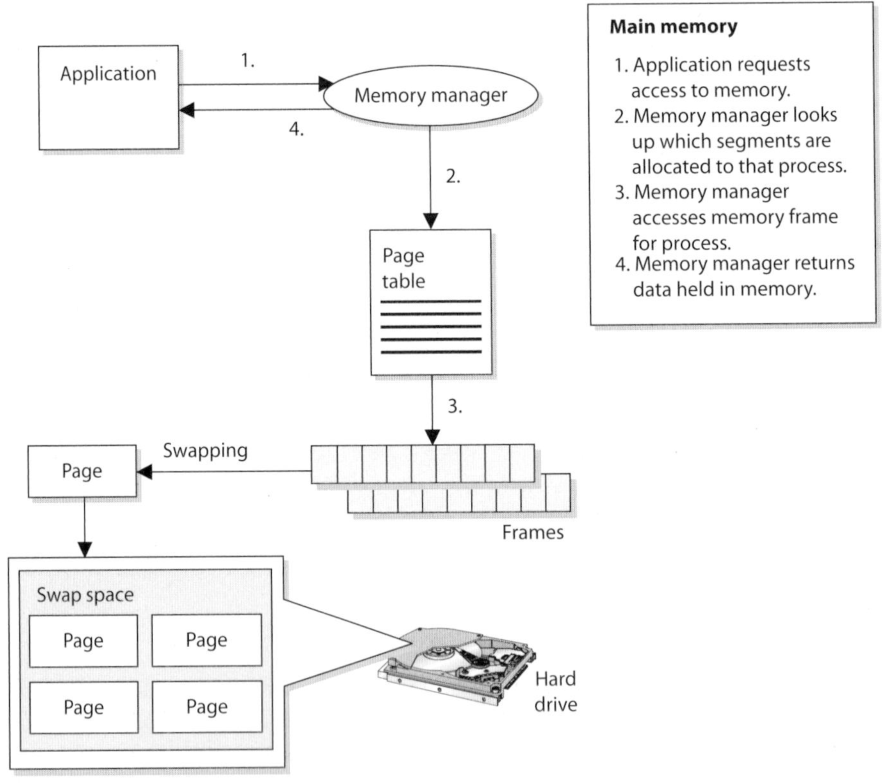

Figure 3-14 Combining RAM and secondary storage to create virtual memory

CAUTION If a program, file, or data is encrypted and saved on the hard drive, it will be decrypted when used by the controlling program. While this unencrypted data is sitting in RAM, the system could write out the data to the swap space on the hard drive in its unencrypted state. This is also true for secret and private keys being held in RAM. Attackers have figured out how to gain access to this space in unauthorized manners.

Input/Output Device Management

We have covered a lot of operating system responsibilities up to now, and we are not stopping yet. An operating system also has to control all input/output devices. It sends commands to them, accepts their interrupts when they need to communicate with the CPU, and provides an interface between the devices and the applications.

I/O devices are usually considered block or character devices. A block device works with data in fixed-size blocks, each block with its own unique address. A disk drive is an example of a block device. A character device, such as a printer, network interface card (NIC), or mouse, works with streams of characters, without using any fixed sizes. This type of data is not addressable.

When a user chooses to print a document, open a stored file on a hard drive, or save files to a USB drive, these requests go from the application the user is working in, through the operating system, to the device requested. The operating system uses a device driver to communicate with a device controller, which may be a circuit card that fits into an expansion slot on the motherboard. The controller is an electrical component with its own software that provides a communication path that enables the device and operating system to exchange data. The operating system sends commands to the device controller's registers, and the controller then writes data to the peripheral device or extracts data to be processed by the CPU, depending on the given commands. If the command is to extract data from the hard drive, the controller takes the bits and puts them into the necessary block size and carries out a checksum activity to verify the integrity of the data. If the integrity is successfully verified, the data is put into memory for the CPU to interact with.

Interrupts

When an I/O device has completed whatever task was asked of it, it needs to inform the CPU that the necessary data is now in memory for processing. The device's controller sends a signal down a bus, which is detected by the interrupt controller. (This is what it means to use an interrupt. The device signals the interrupt controller and is basically saying, "I am done and need attention now.") If the CPU is busy *and* the device's interrupt is not a higher priority than whatever job is being processed, then the device has to wait. The interrupt controller sends a message to the CPU, indicating what device needs attention. The operating system has a table (called the *interrupt vector*) of all the I/O devices connected to it. The CPU compares the received number with the values within the interrupt vector so it knows which I/O device needs its services. The table has the memory addresses of the different I/O devices. So when the CPU understands that the hard drive needs attention, it looks in the table to find the correct memory address.

This is the new program counter value, which is the initial address of where the CPU should start reading from.

One of the main goals of the operating system software that controls I/O activity is to be device independent. This means a developer can write an application to read (open a file) or write (save a file) to any device (USB drive, hard drive, optical disc drive, etc.). This level of abstraction frees application developers from having to write different procedures to interact with the various I/O devices. If a developer had to write an individual procedure of how to write to an optical disc drive *and* how to write to a USB drive, how to write to a hard disk, and so on, each time a new type of I/O device was developed, all of the applications would have to be patched or upgraded.

Operating systems can carry out software I/O procedures in various ways. We will look at the following methods:

- Programmed I/O
- Interrupt-driven I/O
- I/O using DMA
- Premapped I/O
- Fully mapped I/O

Programmable I/O If an operating system is using programmable I/O, this means the CPU sends data to an I/O device and polls the device to see if it is ready to accept more data. If the device is not ready to accept more data, the CPU wastes time by waiting for the device to become ready. For example, the CPU would send a byte of data (a character) to the printer and then ask the printer if it is ready for another byte. The CPU sends the text to be printed 1 byte at a time. This is a very slow way of working and wastes precious CPU time. So the smart people figured out a better way: interrupt-driven I/O.

Interrupt-Driven I/O If an operating system is using interrupt-driven I/O, this means the CPU sends a character over to the printer and then goes and works on another process's request. When the printer is done printing the first character, it sends an interrupt to the CPU. The CPU stops what it is doing, sends another character to the printer, and moves to another job. This process (send character—go do something else—interrupt—send another character) continues until the whole text is printed. Although the CPU is not waiting for each byte to be printed, this method does waste a lot of time dealing with all the interrupts. So we excused those smart people and brought in some new smarter people, who came up with I/O using DMA.

I/O Using DMA *Direct memory access (DMA)* is a way of transferring data between I/O devices and the system's memory without using the CPU. This speeds up data transfer rates significantly. When used in I/O activities, the DMA controller feeds the characters to the printer without bothering the CPU. This method is sometimes referred to as *unmapped I/O.*

Premapped I/O Premapped I/O and fully mapped I/O (described next) do not pertain to performance, as do the earlier methods, but provide two approaches that

can directly affect security. In a premapped I/O system, the CPU sends the physical memory address of the requesting process to the I/O device, and the I/O device is trusted enough to interact with the contents of memory directly, so the CPU does not control the interactions between the I/O device and memory. The operating system trusts the device to behave properly. Scary.

Fully Mapped I/O Under fully mapped I/O, the operating system does not trust the I/O device. The physical address is not given to the I/O device. Instead, the device works purely with logical addresses and works on behalf (under the security context) of the requesting process, so the operating system does not trust the device to interact with memory directly. The operating system does not trust the process or device, and it acts as the broker to control how they communicate with each other.

CPU Architecture Integration

An operating system and a CPU have to be compatible and share a similar architecture to work together. While an operating system is software and a CPU is hardware, they actually work so closely together when a computer is running that this delineation gets blurred. An operating system has to be able to "fit into" a CPU like a hand in a glove. Once a hand is inside of a glove, they both move together as a single entity.

An operating system and a CPU must be able to communicate through an instruction set. You may have heard of x86, which is a family of instruction sets. An *instruction set* is a language an operating system must be able to speak to properly communicate to a CPU. As an analogy, if you want Jimmy to carry out some tasks for you, you will have to tell him the instructions in a language that he understands.

The *microarchitecture* contains the things that make up the physical CPU (registers, logic gates, ALU, cache, etc.). The CPU knows mechanically how to use all of these parts; it just needs to know what the operating system wants it to do. A chef knows how to use all of his pots, pans, spices, and ingredients, but he needs an order from the menu so he knows how to use all of these properly to achieve the requested outcome. Similarly, the CPU has a "menu" of operations the operating system can "order" from, which is the instruction set. The operating system puts in its order (render graphics on screen, print to printer, encrypt data, etc.), and the CPU carries out the request and provides the result.

TIP The most common instruction set in use today (x86) can be used within different microarchitectures (Intel, AMD, etc.) and with different operating systems (Windows, OS X, Linux, etc.).

Along with sharing this same language (instruction set), the operating system and CPU have to work within the same ringed architecture. Let's approach this from the top and work our way down. If an operating system is going to be stable, it must be able to protect itself from its users and their applications. This requires the capability to distinguish between operations performed on behalf of the operating system itself and operations performed on behalf of the users or applications. This can be complex because the operating system software may be accessing memory segments, sending instructions to the CPU for processing, accessing secondary storage devices, communicating with

peripheral devices, dealing with networking requests, and more at the same time. Each user application (e-mail client, antimalware program, web browser, word processor, personal firewall, and so on) may also be attempting the same types of activities at the same time. The operating system must keep track of all of these events and ensure none of them puts the system at risk.

The operating system has several protection mechanisms to ensure processes do not negatively affect each other or the critical components of the system itself. One has already been mentioned: memory protection. Another security mechanism the system uses is a ring-based architecture.

The architecture of the CPU dictates how many rings are available for an operating system to use. As shown in Figure 3-15, the rings act as containers and barriers. They are containers in that they provide an execution environment for processes to be able to carry out their functions, and barriers in that the different processes are "walled off" from each other based upon the trust the operating system has in them.

Suppose you build a facility based upon this type of ring structure. Your crown jewels are stored in the center of the facility (ring 0), so you are not going to allow just anyone in this section of your building—only the people you really trust. You will allow the people you kind of trust in the next level of your facility (ring 1). If you don't trust a particular person at all, you are going keep that person in ring 3 so that he is as far from your crown jewels as possible. This is how the ring structure of a CPU works. Ring 0 is for the most trusted components of the operating system itself. This is because processes that are allowed to work in ring 0 can access very critical components in the system. Ring 0

Figure 3-15 More-trusted processes operate within lower-numbered rings.

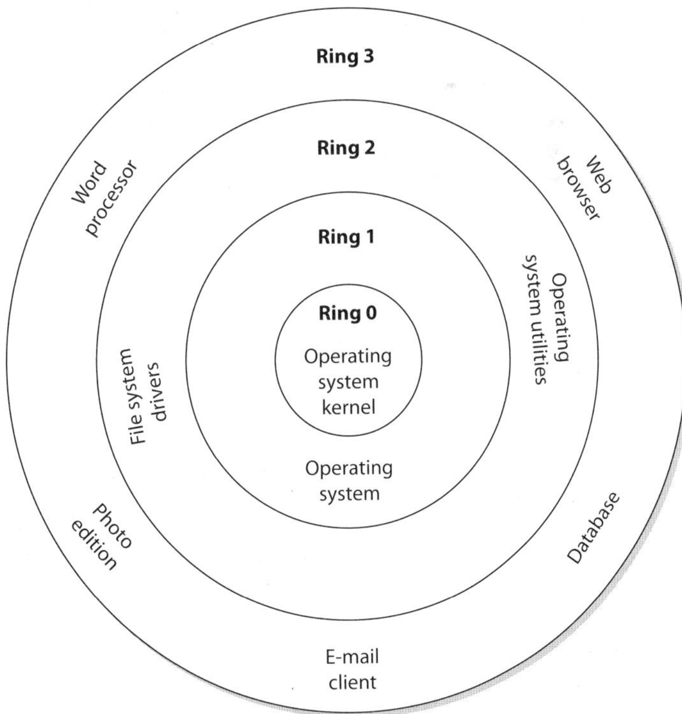

is where the operating system's kernel (most trusted and powerful processes) works. Less trusted processes, as in operating system utilities, can work in ring 1, and the least trusted processes (applications) work in the farthest ring, ring 3. This layered approach provides a self-protection mechanism for the operating system.

Operating system components that operate in ring 0 have the most access to memory locations, peripheral devices, system drivers, and sensitive configuration parameters. Because this ring provides much more dangerous access to critical resources, it is the most protected. Applications usually operate in ring 3, which limits the type of memory, peripheral device, and driver access activity and is controlled through the operating system services and system calls. The type of commands and instructions sent to the CPU from applications in the outer rings are more restrictive in nature. If an application tries to send instructions to the CPU that fall outside its permission level, the CPU treats this violation as an exception and may show a general protection fault or exception error and attempt to shut down the offending application.

These protection rings provide an intermediate layer between processes and are used for access control when one process tries to access another process or interact with system resources. The ring number determines the access level a process has—the lower the ring number, the greater the amount of privilege given to the process running within that ring. A process in ring 3 cannot directly access a process in ring 1, but processes in ring 1 can directly access processes in ring 3. Entities cannot directly communicate with objects in higher rings.

If we go back to our facility analogy, people in ring 0 can go and talk to any of the other people in the different areas (rings) of the facility. You trust them and you will let them do what they need to do. But if people in ring 3 of your facility want to talk to people in ring 2, you cannot allow this to happen in an unprotected manner. You don't trust these people and do not know what they will do. Someone from ring 3 might try to punch someone from ring 2 in the face and then everyone will be unhappy. So if someone in ring 3 needs to communicate to someone in ring 2, she has to write down her message on a piece of paper and give it to the guard. The guard will review it and hand it to the person in ring 2 if it is safe and acceptable.

In an operating system, the less trusted processes that are working in ring 3 send their communication requests to an API provided by the operating system specifically for this purpose (guard). The communication request is passed to the more trusted process in ring 2 in a controlled and safe manner.

Application Programming Interface

An API is the doorway to a protocol, operating service, process, or DLL. When one piece of software needs to send information to another piece of software, it must format its communication request in a way that the receiving software understands. An application may send a request to an operating system's cryptographic DLL, which will in turn carry out the requested cryptographic functionality for the application.

(Continued)

We will cover APIs in more depth in Chapter 8, but for now understand that an API is a type of guard that provides access control between the trusted and nontrusted processes within an operating system. If an application (nontrusted) process needs to send a message to the operating system's network protocol stack, it will send the information to the operating system's networking service. The application sends the request in a format that will be accepted by the service's API. APIs must be properly written by the operating system developers to ensure dangerous data cannot pass through this communication channel. If suspicious data gets past an API, the service could be compromised and execute code in a privileged context.

CPU Operation Modes

As stated earlier, the CPU provides the ring structure architecture, and the operating system assigns its processes to the different rings. When a process is placed in ring 0, its activities are carried out in kernel mode, which means it can access the most critical resources in a nonrestrictive manner. The process is assigned a status level by the operating system (stored as PSW), and when the process needs to interact with the CPU, the CPU checks its status to know what it can and cannot allow the process to do. If the process has the status of user mode, the CPU will limit the process's access to system resources and restrict the functions it can carry out on these resources.

Attackers have found many ways around this protection scheme and have tricked operating systems into loading their malicious code into ring 0, which is very dangerous. Attackers have fooled operating systems by creating their malicious code to mimic system-based DLLs, loadable kernel modules, or other critical files. The operating system then loads the malicious code into ring 0, and it runs in kernel mode. At this point the code could carry out almost any activity within the operating system in an unprotected manner. The malicious code can install key loggers, sniffers, code injection tools, and Trojaned files. The code could delete files on the hard drive, install back doors, or send sensitive data to the attacker's computer using the compromised system's network protocol stack.

NOTE The actual ring numbers available in a CPU architecture are dictated by the CPU itself. Some processors provide four rings and some provide eight or more. The operating systems do not have to use each available ring in the architecture; for example, Windows, OS X, and most versions of Linux commonly use only rings 0 and 3 and do not use ring 1 or ring 2. The vendor of the CPU determines the number of available rings, and the vendor of the operating system determines how it will use these rings.

Process Domain

The term *domain* just means a collection of resources. A process has a collection of resources assigned to it when it is loaded into memory (run time), as in memory addresses, files it can interact with, system services available to it, peripheral devices, etc. The higher the ring level that the process executes within, the larger the domain of resources that is available to it.

It is the responsibility of the operating system to provide a safe execution domain for the different processes it serves. This means that when a process is carrying out its activities, the operating system provides a safe, predictable, and stable environment. The execution domain is a combination of where the process can carry out its functions (memory segment), the tools available to it, and the boundaries involved to keep it in a safe and confined area.

Operating System Architectures

We started this chapter by looking at *system* architecture approaches. Remember that a system is made up of *all* the necessary pieces for computation: hardware, firmware, and software components. We then moved into the architecture of a CPU, looking only at the processor. Now we will look at operating system architectures, which deal specifically with the software components of a system.

Operating system architectures have gone through quite an evolutionary process based upon industry functionality and security needs. The architecture is the framework that dictates how the pieces and parts of the operating system interact with each other and provide the functionality that the applications and users require of it. This section looks at the monolithic, layered, microkernel, and hybrid microkernel architectures.

While operating systems are very complex, some main differences in the architectural approaches have come down to what is running in kernel mode and what is not. In a *monolithic architecture*, all of the operating system processes work in kernel mode, as illustrated in Figure 3-16. The services provided by the operating system (memory management, I/O management, process scheduling, file management, etc.) are available to applications through system calls.

Earlier operating systems, such as MS-DOS, were based upon a monolithic design. The whole operating system acted as one software layer between the user applications and the hardware level. There are several problems with this approach: complexity, portability, extensibility, and security. Since the functionality of the code is spread throughout the system, it is hard to test and debug. If there is a flaw in a software component, it is difficult to localize and easily fix. Many pieces of this spaghetti bowl of code had to be modified just to address one issue.

This type of operating system is also hard to port from one hardware platform to another because the hardware interfaces are implemented throughout the software. If the operating system has to work on new hardware, extensive rewriting of the code is required. Too many components interact directly with the hardware, which increased the complexity.

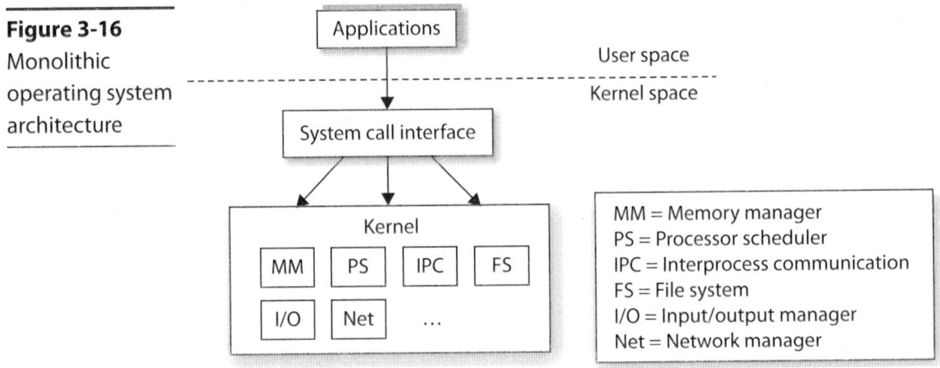

Figure 3-16 Monolithic operating system architecture

Since the monolithic system is not modular in nature, it is difficult to add and subtract functionality. As we will see in this section, later operating systems became more modular in nature to allow for functionality to be added as needed. And since all the code ran in a privileged state (kernel mode), user mistakes could cause drastic effects and malicious activities could take place more easily.

In the next generation of operating system architecture, system architects add more organization to the system. The *layered operating system* architecture separates system functionality into hierarchical layers. For example, a system that followed a layered architecture was, strangely enough, called THE (Technische Hogeschool Eindhoven) multiprogramming system. THE had five layers of functionality. Layer 0 controlled access to the processor and provided multiprogramming functionality, layer 1 carried out memory management, layer 2 provided interprocess communication, layer 3 dealt with I/O devices, and layer 4 was where the applications resided. The processes at the different layers each had interfaces to be used by processes in layers below and above them.

This layered approach, illustrated in Figure 3-17, had the full operating system still working in kernel mode (ring 0). The main difference between the monolithic approach

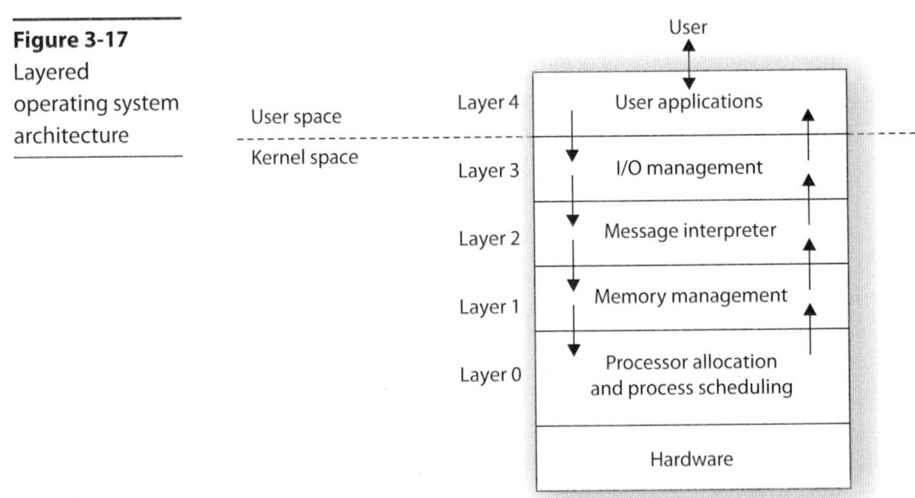

Figure 3-17 Layered operating system architecture

and this layered approach is that the functionality within the operating system was laid out in distinctive layers that called upon each other.

In the monolithic architecture, software modules communicate to each other in an ad hoc manner. In the layered architecture, module communication takes place in an organized, hierarchical structure. Routines in one layer only facilitate the layer directly below it, so no layer is missed.

Layered operating systems provide *data hiding*, which means that instructions and data (packaged up as procedures) at the various layers do not have direct access to the instructions and data at any other layers. Each procedure at each layer has access only to its own data and a set of functions that it requires to carry out its own tasks. Allowing a procedure to access more procedures than it really needs opens the door for more successful compromises. For example, if an attacker is able to compromise and gain control of one procedure and this procedure has direct access to all other procedures, the attacker could compromise a more privileged procedure and carry out more devastating activities.

A monolithic operating system provides only one layer of security. In a layered system, each layer should provide its own security and access control. If one layer contains the necessary security mechanisms to make security decisions for all the other layers, then that one layer knows too much about (and has access to) too many objects at the different layers. This directly violates the data-hiding concept. Modularizing software and its code increases the assurance level of the system because if one module is compromised, it does not mean all other modules are now vulnerable.

Since this layered approach provides more modularity, it allows for functionality to be added to and subtracted from the operating systems more easily. (You experience this type of modularity when you load new kernel modules into Linux-based systems or DLLs in Windows.) The layered approach also introduces the idea of having an abstraction level added to the lower portion of the operating system. This abstraction level allows the operating system to be more portable from one hardware platform to the next. (In Windows environments you know this invention as the Hardware Abstraction Layer, or HAL). Examples of layered operating systems are THE, VAX/VMS, Multics, and Unix (although THE and Multics are no longer in use).

The downfalls with this layered approach are performance, complexity, and security. If several layers of execution have to take place for even simple operating system activities, there can be a performance hit. The security issues mainly deal with so much code still running in kernel mode. The more processes that are running in a privileged state, the higher the likelihood of compromises that have high impact. The attack surface of the operating system overall needs to be reduced.

As the evolution of operating system development marches forward, the system architects reduce the number of required processes that made up the kernel (critical operating system components) and some operating system types move from a monolithic model to a *microkernel* model. The microkernel is a smaller subset of critical kernel processes, which focus mainly on memory management and interprocess communication, as shown in Figure 3-18. Other operating system components, such as protocols, device drivers, and file systems, are not included in the microkernel and work in user mode. The goal is to limit the processes that run in kernel mode so that the overall system is more secure, complexity is reduced, and portability of the operating system is increased.

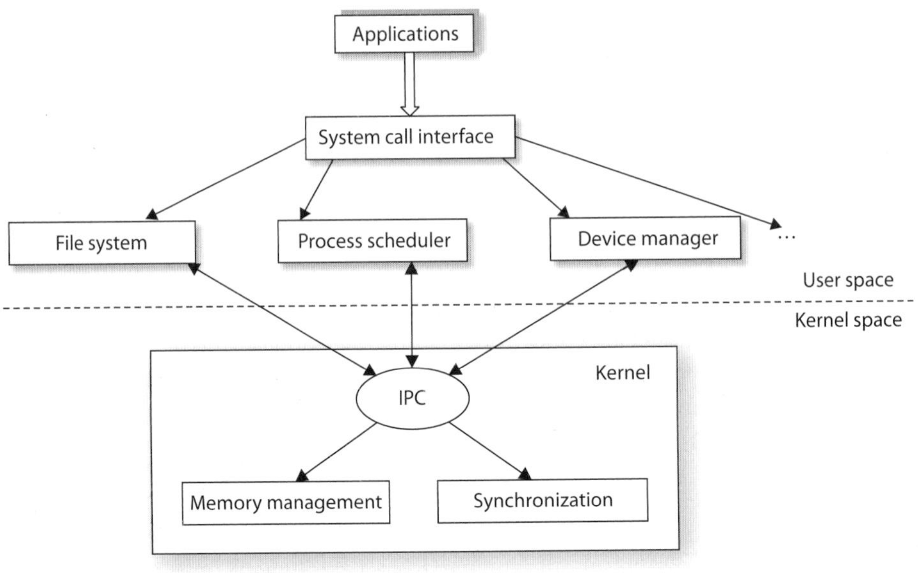

Figure 3-18 Microkernel architecture

Operating system vendors found that having just a stripped-down microkernel working in kernel mode had a lot of performance issues because processing required so many mode transitions. A *mode transition* takes place every time a CPU has to move between executing instructions for processes that work in kernel mode versus user mode. As an analogy, suppose you have to set up a different office environment for two employees, Sam and Vicky, when they come to the office to work. There is only one office with one desk, one computer, and one file cabinet (just like the computer only has one CPU). Before Sam gets to the office you have to put out the papers for his accounts, fill the file cabinet with files relating to his tasks, configure the workstation with his user profile, and make sure his coffee cup is available. When Sam leaves and before Vicky gets to the office, you have to change out all the papers, files, user profile, and coffee cup. Your responsibility is to provide the different employees with the right environment so that they can get right down to work when they arrive at the office, but constantly changing out all the items is time consuming. In essence, this is what a CPU has to do when an interrupt takes place and a process from a different mode (kernel or user) needs its instructions executed. The current process information has to be stored and saved so the CPU can come back and complete the original process's requests. The new process information (memory addresses, program counter value, PSW, etc.) has to be moved into the CPU registers. Once this is completed, then the CPU can start executing the process's instruction set. This back and forth has to happen because it is a multitasking system that is sharing one resource—the CPU.

So the industry went from a bloated kernel (whole operating system) to a small kernel (microkernel), but the performance hit was too great. There has to be a compromise between the two, which is referred to as the hybrid microkernel architecture.

In a *hybrid microkernel architecture*, the microkernel still exists and carries out mainly interprocess communication and memory management responsibilities. All of the other operating services work in a client\server model. The operating system services are the servers, and the application processes are the clients. When a user's application needs the operating system to carry out some type of functionality for it (file system interaction, peripheral device communication, network access, etc.), it makes a request to the specific API of the system's server service. This operating system service carries out the activity for the application and returns the result when finished. The separation of a microkernel and the other operating system services within a hybrid microkernel architecture is illustrated in Figure 3-19, which is the basic structure of a Windows environment. The services that run outside the microkernel are collectively referred to as the executive services.

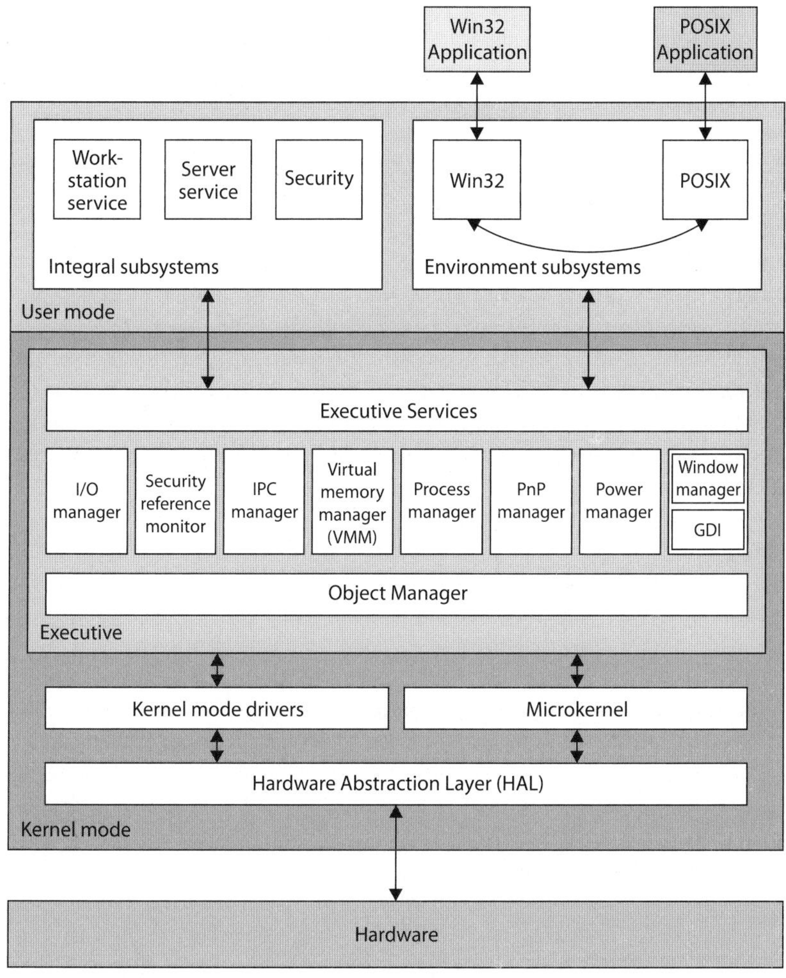

Figure 3-19 Windows hybrid microkernel architecture

The basic core definitions of the different architecture types are as follows:

- **Monolithic** All operating system processes run in kernel mode.
- **Layered** All operating system processes run in a hierarchical model in kernel mode.
- **Microkernel** Core operating system processes run in kernel mode and the remaining ones run in user mode.
- **Hybrid microkernel** All operating system processes run in kernel mode. Core processes run within a microkernel and others run in a client\server model.

The main architectures that are used in systems today are illustrated in Figure 3-20.

Cause for Confusion

If you continue your studies in operating system architecture, you will undoubtedly run into some of the confusion and controversy surrounding these families of architectures. The intricacies and complexities of these arguments are out of scope for the CISSP exam, but a little insight is worth noting.

Today, the terms monolithic operating system and monolithic kernel are used interchangeably, which invites confusion. The industry started with monolithic *operating systems*, as in MS-DOS, which did not clearly separate out kernel and non-kernel processes. As operating systems advanced, the kernel components became more organized, isolated, protected, and focused. The hardware-facing code became more virtualized to allow for portability, and the code became more modular so functionality components (loadable kernel modules, DLLs) could be loaded and unloaded as needed. So while a Unix system today may follow a monolithic *kernel* model, it does not mean that it is as rudimentary as MS-DOS, which was a monolithic *operating system*. The core definition of monolithic stayed the same, which just means the whole operating system runs in kernel mode, but operating systems that fall under this umbrella term advanced over time.

Different operating systems (BSD, Solaris, Linux, Windows, OS X, etc.) have different flavors and versions, and while some cleanly fit into the classic architecture buckets, some do not because the vendors have had to develop their systems to meet their specific customer demands. Some operating systems only got more lean and stripped of functionality so that they could work in embedded systems, real-time systems, or dedicated devices (firewalls, VPN concentrators), and some got more bloated to provide extensive functionality (Windows, Linux). Operating systems moved from cooperative multitasking to preemptive, improved memory management; some changed file system types (FAT to NTFS); I/O management matured; networking components were added; and there was allowance for distributed computing and multiprocessing. So in reality, we cannot think that architectural advancement *just* had to do with what code ran in kernel mode and what did not, but these design families are ways for us to segment operating system advancements at a macro level.

You do not need to know the architecture types specific operating systems follow for the CISSP exam, but just the architecture types in general. Remember that the CISSP exam is a nonvendor and high-level exam.

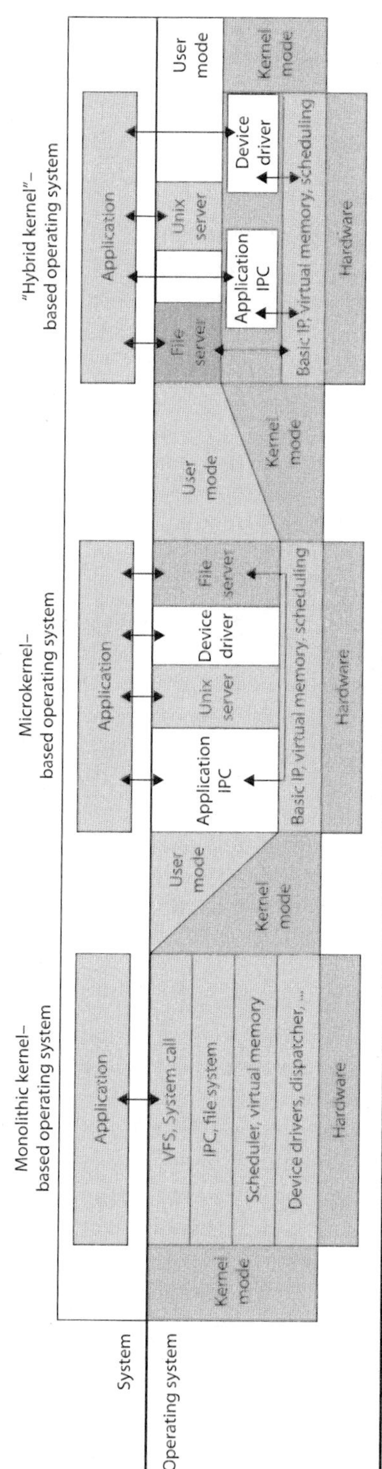

Figure 3-20 Major operating system kernel architectures

Operating system architecture is critical when it comes to the security of a system overall. Systems can be patched, but this is only a Band-Aid approach. Security should be baked in from the beginning and then thought through in every step of the development life cycle.

Virtual Machines

If you have been into computers for a while, you might remember computer games that did not have the complex, lifelike graphics of today's games. *Pong* and *Asteroids* were what we had to play with when we were younger. In those simpler times, the games were 16-bit and were written to work in a 16-bit MS-DOS environment. When our Windows operating systems moved from 16-bit to 32-bit, the 32-bit operating systems were written to be backward compatible, so someone could still load and play a 16-bit game in an environment that the game did not understand. The continuation of this little life pleasure was available to users because the operating systems created virtual environments for the games to run in. Backward compatibility was also introduced with 64-bit operating systems.

When a 32-bit application needs to interact with a 64-bit operating system, it has been developed to make system calls and interact with the computer's memory in a way that would only work within a 32-bit operating system—not a 64-bit system. So, the virtual environment simulates a 32-bit operating system, and when the application makes a request, the operating system converts the 32-bit request into a 64-bit request (this is called *thunking*) and reacts to the request appropriately. When the system sends a reply to this request, it changes the 64-bit reply into a 32-bit reply so the application understands it.

Today, virtual environments are much more advanced. Basic *virtualization* enables single hardware equipment to run multiple operating system environments simultaneously, greatly enhancing processing power utilization, among other benefits. Creating virtual instances of operating systems, applications, and storage devices is known as *virtualization*.

In today's jargon, a virtual instance of an operating system is known as a *virtual machine*. A virtual machine is commonly referred to as a *guest* that is executed in the *host* environment. Virtualization allows a single host environment to execute multiple guests at once, with multiple virtual machines dynamically pooling resources from a common physical system. Computer resources such as RAM, processors, and storage are emulated through the host environment. The virtual machines do not directly access these resources; instead, they communicate with a *hypervisor* within the host environment, which is responsible for managing system resources. The hypervisor is the central program that controls the execution of the various guest operating systems and provides the abstraction level between the guest and host environments, as shown in Figure 3-21.

What this means is that you can have one computer running several different operating systems at one time. For example, you can run a system with Windows 10, Linux, Unix, and Windows 2008 on one computer. Think of a house that has different rooms. Each operating system gets its own room, but each shares the same resources that the house provides—a foundation, electricity, water, roof, and so on. An operating system

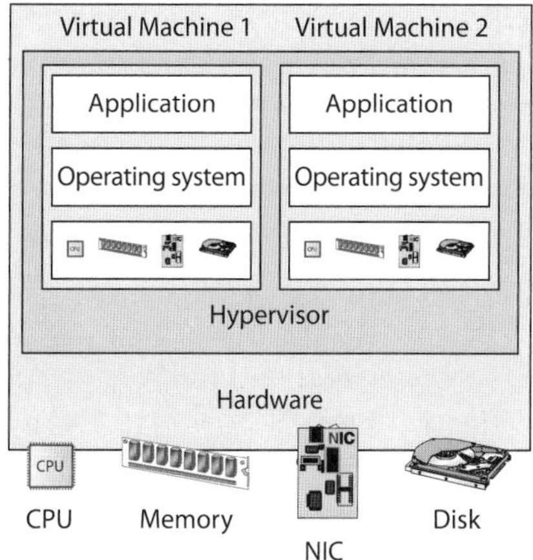

Figure 3-21 The hypervisor controls virtual machine instances.

that is "living" in a specific room does not need to know about or interact with another operating system in another room to take advantage of the resources provided by the house. The same concept happens in a computer: Each operating system shares the resources provided by the physical system (as in memory, processor, buses, and so on). They "live" and work in their own "rooms," which are the guest virtual machines. The physical computer itself is the host.

Why do this? One reason is that it is cheaper than having a full physical system for each and every operating system. If they can all live on one system and share the same physical resources, your costs are reduced immensely. This is the same reason people get roommates. The rent can be split among different people, and all can share the same house and resources. Another reason to use virtualization is security. Providing software their own "clean" environments to work within reduces the possibility of them negatively interacting with each other.

The following useful list, from "An Introduction to Virtualization" by Amit Singh (available at www.kernelthread.com/publications/virtualization), pertains to the different reasons for using virtualization in various environments. It was written years ago (2004), but is still very applicable to today's needs and the CISSP exam.

- *Virtual machines can be used to consolidate the workloads of several under-utilized servers to fewer machines, perhaps a single machine (server consolidation). Related benefits (perceived or real, but often cited by vendors) are savings on hardware, environmental costs, management, and administration of the server infrastructure.*
- *The need to run legacy applications is served well by virtual machines. A legacy application might simply not run on newer hardware and/or operating systems. Even if it does, if may under-utilize the server, so as above, it makes sense to consolidate several applications. This may be difficult without virtualization as such applications are usually not written to co-exist within a single execution environment.*

- *Virtual machines can be used to provide secure, isolated sandboxes for running untrusted applications. You could even create such an execution environment dynamically—on the fly—as you download something from the Internet and run it. Virtualization is an important concept in building secure computing platforms.*
- *Virtual machines can be used to create operating systems, or execution environments with resource limits, and given the right schedulers, resource guarantees. Partitioning usually goes hand-in-hand with quality of service in the creation of QoS-enabled operating systems.*
- *Virtual machines can provide the illusion of hardware, or hardware configuration that you do not have (such as SCSI devices, multiple processors, …). Virtualization can also be used to simulate networks of independent computers.*
- *Virtual machines can be used to run multiple operating systems simultaneously: different versions, or even entirely different systems, which can be on hot standby. Some such systems may be hard or impossible to run on newer real hardware.*
- *Virtual machines allow for powerful debugging and performance monitoring. You can put such tools in the virtual machine monitor, for example. Operating systems can be debugged without losing productivity, or setting up more complicated debugging scenarios.*
- *Virtual machines can isolate what they run, so they provide fault and error containment. You can inject faults proactively into software to study its subsequent behavior.*
- *Virtual machines make software easier to migrate, thus aiding application and system mobility.*
- *You can treat application suites as appliances by "packaging" and running each in a virtual machine.*
- *Virtual machines are great tools for research and academic experiments. Since they provide isolation, they are safer to work with. They encapsulate the entire state of a running system: you can save the state, examine it, modify it, reload it, and so on. The state also provides an abstraction of the workload being run.*
- *Virtualization can enable existing operating systems to run on shared memory multiprocessors.*
- *Virtual machines can be used to create arbitrary test scenarios, and can lead to some very imaginative, effective quality assurance.*
- *Virtualization can be used to retrofit new features in existing operating systems without "too much" work.*
- *Virtualization can make tasks such as system migration, backup, and recovery easier and more manageable.*
- *Virtualization can be an effective means of providing binary compatibility.*
- *Virtualization on commodity hardware has been popular in co-located hosting. Many of the above benefits make such hosting secure, cost-effective, and appealing in general.*
- *Virtualization is fun.*

System Security Architecture

Up to this point we have looked at system architectures, CPU architectures, and operating system architectures. Remember that a system architecture has several views to it, depending upon the stakeholder's individual concerns. Since our main concern is security, we are going to approach system architecture from a security point of view and drill down into the core components that are part of most computing systems today. But first we need to understand how the goals for the individual system security architectures are defined.

Security Policy

In life we set goals for ourselves, our teams, companies, and families to meet. Setting a goal defines the desired end state. We might define a goal for our company to make $2 million by the end of the year. We might define a goal of obtaining three government contracts for our company within the next six months. A goal could be that we lose 30 pounds in 12 months or save enough money for our child to be able to go off to college when she turns 18 years old. The point is that we have to define a desired end state and from there we can lay out a structured plan on how to accomplish those goals, punctuated with specific action items and a defined time line.

It is not usually helpful to have vague goal statements, as in "save money" or "lose weight" or "become successful." Our goals need to be specific, or how do we know when we accomplish them? This is also true in computer security. If your boss were to give you a piece of paper that had a simple goal written on it, "Build a secure system," where would you start? What is the definition of a "system"? What is the definition of "secure"? You'd have no way of knowing whether you accomplished the goal. Now if your boss were to hand you the same paper with the following list included, you'd be in business:

- Discretionary access control–based operating system
- Provides role-based access control functionality
- Capability of protecting data classified at "public" and "confidential" levels
- Does not allow unauthorized access to sensitive data or critical system functions
- Enforces least privilege and separation of duties
- Provides auditing capabilities
- Implements trusted paths and trusted shells for sensitive processing activities
- Enforces identification, authentication, and authorization of trusted subjects
- Implements a capability-based authentication methodology
- Does not contain covert channels
- Enforces integrity rules on critical files

Now you have more direction on what it is that your boss wants you to accomplish, and you can work with your boss to form the overall security goals for the system you will be designing and developing. All of these goals need to be captured and outlined in a security policy.

Security starts at a policy level, with high-level directives that provide the foundational goals for a system overall and the components that make it up from a security perspective. A *security policy* is a strategic tool that dictates how sensitive information and resources are to be managed and protected. A security policy expresses exactly what the security level should be by setting the goals of what the security mechanisms are supposed to accomplish. This is an important element that has a major role in defining the architecture and design of the system. The security policy is a foundation for the specifications of a system and provides the baseline for evaluating a system after it is built. The evaluation is carried out to make sure that the goals that were laid out in the security policy were accomplished.

Security Architecture Requirements

In the 1970s computer systems were moving from single-user, stand-alone, centralized, and closed systems to multiuser systems that had multiprogramming functionality and networking capabilities. The U.S. government needed to ensure that all of the systems that it was purchasing and implementing were properly protecting its most secret secrets. The government had various levels of classified data (secret, top secret) and users with different clearance levels (Secret, Top Secret). It needed to come up with a way to instruct vendors on how to build computer systems to meet their security needs and in turn a way to test the products these vendors developed based upon those same security needs.

In 1972, the U.S. government released a report (Computer Security Technology Planning Study) that outlined basic and foundational security requirements of computer systems that it would deem acceptable for purchase and deployment. These requirements were further defined and built upon, which resulted in the Trusted Computer System Evaluation Criteria, which shaped the security architecture of almost all of the systems in use today. Some of the core tenets of these requirements were the trusted computing base, security perimeter, reference monitor, and security kernel.

Trusted Computing Base

The *trusted computing base (TCB)* is a collection of all the hardware, software, and firmware components within a system that provides some type of security and enforces the system's security policy. The TCB does not address *only* operating system components, because a computer system is not made up of *only* an operating system. Hardware, software components, and firmware components can affect the system in a negative or positive manner, and each has a responsibility to support and enforce the security policy of that particular system. Some components and mechanisms have direct responsibilities in supporting the security policy, such as firmware that will not let a user boot a computer from a USB drive, or the memory manager that will not let processes overwrite other processes' data. Then there are components that do not enforce the security policy but must behave properly and not violate the trust of a system. Examples of the ways in which a component could violate the system's security policy include an application that is allowed to make a direct call to a piece of hardware instead of using the proper system calls through the operating system, a process that is allowed to read data outside of its approved memory space, or a piece of software that does not properly release resources after use.

The operating system's kernel is made up of hardware, software, and firmware, so in a sense the kernel is the TCB. But the TCB can include other components, such as trusted commands, programs, and configuration files that can directly interact with the kernel. For example, when installing a Unix system, the administrator can choose to install the TCB configuration during the setup procedure. If the TCB is enabled, then the system has a trusted path, a trusted shell, and system integrity–checking capabilities. A *trusted path* is a communication channel between the user, or program, and the TCB. The TCB provides protection resources to ensure this channel cannot be compromised in any way. A *trusted shell* means that someone who is working in that shell (command interpreter) cannot "bust out of it" and other processes cannot "bust into it."

Every operating system has specific components that would cause the system grave danger if they were compromised. The components that make up the TCB provide extra layers of protection around these mechanisms to help ensure they are *not* compromised, so the system will always run in a safe and predictable manner. While the TCB components can provide extra layers of protection for sensitive processes, they themselves have to be developed securely. The BIOS function should have a password protection capability and be tamperproof. The subsystem within a Windows operating system that generates access tokens should not be able to be hijacked and be used to produce fake tokens for malicious processes. Before a process can interact with a system configuration file, it must be authenticated by the security kernel. Device drivers should not be able to be modified in an unauthorized manner. Basically, any piece of a system that could be used to compromise the system or put it into an unstable condition is considered to be part of the TCB, and it must be developed and controlled very securely.

You can think of the TCB as a building. You want the building to be strong and safe, so there are certain components that *absolutely* have to be built and installed properly. The right types of construction nails need to be used, not the flimsy ones we use at home to hold up pictures of our grandparents. The beams in the walls need to be made out of steel and properly placed. The concrete in the foundation needs to be made of the right concentration of gravel and water. The windows need to be shatterproof. The electrical wiring needs to be of proper grade and grounded.

An operating system also has critical pieces that absolutely have to be built and installed properly. The memory manager has to be tamperproof and properly protect shared memory spaces. When working in kernel mode, the CPU must have all logic gates in the proper place. Operating system APIs must only accept secure service requests. Access control lists on objects cannot be modified in an unauthorized manner. Auditing must take place, and the audit trails cannot be modified in an unauthorized manner. Interprocess communication must take place in an approved and controlled manner.

The processes within the TCB are the components that protect the system overall. So the developers of the operating system must make sure these processes have their own *execution domain*. This means they reside in ring 0, their instructions are executed in privileged state, and no less trusted processes can directly interact with them. The developers need to ensure the operating system maintains an isolated execution domain, so their processes cannot be compromised or tampered with. The resources that the TCB processes use must also be isolated, so tight access control can be provided and all access requests and operations can be properly audited. So basically, the operating system ensures that all the non-TCB processes and TCB processes interact in a secure manner.

When a system goes through an evaluation process, part of the process is to identify the architecture, security services, and assurance mechanisms that make up the TCB.

During the evaluation process, the tests must show how the TCB is protected from accidental or intentional tampering and compromising activity. For systems to achieve a higher trust level rating, they must meet well-defined TCB requirements, and the details of their operational states, development stages, testing procedures, and documentation will be reviewed with more granularity than systems attempting to achieve a lower trust rating.

Security Perimeter

As stated previously, not every process and resource falls within the TCB, so some of these components fall outside of an imaginary boundary referred to as the *security perimeter.* A security perimeter is a boundary that divides the trusted from the untrusted. For the system to stay in a secure and trusted state, precise communication standards must be developed to ensure that when a component within the TCB needs to communicate with a component outside the TCB, the communication cannot expose the system to unexpected security compromises. This type of communication is handled and controlled through interfaces.

For example, a resource that is within the boundary of the security perimeter is considered to be a part of the TCB and must not allow less trusted components access to critical system resources in an insecure manner. The processes within the TCB must also be careful about the commands and information they accept from less trusted resources. These limitations and restrictions are built into the interfaces that permit this type of communication to take place and are the mechanisms that enforce the security perimeter. Communication between trusted components and untrusted components needs to be controlled to ensure that the system stays stable and safe.

Recall that when we covered CPU architectures, we went through the various rings a CPU provides. The operating system places its software components within those rings. The most trusted components would go inside ring 0, and the less trusted components would go into the other rings. Strict and controlled communication has to be put into place to make sure a less trusted component does not compromise a more trusted component. This control happens through APIs. The APIs are like bouncers at bars. The bouncers only allow individuals who are safe into the bar environment and keep the others out. This is the same idea of a security perimeter. Strict interfaces need to be put into place to control the communication between the items within and outside the TCB.

TIP The TCB and security perimeter are not physical entities, but conceptual constructs used by system architects and developers to delineate between trusted and untrusted components and how they communicate.

Reference Monitor

Up to this point we have a CPU that provides a ringed structure and an operating system that places its components in the different rings based upon the trust level of each component. We have a defined security policy, which outlines the level of security we want our system to provide. We have chosen the mechanisms that will enforce the security policy (TCB) and implemented security perimeters (interfaces) to make sure these mechanisms communicate securely. Now we need to develop and implement a mechanism that ensures that the subjects that access objects within the operating system have been given the necessary permissions to do so. This means we need to develop and implement a reference monitor.

The *reference monitor* is an abstract machine that mediates all access subjects have to objects, both to ensure that the subjects have the necessary access rights and to protect the objects from unauthorized access and destructive modification. For a system to achieve a higher level of trust, it must require subjects (programs, users, processes) to be fully authorized prior to accessing an object (file, program, resource). A subject must not be allowed to use a requested resource until the subject has proven it has been granted access privileges to use the requested object. The reference monitor is an access control concept, not an actual physical component, which is why it is normally referred to as the "reference monitor concept" or an "abstract machine."

The reference monitor defines the design requirements a reference validation mechanism must meet so that it can properly enforce the specifications of a system-based access control policy. Access control is made up of rules, which specify what subjects (processes, programs, users, etc.) can communicate with which objects (files, processes, peripheral devices, etc.) and what operations can be performed (read, write, execute, etc.). If you think about it, almost everything that takes place within an operating system is made up of subject-to-object communication and it has to be tightly controlled, or the whole system could be put at risk. If the access rules of the reference monitor are not properly enforced, a process could potentially misuse an object, which could result in corruption or compromise.

The reference monitor provides direction on how all access control decisions should be made and controlled in a central, concerted manner within a system. Instead of having distributed components carrying out subject-to-object access decisions individually and independently, all access decisions should be made by a core-trusted, tamperproof component of the operating system that works within the system's kernel, which is the role of the security kernel.

Security Kernel

The *security kernel* is made up of hardware, software, and firmware components that fall within the TCB, and it implements and enforces the reference monitor concept. The security kernel mediates all access and functions between subjects and objects. The security kernel is the core of the TCB and is the most commonly used approach to building trusted computing systems. The security kernel has three main requirements:

- It must provide isolation for the processes carrying out the reference monitor concept, and the processes must be tamperproof.
- It must be invoked for every access attempt and must be impossible to circumvent. Thus, the security kernel must be implemented in a complete and foolproof way.
- It must be small enough to be tested and verified in a complete and comprehensive manner.

These are the requirements of the reference monitor; therefore, they are the requirements of the components that provide and enforce the reference monitor concept—the security kernel.

These issues work in the abstract but are implemented in the physical world of hardware devices and software code. The assurance that the components are enforcing the abstract idea of the reference monitor is proved through testing and evaluations.

EXAM TIP The reference monitor is a concept in which an abstract machine mediates all access to objects by subjects. The security kernel is the hardware, firmware, and software of the TCB that implements this concept. The TCB is the totality of protection mechanisms within a computer system that work together to enforce a security policy. It contains the security kernel and all other security protection mechanisms.

The following is a quick analogy to show you the relationship between the processes that make up the security kernel, the security kernel itself, and the reference monitor concept. Individuals (processes) make up a society (security kernel). For a society to have a certain standard of living, its members must interact in specific ways, which is why we have laws. The laws represent the reference monitor, which enforces proper activity. Each individual is expected to stay within the bounds of the laws and act in specific ways so society as a whole is not adversely affected and the standard of living is not threatened. The components within a system must stay within the bounds of the reference monitor's laws so they will not adversely affect other components and threaten the security of the system.

For a system to provide an acceptable level of trust, it must be based on an architecture that provides the capabilities to protect itself from untrusted processes, intentional or accidental compromises, and attacks at different layers of the system. A majority of the trust ratings obtained through formal evaluations require a defined subset of subjects and objects, explicit domains, and the isolation of processes so their access can be controlled and the activities performed on them can be audited.

Let's regroup. We know that a system's trust is defined by how it enforces its own security policy. When a system is tested against specific criteria, a rating is assigned to the system and this rating is used by customers, vendors, and the computing society as a whole. The criteria will determine if the security policy is being properly supported and enforced. The security policy lays out the rules and practices pertaining to how a system will manage, protect, and allow access to sensitive resources. The reference monitor is a concept that says all subjects must have proper authorization to access objects, and this concept is implemented by the security kernel. The security kernel comprises all the resources that supervise system activity in accordance with the system's security policy and is part of the operating system that controls access to system resources. For the security kernel to work correctly, the individual processes must be isolated from each other and domains must be defined to dictate which objects are available to which subjects.

NOTE Security policies that prevent information from flowing from a high security level to a lower security level are called *multilevel security policies*. These types of policies permit a subject to access an object only if the subject's security level is higher than or equal to the object's classification.

As previously stated, many of the concepts covered in the previous sections are abstract ideas that will be manifested in physical hardware components, firmware, software code, and activities through designing, building, and implementing a system. Operating systems implement access rights, permissions, access tokens, mandatory integrity levels, access control lists, access control entities, memory protection, sandboxes, virtualization, and more to meet the requirements of these abstract concepts.

Security Models

A security model maps the abstract goals of the policy to information system terms by specifying explicit data structures and techniques necessary to enforce the security policy. A security model is usually represented in mathematics and analytical ideas, which are mapped to system specifications and then developed by programmers through programming code. So we have a policy that encompasses security goals, such as "each subject must be authenticated and authorized before accessing an object." The security model takes this requirement and provides the necessary mathematical formulas, relationships, and logic structure to be followed to accomplish this goal. From there, specifications are developed per operating system type (Unix, Windows, OS X, and so on), and individual vendors can decide how they are going to implement mechanisms that meet these necessary specifications.

A security policy outlines goals without regard to how they will be accomplished. A model is a framework that gives the policy form and solves security access problems for particular situations. Several security models have been developed to enforce security policies. The following sections provide overviews of the models with which you must be familiar as a CISSP.

Bell-LaPadula Model

The *Bell-LaPadula model* enforces the *confidentiality* aspects of access control. It was developed in the 1970s to prevent secret information from being accessed in an unauthorized manner. It was the first mathematical model of a multilevel security policy used to define the concept of secure modes of access and outlined rules of access. Its development was funded by the U.S. government to provide a framework for computer systems that would be used to store and process sensitive information. A system that employs the Bell-LaPadula model is called a *multilevel security system* because users with different clearances use the system, and the system processes data at different classification levels.

EXAM TIP The Bell-LaPadula model was developed to make sure secrets stay secret; thus, *it provides and addresses confidentiality only.* This model does not address the integrity of the data the system maintains—only who can and cannot access the data and what operations can be carried out.

Three main rules are used and enforced in the Bell-LaPadula model:

- Simple security rule
- *-property (star property) rule
- Strong star property rule

The *simple security rule* states that a subject at a given security level cannot read data that resides at a higher security level. For example, if Bob is given the security clearance of secret, this rule states he cannot *read* data classified as top secret. If the organization wanted Bob to be able to read top-secret data, it would have given him that clearance in the first place.

The **-property rule* (star property rule) states that a subject in a given security level cannot *write* information to a lower security level. The simple security rule is referred to as the "no read up" rule, and the *-property rule is referred to as the "no write down" rule.

The *strong star property rule* states that a subject who has read and write capabilities can only perform both of those functions at the same security level; nothing higher and nothing lower. So, for a subject to be able to read and write to an object, the subject's clearance and the object classification must be equal.

Biba Model

The *Biba model* is a security model that addresses the *integrity* of data within a system. It is not concerned with security levels and confidentiality. The Biba model uses integrity levels to prevent data at any integrity level from flowing to a higher integrity level. Biba has three main rules to provide this type of protection:

- ***-integrity axiom** A subject cannot write data to an object at a higher integrity level (referred to as "no write up").
- **Simple integrity axiom** A subject cannot read data from a lower integrity level (referred to as "no read down").
- **Invocation property** A subject cannot request service (invoke) at a higher integrity.

A simple example might help illustrate how the Biba model could be used in a real context. Suppose that Indira and Erik are on a project team and are writing two documents: Indira is drafting meeting notes for internal use and Erik is writing a report for the CEO. The information Erik uses in writing his report must be very accurate and reliable, which is to say it must have a high level of integrity. Indira, on the other hand, is just documenting the internal work being done by the team, including ideas, opinions, and hunches. She could use unconfirmed and maybe even unreliable sources when writing her document. The **-integrity axiom* dictates that Indira would not be able to contribute (write) material to Erik's report, though there's nothing to say she couldn't use Erik's (higher integrity) information in her own document. The *simple integrity axiom*, on the other hand, would prevent Erik from even reading Indira's document because it could potentially introduce lower integrity information into his own (high integrity) report.

The *invocation property* in the Biba model states that a subject cannot invoke (call upon) a subject at a higher integrity level. How is this different from the other two Biba rules? The *-integrity axiom (no write up) dictates how subjects can *modify* objects. The simple integrity axiom (no read down) dictates how subjects can *read* objects. The invocation property dictates how one subject can communicate with and initialize other subjects at run time. An example of a subject invoking another subject is when a process sends a request to a procedure to carry out some type of task. Subjects are only allowed to invoke tools at a lower integrity level. With the invocation property, the system is making sure a dirty subject cannot invoke a clean tool to contaminate a clean object.

Bell-LaPadula vs. Biba

The Bell-LaPadula and Biba models are informational flow models because they are most concerned about data flowing from one level to another. Bell-LaPadula uses security levels to provide data *confidentiality*, and Biba uses integrity levels to provide data *integrity*.

It is important for CISSP test takers to know the rules of Bell-LaPadula and Biba, and their rules sound similar. Both have "simple" and "* (star)" rules—one writing one way and one reading another way. A tip for how to remember them is if the word "simple" is used, the rule is about *reading*. If the rule uses * or "star," it is about *writing*. So now you just need to remember the reading and writing directions per model.

Clark-Wilson Model

The *Clark-Wilson model* was developed after Biba and takes some different approaches to protecting the integrity of information. This model uses the following elements:

- **Users** Active agents
- **Transformation procedures (TPs)** Programmed abstract operations, such as read, write, and modify
- **Constrained data items (CDIs)** Can be manipulated only by TPs
- **Unconstrained data items (UDIs)** Can be manipulated by users via primitive read and write operations
- **Integrity verification procedures (IVPs)** Check the consistency of CDIs with external reality

A distinctive feature of the Clark-Wilson model is that it focuses on well-formed transactions and separation of duties. A *well-formed transaction* is a series of operations that transform a data item from one consistent state to another. Think of a consistent state as one wherein we know the data is reliable. This consistency ensures the integrity of the data and is the job of the TPs. Separation of duties is implemented in the model by adding a type of procedure (the IVPs) that audits the work done by the TPs and validates the integrity of the data.

When a system uses the Clark-Wilson model, it separates data into one subset that needs to be highly protected, which is referred to as a constrained data item (CDI), and another subset that does not require a high level of protection, which is called an unconstrained data item (UDI). Users cannot modify critical data (CDI) directly. Instead, software procedures (TPs) will carry out the operations on behalf of the user. This is referred to as *access triple:* subject (user), program (TP), and object (CDI). A user cannot modify a CDI without using a TP. The UDI does not require such a high level of protection and can be manipulated directly by the user.

Remember that this is an integrity model, so it must have something that ensures that specific integrity rules are being carried out. This is the job of the IVP. The IVP ensures that all critical data (CDI) manipulation follows the application's defined integrity rules.

Noninterference Model

Multilevel security properties can be expressed in many ways, one being *noninterference*. This concept is implemented to ensure any actions that take place at a higher security level do not affect, or interfere with, actions that take place at a lower level. This type of model does not concern itself with the flow of data, but rather with what a subject knows about the state of the system. So, if an entity at a higher security level performs an action, it cannot change the state for the entity at the lower level. If a lower-level entity was aware of a certain activity that took place by an entity at a higher level and the state of the system changed for this lower-level entity, the entity might be able to deduce too much information about the activities of the higher state, which, in turn, is a way of leaking information.

Let's say that Tom and Kathy are both working on a multilevel mainframe at the same time. Tom has the security clearance of secret and Kathy has the security clearance of top secret. Since this is a central mainframe, the terminal Tom is working at has the context of secret, and Kathy is working at her own terminal, which has a context of top secret. This model states that nothing Kathy does at her terminal should directly or indirectly affect Tom's domain (available resources and working environment). The commands she executes or the resources she interacts with should not affect Tom's experience of working with the mainframe in any way. The real intent of the noninterference model is to address covert channels. The model looks at the shared resources that the different users of a system will access and tries to identify how information can be passed from a process working at a higher security clearance to a process working at a lower security clearance. Since Tom and Kathy are working on the same system at the same time, they will most likely have to share some types of resources. So the model is made up of rules to ensure that Kathy cannot pass data to Tom through covert channels.

Covert Channels

A *covert channel* is a way for an entity to receive information in an unauthorized manner. These communications can be very difficult to detect. Covert channels are of two types: storage and timing. In a *covert storage channel,* processes are able to communicate through some type of storage space on the system. For example, suppose Adam wants to leak classified information to Bob. Adam could create a user account on a web system. Bob pretends he will create an account on the same system and checks to see if the username is available. If it is available, that is the equivalent of a zero (no account existed). Otherwise, he records a one, and aborts the creation of the account. Either way, Bob waits a given amount of time. Adam either removes the account, effectively writing a zero, or ensures one exists (which would be a one). Bob tries again, recording the next bit of covertly communicated information.

In a *covert timing channel,* one process relays information to another by modulating its use of system resources. Adam could tie up a shared resource (such as a communications bus). Bob tries to access the resource and, if successful, records it as a zero bit (no wait). Otherwise, he records a one and waits a predetermined amount of time. Adam, meanwhile is encoding his covert message by selectively tying up or freeing the shared resource. Think of this as a type of Morse code, but using some type of system resource.

Brewer and Nash Model

The *Brewer and Nash model,* also called the *Chinese Wall model,* states that a subject can write to an object if, and only if, the subject cannot read another object that is in a different dataset. It was created to provide access controls that can change dynamically depending upon a user's previous actions. The main goal of the model is to protect against conflicts of interest by users' access attempts. Suppose Maria is a broker at an investment firm that also provides other services to Acme Corporation. If Maria were able to access Acme information from the other service areas, she could learn of a phenomenal earnings report that is about to be released. Armed with that information, she could encourage her clients to buy shares of Acme, confident that the price will go up shortly. The Brewer and Nash Model is designed to mitigate the risk of this situation happening.

Graham-Denning Model

Remember that these are all models, so they are not very specific in nature. Each individual vendor must decide how it is going to actually meet the rules outlined in the chosen model. Bell-LaPadula and Biba do not define how the security and integrity levels are defined and modified, nor do they provide a way to delegate or transfer access rights. The *Graham-Denning model* addresses some of these issues and defines a set of basic rights in terms of commands that a specific subject can execute on an object. This model has eight primitive protection rights, or rules of how these types of functionalities should take place securely:

- How to securely create an object
- How to securely create a subject
- How to securely delete an object
- How to securely delete a subject
- How to securely provide the read access right
- How to securely provide the grant access right
- How to securely provide the delete access right
- How to securely provide transfer access rights

These functionalities may sound insignificant, but when you're building a secure system, they are critical. If a software developer does not integrate these functionalities in a secure manner, they can be compromised by an attacker and the whole system can be at risk.

Harrison-Ruzzo-Ullman Model

The *Harrison-Ruzzo-Ullman (HRU)* model deals with access rights of subjects and the integrity of those rights. A subject can carry out only a finite set of operations on an object. Since security loves simplicity, it is easier for a system to allow or disallow authorization of operations if one command is restricted to a single operation. For example, if a subject sent command X that only requires the operation of Y, this is pretty straightforward and the system can allow or disallow this operation to take place. But, if a subject sent a command M and to fulfill that command, operations N, B, W, and P have to be carried out, then there is much more complexity for the system to decide if this command should be authorized. Also the integrity of the access rights needs to be ensured; thus, in this example, if one operation cannot be processed properly, the whole command fails. So although it is easy to dictate that subject A can only read object B, it is not always so easy to ensure each and every function supports this high-level statement. The HRU model is used by software designers to ensure that no unforeseen vulnerability is introduced and the stated access control goals are achieved.

Security Models Recap

All of these models can seem confusing. Most people are not familiar with all of them, which can make the information even harder to absorb. The following are the core concepts of the different models.

Bell-LaPadula Model This is the first mathematical model of a multilevel security policy that defines the concept of a secure state and necessary modes of access. It ensures that information only flows in a manner that does not violate the system policy and is confidentiality focused.

- **The simple security rule** A subject cannot read data within an object that resides at a higher security level (no read up).
- **The *-property rule** A subject cannot write to an object at a lower security level (no write down).
- **The strong star property rule** For a subject to be able to read and write to an object, the subject's clearance and the object's classification must be equal.

Biba Model A model that describes a set of access control rules designed to ensure data integrity.

- **The simple integrity axiom** A subject cannot read data at a lower integrity level (no read down).
- **The *-integrity axiom** A subject cannot modify an object at a higher integrity level (no write up).

Clark-Wilson Model This integrity model is implemented to protect the integrity of data and to ensure that properly formatted transactions take place. It addresses all three goals of integrity:

- Subjects can access objects only through authorized programs (access triple).
- Separation of duties is enforced.
- Auditing is required.

Noninterference Model This formal multilevel security model states that commands and activities performed at one security level should not be seen by, or affect, subjects or objects at a different security level.

Brewer and Nash Model This model allows for dynamically changing access controls that protect against conflicts of interest. Also known as the Chinese Wall model.

Graham-Denning Model This model shows how subjects and objects should be created and deleted. It also addresses how to assign specific access rights.

Harrison-Ruzzo-Ullman Model This model shows how a finite set of procedures can be available to edit the access rights of a subject.

Systems Evaluation

An *assurance evaluation* examines the security-relevant parts of a system, meaning the TCB, access control mechanisms, reference monitor, kernel, and protection mechanisms. The relationship and interaction between these components are also evaluated in order to determine the level of protection required and provided by the system. Historically, there were different methods of evaluating and assigning assurance levels to systems. Today, however, a framework known as the Common Criteria is the only one of global significance.

Common Criteria

In 1990, the International Organization for Standardization (ISO) identified the need for international standard evaluation criteria to be used globally. The Common Criteria project started in 1993 when several organizations came together to combine and align existing and emerging evaluation criteria. The Common Criteria was developed through collaboration among national security standards organizations within the United States, Canada, France, Germany, the United Kingdom, and the Netherlands. It is codified as international standard ISO/IEC 15408, which is in version 3.1 as of this writing.

The benefit of having a globally recognized and accepted set of criteria is that it helps consumers by reducing the complexity of the ratings and eliminating the need to understand the definition and meaning of different ratings within various evaluation schemes. This also helps vendors, because now they can build to one specific set of requirements if they want to sell their products internationally, instead of having to meet several different ratings with varying rules and requirements.

The *Common Criteria* is a framework within which users specify their security requirements and vendors make claims about how they satisfy those requirements, and independent labs can verify those claims. Under the Common Criteria model, an evaluation is carried out on a product and it is assigned an *Evaluation Assurance Level (EAL)*. The thorough and stringent testing increases in detailed-oriented tasks as the assurance levels increase. The Common Criteria has seven assurance levels. The range is from EAL1, where functionality testing takes place, to EAL7, where thorough testing is performed and the system design is verified. The different EAL packages are

- **EAL1** Functionally tested
- **EAL2** Structurally tested
- **EAL3** Methodically tested and checked
- **EAL4** Methodically designed, tested, and reviewed
- **EAL5** Semiformally designed and tested
- **EAL6** Semiformally verified design and tested
- **EAL7** Formally verified design and tested

TIP When a system is "formally verified," this means it is based on a model that can be mathematically proven.

The Common Criteria uses *protection profiles* in its evaluation process. This is a mechanism used to describe types of products independent of their actual implementation. The protection profile contains the set of security requirements, their meaning and reasoning, and the corresponding EAL rating that the intended product will require. The protection profile describes the environmental assumptions, the objectives, and the functional and assurance level expectations. Each relevant threat is listed along with how it is to be controlled by specific objectives. The protection profile also justifies the assurance level and requirements for the strength of each protection mechanism.

The protection profile provides a means for a consumer, or others, to identify specific security needs; this is the security problem to be conquered. If someone identifies a security need that is not currently being addressed by any current product, that person can write a protection profile describing the product that would be a solution for this real-world problem. The protection profile goes on to provide the necessary goals and protection mechanisms to achieve the required level of security, as well as a list of things that could go wrong during this type of system development. This list is used by the engineers who develop the system, and then by the evaluators to make sure the engineers dotted every *i* and crossed every *t*.

The Common Criteria was developed to stick to evaluation classes, but also to retain some degree of flexibility. Protection profiles were developed to describe the functionality, assurance, description, and rationale of the product requirements.

Like other evaluation criteria before it, the Common Criteria works to answer two basic questions about products being evaluated: What does its security mechanisms do (functionality), and how sure are you of that (assurance)? This system sets up a framework that enables consumers to clearly specify their security issues and problems, developers to specify their security solution to those problems, and evaluators to unequivocally determine what the product actually accomplishes.

A protection profile typically contains the following sections:

- **Security problem description** Lays out the specific problems (i.e., threats) that any compliant product must address.
- **Security objectives** Lists the functionality (i.e., controls) that compliant products must provide in order to address the security problems.
- **Security requirements** These are very specific requirements for compliant products. They are detailed enough for implementation by system developers, and for evaluation by independent laboratories.

The evaluation process is just one leg of determining the functionality and assurance of a product. Once a product achieves a specific rating, it only applies to that particular version and only to certain configurations of that product. So if a company buys a firewall product because it has a high assurance rating, the company has no guarantee the next version of that software will have that rating. The next version will need to go through its own evaluation review. If this same company buys the firewall product and installs it with configurations that are not recommended, the level of security the company was hoping to achieve can easily go down the drain. So, all of this rating stuff is a formalized method of reviewing a system being evaluated in a lab. When the product is implemented in a real environment, factors other than its rating need to be addressed and assessed to ensure it is properly protecting resources and the environment.

CAUTION When a product is assigned an assurance rating, this means it has the *potential* of providing this level of protection. The customer has to properly configure the product to actually obtain this level of security. The vendor should provide the necessary configuration documentation, and it is up to the customer to keep the product properly configured at all times.

Different Components of the Common Criteria

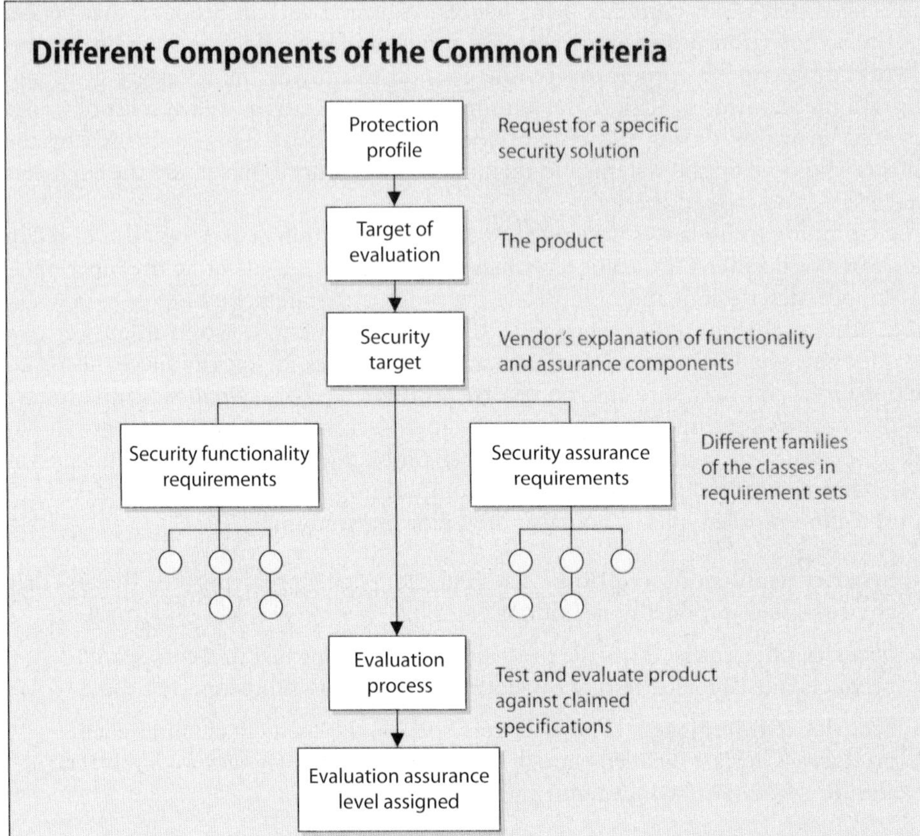

- **Protection profile (PP)** Description of a needed security solution.
- **Target of evaluation (TOE)** Product proposed to provide a needed security solution.
- **Security target** Vendor's written explanation of the security functionality and assurance mechanisms that meet the needed security solution—in other words, "This is what our product does and how it does it."
- **Security functional requirements** Individual security functions that must be provided by a product.
- **Security assurance requirements** Measures taken during development and evaluation of the product to assure compliance with the claimed security functionality.
- **Packages—EALs** Functional and assurance requirements are bundled into packages for reuse. This component describes what must be met to achieve specific EAL ratings.

ISO/IEC 15408 is the international standard that is used as the basis for the evaluation of security properties of products under the CC framework. It actually has three main parts:

- **ISO/IEC 15408-1** Introduction and general model
- **ISO/IEC 15408-2** Security functional components
- **ISO/IEC 15408-3** Security assurance components

ISO/IEC 15408-1 lays out the general concepts and principles of the CC evaluation model. This part defines terms, establishes the core concept of the TOE, describes the evaluation context, and identifies the necessary audience. It provides the key concepts for PP, security requirements, and guidelines for the security target.

ISO/IEC 15408-2 defines the security functional requirements that will be assessed during the evaluation. It contains a catalog of predefined security functional components that maps to most security needs. These requirements are organized in a hierarchical structure of classes, families, and components. It also provides guidance on the specification of customized security requirements if no predefined security functional component exists.

ISO/IEC 15408-3 defines the assurance requirements, which are also organized in a hierarchy of classes, families, and components. This part outlines the evaluation assurance levels, which is a scale for measuring assurance of TOEs, and it provides the criteria for evaluation of protection profiles and security targets.

So product vendors follow these standards when building products that they will put through the CC evaluation process, and the product evaluators follow these standards when carrying out the evaluation processes.

Why Put a Product Through Evaluation?

Submitting a product to be evaluated against the Common Criteria is no walk in the park for a vendor. In fact, it is a really painful and long process, and no one wakes up in the morning thinking, "Yippee! I have to complete all of the paperwork so my product can be certified!" So, before we go through these different criteria, let's look at *why* anyone would even put themselves through this process.

If you were going shopping to buy a firewall, how would you know what level of protection each provides and which is the best product for your environment? You could listen to the vendor's marketing hype and believe the salesperson who informs you that a particular product will solve all of your life problems in one week. Or you could listen to the advice of an independent third party who has fully tested the product and does not have any bias toward it. If you choose the second option, then you join a world of people who work within the realm of assurance ratings in one form or another.

Vendors realize that going through a CC evaluation can give them a competitive advantage. This alone would make the evaluation, as painful as it is, attractive to vendors. However, many governments are increasingly requiring CC evaluations before purchasing security-critical products. Since governments tend to be big buyers, it makes financial sense to follow the CC for certain types of systems.

This evaluation process is very time consuming and expensive for the vendor. Not every vendor puts its product through this process because of the expense and delayed date to get it to market. Typically, a vendor would put its product through this process if its main customer base will be making purchasing decisions based on assurance ratings. In the United States, the Department of Defense *is* the largest customer, so major vendors put their main products through this process with the hope that the Department of Defense (and others) will purchase their products.

Certification vs. Accreditation

We have gone through the evaluation criteria that a system can be appraised against to receive a specific rating. This is a very formalized process, following which the evaluated system or product will be assigned an EAL indicating what rating it achieved. Consumers can check this and compare the different products and systems to see how they rank against each other in the property of protection. However, once a consumer buys this product and sets it up in their environment, security is not guaranteed. Security is made up of system administration, physical security, installation, configuration mechanisms within the environment, and continuous monitoring. To fairly say a system is secure, all of these items must be taken into account. The rating is just one piece in the puzzle of security.

Certification

Certification is the comprehensive technical evaluation of the security components and their compliance for the purpose of accreditation. A certification process may use safeguard evaluation, risk analysis, verification, testing, and auditing techniques to assess the appropriateness of a specific system. For example, suppose Dan is the security officer for a company that just purchased new systems to be used to process its confidential data. He wants to know if these systems are appropriate for these tasks and if they are going to provide the necessary level of protection. He also wants to make sure they are compatible with his current environment, do not reduce productivity, and do not open doors to new threats—basically, he wants to know if these are the right products for his company. He could pay a company that specializes in these matters to perform the necessary procedures to certify the systems, but he wants to carry out the process internally. The evaluation team will perform tests on the software configurations, hardware, firmware, design, implementation, system procedures, and physical and communication controls.

The goal of a certification process is to ensure that a system, product, or network is right for the customer's purposes. Customers will rely upon a product for slightly different reasons, and environments will have various threat levels. So a particular product is not necessarily the best fit for every single customer out there. (Of course, vendors will try to convince you otherwise.) The product has to provide the right functionality and security for the individual customer, which is the whole purpose of a certification process.

The certification process and corresponding documentation will indicate the good, the bad, and the ugly about the product and how it works within the given environment. Dan will take these results and present them to his management for the accreditation process.

Accreditation

Accreditation is the formal acceptance of the adequacy of a system's overall security and functionality by management. The certification information is presented to management, or the responsible body, and it is up to management to ask questions, review the reports and findings, and decide whether to accept the product and whether any corrective action needs to take place. Once satisfied with the system's overall security as presented, management makes a formal accreditation statement. By doing this, management is stating it understands the level of protection the system will provide in its current environment and understands the security risks associated with installing and maintaining this system.

NOTE *Certification* is a technical review that assesses the security mechanisms and evaluates their effectiveness. *Accreditation* is management's official acceptance of the information in the certification process findings.

Because software, systems, and environments continually change and evolve, the certification and accreditation should also continue to take place. Any major addition of software, changes to the system, or modification of the environment should initiate a new certification and accreditation cycle.

No More Pencil Whipping

Many organizations are taking the accreditation process more seriously than they did in the past. Unfortunately, sometimes when a certification process is completed and the documentation is sent to management for review and approval, management members just blindly sign the necessary documentation without really understanding what they are signing. Accreditation means management is accepting the *risk* that is associated with allowing this new product to be introduced into the organization's environment. When a large security compromise takes place, the buck stops at the individual who signed off on the offending item. So as these management members are being held more accountable for what they sign off on, and as more regulations make executives personally responsible for security, the pencil whipping of accreditation papers is decreasing.

(*Continued*)

Certification and accreditation (C&A) really came into focus within the United States when the Federal Information Security Management Act of 2002 (FISMA) was passed as federal law. The act requires each federal agency to develop an agency-wide program to ensure the security of its information and information systems. It also requires an annual review of the agency's security program and a report of the results to be sent to the Office of Management and Budget (OMB). OMB then sends this information to the U.S. Congress to illustrate the individual agency's compliance levels.

C&A is a core component of FISMA compliance, but the manual processes of reviewing each and every system is laborious, time consuming, and error prone. FISMA requirements are now moving to continuous monitoring, which means that systems have to be continuously scanned and monitored instead of having one C&A process carried out per system every couple of years.

Open vs. Closed Systems

Computer systems can be developed to integrate easily with other systems and products (open systems), or they can be developed to be more proprietary in nature and work with only a subset of other systems and products (closed systems). The following sections describe the difference between these approaches.

Open Systems

Systems described as *open* are built upon standards, protocols, and interfaces that have published specifications. This type of architecture provides interoperability between products created by different vendors. This interoperability is provided by all the vendors involved who follow specific standards and provide interfaces that enable each system to easily communicate with other systems and allow add-ons to hook into the system easily.

A majority of the systems in use today are open systems. The reason an administrator can have Windows, OS X, and Unix computers communicating easily on the same network is because these platforms are open. If a software vendor creates a closed system, it is restricting its potential sales to proprietary environments.

Closed Systems

Systems referred to as *closed* use an architecture that does not follow industry standards. Interoperability and standard interfaces are not employed to enable easy communication between different types of systems and add-on features. *Closed systems* are proprietary, meaning the system can only communicate with like systems.

A closed architecture can potentially provide more security to the system because it may operate in a more secluded environment than open environments. Because a closed system is proprietary, there are not as many predefined tools to thwart the security mechanisms and not as many people who understand its design, language, and security weaknesses and thus attempt to exploit them. But just relying upon something being proprietary as its security control is practicing security through obscurity (introduced in Chapter 1). Attackers can find flaws in proprietary systems or open systems, so each type should be built securely and maintained securely.

A majority of the systems today are built with open architecture to enable them to work with other types of systems, easily share information, and take advantage of the functionality that third-party add-ons bring.

Distributed System Security

A distributed system is one in which multiple computers work together to do something. When you visit a website, the web server provides the content, your device renders it and allows you to interact with it, and the network devices in between take care of moving the data back and forth. It is this collaboration that defines a distributed system. We could then say that a *distributed system* is a system in which multiple computing nodes, interconnected by a network, exchange information for the accomplishment of collective tasks.

Distributed systems pose special challenges in terms of security simply because of the number of devices that are involved. In our (seemingly) simple example of visiting a website, we would have to secure at least three nodes: the client, the server, and the network device in between. In reality, rendering just one page could involve dozens of devices owned by different entities in multiple countries. As we will discuss in Chapter 4, an adversary can insert an unauthorized node in the network and get between you and your destination in what's called a man-in-the-middle attack. Even without this attacker, we would have to concern ourselves with the security of domain name servers, load balancers, database servers, proxy servers, and potentially many other devices that are normally transparent to the user. This complexity that is inherent to distributed systems increases the security risks they pose.

To tackle these challenges, we can start by grouping distributed systems according to their architectures. As you will see, each type of distributed system has specific issues that we need to address, which gives us a bit of focus and allows us to zero in on the things we care about. What follows is a brief overview of some of the most common distributed systems in use today.

Cloud Computing

If you were asked to install a brand-new server room for your organization, you would probably have to clear your calendar for weeks (or longer) to address the many tasks that would be involved. From power and environmental controls to hardware acquisition, installation, and configuration to software builds, the list is long and full of headaches. Now, imagine that you can provision all the needed servers in minutes using a simple graphical interface or a short script, and that you can get rid of them just as quickly when you no longer need them. This is one of the benefits of cloud computing.

Cloud computing is the use of shared, remote computing devices for the purpose of providing improved efficiencies, performance, reliability, scalability, and security. These devices are usually based on virtual machines and can be outsourced to a third-party provider or provided in house. Generally speaking, there are three models for cloud computing services:

- **Software as a Service (SaaS)** The user of SaaS is allowed to use a specific application that executes on the service provider's environment. An example of this would be subscribing to a word processing application that you would then access via a web interface.
- **Platform as a Service (PaaS)** In this model, the user gets access to a computing platform that is typically built on a server operating system. An example of this would be spawning an instance of Windows Server 2012R2 to provide a web server. The service provider is normally responsible for configuring and securing the platform, however, so the user normally doesn't get administrative privileges over the entire platform.
- **Infrastructure as a Service (IaaS)** If you want full, unfettered access to (and responsibility for securing) the cloud devices, you would need to subscribe under an IaaS model. Following up on the previous example, this would allow you to manage the patching of the Windows Server 2012R2 instance. The catch is that the service provider has no responsibility for security; it's all on you.

If you are a user of IaaS, then you will probably not do things too differently than you already do in securing your systems. The only exception would be that you wouldn't have physical access to the computers if a provider hosts them. If, on the other hand, you use SaaS or PaaS, the security of your systems will almost always rely on the policies and contracts that you put into place. The policies will dictate how your users interact with the cloud services. This would include the information classification levels that would be allowed on those services, terms of use, and other policies. The contract will specify the quality of service and what the service provider will do with or for you in responding to security events.

CAUTION It is imperative that you carefully review the terms of service when evaluating a potential contract for cloud services and consider them in the context of your organization's security. Though the industry is getting better all the time, security provisions are oftentimes lacking in these contracts at this time.

Parallel Computing

As we discussed earlier in this chapter, most CPUs can only execute a single instruction at a time. This feature can create bottlenecks, particularly when processing very large amounts of data. A way to get around this limitation is to pool multiple CPUs or computers and divide large tasks among them. Obviously, you'd need a conductor to synchronize their efforts, but the concept is otherwise pretty simple. *Parallel computing* is the simultaneous use of multiple computers to solve a specific task by dividing it among the available computers.

This division of labor can happen at one of three levels: bit, instruction, or task. *Bit-level parallelism* takes place in every computing device we use these days. When the CPU performs an instruction on a value stored in a register, each bit is processed separately through a set of parallel gates. This is one of the reasons why 64-bit processors can be faster than 32-bit ones: they operate on twice the amount of data on each cycle.

Instruction-level parallelism allows two or more program instructions to be executed simultaneously. Obviously, this requires that two or more processors are available and synchronized. Most commercially available multicore processors manufactured since 2010 support this type of parallelism. In fact, it is difficult to find new computers that do not have a multicore architecture, and even the latest mobile devices are shipping with dual-core chips as of this writing. Now, to be clear, just because you have a multicore processor in your computer does not necessarily mean that you'll benefit from parallelism. Although the operating system will automatically look for opportunities to execute instructions in parallel, you only get maximum benefit from this capability by executing programs that have been specifically designed to take advantage of multiple cores. This is becoming increasingly common, particularly among developers of bandwidth- or processor-intensive applications such as games and scientific analysis tools.

Task-level parallelism takes place at a higher level of abstraction. In it we divide a program into tasks or threads and run each in parallel. For instance, you may have a program that computes weather forecasts, which is a very computationally intensive process. You could divide the country into sectors and have the tasks of developing each sector's forecast performed in parallel. After you complete these tasks, you could have another set of parallel tasks that determines the effects of adjacent sectors on a given sector's weather. Though we are simplifying things a bit, this is the process by which most weather forecasts are developed. This would take too long to accomplish if we were not able to use parallel computing.

Finally, *data parallelism* describes the distribution of data among different nodes that then process it in parallel. It is related to task parallelism, but is focused on the data. This kind of parallelism is receiving a lot of attention these days, because it enables a lot of the advances in big data processing. For instance, if you had to find every instance of a malware signature among petabytes of captured network data, you could divide the data among computing nodes that were part of a cluster and have each look at a different part of the data.

NOTE Data parallelism can leverage the advantages of cloud computing in that you can easily spin up hundreds of instances of computing nodes only for the specific time you need them in order to process your data. This provides tremendous capability at a fraction of the cost of doing it in house.

Databases

The two main database security issues this section addresses are aggregation and inference. *Aggregation* happens when a user does not have the clearance or permission to access specific information, but she does have the permission to access components of this information. She can then figure out the rest and obtain restricted information. She can learn of information from different sources and combine it to learn something she does not have the clearance to know.

NOTE *Aggregation* is the act of combining information from separate sources. The combination of the data forms new information, which the subject does not have the necessary rights to access. The combined information has a sensitivity that is greater than that of the individual parts.

The following is a silly conceptual example. Let's say a database administrator does not want anyone in the Users group to be able to figure out a specific sentence, so he segregates the sentence into components and restricts the Users group from accessing it, as represented in Figure 3-22. However, Emily can access components A, C, and F. Because she is particularly bright, she figures out the sentence and now knows the restricted secret.

To prevent aggregation, the subject, and any application or process acting on the subject's behalf, needs to be prevented from gaining access to the whole collection, including the independent components. The objects can be placed into containers, which are classified at a higher level to prevent access from subjects with lower-level permissions or clearances. A subject's queries can also be tracked, and context-dependent access control can be enforced. This would keep a history of the objects that a subject has accessed and restrict an access attempt if there is an indication that an aggregation attack is under way.

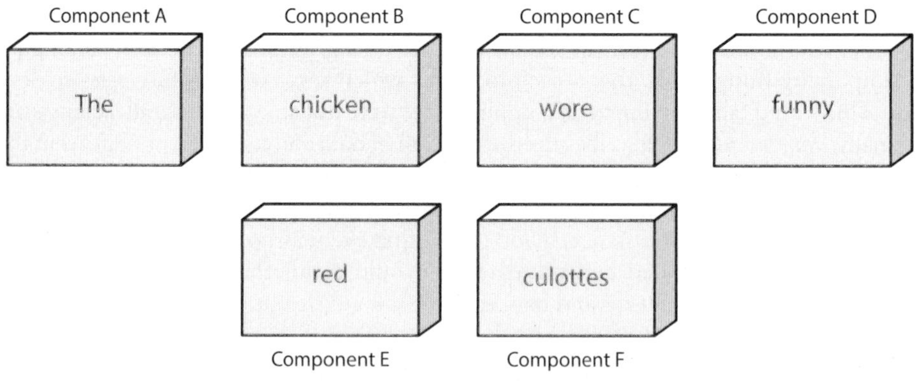

Figure 3-22 Because Emily has access to components A, C, and F, she can figure out the secret sentence through aggregation.

The other security issue is *inference*, which is the intended result of aggregation. The inference problem happens when a subject deduces the full story from the pieces he learned of through aggregation. This is seen when data at a lower security level indirectly portrays data at a higher level.

TIP *Inference* is the ability to derive information not explicitly available.

For example, if a clerk were restricted from knowing the planned movements of troops based in a specific country but did have access to food shipment requirement forms and tent allocation documents, he could figure out that the troops were moving to a specific place because that is where the food and tents are being shipped. The food shipment and tent allocation documents were classified as confidential, and the troop movement was classified as top secret. Because of the varying classifications, the clerk could access and ascertain top-secret information he was not supposed to know.

The trick is to prevent the subject, or any application or process acting on behalf of that subject, from indirectly gaining access to the inferable information. This problem is usually dealt with in the development of the database by implementing content- and context-dependent access control rules. *Content-dependent access control* is based on the sensitivity of the data. The more sensitive the data, the smaller the subset of individuals who can gain access to the data.

Context-dependent access control means that the software "understands" what actions should be allowed based upon the state and sequence of the request. So what does that mean? It means the software must keep track of previous access attempts by the user and understand what sequences of access steps are allowed. Content-dependent access control can go like this: "Does Julio have access to File A?" The system reviews the ACL on File A and returns with a response of "Yes, Julio can access the file, but can only read it." In a context-dependent access control situation, it would be more like this: "Does Julio have access to File A?" The system then reviews several pieces of data: What other access attempts has Julio made? Is this request out of sequence of how a safe series of requests takes place? Does this request fall within the allowed time period of system access (8 A.M. to 5 P.M.)? If the answers to all of these questions are within a set of preconfigured parameters, Julio can access the file. If not, he can't.

If context-dependent access control is being used to protect against inference attacks, the database software would need to keep track of what the user is requesting. So Julio makes a request to see field 1, then field 5, then field 20, which the system allows, but once he asks to see field 15, the database does not allow this access attempt. The software must be preprogrammed (usually through a rule-based engine) as to what sequence and how much data Julio is allowed to view. If he is allowed to view more information, he may have enough data to infer something we don't want him to know.

Obviously, content-dependent access control is not as complex as context-dependent control because of the number of items that need to be processed by the system.

Some other common attempts to prevent inference attacks are cell suppression, partitioning the database, and noise and perturbation. *Cell suppression* is a technique used to hide specific cells that contain information that could be used in inference attacks. *Partitioning* a database involves dividing the database into different parts, which makes it much harder for an unauthorized individual to find connecting pieces of data that can be brought together and other information that can be deduced or uncovered. *Noise and perturbation* is a technique of inserting bogus information in the hopes of misdirecting an attacker or confusing the matter enough that the actual attack will not be fruitful.

Often, security is not integrated into the planning and development of a database. Security is an afterthought, and a trusted front end is developed to be used with the database instead. This approach is limited in the granularity of security and in the types of security functions that can take place.

A common theme in security is a balance between effective security and functionality. In many cases, the more you secure something, the less functionality you have. Although this could be the desired result, it is important not to excessively impede user productivity when security is being introduced.

Web Applications

Considering their exposed nature, websites are primary targets during an attack. It is, therefore, essential for web developers to abide by the time-honored and time-tested principles to provide the maximum level of deterrence to attackers. Web application security principles are meant to govern programming practices to regulate programming styles and strategically reduce the chances of repeating known software bugs and logical flaws.

A good number of websites are exploited on the basis of vulnerabilities arising from reckless programming. With the rapidly growing number of websites out there, the possibility of exploiting such coding errors is vast.

The first pillar of implementing security principles is analyzing the website architecture. The clearer and simpler a website is, the easier it is to analyze its various security aspects. Once a website has been strategically analyzed, the user-generated input fed into the website also needs to be critically scrutinized. As a rule, all input must be considered unsafe, or rogue, and ought to be sanitized before being processed. Likewise, all output generated by the system should also be filtered to ensure private or sensitive data is not being disclosed.

In addition, using encryption helps secure the input/output operations of a web application. Though encrypted data may be intercepted by malicious users, that data should only be readable, or modifiable, by those with the secret key used to encrypt it.

In the event of an error, websites ought to be designed to behave in a predictable and noncompromising manner. This is also generally referred to as *failing securely*. Systems that fail securely display friendly error messages without revealing internal system details.

An important element in designing security functionality is keeping in perspective the human element. Though programmers may be tempted to prompt users for passwords on every mouse click to keep security effective, web developers must maintain a state of equilibrium between functionality and security. Tedious authentication techniques usually do not stay in practice for too long. Experience has shown that the best security measures are those that are simple, intuitive, and psychologically acceptable.

As discussed in Chapter 1, a commonly ineffective approach to security implementation is the use of *security through obscurity*, which assumes that creating overly complex or perplexing programs can reduce the chances of interventions in the software. Though obscure programs may take a tad longer to dissect, this does not guarantee protection from resolute and determined attackers. Protective measures, hence, cannot consist solely of obfuscation.

An effective approach to securing web applications is the use of web application firewalls (WAFs). These are systems that inspect the traffic going to (or coming from) a web application in order to filter out potentially malicious content. Since the WAF is separate from the web application, it provides an added layer of defense that can be independently tuned without having to rewrite or reconfigure the web application.

At the end, it is important to realize that the implementation of even the most beefy security techniques, without tactical considerations, will cause a website to remain as weak as its weakest link.

Mobile Devices

Many corporations do not incorporate the use of portable devices and mobile cell phone technologies into their security policies or overarching security program. This was all right when phones were just phones, but today they are small computers that can connect to websites and various devices, and thus are new entry points for malicious activities.

Since mobile devices are basically small computers, most of the same security vulnerabilities, threats, and risks carry over for this emerging technology. They are penetrated through various attack vectors, they are compromised by malware, sensitive data is stolen from them, denial-of-service attacks can take place, and now that individuals and companies are carrying out credit card transactions on them, they are new and more vulnerable points of presence.

The largest hurdle of securing any mobile or portable device is that people do not always equate them to providing as much risk as a workstation or laptop. People do not usually install antimalware software on these devices and ensure that the software is up to date, and they are constantly installing apps with an amazing amount of functionality from any Internet-based website handing them out. The failure to secure mobile devices not only puts the data on the devices at risk, but also puts at risk the workstations and laptops to which many people connect their mobile devices to allow for synchronization. This provides a jumping point from the mobile device to a computer system that may be directly connected to the corporate network.

Since mobile devices have large hard drives and extensive applications available, users commonly store spreadsheets, word documents, small databases, and more on them. This means the devices are another means of data leakage.

It is important to be aware that cell phones move their data over the airwaves and then the data is put on a wired network by the telephone company or service provider. So, a portion of the distance that the traffic must travel over is wireless, but then the remaining distance may take place over a wired environment. Thus, while mobile carriers typically encrypt their users' data, typically it is encrypted only while it is traveling over the wireless portion of the network. Once it hits the wired portion of the network, it may no longer be encrypted. So encrypting data for transmission on a cell phone or portable device does not necessarily promise end-to-end encryption.

Unfortunately, these types of attacks on cell phones will never really stop. We will come up with more countermeasures, and the bad guys will come up with new ways to exploit vulnerabilities that we did not think of. It is the same cat and mouse game that is carried out in the traditional network world. But the main issue pertaining to cell phone attacks is that they are not usually included in a corporation's security program or even recognized as a threat. This will change as more attacks take place through this new entry point and more viruses are written and spread through the interactions of cell phones and portable devices and the corporate network. The following are some of the issues with using mobile devices in an enterprise:

- False base stations can be created.
- Confidential data can be stolen.
- Camera and microphone functionality can be used improperly.
- Internet sites can be accessed in violation of company policies.
- Malicious code can be downloaded.
- Encryption can be weak and not end to end.

Some mobile phone providers have enterprise-wide solutions, which allow the network administrator to create profiles that are deployed to each approved phone. The following is a short list of items that should be put into place for enterprise mobile device security:

- Only devices that can be centrally managed should be allowed access to corporate resources.
- Remote policies should be pushed to each device, and user profiles should be encrypted with no local options for modification.
- Data encryption, idle timeout locks, screen-saver lockouts, authentication, and remote wipe should be enabled.
- Bluetooth capabilities should be locked down, only allowed applications should be installed, camera policies should be enforced, and restrictions for social media sites (Facebook, Twitter, etc.) should be enabled.
- Endpoint security should expand to mobile endpoints.
- 802.1X should be implemented on wireless VoIP clients on mobile devices.

Implementing security and maintaining it on each and every mobile device is very difficult, so a hybrid approach of "device lockdown" and perimeter control and filtering should be put into place and monitored.

Cyber-Physical Systems

It is almost impossible to distance ourselves from computers because they are part and parcel of virtually every activity in which we engage. This is because we discovered a long time ago that it was oftentimes easier, better, faster, and cheaper for computers to control physical devices and systems than for people to do so. From thermostats and traffic lights to cars, airplanes, and spacecraft, computers control many of the things that make our lives safe and comfortable. Any system in which computers and physical devices collaborate via the exchange of inputs and outputs to accomplish a task or objective is a *cyber-physical system*. Broadly speaking, these systems fall into two classes, which we describe as follows.

Embedded Systems

The simplest form of cyber-physical system is the embedded system. These systems are cheap, rugged, small, and use very little power. The computing device is part of (or embedded into) a mechanical or electrical device or system. A digital thermometer is an example of a very simple embedded system, and other examples of embedded systems include traffic lights and factory assembly line controllers. Embedded systems are usually built around microcontrollers, which are specialized devices that consist of a CPU, memory, and peripheral control interfaces. Microcontrollers have a very basic operating system, if they have one at all.

Some of the very features that make embedded systems useful are also the source of many vulnerabilities. If you think about it, they are meant to be invisible. You are not supposed to think that when you put a load of laundry in your washing machine and start it you are actually executing a program on a tiny computer that will regulate the flow of water and the movements of the motor. When was the last time you thought about how secure the embedded system in your washing machine is? Now, if you transpose that to your workplace, you will find that there are probably dozens, if not hundreds, of embedded systems with which you interact each day.

The main challenge in securing embedded systems is that of ensuring the security of the software that drives them. Many vendors build their embedded systems around commercially available microprocessors, but use their own proprietary code that is difficult, if not impossible, for a customer to audit. Depending on the risk tolerance of your organization, this may be acceptable as long as the embedded systems are stand-alone. The problem is that these systems are increasingly shipping with some sort of network connectivity. For example, one organization recently discovered that one of its embedded devices had a "phone home" feature that was not documented, but that resulted in potentially sensitive information being transmitted unencrypted to the manufacturer. If a full audit of the embedded device security is not possible, at a very minimum you should ensure you see what data flows in and out of it across any network.

Internet of Things

The Internet of Things (IoT) is the global network of connected embedded systems. What distinguishes the IoT is that each node is connected to the Internet and is uniquely addressable. By different accounts, this network is expected to reach anywhere between 5 billion and over 1 trillion devices, which makes this a booming sector of the global economy. Perhaps the most visible aspect of this explosion is in the area of smart homes in which lights, furnaces, and even refrigerators collaborate to create the best environment for the residents.

With this level of connectivity and access to physical devices, the IoT poses many security challenges. Among the issues to address by anyone considering adoption of IoT devices are the following:

- **Authentication** Embedded devices are not known for incorporating strong authentication support, which is the reason why most IoT devices have very poor (if any) authentication.
- **Encryption** Cryptography is typically expensive in terms of processing power and memory requirements, both of which are very limited in IoT devices. The fallout of this is that data at rest and data in motion can be vulnerable in many parts of the IoT.
- **Updates** Though IoT devices are networked, many vendors in this fast-moving sector do not provide functionality to automatically update their software and firmware when patches are available.

Industrial Control Systems

Industrial control systems (ICS) consist of information technology that is specifically designed to control physical devices in industrial processes. ICS exist on factory floors to control conveyor belts and industrial robots. They exist in the power and water infrastructures to control the flows of these utilities. Due to the roles they typically fulfill in manufacturing and infrastructure, maintaining efficiency is key to effective ICS. Another important consideration is that these systems, unlike the majority of other IT systems, control things that can directly cause physical harm to humans. For these two reasons (efficiency and safety), securing ICS requires a slightly different approach than traditional IT systems. A good resource for this is the NIST Special Publication 800-82, "Guide to Industrial Control Systems (ICS) Security."

ICS is really an umbrella term covering a number of somewhat different technologies that were developed independently to solve different problems. Today, however, it can be hard to tell some of these apart as the ICS technologies continue to converge. In the interest of correctness, we discuss each of the three major categories of ICS in the following sections, but it is important to keep in mind that it is becoming increasingly more difficult to find systems that fit perfectly into only one category.

Programmable Logic Controllers (PLC) When automation (the physical kind, not the computing kind to which we're accustomed) first showed up on factory floors, it was bulky, brittle, and difficult to maintain. If, for instance, you wanted an automatic hammer to drive nails into boxes moving through a conveyor belt, you would arrange a series of electrical relays such that they would sequentially actuate the hammer, retrieve it, and then wait for the next box. Whenever you wanted to change your process or repurpose the hammer, you would have to suffer through a complex and error-prone reconfiguration process.

Programmable logic controllers (PLCs) are computers designed to control electromechanical processes such assembly lines, elevators, roller coasters, and nuclear centrifuges. The idea is that a PLC can be used in one application today and then easily reprogrammed to control something else tomorrow. PLCs normally connect to the devices they control over a standard interface such as RS-232. The communications protocols themselves, however, are not always standard. While this creates additional challenges to securing PLCs, we are seeing a trend toward standardization of these serial connection protocols. While early PLCs had limited or no network connectivity, it is now rare to see one that is not network-enabled.

Distributed Control System (DCS) Once relay boxes were replaced with PLCs, the next evolution was to integrate these devices into a system. A *distributed control system (DCS)* is a network of control devices within fairly close proximity that are part of one or more industrial processes. DCS usage is very common in manufacturing plants, oil refineries, and power plants, and is characterized by decisions being made in a concerted manner, but by different nodes within the system.

You can think of a DCS as a hierarchy of devices. At the bottom level, you will find the physical devices that are being controlled or that provide inputs to the system. One level up, you will find the microcontrollers and PLCs that directly interact with the physical devices, but also communicate with higher-level controllers. Above the PLCs are the supervisory computers that control, for example, a given production line. You can also have a higher level that deals with plant-wide controls, which would require some coordination among different production lines.

As you can see, the concept of a DCS was born from the need to control fairly localized physical processes. Because of this, the communications protocols in use are not optimized for wide-area communications or for security. Another byproduct of this localized approach is that DCS users felt for many years that all they needed in order to secure their systems was to provide physical security. If the bad guys can't get into the plant, it was thought, then they can't break our systems. This is because, typically, a DCS consists of devices within the same plant. However, technological advances and converging technologies are blurring the line between a DCS and a SCADA system.

Supervisory Control and Data Acquisition (SCADA) While DCS technology is well suited for local processes such as those in a manufacturing plant, it was never intended to operate across great distances. The *supervisory control and data acquisition (SCADA)* systems were developed to control large-scale physical processes involving nodes separated by significant distances. The main conceptual differences between DCS and SCADA are size and distances. So, while the control of a power plant is perfectly suited for a traditional DCS, the distribution of the generated power across a power grid would require a SCADA system.

SCADA systems typically involve three kinds of devices: endpoints, backends, and user stations. A *remote terminal unit (RTU)* is an endpoint that connects directly to sensors and/or actuators. Though there are still plenty of RTUs in use, many of these have now been replaced with PLCs. The *data acquisition servers (DAS)* are backends that receive all data from the endpoints through a telemetry system, and perform whatever correlation or analysis may be necessary. Finally, the users in charge of controlling the system interact with it through the use of a *human-machine interface (HMI)*, the user station, that displays the data from the endpoints and allows the users to issue commands to the actuators (e.g., to close a valve or open a switch).

One of the main challenges with operating at great distances is effective communications, particularly when parts of the process occur in areas with limited, spotty, or nonexistent telecommunications infrastructures. SCADA systems commonly use dedicated cables and radio links to cover these large expanses. Many legacy SCADA implementations rely on older proprietary communications protocols and devices. For many years, this led this community to feel secure because only someone with detailed knowledge of an obscure protocol and access to specialized communications gear could compromise the system. In part, this assumption is one of the causes of the lack of effective security controls on legacy SCADA communications. While this thinking may have been arguable in the past, today's convergence on IP-based protocols makes it clear that this is not a secure way of doing business.

ICS Security The single greatest vulnerability in ICS is their increasing connectivity to traditional IT networks. This has two notable side effects: it accelerates convergence towards standard protocols, and it exposes once-private systems to anyone with an Internet connection. NIST SP 800-82 has a variety of recommendations for ICS security, but we highlight some of the most important ones here:

- Apply a risk management process to ICS.
- Segment the network to place IDS/IPS at the subnet boundaries.
- Disable unneeded ports and services on all ICS devices.
- Implement least privilege through the ICS.
- Use encryption wherever feasible.
- Ensure there is a process for patch management.
- Monitor audit trails regularly.

A Few Threats to Review

Now that we have talked about how everything is supposed to work, let's take a quick look at some of the things that can go wrong when designing a system.

Software almost always has bugs and vulnerabilities. The rich functionality demanded by users brings about deep complexity, which usually opens the doors to problems in the computer world. Also, vulnerabilities are always around because attackers continually find ways of using system operations and functionality in a negative and destructive way. Just like there will always be cops and robbers, there will always be attackers and security professionals. It is a game of trying to outwit each other and seeing who will put the necessary effort into winning the game.

NOTE Software quality experts estimate an average of six defects in every 1,000 lines of code written in the U.S. Google's total code base is 2 billion lines of code, which could mean 12 million bugs using this average defect rate.

Maintenance Hooks

In the programming world, *maintenance hooks* are a type of back door. They are instructions within software that only the developer knows about and can invoke, and which give the developer easy access to the code. They allow the developer to view and edit the code without having to go through regular access controls. During the development phase of the software, these can be very useful, but if they are not removed before the software goes into production, they can cause major security issues.

An application that has a maintenance hook enables the developer to execute commands by using a specific sequence of keystrokes. Once this is done successfully, the developer can be inside the application looking directly at the code or configuration files. She might do this to watch problem areas within the code, check variable population, export more code into the program, or fix problems she sees taking place. Although this sounds nice and healthy, if an attacker finds out about this maintenance hook, he can take more sinister actions. So all maintenance hooks need to be removed from software before it goes into production.

NOTE You might be inclined to think that maintenance hooks are a thing of the past because developers are more security minded these days. This is not true. Developers are still using maintenance hooks, either because they lack understanding of or don't care about security issues, and many maintenance hooks still reside in older software that organizations are using.

Countermeasures

Because maintenance hooks are usually inserted by programmers, they are the ones who usually have to take them out before the programs go into production. Code reviews and unit and quality assurance testing should always be on the lookout for back doors in case the programmer overlooked extracting them. Because maintenance hooks are within the code of an application or system, there is not much a user can do to prevent their presence, but when a vendor finds out a back door exists in its product, it usually develops and releases a patch to reduce this vulnerability. Because most vendors sell their software without including the associated source code, it may be very difficult for companies who have purchased software to identify back doors. The following lists some preventive measures against back doors:

- Use a host-based intrusion detection system to watch for any attackers using back doors into the system.
- Use file system encryption to protect sensitive information.
- Implement auditing to detect any type of back door use.

Time-of-Check/Time-of-Use Attacks

Specific attacks can take advantage of the way a system processes requests and performs tasks. A *time-of-check/time-of-use (TOC/TOU) attack* deals with the sequence of steps a system uses to complete a task. This type of attack takes advantage of the dependency on the timing of events that take place in a multitasking operating system.

As stated previously, operating systems and applications are, in reality, just lines and lines of instructions. An operating system must carry out instruction 1, then instruction 2, then instruction 3, and so on. This is how it is written. If an attacker can get in between instructions 2 and 3 and manipulate something, she can control the result of these activities.

An example of a TOC/TOU attack is if process 1 validates the authorization of a user to open a noncritical text file and process 2 carries out the `open` command. If the attacker can change out this noncritical text file with a password file while process 1 is carrying out its task, she has just obtained access to this critical file. (It is a flaw within the code that allows this type of compromise to take place.)

NOTE This type of attack is also referred to as an *asynchronous attack*. Asynchronous describes a process in which the timing of each step may vary. The attacker gets in between these steps and modifies something. Race conditions are also considered TOC/TOU attacks by some in the industry.

A *race condition* is when two different processes need to carry out their tasks on one resource. The processes need to follow the correct sequence. Process 1 needs to carry out its work before process 2 accesses the same resource and carries out its tasks. If process 2 goes before process 1, the outcome could be very different. If an attacker can manipulate the processes so process 2 does its task first, she can control the outcome of the processing procedure. Let's say process 1's instructions are to add 3 to a value and process 2's instructions are to divide by 15. If process 2 carries out its tasks before process 1, the outcome would be different. So if an attacker can make process 2 do its work before process 1, she can control the result.

Looking at this issue from a security perspective, there are several types of race condition attacks that are quite concerning. If a system splits up the authentication and authorization steps, an attacker could be authorized before she is even authenticated. For example, in the normal sequence, process 1 verifies the authentication before allowing a user access to a resource, and process 2 authorizes the user to access the resource. If the attacker makes process 2 carry out its tasks before process 1, she can access a resource without the system making sure she has been authenticated properly.

So although the terms "race condition" and "TOC/TOU attack" are sometimes used interchangeably, in reality, they are two different things. A race condition is an attack in which an attacker makes processes execute out of sequence to control the result. A TOC/TOU attack is when an attacker jumps in between two tasks and modifies something to control the result.

Countermeasures

It would take a dedicated attacker with great precision to perform these types of attacks, but it is possible and has been done. To protect against race condition attacks, it is best to *not* split up critical tasks that can have their sequence altered. This means the system should use atomic operations (where only one system call is used) for access control functions. This would not give the processor the opportunity to switch to another process in between two tasks. Unfortunately, using these types of atomic operations is not always possible.

To avoid TOC/TOU attacks, it is best if the operating system can apply software locks to the items it will use when it is carrying out its "checking" tasks. So if a user requests access to a file, while the system is validating this user's authorization, it should put a software lock on the file being requested. This ensures the file cannot be deleted and replaced with another file. Applying locks can be carried out easily on files, but it is more challenging to apply locks to database components and table entries to provide this type of protection.

Cryptography in Context

Now that you have a pretty good understanding of system architectures, we turn to a topic that has become central to protecting these architectures. *Cryptography* is a method of storing and transmitting data in a form that only those it is intended for can read and process. It is considered a science of protecting information by encoding it into an unreadable format. Cryptography is an effective way of protecting sensitive information as it is stored on media or transmitted through untrusted network communication paths.

One of the goals of cryptography, and the mechanisms that make it up, is to hide information from unauthorized individuals. However, with enough time, resources, and motivation, hackers can successfully attack most cryptosystems and reveal the encoded information. So a more realistic goal of cryptography is to make obtaining the information too work intensive or time consuming to be worthwhile to the attacker.

The History of Cryptography

Cryptography has roots that begin around 2000 B.C. in Egypt, when hieroglyphics were used to decorate tombs to tell the life story of the deceased. The intention of the practice was not so much about hiding the messages themselves; rather, the hieroglyphics were intended to make the life story seem more noble, ceremonial, and majestic.

Encryption methods evolved from being mainly for show into practical applications used to hide information from others.

A Hebrew cryptographic method required the alphabet to be flipped so each letter in the original alphabet was mapped to a different letter in the flipped, or shifted, alphabet. The encryption method was called atbash, which was used to hide the true meaning of messages. An example of an encryption key used in the atbash encryption scheme is shown here:

```
ABCDEFGHIJKLMNOPQRSTUVWXYZ
ZYXWVUTSRQPONMLKJIHGFEDCBA
```

For example, the word "security" is encrypted into "hvxfirgb." What does "xrhhk" come out to be?

This is an example of a *substitution cipher* because each character is replaced with another character. This type of substitution cipher is referred to as a *monoalphabetic substitution cipher* because it uses only one alphabet, whereas a *polyalphabetic substitution cipher* uses multiple alphabets.

TIP Cipher is another term for algorithm.

This simplistic encryption method worked for its time and for particular cultures, but eventually more complex mechanisms were required.

Around 400 B.C., the Spartans used a system of encrypting information in which they would write a message on a sheet of papyrus (a type of paper) that was wrapped around a staff (a stick or wooden rod), which was then delivered and wrapped around a different staff by the recipient. The message was only readable if it was wrapped around the correct size staff, which made the letters properly match up, as shown in Figure 3-23. This is referred to as the *scytale cipher*. When the papyrus was not wrapped around the staff, the writing appeared as just a bunch of random characters.

Later, in Rome, Julius Caesar (100–44 B.C.) developed a simple method of shifting letters of the alphabet, similar to the atbash scheme. He simply shifted the alphabet by three positions. The following example shows a standard alphabet and a shifted alphabet. The alphabet serves as the algorithm, and the key is the number of locations it has been shifted during the encryption and decryption process.

- **Standard Alphabet:**
  `ABCDEFGHIJKLMNOPQRSTUVWXYZ`
- **Cryptographic Alphabet:**
  `DEFGHIJKLMNOPQRSTUVWXYZABC`

As an example, suppose we need to encrypt the message "Logical Security." We take the first letter of this message, *L*, and shift up three locations within the alphabet. The encrypted version of this first letter is *O*, so we write that down. The next letter to be encrypted is *O*, which matches *R* when we shift three spaces. We continue this process for the whole message. Once the message is encrypted, a carrier takes the encrypted version to the destination, where the process is reversed.

- **Plaintext:**
  `LOGICAL SECURITY`
- **Ciphertext:**
  `ORJLFDO VHFXULWB`

Today, this technique seems too simplistic to be effective, but in the time of Julius Caesar, not very many people could read in the first place, so it provided a high level of protection. The Caesar cipher is an example of a monoalphabetic cipher. Once more people could read and reverse-engineer this type of encryption process, the cryptographers of that day increased the complexity by creating polyalphabetic ciphers.

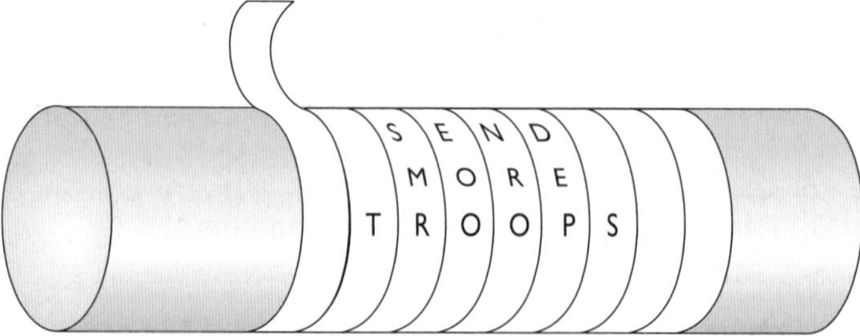

Figure 3-23 The scytale was used by the Spartans to decipher encrypted messages.

ROT13

A more recent encryption method used in the 1980s, *ROT13* was really the same thing as a Caesar cipher. Instead of shifting 3 spaces in the alphabet, the encryption process shifted 13 spaces. It was not really used to protect data because our society could already easily handle this task. Instead, it was used in online forums (or bulletin boards) when "inappropriate" material, as in nasty jokes, were shared among users. The idea was that if you were interested in reading something potentially "offensive" you could simply use the shift-13 approach and read the material. Other people who did not want to view it would not be offended, because they would just leave the text and not decrypt it.

In the 16th century in France, Blaise de Vigenère developed a polyalphabetic substitution cipher for Henry III. This was based on the Caesar cipher, but it increased the difficulty of the encryption and decryption process.

As shown in Figure 3-24, we have a message that needs to be encrypted, which is SYSTEM SECURITY AND CONTROL. We have a key with the value of SECURITY. We also have a Vigenère table, or algorithm, which is really the Caesar cipher on steroids. Whereas the Caesar cipher used a 1-shift alphabet (letters were shifted up three places), the Vigenère cipher has 27 shift alphabets and the letters are shifted up only one place.

NOTE Plaintext is the readable version of a message. After an encryption process, the resulting text is referred to as *ciphertext*.

So, looking at the example in Figure 3-24, we take the first value of the key, *S*, and starting with the first alphabet in our algorithm, trace over to the *S* column. Then we look at the first value of plaintext that needs to be encrypted, which is *S*, and go down to the *S* row. We follow the column and row and see that they intersect on the value *K*. That is the first encrypted value of our message, so we write down *K*. Then we go to the next value in our key, which is *E*, and the next value of plaintext, which is *Y*. We see that the *E* column and the *Y* row intersect at the cell with the value of *C*. This is our second encrypted value, so we write that down. We continue this process for the whole message (notice that the key repeats itself, since the message is longer than the key). The resulting ciphertext is the encrypted form that is sent to the destination. The destination must have the same algorithm (Vigenère table) and the same key (SECURITY) to properly reverse the process to obtain a meaningful message.

The evolution of cryptography continued as countries refined it using new methods, tools, and practices throughout the Middle Ages. By the late 1800s, cryptography was commonly used in the methods of communication between military factions.

During World War II, encryption devices were used for tactical communication, which drastically improved with the mechanical and electromechanical technology that provided the world with telegraphic and radio communication. The rotor cipher machine,

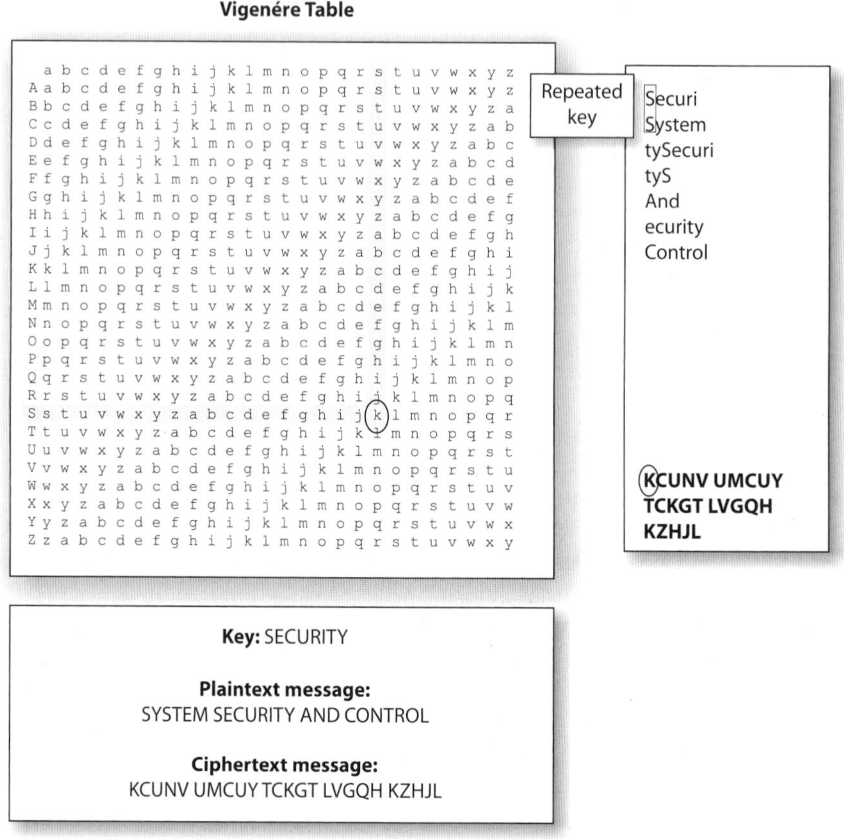

Figure 3-24 Polyalphabetic algorithms were developed to increase encryption complexity.

which is a device that substitutes letters using different rotors within the machine, was a huge breakthrough in military cryptography that provided complexity that proved difficult to break. This work gave way to the most famous cipher machine in history to date: Germany's *Enigma* machine. The Enigma machine had separate rotors, a plug board, and a reflecting rotor.

The originator of the message would configure the Enigma machine to its initial settings before starting the encryption process. The operator would type in the first letter of the message, and the machine would substitute the letter with a different letter and present it to the operator. This encryption was done by moving the rotors a predefined number of times. So, if the operator typed in a *T* as the first character, the Enigma machine might present an *M* as the substitution value. The operator would write down the letter *M* on his sheet. The operator would then advance the rotors and enter the next letter. Each time a new letter was to be encrypted, the operator would advance the rotors to a new setting. This process was followed until the whole message was encrypted. Then the encrypted text was transmitted over the airwaves, most likely to a German U-boat.

The chosen substitution for each letter was dependent upon the rotor setting, so the crucial and secret part of this process (the key) was the initial setting and how the operators advanced the rotors when encrypting and decrypting a message. The operators at each end needed to know this sequence of increments to advance each rotor in order to enable the German military units to properly communicate.

Although the mechanisms of the Enigma were complicated for the time, a team of Polish cryptographers broke its code and gave Britain insight into Germany's attack plans and military movement. It is said that breaking this encryption mechanism shortened World War II by two years. After the war, details about the Enigma machine were published—one of the machines is exhibited at the Smithsonian Institute.

Cryptography has a deep, rich history. Mary, Queen of Scots, lost her life in the 16th century when an encrypted message she sent was intercepted. During the Revolutionary War, Benedict Arnold used a codebook cipher to exchange information on troop movement and strategic military advancements. Militaries have always played a leading role in using cryptography to encode information and to attempt to decrypt the enemy's encrypted information. William Frederick Friedman, who published *The Index of Coincidence and Its Applications in Cryptography* in 1920, is called the "Father of Modern Cryptography" and broke many messages intercepted during World War II. Encryption has been used by many governments and militaries and has contributed to great victory for some because it enabled them to execute covert maneuvers in secrecy. It has also contributed to great defeat for others, when their cryptosystems were discovered and deciphered.

When computers were invented, the possibilities for encryption methods and devices expanded exponentially and cryptography efforts increased dramatically. This era brought unprecedented opportunity for cryptographic designers to develop new encryption techniques. A well-known and successful project was *Lucifer*, which was developed at IBM. Lucifer introduced complex mathematical equations and functions that were later adopted and modified by the U.S. National Security Agency (NSA) to establish the U.S. Data Encryption Standard (DES) in 1976, a federal government standard. DES was used worldwide for financial and other transactions, and was embedded into numerous commercial applications. Though it is no longer considered secure, it lives on as Triple DES, which uses three rounds of DES encryption and is still in use today.

A majority of the protocols developed at the dawn of the computing age have been upgraded to include cryptography and to add necessary layers of protection. Encryption is used in hardware devices and in software to protect data, banking transactions, corporate extranet transmissions, e-mail messages, web transactions, wireless communications, the storage of confidential information, faxes, and phone calls.

The code breakers and cryptanalysis efforts and the amazing number-crunching capabilities of the microprocessors hitting the market each year have quickened the evolution of cryptography. As the bad guys get smarter and more resourceful, the good guys must increase their efforts and strategy. *Cryptanalysis* is the science of studying and breaking the secrecy of encryption processes, compromising authentication schemes, and reverse-engineering algorithms and keys. Cryptanalysis is an important piece of cryptography and cryptology. When carried out by the "good guys," cryptanalysis is intended to identify flaws and weaknesses so developers can go back to the drawing board and improve the components. It is also performed by curious and motivated hackers to identify the same types of flaws, but with the goal of obtaining the encryption key for unauthorized access to confidential information.

NOTE Cryptanalysis is a very sophisticated science that encompasses a wide variety of tests and attacks. We will cover these types of attacks later in this chapter. Cryptology, on the other hand, is the study of cryptanalysis and cryptography.

Different types of cryptography have been used throughout civilization, but today cryptography is deeply rooted in every part of our communications and computing world. Automated information systems and cryptography play a huge role in the effectiveness of militaries, the functionality of governments, and the economics of private businesses. As our dependency upon technology increases, so does our dependency upon cryptography, because secrets will always need to be kept.

Cryptography Definitions and Concepts

Encryption is a method of transforming readable data, called *plaintext*, into a form that appears to be random and unreadable, which is called *ciphertext*. Plaintext is in a form that can be understood either by a person (a document) or by a computer (executable code). Once it is transformed into ciphertext, neither human nor machine can properly process it until it is decrypted. This enables the transmission of confidential information over insecure channels without unauthorized disclosure. When data is stored on a computer, it is usually protected by logical and physical access controls. When this same sensitive information is sent over a network, it can no longer take advantage of these controls and is in a much more vulnerable state.

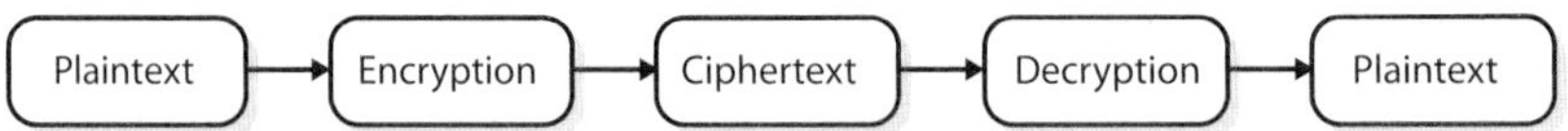

A system or product that provides encryption and decryption is referred to as a *cryptosystem* and can be created through hardware components or program code in an application. The cryptosystem uses an encryption algorithm (which determines how simple or complex the encryption process will be), keys, and the necessary software components and protocols. Most algorithms are complex mathematical formulas that are applied in a specific sequence to the plaintext. Most encryption methods use a secret value called a key (usually a long string of bits), which works with the algorithm to encrypt and decrypt the text.

The *algorithm*, the set of rules also known as the *cipher*, dictates how enciphering and deciphering take place. Many of the mathematical algorithms used in computer systems today are publicly known and are not the secret part of the encryption process. If the internal mechanisms of the algorithm are not a secret, then something must be. The secret piece of using a well-known encryption algorithm is the key. A common analogy used to illustrate this point is the use of locks you would purchase from your local hardware store. Let's say 20 people bought the same brand of lock. Just because these people share the same type and brand of lock does not mean they can now unlock each other's doors and gain access to their private possessions. Instead, each lock comes with its own key, and that one key can only open that one specific lock.

In encryption, the *key* (cryptovariable) is a value that comprises a large sequence of random bits. Is it just any random number of bits crammed together? Not really. An algorithm contains a *keyspace*, which is a range of values that can be used to construct a key. When the algorithm needs to generate a new key, it uses random values from this keyspace. The larger the keyspace, the more available values that can be used to represent different keys—and the more random the keys are, the harder it is for intruders to figure them out. For example, if an algorithm allows a key length of 2 bits, the keyspace for that algorithm would be 4, which indicates the total number of different keys that would be possible. (Remember that we are working in binary and that 2^2 equals 4.) That would not be a very large keyspace, and certainly it would not take an attacker very long to find the correct key that was used.

A large keyspace allows for more possible keys. (Today, we are commonly using key sizes of 128, 256, 512, or even 1,024 bits and larger.) So a key size of 512 bits would provide 2^{512} possible combinations (the keyspace). The encryption algorithm should use the entire keyspace and choose the values to make up the keys as randomly as possible. If a smaller keyspace were used, there would be fewer values to choose from when generating a key, as shown in Figure 3-25. This would increase an attacker's chances of figuring out the key value and deciphering the protected information.

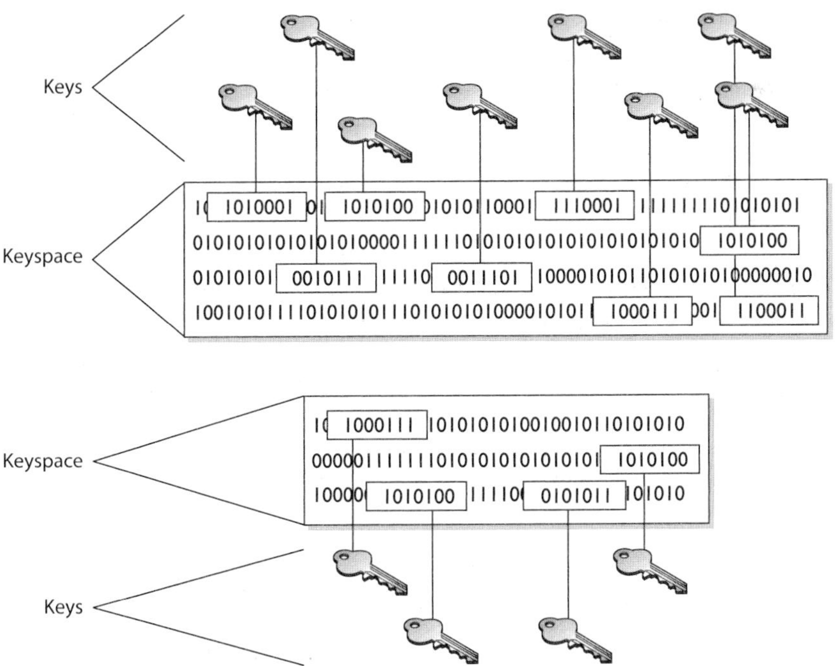

Figure 3-25 Larger keyspaces permit a greater number of possible key values.

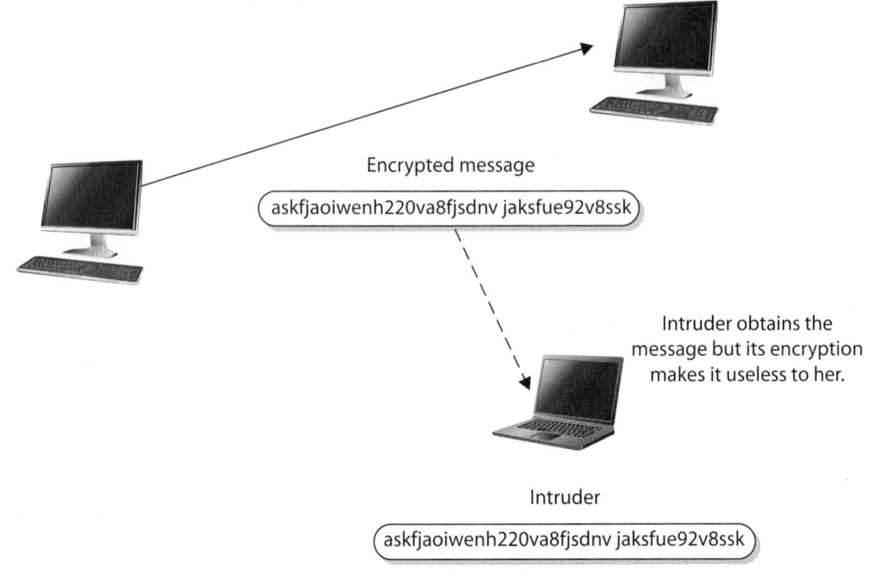
Encrypted message
askfjaoiwenh220va8fjsdnv jaksfue92v8ssk
Intruder obtains the message but its encryption makes it useless to her.
Intruder
askfjaoiwenh220va8fjsdnv jaksfue92v8ssk

Figure 3-26 Without the right key, the captured message is useless to an attacker.

If an eavesdropper captures a message as it passes between two people, she can view the message, but it appears in its encrypted form and is therefore unusable. Even if this attacker knows the algorithm that the two people are using to encrypt and decrypt their information, without the key, this information remains useless to the eavesdropper, as shown in Figure 3-26.

Cryptosystems

A *cryptosystem* encompasses all of the necessary components for encryption and decryption to take place. Pretty Good Privacy (PGP) is just one example of a cryptosystem. A cryptosystem is made up of at least the following:

- Software
- Protocols
- Algorithms
- Keys

Kerckhoffs' Principle

Auguste Kerckhoffs published a paper in 1883 stating that the only secrecy involved with a cryptography system should be the key. He claimed that the algorithm should be publicly known. He asserted that if security were based on too many secrets, there would be more vulnerabilities to possibly exploit.

So, why do we care what some guy said over 120 years ago? Because this debate is still going on. Cryptographers in certain sectors agree with *Kerckhoffs' principle*, because making an algorithm publicly available means that many more people can view the source code, test it, and uncover any type of flaws or weaknesses. It is the attitude of "many heads are better than one." Once someone uncovers some type of flaw, the developer can fix the issue and provide society with a much stronger algorithm.

But not everyone agrees with this philosophy. Governments around the world create their own algorithms that are not released to the public. Their stance is that if a smaller number of people know how the algorithm actually works, then a smaller number of people will know how to possibly break it. Cryptographers in the private sector do not agree with this practice and do not commonly trust algorithms they cannot examine.

It is basically the same as the open-source versus compiled software debate that is in full force today.

The Strength of the Cryptosystem

The *strength* of an encryption method comes from the algorithm, the secrecy of the key, the length of the key, the initialization vectors, and how they all work together within the cryptosystem. When strength is discussed in encryption, it refers to how hard it is to figure out the algorithm or key, whichever is not made public. Attempts to break a cryptosystem usually involve processing an amazing number of possible values in the hopes of finding the one value (key) that can be used to decrypt a specific message. The strength of an encryption method correlates to the amount of necessary processing power, resources, and time required to break the cryptosystem or to figure out the value of the key. Breaking a cryptosystem can be accomplished by a brute-force attack, which means trying every possible key value until the resulting plaintext is meaningful. Depending on the algorithm and length of the key, this can be an easy task or one that is close to impossible. If a key can be broken with a Pentium Core i5 processor in three hours, the cipher is not strong at all. If the key can only be broken with the use of a thousand multiprocessing systems over 1.2 million years, then it is pretty darn strong. The introduction of multicore processors has really increased the threat of brute-force attacks.

NOTE Attacks are measured in the number of instructions a million-instruction-per-second (MIPS) system can execute within a year's time.

The goal when designing an encryption method is to make compromising it too expensive or too time consuming. Another name for cryptography strength is *work factor*, which is an estimate of the effort and resources it would take an attacker to penetrate a cryptosystem.

How strong a protection mechanism is required depends on the sensitivity of the data being protected. It is not necessary to encrypt information about a friend's Saturday barbeque with a top-secret encryption algorithm. Conversely, it is not a good idea to send intercepted spy information using PGP. Each type of encryption mechanism has its place and purpose.

Even if the algorithm is very complex and thorough, other issues within encryption can weaken encryption methods. Because the key is usually the secret value needed to actually encrypt and decrypt messages, improper protection of the key can weaken the encryption. Even if a user employs an algorithm that has all the requirements for strong encryption, including a large keyspace and a large and random key value, if she shares her key with others, the strength of the algorithm becomes almost irrelevant.

Important elements of encryption are to use an algorithm without flaws, use a large key size, use all possible values within the keyspace selected as randomly as possible, and protect the actual key. If one element is weak, it could be the link that dooms the whole process.

Services of Cryptosystems

Cryptosystems can provide the following services:

- **Confidentiality** Renders the information unintelligible except by authorized entities.
- **Integrity** Data has not been altered in an unauthorized manner since it was created, transmitted, or stored.
- **Authentication** Verifies the identity of the user or system that created the information.
- **Authorization** Upon proving identity, the individual is then provided with the key or password that will allow access to some resource.
- **Nonrepudiation** Ensures that the sender cannot deny sending the message.

As an example of how these services work, suppose your boss sends you a message telling you that you will be receiving a raise that doubles your salary. The message is encrypted, so you can be sure it really came from your boss (authenticity), that someone did not alter it before it arrived at your computer (integrity), that no one else was able to read it as it traveled over the network (confidentiality), and that your boss cannot deny sending it later when he comes to his senses (nonrepudiation).

Different types of messages and transactions require higher or lower degrees of one or all of the services that cryptography methods can supply. Military and intelligence agencies are very concerned about keeping information confidential, so they would choose encryption mechanisms that provide a high degree of secrecy. Financial institutions care about confidentiality, but they also care about the integrity of the data being transmitted, so the encryption mechanism they would choose may differ from the military's encryption methods. If messages were accepted that had a misplaced decimal point or zero, the ramifications could be far reaching in the financial world. Legal agencies may care most about the authenticity of the messages they receive. If information received ever needed to be presented in a court of law, its authenticity would certainly be questioned; therefore, the encryption method used must ensure authenticity, which confirms who sent the information.

NOTE If David sends a message and then later claims he did not send it, this is an act of repudiation. When a cryptography mechanism provides nonrepudiation, the sender cannot later deny he sent the message (well, he can try to deny it, but the cryptosystem proves otherwise). It's a way of keeping the sender honest.

The types and uses of cryptography have increased over the years. At one time, cryptography was mainly used to keep secrets secret (confidentiality), but today we use cryptography to ensure the integrity of data, to authenticate messages, to confirm that a message was received, to provide access control, and much more. In this chapter we cover the different types of cryptography that provide these different types of functionality, along with any related security issues.

One-Time Pad

A *one-time pad* is a perfect encryption scheme because it is considered unbreakable if implemented properly. It was invented by Gilbert Vernam in 1917, so sometimes it is referred to as the Vernam cipher.

This cipher does not use shift alphabets, as do the Caesar and Vigenère ciphers discussed earlier, but instead uses a pad made up of random values, as shown in Figure 3-27. Our plaintext message that needs to be encrypted has been converted into bits, and our one-time pad is made up of random bits. This encryption process uses a binary mathematic function called exclusive-OR, usually abbreviated as XOR.

XOR is an operation that is applied to 2 bits and is a function commonly used in binary mathematics and encryption methods. When combining the bits, if both values are the same, the result is 0 (1 XOR 1 = 0). If the bits are different from each other, the result is 1 (1 XOR 0 = 1). For example:

Message stream: `1001010111`

Keystream: `0011101010`

Ciphertext stream: `1010111101`

So in our example, the first bit of the message is XORed to the first bit of the one-time pad, which results in the ciphertext value 1. The second bit of the message is XORed with the second bit of the pad, which results in the value 0. This process continues until the whole message is encrypted. The result is the encrypted message that is sent to the receiver.

In Figure 3-27, we also see that the receiver must have the same one-time pad to decrypt the message by reversing the process. The receiver takes the first bit of the encrypted message and XORs it with the first bit of the pad. This results in the plaintext value. The receiver continues this process for the whole encrypted message until the entire message is decrypted.

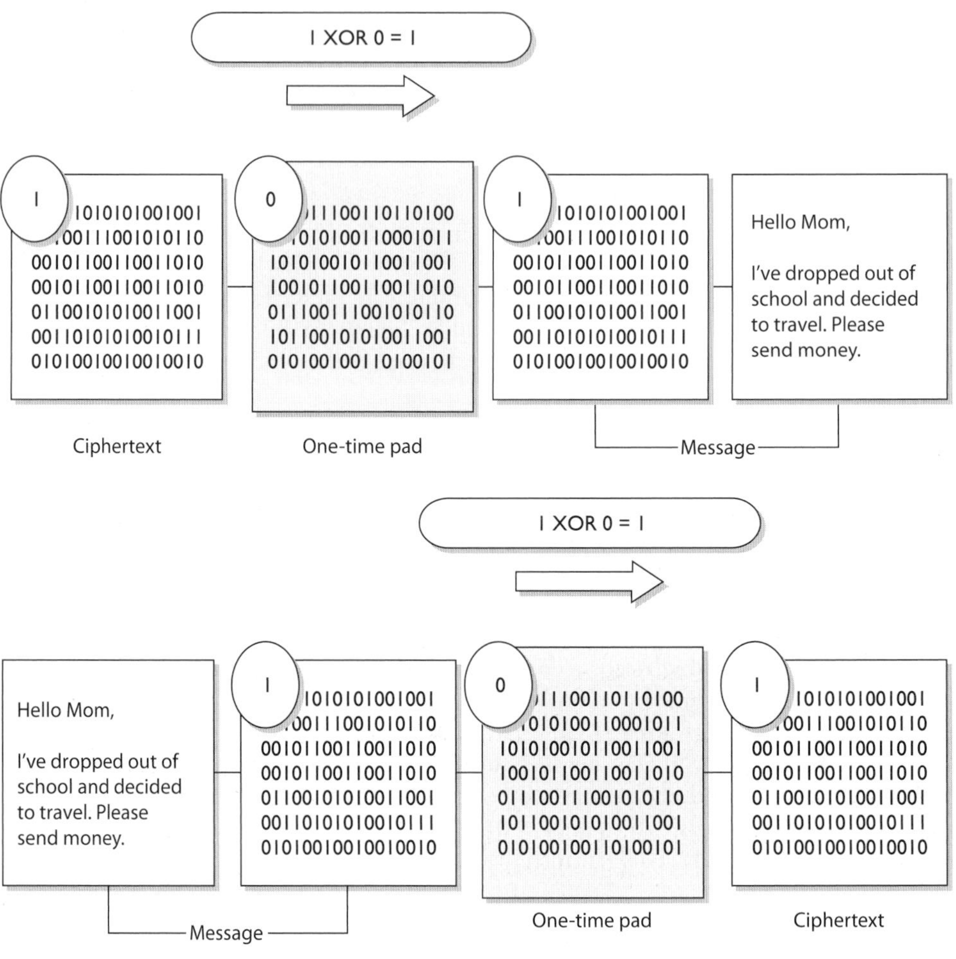

Figure 3-27 A one-time pad

The one-time pad encryption scheme is deemed unbreakable only if the following things are true about the implementation process:

- *The pad must be used only one time.* If the pad is used more than one time, this might introduce patterns in the encryption process that will aid the eavesdropper in his goal of breaking the encryption.
- *The pad must be as long as the message.* If it is not as long as the message, the pad will need to be reused to cover the whole message. This would be the same thing as using a pad more than one time, which could introduce patterns.
- *The pad must be securely distributed and protected at its destination.* This is a very cumbersome process to accomplish, because the pads are usually just individual pieces of paper that need to be delivered by a secure courier and properly guarded at each destination.

- *The pad must be made up of truly random values.* This may not seem like a difficult task, but even our computer systems today do not have truly random number generators; rather, they have pseudorandom number generators.

NOTE A *number generator* is used to create a stream of random values and must be seeded by an initial value. This piece of software obtains its seeding value from some component within the computer system (time, CPU cycles, and so on). Although a computer system is complex, it is a predictable environment, so if the seeding value is predictable in any way, the resulting values created are not truly random—but *pseudorandom*.

Although the one-time pad approach to encryption can provide a very high degree of security, it is impractical in most situations because of all of its different requirements. Each possible pair of entities that might want to communicate in this fashion must receive, in a secure fashion, a pad that is as long as, or longer than, the actual message. This type of key management can be overwhelming and may require more overhead than it is worth. The distribution of the pad can be challenging, and the sender and receiver must be perfectly synchronized so each is using the same pad.

One-time pads have been used throughout history to protect different types of sensitive data. Today, they are still in place for many types of militaries as a backup encryption option if current encryption processes (which require computers and a power source) are unavailable for reasons of war or attacks.

One-Time Pad Requirements

For a one-time pad encryption scheme to be considered unbreakable, each pad in the scheme must be

- Made up of truly random values
- Used only one time
- Securely distributed to its destination
- Secured at sender's and receiver's sites
- At least as long as the message

Running and Concealment Ciphers

Two spy-novel-type ciphers are the running key cipher and the concealment cipher. The *running key cipher* could use a key that does not require an electronic algorithm and bit alterations, but cleverly uses components in the physical world around you. For instance, the algorithm could be a set of books agreed upon by the sender and receiver. The key in this type of cipher could be a book page, line number, and column count. If you get a message from your supersecret spy buddy and the message reads "149l6c7.299l3c7.911l5c8," this could mean for you to look at the 1st book in your predetermined series of books, the 49th page, 6th line down the page, and the 7th column. So you write down the letter in that column, which is *h*. The second set of numbers starts with 2, so you go to the 2nd book, 99th page, 3rd line down, and then to the 7th column, which is *o*. The last letter you get from the 9th book, 11th page, 5th line, 8th column, which is *t*. So now you have come up with your important secret message, which is *hot*. Running key ciphers can be used in different and more complex ways, but this simple example illustrates the point.

A *concealment cipher* is a message within a message. If your supersecret spy buddy and you decide your key value is every third word, then when you get a message from him, you will pick out every third word and write it down. Suppose he sends you a message that reads, "The saying, 'The time is right' is not cow language, so is now a dead subject." Because your key is every third word, you come up with "The right cow is dead."

NOTE A concealment cipher, also called a null cipher, is a type of steganography method. Steganography is described later in this chapter.

No matter which of these two types of cipher is used, the roles of the algorithm and key are the same, even if they are not mathematical equations. In the running key cipher, the algorithm may be a predefined set of books. The key indicates the book, page, line, and word within that line. In substitution ciphers, the algorithm dictates that substitution will take place using a predefined alphabet or sequence of characters, and the key indicates that each character will be replaced with another character, as in the third character that follows it in that sequence of characters. In actual mathematical structures, the algorithm is a set of mathematical functions that will be performed on the message, and the key can indicate in which order these functions take place. So even if an attacker knows the algorithm, and we have to assume he does, if he does not know the key, the message is still useless to him.

Steganography

Steganography is a method of hiding data in another media type so the very existence of the data is concealed. Common steps are illustrated in Figure 3-28. Only the sender and receiver are supposed to be able to see the message because it is secretly hidden in a graphic, Wave file, document, or other type of media. The message is often, but not necessarily, encrypted, just hidden. Encrypted messages can draw attention because it tells the bad guy, "This is something sensitive." A message hidden in a picture of your grandmother would not attract this type of attention, even though the same secret message can be embedded into this image. Steganography is a type of security through obscurity.

Steganography includes the concealment of information within computer files. In digital steganography, electronic communications may include steganographic coding inside of a document file, image file, program, or protocol. Media files are ideal for steganographic transmission because of their large size. As a simple example, a sender might

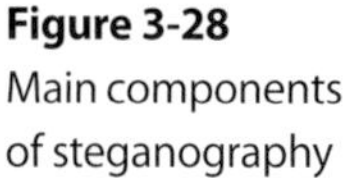

Figure 3-28
Main components of steganography

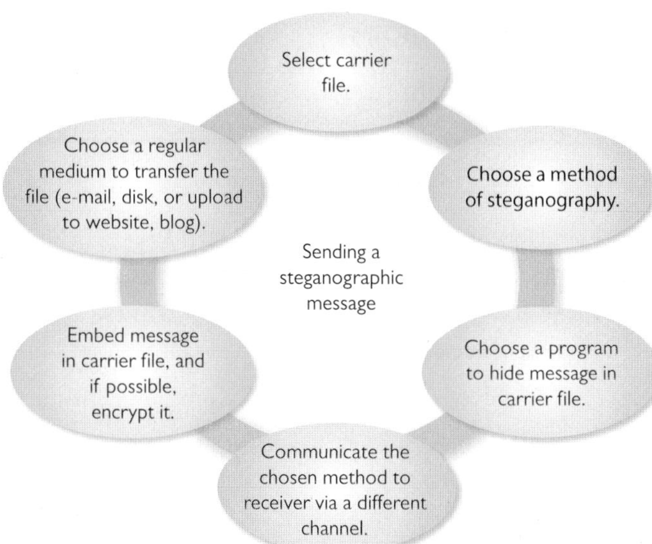
Select carrier file.
Choose a method of steganography.
Choose a program to hide message in carrier file.
Communicate the chosen method to receiver via a different channel.
Embed message in carrier file, and if possible, encrypt it.
Choose a regular medium to transfer the file (e-mail, disk, or upload to website, blog).
Sending a steganographic message

start with an innocuous image file and adjust the color of every 100th pixel to correspond to a letter in the alphabet, a change so subtle that someone not specifically looking for it is unlikely to notice it.

Let's look at the components that are involved with steganography:

- **Carrier** A signal, data stream, or file that has hidden information (payload) inside of it
- **Stegomedium** The medium in which the information is hidden
- **Payload** The information that is to be concealed and transmitted

A method of embedding the message into some types of media is to use the *least significant bit (LSB).* Many types of files have some bits that can be modified and not affect the file they are in, which is where secret data can be hidden without altering the file in a visible manner. In the LSB approach, graphics with a high resolution or an audio file that has many different types of sounds (high bit rate) are the most successful for hiding information within. There is commonly no noticeable distortion, and the file is usually not increased to a size that can be detected. A 24-bit bitmap file will have 8 bits representing each of the three color values, which are red, green, and blue. These 8 bits are within each pixel. If we consider just the blue, there will be 2^8 different values of blue. The difference between 11111111 and 11111110 in the value for blue intensity is likely to be undetectable by the human eye. Therefore, the least significant bit can be used for something other than color information.

A digital graphic is just a file that shows different colors and intensities of light. The larger the file, the more bits that can be modified without much notice or distortion.

Several different types of tools can be used to hide messages within the carrier. Figure 3-29 illustrates one such tool that allows the user to encrypt the message along with hiding it within a file.

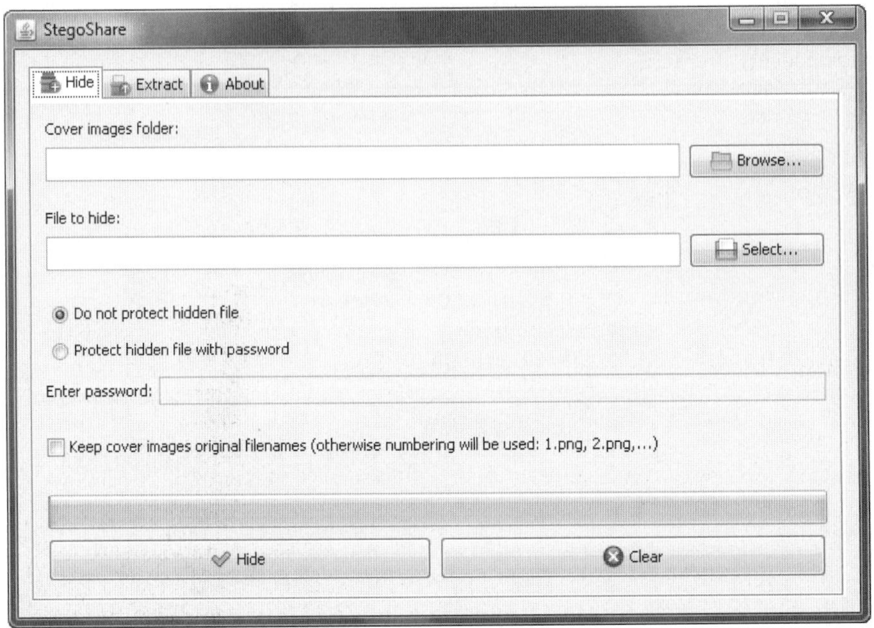

Figure 3-29 Embedding secret material

A concealment cipher (null cipher), explained earlier, is an example of a type of steganography method. The null values are not part of the secret message, but are used to hide the secret message. Let's look at an example. If your spy buddy sends you the message used in the example earlier, "The saying, 'The time is right' is not cow language, so is now a dead subject," you would think he was nuts. If you knew the secret message was made up of every third word, you would be able to extract the secret message from the null values. So the secret message is "The right cow is dead." And you still think he's nuts.

What if you wanted to get a secret message to your buddy in a nondigital format? You would use a physical method of sending secret messages instead of your computers. You could write the message in invisible ink, and he would need to have the necessary chemical to make it readable. You could create a very small photograph of the message, called a *microdot*, and put it within the ink of a stamp. Another physical steganography method is to send your buddy a very complex piece of art, which has the secret message in it that can be seen if it is held at the right angle and has a certain type of light shown on it. These are just some examples of the many ways that steganography can be carried out in the nondigital world.

Types of Ciphers

Symmetric encryption algorithms use a combination of two basic types of ciphers: substitution and transposition (permutation). The *substitution cipher* replaces bits, characters, or blocks of characters with different bits, characters, or blocks. The *transposition cipher* does not replace the original text with different text, but rather moves the original values around. It rearranges the bits, characters, or blocks of characters to hide the original meaning.

Substitution Ciphers

A substitution cipher uses a key to dictate how the substitution should be carried out. In the *Caesar cipher*, each letter is replaced with the letter three places beyond it in the alphabet. The algorithm is the alphabet, and the key is the instruction "shift up three."

As a simple example, if George uses the Caesar cipher with the English alphabet to encrypt the important message "meow," the encrypted message would be "phrz." Substitution is used in today's symmetric algorithms, but it is extremely complex compared to this example, which is only meant to show you the concept of how a substitution cipher works in its most simplistic form.

Transposition Ciphers

In a transposition cipher, the values are scrambled, or put into a different order. The key determines the positions the values are moved to, as illustrated in Figure 3-30.

This is a simplistic example of a transposition cipher and only shows one way of performing transposition. When implemented with complex mathematical functions, transpositions can become quite sophisticated and difficult to break. Symmetric algorithms employed today use both long sequences of complicated substitutions and transpositions on messages. The algorithm contains the possible ways that substitution and transposition processes *can* take place (represented in mathematical formulas). The key is used as

Figure 3-30 A transposition cipher

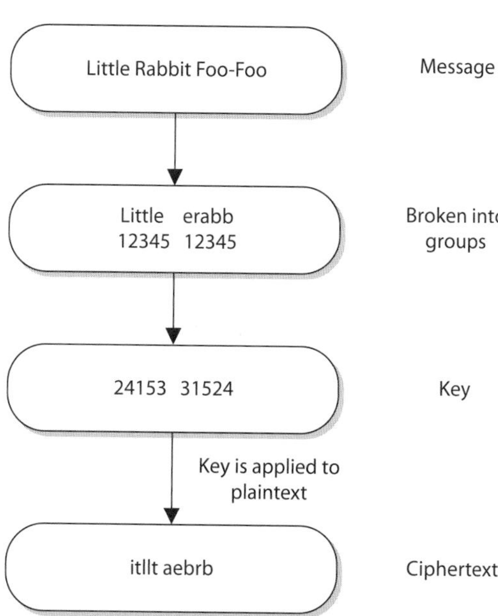

the instructions for the algorithm, dictating exactly how these processes *will* happen and in what order. To understand the relationship between an algorithm and a key, let's look at Figure 3-31. Conceptually, an algorithm is made up of different boxes, each of which has a different set of mathematical formulas that dictate the substitution and transposition steps that will take place on the bits that enter the box. To encrypt our message, the bit values must go through these different boxes. If each of our messages goes through each of these different boxes in the same order with the same values, the eavesdropper will be able to easily reverse-engineer this process and uncover our plaintext message.

To foil an eavesdropper, we use a key, which is a set of values that indicates which box should be used, in what order, and with what values. So if message A is encrypted with key 1, the key will make the message go through boxes 1, 6, 4, and then 5. When we need to encrypt message B, we will use key 2, which will make the message go through boxes 8, 3, 2, and then 9. It is the key that adds the randomness and the secrecy to the encryption process.

Simple substitution and transposition ciphers are vulnerable to attacks that perform *frequency analysis*. In every language, some words and patterns are used more often than others. For instance, in the English language, the most commonly used letter is *E*. If Mike is carrying out frequency analysis on a message, he will look for the most frequently repeated pattern of 8 bits (which makes up a character). So, if Mike sees that there are 12 patterns of 8 bits and he knows that *E* is the most commonly used letter in

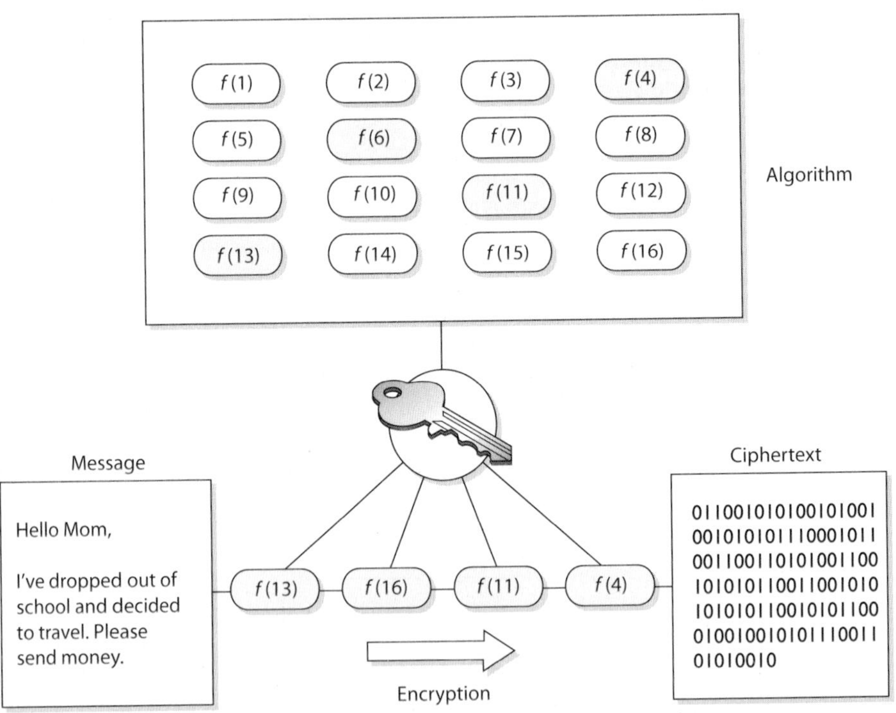

Figure 3-31 The algorithm and key relationship

the language, he will replace these bits with this vowel. This allows him to gain a foothold on the process, which will allow him to reverse-engineer the rest of the message.

Today's symmetric algorithms use substitution and transposition methods in their encryption processes, but the mathematics used are (or should be) too complex to allow for simplistic frequency-analysis attacks to be successful.

Key Derivation Functions

For complex keys to be generated, a master key is commonly created, and then symmetric keys are generated from it. For example, if an application is responsible for creating a session key for each subject that requests one, it should not be giving out the same instance of that one key. Different subjects need to have different symmetric keys to ensure that the window for the adversary to capture and uncover that key is smaller than if the same key were to be used over and over again. When two or more keys are created from a master key, they are called *subkeys*.

Key Derivation Functions (KDFs) are used to generate keys that are made up of random values. Different values can be used independently or together as random key material. The algorithm is created to use specific hash, password, and/or salt values, which will go through a certain number of rounds of mathematical functions dictated by the algorithm. The more rounds that this keying material goes through, the more assurance and security for the cryptosystem overall.

It is important to remember that the algorithm stays static and the randomness provided by cryptography is mainly by means of the keying material.

Methods of Encryption

Although there can be several pieces to an encryption process, the two main pieces are the algorithms and the keys. As stated earlier, algorithms used in computer systems are complex mathematical formulas that dictate the rules of how the plaintext will be turned into ciphertext. A key is a string of random bits that will be used by the algorithm to add to the randomness of the encryption process. For two entities to be able to communicate via encryption, they must use the same algorithm and, many times, the same key. In some encryption technologies, the receiver and the sender use the same key, and in other encryption technologies, they must use different but related keys for encryption and decryption purposes. The following sections explain the differences between these two types of encryption methods.

Symmetric vs. Asymmetric Algorithms

Cryptography algorithms are either *symmetric algorithms*, which use symmetric keys (also called secret keys), or *asymmetric algorithms*, which use asymmetric keys (also called public and private keys). As if encryption were not complicated enough, the terms used to describe the key types only make it worse. Just pay close attention and you will get through this fine.

Symmetric Cryptography

In a cryptosystem that uses symmetric cryptography, the sender and receiver use two instances of the same key for encryption and decryption, as shown in Figure 3-32. So the key has dual functionality, in that it can carry out both encryption and decryption processes. Symmetric keys are also called *secret* keys, because this type of encryption relies on each user to keep the key a secret and properly protected. If an intruder were to get this key, they could decrypt any intercepted message encrypted with it.

Each pair of users who want to exchange data using symmetric key encryption must have two instances of the same key. This means that if Dan and Iqqi want to communicate, both need to obtain a copy of the same key. If Dan also wants to communicate using symmetric encryption with Norm and Dave, he needs to have three separate keys, one for each friend. This might not sound like a big deal until Dan realizes that he may communicate with hundreds of people over a period of several months, and keeping track and using the correct key that corresponds to each specific receiver can become a daunting task. If 10 people needed to communicate securely with each other using symmetric keys, then 45 keys would need to be kept track of. If 100 people were going to communicate, then 4,950 keys would be involved. The equation used to calculate the number of symmetric keys needed is

$$N(N - 1)/2 = \text{number of keys}$$

When using symmetric algorithms, the sender and receiver use the same key for encryption and decryption functions. The security of the symmetric encryption method is completely dependent on how well users protect the key. This should raise red flags for you if you have ever had to depend on a whole staff of people to keep a secret. If a key is compromised, then all messages encrypted with that key can be decrypted and read by an intruder. This is complicated further by how symmetric keys are actually shared and

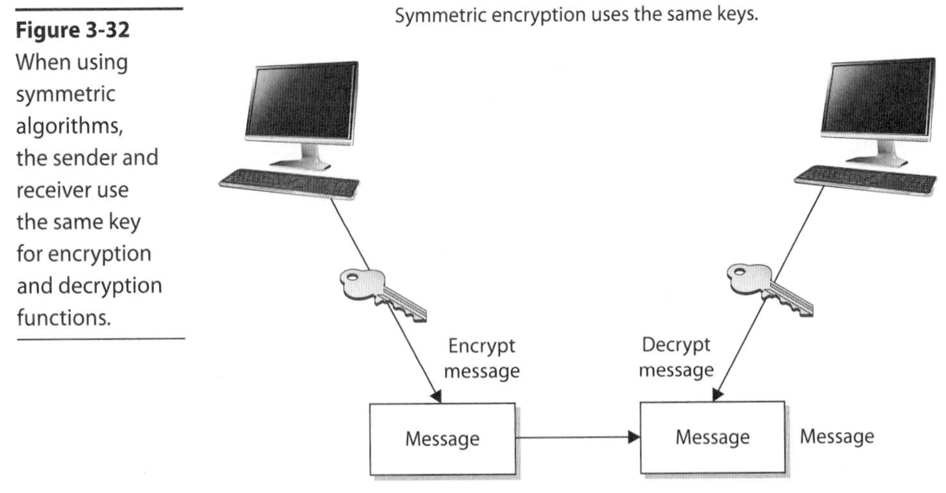

Figure 3-32 When using symmetric algorithms, the sender and receiver use the same key for encryption and decryption functions.

updated when necessary. If Dan wants to communicate with Norm for the first time, Dan has to figure out how to get the right key to Norm securely. It is not safe to just send it in an e-mail message, because the key is not protected and can be easily intercepted and used by attackers. Thus, Dan must get the key to Norm through an *out-of-band method.* Dan can save the key on a thumb drive and walk over to Norm's desk, or have a secure courier deliver it to Norm. This is a huge hassle, and each method is very clumsy and insecure.

Because both users employ the same key to encrypt and decrypt messages, symmetric cryptosystems can provide confidentiality, but they cannot provide authentication or nonrepudiation. There is no way to prove through cryptography who actually sent a message if two people are using the same key.

If symmetric cryptosystems have so many problems and flaws, why use them at all? Because they are very fast and can be hard to break. Compared with asymmetric systems, symmetric algorithms scream in speed. They can encrypt and decrypt relatively quickly large amounts of data that would take an unacceptable amount of time to encrypt and decrypt with an asymmetric algorithm. It is also difficult to uncover data encrypted with a symmetric algorithm if a large key size is used. For many of our applications that require encryption, symmetric key cryptography is the only option.

The following list outlines the strengths and weakness of symmetric key systems:

Strengths:

- Much faster (less computationally intensive) than asymmetric systems.
- Hard to break if using a large key size.

Weaknesses:

- Requires a secure mechanism to deliver keys properly.
- Each pair of users needs a unique key, so as the number of individuals increases, so does the number of keys, possibly making key management overwhelming.
- Provides confidentiality but not authenticity or nonrepudiation.

The following are examples of symmetric algorithms, which will be explained later in the "Block and Stream Ciphers" section:

- Data Encryption Standard (DES)
- Triple-DES (3DES)
- Blowfish
- International Data Encryption Algorithm (IDEA)
- RC4, RC5, and RC6
- Advanced Encryption Standard (AES)

Asymmetric Cryptography

In symmetric key cryptography, a single secret key is used between entities, whereas in public key systems, each entity has different keys, or *asymmetric keys*. The two different asymmetric keys are mathematically related. If a message is encrypted by one key, the other key is required in order to decrypt the message.

In a public key system, the pair of keys is made up of one public key and one private key. The *public key* can be known to everyone, and the *private key* must be known and used only by the owner. Many times, public keys are listed in directories and databases of e-mail addresses so they are available to anyone who wants to use these keys to encrypt or decrypt data when communicating with a particular person. Figure 3-33 illustrates the use of the different keys.

The public and private keys of an asymmetric cryptosystem are mathematically related, but if someone gets another person's public key, she should not be able to figure out the corresponding private key. This means that if an eavesdropper gets a copy of Bob's public key, she can't employ some mathematical magic and find out Bob's private key. But if someone gets Bob's private key, then there is big trouble—no one other than the owner should have access to a private key.

If Bob encrypts data with his private key, the receiver must have a copy of Bob's public key to decrypt it. The receiver can decrypt Bob's message and decide to reply to Bob in an encrypted form. All the receiver needs to do is encrypt her reply with Bob's public key, and then Bob can decrypt the message with his private key. It is not possible to encrypt and decrypt using the same key when using an asymmetric key encryption technology because, although mathematically related, the two keys are not the same key, as they are in symmetric cryptography. Bob can encrypt data with his private key, and the receiver can then decrypt it with Bob's public key. By decrypting the message with Bob's public key, the receiver can be sure the message really came from Bob. A message can be decrypted with a public key only if the message was encrypted with the corresponding private key. This provides authentication, because Bob is the only one who is supposed

Figure 3-33 An asymmetric cryptosystem

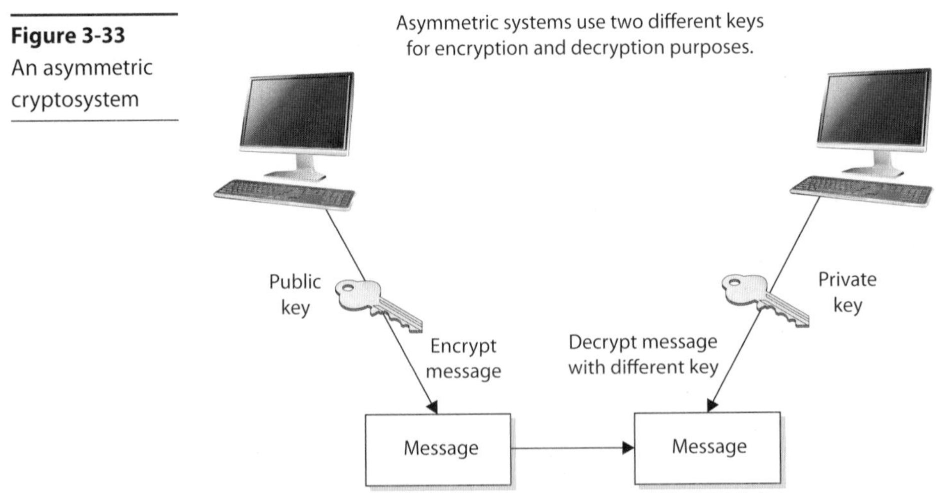

to have his private key. If the receiver wants to make sure Bob is the only one who can read her reply, she will encrypt the response with his public key. Only Bob will be able to decrypt the message because he is the only one who has the necessary private key.

The receiver can also choose to encrypt data with her private key instead of using Bob's public key. Why would she do that? Authentication—she wants Bob to know that the message came from her and no one else. If she encrypted the data with Bob's public key, it does not provide authenticity because anyone can get Bob's public key. If she uses her private key to encrypt the data, then Bob can be sure the message came from her and no one else. Symmetric keys do not provide authenticity, because the same key is used on both ends. Using one of the secret keys does not ensure the message originated from a specific individual.

If confidentiality is the most important security service to a sender, she would encrypt the file with the receiver's public key. This is called a *secure message format* because it can only be decrypted by the person who has the corresponding private key.

If authentication is the most important security service to the sender, then she would encrypt the data with her private key. This provides assurance to the receiver that the only person who could have encrypted the data is the individual who has possession of that private key. If the sender encrypted the data with the receiver's public key, authentication is not provided because this public key is available to anyone.

Encrypting data with the sender's private key is called an *open message format* because anyone with a copy of the corresponding public key can decrypt the message. Confidentiality is not ensured.

Each key type can be used to encrypt and decrypt, so do not get confused and think the public key is only for encryption and the private key is only for decryption. They both have the capability to encrypt and decrypt data. However, if data is encrypted with a private key, it cannot be decrypted with a private key. If data is encrypted with a private key, it must be decrypted with the corresponding public key.

An asymmetric algorithm works much more slowly than a symmetric algorithm, because symmetric algorithms carry out relatively simplistic mathematical functions on the bits during the encryption and decryption processes. They substitute and scramble (transposition) bits, which is not overly difficult or processor intensive. The reason it is hard to break this type of encryption is that the symmetric algorithms carry out this type of functionality over and over again. So a set of bits will go through a long series of being substituted and scrambled.

Asymmetric algorithms are slower than symmetric algorithms because they use much more complex mathematics to carry out their functions, which requires more processing time. Although they are slower, asymmetric algorithms can provide authentication and nonrepudiation, depending on the type of algorithm being used. Asymmetric systems also provide for easier and more manageable key distribution than symmetric systems and do not have the scalability issues of symmetric systems. The reason for these differences is that, with asymmetric systems, you can send out your public key to all of the people you need to communicate with, instead of keeping track of a unique key for each one of them. The "Hybrid Encryption Methods" section later in this chapter shows how these two systems can be used together to get the best of both worlds.

TIP Public key cryptography is asymmetric cryptography. The terms can be used interchangeably.

The following list outlines the strengths and weaknesses of asymmetric key algorithms:

Strengths:

- Better key distribution than symmetric systems.
- Better scalability than symmetric systems.
- Can provide authentication and nonrepudiation.

Weaknesses:

- Works much more slowly than symmetric systems.
- Mathematically intensive tasks.

The following are examples of asymmetric key algorithms:

- Rivest-Shamir-Adleman (RSA)
- Elliptic curve cryptosystem (ECC)
- Diffie-Hellman
- El Gamal
- Digital Signature Algorithm (DSA)

These algorithms will be explained further in the "Types of Asymmetric Systems" section later in the chapter.

Table 3-1 summarizes the differences between symmetric and asymmetric algorithms.

Attribute	Symmetric	Asymmetric
Keys	One key is shared between two or more entities.	One entity has a public key, and the other entity has the corresponding private key.
Key exchange	Out-of-band through secure mechanisms.	A public key is made available to everyone, and a private key is kept secret by the owner.
Speed	Algorithm is less complex and faster.	The algorithm is more complex and slower.
Use	Bulk encryption, which means encrypting files and communication paths.	Key distribution and digital signatures.
Security service provided	Confidentiality	Confidentiality, authentication, and nonrepudiation.

Table 3-1 Differences Between Symmetric and Asymmetric Systems

NOTE Digital signatures will be discussed later in the section "Digital Signatures."

Block and Stream Ciphers

The two main types of symmetric algorithms are block ciphers, which work on blocks of bits, and stream ciphers, which work on one bit at a time.

Block Ciphers

When a *block cipher* is used for encryption and decryption purposes, the message is divided into blocks of bits. These blocks are then put through mathematical functions, one block at a time. Suppose you need to encrypt a message you are sending to your mother and you are using a block cipher that uses 64 bits. Your message of 640 bits is chopped up into 10 individual blocks of 64 bits. Each block is put through a succession of mathematical formulas, and what you end up with is 10 blocks of encrypted text.

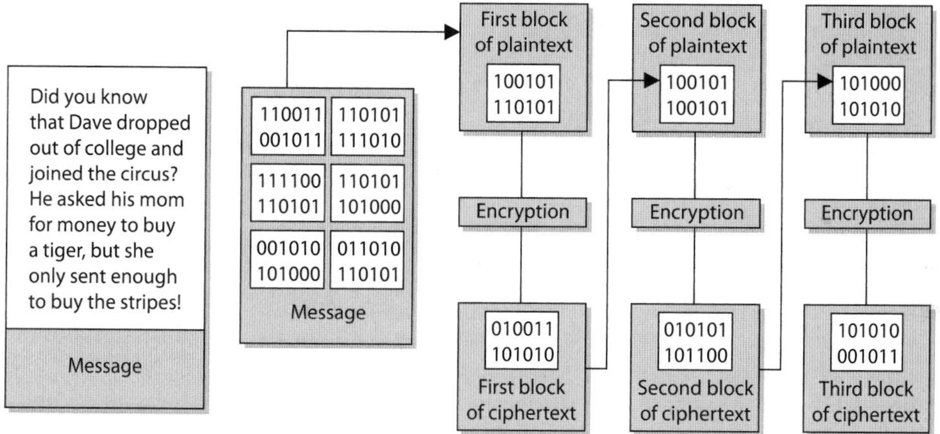

You send this encrypted message to your mother. She has to have the same block cipher and key, and those 10 ciphertext blocks go back through the algorithm in the reverse sequence and end up in your plaintext message.

A strong cipher contains the right level of two main attributes: confusion and diffusion. *Confusion* is commonly carried out through substitution, while *diffusion* is carried out by using transposition. For a cipher to be considered strong, it must contain both of these attributes to ensure that reverse-engineering is basically impossible. The randomness of the key values and the complexity of the mathematical functions dictate the level of confusion and diffusion involved.

In algorithms, diffusion takes place as individual bits of a block are scrambled, or diffused, throughout that block. Confusion is provided by carrying out complex substitution functions so the eavesdropper cannot figure out how to substitute the right values and come up with the original plaintext. Suppose you have 500 wooden blocks with individual letters written on them. You line them all up to spell out a paragraph (plaintext). Then you substitute 300 of them with another set of 300 blocks (confusion through substitution). Then you scramble all of these blocks up (diffusion through transposition) and leave them in a pile. For someone else to figure out your original message, they would have to substitute the correct blocks and then put them back in the right order. Good luck.

Confusion pertains to making the relationship between the key and resulting ciphertext as complex as possible so the key cannot be uncovered from the ciphertext. Each ciphertext value should depend upon several parts of the key, but this mapping between the key values and the ciphertext values should seem completely random to the observer.

Diffusion, on the other hand, means that a single plaintext bit has influence over several of the ciphertext bits. Changing a plaintext value should change many ciphertext values, not just one. In fact, in a strong block cipher, if one plaintext bit is changed, it will change every ciphertext bit with the probability of 50 percent. This means that if one plaintext bit changes, then about half of the ciphertext bits will change.

A very similar concept of diffusion is the *avalanche effect*. If an algorithm follows a strict avalanche effect criteria, this means that if the input to an algorithm is slightly modified, then the output of the algorithm is changed significantly. So a small change to the key or the plaintext should cause drastic changes to the resulting ciphertext. The ideas of diffusion and avalanche effect are basically the same—they were just derived from different people. Horst Feistel came up with the avalanche term, while Claude Shannon came up with the diffusion term. If an algorithm does not exhibit the necessary degree of the avalanche effect, then the algorithm is using poor randomization. This can make it easier for an attacker to break the algorithm.

Block ciphers use diffusion and confusion in their methods. Figure 3-34 shows a conceptual example of a simplistic block cipher. It has four block inputs, and each block is made up of 4 bits. The block algorithm has two layers of 4-bit substitution boxes called *S-boxes*. Each S-box contains a lookup table used by the algorithm as instructions on how the bits should be encrypted.

Figure 3-34 shows that the key dictates what S-boxes are to be used when scrambling the original message from readable plaintext to encrypted nonreadable ciphertext. Each S-box contains the different substitution methods that can be performed on each block. This example is simplistic—most block ciphers work with blocks of 32, 64, or 128 bits in size, and many more S-boxes are usually involved.

Stream Ciphers

As stated earlier, a block cipher performs mathematical functions on blocks of bits. A stream cipher, on the other hand, does not divide a message into blocks. Instead, a *stream cipher* treats the message as a stream of bits and performs mathematical functions on each bit individually.

When using a stream cipher, a plaintext bit will be transformed into a different ciphertext bit each time it is encrypted. Stream ciphers use *keystream generators*, which produce a stream of bits that is XORed with the plaintext bits to produce ciphertext, as shown in Figure 3-35.

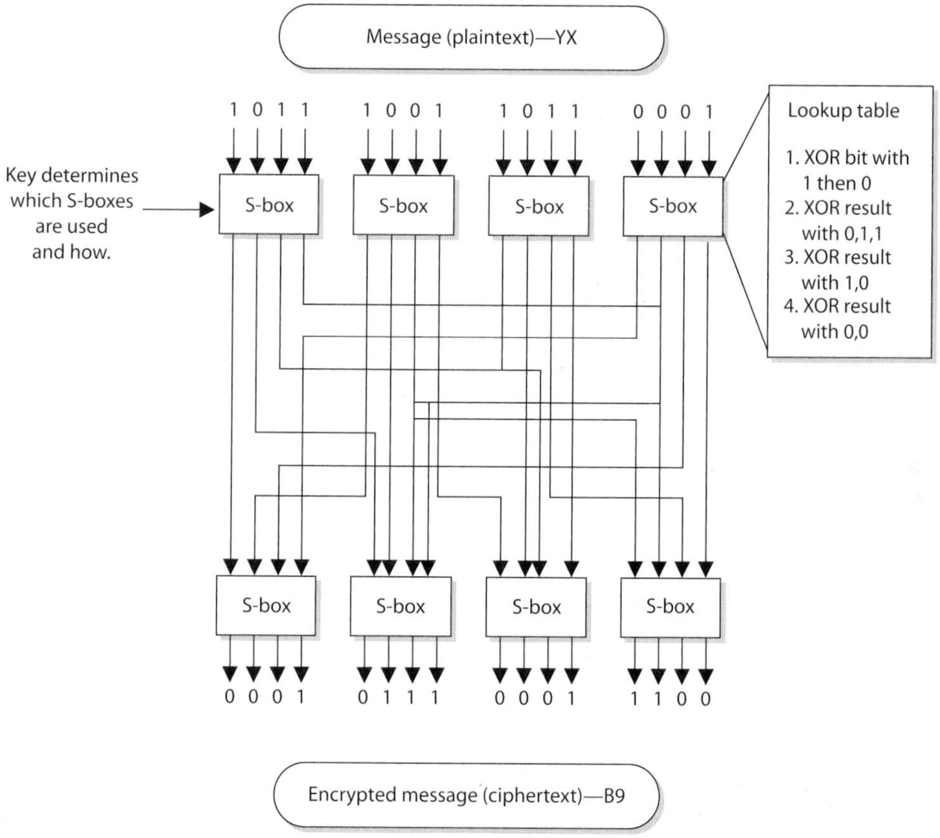

Message (plaintext)—YX
1 0 1 1
1 0 0 1
1 0 1 1
0 0 0 1
Key determines which S-boxes are used and how.
S-box
S-box
S-box
S-box
Lookup table
1. XOR bit with 1 then 0
2. XOR result with 0,1,1
3. XOR result with 1,0
4. XOR result with 0,0
S-box
S-box
S-box
S-box
0 0 0 1
0 1 1 1
0 0 0 1
1 1 0 0
Encrypted message (ciphertext)—B9

Figure 3-34 A message is divided into blocks of bits, and substitution and transposition functions are performed on those blocks.

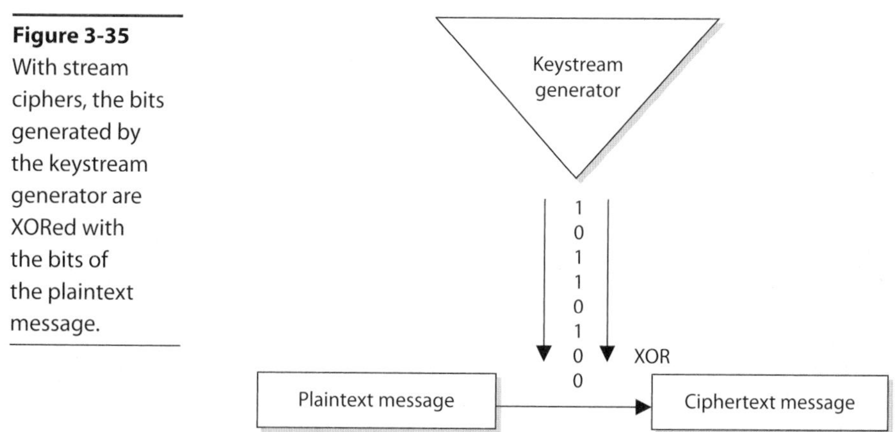

Figure 3-35 With stream ciphers, the bits generated by the keystream generator are XORed with the bits of the plaintext message.

Keystream generator
1
0
1
1
0
1
0
0
XOR
Plaintext message
Ciphertext message

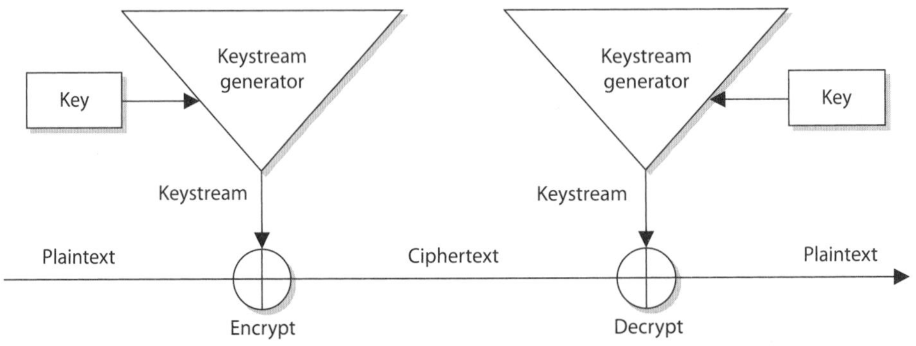

Figure 3-36 The sender and receiver must have the same key to generate the same keystream.

NOTE This process is very similar to the one-time pad explained earlier. The individual bits in the one-time pad are used to encrypt the individual bits of the message through the XOR function, and in a stream algorithm the individual bits created by the keystream generator are used to encrypt the bits of the message through XOR also.

In block ciphers, it is the key that determines what functions are applied to the plaintext and in what order. The key provides the randomness of the encryption process. As stated earlier, most encryption algorithms are public, so people know how they work. The secret to the secret sauce is the key. In stream ciphers, the key also provides randomness, so that the stream of bits that is XORed to the plaintext is as random as possible. This concept is shown in Figure 3-36. As you can see in this graphic, both the sending and receiving ends must have the same key to generate the same keystream for proper encryption and decryption purposes.

Stream Ciphers vs. One-Time Pads

Stream ciphers were developed to provide the same type of protection one-time pads do, which is why they work in such a similar manner. In reality, stream ciphers cannot provide the level of protection one-time pads do, but because stream ciphers are implemented through software and automated means, they are much more practical.

Initialization Vectors

Initialization vectors (IVs) are random values that are used with algorithms to ensure patterns are not created during the encryption process. They are used with keys and do not need to be encrypted when being sent to the destination. If IVs are not used, then two identical plaintext values that are encrypted with the same key will create the same ciphertext. Providing attackers with these types of patterns can make their job easier in breaking the encryption method and uncovering the key. For example, if we have the plaintext value of "See Spot run" two times within our message, we need to make sure that even though there is a pattern in the plaintext message, a pattern in the resulting ciphertext will not be created. So the IV and key are both used by the algorithm to provide more randomness to the encryption process.

A strong and effective stream cipher contains the following characteristics:

- **Easy to implement in hardware** Complexity in the hardware design makes it more difficult to verify the correctness of the implementation and can slow it down.
- **Long periods of no repeating patterns within keystream values** Bits generated by the keystream are not truly random in most cases, which will eventually lead to the emergence of patterns; we want these patterns to be rare.
- **A keystream not linearly related to the key** If someone figures out the keystream values, that does not mean she now knows the key value.
- **Statistically unbiased keystream (as many zeroes as ones)** There should be no dominance in the number of zeroes or ones in the keystream.

Stream ciphers require a lot of randomness and encrypt individual bits at a time. This requires more processing power than block ciphers require, which is why stream ciphers are better suited to be implemented at the hardware level. Because block ciphers do not require as much processing power, they can be easily implemented at the software level.

Overall, stream ciphers are considered less secure than block ciphers and are used less frequently. One difficulty in proper stream cipher implementation is generating a truly random and unbiased keystream. Many stream ciphers have been broken because it was uncovered that their keystreams had redundancies. One way in which stream ciphers are advantageous compared to block ciphers is when streaming communication data needs to be encrypted. Stream ciphers can encrypt and decrypt more quickly and are able to scale better within increased bandwidth requirements. When real-time applications, as in VoIP or multimedia, have encryption requirements, it is common that stream ciphers are implemented to accomplish this task. It is also worth pointing out that a computational error in a block encryption may render one block undecipherable, whereas a single computation error in stream encryption will propagate through the remainder of the stream.

Cryptographic Transformation Techniques

We have covered diffusion, confusion, avalanche, IVs, and random number generation. Some other techniques used in algorithms to increase their cryptographic strength are listed here:

- **Compression** Reduce redundancy before plaintext is encrypted. Compression functions are run on the text before it goes into the encryption algorithm.
- **Expansion** Expanding the plaintext by duplicating values. Commonly used to increase the plaintext size to map to key sizes.
- **Padding** Adding material to plaintext data before it is encrypted.
- **Key mixing** Using a portion (subkey) of a key to limit the exposure of the key. Key schedules are used to generate subkeys from master keys.

Hybrid Encryption Methods

Up to this point, we have figured out that symmetric algorithms are fast but have some drawbacks (lack of scalability, difficult key management, and they provide only confidentiality). Asymmetric algorithms do not have these drawbacks but are very slow. We just can't seem to win. So we turn to a hybrid system that uses symmetric and asymmetric encryption methods together.

Asymmetric and Symmetric Algorithms Used Together

Public key cryptography uses two keys (public and private) generated by an asymmetric algorithm for protecting encryption keys and key distribution, and a secret key is generated by a symmetric algorithm and used for bulk encryption. This is a hybrid use of the two different algorithms: asymmetric and symmetric. Each algorithm has its pros and cons, so using them together can be the best of both worlds.

In the hybrid approach, the two technologies are used in a complementary manner, with each performing a different function. A symmetric algorithm creates keys used for encrypting bulk data, and an asymmetric algorithm creates keys used for automated key distribution.

When a symmetric key is used for bulk data encryption, this key is used to encrypt the message you want to send. When your friend gets the message you encrypted, you want him to be able to decrypt it, so you need to send him the necessary symmetric key to use to decrypt the message. You do not want this key to travel unprotected, because if the message were intercepted and the key were not protected, an eavesdropper could intercept the message that contains the necessary key to decrypt your message and read your information. If the symmetric key needed to decrypt your message is not protected, there is no use in encrypting the message in the first place. So you should use an asymmetric algorithm to encrypt the symmetric key, as depicted in Figure 3-37. Why use the symmetric key on the message and the asymmetric key on the symmetric key? As stated earlier, the asymmetric algorithm takes longer because the math is more complex. Because your message is most likely going to be longer than the length of the key, you use the faster algorithm (symmetric) on the message and the slower algorithm (asymmetric) on the key.

How does this actually work? Let's say Bill is sending Paul a message that Bill wants only Paul to be able to read. Bill encrypts his message with a secret key, so now Bill has ciphertext and a symmetric key. The key needs to be protected, so Bill encrypts the symmetric key with an asymmetric key. Remember that asymmetric algorithms use private and public keys, so Bill will encrypt the symmetric key with Paul's public key. Now Bill has ciphertext from the message and ciphertext from the symmetric key. Why did Bill encrypt the symmetric key with Paul's public key instead of his own private key? Because if Bill encrypted it with his own private key, then anyone with Bill's public key could decrypt it and retrieve the symmetric key. However, Bill does not want anyone who has his public key to read his message to Paul. Bill only wants Paul to be able to read it. So Bill encrypts the symmetric key with Paul's public key. If Paul has done a good job protecting his private key, he will be the only one who can read Bill's message.

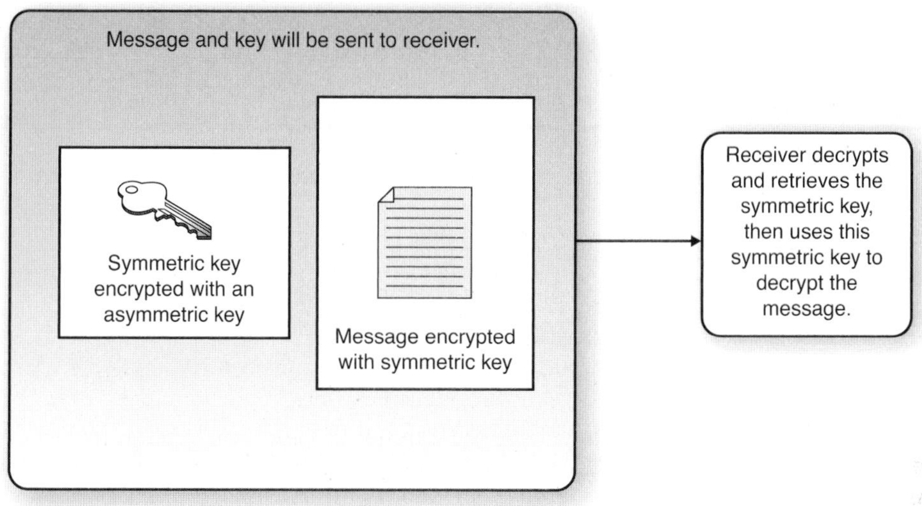

Figure 3-37 In a hybrid system, the asymmetric key is used to encrypt the symmetric key, and the symmetric key is used to encrypt the message

Paul receives Bill's message, and Paul uses his private key to decrypt the symmetric key. Paul then uses the symmetric key to decrypt the message. Paul then reads Bill's very important and confidential message that asks Paul how his day is.

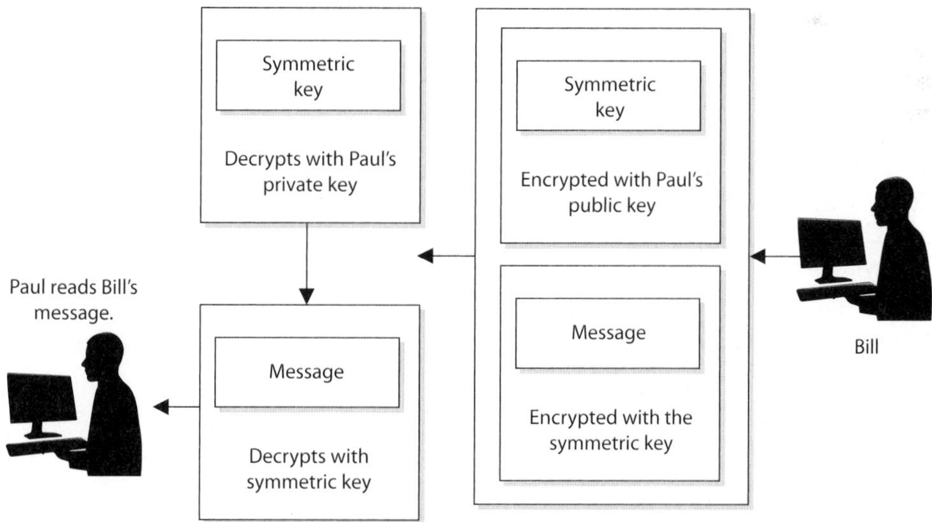

Now when we say that Bill is using this key to encrypt and that Paul is using that key to decrypt, those two individuals do not necessarily need to find the key on their hard drive and know how to properly apply it. We have software to do this for us—thank goodness.

If this is your first time with these issues and you are struggling, don't worry. Just remember the following points:

- An asymmetric algorithm performs encryption and decryption by using public and private keys that are related to each other mathematically.
- A symmetric algorithm performs encryption and decryption by using a shared secret key.
- A symmetric key is used to encrypt and/or decrypt the actual message.
- Public keys are used to encrypt the symmetric key for secure key exchange.
- A secret key is synonymous with a symmetric key.
- An asymmetric key refers to a public or private key.

So, that is how a hybrid system works. The symmetric algorithm uses a secret key that will be used to encrypt the bulk, or the message, and the asymmetric key encrypts the secret key for transmission.

Now to ensure that some of these concepts are driven home, ask these questions of yourself without reading the answers provided:

1. If a symmetric key is encrypted with a receiver's public key, what security service(s) is (are) provided?
2. If data is encrypted with the sender's private key, what security service(s) is (are) provided?
3. If the sender encrypts data with the receiver's private key, what security services(s) is (are) provided?
4. Why do we encrypt the message with the symmetric key?
5. Why don't we encrypt the symmetric key with another symmetric key?

Answers:

1. Confidentiality, because only the receiver's private key can be used to decrypt the symmetric key, and only the receiver should have access to this private key.
2. Authenticity of the sender and nonrepudiation. If the receiver can decrypt the encrypted data with the sender's public key, then she knows the data was encrypted with the sender's private key.
3. None, because no one but the owner of the private key should have access to it. Trick question.
4. Because the asymmetric key algorithm is too slow.
5. We need to get the necessary symmetric key to the destination securely, which can only be carried out through asymmetric cryptography via the use of public and private keys to provide a mechanism for secure transport of the symmetric key.

Digital Envelopes

When cryptography is new to people, the process of using symmetric and asymmetric cryptography together can be a bit confusing. But it is important to understand these concepts, because they really are the core, fundamental concepts of all cryptography. This process is not just used in an e-mail client or in a couple of products—this is how it is done when data and a symmetric key must be protected in transmission.

The use of these two technologies together can be referred to as a hybrid approach, but more commonly as a *digital envelope.*

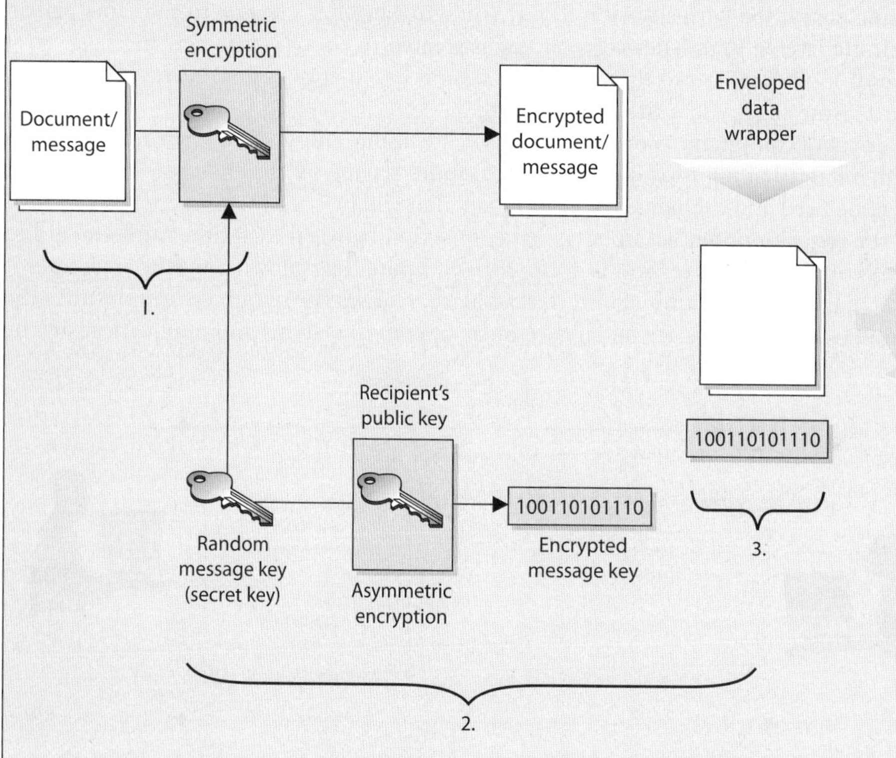

Session Keys

A *session key* is a single-use symmetric key that is used to encrypt messages between two users during a communication session. A session key is no different from the symmetric key described in the previous section, but it is only good for one communication session between users.

If Tanya has a symmetric key she uses to always encrypt messages between Lance and herself, then this symmetric key would not be regenerated or changed. They would use the same key every time they communicated using encryption. However, using the same

key repeatedly increases the chances of the key being captured and the secure communication being compromised. If, on the other hand, a new symmetric key were generated each time Lance and Tanya wanted to communicate, as shown in Figure 3-38, it would be used only during their one dialogue and then destroyed. If they wanted to communicate an hour later, a new session key would be created and shared.

A session key provides more protection than static symmetric keys because it is valid for only one session between two computers. If an attacker were able to capture the session key, she would have a very small window of time to use it to try to decrypt messages being passed back and forth.

In cryptography, almost all data encryption takes place through the use of session keys. When you write an e-mail and encrypt it before sending it over the wire, it is actually being encrypted with a session key. If you write another message to the same person one minute later, a brand-new session key is created to encrypt that new message. So if an eavesdropper happens to figure out one session key, that does not mean she has access to all other messages you write and send off.

When two computers want to communicate using encryption, they must first go through a handshaking process. The two computers agree on the encryption algorithms that will be used and exchange the session key that will be used for data encryption. In a sense, the two computers set up a virtual connection between each other and are said to be in session. When this session is done, each computer tears down any data structures it built to enable this communication to take place, releases the resources, and destroys the session key. These things are taken care of by operating systems and applications in the

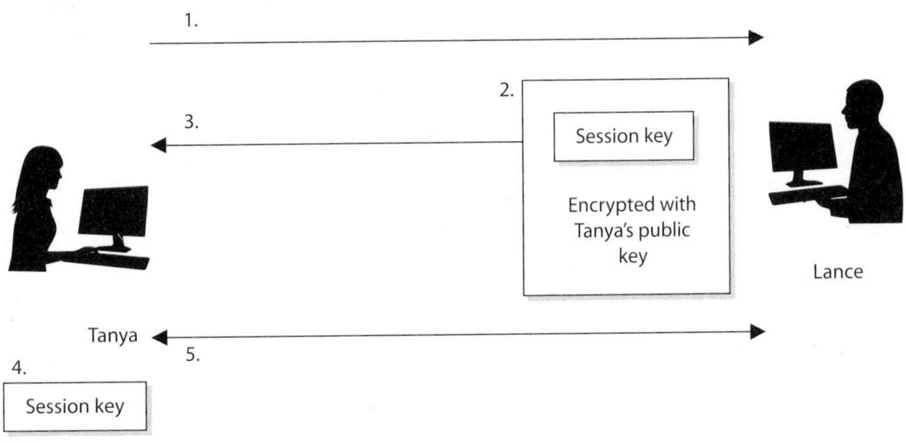

1) Tanya sends Lance her public key.
2) Lance generates a random session key and encrypts it using Tanya's public key.
3) Lance sends the session key, encrypted with Tanya's public key, to Tanya.
4) Tanya decrypts Lance's message with her private key and now has a copy of the session key.
5) Tanya and Lance use this session key to encrypt and decrypt messages to each other.

Figure 3-38 A session key is generated so all messages can be encrypted during one particular session between users.

background, so a user would not necessarily need to be worried about using the wrong type of key for the wrong reason. The software will handle this, but it is important for security professionals to understand the difference between the key types and the issues that surround them.

CAUTION Private and symmetric keys should not be available in cleartext. This may seem obvious to you, but there have been several implementations over time that have allowed for this type of compromise to take place.

Unfortunately, we don't always seem to be able to call an apple an apple. In many types of technology, the exact same thing can have more than one name. You could see symmetric cryptography referred to as any of the following:

- Secret key cryptography
- Session key cryptography
- Private key cryptography
- Shared-key cryptography

We know the difference between secret keys (static) and session keys (dynamic), but what is this "single key" and "private key" mess? Well, using the term "single key" makes sense, because the sender and receiver are using one single key. It's unfortunate that the term "private key" can be used to describe symmetric cryptography, because it only adds more confusion to the difference between symmetric cryptography (where one symmetric key is used) and asymmetric cryptography (where both a private and public key are used). You just need to remember this little quirk and still understand the difference between symmetric and asymmetric cryptography.

Types of Symmetric Systems

Several types of symmetric algorithms are used today. They have different methods of providing encryption and decryption functionality. The one thing they all have in common is that they are symmetric algorithms, meaning the sender and receiver are using two instances of the same key.

In this section, we will be walking through many of the following algorithms and their characteristics:

- Data Encryption Standard (DES)
- Triple-DES (3DES)
- Advanced Encryption Standard (AES)
- International Data Encryption Algorithm (IDEA)
- Blowfish
- RC4, RC5, and RC6

Data Encryption Standard

Data Encryption Standard (DES) has had a long and rich history within the computer community. The National Institute of Standards and Technology (NIST) researched the need for the protection of sensitive but unclassified data during the 1960s and initiated a cryptography program in the early 1970s. NIST invited vendors to submit data encryption algorithms to be used as a cryptographic standard. IBM had already been developing encryption algorithms to protect financial transactions. In 1974, IBM's 128-bit algorithm, named Lucifer, was submitted and accepted. The NSA modified this algorithm to use a key size of 64 bits (with 8 bits used for parity, resulting in an effective key length of 56 bits) instead of the original 128 bits, and named it the *Data Encryption Algorithm (DEA).* Controversy arose about whether the NSA weakened Lucifer on purpose to enable it to decrypt messages not intended for it, but in the end the modified Lucifer became a national cryptographic standard in 1977 and an American National Standards Institute (ANSI) standard in 1978.

EXAM TIP DEA is the algorithm that fulfills DES, which is really just a standard. So DES is the standard and DEA is the algorithm, but in the industry we usually just refer to it as DES. The CISSP exam may refer to the algorithm by either name, so remember both.

DES has been implemented in a majority of commercial products using cryptography functionality and in the applications of almost all government agencies. It was tested and approved as one of the strongest and most efficient cryptographic algorithms available. The continued overwhelming support of the algorithm is what caused the most confusion when the NSA announced in 1986 that, as of January 1988, the agency would no longer endorse DES and that DES-based products would no longer fall under compliance with Federal Standard 1027. The NSA felt that because DES had been so popular for so long, it would surely be targeted for penetration and become useless as an official standard. Many researchers disagreed, but the NSA wanted to move on to a newer, more secure, and less popular algorithm as the new standard.

The NSA's decision to drop its support for DES caused major concern and negative feedback. At that time, it was shown that DES still provided the necessary level of protection; that projections estimated a computer would require thousands of years to crack DES; that DES was already embedded in thousands of products; and that there was no equivalent substitute. The NSA reconsidered its decision, and NIST ended up recertifying DES for another five years.

In 1998, the Electronic Frontier Foundation built a computer system for $250,000 that broke DES in three days by using a brute-force attack against the keyspace. It contained 1,536 microprocessors running at 40 MHz, which performed 60 million test decryptions per second per chip. Although most people do not have these types of systems to conduct such attacks, the rise of technologies such as botnets and cloud computing make this feasible for the average attacker. This brought about 3DES, which provides stronger protection, as discussed later in the chapter.

DES was later replaced by the *Rijndael* algorithm as the *Advanced Encryption Standard (AES)* by NIST. This means that Rijndael is the new approved method of encrypting sensitive but unclassified information for the U.S. government; it has been accepted by, and is widely used in, the public arena today.

How Does DES Work?

DES is a symmetric block encryption algorithm. When 64-bit blocks of plaintext go in, 64-bit blocks of ciphertext come out. It is also a symmetric algorithm, meaning the same key is used for encryption and decryption. It uses a 64-bit key: 56 bits make up the true key, and 8 bits are used for parity.

When the DES algorithm is applied to data, it divides the message into blocks and operates on them one at a time. The blocks are put through 16 rounds of transposition and substitution functions. The order and type of transposition and substitution functions depend on the value of the key used with the algorithm. The result is 64-bit blocks of ciphertext.

What Does It Mean When an Algorithm Is Broken?

As described in an earlier section, DES was finally broken with a dedicated computer (lovingly named the DES Cracker, aka Deep Crack). But what does "broken" really mean?

In most instances, an algorithm is broken if someone is able to uncover a key that was used during an encryption process. So let's say Kevin encrypted a message and sent it to Valerie. Marc captures this encrypted message and carries out a brute-force attack on it, which means he tries to decrypt the message with different keys until he uncovers the right one. Once he identifies this key, the algorithm is considered broken. So does that mean the algorithm is worthless? It depends on who your enemies are.

If an algorithm is broken through a brute-force attack, this just means the attacker identified the one key that was used for one instance of encryption. But in proper implementations, we should be encrypting data with session keys, which are good only for that one session. So even if the attacker uncovers one session key, it may be useless to the attacker, in which case he now has to work to identify a new session key.

If your information is of sufficient value that enemies or thieves would exert a lot of resources to break the encryption (as may be the case for financial transactions or military secrets), you would not use an algorithm that has been broken. If you are encrypting messages to your mother about a meatloaf recipe, you likely are not going to worry about whether the algorithm has been broken.

So defeating an algorithm can take place through brute-force attacks or by identifying weaknesses in the algorithm itself. Brute-force attacks have increased in potency because of the increased processing capacity of computers today. An algorithm that uses a 40-bit key has around 1 trillion possible key values. If a 56-bit key is used, then there are approximately 72 quadrillion different key values. This may seem like a lot, but relative to today's computing power, these key sizes do not provide much protection at all.

On a final note, algorithms are built on the current understanding of mathematics. As the human race advances in mathematics, the level of protection that today's algorithms provide may crumble.

DES Modes

Block ciphers have several modes of operation. Each mode specifies how a block cipher will operate. One mode may work better in one type of environment for specific functionality, whereas another mode may work better in another environment with totally different requirements. It is important that vendors who employ DES (or any block cipher) understand the different modes and which one to use for which purpose.

DES and other symmetric block ciphers have several distinct modes of operation that are used in different situations for different results. You just need to understand five of them:

- Electronic Code Book (ECB)
- Cipher Block Chaining (CBC)
- Cipher Feedback (CFB)
- Output Feedback (OFB)
- Counter (CTR)

Electronic Code Book (ECB) Mode *ECB* mode operates like a code book. A 64-bit data block is entered into the algorithm with a key, and a block of ciphertext is produced. For a given block of plaintext and a given key, the same block of ciphertext is always produced. Not all messages end up in neat and tidy 64-bit blocks, so ECB incorporates padding to address this problem. ECB is the easiest and fastest mode to use, but as we will see, it has its dangers.

A key is basically instructions for the use of a code book that dictates how a block of text will be encrypted and decrypted. The code book provides the recipe of substitutions and permutations that will be performed on the block of plaintext. The security issue with using ECB mode is that each block is encrypted with the exact same key, and thus the exact same code book. So, two bad things can happen here: an attacker could uncover the key and thus have the key to decrypt all the blocks of data, or an attacker could gather the ciphertext and plaintext of each block and build the code book that was used, without needing the key.

The crux of the problem is that there is not enough randomness to the process of encrypting the independent blocks, so if this mode is used to encrypt a large amount of data, it could be cracked more easily than the other modes that block ciphers can work in. So the next question to ask is, why even use this mode? This mode is the fastest and easiest, so we use it to encrypt small amounts of data, such as PINs, challenge-response values in authentication processes, and encrypting keys.

Because this mode works with blocks of data independently, data within a file does not have to be encrypted in a certain order. This is very helpful when using encryption in databases. A database has different pieces of data accessed in a random fashion. If it is encrypted in ECB mode, then any record or table can be added, encrypted, deleted, or decrypted independently of any other table or record. Other DES modes are dependent upon the text encrypted before them. This dependency makes it harder to encrypt and decrypt smaller amounts of text, because the previous encrypted text would need to be decrypted first. (After we cover chaining in the next section, this dependency will make more sense.)

ECB mode does not use chaining, so you should not use it to encrypt large amounts of data because patterns would eventually show themselves.

Some important characteristics of ECB mode encryption are as follows:

- Operations can be run in parallel, which decreases processing time.
- Errors are contained. If an error takes place during the encryption process, it only affects one block of data.
- It is only usable for the encryption of short messages.
- It cannot carry out preprocessing functions before receiving plaintext.

Cipher Block Chaining (CBC) Mode In ECB mode, a block of plaintext and a key will always give the same ciphertext. This means that if the word "balloon" were encrypted and the resulting ciphertext was "hwicssn," each time it was encrypted using the same key, the same ciphertext would always be given. This can show evidence of a pattern, enabling an eavesdropper, with some effort, to discover the pattern and get a step closer to compromising the encryption process.

Cipher Block Chaining (CBC) mode does not reveal a pattern because each block of text, the key, and the value based on the previous block are processed in the algorithm and applied to the next block of text, as shown in Figure 3-39. This results in more random ciphertext. Ciphertext is extracted and used from the previous block of text. This provides dependence between the blocks, in a sense chaining them together. This is where the name Cipher Block Chaining comes from, and it is this chaining effect that hides any patterns.

The results of one block are XORed with the next block before it is encrypted, meaning each block is used to modify the following block. This chaining effect means that a particular ciphertext block is dependent upon all blocks before it, not just the previous block.

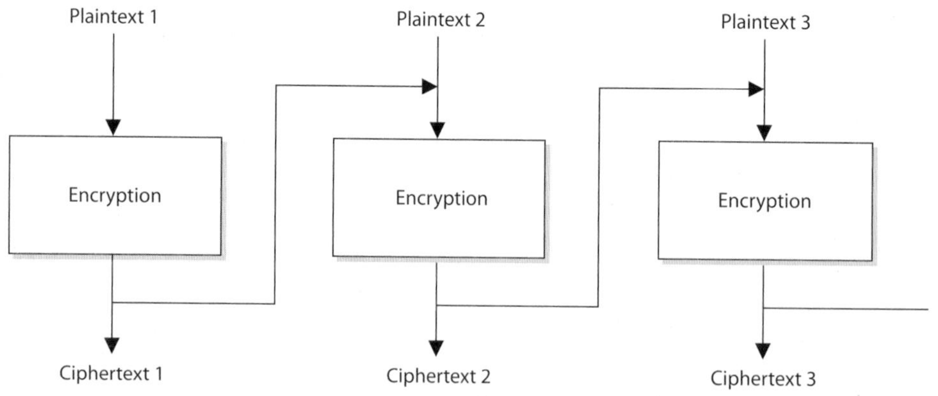

Figure 3-39 In CBC mode, the ciphertext from the previous block of data is used in encrypting the next block of data.

As an analogy, let's say you have five buckets of marbles. Each bucket contains a specific color of marbles: red, blue, yellow, black, and green. You shake and tumble (encrypt) the first bucket of red marbles (block of bits) to get them all mixed up. Then you take the second bucket of marbles, which are blue, and pour in the red marbles and go through the same exercise of shaking and tumbling them. You pour this bucket of red and blue marbles into your next bucket of yellow marbles and shake them all up. This illustrates the incorporated randomness that is added when using chaining in a block encryption process.

When we encrypt our very first block using CBC, we do not have a previous block of ciphertext to "dump in" and use to add the necessary randomness to the encryption process. If we do not add a piece of randomness when encrypting this first block, then the bad guys could identify patterns, work backward, and uncover the key. So, we use an initialization vector (IVs were introduced previously in the "Initialization Vectors" section). The 64-bit IV is XORed with the first block of plaintext, and then it goes through its encryption process. The result of that (ciphertext) is XORed with the second block of plaintext, and then the second block is encrypted. This continues for the whole message. It is the chaining that adds the necessary randomness that allows us to use CBC mode to encrypt large files. Neither the individual blocks nor the whole message will show patterns that will allow an attacker to reverse-engineer and uncover the key.

If we choose a different IV each time we encrypt a message, even if it is the same message, the ciphertext will always be unique. This means that if you send the same message out to 50 people and encrypt each message using a different IV, the ciphertext for each message will be different. Pretty nifty.

Cipher Feedback (CFB) Mode Sometimes block ciphers can emulate a stream cipher. Before we dig into how this would happen, let's first look at why. If you are going to send an encrypted e-mail to your boss, your e-mail client will use a symmetric block cipher working in CBC mode. The e-mail client would not use ECB mode because most messages are long enough to show patterns that can be used to reverse-engineer the process and uncover the encryption key. The CBC mode is great to use when you need to send large chunks of data at a time. But what if you are not sending large chunks of data at one time, but instead are sending a steady stream of data to a destination? If you are working on a terminal that communicates with a back-end terminal server, what is really going on is that each keystroke and mouse movement you make is sent to the back-end server in chunks of 8 bits to be processed. So even though it seems as though the computer you are working on is carrying out your commands and doing the processing you are requesting, it is not—this is happening on the server. Thus, if you need to encrypt the data that goes from your terminal to the terminal server, you could not use CBC mode because it only encrypts blocks of data 64 bits in size. You have blocks of 8 bits that you need to encrypt. So what do you do now? We have just the mode for this type of situation!

Figure 3-40 illustrates how *Cipher Feedback (CFB)* mode works, which is really a combination of a block cipher and a stream cipher. For the first block of 8 bits that needs to be encrypted, we do the same thing we did in CBC mode, which is to use an IV. Recall how stream ciphers work: The key and the IV are used by the algorithm to create

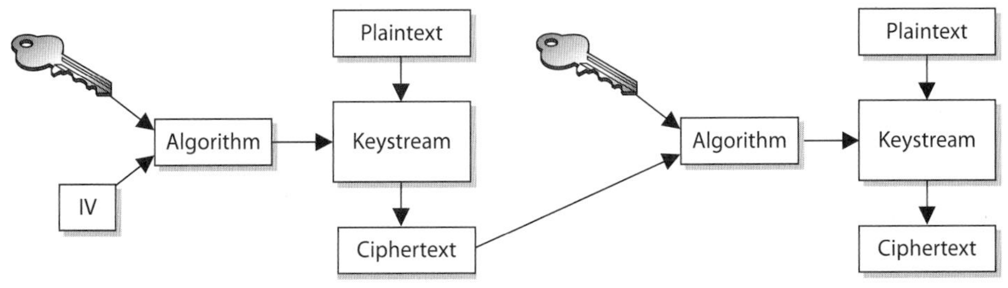

Figure 3-40 A block cipher working in CFB mode

a keystream, which is just a random set of bits. This set of bits is XORed to the block of plaintext, which results in the same size block of ciphertext. So the first block (8 bits) is XORed to the set of bits created through the keystream generator. Two things take place with this resulting 8-bit block of ciphertext. One copy goes over the wire to the destination (in our scenario, to the terminal server), and another copy is used to encrypt the next block of 8-bit plaintext. Adding this copy of ciphertext to the encryption process of the next block adds more randomness to the encryption process.

We walked through a scenario where 8-bit blocks needed to be encrypted, but in reality, CFB mode can be used to encrypt any size blocks, even blocks of just 1 bit. But since most of our encoding maps 8 bits to one character, using CFB to encrypt 8-bit blocks is very common.

NOTE When using CBC mode, it is a good idea to use a unique IV value per message, but this is not necessary since the message being encrypted is usually very large. When using CFB mode, you are encrypting a smaller amount of data, so it is imperative a new IV value be used to encrypt each new stream of data.

Output Feedback (OFB) Mode As you have read, you can use ECB mode for the process of encrypting small amounts of data, such as a key or PIN value. These components will be around 64 bits or more, so ECB mode works as a true block cipher. You can use CBC mode to encrypt larger amounts of data in block sizes of 64 bits. In situations where you need to encrypt a smaller amount of data, you need the cipher to work like a stream cipher and to encrypt individual bits of the blocks, as in CFB. In some cases, you still need to encrypt a small amount of data at a time (1 to 8 bits), but you need to ensure possible errors do not affect your encryption and decryption processes.

If you look back at Figure 3-40, you see that the ciphertext from the previous block is used to encrypt the next block of plaintext. What if a bit in the first ciphertext gets corrupted? Then we have corrupted values going into the process of encrypting the next block of plaintext, and this problem just continues because of the use of chaining in this mode. Now look at Figure 3-41. It looks terribly similar to Figure 3-40, but notice that the values used to encrypt the next block of plaintext are coming directly from the keystream, not from the resulting ciphertext. This is the difference between the two modes.

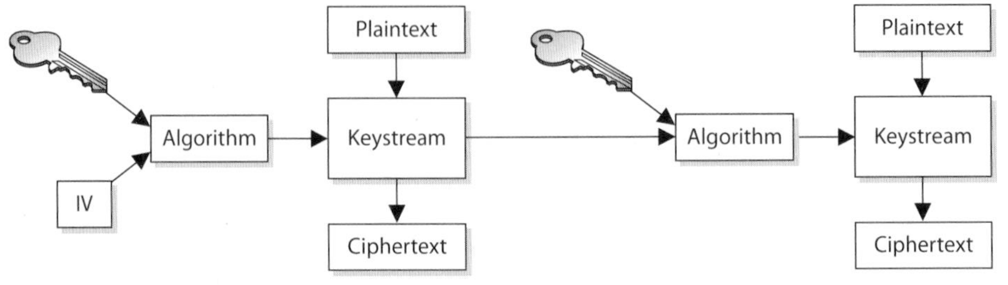

Figure 3-41 A block cipher working in OFB mode

If you need to encrypt something that would be very sensitive to these types of errors, such as digitized video or digitized voice signals, you should not use CFB mode. You should use OFB mode instead, which reduces the chance that these types of bit corruptions can take place.

So *Output Feedback (OFB)* is a mode that a block cipher can work in when it needs to emulate a stream because it encrypts small amounts of data at a time, but it has a smaller chance of creating and extending errors throughout the full encryption process.

To ensure OFB and CFB are providing the most protection possible, the size of the ciphertext (in CFB) or keystream values (in OFB) needs to be the same size as the block of plaintext being encrypted. This means that if you are using CFB and are encrypting 8 bits at a time, the ciphertext you bring forward from the previous encryption block needs to be 8 bits. Otherwise, you are repeating values over and over, which introduces patterns. (This is the same reason why a one-time pad should be used only one time and should be as long as the message itself.)

Counter (CTR) Mode *Counter (CTR)* mode is very similar to OFB mode, but instead of using a randomly unique IV value to generate the keystream values, this mode uses an IV counter that increments for each plaintext block that needs to be encrypted. The unique counter ensures that each block is XORed with a unique keystream value.

The other difference is that there is no chaining involved, which means no ciphertext is brought forward to encrypt the next block. Since there is no chaining, the encryption of the individual blocks can happen in parallel, which increases the performance. The main reason CTR mode would be used instead of the other modes is performance.

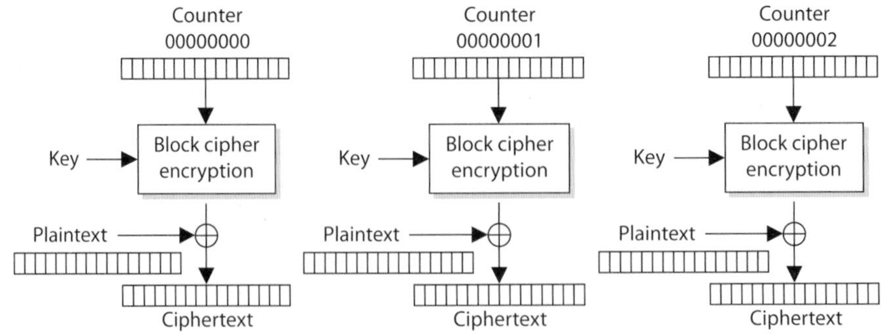

CTR mode has been around for quite some time and is used in encrypting ATM cells for virtual circuits, in IPSec, and in the wireless security standard IEEE 802.11i. A developer would choose to use this mode in these situations because individual ATM cells or packets going through an IPSec tunnel or over radio frequencies may not arrive at the destination in order. Since chaining is not involved, the destination can decrypt and begin processing the packets without having to wait for the full message to arrive and *then* decrypt all the data.

Synchronous vs. Asynchronous

Synchronous cryptosystems use keystreams to encrypt plaintext one bit at a time. The keystream values are "in sync" with the plaintext values. An *asynchronous* cryptosystem uses previously generated output to encrypt the current plaintext values. So a stream algorithm would be considered synchronous, while a block algorithm using chaining would be considered asynchronous.

Triple-DES

We went from DES to *Triple-DES (3DES)*, so it might seem we skipped Double-DES. We did. Double-DES has a key length of 112 bits, but there is a specific attack against Double-DES that reduces its work factor to about the same as DES. Thus, it is no more secure than DES. So let's move on to 3DES.

Many successful attacks against DES and the realization that the useful lifetime of DES was about up brought much support for 3DES. NIST knew that a new standard had to be created, which ended up being AES (discussed in the next section), but a quick fix was needed in the meantime to provide more protection for sensitive data. The result: 3DES (aka TDEA—Triple Data Encryption Algorithm).

3DES uses 48 rounds in its computation, which makes it highly resistant to differential cryptanalysis. However, because of the extra work 3DES performs, there is a heavy performance hit. It can take up to three times longer than DES to perform encryption and decryption.

Although NIST has selected the Rijndael algorithm to replace DES as *the* AES, NIST and others expect 3DES to be around and used for quite some time.

3DES can work in different modes, and the mode chosen dictates the number of keys used and what functions are carried out:

- **DES-EEE3** Uses three different keys for encryption, and the data is encrypted, encrypted, encrypted.
- **DES-EDE3** Uses three different keys for encryption, and the data is encrypted, decrypted, encrypted.
- **DES-EEE2** The same as DES-EEE3, but uses only two keys, and the first and third encryption processes use the same key.
- **DES-EDE2** The same as DES-EDE3, but uses only two keys, and the first and third encryption processes use the same key.

EDE may seem a little odd at first. How much protection could be provided by encrypting something, decrypting it, and encrypting it again? The decrypting portion here is decrypted with a different key. When data is encrypted with one symmetric key and decrypted with a different symmetric key, it is jumbled even more. So the data is not actually decrypted in the middle function; it is just run through a decryption process with a different key. Pretty tricky.

Advanced Encryption Standard

After DES was used as an encryption standard for over 20 years and it was cracked in a relatively short time once the necessary technology was available, NIST decided a new standard, the *Advanced Encryption Standard (AES)*, needed to be put into place. In January 1997, NIST announced its request for AES candidates and outlined the requirements in FIPS PUB 197. AES was to be a symmetric block cipher supporting key sizes of 128, 192, and 256 bits. The following five algorithms were the finalists:

- **MARS** Developed by the IBM team that created Lucifer
- **RC6** Developed by RSA Laboratories
- **Serpent** Developed by Ross Anderson, Eli Biham, and Lars Knudsen
- **Twofish** Developed by Counterpane Systems
- **Rijndael** Developed by Joan Daemen and Vincent Rijmen

Out of these contestants, Rijndael was chosen. The block sizes that Rijndael supports are 128, 192, and 256 bits. The number of rounds depends upon the size of the block and the key length:

- If both the key and block size are 128 bits, there are 10 rounds.
- If both the key and block size are 192 bits, there are 12 rounds.
- If both the key and block size are 256 bits, there are 14 rounds.

Rijndael works well when implemented in software and hardware in a wide range of products and environments. It has low memory requirements and has been constructed to easily defend against timing attacks.

Rijndael was NIST's choice to replace DES. It is now the algorithm required to protect sensitive but unclassified U.S. government information.

TIP DEA is the algorithm used within DES, and Rijndael is the algorithm used in AES. In the industry, we refer to these as DES and AES instead of by the actual algorithms.

International Data Encryption Algorithm

International Data Encryption Algorithm (IDEA) is a block cipher and operates on 64-bit blocks of data. The 64-bit data block is divided into 16 smaller blocks, and each has eight rounds of mathematical functions performed on it. The key is 128 bits long, and IDEA is faster than DES when implemented in software.

The IDEA algorithm offers different modes similar to the modes described in the DES section, but it is considered harder to break than DES because it has a longer key size. IDEA is used in PGP and other encryption software implementations. It was thought to replace DES, but it is patented, meaning that licensing fees would have to be paid to use it.

As of this writing, there have been no successful practical attacks against this algorithm, although there have been numerous attempts.

Blowfish

Blowfish is a block cipher that works on 64-bit blocks of data. The key length can be anywhere from 32 bits up to 448 bits, and the data blocks go through 16 rounds of cryptographic functions. It was intended as a replacement to the aging DES. While many of the other algorithms have been proprietary and thus encumbered by patents or kept as government secrets, this isn't the case with Blowfish. Bruce Schneier, the creator of Blowfish, has stated, "Blowfish is unpatented, and will remain so in all countries. The algorithm is hereby placed in the public domain, and can be freely used by anyone." Nice guy.

RC4

RC4 is one of the most commonly implemented stream ciphers. It has a variable key size, is used in the Secure Sockets Layer (SSL) protocol, and was (improperly) implemented in the 802.11 WEP protocol standard. RC4 was developed in 1987 by Ron Rivest and was considered a trade secret of RSA Data Security, Inc., until someone posted the source code on a mailing list. Since the source code was released nefariously, the stolen algorithm is sometimes implemented and referred to as ArcFour or ARC4 because the title RC4 is trademarked.

The algorithm is very simple, fast, and efficient, which is why it became so popular. But it is vulnerable to modification attacks. This is one reason that IEEE 802.11i moved from the RC4 algorithm to the AES algorithm.

RC5

RC5 is a block cipher that has a variety of parameters it can use for block size, key size, and the number of rounds used. It was created by Ron Rivest. The block sizes used in this algorithm are 32, 64, or 128 bits, and the key size goes up to 2,048 bits. The number of rounds used for encryption and decryption is also variable. The number of rounds can go up to 255.

RC6

RC6 is a block cipher that was built upon RC5, so it has all the same attributes as RC5. The algorithm was developed mainly to be submitted as AES, but Rijndael was chosen instead. There were some modifications of the RC5 algorithm to increase the overall speed, the result of which is RC6.

Cryptography Notation

In some resources, you may run across *rc5-w/r/b* or *RC5-32/12/16*. This is a type of shorthand that describes the configuration of the algorithm:

- *w* = Word size, in bits, which can be 16, 32, or 64 bits in length
- *r* = Number of rounds, which can be 0 to 255
- *b* = Key size, in bytes

So *RC5-32/12/16* would mean the following:

- 32-bit words, which means it encrypts 64-bit data blocks
- Using 12 rounds
- With a 16-byte (128-bit) key

A developer configures these parameters (words, number of rounds, key size) for the algorithm for specific implementations. The existence of these parameters gives developers extensive flexibility.

Types of Asymmetric Systems

As described earlier in the chapter, using purely symmetric key cryptography has three drawbacks, which affect the following:

- **Security services** Purely symmetric key cryptography provides confidentiality only, not authentication or nonrepudiation.
- **Scalability** As the number of people who need to communicate increases, so does the number of symmetric keys required, meaning more keys must be managed.
- **Secure key distribution** The symmetric key must be delivered to its destination through a secure courier.

Despite these drawbacks, symmetric key cryptography was all that the computing society had available for encryption for quite some time. Symmetric and asymmetric cryptography did not arrive on the same day or even in the same decade. We dealt with the issues surrounding symmetric cryptography for quite some time, waiting for someone smarter to come along and save us from some of this grief.

Diffie-Hellman Algorithm

The first group to address the shortfalls of symmetric key cryptography decided to attack the issue of secure distribution of the symmetric key. Whitfield Diffie and Martin Hellman worked on this problem and ended up developing the first asymmetric key agreement algorithm, called, naturally, Diffie-Hellman.

To understand how *Diffie-Hellman* works, consider an example. Let's say that Tanya and Erika would like to communicate over an encrypted channel by using Diffie-Hellman. They would both generate a private and public key pair and exchange public keys. Tanya's software would take her private key (which is just a numeric value) and Erika's public key (another numeric value) and put them through the Diffie-Hellman algorithm. Erika's software would take her private key and Tanya's public key and insert them into the Diffie-Hellman algorithm on her computer. Through this process, Tanya and Erika derive the same shared value, which is used to create instances of symmetric keys.

So, Tanya and Erika exchanged information that did not need to be protected (their public keys) over an untrusted network, and in turn generated the exact same symmetric key on each system. They both can now use these symmetric keys to encrypt, transmit, and decrypt information as they communicate with each other.

NOTE The preceding example describes key *agreement*, which is different from key *exchange*, the functionality used by the other asymmetric algorithms that will be discussed in this chapter. With key exchange functionality, the sender encrypts the symmetric key with the receiver's public key before transmission.

The Diffie-Hellman algorithm enables two systems to generate a symmetric key securely without requiring a previous relationship or prior arrangements. The algorithm allows for key distribution, but does not provide encryption or digital signature functionality. The algorithm is based on the difficulty of calculating discrete logarithms in a finite field.

The original Diffie-Hellman algorithm is vulnerable to a man-in-the-middle attack, because no authentication occurs before public keys are exchanged. In our example, when Tanya sends her public key to Erika, how does Erika really know it is Tanya's public key? What if Lance spoofed his identity, told Erika he was Tanya, and sent over his key? Erika would accept this key, thinking it came from Tanya. Let's walk through the steps of how this type of attack would take place, as illustrated in Figure 3-42:

1. Tanya sends her public key to Erika, but Lance grabs the key during transmission so it never makes it to Erika.
2. Lance spoofs Tanya's identity and sends over his public key to Erika. Erika now thinks she has Tanya's public key.
3. Erika sends her public key to Tanya, but Lance grabs the key during transmission so it never makes it to Tanya.
4. Lance spoofs Erika's identity and sends over his public key to Tanya. Tanya now thinks she has Erika's public key.
5. Tanya combines her private key and Lance's public key and creates symmetric key S1.

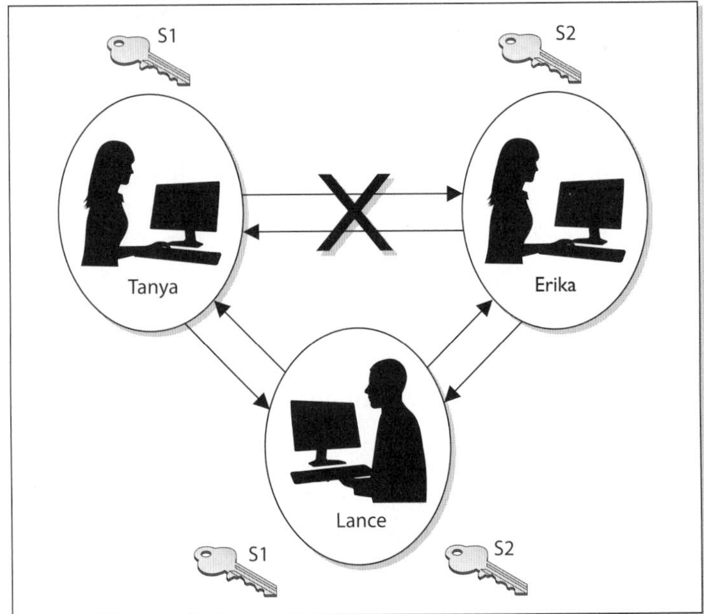

Figure 3-42 A man-in-the-middle attack

6. Lance combines his private key and Tanya's public key and creates symmetric key S1.
7. Erika combines her private key and Lance's public key and creates symmetric key S2.
8. Lance combines his private key and Erika's public key and creates symmetric key S2.
9. Now Tanya and Lance share a symmetric key (S1) and Erika and Lance share a different symmetric key (S2). Tanya and Erika think they are sharing a key between themselves and do not realize Lance is involved.
10. Tanya writes a message to Erika, uses her symmetric key (S1) to encrypt the message, and sends it.
11. Lance grabs the message and decrypts it with symmetric key S1, reads or modifies the message and re-encrypts it with symmetric key S2, and then sends it to Erika.
12. Erika takes symmetric key S2 and uses it to decrypt and read the message.

The countermeasure to this type of attack is to have authentication take place before accepting someone's public key. The basic idea is that we use some sort of certificate to attest the identity of the party on the other side before trusting the data we receive from it. One of the most common ways to do this authentication is through the use of the RSA cryptosystem, which we describe next.

NOTE *MQV* (Menezes-Qu-Vanstone) is an authentication key agreement cryptography function very similar to Diffie-Hellman. The users' public keys are exchanged to create session keys. It provides protection from an attacker figuring out the session key because the attacker would need to have both users' private keys.

What Is the Difference Between Public Key Cryptography and Public Key Infrastructure?

Public key cryptography is the use of an asymmetric algorithm. Thus, the terms asymmetric algorithm and public key cryptography are interchangeable. Examples of asymmetric algorithms are RSA, elliptic curve cryptosystems (ECC), Diffie-Hellman, El Gamal, and knapsack. These algorithms are used to create public/private key pairs, perform key exchange or agreement, and generate and verify digital signatures.

Public key infrastructure (PKI) is a different animal. It is not an algorithm, a protocol, or an application—it is an infrastructure based on public key cryptography.

RSA

RSA, named after its inventors Ron Rivest, Adi Shamir, and Leonard Adleman, is a public key algorithm that is the most popular when it comes to asymmetric algorithms. RSA is a worldwide de facto standard and can be used for digital signatures, key exchange, and encryption. It was developed in 1978 at MIT and provides authentication as well as key encryption.

The security of this algorithm comes from the difficulty of factoring large numbers into their original prime numbers. The public and private keys are functions of a pair of large prime numbers, and the necessary activity required to decrypt a message from ciphertext to plaintext using a private key is comparable to factoring a product into two prime numbers.

NOTE A prime number is a positive whole number whose only factors (i.e., integer divisors) are 1 and the number itself.

One advantage of using RSA is that it can be used for encryption and digital signatures. Using its one-way function, RSA provides encryption and signature verification, and the inverse direction performs decryption and signature generation.

RSA has been implemented in applications; in operating systems by Microsoft, Apple, Sun, and Novell; and at the hardware level in network interface cards, secure telephones, and smart cards. It can be used as a *key exchange protocol*, meaning it is used to encrypt the symmetric key to get it securely to its destination. RSA has been most commonly used with the symmetric algorithm DES, which is quickly being replaced with AES. So, when RSA is used as a key exchange protocol, a cryptosystem generates a symmetric key using either the DES or AES algorithm. Then the system encrypts the symmetric key with the receiver's public key and sends it to the receiver. The symmetric key is protected because only the individual with the corresponding private key can decrypt and extract the symmetric key.

Diving into Numbers

Cryptography is really all about using mathematics to scramble bits into an undecipherable form and then using the same mathematics in reverse to put the bits back into a form that can be understood by computers and people. RSA's mathematics are based on the difficulty of factoring a large integer into its two prime factors. Put on your nerdy hat with the propeller and let's look at how this algorithm works.

The algorithm creates a public key and a private key from a function of large prime numbers. When data is encrypted with a public key, only the corresponding private key can decrypt the data. This act of decryption is basically the same as factoring the product of two prime numbers. So, let's say Ken has a secret (encrypted message), and for you to be able to uncover the secret, you have to take a specific large number and factor it and come up with the two numbers Ken has written down on a piece of paper. This may sound simplistic, but the number you must properly factor can be 2^{2048} in size. Not as easy as you may think.

The following sequence describes how the RSA algorithm comes up with the keys in the first place:

1. Choose two random large prime numbers, p and q.
2. Generate the product of these numbers: $n = pq$.
   n is used as the modulus.
3. Choose a random integer e (the public key) that is greater than 1 but less than $(p - 1)(q - 1)$. Make sure that e and $(p - 1)(q - 1)$ are relatively prime.
4. Compute the corresponding private key, d, such that $de - 1$ is a multiple of $(p - 1)(q - 1)$.
5. The public key = (n, e).
6. The private key = (n, d).
7. The original prime numbers p and q are discarded securely.

We now have our public and private keys, but how do they work together?

If you need to encrypt message m with your public key (e, n), the following formula is carried out:

$$C = m^e \bmod n$$

Then you need to decrypt the message with your private key (d), so the following formula is carried out:

$$M = c^d \bmod n$$

You may be thinking, "Well, I don't understand these formulas, but they look simple enough. Why couldn't someone break these small formulas and uncover the encryption key?" Maybe someone will one day. As the human race advances in its understanding of mathematics and as processing power increases and cryptanalysis evolves, the RSA algorithm may be broken one day. If we were to figure out how to quickly and more easily factor large numbers into their original prime values, all of these cards would fall down, and this algorithm would no longer provide the security it does today. But we have not hit that bump in the road yet, so we are all happily using RSA in our computing activities.

One-Way Functions

A *one-way function* is a mathematical function that is easier to compute in one direction than in the opposite direction. An analogy of this is when you drop a glass on the floor. Although dropping a glass on the floor is easy, putting all the pieces back together again to reconstruct the original glass is next to impossible. This concept is similar to how a one-way function is used in cryptography, which is what the RSA algorithm, and all other asymmetric algorithms, are based upon.

The easy direction of computation in the one-way function that is used in the RSA algorithm is the process of multiplying two large prime numbers. Multiplying the two numbers to get the resulting product is much easier than factoring the product and recovering the two initial large prime numbers used to calculate the obtained product, which is the difficult direction. RSA is based on the difficulty of factoring large numbers that are the product of two large prime numbers. Attacks on these types of cryptosystems do not necessarily try every possible key value, but rather try to factor the large number, which will give the attacker the private key.

When a user encrypts a message with a public key, this message is encoded with a one-way function (breaking a glass). This function supplies a *trapdoor* (knowledge of how to put the glass back together), but the only way the trapdoor can be taken advantage of is if it is known about and the correct code is applied. The private key provides this service. The private key knows about the trapdoor, knows how to derive the original prime numbers, and has the necessary programming code to take advantage of this secret trapdoor to unlock the encoded message (reassembling the broken glass). Knowing about the trapdoor and having the correct functionality to take advantage of it are what make the private key private.

When a one-way function is carried out in the easy direction, encryption and digital signature verification functionality are available. When the one-way function is carried out in the hard direction, decryption and signature generation functionality are available. This means only the public key can carry out encryption and signature verification and only the private key can carry out decryption and signature generation.

As explained earlier in this chapter, *work factor* is the amount of time and resources it would take for someone to break an encryption method. In asymmetric algorithms, the work factor relates to the difference in time and effort that carrying out a one-way function in the easy direction takes compared to carrying out a one-way function in the hard direction. In most cases, the larger the key size, the longer it would take for the bad guy to carry out the one-way function in the hard direction (decrypt a message).

The crux of this section is that all asymmetric algorithms provide security by using mathematical equations that are easy to perform in one direction and next to impossible to perform in the other direction. The "hard" direction is based on a "hard" mathematical problem. RSA's hard mathematical problem requires factoring large numbers into their original prime numbers. Diffie-Hellman and El Gamal are based on the difficulty of calculating logarithms in a finite field.

El Gamal

El Gamal is a public key algorithm that can be used for digital signatures, encryption, and key exchange. It is based not on the difficulty of factoring large numbers, but on calculating discrete logarithms in a finite field. A discrete logarithm is the power to which we must raise a given integer in order to get another given integer. In other words, if b and g are integers, then k is the logarithm in the equation $b^k = g$. When the numbers are large, calculating the logarithm becomes very difficult. In fact, we know of no efficient way of doing this using modern computers. This is what makes discrete logarithms useful in cryptography. El Gamal is actually an extension of the Diffie-Hellman algorithm.

Although El Gamal provides the same type of functionality as some of the other asymmetric algorithms, its main drawback is performance. When compared to other algorithms, this algorithm is usually the slowest.

Elliptic Curve Cryptosystems

Elliptic curves are rich mathematical structures that have shown usefulness in many different types of applications. An *elliptic curve cryptosystem (ECC)* provides much of the same functionality RSA provides: digital signatures, secure key distribution, and encryption. One differing factor is ECC's efficiency. ECC is more efficient than RSA and any other asymmetric algorithm.

Figure 3-43 is an example of an elliptic curve. In this field of mathematics, points on the curve compose a structure called a group. These points are the values used in mathematical formulas for ECC's encryption and decryption processes. The algorithm computes discrete logarithms of elliptic curves, which is different from calculating discrete logarithms in a finite field (which is what Diffie-Hellman and El Gamal use).

Some devices have limited processing capacity, storage, power supply, and bandwidth, such as wireless devices and cellular telephones. With these types of devices, efficiency of resource use is very important. ECC provides encryption functionality, requiring a smaller percentage of the resources compared to RSA and other algorithms, so it is used in these types of devices.

Figure 3-43
Elliptic curve

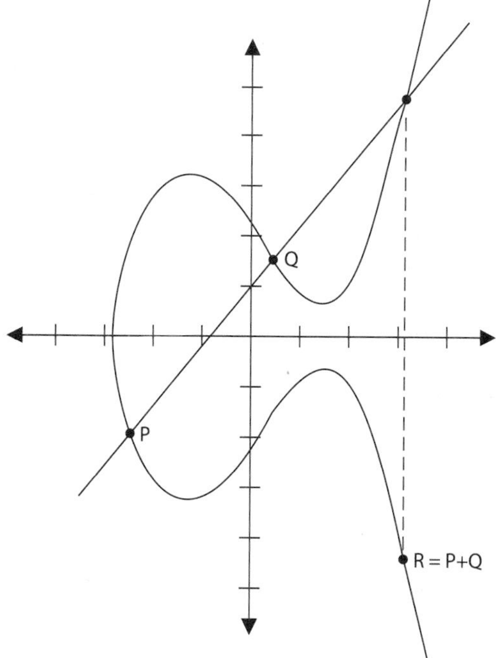

In most cases, the longer the key, the more protection that is provided, but ECC can provide the same level of protection with a key size that is shorter than what RSA requires. Because longer keys require more resources to perform mathematical tasks, the smaller keys used in ECC require fewer resources of the device.

Knapsack

Over the years, different versions of *knapsack* algorithms have arisen. The first to be developed, Merkle-Hellman, could be used only for encryption, but it was later improved upon to provide digital signature capabilities. These types of algorithms are based on the "knapsack problem," a mathematical dilemma that poses the following question: If you have several different items, each having its own weight, is it possible to add these items to a knapsack so the knapsack has a specific weight?

This algorithm was discovered to be insecure and is not currently used in cryptosystems.

Zero Knowledge Proof

When military representatives are briefing the news media about some big world event, they have one goal in mind: Tell the story that the public is supposed to hear and nothing more. Do not provide extra information that someone could use to infer more information than they are supposed to know. The military has this goal because it knows that not just the good guys are watching CNN. This is an example of *zero knowledge proof*. You tell someone just the information they need to know without "giving up the farm."

Zero knowledge proof is used in cryptography also. For example, if Irene encrypts something with her private key, you can verify her private key was used by decrypting the data with her public key. By encrypting something with her private key, Irene is proving to you that she has her private key—but she does not give or show you her private key. Irene does not "give up the farm" by disclosing her private key. In a zero knowledge proof, the verifier cannot prove to another entity that this proof is real because the verifier does not have the private key to prove it. So, only the owner of the private key can prove she has possession of the key.

Message Integrity

Parity bits and cyclic redundancy check (CRC) functions have been used in protocols to detect modifications in streams of bits as they are passed from one computer to another, but they can usually detect only unintentional modifications. Unintentional modifications can happen if a spike occurs in the power supply, if there is interference or attenuation on a wire, or if some other type of physical condition happens that causes the corruption of bits as they travel from one destination to another. Parity bits cannot identify whether a message was captured by an intruder, altered, and then sent on to the intended destination. The intruder can just recalculate a new parity value that includes his changes, and the receiver would never know the difference. For this type of protection, hash algorithms are required to successfully detect intentional and unintentional unauthorized modifications to data. We will now dive into hash algorithms and their characteristics.

The One-Way Hash

A *one-way hash* is a function that takes a variable-length string (a message) and produces a fixed-length value called a hash value. For example, if Kevin wants to send a message to Maureen and he wants to ensure the message does not get altered in an unauthorized fashion while it is being transmitted, he would calculate a hash value for the message and append it to the message itself. When Maureen receives the message, she performs the same hashing function Kevin used and then compares her result with the hash value sent with the message. If the two values are the same, Maureen can be sure the message was not altered during transmission. If the two values are different, Maureen knows the message was altered, either intentionally or unintentionally, and she discards the message.

The hashing algorithm is not a secret—it is publicly known. The secrecy of the one-way hashing function is its "one-wayness." The function is run in only one direction, not the other direction. This is different from the one-way function used in public key cryptography, in which security is provided based on the fact that, without knowing a trapdoor, it is very hard to perform the one-way function backward on a message and come up with readable plaintext. However, one-way hash functions are never used in reverse; they create a hash value and call it a day. The receiver does not attempt to reverse the process at the other end, but instead runs the same hashing function one way and compares the two results.

The hashing one-way function takes place without the use of any keys. This means, for example, that if Cheryl writes a message, calculates a message digest, appends the digest to the message, and sends it on to Scott, Bruce can intercept this message, alter Cheryl's message, recalculate another message digest, append it to the message, and send it on to Scott. When Scott receives it, he verifies the message digest, but never knows the message was actually altered by Bruce. Scott thinks the message came straight from Cheryl and was never modified because the two message digest values are the same. If Cheryl wanted more protection than this, she would need to use *message authentication code (MAC).*

A MAC function is an authentication scheme derived by applying a secret key to a message in some form. This does not mean the symmetric key is used to encrypt the message, though. You should be aware of three basic types of MAC functions: a hash MAC (HMAC), CBC-MAC, and CMAC.

HMAC

In the previous example, if Cheryl were to use an HMAC function instead of just a plain hashing algorithm, a symmetric key would be concatenated with her message. The result of this process would be put through a hashing algorithm, and the result would be a MAC value. This MAC value would then be appended to her message and sent to Scott. If Bruce were to intercept this message and modify it, he would not have the necessary symmetric key to create the MAC value that Scott will attempt to generate. Figure 3-44 walks through these steps.

The top portion of Figure 3-44 shows the steps of a hashing process:

1. The sender puts the message through a hashing function.
2. A message digest value is generated.
3. The message digest is appended to the message.
4. The sender sends the message to the receiver.
5. The receiver puts the message through a hashing function.
6. The receiver generates her own message digest value.
7. The receiver compares the two message digest values. If they are the same, the message has not been altered.

The bottom half of Figure 3-44 shows the steps of an HMAC function:

1. The sender concatenates a symmetric key with the message.
2. The result is put through a hashing algorithm.

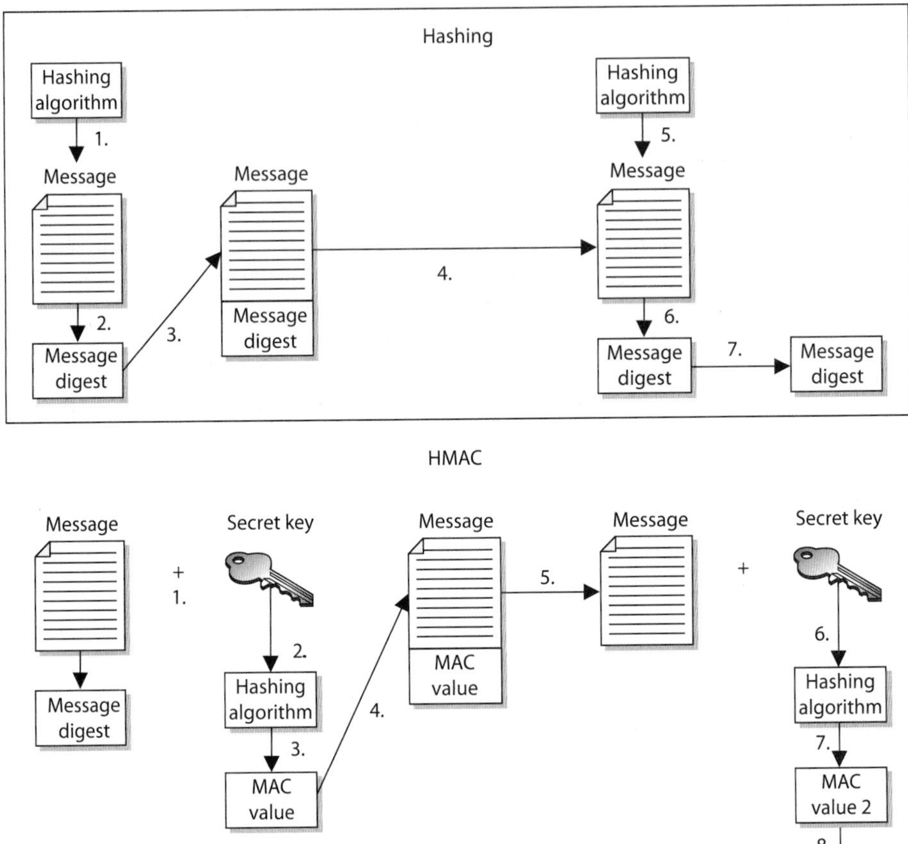

Figure 3-44 The steps involved in using a hashing algorithm and HMAC function

3. A MAC value is generated.
4. The MAC value is appended to the message.
5. The sender sends the message to the receiver. (Just the message with the attached MAC value. The sender does not send the symmetric key with the message.)
6. The receiver concatenates a symmetric key with the message.
7. The receiver puts the results through a hashing algorithm and generates her own MAC value.
8. The receiver compares the two MAC values. If they are the same, the message has not been modified.

Now, when we say that the message is concatenated with a symmetric key, we don't mean a symmetric key is used to encrypt the message. The message is not encrypted in an HMAC function, so there is no confidentiality being provided. Think about throwing a message in a bowl and then throwing a symmetric key in the same bowl. If you dump the contents of the bowl into a hashing algorithm, the result will be a MAC value.

This type of technology requires the sender and receiver to have the same symmetric key. The HMAC function does not involve getting the symmetric key to the destination securely. That would have to happen through one of the other technologies we have discussed already (Diffie-Hellman and key agreement, or RSA and key exchange).

CBC-MAC

If a *Cipher Block Chaining Message Authentication Code (CBC-MAC)* is being used, the message is encrypted with a symmetric block cipher in CBC mode, and the output of the final block of ciphertext is used as the MAC. The sender does not send the encrypted version of the message, but instead sends the plaintext version and the MAC attached to the message. The receiver receives the plaintext message and encrypts it with the same symmetric block cipher in CBC mode and calculates an independent MAC value. The receiver compares the new MAC value with the MAC value sent with the message. This method does not use a hashing algorithm as does HMAC.

The use of the symmetric key ensures that the only person who can verify the integrity of the message is the person who has a copy of this key. No one else can verify the data's integrity, and if someone were to make a change to the data, he could not generate the MAC value (HMAC or CBC-MAC) the receiver would be looking for. Any modifications would be detected by the receiver.

Now the receiver knows that the message came from the system that has the other copy of the same symmetric key, so MAC provides a form of authentication. It provides *data origin authentication*, sometimes referred to as *system authentication*. This is different from user authentication, which would require the use of a private key. A private key is bound to an individual; a symmetric key is not. MAC authentication provides the weakest form of authentication because it is not bound to a user, just to a computer or device.

CAUTION The same key should not be used for authentication and encryption.

As with most things in security, the industry found some security issues with CBC-MAC and created *Cipher-Based Message Authentication Code (CMAC)*. CMAC provides the same type of data origin authentication and integrity as CBC-MAC, but is more secure mathematically. CMAC is a variation of CBC-MAC. It is approved to work with

AES and Triple-DES. CRCs are used to identify data modifications, but these are commonly used lower in the network stack. Since these functions work lower in the network stack, they are used to identify modifications (as in corruption) when the packet is transmitted from one computer to another. HMAC, CBC-MAC, and CMAC work higher in the network stack and can identify not only transmission errors (accidental), but also more nefarious modifications, as in an attacker messing with a message for her own benefit. This means all of these technologies (except CRC) can identify intentional, unauthorized modifications and accidental changes—three in one!

So here is how CMAC works: The symmetric algorithm (AES or 3DES) creates the symmetric key. This key is used to create subkeys. The subkeys are used individually to encrypt the individual blocks of a message as shown in Figure 3-45. This is exactly how CBC-MAC works, but with some better math that works underneath the hood. The math that is underneath is too deep for the CISSP exam. To understand more about this math, please visit http://csrc.nist.gov/publications/nistpubs/800-38B/SP_800-38B.pdf.

Although digging into the CMAC mathematics is too deep for the CISSP exam, what you do need to know is that it is a block cipher–based message authentication code algorithm and how the foundations of the algorithm type works.

NOTE A newer block mode combines CTR mode and CBC-MAC and is called *CCM*. The goal of using this mode is to provide both data origin authentication and encryption through the use of the same key. One key value is used for the counter values for CTR mode encryption and the IV value for CBC-MAC operations. The IEEE 802.11i wireless security standard outlines the use of CCM mode for the block cipher AES.

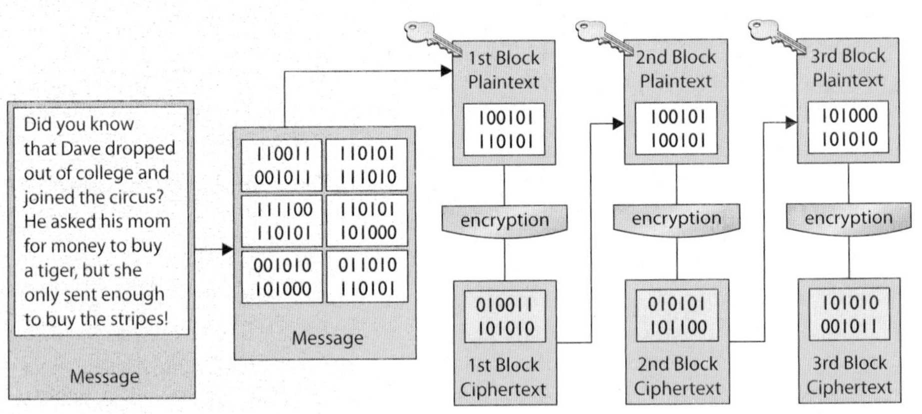

Figure 3-45 Cipher block chaining mode process

Hashes, HMACs, CBC-MACs, CMACs—Oh My!

MACs and hashing processes can be confusing. The following table simplifies the differences between them.

Function	Steps	Security Service Provided
Hash	**1.** Sender puts a message through a hashing algorithm and generates a message digest (MD) value. **2.** Sender sends message and MD value to receiver. **3.** Receiver runs just the message through the same hashing algorithm and creates an independent MD value. **4.** Receiver compares both MD values. If they are the same, the message was not modified.	Integrity; not confidentiality or authentication. Can detect only unintentional modifications.
HMAC	**1.** Sender concatenates a message and secret key and puts the result through a hashing algorithm. This creates a MAC value. **2.** Sender appends the MAC value to the message and sends it to the receiver. **3.** The receiver takes just the message and concatenates it with her own symmetric key. This results in an independent MAC value. **4.** The receiver compares the two MAC values. If they are the same, the receiver knows the message was not modified and knows from which system it came.	Integrity and data origin authentication; confidentiality is not provided.
CBC-MAC	**1.** Sender encrypts a message with a symmetric block algorithm in CBC mode. **2.** The last block is used as the MAC. **3.** The plaintext message and the appended MAC are sent to the receiver. **4.** The receiver encrypts the message, creates a new MAC, and compares the two values. If they are the same, the receiver knows the message was not modified and from which system it came.	Integrity and data origin authentication; confidentiality is not provided.
CMAC	CMAC works the same way as CBC-MAC, but is based on more complex logic and mathematical functions.	

Various Hashing Algorithms

As stated earlier, the goal of using a one-way hash function is to provide a fingerprint of the message. If two different messages produce the same hash value, it would be easier for an attacker to break that security mechanism because patterns would be revealed.

A strong one-hash function should not provide the same hash value for two or more different messages. If a hashing algorithm takes steps to ensure it does not create the same hash value for two or more messages, it is said to be *collision free*.

Strong cryptographic hash functions have the following characteristics:

- The hash should be computed over the entire message.
- The hash should be a one-way function so messages are not disclosed by their values.
- Given a message and its hash value, computing another message with the same hash value should be impossible.
- The function should be resistant to birthday attacks (explained in the upcoming section "Attacks Against One-Way Hash Functions").

Table 3-2 and the following sections quickly describe some of the available hashing algorithms used in cryptography today.

MD4

MD4 is a one-way hash function designed by Ron Rivest. It also produces a 128-bit message digest value. It was used for high-speed computation in software implementations and was optimized for microprocessors. It is no longer considered secure.

MD5

MD5 was also created by Ron Rivest and is the newer version of MD4. It still produces a 128-bit hash, but the algorithm is more complex, which makes it harder to break.

MD5 added a fourth round of operations to be performed during the hashing functions and makes several of its mathematical operations carry out more steps or more complexity to provide a higher level of security. Recent research has shown MD5 to be subject to collision attacks, and it is therefore no longer suitable for applications like SSL certificates and digital signatures that require collision attack resistance. It is still

Algorithm	**Description**
Message Digest 4 (MD4) algorithm	Produces a 128-bit hash value.
Message Digest 5 (MD5) algorithm	Produces a 128-bit hash value. More complex than MD4.
Secure Hash Algorithm (SHA)	Produces a 160-bit hash value. Used with Digital Signature Algorithm (DSA).
SHA-1, SHA-256, SHA-384, SHA-512	Updated version of SHA. SHA-1 produces a 160-bit hash value, SHA-256 creates a 256-bit value, and so on.

Table 3-2 Various Hashing Algorithms Available

commonly used for file integrity checksums, such as those required by some intrusion detection systems, as well as for forensic evidence integrity.

SHA

SHA was designed by NSA and published by NIST to be used with the Digital Signature Standard (DSS), which is discussed a bit later in more depth. SHA was designed to be used in digital signatures and was developed when a more secure hashing algorithm was required for U.S. government applications.

SHA produces a 160-bit hash value, or message digest. This is then inputted into an asymmetric algorithm, which computes the signature for a message.

SHA is similar to MD4. It has some extra mathematical functions and produces a 160-bit hash instead of a 128-bit hash, which makes it more resistant to brute-force attacks, including birthday attacks.

SHA was improved upon and renamed SHA-1. Recently, SHA-1 was found to be vulnerable to collisions and is no longer considered secure for applications requiring collision resistance. Newer versions of this algorithm (collectively known as the SHA-2 and SHA-3 families) have been developed and released: SHA-256, SHA-384, and SHA-512. The SHA-2 and SHA-3 families are considered secure for all uses.

Attacks Against One-Way Hash Functions

A strong hashing algorithm does not produce the same hash value for two different messages. If the algorithm does produce the same value for two distinctly different messages, this is called a *collision*. An attacker can attempt to force a collision, which is referred to as a *birthday attack*. This attack is based on the mathematical birthday paradox that exists in standard statistics. Now hold on to your hat while we go through this—it is a bit tricky:

How many people must be in the same room for the chance to be greater than even that another person has the same birthday as you?

Answer: 253

How many people must be in the same room for the chance to be greater than even that at least two people share the same birthday?

Answer: 23

This seems a bit backward, but the difference is that in the first instance, you are looking for someone with a specific birthday date that matches yours. In the second instance, you are looking for any two people who share the same birthday. There is a higher probability of finding two people who share a birthday than of finding another person who shares your birthday. Or, stated another way, it is easier to find two matching values in a sea of values than to find a match for just one specific value.

Why do we care? The birthday paradox can apply to cryptography as well. Since any random set of 23 people most likely (at least a 50 percent chance) includes two people who share a birthday, by extension, if a hashing algorithm generates a message digest of 60 bits, there is a high likelihood that an adversary can find a collision using only 2^{30} inputs.

The main way an attacker can find the corresponding hashing value that matches a specific message is through a brute-force attack. If he finds a message with a specific hash value, it is equivalent to finding someone with a specific birthday. If he finds two messages with the same hash values, it is equivalent to finding two people with the same birthday.

The output of a hashing algorithm is n, and to find a message through a brute-force attack that results in a specific hash value would require hashing 2^n random messages. To take this one step further, finding two messages that hash to the same value would require review of only $2^{n/2}$ messages.

How Would a Birthday Attack Take Place?

Sue and Joe are going to get married, but before they do, they have a prenuptial contract drawn up that states if they get divorced, then Sue takes her original belongings and Joe takes his original belongings. To ensure this contract is not modified, it is hashed and a message digest value is created.

One month after Sue and Joe get married, Sue carries out some devious activity behind Joe's back. She makes a copy of the message digest value without anyone knowing. Then she makes a new contract that states that if Joe and Sue get a divorce, Sue owns both her own original belongings and Joe's original belongings. Sue hashes this new contract and compares the new message digest value with the message digest value that correlates with the contract. They don't match. So Sue tweaks her contract ever so slightly and creates another message digest value and compares them. She continues to tweak her contract until she forces a collision, meaning her contract creates the same message digest value as the original contract. Sue then changes out the original contract with her new contract and quickly divorces Joe. When Sue goes to collect Joe's belongings and he objects, she shows him that no modification could have taken place on the original document because it still hashes out to the same message digest. Sue then moves to an island.

Hash algorithms usually use message digest sizes (the value of n) that are large enough to make collisions difficult to accomplish, but they are still possible. An algorithm that has 160-bit output, like SHA-1, may require approximately 2^{80} computations to break. This means there is a less than 1 in 2^{80} chance that someone could carry out a successful birthday attack.

The main point of discussing this paradox is to show how important longer hashing values truly are. A hashing algorithm that has a larger bit output is less vulnerable to brute-force attacks such as a birthday attack. This is the primary reason why the new versions of SHA have such large message digest values.

Digital Signatures

A *digital signature* is a hash value that has been encrypted with the sender's private key. The act of signing means encrypting the message's hash value with a private key, as shown in Figure 3-46.

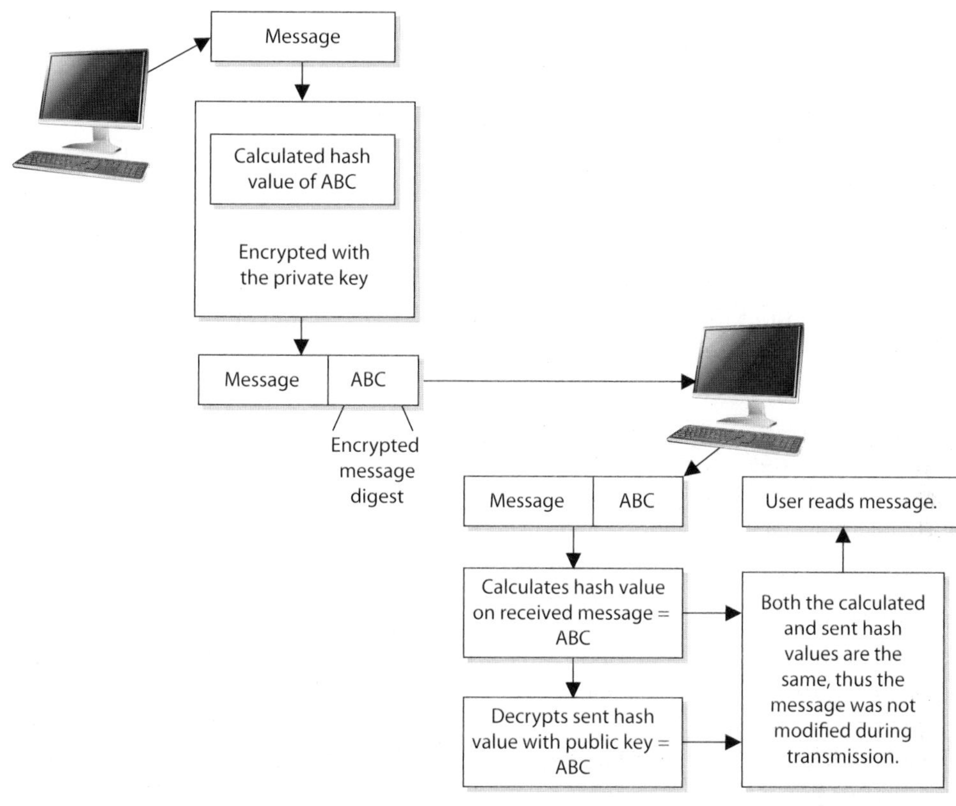

Figure 3-46 Creating a digital signature for a message

From our earlier example in the section "The One-Way Hash," if Kevin wants to ensure that the message he sends to Maureen is not modified *and* he wants her to be sure it came only from him, he can digitally sign the message. This means that a one-way hashing function would be run on the message, and then Kevin would encrypt that hash value with his private key.

When Maureen receives the message, she will perform the hashing function on the message and come up with her own hash value. Then she will decrypt the sent hash value (digital signature) with Kevin's public key. She then compares the two values, and if they are the same, she can be sure the message was not altered during transmission. She is also sure the message came from Kevin because the value was encrypted with his private key.

The hashing function ensures the integrity of the message, and the signing of the hash value provides authentication and nonrepudiation. The act of signing just means the value was encrypted with a private key.

We need to be clear on all the available choices within cryptography, because different steps and algorithms provide different types of security services:

- A message can be encrypted, which provides confidentiality.
- A message can be hashed, which provides integrity.

- A message can be digitally signed, which provides authentication, nonrepudiation, and integrity.
- A message can be encrypted and digitally signed, which provides confidentiality, authentication, nonrepudiation, and integrity.

Some algorithms can only perform encryption, whereas others support digital signatures and encryption. When hashing is involved, a hashing algorithm is used, not an encryption algorithm.

It is important to understand that not all algorithms can necessarily provide all security services. Most of these algorithms are used in some type of combination to provide all the necessary security services required of an environment. Table 3-3 shows the services provided by the algorithms.

Digital Signature Standard

Because digital signatures are so important in proving who sent which messages, the U.S. government decided to establish standards pertaining to their functions and acceptable use. In 1991, NIST proposed a federal standard called the *Digital Signature Standard (DSS)*. It was developed for federal departments and agencies, but most vendors also designed their products to meet these specifications. The federal government requires its departments to use DSA, RSA, or the elliptic curve digital signature algorithm (ECDSA)

Algorithm Type	Encryption	Digital Signature	Hashing Function	Key Distribution
Asymmetric Key				
RSA	X	X		X
ECC	X	X		X
Diffie-Hellman				X
El Gamal	X	X		X
DSA		X		
Knapsack	X	X		X
Symmetric Key				
DES	X			
3DES	X			
Blowfish	X			
IDEA	X			
RC4	X			
Hashing				
Ron Rivest family of hashing functions: MD4 and MD5			X	
SHA family			X	

Table 3-3 Various Functions of Different Algorithms

and SHA. SHA creates a 160-bit message digest output, which is then inputted into one of the three mentioned digital signature algorithms. SHA is used to ensure the integrity of the message, and the other algorithms are used to digitally sign the message. This is an example of how two different algorithms are combined to provide the right combination of security services.

RSA and DSA are the best known and most widely used digital signature algorithms. DSA was developed by the NSA. Unlike RSA, DSA can be used only for digital signatures, and DSA is slower than RSA in signature verification. RSA can be used for digital signatures, encryption, and secure distribution of symmetric keys.

Public Key Infrastructure

Public key infrastructure (PKI) consists of programs, data formats, procedures, communication protocols, security policies, and public key cryptographic mechanisms working in a comprehensive manner to enable a wide range of dispersed people to communicate in a secure and predictable fashion. In other words, a PKI establishes a level of trust within an environment. PKI is an ISO authentication framework that uses public key cryptography and the X.509 standard. The framework was set up to enable authentication to happen across different networks and the Internet. Particular protocols and algorithms are not specified, which is why PKI is called a framework and not a specific technology.

PKI provides authentication, confidentiality, nonrepudiation, and integrity of the messages exchanged. It is a *hybrid* system of symmetric and asymmetric key algorithms and methods, which were discussed in earlier sections.

There is a difference between public key cryptography and PKI. Public key cryptography is another name for asymmetric algorithms, while PKI is what its name states—it is an infrastructure. The infrastructure assumes that the receiver's identity can be positively ensured through certificates and that an asymmetric algorithm will automatically carry out the process of key exchange. The infrastructure therefore contains the pieces that will identify users, create and distribute certificates, maintain and revoke certificates, distribute and maintain encryption keys, and enable all technologies to communicate and work together for the purpose of encrypted communication and authentication.

Public key cryptography is one piece in PKI, but many other pieces make up this infrastructure. An analogy can be drawn with the e-mail protocol Simple Mail Transfer Protocol (SMTP). SMTP is the technology used to get e-mail messages from here to there, but many other things must be in place before this protocol can be productive. We need e-mail clients, e-mail servers, and e-mail messages, which together build a type of infrastructure—an e-mail infrastructure. PKI is made up of many different parts: certificate authorities, registration authorities, certificates, keys, and users. The following sections explain these parts and how they all work together.

Certificate Authorities

Each person who wants to participate in a PKI requires a digital certificate, which is a credential that contains the public key for that individual along with other identifying information. The certificate is created and signed (digital signature) by a trusted third party, which is a *certificate authority (CA)*. When the CA signs the certificate, it binds the individual's identity to the public key, and the CA takes liability for the authenticity of that individual. It is this trusted third party (the CA) that allows people who have never met to authenticate to each other and to communicate in a secure method. If Kevin has never met Dave but would like to communicate securely with him, and they both trust the same CA, then Kevin could retrieve Dave's digital certificate and start the process.

A CA is a trusted organization (or server) that maintains and issues digital certificates. When a person requests a certificate, the *registration authority (RA)* verifies that individual's identity and passes the certificate request off to the CA. The CA constructs the certificate, signs it, sends it to the requester, and maintains the certificate over its lifetime. When another person wants to communicate with this person, the CA will basically vouch for that person's identity. When Dave receives a digital certificate from Kevin, Dave will go through steps to validate it. Basically, by providing Dave with his digital certificate, Kevin is stating, "I know you don't know or trust me, but here is this document that was created by someone you do know and trust. The document says I am a good guy and you should trust me."

Once Dave validates the digital certificate, he extracts Kevin's public key, which is embedded within it. Now Dave knows this public key is bound to Kevin. He also knows that if Kevin uses his private key to create a digital signature and Dave can properly decrypt it using this public key, it did indeed come from Kevin.

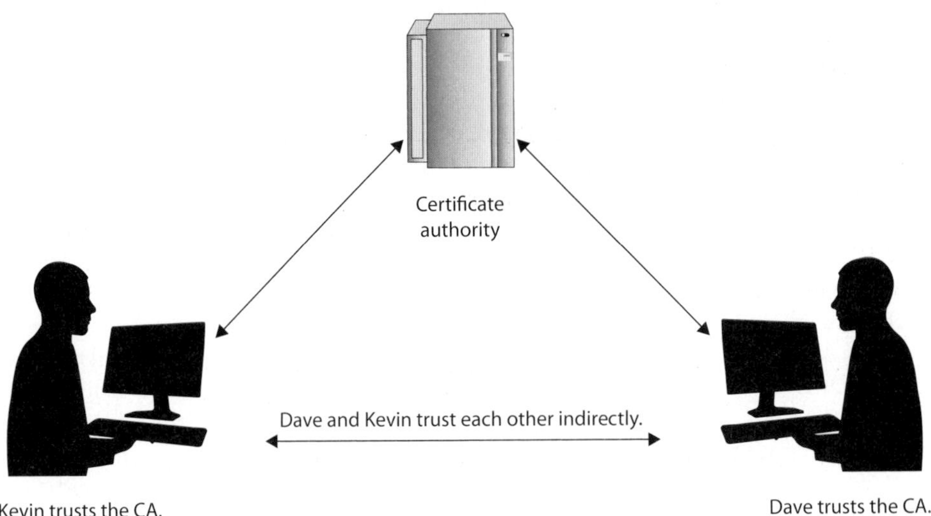
Certificate authority
Dave and Kevin trust each other indirectly.
Kevin trusts the CA.
Dave trusts the CA.

TIP Remember the man-in-the-middle attack covered earlier in the section "The Diffie-Hellman Algorithm"? This attack is possible if two users are not working in a PKI environment and do not truly know the identity of the owners of the public keys. Exchanging digital certificates can thwart this type of attack.

The CA can be internal to an organization. Such a setup would enable the company to control the CA server, configure how authentication takes place, maintain the certificates, and recall certificates when necessary. Other CAs are organizations dedicated to this type of service, and other individuals and companies pay them to supply it. Some well-known CAs are Entrust and VeriSign. All browsers have several well-known CAs configured by default. Most are configured to trust dozens or hundreds of CAs.

NOTE More and more organizations are setting up their own internal PKIs. When these independent PKIs need to interconnect to allow for secure communication to take place (either between departments or between different companies), there must be a way for the two root CAs to trust each other. The two CAs do not have a CA above them they can both trust, so they must carry out cross certification. *Cross certification* is the process undertaken by CAs to establish a trust relationship in which they rely upon each other's digital certificates and public keys as if they had issued them themselves. When this is set up, a CA for one company can validate digital certificates from the other company and vice versa.

The CA is responsible for creating and handing out certificates, maintaining them, and revoking them if necessary. Revocation is handled by the CA, and the revoked certificate information is stored on a *certificate revocation list (CRL)*. This is a list of every certificate that has been revoked. This list is maintained and updated periodically. A certificate may be revoked because the key holder's private key was compromised or because the CA discovered the certificate was issued to the wrong person. An analogy for the use of a CRL is how a driver's license is used by a police officer. If an officer pulls over Sean for speeding, the officer will ask to see Sean's license. The officer will then run a check on the license to find out if Sean is wanted for any other infractions of the law and to verify the license has not expired. The same thing happens when a person compares a certificate to a CRL. If the certificate became invalid for some reason, the CRL is the mechanism for the CA to let others know this information.

CAUTION CRLs are the thorn in the side of many PKI implementations. They are challenging for a long list of reasons. By default, web browsers do not check a CRL to ensure that a certificate is not revoked. So when you are setting up an SSL connection to do e-commerce over the Internet, you could be relying on a certificate that has actually been revoked. Not good.

Online Certificate Status Protocol (OCSP) is being used more and more rather than the cumbersome CRL approach. When using just a CRL, either the user's browser must check a central CRL to find out if the certification has been revoked, or the CA has to continually push out CRL values to the clients to ensure they have an updated CRL. If OCSP is implemented, it does this work automatically in the background. It carries out real-time validation of a certificate and reports back to the user whether the certificate is valid, invalid, or unknown. OCSP checks the CRL that is maintained by the CA. So the CRL is still being used, but now we have a protocol developed specifically to check the CRL during a certificate validation process.

Certificates

One of the most important pieces of a PKI is its digital certificate. A *certificate* is the mechanism used to associate a public key with a collection of components in a manner that is sufficient to uniquely identify the claimed owner. The standard for how the CA creates the certificate is *X.509*, which dictates the different fields used in the certificate and the valid values that can populate those fields. The most commonly used version is 3 of this standard, which is often denoted as X.509v3. Many cryptographic protocols use this type of certificate, including SSL.

The certificate includes the serial number, version number, identity information, algorithm information, lifetime dates, and the signature of the issuing authority, as shown in Figure 3-47.

The Registration Authority

The *registration authority (RA)* performs the certification registration duties. The RA establishes and confirms the identity of an individual, initiates the certification process with a CA on behalf of an end user, and performs certificate life-cycle management functions. The RA cannot issue certificates, but can act as a broker between the user and the CA. When users need new certificates, they make requests to the RA, and the RA verifies all necessary identification information before allowing a request to go to the CA.

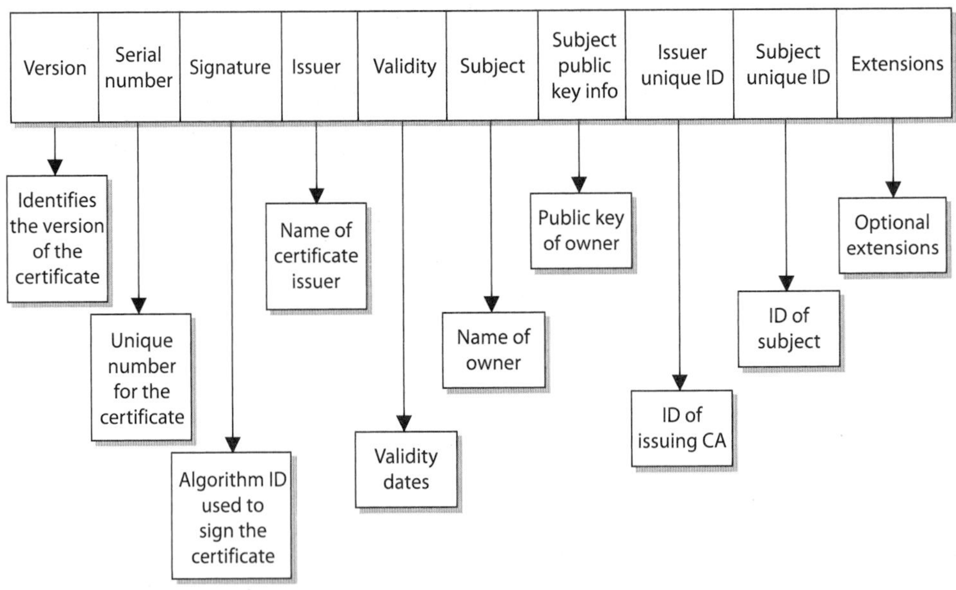

Figure 3-47 Each certificate has a structure with all the necessary identifying information in it.

PKI Steps

Now that we know some of the main pieces of a PKI and how they actually work together, let's walk through an example. First, suppose that John needs to obtain a digital certificate for himself so he can participate in a PKI. The following are the steps to do so:

1. John makes a request to the RA.
2. The RA requests certain identification information from John, such as a copy of his driver's license, his phone number, his address, and other identifying information.
3. Once the RA receives the required information from John and verifies it, the RA sends his certificate request to the CA.
4. The CA creates a certificate with John's public key and identity information embedded. (The private/public key pair is generated either by the CA or on John's machine, which depends on the systems' configurations. If it is created at the CA, his private key needs to be sent to him by secure means. In most cases, the user generates this pair and sends in his public key during the registration process.)

Now John is registered and can participate in a PKI. John and Diane decide they want to communicate, so they take the following steps, shown in Figure 3-48:

1. John requests Diane's public key from a public directory.
2. The directory, sometimes called a repository, sends Diane's digital certificate.
3. John verifies the digital certificate and extracts her public key. John uses this public key to encrypt a session key that will be used to encrypt their messages. John sends the encrypted session key to Diane. John also sends his certificate, containing his public key, to Diane.
4. When Diane receives John's certificate, her browser looks to see if it trusts the CA that digitally signed this certificate. Diane's browser trusts this CA and, after she verifies the certificate, both John and Diane can communicate using encryption.

Figure 3-48 CA and user relationships

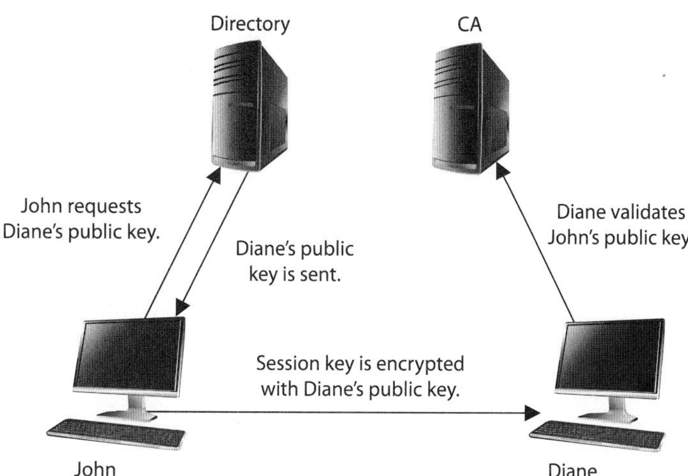
Directory
CA
John requests Diane's public key.
Diane's public key is sent.
Diane validates John's public key.
Session key is encrypted with Diane's public key.
John
Diane

A PKI may be made up of the following entities and functions:

- Certification authority
- Registration authority
- Certificate repository
- Certificate revocation system
- Key backup and recovery system
- Automatic key update
- Management of key histories
- Timestamping
- Client-side software

PKI supplies the following security services:

- Confidentiality
- Access control
- Integrity
- Authentication
- Nonrepudiation

A PKI must retain a key history, which keeps track of all the old and current public keys that have been used by individual users. For example, if Kevin encrypted a symmetric key with Dave's old public key, there should be a way for Dave to still access this data. This can only happen if the CA keeps a proper history of Dave's old certificates and keys.

NOTE Another important component that must be integrated into a PKI is a reliable time source that provides a way for secure timestamping. This comes into play when true nonrepudiation is required.

Key Management

Cryptography can be used as a security mechanism to provide confidentiality, integrity, and authentication, but not if the keys are compromised in any way. The keys can be captured, modified, corrupted, or disclosed to unauthorized individuals. Cryptography is based on a trust model. Individuals must trust each other to protect their own keys; trust the administrator who is maintaining the keys; and trust a server that holds, maintains, and distributes the keys.

Many administrators know that key management causes one of the biggest headaches in cryptographic implementation. There is more to key maintenance than using them to encrypt messages. The keys must be distributed securely to the right entities and updated continuously. They must also be protected as they are being transmitted and while they are being stored on each workstation and server. The keys must be generated, destroyed, and recovered properly. Key management can be handled through manual or automatic processes.

The keys are stored before and after distribution. When a key is distributed to a user, it does not just hang out on the desktop. It needs a secure place within the file system to be stored and used in a controlled method. The key, the algorithm that will use the key, configurations, and parameters are stored in a module that also needs to be protected. If an attacker is able to obtain these components, she could masquerade as another user and decrypt, read, and re-encrypt messages not intended for her.

Historically, physical cryptographic keys were kept in secured boxes and delivered by escorted couriers. The keys could be distributed to a main server, and then the local administration would distribute them, or the courier would visit each computer individually. Some implementations distributed a master key to a site, and then that key was used to generate unique secret keys to be used by individuals at that location. Today, most key distributions are handled by a protocol through automated means and not manually by an individual. A company must evaluate the overhead of key management, the required security level, and cost-benefit issues to decide how it will conduct key management, but overall, automation provides a more accurate and secure approach.

When using the Kerberos protocol (which we will describe in Chapter 5), a Key Distribution Center (KDC) is used to store, distribute, and maintain cryptographic session and secret keys. This method provides an automated method of key distribution. The computer that wants to access a service on another computer requests access via the KDC. The KDC then generates a session key to be used between the requesting computer and the computer providing the requested resource or service. The automation of this process reduces the possible errors that can happen through a manual process, but if the ticket-granting service (TGS) portion of the KDC gets compromised in any way, then all the computers and their services are affected and possibly compromised.

In some instances, keys are still managed through manual means. Unfortunately, although many companies use cryptographic keys, they rarely, if ever, change them, either because of the hassle of key management or because the network administrator is already overtaxed with other tasks or does not realize the task actually needs to take place. The frequency of use of a cryptographic key has a direct correlation to how often the key should be changed. The more a key is used, the more likely it is to be captured and compromised. If a key is used infrequently, then this risk drops dramatically. The necessary level of security and the frequency of use can dictate the frequency of key updates. A mom-and-pop diner might only change its cryptography keys every month, whereas an information warfare military unit might change them every day or every week. The important thing is to change the keys using a secure method.

Key management is the most challenging part of cryptography and also the most crucial. It is one thing to develop a very complicated and complex algorithm and key method, but if the keys are not securely stored and transmitted, it does not really matter how strong the algorithm is.

Key Management Principles

Keys should not be in cleartext outside the cryptography device. As stated previously, many cryptography algorithms are known publicly, which puts more stress on protecting the secrecy of the key. If attackers know how the actual algorithm works, in many cases, all they need to figure out is the key to compromise a system. This is why keys should not be available in cleartext—the key is what brings secrecy to encryption.

These steps, and all of key distribution and maintenance, should be automated and hidden from the user. These processes should be integrated into software or the operating system. It only adds complexity and opens the doors for more errors when processes are done manually and depend upon end users to perform certain functions.

Keys are at risk of being lost, destroyed, or corrupted. Backup copies should be available and easily accessible when required. If data is encrypted and then the user accidentally loses the necessary key to decrypt it, this information would be lost forever if there were not a backup key to save the day. The application being used for cryptography may have key recovery options, or it may require copies of the keys to be kept in a secure place.

Different scenarios highlight the need for key recovery or backup copies of keys. For example, if Bob has possession of all the critical bid calculations, stock value information, and corporate trend analysis needed for tomorrow's senior executive presentation, and Bob has an unfortunate confrontation with a bus, someone is going to need to access this data after the funeral. As another example, if an employee leaves the company and has encrypted important documents on her computer before departing, the company would probably still want to access that data later. Similarly, if the vice president did not know that running a large magnet over the USB drive that holds his private key was not a good idea, he would want his key replaced immediately instead of listening to a lecture about electromagnetic fields and how they rewrite sectors on media.

Of course, having more than one key increases the chance of disclosure, so a company needs to decide whether it wants to have key backups and, if so, what precautions to put into place to protect them properly. A company can choose to have multiparty control for emergency key recovery. This means that if a key must be recovered, more than one person is needed for this process. The key recovery process could require two or more other individuals to present their private keys or authentication information. These individuals should not all be members of the IT department. There should be a member from management, an individual from security, and one individual from the IT department, for example. All of these requirements reduce the potential for abuse and would require collusion for fraudulent activities to take place.

Rules for Keys and Key Management

Key management is critical for proper protection. The following are responsibilities that fall under the key management umbrella:

- The key length should be long enough to provide the necessary level of protection.
- Keys should be stored and transmitted by secure means.
- Keys should be extremely random, and the algorithm should use the full spectrum of the keyspace.
- The key's lifetime should correspond with the sensitivity of the data it is protecting. (Less secure data may allow for a longer key lifetime, whereas more sensitive data might require a shorter key lifetime.)
- The more the key is used, the shorter its lifetime should be.
- Keys should be backed up or escrowed in case of emergencies.
- Keys should be properly destroyed when their lifetime comes to an end.

Key escrow is a process or entity that can recover lost or corrupted cryptographic keys; thus, it is a common component of key recovery operations. When two or more entities are required to reconstruct a key for key recovery processes, this is known as *multiparty key recovery*. Multiparty key recovery implements dual control, meaning that two or more people have to be involved with a critical task.

Trusted Platform Module

The *Trusted Platform Module (TPM)* is a microchip installed on the motherboard of modern computers and is dedicated to carrying out security functions that involve the storage and processing of symmetric and asymmetric keys, hashes, and digital certificates. The TPM was devised by the Trusted Computing Group (TCG), an organization that promotes open standards to help strengthen computing platforms against security weaknesses and attacks.

The essence of the TPM lies in a protected and encapsulated microcontroller security chip that provides a safe haven for storing and processing security-intensive data such as keys, passwords, and digital certificates.

The use of a dedicated and encoded hardware-based platform drastically improves the Root of Trust of the computing system while allowing for a vastly superior implementation and integration of security features. The introduction of TPM has made it much harder to access information on computing devices without proper authorization and allows for effective detection of malicious configuration changes to a computing platform.

TPM Uses

The most common usage scenario of the TPM is to *bind* a hard disk drive, where the content of a given hard disk drive is affixed with a particular computing system. The content of the hard disk drive is encrypted, and the decryption key is stored away in the TPM chip. To ensure safe storage of the decryption key, it is further "wrapped" with another encryption key. Binding a hard disk drive makes its content basically inaccessible to other systems, and any attempt to retrieve the drive's content by attaching it to another system will be very difficult. However, in the event of the TPM chip's failure, the hard drive's content will be rendered useless, unless a backup of the key has been escrowed.

Another application of the TPM is *sealing* a system's state to a particular hardware and software configuration. Sealing a computing system through TPM is used to deter any attempts to tamper with a system's configurations. In practice, this is similar to how hashes are used to verify the integrity of files shared over the Internet (or any other untrusted medium).

Sealing a system is fairly straightforward. The TPM generates hash values based on the system's configuration files and stores them in its memory. A sealed system will only be activated once the TPM verifies the integrity of the system's configuration by comparing it with the original "sealing" value.

The TPM is essentially a securely designed microcontroller with added modules to perform cryptographic functions. These modules allow for accelerated and storage processing of cryptographic keys, hash values, and pseudonumber sequences. The TPM's internal storage is based on nonvolatile random access memory (NVRAM), which retains its information when power is turned off and is therefore termed *nonvolatile*.

TPM's internal memory is divided into two different segments: persistent (static) and versatile (dynamic) memory modules.

Persistent Memory

Two kinds of keys are present in the static memory:

- **Endorsement Key (EK)** A public/private key pair that is installed in the TPM at the time of manufacture and cannot be modified. The private key is always present inside the TPM, while the public key is used to verify the authenticity of the TPM itself. The EK, installed in the TPM, is unique to that TPM and its platform.
- **Storage Root Key (SRK)** The master wrapping key used to secure the keys stored in the TPM.

Versatile Memory

Three kinds of keys (or values) are present in the versatile memory:

- **Attestation Identity Key (AIK)** Used for the attestation of the TPM chip itself to service providers. The AIK is linked to the TPM's identity at the time of development, which in turn is linked to the TPM's Endorsement Key. Therefore, the AIK ensures the integrity of the EK.

- **Platform Configuration Registers (PCR)** Used to store cryptographic hashes of data used for TPM's "sealing" functionality.
- **Storage keys** Used to encrypt the storage media of the computer system.

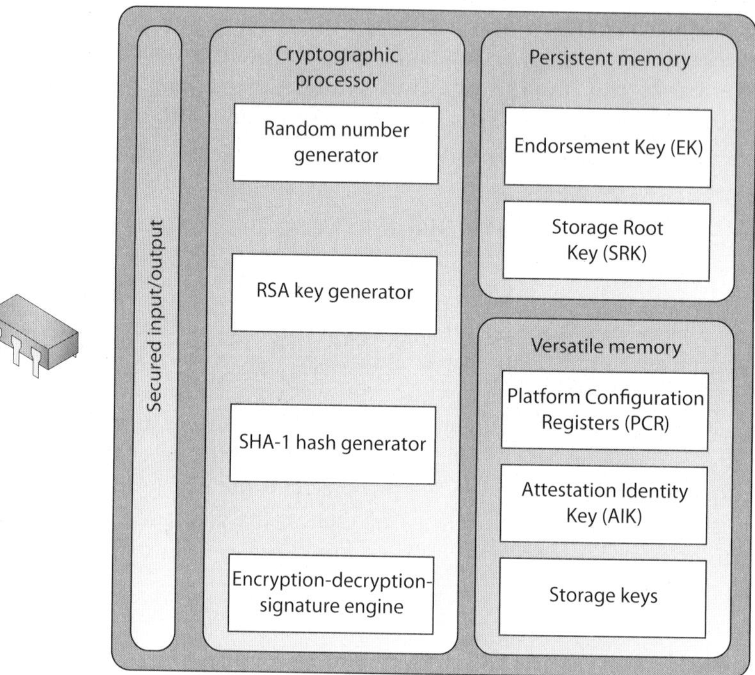

Attacks on Cryptography

Eavesdropping and sniffing data as it passes over a network are considered *passive attacks* because the attacker is not affecting the protocol, algorithm, key, message, or any parts of the encryption system. Passive attacks are hard to detect, so in most cases methods are put in place to try to prevent them rather than to detect and stop them.

Altering messages, modifying system files, and masquerading as another individual are acts that are considered *active attacks* because the attacker is actually doing something instead of sitting back and gathering data. Passive attacks are usually used to gain information prior to carrying out an active attack.

The common attack vectors in cryptography are key, algorithm, implementation, data, and people. We should assume that the attacker knows what algorithm we are using and that the attacker has access to all encrypted text. The following sections address some active attacks that relate to cryptography.

Ciphertext-Only Attacks

In this type of attack, the attacker has the ciphertext of several messages. Each of the messages has been encrypted using the same encryption algorithm. The attacker's goal is to discover the key used in the encryption process. Once the attacker figures out the key, she can decrypt all other messages encrypted with the same key.

A *ciphertext-only attack* is the most common type of active attack because it is very easy to get ciphertext by sniffing someone's traffic, but it is the hardest attack to actually be successful at because the attacker has so little information about the encryption process.

Known-Plaintext Attacks

In *known-plaintext attacks*, the attacker has the plaintext and corresponding ciphertext of one or more messages. Again, the goal is to discover the key used to encrypt the messages so other messages can be deciphered and read.

Messages usually start with the same type of beginning and close with the same type of ending. An attacker might know that each message a general sends out to his commanders always starts with certain greetings and ends with specific salutations and the general's name and contact information. In this instance, the attacker has some of the plaintext (the data that is the same on each message) and can capture an encrypted message, and therefore capture the ciphertext. Once a few pieces of the puzzle are discovered, the rest is accomplished by reverse-engineering, frequency analysis, and brute-force attempts. Known-plaintext attacks were used by the United States against the Germans and the Japanese during World War II.

Chosen-Plaintext Attacks

In *chosen-plaintext attacks*, the attacker has the plaintext and ciphertext, but can choose the plaintext that gets encrypted to see the corresponding ciphertext. This gives the attacker more power and possibly a deeper understanding of the way the encryption process works so she can gather more information about the key being used. Once the key is discovered, other messages encrypted with that key can be decrypted.

How would this be carried out? Doris can e-mail a message to you that she thinks you not only will believe, but will also panic about, encrypt, and send to someone else. Suppose Doris sends you an e-mail that states, "The meaning of life is 42." You may think you have received an important piece of information that should be concealed from others, everyone except your friend Bob, of course. So you encrypt Doris's message and send it to Bob. Meanwhile Doris is sniffing your traffic and now has a copy of the plaintext of the message, because she wrote it, and a copy of the ciphertext.

Chosen-Ciphertext Attacks

In *chosen-ciphertext attacks*, the attacker can choose the ciphertext to be decrypted and has access to the resulting decrypted plaintext. Again, the goal is to figure out the key. This is a harder attack to carry out compared to the previously mentioned attacks, and the attacker may need to have control of the system that contains the cryptosystem.

NOTE All of these attacks have a derivative form, the names of which are the same except for putting the word "adaptive" in front of them, such as adaptive chosen-plaintext and adaptive chosen-ciphertext. What this means is that the attacker can carry out one of these attacks and, depending upon what she gleaned from that first attack, modify her next attack. This is the process of reverse-engineering or cryptanalysis attacks: using what you learned to improve your next attack.

Differential Cryptanalysis

This type of attack also has the goal of uncovering the key that was used for encryption purposes. This attack looks at ciphertext pairs generated by encryption of plaintext pairs with specific differences and analyzes the effect and result of those differences. One such attack was invented in 1990 as an attack against DES, and it turned out to be an effective and successful attack against DES and other block algorithms.

The attacker takes two messages of plaintext and follows the changes that take place to the blocks as they go through the different S-boxes. (Each message is being encrypted with the same key.) The differences identified in the resulting ciphertext values are used to map probability values to different possible key values. The attacker continues this process with several more sets of messages and reviews the common key probability values. One key value will continue to show itself as the most probable key used in the encryption processes. Since the attacker chooses the different plaintext messages for this attack, it is considered a type of chosen-plaintext attack.

Public vs. Secret Algorithms

The public mainly uses algorithms that are known and understood versus the secret algorithms where the internal processes and functions are not released to the public. In general, cryptographers in the public sector feel as though the strongest and best-engineered algorithms are the ones released for peer review and public scrutiny, because a thousand brains are better than five, and many times some smarty-pants within the public population can find problems within an algorithm that the developers did not think of. This is why vendors and companies have competitions to see if anyone can break their code and encryption processes. If someone does break it, that means the developers must go back to the drawing board and strengthen this or that piece.

Not all algorithms are released to the public, such as the ones developed by the NSA. Because the sensitivity level of what the NSA encrypts is so important, it wants as much of the process to be as secret as possible. The fact that the NSA does not release its algorithms for public examination and analysis does not mean its algorithms are weak. Its algorithms are developed, reviewed, and tested by many of the top cryptographic pros around, and are of very high quality.

Linear Cryptanalysis

Linear cryptanalysis is another type of attack that carries out functions to identify the highest probability of a specific key employed during the encryption process using a block algorithm. The attacker carries out a known-plaintext attack on several different messages encrypted with the same key. The more messages the attacker can use and put through this type of attack, the higher the confidence level in the probability of a specific key value.

The attacker evaluates the input and output values for each S-box. He evaluates the probability of input values ending up in a specific combination. Identifying specific output combinations allows him to assign probability values to different keys until one shows a continual pattern of having the highest probability.

Side-Channel Attacks

All of the attacks we have covered thus far have been based mainly on the mathematics of cryptography. Using plaintext and ciphertext involves high-powered mathematical tools that are needed to uncover the key used in the encryption process.

But what if we took a different approach? Let's say we see something that looks like a duck, walks like a duck, sounds like a duck, swims in water, and eats bugs and small fish. We could confidently conclude that this is a duck. Similarly, in cryptography, we can review facts and infer the value of an encryption key. For example, we could detect how much power consumption is used for encryption and decryption (the fluctuation of electronic voltage). We could also intercept the radiation emissions released and then calculate how long the processes took. Looking around the cryptosystem, or its attributes and characteristics, is different from looking into the cryptosystem and trying to defeat it through mathematical computations.

If Omar wants to figure out what you do for a living, but he doesn't want you to know he is doing this type of reconnaissance work, he won't ask you directly. Instead, he will find out when you go to work and when you come home, the types of clothing you wear, the items you carry, and whom you talk to—or he can just follow you to work. These are examples of *side channels*.

So, in cryptography, gathering "outside" information with the goal of uncovering the encryption key is just another way of attacking a cryptosystem.

An attacker could measure power consumption, radiation emissions, and the time it takes for certain types of data processing. With this information, he can work backward by reverse-engineering the process to uncover an encryption key or sensitive data. A power attack reviews the amount of heat released. This type of attack has been successful in uncovering confidential information from smart cards. In 1995, RSA private keys were uncovered by measuring the relative time cryptographic operations took.

The idea is that instead of attacking a device head on, just watch how it performs to figure out how it works. In biology, scientists can choose to carry out a noninvasive experiment, which will watch an organism eat, sleep, mate, and so on. This type of approach learns about the organism through understanding its behaviors instead of killing it and looking at it from the inside out.

Replay Attacks

A big concern in distributed environments is the *replay attack*, in which an attacker captures some type of data and resubmits it with the hopes of fooling the receiving device into thinking it is legitimate information. Many times, the data captured and resubmitted is authentication information, and the attacker is trying to authenticate herself as someone else to gain unauthorized access.

Timestamps and sequence numbers are two countermeasures to replay attacks. Packets can contain sequence numbers, so each machine will expect a specific number on each receiving packet. If a packet has a sequence number that has been previously used, this is an indication of a replay attack. Packets can also be timestamped. A threshold can be set on each computer to only accept packets within a certain timeframe. If a packet is received that is past this threshold, it can help identify a replay attack.

Algebraic Attacks

Algebraic attacks analyze the vulnerabilities in the mathematics used within the algorithm and exploit the intrinsic algebraic structure. For instance, attacks on the "textbook" version of the RSA cryptosystem exploit properties of the algorithm, such as the fact that the encryption of a raw "0" message is "0."

Analytic Attacks

Analytic attacks identify algorithm structural weaknesses or flaws, as opposed to brute-force attacks, which simply exhaust all possibilities without respect to the specific properties of the algorithm. Examples include the Double DES attack and RSA factoring attack.

Statistical Attacks

Statistical attacks identify statistical weaknesses in algorithm design for exploitation—for example, if statistical patterns are identified, as in the number of zeros compared to the number of ones. For instance, a random number generator (RNG) may be biased. If keys are taken directly from the output of the RNG, then the distribution of keys would also be biased. The statistical knowledge about the bias could be used to reduce the search time for the keys.

Social Engineering Attacks

Attackers can trick people into providing their cryptographic key material through various social engineering attack types. Social engineering attacks are carried out on people with the goal of tricking them into divulging some type of sensitive information that can be used by the attacker. The attacker may convince the victim that he is a security administrator that requires the cryptographic data for some type of operational effort. The attacker could then use the data to decrypt and gain access to sensitive data. The attacks can be carried out through persuasion, coercion (rubber-hose cryptanalysis), or bribery (purchase-key attack).

Meet-in-the-Middle Attacks

This term refers to a mathematical analysis used to try and break a math problem from both ends. It is a technique that works on the forward mapping of a function and the inverse of the second function at the same time. The attack works by encrypting from one end and decrypting from the other end, thus *meeting in the middle.*

Site and Facility Security

Let's recap briefly where we've been so far in this chapter. We covered a variety of computing architectures and how to evaluate the security of systems built upon them. Since it is critical to protect not only our computing systems but also the information that makes them useful to us, we included a lengthy discussion on cryptography. This gives us a very solid base on which to engineer security into our systems. (We defer the discussion on network issues until the next chapter.) Unfortunately, this is not enough. If skilled attackers can have "alone time" with our systems, the odds are very good that they will be able to compromise the security of those systems. We must then ensure that we make it difficult for unauthorized persons to gain physical access in the first place.

Many people in the information security field do not think as much about *physical* security as they do about *information* and *computer* security and the associated hackers, ports, malware, and technology-oriented security countermeasures. But information security without proper physical security could be a waste of time.

Physical security has a different set of vulnerabilities, threats, and countermeasures from that of computer and information security. The set for physical security has more to do with physical destruction, intruders, environmental issues, theft, and vandalism. When security professionals look at *information* security, they think about how someone can enter an environment in an unauthorized manner through a port, wireless access point, or software exploitation. When security professionals look at *physical* security, they are concerned with how people can physically enter an environment and cause an array of damages.

The threats that an organization faces fall into these broad categories:

- **Natural environmental threats** Floods, earthquakes, storms and tornadoes, fires, extreme temperature conditions, and so forth
- **Supply system threats** Power distribution outages, communications interruptions, and interruption of other resources such as water, gas, air filtration, and so on
- **Manmade threats** Unauthorized access (both internal and external), explosions, damage by disgruntled employees, employee errors and accidents, vandalism, fraud, theft, and others
- **Politically motivated threats** Strikes, riots, civil disobedience, terrorist attacks, bombings, and so forth

In all situations, the primary consideration, above all else, is that nothing should impede *life safety* goals. When we discuss life safety, protecting human life is the first priority. Good planning helps balance life safety concerns and other security measures. For example, barring a door to prevent unauthorized physical intrusion might prevent individuals from being able to escape in the event of a fire. Life safety goals should always take precedence over all other types of goals; thus, this door might allow insiders to exit through it after pushing an emergency bar, but not allow external entities in.

As we consider site and facility security, we must implement *layered defense models*, which means that physical controls should work together in a tiered architecture. The concept is that if one layer fails, other layers will protect the valuable asset. Layers would be implemented moving from the perimeter toward the asset. For example, you would have a fence, then your facility walls, then an access control card device, then a guard, then an IDS, and then locked computer cases and safes. This series of layers will protect the company's most sensitive assets, which would be placed in the innermost control zone of the environment. So if the bad guy were able to climb over your fence and outsmart the security guard, he would still have to circumvent several layers of controls before getting to your precious resources and systems.

Security needs to protect all the assets of the organization and enhance productivity by providing a secure and predictable environment. Good security enables employees to focus on their tasks at hand and encourages attackers to move on to an easier target. We'll next look at physical security that can affect the *availability* of company resources, the *integrity* of the assets and environment, and the *confidentiality* of the data and business processes.

The Site Planning Process

A designer, or team of designers, needs to be identified to create or improve upon an organization's current site and facility security program. The team must work with management to define the objectives of the program, design the program, and develop performance-based metrics and evaluation processes to ensure the objectives are continually being met.

The objectives of the site and facility security program depend upon the level of protection required for the various assets and the company as a whole. And this required level of protection, in turn, depends upon the organization's acceptable risk level. This acceptable risk level should be derived from the laws and regulations with which the organization must comply and from the threat profile of the organization overall. This requires identifying who and what could damage business assets, identifying the types of attacks and crimes that could take place, and understanding the business impact of these threats. The type of physical countermeasures required and their adequacy or inadequacy need to be measured against the organization's threat profile. A financial institution has a much different threat profile, and thus a much different acceptable risk level, when compared to a grocery store. The threat profile of a hospital is different from the threat profile of a military base or a government agency. The team must understand the types of adversaries it must consider, the capabilities of these adversaries, and the resources and tactics these individuals would use. (Review Chapter 1 for a discussion of acceptable risk-level concepts.)

Physical security is a combination of people, processes, procedures, technology, and equipment to protect resources. The design of a solid physical security program should be methodical and should weigh the objectives of the program and the available resources. Although every organization is different, the approach to constructing and maintaining a physical security program is the same. The organization must first define the vulnerabilities, threats, threat agents, and targets.

NOTE Remember that a vulnerability is a weakness and a threat is the potential that someone will identify this weakness and use it against you. The threat agent is the person or mechanism that actually exploits this identified vulnerability.

Threats can be grouped into categories such as internal and external threats. Internal threats may include faulty technology, fire hazards, or employees who aim to damage the company in some way. Employees have intimate knowledge of the company's facilities and assets, which is usually required to perform tasks and responsibilities—but this makes it easier for the insider to carry out damaging activity without being noticed. Unfortunately, a large threat to companies can be their own security guards, which is usually not realized until it is too late. These people have keys and access codes to all portions of a facility and usually work during employee off-hours. This gives the guards ample windows of opportunity to carry out their crimes. It is critical for a company to carry out a background investigation, or to pay a company to perform this service, before hiring a security guard. If you hire a wolf to guard the chicken coop, things can get ugly.

External threats come in many different forms as well. Government buildings are usually chosen targets for some types of political revenge. If a company performs abortions or conducts animal research, then activists are usually a large and constant threat. And, of course, banks and armored cars are tempting targets for organized crime members.

A threat that is even trickier to protect against is *collusion*, in which two or more people work together to carry out fraudulent activity. Many criminal cases have uncovered insiders working with outsiders to defraud or damage a company. The types of controls for this type of activity are procedural protection mechanisms. This may include separation of duties, preemployment background checks, rotations of duties, and supervision.

As with any type of security, most attention and awareness surrounds the exciting and headline-grabbing tidbits about large crimes being carried out and criminals being captured. In information security, most people are aware of viruses and hackers, but not of the components that make up a corporate security program. The same is true for physical security. Many people talk about current robberies, murders, and other criminal activity at the water cooler, but do not pay attention to the necessary framework that should be erected and maintained to reduce these types of activities. An organization's physical security program should address the following goals:

- **Crime and disruption prevention through deterrence** Fences, security guards, warning signs, and so forth
- **Reduction of damage through the use of delaying mechanisms** Layers of defenses that slow down the adversary, such as locks, security personnel, and barriers

- **Crime or disruption detection** Smoke detectors, motion detectors, CCTV, and so forth
- **Incident assessment** Response of security guards to detected incidents and determination of damage level
- **Response procedures** Fire suppression mechanisms, emergency response processes, law enforcement notification, and consultation with outside security professionals

So, an organization should try to prevent crimes and disruptions from taking place, but must also plan to deal with them when they do happen. A criminal should be delayed in her activities by having to penetrate several layers of controls before gaining access to a resource. All types of crimes and disruptions should be able to be detected through components that make up the physical security program. Once an intrusion is discovered, a security guard should be called upon to assess the situation. The security guard must then know how to properly respond to a large range of potentially dangerous activities. The emergency response activities could be carried out by the organization's internal security team or by outside experts.

This all sounds straightforward enough, until the team responsible for developing the physical security program looks at all the possible threats, the finite budget that the team has to work with, and the complexity of choosing the right combination of countermeasures and ensuring that they all work together in a manner that ensures no gaps of protection. All of these components must be understood in depth before the design of a physical security program can begin.

As with all security programs, it is possible to determine how beneficial and effective your physical security program is only if it is monitored through a *performance-based approach*. This means you should devise measurements and metrics to gauge the effectiveness of your countermeasures. This enables management to make informed business decisions when investing in the protection of the organization's physical security. The goal is to increase the performance of the physical security program and decrease the risk to the company in a cost-effective manner. You should establish a baseline of performance and thereafter continually evaluate performance to make sure that the company's protection objectives are being met. The following list provides some examples of possible performance metrics:

- Number of successful crimes
- Number of successful disruptions
- Number of unsuccessful crimes
- Number of unsuccessful disruptions
- Time between detection, assessment, and recovery steps
- Business impact of disruptions
- Number of false-positive detection alerts

- Time it took for a criminal to defeat a control
- Time it took to restore the operational environment
- Financial loss of a successful crime
- Financial loss of a successful disruption

Capturing and monitoring these types of metrics enables the organization to identify deficiencies, evaluate improvement measures, and perform cost/benefit analyses.

NOTE Metrics are becoming more important in all domains of security because organizations need to allocate the necessary controls and countermeasures to mitigate risks in a cost-beneficial manner. You can't manage what you can't measure.

The physical security team needs to carry out a risk analysis, which will identify the organization's vulnerabilities, threats, and business impacts. The team should present these findings to management and work with management to define an acceptable risk level for the physical security program. From there, the team must develop baselines (minimum levels of security) and metrics in order to evaluate and determine if the baselines are being met by the implemented countermeasures. Once the team identifies and implements the countermeasures, the performance of these countermeasures should be continually evaluated and expressed in the previously created metrics. These performance values are compared to the set baselines. If the baselines are continually maintained, then the security program is successful because the company's acceptable risk level is not being exceeded. This is illustrated in Figure 3-49.

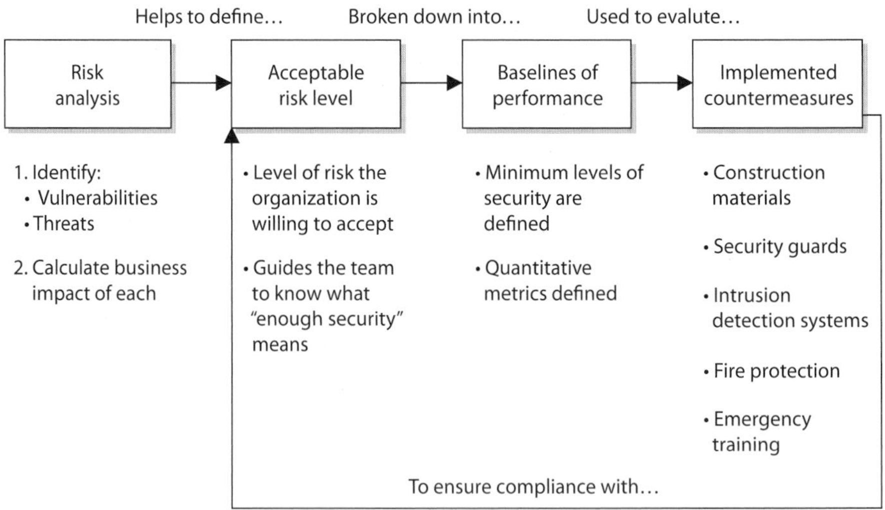

Figure 3-49 Relationships of risk, baselines, and countermeasures

Similarities in Approaches

The risk analysis steps that need to take place for the development of a physical security program are similar to the steps outlined for the development of an organizational security program and for business impact analysis (both covered in Chapter 1), because each of these processes (development of an information security program, a physical security program, or a business continuity plan) accomplishes goals that are similar to the goals of the other two processes, but with different focuses. Each process requires a team to carry out a risk analysis to determine the company's threats and risks. An information security program looks at the internal and external threats to resources and data through business processes and technological means. Business continuity planning looks at how natural disasters and disruptions could damage the organization, while a physical security program looks at internal and external physical threats to the company resources.

Each requires a solid risk analysis process. Review Chapter 1 to understand the core components of every risk analysis.

So, before an effective physical security program can be rolled out, the following steps must be taken:

1. Identify a team of internal employees and/or external consultants who will build the physical security program through the following steps.
2. Define the scope of the effort: site or facility.
3. Carry out a risk analysis to identify the vulnerabilities and threats and to calculate the business impact of each threat.
4. Identify regulatory and legal requirements that the organization must meet and maintain.
5. Work with management to define an acceptable risk level for the physical security program.
6. Derive the required performance baselines from the acceptable risk level.
7. Create countermeasure performance metrics.
8. Develop criteria from the results of the analysis, outlining the level of protection and performance required for the following categories of the security program:
   - Deterrence
   - Delaying
   - Detection
   - Assessment
   - Response

9. Identify and implement countermeasures for each program category.
10. Continuously evaluate countermeasures against the set baselines to ensure the acceptable risk level is not exceeded.

Legal Requirements

In physical security there are some regulatory and high-level legal requirements that must be met, but many of them just have high-level statements, as in "protect personnel" or "implement lifesaving controls." It is up to the organization to figure out how to actually meet these requirements in a practical manner. In the United States there is a lot of case law that pertains to physical security requirements, which is built upon precedence. This means that there have been lawsuits pertaining to specific physical security instances and a judgment was made on liability. For example, there is no law that dictates that you must put up a yellow sign indicating that a floor is wet. Many years ago someone somewhere slipped on a wet floor and sued the company, and the judge ruled that the company was negligent and liable for the person's injuries. Now it is built into many company procedures that after a floor is mopped or there is a spill, this yellow sign is put in place so no one will fall and sue the company. It is hard to think about and cover all of these issues since there is no specific checklist to follow. This is why it is a good idea to consult with a physical security expert when developing a physical security program.

Once these steps have taken place then the team is ready to move forward in its actual design phase. The design will incorporate the controls required for each category of the program: deterrence, delaying, detection, assessment, and response. We will dig deeper into these categories and their corresponding controls later in the chapter in the section "Designing a Physical Security Program."

One of the most commonly used approaches in physical security program development is described in the following section.

Crime Prevention Through Environmental Design

Crime Prevention Through Environmental Design (CPTED) is a discipline that outlines how the proper design of a physical environment can reduce crime by directly affecting human behavior. It provides guidance in loss and crime prevention through proper facility construction and environmental components and procedures.

CPTED concepts were developed in the 1960s. They have been expanded upon and have matured as our environments and crime types have evolved. CPTED has been used not just to develop corporate physical security programs, but also for large-scale activities such as development of neighborhoods, towns, and cities. It addresses landscaping, entrances, facility and neighborhood layouts, lighting, road placement, and traffic circulation patterns. It looks at microenvironments, such as offices and restrooms, and macroenvironments, like campuses and cities. The crux of CPTED is that the physical environment can be manipulated to create behavioral effects that will reduce crime and the fear of crime. It looks at the components that make up the relationship between humans and their environment. This encompasses the physical, social, and psychological needs of the users of different types of environments and predictable behaviors of these users and offenders.

CPTED provides guidelines on items some of us might not consider. For example, hedges and planters around a facility should not be higher than 2.5 feet tall so they cannot be used to gain access to a window. A data center should be located at the center of a facility so the facility's walls will absorb any damages from external forces, instead of the data center itself. Street furnishings (benches and tables) encourage people to sit and watch what is going on around them, which discourages criminal activity. A corporation's landscape should not include wooded areas or other places where intruders can hide. CCTV cameras should be mounted in full view so that criminals know their activities will be captured and other people know that the environment is well monitored and thus safer.

CPTED and target hardening are two different approaches. *Target hardening* focuses on denying access through physical and artificial barriers (alarms, locks, fences, and so on). Traditional target hardening can lead to restrictions on the use, enjoyment, and aesthetics of an environment. Sure, we can implement hierarchies of fences, locks, and intimidating signs and barriers—but how pretty would that be? If your environment is a prison, this look might be just what you need. But if your environment is an office building, you're not looking for Fort Knox décor. Nevertheless, you still must provide the necessary levels of protection, but your protection mechanisms should be more subtle and unobtrusive.

Let's say your organization's team needs to protect a side door at your facility. The traditional target-hardening approach would be to put locks, alarms, and cameras on the door; install an access control mechanism, such as a proximity reader; and instruct security guards to monitor this door. The CPTED approach would be to ensure there is no sidewalk leading to this door from the front of the building if you don't want customers using it. The CPTED approach would also ensure no tall trees or bushes block the ability to view someone using this door. Barriers such as trees and bushes may make intruders feel more comfortable in attempting to break in through a secluded door.

The best approach is usually to build an environment from a CPTED approach and then apply the target-hardening components on top of the design where needed.

If a parking garage were developed using the CPTED approach, the stair towers and elevators within the garage might have glass windows instead of metal walls, so people would feel safer, and potential criminals would not carry out crimes in this more visible environment. Pedestrian walkways would be created such that people could look out across the rows of cars and see any suspicious activities. The different rows for cars to park in would be separated by low walls and structural pillars, instead of solid walls, to allow pedestrians to view activities within the garage. The goal is to not provide any hidden areas where criminals can carry out their crimes and to provide an open-viewed area so if a criminal does attempt something malicious, there is a higher likelihood of someone seeing it.

CPTED provides three main strategies to bring together the physical environment and social behavior to increase overall protection: natural access control, natural surveillance, and natural territorial reinforcement.

Natural Access Control

Natural access control is the guidance of people entering and leaving a space by the placement of doors, fences, lighting, and even landscaping. For example, an office building may have external bollards with lights in them, as shown in Figure 3-50. These bollards actually carry out different safety and security services. The bollards themselves protect the facility from physical destruction by preventing people from driving their cars into the building. The light emitted helps ensure that criminals do not have a dark place to hide. And the lights and bollard placement guide people along the sidewalk to the entrance, instead of using signs or railings. As shown in Figure 3-50, the landscape, sidewalks, lighted bollards, and clear sight lines are used as natural access controls. They work together to give individuals a feeling of being in a safe environment and help dissuade criminals by working as deterrents.

NOTE Bollards are short posts commonly used to prevent vehicular access and to protect a building or people walking on a sidewalk from vehicles. They can also be used to direct foot traffic.

Figure 3-50 Sidewalks, lights, and landscaping can be used for protection.

Clear lines of sight and transparency can be used to discourage potential offenders, because of the absence of places to hide or carry out criminal activities.

The CPTED model shows how *security zones* can be created. An environment's space should be divided into zones with different security levels, depending upon who needs to be in that zone and the associated risk. The zones can be labeled as controlled, restricted, public, or sensitive. This is conceptually similar to information classification, as described in Chapter 2. In a data classification program, different classifications are created, along with data handling procedures and the level of protection that each classification requires. The same is true of physical zones. Each zone should have a specific protection level required of it, which will help dictate the types of controls that should be put into place.

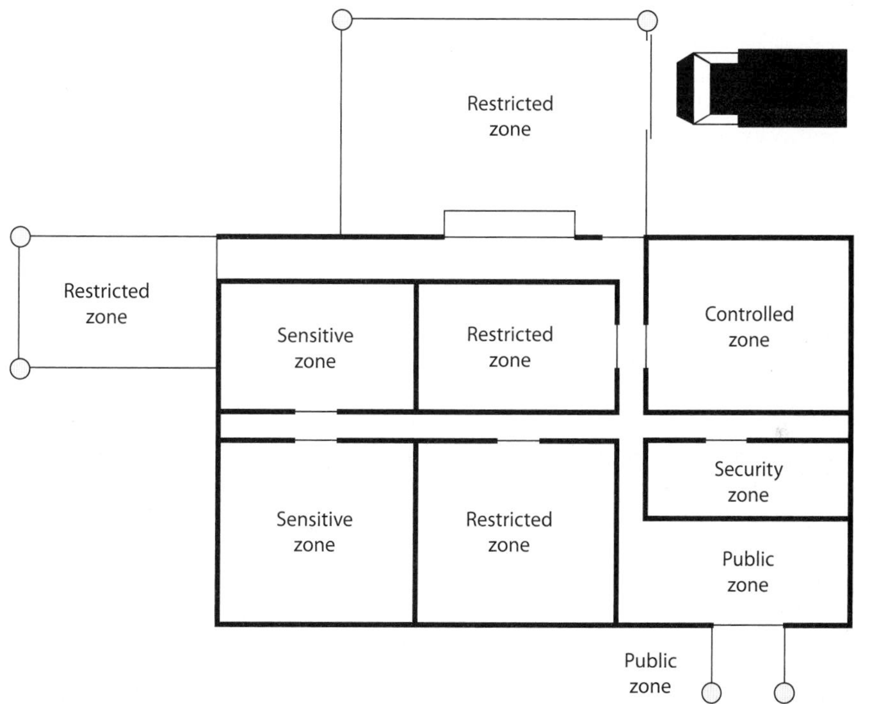

Access control should be in place to control and restrict individuals from going from one security zone to the next. Access control should also be in place for all facility entrances and exits. The security program development team needs to consider other ways in which intruders can gain access to buildings, such as by climbing adjacent trees to access skylights, upper-story windows, and balconies. The following controls are commonly used for access controls within different organizations:

- Limit the number of entry points.
- Force all guests to go to a front desk and sign in before entering the environment.

- Reduce the number of entry points even further after hours or during the weekend, when not as many employees are around.
- Implement sidewalks and landscaping to guide the public to a main entrance.
- Implement a back driveway for suppliers and deliveries that is not easily accessible to the public.
- Provide lighting for the pathways the public should follow to enter a building to help encourage use of only one entry for access.
- Implement sidewalks and grassy areas to guide vehicle traffic to only enter and exit through specific locations.
- Provide parking in the front of the building (not the back or sides) so people will be directed to enter the intended entrance.

These types of access controls are used all of the time, and we usually do not think about them. They are built into the natural environment to manipulate us into doing what the owner of the facility wants us to do. When you are walking on a sidewalk that leads to an office front door and there are pretty flowers on both sides of the sidewalk, know that they are put there because people tend not to step off a sidewalk and crush pretty flowers. Flowers are commonly placed on both sides of a sidewalk to help ensure that people stay on the sidewalk. Subtle and sneaky, but these control mechanisms work.

More obvious access barriers can be naturally created (cliffs, rivers, hills), existing manmade elements (railroad tracks, highways), or artificial forms designed specifically to impede movement (fences, closing streets). These can be used in tandem or separately to provide the necessary level of access control.

Natural Surveillance

Surveillance can also take place through organized means (security guards), mechanical means (CCTV), and natural strategies (straight lines of sight, low landscaping, raised entrances). The goal of *natural surveillance* is to make criminals feel uncomfortable by providing many ways observers could potentially see them and to make all other people feel safe and comfortable by providing an open and well-designed environment.

Natural surveillance is the use and placement of physical environmental features, personnel walkways, and activity areas in ways that maximize visibility. Figure 3-51 illustrates a stairway in a parking garage designed to be open and allow easy observation.

Next time you are walking down a street and see a bench next to a building or you see a bench in a park, know that the city has not allocated funds for these benches just in case your legs get tired. These benches are strategically placed so that people will sit and watch other people. This is a very good surveillance system. The people who are watching others do not realize that they are actually protecting the area, but many criminals will identify them and not feel as confident in carrying out some type of malicious deed.

Walkways and bicycle paths are commonly installed so that there will be a steady flow of pedestrians who could identify malicious activity. Buildings might have large windows that overlook sidewalks and parking lots for the same reason. Shorter fences might be

Figure 3-51 Open areas reduce the likelihood of criminal activity.

installed so people can see what is taking place on both sides of the fence. Certain high-risk areas have more lighting than what is necessary so that people from a distance can see what is going on. These high-risk areas could be stairs, parking areas, bus stops, laundry rooms, children's play areas, dumpsters, and recycling stations. These constructs help people protect people without even knowing it.

Natural Territorial Reinforcement

The third CPTED strategy is natural *territorial reinforcement*, which creates physical designs that emphasize or extend the company's physical sphere of influence so legitimate users feel a sense of ownership of that space. Territorial reinforcement can be implemented through the use of walls, fences, landscaping, light fixtures, flags, clearly marked addresses, and decorative sidewalks. The goal of territorial reinforcement is to create a sense of a dedicated community. Companies implement these elements so employees feel proud of their environment and have a sense of belonging, which they will defend if required to do so. These elements are also implemented to give potential offenders the impression that they do not belong there, that their activities are at risk of being observed, and that their illegal activities will not be tolerated or ignored.

Most corporate environments use a mix of the CPTED and target-hardening approaches. CPTED deals mainly with the construction of the facility, its internal and external designs, and exterior components such as landscaping and lighting. If the environment is built based on CPTED, then the target hardening is like icing on the cake. The target-hardening approach applies more granular protection mechanisms, such as locks and motion detectors. The rest of the chapter looks at physical controls that can be used in both models.

Designing a Physical Security Program

If a team is organized to assess the protection level of an existing facility, it needs to investigate the following:

- Construction materials of walls and ceilings
- Power distribution systems
- Communication paths and types (copper, telephone, fiber)
- Surrounding hazardous materials
- Exterior components:
  - Topography
  - Proximity to airports, highways, railroads
  - Potential electromagnetic interference from surrounding devices
  - Climate
  - Soil
  - Existing fences, detection sensors, cameras, barriers
  - Operational activities that depend upon physical resources
  - Vehicle activity
  - Neighbors

To properly obtain this information, the team should do physical surveys and interview various employees. All of this collected data will help the team to evaluate the current controls, identify weaknesses, and ensure operational productivity is not negatively affected by implementing new controls.

Although there are usually written policies and procedures on what *should* be taking place pertaining to physical security, policies and reality do not always match up. It is important for the team to observe how the facility is used, note daily activities that could introduce vulnerabilities, and determine how the facility is protected. This information should be documented and compared to the information within the written policy and procedures. In most cases, existing gaps must be addressed and fixed. Just writing out a policy helps no one if it is not actually followed.

Every organization must comply with various regulations, whether they be safety and health regulations; fire codes; state and local building codes; Departments of Defense, Energy, or Labor requirements; or some other agency's regulations. The organization may also have to comply with requirements of the Occupational Safety and Health Administration (OSHA) and the Environmental Protection Agency (EPA), if it is operating in the United States, or with the requirements of equivalent organizations within another country. The physical security program development team must understand all the regulations the organization must comply with and how to reach compliance through physical security and safety procedures.

Legal issues must be understood and properly addressed as well. These issues may include access availability for the disabled, liability issues, the failure to protect assets, and so on. This long laundry list of items can get a company into legal trouble if it is not doing what it is supposed to. Occasionally, the legal trouble may take the form of a criminal case—for example, if doors default to being locked when power is lost and, as a result, several employees are trapped and killed during a fire, criminal negligence may be alleged. Legal trouble can also come in the form of civil cases—for instance, if a company does not remove the ice on its sidewalks and a pedestrian falls and breaks his ankle, the pedestrian may sue the company. The company may be found negligent and held liable for damages.

Every organization should have a *facility safety officer*, whose main job is to understand all the components that make up the facility and what the company needs to do to protect its assets and stay within compliance. This person should oversee facility management duties day in and day out, but should also be heavily involved with the team that has been organized to evaluate the organization's physical security program.

A physical security program is a collection of controls that are implemented and maintained to provide the protection levels necessary to be in compliance with the physical security policy. The policy should embody all the regulations and laws that must be adhered to and should set the risk level the company is willing to accept.

By this point, the team has carried out a risk analysis, which consisted of identifying the company's vulnerabilities, threats, and business impact pertaining to the identified threats. The program design phase should begin with a structured outline, which will evolve into a framework. This framework will then be fleshed out with the necessary controls and countermeasures. The outline should contain the program categories and the necessary countermeasures. The following is a simplistic example:

I. Deterrence of criminal activity
- **A.** Fences
- **B.** Warning signs
- **C.** Security guards
- **D.** Dogs

II. Delay of intruders to help ensure they can be caught
- **A.** Locks
- **B.** Defense-in-depth measures
- **C.** Access controls

III. Detection of intruders

  A. External intruder sensors

  B. Internal intruder sensors

IV. Assessment of situations

  A. Security guard procedures

  B. Damage assessment criteria

V. Response to intrusions and disruptions

  A. Communication structure (calling tree)

  B. Response force

  C. Emergency response procedures

  D. Police, fire, medical personnel

The team can then start addressing each phase of the security program, usually starting with the facility.

Facility

When a company decides to erect a building, it should consider several factors before pouring the first batch of concrete. Of course, it should review land prices, customer population, and marketing strategies, but as security professionals, we are more interested in the confidence and protection that a specific location can provide. Some organizations that deal with top-secret or confidential information and processes make their facilities unnoticeable so they do not attract the attention of would-be attackers. The building may be hard to see from the surrounding roads, the company signs and logos may be small and not easily noticed, and the markings on the building may not give away any information that pertains to what is going on inside that building. It is a type of urban camouflage that makes it harder for the enemy to seek out that company as a target. This is very common for telecommunication facilities that contain critical infrastructure switches and other supporting technologies. When driving down the road you might pass three of these buildings, but because they have no features that actually stand out, you likely would not even give them a second thought—which is the goal.

A company should evaluate how close the facility would be to a police station, fire station, and medical facilities. Many times, the proximity of these entities raises the real estate value of properties, but for good reason. If a chemical company that manufactures highly explosive materials needs to build a new facility, it may make good business sense to put it near a fire station. (Although the fire station might not be so happy.) If another company that builds and sells expensive electronic devices is expanding and needs to move operations into another facility, police reaction time may be looked at when choosing one facility location over another. Each of these issues—police station, fire station, and medical facility proximity—can also reduce insurance rates and must be looked at carefully. Remember that the ultimate goal of physical security is to ensure the safety of personnel. Always keep that in mind when implementing any sort of physical security control. Protect your fellow humans, be your brother's keeper, and *then* run.

Some buildings are placed in areas surrounded by hills or mountains to help prevent eavesdropping of electrical signals emitted by the facility's equipment. In some cases, the organization itself will build hills or use other landscaping techniques to guard against eavesdropping. Other facilities are built underground or right into the side of a mountain for concealment and disguise in the natural environment, and for protection from radar tools, spying activities, and aerial bomb attacks.

In the United States there is an Air Force base built into the Cheyenne Mountain close to Colorado Springs, Colorado. The base was built into the mountain and is made up of an inner complex of buildings, rooms, and tunnels. It has its own air intake supply, as well as water, fuel, and sewer lines. This is where the North American Aerospace Defense Command carries out its mission and apparently, according to many popular movies, is where you should be headed if the world is about to be blown up.

Construction

Physical construction materials and structure composition need to be evaluated for their appropriateness to the site environment, their protective characteristics, their utility, and their costs and benefits. Different building materials provide various levels of fire protection and have different rates of combustibility, which correlate with their fire ratings. When making structural decisions, the decision of what type of construction material to use (wood, concrete, or steel) needs to be considered in light of what the building is going to be used for. If an area will be used to store documents and old equipment, it has far different needs and legal requirements than if it is going to be used for employees to work in every day.

The *load* (how much weight can be held) of a building's walls, floors, and ceilings needs to be estimated and projected to ensure the building will not collapse in different situations. In most cases, this is dictated by local building codes. The walls, ceilings, and floors must contain the necessary materials to meet the required fire rating and to protect against water damage. The windows (interior and exterior) may need to provide ultraviolet (UV) protection, may need to be shatterproof, or may need to be translucent or opaque, depending on the placement of the window and the contents of the building. The doors (exterior and interior) may need to have directional openings, have the same fire rating as the surrounding walls, prohibit forcible entries, display emergency egress markings, and—depending on placement—have monitoring and attached alarms. In most buildings, raised floors are used to hide and protect wires and pipes, and it is important to ensure any raised outlets are properly grounded.

Building codes may regulate all of these issues, but there are still many options within each category that the physical security program development team should review for extra security protection. The right options should accomplish the company's security and functionality needs and still be cost effective.

Ground

If you are holding a power cord plug that has two skinny metal pieces and one fatter, rounder metal piece, which all go into the outlet—what is that fatter, rounder piece for? It is a ground connector, which is supposed to act as the conduit for any excess current to ensure that people and devices are not negatively affected by a spike in electrical current. So, in the wiring of a building, where do you think this ground should be connected? Yep, to the ground. Old mother earth. But many buildings are not wired properly, and the ground connector is connected to nothing. This can be very dangerous, since the extra current has nowhere to escape but into our equipment or ourselves.

When designing and building a facility, the following major items need to be addressed from a physical security point of view.

Walls:

- Combustibility of material (wood, steel, concrete)
- Fire rating
- Reinforcements for secured areas

Doors:

- Combustibility of material (wood, pressed board, aluminum)
- Fire rating
- Resistance to forcible entry
- Emergency marking
- Placement
- Locked or controlled entrances
- Alarms
- Secure hinges
- Directional opening
- Electric door locks that revert to an unlocked state for safe evacuation in power outages
- Type of glass—shatterproof or bulletproof glass requirements

Ceilings:

- Combustibility of material (wood, steel, concrete)
- Fire rating
- Weight-bearing rating
- Drop-ceiling considerations

Windows:

- Translucent or opaque requirements
- Shatterproof
- Alarms
- Placement
- Accessibility to intruders

Flooring:

- Weight-bearing rating
- Combustibility of material (wood, steel, concrete)
- Fire rating
- Raised flooring
- Nonconducting surface and material

Heating, ventilation, and air conditioning:

- Positive air pressure
- Protected intake vents
- Dedicated power lines
- Emergency shutoff valves and switches
- Placement

Electric power supplies:

- Backup and alternative power supplies
- Clean and steady power source
- Dedicated feeders to required areas
- Placement and access to distribution panels and circuit breakers

Water and gas lines:

- Shutoff valves—labeled and brightly painted for visibility
- Positive flow (material flows out of building, not in)
- Placement—properly located and labeled

Fire detection and suppression:

- Placement of sensors and detectors
- Placement of suppression systems
- Type of detectors and suppression agents

The risk analysis results will help the team determine the type of construction material that should be used when constructing a new facility. Several grades of building construction are available. For example, *light frame construction material* provides the least amount of protection against fire and forcible entry attempts. It is composed of untreated lumber that would be combustible during a fire. Light frame construction material is usually used to build homes, primarily because it is cheap, but also because homes typically are not under the same types of fire and intrusion threats that office buildings are.

Heavy timber construction material is commonly used for office buildings. Combustible lumber is still used in this type of construction, but there are requirements on the thickness and composition of the materials to provide more protection from fire. The construction materials must be at least 4 inches in thickness. Denser woods are used and are fastened with metal bolts and plates. Whereas light frame construction material has a fire survival rate of 30 minutes, the heavy timber construction material has a fire survival rate of one hour.

A building could be made up of *incombustible material*, such as steel, which provides a higher level of fire protection than the previously mentioned materials, but loses its strength under extreme temperatures, something that may cause the building to collapse. So, although the steel will not burn, it may melt and weaken. If a building consists of *fire-resistant material*, the construction material is fire retardant and may have steel rods encased inside of concrete walls and support beams. This provides the most protection against fire and forced entry attempts.

The team should choose its construction material based on the identified threats of the organization and the fire codes to be complied with. If a company is just going to have some office workers in a building and has no real adversaries interested in destroying the facility, then the light frame or heavy timber construction material would be used. Facilities for government organizations, which are under threat by domestic and foreign terrorists, would be built with fire-resistant materials. A financial institution would also use fire-resistant and reinforcement material within its building. This is especially true for its exterior walls, through which thieves may attempt to drive vehicles to gain access to the vaults.

Calculations of approximate penetration times for different types of explosives and attacks are based on the thickness of the concrete walls and the gauge of rebar used. (*Rebar*, short for *reinforcing bar*, refers to the steel rods encased within the concrete.) So even if the concrete were damaged, it would take longer to actually cut or break through the rebar. Using thicker rebar and properly placing it within the concrete provides even more protection.

Reinforced walls, rebar, and the use of double walls can be used as delaying mechanisms. The idea is that it will take the bad guy longer to get through two reinforced walls, which gives the response force sufficient time (hopefully) to arrive at the scene and stop the attacker.

Entry Points

Understanding the company needs and types of entry points for a specific building is critical. The various types of entry points may include doors, windows, roof access, fire escapes, chimneys, and service delivery access points. Second and third entry points must also be considered, such as internal doors that lead into other portions of the building and to exterior doors, elevators, and stairwells. Windows at the ground level should be fortified because they could be easily broken. Fire escapes, stairwells to the roof, and chimneys often are overlooked as potential entry points.

NOTE Ventilation ducts and utility tunnels can also be used by intruders and thus must be properly protected with sensors and access control mechanisms.

The weakest portion of the structure, usually its doors and windows, will likely be attacked first. With regard to doors, the weaknesses usually lie within the frames, hinges, and door material. The bolts, frames, hinges, and material that make up the door should all provide the same level of strength and protection. For example, if a company implements a heavy, nonhollow steel door but uses weak hinges that could be easily extracted, the company is just wasting money. The attacker can just remove the hinges and remove this strong and heavy door.

The door and surrounding walls and ceilings should also provide the same level of strength. If another company has an extremely fortified and secure door, but the surrounding wall materials are made out of regular light frame wood, then it is also wasting money on doors. There is no reason to spend a lot of money on one countermeasure that can be easily circumvented by breaking a weaker countermeasure in proximity.

Doors Different door types for various functionalities include the following:

- Vault doors
- Personnel doors
- Industrial doors
- Vehicle access doors
- Bullet-resistant doors

Doors can be hollow-core or solid-core. The team needs to understand the various entry types and the potential forced-entry threats, which will help the team determine what type of door should be implemented. Hollow-core doors can be easily penetrated by kicking or cutting them; thus, they are usually used internally. The team also has a choice of solid-core doors, which are made up of various materials to provide different fire ratings and protection from forced entry. As stated previously, the fire rating and protection level of the door need to match the fire rating and protection level of the surrounding walls.

Bulletproof doors are also an option if there is a threat that damage could be done to resources by shooting through the door. These types of doors are constructed in a manner that involves sandwiching bullet-resistant and bulletproof material between wood or steel veneers to still give the door some aesthetic qualities while providing the necessary levels of protection.

Hinges and strike plates should be secure, especially on exterior doors or doors used to protect sensitive areas. The hinges should have pins that cannot be removed, and the door frames must provide the same level of protection as the door itself.

Fire codes dictate the number and placement of doors with panic bars on them. These are the crossbars that release an internal lock to allow a locked door to open. Panic bars can be on regular entry doors and also on emergency exit doors. Those are the ones that usually have the sign that indicates the door is not an exit point and that an alarm will go off if the door is opened. It might seem like fun and a bit tempting to see if the alarm will *really* go off or not—but don't try it. Security people are not known for their sense of humor.

Mantraps and turnstiles can be used so unauthorized individuals entering a facility cannot get in or out if it is activated. A *mantrap* is a small room with two doors. The first door is locked; a person is identified and authenticated by a security guard, biometric system, smart card reader, or swipe card reader. Once the person is authenticated and access is authorized, the first door opens and allows the person into the mantrap. The first door locks and the person is trapped. The person must be authenticated again before the second door unlocks and allows him into the facility. Some mantraps use biometric systems that weigh the person who enters to ensure that only one person at a time is entering the mantrap area. This is a control to counter piggybacking.

Doorways with automatic locks can be configured to be fail-safe or fail-secure. A *fail-safe* setting means that if a power disruption occurs that affects the automated locking system, the doors default to being unlocked. Fail-safe deals directly with protecting people. If people work in an area in which there is a fire or the power is lost, it is not a good idea to lock them in. A *fail-secure* configuration means that the doors default to being locked if there are any problems with the power. If people do not need to use specific doors for escape during an emergency, then these doors can most likely default to fail-secure settings.

Window Types Though most of us would probably think of doors as the obvious entry points, windows deserve every bit as much attention in the design of secure facilities. Like doors, different types of windows afford various degrees of protection against intrusions. The following sums up the types of windows that can be used:

- **Standard** No extra protection. The cheapest and lowest level of protection.
- **Tempered** Glass is heated and then cooled suddenly to increase its integrity and strength.
- **Acrylic** A type of plastic instead of glass. Polycarbonate acrylics are stronger than regular acrylics.
- **Wired** A mesh of wire is embedded between two sheets of glass. This wire helps prevent the glass from shattering.
- **Laminated** The plastic layer between two outer glass layers. The plastic layer helps increase its strength against breakage.
- **Solar window film** Provides extra security by being tinted and offers extra strength due to the film's material.
- **Security film** Transparent film is applied to the glass to increase its strength.

Internal Compartments

Many components that make up a facility must be looked at from a security point of view. *Internal partitions* are used to create barriers between one area and another. These partitions can be used to segment separate work areas, but should never be used in protected areas that house sensitive systems and devices. Many buildings have dropped ceilings, meaning the interior partitions do not extend to the true ceiling—only to the dropped ceiling. An intruder can lift a ceiling panel and climb over the partition. This example of intrusion is shown in Figure 3-52. In many situations, this would not require forced entry, specialized tools, or much effort. (In some office buildings, this may even be possible from a common public-access hallway.) These types of internal partitions should not be relied upon to provide protection for sensitive areas.

Computer and Equipment Rooms

It used to be necessary to have personnel within the computer rooms for proper maintenance and operations. Today, most servers, routers, switches, mainframes, and other equipment housed in computer rooms can be controlled remotely. This enables computers to live in rooms that have fewer people milling around and spilling coffee. Because the computer rooms no longer have personnel sitting and working in them for long periods, the rooms can be constructed in a manner that is efficient for equipment instead of people.

On the other hand, there are situations in which people may have to be physically in the data center, perhaps for very extended periods of time (equipment installations/upgrades, data center infrastructure upgrades and reconfigurations, incident response, forensic data acquisition, etc.). Consequently, the inhospitable conditions (cold, dry environment; lack of comfortable work spaces; extremely high decibel levels) should be taken into account when deploying such personnel.

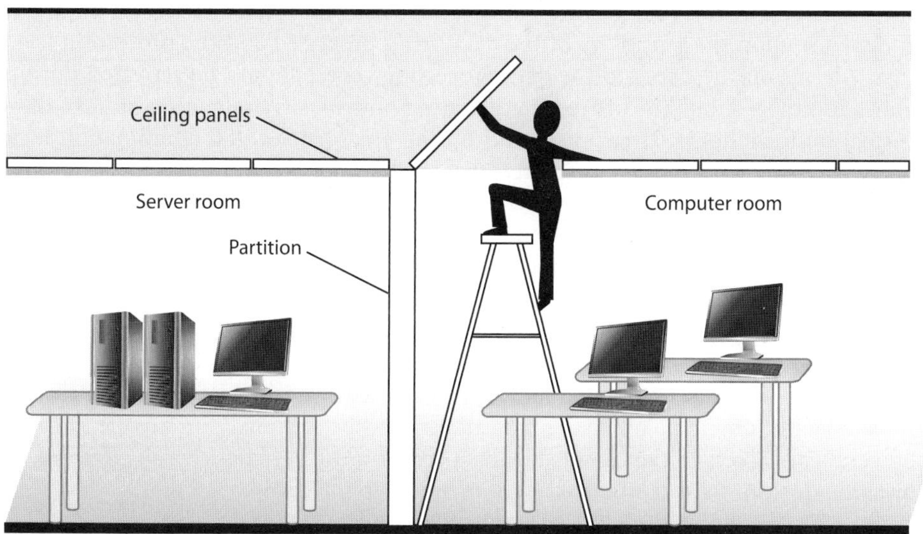

Figure 3-52 An intruder can lift ceiling panels and enter a secured area with little effort.

Smaller systems can be stacked vertically to save space. They should be mounted on racks or placed inside equipment cabinets. The wiring should be close to the equipment to save on cable costs and to reduce tripping hazards.

Data centers, server rooms, and wiring closets should be located in the core areas of a facility, near wiring distribution centers. Strict access control mechanisms and procedures should be implemented for these areas. The access control mechanisms may be smart card readers, biometric readers, or combination locks. These restricted areas should have only one *access* door, but fire code requirements typically dictate there must be at least two doors to most data centers and server rooms. Only one door should be used for daily entry and exit, and the other door should be used only in emergency situations. This second door should not be an access door, which means people should not be able to come in through this door. It should be locked, but should have a panic bar that will release the lock if pressed.

These restricted areas ideally should not be directly accessible from public areas like stairways, corridors, loading docks, elevators, and restrooms. This helps ensure that the people who are by the doors to secured areas have a specific purpose for being there, versus being on their way to the restroom or standing around in a common area gossiping about the CEO.

Because data centers usually hold expensive equipment and the company's critical data, their protection should be thoroughly thought out before implementation. A data center should not be located on an upper floor of a building, because that would make accessing it in a timely fashion in case of a fire more difficult for an emergency crew. By the same token, data centers should not be located in basements where flooding can affect the systems. And if a facility is in a hilly area, the data center should be located well above ground level. Data centers should be located at the core of a building so that if there is some type of attack on the building, the exterior walls and structures will absorb the hit and hopefully the data center will not be damaged.

Which access controls and security measures should be implemented for the data center depends upon the sensitivity of the data being processed and the protection level required. Alarms on the doors to the data processing center should be activated during off-hours, and there should be procedures dictating how to carry out access control during normal business hours, after hours, and during emergencies. If a combination lock is used to enter the data processing center, the combination should be changed at least every six months and also after an employee who knows the code leaves the company.

The various controls discussed next are shown in Figure 3-53. The team responsible for designing a new data center (or evaluating a current data center) should understand all the controls shown in Figure 3-53 and be able to choose what is needed.

The data processing center should be constructed as one room rather than different individual rooms. The room should be away from any of the building's water pipes in case a break in a line causes a flood. The vents and ducts from the HVAC system should be protected with some type of barrier bars and should be too small for anyone to crawl through and gain access to the center. The data center must have positive air pressure, so no contaminants can be sucked into the room and into the computers' fans.

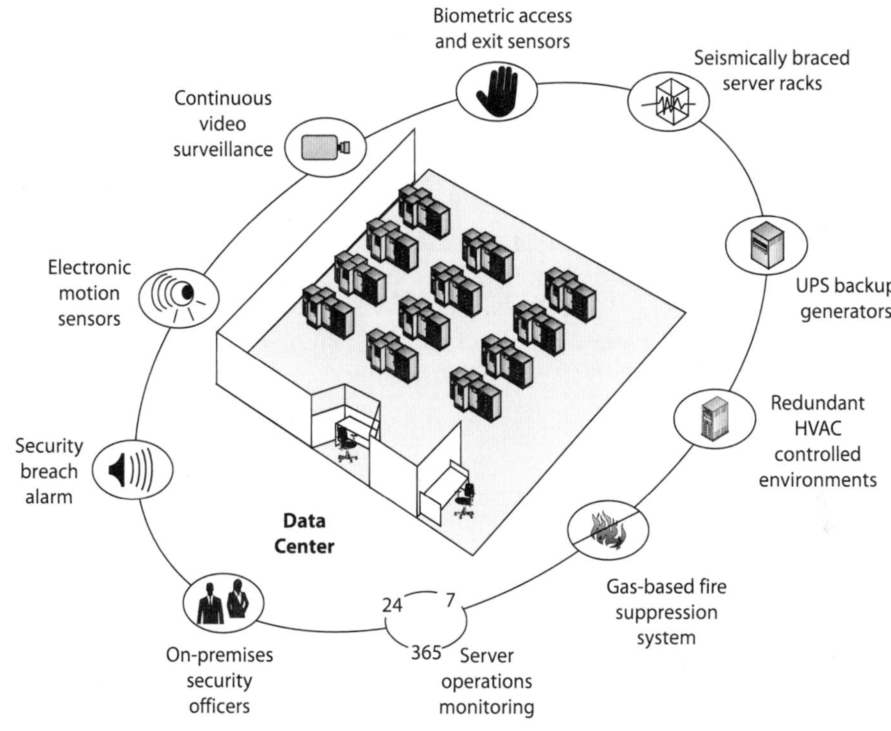

Figure 3-53 A data center should have many physical security controls.

Smoke detectors or fire sensors should be implemented, and portable fire extinguishers should be located close to the equipment and should be easy to see and access (see "Fire Prevention, Detection, and Suppression" later in the chapter for details). Water sensors should be placed under the raised floors. Since most of the wiring and cables run under the raised floors, it is important that water does not get to these places and, if it does, that an alarm sound if water is detected.

TIP If there is any type of water damage in a data center or facility, mold and mildew could easily become a problem. Instead of allowing things to "dry out on their own," many times it is better to use industry-strength dehumidifiers, water movers, and sanitizers to ensure secondary damage does not occur.

Water can cause extensive damage to equipment, flooring, walls, computers, and facility foundations. It is important that an organization be able to detect leaks and unwanted water. The detectors should be under raised floors and on dropped ceilings (to detect leaks from the floor above it). The location of the detectors should be documented and their position marked for easy access. As smoke and fire detectors should be tied to an alarm system, so should water detectors. The alarms usually just alert the necessary staff members and not everyone in the building. The staff members who are responsible for following up when an alarm sounds should be trained properly on how to reduce any potential water damage. Before anyone pokes around to see where water is or is not pooling in places it does not belong, the electricity for that particular zone of the building should be temporarily turned off.

Water detectors can help prevent damage to

- Equipment
- Flooring
- Walls
- Computers
- Facility foundations

Location of water detectors should be

- Under raised floors
- On dropped ceilings

It is important to maintain the proper temperature and humidity levels within data centers, which is why an HVAC system should be implemented specifically for this room. Too high a temperature can cause components to overheat and turn off; too low a temperature can cause the components to work more slowly. If the humidity is high, then corrosion of the computer parts can take place; if humidity is low, then static electricity can be introduced. Because of this, the data center must have its own temperature and humidity controls that are separate from those for the rest of the building.

It is best if the data center is on a different electrical system than the rest of the building, if possible. Thus, if anything negatively affects the main building's power, it will not carry over and affect the center. The data center may require redundant power supplies, which means two or more feeders coming in from two or more electrical substations. The idea is that if one of the power company's substations were to go down, the company would still be able to receive electricity from the other feeder. But just because a company has two or more electrical feeders coming into its facility does not mean true redundancy is automatically in place. Many companies have paid for two feeders to come into their building, only to find out both feeders were coming from the same substation! This defeats the whole purpose of having two feeders in the first place.

Data centers need to have their own backup power supplies, either an uninterrupted power supply (UPS) or generators. The different types of backup power supplies are discussed later in the chapter, but it is important to know at this point that the power backup must be able to support the load of the data center.

Many companies choose to use large glass panes for the walls of the data center so personnel within the center can be viewed at all times. This glass should be shatter-resistant since the window is acting as an exterior wall. The center's doors should not be hollow, but rather secure solid-core doors. Doors should open out rather than in so they don't damage equipment when opened. Best practices indicate that the door frame should be fixed to adjoining wall studs and that there should be at least three hinges per door. These characteristics would make the doors much more difficult to break down.

Protecting Assets

The main threats that physical security components combat are theft, interruptions to services, physical damage, compromised system and environment integrity, and unauthorized access.

Real loss is determined by the cost to replace the stolen items, the negative effect on productivity, the negative effect on reputation and customer confidence, fees for consultants that may need to be brought in, and the cost to restore lost data and production levels. Many times, companies just perform an inventory of their hardware and provide value estimates that are plugged into risk analysis to determine what the cost to the company would be if the equipment were stolen or destroyed. However, the information held within the equipment may be much more valuable than the equipment itself, and proper recovery mechanisms and procedures also need to be plugged into the risk assessment for a more realistic and fair assessment of cost.

Protecting Mobile Devices

Mobile device theft is increasing at incredible rates each year. Mobile devices include laptops, smartphones, and tablets. They have been stolen for years, but in the past they were stolen mainly to sell the hardware. Now mobile devices are also being stolen to gain sensitive data for identity theft crimes. What is important to understand is that this is a rampant, and potentially very dangerous, crime. Many people claim, "My whole life is on my laptop" or possibly their smartphone. Since employees use laptops as they travel, they may have extremely sensitive company or customer data on their systems that can easily fall into the wrong hands. The following list provides many of the protection mechanisms that can be used to protect mobile devices and the data they hold:

- Inventory all mobile devices, including serial numbers, so they can be properly identified if recovered.
- Harden the operating system.
- Password-protect the devices.
- Do not check mobile devices as luggage when flying.
- Never leave a mobile device unattended, and carry it in a nondescript carrying case.
- Engrave the mobile device with a symbol or number for proper identification.

- Use a slot lock with a cable to connect laptops to stationary objects.
- Back up the data from the mobile device and store it on a backup media.
- Use room safes if storing mobile devices in hotel rooms.
- Encrypt all data on mobile devices.

Tracing software can be installed so that your laptop can "phone home" if it is taken from you. Several products offer this tracing capability. Once installed and configured, the software periodically sends in a signal to a tracking center. If you report that your laptop has been stolen, the vendor of this software will work with service providers and law enforcement to track down and return your laptop.

Using Safes

A company may have need for a safe. Safes are commonly used to store backup data tapes, original contracts, or other types of valuables. The safe should be penetration-resistant and provide fire protection. The types of safes an organization can choose from are

- **Wall safe** Embedded into the wall and easily hidden
- **Floor safe** Embedded into the floor and easily hidden
- **Chests** Stand-alone safes
- **Depositories** Safes with slots, which allow the valuables to be easily slipped in
- **Vaults** Safes that are large enough to provide walk-in access

If a safe has a combination lock, it should be changed periodically, and only a small subset of people should have access to the combination or key. The safe should be in a visible location, so anyone who is interacting with the safe can be seen. The goal is to uncover any unauthorized access attempts. Some safes have passive or thermal relocking functionality. If the safe has a *passive relocking* function, it can detect when someone attempts to tamper with it, in which case extra internal bolts will fall into place to ensure it cannot be compromised. If a safe has a *thermal relocking* function, when a certain temperature is met (possibly from drilling), an extra lock is implemented to ensure the valuables are properly protected.

Internal Support Systems

Having a fortified facility with secure compartmentalized areas and protected assets is nice, but also having lights, air conditioning, and water within this facility is even better. Physical security needs to address these support services, because their malfunction or disruption could negatively affect the organization in many ways.

Although there are many incidents of various power losses here and there for different reasons (storms, hurricanes, California nearly running out of electricity), one of the most notable power losses took place in August 2003, when eight East Coast states and portions of Canada lost power for several days. There were rumors about a computer worm causing this disruption, but the official report blamed it on a software bug in GE Energy's XA/21 system. This disaster left over 50 million people without power for days, caused four nuclear power plants to be shut down, and put a lot of companies in insecure and chaotic conditions. Security professionals need to be able to help organizations handle both the small bumps in the road, such as power surges or sags, and the gigantic sinkholes, such as what happened in the United States and Canada on August 14, 2003.

Electric Power

Because computing and communication have become so essential in almost every aspect of life, power failure is a much more devastating event than it was 10 to 15 years ago. Having good plans to fall back on is crucial to ensure that a business will not be drastically affected by storms, high winds, hardware failure, lightning, or other events that can stop or disrupt power supplies. A continuous supply of electricity assures the availability of company resources; thus, a security professional must be familiar with the threats to electric power and the corresponding countermeasures.

Several types of power backup capabilities exist. Before a company chooses one, it should calculate the total cost of anticipated downtime and its effects. This information can be gathered from past records and other businesses in the same area on the same power grid. The total cost per hour for backup power is derived by dividing the annual expenditures by the annual standard hours of use.

Large and small issues can cause power failure or fluctuations. The effects manifest in variations of voltage that can last a millisecond to days. A company can pay to have two different supplies of power to reduce its risks, but this approach can be costly. Other, less expensive mechanisms are to have generators or UPSs in place. Some generators have sensors to detect power failure and will start automatically upon failure. Depending on the type and size of the generator, it might provide power for hours or days. UPSs are usually short-term solutions compared to generators.

Smart Grid

Most of our power grid today is not considered "smart." There are power plants that turn something (e.g., coal) into electricity. The electricity goes through a transmission substation, which puts the electricity on long-haul transmission lines. These lines distribute the electricity to large areas. Before the electricity gets to our home or office, it goes through a power substation and a transformer, which changes the electrical current and voltage to the proper levels, and the electricity travels over power lines (usually on poles) and connects to our buildings. So our current power grid is similar to a system of rivers and streams—electricity gets to where it needs to go without much technological intelligence involved. This "dumb" system makes it hard to identify disruptions when they happen, deal with high-peak demands, use

(Continued)

renewable energy sources, react to attacks, and deploy solutions that would make our overall energy consumption more efficient.

We are moving to smart grids, which means that there is a lot more computing software and technology embedded into the grids to optimize and automate these functions. Some of the goals of a smart grid are self-healing, resistant to physical and cyberattacks, bidirectional communication capabilities, increased efficiency, and better integration of renewable energy sources. We want our grids to be more reliable, resilient, flexible, and efficient. While all of this is wonderful and terrific, it means that almost every component of the new power grid has to be computerized in some manner (smart meters, smart thermostats, automated control software, automated feedback loops, digital scheduling and load shifting, etc.).

The actual definition of "smart grid" is nebulous because it is hard to delineate between what falls within and outside the grid's boundaries, many different technologies are involved, and it is in an immature evolutionary stage. From a security point of view, while the whole grid will be more resilient and centrally controlled, now there could be more attack vectors because most pieces will have some type of technology embedded.

In the past our telephones were "dumb," but now they are small computers, so they are "smart." The increased functionality and intelligence open the doors for more attacks on our individual smartphones. The smart grid is similar to our advances in telephony. We can secure the core infrastructure, but it is the end points that are very difficult to secure. And while telephones are important, power grids are part of every nation's critical infrastructure.

Power Protection

Protecting power can be done in three ways: through UPSs, power line conditioners, and backup sources. UPSs use battery packs that range in size and capacity. A UPS can be online or standby. *Online UPS systems* use AC line voltage to charge a bank of batteries. When in use, the UPS has an inverter that changes the DC output from the batteries into the required AC form and regulates the voltage as it powers computer devices. This conversion process is shown in Figure 3-54. Online UPS systems have the normal primary power passing through them day in and day out. They constantly provide power from their own inverters, even when the electric power is in proper use. Since the environment's electricity passes through this type of UPS all the time, the UPS device is able to quickly detect when a power failure takes place. An online UPS can provide the necessary electricity and picks up the load after a power failure much more quickly than a standby UPS.

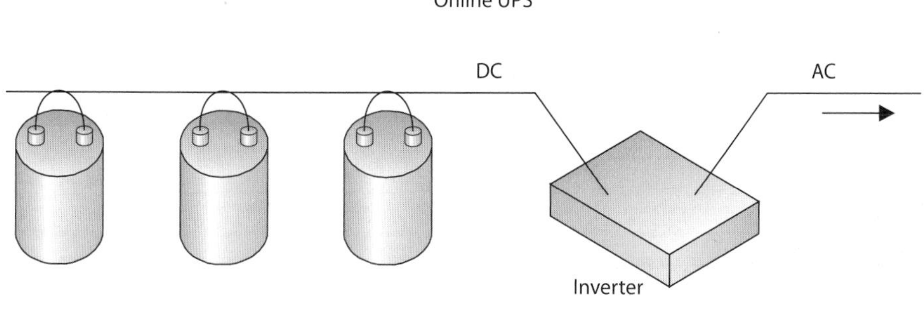

Figure 3-54 A UPS device converts DC current from its internal or external batteries to usable AC by using an inverter.

Standby UPS devices stay inactive until a power line fails. The system has sensors that detect a power failure, and the load is switched to the battery pack. The switch to the battery pack is what causes the small delay in electricity being provided. So an online UPS picks up the load much more quickly than a standby UPS, but costs more, of course.

Backup power supplies are necessary when there is a power failure and the outage will last longer than a UPS can last. Backup supplies can be a redundant line from another electrical substation or from a motor generator, and can be used to supply main power or to charge the batteries in a UPS system.

A company should identify critical systems that need protection from interrupted power supplies and then estimate how long secondary power would be needed and how much power is required per device. Some UPS devices provide just enough power to allow systems to shut down gracefully, whereas others allow the systems to run for a longer period. A company needs to determine whether systems should only have a big enough power supply to allow them to shut down properly or to keep them up and running so critical operations remain available.

Just having a generator in the closet should not give a company that warm fuzzy feeling of protection. An alternative power source should be tested periodically to make sure it works and to the extent expected. It is never good to find yourself in an emergency only to discover the generator does not work or someone forgot to buy the gas necessary to keep the thing running.

Electric Power Issues

Electric power enables us to be productive and functional in many different ways, but if it is not installed, monitored, and respected properly, it can do us great harm.

When *clean* power is being provided, the power supply contains no interference or voltage fluctuation. The possible types of interference (*line noise*) are *electromagnetic interference (EMI)* and *radio frequency interference (RFI)*, which can cause disturbance to the flow of electric power while it travels across a power line, as shown in Figure 3-55. EMI can be created by the difference between three wires: hot, neutral, and ground, and the magnetic field they create. Lightning and electrical motors can induce EMI, which could then interrupt the proper flow of electrical current as it travels over wires

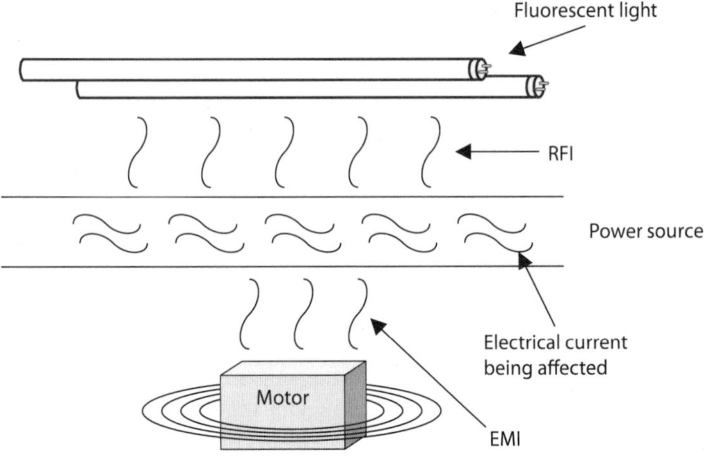

Figure 3-55 RFI and EMI can cause line noise on power lines.

to, from, and within buildings. RFI can be caused by anything that creates radio waves. Fluorescent lighting is one of the main causes of RFI within buildings today, so does that mean we need to rip out all the fluorescent lighting? That's one choice, but we could also just use shielded cabling where fluorescent lighting could cause a problem. If you take a break from your reading, climb up into your office's dropped ceiling, and look around, you would probably see wires bundled and tied up to the *true* ceiling. If your office is using fluorescent lighting, the power and data lines should not be running over, or on top of, the fluorescent lights. This is because the radio frequencies being given off can interfere with the data or power current as it travels through these wires. Now, get back down from the ceiling. We have work to do.

Interference interrupts the flow of an electrical current, and fluctuations can actually deliver a different level of voltage than what was expected. Each fluctuation can be damaging to devices and people. The following explains the different types of voltage fluctuations possible with electric power:

Power excess:

- **Spike** Momentary high voltage
- **Surge** Prolonged high voltage

Power loss:

- **Fault** Momentary power outage
- **Blackout** Prolonged, complete loss of electric power

Power degradation:

- **Sag/dip** Momentary low-voltage condition, from one cycle to a few seconds
- **Brownout** Prolonged power supply that is below normal voltage
- **In-rush current** Initial surge of current required to start a load

When an electrical device is turned on, it can draw a large amount of current, which is referred to as *in-rush current*. If the device sucks up enough current, it can cause a *sag* in the available power for surrounding devices. This could negatively affect their performance. As stated earlier, it is a good idea to have the data processing center and devices on a different electrical wiring segment from that of the rest of the facility, if possible, so the devices will not be affected by these issues. For example, if you are in a building or house without efficient wiring and you turn on a vacuum cleaner or microwave, you may see the lights quickly dim because of this in-rush current. The drain on the power supply caused by in-rush currents still happens in other environments when these types of electrical devices are used—you just might not be able to see the effects. Any type of device that would cause such a dramatic in-rush current should not be used on the same electrical segment as data processing systems.

Because these and other occurrences are common, mechanisms should be in place to detect unwanted power fluctuations and protect the integrity of your data processing environment. *Voltage regulators* and *line conditioners* can be used to ensure a clean and smooth distribution of power. The primary power runs through a regulator or conditioner. They have the capability to absorb extra current if there is a spike and to store energy to add current to the line if there is a sag. The goal is to keep the current flowing at a nice, steady level so neither motherboard components nor employees get fried.

Many data centers are constructed to take power-sensitive equipment into consideration. Because surges, sags, brownouts, blackouts, and voltage spikes frequently cause data corruption, the centers are built to provide a high level of protection against these events. Other types of environments usually are not built with these things in mind and do not provide this level of protection. Offices usually have different types of devices connected and plugged into the same outlets. Outlet strips are plugged into outlet strips, which are connected to extension cords. This causes more line noise and a reduction of voltage to each device. Figure 3-56 depicts an environment that can cause line noise, voltage problems, and possibly a fire hazard.

Figure 3-56 This configuration can cause a lot of line noise and poses a fire hazard.

Preventive Measures and Good Practices

When dealing with electric power issues, the following items can help protect devices and the environment:

- Employ surge protectors to protect from excessive current.
- Shut down devices in an orderly fashion to help avoid data loss or damage to devices due to voltage changes.
- Employ power line monitors to detect frequency and voltage amplitude changes.
- Use regulators to keep voltage steady and the power clean.
- Protect distribution panels, master circuit breakers, and transformer cables with access controls.
- Provide protection from magnetic induction through shielded lines.
- Use shielded cabling for long cable runs.
- Do not run data or power lines directly over fluorescent lights.
- Use three-prong connections or adapters if using two-prong connections.
- Do not plug outlet strips and extension cords into each other.

Environmental Issues

Improper environmental controls can cause damage to services, hardware, and lives. Interruption of some services can cause unpredicted and unfortunate results. Power, heating, ventilation, air-conditioning, and air-quality controls can be complex and contain many variables. They all need to be operating properly and to be monitored regularly.

During facility construction, the physical security team must make certain that water, steam, and gas lines have proper shutoff valves, as shown in Figure 3-57, and *positive drains*, which means their contents flow out instead of in. If there is ever a break in a main water pipe, the valve to shut off water flow must be readily accessible. Similarly, in case of fire in a building, the valve to shut off the gas lines must be readily accessible. In case of a flood, a company wants to ensure that material cannot travel up through the water pipes and into its water supply or facility. Facility, operations, and security personnel should know where these shutoff valves are, and there should be strict procedures to follow in these types of emergencies. This will help reduce the potential damage.

Most electronic equipment must operate in a climate-controlled atmosphere. Although it is important to keep the atmosphere at a proper working temperature, it is important to understand that the components within the equipment can suffer from overheating even in a climate-controlled atmosphere if the internal computer fans are not cleaned or are blocked. When devices are overheated, the components can expand and contract, which causes components to change their electronic characteristics, reducing their effectiveness or damaging the system overall.

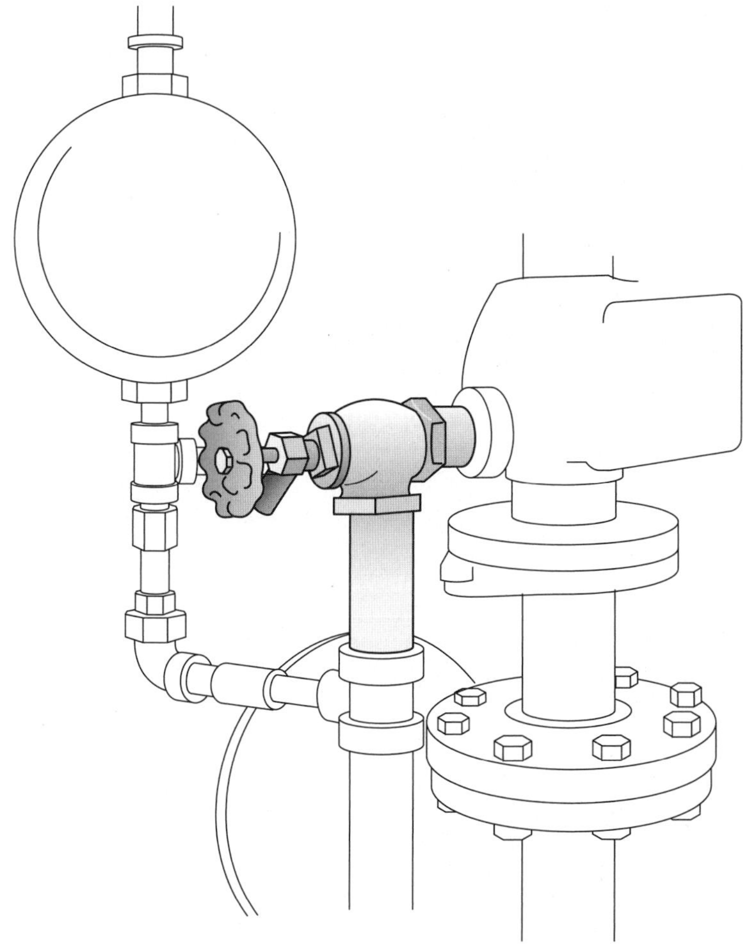

Figure 3-57 Water, steam, and gas lines should have emergency shutoff valves.

NOTE The climate issues involved with a data processing environment are why it needs its own separate HVAC system. Maintenance procedures should be documented and properly followed. HVAC activities should be recorded and reviewed annually.

Maintaining appropriate temperature and humidity is important in any facility, especially facilities with computer systems. Improper levels of either can cause damage to computers and electrical devices. High humidity can cause corrosion, and low humidity can cause excessive static electricity. This static electricity can short out devices and cause the loss of information.

Table 3-4 Components Affected by Specific Temperatures

Material or Component	Damaging Temperature
Computer systems and peripheral devices	175°F
Magnetic storage devices	100°F
Paper products	350°F

Lower temperatures can cause mechanisms to slow or stop, and higher temperatures can cause devices to use too much fan power and eventually shut down. Table 3-4 lists different components and their corresponding damaging temperature levels.

In drier climates, or during the winter, the air contains less moisture, which can cause static electricity when two dissimilar objects touch each other. This electricity usually travels through the body and produces a spark from a person's finger that can release several thousand volts. This can be more damaging than you would think. Usually the charge is released on a system casing and is of no concern, but sometimes it is released directly to an internal computer component and causes damage. People who work on the internal parts of a computer usually wear antistatic armbands to reduce the chance of this happening.

In more humid climates, or during the summer, more humidity is in the air, which can also affect components. Particles of silver can begin to move away from connectors onto copper circuits, which cement the connectors into their sockets. This can adversely affect the electrical efficiency of the connection. A *hygrometer* is usually used to monitor humidity. It can be manually read, or an automatic alarm can be set up to go off if the humidity passes a set threshold.

Fire Prevention, Detection, and Suppression

The subject of physical security would not be complete without a discussion on fire safety. A company must meet national and local standards pertaining to fire prevention, detection, and suppression methods. *Fire prevention* includes training employees on how to react properly when faced with a fire, supplying the right equipment and ensuring it is in working order, making sure there is an easily reachable fire suppression supply, and storing combustible elements in the proper manner. Fire prevention may also include using proper noncombustible construction materials and designing the facility with containment measures that provide barriers to minimize the spread of fire and smoke. These thermal or fire barriers can be made up of different types of construction material that is noncombustible and has a fire-resistant coating applied.

Fire detection response systems come in many different forms. Manual detection response systems are the red pull boxes you see on many building walls. Automatic detection response systems have sensors that react when they detect the presence of fire or smoke. We will review different types of detection systems in the next section.

Fire suppression is the use of a suppression agent to put out a fire. Fire suppression can take place manually through handheld portable extinguishers or through automated systems such as water sprinkler systems or CO_2 discharge systems. The upcoming

"Fire Suppression" section reviews the different types of suppression agents and where they are best used. Automatic sprinkler systems are widely used and highly effective in protecting buildings and their contents. When deciding upon the type of fire suppression systems to install, a company needs to evaluate many factors, including an estimate of the occurrence rate of a possible fire, the amount of damage that could result, the types of fires that would most likely take place, and the types of suppression systems to choose from.

Fire protection processes should consist of implementing early smoke or fire detection devices and shutting down systems until the source of the fire is eliminated. A warning signal may be sounded by a smoke or fire detector before the suppression agent is released so that if it is a false alarm or a small fire that can be handled without the automated suppression system, someone has time to shut down the suppression system.

Types of Fire Detection

Fires present a dangerous security threat because they can damage hardware and data and risk human life. Smoke, high temperatures, and corrosive gases from a fire can cause devastating results. It is important to evaluate the fire safety measurements of a building and the different sections within it.

A fire begins because something ignited it. Ignition sources can be failure of an electrical device, improper storage of combustible materials, carelessly discarded cigarettes, malfunctioning heating devices, and arson. A fire needs fuel (paper, wood, liquid, and so on) and oxygen to continue to burn and grow. The more fuel per square foot, the more intense the fire will become. A facility should be built, maintained, and operated to minimize the accumulation of fuels that can feed fires.

There are four classes (A, B, C, and D) of fire, which are explained in the "Fire Suppression" section. You need to know the differences between the types of fire so you know how to properly extinguish each type. Portable fire extinguishers have markings that indicate what type of fire they should be used on, as illustrated in Figure 3-58. The markings denote what types of chemicals are within the canisters and what types of fires

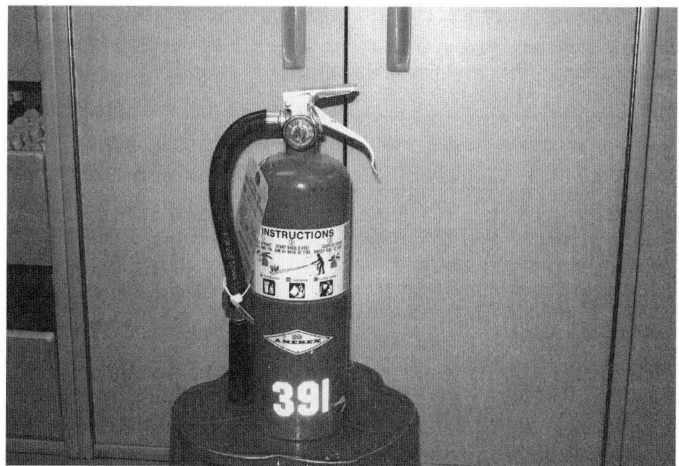

Figure 3-58 Portable extinguishers are marked to indicate what type of fire they should be used on.

they have been approved to be used on. Portable fire extinguishers should be located within 50 feet of any electrical equipment and also near exits. The extinguishers should be marked clearly, with an unobstructed view. They should be easily reachable and operational by employees and inspected quarterly.

Fire Resistance Ratings

Fire resistance ratings are the result of tests carried out in laboratories using specific configurations of environmental settings. The American Society for Testing and Materials (ASTM) is the organization that creates the standards that dictate how these tests should be performed and how to properly interpret the test results. ASTM accredited testing centers carry out the evaluations in accordance with these standards and assign fire resistance ratings that are then used in federal and state fire codes. The tests evaluate the fire resistance of different types of materials in various environmental configurations. Fire resistance represents the ability of a laboratory-constructed assembly to contain a fire for a specific period. For example, a 5/8-inch-thick drywall sheet installed on each side of a wood stud provides a one-hour rating. If the thickness of this drywall is doubled, then this would be given a two-hour rating. The rating system is used to classify different building components.

A lot of computer systems are made of components that are not combustible but that will melt or char if overheated. Most computer circuits use only 2 to 5 volts of direct current, which usually cannot start a fire. If a fire does happen in a computer room, it will most likely be an electrical fire caused by overheating of wire insulation or by overheating components that ignite surrounding plastics. Prolonged smoke usually occurs before combustion.

Several types of detectors are available, each of which works in a different way. The detector can be activated by smoke or heat.

Smoke Activated Smoke-activated detectors are good for early warning devices. They can be used to sound a warning alarm before the suppression system activates. A *photoelectric device*, also referred to as an optical detector, detects the variation in light intensity. The detector produces a beam of light across a protected area, and if the beam is obstructed, the alarm sounds. Figure 3-59 illustrates how a photoelectric device works.

Another type of photoelectric device samples the surrounding air by drawing air into a pipe. If the light source is obscured, the alarm will sound.

Heat Activated Heat-activated detectors can be configured to sound an alarm either when a predefined temperature (fixed temperature) is reached or when the temperature increases over time (rate-of-rise). Rate-of-rise temperature sensors usually provide a quicker warning than fixed-temperature sensors because they are more sensitive, but they can also cause more false alarms. The sensors can either be spaced uniformly throughout a facility or implemented in a line type of installation, which is operated by a heat-sensitive cable.

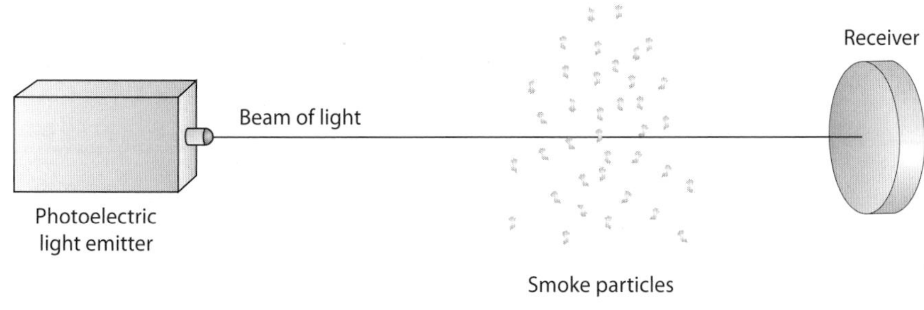

Figure 3-59 A photoelectric device uses a light emitter and a receiver.

It is not enough to have these fire and smoke detectors installed in a facility; they must be installed in the right places. Detectors should be installed both on and above suspended ceilings and raised floors because companies run many types of wires in both places that could start an electrical fire. No one would know about the fire until it broke through the floor or dropped ceiling if detectors were not placed in these areas. Detectors should also be located in enclosures and air ducts because smoke can gather in these areas before entering other spaces. It is important that people are alerted about a fire as quickly as possible so damage may be reduced, fire suppression activities may start quickly, and lives may be saved. Figure 3-60 illustrates the proper placement of smoke detectors.

Figure 3-60 Smoke detectors should be located above suspended ceilings, below raised floors, and in air vents.

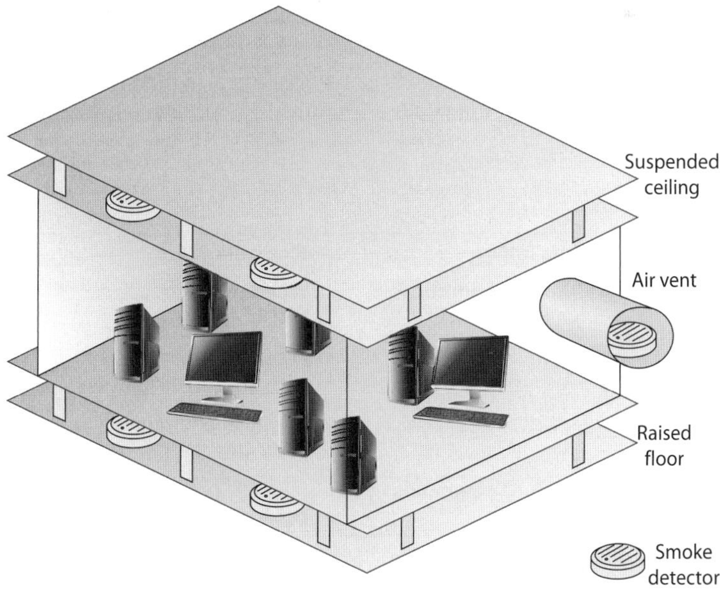

Fire Suppression

It is important to know the different types of fires and what should be done to properly suppress them. Each fire type has a rating that indicates what materials are burning. Table 3-5 shows the four types of fires and their suppression methods, which all employees should know.

You can suppress a fire in several ways, all of which require that certain precautions be taken. In many buildings, suppression agents located in different areas are designed to initiate after a specific trigger has been set off. Each agent has a zone of coverage, meaning an area that the agent supplier is responsible for. If a fire ignites within a certain zone, it is the responsibility of that suppression agent device to initiate and then suppress that fire. Different types of suppression agents available include water, foams, CO_2, and dry powders. CO_2 is good for putting out fires but bad for many types of life forms. If an organization uses CO_2, the suppression-releasing device should have a delay mechanism within it that makes sure the agent does not start applying CO_2 to the area until after an audible alarm has sounded and people have been given time to evacuate. CO_2 is a colorless, odorless substance that is potentially lethal because it removes oxygen from the air. Gas masks do not provide protection against CO_2. This type of fire suppression mechanism is best used in unattended facilities and areas.

For Class B and C fires, specific types of dry powders can be used, which include sodium or potassium bicarbonate, calcium carbonate, or monoammonium phosphate. The first three powders interrupt the chemical combustion of a fire. Monoammonium phosphate melts at low temperatures and excludes oxygen from the fuel.

Foams are mainly water-based and contain a foaming agent that allows them to float on top of a burning substance to exclude the oxygen.

TIP There is actually a Class K fire, for commercial kitchens. These fires should be put out with a wet chemical, which is usually a solution of potassium acetate. This chemical works best when putting out cooking oil fires.

Fire Class	Type of Fire	Elements of Fire	Suppression Method
A	Common combustibles	Wood products, paper, and laminates	Water, foam
B	Liquid	Petroleum products and coolants	Gas, CO_2, foam, dry powders
C	Electrical	Electrical equipment and wires	Gas, CO_2, dry powders
D	Combustible metals	Magnesium, sodium, potassium	Dry powder

Table 3-5 Four Types of Fires and Their Suppression Methods

Combustion Element	Suppression Method	How Suppression Works
Fuel	Soda acid	Removes fuel
Oxygen	Carbon dioxide	Removes oxygen
Temperature	Water	Reduces temperature
Chemical combustion	Gas—Halon substitute	Interferes with the chemical reactions between elements

Table 3-6 How Different Substances Interfere with Elements of Fire

A fire needs fuel, oxygen, and high temperatures. Table 3-6 shows how different suppression substances interfere with these elements of fire.

NOTE Halon has not been manufactured since January 1, 1992, by international agreement. The Montreal Protocol banned halon in 1987, and countries were given until 1992 to comply with these directives. The most effective replacement for halon is FM-200, which is similar to halon but does not damage the ozone.

The HVAC system should be connected to the fire alarm and suppression system so it properly shuts down if a fire is identified. A fire needs oxygen, and this type of system can feed oxygen to the fire. Plus, the HVAC system can spread deadly smoke into all areas of the building. Many fire systems can configure the HVAC system to shut down if a fire alarm is triggered.

Plenum Area

Wiring and cables are strung through *plenum areas*, such as the space above dropped ceilings, the space in wall cavities, and the space under raised floors. Plenum areas should have fire detectors. Also, only plenum-rated cabling should be used in plenum areas, which is cabling that is made out of material that does not let off hazardous gases if it burns.

Water Sprinklers

Water sprinklers typically are simpler and less expensive than FM-200 system, but can cause water damage. In an electrical fire, the water can increase the intensity of the fire because it can work as a conductor for electricity—only making the situation worse. If water is going to be used in any type of environment with electrical equipment, the electricity must be turned off before the water is released. Sensors should be used to shut down the electric power before water sprinklers activate. Each sprinkler head should activate individually to avoid wide-area damage, and there should be shutoff valves so the water supply can be stopped if necessary.

A company should take great care in deciding which suppression agent and system is best for it. Four main types of water sprinkler systems are available:

- **Wet pipe** Wet pipe systems always contain water in the pipes and are usually discharged by temperature control–level sensors. One disadvantage of wet pipe systems is that the water in the pipes may freeze in colder climates. Also, if there is a nozzle or pipe break, it can cause extensive water damage. These types of systems are also called closed-head systems.
- **Dry pipe** In dry pipe systems, the water is not actually held in the pipes. The water is contained in a "holding tank" until it is released. The pipes hold pressurized air, which is reduced when a fire or smoke alarm is activated, allowing the water valve to be opened by the water pressure. Water is not allowed into the pipes that feed the sprinklers until an actual fire is detected. First, a heat or smoke sensor is activated; then, the water fills the pipes leading to the sprinkler heads, the fire alarm sounds, the electric power supply is disconnected, and finally water is allowed to flow from the sprinklers. These pipes are best used in colder climates because the pipes will not freeze. Figure 3-61 depicts a dry pipe system.
- **Preaction** Preaction systems are similar to dry pipe systems in that the water is not held in the pipes, but is released when the pressurized air within the pipes is reduced. Once this happens, the pipes are filled with water, but it is not released right away. A thermal-fusible link on the sprinkler head has to melt before the water is released. The purpose of combining these two techniques is to give people more time to respond to false alarms or to small fires that can be handled by other means. Putting out a small fire with a handheld extinguisher is better than losing a lot of electrical equipment to water damage. These systems are usually used only in data processing environments rather than the whole building because of the higher cost of these types of systems.
- **Deluge** A deluge system has its sprinkler heads wide open to allow a larger volume of water to be released in a shorter period. Because the water being released is in such large volumes, these systems are usually not used in data processing environments.

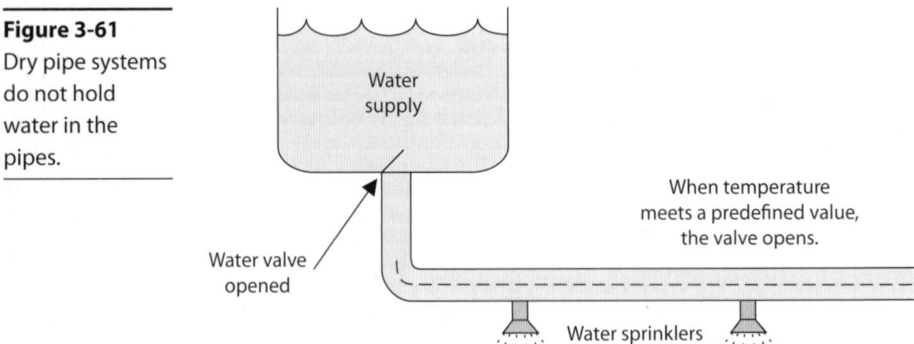
Water
supply
When temperature
meets a predefined value,
the valve opens.
Water valve
opened
Water sprinklers

Figure 3-61 Dry pipe systems do not hold water in the pipes.

Summary

Central to security engineering are the architectures of the systems and subsystems upon which we are building. The architecture of a computer system is very important and comprises many topics. The system has to ensure that memory is properly segregated and protected, ensure that only authorized subjects access objects, ensure that untrusted processes cannot perform activities that would put other processes at risk, control the flow of information, and define a domain of resources for each subject. It also must ensure that if the computer experiences any type of disruption, it will not result in an insecure state. Many of these issues are dealt with in the system's security policy.

Once the security policy and architecture have been developed, the computer operating system or product must be built, tested, evaluated, and rated. An evaluation is done by comparing the system to predefined criteria. The rating assigned to the system depends upon how it fulfills the requirements of the criteria. Customers use this rating to understand what they are really buying and how much they can trust this new product. Once the customer buys the product, it must be tested within their own environment to make sure it meets their company's needs, which takes place through certification and accreditation processes.

Cryptographic algorithms provide the underlying tools to most security protocols used in today's infrastructures. They are, therefore, an integral part of security engineering. The cryptographic algorithms work off of mathematical functions and provide various types of functionality and levels of security. A big leap was made when encryption went from purely symmetric key use to public key cryptography. This evolution provided users and maintainers much more freedom and flexibility when it came to communicating with a variety of users all over the world.

On a more local scale, every organization should develop, implement, and maintain site and facility security programs that contain the following control categories: deterrence, delay, detection, assessment, and response. It is up to the organization to determine its acceptable risk level and the specific controls required to fulfill the responsibility of each category. Physical security is not often considered when people think of organizational security and company asset protection, but real threats and risks need to be addressed and planned for. Who cares if a hacker can get through an open port on the web server if the building is burning down?

Quick Tips

- System architecture is a formal tool used to design computer systems in a manner that ensures each of the stakeholders' concerns is addressed.
- A system's architecture is made up of different views, which are representations of system components and their relationships. Each view addresses a different aspect of the system (functionality, performance, interoperability, security).
- ISO/IEC 42010 is an international standard that outlines how system architecture frameworks and their description languages are to be used.

- A CPU contains a control unit, which controls the timing of the execution of instructions and data, and an ALU, which performs mathematical functions and logical operations.
- Memory managers use various memory protection mechanisms, as in base (beginning) and limit (ending) addressing, address space layout randomization, and data execution prevention.
- Operating systems use absolute (hardware addresses), logical (indexed addresses), and relative address (indexed addresses, including offsets) memory schemes.
- Buffer overflow vulnerabilities are best addressed by implementing bounds checking.
- A garbage collector is a software tool that releases unused memory segments to help prevent "memory starvation."
- Different processor families work within different microarchitectures to execute specific instruction sets.
- Early operating systems were considered "monolithic" because all of the code worked within one layer and ran in kernel mode, and components communicated in an ad hoc manner.
- Operating systems can work within the following architectures: monolithic kernel, layered, microkernel, or hybrid kernel.
- Mode transition is when a CPU has to switch from executing one process's instructions running in user mode to another process's instructions running in kernel mode.
- CPUs provide a ringed architecture, which operating systems run within. The more trusted processes run in the lower-numbered rings and have access to all or most of the system resources. Nontrusted processes run in higher-numbered rings and have access to a smaller amount of resources.
- Operating system processes are executed in privileged mode (also called kernel or supervisor mode), and applications are executed in user mode, also known as "problem state."
- Virtual memory combines RAM and secondary storage so the system seems to have a larger bank of memory.
- The more complex a security mechanism is, the less amount of assurance it can usually provide.
- The trusted computing base (TCB) is a collection of system components that enforces the security policy directly and protects the system. These components are within the security perimeter.
- Components that make up the TCB are hardware, software, and firmware that provide some type of security protection.
- A security perimeter is an imaginary boundary that has trusted components within it (those that make up the TCB) and untrusted components outside it.

- The reference monitor concept is an abstract machine that ensures all subjects have the necessary access rights before accessing objects. Therefore, it mediates all access to objects by subjects.
- The security kernel is the mechanism that actually enforces the rules of the reference monitor concept.
- The security kernel must isolate processes carrying out the reference monitor concept, must be tamperproof, must be invoked for each access attempt, and must be small enough to be properly tested.
- Processes need to be isolated, which can be done through segmented memory addressing, encapsulation of objects, time multiplexing of shared resources, naming distinctions, and virtual mapping.
- The level of security a system provides depends upon how well it enforces its security policy.
- A closed system is often proprietary to the manufacturer or vendor, whereas an open system allows for more interoperability.
- The Common Criteria was developed to provide globally recognized evaluation criteria.
- The Common Criteria uses protection profiles, security targets, and ratings (EAL1 to EAL7) to provide assurance ratings for targets of evaluation (TOEs).
- Certification is the technical evaluation of a system or product and its security components. Accreditation is management's formal approval and acceptance of the security provided by a system.
- ISO/IEC 15408 is the international standard that is used as the basis for the evaluation of security properties of products under the CC framework.
- Process isolation ensures that multiple processes can run concurrently and the processes will not interfere with each other or affect each other's memory segments.
- TOC/TOU stands for time-of-check/time-of-use. This is a class of asynchronous attacks.
- A distributed system is a system in which multiple computing nodes, interconnected by a network, exchange information for the accomplishment of collective tasks.
- Cloud computing is the use of shared, remote computing devices for the purpose of providing improved efficiencies, performance, reliability, scalability, and security.
- Software as a Service (SaaS) is a cloud computing model that provides users access to a specific application that executes on the service provider's environment.
- Platform as a Service (PaaS) is a cloud computing model that provides users access to a computing platform that is typically built on a server operating system, but not the virtual machine on which it runs.

- Infrastructure as a Service (IaaS) is a cloud computing model that provides users unfettered access to a cloud device, such as an instance of a server, which includes both the operating system and the virtual machine on which it runs.
- Parallel computing is the simultaneous use of multiple computers to solve a specific task by dividing it among the available computers.
- Any system in which computers and physical devices collaborate via the exchange of inputs and outputs to accomplish a task or objective is a cyber-physical system.
- Cryptography is the science of protecting information by encoding it into an unreadable format.
- The most famous rotor encryption machine is the Enigma used by the Germans in World War II.
- A readable message is in a form called plaintext, and once it is encrypted, it is in a form called ciphertext.
- Cryptographic algorithms are the mathematical rules that dictate the functions of enciphering and deciphering.
- Cryptanalysis is the study of breaking cryptosystems.
- Nonrepudiation is a service that ensures the sender cannot later falsely deny sending a message.
- Key clustering is an instance in which two different keys generate the same ciphertext from the same plaintext.
- The range of possible keys is referred to as the keyspace. A larger keyspace and the full use of the keyspace allow for more random keys to be created. This provides more protection.
- The two basic types of encryption mechanisms used in symmetric ciphers are substitution and transposition. Substitution ciphers change a character (or bit) out for another, while transposition ciphers scramble the characters (or bits).
- A polyalphabetic cipher uses more than one alphabet to defeat frequency analysis.
- Steganography is a method of hiding data within another media type, such as a graphic, WAV file, or document. This method is used to hide the existence of the data.
- A key is a random string of bits inserted into an encryption algorithm. The result determines what encryption functions will be carried out on a message and in what order.
- In symmetric key algorithms, the sender and receiver use the same key for encryption and decryption purposes.
- In asymmetric key algorithms, the sender and receiver use different keys for encryption and decryption purposes.
- Symmetric key processes provide barriers of secure key distribution and scalability. However, symmetric key algorithms perform much faster than asymmetric key algorithms.

- Symmetric key algorithms can provide confidentiality, but not authentication or nonrepudiation.
- Examples of symmetric key algorithms include DES, 3DES, Blowfish, IDEA, RC4, RC5, RC6, and AES.
- Asymmetric algorithms are used to encrypt keys, and symmetric algorithms are used to encrypt bulk data.
- Asymmetric key algorithms are much slower than symmetric key algorithms, but can provide authentication and nonrepudiation services.
- Examples of asymmetric key algorithms include RSA, ECC, Diffie-Hellman, El Gamal, knapsack, and DSA.
- Two main types of symmetric algorithms are stream ciphers and block ciphers. Stream ciphers use a keystream generator and encrypt a message one bit at a time. A block cipher divides the message into groups of bits and encrypts them.
- Many algorithms are publicly known, so the secret part of the process is the key. The key provides the necessary randomization to encryption.
- Data Encryption Standard (DES) is a block cipher that divides a message into 64-bit blocks and employs S-box-type functions on them.
- Because technology has allowed the DES keyspace to be successfully broken, Triple-DES (3DES) was developed to be used instead. 3DES uses 48 rounds of computation and up to three different keys.
- International Data Encryption Algorithm (IDEA) is a symmetric block cipher with a key of 128 bits.
- RSA is an asymmetric algorithm developed by Rivest, Shamir, and Adleman and is the de facto standard for digital signatures.
- Elliptic curve cryptosystems (ECCs) are used as asymmetric algorithms and can provide digital signature, secure key distribution, and encryption functionality. They use fewer resources, which makes them better for wireless device and cell phone encryption use.
- When symmetric and asymmetric key algorithms are used together, this is called a hybrid system. The asymmetric algorithm encrypts the symmetric key, and the symmetric key encrypts the data.
- A session key is a symmetric key used by the sender and receiver of messages for encryption and decryption purposes. The session key is only good while that communication session is active and then it is destroyed.
- A public key infrastructure (PKI) is a framework of programs, procedures, communication protocols, and public key cryptography that enables a diverse group of individuals to communicate securely.
- A certificate authority (CA) is a trusted third party that generates and maintains user certificates, which hold their public keys.

- The CA uses a certification revocation list (CRL) to keep track of revoked certificates.
- A certificate is the mechanism the CA uses to associate a public key to a person's identity.
- A registration authority (RA) validates the user's identity and then sends the request for a certificate to the CA. The RA cannot generate certificates.
- A one-way function is a mathematical function that is easier to compute in one direction than in the opposite direction.
- RSA is based on a one-way function that factors large numbers into prime numbers. Only the private key knows how to use the trapdoor and how to decrypt messages that were encrypted with the corresponding public key.
- Hashing algorithms provide data integrity only.
- When a hash algorithm is applied to a message, it produces a message digest, and this value is signed with a private key to produce a digital signature.
- Some examples of hashing algorithms include SHA-1, SHA-2, SHA-3, MD4, and MD5.
- SHA produces a 160-bit hash value and is used in DSS.
- A birthday attack is an attack on hashing functions through brute force. The attacker tries to create two messages with the same hashing value.
- A one-time pad uses a pad with random values that are XORed against the message to produce ciphertext. The pad is at least as long as the message itself and is used once and then discarded.
- A digital signature is the result of a user signing a hash value with a private key. It provides authentication, data integrity, and nonrepudiation. The act of signing is the actual encryption of the value with the private key.
- Examples of algorithms used for digital signatures include RSA, El Gamal, ECDSA, and DSA.
- Key management is one of the most challenging pieces of cryptography. It pertains to creating, maintaining, distributing, and destroying cryptographic keys.
- Crime Prevention Through Environmental Design (CPTED) combines the physical environment and sociology issues that surround it to reduce crime rates and the fear of crime.
- The value of property within the facility and the value of the facility itself need to be ascertained to determine the proper budget for physical security so that security controls are cost effective.
- Some physical security controls may conflict with the safety of people. These issues need to be addressed; human life is always more important than protecting a facility or the assets it contains.
- When looking at locations for a facility, consider local crime; natural disaster possibilities; and distance to hospitals, police and fire stations, airports, and railroads.

- Exterior fencing can be costly and unsightly, but can provide crowd control and help control access to the facility.
- If interior partitions do not go all the way up to the true ceiling, an intruder can remove a ceiling tile and climb over the partition into a critical portion of the facility.
- The primary power source is what is used in day-to-day operations, and the alternative power source is a backup in case the primary source fails.
- Smoke detectors should be located on and above suspended ceilings, below raised floors, and in air ducts to provide maximum fire detection.
- A fire needs high temperatures, oxygen, and fuel. To suppress it, one or more of those items needs to be reduced or eliminated.
- Gases like FM-200 and other halon substitutes interfere with the chemical reaction of a fire.
- Portable fire extinguishers should be located within 50 feet of electrical equipment and should be inspected quarterly.
- CO_2 is a colorless, odorless, and potentially lethal substance because it removes the oxygen from the air in order to suppress fires.
- CPTED provides three main strategies, which are natural access control, natural surveillance, and natural territorial reinforcement.
- Window types that should be understood are standard, tempered, acrylic, wired, and laminated.

Questions

Please remember that these questions are formatted and asked in a certain way for a reason. Keep in mind that the CISSP exam is asking questions at a conceptual level. Questions may not always have the perfect answer, and the candidate is advised against always looking for the perfect answer. Instead, the candidate should look for the best answer in the list.

1. What is the final step in authorizing a system for use in an environment?

  A. Certification

  B. Security evaluation and rating

  C. Accreditation

  D. Verification

2. What feature enables code to be executed without the usual security checks?

  A. Temporal isolation

  B. Maintenance hook

  C. Race conditions

  D. Process multiplexing

3. If a component fails, a system should be designed to do which of the following?
   A. Change to a protected execution domain
   B. Change to a problem state
   C. Change to a more secure state
   D. Release all data held in volatile memory
4. The trusted computing base (TCB) contains which of the following?
   A. All trusted processes and software components
   B. All trusted security policies and implementation mechanisms
   C. All trusted software and design mechanisms
   D. All trusted software and hardware components
5. What is the imaginary boundary that separates components that maintain security from components that are not security related?
   A. Reference monitor
   B. Security kernel
   C. Security perimeter
   D. Security policy
6. What is the best description of a security kernel from a security point of view?
   A. Reference monitor
   B. Resource manager
   C. Memory mapper
   D. Security perimeter
7. In secure computing systems, why is there a logical form of separation used between processes?
   A. Processes are contained within their own security domains so each does not make unauthorized accesses to other processes or their resources.
   B. Processes are contained within their own security perimeter so they can only access protection levels above them.
   C. Processes are contained within their own security perimeter so they can only access protection levels equal to them.
   D. The separation is hardware and not logical in nature.
8. What type of rating is used within the Common Criteria framework?
   A. PP
   B. EPL
   C. EAL
   D. A–D

9. Which of the following is a true statement pertaining to memory addressing?

   A. The CPU uses absolute addresses. Applications use logical addresses. Relative addresses are based on a known address and an offset value.

   B. The CPU uses logical addresses. Applications use absolute addresses. Relative addresses are based on a known address and an offset value.

   C. The CPU uses absolute addresses. Applications use relative addresses. Logical addresses are based on a known address and an offset value.

   D. The CPU uses absolute addresses. Applications use logical addresses. Absolute addresses are based on a known address and an offset value.

10. Pete is a new security manager at a financial institution that develops its own internal software for specific proprietary functionality. The financial institution has several locations distributed throughout the world and has bought several individual companies over the last ten years, each with its own heterogeneous environment. Since each purchased company had its own unique environment, it has been difficult to develop and deploy internally developed software in an effective manner that meets all the necessary business unit requirements. Which of the following best describes a standard that Pete should ensure the software development team starts to implement so that various business needs can be met?

   A. ISO/IEC 42010

   B. Common Criteria

   C. ISO/IEC 43010

   D. ISO/IEC 15408

11. Which of the following is an incorrect description pertaining to the common components that make up computer systems?

   i. General registers are commonly used to hold temporary processing data, while special registers are used to hold process-characteristic data as in condition bits.

   ii. A processor sends a memory address and a "read" request down an address bus and a memory address and a "write" request down an I/O bus.

   iii. Process-to-process communication commonly takes place through memory stacks, which are made up of individually addressed buffer locations.

   iv. A CPU uses a stack return pointer to keep track of the next instruction sets it needs to process.

   A. i

   B. i, ii

   C. ii, iii

   D. ii, iv

12. Mark is a security administrator who is responsible for purchasing new computer systems for a co-location facility his company is starting up. The company has several time-sensitive applications that require extensive processing capabilities. The co-location facility is not as large as the main facility, so it can only fit a smaller number of computers, which still must carry the same processing load as the systems in the main building. Which of the following best describes the most important aspects of the products Mark needs to purchase for these purposes?
    - **A.** Systems must provide symmetric multiprocessing capabilities and virtualized environments.
    - **B.** Systems must provide asymmetric multiprocessing capabilities and virtualized environments.
    - **C.** Systems must provide multiprogramming multiprocessing capabilities and virtualized environments.
    - **D.** Systems must provide multiprogramming multiprocessing capabilities and symmetric multiprocessing environments.

Use the following scenario to answer Questions 13–14. Tom is a new security manager who is responsible for reviewing the current software that the company has developed internally. He finds that some of the software is outdated, which causes performance and functionality issues. During his testing procedures he sees that when one program stops functioning, it negatively affects other programs on the same system. He also finds out that as systems run over a period of a month, they start to perform more slowly, but by rebooting the systems this issue goes away.

13. Which of the following best describes a characteristic of the software that may be causing issues?
    - **A.** Cooperative multitasking
    - **B.** Preemptive multitasking
    - **C.** Maskable interrupt use
    - **D.** Nonmaskable interrupt use
14. Which of the following best describes why rebooting helps with system performance in the situation described in this scenario?
    - **A.** Software is not using cache memory properly.
    - **B.** Software is carrying out too many mode transitions.
    - **C.** Software is working in ring 0.
    - **D.** Software is not releasing unused memory.

Use the following scenario to answer Questions 15–17. Steve has found out that the software product that his team submitted for evaluation did not achieve the actual rating they were hoping for. He was confused about this issue since the software passed the necessary certification and accreditation processes before being deployed. Steve was told that the system allows for unauthorized device drivers to be loaded and that there was a key sequence that could be used to bypass the software access control protection mechanisms. Some feedback Steve received from the product testers is that it should implement address space layout randomization and data execution protection.

15. Which of the following best describes Steve's confusion?
    - A. Certification must happen first before the evaluation process can begin.
    - B. Accreditation is the acceptance from management, which must take place before the evaluation process.
    - C. Evaluation, certification, and accreditation are carried out by different groups with different purposes.
    - D. Evaluation requirements include certification and accreditation components.
16. Which of the following best describes an item the software development team needs to address to ensure that drivers cannot be loaded in an unauthorized manner?
    - A. Improved security kernel processes
    - B. Improved security perimeter processes
    - C. Improved application programming interface processes
    - D. Improved garbage collection processes
17. Which of the following best describes some of the issues that the evaluation testers most likely ran into while testing the submitted product?
    - A. Nonprotected ROM sections
    - B. Vulnerabilities that allowed malicious code to execute in protected memory sections
    - C. Lack of a predefined and implemented trusted computing base
    - D. Lack of a predefined and implemented security kernel
18. John has been told that one of the applications installed on a web server within the DMZ accepts any length of information that a customer using a web browser inputs into the form the web server provides to collect new customer data. Which of the following describes an issue that John should be aware of pertaining to this type of vulnerability?
    - A. Application is written in the C programming language.
    - B. Application is not carrying out enforcement of the trusted computing base.
    - C. Application is running in ring 3 of a ring-based architecture.
    - D. Application is not interacting with the memory manager properly.
19. What is the goal of cryptanalysis?
    - A. To determine the strength of an algorithm
    - B. To increase the substitution functions in a cryptographic algorithm

C. To decrease the transposition functions in a cryptographic algorithm

D. To determine the permutations used

20. Why has the frequency of successful brute-force attacks increased?

A. The use of permutations and transpositions in algorithms has increased.

B. As algorithms get stronger, they get less complex, and thus more susceptible to attacks.

C. Processor speed and power have increased.

D. Key length reduces over time.

21. Which of the following is not a property or characteristic of a one-way hash function?

A. It converts a message of arbitrary length into a value of fixed length.

B. Given the digest value, it should be computationally infeasible to find the corresponding message.

C. It should be impossible or rare to derive the same digest from two different messages.

D. It converts a message of fixed length to an arbitrary length value.

22. What would indicate that a message had been modified?

A. The public key has been altered.

B. The private key has been altered.

C. The message digest has been altered.

D. The message has been encrypted properly.

23. Which of the following is a U.S. federal government algorithm developed for creating secure message digests?

A. Data Encryption Algorithm

B. Digital Signature Standard

C. Secure Hash Algorithm

D. Data Signature Algorithm

24. Which of the following best describes the difference between HMAC and CBC-MAC?

A. HMAC creates a message digest and is used for integrity; CBC-MAC is used to encrypt blocks of data for confidentiality.

B. HMAC uses a symmetric key and a hashing algorithm; CBC-MAC uses the first block for the checksum.

C. HMAC provides integrity and data origin authentication; CBC-MAC uses a block cipher for the process of creating a MAC.

D. HMAC encrypts a message with a symmetric key and then puts the result through a hashing algorithm; CBC-MAC encrypts the whole message.

25. What is an advantage of RSA over DSA?
    - A. It can provide digital signature and encryption functionality.
    - B. It uses fewer resources and encrypts faster because it uses symmetric keys.
    - C. It is a block cipher rather than a stream cipher.
    - D. It employs a one-time encryption pad.
26. What is used to create a digital signature?
    - A. The receiver's private key
    - B. The sender's public key
    - C. The sender's private key
    - D. The receiver's public key
27. Which of the following best describes a digital signature?
    - A. A method of transferring a handwritten signature to an electronic document
    - B. A method to encrypt confidential information
    - C. A method to provide an electronic signature and encryption
    - D. A method to let the receiver of the message prove the source and integrity of a message
28. How many bits make up the effective length of the DES key?
    - A. 56
    - B. 64
    - C. 32
    - D. 16
29. Why would a certificate authority revoke a certificate?
    - A. If the user's public key has become compromised
    - B. If the user changed over to using the PEM model that uses a web of trust
    - C. If the user's private key has become compromised
    - D. If the user moved to a new location
30. What does DES stand for?
    - A. Data Encryption System
    - B. Data Encryption Standard
    - C. Data Encoding Standard
    - D. Data Encryption Signature

31. Which of the following best describes a certificate authority?
    - A. An organization that issues private keys and the corresponding algorithms
    - B. An organization that validates encryption processes
    - C. An organization that verifies encryption keys
    - D. An organization that issues certificates
32. What does DEA stand for?
    - A. Data Encoding Algorithm
    - B. Data Encoding Application
    - C. Data Encryption Algorithm
    - D. Digital Encryption Algorithm
33. Who was involved in developing the first public key algorithm?
    - A. Adi Shamir
    - B. Ross Anderson
    - C. Bruce Schneier
    - D. Martin Hellman
34. What process usually takes place after creating a DES session key?
    - A. Key signing
    - B. Key escrow
    - C. Key clustering
    - D. Key exchange
35. DES performs how many rounds of transposition/permutation and substitution?
    - A. 16
    - B. 32
    - C. 64
    - D. 56
36. Which of the following is a true statement pertaining to data encryption when it is used to protect data?
    - A. It verifies the integrity and accuracy of the data.
    - B. It requires careful key management.
    - C. It does not require much system overhead in resources.
    - D. It requires keys to be escrowed.

37. If different keys generate the same ciphertext for the same message, what is this called?
    A. Collision
    B. Secure hashing
    C. MAC
    D. Key clustering
38. What is the definition of an algorithm's work factor?
    A. The time it takes to encrypt and decrypt the same plaintext
    B. The time it takes to break the encryption
    C. The time it takes to implement 16 rounds of computation
    D. The time it takes to apply substitution functions
39. What is the primary purpose of using one-way hashing on user passwords?
    A. It minimizes the amount of primary and secondary storage needed to store passwords.
    B. It prevents anyone from reading passwords in plaintext.
    C. It avoids excessive processing required by an asymmetric algorithm.
    D. It prevents replay attacks.
40. Which of the following is based on the fact that it is hard to factor large numbers into two original prime numbers?
    A. ECC
    B. RSA
    C. DES
    D. Diffie-Hellman
41. Which of the following describes the difference between the Data Encryption Standard and the Rivest-Shamir-Adleman algorithm?
    A. DES is symmetric, while RSA is asymmetric.
    B. DES is asymmetric, while RSA is symmetric.
    C. They are hashing algorithms, but RSA produces a 160-bit hashing value.
    D. DES creates public and private keys, while RSA encrypts messages.
42. Which of the following uses a symmetric key and a hashing algorithm?
    A. HMAC
    B. Triple-DES
    C. ISAKMP-OAKLEY
    D. RSA

43. The generation of keys that are made up of random values is referred to as Key Derivation Functions (KDFs). What values are not commonly used in this key generation process?
    A. Hashing values
    B. Asymmetric values
    C. Salts
    D. Passwords
44. When should a Class C fire extinguisher be used instead of a Class A fire extinguisher?
    A. When electrical equipment is on fire
    B. When wood and paper are on fire
    C. When a combustible liquid is on fire
    D. When the fire is in an open area
45. Which of the following is not a main component of CPTED?
    A. Natural access control
    B. Natural surveillance
    C. Territorial reinforcement
    D. Target hardening
46. Which problems may be caused by humidity in an area with electrical devices?
    A. High humidity causes excess electricity, and low humidity causes corrosion.
    B. High humidity causes corrosion, and low humidity causes static electricity.
    C. High humidity causes power fluctuations, and low humidity causes static electricity.
    D. High humidity causes corrosion, and low humidity causes power fluctuations.
47. What does positive pressurization pertaining to ventilation mean?
    A. When a door opens, the air comes in.
    B. When a fire takes place, the power supply is disabled.
    C. When a fire takes place, the smoke is diverted to one room.
    D. When a door opens, the air goes out.
48. Which of the following answers contains a category of controls that does not belong in a physical security program?
    A. Deterrence and delaying
    B. Response and detection
    C. Assessment and detection
    D. Delaying and lighting

Answers

1. **C.** Certification is a technical review of a product, and accreditation is management's formal approval of the findings of the certification process. This question asked you which step was the final step in authorizing a system before it is used in an environment, and that is what accreditation is all about.
2. **B.** Maintenance hooks get around the system's or application's security and access control checks by allowing whoever knows the key sequence to access the application and most likely its code. Maintenance hooks should be removed from any code before it gets into production.
3. **C.** The state machine model dictates that a system should start up securely, carry out secure state transitions, and even fail securely. This means that if the system encounters something it deems unsafe, it should change to a more secure state for self-preservation and protection.
4. **D.** The TCB contains and controls all protection mechanisms within the system, whether they are software, hardware, or firmware.
5. **C.** The security perimeter is a boundary between items that are within the TCB and items that are outside the TCB. It is just a mark of delineation between these two groups of items.
6. **A.** The security kernel is a portion of the operating system's kernel and enforces the rules outlined in the reference monitor. It is the enforcer of the rules and is invoked each time a subject makes a request to access an object.
7. **A.** Processes are assigned their own variables, system resources, and memory segments, which make up their domain. This is done so they do not corrupt each other's data or processing activities.
8. **C.** The Common Criteria uses a different assurance rating system than the previously used criteria. It has packages of specifications that must be met for a product to obtain the corresponding rating. These ratings and packages are called Evaluation Assurance Levels (EALs). Once a product achieves any type of rating, customers can view this information on an Evaluated Products List (EPL).
9. **A.** The physical memory addresses that the CPU uses are called absolute addresses. The indexed memory addresses that software uses are referred to as logical addresses. A relative address is a logical address that incorporates the correct offset value.
10. **A.** ISO/IEC 42010 is an international standard that outlines specifications for system architecture frameworks and architecture languages. It allows for systems to be developed in a manner that addresses all of the stakeholder's concerns.
11. **D.** A processer sends a memory address and a "read" request down an address bus. The system reads data from that memory address and puts the requested data on the data bus. A CPU uses a program counter to keep track of the memory addresses containing the instruction sets it needs to process in sequence. A stack pointer is a component used within memory stack communication processes. An I/O bus is used by a peripheral device.

12. **B.** When systems provide asymmetric multiprocessing, this means multiple CPUs can be used for processing. Asymmetric indicates the capability of assigning specific applications to one CPU so that they do not have to share computing capabilities with other competing processes, which increases performance. Since a smaller number of computers can fit in the new location, virtualization should be deployed to allow for several different systems to share the same physical computer platforms.
13. **A.** Cooperative multitasking means that a developer of an application has to properly code his software to release system resources when the application is finished using them, or the other software running on the system could be negatively affected. In this type of situation an application could be poorly coded and not release system resources, which would negatively affect other software running on the system. In a preemptive multitasking environment, the operating system would have more control of system resource allocation and provide more protection for these types of situations.
14. **D.** When software is poorly written, it could be allocating memory and not properly releasing it. This can affect the performance of the whole system, since all software processes have to share a limited supply of memory. When a system is rebooted, the memory allocation constructs are reset.
15. **C.** Evaluation, certification, and accreditation are carried out by different groups with different purposes. Evaluations are carried out by qualified third parties who use specific evaluation criteria (e.g., Common Criteria) to assign an assurance rating to a tested product. A certification process is a technical review commonly carried out internally to an organization, and accreditation is management's formal acceptance that is carried out after the certification process. A system can be certified internally by a company and not pass an evaluation testing process because they are completely different things.
16. **A.** If device drivers can be loaded improperly, then either the access control rules outlined within the reference monitor need to be improved upon or the current rules need to be better enforced through the security kernel processes. Only authorized subjects should be able to install sensitive software components that run within ring 0 of a system.
17. **B.** If testers suggested to the team that address space layout randomization and data execution protection should be integrated, this is most likely because the system allows for malicious code to easily execute in memory sections that would be dangerous to the system. These are both memory protection approaches.
18. **A.** The C language is susceptible to buffer overflow attacks because it allows for direct pointer manipulations to take place. Specific commands can provide access to low-level memory addresses without carrying out bounds checking.
19. **A.** Cryptanalysis is the process of trying to reverse-engineer a cryptosystem, with the possible goal of uncovering the key used. Once this key is uncovered, all other messages encrypted with this key can be accessed. Cryptanalysis is carried out by the white hats to test the strength of the algorithm.

20. **C.** A brute-force attack is resource-intensive. It tries all values until the correct one is obtained. As computers have more powerful processors added to them, attackers can carry out more powerful brute-force attacks.

21. **D.** A hashing algorithm will take a string of variable length (the message can be any size) and compute a fixed-length value. The fixed-length value is the message digest. The MD family creates the fixed-length value of 128 bits, and SHA creates one of 160 bits.

22. **C.** Hashing algorithms generate message digests to detect whether modification has taken place. The sender and receiver independently generate their own digests, and the receiver compares these values. If they differ, the receiver knows the message has been altered.

23. **C.** SHA was created to generate secure message digests. Digital Signature Standard (DSS) is the standard to create digital signatures, which dictates that SHA must be used. DSS also outlines the digital signature algorithms that can be used with SHA: RSA, DSA, and ECDSA.

24. **C.** In an HMAC operation, a message is concatenated with a symmetric key and the result is put through a hashing algorithm. This provides integrity and system or data authentication. CBC-MAC uses a block cipher to create a MAC, which is the last block of ciphertext.

25. **A.** RSA can be used for data encryption, key exchange, and digital signatures. DSA can be used only for digital signatures.

26. **C.** A digital signature is a message digest that has been encrypted with the sender's private key. A sender, or anyone else, should never have access to the receiver's private key.

27. **D.** A digital signature provides authentication (knowing who really sent the message), integrity (because a hashing algorithm is involved), and nonrepudiation (the sender cannot deny sending the message).

28. **A.** DES has a key size of 64 bits, but 8 bits are used for parity, so the true key size is 56 bits. Remember that DEA is the algorithm used for the DES standard, so DEA also has a true key size of 56 bits, because we are actually talking about the same algorithm here. DES is really the standard, and DEA is the algorithm.

29. **C.** The reason a certificate is revoked is to warn others who use that person's public key that they should no longer trust the public key because, for some reason, that public key is no longer bound to that particular individual's identity. This could be because an employee left the company or changed his name and needed a new certificate, but most likely it is because the person's private key was compromised.

30. **B.** Data Encryption Standard was developed by NIST and the NSA to encrypt sensitive but unclassified government data.

31. **D.** A registration authority (RA) accepts a person's request for a certificate and verifies that person's identity. Then the RA sends this request to a certificate authority (CA), which generates and maintains the certificate.

32. **C.** DEA is the algorithm that fulfilled the DES standard. So DEA has all of the attributes of DES: a symmetric block cipher that uses 64-bit blocks, 16 rounds, and a 56-bit key.

33. **D.** The first released public key cryptography algorithm was developed by Whitfield Diffie and Martin Hellman.

34. **D.** After a session key has been created, it must be exchanged securely. In most cryptosystems, an asymmetric key (the receiver's public key) is used to encrypt this session key, and it is sent to the receiver.

35. **A.** DES carries out 16 rounds of mathematical computation on each 64-bit block of data it is responsible for encrypting. A round is a set of mathematical formulas used for encryption and decryption processes.

36. **B.** Data encryption always requires careful key management. Most algorithms are so strong today that it is much easier to go after key management than to launch a brute-force attack. Hashing algorithms are used for data integrity, encryption does require a good amount of resources, and keys do not have to be escrowed for encryption.

37. **D.** Message A was encrypted with key A and the result is ciphertext Y. If that same message A were encrypted with key B, the result should not be ciphertext Y. The ciphertext should be different because a different key was used. But if the ciphertext is the same, this occurrence is referred to as key clustering.

38. **B.** The work factor of a cryptosystem is the amount of time and resources necessary to break the cryptosystem or its encryption process. The goal is to make the work factor so high that an attacker could not be successful in breaking the algorithm or cryptosystem.

39. **B.** Passwords are usually run through a one-way hashing algorithm so the actual password is not transmitted across the network or stored on a system in plaintext. This greatly reduces the risk of an attacker being able to obtain the actual password.

40. **B.** The RSA algorithm's security is based on the difficulty of factoring large numbers into their original prime numbers. This is a one-way function. It is easier to calculate the product than it is to identify the prime numbers used to generate that product.

41. **A.** DES is a symmetric algorithm. RSA is an asymmetric algorithm. DES is used to encrypt data, and RSA is used to create public/private key pairs.

42. **A.** When an HMAC function is used, a symmetric key is combined with the message, and then that result is put though a hashing algorithm. The result is an HMAC value. HMAC provides data origin authentication and data integrity.

43. **B.** Different values can be used independently or together to play the role of random key material. The algorithm is created to use specific hash, password, and\or salt value, which will go through a certain number of rounds of mathematical functions dictated by the algorithm.

44. **A.** A Class C fire is an electrical fire. Thus, an extinguisher with the proper suppression agent should be used. The following table shows the fire types, their attributes, and suppression methods:

Fire Class	Type of Fire	Elements of Fire	Suppression Method
A	Common combustibles	Wood products, paper, and laminates	Water, foam
B	Liquid	Petroleum products and coolants	Gas, CO_2, foam, dry powders
C	Electrical	Electrical equipment and wires	Gas, CO_2, dry powders
D	Combustible metals	Magnesium, sodium, potassium	Dry powder

45. **D.** Natural access control is the use of the environment to control access to entry points, such as using landscaping and bollards. An example of natural surveillance is the construction of pedestrian walkways so there is a clear line of sight of all the activities in the surroundings. Territorial reinforcement gives people a sense of ownership of a property, giving them a greater tendency to protect it. These concepts are all parts of CPTED. Target hardening has to do with implementing locks, security guards, and proximity devices.

46. **B.** High humidity can cause corrosion, and low humidity can cause excessive static electricity. Static electricity can short out devices or cause loss of information.

47. **D.** Positive pressurization means that when someone opens a door, the air goes out, and outside air does not come in. If a facility were on fire and the doors were opened, positive pressure would cause the smoke to go out instead of being pushed back into the building.

48. **D.** The categories of controls that should make up any physical security program are deterrence, delaying, detection, assessment, and response. Lighting is a control itself, not a category of controls.

CHAPTER 4

Communication and Network Security

This chapter presents the following:

- OSI and TCP/IP models
- Protocol types and security issues
- LAN, WAN, MAN, intranet, and extranet technologies
- Cable types and data transmission types
- Network devices and services
- Communications security management
- Telecommunications devices and technologies
- Remote connectivity technologies
- Wireless technologies
- Network encryption
- Threats and attacks
- Software-defined routing
- Content distribution networks
- Multilayer protocols
- Convergent network technologies

The Internet… it's a series of tubes.

—Ted Stevens

Telecommunications and networking use various mechanisms, devices, software, and protocols that are interrelated and integrated. Networking is one of the more complex topics in the computer field, mainly because so many technologies are involved and are evolving. Our current technologies are constantly evolving, and every month there seems to be new "emerging" technologies that we have to learn, understand, implement, and secure. A network administrator must know how to configure networking software, protocols and services, and devices; deal with interoperability issues; install, configure, and interface with telecommunications software and devices; and troubleshoot effectively. A security professional must understand these issues and be able to analyze them a few levels deeper to recognize fully where vulnerabilities can arise within each of these components and then know what to do about them. This can be a challenging task. However, if you are knowledgeable, have a solid practical skill set, and are willing to continue to learn, you can have more career opportunities than you know what to do with.

While almost every country in the world has had to deal with hard economic times, one industry that has not been greatly affected by the downward economies is information security. Organizations and government agencies do not have a large enough pool of people with the necessary skill set to hire from, and the attacks against these entities are only increasing and becoming more critical. Security is a good business to be in, if you are truly knowledgeable, skilled, and disciplined.

Ten years ago, it seemed possible to understand a network and everything that resided within it. As technology grew in importance in every aspect of our lives over the years, however, almost every component that made up a traditional network grew in complexity. We still need to know the basics (routers, firewalls, TCP/IP protocols, cabling, switching technologies, etc.), but now we also need to understand data loss prevention, web and e-mail security, mobile technologies, antimalware products, virtualization, cloud computing, endpoint security solutions, radio-frequency identification (RFID), virtual private network protocols, social networking threats, wireless technologies, continuous monitoring capabilities, and more. Our society has come up with so many different real-time communication technologies (instant messaging, IP telephony, video conferencing, SMS, etc.), we had to develop unified communication models to allow for interoperability and optimization. The IEEE (Institute of Electrical and Electronics Engineers) standards that define various editions and components of wireless local area network (WLAN) technologies have gone through the whole alphabet (802.11a, 802.11b, 802.11c, 802.11d, 802.11e, 802.11f, etc.) and we have had to start doubling up on our letters, as in IEEE 802.11ac. Mobile communication technology has gone from 1G to 4G, with some half G's in between (2.5G, 3.5G). And as the technology increases in complexity and the attackers become more determined and creative, we need to understand not only basic attack types (buffer overflows, fragmentation attacks, DoS, viruses, social engineering), but also the more advanced attack types (client-side, injection, fuzzing, pointer manipulation, cache poisoning, etc.).

A network used to be a construct with boundaries, but today most environments do not have clear-cut boundaries. Most communication gadgets are some type of computer (smartphones, tablets, medical devices and appliances, etc.) and these devices do not stay within the walls of an office as people hit the road, telecommute, and work from virtual offices. The increased use of outsourcing also increases the boundaries of our traditional networks and with so many entities needing access, the boundaries are commonly porous in nature.

As our technologies continue to explode with complexity, the threats of compromise from attackers continue to increase—not just in volume but in criticality. Today's attackers are commonly part of organized crime rings or funded by nation-states (and sometimes both). This means that the attackers are trained, organized, and very focused. Various ways of stealing funds (siphoning, identity theft, money mules, carding) are rampant; stealing intellectual property is continuously on the rise, and cyber warfare is becoming more well known. When the Stuxnet worm negatively affected Iran's uranium enrichment infrastructure in 2010 and was widely reported in the news, the world became more aware of what malware is capable of.

Today's security professional needs to understand many things on many different levels because the world of technology is only getting more complex and the risks are only increasing. In this chapter we will start with the basics of networking and telecommunications and build upon them and identify many of the security issues that are involved.

Telecommunications

Telecommunications is the electromagnetic transmission of data among systems, whether through analog, digital, or wireless transmission types. The data can flow through copper wires; coaxial cable; airwaves; the telephone company's public-switched telephone network (PSTN); and a service provider's fiber cables, switches, and routers. Definitive lines exist between the media used for transmission, the technologies, the protocols, and whose equipment is being used. However, the definitive lines get blurry when one follows how data created on a user's workstation flows within seconds through a complex path of Ethernet cables, to a router that divides the company's network and the rest of the world, through the Asynchronous Transfer Mode (ATM) switch provided by the service provider, to the many switches the packets traverse throughout the ATM cloud, on to another company's network, through its router, and to another user's workstation. Each piece is interesting, but when they are all integrated and work together, it is awesome.

Telecommunications usually refers to telephone systems, service providers, and carrier services. Most telecommunications systems are regulated by governments and international organizations. In the United States, the Federal Communications Commission (FCC) regulates telecommunications systems, which includes voice and data transmissions. In Canada, Industry Canada regulates telecommunications systems through the Spectrum, Information Technologies and Telecommunications (SITT) service standard. Globally, organizations develop policies, recommend standards, and work together to provide standardization and the capability for different technologies to properly interact.

The main standards organizations are the International Telecommunication Union (ITU) and the International Standards Organization (ISO). Their models and standards have shaped our technology today, and the technological issues governed by these organizations are addressed throughout this chapter.

Open Systems Interconnection Reference Model

ISO is a worldwide federation that works to provide international standards. In the early 1980s, ISO worked to develop a protocol set that would be used by all vendors throughout the world to allow the interconnection of network devices. This movement was fueled with the hopes of ensuring that all vendor products and technologies could communicate and interact across international and technical boundaries. The actual protocol set did not catch on as a standard, but the model of this protocol set, the *Open Systems Interconnection (OSI) reference model*, was adopted and is used as an abstract framework to which most operating systems and protocols adhere.

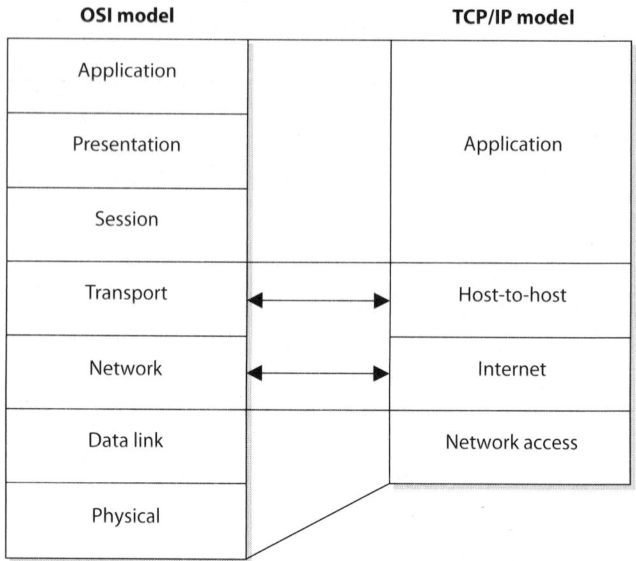

Figure 4-1 The OSI and TCP/IP networking models

Many people think that the OSI reference model arrived at the beginning of the computing age as we know it and helped shape and provide direction for many, if not all, networking technologies. However, this is not true. In fact, it was introduced in 1984, at which time the basics of the Internet had already been developed and implemented, and the basic Internet protocols had been in use for many years. The Transmission Control Protocol/Internet Protocol (TCP/IP) suite actually has its own model that is often used today when examining and understanding networking issues. Figure 4-1 shows the differences between the OSI and TCP/IP networking models. In this chapter, we will focus more on the OSI model.

NOTE The host-to-host layer is sometimes called the transport layer in the TCP/IP model. The application layer in the TCP/IP architecture model is equivalent to a combination of the application, presentation, and session layers in the OSI model.

Protocol

A network protocol is a standard set of rules that determines how systems will communicate across networks. Two different systems that use the same protocol can communicate and understand each other despite their differences, similar to how two people can communicate and understand each other by using the same language.

The OSI reference model, as described by ISO Standard 7498-1, provides important guidelines used by vendors, engineers, developers, and others. The model segments the networking tasks, protocols, and services into different layers. Each layer has its own responsibilities regarding how two computers communicate over a network. Each layer has certain functionalities, and the services and protocols that work within that layer fulfill them.

The OSI model's goal is to help others develop products that will work within an open network architecture. An *open network* architecture is one that no vendor owns, that is not proprietary, and that can easily integrate various technologies and vendor implementations of those technologies. Vendors have used the OSI model as a jumping-off point for developing their own networking frameworks. These vendors use the OSI model as a blueprint and develop their own protocols and services to produce functionality that is different from, or overlaps, that of other vendors. However, because these vendors use the OSI model as their starting place, integration of other vendor products is an easier task, and the interoperability issues are less burdensome than if the vendors had developed their own networking framework from scratch.

Although computers communicate in a physical sense (electronic signals are passed from one computer over a wire to the other computer), they also communicate through logical channels. Each protocol at a specific OSI layer on one computer communicates with a corresponding protocol operating at the same OSI layer on another computer. This happens through *encapsulation*.

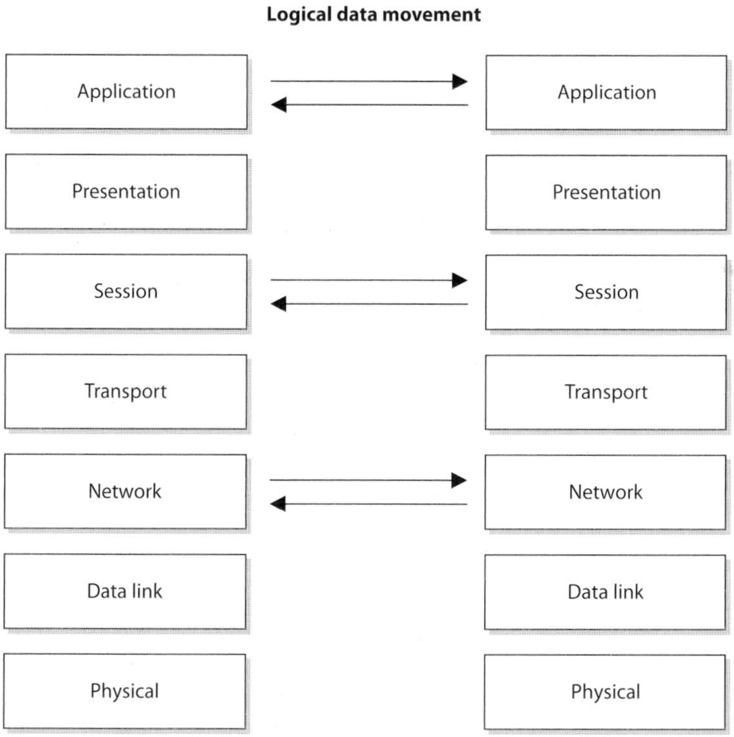

Logical data movement

Application	⇄	Application
Presentation		Presentation
Session	⇄	Session
Transport		Transport
Network	⇄	Network
Data link		Data link
Physical		Physical

Here's how encapsulation works: A message is constructed within a program on one computer and is then passed down through the network protocol's stack. A protocol at each layer adds its own information to the message; thus, the message grows in size as it goes down the protocol stack. The message is then sent to the destination computer, and the encapsulation is reversed by taking the packet apart through the same steps used by the source computer that encapsulated it. At the data link layer, only the information pertaining to the data link layer is extracted, and the message is sent up to the next layer. Then at the network layer, only the network layer data is stripped and processed, and the packet is again passed up to the next layer, and so on. This is how computers communicate logically. The information stripped off at the destination computer informs it how to interpret and process the packet properly. Data encapsulation is shown in Figure 4-2.

A protocol at each layer has specific responsibilities and control functions it performs, as well as data format syntaxes it expects. Each layer has a special interface (connection point) that allows it to interact with three other layers: (1) communications from the interface of the layer above it, (2) communications to the interface of the layer below it, and (3) communications with the same layer in the interface of the target packet address. The control functions, added by the protocols at each layer, are in the form of headers and trailers of the packet.

The benefit of modularizing these layers, and the functionality within each layer, is that various technologies, protocols, and services can interact with each other and provide the proper interfaces to enable communications. This means a computer can use an application protocol developed by Novell, a transport protocol developed by Apple, and a data link protocol developed by IBM to construct and send a message over a network. The protocols, technologies, and computers that operate within the OSI model are considered *open systems*. Open systems are capable of communicating with other open systems because they implement international standard protocols and interfaces.

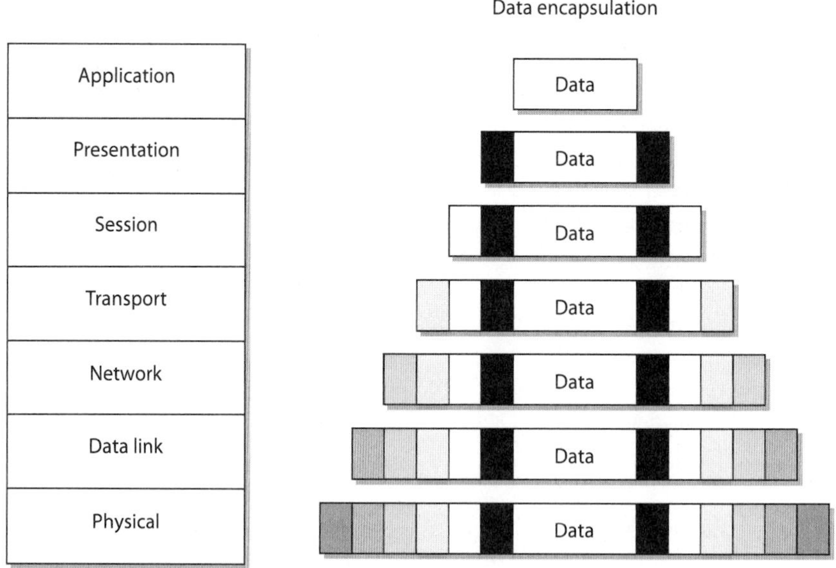

Figure 4-2 Each OSI layer protocol adds its own information to the data packet.

The specification for each layer's interface is very structured, while the actual code that makes up the internal part of the software layer is not defined. This makes it easy for vendors to write plug-ins in a modularized manner. Systems are able to integrate the plug-ins into the network stack seamlessly, gaining the vendor-specific extensions and functions.

Understanding the functionalities that take place at each OSI layer and the corresponding protocols that work at those layers helps you understand the overall communication process between computers. Once you understand this process, a more detailed look at each protocol will show you the full range of options each protocol provides and the security weaknesses embedded into each of those options.

Attacks at Different Layers

As we examine the different layers of a common network stack, we will also look at the specific attack types that can take place at each layer. One concept to understand at this point is that a network can be used as a *channel for an attack*, or the network can be the *target of an attack*. If the network is a channel for an attack, this means the attacker is using the network as a resource. For example, when an attacker sends a virus from one system to another system, the virus travels through the network channel. If an attacker carries out a denial-of-service (DoS) attack, which sends a large amount of bogus traffic over a network link to bog it down, then the network itself is the target. As you will see throughout this chapter, it is important to understand how attacks take place and where they take place so that the correct countermeasures can be put into place.

Application Layer

The *application layer*, layer 7, works closest to the user and provides file transmissions, message exchanges, terminal sessions, and much more. This layer does not include the actual applications, but rather the protocols that support the applications. When an application needs to send data over the network, it passes instructions and the data to the protocols that support it at the application layer. This layer processes and properly formats the data and passes it down to the next layer within the OSI model. This happens until the data the application layer constructed contains the essential information from each layer necessary to transmit the data over the network. The data is then put on the network cable and transmitted until it arrives at the destination computer.

As an analogy, let's say that you write a letter that you would like to send to your congressman. Your job is to write the letter, your clerk's job is to figure out how to get it to him, and the congressman's job is to read your letter and respond to it. You (the application) create the content (message) and hand it to your assistant (application layer protocol). Your assistant puts the content into an envelope, writes the congressman's address on the envelope (inserts headers and trailers), and puts it into the mailbox (passes it on to the next protocol in the network stack). When your assistant checks the mailbox a week later, there is a letter from the congressman (the remote application) addressed to

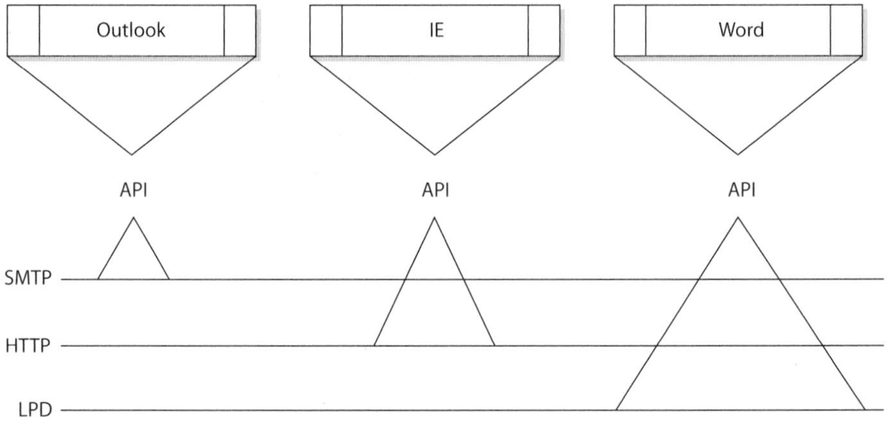

Figure 4-3 Applications send requests to an API, which is the interface to the supporting protocol.

you. Your assistant opens the envelope (strips off headers and trailers) and gives you the message (passes the message up to the application).

Some examples of the protocols working at this layer are the Simple Mail Transfer Protocol (SMTP), Hypertext Transfer Protocol (HTTP), Domain Name System (DNS), Internet Relay Chat (IRC) protocol, and the Line Printer Daemon (LDP) protocol. Figure 4-3 shows how applications communicate with the underlying protocols through application programming interfaces (APIs). If a user makes a request to send an e-mail message through her e-mail client Outlook, the e-mail client sends this information to SMTP. SMTP adds its information to the user's message and passes it down to the presentation layer.

Presentation Layer

The *presentation layer*, layer 6, receives information from the application layer protocol and puts it in a format that any process operating at the same layer on a destination computer following the OSI model can understand. This layer provides a common means of representing data in a structure that can be properly processed by the end system. This means that when a user creates a Word document and sends it out to several people, it does not matter whether the receiving computers have different word processing programs; each of these computers will be able to receive this file and understand and present it to its user as a document. It is the data representation processing that is done at the presentation layer that enables this to take place. For example, when a Windows 8 computer receives a file from another computer system, information within the file's header indicates what type of file it is. The Windows 8 operating system has a list of file types it understands and a table describing what program should be used to open and manipulate each of these file types. For example, the sender could create a Portable Document Format (PDF) file in Word 2010, while the receiver uses a Linux system. The receiver can open this file because the presentation layer on the sender's system encoded the file and added a descriptive header in accordance with the Multipurpose Internet

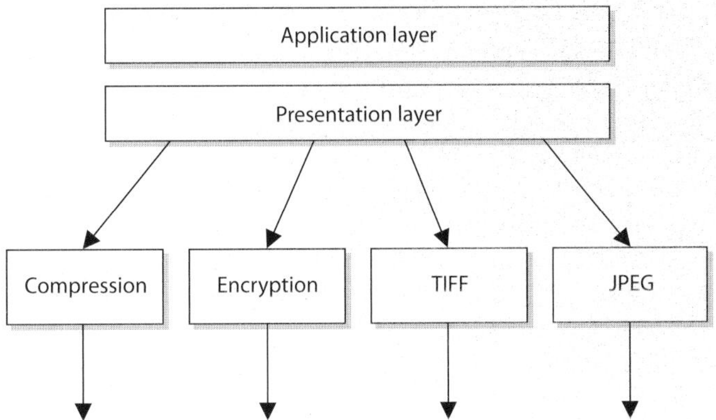

Figure 4-4 The presentation layer receives data from the application layer and puts it into a standard format.

Mail Extensions (MIME) standards, and the receiver's computer interprets the header's MIME type (Content-Type: application/pdf), decodes the file, and knows to open it with its PDF viewer application.

The presentation layer is not concerned with the meaning of data, but with the syntax and format of that data. It works as a translator, translating the format an application is using to a standard format used for passing messages over a network. If a user uses a Corel application to save a graphic, for example, the graphic could be a Tagged Image File Format (TIFF), Graphic Interchange Format (GIF), or Joint Photographic Experts Group (JPEG) format. The presentation layer adds information to tell the destination computer the file type and how to process and present it. This way, if the user sends this graphic to another user who does not have the Corel application, the user's operating system can still present the graphic because it has been saved into a standard format. Figure 4-4 illustrates the conversion of a file into different standard file types.

This layer also handles data compression and encryption issues. If a program requests a certain file to be compressed and encrypted before being transferred over the network, the presentation layer provides the necessary information for the destination computer. It provides information on how the file was encrypted and/or compressed so that the receiving system knows what software and processes are necessary to decrypt and decompress the file. Let's say Sara compresses a file using WinZip and sends it to you. When your system receives this file, it looks at data within the header (Content-Type: application/zip) and knows what application can decompress the file. If your system has WinZip installed, then the file can be decompressed and presented to you in its original form. If your system does not have an application that understands the compression/decompression instructions, the file will be presented to you with an unassociated icon.

Session Layer

When two applications need to communicate or transfer data between themselves, a connection may need to be set up between them. The *session layer*, layer 5, is responsible for establishing a connection between the two applications, maintaining it during the transfer of data, and controlling the release of this connection. A good analogy for the functionality within this layer is a telephone conversation. When Kandy wants to call a friend, she uses the telephone. The telephone network circuitry and protocols set up the connection over the telephone lines and maintain that communication path, and when Kandy hangs up, they release all the resources they were using to keep that connection open.

Similar to how telephone circuitry works, the session layer works in three phases: connection establishment, data transfer, and connection release. It provides session restart and recovery if necessary and provides the overall maintenance of the session. When the conversation is over, this path is broken down and all parameters are set back to their original settings. This process is known as *dialog management*. Figure 4-5 depicts the three phases of a session. Some protocols that work at this layer are the Password Authentication Protocol (PAP), Point-to-Point Tunneling Protocol (PPTP), Network Basic Input Output System (NetBIOS), and Remote Procedure Call (RPC).

The session layer protocol can enable communication between two applications to happen in three different modes:

- **Simplex** Communication takes place in one direction, though in practice this is very seldom the case.
- **Half-duplex** Communication takes place in both directions, but only one application can send information at a time.
- **Full-duplex** Communication takes place in both directions, and both applications can send information at the same time.

Figure 4-5 The session layer sets up the connection, maintains it, and tears it down once communication is completed.

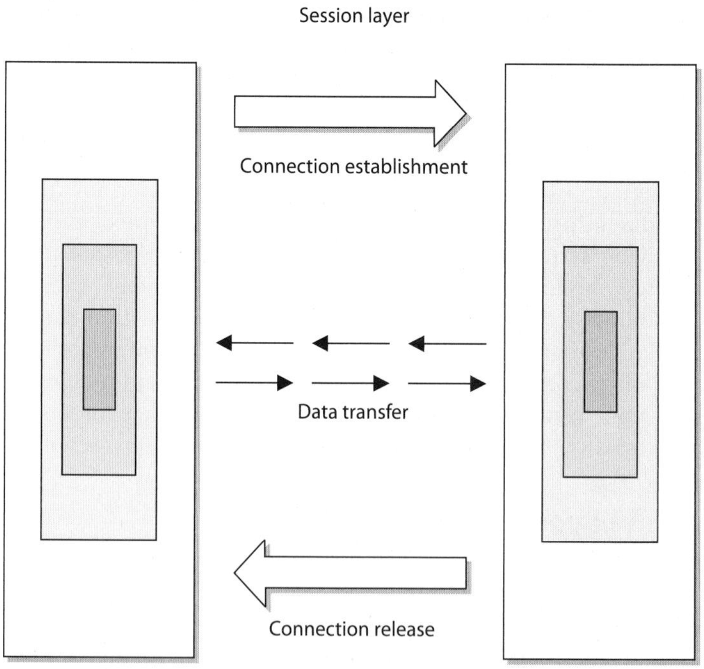

Many people have a hard time understanding the difference between what takes place at the session layer versus the transport layer because their definitions sound similar. Session layer protocols control application-to-application communication, whereas the transport layer protocols handle computer-to-computer communication. For example, if you are using a product that is working in a client/server model, in reality you have a small piece of the product on your computer (client portion) and the larger piece of the software product is running on a different computer (server portion). The communication between these two pieces of the same software product needs to be controlled, which is why session layer protocols even exist. Session layer protocols take on the functionality of middleware, which allows software on two different computers to communicate.

Session layer protocols provide interprocess communication channels, which allow a piece of software on one system to call upon a piece of software on another system without the programmer having to know the specifics of the software on the receiving system. The programmer of a piece of software can write a function call that calls upon a subroutine. The subroutine could be local to the system or be on a remote system. If the subroutine is on a remote system, the request is carried over a session layer protocol. The result that the remote system provides is then returned to the requesting system over the same session layer protocol. This is how RPC works. A piece of software can execute components that reside on another system. This is the core of distributed computing.

CAUTION One security issue common to RPC (and similar interprocess communication software) is the lack of authentication or the use of weak authentication. *Secure RPC (SRPC)* can be implemented, which requires authentication to take place before two computers located in different locations can communicate with each other. Authentication can take place using shared secrets, public keys, or Kerberos tickets. Session layer protocols need to provide secure authentication capabilities.

Session layer protocols are the least used protocols in a network environment; thus, many of them should be disabled on systems to decrease the chance of them getting exploited. RPC, NetBIOS, and similar distributed computing calls usually only need to take place within a network; thus, firewalls should be configured so this type of traffic is not allowed into or out of a network. Firewall filtering rules should be in place to stop this type of unnecessary and dangerous traffic.

Transport Layer

When two computers are going to communicate through a connection-oriented protocol, they will first agree on how much information each computer will send at a time, how to verify the integrity of the data once received, and how to determine whether a packet was lost along the way. The two computers agree on these parameters through a handshaking process at the *transport layer*, layer 4. The agreement on these issues before transferring data helps provide more reliable data transfer, error detection, correction, recovery, and flow control, and it optimizes the network services needed to perform these tasks. The transport layer provides end-to-end data transport services and establishes the logical connection between two communicating computers.

NOTE Connection-oriented protocols, such as Transmission Control Protocol (TCP), provide reliable data transmission when compared to connectionless protocols, such as User Datagram Protocol (UDP). This distinction is covered in more detail in the "TCP/IP Model" section, later in the chapter.

The functionality of the session and transport layers is similar insofar as they both set up some type of session or virtual connection for communication to take place. The difference is that protocols that work at the session layer set up connections between *applications*, whereas protocols that work at the transport layer set up connections between *computer systems*. For example, we can have three different applications on computer A communicating with three applications on computer B. The session layer protocols keep track of these different sessions. You can think of the transport layer protocol as the bus. It does not know or care what applications are communicating with each other. It just provides the mechanism to get the data from one system to another.

The transport layer receives data from many different applications and assembles the data into a stream to be properly transmitted over the network. The main protocols that work at this layer are TCP and UDP. Information is passed down from different entities at higher layers to the transport layer, which must assemble the information into a stream, as shown in Figure 4-6. The stream is made up of the various data segments passed to it. Just like a bus can carry a variety of people, the transport layer protocol can carry a variety of application data types.

TIP Different references can place specific protocols at different layers. For example, many references place the Transport Layer Security (TLS) protocol in the session layer, while other references place it in the transport layer. It is not that one is right or wrong. The OSI model tries to draw boxes around reality, but some protocols straddle the different layers.

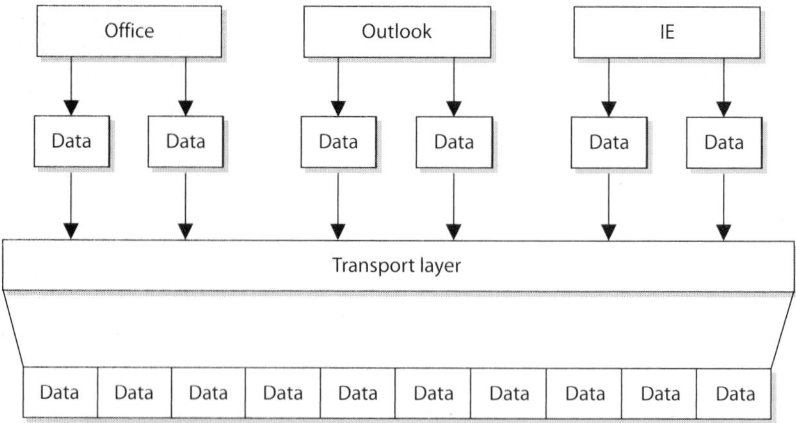

Figure 4-6 TCP formats data from applications into a stream to be prepared for transmission.

Network Layer

The main responsibilities of the *network layer*, layer 3, are to insert information into the packet's header so it can be properly addressed and routed, and then to actually route the packets to their proper destination. In a network, many routes can lead to one destination. The protocols at the network layer must determine the best path for the packet to take. Routing protocols build and maintain their routing tables. These tables are maps of the network, and when a packet must be sent from computer A to computer M, the protocols check the routing table, add the necessary information to the packet's header, and send it on its way.

The protocols that work at this layer do not ensure the delivery of the packets. They depend on the protocols at the transport layer to catch any problems and resend packets if necessary. The Internet Protocol (IP) is a common protocol working at the network layer, although other routing and routed protocols work there as well. Some of the other protocols are the Internet Control Message Protocol (ICMP), Routing Information Protocol (RIP), Open Shortest Path First (OSPF), Border Gateway Protocol (BGP), and Internet Group Management Protocol (IGMP). Figure 4-7 shows that a packet can take many routes and that the network layer enters routing information into the header to help the packet arrive at its destination.

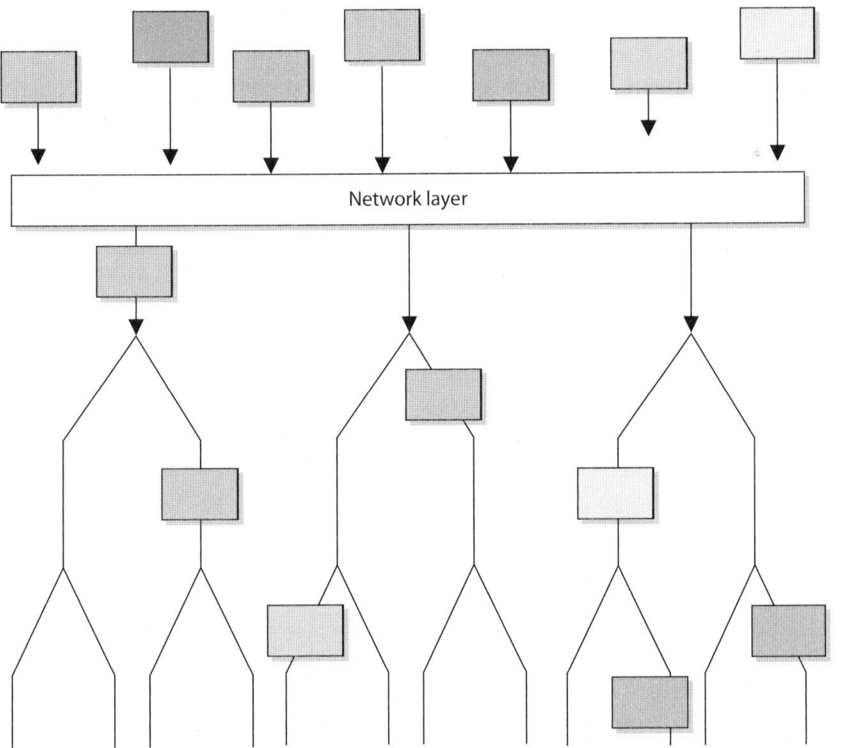

Figure 4-7 The network layer determines the most efficient path for each packet to take.

Data Link Layer

As we continue down the protocol stack, we are getting closer to the actual transmission channel (i.e., network wire) over which all the data will travel. The outer format of the data packet changes slightly at each layer, and it comes to a point where it needs to be translated into the LAN or wide area network (WAN) technology binary format for proper line transmission. This happens at the *data link layer*, layer 2.

LAN and WAN technologies can use different protocols, network interface cards (NICs), cables, and transmission methods. Each of these components has a different header data format structure, and they interpret electromagnetic signals in different ways. The data link layer is where the network stack knows in what format the data frame must be in order to transmit it properly over Token Ring, Ethernet, ATM, or Fiber Distributed Data Interface (FDDI) networks. If the network is an Ethernet network, for example, all the computers will expect packet headers to be a certain length, the flags to be positioned in certain field locations within the header, and the trailer information to be in a certain place with specific fields. Compared to Ethernet, Token Ring network technology has different frame header lengths, flag values, and header formats.

The data link layer is divided into two functional sublayers: the *Logical Link Control (LLC)* and the *Media Access Control (MAC)*. The LLC, which was originally defined in the IEEE 802.2 specification for Ethernet networks and is now also the ISO/IEC 8802-2 standard, communicates with the protocol immediately above it, the network layer. The MAC will have the appropriately loaded protocols to interface with the protocol requirements of the physical layer.

As data is passed down the network stack, it has to go from the network layer to the data link layer. The protocol at the network layer does not know if the underlying network is Ethernet, Token Ring, or ATM—it does not need to have this type of insight. The protocol at the network layer just adds its header and trailer information to the packet and passes it on to the next layer, which is the LLC sublayer. The LLC sublayer takes care of flow control and error checking. Data coming from the network layer passes down through the LLC sublayer and goes to the MAC. The technology at the MAC sublayer knows if the network is Ethernet, Token Ring, or ATM, so it knows how to put the last header and trailer on the packet before it "hits the wire" for transmission.

The IEEE MAC specification for Ethernet is 802.3, Token Ring is 802.5, wireless LAN is 802.11, and so on. So when you see a reference to an IEEE standard, such as 802.11, 802.16, or 802.3, it refers to the protocol working at the MAC sublayer of the data link layer of a protocol stack.

Some of the protocols that work at the data link layer are the Point-to-Point Protocol (PPP), ATM, Layer 2 Tunneling Protocol (L2TP), FDDI, Ethernet, and Token Ring. Figure 4-8 shows the two sublayers that make up the data link layer.

Each network technology (Ethernet, ATM, FDDI, and so on) defines the compatible physical transmission type (coaxial, twisted pair, fiber, wireless) that is required to enable network communication. Each network technology also has defined electronic signaling and encoding patterns. For example, if the MAC sublayer received a bit with the value of 1 that needed to be transmitted over an Ethernet network, the MAC sublayer technology would tell the physical layer to create a +0.5-volt electric signal. In the "language of

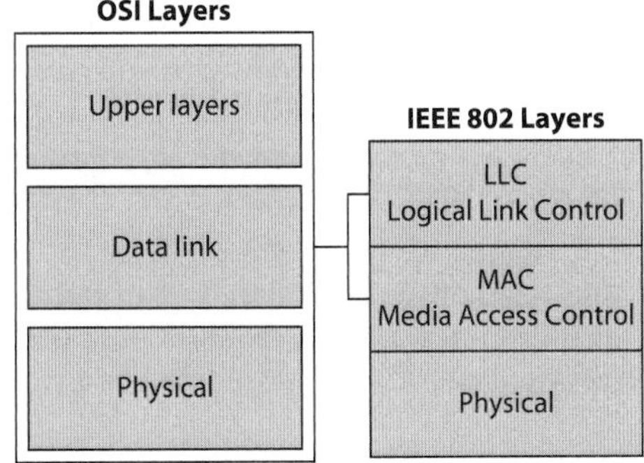

Figure 4-8 The data link layer is made up of two sublayers.

Ethernet" this means that 0.5 volts is the encoding value for a bit with the value of 1. If the next bit the MAC sublayer receives is 0, the MAC layer would tell the physical layer to transmit 0 volts. The different network types will have different encoding schemes. So a bit value of 1 in an ATM network might actually be encoded to the voltage value of 0.85. It is just a sophisticated Morse code system. The receiving end will know when it receives a voltage value of 0.85 that a bit with the value of 1 has been transmitted.

Network cards bridge the data link and physical layers. Data is passed down through the first six layers and reaches the network card driver at the data link layer. Depending on the network technology being used (Ethernet, Token Ring, FDDI, and so on), the network card driver encodes the bits at the data link layer, which are then turned into electricity states at the physical layer and placed onto the wire for transmission.

EXAM TIP When the data link layer applies the last header and trailer to the data message, this is referred to as *framing*. The unit of data is now called a *frame*.

Physical Layer

The *physical layer*, layer 1, converts bits into voltage for transmission. Signals and voltage schemes have different meanings for different LAN and WAN technologies, as covered earlier. If a user sends data through his dial-up software and out his modem onto a telephone line, the data format, electrical signals, and control functionality are much different than if that user sends data through the NIC and onto a unshielded twisted pair (UTP) wire for LAN communication. The mechanisms that control this data going onto the telephone line, or the UTP wire, work at the physical layer. This layer controls synchronization, data rates, line noise, and transmission techniques. Specifications for the physical layer include the timing of voltage changes, voltage levels, and the physical connectors for electrical, optical, and mechanical transmission.

EXAM TIP To remember all the layers within the OSI model in the correct order, memorize "All People Seem To Need Data Processing." Remember that you are starting at layer 7, the application layer, at the top.

Functions and Protocols in the OSI Model

For the CISSP exam, you will need to know the functionality that takes place at the different layers of the OSI model, along with specific protocols that work at each layer. The following is a quick overview of each layer and its components.

Application

The protocols at the application layer handle file transfer, virtual terminals, network management, and fulfilling networking requests of applications. A few of the protocols that work at this layer include

- File Transfer Protocol (FTP)
- Trivial File Transfer Protocol (TFTP)
- Simple Network Management Protocol (SNMP)
- Simple Mail Transfer Protocol (SMTP)
- Telnet
- Hypertext Transfer Protocol (HTTP)

Presentation

The services of the presentation layer handle translation into standard formats, data compression and decompression, and data encryption and decryption. No protocols work at this layer, just services. The following lists some of the presentation layer standards:

- American Standard Code for Information Interchange (ASCII)
- Extended Binary-Coded Decimal Interchange Mode (EBCDIC)
- Tagged Image File Format (TIFF)
- Joint Photographic Experts Group (JPEG)
- Motion Picture Experts Group (MPEG)
- Musical Instrument Digital Interface (MIDI)

Session

The session layer protocols set up connections between applications; maintain dialog control; and negotiate, establish, maintain, and tear down the communication channel. Some of the protocols that work at this layer include

- Network Basic Input Output System (NetBIOS)
- Password Authentication Protocol (PAP)
- Point-to-Point Tunneling Protocol (PPTP)
- Remote Procedure Call (RPC)

Transport

The protocols at the transport layer handle end-to-end transmission and segmentation of a data stream. The following protocols work at this layer:

- Transmission Control Protocol (TCP)
- User Datagram Protocol (UDP)
- Sequenced Packet Exchange (SPX)

Network

The responsibilities of the network layer protocols include internetworking service, addressing, and routing. The following lists some of the protocols that work at this layer:

- Internet Protocol (IP)
- Internet Control Message Protocol (ICMP)
- Internet Group Management Protocol (IGMP)
- Routing Information Protocol (RIP)
- Open Shortest Path First (OSPF)
- Internetwork Packet Exchange (IPX)

Data Link

The protocols at the data link layer convert data into LAN or WAN frames for transmission and define how a computer accesses a network. This layer is divided into the Logical Link Control (LLC) and the Media Access Control (MAC) sublayers. Some protocols that work at this layer include the following:

- Address Resolution Protocol (ARP)
- Reverse Address Resolution Protocol (RARP)
- Point-to-Point Protocol (PPP)
- Serial Line Internet Protocol (SLIP)
- Ethernet (IEEE 802.3)
- Token Ring (IEEE 802.5)
- Wireless Ethernet (IEEE 802.11)

Physical

Network interface cards and drivers convert bits into electrical signals and control the physical aspects of data transmission, including optical, electrical, and mechanical requirements. The following are some of the standard interfaces at this layer:

- RS/EIA/TIA-422, RS/EIA/TIA-423, RS/EIA/TIA-449, RS/EIA/TIA-485
- 10Base-T, 10Base2, 10Base5, 100Base-TX, 100Base-FX, 100Base-T, 1000Base-T, 1000Base-SX

- Integrated Services Digital Network (ISDN)
- Digital subscriber line (DSL)
- Synchronous Optical Networking (SONET)

Tying the Layers Together

The OSI model is used as a framework for many network-based products and is used by many types of vendors. Various types of devices and protocols work at different parts of this seven-layer model. The main reason that a Cisco switch, Microsoft web server, a Barracuda firewall, and a Belkin wireless access point can all communicate properly on one network is because they all work within the OSI model. They do not have their own individual ways of sending data; they follow a standardized manner of communication, which allows for interoperability and allows a network to be a network. If a product does not follow the OSI model, it will not be able to communicate with other devices on the network because the other devices will not understand its proprietary way of communicating.

The different device types work at specific OSI layers. For example, computers can interpret and process data at each of the seven layers, but routers can understand information only up to the network layer because a router's main function is to route packets, which does not require knowledge about any further information within the packet. A router peels back the header information until it reaches the network layer data, where the routing and IP address information is located. The router looks at this information to make its decisions on where the packet should be routed. Bridges and switches understand only up to the data link layer, and repeaters understand traffic only at the physical layer. So if you hear someone mention a "layer 3 device," the person is referring to a device that works at the network layer. A "layer 2 device" works at the data link layer. Figure 4-9 shows what layer of the OSI model each type of device works within.

NOTE Some techies like to joke that all computer problems reside at layer 8. The OSI model does not have an eighth layer, and what these people are referring to is the user of a computer. So if someone states that there is a problem at layer 8, this is code for "the user is the problem."

Let's walk through an example. You open an FTP client on your computer and connect to an FTP server on your network. In your FTP client you choose to download a photo from a server. The FTP server now has to move this file over the network to your computer. The server sends this document to the FTP application protocol on its network stack. This FTP protocol puts headers and trailers on the document and passes it down to the presentation layer. A service at the presentation layer adds a header that indicates this document is in JPEG format so that your system knows how to open the file when it is received.

This bundle is then handed to the transport layer TCP, which also adds a header and trailer, which include source and destination port values. The bundle continues down

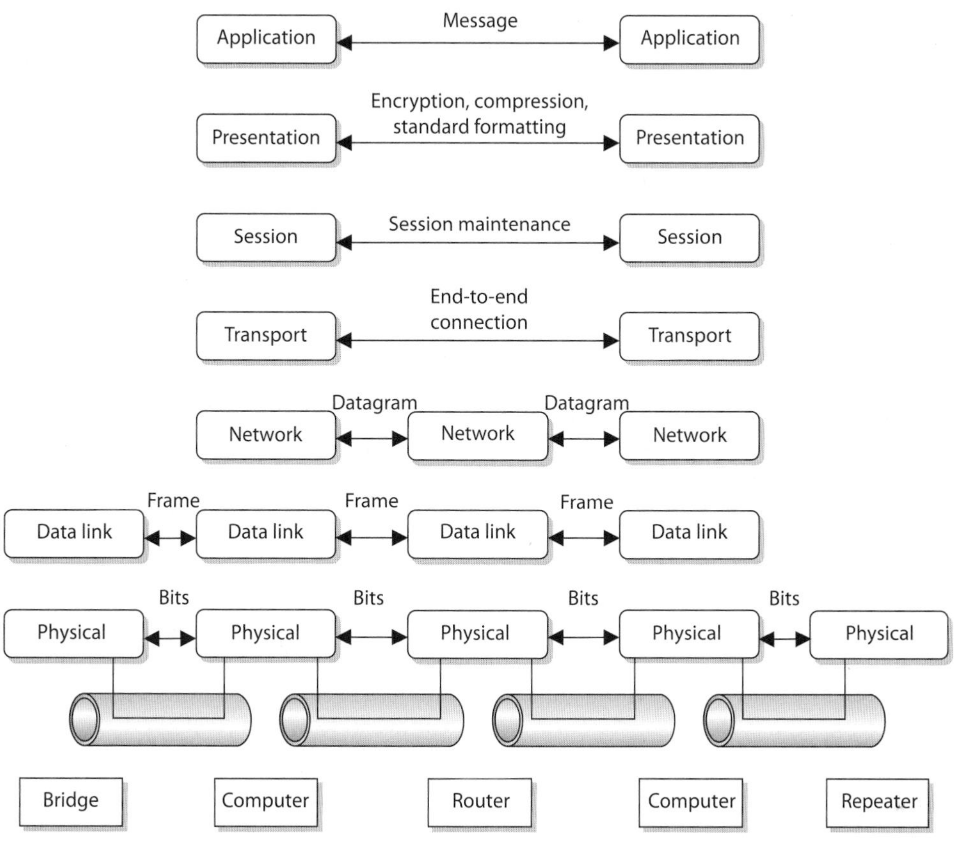

Figure 4-9 Each device works at a particular layer within the OSI model.

the network stack to the IP protocol, which provides a source IP address (FTP server) and a destination IP address (your system). The bundle goes to the data link layer, and the server's NIC driver encodes the bundle to be able to be transmitted over the Ethernet connection between the server and your system.

Multilayer Protocols

Not all protocols fit neatly within the layers of the OSI model. This is particularly evident among devices and networks that were never intended to interoperate with the Internet. For this same reason, they tend to lack robust security features aimed at protecting the availability, integrity, and confidentiality of the data they communicate. The problem is that as the Internet of old becomes the Internet of Things (IoT), these previously isolated devices and networks find themselves increasingly connected to a host of threats they were never meant to face.

As security professionals, we need to be aware of these nontraditional protocols and their implications for the security of the networks to which they are connected. In particular, we should be vigilant when it comes to identifying nonobvious cyber-physical systems. In December 2015, attackers were able to cut power to over 80,000 homes in Ukraine apparently by compromising the utilities' supervisory control and data acquisition (SCADA) systems in what is considered the first known blackout caused by a cyberattack. At the heart of most SCADA systems used by power and water utilities is a multilayer protocol known as DNP3.

Distributed Network Protocol 3

The Distributed Network Protocol 3 (DNP3) is a communications protocol designed for use in SCADA systems, particularly those within the power sector. It is not a general-purpose protocol like IP, nor does it incorporate routing functionality. SCADA systems typically have a very flat hierarchical architecture in which sensors and actuators are connected to remote terminal units (RTUs). The RTUs aggregate data from one or more of these devices and relay it to the SCADA master, which includes a human-machine interface (HMI) component. Control instructions and configuration changes are sent from the SCADA master to the RTUs and then on to the sensors and actuators.

At the time DNP3 was designed, there wasn't a need to route traffic among the components (most of which were connected with point-to-point circuits), so networking was not needed or supported in DNP3. Instead of using the OSI seven-layer model, its developers opted for a simpler three-layer model called the Enhanced Performance Architecture (EPA) that roughly corresponds to layers 2, 4, and 7 of the OSI model. There was no encryption or authentication, since the developers did not think network attacks were feasible on a system consisting of devices connected to each other and to nothing else.

Over time, SCADA systems were connected to other networks and then to the Internet for a variety of very valid business reasons. Unfortunately, security wasn't considered until much later. Encryption and authentication features were added as an afterthought, though not all implementations have been thus updated. Network segmentation is not always present either, even in some critical installations. Perhaps most concerning is the shortage of effective intrusion prevention systems (IPSs) and intrusion detection systems (IDSs) that understand the interconnections between DNP3 and IP networks and can identify DNP3-based attacks.

Controller Area Network Bus

Another multilayer protocol that had almost no security features until very recently is the one that runs most automobiles worldwide. The Controller Area Network bus (CAN bus) is a protocol designed to allow microcontrollers and other embedded devices to communicate with each other on a shared bus. Over time, these devices have diversified so that today they can control almost every aspect of a vehicle's functions, including steering, braking, and throttling. CAN bus was never meant to communicate with anything outside the vehicle except for a mechanic's maintenance computer, so there never appeared to be a need for security features.

As cars started getting connected via Wi-Fi and cellular data networks, their designers didn't fully consider the new attack vectors this would introduce to an otherwise undefended system. That is, until Charlie Miller and Chris Valasek famously hacked a Jeep in 2015 by connecting to it over a cellular data network and bridging the head unit (which controls the sound system and GPS) to the CAN bus (which controls all the vehicle sensors and actuators) and causing it to run off a road. As cars become more autonomous, security of the CAN bus will become increasingly important.

TCP/IP Model

The *Transmission Control Protocol/Internet Protocol (TCP/IP)* is a suite of protocols that governs the way data travels from one device to another. Besides its eponymous two main protocols, TCP/IP includes other protocols as well, which we will cover in this chapter.

IP is a network layer protocol and provides datagram routing services. IP's main task is to support internetwork addressing and packet routing. It is a connectionless protocol that envelops data passed to it from the transport layer. The IP protocol addresses the datagram with the source and destination IP addresses. The protocols within the TCP/IP suite work together to break down the data passed from the application layer into pieces that can be moved along a network. They work with other protocols to transmit the data to the destination computer and then reassemble the data back into a form that the application layer can understand and process.

Two main protocols work at the transport layer: TCP and UDP. *TCP* is a reliable and *connection-oriented protocol*, which means it ensures packets are delivered to the destination computer. If a packet is lost during transmission, TCP has the ability to identify this issue and resend the lost or corrupted packet. TCP also supports packet sequencing (to ensure each and every packet was received), flow and congestion control, and error detection and correction. *UDP*, on the other hand, is a *best-effort* and *connectionless protocol*. It has neither packet sequencing nor flow and congestion control, and the destination does not acknowledge every packet it receives.

IP

IP is a connectionless protocol that provides the addressing and routing capabilities for each package of data.

The data, IP, and network relationship can be compared to the relationship between a letter and the postal system:

- Data = Letter
- IP = Addressed envelope
- Network = Postal system

The message is the letter, which is enveloped and addressed by IP, and the network and its services enable the message to be sent from its origin to its destination, like the postal system.

TCP

TCP is referred to as a connection-oriented protocol because before any user data is actually sent, handshaking takes place between the two systems that want to communicate. Once the handshaking completes successfully, a virtual connection is set up between the two systems. UDP is considered a connectionless protocol because it does not go through these steps. Instead, UDP sends out messages without first contacting the destination computer and does not know if the packets were received properly or dropped. Figure 4-10 shows the difference between a connection-oriented protocol and a connectionless protocol.

UDP and TCP sit together on the transport layer, and developers can choose which to use when developing applications. Many times, TCP is the transport protocol of choice because it provides reliability and ensures the packets are delivered. For example, SMTP is used to transmit e-mail messages and uses TCP because it must make sure the data is delivered. TCP provides a full-duplex, reliable communication mechanism, and if any packets are lost or damaged, they are re-sent; however, TCP requires a lot of system overhead compared to UDP.

If a programmer knows that data being dropped during transmission is not detrimental to the application, he may choose to use UDP because it is faster and requires fewer resources. For example, UDP is a better choice than TCP when a server sends status information to all listening nodes on the network. A node will not be negatively affected if, by some chance, it did not receive this status information, because the information will be re-sent every 60 seconds.

UDP and TCP are transport protocols that applications use to get their data across a network. They both use *ports* to communicate with upper OSI layers and to keep track of various conversations that take place simultaneously. The ports are also the mechanism

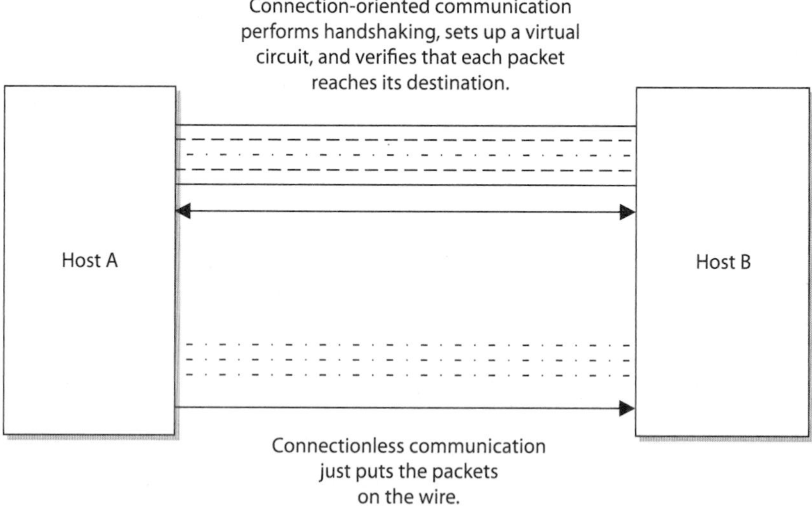

Figure 4-10 Connection-oriented protocol vs. connectionless protocol functionality

used to identify how other computers access services. When a TCP or UDP message is formed, source and destination ports are contained within the header information along with the source and destination IP addresses. The combination of protocol (TCP or UDP), port, and IP address makes up a *socket*, and is how packets know where to go (by the address) and how to communicate with the right service or protocol on the other computer (by the port number). The IP address acts as the doorway to a computer, and the port acts as the doorway to the actual protocol or service. To communicate properly, the packet needs to know these doors. Figure 4-11 shows how packets communicate with applications and services through ports.

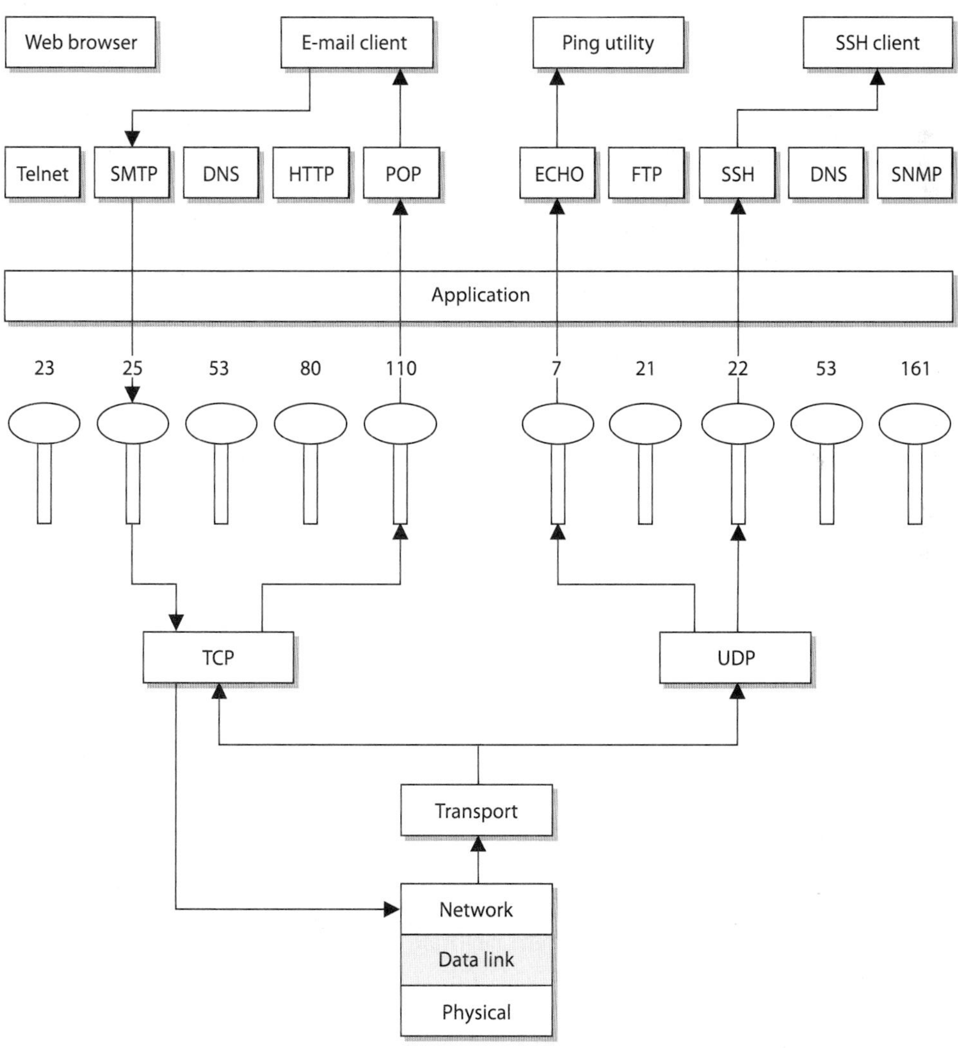

Figure 4-11 The packet can communicate with upper-layer protocols and services through a port.

The difference between TCP and UDP can also be seen in the message formats. Because TCP offers more services than UDP, it must contain much more information within its packet header format, as shown in Figure 4-12. Table 4-1 lists the major differences between TCP and UDP.

Port Types

Port numbers up to 1023 (0 to 1023) are called *well-known ports*, and almost every computer in the world has the exact same protocol mapped to the exact same port number. That is why they are called well known—everyone follows this same standardized approach. This means that on almost every computer, port 25 is mapped to SMTP, port 21 is mapped to FTP, port 80 is mapped to HTTP, and so on. This mapping between lower-numbered ports and specific protocols is a de facto standard, which just means that we all do this and that we do not have a standards body dictating that it absolutely has to be done this way. The fact that almost everyone follows this approach translates to more interoperability among systems all over the world.

Because this is a de facto standard and not a standard that absolutely must be followed, administrators can map different protocols to different port numbers if that fits their purpose. However, one thing to note is that ports 0 to 1023 can be used only by privileged system or root processes.

The following shows some of the most commonly used protocols and the ports to which they are usually mapped:

- Telnet port 23
- SMTP port 25
- HTTP port 80
- SNMP ports 161 and 162
- FTP ports 21 and 20

Registered ports are 1024 to 49151, which can be registered with the Internet Corporation for Assigned Names and Numbers (ICANN) for a particular use. Vendors register specific ports to map to their proprietary software. *Dynamic ports* are 49152 to 65535 and are available to be used by any application on an "as needed" basis.

TCP Handshake

TCP must set up a virtual connection between two hosts before any data is sent. This means the two hosts must agree on certain parameters, data flow, windowing, error detection, and options. These issues are negotiated during the handshaking phase, as shown in Figure 4-13.

The host that initiates communication sends a synchronous (SYN) packet to the receiver. The receiver acknowledges this request by sending a SYN/ACK packet. This packet translates into, "I have received your request and am ready to communicate with you." The sending host acknowledges this with an acknowledgment (ACK) packet, which translates into, "I received your acknowledgment. Let's start transmitting our data."

Source port			Destination port	
Sequence number				
Acknowledgment number				
Offset	Reserved	Flags	Window	
Checksum			Urgent pointer	
Options				Padding
Data				

TCP format

Source port	Destination port
Length	Checksum
Data	

UDP format

Figure 4-12 TCP carries a lot more information within its segment because it offers more services than UDP.

Property	TCP	UDP
Reliability	Ensures that packets reach their destinations, returns ACKs when packets are received, and is a reliable protocol.	Does not return ACKs and does not guarantee that a packet will reach its destination. Is an unreliable protocol.
Connection	Connection-oriented. It performs handshaking and develops a virtual connection with the destination computer.	Connectionless. It does no handshaking and does not set up a virtual connection.
Packet sequencing	Uses sequence numbers within headers to make sure each packet within a transmission is received.	Does not use sequence numbers.
Congestion controls	The destination computer can tell the source if it is overwhelmed and thus slow the transmission rate.	The destination computer does not communicate back to the source computer about flow control.
Usage	Used when reliable delivery is required. Intended for relatively small amounts of data transmission.	Used when reliable delivery is not required and high volumes of data need to be transmitted, such as in streaming video and status broadcasts.
Speed and overhead	Uses a considerable amount of resources and is slower than UDP.	Uses fewer resources and is faster than TCP.

Table 4-1 Major Differences Between TCP and UDP

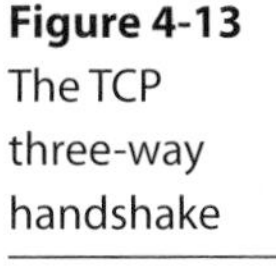

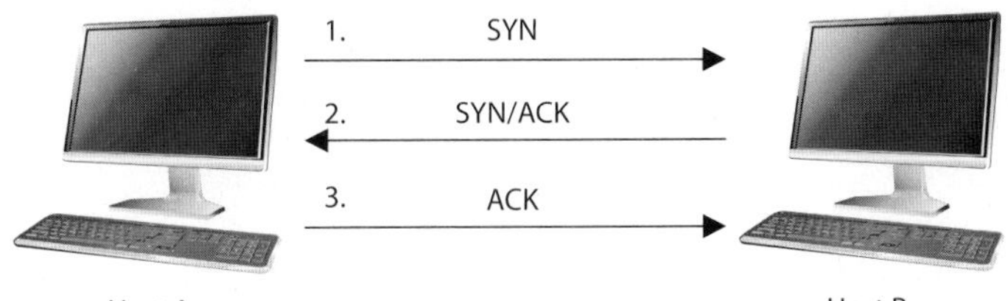

Figure 4-13 The TCP three-way handshake

This completes the handshaking phase, after which a virtual connection is set up, and actual data can now be passed. The connection that has been set up at this point is considered *full duplex*, which means transmission in both directions is possible using the same transmission line.

If an attacker sends a target system SYN packets with a spoofed address, then the victim system replies to the spoofed address with SYN/ACK packets. Each time the victim system receives one of these SYN packets, it sets aside resources to manage the new connection. If the attacker floods the victim system with SYN packets, eventually the victim system allocates all of its available TCP connection resources and can no longer process new requests. This is a type of DoS that is referred to as a *SYN flood.* To thwart this type of attack you can use a number of mitigations, the most common of which are described in Internet Engineering Task Force's (IETF) Request for Comments (RFC) 4987. One of the most effective techniques described in RFC 4987 is the use of SYN caches, which delays the allocation of a socket until the handshake is completed.

Another attack vector we need to understand is TCP sequence numbers. One of the values that is agreed upon during a TCP handshake between two systems is the sequence numbers that will be inserted into the packet headers. Once the sequence number is agreed upon, if a receiving system receives a packet from the sending system that does not have this predetermined value, it will disregard the packet. This means that an attacker cannot just spoof the address of a sending system to fool a receiving system; the attacker has to spoof the sender's address and use the correct sequence number values. If an attacker can correctly predict the TCP sequence numbers that two systems will use, then she can create packets containing those numbers and fool the receiving system into thinking that the packets are coming from the authorized sending system. She can then take over the TCP connection between the two systems, which is referred to as *TCP session hijacking.*

Data Structures

As stated earlier, the message is formed and passed to the application layer from a program and sent down through the protocol stack. Each protocol at each layer adds its own information to the message and passes it down to the next layer. This activity is referred to as *data encapsulation*. As the message is passed down the stack, it goes through a sort of evolution, and each stage has a specific name that indicates what is taking place. When an application formats data to be transmitted over the network, the data is called a *message* or *data*. The message is sent to the transport layer, where TCP does its magic on it. The bundle of data is now a *segment*. The segment is sent to the network layer. The network layer adds routing and addressing, and now the bundle is called a *packet*. The network layer passes off the packet to the data link layer, which frames the packet with a header and a trailer, and now it is called a *frame*. Figure 4-14 illustrates these stages.

EXAM TIP If the message is being transmitted over TCP, it is referred to as a "segment." If it is being transmitted over UDP, it is referred to as a "datagram."

Sometimes when an author refers to a segment, she is specifying the stage in which the data is located within the protocol stack. If the literature is describing routers, which

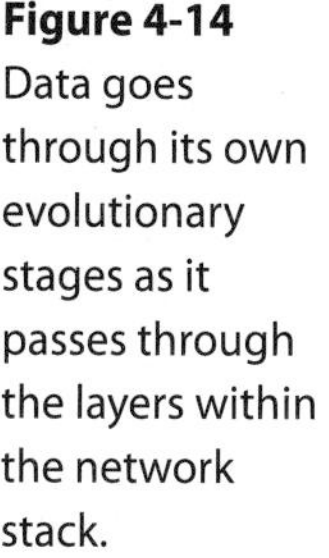

Figure 4-14 Data goes through its own evolutionary stages as it passes through the layers within the network stack.

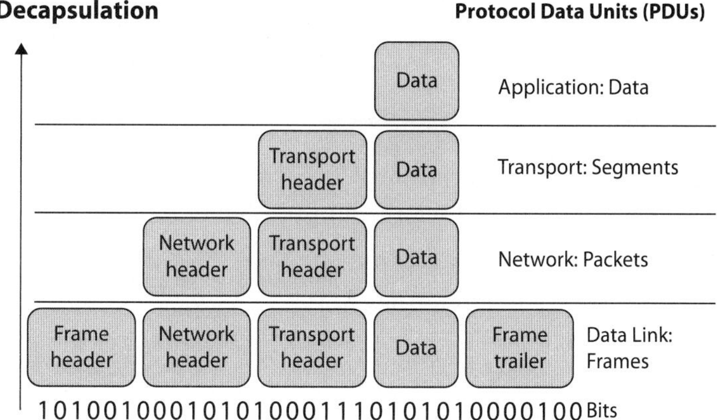

work at the network layer, the author might use the word "packet" because the data at this layer has routing and addressing information attached. If an author is describing network traffic and flow control, she might use the word "frame" because all data actually ends up in the frame format before it is put on the network wire.

The important thing here is that you understand the various steps a data package goes through when it moves up and down the protocol stack.

IP Addressing

Each node on a network must have a unique IP address. Today, the most commonly used version of IP is *IP version 4 (IPv4)*, but its addresses are in such high demand that their supply has started to run out. *IP version 6 (IPv6)* was created to address this shortage. (IPv6 also has many security features built into it that are not part of IPv4.) IPv6 is covered later in this chapter.

IPv4 uses 32 bits for its addresses, whereas IPv6 uses 128 bits; thus, IPv6 provides more possible addresses with which to work. Each address has a host portion and a network portion, and the addresses are grouped into *classes* and then into *subnets*. The subnet mask of the address differentiates the groups of addresses that define the subnets of a network. IPv4 address classes are listed in Table 4-2.

Class	Address Range	Description
A	0.0.0.0 to 127.255.255.255	The first byte is the network portion, and the remaining 3 bytes are the host portion.
B	128.0.0.0 to 191.255.255.255	The first 2 bytes are the network portion, and the remaining 2 bytes are the host portion.
C	192.0.0.0 to 223.255.255.255	The first 3 bytes are the network portion, and the remaining 1 byte is the host portion.
D	224.0.0.0 to 239.255.255.255	Used for multicast addresses.
E	240.0.0.0 to 255.255.255.255	Reserved for research.

Table 4-2 IPv4 Addressing

For any given IP network within an organization, all nodes connected to the network can have different host addresses but a common network address. The host address identifies every individual node, whereas the network address is the identity of the network all the nodes are connected to; therefore, it is the same for each one of them. Any traffic meant for nodes on this network will be sent to the prescribed network address.

A *subnet* is created from the host portion of an IP address to designate a "sub" network. This allows us to further break the host portion of the address into two or more logical groupings, as shown in Figure 4-15. A network can be logically partitioned to reduce administration headaches, traffic performance, and potentially security. As an analogy, let's say you work at Toddlers R Us and you are responsible for babysitting 100 toddlers. If you kept all 100 toddlers in one room, you would probably end up crazy. To better manage these kids, you could break them up into groups. The three-year-olds go in the yellow room, the four-year-olds go in the green room, and the five-year-olds go in the blue room. This is what a network administrator would do—break up and separate computer nodes to be able to better control them. Instead of putting them into physical rooms, the administrator puts them into logical rooms (subnets).

To continue with our analogy, when you put your toddlers in different rooms, you would have physical barriers that separate them—walls. Network subnetting is not physical; it is logical. This means you would not have physical walls separating your individual subnets, so how do you keep them separate? This is where subnet masks

Figure 4-15 Subnets create logical partitions.

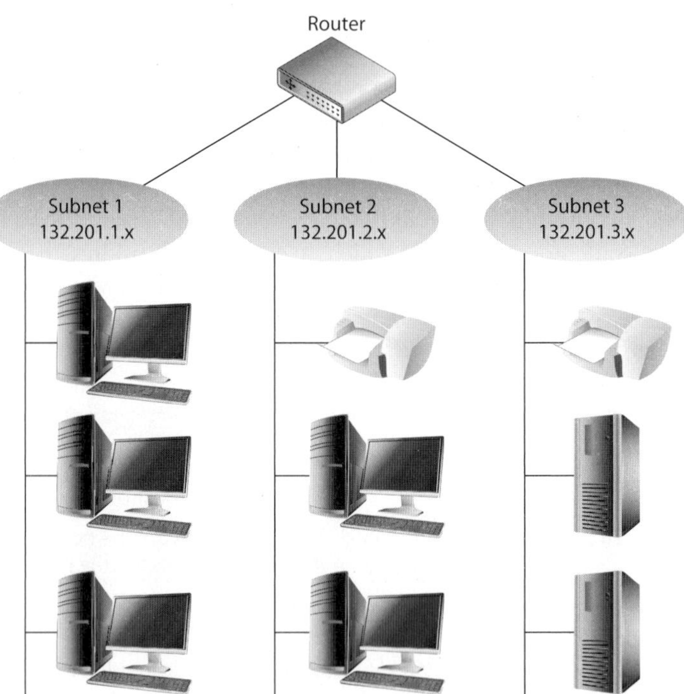

come into play. A subnet mask defines smaller networks inside a larger network, just like individual rooms are defined within a building.

Subnetting allows larger IP ranges to be divided into smaller, logical, and more tangible network segments. Consider an organization with several divisions, such as IT, Accounting, HR, and so on. Creating subnets for each division breaks the networks into logical partitions that route traffic directly to recipients without dispersing data all over the network. This drastically reduces the traffic load across the network, reducing the possibility of network congestion and excessive broadcast packets in the network. Implementing network security policies is also much more effective across logically categorized subnets with a demarcated perimeter, as compared to a large, cluttered, and complex network.

Subnetting is particularly beneficial in keeping down routing table sizes because external routers can directly send data to the actual network segment without having to worry about the internal architecture of that network and getting the data to individual hosts. This job can be handled by the internal routers, which can determine the individual hosts in a subnetted environment and save the external routers the hassle of analyzing all 32 bits of an IP address and just look at the "masked" bits.

TIP You should not have to calculate any subnets for the CISSP exam, but for a better understanding of how this stuff works under the hood, visit http://compnetworking.about.com/od/workingwithipaddresses/a/subnetmask.htm.

If the traditional subnet masks are used, they are referred to as *classful* or *classical* IP addresses. If an organization needs to create subnets that do not follow these traditional sizes, then it would use *classless* IP addresses. This just means a different subnet mask would be used to define the network and host portions of the addresses. After it became clear that available IP addresses were running out as more individuals and corporations participated on the Internet, *classless interdomain routing (CIDR)* was created. A Class B address range is usually too large for most companies, and a Class C address range is too small, so CIDR provides the flexibility to increase or decrease the class sizes as necessary. CIDR is the method to specify more flexible IP address classes. CIDR is also referred to as *supernetting*.

NOTE To better understand CIDR, visit the following resource: www.tcpipguide.com/free/t_IPClasslessAddressingClasslessInterDomainRoutingCI.htm.

Although each node has an IP address, people usually refer to their hostname rather than their IP address. Hostnames, such as www.mcgraw-hill.com, are easier for humans to remember than IP addresses, such as 198.105.254.228. However, the use of these two nomenclatures requires mapping between the hostnames and IP addresses because the computer understands only the numbering scheme. This process is addressed in the "Domain Name Service" section later in this chapter.

NOTE IP provides addressing, packet fragmentation, and packet timeouts. To ensure that packets do not continually traverse a network forever, IP provides a *Time to Live (TTL)* value that is decremented every time the packet passes through a router. IP can also provide a *Type of Service (ToS)* capability, which means it can prioritize different packets for time-sensitive functions.

IPv6

IPv6, also called *IP next generation (IPng)*, not only has a larger address space than IPv4 to support more IP addresses; it has some capabilities that IPv4 does not and it accomplishes some of the same tasks differently. All of the specifics of the new functions within IPv6 are beyond the scope of this book, but we will look at a few of them, because IPv6 is the way of the future. IPv6 allows for scoped addresses, which enables an administrator to restrict specific addresses for specific servers or file and print sharing, for example. IPv6 has Internet Protocol Security (IPSec) integrated into the protocol stack, which provides end-to-end secure transmission and authentication. IPv6 has more flexibility and routing capabilities and allows for Quality of Service (QoS) priority values to be assigned to time-sensitive transmissions. The protocol offers autoconfiguration, which makes administration much easier, and it does not require network address translation (NAT) to extend its address space.

NAT was developed because IPv4 addresses were running out. Although the NAT technology is extremely useful, it has caused a lot of overhead and transmission problems because it breaks the client/server model that many applications use today. One reason the industry did not jump on the IPv6 bandwagon when it came out years ago is that NAT was developed, which reduced the speed at which IP addresses were being depleted. Although the conversion rate from IPv4 to IPv6 is slow in some parts of the world and the implementation process is quite complicated, the industry is making the shift because of all the benefits that IPv6 brings to the table.

NOTE NAT is covered in the "Network Address Translation" section later in this chapter.

The IPv6 specification, as outlined in RFC 2460, lays out the differences and benefits of IPv6 over IPv4. A few of the differences are as follows:

- IPv6 increases the IP address size from 32 bits to 128 bits to support more levels of addressing hierarchy, a much greater number of addressable nodes, and simpler autoconfiguration of addresses.
- The scalability of multicast routing is improved by adding a "scope" field to multicast addresses. Also, a new type of address called an *anycast address* is defined, which is used to send a packet to any one of a group of nodes.

- Some IPv4 header fields have been dropped or made optional to reduce the common-case processing cost of packet handling and to limit the bandwidth cost of the IPv6 header. This is illustrated in Figure 4-16.
- Changes in the way IP header options are encoded allow for more efficient forwarding, less stringent limits on the length of options, and greater flexibility for introducing new options in the future.
- A new capability is added to enable the labeling of packets belonging to particular traffic "flows" for which the sender requests special handling, such as nondefault QoS or "real-time" service.
- Extensions to support authentication, data integrity, and (optional) data confidentiality are also specified for IPv6.

IPv4 limits packets to 65,535 bytes of payload, and IPv6 extends this size to 4,294,967,295 bytes. These larger packets are referred to as *jumbograms* and improve performance over high-maximum transmission unit (MTU) links. Currently most of the world still uses IPv4, but IPv6 is being deployed more rapidly. This means that there are "pockets" of networks using IPv4 and "pockets" of networks using IPv6 that still need to communicate. This communication takes place through different tunneling techniques, which either encapsulate IPv6 packets within IPv4 packets or carry out

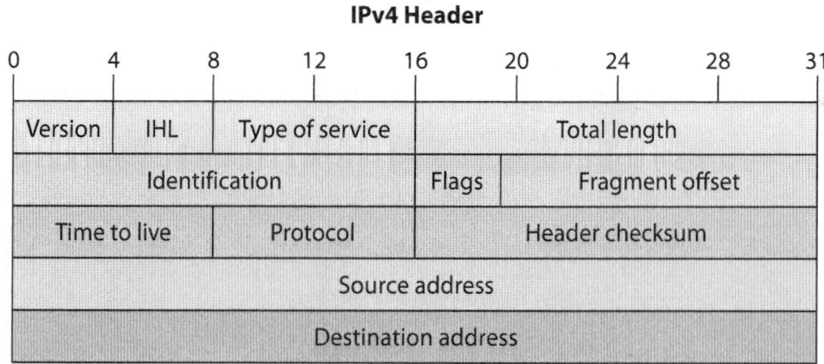

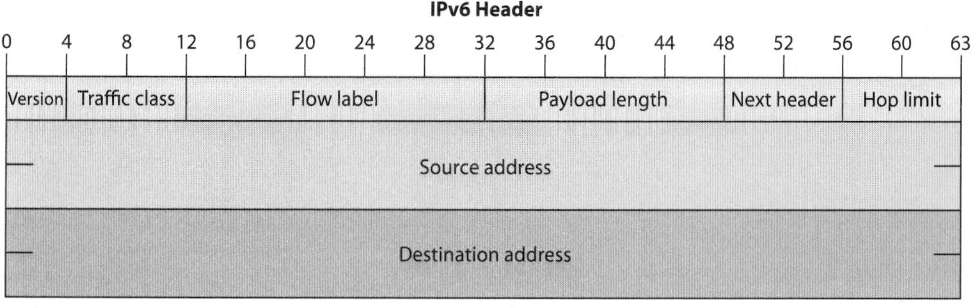

Figure 4-16 IPv4 vs. IPv6 headers

automated address translations. *Automatic tunneling* is a technique where the routing infrastructure automatically determines the tunnel endpoints so that protocol tunneling can take place without preconfiguration. In the *6to4* tunneling method, the tunnel endpoints are determined by using a well-known IPv4 anycast address on the remote side and embedding IPv4 address data within IPv6 addresses on the local side. *Teredo* is another automatic tunneling technique that uses UDP encapsulation so that NAT address translations are not affected. *Intra-Site Automatic Tunnel Addressing Protocol (ISATAP)* treats the IPv4 network as a virtual IPv6 local link, with mappings from each IPv4 address to a link-local IPv6 address.

The 6to4 and Teredo are *intersite* tunneling mechanisms, and ISATAP is an *intrasite* mechanism. So the first two are used for connectivity between different networks, and ISATAP is used for connectivity of systems within a specific network. Notice in Figure 4-17 that 6to4 and Teredo are used on the Internet and ISATAP is used within an intranet.

While many of these automatic tunneling techniques reduce administration overhead, because network administrators do not have to configure each and every system and network device with two different IP addresses, there are security risks that need to be understood. Many times users and network administrators do not know that automatic tunneling capabilities are enabled, and thus they do not ensure that these different tunnels are secured and/or are being monitored. If you are an administrator of a network and have intrusion detection systems (IDSs), intrusion prevention systems (IPSs), and

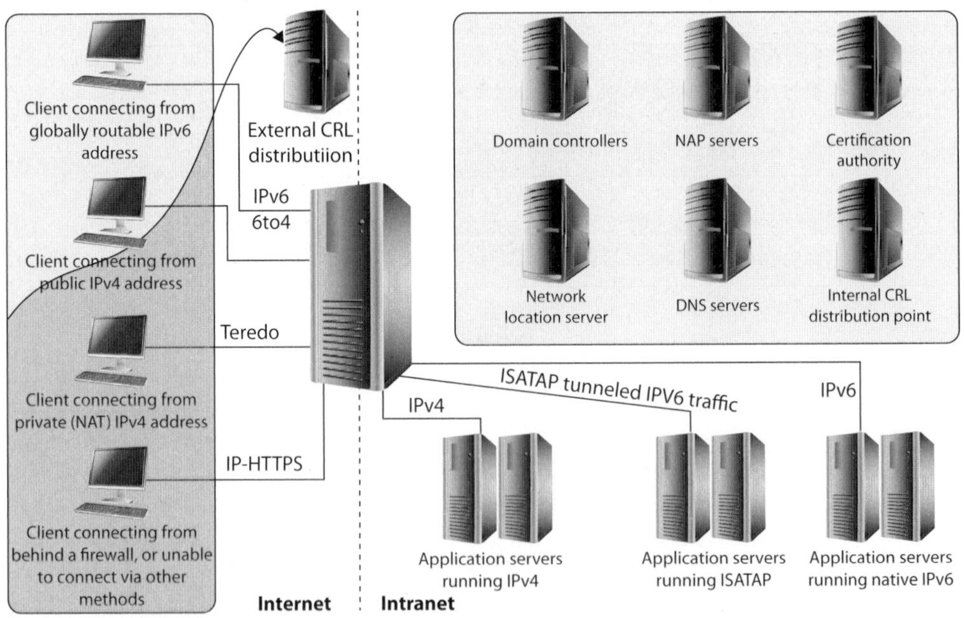

Figure 4-17 Various IPv4 to IPv6 tunneling techniques

firewalls that are only configured to monitor and restrict IPv4 traffic, then all IPv6 traffic could be traversing your network insecurely. Attackers use these protocol tunnels and misconfigurations to get past these types of security devices so that malicious activities can take place unnoticed. If you are a user and have a host-based firewall that only understands IPv4 and your operating system has a dual IPv4/IPv6 networking stack, traffic could be bypassing your firewall without being monitored and logged. The use of Teredo can actually open ports in NAT devices that allow for unintended traffic in and out of a network. It is critical that people who are responsible for configuring and maintaining systems and networks understand the differences between IPv4 and IPv6 and how the various tunneling mechanisms work so that all vulnerabilities are identified and properly addressed. Products and software may need to be updated to address both traffic types, proxies may need to be deployed to manage traffic communication securely, IPv6 should be disabled if not needed, and security appliances need to be configured to monitor all traffic types.

Layer 2 Security Standards

As frames pass from one network device to another device, attackers could sniff the data; modify the headers; redirect the traffic; spoof traffic; carry out man-in-the-middle attacks, DoS attacks, and replay attacks; and indulge in other malicious activities. It has become necessary to secure network traffic at the frame level, which is layer 2 of the OSI model.

802.1AE is the IEEE MAC Security standard (MACSec), which defines a security infrastructure to provide data confidentiality, data integrity, and data origin authentication. Where a virtual private network (VPN) connection provides protection at the higher networking layers, MACSec provides hop-by-hop protection at layer 2, as shown in Figure 4-18.

MACSec integrates security protection into wired Ethernet networks to secure LAN-based traffic. Only authenticated and trusted devices on the network can communicate with each other. Unauthorized devices are prevented from communicating via the network, which helps prevent attackers from installing rogue devices and redirecting traffic between nodes in an unauthorized manner. When a frame arrives at a device that is configured with MACSec, the MACSec Security Entity (SecY) decrypts the frame if necessary and computes an integrity check value (ICV) on the frame and compares it with the ICV that was sent with the frame. If the ICVs match, the device processes the

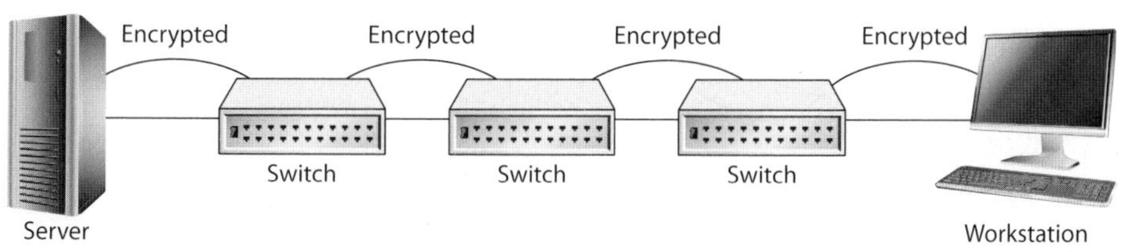

Figure 4-18 MACSec provides layer 2 frame protection.

frame. If they do not match, the device handles the frame according to a preconfigured policy, such as discarding it.

The *IEEE 802.1AR* standard specifies unique per-device identifiers (DevID) and the management and cryptographic binding of a device (router, switch, access point) to its identifiers. A verifiable unique device identity allows establishment of the trustworthiness of devices, and thus facilitates secure device provisioning.

As a security administrator you really only want devices that are allowed on your network to be plugged into your network. But how do you properly and uniquely identify devices? The manufacture serial number is not available for a protocol to review. MAC, hostnames, and IP addresses are easily spoofed. 802.1AR defines a globally unique per-device secure identifier cryptographically bound to the device through the use of public cryptography and digital certificates. These unique hardware-based credentials can be used with the Extensible Authentication Protocol-Transport Layer Security (EAP-TLS) authentication framework. Each device that is compliant with IEEE 802.1AR comes with a single built-in initial secure device identity (iDevID). The iDevID is an instance of the general concept of a DevID, which is intended to be used with authentication protocols such as EAP, which is supported by IEEE 802.1X.

So 802.1AR provides a unique ID for a device. 802.1AE provides data encryption, integrity, and origin authentication functionality. 802.1AF carries out key agreement functions for the session keys used for data encryption. Each of these standards provides specific parameters to work within an 802.1X EAP-TLS framework, as shown in Figure 4-19.

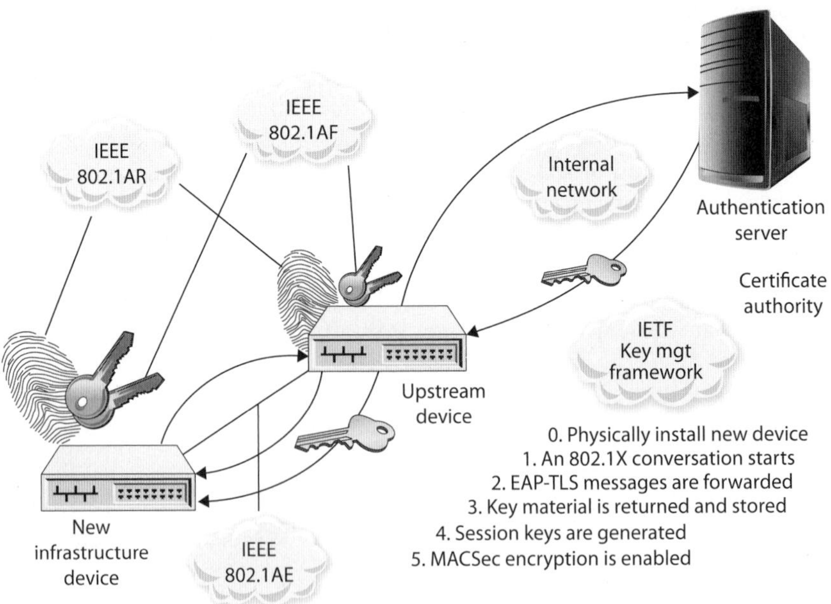

Figure 4-19 Layer 2 security protocols

As Figure 4-19 shows, when a new device is installed on the network, it cannot just start communicating with other devices, receive an IP address from a Dynamic Host Configuration Protocol (DHCP) server, resolve names with the DNS server, etc. The device cannot carry out any network activity until it is authorized to do so. So 802.1X port authentication kicks in, which means that only authentication data is allowed to travel from the new device to the authenticating server. The authentication data is the digital certificate and hardware identity associated with that device (802.1AR), which is processed by EAP-TLS. Once the device is authenticated, usually by a Remote Authentication Dial-In User Server (RADIUS) server, encryption keying material is negotiated and agreed upon between surrounding network devices. Once the keying material is installed, then data encryption and frame integrity checking can take place (802.1AE) as traffic goes from one network device to the next.

These IEEE standards are new and evolving and at different levels of implementation by various vendors. One way the unique hardware identity and cryptographic material are embedded in new network devices is through the use of a Trusted Platform Module (TPM; described in Chapter 3).

Converged Protocols

Converged protocols are those that started off independent and distinct from one another but over time converged to become one. How is this possible? Think about the phone and data networks. Once upon a time, these were two different entities and each had its own protocols and transmission media. For a while, in the 1990s, data networks sometimes rode over voice networks using data modems. This was less than ideal, which is why we flipped it around and started using data networks as the carrier for voice communications. Over time, the voice protocols converged onto the data protocols, which paved the way for Voice over IP (VoIP).

Technically, the term *converged* implies that the two protocols became one. Oftentimes, however, the term is used to describe cases in which one protocol was originally independent of another, but over time started being encapsulated (or tunneled) within that other one. The following are examples of converged protocols:

- **Fibre Channel over Ethernet (FCoE)** This is a protocol encapsulation that allows Fibre Channel (FC) frames to ride over Ethernet networks. FC was developed by ANSI in 1988 as a way to connect supercomputers using optical fibers. Nowadays FCoE is used in some storage area networks (SANs), but is not common.
- **Multiprotocol Label Switching (MPLS)** MPLS was originally developed to improve routing performance, but is frequently used for its ability to create VPNs over a variety of layer 2 protocols. It has elements of both layer 2 (data link) and layer 3 (networking), and so is commonly referred to as a layer 2.5 protocol. MPLS is considered a converged protocol because it can encapsulate any higher-layer protocol and tunnel it over a variety of links.

- **Internet Small Computer System Interface (iSCSI)** iSCSI encapsulates SCSI data in TCP segments. SCSI is a set of technologies that allows peripherals to be connected to computers. The problem with the original SCSI was that it has limited range, which means that connecting a remote peripheral (e.g., camera or storage device) is not normally possible. The solution was to let SCSI ride on TCP segments so a peripheral device could be literally anywhere in the world and still appear as local to a computer.

IP convergence, which addresses a specific type of converged protocols, is the transition of services from disparate transport media and protocols to IP. The earlier example of VoIP is also a case of IP convergence. It is not hard to see that IP has emerged as the dominant standard for networking, so it makes sense that any new protocols would leverage this existing infrastructure rather than create a separate one.

Types of Transmission

Physical data transmission can happen in different ways (analog or digital); can use different synchronization schemes (synchronous or asynchronous); can use either one sole channel over a transmission medium (baseband) or several different channels over a transmission medium (broadband); and can take place as electrical voltage, radio wave, or optical signals. These transmission types and their characteristics are described in the following sections.

Analog and Digital

A *signal* is just some way of moving information in a physical format from one point to another point. You can signal a message to another person through nodding your head, waving your hand, or giving a wink. Somehow you are transmitting data to that person through your signaling method. In the world of technology, we have specific carrier signals that are in place to move data from one system to another system. The carrier signal is like a horse, which takes a rider (data) from one place to another place. Data can be transmitted through analog or digital signaling formats. If you are moving data through an analog transmission technology (e.g., radio), then the data is represented by the characteristics of the waves that are carrying it. For example, a radio station uses a transmitter to put its data (music) onto a radio wave that will travel all the way to your antenna. The information is stripped off by the receiver in your radio and presented to you in its original format—a song. The data is encoded onto the carrier signal and is represented by various amplitude and frequency values, as shown in Figure 4-20.

Data being represented in wave values (analog) is different from data being represented in discrete voltage values (digital). As an analogy, compare an analog clock and a digital clock. An analog clock has hands that continuously rotate on the face of the clock. To figure out what time it is, you have to interpret the position of the hands and map their positions to specific values. So you have to know that if the large hand is on the number 1 and the small hand is on the number 6, this actually means 1:30. The individual and specific location of the hands corresponds to a value. A digital clock does not take this much work. You just look at it and it gives you a time value in the format of

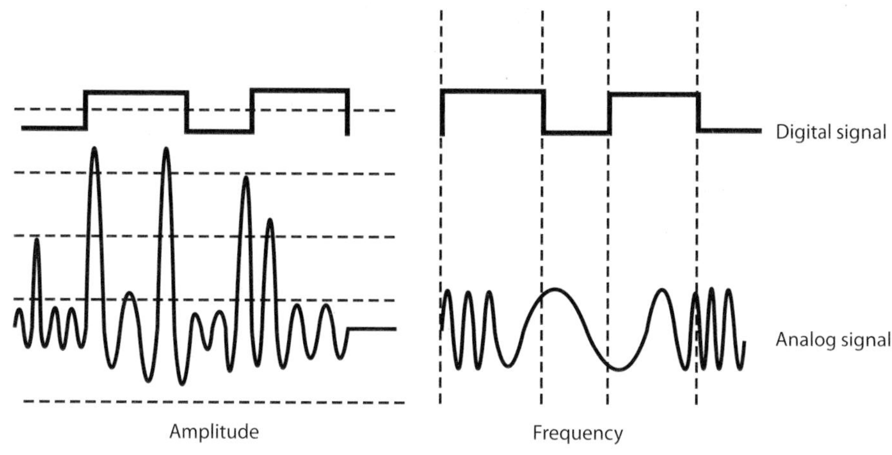

Figure 4-20 Analog signals are measured in amplitude and frequency, whereas digital signals represent binary digits as electrical pulses.

number:number. There is no mapping work involved with a digital clock because it provides you with data in clear-cut formats.

An analog clock can represent different values as the hands move forward—1:35 and 1 second, 1:35 and 2 seconds, 1:35 and 3 seconds. Each movement of the hands represents a specific value just like the individual data points on a wave in an analog transmission. A digital clock provides discrete values without having to map anything. The same is true with digital transmissions: the value is always either a 1 or a 0—no need for mapping to find the actual value.

Computers have always worked in a binary and digital manner (1 or 0). When our telecommunication infrastructure was purely analog, each system that needed to communicate over a telecommunication line had to have a modem (modulator/demodulator), which would modulate the digital data into an analog signal. The sending system's modem would modulate the data on to the signal, and the receiving system's modem would demodulate the data off the signal.

Digital signals are more reliable than analog signals over a long distance and provide a clear-cut and efficient signaling method because the voltage is either on (1) or not on (0), compared to interpreting the waves of an analog signal. Extracting digital signals from a noisy carrier is relatively easy. It is difficult to extract analog signals from background noise because the amplitudes and frequencies of the waves slowly lose form. This is because an analog signal could have an infinite number of values or states, whereas a digital signal exists in discrete states. A digital signal is a square wave, which does not have all of the possible values of the different amplitudes and frequencies of an analog signal. Digital systems can implement compression mechanisms to increase data throughput, provide signal integrity through repeaters that "clean up" the transmissions, and multiplex different types of data (voice, data, video) onto the same transmission channel. As we will see in following sections, most telecommunication technologies have moved from analog to digital transmission technologies.

EXAM TIP *Bandwidth* refers to the number of electrical pulses that can be transmitted over a link within a second, and these electrical pulses carry individual *bits* of information. Bandwidth is the data transfer *capability* of a connection and is commonly associated with the amount of available frequencies and speed of a link. *Data throughput* is the actual amount of data that can be carried over this connection. Data throughput values can be higher than bandwidth values if compression mechanisms are implemented. But if links are highly congested or there are interference issues, the data throughput values can be lower. Both bandwidth and data throughput are measured in bits per second.

Asynchronous and Synchronous

Analog and digital transmission technologies deal with the characteristics of the physical carrier on which data is moved from one system to another. Asynchronous and synchronous transmission types are similar to the cadence rules we use for conversation *synchronization*. Asynchronous and synchronous network technologies provide synchronization rules to govern how systems communicate to each other. If you have ever spoken over a satellite phone, you have probably experienced problems with communication synchronization. You and the other person talking do not allow for the necessary delay that satellite communication requires, so you "speak over" one another. Once you figure out the delay in the connection, you resynchronize your timing so that only one person's data (voice) is transmitting at one time so that each person can properly understand the full conversation. Proper pauses frame your words in a way to make them understandable.

Synchronization through communication also happens when we write messages to each other. Properly placed commas, periods, and semicolons provide breaks in text so that the person reading the message can better understand the information. If you see "stickwithmekidandyouwillweardiamonds" without the proper punctuation, it is more difficult for you to understand. This is why we have grammar rules. If someone writes you a letter starting from the bottom and right side of a piece of paper and you do not know this, you will not be able to read his message properly.

Technological communication protocols also have their own grammar and synchronization rules when it comes to the transmission of data. If two systems are communicating over a network protocol that employs asynchronous timing, then start and stop bits are used. The sending system sends a "start" bit, then sends its character, and then sends a "stop" bit. This happens for the whole message. The receiving system knows when a character is starting and stopping; thus, it knows how to interpret each character of the message. This is akin to our previous example of using punctuation marks in written communications to convey pauses. If the systems are communicating over a network protocol that uses synchronous timing, then no start and stop bits are added. The whole message is sent without artificial breaks, but with a common timing signal that allows the receiver to know how to interpret the information without these bits. This is similar to our satellite phone example in which we use a timing signal (i.e., we count off seconds in our head) to ensure we don't step all over the other person's speech.

If two systems are going to communicate using a synchronous transmission technology, they do not use start and stop bits, but the synchronization of the transfer of data takes place through a timing sequence, which is initiated by a clock pulse.

It is the data link protocol that has the synchronization rules embedded into it. So when a message goes down a system's network stack, if a data link protocol, such as High-level Data Link Control (HDLC, described later in the chapter), is being used, then a clocking sequence is in place. (The receiving system has to also be using this protocol so it can interpret the data.) If the message is going down a network stack and a protocol such as Asynchronous Transfer Mode (ATM) is at the data link layer, then the message is framed with start and stop indicators.

Data link protocols that employ synchronous timing mechanisms are commonly used in environments that have systems that transfer large amounts of data in a predictable manner (i.e., mainframe environment). Environments that contain systems that send data in a nonpredictable manner (i.e., Internet connections) commonly have systems with protocols that use asynchronous timing mechanisms.

So, synchronous communication protocols transfer data as a stream of bits instead of framing it in start and stop bits. The synchronization can happen between two systems using a clocking mechanism, or a signal can be encoded into the data stream to let the receiver synchronize with the sender of the message. This synchronization needs to take place before the first message is sent. The sending system can transmit a digital clock pulse to the receiving system, which translates into, "We will start here and work in this type of synchronization scheme." Many modern bulk communication systems, such as high-bandwidth satellite links, use Global Positioning System (GPS) clock signals to synchronize their communications without the need to include a separate channel for timing.

Communication Characteristics

Asynchronous:

- No timing component
- Surrounds each byte with processing bits
- Parity bit used for error control
- Each byte requires three bits of instruction (start, stop, parity)

Synchronous:

- Timing component for data transmission synchronization
- Robust error checking, commonly through cyclic redundancy checking (CRC)
- Used for high-speed, high-volume transmissions
- Minimal overhead compared to asynchronous communication

Broadband and Baseband

So analog transmission means that data is being moved as waves, and digital transmission means that data is being moved as discrete electric pulses. Synchronous transmission means that two devices control their conversations with a clocking mechanism, and asynchronous means that systems use start and stop bits for communication synchronization. Now let's look at how many individual communication sessions can take place at one time.

A *baseband* technology uses the entire communication channel for its transmission, whereas a *broadband* technology divides the communication channel into individual and independent subchannels so that different types of data can be transmitted simultaneously. Baseband permits only one signal to be transmitted at a time, whereas broadband carries several signals over different subchannels. For example, a coaxial cable TV (CATV) system is a broadband technology that delivers multiple television channels over the same cable. This system can also provide home users with Internet access, but this data is transmitted at a different frequency range than the TV channels.

As an analogy, baseband technology only provides a one-lane highway for data to get from one point to another point. A broadband technology provides a data highway made up of many different lanes, so that not only can more data be moved from one point to another point, but different types of data can travel over the individual lanes.

Any transmission technology that "chops up" one communication channel into multiple channels is considered broadband. The communication channel is usually a specific range of frequencies, and the broadband technology provides delineation between these frequencies and techniques on how to modulate the data onto the individual subchannels. To continue with our analogy, we could have one large highway that *could* fit eight individual lanes—but unless we have something that defines these lanes and there are rules for how these lanes are used, this is a baseband connection. If we take the same highway and lay down painted white lines, traffic signs, on and off ramps, and rules that drivers have to follow, now we are talking about broadband.

A digital subscriber line (DSL) uses one single phone line and constructs a set of high-frequency channels for Internet data transmissions. A cable modem uses the available frequency spectrum that is provided by a cable TV carrier to move Internet traffic to and from a household. Mobile broadband devices implement individual channels over a cellular connection, and Wi-Fi broadband technology moves data to and from an access point over a specified frequency set. We will cover these technologies in more depth throughout the chapter, but for now you just need to understand that they are different ways of cutting up one channel into individual channels for higher data transfer and that they provide the capability to move different types of traffic at the same time.

How Do These Technologies Work Together?

If you are new to networking, it can be hard to understand how the OSI model, analog and digital, synchronous and asynchronous, and baseband and broadband technologies interrelate and differentiate. You can think of the OSI model as a structure to build different languages. If you and Luigi are going to speak to each other in

English, you have to follow the rules of this language to be able to understand each other. If you are going to speak French, you still have to follow the rules of language (OSI model), but the individual letters that make up the words are in a different order. The OSI model is a generic structure that can be used to define many different "languages" for devices to be able to talk to each other. Once you and Luigi agree that you are going to communicate using English, you can *speak* your message to Luigi, and thus your words move over continuous airwaves (analog). Or you can choose to send your message to Luigi through Morse code, which uses individual discrete values (digital). You can send Luigi all of your words with no pauses or punctuation (synchronous) or insert pauses and punctuation (asynchronous). If you are the only one speaking to Luigi at a time, this would be analogous to baseband. If ten people are speaking to Luigi at one time, this would be broadband.

Next, let's look at the different ways we connect the many devices that make up small and large networks around the world.

Cabling

Electrical signals travel as currents through cables and can be negatively affected by many factors within the environment, such as motors, fluorescent lighting, magnetic forces, and other electrical devices. These items can corrupt the data as it travels through the cable, which is why cable standards are used to indicate cable type, shielding, transmission rates, and maximum distance a particular type of cable can be used.

Cabling has bandwidth values associated with it, which is different from data throughput values. Although these two terms are related, they are indeed different. The bandwidth of a cable indicates the highest frequency range it uses—for instance, 10Base-T uses 10 MHz, 100Base-TX uses 80 MHz, and 1000Base-T uses 100 MHz. This is different from the actual amount of data that can be pushed through a cable. The data throughput rate is the actual amount of data that goes through the wire after compression and encoding have been used. 10Base-T has a data rate of 10 Mbps, 100Base-TX has a data rate of 100 Mbps, and 1000Base-T has a data rate of 1 Gbps. The bandwidth can be thought of as the size of the pipe, and the data throughput rate is the actual amount of data that travels per second through that pipe.

Bandwidth is just one of the characteristics we will look at as we cover various cabling types in the following sections.

Coaxial Cable

Coaxial cable has a copper core that is surrounded by a shielding layer and grounding wire, as shown in Figure 4-21. This is all encased within a protective outer jacket. Compared to twisted-pair cable, coaxial cable is more resistant to electromagnetic interference

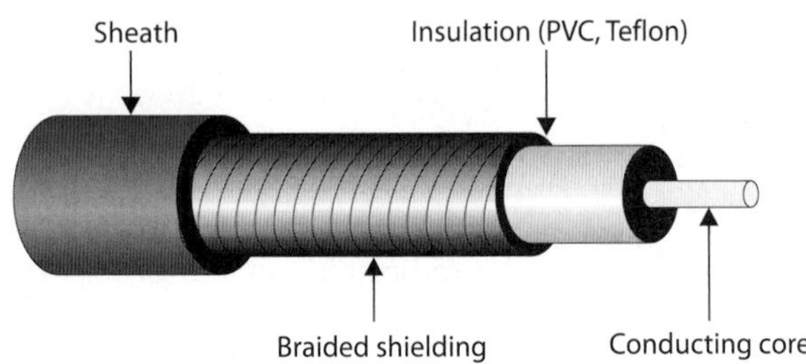

Figure 4-21 Coaxial cable

(EMI), provides a higher bandwidth, and supports the use of longer cable lengths. So, why is twisted-pair cable more popular? Twisted-pair cable is cheaper and easier to work with, and the move to switched environments that provide hierarchical wiring schemes has overcome the cable-length issue of twisted-pair cable.

Coaxial cabling is used as a transmission line for radio frequency signals. If you have cable TV, you have coaxial cabling entering your house and the back of your TV. The various TV channels are carried over different radio frequencies. We will cover cable modems later in this chapter, which is a technology that allows you to use some of the "empty" TV frequencies for Internet connectivity.

Twisted-Pair Cable

Twisted-pair cabling has insulated copper wires surrounded by an outer protective jacket. If the cable has an outer foil shielding, it is referred to as *shielded twisted pair (STP)*, which adds protection from radio frequency interference (RFI) and EMI. Twisted-pair cabling, which does not have this extra outer shielding, is called *unshielded twisted pair (UTP)*.

The twisted-pair cable contains copper wires that twist around each other, as shown in Figure 4-22. This twisting of the wires protects the integrity and strength of the signals they carry. Each wire forms a balanced circuit, because the voltage in each pair uses the same amplitude, just with opposite phases. The tighter the twisting of the wires, the more resistant the cable is to interference and attenuation. UTP has several categories of cabling, each of which has its own unique characteristics.

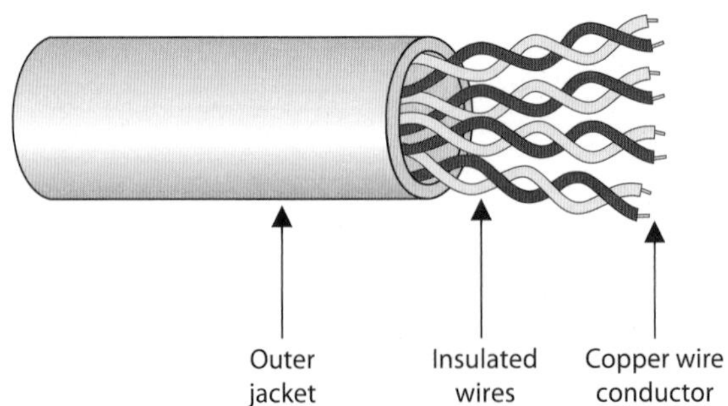

Figure 4-22 Twisted-pair cabling uses copper wires.

UTP Category	Characteristics	Usage
Category 1	Voice-grade telephone cable for up to 1 Mbps transmission rate	Not recommended for network use, but modems can communicate over it.
Category 2	Data transmission up to 4 Mbps	Used in mainframe and minicomputer terminal connections, but not recommended for high-speed networking.
Category 3	10 Mbps for Ethernet and 4 Mbps for Token Ring	Used in 10Base-T network installations.
Category 4	16 Mbps	Normally used in Token Ring networks.
Category 5	100 Mbps; has high twisting and thus low crosstalk	Used in 100Base-TX, CDDI, Ethernet, and ATM installations; most widely used in network installations.
Category 6	1 Gbps	Used in new network installations requiring high-speed transmission. Standard for Gigabit Ethernet.
Category 7	10 Gbps	Used in new network installations requiring higher-speed transmission.

Table 4-3 UTP Cable Ratings

The twisting of the wires, the type of insulation used, the quality of the conductive material, and the shielding of the wire determine the rate at which data can be transmitted. The UTP ratings indicate which of these components were used when the cables were manufactured. Some types are more suitable and effective for specific uses and environments. Table 4-3 lists the cable ratings.

Copper cable has been around for many years. It is inexpensive and easy to use. A majority of the telephone systems today use copper cabling with the rating of voice grade. Twisted-pair wiring is the preferred network cabling, but it also has its drawbacks. Copper actually resists the flow of electrons, which causes a signal to degrade after it has traveled a certain distance. This is why cable lengths are recommended for copper cables; if these recommendations are not followed, a network could experience signal loss and data corruption. Copper also radiates energy, which means information can be monitored and captured by intruders. UTP is the least secure networking cable compared to coaxial and fiber. If a company requires higher speed, higher security, and cables to have longer runs than what is allowed in copper cabling, fiber-optic cable may be a better choice.

Fiber-Optic Cable

Twisted-pair cable and coaxial cable use copper wires as their data transmission media, but fiber-optic cable uses a type of glass that carries light waves, which represent the data being transmitted. The glass core is surrounded by a protective cladding, which in turn is encased within an outer jacket.

Because it uses glass, *fiber-optic* cabling has higher transmission speeds that allow signals to travel over longer distances. Fiber cabling is not as affected by attenuation and EMI when compared to cabling that uses copper. It does not radiate signals, as does

UTP cabling, and is difficult to eavesdrop on; therefore, fiber-optic cabling is much more secure than UTP, STP, or coaxial.

Using fiber-optic cable sounds like the way to go, so you might wonder why you would even bother with UTP, STP, or coaxial. Unfortunately, fiber-optic cable is expensive and difficult to work with. It is usually used in backbone networks and environments that require high data transfer rates. Most networks use UTP and connect to a backbone that uses fiber.

NOTE The price of fiber and the cost of installation have been continuously decreasing, while the demand for more bandwidth only increases. More organizations and service providers are installing fiber directly to the end user.

Fiber Components

Fiber-optic cables are made up of a light source, an optical fiber cable, and a light detector.

Light sources Convert electrical signal into light signal.

- Light-emitting diodes (LEDs)
- Diode lasers

Optical fiber cable Data travels as light.

- **Single mode** Small glass core, and are used for high-speed data transmission over long distances. They are less susceptible to attenuation than multimode fibers.
- **Multimode** Large glass cores, and are able to carry more data than single-core fibers, though they are best for shorter distances because of their higher attenuation levels.

Light detector Converts light signal back into electrical signal.

Cabling Problems

Cables are extremely important within networks, and when they experience problems, the whole network could experience problems. This section addresses some of the more common cabling issues many networks experience.

Noise

Noise on a line is usually caused by surrounding devices or by characteristics of the wiring's environment. Noise can be caused by motors, computers, copy machines, fluorescent lighting, and microwave ovens, to name a few. This background noise can

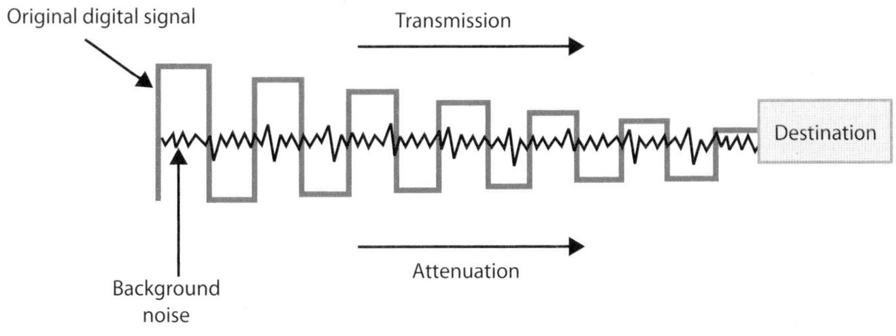

Figure 4-23 Background noise can merge with an electronic signal and alter the signal's integrity.

combine with the data being transmitted over the cable and distort the signal, as shown in Figure 4-23. The more noise there is interacting with the cable, the more likely the receiving end will not receive the data in the form originally transmitted.

Attenuation

Attenuation is the loss of signal strength as it travels. This is akin to rolling a ball down the floor; as it travels, air causes resistance that slows it down and eventually stops it. In the case of electricity, the metal in the wire also offers resistance to the flow of electricity. Though some materials such as copper and gold offer very little resistance, it is still there. The longer a wire, the more attenuation occurs, which causes the signal carrying the data to deteriorate. This is why standards include suggested cable-run lengths.

The effects of attenuation increase with higher frequencies; thus, 100Base-TX at 80 MHz has a higher attenuation rate than 10Base-T at 10 MHz. This means that cables used to transmit data at higher frequencies should have shorter cable runs to ensure attenuation does not become an issue.

If a networking cable is too long, attenuation will become a problem. Basically, the data is in the form of electrons, and these electrons have to "swim" through a copper wire. However, this is more like swimming upstream, because there is a lot of resistance on the electrons working in this media. After a certain distance, the electrons start to slow down and their encoding format loses form. If the form gets too degraded, the receiving system cannot interpret them any longer. If a network administrator needs to run a cable longer than its recommended segment length, she needs to insert a repeater or some type of device that will amplify the signal and ensure it gets to its destination in the right encoding format.

Attenuation can also be caused by cable breaks and malfunctions. This is why cables should be tested. If a cable is suspected of attenuation problems, cable testers can inject signals into the cable and read the results at the end of the cable.

Crosstalk

Crosstalk is a phenomenon that occurs when electrical signals of one wire spill over to the signals of another wire. When electricity flows through a wire, it generates a magnetic field around it. If another wire is close enough, the second wire acts as an antenna that turns this magnetic field into an electric current. When the different electrical signals mix, their integrity degrades and data corruption can occur. UTP is much more vulnerable to crosstalk than STP or coaxial because it does not have extra layers of shielding to help protect against it.

Fire Rating of Cables

Just as buildings must meet certain fire codes, so must wiring schemes. A lot of companies string their network wires in drop ceilings—the space between the ceiling and the next floor—or under raised floors. This hides the cables and prevents people from tripping over them. However, when wires are strung in places like this, they are more likely to catch on fire without anyone knowing about it. Some cables produce hazardous gases when on fire that would spread throughout the building quickly. Network cabling that is placed in these types of areas, called *plenum space*, must meet a specific fire rating to ensure it will not produce and release harmful chemicals in case of a fire. A ventilation system's components are usually located in this plenum space, so if toxic chemicals were to get into that area, they could easily spread throughout the building in minutes.

Nonplenum cables usually have a polyvinyl chloride (PVC) jacket covering, whereas plenum-rated cables have jacket covers made of fluoropolymers. When setting up a network or extending an existing network, it is important you know which wire types are required in which situation.

Cables should be installed in unexposed areas so they are not easily tripped over, damaged, or eavesdropped upon. The cables should be strung behind walls and in the protected spaces as in dropped ceilings. In environments that require extensive security, wires can be encapsulated within *pressurized conduits* so if someone attempts to access a wire, the pressure of the conduit will change, causing an alarm to sound and a message to be sent to the security staff. A better approach to high-security requirements is probably to use fiber-optic cable, which is much more difficult to covertly tap.

NOTE While a lot of the world's infrastructure is wired and thus uses one of these types of cables, remember that a growing percentage of our infrastructure is not wired. We will cover these technologies later in the chapter (mobile, wireless, satellite, etc.).

Networking Foundations

Networking has made amazing advances in just a short period of time. In the beginning of the Computer Age, mainframes were the name of the game. They were isolated powerhouses, and many had "dumb" terminals hanging off them. However, this was not true networking. In the late 1960s and early 1970s, some technical researchers came up with ways of connecting all the mainframes and Unix systems to enable them to communicate. This marked the Internet's baby steps.

Microcomputers evolved and were used in many offices and work areas. Slowly, dumb terminals got a little smarter and more powerful as users needed to share office resources. And bam! Ethernet was developed, which allowed for true networking. There was no turning back after this.

While access to shared resources was a major drive in the evolution of networking, today the infrastructure that supports these shared resources and the services these components provide is really the secret to the secret sauce. As we will see, networks are made up of routers, switches, web servers, proxies, firewalls, name resolution technologies, protocols, IDS, IPS, storage systems, antimalware software, virtual private networks, demilitarized zones (DMZs), data loss prevention solutions, e-mail systems, cloud computing, web services, authentication services, redundant technologies, public key infrastructure, private branch exchange (PBX), and more. While functionality is critical, there are other important requirements that need to be understood when architecting a network, such as scalability, redundancy, performance, security, manageability, and maintainability.

Infrastructure provides foundational capabilities that support almost every aspect of our lives. When most people think of technology, they focus on the end systems that they interact with—laptops, mobile phones, tablet PCs, workstations, etc.—or the applications they use, such as e-mail, fax, Facebook, websites, instant messaging, Twitter, and online banking. Most people do not even give a thought to how this stuff works under the covers, and many people do not fully realize all the other stuff that is dependent upon technology: medical devices, critical infrastructure, weapon systems, transportation, satellites, telephony, etc. People say it is love that makes the world go around, but let them experience one day without the Internet. We are all more dependent upon the Matrix than we fully realize, and as security professionals we need to not only understand the Matrix, but also secure it.

Network Topology

The arrangement of computers and devices is called a *network topology*. Topology refers to the manner in which a network is physically connected and shows the layout of resources and systems. A difference exists between the physical network topology and the logical topology. A network can be configured as a physical star but work logically as a ring, as in the Token Ring technology.

The best topology for a particular network depends on such things as how nodes are supposed to interact; which protocols are used; the types of applications that are available; the reliability, expandability, and physical layout of a facility; existing wiring; and the technologies implemented. The wrong topology or combination of topologies can negatively affect the network's performance, productivity, and growth possibilities.

This section describes the basic types of network topologies. Most networks are much more complex and are usually implemented using a combination of topologies.

Ring Topology

A *ring topology* has a series of devices connected by unidirectional transmission links, as shown in Figure 4-24. These links form a closed loop and do not connect to a central system, as in a star topology (discussed later). In a physical ring formation, each node is dependent upon the preceding nodes. In simple networks, if one system fails, all other systems could be negatively affected because of this interdependence. Today, most networks have redundancy in place or other mechanisms that will protect a whole network from being affected by just one workstation misbehaving, but one disadvantage of using a ring topology is that this possibility exists.

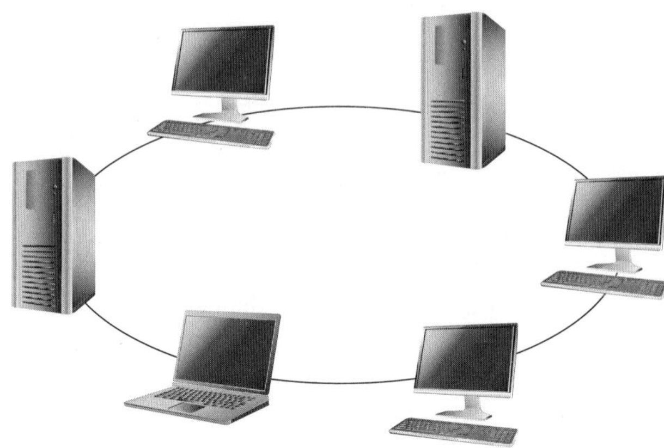

Figure 4-24 A ring topology forms a closed-loop connection.

Bus Topology

In a simple *bus topology*, a single cable runs the entire length of the network. Nodes are attached to the network through drop points on this cable. Data communications transmit the length of the medium, and each packet transmitted has the capability of being "looked at" by all nodes. Each node decides to accept or ignore the packet, depending upon the packet's destination address.

Bus topologies are of two main types: linear and tree. The *linear bus topology* has a single cable with nodes attached. A *tree topology* has branches from the single cable, and each branch can contain many nodes.

In simple implementations of a bus topology, if one workstation fails, other systems can be negatively affected because of the degree of interdependence. In addition, because all nodes are connected to one main cable, the cable itself becomes a potential single point of failure. Traditionally, Ethernet uses bus and star topologies.

Star Topology

In a *star topology*, all nodes connect to a central device such as a switch. Each node has a dedicated link to the central device. The central device needs to provide enough throughput that it does not turn out to be a detrimental bottleneck for the network as a whole. Because a central device is required, it is a potential single point of failure, so redundancy may need to be implemented. Switches can be configured in flat or hierarchical implementations so larger organizations can use them.

When one workstation fails on a star topology, it does not affect other systems, as in the ring or bus topologies. In a star topology, each system is not as dependent on others as it is dependent on the central connection device. This topology generally requires less cabling than other types of topologies. As a result, cut cables are less likely, and detecting cable problems is an easier task.

Not many networks use true linear bus and ring topologies anymore. A ring topology can be used for a backbone network, but most networks are constructed in a star topology because it enables the network to be more resilient and not as affected if an individual node experiences a problem.

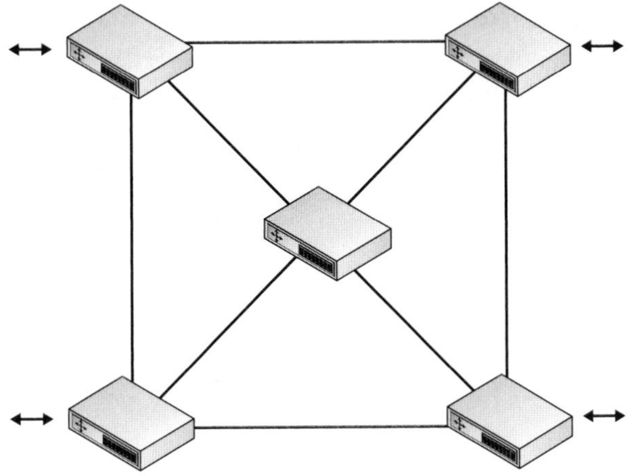

Figure 4-25 In a mesh topology, each node is connected to all other nodes, which provides for redundant paths.

Mesh Topology

In a *mesh topology*, all systems and resources are connected to each other in a way that does not follow the uniformity of the previous topologies, as shown in Figure 4-25. This arrangement is usually a network of interconnected routers and switches that provides multiple paths to all the nodes on the network. In a full mesh topology, every node is directly connected to every other node, which provides a great degree of redundancy. In a partial mesh topology, every node is not directly connected. The Internet is an example of a partial mesh topology.

A summary of the different network topologies and their important characteristics is provided in Table 4-4.

Topology	Characteristics	Problems
Bus	Uses a linear, single cable for all computers attached. All traffic travels the full cable and can be viewed by all other computers.	If one station experiences a problem, it can negatively affect surrounding computers on the same cable.
Ring	All computers are connected by a unidirectional transmission link, and the cable is in a closed loop.	If one station experiences a problem, it can negatively affect surrounding computers on the same ring.
Star	All computers are connected to a central device, which provides more resilience for the network.	The central device is a single point of failure.
Tree	A bus topology with branches off of the main cable.	Multiple single points of failure.
Mesh	Computers are connected to each other, which provides redundancy.	Requires more expense in cabling and extra effort to track down cable faults.

Table 4-4 Summary of Network Topologies

Media Access Technologies

The physical topology of a network is the lower layer, or foundation, of a network. It determines what type of media will be used and how the media will be connected between different systems. Media access technologies deal with how these systems communicate over this media and are usually represented in protocols, NIC drivers, and interfaces. LAN access technologies set up the rules of how computers will communicate on a network, how errors are handled, the maximum transmission unit (MTU) size of frames, and much more. These rules enable all computers and devices to communicate and recover from problems, and enable users to be productive in accomplishing their networking tasks. Each participating entity needs to know how to communicate properly so all other systems will understand the transmissions, instructions, and requests. This is taken care of by the LAN media access technology.

NOTE An MTU is a parameter that indicates how much data a frame can carry on a specific network. Recall that a data frame is the data encapsulation structure that exists at layer 2 (data link) of the OSI model. Different types of network technologies may require different MTU sizes, which is why frames are sometimes fragmented.

These technologies reside at the data link layer of the OSI model. Remember that as a message is passed down through a network stack, it is encapsulated by the protocols and services at each layer. When the data message reaches the data link layer, the protocol at this layer adds the necessary headers and trailers that will allow the message to traverse a specific type of network (Ethernet, Token Ring, FDDI, etc.) The protocol and network driver work at the data link layer, and the NIC works at the physical layer, but they have to work together and be compatible. If you install a new server on an Ethernet network, you must implement an Ethernet NIC and driver.

The LAN-based technologies we will cover in the next sections are Ethernet, Token Ring, and FDDI. We will cover wireless networking technologies later in the chapter.

A *local area network (LAN)* is a network that provides shared communication and resources in a relatively small area. What defines a LAN, as compared to a WAN, depends on the physical medium, encapsulation protocols, and media access technology. For example, a LAN could use 10Base-T cabling, TCP/IP protocols, and Ethernet media access technology, and it could enable users who are in the same local building to communicate. A WAN, on the other hand, could use fiber-optic cabling, the L2TP encapsulation protocol, and ATM media access technology and could enable users from one building to communicate with users in another building in another state (or country). A WAN connects LANs over great distances geographically. Most of the differences between these technologies are found at the data link layer.

Media Sharing

No matter what type of media access technology is being used, the main resource that has to be shared by all systems and devices on the network is the network transmission channel. This transmission channel could be Token Ring over coaxial cabling, Ethernet over UTP, FDDI over fiber, or Wi-Fi over radio waves. There must be methods in place to make sure that each system gets access to the channel, that the system's data is not corrupted during transmission, and that there is a way to control traffic in peak times.

The different media access technologies covered in the previous sections have their own specific media-sharing capabilities, which are covered next.

Token Passing A token is a 24-bit control frame used to control which computers communicate at what intervals. The token is passed from computer to computer, and only the computer that has the token can actually put frames onto the wire. The token grants a computer the right to communicate. The token contains the data to be transmitted and source and destination address information. When a system has data it needs to transmit, it has to wait to receive the token. The computer then connects its message to the token and puts it on the wire. Each computer checks this message to determine whether it is addressed to it, which continues until the destination computer receives the message. The destination computer makes a copy of the message and flips a bit to tell the source computer it did indeed get its message. Once this gets back to the source computer, it removes the frames from the network. The destination computer makes a copy of the message, but only the originator of the message can remove the message from the token and the network.

If a computer that receives the token does not have a message to transmit, it sends the token to the next computer on the network. An empty token has a header, data field, and trailer, but a token that has an actual message has a new header, destination address, source address, and a new trailer.

This type of media-sharing method is used by Token Ring and FDDI technologies.

NOTE Some applications and network protocols work better if they can communicate at determined intervals, instead of "whenever the data arrives." In token-passing technologies, traffic arrives in this type of deterministic nature because not all systems can communicate at one time; only the system that has control of the token can communicate.

CSMA Ethernet protocols define how nodes are to communicate, recover from errors, and access the shared network cable. Ethernet uses CSMA to provide media-sharing capabilities. There are two distinct types of CSMA: CSMA/CD and CSMA/CA.

A transmission is called a *carrier*, so if a computer is transmitting frames, it is performing a carrier activity. When computers use the *carrier sense multiple access with collision detection (CSMA/CD)* protocol, they monitor the transmission activity, or carrier activity, on the wire so they can determine when would be the best time to transmit data. Each node monitors the wire continuously and waits until the wire is free before it transmits its data. As an analogy, consider several people gathered in a group talking here and there about this and that. If a person wants to talk, she usually listens to the current conversation and waits for a break before she proceeds to talk. If she does not wait for the first person to stop talking, she will be speaking at the same time as the other person, and the people around them may not be able to understand fully what each is trying to say.

When using the CSMA/CD access method, computers listen for the absence of a carrier tone on the cable, which indicates that no other system is transmitting data. If two computers sense this absence and transmit data at the same time, a collision can take place. A *collision* happens when two or more frames collide, which most likely corrupts both frames. If a computer puts frames on the wire and its frames collide with another computer's frames, it will abort its transmission and alert all other stations that a collision just took place. All stations will execute a random collision timer to force a delay before they attempt to transmit data. This random collision timer is called the *back-off algorithm.*

NOTE Collisions are usually reduced by dividing a network with routers or switches.

Carrier sense multiple access with collision avoidance (CSMA/CA) is a medium-sharing method in which each computer signals its intent to transmit data before it actually does so. This tells all other computers on the network not to transmit data right now because doing so could cause a collision. Basically, a system listens to the shared medium to determine whether it is busy or free. Once the system identifies that the "coast is clear" and it can put its data on the wire, it sends out a broadcast to all other systems, telling them it is going to transmit information. It is similar to saying, "Everyone shut up. I am going to talk now." Each system will wait a period of time before attempting to transmit data to ensure collisions do not take place. The wireless LAN technology 802.11 uses CSMA/CA for its media access functionality.

Carrier-Sensing and Token-Passing Access Methods

Overall, carrier-sensing access methods are faster than token-passing access methods, but the former do have the problem of collisions. A network segment with many devices can cause too many collisions and slow down the network's performance. Token-passing technologies do not have problems with collisions, but they do not perform at the speed of carrier-sensing technologies. Network routers can help significantly in isolating the network resources for both the CSMA/CD and the token-passing methods.

NOTE When there is just one transmission medium (i.e., UTP cable) that has to be shared by all nodes and devices in a network, this is referred to as a *contention-based* environment. Each system has to "compete" to use the transmission line, which can cause contention.

Collision Domains As indicated in the preceding section, a collision occurs on Ethernet networks when two computers transmit data at the same time. Other computers on the network detect this collision because the overlapping signals of the collision increase the voltage of the signal above a specific threshold. The more devices on a contention-based network, the more likely collisions will occur, which increases network latency (data transmission delays). A collision domain is a group of computers that are contending, or competing, for the same shared communication medium.

An unacceptable amount of collisions can be caused by a highly populated network, a damaged cable or connector, too many repeaters, or cables that exceed the recommended length. If a cable is longer than what is recommended by the Ethernet specification, two computers on opposite ends of the cable may transmit data at the same time. Because the computers are so far away from each other, they may both transmit data and not realize that a collision took place. The systems then go merrily along with their business, unaware that their packets have been corrupted. If the cable is too long, the computers may not listen long enough for evidence of a collision. If the destination computers receive these corrupted frames, they then have to send a request to the source system to retransmit the message, causing even more traffic.

These types of problems are dealt with mainly by implementing collision domains. An Ethernet network has broadcast and collision domains. One subnet will be on the same broadcast and collision domain if it is not separated by routers or bridges. If the same subnet is divided by bridges, the bridges can enable the broadcast traffic to pass between the different parts of a subnet, but not the collisions, as shown in Figure 4-26. This is

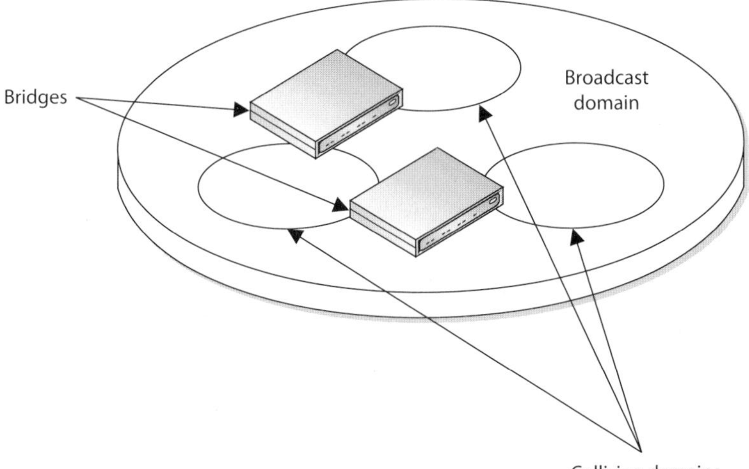

Figure 4-26 Collision domains within one broadcast domain

how collision domains are formed. Isolating collision domains reduces the amount of collisions that take place on a network and increases its overall performance.

EXAM TIP *Broadcast domains* are sets of computing nodes that all receive a layer 2 broadcast frame. These are normally all nodes that are interconnected by switches, hubs, or bridges but with no routers in between them. *Collision domains* are sets of computing nodes that may produce collisions when they transmit data. These are normally nodes connected by hubs, repeaters, or wireless access points.

Another benefit of restricting and controlling broadcast and collision domains is that it makes sniffing the network and obtaining useful information more difficult for an intruder as he traverses the network. A useful tactic for attackers is to install a Trojan horse that sets up a network sniffer on the compromised computer. The sniffer is usually configured to look for a specific type of information, such as usernames and passwords. If broadcast and collision domains are in effect, the compromised system will have access only to the broadcast and collision traffic within its specific subnet or broadcast domain. The compromised system will not be able to listen to traffic on other broadcast and collision domains, and this can greatly reduce the amount of traffic and information available to an attacker.

Polling The third type of media-sharing method is polling. In an environment where a *polling* LAN media access and sharing method is used, some systems are configured as primary stations and others are configured as secondary stations. At predefined intervals, the primary station asks the secondary station if it has anything to transmit. This is the only time a secondary station can communicate.

Polling is a method of monitoring multiple devices and controlling network access transmission. If polling is used to monitor devices, the primary device communicates with each secondary device in an interval to check its status. The primary device then logs the response it receives and moves on to the next device. If polling is used for network access, the primary station asks each device if it has something to communicate to another device. Network access transmission polling is used mainly with mainframe environments.

So remember that there are different media access technologies (Ethernet, Token Ring, FDDI, Wi-Fi) that work at the data link and physical layers of the OSI model. These technologies define the data link protocol, NIC and NIC driver specifications, and media interface requirements. These individual media access technologies have their own way of allowing systems to share the one available network transmission medium—Ethernet uses CSMA\CD, Token Ring uses tokens, FDDI uses tokens, Wi-Fi uses CSMA\CA, and mainframe media access technology uses polling. The media-sharing technology is a subcomponent of the media access technology.

When Is a LAN No Longer a LAN?

When two distinct LANs are connected by a router, the result is an internetwork, not a larger LAN. Each distinct LAN has its own addressing scheme, broadcast domain, and communication mechanisms. If two LANs are connected by a different data link layer technology, such as frame relay or ATM, they are considered a WAN.

The term "local" in the context of a LAN refers not so much to the geographical area as to the limitations of a LAN with regard to the shared medium, the number of devices and computers that can be connected to it, the transmission rates, the types of cable that can be used, and the compatible devices. If a network administrator develops a very large LAN that would more appropriately be multiple LANs, too much traffic could result in a big performance hit, or the cabling could be too long, in which case attenuation (signal loss) becomes a factor. Environments where there are too many nodes, routers, and switches may be overwhelmed, and administration of these networks could get complex, which opens the door for errors, collisions, and security holes. The network administrator should follow the specifications of the technology he is using, and once he has maxed out these numbers, he should consider implementing two or more LANs instead of one large LAN. LANs are defined by their physical topologies, data link layer technologies, protocols, and devices used. The following sections cover these topics and how they interrelate.

Ethernet

Ethernet is a set of technologies that enables several devices to communicate on the same network. Ethernet usually uses a bus or star topology. If a linear bus topology is used, all devices connect to one cable. If a star topology is used, each device is connected to a cable that is connected to a centralized device, such as a switch. Ethernet was developed in the 1970s, became commercially available in 1980, and was officially defined through the IEEE 802.3 standard.

Ethernet has seen quite an evolution in its short history, from purely coaxial cable installations that worked at 10 Mbps to mostly Category 5 twisted-pair cable that works at speeds of 100 Mbps, 1,000 Mbps (1 Gbps), and 10 Gbps.

Ethernet is defined by the following characteristics:

- Contention-based technology (all resources use the same shared communication medium)
- Uses broadcast and collision domains
- Uses the carrier sense multiple access with collision detection (CSMA/CD) access method
- Supports full-duplex communication
- Can use coaxial, twisted-pair, or fiber-optic cabling types
- Is defined by standard IEEE 802.3

Ethernet Type	Cable Type (minimum)	Speed
10Base-T	Cat3 UTP	10 Mbps
100Base-TX, Fast Ethernet	Cat5 UTP	100 Mbps
1000Base-T, Gigabit Ethernet	Cat5 UTP	1,000 Mbps
10GBase-T	Cat6a UTP	10,000 Mbps

Table 4-5 Ethernet Implementation Types

Ethernet addresses how computers share a common network and how they deal with collisions, data integrity, communication mechanisms, and transmission controls. These are the common characteristics of Ethernet, but Ethernet does vary in the type of cabling schemes and transfer rates it can supply. Several types of Ethernet implementations are available, as outlined in Table 4-5. The following sections discuss 10Base-T, 100BaseTX, 1000Base-T, and 10GBase-T, which are common implementations.

10Base-T 10Base-T uses twisted-pair copper wiring instead of coaxial cabling. Twisted-pair wiring uses one wire to transmit data and the other to receive data. 10Base-T is usually implemented in a star topology, which provides easy network configuration. In a star topology, all systems are connected to centralized devices, which can be in a flat or hierarchical configuration.

10Base-T networks have RJ-45 connector faceplates to which the computer connects. The wires usually run behind walls and connect the faceplate to a punchdown block within a wiring closet. The punchdown block is often connected to a 10Base-T hub that serves as a doorway to the network's backbone cable or to a central switch. This type of configuration is shown in Figure 4-27.

100Base-TX Not surprisingly, 10 Mbps was considered heaven-sent when it first arrived on the networking scene, but soon many users were demanding more speed and power. The smart people had to gather into small rooms and hit the whiteboards with ideas, calculations, and new technologies. The result of these meetings, computations, engineering designs, and testing was Fast Ethernet.

Fast Ethernet is regular Ethernet, except that it runs at 100 Mbps over twisted-pair wiring instead of at 10 Mbps. Around the same time Fast Ethernet arrived, another 100-Mbps technology was developed: 100-VG-AnyLAN. This technology did not use Ethernet's traditional CSMA/CD and did not catch on like Fast Ethernet did.

Fast Ethernet uses the traditional CSMA/CD (explained in the "CSMA" section later in the chapter) and the original frame format of Ethernet. This is why it is used in many enterprise LAN environments today. One environment can run 10- and 100-Mbps network segments that can communicate via 10/100 hubs or switches.

1000Base-T Improved Ethernet technology has allowed for gigabit speeds over a Category 5 wire. In the 1000Base-T version, all four pairs of twisted unshielded cable pairs are used for simultaneous transmission in both directions for a maximum distance of 100 meters. Negotiation takes place on two pairs, and if two Gigabit Ethernet devices

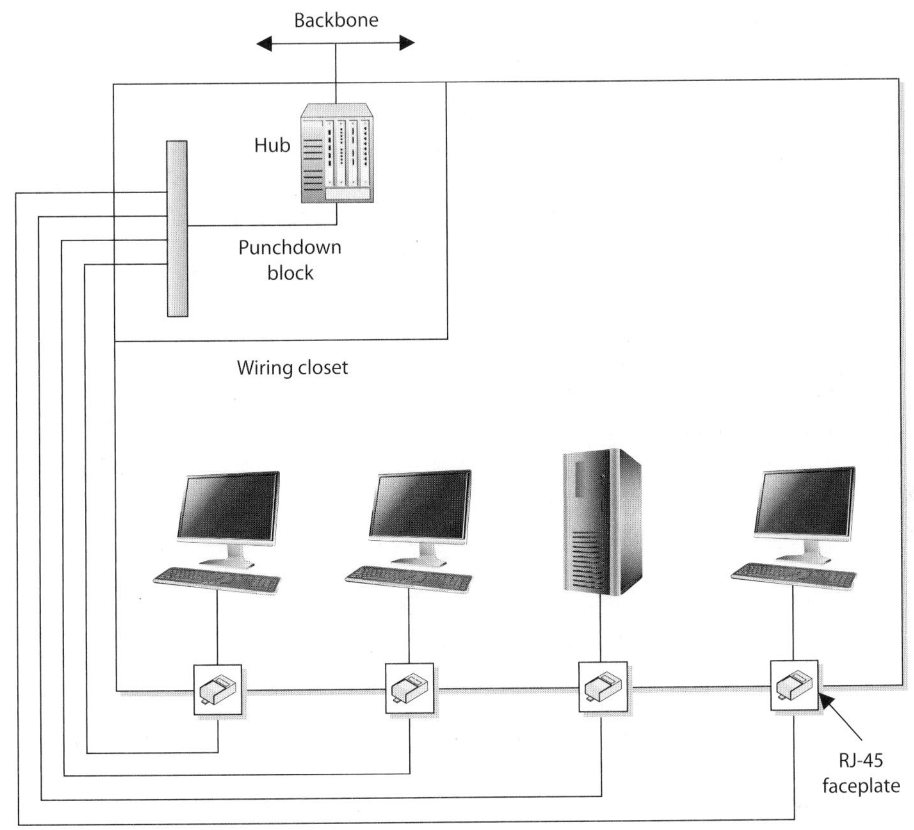

Figure 4-27 Ethernet hosts connect to a punchdown block within the wiring closet, which is connected to the backbone via a hub or switch.

are connected through a cable with only two pairs, the devices will successfully choose "gigabit" as the highest common denominator.

10GBase-T Naturally, the need for faster network protocols continues unabated. After Gigabit Ethernet, the next step was to increase the performance tenfold in order to achieve 10 Gigabit throughputs. In order to do this, engineers had to do away with the venerable CSMA/CD technology that had been at the heart of the 802.3 standards. They also used sophisticated digital signal processing schemes to mitigate the effects of crosstalk and noise, which become increasingly problematic as the data rates increase.

10G Ethernet has not seen the rapid and widespread adoption of Gigabit Ethernet, primarily because of its cost-to-performance ratio. Still, it continues to grow steadily in the enterprise, particularly for interconnecting servers and network storage devices.

We will touch upon Ethernet again later in the chapter because it has beat out many of the other competing media access technologies. While Ethernet started off as just a

LAN technology, it has evolved and is commonly used in metropolitan area networks (MANs) also.

Token Ring

Like Ethernet, *Token Ring* is a LAN media access technology that enables the communication and sharing of networking resources. The Token Ring technology was originally developed by IBM and then defined by the IEEE 802.5 standard. At first, Token Ring technology had the ability to transmit data at 4 Mbps. Later, it was improved to transmit at 16 Mbps. It uses a token-passing technology with a star-configured topology. The *ring* part of the name pertains to how the signals travel, which is in a logical ring. Each computer is connected to a central hub, called a *Multistation Access Unit (MAU).* Physically, the topology can be a star, but the signals and transmissions are passed in a logical ring.

A *token-passing technology* is one in which a device cannot put data on the network wire without having possession of a *token,* a control frame that travels in a logical circle and is "picked up" when a system needs to communicate. This is different from Ethernet, in which all the devices attempt to communicate at the same time. This is why Ethernet is referred to as a "chatty protocol" and has collisions. Token Ring does not endure collisions, since only one system can communicate at a time, but this also means communication takes place more slowly compared to Ethernet.

Token Ring employs a couple of mechanisms to deal with problems that can occur on this type of network. The *active monitor* mechanism removes frames that are continuously circulating on the network. This can occur if a computer locks up or is taken offline for one reason or another and cannot properly receive a token destined for it. With the *beaconing* mechanism, if a computer detects a problem with the network, it sends a beacon frame. This frame generates a failure domain, which is between the computer that issued the beacon and its neighbor downstream. The computers and devices within this failure domain will attempt to reconfigure certain settings to try to work around the detected fault. Figure 4-28 depicts a Token Ring network in a physical star configuration.

Token Ring networks were popular in the 1980s and 1990s, and although some are still around, Ethernet has become much more popular and has taken over the LAN networking market.

FDDI

Fiber Distributed Data Interface (FDDI) technology, developed by the American National Standards Institute (ANSI), is a high-speed, token-passing, media access technology. FDDI has a data transmission speed of up to 100 Mbps and is usually used as a backbone network using fiber-optic cabling. FDDI also provides fault tolerance by offering a second counter-rotating fiber ring. The primary ring has data traveling clockwise and is used for regular data transmission. The second ring transmits data in a counterclockwise fashion and is invoked only if the primary ring goes down. Sensors watch the primary ring and, if it goes down, invoke a ring *wrap* so the data will be diverted to the second ring. Each node on the FDDI network has relays that are connected to both rings, so if a break in the ring occurs, the two rings can be joined.

When FDDI is used as a backbone network, it usually connects several different networks, as shown in Figure 4-29.

Figure 4-28 A Token Ring network

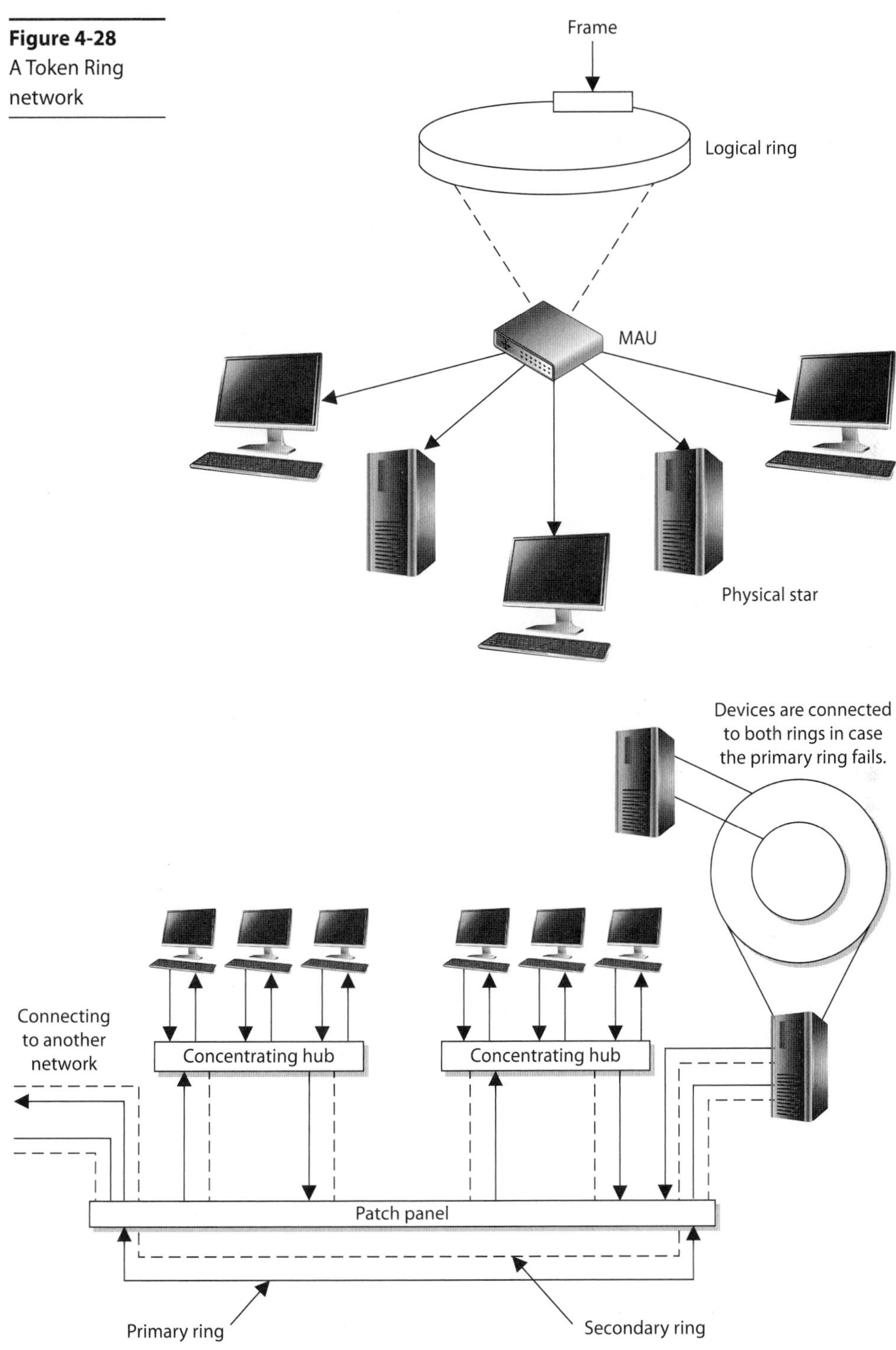

Figure 4-29 FDDI rings can be used as backbones to connect different LANs.

Before Fast Ethernet and Gigabit Ethernet hit the market, FDDI was used mainly as campus and service provider backbones. Because FDDI can be employed for distances up to 100 kilometers, it was often used in MANs. The benefit of FDDI is that it can work over long distances and at high speeds with minimal interference. It enables several tokens to be present on the ring at the same time, causing more communication to take place simultaneously, and it provides predictable delays that help connected networks and devices know what to expect and when.

NOTE FDDI-2 provides fixed bandwidth that can be allocated for specific applications. This makes it work more like a broadband connection with QoS capabilities, which allows for voice, video, and data to travel over the same lines.

A version of FDDI, *Copper Distributed Data Interface (CDDI)*, can work over UTP cabling. Whereas FDDI would be used more as a MAN, CDDI can be used within a LAN environment to connect network segments.

Devices that connect to FDDI rings fall into one of the following categories:

- **Single-attachment station (SAS)** Attaches to only one ring (the primary) through a concentrator
- **Dual-attachment station (DAS)** Has two ports and each port provides a connection for both the primary and the secondary rings
- **Single-attached concentrator (SAC)** Concentrator that connects an SAS device to the primary ring
- **Dual-attached concentrator (DAC)** Concentrator that connects DAS, SAS, and SAC devices to both rings

The different FDDI device types are illustrated in Figure 4-30.

NOTE Ring topologies are considered deterministic, meaning that the rate of the traffic flow can be predicted. Since traffic can only flow if a token is in place, the maximum time that a node will have to wait to receive traffic can be determined. This can be beneficial for time-sensitive applications.

Table 4-6 sums up the important characteristics of the technologies described in the preceding sections.

Transmission Methods

A packet may need to be sent to only one workstation, to a set of workstations, or to all workstations on a particular subnet. If a packet needs to go from the source computer to one particular system, a *unicast* transmission method is used. If the packet needs to go to a specific group of systems, the sending system uses the *multicast* method. If a system wants all computers on its subnet to receive a message, it will use the *broadcast* method.

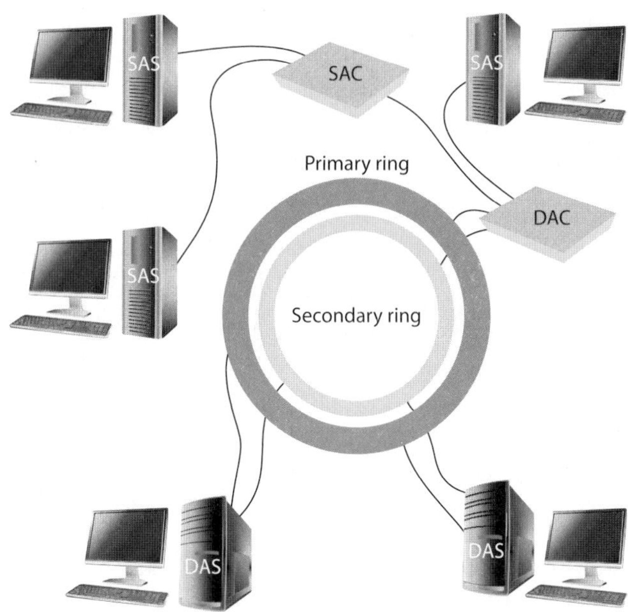

Figure 4-30 FDDI device types

Unicast is pretty simple because it has a source address and a destination address. The data goes from point A to Z, it is a one-to-one transmission, and everyone is happy. Multicast is a bit different in that it is a one-to-many transmission. Multicasting enables one computer to send data to a selective group of computers. A good example of multicasting is tuning into a radio station on a computer. Some computers have software that enables the user to determine whether she wants to listen to country western, pop, or a talk radio station, for example. Once the user selects one of these genres, the software

LAN Implementation	Standard	Characteristics
Ethernet	IEEE 802.3	• Uses broadcast and collision domains. • Uses CSMA/CD access method. • Can use coaxial, twisted-pair, or fiber-optic media. • Transmission speeds of 10 Mbps to 1 Gbps.
Token Ring	IEEE 802.5	• Token-passing media access method. • Transmission speeds of 4 to 16 Mbps. • Uses an active monitor and beaconing. • Effectively defunct.
FDDI	ANSI standard Based on IEEE 802.4	• Dual counter-rotating rings for fault tolerance. • Transmission speeds of 100 Mbps. • Operates over long distances at high speeds and is therefore used as a backbone. • CDDI works over UTP. • Very rarely seen in the enterprise.

Table 4-6 LAN Media Access Methods

must tell the NIC driver to pick up not only packets addressed to its specific MAC address, but also packets that contain a specific multicast address.

The difference between broadcast and multicast is that in a broadcast one-to-all transmission, everyone gets the data, whereas in a multicast, only certain nodes receive the data. So how does a server three states away multicast to one particular computer on a specific network and no other networks in between? Suppose a user tunes in to her favorite Internet radio station. An application running on her computer (say, a web browser) has to tell her local router she wants to get frames with this particular multicast address passed her way. The local router must tell the router upstream, and this process continues so each router between the source and destination knows where to pass this multicast data. This ensures that the user can get her rock music without other networks being bothered with this extra data.

IPv4 multicast protocols use a Class D address (224.0.0.0 to 239.255.255.255), which is a special address space reserved for multicasting. IPv6 multicast addresses start with eight 1's (that is, 1111 1111). Multicasting can be used to send out information; multimedia data; and even real-time video, music, and voice clips.

Internet Group Management Protocol (IGMP) is used to report multicast group memberships to routers. When a user chooses to accept multicast traffic, she becomes a member of a particular multicast group. IGMP is the mechanism that allows her computer to inform the local routers that she is part of this group and to send traffic with a specific multicast address to her system. IGMP can be used for online streaming video and gaming activities. The protocol allows for efficient use of the necessary resources when supporting these types of applications.

Like most protocols, IGMP has gone through a few different versions, each improving upon the earlier one. In version 1, multicast agents periodically send queries to systems on the network they are responsible for and update their databases, indicating which system belongs to which group membership. Version 2 provides more granular query types and allows a system to signal to the agent when it wants to leave a group. Version 3 allows the systems to specify the sources it wants to receive multicast traffic from.

NOTE The previous statements are true pertaining to IPv4. IPv6 is more than just an upgrade to the original IP protocol; it functions differently in many respects, including how it handles multicasting, which has caused many interoperability issues and delay in its full deployment.

Network Protocols and Services

Some protocols, such as UDP, TCP, IP, and IGMP, were addressed in earlier sections. Networks are made up of these and many other types of protocols that provide an array of functionality. Networks are also made up of many different services, as in DHCP, DNS, e-mail, and others. The services that network infrastructure components provide directly support the functionality required of the users of the network. Protocols usually provide a communication channel for these services to use so that they can carry out their jobs. Networks are complex because there are layers of protocols and services that all work together simultaneously and, hopefully, seamlessly. We will cover some of the core protocols and services that are used in all networks today.

Address Resolution Protocol

On a TCP/IP network, each computer and network device requires a unique IP address and a unique physical hardware address. Each NIC has a unique physical address that is programmed by the manufacturer into the ROM chips on the card. The physical address is also referred to as the *Media Access Control (MAC)* address. The network layer works with and understands IP addresses, and the data link layer works with and understands physical MAC addresses. So, how do these two types of addresses work together while operating at different layers?

NOTE A MAC address is unique because the first 24 bits represent the manufacturer code and the last 24 bits represent the unique serial number assigned by the manufacturer.

When data comes from the application layer, it goes to the transport layer for sequence numbers, session establishment, and streaming. The data is then passed to the network layer, where routing information is added to each packet and the source and destination IP addresses are attached to the data bundle. Then this goes to the data link layer, which must find the MAC address and add it to the header portion of the frame. When a frame hits the wire, it only knows what MAC address it is heading toward. At this lower layer of the OSI model, the mechanisms do not even understand IP addresses. So if a computer cannot resolve the IP address passed down from the network layer to the corresponding MAC address, it cannot communicate with that destination computer.

NOTE A *frame* is data that is fully encapsulated, with all of the necessary headers and trailers.

MAC and IP addresses must be properly mapped so they can be correctly resolved. This happens through the *Address Resolution Protocol (ARP)*. When the data link layer receives a frame, the network layer has already attached the destination IP address to it, but the data link layer cannot understand the IP address and thus invokes ARP for help. ARP broadcasts a frame requesting the MAC address that corresponds with the destination IP address. Each computer on the broadcast domain receives this frame, and all but the computer that has the requested IP address ignore it. The computer that has the destination IP address responds with its MAC address. Now ARP knows what hardware address corresponds with that specific IP address. The data link layer takes the frame, adds the hardware address to it, and passes it on to the physical layer, which enables the frame to hit the wire and go to the destination computer. ARP maps the hardware address and associated IP address and stores this mapping in its table for a predefined amount of time. This caching is done so that when another frame destined for the same IP address needs to hit the wire, ARP does not need to broadcast its request again. It just looks in its table for this information.

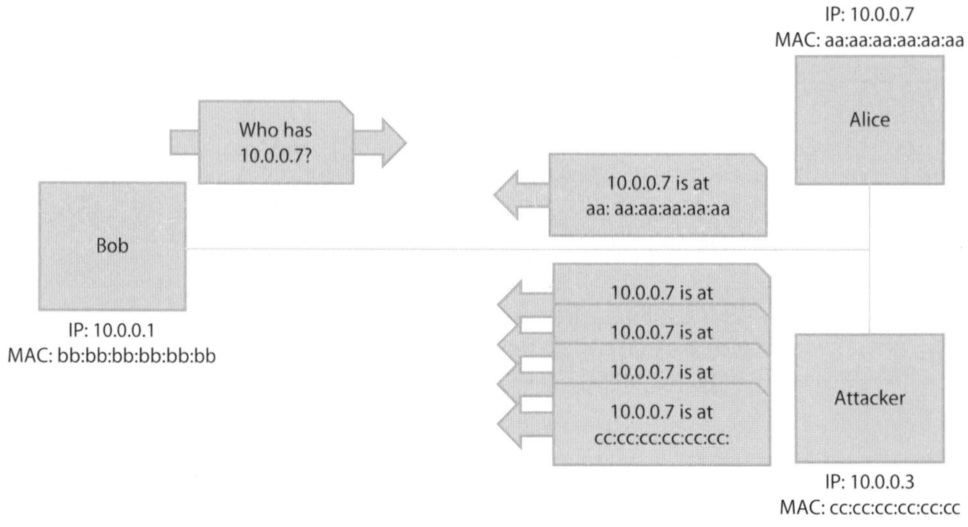

Figure 4-31 ARP poisoning attack

Sometimes attackers alter a system's ARP table so it contains incorrect information. This is called *ARP table cache poisoning*. The attacker's goal is to receive packets intended for another computer. This is a type of masquerading attack. For example, let's say that Bob's computer has an IP of 10.0.0.1 and a MAC address of bb:bb:bb:bb:bb:bb, Alice's computer has an IP of 10.0.0.7 and MAC address of aa:aa:aa:aa:aa:aa, and an attacker has an IP address of 10.0.0.3 and a MAC address of cc:cc:cc:cc:cc:cc, as shown in Figure 4-31. Suppose Bob wants to send a message to Alice. The message is encapsulated at the IP layer with information including Alice's IP address and then handed off to the data link layer. If this is the first message for Alice's computer, the data link process on Bob's computer has no way of knowing her MAC address, so it crafts an ARP query that (literally) says "who has 10.0.0.7?" This ARP frame is broadcast to the network, where it is received by both Alice's computer and the attacker's computer. Both respond claiming to be the rightful owners of that IP address. What does Bob's computer do when faced with multiple different responses? The answer in most cases is that the most recent response is used. If the attacker wants to ensure that Bob's ARP table remains poisoned, then he will have to keep pumping out bogus ARP replies.

So ARP is critical for a system to communicate, but it can be manipulated to allow traffic to be sent to unintended systems. ARP is a rudimentary protocol and does not have any security measures built in to protect itself from these types of attacks. Networks should have IDS sensors monitoring for this type of activity so that administrators can be alerted if this type of malicious activity is underway. This is not difficult to detect, since, as already noted, the attacker will have to constantly (or at least frequently) transmit bogus ARP replies.

Dynamic Host Configuration Protocol

A computer can receive its IP addresses in a few different ways when it first boots up. If it has a statically assigned address, nothing needs to happen. It already has the configuration settings it needs to communicate and work on the intended network. If a computer depends upon a DHCP server to assign it the correct IP address, it boots up and makes a request to the DHCP server. The DHCP server assigns the IP address, and everyone is happy.

DHCP is a UDP-based protocol that allows servers to assign IP addresses to network clients in real time. Unlike static IP addresses, where IP addresses are manually configured, the DHCP server automatically checks for available IP addresses and correspondingly assigns an IP address to the client. This eliminates the possibility of IP address conflicts that occur if two systems are assigned identical IP addresses, which could cause loss of service. On the whole, DHCP considerably reduces the effort involved in managing large-scale IP networks.

The DHCP server assigns IP addresses in real time from a specified range when a client connects to the network; this is different from static addresses, where each system is individually assigned a specific IP address when coming online. In a standard DHCP-based network, the client computer broadcasts a DHCPDISCOVER message on the network in search of the DHCP server. Once the respective DHCP server receives the DHCPDISCOVER request, the server responds with a DHCPOFFER packet, offering the client an IP address. The server assigns the IP address based on the subject of the availability of that IP address and in compliance with its network administration policies. The DHCPOFFER packet that the server responds with contains the assigned IP address information and configuration settings for client-side services.

Once the client receives the settings sent by the server through the DHCPOFFER, it responds to the server with a DHCPREQUEST packet confirming its acceptance of the allotted settings. The server now acknowledges with a DHCPACK packet, which includes the validity period (lease) for the allocated parameters.

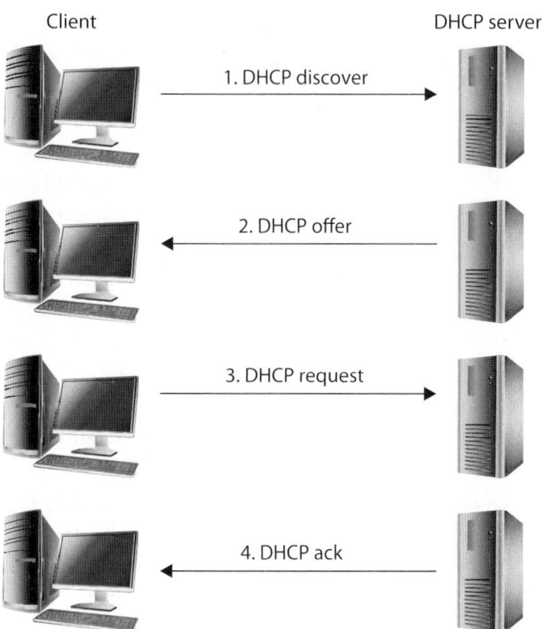

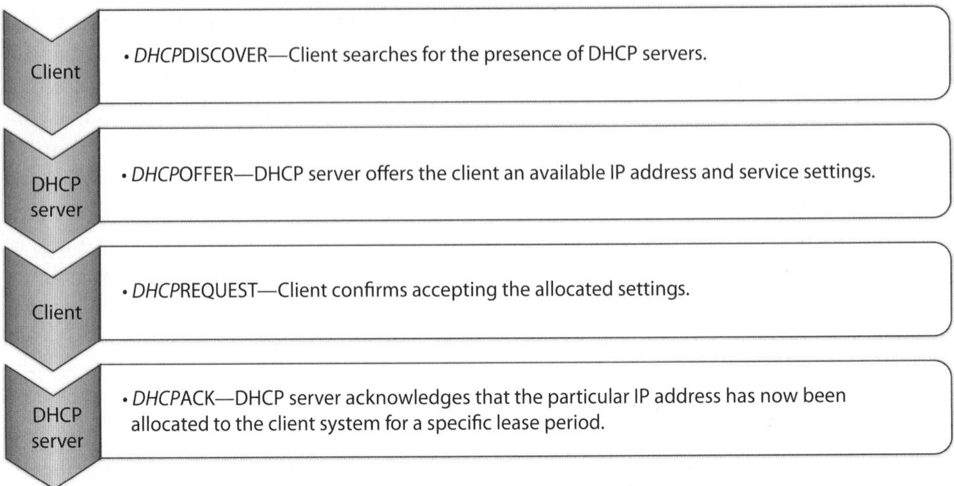

Figure 4-32 The four stages of the Discover, Offer, Request, and Acknowledgment (D-O-R-A) process

So as shown in Figure 4-32, the DHCP client yells out to the network, "Who can help me get an address?" The DHCP server responds with an offer: "Here is an address and the parameters that go with it." The client accepts this gracious offer with the DHCPREQUEST message, and the server acknowledges this message. Now the client can start interacting with other devices on the network and the user can surf the Web and check her e-mail.

Unfortunately, both the client and server segments of the DHCP are vulnerable to falsified identity. On the client end, attackers can masquerade their systems to appear as valid network clients. This enables rogue systems to become a part of an organization's network and potentially infiltrate other systems on the network. An attacker may create an unauthorized DHCP server on the network and start responding to clients searching for a DHCP server. A DHCP server controlled by an attacker can compromise client system configurations, carry out man-in-the-middle attacks, route traffic to unauthorized networks, and a lot more, with the end result of jeopardizing the entire network.

An effective method to shield networks from unauthenticated DHCP clients is through the use of *DHCP snooping* on network switches. DHCP snooping ensures that DHCP servers can assign IP addresses to only selected systems, identified by their MAC addresses. Also, advanced network switches have the capability to direct clients toward legitimate DHCP servers to get IP addresses and restrict rogue systems from becoming DHCP servers on the network.

Diskless workstations do not have a full operating system but have just enough code to know how to boot up and broadcast for an IP address, and they may have a pointer to the server that holds the operating system. The diskless workstation knows its hardware address, so it broadcasts this information so that a listening server can assign it the correct IP address. As with ARP, *Reverse Address Resolution Protocol (RARP)* frames go to all systems on the subnet, but only the RARP server responds. Once the RARP server receives this request, it looks in its table to see which IP address matches the broadcast hardware address. The server then sends a message that contains its IP address back to the requesting computer. The system now has an IP address and can function on the network.

The *Bootstrap Protocol (BOOTP)* was created after RARP to enhance the functionality that RARP provides for diskless workstations. The diskless workstation can receive its IP address, the name server address for future name resolutions, and the default gateway address from the BOOTP server. BOOTP usually provides more functionality to diskless workstations than does RARP.

Internet Control Message Protocol

The *Internet Control Message Protocol (ICMP)* is basically IP's "messenger boy." ICMP delivers status messages, reports errors, replies to certain requests, and reports routing information and is used to test connectivity and troubleshoot problems on IP networks.

The most commonly understood use of ICMP is through the use of the *ping* utility. When a person wants to test connectivity to another system, he may ping it, which sends out ICMP Echo Request frames. The replies on his screen that are returned to the ping utility are called ICMP Echo Reply frames and are responding to the Echo Request frames. If a reply is not returned within a predefined time period, the ping utility sends more Echo Request frames. If there is still no reply, ping indicates the host is unreachable.

ICMP also indicates when problems occur with a specific route on the network and tells surrounding routers about better routes to take based on the health and congestion of the various pathways. Routers use ICMP to send messages in response to packets that could not be delivered. The router selects the proper ICMP response and sends it back to the requesting host, indicating that problems were encountered with the transmission request.

ICMP is used by other connectionless protocols, not just IP, because connectionless protocols do not have any way of detecting and reacting to transmission errors, as do connection-oriented protocols. In these instances, the connectionless protocol may use ICMP to send error messages back to the sending system to indicate networking problems.

As you can see in Table 4-7, ICMP is used for many different networking purposes. This table lists the various messages that can be sent to systems and devices through ICMP.

Attacks Using ICMP ICMP was developed to send status messages, not to hold or transmit user data. But someone figured out how to insert some data inside of an ICMP packet, which can be used to communicate to an already compromised system. This technique is called *ICMP tunneling*, and is an older, but still effective, client/server approach that can be used by hackers to set up and maintain covert communication channels to compromised systems. The attacker would target a computer and install the server portion of the tunneling software. This server portion would "listen" on a port, which is the back door an attacker can use to access the system. To gain access and open a remote shell to this computer, an attacker would send commands inside of ICMP

Type	Name
0	Echo Reply
1	Unassigned
2	Unassigned
3	Destination Unreachable
4	Source Quench
5	Redirect
6	Alternate Host Address
7	Unassigned
8	Echo Request
9	Router Advertisement
10	Router Solicitation
11	Time Exceeded
12	Parameter Problem
13	Timestamp
14	Timestamp Reply
15	Information Request
16	Information Reply
17	Address Mask Request
18	Address Mask Reply
19	Reserved (for Security)
20–29	Reserved (for Robustness Experiment)
30	Traceroute
31	Datagram Conversion Error
32	Mobile Host Redirect
33	IPv6 Where-Are-You
34	IPv6 I-Am-Here
35	Mobile Registration Request
36	Mobile Registration Reply
37	Domain Name Request
38	Domain Name Reply
39	SKIP
40	Photuris (Disambiguation)
41	ICMP messages utilized by experimental mobility protocols such as Seamoby

Table 4-7 ICMP Message Types

packets. This is usually successful because many routers and firewalls are configured to allow ICMP traffic to come and go out of the network, based on the assumption that this is safe because ICMP was developed to not hold any data or a payload.

Just as any tool that can be used for good can also be used for evil, attackers commonly use ICMP to redirect traffic. The redirected traffic can go to the attacker's dedicated system, or it can go into a "black hole." Routers use ICMP messages to update each other on network link status. An attacker could send a bogus ICMP message with incorrect information, which could cause the routers to divert network traffic to where the attacker indicates it should go.

ICMP is also used as the core protocol for a network tool called Traceroute. Traceroute is used to diagnose network connections, but since it gathers a lot of important network statistics, attackers use the tool to map out a victim's network. This is similar to a burglar "casing the joint," meaning that the more the attacker learns about the environment, the easier it can be for her to exploit some critical targets. So while the Traceroute tool is a valid networking program, a security administrator might configure the IDS sensors to monitor for extensive use of this tool because it could indicate that an attacker is attempting to map out the network's architecture.

The countermeasures to these types of attacks are to use firewall rules that only allow the necessary ICMP packets into the network and the use of IDS or IPS to watch for suspicious activities. Host-based protection (host firewalls and host IDS) can also be installed and configured to identify this type of suspicious behavior.

Simple Network Management Protocol

Simple Network Management Protocol (SNMP) was released to the networking world in 1988 to help with the growing demand of managing network IP devices. Companies use many types of products that use SNMP to view the status of their network, traffic flows, and the hosts within the network. Since these tasks are commonly carried out using graphical user interface (GUI)–based applications, many people do not have a full understanding of how the protocol actually works. The protocol is important to understand because it can provide a wealth of information to attackers, and you should understand the amount of information that is available to the ones who wish to do you harm, how they actually access this data, and what can be done with it.

The two main components within SNMP are managers and agents. The manager is the server portion, which polls different devices to check status information. The server component also receives trap messages from agents and provides a centralized place to hold all network-wide information.

The agent is a piece of software that runs on a network device, which is commonly integrated into the operating system. The agent has a list of objects that it is to keep track of, which is held in a database-like structure called the *Management Information Base (MIB)*. An MIB is a logical grouping of managed objects that contain data used for specific management tasks and status checks.

When the SNMP manager component polls the individual agent installed on a specific device, the agent pulls the data it has collected from the MIB and sends it to the manager. Figure 4-33 illustrates how data pulled from different devices is located in one

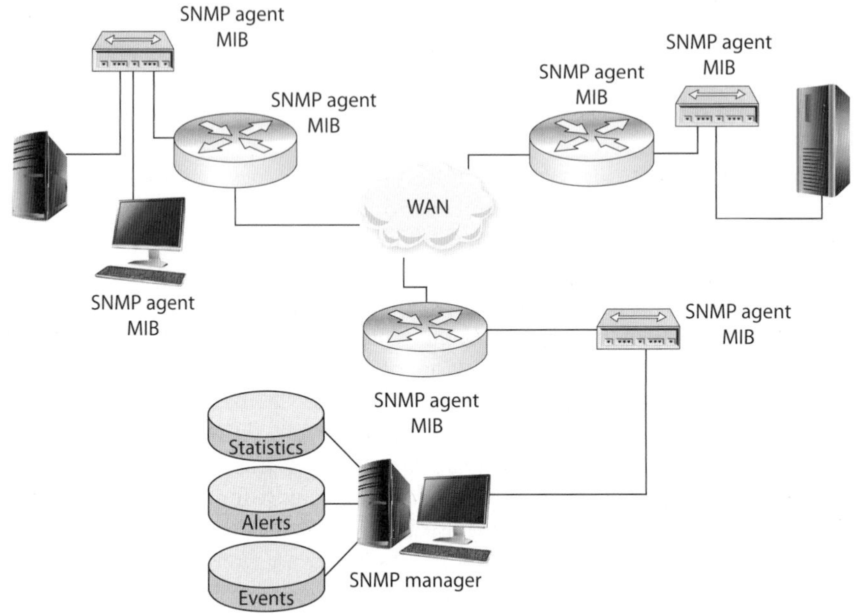

Figure 4-33 Agents provide the manager with SNMP data.

centralized location (SNMP manager). This allows the network administrator to have a holistic view of the network and the devices that make up that network.

NOTE The trap operation allows the agent to inform the manager of an event, instead of having to wait to be polled. For example, if an interface on a router goes down, an agent can send a trap message to the manager. This is the only way an agent can communicate with the manager without first being polled.

It might be necessary to restrict which managers can request information of an agent, so *communities* were developed to establish a trust between specific agents and managers. A *community string* is basically a password a manager uses to request data from the agent, and there are two main community strings with different levels of access: read-only and read-write. As the names imply, the read-only community string allows a manager to read data held within a device's MIB, and the read-write string allows a manager to read the data and modify it. If an attacker can uncover the read-write string, she could change values held within the MIB, which could reconfigure the device.

Since the community string is a password, it should be hard to guess and be protected. It should contain mixed-case alphanumeric strings that are not dictionary words. This is not always the case in many networks. The usual default read-only community string is "public" and the read-write string is "private." Many companies do not change these, so anyone who can connect to port 161 can read the status information of a device and potentially reconfigure it. Different vendors may put in their own default community string values, but companies may still not take the necessary steps to change them. Attackers usually have lists of default vendor community string values, so they can be easily discovered and used against networks.

To make matters worse, the community strings are sent in cleartext in SNMP v1 and v2, so even if a company does the right thing by changing the default values, they are still easily accessible to any attacker with a sniffer. For the best protection, community strings should be changed often, and different network segments should use different community strings, so that if one string is compromised an attacker cannot gain access to all the devices in the network. The SNMP ports (161 and 162) should not be open to untrusted networks, like the Internet, and if needed they should be filtered to ensure only authorized individuals can connect to them. If these ports need to be available to an untrusted network, configure the router or firewall to only allow UDP traffic to come and go from preapproved network-management stations. While versions 1 and 2 of this protocol send the community string values in cleartext, version 3 has cryptographic functionality, which provides encryption, message integrity, and authentication security. So, SNMP v3 should be implemented for more granular protection.

If the proper countermeasures are not put into place, then an attacker can gain access to a wealth of device-oriented data that can be used in her follow-up attacks. The following are just some data sets held within MIB SNMP objects that attackers would be interested in:

.server.svSvcTable.svSvcEntry.svSvcName	Running services
.server.svShareTable.svShareEntry.svShareName	Share names
.server.sv.ShareTable.svShareEntry.svSharePath	Share paths
.server.sv.ShareTable.svShareEntry.svShareComment	Comments on shares
.server.svUserTable.svUserEntry.svUserName	Usernames
.domain.domPrimaryDomain8	Domain names

Gathering this type of data allows an attacker to map out the target network and enumerate the nodes that make up the network.

As with all tools, SNMP is used for good purposes (network management) and for bad purposes (target mapping, device reconfiguration). We need to understand both sides of all tools available to us.

Domain Name Service

Imagine how hard it would be to use the Internet if we had to remember actual specific IP addresses to get to various websites. The *Domain Name Service (DNS)* is a method of resolving hostnames to IP addresses so names can be used instead of IP addresses within networked environments.

TIP DNS provides hostname-to-IP address translation similarly to how the yellow pages provide a person's name to their corresponding phone number. We remember people and company names better than phone numbers or IP addresses.

The first iteration of the Internet was made up of about 100 computers (versus over 3 billion now), and a list was kept that mapped every system's hostname to their IP address. This list was kept on an FTP server so everyone could access it. It did not take long for the task of maintaining this list to become overwhelming, and the computing community looked to automate it.

When a user types a uniform resource locator (URL) into his web browser, the URL is made up of words or letters that are in a sequence that makes sense to that user, such as www.google.com. However, these words are only for humans—computers work with IP addresses. So after the user enters this URL and presses ENTER, behind the scenes his computer is actually being directed to a DNS server that will resolve this URL, or hostname, into an IP address that the computer understands. Once the hostname has been resolved into an IP address, the computer knows how to get to the web server holding the requested web page.

Many companies have their own DNS servers to resolve their internal hostnames. These companies usually also use the DNS servers at their Internet service providers (ISPs) to resolve hostnames on the Internet. An internal DNS server can be used to resolve hostnames on the entire LAN, but usually more than one DNS server is used so the load can be split up and so redundancy and fault tolerance are in place.

Within DNS servers, DNS namespaces are split up administratively into *zones*. One zone may contain all hostnames for the marketing and accounting departments, and another zone may contain hostnames for the administration, research, and legal departments. The DNS server that holds the files for one of these zones is said to be the *authoritative* name server for that particular zone. A zone may contain one or more domains, and the DNS server holding those host records is the authoritative name server for those domains.

The DNS server contains records that map hostnames to IP addresses, which are referred to as *resource records*. When a user's computer needs to resolve a hostname to an IP address, it looks to its networking settings to find its DNS server. The computer then sends a request, containing the hostname, to the DNS server for resolution. The DNS server looks at its resource records and finds the record with this particular hostname, retrieves the address, and replies to the computer with the corresponding IP address.

It is recommended that a primary and a secondary DNS server cover each zone. The primary DNS server contains the actual resource records for a zone, and the secondary DNS server contains copies of those records. Users can use the secondary DNS server to resolve names, which takes a load off of the primary server. If the primary server goes down for any reason or is taken offline, users can still use the secondary server for name resolution. Having both a primary DNS server and a secondary DNS server provides fault tolerance and redundancy to ensure users can continue to work if something happens to one of these servers.

The primary and secondary DNS servers synchronize their information through a *zone transfer*. After changes take place to the primary DNS server, those changes must be replicated to the secondary DNS server. It is important to configure the DNS server to allow zone transfers to take place only between the specific servers. For years now, attackers have been carrying out unauthorized zone transfers to gather very useful network information from victims' DNS servers. An unauthorized zone transfer provides the attacker with information on almost every system within the network. The attacker now knows the hostname and IP address of each system, system alias names, PKI server, DHCP server, DNS servers, etc. This allows an attacker to carry out very targeted attacks on specific systems. If you were the attacker and you had a new exploit for DHCP software, now you would know the IP address of the company's DHCP server and could send your attack parameters directly to that system. Also, since the zone transfer can provide data on all of the systems in the network, the attacker can map out the network. He knows what subnets are being used, which systems are in each subnet, and where the critical network systems reside. This is analogous to you allowing a burglar into your house with the freedom of identifying where you keep your jewels, expensive stereo equipment, piggy bank, and keys to your car, which will allow him to more easily steal these items when you are on vacation. Unauthorized zone transfers can take place if the DNS servers are not properly configured to restrict this type of activity.

Internet DNS and Domains

Networks on the Internet are connected in a hierarchical structure, as are the different DNS servers, as shown in Figure 4-34. While performing routing tasks, if a router does not know the necessary path to the requested destination, that router passes the packet up to a router above it. The router above it knows about all the routers below it. This router has a broader view of the routing that takes place on the Internet and has a better chance of getting the packet to the correct destination. This holds true with DNS servers also. If one DNS server does not know which DNS server holds the necessary resource record to resolve a hostname, it can pass the request up to a DNS server above it.

The naming scheme of the Internet resembles an inverted tree with the root servers at the top. Lower branches of this tree are divided into top-level domains, with second-level domains under each. The most common top-level domains are as follows:

- **COM** Commercial
- **EDU** Education
- **MIL** U.S. military organization
- **INT** International treaty organization
- **GOV** Government
- **ORG** Organizational
- **NET** Networks

So how do all of these DNS servers play together in the Internet playground? When a user types in a URL to access a website that sells computer books, for example, his

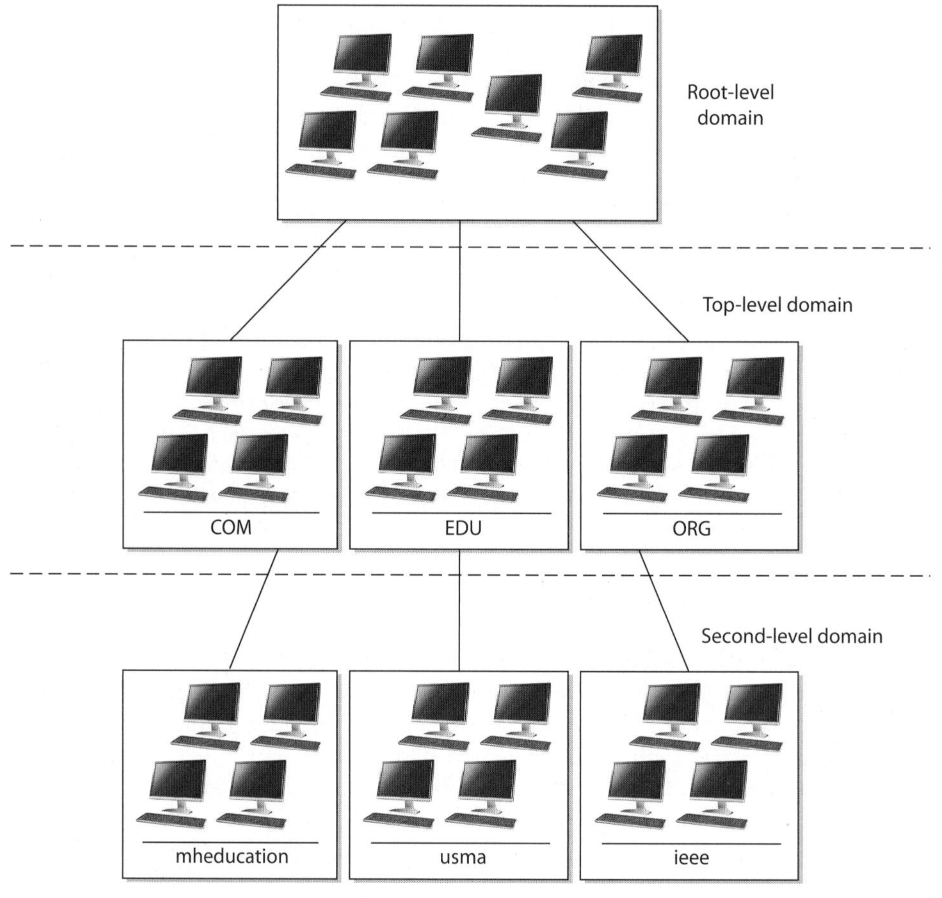

Figure 4-34 The DNS naming hierarchy is similar to the routing hierarchy on the Internet.

computer asks its local DNS server if it can resolve this hostname to an IP address. If the primary DNS server cannot resolve the hostname, it must query a higher-level DNS server, ultimately ending at an authoritative DNS server for the specified domain. Because this website is most likely not on the corporate network, the local LAN DNS server will not usually know the necessary IP address of that website. The DNS server does not reject the user's request, but rather passes it on to another DNS server on the Internet. The request for this hostname resolution continues through different DNS servers until it reaches one that knows the IP address. The requested host's IP information is reported back to the user's computer. The user's computer then attempts to access the website using the IP address, and soon the user is buying computer books, happy as a clam.

DNS server and hostname resolution is extremely important in corporate networking and Internet use. Without it, users would have to remember and type in the IP address for each website and individual system instead of the name. That would be a mess.

DNS Resolution Components

Your computer has a *DNS resolver*, which is responsible for sending out requests to DNS servers for host IP address information. If your system did not have this resolver, when you type in www.google.com in your browser, you would not get to this website because your system does not actually know what www.google.com means. When you type in this URL, your system's resolver has the IP address of a DNS server it is supposed to send its hostname-to-IP address request to. Your resolver can send out a nonrecursive query or a recursive query to the DNS server. A *nonrecursive query* means that the request just goes to that specified DNS server and either the answer is returned to the resolver or an error is returned. A *recursive query* means that the request can be passed on from one DNS server to another one until the DNS server with the correct information is identified. In the following illustration, you can follow the succession of requests that commonly takes place. Your system's resolver first checks to see if it already has the necessary hostname-to-IP address mapping cached or if it is in a local HOSTS file. If the necessary information is not found, the resolver sends the request to the local DNS server. If the local DNS server does not have the information, it sends the request to a different DNS server.

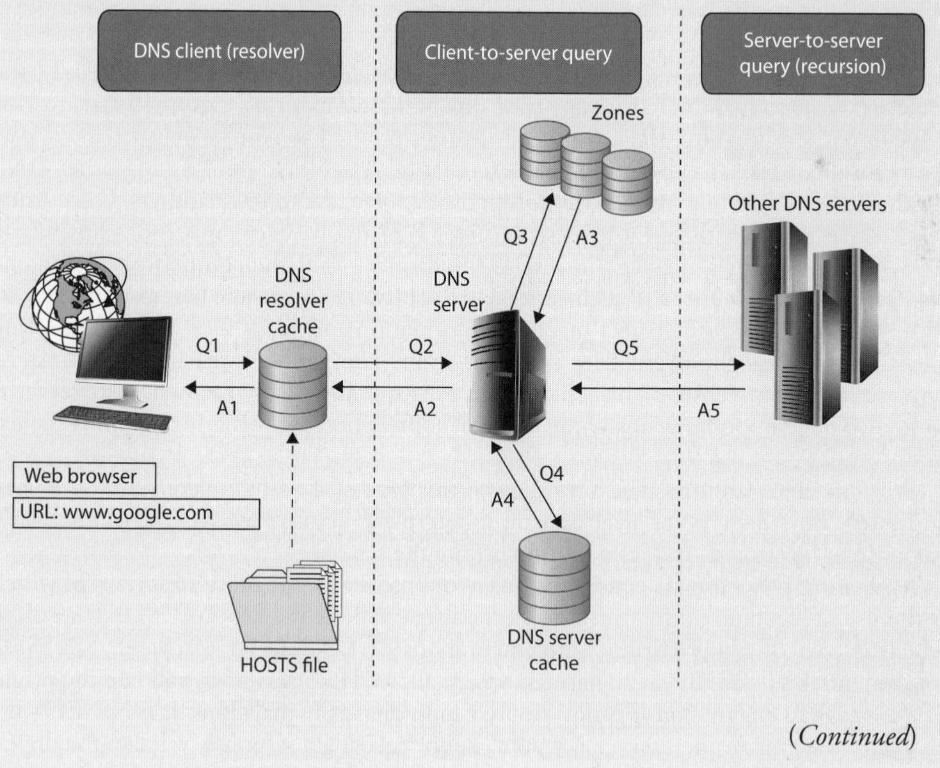

(Continued)

The HOSTS file resides on the local computer and can contain static hostname-to-IP address mapping information. If you do not want your system to query a DNS server, you can add the necessary data in the HOSTS file, and your system will check its contents before reaching out to a DNS server. HOSTS files are like two-edged swords: on the one hand they offer a degree of security by ensuring that certain hosts resolve to specific IP addresses, but on the other hand they are attractive targets for attackers who want to redirect your traffic to specific hosts. They key, as always, is to carefully analyze and mitigate the risks.

DNS Threats

As stated earlier, not every DNS server knows the IP address of every hostname it is asked to resolve. When a request for a hostname-to-IP address mapping arrives at a DNS server (server A), the server reviews its resource records to see if it has the necessary information to fulfill this request. If the server does not have a resource record for this hostname, it forwards the request to another DNS server (server B), which in turn reviews its resource records and, if it has the mapping information, sends the information back to server A. Server A caches this hostname-to-IP address mapping in its memory (in case another client requests it) and sends the information on to the requesting client.

With the preceding information in mind, consider a sample scenario. Andy the attacker wants to make sure that any time one of his competitor's customers tries to visit the competitor's website, the customer is instead pointed to Andy's website. Therefore, Andy installs a tool that listens for requests that leave DNS server A asking other DNS servers if they know how to map the competitor's hostname to its IP address. Once Andy sees that server A sends out a request to server B to resolve the competitor's hostname, Andy quickly sends a message to server A indicating that the competitor's hostname resolves to Andy's website's IP address. Server A's software accepts the first response it gets, so server A caches this incorrect mapping information and sends it on to the requesting client. Now when the client tries to reach Andy's competitor's website, she is instead pointed to Andy's website. This will happen subsequently to any user who uses server A to resolve the competitor's hostname to an IP address because this information is cached on server A.

Previous vulnerabilities that have allowed this type of activity to take place have been addressed, but this type of attack is still taking place because when server A receives a response to its request, it does not authenticate the sender.

Mitigating DNS threats consists of numerous measures, the most important of which is the use of stronger authentication mechanisms such as the *DNSSEC* (DNS security, which is part of many current implementations of DNS server software). DNSSEC implements PKI and digital signatures, which allows DNS servers to validate the origin of a message to ensure that it is not spoofed and potentially malicious. If DNSSEC were enabled on server A, then server A would, upon receiving a response, validate the digital signature on the message before accepting the information to make sure that the response

is from an authorized DNS server. So even if an attacker sends a message to a DNS server, the DNS server would discard it because the message would not contain a valid digital signature. DNSSEC allows DNS servers to send and receive authorized messages between themselves and thwarts the attacker's goal of poisoning a DNS cache table.

This sounds simple enough, but for DNSSEC to be rolled out properly, all of the DNS servers on the Internet would have to participate in a PKI to be able to validate digital signatures. The implementation of Internet-wide PKIs simultaneously and seamlessly has proved to be difficult.

Despite the fact that DNSSEC requires more resources than the traditional DNS, more and more organizations globally are opting to use DNSSEC. The U.S. government has committed to using DNSSEC for all its top-level domains (.gov, .mil). Countries such as Brazil, Sweden, and Bulgaria have already implemented DNSSEC on their top-level domains. In addition, ICANN has made an agreement with VeriSign to implement DNSSEC on all of its top-level domains (.com, .net, .org, and so on). So we are getting there, slowly but surely.

DNS Splitting

Organizations should implement *split DNS*, which means a DNS server in the DMZ handles external hostname-to-IP address resolution requests, while an internal DNS server handles only internal requests. This helps ensure that the internal DNS server has layers of protection and is not exposed by being "Internet facing." The internal DNS server should only contain resource records for the internal computer systems, and the external DNS server should only contain resource records for the systems the organization wants the outside world to be able to connect to. If the external DNS server is compromised and it has the resource records for all of the internal systems, now the attacker has a lot of "inside knowledge" and can carry out targeted attacks. External DNS servers should only contain information on the systems within the DMZ that the organization wants others on the Internet to be able to communicate with (web servers, external mail server, etc.).

Now let's discuss another (indirectly related) predicament in securing DNS traffic—that is, the manipulation of the HOSTS file, a technique frequently used by malware. The HOSTS file is used by the operating system to map hostnames to IP addresses as described before. The HOSTS file is a plaintext file located in the *%systemroot%\system32\i386\drivers\etc/* folder in Windows and at */etc/hosts* in UNIX/Linux systems. The file simply consists of a list of IP addresses with their corresponding hostnames.

Depending on its configuration, the computer refers to the HOSTS file before issuing a DNS request to a DNS server. Most operating systems give preference to HOSTS file–returned IP addresses' details rather than the ones from the DNS server because the HOSTS file is generally under the direct control of the local system administrator.

As covered previously, in the early days of the Internet and prior to the adoption of DNS, HOSTS files were the primary source of determining a host's network addresses

from its hostname. With the increase in the number of hosts connected to the Internet, maintaining HOSTS files became next to impossible and ultimately led to the creation of DNS.

Due to the important role of HOSTS files, they are frequently targeted by malware to propagate across systems connected on a local network. Once a malicious program takes over the HOSTS file, it can divert traffic from its intended destination to websites hosting malicious content, for example. A common example of HOSTS file manipulation carried out by malware involves blocking users from visiting antivirus update websites. This is usually done by mapping target hostnames to the loopback interface IP address 127.0.0.1. The most effective technique for preventing HOSTS file intrusions is to set it as a read-only file and implement a host-based IDS that watches for critical file modification attempts.

Attackers don't always have to go through all this trouble to divert traffic to rogue destinations. They can also use some very simple techniques that are surprisingly effective in routing naive users to unintended destinations. The most common approach is known as *URL hiding*. Hypertext Markup Language (HTML) documents and e-mail messages allow users to attach or embed hyperlinks in any given text, such as the "Click Here" links you commonly see in e-mail messages or web pages. Attackers misuse hyperlinks to deceive unsuspecting users into clicking rogue links.

Let's say a malicious attacker creates an unsuspicious text, www.good.site, but embeds the link to an abusive website, www.bad.site. People are likely to click the www.good.site link without knowing that they are actually being taken to the bad site. In addition, attackers also use character encoding to obscure web addresses that may arouse user suspicion.

Domain Name Registration Issues

We'll now have a look at some legal aspects of domain registration. Although these do not pose a direct security risk to your DNS servers or your IT infrastructure, ignorance of them may risk your very domain name on the Internet, thus jeopardizing your entire online presence. Awareness of *domain grabbing* and *cyber squatting* issues will help you better plan out your online presence and allow you to steer clear of these traps.

ICANN promotes a governance model that follows a first-come, first-serve policy when registering domain names, regardless of trademark considerations. This has led to a race among individuals to secure attractive and prominent domains. Among these are *cyber squatters*, individuals who register prominent or established names, hoping to sell these later to real-world businesses that may require these names to establish their online presence. So if you were preparing to launch a huge business called SecurityRUS, a cyber squatter could go purchase this domain name, and its various formats, at a low price. This person knows you will need this domain name for your website, so they will mark up the price by 1,000 percent and force you to pay this higher rate.

Another tactic employed by cyber squatters is to watch for top-used domain names that are approaching their re-registration date. If you forget to re-register the domain name you have used for the last ten years, a cyber squatter can purchase the name and then require you to pay a huge amount of money just to use the name you have owned and used for years. These are opportunist types of attacks.

To protect your organization from these threats, it is essential that you register a domain as soon as your company conceives of launching a new brand or applies for a new trademark. Registering important domains for longer periods, such as for five or ten years, instead of annually renewing them, reduces the chances of domains slipping out to cyber squatters. Another technique is to register nearby domains as well. For example, if you own the domain something.com, registering some-thing.com and something.net may be a good idea because this will prevent someone else from occupying these domains for furtive purposes.

E-mail Services

A user has an e-mail client that is used to create, modify, address, send, receive, and forward messages. This e-mail client may provide other functionality, such as a personal address book and the ability to add attachments, set flags, recall messages, and store messages within different folders.

A user's e-mail message is of no use unless it can actually be sent somewhere. This is where *Simple Mail Transfer Protocol (SMTP)* comes in. In e-mail clients, SMTP works as a message transfer agent, as shown in Figure 4-35, and moves the message from the user's computer to the mail server when the user clicks the Send button. SMTP also functions as a message transfer protocol between e-mail servers. Lastly, SMTP is a message-exchange addressing standard, and most people are used to seeing its familiar addressing scheme: something@somewhere.com.

Many times, a message needs to travel throughout the Internet and through different mail servers before it arrives at its destination mail server. SMTP is the protocol that carries this message, and it works on top of TCP because it is a reliable protocol and provides sequencing and acknowledgments to ensure the e-mail message arrived successfully at its destination.

The user's e-mail client must be SMTP-compliant to be properly configured to use this protocol. The e-mail client provides an interface to the user so the user can create and modify messages as needed, and then the client passes the message off to the SMTP

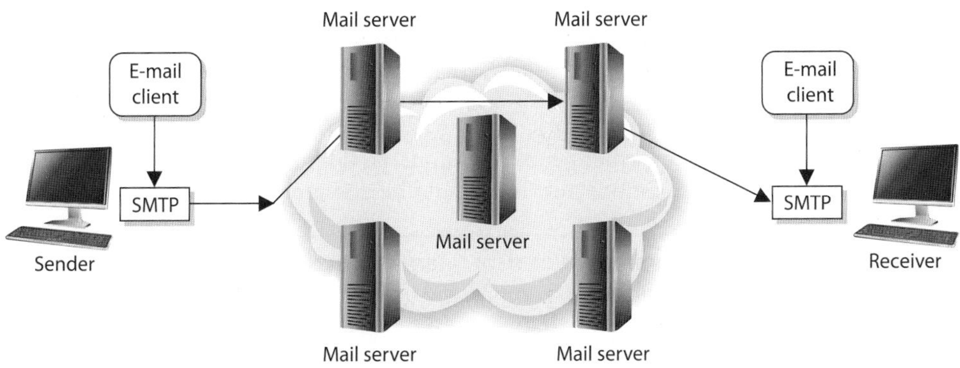

Figure 4-35 SMTP works as a transfer agent for e-mail messages.

application layer protocol. So, to use the analogy of sending a letter via the post office, the e-mail client is the typewriter that a person uses to write the message, SMTP is the mail courier who picks up the mail and delivers it to the post office, and the post office is the mail server. The mail server has the responsibility of understanding where the message is heading and properly routing the message to that destination.

The mail server is often referred to as an SMTP server. The most common SMTP server software within the UNIX world is Sendmail, which is actually an e-mail server application. This means that UNIX uses Sendmail software to store, maintain, and route e-mail messages. Within the Microsoft world, Microsoft Exchange is mostly used, and in Novell, GroupWise is the common SMTP server. SMTP works closely with two mail server protocols, POP and IMAP, which are explained in the following sections.

POP

Post Office Protocol (POP) is an Internet mail server protocol that supports incoming and outgoing messages. A mail server that uses POP, apart from storing and forwarding e-mail messages, works with SMTP to move messages between mail servers.

A smaller company may have one POP server that holds all employee mailboxes, whereas larger companies may have several POP servers, one for each department within the organization. There are also Internet POP servers that enable people all over the world to exchange messages. This system is useful because the messages are held on the mail server until users are ready to download their messages, instead of trying to push messages right to a person's computer, which may be down or offline.

The e-mail server can implement different authentication schemes to ensure an individual is authorized to access a particular mailbox, but this is usually handled through usernames and passwords.

IMAP

Internet Message Access Protocol (IMAP) is also an Internet protocol that enables users to access mail on a mail server. IMAP provides all the functionalities of POP, but has more capabilities. If a user is using POP, when he accesses his mail server to see if he has received any new messages, all messages are automatically downloaded to his computer. Once the messages are downloaded from the POP server, they are usually deleted from that server, depending upon the configuration. POP can cause frustration for mobile users because the messages are automatically pushed down to their computer or device and they may not have the necessary space to hold all the messages. This is especially true for mobile devices that can be used to access e-mail servers. This is also inconvenient for people checking their mail on other people's computers. If Christina checks her e-mail on Jessica's computer, all of Christina's new mail could be downloaded to Jessica's computer.

NOTE POP is commonly used for Internet-based e-mail accounts (Gmail, Yahoo!, etc.), while IMAP is commonly used for corporate e-mail accounts.

If a user uses IMAP instead of POP, she can download all the messages or leave them on the mail server within her remote message folder, referred to as a mailbox. The user can also manipulate the messages within this mailbox on the mail server as if the messages resided on her local computer. She can create or delete messages, search for specific messages, and set and clear flags. This gives the user much more freedom and keeps the messages in a central repository until the user specifically chooses to download all messages from the mail server.

IMAP is a store-and-forward mail server protocol that is considered POP's successor. IMAP also gives administrators more capabilities when it comes to administering and maintaining the users' messages.

E-mail Authorization

POP has gone through a few version updates and is currently on POP3. POP3 has the capability to integrate *Simple Authentication and Security Layer (SASL)*, a protocol-independent framework for performing authentication. This means that any protocol that knows how to interact with SASL can use its various authentication mechanisms without having to actually embed the authentication mechanisms within its code.

To use SASL, a protocol includes a command for identifying and authenticating a user to an authentication server and for optionally negotiating protection of subsequent protocol interactions. If its use is negotiated, a security layer is inserted between the protocol and the connection. The data security layer can provide data integrity, data confidentiality, and other services. SASL's design is intended to allow new protocols to reuse existing mechanisms without requiring redesign of the mechanisms, and allows existing protocols to make use of new mechanisms without redesign of protocols.

The use of SASL is not unique just to POP; other protocols, such as IMAP, Internet Relay Chat (IRC), Lightweight Directory Access Protocol (LDAP), and SMTP, can also use SASL and its functionality.

E-mail Relaying

Most companies have their public mail servers in their DMZ and may have one or more mail servers within their internal LAN. The mail servers in the DMZ are in this protected space because they are directly connected to the Internet. These servers should be tightly locked down and their relaying mechanisms should be correctly configured. Mail servers use a *relay agent* to send a message from one mail server to another. This relay agent needs to be properly configured so a company's mail server is not used by a malicious entity for spamming activity.

Spamming usually is illegal, so the people doing the spamming do not want the traffic to seem as though it originated from their equipment. They will find mail servers on the Internet, or within company DMZs, that have loosely configured relaying mechanisms and use these servers to send their spam. If relays are configured "wide open" on a mail server, the mail server can be used to receive *any* mail message and send it on to *any* intended recipients, as shown in Figure 4-36. This means that if a company does not properly configure its mail relaying, its server can be used to distribute advertisements for other companies, spam messages, and pornographic material. It is important that mail servers have proper antispam features enabled, which are actually antirelaying features. A company's mail server should only accept mail destined for its domain and should not forward messages to other mail servers and domains that may be suspicious.

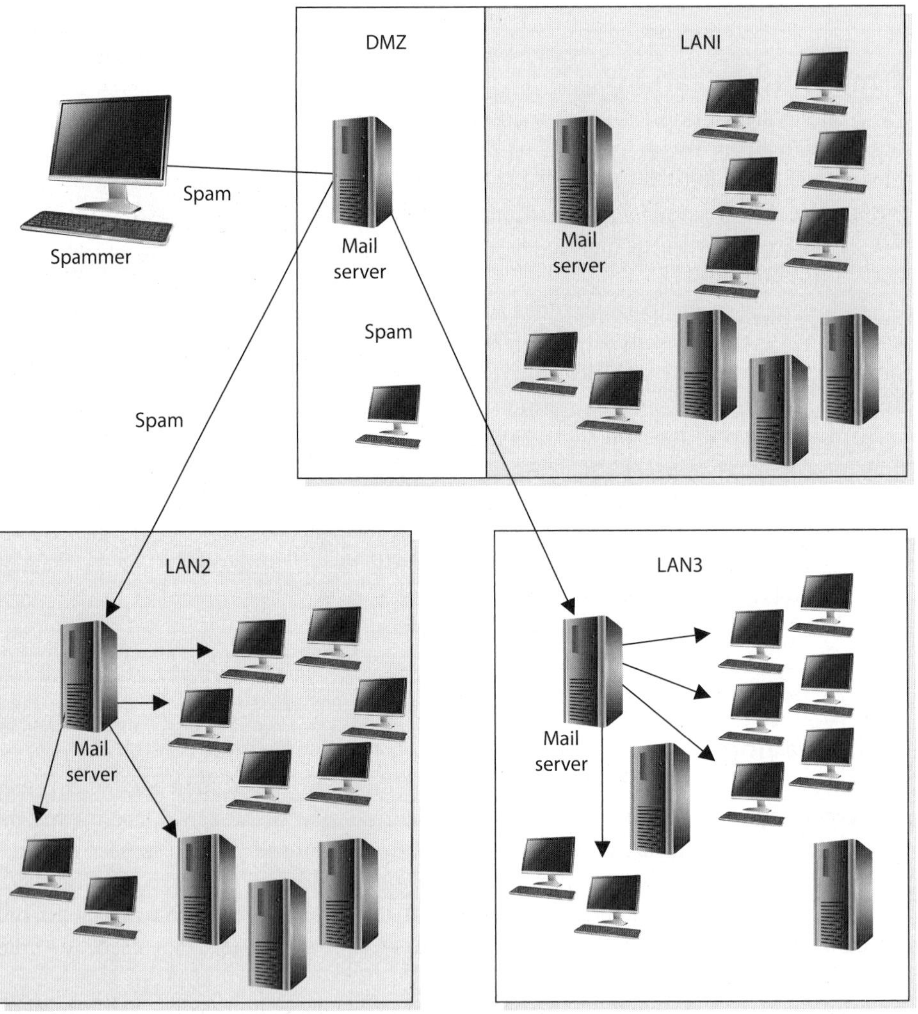

Figure 4-36 Mail servers can be used for relaying spam if relay functionality is not properly configured.

Many companies also employ antivirus and content-filtering applications on their mail servers to try and stop the spread of malicious code and not allow unacceptable messages through the e-mail gateway. It is important to filter both incoming and outgoing messages. This helps ensure that inside employees are not spreading viruses or sending out messages that are against company policy.

E-mail Threats

E-mail spoofing is a technique used by malicious users to forge an e-mail to make it appear to be from a legitimate source. Usually, such e-mails appear to be from known and trusted e-mail addresses when they are actually generated from a malicious source. This technique is widely used by attackers these days for spamming and phishing purposes. An attacker tries to acquire the target's sensitive information, such as username and password or bank account credentials. Sometimes, the e-mail messages contain a link of a known website when it is actually a fake website used to trick the user into revealing his information.

E-mail spoofing is done by modifying the fields of e-mail headers, such as the From, Return-Path, and Reply-To fields, so the e-mail appears to be from a trusted source. This results in an e-mail looking as though it is from a known e-mail address. Mostly the From field is spoofed, but some scams have modified the Reply-To field to the attacker's e-mail address. E-mail spoofing is caused by the lack of security features in SMTP. When SMTP technologies were developed, the concept of e-mail spoofing didn't exist, so countermeasures for this type of threat were not embedded into the protocol. A user could use an SMTP server to send e-mail to anyone from any e-mail address.

SMTP authentication (SMTP-AUTH) was developed to provide an access control mechanism. This extension comprises an authentication feature that allows clients to authenticate to the mail server before an e-mail is sent. Servers using the SMTP-AUTH extension are configured in such a manner that their clients are obliged to use the extension so that the sender can be authenticated.

E-mail spoofing can be mitigated in several ways. The SMTP server can be configured to prevent unauthenticated users from sending e-mails. It is important to always log all the connections to your mail servers so that unsolicited e-mails can be traced and tracked. It's also advised that you filter incoming and outgoing traffic toward mail servers through a firewall to prevent generic network-level attacks, such as packet spoofing, distributed denial-of-service (DDoS) attacks, and so on. Important e-mails can be communicated over encrypted channels so that the sender and receiver are properly authenticated.

Another way to deal with the problem of forged e-mail messages is by using *Sender Policy Framework (SPF)*, which is an e-mail validation system designed to prevent e-mail spam by detecting e-mail spoofing by verifying the sender's IP address. SPF allows administrators to specify which hosts are allowed to send e-mail from a given domain by creating a specific SPF record in DNS. Mail exchanges use DNS to check that mail from a given domain is being sent by a host sanctioned by that domain's administrators.

Phishing is a social engineering attack that is commonly carried out through maliciously crafted e-mail messages. The goal is to get someone to click a malicious link or for the victim to send the attacker some confidential data (Social Security number, account number, etc.). The attacker crafts an e-mail that seems to originate from a trusted source and sends it out to many victims at one time. A *spear phishing* attack zeroes in on specific people. So if an attacker wants your specific information because she wants to break into your bank account, she could gather information about you via Facebook, LinkedIn, or other resources and create an e-mail purporting to be from someone she thinks you will trust. A similar attack is called whaling. In a *whaling attack* an attacker usually identifies some "big fish" in an organization (CEO, CFO, COO, CSO) and targets them because they have access to some of the most sensitive data in the organization. The attack is finely tuned to achieve the highest likelihood of success.

E-mail is, of course, a critical communication tool, but is the most commonly misused channel for malicious activities.

Network Address Translation

When computers need to communicate with each other, they must use the same type of addressing scheme so everyone understands how to find and talk to one another. The Internet uses the IP address scheme as discussed earlier in the chapter, and any computer or network that wants to communicate with other users on the network must conform to this scheme; otherwise, that computer will sit in a virtual room with only itself to talk to.

However, IP addresses have become scarce (until the full adoption of IPv6) and expensive. So some smart people came up with *network address translation (NAT)*, which enables a network that does not follow the Internet's addressing scheme to communicate over the Internet.

Private IP addresses have been reserved for internal LAN address use, as outlined in RFC 1918. These addresses can be used within the boundaries of a company, but they cannot be used on the Internet because they will not be properly routed. NAT enables a company to use these private addresses and still be able to communicate transparently with computers on the Internet.

The following lists current private IP address ranges:

- 10.0.0.0–10.255.255.255 Class A networks
- 172.16.0.0–172.31.255.255 Class B networks
- 192.168.0.0–192.168.255.255 Class C networks

NAT is a gateway that lies between a network and the Internet (or another network) that performs transparent routing and address translation. Because IP addresses were depleting fast, IPv6 was developed in 1999, and was intended to be the long-term fix to the address shortage problem. NAT was developed as the short-term fix to enable more companies to participate on the Internet. However, to date, IPv6 is slow in acceptance and implementation, while NAT has caught on like wildfire. Many firewall vendors have implemented NAT into their products, and it has been found that NAT actually provides a great security benefit. When attackers want to hack a network, they first do what they can to learn all about the network and its topology, services, and addresses. Attackers cannot easily find out a company's address scheme and its topology when NAT is in place, because NAT acts like a large nightclub bouncer by standing in front of the network and hiding the true IP scheme.

NAT hides internal addresses by centralizing them on one device, and any frames that leave that network have only the source address of that device, not of the actual internal computer that sends the message. So when a message comes from an internal computer with the address of 10.10.10.2, for example, the message is stopped at the device running NAT software, which happens to have the IP address of 1.2.3.4. NAT changes the header of the packet from the internal address, 10.10.10.2, to the IP address of the NAT device, 1.2.3.4. When a computer on the Internet replies to this message, it replies to the address 1.2.3.4. The NAT device changes the header on this reply message to 10.10.10.2 and puts it on the wire for the internal user to receive.

Three basic types of NAT implementations can be used:

- **Static mapping** The NAT software has a pool of public IP addresses configured. Each private address is statically mapped to a specific public address. So computer A always receives the public address x, computer B always receives the public address y, and so on. This is generally used for servers that need to keep the same public address at all times.
- **Dynamic mapping** The NAT software has a pool of IP addresses, but instead of statically mapping a public address to a specific private address, it works on a first-come, first-served basis. So if Bob needs to communicate over the Internet, his system makes a request to the NAT server. The NAT server takes the first IP address on the list and maps it to Bob's private address. The balancing act is to estimate how many computers will most likely need to communicate outside the internal network at one time. This estimate is the number of public addresses the company purchases, instead of purchasing one public address for each computer.
- **Port address translation (PAT)** The company owns and uses only one public IP address for all systems that need to communicate outside the internal network. How in the world could all computers use the exact same IP address? Good question. Here's an example: The NAT device has an IP address of 127.50.41.3. When computer A needs to communicate with a system on the Internet, the NAT device documents this computer's private address and source port number (10.10.44.3; port 43,887). The NAT device changes the IP address in the computer's packet header to 127.50.41.3, with the source port 40,000. When computer B also needs to communicate with a system on the Internet, the NAT device documents the private address and source port number (10.10.44.15; port 23,398) and changes the header information to 127.50.41.3 with source port 40,001. So when a system responds to computer A, the packet first goes to the NAT device, which looks up the port number 40,000 and sees that it maps to computer A's real information. So the NAT device changes the header information to address 10.10.44.3 and port 43,887 and sends it to computer A for processing. A company can save a lot more money by using PAT because the company needs to buy only a few public IP addresses, which are used by all systems in the network.

Most NAT implementations are *stateful*, meaning they keep track of a communication between the internal host and an external host until that session is ended. The NAT device needs to remember the internal IP address and port to send the reply messages back. This stateful characteristic is similar to stateful-inspection firewalls, but NAT does not perform scans on the incoming packets to look for malicious characteristics. Instead, NAT is a service usually performed on routers or gateway devices within a company's screened subnet.

Although NAT was developed to provide a quick fix for the depleting IP address problem, it has actually put the problem off for quite some time. The more companies that implement private address schemes, the less likely IP addresses will become scarce. This has been helpful to NAT and the vendors that implement this technology, but it has put the acceptance and implementation of IPv6 much farther down the road.

Routing Protocols

Individual networks on the Internet are referred to as *autonomous systems (ASs)*. These ASs are independently controlled by different service providers and organizations. An AS is made up of routers, which are administered by a single entity and use a common Interior Gateway Protocol (IGP) within the boundaries of the AS. The boundaries of these ASs are delineated by border routers. These routers connect to the border routers of other ASs and run interior and exterior routing protocols. Internal routers connect to other routers within the same AS and run interior routing protocols. So, in reality, the Internet is just a network made up of ASs and routing protocols.

NOTE As an analogy, just as the world is made up of different countries, the Internet is made up of different ASs. Each AS has delineation boundaries just as countries do. Countries can have their own languages (Spanish, Arabic, Russian). Similarly, ASs have their own internal routing protocols. Countries that speak different languages need to have a way of communicating to each other, which could happen through interpreters. ASs need to have a standardized method of communicating and working together, which is where external routing protocols come into play.

The architecture of the Internet that supports these various ASs is created so that no entity that needs to connect to a specific AS has to know or understand the interior routing protocols that are being used. Instead, for ASs to communicate, they just have to be using the same exterior routing protocols (see Figure 4-37). As an analogy, suppose you want to deliver a package to a friend who lives in another state. You give the package to your brother, who is going to take a train to the edge of the state and hand it to the postal system at that junction. Thus, you know how your brother will arrive at the edge of the state—by train. You do not know how the postal system will then deliver your package to your friend's house (truck, car, bus), but that is not your concern. It will get to its destination without your participation. Similarly, when one network communicates with another network, the first network puts the data packet (package) on an exterior protocol (train), and when the data packet gets to the border router (edge of the state), the data is transferred to whatever interior protocol is being used on the receiving network.

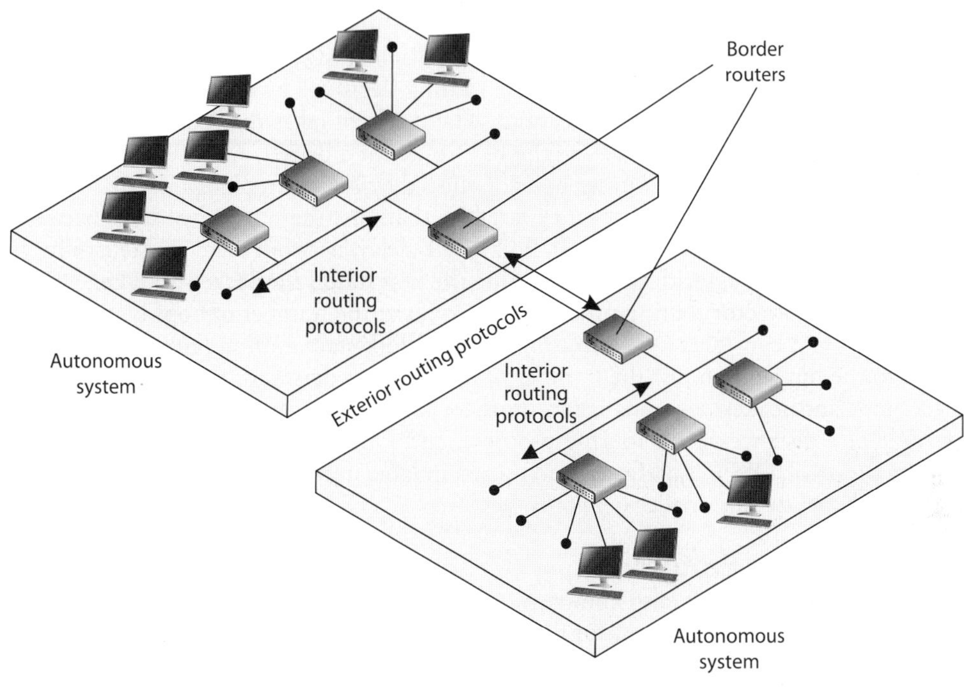

Figure 4-37 Autonomous systems

NOTE Routing protocols are used by routers to identify a path between the source and destination systems.

Dynamic vs. Static

Routing protocols can be dynamic or static. A *dynamic routing protocol* can discover routes and build a routing table. Routers use these tables to make decisions on the best route for the packets they receive. A dynamic routing protocol can change the entries in the routing table based on changes that take place to the different routes. When a router that is using a dynamic routing protocol finds out that a route has gone down or is congested, it sends an update message to the other routers around it. The other routers use this information to update their routing table, with the goal of providing efficient routing functionality. A *static routing protocol* requires the administrator to manually configure the router's routing table. If a link goes down or there is network congestion, the routers cannot tune themselves to use better routes.

NOTE *Route flapping* refers to the constant changes in the availability of routes. Also, if a router does not receive an update that a link has gone down, the router will continue to forward packets to that route, which is referred to as a *black hole*.

Distance-Vector vs. Link-State

Two main types of routing protocols are used: distance-vector and link-state routing. *Distance-vector routing protocols* make their routing decisions based on the distance (or number of hops) and a vector (a direction). The protocol takes these variables and uses them with an algorithm to determine the best route for a packet. *Link-state routing protocols* build a more accurate routing table because they build a topology database of the network. These protocols look at more variables than just the number of hops between two destinations. They use packet size, link speed, delay, network load, and reliability as the variables in their algorithms to determine the best routes for packets to take.

So, a distance-vector routing protocol only looks at the number of hops between two destinations and considers each hop to be equal. A link-state routing protocol sees more pieces to the puzzle than just the number of hops, but understands the status of each of those hops and makes decisions based on these factors also. As you will see, RIP is an example of a distance-vector routing protocol, and OSPF is an example of a link-state routing protocol. OSPF is preferred and is used in large networks. RIP is still around but should only be used in smaller networks.

Interior Routing Protocols

Interior Routing Protocols (also known as Interior Gateway Protocols) route traffic within the same AS. Just like the process for flying from one airport to another is different if you travel domestically or internationally, routing protocols are designed differently depending on which side of the AS boundary they operate. De facto and proprietary interior protocols are being used today. The following are just a few of them:

- **Routing Information Protocol** RIP is a standard that outlines how routers exchange routing table data and is considered a distance-vector protocol, which means it calculates the shortest distance between the source and destination. It is considered a legacy protocol because of its slow performance and lack of functionality. It should only be used in small networks. RIP version 1 has no authentication, and RIP version 2 sends passwords in cleartext or hashed with MD5. RIPng is the third generation of this venerable protocol. It is very similar to the version 2, but is designed for IPv6 routing.
- **Open Shortest Path First** OSPF uses link-state algorithms to send out routing table information. The use of these algorithms allows for smaller, more frequent routing table updates to take place. This provides a more stable network than RIP, but requires more memory and CPU resources to support this extra processing. OSPF allows for a hierarchical routing network that has a backbone link connecting all subnets together. OSPF has replaced RIP in many networks today. Authentication can take place with cleartext passwords or hashed passwords, or you can choose to configure no authentication on the routers using this protocol. The latest OSPF is version 3. Though it was designed to support IPv6, it also supports IPv4. Among the most important improvements is that OSPFv3 uses IPSec for authentication.

- **Interior Gateway Routing Protocol** IGRP is a distance-vector routing protocol that was developed by, and is proprietary to, Cisco Systems. Whereas RIP uses one criterion to find the best path between the source and destination, IGRP uses five criteria to make a "best route" decision. A network administrator can set weights on these different metrics so that the protocol works best in that specific environment.
- **Enhanced Interior Gateway Routing Protocol** EIGRP is a Cisco-proprietary and advanced distance-vector routing protocol. It allows for faster router table updates than its predecessor IGRP and minimizes routing instability, which can occur after topology changes. Routers exchange messages that contain information about bandwidth, delay, load, reliability, and MTU of the path to each destination as known by the advertising router. The latest version is 4, which is able to support multiple network protocols such as IPv4, IPv6, IPX, and AppleTalk.
- **Virtual Router Redundancy Protocol** VRRP is used in networks that require high availability where routers as points of failure cannot be tolerated. It is designed to increase the availability of the default gateway by advertising a "virtual router" as a default gateway. Two physical routers (primary and secondary) are mapped to one virtual router. If one of the physical routers fails, the other router takes over the workload.
- **Intermediate System to Intermediate System** IS-IS is a link-state protocol that allows each router to independently build a database of a network's topology. Similar to the OSPF protocol, it computes the best path for traffic to travel. It is a classless and hierarchical routing protocol that is vendor neutral. Unlike other protocols (e.g., RIP and OSPF), IS-IS does not use IP addresses. Instead, it uses ISO addresses, which means that the protocol didn't have to be redesigned to support IPv6.

TIP Although most routing protocols have authentication functionality, many routers do not have this functionality enabled.

Exterior Routing Protocols

The exterior routing protocols used by routers connecting different ASs are generically referred to as *exterior gateway protocols (EGPs)*. The *Border Gateway Protocol (BGP)* enables routers on different ASs to share routing information to ensure effective and efficient routing between the different AS networks. BGP is commonly used by Internet service providers to route data from one location to the next on the Internet.

NOTE There is an exterior routing protocol called Exterior Gateway Protocol, but it has been widely replaced by BGP, and now the term "exterior gateway protocol" and the acronym EGP are used to refer generically to a type of protocol rather than to specify the outdated protocol.

BGP uses a combination of link-state and distance-vector routing algorithms. It creates a network topology by using its link-state functionality and transmits updates on a periodic basis instead of continuously, which is how distance-vector protocols work. Network administrators can apply weights to the different variables used by link-state routing protocols when determining the best routes. These configurations are collectively called the *routing policy*.

Routing Protocol Attacks

Several types of attacks can take place on routers through their routing protocols. A majority of the attacks have the goal of misdirecting traffic through the use of spoofed ICMP messages. An attacker can masquerade as another router and submit routing table information to the victim router. After the victim router integrates this new information, it may be sending traffic to the wrong subnets or computers, or even to a nonexistent address (black hole). These attacks are successful mainly when routing protocol authentication is not enabled. When authentication is not required, a router can accept routing updates without knowing whether or not the sender is a legitimate router. An attacker could divert a company's traffic to reveal confidential information or to just disrupt traffic, which would be considered a DoS attack.

Other types of DoS attacks exist, such as flooding a router port, buffer overflows, and SYN floods. Since there are many different types of attacks that can take place, there are just as many countermeasures to be aware of to thwart these types of attacks. Most of these countermeasures involve authentication and encryption of routing data as it is transmitted back and forth through the use of shared keys or IPSec.

Wormhole Attack

An attacker can capture a packet at one location in the network and tunnel it to another location in the network. In this type of attack, there are two attackers, one at each end of the tunnel (referred to as a *wormhole*). Attacker A could capture an authentication token that is being sent to an authentication server and then send this token to the other attacker, who then uses it to gain unauthorized access to a resource. This can take place on a wired or wireless network, but it is easier to carry out on a wireless network because the attacker does not need to actually penetrate a physical wire.

The countermeasure to this type of attack is to use a *leash*, which is just data that is put into a header of the individual packets. The leash restricts the packet's maximum allowed transmission distance. The leash can be either *geographical*, which ensures that a packet stays within a certain distance of the sender, or *temporal*, which limits the lifetime of the packet.

It is like the idea of using leashes for your pets. You put a collar (leash) on your dog (packet) and it prevents him from leaving your yard (network segment).

Networking Devices

Several types of devices are used in LANs, MANs, and WANs to provide intercommunication among computers and networks. We need to have physical devices throughout the network to actually use all the protocols and services we have covered up to this point. The different networking devices vary according to their functionality, capabilities, intelligence, and network placement. We will look at the following devices:

- Repeaters
- Bridges
- Routers
- Switches

Repeaters

A *repeater* provides the simplest type of connectivity because it only repeats electrical signals between cable segments, which enables it to extend a network. Repeaters work at the physical layer and are add-on devices for extending a network connection over a greater distance. The device amplifies signals because signals attenuate the farther they have to travel.

Repeaters can also work as line conditioners by actually cleaning up the signals. This works much better when amplifying digital signals than when amplifying analog signals because digital signals are discrete units, which makes extraction of background noise from them much easier for the amplifier. If the device is amplifying analog signals, any accompanying noise often is amplified as well, which may further distort the signal.

A *hub* is a multiport repeater. A hub is often referred to as a *concentrator* because it is the physical communication device that allows several computers and devices to communicate with each other. A hub does not understand or work with IP or MAC addresses. When one system sends a signal to go to another system connected to it, the signal is broadcast to all the ports, and thus to all the systems connected to the concentrator.

Bridges

A *bridge* is a LAN device used to connect LAN segments. It works at the data link layer and therefore works with MAC addresses. A repeater does not work with addresses; it just forwards all signals it receives. When a frame arrives at a bridge, the bridge determines whether or not the MAC address is on the local network segment. If the MAC address is not on the local network segment, the bridge forwards the frame to the necessary network segment.

A bridge is used to divide overburdened networks into smaller segments to ensure better use of bandwidth and traffic control. A bridge amplifies the electrical signal, as does a repeater, but it has more intelligence than a repeater and is used to extend a LAN and enable the administrator to filter frames so he can control which frames go where.

When using bridges, you have to watch carefully for *broadcast storms*. Because bridges can forward all traffic, they forward all broadcast packets as well. This can overwhelm the network and result in a broadcast storm, which degrades the network bandwidth and performance.

Three main types of bridges are used: local, remote, and translation. A *local bridge* connects two or more LAN segments within a local area, which is usually a building. A *remote bridge* can connect two or more LAN segments over a MAN by using telecommunications links. A remote bridge is equipped with telecommunications ports, which enable it to connect two or more LANs separated by a long distance and can be brought together via telephone or other types of transmission lines. A *translation bridge* is needed if the two LANs being connected are different types and use different standards and protocols. For example, consider a connection between a Token Ring network and an Ethernet network. The frames on each network type are different sizes, the fields contain different protocol information, and the two networks transmit at different speeds. If a regular bridge were put into place, Ethernet frames would go to the Token Ring network, and vice versa, and neither would be able to understand messages that came from the other network segment. A translation bridge does what its name implies—it translates between the two network types.

The following list outlines the functions of a bridge:

- Segments a large network into smaller, more controllable pieces.
- Uses filtering based on MAC addresses.
- Joins different types of network links while retaining the same broadcast domain.
- Isolates collision domains within the same broadcast domain.
- Bridging functionality can take place locally within a LAN or remotely to connect two distant LANs.
- Can translate between protocol types.

EXAM TIP Do not confuse routers with bridges. Routers work at the network layer and filter packets based on IP addresses, whereas bridges work at the data link layer and filter frames based on MAC addresses. Routers usually do not pass broadcast information, but bridges do pass broadcast information.

Forwarding Tables

A bridge must know how to get a frame to its destination—that is, it must know to which port the frame must be sent and where the destination host is located. Years ago, network administrators had to type route paths into bridges so the bridges had static paths indicating where to pass frames that were headed for different destinations. This was a tedious task and prone to errors. Today, bridges use *transparent bridging*.

If transparent bridging is used, a bridge starts to learn about the network's environment as soon as it is powered on and as the network changes. It does this by examining frames and making entries in its forwarding tables. When a bridge receives a frame from a new source computer, the bridge associates this new source address and the port on which it arrived. It does this for all computers that send frames on the network. Eventually, the bridge knows the address of each computer on the various network segments and to which port each is connected. If the bridge receives a request to send a frame to a destination that is not in its forwarding table, it sends out a query frame on each network segment except for the source segment. The destination host is the only one that replies to this query. The bridge updates its table with this computer address and the port to which it is connected and forwards the frame.

Many bridges use the *Spanning Tree Algorithm (STA)*, which adds more intelligence to the bridges. STA ensures that frames do not circle networks forever, provides redundant paths in case a bridge goes down, assigns unique identifiers to each bridge, assigns priority values to these bridges, and calculates path costs. This creates much more efficient frame-forwarding processes by each bridge. STA also enables an administrator to indicate whether he wants traffic to travel certain paths instead of others.

If *source routing* is allowed, the packets contain the necessary information within them to tell the bridge or router where they should go. The packets hold the forwarding information so they can find their way to their destination without needing bridges and routers to dictate their paths. If the computer wants to dictate its forwarding information instead of depending on a bridge, how does it know the correct route to the destination computer? The source computer sends out explorer packets that arrive at the destination computer. These packets contain the route information the packets had to take to get to the destination, including what bridges and/or routers they had to pass through. The destination computer then sends these packets back to the source computer, and the source computer strips out the routing information, inserts it into the packets, and sends them on to the destination.

Connecting Two LANS: Bridge vs. Router

What is the difference between two LANs connected via a bridge versus two LANs connected via a router? If two LANs are connected with a bridge, the LANs have been extended because they are both in the same broadcast domain. A router separates broadcast domains, so if two LANs are connected with a router, an internetwork results. An internetwork is a group of networks connected in a way that enables any node on any network to communicate with any other node. The Internet is an example of an internetwork.

CAUTION External devices and border routers should not accept packets with source routing information within their headers, because that information will override what is laid out in the forwarding and routing tables configured on the intermediate devices. You want to control how traffic traverses your network; you don't want packets to have this type of control and be able to go wherever they want. Source routing can be used by attackers to get around certain bridge and router filtering rules.

Routers

We are going up the chain of the OSI layers while discussing various networking devices. Repeaters work at the physical layer, bridges work at the data link layer, and routers work at the network layer. As we go up each layer, each corresponding device has more intelligence and functionality because it can look deeper into the frame. A repeater looks at the electrical signal. The bridge can look at the MAC address within the header. The router can peel back the first header information and look farther into the frame and find out the IP address and other routing information. The farther a device can look into a frame, the more decisions it can make based on the information within the frame.

Routers are layer 3, or network layer, devices that are used to connect similar or different networks. (For example, they can connect two Ethernet LANs or an Ethernet LAN to a Token Ring LAN.) A router is a device that has two or more interfaces and a routing table so it knows how to get packets to their destinations. It can filter traffic based on access control lists (ACLs), and it fragments packets when necessary. Because routers have more network-level knowledge, they can perform higher-level functions, such as calculating the shortest and most economical path between the sending and receiving hosts.

A router discovers information about routes and changes that take place in a network through its routing protocols (RIP, BGP, OSPF, and others). These protocols tell routers if a link has gone down, if a route is congested, and if another route is more economical. They also update routing tables and indicate if a router is having problems or has gone down.

The router may be a dedicated appliance or a computer running a networking operating system that is dual-homed. When packets arrive at one of the interfaces, the router compares those packets to its ACLs. This list indicates what packets are allowed in and what packets are denied. Access decisions are based on source and destination IP addresses, protocol type, and source and destination ports. An administrator may block all packets coming from the 10.10.12.0 network, any FTP requests, or any packets headed toward a specific port on a specific host, for example. This type of control is provided by the ACLs, which the administrator must program and update as necessary.

What actually happens inside the router when it receives a packet? Let's follow the steps:

1. A packet is received on one of the interfaces of a router. The router views the routing data.
2. The router retrieves the destination IP network address from the packet.
3. The router looks at its routing table to see which port matches the requested destination IP network address.
4. If the router does not have information in its table about the destination address, it sends out an ICMP error message to the sending computer indicating that the message could not reach its destination.
5. If the router does have a route in its routing table for this destination, it decrements the TTL value and sees whether the MTU is different for the destination network. If the destination network requires a smaller MTU, the router fragments the datagram.

Bridge	Router
Reads header information, but does not alter it	Creates a new header for each packet
Builds forwarding tables based on MAC addresses	Builds routing tables based on IP addresses
Uses the same network address for all ports	Assigns a different network address per port
Filters traffic based on MAC addresses	Filters traffic based on IP addresses
Forwards broadcast packets	Does not forward broadcast packets
Forwards traffic if a destination address is unknown to the bridge	Does not forward traffic that contains a destination address unknown to the router

Table 4-8 Main Differences Between Bridges and Routers

6. The router changes header information in the packet so the packet can go to the next correct router, or if the destination computer is on a connecting network, the changes made enable the packet to go directly to the destination computer.
7. The router sends the packet to its output queue for the necessary interface.

Table 4-8 provides a quick review of the differences between routers and bridges.

When is it best to use a repeater, bridge, or router? A repeater is used if an administrator needs to expand a network and amplify signals so they do not weaken on longer cables. However, a repeater will also extend collision and broadcast domains.

Bridges work at the data link layer and have a bit more intelligence than a repeater. Bridges can do simple filtering and separate collision domains, but not broadcast domains. A bridge should be used when an administrator wants to divide a network into segments to reduce traffic congestion and excessive collisions.

A router splits up a network into collision domains and broadcast domains. A router gives more of a clear-cut division between network segments than repeaters or bridges. A router should be used if an administrator wants to have more defined control of where the traffic goes because more sophisticated filtering is available with routers, and when a router is used to segment a network, the result is more controllable sections.

A router is used when an administrator wants to divide a network along the lines of departments, workgroups, or other business-oriented divisions. A bridge divides segments based more on the traffic type and load.

Switches

Switches combine the functionality of a repeater and the functionality of a bridge. A switch amplifies the electrical signal, like a repeater, and has the built-in circuitry and intelligence of a bridge. It is a multiport connection device that provides connections for individual computers or other hubs and switches. Any device connected to one port can communicate with a device connected to another port with its own virtual private link. How does this differ from the way in which devices communicate using a bridge or a hub? When a frame comes to a hub, the hub sends the frame out through all of its ports. When a frame comes to a bridge, the bridge sends the frame to the port to which the destination network segment is connected. When a frame comes to a switch, the switch sends the frame directly to the destination computer or network, which results in a reduction of traffic. Figure 4-38 illustrates a network configuration that has computers directly connected to their corresponding switches.

On Ethernet networks, computers have to compete for the same shared network medium. Each computer must listen for activity on the network and transmit its data when it thinks the coast is clear. This contention and the resulting collisions cause traffic delays and use up precious bandwidth. When switches are used, contention and collisions are not issues, which results in more efficient use of the network's bandwidth and decreased latency. Switches reduce or remove the sharing of the network medium and the problems that come with it.

A switch is a multiport bridging device, and each port provides dedicated bandwidth to the device attached to it. A port is bridged to another port so the two devices have an end-to-end private link. The switch employs full-duplex communication, so one wire pair is used for sending and another pair is used for receiving. This ensures the two connected devices do not compete for the same bandwidth.

Basic switches work at the data link layer and forward traffic based on MAC addresses. However, today's layer 3, layer 4, and other layer switches have more enhanced functionality than layer 2 switches. These higher-level switches offer routing functionality, packet inspection, traffic prioritization, and QoS functionality. These switches are referred to as *multilayered switches* because they combine data link layer, network layer, and other layer functionalities.

Multilayered switches use hardware-based processing power, which enables them to look deeper within the packet, to make more decisions based on the information found within the packet, and then to provide routing and traffic management tasks. Usually

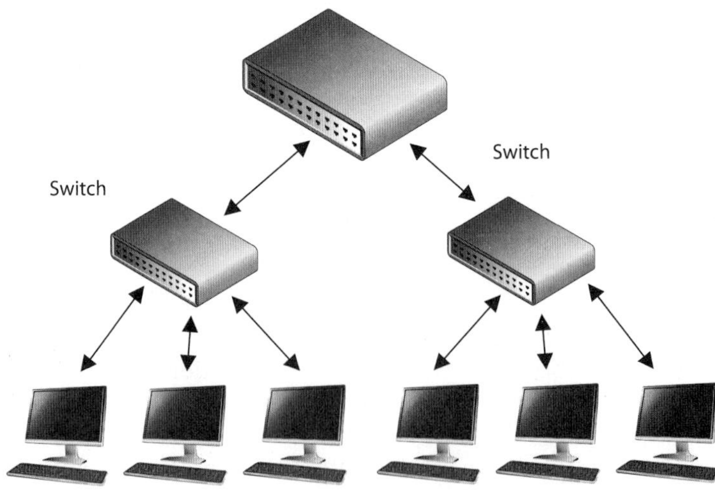

Figure 4-38 Switches enable devices to communicate with each other via their own virtual link.

this amount of work creates a lot of overhead and traffic delay, but multilayered switches perform these activities within an application-specific integrated circuit (ASIC). This means that most of the functions of the switch are performed at the hardware and chip level rather than at the software level, making it much faster than routers.

CAUTION While it is harder for attackers to sniff traffic on switched networks, they should not be considered safe just because switches are involved. Attackers commonly poison cache memory used on switches to divert traffic to their desired location.

Layer 3 and 4 Switches

Layer 2 switches only have the intelligence to forward a frame based on its MAC address and do not have a higher understanding of the network as a whole. A layer 3 switch has the intelligence of a router. It not only can route packets based on their IP addresses, but also can choose routes based on availability and performance. A layer 3 switch is basically a router on steroids, because it moves the route lookup functionality to the more efficient switching hardware level.

The basic distinction between layer 2, 3, and 4 switches is the header information the device looks at to make forwarding or routing decisions (data link, network, or transport OSI layers). But layer 3 and 4 switches can use tags, which are assigned to each destination network or subnet. When a packet reaches the switch, the switch compares the destination address with its tag information base, which is a list of all the subnets and their corresponding tag numbers. The switch appends the tag to the packet and sends it to the next switch. All the switches in between this first switch and the destination host just review this tag information to determine which route it needs to take, instead of analyzing the full header. Once the packet reaches the last switch, this tag is removed and the packet is sent to the destination. This process increases the speed of routing of packets from one location to another.

The use of these types of tags, referred to as *Multiprotocol Label Switching (MPLS)*, not only allows for faster routing, but also addresses service requirements for the different packet types. Some time-sensitive traffic (such as video conferencing) requires a certain level of service (QoS) that guarantees a minimum rate of data delivery to meet the requirements of a user or application. When MPLS is used, different priority information is placed into the tags to help ensure that time-sensitive traffic has a higher priority than less sensitive traffic, as shown in Figure 4-39.

Many enterprises today use a switched network in which computers are connected to dedicated ports on Ethernet switches, Gigabit Ethernet switches, ATM switches, and more. This evolution of switches, added services, and the capability to incorporate repeater, bridge, and router functionality have made switches an important part of today's networking world.

Because security requires control over who can access specific resources, more intelligent devices can provide a higher level of protection because they can make more detail-oriented decisions regarding who can access resources. When devices can look deeper into the packets, they have access to more information to make access decisions, which provides more granular access control.

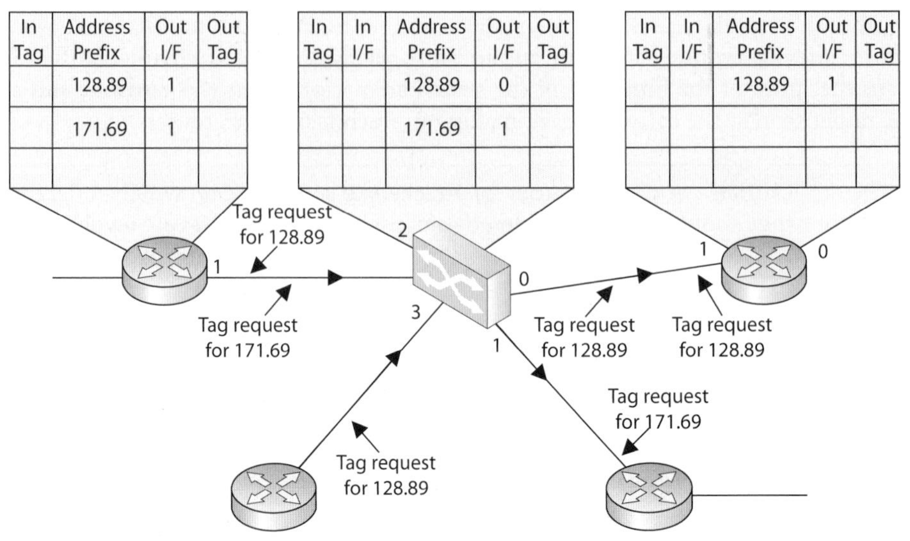

Figure 4-39 MPLS uses tags and tables for routing functions.

As previously stated, switching makes it more difficult for intruders to sniff and monitor network traffic because no broadcast and collision information is continually traveling throughout the network. Switches provide a security service that other devices cannot provide. *Virtual LANs (VLANs)* are an important part of switching networks, because they enable administrators to have more control over their environment and they can isolate users and groups into logical and manageable entities. VLANs are described in the next section.

VLANs

The technology within switches has introduced the capability to use VLANs. VLANs enable administrators to separate and group computers logically based on resource requirements, security, or business needs instead of the standard physical location of the systems. When repeaters, bridges, and routers are used, systems and resources are grouped in a manner dictated by their physical location. Figure 4-40 shows how computers that are physically located next to each other can be grouped logically into different VLANs. Administrators can form these groups based on the users' and company's needs instead of the physical location of systems and resources.

An administrator may want to place the computers of all users in the marketing department in the same VLAN network, for example, so all users receive the same broadcast messages and can access the same types of resources. This arrangement could get tricky if a few of the users are located in another building or on another floor, but VLANs provide the administrator with this type of flexibility. VLANs also enable an administrator to apply particular security policies to respective logical groups. This way, if tighter security is required for the payroll department, for example, the administrator can develop a policy, add all payroll systems to a specific VLAN, and apply the security policy only to the payroll VLAN.

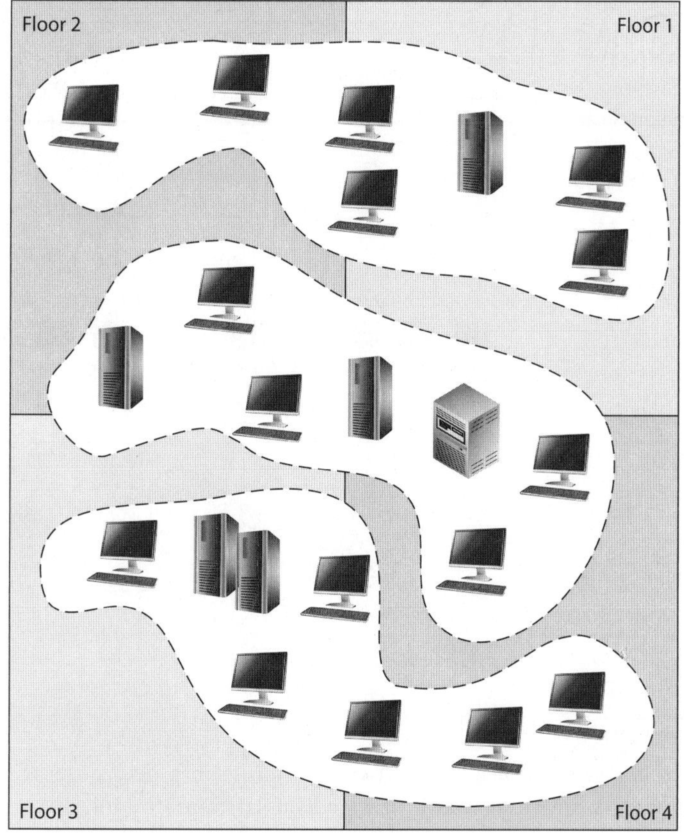

Figure 4-40 VLANs enable administrators to manage logical networks.

A VLAN exists on top of the physical network, as shown in Figure 4-41. If workstation P1 wants to communicate with workstation D1, the message has to be routed—even though the workstations are physically next to each other—because they are on different logical networks.

NOTE The IEEE standard that defines how VLANs are to be constructed and how tagging should take place to allow for interoperability is IEEE 802.1Q.

While VLANs are used to segment traffic, attackers can still gain access to traffic that is supposed to be "walled off" in another VLAN segment. *VLAN hopping attacks* allow attackers to gain access to traffic in various VLAN segments. An attacker can have a system act as though it is a switch. The system understands the tagging values being used in the network and the trunking protocols and can insert itself between other VLAN devices and gain access to the traffic going back and forth. This is called a *switch spoofing attack*. An attacker can also insert VLAN tags to manipulate the control of traffic at the data link layer in what is known as a *double tagging attack*. Proper configuration of all switches mitigate VLAN hopping attacks.

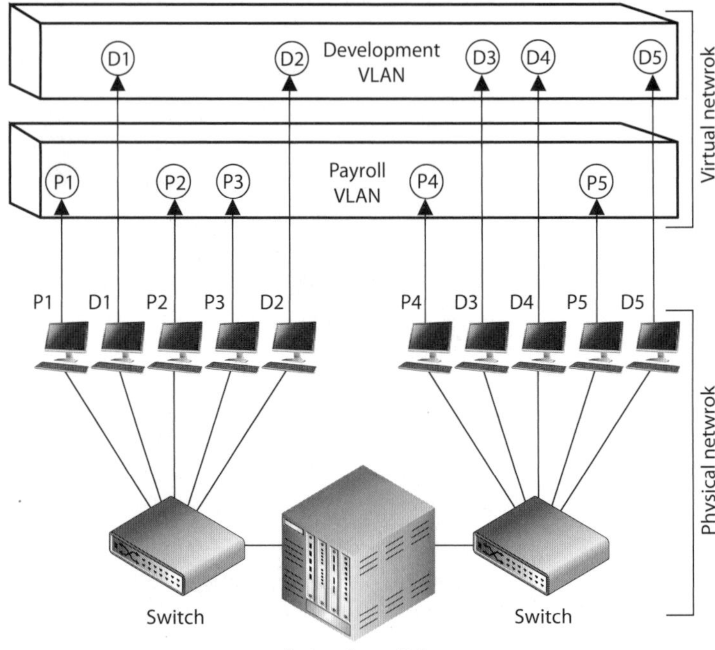

Figure 4-41 VLANs exist on a higher level than the physical network and are not bound to it.

Gateways

Gateway is a general term for software running on a device that connects two different environments and that many times acts as a translator for them or somehow restricts their interactions. Usually a gateway is needed when one environment speaks a different language, meaning it uses a certain protocol that the other environment does not understand. The gateway can translate Internetwork Packet Exchange (IPX) protocol packets to IP packets, accept mail from one type of mail server, and format it so another type of mail server can accept and understand it, or it can connect and translate different data link technologies such as FDDI to Ethernet.

Gateways perform much more complex tasks than connection devices such as routers and bridges. However, some people refer to routers as gateways when they connect two unlike networks (Token Ring and Ethernet) because the router has to translate between the data link technologies. Figure 4-42 shows how a network access server (NAS) functions as a gateway between telecommunications and network connections.

When networks connect to a backbone, a gateway can translate the different technologies and frame formats used on the backbone network versus the connecting LAN protocol frame formats. If a bridge were set up between an FDDI backbone and an Ethernet LAN, the computers on the LAN would not understand the FDDI protocols and frame formats. In this case, a LAN gateway would be needed to translate the protocols used between the different networks.

A popular type of gateway is an *electronic mail* gateway. Because several e-mail vendors have their own syntax, message format, and way of dealing with message transmission,

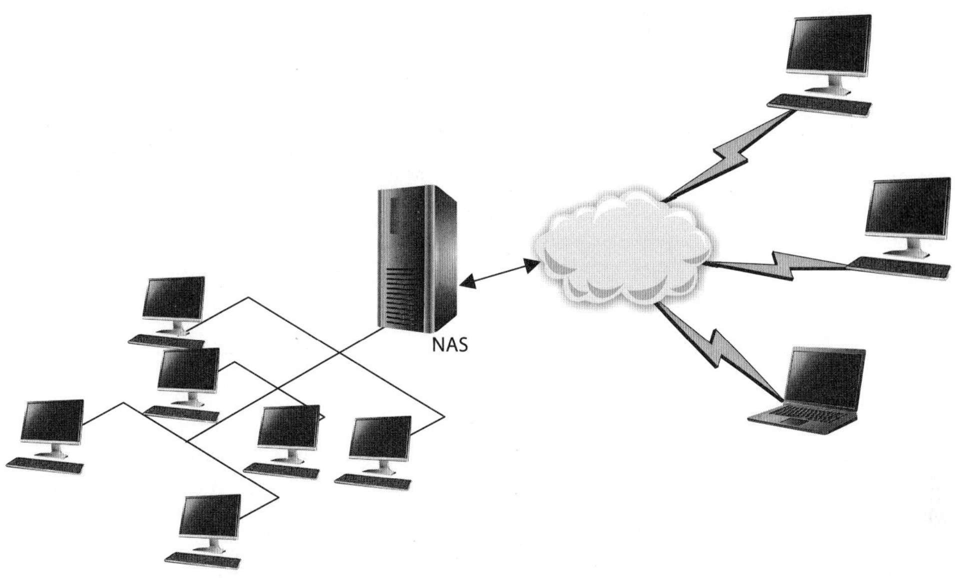

Figure 4-42 Several types of gateways can be used in a network. A NAS is one example.

e-mail gateways are needed to convert messages between e-mail server software. For example, suppose that David, whose corporate network uses Sendmail, writes an e-mail message to Dan, whose corporate network uses Microsoft Exchange. The e-mail gateway will convert the message into a standard that all mail servers understand—usually X.400—and pass it on to Dan's mail server.

Another example of a gateway is a voice and media gateway. Recently, there has been a drive to combine voice and data networks. This provides for a lot of efficiency because the same medium can be used for both types of data transfers. However, voice is a streaming technology, whereas data is usually transferred in packets. So, this shared medium eventually has to communicate with two different types of networks: the telephone company's PSTN, and routers that will take the packet-based data off to the Internet. This means that a gateway must separate the combined voice and data information and put it into a form that each of the networks can understand.

Table 4-9 lists the devices covered in this "Networking Devices" section and points out their important characteristics.

PBXs

Telephone companies use switching technologies to transmit phone calls to their destinations. A telephone company's central office houses the switches that connect towns, cities, and metropolitan areas through the use of optical fiber rings. So, for example, when Dusty makes a phone call from his house, the call first hits the local central office of the telephone company that provides service to Dusty, and then the switch within that office decides whether it is a local or long-distance call and where it needs to go from there.

Device	OSI Layer	Functionality
Repeater	Physical	Amplifies the signal and extends networks.
Bridge	Data link	Forwards packets and filters based on MAC addresses; forwards broadcast traffic, but not collision traffic.
Router	Network	Separates and connects LANs creating internetworks; routers filter based on IP addresses.
Switch	Data link	Provides a private virtual link between communicating devices; allows for VLANs; reduces collisions; impedes network sniffing.
Gateway	Application	Connects different types of networks; performs protocol and format translations.

Table 4-9 Network Device Differences

A *Private Branch Exchange (PBX)* is a private telephone switch that is located on a company's property. This switch performs some of the same switching tasks that take place at the telephone company's central office. The PBX has a dedicated connection to its local telephone company's central office, where more intelligent switching takes place.

A PBX can interface with several types of devices and provides a number of telephone services. The voice data is multiplexed onto a dedicated line connected to the telephone company's central office. Figure 4-43 shows how data from different data sources can be placed on one line at the PBX and sent to the telephone company's switching facility.

PBXs use digital switching devices that can control analog and digital signals. Older PBXs may support only analog devices, but most PBXs have been updated to digital. This move to digital systems and signals has reduced a number of the PBX and telephone security vulnerabilities that used to exist. However, that in no way means PBX fraud does not take place today. Many companies, for example, have modems hanging off their PBX (or other transmission access methods) to enable the vendor to dial in and perform

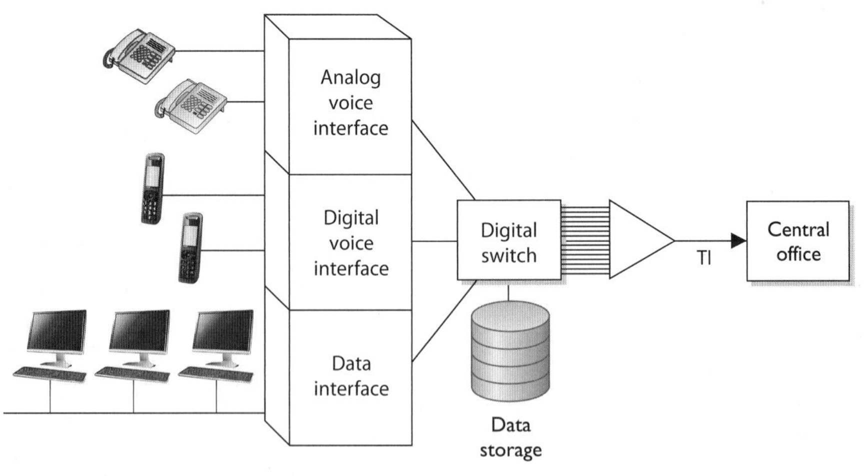

Figure 4-43 A PBX combines different types of data on the same lines.

maintenance to the system. These modems are usually unprotected doorways into a company's network. The modem should be activated only when a problem requires the vendor to dial in. It should be disabled otherwise.

In addition, many PBX systems have system administrator passwords that are hardly ever changed. These passwords are set by default; therefore, if 100 companies purchased and implemented 100 PBX systems from the PBX vendor ABC and they do not reset the password, a *phreaker* (a phone hacker) who knows this default password would now have access to 100 PBX systems. Once a phreaker breaks into a PBX system, she can cause mayhem by rerouting calls, reconfiguring switches, or configuring the system to provide her and her friends with free long-distance calls. This type of fraud happens more often than most companies realize because many companies do not closely watch their phone bills. Though the term is not used as much nowadays, phreakers are very much an issue to our telecommunications systems. Toll fraud (as most of their activities are called) is estimated to cost $1 billion in annual losses worldwide.

PBX systems are also vulnerable to brute force and other types of attacks, in which phreakers use scripts and dictionaries to guess the necessary credentials to gain access to the system. In some cases, phreakers have listened to and changed people's voice messages. So, for example, when people call to leave Bob a message, they might not hear his usual boring message, but a new message that is screaming obscenities and insults.

NOTE Unfortunately, many security people do not even think about a PBX when they are assessing a network's vulnerabilities and security level. This is because telecommunication devices have historically been managed by service providers and/or by someone on the staff who understands telephony. The network administrator is usually not the person who manages the PBX, so the PBX system commonly does not even get assessed. The PBX is just a type of switch and it is directly connected to the company's infrastructure; thus, it is a doorway for the bad guys to exploit and enter. These systems need to be assessed and monitored just like any other network device.

Network Diagramming

In many cases, you cannot capture a full network in a diagram because of the complexity of most organizations' networks. Sometimes we have a false sense of security when we have a pretty network diagram that we can all look at and be proud of, but let's dig deeper into why this can be deceiving. From what perspective should you look at a network? There can be a cabling diagram that shows you how everything is physically connected (coaxial, UTP, fiber) and a wireless portion that describes the WLAN structure. There can be a network diagram that illustrates the network in infrastructure layers of access, aggregation, edge, and core. You can have a diagram that illustrates how the various networking routing takes place (VLANs, MPLS connections, OSPF, IGRP, and BGP links). You can have a diagram that shows you how different data flows take place (FTP, IPSec, HTTP, TLS, L2TP, PPP, Ethernet, FDDI, ATM, etc.). You can have a diagram that separates workstations and the core server types that almost every network uses (DNS,

DHCP, web farm, storage, print, SQL, PKI, mail, domain controllers, RADIUS, etc.). You can look at a network based upon trust zones, which are enforced by filtering routers, firewalls, and DMZ structures. You can look at a network based upon its IP subnet structure. But what if you look at a network diagram from a Microsoft perspective, which illustrates many of these things but in forest, tree, domain, and OU containers? Then you need to show remote access connections, VPN concentrators, extranets, and the various MAN and WAN connections. How do we illustrate our IP telephony structure? How do we integrate our mobile device administration servers into the diagram? How do we document our new cloud computing infrastructure? How do we show the layers of virtualization within our database? How are redundant lines and fault-tolerance solutions marked? How does this network correlate and interact with our offsite location that carries out parallel processing? And we have not even gotten to our security components (firewalls, IDS, IPS, DLP, antimalware, content filters, etc.). And in the real world whatever network diagrams a company does have are usually out of date because they take a lot of effort to create and maintain.

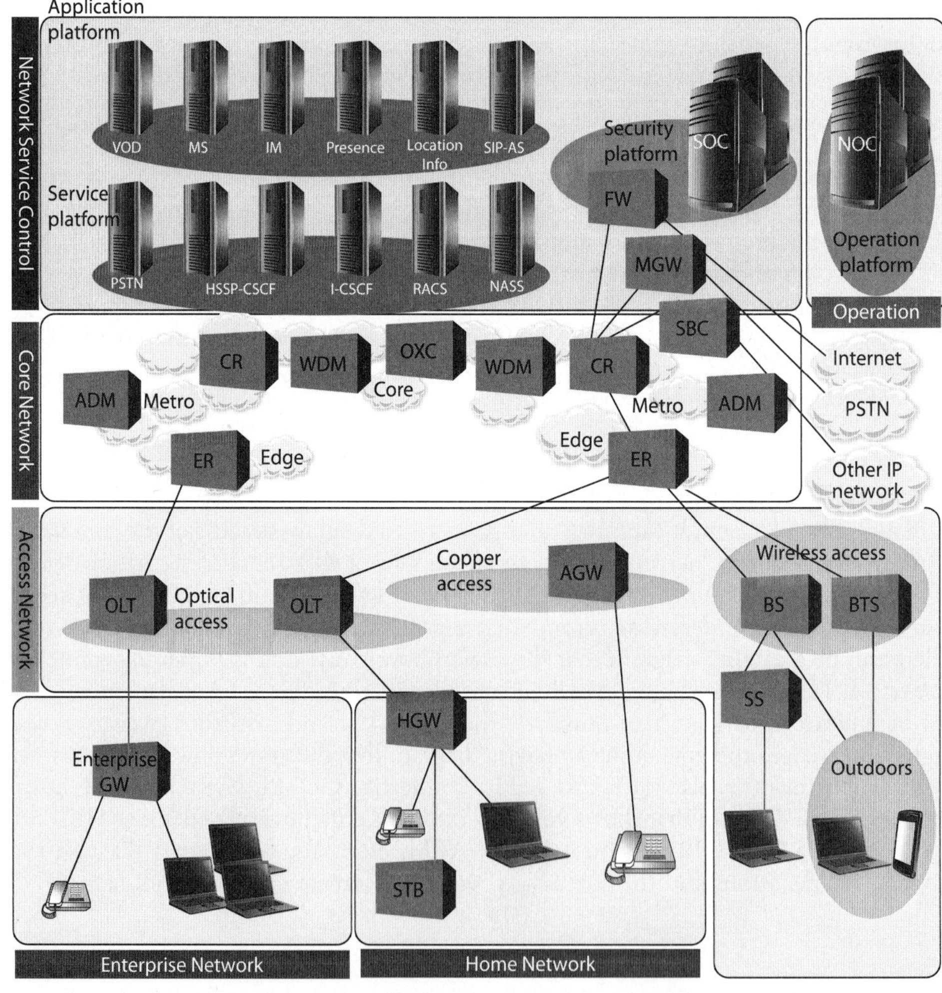

The point is that a network is a complex beast that cannot really be captured on one piece of paper. Compare it to a human body. When you go into the doctor's office you see posters on the wall. One poster shows the circulatory system, one shows the muscles, one shows bones, another shows organs, another shows tendons and ligaments; a dentist office has a bunch of posters on teeth; if you are at an acupuncture clinic, there will be a poster on acupuncture and reflexology points. And then there is a ton of stuff no one makes posters for: hair follicles, skin, toenails, eyebrows, but these are all part of one system.

So what does this mean to the security professional? You have to understand a network from many different aspects if you are actually going to secure it. You start by learning all this network stuff in a modular fashion, but you need to quickly understand how it all works together under the covers. You can be a complete genius on how everything works within your current environment but not fully understand that when an employee connects her iPhone to her company laptop that is connected to the corporate network and uses it as a modem, this is an unmonitored WAN connection that can be used as a doorway by an attacker. Security is complex and demanding, so do not ever get too cocky, and always remember that a diagram is just showing a perspective of a network, not the whole network.

Firewalls

Firewalls are used to restrict access to one network from another network. Most companies use firewalls to restrict access to their networks from the Internet. They may also use firewalls to restrict one internal network segment from accessing another internal segment. For example, if the security administrator wants to make sure employees cannot access the research and development network, he would place a firewall between this network and all other networks and configure the firewall to allow only the type of traffic he deems acceptable.

A firewall device supports and enforces the company's network security policy. An organizational security policy provides high-level directives on acceptable and unacceptable actions as they pertain to protecting critical assets. The firewall has a more defined and granular security policy that dictates what services are allowed to be accessed, what IP addresses and ranges are to be restricted, and what ports can be accessed. The firewall is described as a "choke point" in the network because all communication should flow through it, and this is where traffic is inspected and restricted.

A firewall may be a server running a firewall software product or a specialized hardware appliance. It monitors packets coming into and out of the network it is protecting. It can discard packets, repackage them, or redirect them, depending upon the firewall configuration. Packets are filtered based on their source and destination addresses, and ports by service, packet type, protocol type, header information, sequence bits, and much more. Many times, companies set up firewalls to construct a *demilitarized zone (DMZ)*, which is a network segment located between the protected and unprotected networks. The DMZ provides a buffer zone between the dangerous Internet and the goodies within the internal network that the company is trying to protect. As shown in Figure 4-44, two firewalls are usually installed to form the DMZ. The DMZ usually contains web,

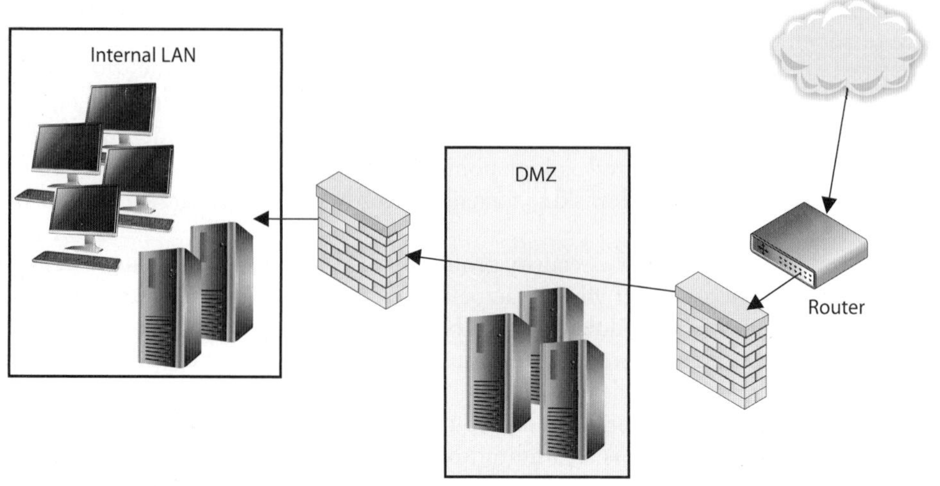

Figure 4-44 At least two firewalls, or firewall interfaces, are generally used to construct a DMZ.

mail, and DNS servers, which must be hardened systems because they would be the first in line for attacks. Many DMZs also have an IDS sensor that listens for malicious and suspicious behavior.

Many different types of firewalls are available, because each environment may have unique requirements and security goals. Firewalls have gone through an evolution of their own and have grown in sophistication and functionality. The following sections describe the various types of firewalls.

The types of firewalls we will review are

- Packet filtering
- Stateful
- Proxy
- Dynamic packet filtering
- Kernel proxy

We will then dive into the three main firewall architectures, which are

- Screened host
- Multihome
- Screened subnet

Packet-Filtering Firewalls

Packet filtering is a firewall technology that makes access decisions based upon network-level protocol header values. The device that is carrying out packet-filtering processes is

configured with ACLs, which dictate the type of traffic that is allowed into and out of specific networks.

Packet filtering was the first generation of firewalls, and it is the most rudimentary type of all of the firewall technologies. The filters only have the capability of reviewing protocol header information at the network and transport layers and carrying out permit or deny actions on individual packets. This means the filters can make access decisions based upon the following basic criteria:

- Source and destination IP addresses
- Source and destination port numbers
- Protocol types
- Inbound and outbound traffic direction

Packet filtering is built into a majority of the firewall products today and is a capability that many routers perform. The ACL filtering rules are enforced at the network interface of the device, which is the doorway into or out of a network. As an analogy, you could have a list of items you look for before allowing someone into your office premises through your front door. Your list can indicate that a person must be 18 years or older, have an access badge, and be wearing pants. When someone knocks on the door, you grab your list, which you will use to decide if this person can or cannot come inside. So your front door is one interface into your office premises. You can also have a list that outlines who can exit your office premises through your back door, which is another interface. As shown in Figure 4-45, a router has individual interfaces with their own unique addresses,

Figure 4-45 ACLs are enforced at the network interface level.

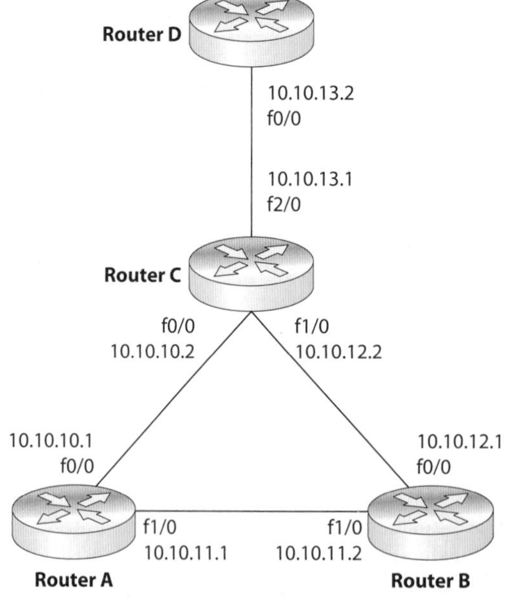

which provide doorways into and out of a network. Each interface can have its own ACL values, which indicate what type of traffic is allowed in and out of that specific interface.

We will cover some basic ACL rules to illustrate how packet filtering is implemented and enforced. The following router configuration allows SMTP traffic to travel from system 10.1.1.2 to system 172.16.1.1:

```
permit tcp host 10.1.1.2 host 172.16.1.1 eq smtp
```

This next rule permits UDP traffic from system 10.1.1.2 to 172.16.1.1:

```
permit udp host 10.1.1.2 host 172.16.1.1
```

If you want to ensure that no ICMP traffic enters through a certain interface, the following ACL can be configured and deployed:

```
deny icmp any any
```

If you want to allow standard web traffic (that is, to a web server listening on port 80) from system 1.1.1.1 to system 5.5.5.5, you can use the following ACL:

```
permit tcp host 1.1.1.1 host 5.5.5.5 eq www
```

NOTE Filtering inbound traffic is known as *ingress filtering*. Outgoing traffic can also be filtered using a process referred to as *egress filtering*.

So when a packet arrives at a packet-filtering device, the device starts at the top of its ACL and compares the packet's characteristics to each rule set. If a successful match (permit or deny) is found, then the remaining rules are not processed. If no matches are found when the device reaches the end of the list, the traffic should be denied, but each product is different. So if you are configuring a packet-filtering device, make sure that if no matches are identified, then the traffic is denied.

Packet filtering is also known as *stateless inspection* because the device does not understand the context that the packets are working within. This means that the device does not have the capability to understand the "full picture" of the communication that is taking place between two systems, but can only focus on individual packet characteristics. As we will see in a later section, stateful firewalls understand and keep track of a full communication session, not just the individual packets that make it up. Stateless firewalls make their decisions for each packet based solely on the data contained in that individual packet. Stateful firewalls accumulate data about the packets they see and use that data in an attempt to match incoming and outgoing packets to determine which packets may be part of the same network communications session. By evaluating a packet in the larger context of a network communications session, a stateful firewall has much more complete information than a stateless firewall and can therefore more readily recognize and reject packets that may be part of a network protocol–based attack.

Packet-filtering devices can block many types of attacks at the network protocol level, but they are not effective at protecting against attacks that exploit application-specific vulnerabilities. That is because filtering only examines a packet's header (i.e., delivery information) and not the data moving between the applications. Thus, a packet-filtering

firewall cannot protect against packet content that could, for example, probe for and exploit a buffer overflow in a given piece of software.

The lack of sophistication in packet filtering means that an organization should not solely depend upon this type of firewall to protect its infrastructure and assets, but it does not mean that this technology should not be used at all. Packet filtering is commonly carried out at the edge of a network to strip out all of the obvious "junk" traffic. Since the rules are simple and only header information is analyzed, this type of filtering can take place quickly and efficiently. After traffic is passed through a packet-filtering device, it is usually then processed by a more sophisticated firewall, which digs deeper into the packet contents and can identify application-based attacks.

Some of the weaknesses of packet-filtering firewalls are as follows:

- They cannot prevent attacks that employ application-specific vulnerabilities or functions.
- They have limited logging functionality.
- Most packet-filtering firewalls do not support advanced user authentication schemes.
- Many packet-filtering firewalls cannot detect spoofed addresses.
- They may not be able to detect packet fragmentation attacks.

The advantages to using packet-filtering firewalls are that they are scalable, they are not application dependent, and they have high performance because they do not carry out extensive processing on the packets. They are commonly used as the first line of defense to strip out all the network traffic that is obviously malicious or unintended for a specific network. The network traffic usually then has to be processed by more sophisticated firewalls that will identify the not-so-obvious security risks.

Stateful Firewalls

When packet filtering is used, a packet arrives at the firewall, and it runs through its ACLs to determine whether this packet should be allowed or denied. If the packet is allowed, it is passed on to the destination host, or to another network device, and the packet-filtering device forgets about the packet. This is different from stateful inspection, which remembers and keeps track of what packets went where until each particular connection is closed.

A *stateful firewall* is like a nosy neighbor who gets into people's business and conversations. She keeps track of the suspicious cars that come into the neighborhood, who is out of town for the week, and the postman who stays a little too long at the neighbor lady's house. This can be annoying until your house is burglarized. Then you and the police will want to talk to the nosy neighbor, because she knows everything going on in the neighborhood and would be the one most likely to know something unusual happened. A stateful-inspection firewall is nosier than a regular filtering device because it keeps track of what computers say to each other. This requires that the firewall maintain a *state table*, which is like a score sheet of who said what to whom.

Keeping track of the state of a protocol connection requires keeping track of many variables. Most people understand the three-step handshake a TCP connection goes

through (SYN, SYN/ACK, ACK), but what does this really mean? If Quincy's system wants to communicate with your system using TCP, it will send your system a packet and in the TCP header the SYN flag value will be set to 1. This makes this packet a SYN packet. If your system accepts Quincy's system's connection request, it will send back a packet that has both the SYN and ACK flags within the packet header set to 1. This is a SYN/ACK packet. While many people know about these three steps of setting up a TCP connection, they are not always familiar with all of the other items that are being negotiated at this time. For example, your system and Quincy's system will agree upon sequence numbers, how much data to send at a time (window size), how potential transmission errors will be identified (CRC values), etc. Figure 4-46 shows all of the values that make up a TCP header. So there is a lot of information going back and forth between your systems just in this one protocol—TCP. There are other protocols that are involved with networking that a stateful firewall has to be aware of and keep track of.

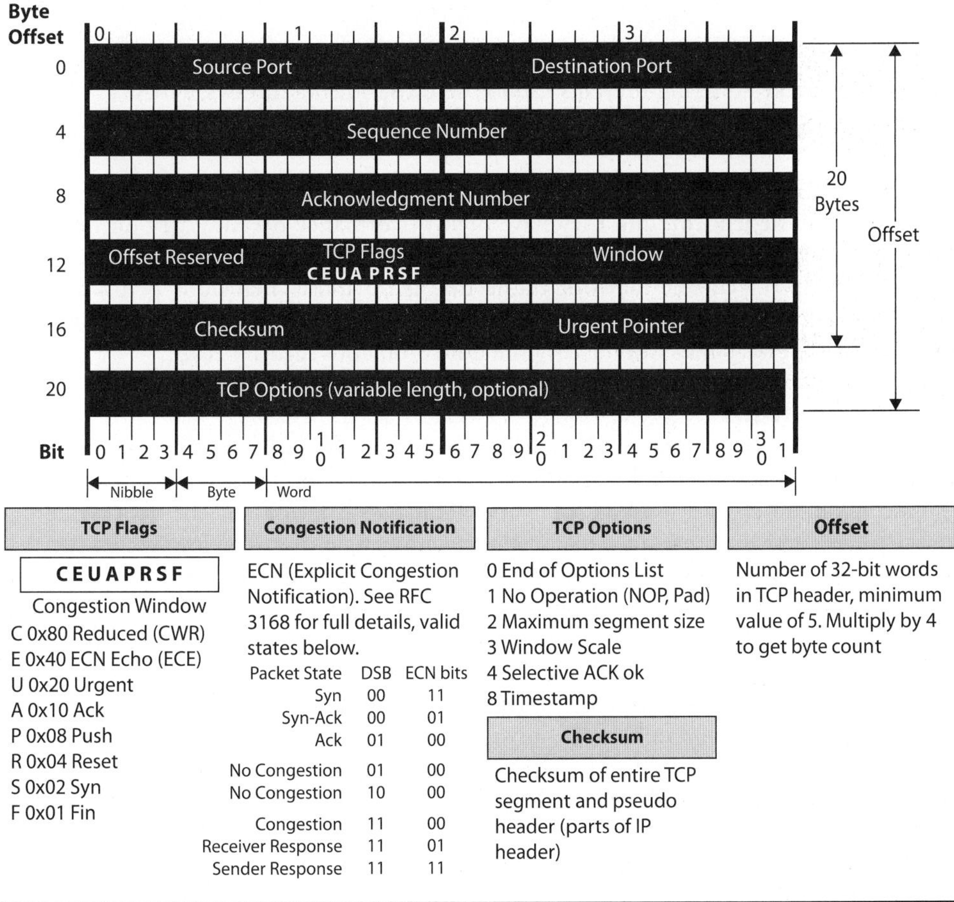

Figure 4-46 TCP header

So "keeping state of a connection" means to keep a scorecard of all the various protocol header values as packets go back and forth between systems. The values not only have to be correct—they have to happen in the right sequence. For example, if a stateful firewall receives a packet that has all TCP flag values turned to 1, something malicious is taking place. Under no circumstances during a legitimate TCP connection should all of these values be turned on like this. Attackers send packets with all of these values turned to 1 with the hopes that the firewall does not understand or check these values and just forwards the packets onto the target system.

In another situation, if Gwen's system sends your system a SYN/ACK packet and your system did not first send a SYN packet to Gwen's system, this, too, is against the protocol rules. The protocol communication steps have to follow the proper sequence. Attackers send SYN/ACK packets to target systems hoping that the firewall interprets this as an already established connection and just allows the packets to go to the destination system without inspection. A stateful firewall will not be fooled by such actions because it keeps track of each step of the communication. It knows how protocols are supposed to work, and if something is out of order (incorrect flag values, incorrect sequence, etc.), it does not allow the traffic to pass through.

When a connection begins between two systems, the firewall investigates *all* elements of the packet (all headers, payload, and trailers). All of the necessary information about the specific connection is stored in the state table (source and destination IP addresses, source and destination ports, protocol type, header flags, sequence numbers, timestamps, etc.). Once the initial packets go through this in-depth inspection and everything is deemed safe, the firewall then just reviews the network and transport header portions for the rest of the session. The values of each header for each packet are compared to what is in the current state table, and the table is updated to reflect the progression of the communication process. Scaling down the inspection of the full packet to just the headers for each packet is done to increase performance.

TCP is considered a connection-oriented protocol, and the various steps and states this protocol operates within are very well defined. A connection progresses through a series of states during its lifetime. The states are LISTEN, SYN-SENT, SYN-RECEIVED, ESTABLISHED, FIN-WAIT-1, FIN-WAIT-2, CLOSE-WAIT, CLOSING, LAST-ACK, TIME-WAIT, and the fictional state CLOSED. A stateful firewall keeps track of each of these states for each packet that passes through, along with the corresponding acknowledgment and sequence numbers. If the acknowledgment and/or sequence numbers are out of order, this could imply that a replay attack is underway, and the firewall will protect the internal systems from this activity.

Nothing is ever simple in life, including the standardization of network protocol communication. While the previous statements are true pertaining to the states of a TCP connection, in some situations an application layer protocol has to change these basic steps. For example, FTP uses an unusual communication exchange when initializing its data channel compared to all of the other application layer protocols. FTP basically sets up two sessions just for one communication exchange between two computers. The states of the two individual TCP connections that make up an FTP session can be tracked in the normal fashion, but the state of the FTP connection follows different rules. For a stateful device to be able to properly monitor the traffic of an FTP session, it must be able to take into account the way that FTP uses one outbound connection for the control channel and one inbound connection for the data channel. If you were configuring a stateful firewall, you would need to understand the particulars of some specific protocols to ensure that each is being properly inspected and controlled.

Since TCP is a connection-oriented protocol, it has clearly defined states during the connection establishment, maintenance, and tearing-down stages. UDP is a connectionless protocol, which means that none of these steps take place. UDP holds no state, which makes it harder for a stateful firewall to keep track of. For connectionless protocols, a stateful firewall keeps track of source and destination addresses, UDP header values, and some ACL rules. This connection information is also stored in the state table and tracked. Since the protocol does not have a specific tear-down stage, the firewall will just time out the connection after a period of inactivity and remove the data being kept pertaining to that connection from the state table.

An interesting complexity of stateful firewalls and UDP connections is how ICMP comes into play. Since UDP is connectionless, it does not provide a mechanism to allow the receiving computer to tell the sending computer that data is coming too fast. In TCP, the receiving computer can alter the window value in its header, which tells the sending computer to reduce the amount of data that is being sent. The message is basically, "You are overwhelming me and I cannot process the amount of data you are sending me. Slow down." UDP does not have a window value in its header, so instead the receiving computer sends an ICMP packet that provides the same function. But now this means that the stateful firewall must keep track of and allow associated ICMP packets with specific UDP connections. If the firewall does not allow the ICMP packets to get to the sending system, the receiving system could get overwhelmed and crash. This is just one example of the complexity that comes into play when a firewall has to do more than just packet filtering. Although stateful inspection provides an extra step of protection, it also adds more complexity because this device must now keep a dynamic state table and remember connections.

Stateful-inspection firewalls unfortunately have been the victims of many types of DoS attacks. Several types of attacks are aimed at flooding the state table with bogus information. The state table is a resource, similar to a system's hard drive space, memory, and CPU. When the state table is stuffed full of bogus information, a poorly designed device may either freeze or reboot.

Stateful-Inspection Firewall Characteristics

The following lists some important characteristics of a stateful-inspection firewall:

- Maintains a state table that tracks each and every communication session
- Provides a high degree of security and does not introduce the performance hit that application proxy firewalls introduce
- Is scalable and transparent to users
- Provides data for tracking connectionless protocols such as UDP and ICMP
- Stores and updates the state and context of the data within the packets

Proxy Firewalls

A *proxy* is a middleman. It intercepts and inspects messages before delivering them to the intended recipients. Suppose you need to give a box and a message to the president of the United States. You couldn't just walk up to the president and hand over these items. Instead, you would have to go through a middleman, likely the Secret Service, who would accept the box and message and thoroughly inspect the box to ensure nothing dangerous was inside. This is what a proxy firewall does—it accepts messages either entering or leaving a network, inspects them for malicious information, and, when it decides the messages are okay, passes the data on to the destination computer.

A *proxy firewall* stands between a trusted and untrusted network and makes the connection, each way, on behalf of the source. What is important is that a proxy firewall breaks the communication channel; there is no *direct* connection between the two communicating devices. Where a packet-filtering device just monitors traffic as it is traversing a network connection, a proxy ends the communication session and restarts it on behalf of the sending system. Figure 4-47 illustrates the steps of a proxy-based firewall. Notice that the firewall is not just applying ACL rules to the traffic, but stops the user connection at the internal interface of the firewall itself and then starts a new session on behalf of this user on the external interface. When the external web server replies to the request, this reply goes to the external interface of the proxy firewall and ends. The proxy firewall examines the reply information and, if it is deemed safe, starts a new session from itself to the internal system. This is just like our analogy of what the delivery man does between you and the president.

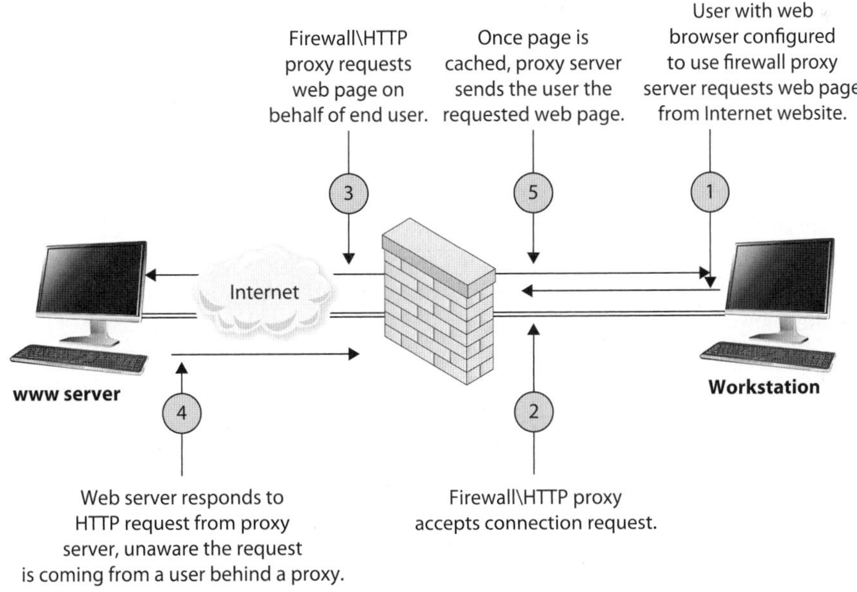

Figure 4-47 Proxy firewall breaks connection

Now a proxy technology can actually work at different layers of a network stack. A proxy-based firewall that works at the lower layers of the OSI model is referred to as a circuit-level proxy. A proxy-based firewall that works at the application layer is, strangely enough, called an application-level proxy.

A *circuit-level proxy* creates a connection (circuit) between the two communicating systems. It works at the session layer of the OSI model and monitors traffic from a network-based view. This type of proxy cannot "look into" the contents of a packet; thus, it does not carry out deep-packet inspection. It can only make access decisions based upon protocol header and session information that is available to it. While this means that it cannot provide as much protection as an application-level proxy, because it does not have to understand application layer protocols, it is considered application independent. So it cannot provide the detail-oriented protection that a proxy working at a higher level can, but this allows it to provide a broader range of protection where application layer proxies may not be appropriate or available.

NOTE Traffic sent to the receiving computer through a circuit-level proxy appears to have originated from the firewall instead of the sending system. This is useful for hiding information about the internal computers on the network the firewall is protecting.

Application-level proxies inspect the packet up through the application layer. Where a circuit-level proxy only has insight up to the session layer, an application-level proxy understands the packet as a whole and can make access decisions based on the content of the packets. Application-level proxies understand various services and protocols and the commands that are used by them. An application-level proxy can distinguish between an FTP GET command and an FTP PUT command, for example, and make access decisions based on this granular level of information; on the other hand, packet-filtering firewalls and circuit-level proxies can allow or deny FTP requests only as a whole, not by the commands used within FTP.

An application-level proxy firewall has one proxy per protocol. A computer can have many types of protocols (FTP, NTP, SMTP, HTTP, and so on). Thus, one application-level proxy per protocol is required. This does not mean one proxy firewall per service is required, but rather that one portion of the firewall product is dedicated to understanding how a specific protocol works and how to properly filter it for suspicious data.

Providing application-level proxy protection can be a tricky undertaking. The proxy must totally understand how specific protocols work and what commands within that protocol are legitimate. This is a lot to know and look at during the transmission of data. As an analogy, picture a screening station at an airport that is made up of many employees, all with the job of interviewing people before they are allowed into the airport and onto an airplane. These employees have been trained to ask specific questions and detect suspicious answers and activities, and have the skill set and authority to detain suspicious individuals. Now, suppose each of these employees speaks a different language because the people they interview come from different parts of the world. So, one employee who speaks German could not understand and identify suspicious answers of a person from Italy because they do not speak the same language. This is the same for an application-level proxy firewall.

Each proxy is a piece of software that has been designed to understand how a specific protocol "talks" and how to identify suspicious data within a transmission using that protocol.

NOTE If the application-level proxy firewall does not understand a certain protocol or service, it cannot protect this type of communication. In this scenario, a circuit-level proxy is useful because it does not deal with such complex issues. An advantage of a circuit-level proxy is that it can handle a wider variety of protocols and services than an application-level proxy can, but the downfall is that the circuit-level proxy cannot provide the degree of granular control that an application-level proxy provides. Life is just full of compromises.

A circuit-level proxy works similarly to a packet filter in that it makes access decisions based on address, port, and protocol type header values. It looks at the data within the packet header rather than the data at the application layer of the packet. It does not know whether the contents within the packet are safe or unsafe; it only understands the traffic from a network-based view.

An application-level proxy, on the other hand, is dedicated to a particular protocol or service. At least one proxy is used per protocol because one proxy could not properly interpret all the commands of all the protocols coming its way. A circuit-level proxy works at a lower layer of the OSI model and does not require one proxy per protocol because it does not look at such detailed information.

Application-Level Proxy Firewalls

Application-level proxy firewalls, like all technologies, have their pros and cons. It is important to fully understand all characteristics of this type of firewall before purchasing and deploying this type of solution.

Characteristics of application-level proxy firewalls:

- They have extensive logging capabilities due to the firewall being able to examine the entire network packet rather than just the network addresses and ports.
- They are capable of authenticating users directly, as opposed to packet-filtering firewalls and stateful-inspection firewalls, which can usually only carry out system authentication.
- Since they are not simply layer 3 devices, they can address spoofing attacks and other sophisticated attacks.

Disadvantages of using application-level proxy firewalls:

- They are not generally well suited to high-bandwidth or real-time applications.
- They tend to be limited in terms of support for new network applications and protocols.
- They create performance issues because of the necessary per-packet processing requirements.

SOCKS is an example of a circuit-level proxy gateway that provides a secure channel between two computers. When a SOCKS-enabled client sends a request to access a computer on the Internet, this request actually goes to the network's SOCKS proxy firewall, as shown in Figure 4-48, which inspects the packets for malicious information and checks its policy rules to see whether this type of connection is allowed. If the packet is acceptable and this type of connection is allowed, the SOCKS firewall sends the message to the destination computer on the Internet. When the computer on the Internet responds, it sends its packets to the SOCKS firewall, which again inspects the data and then passes the packets on to the client computer.

The SOCKS firewall can screen, filter, audit, log, and control data flowing in and out of a protected network. Because of its popularity, many applications and protocols have been configured to work with SOCKS in a manner that takes less configuration on the administrator's part, and various firewall products have integrated SOCKS software to provide circuit-based protection.

NOTE Remember that whether an application- or circuit-level proxy firewall is being used, it is still acting as a proxy. Both types of proxy firewalls deny actual end-to-end connectivity between the source and destination systems. In attempting a remote connection, the client connects to and communicates with the proxy; the proxy, in turn, establishes a connection to the destination system and makes requests to it on the client's behalf. The proxy maintains two independent connections for every one network transmission. It essentially turns a two-party session into a four-party session, with the middle process emulating the two real systems.

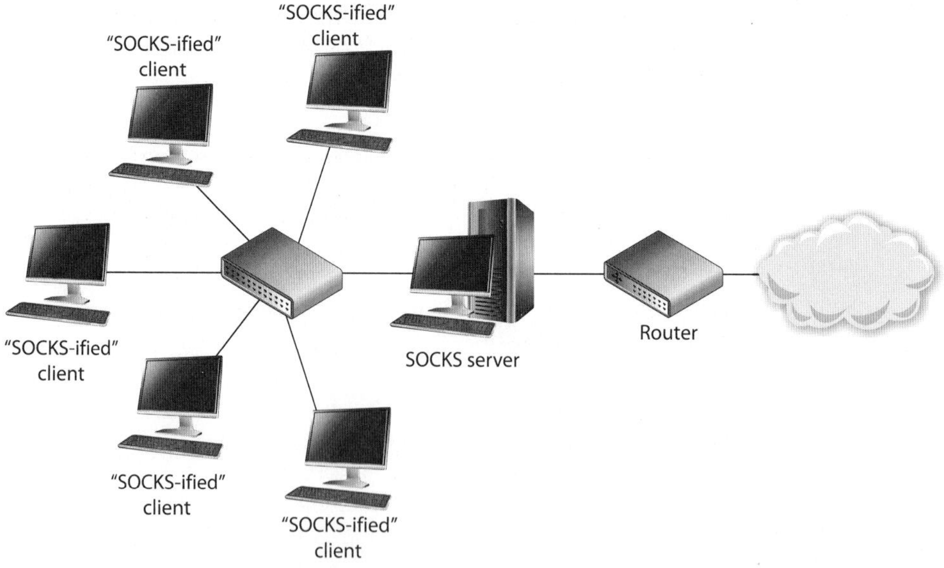

Figure 4-48 Circuit-level proxy firewall

Application-Level vs. Circuit-Level Proxy Firewall Characteristics

Characteristics of application-level proxy firewalls:

- Each protocol that is to be monitored must have a unique proxy.
- They provide more protection than circuit-level proxy firewalls.
- They require more processing per packet and thus are slower than circuit-level proxy firewalls.

Characteristics of circuit-level proxy firewalls:

- They do not require a proxy for each and every protocol.
- They do not provide the deep-inspection capabilities of an application-level proxy firewall.
- They provide security for a wider range of protocols.

Dynamic Packet-Filtering Firewalls

When an internal system needs to communicate with an entity outside its trusted network, it must choose a source port so the receiving system knows how to respond properly. Ports up to 1023 are called *well-known ports* and are reserved for specific server-side services. The sending system must choose a dynamic port higher than 1023 when it sets up a connection with another entity. The *dynamic packet-filtering firewall* then creates an ACL that allows the external entity to communicate with the internal system via this high-numbered port. If this were not an available option for your dynamic packet-filtering firewall, you would have to allow "punch holes" in your firewalls for all ports above 1023, because the client side chooses these ports dynamically and the firewall would never know exactly on which port to allow or disallow traffic.

NOTE The standard port for HTTP is 80, which means a server will have a service listening on port 80 for HTTP traffic. HTTP (and most other protocols) works in a type of client/server model. The server portion uses the well-known ports (FTP uses 20 and 21; SMTP uses 25) so everyone knows how to connect to those services. A client will not use one of these well-known port numbers for itself, but will choose a random, higher port number.

An internal system could choose a source port of 11,111 for its message to the outside system. This frame goes to the dynamic packet-filtering firewall, which builds an ACL, as illustrated in Figure 4-49, that indicates a response from the destination computer to this internal system's IP address and port 11,111 is to be allowed. When the destination system sends a response, the firewall allows it. These ACLs are dynamic in nature, so once the connection is finished (either a FIN or RST packet is received), the ACL is removed

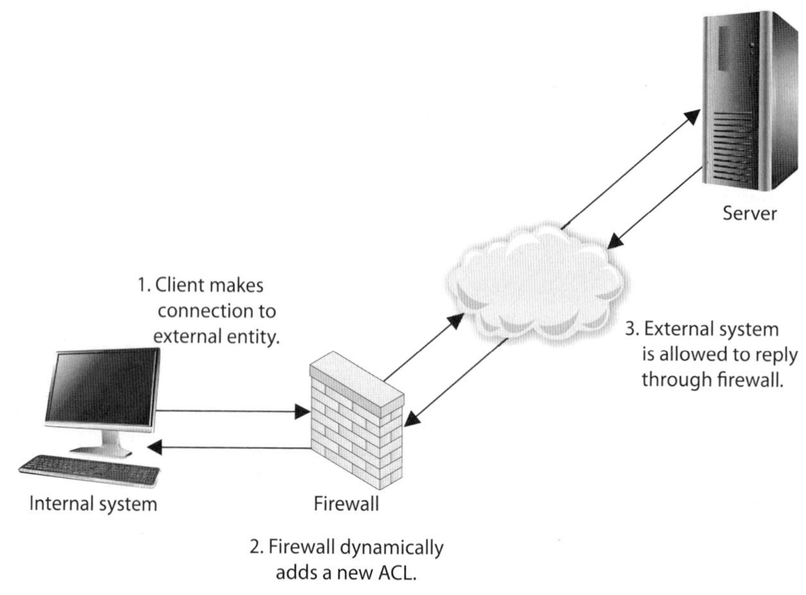

Figure 4-49 Dynamic packet filtering adds ACLs when connections are created.

from the list. On connectionless protocols, such as UDP, the connection times out and then the ACL is removed.

The benefit of a dynamic packet-filtering firewall is that it gives you the option of allowing any type of traffic outbound and permitting only response traffic inbound.

Kernel Proxy Firewalls

A *kernel proxy firewall* is considered a fifth-generation firewall. It differs from all the previously discussed firewall technologies because it creates dynamic, customized network stacks when a packet needs to be evaluated.

When a packet arrives at a kernel proxy firewall, a new virtual network stack is created, which is made up of only the protocol proxies necessary to examine this specific packet properly. If it is an FTP packet, then the FTP proxy is loaded in the stack. The packet is scrutinized at every layer of the stack. This means the data link header will be evaluated along with the network header, transport header, session layer information, and the application layer data. If anything is deemed unsafe at any of these layers, the packet is discarded.

Kernel proxy firewalls are faster than application-level proxy firewalls because all of the inspection and processing takes place in the kernel and does not need to be passed up to a higher software layer in the operating system. It is still a proxy-based system, so the connection between the internal and external entity is broken by the proxy acting as a middleman, and it can perform NAT by changing the source address, as do the preceding proxy-based firewalls.

Appliances

A firewall may take the form of either software installed on a regular computer using a regular operating system or a dedicated hardware appliance that has its own operating system. The second choice is usually more secure, because the vendor uses a stripped-down version of an operating system (usually Linux or BSD Unix). Operating systems are full of code and functionality that are not necessary for a firewall. This extra complexity opens the doors for vulnerabilities. If a hacker can exploit and bring down a company's firewall, then the company is very exposed and in danger.

In today's jargon, dedicated hardware devices that have stripped-down operating systems and limited and focused software capabilities are called *appliances*. Where an operating system has to provide a vast array of functionality, an appliance provides very focused functionality—as in just being a firewall.

If a software-based firewall is going to run on a regular system, then the unnecessary user accounts should be disabled, unnecessary services deactivated, unused subsystems disabled, unneeded ports closed, etc. If firewall software is going to run on a regular system and not a dedicated appliance, then the system needs to be fully locked down.

Next-Generation Firewalls

A *next-generation firewall (NGFW)* combines the best attributes of the previously discussed firewalls, but adds a number of important improvements. Most importantly, it incorporates a signature-based IPS engine. This means that, in addition to ensuring that the traffic is behaving in accordance with the rules of the applicable protocols, the firewall can look for specific indicators of attack even in otherwise well-behaved traffic. Some of the most advanced NGFWs include features that allow them to share signatures with a cloud-based aggregator so that once a new attack is detected by one firewall, all other firewalls manufactured by that vendor become aware of the attack signature.

Another characteristic of an NGFW is its ability to connect to external data sources such as Active Directory, whitelists, blacklists, and policy servers. This features allows controls to be defined in one place and pulled by every NGFW on the network, which reduces the chances of inconsistent settings on the various firewalls that typically exist in large networks.

For all their power, NGFWs are not for everyone. The typical cost of ownership alone tends to make these infeasible for small or even medium-sized networks. Organizations need to ensure that the correct firewall technology is in place to monitor specific network traffic types and protect unique resource types. The firewalls also have to be properly placed; we will cover this topic in the next section.

NOTE Firewall technology has evolved as attack types have evolved. The first-generation firewalls could only monitor network traffic. As attackers moved from just carrying out network-based attacks (DoS, fragmentation, spoofing, etc.) to software-based attacks (buffer overflows, injections, malware, etc.), new generations of firewalls were developed to monitor for these types of attacks.

Firewall Type	OSI Layer	Characteristics
Packet filtering	Network layer	Looks at destination and source addresses, ports, and services requested. Routers using ACLs to monitor network traffic.
Stateful	Network layer	Looks at the state and context of packets. Keeps track of each conversation using a state table.
Application-level proxy	Application layer	Looks deep into packets and makes granular access control decisions. It requires one proxy per protocol.
Circuit-level proxy	Session layer	Looks only at the header packet information. It protects a wider range of protocols and services than an application-level proxy, but does not provide the detailed level of control available to an application-level proxy.
Dynamic packet filtering	Network layer	Allows any permitted type of traffic outbound and only response traffic inbound.
Kernel proxy	Application layer	Faster because processing is performed in the kernel. One network stack is created for each packet.
Next-generation firewall	Multiple layers	Very fast and supportive of high bandwidth. Built-in IPS. Able to connect to external services like Active Directory.

Table 4-10 Comparison of Different Types of Firewalls

Table 4-10 lists the important concepts and characteristics of the firewall types discussed in the preceding sections. Although various firewall products can provide a mix of these services and work at different layers of the OSI model, it is important you understand the basic definitions and functionalities of these firewall types.

Firewall Architecture

Firewalls can be placed in a number of areas on a network to meet particular needs. They can protect an internal network from an external network and act as a choke point for all traffic. A firewall can be used to segment and partition network sections and enforce access controls between two or more subnets. Firewalls can also be used to provide a DMZ architecture. And as covered in the previous section, the right firewall type needs to be placed in the right location. Organizations have common needs for firewalls; hence, they keep them in similar places on their networks. We will see more on this topic in the following sections.

Bastion Host

A system is considered a *bastion host* if it is a highly exposed device that is most likely to be targeted by attackers. The closer any system is to an untrusted network, such as the Internet, the more it is considered a target candidate since it has a smaller number of layers of protection guarding it. If a system is on the public side of a

DMZ or is directly connected to an untrusted network, it is considered a bastion host; thus, it needs to be extremely locked down.

The system should have all unnecessary services disabled, unnecessary accounts disabled, unneeded ports closed, unused applications removed, unused subsystems and administrative tools removed, etc. The attack surface of the system needs to be reduced, which means the number of potential vulnerabilities need to be reduced as much as possible.

A bastion host does not have to be a firewall—the term just relates to the position of the system in relation to an untrusted environment and its threat of attack. Different systems can be considered bastion hosts (mail, web, DNS) since many of these are placed on the outer edges of networks.

Dual-Homed Firewall *Dual-homed* refers to a device that has two interfaces: one connected to one network and the other connected to a different network. If firewall software is installed on a dual-homed device—and it usually is—the underlying operating system should have packet forwarding and routing turned off for security reasons. If they are enabled, the computer may not apply the necessary ACLs, rules, or other restrictions required of a firewall. When a packet comes to the external NIC from an untrusted network on a dual-homed firewall and the operating system has forwarding enabled, the operating system will forward the traffic instead of passing it up to the firewall software for inspection.

Many network devices today are *multihomed*, which just means they have several NICs that are used to connect several different networks. Multihomed devices are commonly used to house firewall software, since the job of a firewall is to control the traffic as it goes from one network to another. A common multihomed firewall architecture allows a company to have several DMZs. One DMZ may hold devices that are shared between companies in an extranet, another DMZ may house the company's DNS and mail servers, and yet another DMZ may hold the company's web servers. Different DMZs are used for two reasons: to control the different traffic types (for example, to make sure HTTP traffic only goes toward the web servers and ensure DNS requests go toward the DNS server), and to ensure that if one system on one DMZ is compromised, the other systems in the rest of the DMZs are not accessible to this attacker.

If a company depends solely upon a multihomed firewall with no redundancy, this system could prove to be a single point of failure. If it goes down, then all traffic flow stops. Some firewall products have embedded redundancy or fault-tolerance capabilities. If a company uses a firewall product that does not have these capabilities, then the network should have redundancy built into it.

Along with potentially being a single point of failure, another security issue that should be understood is the lack of defense in depth. If the company depends upon just one firewall, no matter what architecture is being used or how many interfaces the device has, there is only one layer of protection. If an attacker can compromise the one firewall, then she can gain direct access to company network resources.

Screened Host A *screened host* is a firewall that communicates directly with a perimeter router and the internal network. Figure 4-50 shows this type of architecture.

Traffic received from the Internet is first filtered via packet filtering on the outer router. The traffic that makes it past this phase is sent to the screened-host firewall, which applies more rules to the traffic and drops the denied packets. Then the traffic moves to the internal destination hosts. The screened host (the firewall) is the only device that receives traffic directly from the router. No traffic goes directly from the Internet, through the router, and to the internal network. The screened host is always part of this equation.

If the firewall is an application-based system, protection is provided at the network layer by the router through packet filtering, and at the application layer by the firewall. This arrangement offers a high degree of security, because for an attacker to be successful, she would have to compromise two systems.

What does the word "screening" mean in this context? As shown in Figure 4-50, the router is a screening device and the firewall is the screened host. This just means there is a layer that scans the traffic and gets rid of a lot of the "junk" before it is directed toward the firewall. A screened host is different from a screened subnet, which is described next.

Screened Subnet A *screened-subnet* architecture adds another layer of security to the screened-host architecture. The external firewall screens the traffic entering the DMZ network. However, instead of the firewall then redirecting the traffic to the internal network, an interior firewall also filters the traffic. The use of these two physical firewalls creates a DMZ.

In an environment with only a screened host, if an attacker successfully breaks through the firewall, nothing lies in her way to prevent her from having full access to the internal network. In an environment using a screened subnet, the attacker would have

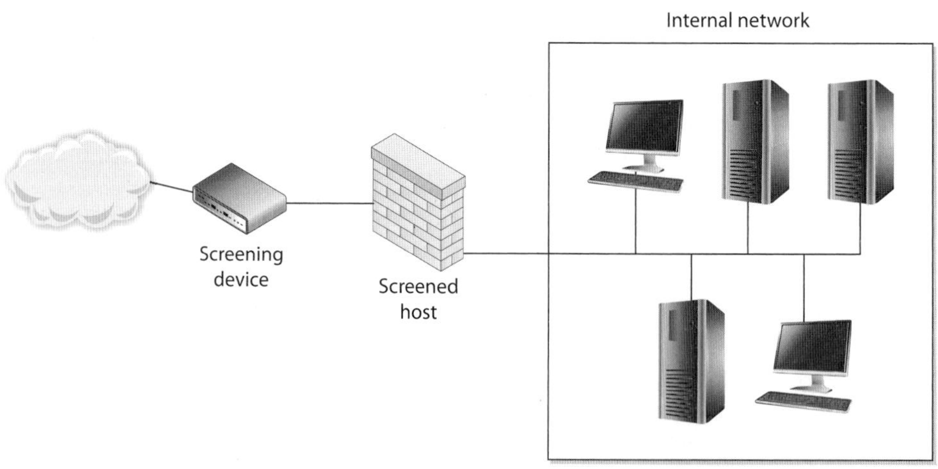

Figure 4-50 A screened host is a firewall that is screened by a router.

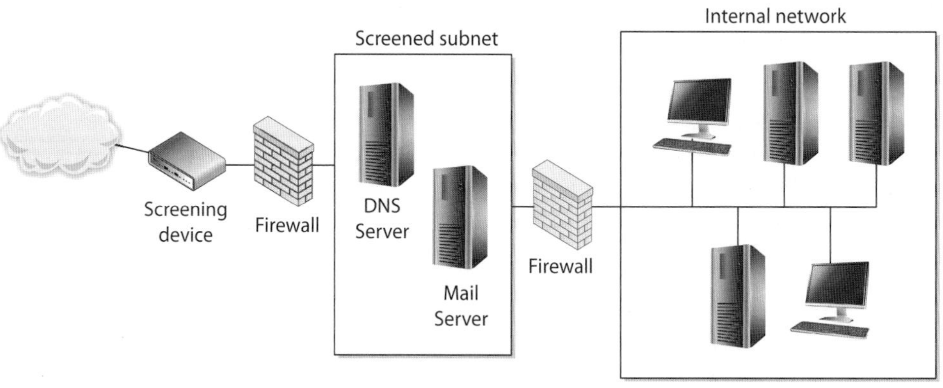

Figure 4-51 With a screened subnet, two firewalls are used to create a DMZ.

to hack through another firewall to gain access. In this layered approach to security, the more layers provided, the better the protection. Figure 4-51 shows a simple example of a screened subnet.

The examples shown in the figures are simple in nature. Often, more complex networks and DMZs are implemented in real-world systems. Figures 4-52 and 4-53 show some other possible architectures of screened subnets and their configurations.

The screened-subnet approach provides more protection than a stand-alone firewall or a screened-host firewall because three devices are working together and all three devices must be compromised before an attacker can gain access to the internal network. This architecture also sets up a DMZ between the two firewalls, which functions as a small network isolated among the trusted internal and untrusted external networks. The internal users usually have limited access to the servers within this area. Web, e-mail, and other public servers often are placed within the DMZ. Although this solution provides the highest security, it also is the most complex. Configuration and maintenance can prove to be difficult in this setup, and when new services need to be added, three systems may need to be reconfigured instead of just one.

TIP Sometimes a screened-host architecture is referred to as a single-tiered configuration and a screened subnet is referred to as a two-tiered configuration. If three firewalls create two separate DMZs, this may be called a three-tiered configuration.

Virtualized Firewalls

A lot of the network functionality we have covered up to this point can take place in virtual environments. Most people understand that a host system can have virtual guest systems running on it, enabling multiple operating systems to run on the same hardware platform simultaneously. But the industry has advanced much further than this when it comes to virtualized technology. Routers and switches can be virtualized, which means you do not actually purchase a piece of hardware and plug it into your network, but instead you deploy software products that carry out routing and switching functionality.

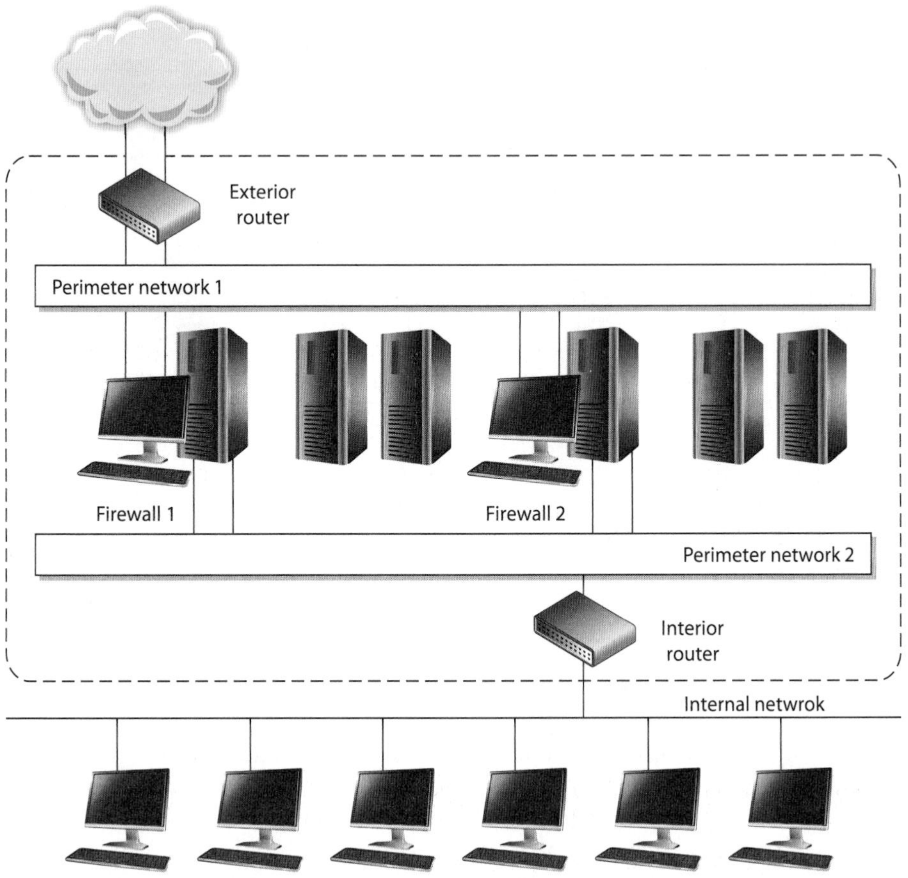

Figure 4-52 A screened subnet can have different networks within it and different firewalls that filter for specific threats.

Firewall Architecture Characteristics

It is important to understand the following characteristics of these firewall architecture types:

Dual-homed:

- A single computer with separate NICs connected to each network.
- Used to divide an internal trusted network from an external untrusted network.
- Must disable a computer's forwarding and routing functionality so the two networks are truly segregated.

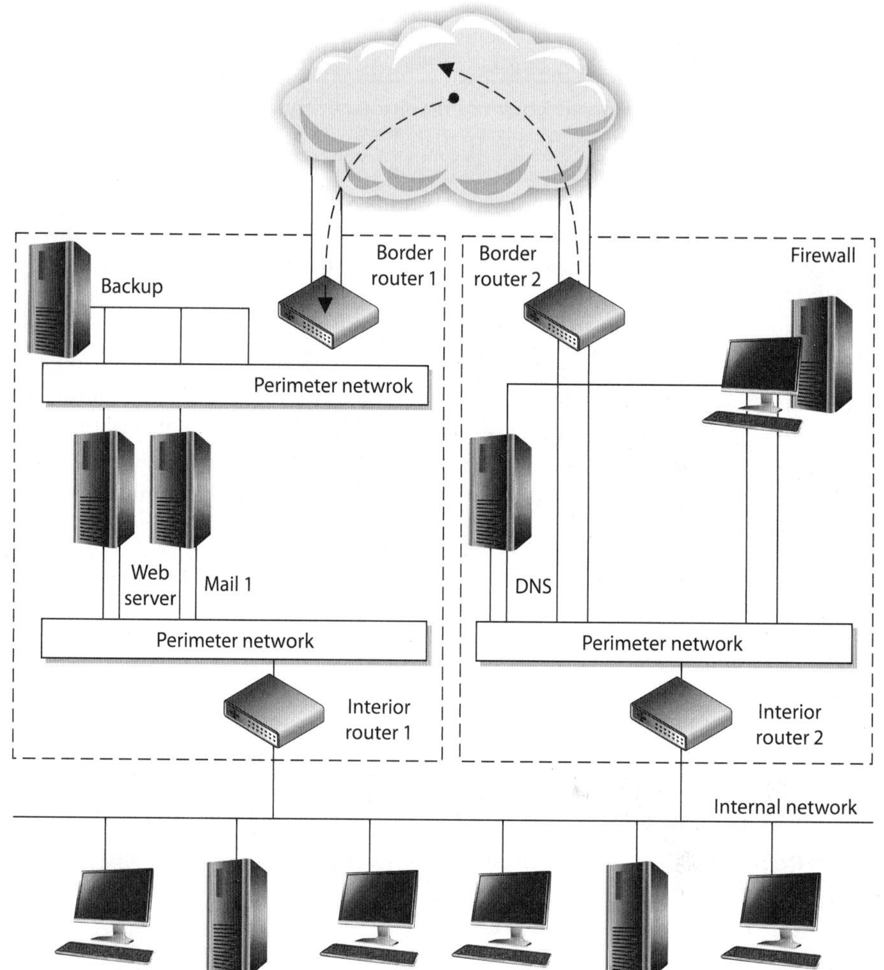

Figure 4-53 Some architectures have separate screened subnets with different server types in each.

> **Screened host:**
>
> - A router filters (screens) traffic before it is passed to the firewall.
>
> **Screened subnet:**
>
> - An external router filters (screens) traffic before it enters the subnet. Traffic headed toward the internal network then goes through two firewalls.

We used to deploy a piece of hardware for every network function needed (DNS, mail, routers, switches, storage, Web), but today many of these items run within virtual machines on a smaller number of hardware machines. This reduces software and hardware costs and allows for more centralized administration, but these components still need to be protected from each other and external malicious entities. As an analogy, let's say that 15 years ago each person lived in their own house and a police officer was placed between each house so that the people in the houses could not attack each other. Then last year, many of these people moved in together so that now at least five people live in the same physical house. These people still need to be protected from each other, so some of the police officers had to be moved inside the houses to enforce the laws and keep the peace. This is the same thing that virtualized firewalls do—they have "moved into" the virtualized environments to provide the necessary protection between virtualized entities.

As illustrated in Figure 4-54, a network can have a traditional physical firewall on the physical network and *virtual firewalls* within the individual virtual environments.

Virtual firewalls can provide bridge-type functionality in which individual traffic links are monitored between virtual machines, or they can be integrated within the hypervisor.

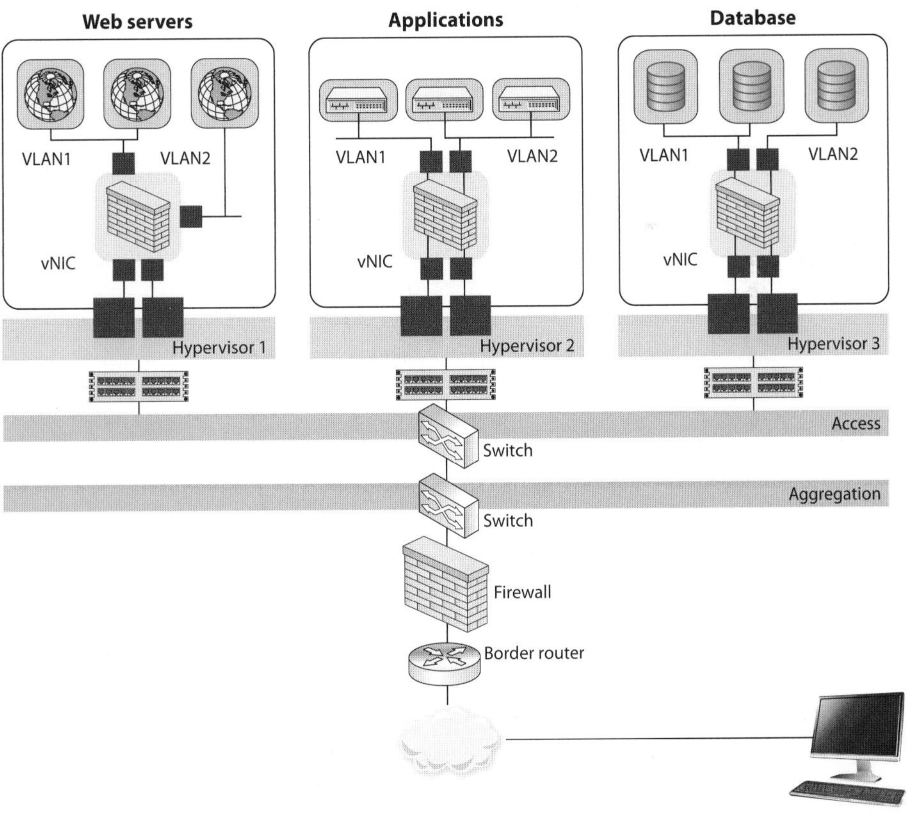

Figure 4-54 Virtual firewalls

The hypervisor is the software component that carries out virtual machine management and oversees guest system software execution. If the firewall is embedded within the hypervisor, then it can "see" and monitor all the activities taking place within the system.

The "Shoulds" of Firewalls

The default action of any firewall should be to implicitly deny any packets not explicitly allowed. This means that if no rule states that the packet can be accepted, that packet should be denied, no questions asked. Any packet entering the network that has a source address of an internal host should be denied. *Masquerading*, or *spoofing*, is a popular attacking trick in which the attacker modifies a packet header to have the source address of a host inside the network she wants to attack. This packet is spoofed and illegitimate. There is no reason a packet coming from the Internet should have an internal source network address, so the firewall should deny it. The same is true for outbound traffic. No traffic should be allowed to leave a network that does not have an internal source address. If this occurs, it means someone, or some program, on the internal network is spoofing traffic. This is how *zombies* work—the agents used in distributed DoS (DDoS) attacks. If packets are leaving a network with different source addresses, these packets are spoofed and the network is most likely being used as an accomplice in a DDoS attack.

Firewalls should reassemble fragmented packets before sending them on to their destination. In some types of attacks, the hackers alter the packets and make them seem to be something they are not. When a fragmented packet comes to a firewall, the firewall is seeing only part of the picture. It will make its best guess as to whether this piece of a packet is malicious or not. Because these fragments contain only a part of the full packet, the firewall is making a decision without having all the facts. Once all fragments are allowed through to a host computer, they can be reassembled into malicious packages that can cause a lot of damage. A firewall should accept each fragment, assemble the fragments into a complete packet, and then make an access decision based on the whole packet. The drawback to this, however, is that firewalls that do reassemble packet fragments before allowing them to go on to their destination computer cause traffic delay and more overhead. It is up to the organization to decide whether this configuration is necessary and whether the added traffic delay is acceptable.

Fragmentation Attacks

Attackers have constructed several exploits that take advantage of some of the packet fragmentation steps within networking protocols. The following are three such examples:

- **IP fragmentation** Fragmentation and reassembly flaws within IP are exploited, which causes DoS.
- **Teardrop attack** Malformed fragments are created by the attacker, and once they are reassembled, they could cause the victim system to become unstable.
- **Overlapping fragment attack** Used to subvert packet filters that do not reassemble packet fragments before inspection. A malicious fragment overwrites a previously approved fragment and executes an attack on the victim's system.

Many companies choose to deny network entrance to packets that contain source routing information, which was mentioned earlier. Source routing means the packet decides how to get to its destination, not the routers in between the source and destination computer. Source routing moves a packet throughout a network on a predetermined path. The sending computer must know about the topology of the network and how to route data properly. This is easier for the routers and connection mechanisms in between, because they do not need to make any decisions on how to route the packet. However, it can also pose a security risk. When a router receives a packet that contains source routing information, the router assumes the packet knows what needs to be done and passes the packet on. In some cases, not all filters may be applied to the packet, and a network administrator may want packets to be routed only through a certain path and not the route a particular packet dictates. To make sure none of this misrouting happens, many firewalls are configured to check for source routing information within the packet and deny it if it is present.

Some common firewall rules that should be implemented are as follows:

- **Silent rule** Drops "noisy" traffic without logging it. This reduces log sizes by not responding to packets that are deemed unimportant.
- **Stealth rule** Disallows access to firewall software from unauthorized systems.
- **Cleanup rule** Last rule in rule base, drops and logs any traffic that does not meet preceding rules.
- **Negate rule** Used instead of the broad and permissive "any rules," provides tighter permission rights by specifying what system can be accessed and how.

Firewalls are not effective "right out of the box." You really need to understand the type of firewall being implemented and its configuration ramifications. For example, a firewall may have implied rules, which are used before the rules you configure. These implied rules might contradict your rules and override them. In this case you think a certain traffic type is being restricted, but the firewall may allow that type of traffic into your network by default.

Unfortunately, once a company erects a firewall, it may have a false sense of security. Firewalls are only one piece of the puzzle, and security has a lot of pieces.

The following list addresses some of the issues that need to be understood as they pertain to firewalls:

- Most of the time a distributed approach needs to be used to control all network access points, which cannot happen through the use of just one firewall.
- Firewalls can present a potential bottleneck to the flow of traffic and a single point of failure threat.
- Some firewalls do not provide protection from malware and can be fooled by the more sophisticated attack types.
- Firewalls do not protect against sniffers or rogue wireless access points and provide little protection against insider attacks.

The role of firewalls is becoming more and more complex as they evolve and take on more functionality and responsibility. At times, this complexity works against security professionals because it requires them to understand and properly implement additional functionality. Without an understanding of the different types of firewalls and architectures available, many more security holes can be introduced, which lays out the welcome mat for attackers.

Proxy Servers

Earlier we covered two types of proxy-based firewalls, which are different from proxy servers. *Proxy servers* act as an intermediary between the clients that want access to certain services and the servers that provide those services. As a security administrator, you do not want internal systems to directly connect to external servers without some type of control taking place. For example, if users on your network could connect directly to websites without some type of filtering and rules in place, the users could allow malicious traffic into the network or could surf websites your company deems inappropriate. In this situation, all internal web browsers would be configured to send their web requests to a web proxy server. The proxy server validates that the request is safe and then sends an independent request to the website on behalf of the user. A very basic proxy server architecture is shown in Figure 4-55.

The proxy server may cache the response it receives from the server so that when other clients make the same request, a connection does not have to go out to the actual web server again, but the necessary data is served up directly from the proxy server. This drastically reduces latency and allows the clients to get the data they need much more quickly.

There are different types of proxies that provide specific services. A *forwarding proxy* is one that allows the client to specify the server it wants to communicate with, as in our scenario earlier. An *open proxy* is a forwarding proxy that is open for anyone to use.

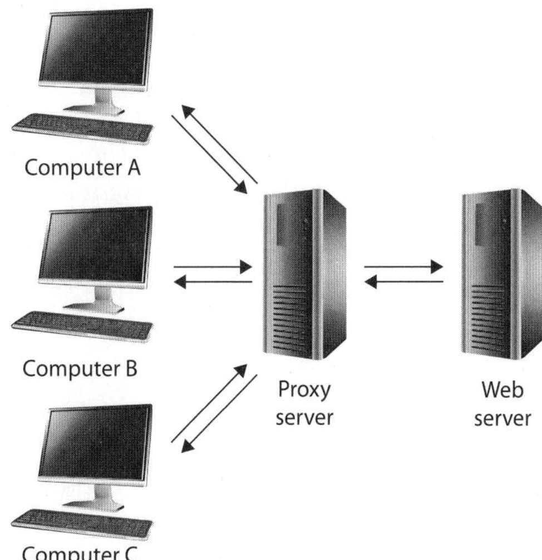

Figure 4-55 Proxy servers control traffic between clients and servers.

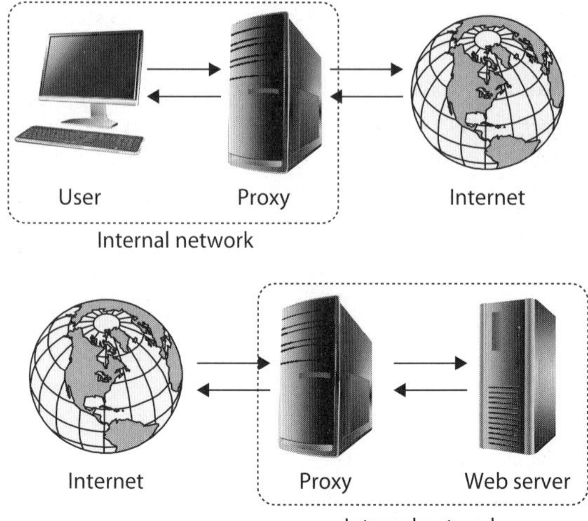

Figure 4-56 Forward vs. reverse proxy services

An anonymous open proxy allows users to conceal their IP address while browsing websites or using other Internet services. A *reverse proxy* appears to the clients as the original server. The client sends a request to what it thinks is the original server, but in reality this reverse proxy makes a request to the actual server and provides the client with the response. The forwarding and reverse proxy functionality seems similar, but as Figure 4-56 illustrates, a forwarding proxy server is commonly on an internal network controlling traffic that is exiting the network. A reverse proxy server is commonly on the network that fulfills clients' requests; thus, it is handling traffic that is entering its network. The reverse proxy can carry out load balancing, encryption acceleration, security, and caching.

Web proxy servers are commonly used to carry out content filtering to ensure that Internet use conforms to the organization's acceptable-use policy. These types of proxies can block unacceptable web traffic, provide logs with detailed information pertaining to the websites specific users visited, monitor bandwidth usage statistics, block restricted website usage, and screen traffic for specific keywords (e.g., porn, confidential, Social Security numbers). The proxy servers can be configured to act mainly as caching servers, which keep local copies of frequently requested resources, allowing organizations to significantly reduce their upstream bandwidth usage and costs while significantly increasing performance.

While it is most common to use proxy servers for web-based traffic, they can be used for other network functionality and capabilities, as in DNS proxy servers. Proxy servers are a critical component of almost every network today. They need to be properly placed, configured, and monitored.

NOTE The use of proxy servers to allow for online anonymity has increased over the years. Some people use a proxy server to protect their browsing behaviors from others, with the goal of providing personal freedom and privacy. Attackers use the same functionality to help ensure their activities cannot be tracked back to their local systems.

Honeypot

A *honeypot* is a computer that is intended to be exploited by attackers, with the administrator's goal being to gain information on the attack tactics, techniques, and procedures. A honeypot usually sits in the screened subnet, or DMZ, and attempts to lure attackers to it instead of to actual production computers. To make a honeypot system alluring to attackers, administrators may enable services and ports that are popular to exploit. Some honeypot systems *emulate* services, meaning the actual services are not running but software that acts like those services is available. Honeypot systems can get an attacker's attention by advertising themselves as easy targets to compromise. They are configured to look like regular company systems so that attackers will be drawn to them like bears are to honey.

Honeypots can work as early detection mechanisms, meaning that the network staff can be alerted that an intruder is attacking a honeypot system, and they can quickly go into action to make sure no production systems are vulnerable to that specific attack type. If two or more honeypot systems are used together, this is referred to as a *honeynet*.

Organizations use these systems to identify, quantify, and qualify specific traffic types to help determine their danger levels. The systems can gather network traffic statistics and return them to a centralized location for better analysis. So as the systems are being attacked, they gather intelligence information that can help the network staff better understand what is taking place within their environment.

It is important to make sure that the honeypot systems are not connected to production systems and do not provide any "jumping off" points for the attacker. There have been instances where companies improperly implemented honeypots and they were exploited by attackers, who were then able to move from those systems to the company's internal systems. The honeypots need to be properly segmented from any other live systems on the network.

On a smaller scale, companies may choose to implement *tarpits*, which are similar to honeypots in that they appear to be easy targets for exploitation. A tarpit can be configured to appear as a vulnerable service that attackers will commonly attempt to exploit. Once the attackers start to send packets to this "service," the connection to the victim system seems to be live and ongoing, but the response from the victim system is slow and the connection may time out. Most attacks and scanning activities take place through automated tools that require quick responses from their victim systems. If the victim systems do not reply or are very slow to reply, the automated tools may not be successful because the protocol connection times out.

Unified Threat Management

It can be very challenging to manage the long laundry list of security solutions almost every network needs to have in place. The list includes, but is not limited to, firewalls, antimalware, antispam, IDS/IPS, content filtering, data leak prevention, VPN capabilities, and continuous monitoring and reporting. *Unified threat management (UTM)* appliance products have been developed that provide all (or many) of these functionalities in a single network appliance. The goals of UTM are simplicity, streamlined installation and maintenance, centralized control, and the ability to understand a network's security

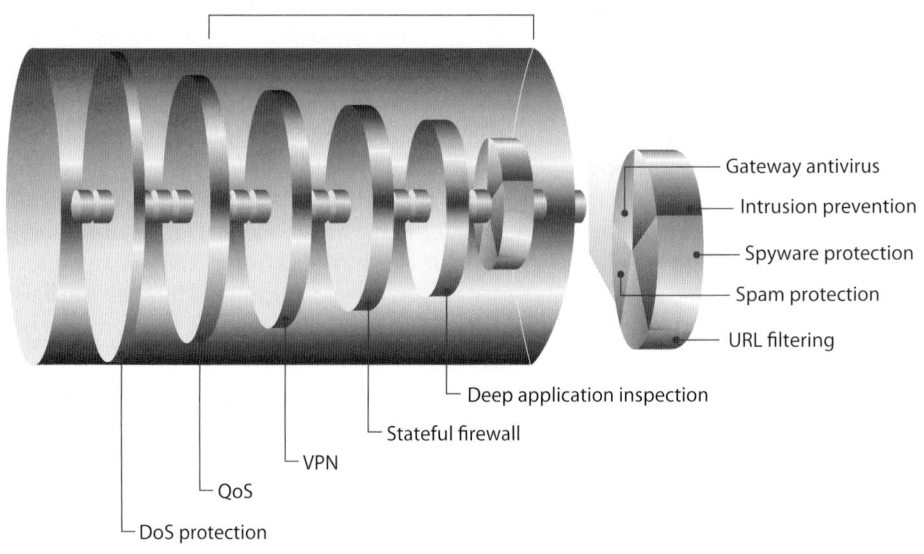

Figure 4-57 Unified threat management

from a holistic point of view. Figure 4-57 illustrates how all of these security functions are applied to traffic as it enters this type of dedicated device.

These products are considered all-in-one devices, and the actual type of functionality that is provided varies between vendors. Some products may be able to carry out this type of security for wired, wireless, and Voice over Internet Protocol (VoIP) types of traffic.

Some issues with implementing UTM products are

- **Single point of failure for traffic** Some type of redundancy should be put into place.
- **Single point of compromise** If the UTM is successfully hacked, there may not be other layers deployed for protection.
- **Performance issues** Latency and bandwidth issues can arise since this is a "choke point" device that requires a lot of processing.

Content Distribution Networks

So far, our discussion of networking has sort of implied that there is *a* (singular) web server, a (singular) database server, and so on. While this simplifies our discussion of network foundations, protocols, and services, we all know that this is a very rare scenario in all but the smallest networks. Instead, we tend to implement multiples of each service, whether to segment systems, provide redundancy, or both. We may have a couple of web servers connected by a load balancer and interfacing with multiple back-end database servers. This sort of redundant deployment can improve performance, but all clients still have to reach the same physical location regardless of where in the world they may be. Wouldn't it be nice if users in Europe did not have to ride transatlantic cables or satellite links to reach a server in the United States and instead could use one closer to them?

A *content distribution network (CDN)* consists of multiple servers distributed across a large region, each of which provides content that is optimized for users closest to it. This optimization can come in many flavors. For example, if you were a large video distribution entity like Netflix, you would want to keep your movie files from having to traverse multiple links between routers, since each hop would incur a delay and potential loss of packets (which could cause jitter in the video). Reducing the number of network hops for your video packets would also usually mean having a server geographically closer to the other node, offering you the opportunity to tailor the content for users in that part of the world. Building on our video example, you could keep movies dubbed in Chinese on servers that are on or closer to Asia and those dubbed in French closer to Europe. So when we talk about optimizing content, we can mean many things.

Another benefit of using CDNs is that they make your Internet presence more resistant to DDoS attacks. We will get into detail on these attacks later in this chapter, but for now you should keep in mind that they rely on having a large number of computers flood a server until it becomes unresponsive to legitimate requests. If an attacker can muster a DDoS attack that can send a million packets per second (admittedly fairly small by today's standards) and aim it at a single server, then it could very well be effective. However, if the attacker tries that against a server that is part of a CDN, the clients will simply start sending their requests to other servers in the network. If the attacker then directs a portion of his attack stream to each server on the CDN in hopes of bringing the whole thing down, the attack will obviously be diffused and would likely require many times more packets. Unsurprisingly, CDNs are how many organizations protect themselves against DDoS attacks.

Software Defined Networking

Software-defined networking (SDN) is an approach to networking that relies on distributed software to provide unprecedented agility and efficiency. Using SDN, it becomes much easier to dynamically route traffic to and from newly provisioned services and platforms. This means a new server can be quickly provisioned using a cloud service provider in response to a spike in service requests and the underlying network can just as quickly adapt to the new traffic patterns. It also means that a service or platform can be quickly moved from one location to another and the SDN will just as quickly update traffic flow rules in response to this change. Unsurprisingly, the three biggest drivers to the adoption of SDN are the growth in cloud computing, big data, and mobile computing.

How does SDN differ from traditional networking? Whereas traditional networking relies on network devices that coordinate with one another in a mostly decentralized manner, SDN centralizes the configuration and control of devices. In a decentralized environment, it takes time for routers to converge onto (or agree on) good routes. These devices must normally be manually configured whenever any changes take place, which is also a time-consuming task. In SDN, on the other hand, all changes are pushed out to the devices either reactively (i.e., in response to requests from the devices) or proactively (i.e., because the admins know a change is being made, such as the addition of 100 servers). Because it is centrally controlled, the SDN approach allows traffic to be routed much more efficiently and securely. Perhaps the most important element of SDN is the abstraction of control and forwarding planes.

Control and Forwarding Planes

The *control plane* is where the internetwork routing decisions are being made. Think of this as the part of your router that runs the routing protocol (e.g., OSPF). (The analogy is not perfect, but it is useful for now.) This part is responsible for discovering the topology of neighboring networks and maintaining a table of routes for outbound packets. Since most networks are pretty dynamic places in which congestion along different routes is always changing, the control plane is a pretty dynamic place as well. New routes are routinely being discovered, just as old routes are dropped or at least flagged as slow or expensive. As you can see, the control plane is mostly interested in effects that are more than one hop away.

The *forwarding plane*, by contrast, is where traffic forwarding decisions are made. Think of this as that part of your router that decides (very quickly) that a packet received on network interface eth0 needs to be forwarded to network interface eth3. How does the forwarding plane decide this? By using the products developed by the control plane. The control plane is the strategic, methodical planner of traffic routing, while the forwarding plane is the tactical, fast executioner of those plans. Unsurprisingly, the forwarding plane is typically implemented in hardware such an application-specific integrated chip (ASIC).

NOTE Because traditional routing decisions are made by the controller in an SDN architecture, the networking devices behave (and are referred to) as switches.

In a traditional network architecture, each networking device has its own control plane and its own forwarding plane, both of which run on some sort of proprietary operating system (e.g., Cisco IOS). The normal way of reconfiguring these traditional devices is via a terminal connection of some sort. This means that an administrator must remotely log into each device in order to change its configuration. Let's suppose that we want to support a distinct QoS for a new user. In order to do this, we'd modify the configuration in each networking device that would be involved in providing services to this user. Even assuming that we are able to do this without making any mistakes, we still face the onerous task of manually changing these parameters whenever the terms of the contract change, or when equipment is replaced or upgraded, or when the network architecture changes. There are exceptions to these challenges, of course, but the point is that making frequent, granular configuration changes is tough.

What About Automation?

One of the challenges of network administration is that most network devices (apart from those that support SDN) do not have comprehensive mechanisms for programmatically and remotely changing the configuration of the device. This is why administrators have to manually log into each device and update the configuration. Reading information is easier because these devices typically support SNMP, but writing meaningful changes to the devices almost always requires manual interaction or some third-party tool that comes with its own set of constraints.

Further complicating the issue of making dynamic changes, vendors typically use their own proprietary operating system, which makes it harder to write a script that makes the same changes to all devices in heterogeneous environments that implement products from multiple vendors. This is the reason why many organizations implement homogeneous network architectures in which all the devices are manufactured by the same vendor. A big downside of this homogeneity is that it leads to vendor lockdown because it is hard (and expensive) to change vendors when that means you must change every single device on your network. Furthermore, homogeneity is bad for security, because an exploit that leverages a vulnerability in a network operating system will likely affect every device in a homogeneous network.

In SDN, by contrast, the control plane is implemented in a central node that is responsible for managing all the devices in the network. For redundancy and efficiency, this node can actually be a federation of nodes that coordinate their activities with one another. The network devices are then left to do what they do best: forward packets very efficiently. So the forwarding plane lives in the network devices and the control plane lives in a centralized SDN controller. This allows us to abstract the network devices (heterogeneous or otherwise) from the applications that rely on them to communicate in much the same way Windows abstracts the hardware details from the applications running on a workstation.

Approaches to SDN

The concept of network abstraction is central to all implementations of SDN. The manner in which this abstraction is implemented, however, varies significantly among flavors of SDN. There are at least three common approaches to SDN, each championed by a different community and delivered primarily through a specific technology:

- **Open** The SDN approach championed by the Open Networking Foundation (ONF) (https://www.opennetworking.org) is, by most accounts, the most common. It relies on open-source code and standards to develop the building blocks of an SDN solution. The controller communicates with the switches using OpenFlow. OpenFlow is a standardized, open-source communications interface between controllers and networking devices in an SDN architecture. It allows the devices implementing the forwarding plane to provide information (such as utilization data) to the controller, while allowing the controller to update the flow tables (akin to traditional routing tables) on the devices. Applications communicate with the controller using the RESTful or Java APIs.

- **API** Another approach to SDN, and one that is championed by Cisco, is built on the premise that OpenFlow is not sufficient to fully leverage the promise of SDN in the enterprise. In addition to OpenFlow, this approach leverages a rich API on proprietary switches that allows greater control over traffic in an SDN. Among the perceived shortcomings that are corrected are the inability of OpenFlow to do deep packet inspection and manipulation, and its reliance on a centralized control plane. This proprietary API approach to SDN is seen as enriching rather than replacing ONF's SDN approach.
- **Overlays** Finally, one can imagine a virtualized network architecture as an overlay on a traditional one. In this approach, we virtualize all network nodes, including switches, routers, and servers, and treat them independently of the physical networks upon which this virtualized infrastructure exists. The SDN exists simply as a virtual overlay on top of a physical (underlay) network.

Intranets and Extranets

Web technologies and their uses have exploded with functionality, capability, and popularity. Companies set up internal websites for centralized business information such as employee phone numbers, policies, events, news, and operations instructions. Many companies have also implemented web-based terminals that enable employees to perform their daily tasks, access centralized databases, make transactions, collaborate on projects, access global calendars, use videoconferencing tools and whiteboard applications, and obtain often-used technical or marketing data.

Web-based clients are different from workstations that log into a network and have their own desktop. Web-based clients limit a user's ability to access the computer's system files, resources, and hard drive space; access back-end systems; and perform other tasks. The web-based client can be configured to provide a GUI with only the buttons, fields, and pages necessary for the users to perform tasks. This gives all users a standard universal interface with similar capabilities.

When a company uses web-based technologies that are only available inside its networks, it is using an *intranet*, a "private" network. The company has web servers and client machines using web browsers, and it uses the TCP/IP protocol suite. The web pages are written in HTML or XML (eXtensible Markup Language) and are accessed via HTTP.

Using web-based technologies has many pluses. They have been around for quite some time, they are easy to implement, no major interoperability issues occur, and with just the click of a link, a user can be taken to the location of the requested resource. Web-based technologies are not platform dependent, meaning all websites and pages may be maintained on various platforms and different flavors of client workstations can access them—they only need a web browser.

An *extranet* extends outside the bounds of the company's network to enable two or more companies to share common information and resources. Business partners commonly set up extranets to accommodate business-to-business communication. An extranet enables business partners to work on projects together; share marketing information; communicate and work collaboratively on issues; post orders; and share catalogs, pricing structures, and information on upcoming events. Trading partners often use *electronic data interchange (EDI)*, which provides structure and organization to electronic documents, orders, invoices, purchase orders, and a data flow. EDI has evolved into web-based technologies to provide easy access and easier methods of communication.

For many businesses, an extranet can create a weakness or hole in their security if the extranet is not implemented and maintained properly. Properly configured firewalls need to be in place to control who can use the extranet communication channels. Extranets used to be based mainly on dedicated transmission lines, which are more difficult for attackers to infiltrate, but today many extranets are set up over the Internet, which requires properly configured VPNs and security policies.

Value-Added Networks

Many different types of companies use EDI for internal communication and for communication with other companies. A very common implementation is between a company and its supplier. For example, some supplier companies provide inventory to many different companies, such as Target, Wal-Mart, and Kmart. Many of these supplies are made in China and then shipped to a warehouse somewhere in a specific country, as in the United States. When Wal-Mart needs to order more inventory, it sends its request through an EDI network, which is basically an electronic form of our paper-based world. Instead of using paper purchase orders, receipts, and forms, EDI provides all of this digitally.

A *value-added network (VAN)* is an EDI infrastructure developed and maintained by a service bureau. A Wal-Mart store tracks its inventory by having employees scan bar codes on individual items. When the inventory of an item becomes low, a Wal-Mart system sends a request for more of that specific item. This request goes to a VAN that Wal-Mart pays to use, and the request is then pushed out to a supplier that provides this type of inventory for Wal-Mart. Because Wal-Mart (and other stores) deals with thousands of suppliers, using a VAN simplifies the ordering process: instead of an employee having to track down the right supplier and submit a purchase order, this all happens in the background through an automated EDI network, which is managed by a VAN company for use by other companies.

EDI is moving away from proprietary VAN EDI structures to standardized communication structures to allow more interoperability and easier maintenance.

(*Continued*)

This means that XML, SOAP (Simple Object Access Protocol), and web services are being used. These are the communication structures used in supply chain infrastructures, as illustrated here.

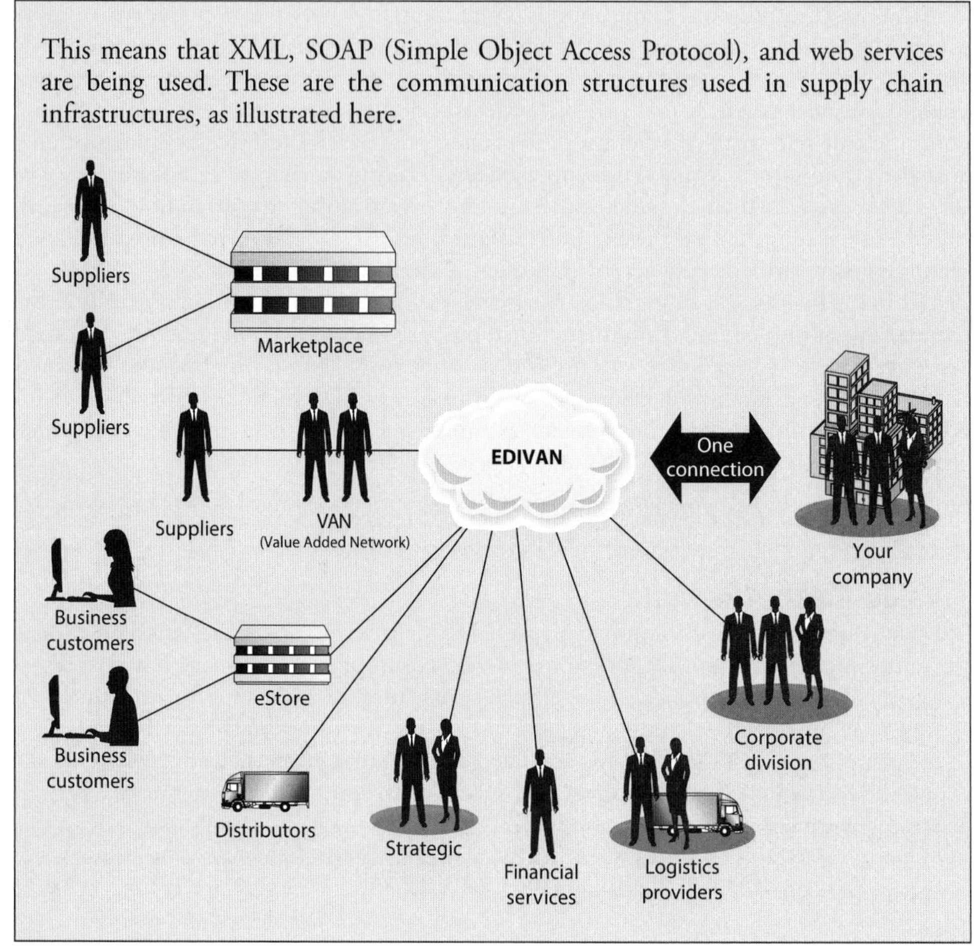

Metropolitan Area Networks

A *metropolitan area network (MAN)* is usually a backbone that connects LANs to each other and LANs to WANs, the Internet, and telecommunications and cable networks. A majority of today's MANs are *Synchronous Optical Networks (SONETs)* or FDDI rings and Metro Ethernet provided by the telecommunications service providers. (FDDI technology was discussed earlier in the chapter.) The SONET and FDDI rings cover a large area, and businesses can connect to the rings via T1, fractional T1, and T3 lines. Figure 4-58 illustrates two companies connected via a SONET ring and the devices usually necessary to make this type of communication possible. This is a simplified example of a MAN. In reality, several businesses are usually connected to one ring.

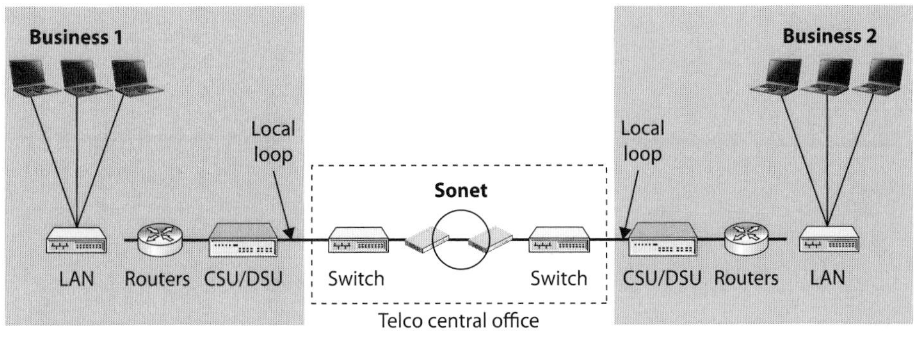

Figure 4-58 A MAN covers a large area and enables businesses to connect to each other, to the Internet, or to other WAN connections.

SONET is a standard for telecommunications transmissions over fiber-optic cables. Carriers and telephone companies have deployed SONET networks for North America, and if they follow the SONET standards properly, these various networks can intercommunicate with little difficulty.

SONET is *self-healing*, meaning that if a break in the line occurs, it can use a backup redundant ring to ensure transmission continues. All SONET lines and rings are fully redundant. The redundant line waits in the wings in case anything happens to the primary ring.

SONET networks can transmit voice, video, and data over optical networks. Slower-speed SONET networks often feed into larger, faster SONET networks, as shown in Figure 4-59. This enables businesses in different cities and regions to communicate.

MANs can be made up of wireless infrastructures, optical fiber, or Ethernet connections. Ethernet has evolved from just being a LAN technology to being used in MAN environments. Due to its prevalent use within organizations' networks, it is easily extended and interfaced into MAN networks. A service provider commonly uses layer 2 and 3 switches to connect optical fibers, which can be constructed in a ring, star, or partial mesh topology.

VLANs are commonly implemented to differentiate between the various logical network connections that run over the same physical network connection. The VLANs allow for the isolation of the different customers' traffic from each other and from the core network internal signaling traffic.

Metro Ethernet

Ethernet has been around for many years and embedded in almost every LAN. Ethernet LANs can connect to previously mentioned MAN technologies, or they can be extended to cover a metropolitan area, which is called *Metro Ethernet*.

Ethernet on the MAN can be used as pure Ethernet or Ethernet integrated with other networking technologies, as in Multiprotocol Label Switching (MPLS). Pure Ethernet is

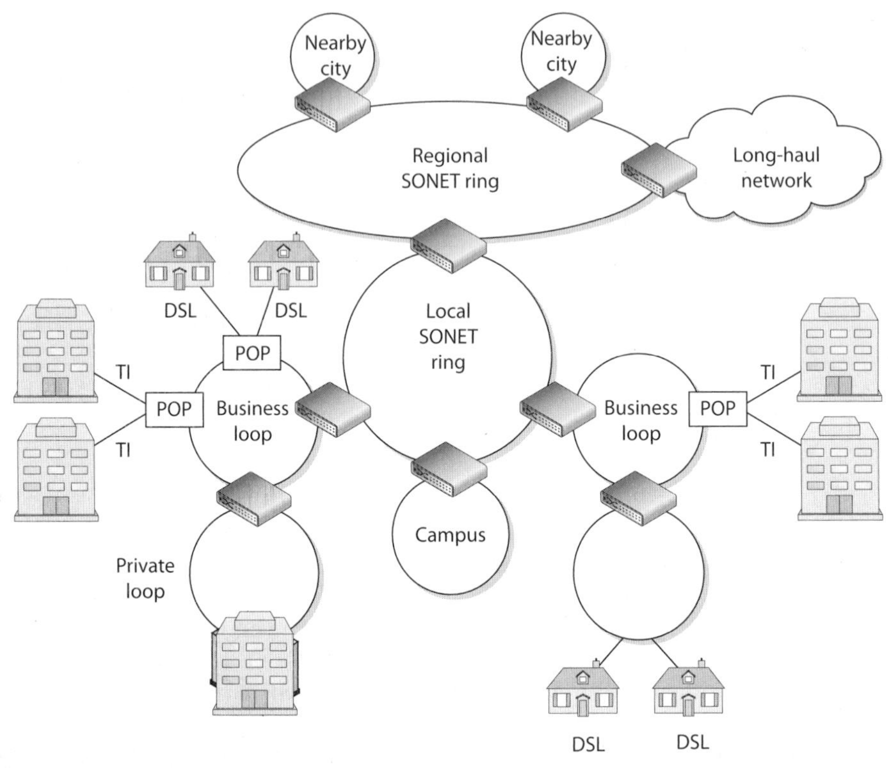

Figure 4-59 Smaller SONET rings connect to larger SONET rings to construct individual MANs.

less expensive but less reliable and scalable. MPLS-based deployments are more expensive but highly reliable and scalable, and are typically used by large service providers.

MAN architectures are commonly built upon the following layers: access, aggregation/distribution, metro, and core, as illustrated in Figure 4-60.

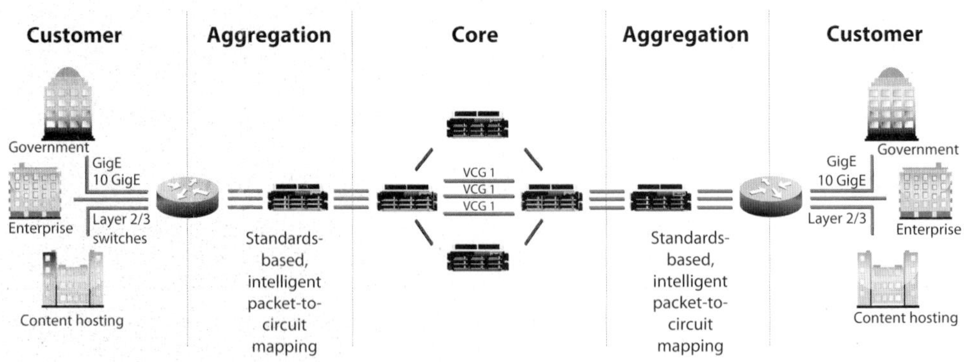

Figure 4-60 MAN architecture

Access devices exist at a customer's premises and connect the customer's equipment to the service provider's network. The service provider's distribution network aggregates the traffic and sends it to the provider's core network. From there, the traffic is moved to the next aggregation network that is closest to the destination. This is similar to how smaller highways are connected to larger interstates with on and off ramps that allow people to quickly travel from one location to a different one.

NOTE A Virtual Private LAN Service (VPLS) is a multipoint, layer 2 VPN that connects two or more customer devices using Ethernet bridging techniques. In other words, VPLS emulates a LAN over a managed IP/MPLS network.

Wide Area Networks

LAN technologies provide communication capabilities over a small geographic area, whereas *wide area network (WAN)* technologies are used when communication needs to travel over a larger geographical area. LAN technologies encompass how a computer puts its data onto a network cable, the rules and protocols of how that data is formatted and transmitted, how errors are handled, and how the destination computer picks up this data from the cable. When a computer on one network needs to communicate with a network on the other side of the country or in a different country altogether, WAN technologies kick in.

The network must have some avenue to other networks, which is most likely a router that communicates with the company's service provider's switches or telephone company facilities. Just as several types of technologies lie within the LAN arena, several technologies lie within the WAN arena. This section touches on many of these WAN technologies.

Telecommunications Evolution

Telephone systems have been around for about 100 years, and they started as copper-based analog systems. Central switching offices connected individual telephones manually (via human operators) at first, and later by using electronic switching equipment. After two telephones were connected, they had an end-to-end connection (end-to-end circuit). Multiple phone calls were divided up and placed on the same wire, which is called multiplexing. *Multiplexing* is a method of combining multiple channels of data over a single transmission path. The transmission is so fast and efficient that the ends do not realize they are sharing a line with many other entities. They think they have the line all to themselves.

In the mid-1960s, digital phone systems emerged with T1 trunks, which carried 24 voice communication calls over two pairs of copper wires. This provided a 1.544-Mbps transmission rate, which brought quicker service, but also the capability to put more multiplexed calls on one wire. When calls take place between switching offices (say, local phone calls), they are multiplexed on trunks such as T1 lines. When more bandwidth is needed, the trunks can be implemented on T3 lines, which can carry up to 28 T1 lines.

The next entity to join the telecommunications party was fiber optics, which enabled even more calls to be multiplexed on one trunk line over longer distances. Then came optical carrier technologies such as SONET, which is a standard for telecommunications transmission over fiber-optic cables. This standard sets up the necessary parameters for transporting digital information over optical systems. Telecommunications carriers used this technology to multiplex lower-speed optical links into higher-speed links, similar to how lower-speed LANs connect to higher-speed WAN links today. Figure 4-61 shows an example of SONET rings connected together and how telecommunications carriers can provide telephone and Internet access to companies and individuals in large areas. The SONET standard enables all carriers to interconnect.

The next evolutionary step in telecommunications history is *Asynchronous Transfer Mode (ATM)*. ATM encapsulates data in fixed cells and can be used to deliver data over a SONET network. The analogy of a highway and cars is used to describe the SONET and ATM relationship. SONET is the highway that provides the foundation (or network) for the cars—the ATM packets—to travel on.

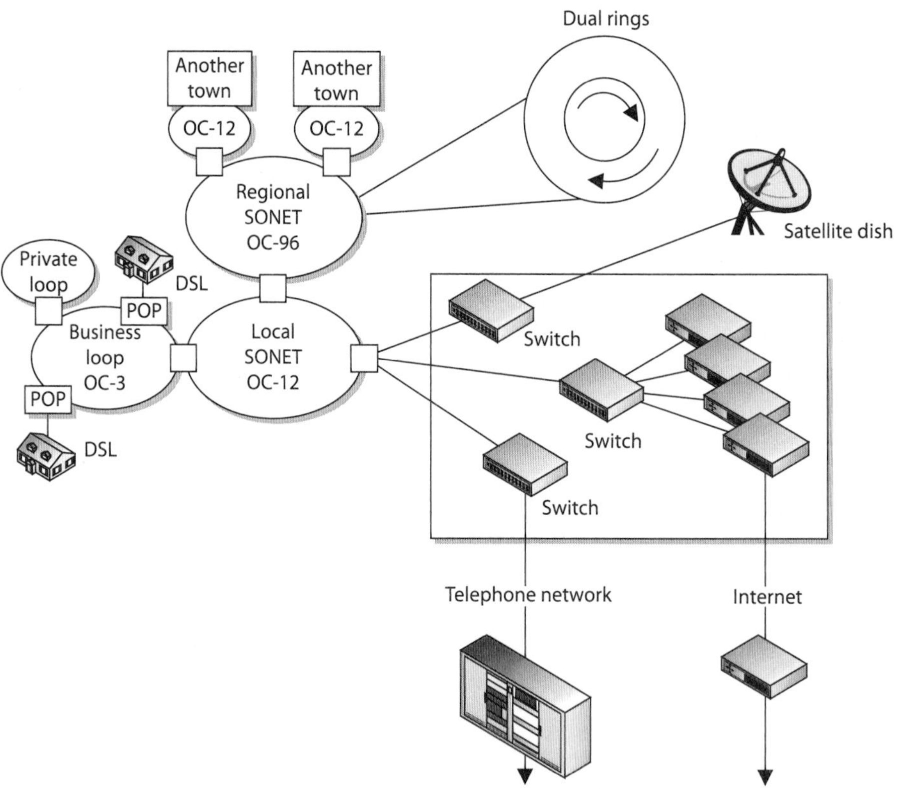

Figure 4-61 SONET technology enables several optical communication loops to communicate.

LAN and WAN Protocols

Communication error rates are lower in LAN environments than in WAN environments, which makes sense when you compare the complexity of each environment. WAN traffic may have to travel hundreds or thousands of miles and pass through several different types of devices, cables, and protocols. Because of this difference, most LAN MAC protocols are connectionless and most WAN communication protocols are connection oriented. Connection-oriented protocols provide reliable transmission because they have the capability of error detection and correction.

ATM is a high-speed network technology that is used in WAN implementations by carriers, ISPs, and telephone companies. ATM uses a fixed cell size instead of the variable frame size employed by earlier technologies. This fixed size provides better performance and a reduced overhead for error handling. (More information on ATM technology is provided in the "ATM" section a little later.)

The following is a quick snapshot of telecommunications history:

- Copper lines carry purely analog signals.
- T1 lines carry up to 24 conversations.
- T3 lines carry up to 28 T1 lines.
- Fiber optics and the SONET network.
- ATM over SONET.

SONET was developed in the United States to achieve a data rate around 50 Mbps to support the data flow from T1 lines (1.544 Mbps) and T3 lines (44.736 Mbps). Data travels over these T-carriers as electronic voltage to the edge of the SONET network. Then the voltage must be converted into light to run over the fiber-optic carrier lines, known as optical carrier (OC) lines. Each OC-1 frame runs at a signaling rate of 51.84 Mbps, with a throughput of 44.738 Mbps.

NOTE Optical carrier lines can provide different bandwidth values: OC-1 = 51.84 Mbps, OC-3 = 155.52 Mbps, OC-12 = 622.08 Mbps, and so on.

Europe has a different infrastructure and chose to use *Synchronous Digital Hierarchy (SDH)*, which supports E1 lines (2.048 Mbps) and E3 lines (34.368 Mbps). SONET is the standard for North America, while SDH is the standard for the rest of the world. SDH and SONET are similar but just different enough to be incompatible. For communication to take place between SDH and SONET lines, a gateway must do the proper signaling translation.

You've had only a quick glimpse at an amazingly complex giant referred to as telecommunications. Many more technologies are being developed and implemented to increase the amount of data that can be efficiently delivered in a short period of time.

Dedicated Links

A *dedicated link* is also called a *leased line* or *point-to-point link*. It is one single link that is pre-established for the purposes of WAN communications between two destinations. It is dedicated, meaning only the destination points can communicate with each other. This link is not shared by any other entities at any time. This was the main way companies communicated in the past, because not as many choices were available as there are today. Establishing a dedicated link is a good idea for two locations that will communicate often and require fast transmission and a specific bandwidth, but it is expensive compared to other possible technologies that enable several companies to share the same bandwidth and also share the cost. This does not mean that dedicated lines are not in use; they definitely are used, but many other options are now available, including X.25, frame relay, MPLS, and ATM technologies.

T-Carriers

T-carriers are dedicated lines that can carry voice and data information over trunk lines. They were developed by AT&T and were initially implemented in the early 1960s to support pulse-code modulation (PCM) voice transmission. This was first used to digitize the voice over a dedicated, point-to-point, high-capacity connection line. The most commonly used T-carriers are T1 lines and T3 lines. Both are digital circuits that multiplex several individual channels into a higher-speed channel.

These lines can have multiplex functionality through *time-division multiplexing (TDM)*. What does this multiplexing stuff really mean? It means that each channel gets to use the path only during a specific time slot. It's like having a time-share property on the beach; each co-owner gets to use it, but only one can do so at a time and can only remain for a fixed number of days. Consider a T1 line, which can multiplex up to 24 channels. If a company has a PBX connected to a T1 line, which in turn connects to the telephone company switching office, 24 calls can be chopped up and placed on the T1 line and transferred to the switching office. If this company did not use a T1 line, it would need 24 individual twisted pairs of wire to handle this many calls.

As shown in Figure 4-62, data is input into these 24 channels and transmitted. Each channel gets to insert up to 8 bits into its established time slot. Twenty-four of these 8-bit

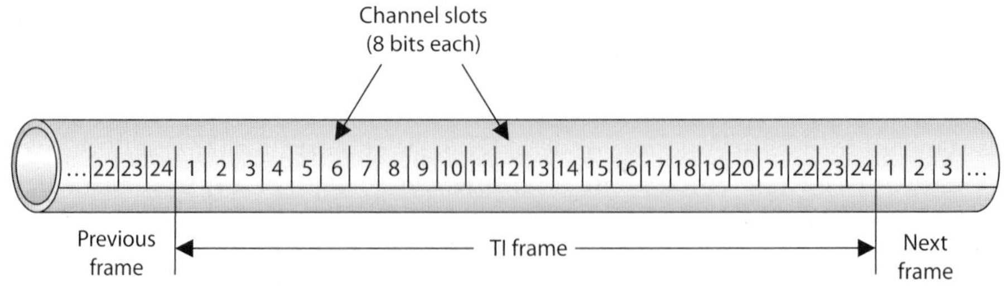

Figure 4-62 Multiplexing puts several phone calls, or data transmissions, on the same wire.

Carrier	# of T1s	# of Channels	Speed (Mbps)
Fractional	1/24	1	0.064
T1	1	24	1.544
T2	4	96	6.312
T3	28	672	44.736
T4	168	4,032	274.760

Table 4-11 A T-Carrier Hierarchy Summary Chart

time slots make up a T1 frame. That does not sound like much information, but 8,000 frames are built per second. Because this happens so quickly, the receiving end does not notice a delay and does not know it is sharing its connection and bandwidth with up to 23 other devices.

Originally, T1 and T3 lines were used by the carrier companies, but they have been replaced mainly with optical lines. Now T1 and T3 lines feed data into these powerful and super-fast optical lines. The T1 and T3 lines are leased to companies and ISPs that need high-capacity transmission capability. Sometimes, T1 channels are split up between companies who do not really need the full bandwidth of 1.544 Mbps. These are called *fractional* T lines. The different carrier lines and their corresponding characteristics are listed in Table 4-11.

As mentioned earlier, dedicated lines have their drawbacks. They are expensive and inflexible. If a company moves to another location, a T1 line cannot easily follow it. A dedicated line is expensive because companies have to pay for a dedicated connection with a lot of bandwidth even when they do not use the bandwidth. Not many companies require this level of bandwidth 24 hours a day. Instead, they may have data to send out here and there, but not continuously.

The cost of a dedicated line is determined by the distance to the destination. A T1 line run from one building to another building 2 miles away is much cheaper than a T1 line that covers 50 miles or a full state.

E-Carriers

E-carriers are similar to T-carrier telecommunication connections, where a single physical wire pair can be used to carry many simultaneous voice conversations by time-division multiplexing. Within this technology 30 channels interleave 8 bits of data in a frame. While the T-carrier and E-carrier technologies are similar, they are not interoperable. E-carriers are used by European countries.

The E-carrier channels and associated rates are shown in Table 4-12.

The most commonly used channels used are E1 and E3 and fractional E-carrier lines.

Table 4-12 E-carrier Characteristics

Signal	Rate
E0	64 Kbps
E1	2.048 Mbps
E2	8.448 Mbps
E3	34.368 Mbps
E4	139.264 Mbps
E5	565.148 Mbps

Optical Carrier

High-speed fiber-optic connections are measured in *optical carrier (OC)* transmission rates. The transmission rates are defined by rate of the bit stream of the digital signal and are designated by an integer value of the multiple of the basic unit of rate. They are generically referred to as OCx, where the "x" represents a multiplier of the basic OC-1 transmission rate, which is 51.84 Mbps. The carrier levels and speeds are shown in Table 4-13.

Small and medium-sized companies that require high-speed Internet connectivity may use OC-3 or OC-12 connections. Service providers that require much larger amounts of bandwidth may use one or more OC-48 connections. OC-192 and greater connections are commonly used for the Internet backbone, which connects the largest networks in the world together.

Table 4-13 OC Transmission Rates

Optical Carrier	Speed
OC-1	51.84 Mbps
OC-3	155.52 Mbps
OC-9	466.56 Mbps
OC-12	622.08 Mbps
OC-19	933.12 Mbps
OC-24	1.244 Gbps
OC-36	1.866 Gbps
OC-48	2.488 Gbps
OC-96	4.977 Gbps
OC-192	9.953 Gbps
OC-768	40 Gbps
OC-3072	160 Gbps

More Multiplexing

Here are some other types of multiplexing functionalities you should be aware of:

Statistical time-division multiplexing (STDM):

- Transmits several types of data simultaneously across a single transmission cable or line (such as a T1 or T3 line).
- STDM analyzes statistics related to the typical workload of each input device (printer, fax, computer) and determines in real time how much time each device should be allocated for data transmission.

Frequency-division multiplexing (FDM):

- An available wireless spectrum is used to move data.
- Available frequency band is divided into narrow frequency bands and used to have multiple parallel channels for data transfer.

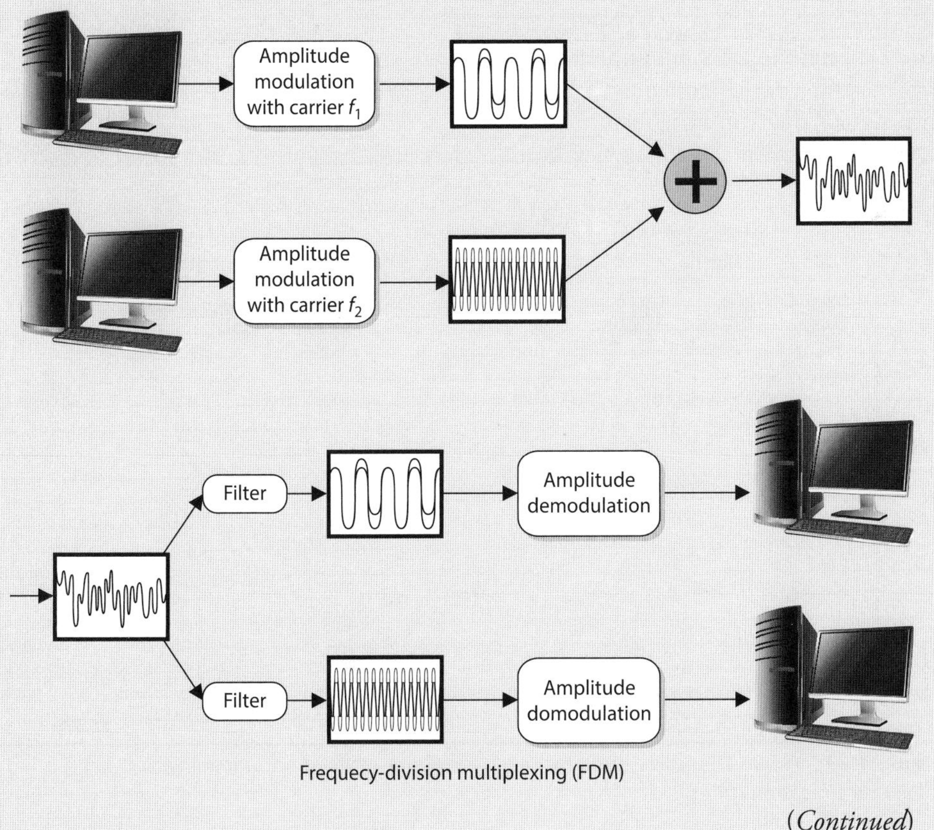

Frequecy-division multiplexing (FDM)

(Continued)

Wave-division multiplexing (WDM):

- Used in fiber-optic communication.
- Multiplexes a number of optical carrier signals onto a single optical fiber.

WAN Technologies

Several varieties of WAN technologies are available to companies today. The information that a company evaluates to decide which is the most appropriate WAN technology for it usually includes functionality, bandwidth demands, service level agreements, required equipment, cost, and what is available from service providers. The following sections go over some of the WAN technologies available today.

CSU/DSU

A *channel service unit/data service unit (CSU/DSU)* is required when digital equipment will be used to connect a LAN to a WAN. This connection can take place with T1 and T3 lines, as shown in Figure 4-63. A CSU/DSU is necessary because the signals and frames can vary between the LAN equipment and the WAN equipment used by service providers.

The DSU device converts digital signals from routers, switches, and multiplexers into signals that can be transmitted over the service provider's digital lines. The DSU device ensures that the voltage levels are correct and that information is not lost during

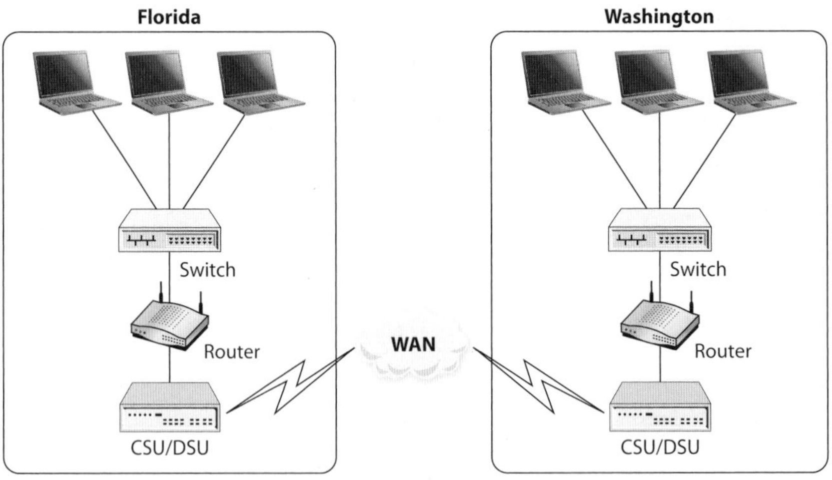

Figure 4-63 A CSU/DSU is required for digital equipment to communicate with telecommunications lines.

the conversion. The CSU connects the network directly to the service provider's line. The CSU/DSU is not always a separate device and can be part of a networking device.

The CSU/DSU provides a digital interface for data terminal equipment (DTE), such as terminals, multiplexers, or routers, and an interface to the data circuit-terminating equipment (DCE) device, such as a carrier's switch. The CSU/DSU basically works as a translator and, at times, as a line conditioner.

Switching

Dedicated links have one single path to traverse; thus, there is no complexity when it comes to determining how to get packets to different destinations. Only two points of reference are needed when a packet leaves one network and heads toward the other. It gets much more complicated when thousands of networks are connected to each other, which is often when switching comes into play.

Two main types of switching can be used: circuit switching and packet switching. *Circuit switching* sets up a virtual connection that acts like a dedicated link between two systems. ISDN and telephone calls are examples of circuit switching, which is shown in the lower half of Figure 4-64.

When the source system makes a connection with the destination system, they set up a communication channel. If the two systems are local to each other, fewer devices need to be involved with setting up this channel. The farther the two systems are from each other, the more the devices are required to be involved with setting up the channel and connecting the two systems.

An example of how a circuit-switching system works is daily telephone use. When one person calls another, the same type of dedicated virtual communication link is set up. Once the connection is made, the devices supporting that communication channel do not dynamically move the call through different devices, which is what takes place in a

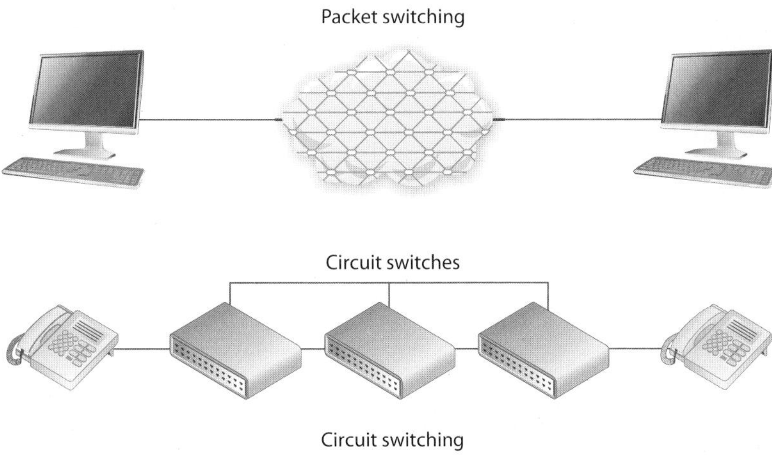

Figure 4-64 Circuit switching provides one road for a communication path, whereas packet switching provides many different possible roads.

packet-switching environment. The channel remains configured at the original devices until the call (connection) is done and torn down.

Packet switching, on the other hand, does not set up a dedicated virtual link, and packets from one connection can pass through a number of different individual devices (see the top of Figure 4-64), instead of all of them following one another through the same devices. Some examples of packet-switching technologies are the Internet, X.25, and frame relay. The infrastructure that supports these methods is made up of routers and switches of different types. They provide multiple paths to the same destinations, which offers a high degree of redundancy.

In a packet-switching network, the data is broken up into packets containing frame check sequence (FCS) numbers. These packets go through different devices, and their paths can be dynamically altered by a router or switch that determines a better route for a specific packet to take. Once the packets are received at the destination computer, all the packets are reassembled according to their FCS numbers and processed.

Because the path a packet will take in a packet-switching environment is not set in stone, there could be variable delays when compared to a circuit-switching technology. This is okay, because packet-switching networks usually carry data rather than voice. Because voice connections clearly detect these types of delays, in many situations a circuit-switching network is more appropriate for voice connections. Voice calls usually provide a steady stream of information, whereas a data connection is "burstier" in nature. When you talk on the phone, the conversation keeps a certain rhythm. You and your friend do not talk extremely fast and then take a few minutes in between conversations to stop talking and create a void with complete silence. However, this is usually how a data connection works. A lot of data is sent from one end to the other at one time, and then dead time occurs until it is time to send more data.

NOTE Voice over IP (VoIP) does move voice data over packet-switched environments. This technology is covered in the section "Multiservice Access Technologies," later in the chapter.

Circuit Switching vs. Packet Switching

The following points provide a concise summary of the differences between circuit- and packet-switching technologies:

Circuit switching:

- Connection-oriented virtual links.
- Traffic travels in a predictable and constant manner.
- Fixed delays.
- Usually carries voice-oriented data.

Packet switching:

- Packets can use many different dynamic paths to get to the same destination.
- Traffic is usually bursty in nature.
- Variable delays.
- Usually carries data-oriented data.

Frame Relay

For a long time, many companies used dedicated links to communicate with other companies. Company A had a pipeline to company B that provided a certain bandwidth 24 hours a day and was not used by any other entities. This was great because only the two companies could use the line, so a certain level of bandwidth was always available, but it was expensive and most companies did not use the full bandwidth each and every hour the link was available. Thus, the companies spent a lot of money for a service they did not use all the time. Later, to avoid this unnecessary cost, companies turned to using frame relay instead of dedicated lines.

EXAM TIP Frame relay is an obsolescent technology. It is still in limited use, however, and you should be familiar with it for the CISSP exam.

Frame relay is a WAN technology that operates at the data link layer. It is a WAN solution that uses packet-switching technology to let multiple companies and networks share the same WAN medium, devices, and bandwidth. Whereas direct point-to-point links have a cost based on the distance between the endpoints, the frame relay cost is based on the amount of bandwidth used. Because several companies and networks use the same medium and devices (routers and switches), the cost can be greatly reduced per company compared to dedicated links.

If a company knows it will usually require a certain amount of bandwidth each day, it can pay a certain fee to make sure this amount of bandwidth is always available to it. If another company knows it will not have a high bandwidth requirement, it can pay a lower fee that does not guarantee the higher bandwidth allocation. This second company will have the higher bandwidth available to it anyway—at least until that link gets busy, and then the bandwidth level will decrease. (Companies that pay more to ensure that a higher level of bandwidth will always be available pay a *committed information rate*, or CIR.)

Two main types of equipment are used in frame relay connections: DTE and DCE, both of which were previously introduced in the discussion of CSU/DSU. The DTE is usually a customer-owned device, such as a router or switch, that provides connectivity between the company's own network and the frame relay network. DCE is the service provider's device, or telecommunications company's device, that does the actual data transmission and switching in the frame relay cloud. So the DTE is a company's ramp onto the frame relay network, and the DCE devices actually do the work within the frame relay cloud.

The frame relay cloud is the collection of DCE devices that provides switching and data communications functionality. Several service providers offer this type of service, and some providers use other providers' equipment—it can all get confusing because a packet can take so many different routes. This collection is called a *cloud* to differentiate it from other types of networks and because when a packet hits this cloud, users do not usually know the route their frames will take. The frames will be sent either through permanent or switched virtual circuits that are defined within the DCE or through carrier switches.

NOTE The term cloud is used in several technologies: Internet cloud, ATM cloud, frame relay cloud, cloud computing, etc. The cloud is like a black box—we know our data goes in and we know it comes out, but we do not normally care about all the complex things that are taking place internally.

Frame relay is an any-to-any service that is shared by many users. As stated earlier, this is beneficial because the costs are much lower than those of dedicated leased lines. Because frame relay is shared, if one subscriber is not using its bandwidth, it is available for others to use. On the other hand, when traffic levels increase, the available bandwidth decreases. This is why subscribers who want to ensure a certain bandwidth is always available to them pay a higher CIR.

Figure 4-65 shows five sites being connected via dedicated lines versus five sites connected through the frame relay cloud. The first solution requires many dedicated lines that are expensive and not flexible. The second solution is cheaper and provides companies much more flexibility.

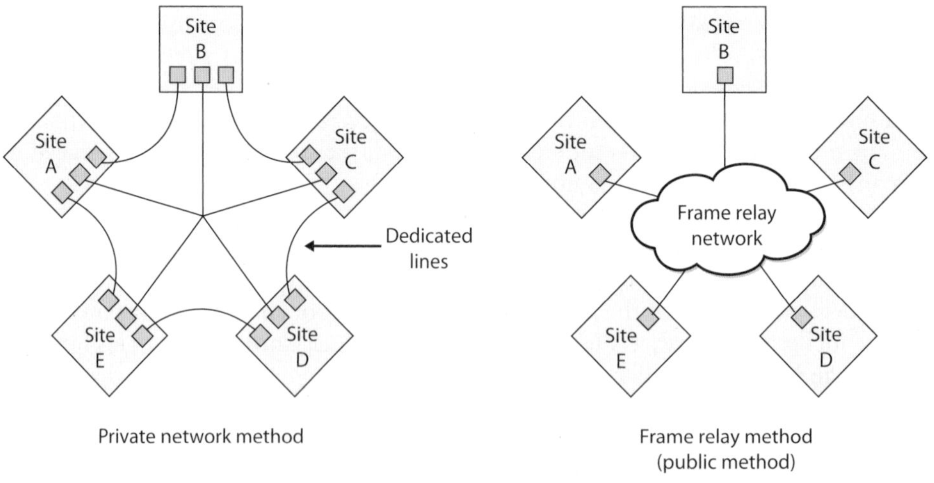

Figure 4-65 A private network connection requires several expensive dedicated links. Frame relay enables users to share a public network.

Virtual Circuits

Frame relay (and X.25) forwards frames across virtual circuits. These circuits can be either *permanent*, meaning they are programmed in advance, or *switched*, meaning the circuit is quickly built when it is needed and torn down when it is no longer needed. The *permanent virtual circuit (PVC)* works like a private line for a customer with an agreed-upon bandwidth availability. When a customer decides to pay for the CIR, a PVC is programmed for that customer to ensure it will always receive a certain amount of bandwidth.

Unlike PVCs, *switched virtual circuits (SVCs)* require steps similar to a dial-up and connection procedure. The difference is that a permanent path is set up for PVC frames, whereas when SVCs are used, a circuit must be built. It is similar to setting up a phone call over the public network. During the setup procedure, the required bandwidth is requested, the destination computer is contacted and must accept the call, a path is determined, and forwarding information is programmed into each switch along the SVC's path. SVCs are used for teleconferencing, establishing temporary connections to remote sites, data replication, and voice calls. Once the connection is no longer needed, the circuit is torn down and the switches forget it ever existed.

Although a PVC provides a guaranteed level of bandwidth, it does not have the flexibility of an SVC. If a customer wants to use her PVC for a temporary connection, as mentioned earlier, she must call the carrier and have it set up, which can take hours.

X.25

X.25 is an older WAN protocol that defines how devices and networks establish and maintain connections. Like frame relay, X.25 is a switching technology that uses carrier switches to provide connectivity for many different networks. It also provides an any-to-any connection, meaning many users use the same service simultaneously. Subscribers are charged based on the amount of bandwidth they use, unlike dedicated links, for which a flat fee is charged.

Data is divided into 128 bytes and encapsulated in High-level Data Link Control (HDLC) frames. The frames are then addressed and forwarded across the carrier switches. Much of this sounds the same as frame relay—and it is—but frame relay is much more advanced and efficient when compared to X.25, because the X.25 protocol was developed and released in the 1970s. During this time, many of the devices connected to networks were dumb terminals and mainframes, the networks did not have built-in functionality and fault tolerance, and the Internet overall was not as foundationally stable and resistant to errors as it is today. When these characteristics were not part of the Internet, X.25 was required to compensate for these deficiencies and to provide many layers of error checking, error correcting, and fault tolerance. This made the protocol fat, which was required back then, but today it slows down data transmission and provides a lower performance rate than frame relay or ATM.

ATM

Asynchronous Transfer Mode (ATM) is another switching technology, but instead of being a packet-switching method, it uses a cell-switching method. ATM is a high-speed networking technology used for LAN, MAN, WAN, and service provider connections. Like frame relay, it is a connection-oriented switching technology, and creates and uses a fixed channel. IP is an example of a connectionless technology. Within the TCP/IP protocol suite, IP is connectionless and TCP is connection oriented. This means IP segments can be quickly and easily routed and switched without each router or switch in between having to worry about whether the data actually made it to its destination—that is TCP's job. TCP works at the source and destination ends to ensure data was properly transmitted, and it resends data that ran into some type of problem and did not get delivered properly. When using ATM or frame relay, the devices in between the source and destination have to ensure that data gets to where it needs to go, unlike when a purely connectionless protocol is being used.

Since ATM is a cell-switching technology rather than a packet-switching technology, data is segmented into fixed-size cells of 53 bytes instead of variable-size packets. This provides for more efficient and faster use of the communication paths. ATM sets up virtual circuits, which act like dedicated paths between the source and destination. These virtual circuits can guarantee bandwidth and QoS. For these reasons, ATM is a good carrier for voice and video transmission.

ATM technology is used by carriers and service providers, and is the core technology of the Internet, but ATM technology can also be used for a company's private use in backbones and connections to the service provider's networks.

Traditionally, companies used dedicated lines, usually T-carrier lines, to connect to the public networks. However, companies have also moved to implementing an ATM switch on their network, which connects them to the carrier infrastructure. Because the fee is based on bandwidth used instead of a continual connection, it can be much cheaper. Some companies have replaced their Fast Ethernet and FDDI backbones with ATM. When a company uses ATM as a private backbone, the company has ATM switches that take the Ethernet, or whatever data link technology is being used, and frame them into the 53-byte ATM cells.

Quality of Service *Quality of Service (QoS)* is a capability that allows a protocol to distinguish between different classes of messages and assign priority levels. Some applications, such as video conferencing, are time sensitive, meaning delays would cause unacceptable performance of the application. A technology that provides QoS allows an administrator to assign a priority level to time-sensitive traffic. The protocol then ensures this type of traffic has a specific or minimum rate of delivery.

QoS allows a service provider to guarantee a level of service to its customers. QoS began with ATM and then was integrated into other technologies and protocols responsible for moving data from one place to another. Four different types of ATM QoS services (listed next) are available to customers. Each service maps to a specific type of data that will be transmitted.

- **Constant bit rate (CBR)** A connection-oriented channel that provides a consistent data throughput for time-sensitive applications, such as voice and video applications. Customers specify the necessary bandwidth requirement at connection setup.

- **Variable bit rate (VBR)** A connection-oriented channel best used for delay-insensitive applications because the data throughput flow is uneven. Customers specify their required peak and sustained rate of data throughput.
- **Unspecified bit rate (UBR)** A connectionless channel that does not promise a specific data throughput rate. Customers cannot, and do not need to, control their traffic rate.
- **Available bit rate (ABR)** A connection-oriented channel that allows the bit rate to be adjusted. Customers are given the bandwidth that remains after a guaranteed service rate has been met.

ATM was the first protocol to provide true QoS, but as the computing society has increased its desire to send time-sensitive data throughout many types of networks, developers have integrated QoS into other technologies.

QoS has three basic levels:

- **Best-effort service** No guarantee of throughput, delay, or delivery. Traffic that has priority classifications goes before traffic that has been assigned this classification. Most of the traffic that travels on the Internet has this classification.
- **Differentiated service** Compared to best-effort service, traffic that is assigned this classification has more bandwidth, shorter delays, and fewer dropped frames.
- **Guaranteed service** Ensures specific data throughput at a guaranteed speed. Time-sensitive traffic (voice and video) is assigned this classification.

Administrators can set the classification priorities (or use a policy manager product) for the different traffic types, which the protocols and devices then carry out.

Controlling network traffic to allow for the optimization or the guarantee of certain performance levels is referred to as *traffic shaping*. Using technologies that have QoS capabilities allows for traffic shaping, which can improve latency and increase bandwidth for specific traffic types, bandwidth throttling, and rate limiting.

SDLC

Synchronous Data Link Control (SDLC) is a protocol used in networks that use dedicated, leased lines with permanent physical connections. It is used mainly for communications with IBM hosts within a Systems Network Architecture (SNA). Developed by IBM in the 1970s, SDLC is a bit-oriented, synchronous protocol that has evolved into other communication protocols, such as HDLC, Link Access Procedure (LAP), and Link Access Procedure-Balanced (LAPB).

SDLC was developed to enable mainframes to communicate with remote locations. The environments that use SDLC usually have primary systems that control secondary stations' communication. SDLC provides the polling media access technology, which is the mechanism that enables secondary stations to communicate on the network. Figure 4-66 shows the primary and secondary stations on an SDLC network.

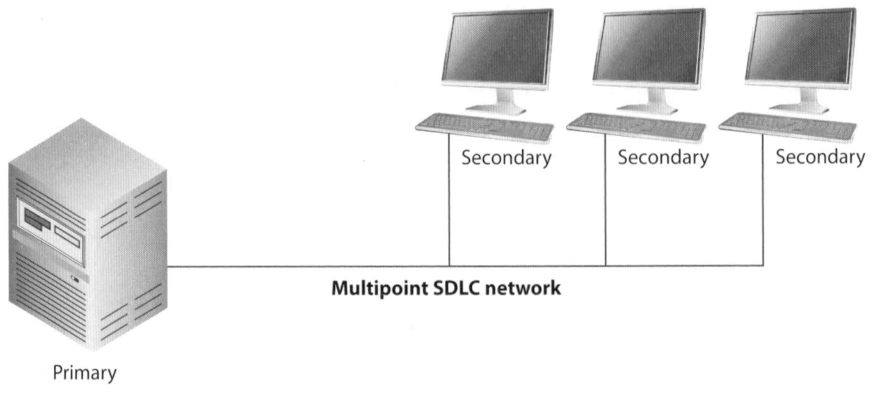

Figure 4-66 SDLC is used mainly in mainframe environments within an SNA network.

HDLC

High-level Data Link Control (HDLC) is a protocol that is also a bit-oriented link layer protocol and is used for serial device-to-device WAN communication. HDLC is an extension of SDLC, which was mainly used in SNA environments. SDLC basically died out as the mainframe environments using SNA reduced greatly in numbers. HDLC stayed around and evolved.

So what does a bit-oriented link layer protocol really mean? If you think back to the OSI model, you remember that at the data link layer packets have to be framed. This means the last header and trailer are added to the packet before it goes onto the wire and is sent over the network. There is a lot of important information that actually has to go into the header. There are flags that indicate if the connection is half or full duplex, switched or not switched, point-to-point or multipoint paths, compression data, authentication data, etc. If you send some frames to Etta and she does not know how to interpret these flags in the frame headers, that means you and Etta are not using the same data link protocol and cannot communicate. If your system puts a PPP header on a frame and sends it to Etta's system, which is only configured with HDLC, her system does not know how to interpret the first header, and thus cannot process the rest of the data. As an analogy, let's say the first step between you and Etta communicating requires that you give her a piece of paper that outlines how she is supposed to talk to you. These are the rules she has to know and follow to be able to communicate with you. You hand this piece of paper to Etta and the necessary information is there, but it is written in Italian. Etta does not know Italian, and thus does not know how to move forward with these communication efforts. She will just stand there and wait for someone else to come and give her a piece of paper with information on it that she can understand and process.

NOTE HDLC is a framing protocol that is used mainly for device-to-device communication, such as two routers communicating over a WAN link.

Point-to-Point Protocol

Point-to-Point Protocol (PPP) is similar to HDLC in that it is a data link protocol that carries out framing and encapsulation for point-to-point connections. A point-to-point connection means there is one connection between one device (point) and another device (point). If the systems on your LAN use the Ethernet protocol, what happens when a system needs to communicate to a server at your ISP for Internet connectivity? This is not an Ethernet connection, so how do the systems know how to communicate with each other if they cannot use Ethernet as their data link protocol? They use a data link protocol they do understand. Telecommunication devices commonly use PPP as their data link protocol.

PPP carries out several functions, including the encapsulation of multiprotocol packets; it has a *Link Control Protocol (LCP)* that establishes, configures, and maintains the connection; *Network Control Protocols (NCPs)* are used for network layer protocol configuration; and it provides user authentication capabilities through Password Authentication Protocol (PAP), Challenge Handshake Authentication Protocol (CHAP), and Extensible Authentication Protocol (EAP).

CAUTION PAP sends passwords in cleartext and is insecure. If you must use PAP, then ensure you do so on an encrypted connection only.

LCP is used to carry out the encapsulation format options, handle varying limits on sizes of packets, detect a looped-back link and other common misconfiguration errors, and terminate the link when necessary. LCP is the generic maintenance component used for each and every connection. So LCP makes sure the foundational functions of an actual connection work properly, and NCP makes sure that PPP can integrate and work with many different protocols. If PPP just moved IP traffic from one place to the other, it would not need NCPs. PPP has to "plug in" and work with different network layer protocols, and various network layer protocol configurations have to change as a packet moves from one network to another one. So PPP uses NCPs to be able to understand and work with different network layer protocols (IP, IPX, NetBEUI, AppleTalk).

How Many Protocols Do We Need?

If you are new to networking, all of these protocols can get quite confusing. For example, this chapter has already covered the following data link protocols: Ethernet, Token Ring, FDDI, ATM, frame relay, SDLC, HDLC, and now PPP and we have not even gotten to PPTP, Wi-Fi, or WiMAX. Why in the world do we need so many data link protocols?

(*Continued*)

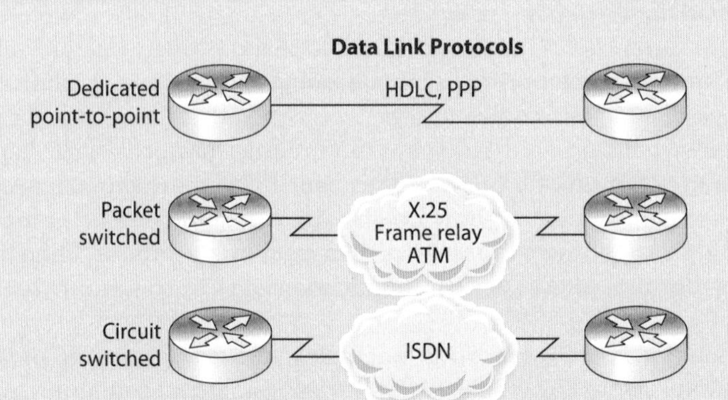

Data link protocols control how devices talk to each other, and networks have a lot of different devices that need to communicate. Some devices work within LAN environments (Ethernet, Token Ring, Wi-Fi), some in MAN environments (FDDI, WiMAX, Metro Ethernet), and some in WAN environments (frame relay, ATM). Some devices communicate directly to each other over point-to-point connections (HDLC, PPP). A computer that has an Ethernet NIC does not know how to talk to a computer that has a Token Ring NIC. A computer that has a Wi-Fi NIC does not know how to talk to a switch that has an ATM NIC. While it might seem like it would be less confusing if all devices just used one data link protocol, it is not possible because each device and each protocol has its own functions and responsibilities.

As an analogy, think about how different professions have their own language and terminology. Medical personnel use terms such as "dacryoadenitis," "macrovascular," and "sacrum." Accounting personnel use words such as "ledger," "trade receivables," and "capital." Techies use terms such as "C++," "cluster," and "parity." Each profession has its own responsibilities, and because each is specialized and complex, it has its own language. You do not want a techie working on your sacrum, a doctor fixing your cluster, or either of them maintaining your ledgers. If your doctor asks you what is wrong and you start telling him that your web server has experienced a buffer overflow, your browser experienced a man-in-the-middle attack, or that your LAN experienced an ARP spoof attack, he can't help you because he can't understand you. Our networking devices also have their own responsibilities and their own languages (data link protocols).

HSSI

High-Speed Serial Interface (HSSI) is an interface used to connect multiplexers and routers to high-speed communications services such as ATM and frame relay. It supports speeds up to 52 Mbps, as in T3 WAN connections, which are usually integrated with router and multiplex devices to provide serial interfaces to the WAN. These interfaces define the electrical and physical interfaces to be used by DTE/DCE devices; thus, HSSI works at the physical layer.

Multiservice Access Technologies

Multiservice access technologies combine several types of communication categories (data, voice, and video) over one transmission line. This provides higher performance, reduced operational costs, and greater flexibility, integration, and control for administrators. The regular phone system is based on a circuit-switched, voice-centric network, called the *public-switched telephone network (PSTN)*. The PSTN uses circuit switching instead of packet switching. When a phone call is made, the call is placed at the PSTN interface, which is the user's telephone. This telephone is connected to the telephone company's local loop via copper wiring. Once the signals for this phone call reach the telephone company's central office (the end of the local loop), they are part of the telephone company's circuit-switching world. A connection is made between the source and the destination, and as long as the call is in session, the data flows through the same switches.

When a phone call is made, the connection has to be set up, signaling has to be controlled, and the session has to be torn down. This takes place through the Signaling System 7 (SS7) protocol. When *Voice over IP (VoIP)* is used, it employs the *Session Initiation Protocol (SIP)*, which sets up and breaks down the call sessions, just as SS7 does for non-IP phone calls. SIP is an application layer protocol that can work over TCP or UDP. SIP provides the foundation to allow the more complex phone-line features that SS7 provides, such as causing a phone to ring, dialing a phone number, generating busy signals, and so on.

The PSTN is being replaced by data-centric, packet-oriented networks that can support voice, data, and video. The new VoIP networks use different switches, protocols, and communication links compared to PSTN. This means VoIP has to go through a tricky transition stage that enables the old systems and infrastructures to communicate with the new systems until the old systems are dead and gone.

High-quality compression is used with VoIP technology, and the identification numbers (phone numbers) are IP addresses. This technology gets around some of the barriers present in the PSTN today. The PSTN interface devices (telephones) have limited embedded functions and logic, and the PSTN environment as a whole is inflexible in that new services cannot be easily added. In VoIP, the interface to the network can be a computer, server, PBX, or anything else that runs a telephone application. This provides more flexibility when it comes to adding new services and provides a lot more control and intelligence to the interfacing devices. The traditional PSTN has basically dumb interfaces (telephones without much functionality), and the telecommunication infrastructure has to provide all the functionality. In VoIP, the interfaces are the "smart ones" and the network just moves data from one point to the next.

Because VoIP is a packet-oriented switching technology, latency delays are possible. This manifests as longer delays within a conversation and a slight loss of synchronicity in the conversation. When someone using VoIP for a phone call experiences these types of lags in the conversation, it means the packets holding the other person's voice message got queued somewhere within the network and are on their way. This is referred to as *jitter*, but protocols are developed to help smooth out these issues and provide a more continuous telephone call experience.

TIP Applications that are time sensitive, such as voice and video signals, need to work over an isochronous network. An isochronous network contains the necessary protocols and devices that guarantee continuous bandwidth without interruption.

Four main components are needed for VoIP: an IP telephony device, a call-processing manager, a voicemail system, and a voice gateway. The *IP telephony device* is just a phone that has the necessary software that allows it to work as a network device. Traditional phone systems require a "smart network" and a "dumb phone." In VoIP, the phone must be "smart" by having the necessary software to take analog signals, digitize them, break them into packets, and create the necessary headers and trailers for the packets to find their destination. The *voicemail system* is a storage place for messages and provides user directory lookups and call-forwarding functionality. A *voice gateway* carries out packet routing and provides access to legacy voice systems and backup calling processes.

When a user makes a call, his "smart phone" will send a message to the *call-processing manager* to indicate a call needs to be set up. When the person at the destination takes her phone off the hook, this notifies the call-processing manager that the call has been accepted. The call-processing manager notifies both the sending and receiving phones that the channel is active, and voice data is sent back and forth over a traditional data network line.

Moving voice data through packets is more involved than moving regular data through packets. This is because data is usually sent in bursts, in which voice data is sent as a constant stream. A delay in data transmission is not noticed as much as is a delay in voice transmission. The VoIP technology, and its supporting protocols, has advanced to provide voice data transmission with increased bandwidth, while reducing variability in delay, round-trip delay, and packet loss issues.

Using VoIP means a company has to pay for and maintain only one network, instead of one network dedicated to data transmission and another network dedicated to voice transmission. This saves money and administration overhead, but certain security issues must be understood and dealt with.

NOTE A media gateway is the translation unit between disparate telecommunications networks. VoIP media gateways perform the conversion between TDM voice to VoIP, for example.

H.323 Gateways

The ITU-T recommendations cover a wide variety of multimedia communication services. *H.323* is part of this family of recommendations, but it is also a standard that deals with video, real-time audio, and data packet–based transmissions where multiple users can be involved with the data exchange. An H.323 environment features terminals, which can be telephones or computers with telephony software, gateways that connect this environment to the PSTN, multipoint control units, and gatekeepers that manage calls and functionality.

Like any type of gateway, H.323 gateways connect different types of systems and devices and provide the necessary translation functionality. The H.323 terminals are connected to these gateways, which in turn can be connected to the PSTN. These gateways translate protocols used on the circuit-based telephone network and the packet-based VoIP network. The gateways also translate the circuit-oriented traffic into packet-oriented traffic and vice versa as required.

Today, it is necessary to implement the gateways that enable the new technology to communicate with the old, but soon the old PSTN may be a thing of the past and all communication may take place over packets instead of circuits.

The newer technology looks to provide transmission mechanisms that will involve much more than just voice. Although we have focused mainly on VoIP, other technologies support the combination of voice and data over the same network, such as Voice over ATM (VoATM) and Voice over Frame Relay (VoFR). ATM and frame relay are connection-oriented protocols, and IP is connectionless. This means frame relay and ATM commonly provide better QoS and less jitter and latency.

The best of both worlds is to combine IP over ATM or frame relay. This allows for packet-oriented communication over a connection-oriented network that will provide an end-to-end connection. IP is at the network layer and is medium independent—it can run over a variety of data link layer protocols and technologies.

VoIP vs. IP Telephony

The terms "IP telephony" and "Voice over IP" are used interchangeably:

- The term "VoIP" is widely used to refer to the actual services offered: caller ID, QoS, voicemail, and so on.
- IP telephony is an umbrella term for all real-time applications over IP, including voice over instant messaging (IM) and videoconferencing.

So, "IP telephony" means that telephone and telecommunications activities are taking place over an IP network instead of the traditional PSTN. "Voice over IP" means voice data is being moved over an IP network instead of the traditional PSTN. They are basically the same thing, but VoIP focuses more on the telephone call services.

Traditionally, a company has on its premises a PBX, which is a switch between the company and the PSTN, and T1 or T3 lines connecting the PBX to the telephone company's central office, which houses switches that act as ramps onto the PSTN. When WAN technologies are used instead of accessing the PSTN through the central office switches, the data is transmitted over the frame relay, ATM, or Internet clouds. An example of this configuration is shown in Figure 4-67.

Because frame relay and ATM utilize PVCs and SVCs, they both have the ability to use SVCs for telephone calls. Remember that a CIR is used when a company wants to

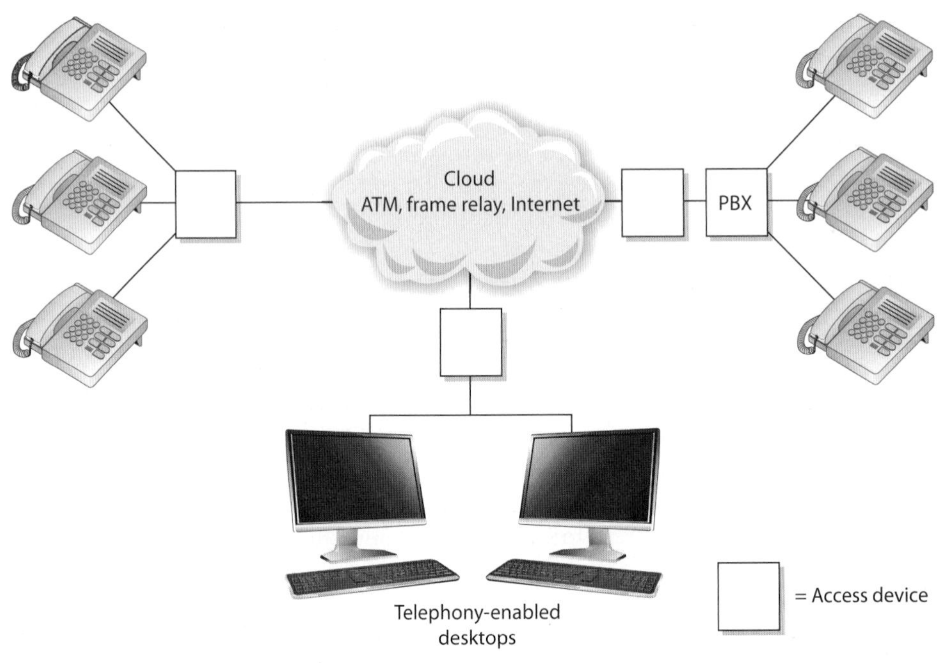

Figure 4-67 Regular telephone calls connect phones to the PSTN. Voice over WAN technologies connect calls to a WAN.

ensure it will always have a certain bandwidth available. When a company pays for this guaranteed bandwidth, it is paying for a PVC for which the switches and routers are programmed to control its connection and for that connection to be maintained. SVCs, on the other hand, are set up on demand and are temporary in nature. They are perfect for making telephone calls or transmitting video during videoconferencing.

Digging Deeper into SIP

As stated earlier, SIP is a signaling protocol widely used for VoIP communications sessions. It is used in applications such as video conferencing, multimedia, instant messaging, and online gaming. It is analogous to the SS7 protocol used in PSTN networks and supports features present in traditional telephony systems.

SIP consists of two major components: the *User Agent Client (UAC)* and *User Agent Server (UAS)*. The UAC is the application that creates the SIP requests for initiating a communication session. UACs are generally messaging tools and soft-phone applications that are used to place VoIP calls. The UAS is the SIP server, which is responsible for handling all routing and signaling involved in VoIP calls.

SIP relies on a three-way-handshake process to initiate a session. To illustrate how an SIP-based call kicks off, let's look at an example of two people, Bill and John, trying to communicate using their VoIP phones. Bill's system starts by sending an INVITE packet to John's system. Since Bill's system is unaware of John's location, the INVITE packet is sent to the SIP server, which looks up John's address in the SIP *registrar* server. Once the location of John's system has been determined, the INVITE packet is forwarded to him.

During this entire process, the server keeps the caller (Bill) updated by sending him a TRYING packet, indicating the process is underway. Once the INVITE packet reaches John's system, it starts ringing. While John's system rings and waits for John to respond, it sends a RINGING packet to Bill's system, notifying Bill that the INVITE packet has been received and John's system is waiting for John to accept the call. As soon as John answers the call, an OK packet is sent to Bill's system (through the server). Bill's system now issues an ACK packet to begin call setup. It is important to note here that SIP itself is not used to stream the conversation because it's just a signaling protocol. The actual voice stream is carried on media protocols such as the *Real-time Transport Protocol (RTP)*. RTP provides a standardized packet format for delivering audio and video over IP networks. Once Bill and John are done communicating, a BYE message is sent from the system terminating the call. The other system responds with an OK, acknowledging the session has ended. This handshake is illustrated in Figure 4-68.

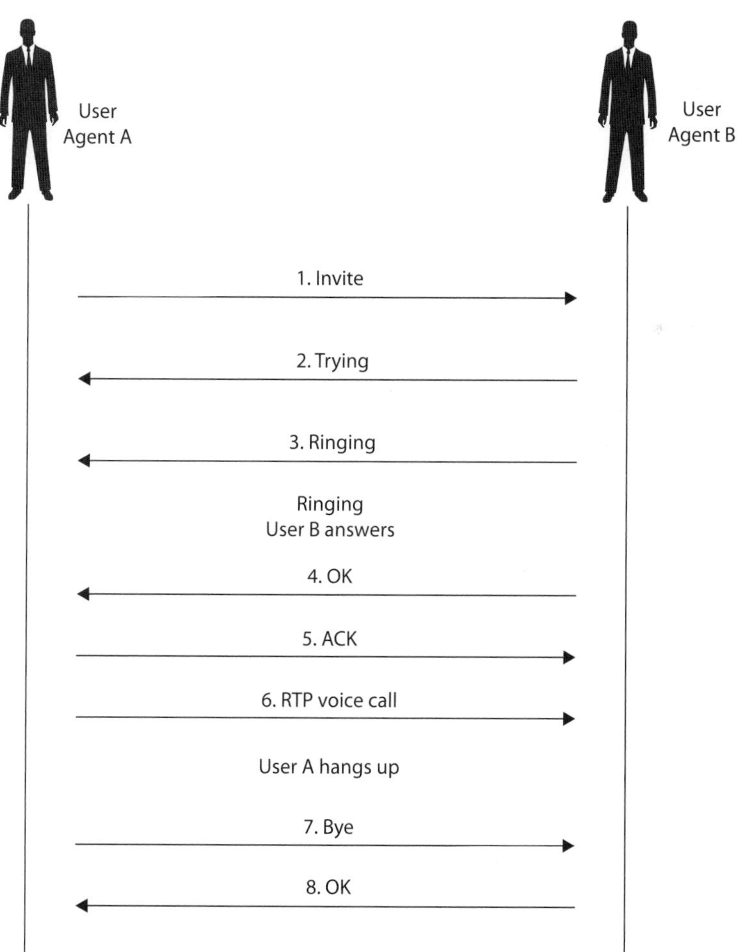

Figure 4-68
SIP handshake

The SIP architecture consists of three different types of servers, which play an integral role in the entire communication process of the VoIP system. These servers are the *proxy* server, the *registrar* server, and the *redirect* server. The proxy server is used to relay packets within a network between the UACs and the UAS. It also forwards requests generated by callers to their respective recipients. Proxy servers are also generally used for name mapping, which allows the proxy server to interlink an external SIP system to an internal SIP client.

The registrar server keeps a centralized record of the updated locations of all the users on the network. These addresses are stored on a location server. The redirect server allows SIP devices to retain their SIP identities despite changes in their geographic location. This allows a device to remain accessible when its location is physically changed and hence while it moves through different networks. The use of redirect servers allows clients to remain within reach while they move through numerous network coverage zones. This configuration is generally known as an *intraorganizational* configuration. Intraorganizational routing enables SIP traffic to be routed within a VoIP network without being transmitted over the PSTN or external network.

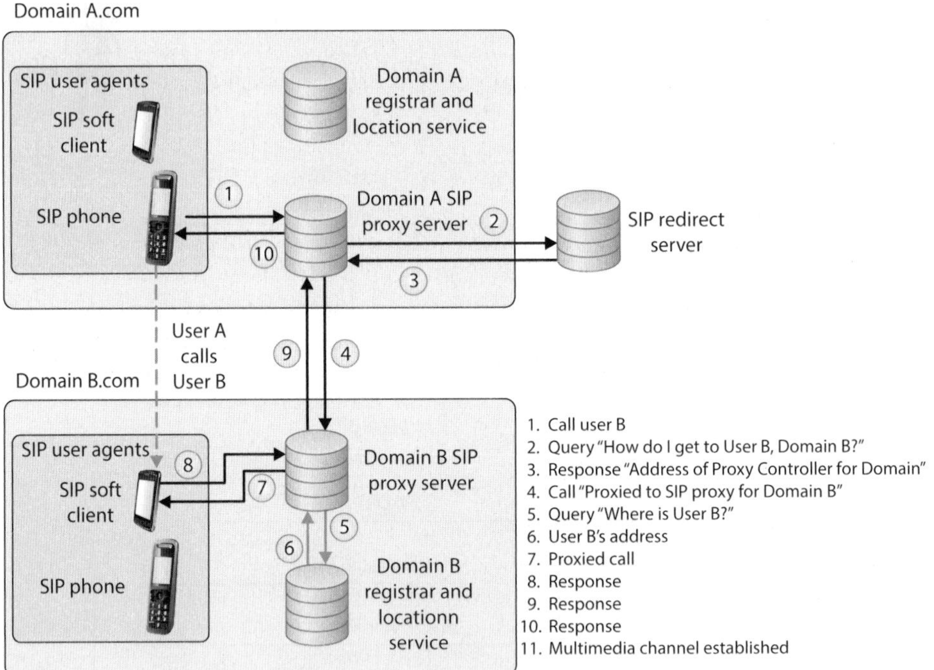

Skype is a popular Internet telephony application that uses a peer-to-peer communication model rather than the traditional client/server approach of VoIP systems. The Skype network does not rely on centralized servers to maintain its user directories. Instead, user records are maintained across distributed member nodes. This is the reason the network can quickly accommodate user surges without having to rely on expensive central infrastructure and computing resources.

Streaming Protocols

RTP is a session layer protocol that carries data in media stream format, as in audio and video, and is used extensively in VoIP, telephony, video conferencing, and other multimedia streaming technologies. It provides end-to-end delivery services and is commonly run over the transport layer protocol UDP. *RTP Control Protocol (RTCP)* is used in conjunction with RTP and is also considered a session layer protocol. It provides out-of-band statistics and control information to provide feedback on QoS levels of individual streaming multimedia sessions.

IP Telephony Issues

VoIP's integration with the TCP/IP protocol has brought about immense security challenges because it allows malicious users to bring their TCP/IP experience into this relatively new platform, where they can probe for flaws in both the architecture and the VoIP systems. Also involved are the traditional security issues associated with networks, such as unauthorized access, exploitation of communication protocols, and the spreading of malware. The promise of financial benefit derived from stolen call time is a strong incentive for most attackers, as we mentioned in the section on PBXs earlier in this chapter. In short, the VoIP telephony network faces all the flaws that traditional computer networks have faced. Moreover, VoIP devices follow architectures similar to traditional computers—that is, they use operating systems, communicate through Internet protocols, and provide a combination of services and applications.

SIP-based signaling suffers from the lack of encrypted call channels and authentication of control signals. Attackers can tap into the SIP server and client communication to sniff out login IDs, passwords/PINs, and phone numbers. Once an attacker gets a hold of such information, he can use it to place unauthorized calls on the network. Toll fraud is considered to be the most significant threat that VoIP networks face. VoIP network implementations will need to ensure that VoIP–PSTN gateways are secure from intrusions to prevent these instances of fraud.

Attackers can also masquerade identities by redirecting SIP control packets from a caller to a forged destination to mislead the caller into communicating with an unintended end system. Like in any networked system, VoIP devices are also vulnerable to DoS attacks. Just as attackers would flood TCP servers with SYN packets on an IP network to exhaust a device's resources, attackers can flood RTP servers with call requests in order to overwhelm its processing capabilities. Attackers have also been known to connect laptops simulating IP phones to the Ethernet interfaces that IP phones use. These systems can then be used to carry out intrusions and DoS attacks. In addition to these circumstances, if attackers are able to intercept voice packets, they may eavesdrop onto ongoing conversations. Attackers can also intercept RTP packets containing the media stream of a communication session to inject arbitrary audio/video data that may be a cause of annoyance to the actual participants.

Attackers can also impersonate a server and issue commands such as BYE, CHECKSYNC, and RESET to VoIP clients. The BYE command causes VoIP devices to close down while in a conversation, the CHECKSYNC command can be used to reboot VoIP terminals, and the RESET command causes the server to reset and reestablish the connection, which takes considerable time.

NOTE Recently, a new variant to traditional e-mail spam has emerged on VoIP networks, commonly known as *SPIT (Spam over Internet Telephony)*. SPIT causes loss of VoIP bandwidth and is a time-wasting nuisance for the people on the attacked network. Because SPIT cannot be deleted like spam on first sight, the victim has to go through the entire message. SPIT is also a major cause of overloaded voicemail servers.

Combating VoIP security threats requires a well-thought-out infrastructure implementation plan. With the convergence of traditional and VoIP networks, balancing security while maintaining unconstrained traffic flow is crucial. The use of authorization on the network is an important step in limiting the possibilities of rogue and unauthorized entities on the network. Authorization of individual IP terminals ensures that only prelisted devices are allowed to access the network. Although not absolutely foolproof, this method is a first layer of defense in preventing possible rogue devices from connecting and flooding the network with illicit packets. In addition to this preliminary measure, it is essential for two communicating VoIP devices to be able to authenticate their identities. Device identification may occur on the basis of fixed hardware identification parameters, such as MAC addresses or other "soft" codes that may be assigned by servers.

VoIP Security Measures Broken Down

Hackers can intercept incoming and outgoing calls, carry out DoS attacks, spoof phone calls, and eavesdrop on sensitive conversations. Many of the countermeasures to these types of attacks are the same ones used with traditional data-oriented networks:

- Keep patches updated on each network device involved with VoIP transmissions:
  - The call manager server
  - The voicemail server
  - The gateway server
- Identify unidentified or rogue telephony devices:
  - Implement authentication so only authorized telephony devices are working on the network
- Install and maintain:
  - Stateful firewalls

- VPN for sensitive voice data
- Intrusion detection
- Disable unnecessary ports and services on routers, switches, PCs, and IP telephones
- Employ real-time monitoring that looks for attacks, tunneling, and abusive call patterns through IDS/IPS:
  - Employ content monitoring
  - Use encryption when data (voice, fax, video) cross an untrusted network
  - Use a two-factor authentication technology
  - Limit the number of calls via media gateways
  - Close the media sessions after completion

The use of secure cryptographic protocols such as TLS ensures that all SIP packets are conveyed within an encrypted and secure tunnel. The use of TLS can provide a secure channel for VoIP client/server communication and prevents the possibility of eavesdropping and packet manipulation.

WAN Technology Summary

We have covered several WAN technologies in the previous sections. Table 4-14 provides a snapshot of the important characteristics of each.

WAN Technology	Characteristics
Dedicated line	• Dedicated, leased line that connects two locations • Expensive compared to other WAN options • Secure because only two locations are using the same medium
Frame relay	• High-performance WAN protocol that uses packet-switching technology, which works over public networks • Shared media among companies • Uses SVCs and PVCs • Fee based on bandwidth used
X.25	• First packet-switching technology developed to work over public networks • Lower speed than frame relay because of its extra overhead • Uses SVCs and PVCs • Basically obsolete and replaced with other WAN protocols
ATM	• High-speed bandwidth switching and multiplexing technology that has a low delay • Uses 53-byte fixed-size cells • Very fast because of the low overhead

Table 4-14 Characteristics of WAN Technologies *(continued)*

WAN Technology	Characteristics
SDLC	• Enables mainframes to communicate with remote offices • Provides a polling mechanism to allow primary and secondary stations to communicate
HDLC	• Data encapsulation method for synchronous serial links • Point-to-point and multipoint communication
PPP	• Data encapsulation method for synchronous and asynchronous links • Point-to-point and multipoint communication
HSSI	• DTE/DCE interface to enable high-speed communication over WAN links

Table 4-14 Characteristics of WAN Technologies

Remote Connectivity

Remote connectivity covers several technologies that enable remote and home users to connect to networks that will grant them access to resources needed for them to perform their tasks. Most of the time, these users must first gain access to the Internet through an ISP, which sets up a connection to the destination network.

For many corporations, remote access is a necessity because it enables users to access centralized network resources; it reduces networking costs by using the Internet as the access medium instead of expensive dedicated lines; and it extends the workplace for employees to their home computers, laptops, or mobile devices. Remote access can streamline access to resources and information through Internet connections and provides a competitive advantage by letting partners, suppliers, and customers have closely controlled links. The types of remote connectivity methods we will cover next are dial-up connections, ISDN, cable modems, DSL, and VPNs.

Dial-up Connections

Since almost every house and office had a telephone line running to it already, the first type of remote connectivity technology that was used took advantage of this in-place infrastructure. Modems were added to computers that needed to communicate with other computers over telecommunication lines.

Each telephone line is made up of UTP copper wires and has an available analog carrier signal and frequency range to move voice data back and forth. A *modem* (modulator-demodulator) is a device that modulates an outgoing digital signal into an analog signal that will be carried over an analog carrier, and demodulates the incoming analog signal into digital signals that can be processed by a computer.

While the individual computers had built-in modems to allow for Internet connectivity, organizations commonly had a pool of modems to allow for remote access into and out of their networks. In some cases the modems were installed on individual servers here and there throughout the network or they were centrally located and managed. Most companies did not properly enforce access control through these modem connections, and they served as easy entry points for attackers. Attackers used programs that carried out war dialing to identify modems that could be compromised. The attackers fed a large bank of phone numbers into the war-dialing tools, which in turn called each number. If a person answered the phone, the war dialer documented that the number was not connected to a computer system and dropped it from its list. If a fax machine answered, it did the same thing. If a modem answered, the war dialer would send signals and attempt to set up a connection between the attacker's system and the target system. If it was successful, the attacker then had direct access to the network.

Most burglars are not going to break into a house through the front door, because there are commonly weaker points of entry that can be more easily compromised (back doors, windows, etc.). Hackers usually try to find "side doors" into a network instead of boldly trying to hack through a fortified firewall. In many environments, remote access points are not as well protected as the more traditional network access points. Attackers know this and take advantage of these situations.

CAUTION Antiquated as they may seem, many organizations have modems enabled that the network staff is unaware of. Therefore, it is important to search for them to ensure no unauthorized modems are attached and operational.

Like most telecommunication connections, dial-up connections take place over PPP, which has authentication capabilities. Authentication should be enabled for the PPP connections, but another layer of authentication should be in place before users are allowed access to network resources. We will cover access control in Chapter 5.

If you find yourself using modems, some of the security measures that you should put in place for dial-up connections include

- Configure the remote access server to call back the initiating phone number to ensure it is a valid and approved number.
- Disable or remove modems if not in use.
- Consolidate all modems into one location and manage them centrally, if possible.
- Implement use of two-factor authentication, VPNs, and personal firewalls for remote access connections.

While dial-up connections using modems still exist in some locations, this type of remote connectivity has been mainly replaced with technologies that can digitize telecommunication connections.

ISDN

Integrated Services Digital Network (ISDN) is a technology provided by telephone companies and ISPs. This technology, and the necessary equipment, enables data, voice, and other types of traffic to travel over a medium in a digital manner previously used only for analog voice transmission. Telephone companies went all digital many years ago, except for the local loops, which consist of the copper wires that connect houses and businesses to their carrier provider's central offices. These central offices contain the telephone company's switching equipment, and it is here the analog-to-digital transformation takes place. However, the local loop is almost always analog, and is therefore slower. ISDN was developed to replace the aging telephone analog systems, but it has yet to catch on to the level expected.

ISDN uses the same wires and transmission medium used by analog dial-up technologies, but it works in a digital fashion. If a computer uses a modem to communicate with an ISP, the modem converts the data from digital to analog to be transmitted over the phone line. If that same computer was configured and had the necessary equipment to utilize ISDN, it would not need to convert the data from digital to analog, but would keep it in a digital form. This, of course, means the receiving end would also require the necessary equipment to receive and interpret this type of communication properly. Communicating in a purely digital form provides higher bit rates that can be sent more economically.

ISDN is a set of telecommunications services that can be used over public and private telecommunications networks. It provides a digital, point-to-point, circuit-switched medium and establishes a circuit between the two communicating devices. An ISDN connection can be used for anything a modem can be used for, but it provides more functionality and higher bandwidth. This digital service can provide bandwidth on an as-needed basis and can be used for LAN-to-LAN on-demand connectivity, instead of using an expensive dedicated link.

ISDN Examined

ISDN breaks the telephone line into different channels and transmits data in a digital form rather than the old analog form. Three ISDN implementations are in use:

- **Basic Rate Interface (BRI) ISDN** This implementation operates over existing copper lines at the local loop and provides digital voice and data channels. It uses two B (at 64 Kbps each) channels and one D (at 16 Kbps) channel with a combined bandwidth of 144 Kbps and is generally used for home and small office subscribers.
- **Primary Rate Interface (PRI) ISDN** This implementation has up to 23 B channels and 1 D channel, at 64 Kbps per channel. The total bandwidth is equivalent to a T1, which is 1.544 Mbps. This would be more suitable for a company that requires a higher amount of bandwidth compared to BRI ISDN.
- **Broadband ISDN (BISDN)** This implementation can handle many different types of services simultaneously and is mainly used within telecommunications carrier backbones. When BISDN is used within a backbone, ATM is commonly employed to encapsulate data at the data link layer into cells, which travel over a SONET network.

Analog telecommunication signals use a full channel for communication, but ISDN can break up this channel into multiple channels to move various types of data, and provide full-duplex communication and a higher level of control and error handling. ISDN provides two basic services: *Basic Rate Interface (BRI)* and *Primary Rate Interface (PRI)*.

BRI has two B channels that enable data to be transferred and one D channel that provides for call setup, connection management, error control, caller ID, and more. The bandwidth available with BRI is 144 Kbps, and BRI service is aimed at small office and home office. The D channel provides for a quicker call setup and process in making a connection compared to dial-up connections. An ISDN connection may require a setup connection time of only 2 to 5 seconds, whereas a modem may require a timeframe of 45 to 90 seconds. This D channel is an out-of-band communication link between the local loop equipment and the user's system. It is considered "out-of-band" because the control data is not mixed in with the user communication data. This makes it more difficult for a would-be defrauder to send bogus instructions back to the service provider's equipment in hopes of causing a DoS, obtaining services not paid for, or conducting some other type of destructive behavior.

PRI has 23 B channels and one D channel, and is more commonly used in corporations. The total bandwidth is equivalent to a T1, which is 1.544 Mbps.

ISDN is not usually the primary telecommunications connection for companies, but it can be used as a backup in case the primary connection goes down. A company can also choose to implement *dial-on-demand routing (DDR)*, which can work over ISDN. DDR allows a company to send WAN data over its existing telephone lines and use the public switched telephone network (PSTN) as a temporary type of WAN link. It is usually implemented by companies that send out only a small amount of WAN traffic and is a much cheaper solution than a real WAN implementation. The connection activates when it is needed and then idles out.

DSL

Digital subscriber line (DSL) is another type of high-speed connection technology used to connect a home or business to the service provider's central office. It can provide 6 to 30 times higher bandwidth speeds than ISDN and analog technologies. It uses existing phone lines and provides a 24-hour connection to the Internet at rates of up to 52 Mbps. This does indeed sound better than sliced bread, but only certain people can get this service because you have to be within a 2.5-mile radius of the DSL service provider's equipment. As the distance between a residence and the central office increases, the transmission rates for DSL decrease.

DSL provides faster transmission rates than an analog dial-up connection because it uses all of the available frequencies available on a voice-grade UTP line. When you call someone, your voice data travels down this UTP line and the service provider "cleans up" the transmission by removing the high and low frequencies. Humans do not use these frequencies when they talk, so if there is anything on these frequencies, it is considered line noise and thus removed. So in reality, the available bandwidth of the line that goes from your house to the telephone company's central office is artificially reduced.

When DSL is used, this does not take place, and therefore the high and low frequencies can be used for data transmission.

DSL offers several types of services. With *symmetric services*, traffic flows at the same speed upstream and downstream (to and from the Internet or destination). With *asymmetric services*, the downstream speed is much higher than the upstream speed. In most situations, an asymmetric connection is fine for residential users because they usually download items from the Web much more often than they upload data.

xDSL

Many different flavors of DSL are available, each with its own characteristics and specific uses:

- **Symmetric DSL (SDSL)** Data travels upstream and downstream at the same rate. Bandwidth can range between 192 Kbps and 1.1 Mbps. Used mainly for business applications that require high speeds in both directions.
- **Asymmetric DSL (ADSL)** Data travels downstream faster than upstream. Upstream speeds are 128 Kbps to 384 Kbps, and downstream speeds can be as fast as 768 Kbps. Generally used by residential users.
- **High-bit-rate DSL (HDSL)** Provides T1 (1.544 Mbps) speeds over regular copper phone wire without the use of repeaters. Requires two twisted pairs of wires, which many voice-grade UTP lines do not have.
- **Very High-Data-Rate Digital Subscriber Line (VDSL)** VDSL is basically ADSL at much higher data rates (13 Mbps downstream and 2 Mbps upstream). It is capable of supporting high-bandwidth applications such as HDTV, telephone services (voice over IP), and general Internet access over a single connection.
- **Rate-Adaptive Digital Subscriber Line (RADSL)** Rate-adaptive feature that will adjust the transmission speed to match the quality and the length of the line.

Cable Modems

The cable television companies have been delivering television services to homes for years, and then they started delivering data transmission services for users who have cable modems and want to connect to the Internet at high speeds.

Cable modems provide high-speed access to the Internet through existing cable coaxial and fiber lines. The cable modem provides upstream and downstream conversions.

Coaxial and fiber cables are used to deliver hundreds of television stations to users, and one or more of the channels on these lines are dedicated to carrying data. The bandwidth is shared between users in a local area; therefore, it will not always stay at a static rate. So, for example, if Mike attempts to download a program from the Internet at 5:30 P.M., he most likely will have a much slower connection than if he had attempted it at 10:00 A.M., because many people come home from work and hit the Internet at the same time. As more people access the Internet within his local area, Mike's Internet access performance drops.

Most cable providers comply with *Data-Over-Cable Service Interface Specifications (DOCSIS)*, which is an international telecommunications standard that allows for the addition of high-speed data transfer to an existing cable TV (CATV) system. DOCSIS includes MAC layer security services in its Baseline Privacy Interface/Security (BPI/SEC) specifications. This protects individual user traffic by encrypting the data as it travels over the provider's infrastructure.

Sharing the same medium brings up a slew of security concerns, because users with network sniffers can easily view their neighbors' traffic and data as both travel to and from the Internet. Many cable companies are now encrypting the data that goes back and forth over shared lines through a type of data link encryption.

Always Connected

Unlike dial-up modems and ISDN connections, DSL lines and cable modems are connected to the Internet and "live" all the time. No dial-up steps are required. This can cause a security issue because these types of connections are always online and available for scanning, probing, hacking, and attacking. These systems are also often used in DDoS attacks. Because the systems are on all the time, attackers attempt to plant Trojan horses that lie dormant until they get the command from the attacker to launch an attack against a victim. Many of the DDoS attacks use as their accomplices systems with DSL and cable modems, and usually the owner of the computer has no idea their system is being used to attack another system.

VPN

A *virtual private network (VPN)* is a secure, private connection through an untrusted network, as shown in Figure 4-69. It is a private connection because the encryption and tunneling protocols are used to ensure the confidentiality and integrity of the data in transit. It is important to remember that VPN technology requires a tunnel to work and it assumes encryption.

We need VPNs because we send so much confidential information from system to system and network to network. The information can be credentials, bank account data, Social Security numbers, medical information, or any other type of data we do not want to share with the world. The demand for securing data transfers has increased over the years, and as our networks have increased in complexity, so have our VPN solutions.

Point-To-Point Tunneling Protocol

For many years the de facto standard VPN software was *Point-To-Point Tunneling Protocol (PPTP)*, which was made most popular when Microsoft included it in its Windows products. Since most Internet-based communication first started over telecommunication

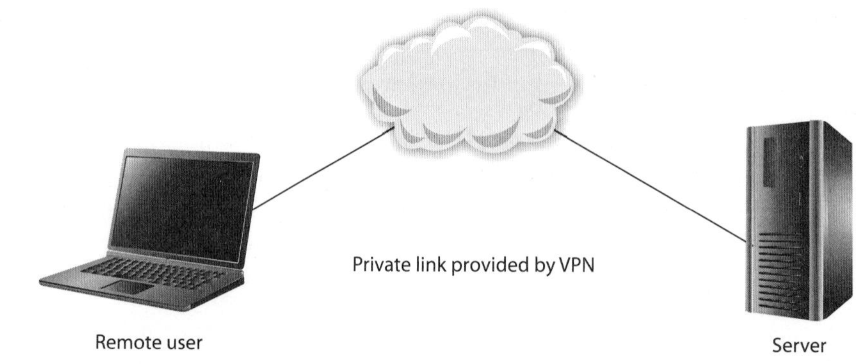

Figure 4-69 A VPN provides a virtual dedicated link between two entities across a public network.

links, the industry needed a way to secure PPP connections. The original goal of PPTP was to provide a way to tunnel PPP connections through an IP network, but most implementations included security features also since protection was becoming an important requirement for network transmissions at that time.

PPTP uses Generic Routing Encapsulation (GRE) and TCP to encapsulate PPP packets and extend a PPP connection through an IP network, as shown in Figure 4-70. In Microsoft implementations, the tunneled PPP traffic can be authenticated with PAP, CHAP, MS-CHAP, or EAP-TLS and the PPP payload is encrypted using Microsoft Point-to-Point Encryption (MPPE). Other vendors have integrated PPTP functionality in their products for interoperability purposes.

The first security technologies that hit the market commonly have security issues and drawbacks identified after their release, and PPTP was no different. The earlier authentication methods that were used with PPTP had some inherent vulnerabilities, which allowed an attacker to easily uncover password values. MPPE also used the symmetric algorithm RC4 in a way that allowed data to be modified in an unauthorized

Figure 4-70 PPTP extends PPP connections over IP networks.

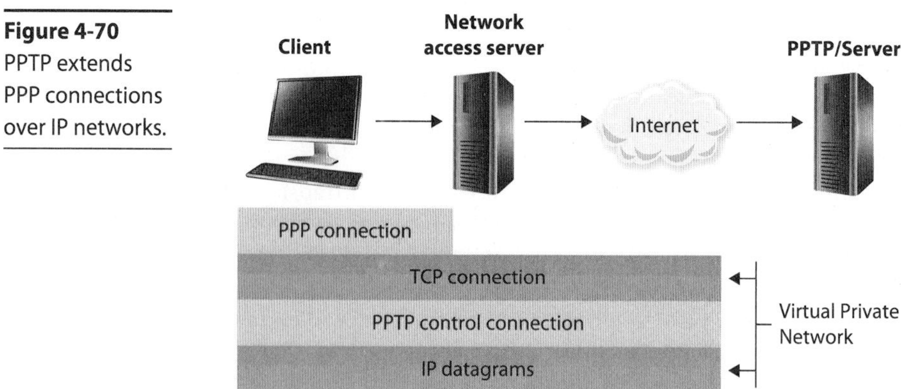

manner, and through the use of certain attack tools, the encryption keys could be uncovered. Later implementations of PPTP addressed these issues, but the protocol still has some limitations that should be understood. For example, PPTP cannot support multiple connections over one VPN tunnel, which means that it can be used for system-to-system communication but not gateway-to-gateway connections that must support many user connections simultaneously. PPTP relies on PPP functionality for a majority of its security features, and because it never became an actual industry standard, incompatibilities through different vendor implementations exist.

Layer 2 Tunneling Protocol

Another VPN solution was developed that combines the features of PPTP and Cisco's Layer 2 Forwarding (L2F) protocol. *Layer 2 Tunneling Protocol (L2TP)* tunnels PPP traffic over various network types (IP, ATM, X.25, etc.); thus, it is not just restricted to IP networks as PPTP is. PPTP and L2TP have very similar focuses, which is to get PPP traffic to an end point that is connected to some type of network that does not understand PPP. Like PPTP, L2TP does not actually provide much protection for the PPP traffic it is moving around, but it integrates with protocols that *do* provide security features. L2TP inherits PPP authentication and integrates with IPSec to provide confidentiality, integrity, and potentially another layer of authentication.

NOTE PPP provides *user* authentication through PAP, CHAP, or EAP-TLS, whereas IPSec provides *system* authentication.

It can get confusing when several protocols are involved with various levels of encapsulation, but if you do not understand how they work together, you cannot identify if certain traffic links lack security. To figure out if you understand how these protocols work together and why, ask yourself these questions:

1. If the Internet is an IP-based network, why do we even need PPP?
2. If PPTP and L2TP do not actually secure data themselves, then why do they exist?
3. If PPTP and L2TP basically do the same thing, why choose L2TP over PPTP?
4. If a connection is using IP, PPP, and L2TP, where does IPSec come into play?

Let's go through the answers together. Let's say that you are a remote user and work from your home office. You do not have a dedicated link from your house to your company's network; instead, your traffic needs to go through the Internet to be able to communicate with the corporate network. The line between your house and your ISP is a point-to-point telecommunications link, one point being your home router and the other point being the ISP's switch, as shown in Figure 4-71. Point-to-point telecommunication devices do not understand IP, so your router has to encapsulate your traffic in a protocol the ISP's device will understand—PPP. Now your traffic is not

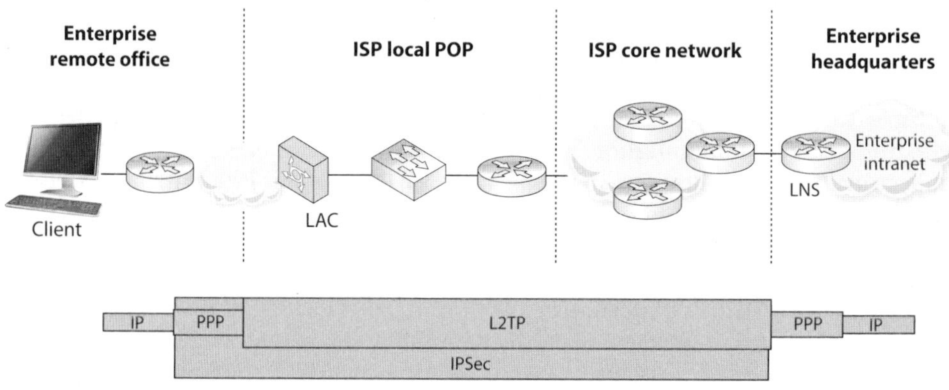

Figure 4-71 IP, PPP, L2TP, and IPSec can work together.

headed toward some website on the Internet; instead, it has a target of your company's corporate network. This means that your traffic has to be "carried through" the Internet to its ultimate destination through a tunnel. The Internet does not understand PPP, so your PPP traffic has to be encapsulated with a protocol that can work on the Internet and create the needed tunnel, as in PPTP or L2TP. If the connection between your ISP and the corporate network will not happen over the regular Internet (IP-based network), but instead over a WAN-based connection (ATM, frame relay), then L2TP has to be used for this PPP tunnel because PPTP cannot travel over non-IP networks.

So your IP packets are wrapped up in PPP, which are then wrapped up in L2TP. But you still have no encryption involved, so your data is actually not protected. This is where IPSec comes in. IPSec is used to encrypt the data that will pass through the L2TP tunnel. Once your traffic gets to the corporate network's perimeter device, it will decrypt the packets, take off the L2TP and PPP headers, add the necessary Ethernet headers, and send these packets to their ultimate destination.

So here are the answers to our questions…

1. If the Internet is an IP-based network, why do we even need PPP?
   Answer: The point-to-point line devices that connect individual systems to the Internet do not understand IP, so the traffic that travels over these links has to be encapsulated in PPP.
2. If PPTP and L2TP do not actually secure data themselves, then why do they exist?
   Answer: They extend PPP connections by providing a tunnel through networks that do not understand PPP.
3. If PPTP and L2TP basically do the same thing, why choose L2TP over PPTP?
   Answer: PPTP only works over IP-based networks. L2TP works over IP-based and WAN-based (ATM, frame relay) connections. If a PPP connection needs to be extended over a WAN-based connection, L2TP must be used.

4. If a connection is using IP, PPP, and L2TP, where does IPSec come into play? Answer: IPSec provides the encryption, data integrity, and system-based authentication.

So here is another question. Does all of this PPP, PPTP, L2TP, and IPSec encapsulation have to happen for every single VPN used on the Internet? No, only when connections over point-to-point connections are involved. When two gateway routers are connected over the Internet and provide VPN functionality, they only have to use IPSec.

Internet Protocol Security

IPSec is a suite of protocols that was developed to specifically protect IP traffic. IPv4 does not have any integrated security, so IPSec was developed to "bolt onto" IP and secure the data the protocol transmits. Where PPTP and L2TP work at the data link layer, IPSec works at the network layer of the OSI model.

The main protocols that make up the IPSec suite and their basic functionality are as follows:

- **Authentication Header (AH)** Provides data integrity, data-origin authentication, and protection from replay attacks
- **Encapsulating Security Payload (ESP)** Provides confidentiality, data-origin authentication, and data integrity
- **Internet Security Association and Key Management Protocol (ISAKMP)** Provides a framework for security association creation and key exchange
- **Internet Key Exchange (IKE)** Provides authenticated keying material for use with ISAKMP

AH and ESP can be used separately or together in an IPSec VPN configuration. The AH protocols can provide data-origin authentication (system authentication) and protection from unauthorized modification, but do not provide encryption capabilities. If the VPN needs to provide confidentiality, then ESP has to be enabled and configured properly.

When two routers need to set up an IPSec VPN connection, they have a list of security attributes that need to be agreed upon through handshaking processes. The two routers have to agree upon algorithms, keying material, protocol types, and modes of use, which will all be used to protect the data that is transmitted between them.

Let's say that you and Juan are routers that need to protect the data you will pass back and forth to each other. Juan send's you a list of items that you will use to process the packets he sends to you. His list contains AES-128, SHA-1, and ESP tunnel mode. You take these parameters and store them in a security association (SA). When Juan sends you packets one hour later, you will go to this SA and follow these parameters so

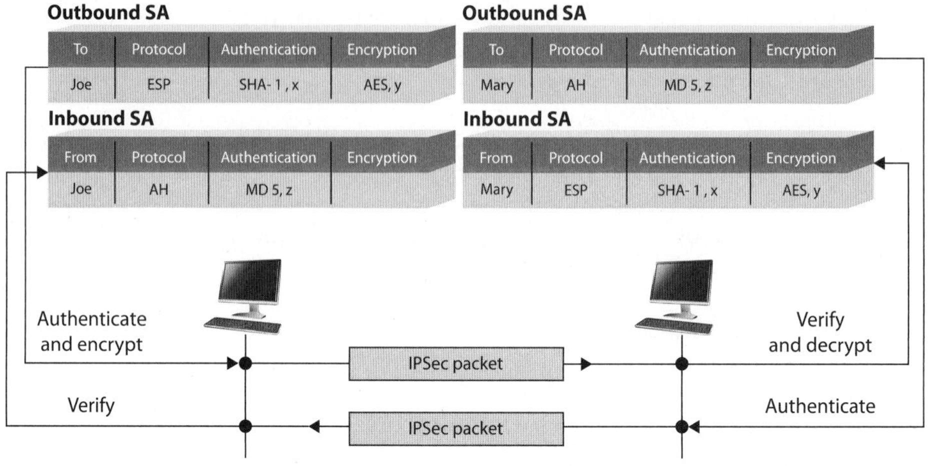

Figure 4-72 IPSec uses security associations to store VPN parameters.

that you know how to process this traffic. You know what algorithm to use to verify the integrity of the packets, the algorithm to use to decrypt the packets, and which protocol to activate and in what mode. Figure 4-72 illustrates how SAs are used for inbound and outbound traffic.

NOTE The U.S. National Security Agency uses a protocol encryptor that is based upon IPSec. A *HAIPE (High Assurance Internet Protocol Encryptor)* is a Type 1 encryption device that is based on IPSec with additional restrictions, enhancements, and capabilities. A HAIPE is typically a secure gateway that allows two enclaves to exchange data over an untrusted or lower-classification network. Since this technology works at the network layer, secure end-to-end connectivity can take place in heterogeneous environments. This technology has largely replaced link layer encryption technology implementations.

Transport Layer Security VPN

A newer VPN technology is *Transport Layer Security (TLS)*, which works at even higher layers in the OSI model than the previously covered VPN protocols. TLS, which we discuss in detail later in this chapter, works at the session layer of the network stack and is used mainly to protect HTTP traffic. TLS capabilities are already embedded into most web browsers, so the deployment and interoperability issues are minimal.

IPSec

IPSec can be configured to provide *transport adjacency*, which just means that more than one security protocol (ESP and AH) is used in a VPN tunnel. IPSec can also be configured to provide *iterated tunneling*, in which an IPSec tunnel is tunneled through another IPSec tunnel, as shown in the following diagram. Iterated tunneling would be used if the traffic needed different levels of protection at different junctions of its path. For example, if the IPSec tunnel started from an internal host and terminated at an internal border router, this may not require encryption, so only the AH protocol would be used. But when that data travels from that border router throughout the Internet to another network, then the data requires more protection. So the first packets travel through a semisecure tunnel until they get ready to hit the Internet and then they go through a very secure second tunnel.

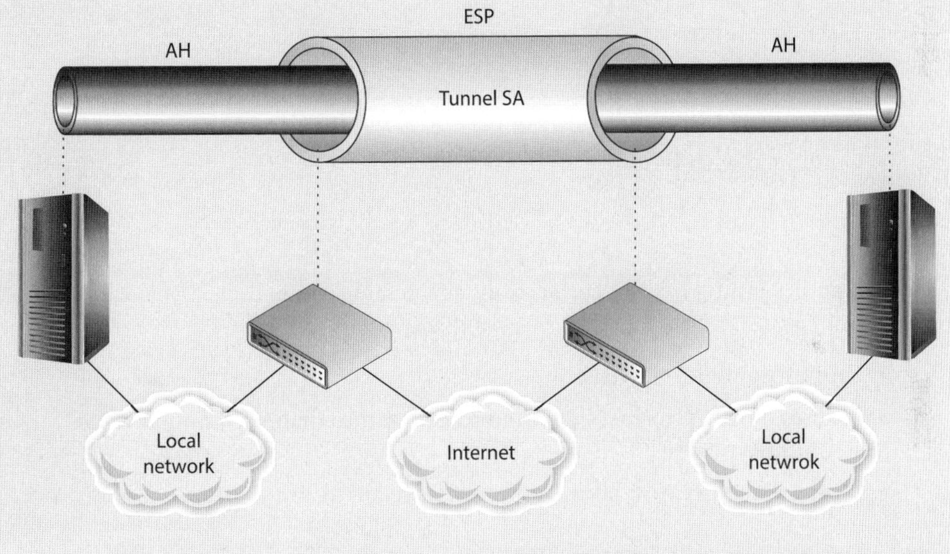

The most common implementation types of TLS VPN are as follows:

- **TLS portal VPN** An individual uses a single standard TLS connection to a website to securely access multiple network services. The website accessed is typically called a portal because it is a single location that provides access to other resources. The remote user accesses the TLS VPN gateway using a web browser, is authenticated, and is then presented with a web page that acts as the portal to the other services.
- **TLS tunnel VPN** An individual uses a web browser to securely access multiple network services, including applications and protocols that are not web-based, through a TLS tunnel. This commonly requires custom programming to allow the services to be accessible through a web-based connection.

Summary of Tunneling Protocols

Point-to-Point Tunneling Protocol (PPTP):

- Works in a client/server model
- Extends and protects PPP connections
- Works at the data link layer
- Transmits over IP networks only

Layer 2 Tunneling Protocol (L2TP):

- Hybrid of L2F and PPTP
- Extends and protects PPP connections
- Works at the data link layer
- Transmits over multiple types of networks, not just IP
- Combined with IPSec for security

IPSec:

- Handles multiple VPN connections at the same time
- Provides secure authentication and encryption
- Supports only IP networks
- Focuses on LAN-to-LAN communication rather than user-to-user communication
- Works at the network layer, and provides security on top of IP

Transport Layer Security (TLS):

- Works at the session layer and protects mainly web and e-mail traffic
- Granular access control and configuration are available
- Easy deployment since TLS is already embedded into web browsers
- Can only protect a small number of protocol types, thus is not an infrastructure-level VPN solution

Since TLS VPNs are closer to the application layer, they can provide more granular access control and security features compared to the other VPN solutions. But since they are dependent on the application layer protocol, there are a smaller number of traffic types that can be protected through this VPN type.

One VPN solution is not necessarily better than the other; they just have their own focused purposes:

- PPTP is used when a PPP connection needs to be extended through an IP-based network.
- L2TP is used when a PPP connection needs to be extended through a non–IP-based network.
- IPSec is used to protect IP-based traffic and is commonly used in gateway-to-gateway connections.
- TLS VPN is used when a specific application layer traffic type needs protection.

Again, what can be used for good can also be used for evil. Attackers commonly encrypt their attack traffic so that countermeasures we put into place to analyze traffic for suspicious activity are not effective. Attackers can use TLS or PPTP to encrypt malicious traffic as it traverses the network. When an attacker compromises and opens up a back door on a system, she will commonly encrypt the traffic that will then go between her system and the compromised system. It is important to configure security network devices to only allow approved encrypted channels.

Authentication Protocols

Password Authentication Protocol (PAP) is used by remote users to authenticate over PPP connections. It provides identification and authentication of the user who is attempting to access a network from a remote system. This protocol requires a user to enter a password before being authenticated. The password and the username credentials are sent over the network to the authentication server after a connection has been established via PPP. The authentication server has a database of user credentials that are compared to the supplied credentials to authenticate users.

PAP is one of the least secure authentication methods because the credentials are sent in cleartext, which renders them easy to capture by network sniffers. Although it is not recommended, some systems revert to PAP if they cannot agree on any other authentication protocol. During the handshake process of a connection, the two entities negotiate how authentication is going to take place, what connection parameters to use, the speed of data flow, and other factors. Both entities will try to negotiate and agree upon the most secure method of authentication; they may start with EAP, and if one computer does not have EAP capabilities, they will try to agree upon CHAP; if one of the computers does not have CHAP capabilities, they may be forced to use PAP. If this type of authentication is unacceptable, the administrator will configure the remote access server (RAS) to accept only CHAP authentication and higher, and PAP cannot be used at all.

Challenge Handshake Authentication Protocol (CHAP) addresses some of the vulnerabilities found in PAP. It uses a challenge/response mechanism to authenticate the user instead of having the user send a password over the wire. When a user wants to establish a PPP connection and both ends have agreed that CHAP will be used for authentication purposes, the user's computer sends the authentication server a logon request. The server sends the user a challenge (nonce), which is a random value. This challenge is encrypted with the use of a predefined password as an encryption key, and the encrypted challenge value is returned to the server. The authentication server also uses the predefined password as an encryption key and decrypts the challenge value, comparing it to the original value sent. If the two results are the same, the authentication server deduces that the user must have entered the correct password, and authentication is granted. The steps that take place in CHAP are depicted in Figure 4-73.

EXAM TIP MS-CHAP is Microsoft's version of CHAP and provides mutual authentication functionality. It has two versions, which are incompatible with each other.

PAP is vulnerable to sniffing because it sends the password and data in plaintext, but it is also vulnerable to man-in-the-middle attacks. CHAP is not vulnerable to man-in-the-middle attacks because it continues this challenge/response activity throughout the connection to ensure the authentication server is still communicating with a user who holds the necessary credentials.

Extensible Authentication Protocol (EAP) is also supported by PPP. Actually, EAP is not a specific authentication protocol as are PAP and CHAP. Instead, it provides a framework to enable many types of authentication techniques to be used when establishing network connections. As the name states, it *extends* the authentication possibilities from the norm (PAP and CHAP) to other methods, such as one-time passwords, token cards, biometrics, Kerberos, digital certificates, and future mechanisms. So when a user connects to an authentication server and both have EAP capabilities, they can negotiate between a longer list of possible authentication methods.

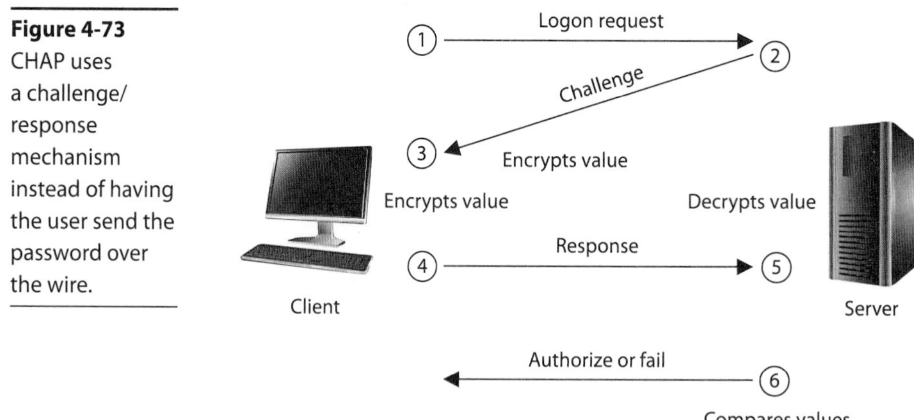

Figure 4-73 CHAP uses a challenge/response mechanism instead of having the user send the password over the wire.

Protocol	Description
Lightweight EAP (LEAP)	Wireless LAN authentication method developed by Cisco Systems
EAP-TLS	Digital certificate–based authentication
EAP-MD5	Weak system authentication based upon hash values
EAP-PSK	Provides mutual authentication and session key derivation using a preshared key
EAP-TTLS	Extends TLS functionality
EAP-IKE2	Provides mutual authentication and session key establishment using asymmetric or symmetric keys or passwords
PEAPv0/EAP-MSCHAPv2	Similar in design to EAP-TTLS but only requires a server-side digital certificate
PEAPv1/EAP-GTC	Cisco variant based on Generic Token Card (GTC) authentication
EAP-FAST	Cisco-proprietary replacement for LEAP based on Flexible Authentication via Secure Tunneling (FAST)
EAP-SIM	For Global System for Mobile Communications (GSM), based on Subscriber Identity Module (SIM), a variant of PEAP for GSM
EAP-AKA	For Universal Mobile Telecommunication System (UMTS) Subscriber Identity Module (USIM) and provides Authentication and Key Agreement (AKA)
EAP-GSS	Based on Generic Security Service (GSS), uses Kerberos

Table 4-15 EAP Variants

NOTE EAP has been defined for use with a variety of technologies and protocols, including PPP, PPTP, L2TP, IEEE 802 wired networks, and wireless technologies such as 802.11 and 802.16.

There are many different variants of EAP, as shown in Table 4-15, because EAP is an extensible framework that can be morphed for different environments and needs.

Wireless Networks

Wireless communications take place much more often than we think, and a wide range of broadband wireless data transmission technologies are used in various frequency ranges. Broadband wireless signals occupy frequency bands that may be shared with microwave, satellite, radar, and ham radio use, for example. We use these technologies for television transmissions, cellular phones, satellite transmissions, spying, surveillance, and garage door openers. As we will see in the next sections, wireless communication takes place over personal area networks; wireless LANs, MANs, and WANs; and via satellite. Each is illustrated in Figure 4-74.

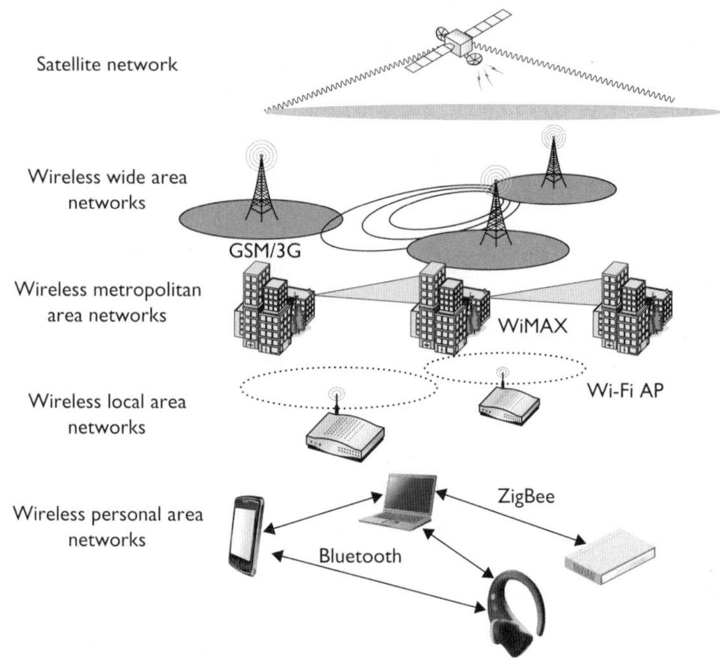

Figure 4-74 Various wireless transmission types

Wireless Communications Techniques

Wireless communication involves transmitting information via radio waves that move through air and space. These signals can be described in a number of ways, but normally are described in terms of *frequency* and *amplitude*. The frequency of a signal dictates the amount of data that can be carried and how far. The higher the frequency, the more data the signal can carry, but the higher the frequency, the more susceptible the signal is to atmospheric interference. Normally, a higher frequency can carry more data, but over a shorter distance.

In a wired network, each computer and device has its own cable connecting it to the network in some fashion. In wireless technologies, each device must instead share the allotted radio frequency spectrum with all other wireless devices that need to communicate. This spectrum of frequencies is finite in nature, which means it cannot grow if more and more devices need to use it. The same thing happens with Ethernet—all the computers on a segment share the same medium, and only one computer can send data at any given time. Otherwise, a collision can take place. Wired networks using Ethernet employ the CSMA/CD (collision detection) technology. Wireless LAN (WLAN) technology is actually very similar to Ethernet, but it uses CSMA/CA (collision avoidance). The wireless device sends out a broadcast indicating it is going to transmit data. This is received by other devices on the shared medium, which causes them to hold off on transmitting information. It is all about trying to eliminate or reduce collisions. (The two versions of CSMA are explained earlier in this chapter in the section "CSMA.")

A number of techniques have been developed to allow wireless devices to access and share this limited amount of medium for communication purposes. We will look at different types of spread spectrum techniques in the next sections. The goal of each of these wireless technologies is to split the available frequency into usable portions, since it is a limited resource, and to allow the devices to share them efficiently.

Spread Spectrum

In the world of wireless communications, certain technologies and industries are allocated specific spectrums, or frequency ranges, to be used for transmissions. In the United States, the Federal Communications Commission (FCC) decides upon this allotment of frequencies and enforces its own restrictions. *Spread spectrum* means that something is distributing individual signals across the allocated frequencies in some fashion. So when a spread spectrum technology is used, the sender spreads its data across the frequencies over which it has permission to communicate. This allows for more effective use of the available bandwidth, because the sending system can use more than one frequency at a time.

Think of it in terms of investments. In conventional radio transmissions, all the data bits are modulated onto a single carrier wave that operates on a specific frequency (as in amplitude modulated [AM] radio systems) or on a narrow band of frequencies (as in frequency modulated [FM] radio). This is akin to investing only in one stock; it is simple and efficient, but may not be ideal in risky environments. The alternative is to diversify your portfolio, which is normally done by investing a bit of your money in each of many stocks across a wide set of industries. This is more complex and inefficient, but can save your bottom line when one of your companies takes a nose-dive. This example is akin to direct sequence spread spectrum (DSSS), which we discuss in an upcoming section. There is in theory another way to minimize your exposure to volatile markets. Suppose the cost of buying and selling was negligible. You could then invest all your money in a single stock, but only for a brief period of time, sell it as soon as you turn a profit, and then reinvest all your proceeds in another stock. By jumping around the market, your exposure to the problems of any one company are minimized. This approach would be comparable to frequency hopping spread spectrum (FHSS). The point is that spread-spectrum communications are used primarily to reduce the effects of adverse conditions such as crowded radio bands, interference, and eavesdropping.

Frequency Hopping Spread Spectrum *Frequency hopping spread spectrum (FHSS)* takes the total amount of bandwidth (spectrum) and splits it into smaller subchannels. The sender and receiver work at one of these subchannels for a specific amount of time and then move to another subchannel. The sender puts the first piece of data on one frequency, the second on a different frequency, and so on. The FHSS algorithm determines the individual frequencies that will be used and in what order, and this is referred to as the sender and receiver's *hop sequence.*

Interference is a large issue in wireless transmissions because it can corrupt signals as they travel. Interference can be caused by other devices working in the same frequency space. The devices' signals step on each other's toes and distort the data being sent. The FHSS approach to this is to hop between different frequencies so that if another device is operating at the same frequency, it will not be drastically affected. Consider another analogy: Suppose George and Marge have to work in the same room. They could get into each other's way and affect each other's work. But if they periodically change rooms, the probability of them interfering with each other is reduced.

A hopping approach also makes it much more difficult for eavesdroppers to listen in on and reconstruct the data being transmitted when used in technologies other than WLAN. FHSS has been used extensively in military wireless communications devices because the only way the enemy could intercept and capture the transmission is by knowing the hopping sequence. The receiver has to know the sequence to be able to obtain the data. But in today's WLAN devices, the hopping sequence is known and does not provide any security.

So how does this FHSS stuff work? The sender and receiver hop from one frequency to another based on a predefined hop sequence. Several pairs of senders and receivers can move their data over the same set of frequencies because they are all using different hop sequences. Let's say you and Marge share a hop sequence of 1, 5, 3, 2, 4, and Nicole and Ed have a sequence of 4, 2, 5, 1, 3. Marge sends her first message on frequency 1, and Nicole sends her first message on frequency 4 at the same time. Marge's next piece of data is sent on frequency 5, the next on 3, and so on until each reaches its destination, which is your wireless device. So your device listens on frequency 1 for a half-second, and then listens on frequency 5, and so on, until it receives all of the pieces of data that are on the line on those frequencies at that time. Ed's device is listening to the same frequencies but at different times and in a different order, so his device ignores Marge's message because it is out of sync with his predefined sequence. Without knowing the right code, Ed treats Marge's messages as background noise and does not process them.

Direct Sequence Spread Spectrum *Direct sequence spread spectrum (DSSS)* takes a different approach by applying sub-bits to a message. The sub-bits are used by the sending system to generate a different format of the data before the data is transmitted. The receiving end uses these sub-bits to reassemble the signal into the original data format. The sub-bits are called *chips*, and the sequence of how the sub-bits are applied is referred to as the *chipping code*.

When the sender's data is combined with the chip, the signal appears as random noise to anyone who does not know the chipping sequence. This is why the sequence is sometimes called a pseudo-noise sequence. Once the sender combines the data with the chipping sequence, the new form of the information is modulated with a radio carrier signal, and it is shifted to the necessary frequency and transmitted. What the heck does that mean? When using wireless transmissions, the data is actually moving over radio signals that work in specific frequencies. Any data to be moved in this fashion must have a carrier signal, and this carrier signal works in its own specific range, which is a frequency. So you can think of it this way: once the data is combined with the chipping code, it is put into a car (carrier signal), and the car travels down its specific road (frequency) to get to its destination.

The receiver basically reverses the process, first by demodulating the data from the carrier signal (removing it from the car). The receiver must know the correct chipping sequence to change the received data into its original format. This means the sender and receiver must be properly synchronized.

The sub-bits provide error-recovery instructions, just as parity does in RAID technologies. If a signal is corrupted using FHSS, it must be re-sent; but by using DSSS, even if the message is somewhat distorted, the signal can still be regenerated because it can be rebuilt from the chipping code bits. The use of this code allows for prevention of interference, allows for tracking of multiple transmissions, and provides a level of error correction.

FHSS vs. DSSS FHSS uses only a portion of the total bandwidth available at any one time, while the DSSS technology uses all of the available bandwidth continuously. DSSS spreads the signals over a wider frequency band, whereas FHSS uses a narrow band carrier that changes frequently across a wide band.

Since DSSS sends data across all frequencies at once, it has a higher data throughput than FHSS. The first wireless WAN standard, 802.11, used FHSS, but as bandwidth requirements increased, DSSS was implemented. By using FHSS, the 802.11 standard can provide a data throughput of only 1 to 2 Mbps. By using DSSS instead, 802.11b provides a data throughput of up to 11 Mbps.

Spread Spectrum Types

This technology transmits data by "spreading" it over a broad range of frequencies:

- FHSS moves data by changing frequencies.
- DSSS takes a different approach by applying sub-bits to a message and uses all of the available frequencies at the same time.

Orthogonal Frequency-Division Multiplexing

The next step in trying to move even more data over wireless frequency signals came in the form of *orthogonal frequency-division multiplexing (OFDM)*. OFDM is a digital multicarrier modulation scheme that compacts multiple modulated carriers tightly together, reducing the required bandwidth. The modulated signals are orthogonal (perpendicular) and do not interfere with each other. OFDM uses a composite of narrow channel bands to enhance its performance in high-frequency bands. OFDM is officially a multiplexing technology and not a spread spectrum technology, but is used in a similar manner.

A large number of closely spaced orthogonal subcarrier signals are used, and the data is divided into several parallel data streams or channels, one for each subcarrier. Channel equalization is simplified because OFDM uses many slowly modulated narrowband signals rather than one rapidly modulated wideband signal.

OFDM is used for several wideband digital communication types such as digital television, audio broadcasting, DSL broadband Internet access, wireless networks, and 4G mobile communications.

WLAN Components

A WLAN uses a transceiver, called an *access point (AP)*, which connects to an Ethernet cable that is the link wireless devices use to access resources on the wired network, as shown in Figure 4-75. When the AP is connected to the LAN Ethernet by a wired cable, it is the component that connects the wired and the wireless worlds. The APs are in fixed locations throughout a network and work as communication beacons. Let's say a wireless user has a device with a wireless NIC, which modulates her data onto radio frequency signals that are accepted and processed by the AP. The signals transmitted from the AP are received by the wireless NIC and converted into a digital format, which the device can understand.

When APs are used to connect wireless and wired networks, this is referred to as an *infrastructure WLAN*, which is used to extend an existing wired network. When there is just one AP and it is not connected to a wired network, it is considered to be in *stand-alone* mode and just acts as a wireless hub.

An *ad hoc WLAN* has no APs; the wireless devices communicate with each other through their wireless NICs instead of going through a centralized device. To construct an ad hoc network, wireless client software on contributing hosts and configured for peer-to-peer operation mode. Then, the user clicks Network in Windows Explorer and the software searches for other hosts operating in this similar mode and shows them to the user.

For a wireless device and AP to communicate, they must be configured to communicate over the same channel. A *channel* is a certain frequency within a given frequency band.

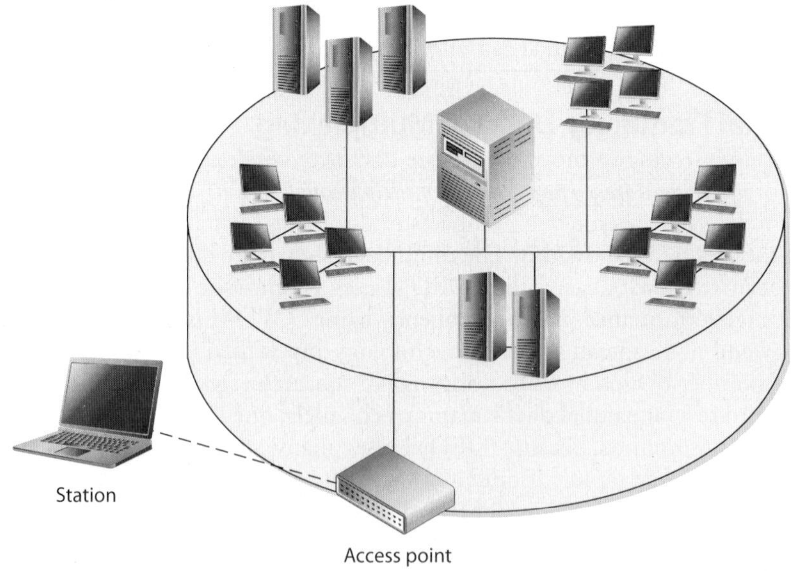

Figure 4-75 Access points allow wireless devices to participate in wired LANs.

The AP is configured to transmit over a specific channel, and the wireless device will "tune" itself to be able to communicate over this same frequency.

Any hosts that wish to participate within a particular WLAN must be configured with the proper *Service Set ID (SSID)*. Various hosts can be segmented into different WLANs by using different SSIDs. The reasons to segment a WLAN into portions are the same reasons wired systems are segmented on a network: the users require access to different resources, have different business functions, or have different levels of trust.

NOTE When wireless devices work in infrastructure mode, the AP and wireless clients form a group referred to as a Basic Service Set (BSS). This group is assigned a name, which is the SSID value.

When WLAN technologies first came out, authentication was this simplistic—your device either had the right SSID value and WEP key or it did not. As wireless communication increased in use and many deficiencies were identified in these simplistic ways of authentication and encryption, many more solutions were developed and deployed.

Evolution of WLAN Security

To say that security was an afterthought in the first WLANs would be a remarkable understatement. As with many new technologies, wireless networks were often rushed to market with a focus on functionality, even if that sometimes came at the expense of security. Over time, vendors and standards bodies caught on and tried to correct these omissions. While we have made significant headway in securing our wireless networks, as security professionals we must acknowledge that whenever we transmit anything over the electromagnetic spectrum, we are essentially putting our data in the hands (or at least within the grasp) of our adversaries.

IEEE Standard 802.11

When wireless LANs (WLANs) were being introduced, there was industry-wide consensus that some measures would have to be taken to assure users that their data (now in the air) would be protected from eavesdropping to the same degree that data on a wired LAN was already protected. This was the genesis of *Wired Equivalent Privacy (WEP)*. This first WLAN standard, codified as IEEE 802.11, had a tremendous number of security flaws. These were found within the core standard itself, as well as in different implementations of this standard. Before we delve into these, it will be useful to spend a bit of time with some of the basics of 802.11.

The wireless devices using this protocol can authenticate to the AP in two main ways: *open system authentication (OSA)* and *shared key authentication (SKA)*. OSA does not require the wireless device to prove to the AP it has a specific cryptographic key to allow for authentication purposes. In many cases, the wireless device needs to provide only the correct SSID value. In OSA implementations, all transactions are in cleartext because no encryption is involved. So an intruder can sniff the traffic, capture the necessary steps of authentication, and walk through the same steps to be authenticated and associated to an AP.

When an AP is configured to use SKA, the AP sends a random value to the wireless device. The device encrypts this value with its cryptographic key and returns it. The AP decrypts and extracts the response, and if it is the same as the original value, the device is authenticated. In this approach, the wireless device is authenticated to the network by proving it has the necessary encryption key.

The three core deficiencies with WEP are the use of static encryption keys, the ineffective use of initialization vectors, and the lack of packet integrity assurance. The WEP protocol uses the RC4 algorithm, which is a stream-symmetric cipher. *Symmetric* means the sender and receiver must use the exact same key for encryption and decryption purposes. The 802.11 standard does not stipulate how to update these keys through an automated process, so in most environments, the RC4 symmetric keys are never changed out. And usually all of the wireless devices and the AP share the exact same key. This is like having everyone in your company use the exact same password. Not a good idea. So that is the first issue—static WEP encryption keys on all devices.

NOTE Cryptography topics are covered in detail in Chapter 3.

The next flaw is how initialization vectors (IVs) are used. An IV is a numeric seeding value that is used with the symmetric key and RC4 algorithm to provide more randomness to the encryption process. Randomness is extremely important in encryption because any patterns can give the bad guys insight into how the process works, which may allow them to uncover the encryption key that was used. The key and IV value are inserted into the RC4 algorithm to generate a key stream. The values (1's and 0's) of the key stream are XORed with the binary values of the individual packets. The result is ciphertext, or encrypted packets.

In most WEP implementations, the same IV values are used over and over again in this process, and since the same symmetric key (or shared secret) is generally used, there is no way to provide effective randomness in the key stream that is generated by the algorithm. The appearance of patterns allows attackers to reverse-engineer the process to uncover the original encryption key, which can then be used to decrypt future encrypted traffic.

So now we are onto the third mentioned weakness, which is the integrity assurance issue. WLAN products that use only the 802.11 standard introduce a vulnerability that is not always clearly understood. An attacker can actually change data within the wireless packets by flipping specific bits and altering the Integrity Check Value (ICV) so the receiving end is oblivious to these changes. The ICV works like a CRC function; the sender calculates an ICV and inserts it into a frame's header. The receiver calculates his own ICV and compares it with the ICV sent with the frame. If the ICVs are the same, the receiver can be assured that the frame was not modified during transmission. If the

ICVs are different, it indicates a modification did indeed take place and thus the receiver discards the frame. In WEP, there are certain circumstances in which the receiver cannot detect whether an alteration to the frame has taken place; thus, there is no true integrity assurance.

So the problems identified with the 802.11 standard include poor authentication, static WEP keys that can be easily obtained by attackers, IV values that are repetitive and do not provide the necessary degree of randomness, and a lack of data integrity. The next section describes the measures taken to remedy these problems.

CAUTION WEP is considered insecure and should not be used.

IEEE Standard 802.11i

IEEE came out with a standard in 2004 that deals with the security issues of the original 802.11 standard, which is called IEEE 802.11i or *Wi-Fi Protected Access II (WPA2)*. Why the number 2? Because while the formal standard was being ratified by the IEEE, the Wi-Fi alliance pushed out WPA (the first one) based on the draft of the standard. For this reason, WPA is sometimes referred to as the *draft* IEEE 802.11i. This rush to push out WPA required the reuse of elements of WEP, which ultimately made WPA vulnerable to some of the same attacks that doomed its predecessor. Let's start off by looking at WPA in depth, since this protocol is still widely used despite its weaknesses.

WPA employs different approaches that provide much more security and protection than the methods used in the original 802.11 standard. This enhancement of security is accomplished through specific protocols, technologies, and algorithms. The first protocol is *Temporal Key Integrity Protocol (TKIP)*, which is backward-compatible with the WLAN devices based upon the original 802.11 standard. TKIP actually works with WEP by feeding it keying material, which is data to be used for generating new dynamic keys. TKIP generates a new key for every frame that is transmitted. WPA also integrates 802.1X port authentication and EAP authentication methods.

NOTE TKIP was developed by the IEEE 802.11i task group and the Wi-Fi Alliance. The goal of this protocol was to increase the strength of WEP or replace it fully without the need for hardware replacement. TKIP provides a key mixing function, which allows the RC4 algorithm to provide a higher degree of protection. It also provides a sequence counter to protect against replay attacks and implements a message integrity check mechanism.

The use of the 802.1X technology in the new 802.11i standard provides access control by restricting network access until full authentication and authorization have been completed, and provides a robust authentication framework that allows for different EAP modules to be plugged in. These two technologies (802.1X and EAP) work together to enforce mutual authentication between the wireless device and authentication server. So what about the static keys, IV value, and integrity issues?

TKIP addresses the deficiencies of WEP pertaining to static WEP keys and inadequate use of IV values. Two hacking tools, AirSnort and WEPCrack, can be used to easily crack WEP's encryption by taking advantage of these weaknesses and the ineffective use of the key scheduling algorithm within the WEP protocol. If a company is using products that implement only WEP encryption and is not using a third-party encryption solution (such as a VPN), these programs can break its encrypted traffic within minutes. There is no "maybe" pertaining to breaking WEP's encryption. Using these tools means it will be broken whether a 40-bit or 128-bit key is being used—it doesn't matter. This is one of the most serious and dangerous vulnerabilities pertaining to the original 802.11 standard.

The use of TKIP provides the ability to rotate encryption keys to help fight against these types of attacks. The protocol increases the length of the IV value and ensures each and every frame has a different IV value. This IV value is combined with the transmitter's MAC address and the original WEP key, so even if the WEP key is static, the resulting encryption key will be different for each and every frame. (WEP key + IV value + MAC address = new encryption key.) So what does that do for us? This brings more randomness to the encryption process, and it is randomness that is necessary to properly thwart cryptanalysis and attacks on cryptosystems. The changing IV values and resulting keys make the resulting key stream less predictable, which makes it much harder for the attacker to reverse-engineer the process and uncover the original key.

TKIP also deals with the integrity issues by using a MIC instead of an ICV function. If you are familiar with a message authentication code (MAC) function, this is the same thing. A symmetric key is used with a hashing function, which is similar to a CRC function but stronger. The use of MIC instead of ICV ensures the receiver will be properly alerted if changes to the frame take place during transmission. The sender and receiver calculate their own separate MIC values. If the receiver generates a MIC value different from the one sent with the frame, the frame is seen as compromised and it is discarded.

The types of attacks that have been carried out on WEP devices and networks that just depend upon WEP are numerous and unnerving. Wireless traffic can be easily sniffed, data can be modified during transmission without the receiver being notified, rogue APs can be erected (which users can authenticate to and communicate with, not knowing it is a malicious entity), and encrypted wireless traffic can be decrypted quickly and easily. Unfortunately, these vulnerabilities usually provide doorways to the actual wired network where the more destructive attacks can begin.

The full 802.11i (WPA2) has a major advantage over WPA by providing encryption protection with the use of the AES algorithm in counter mode with CBC-MAC (CCM), which is referred to as the Counter Mode Cipher Block Chaining Message Authentication Code Protocol (CCM Protocol or CCMP). AES is a more appropriate algorithm for wireless than RC4 and provides a higher level of protection. WPA2 defaults to CCMP, but can switch down to TKIP and RC4 to provide backward compatibility with WPA devices and networks.

NOTE CBC, CCM, and CCMP modes are explained in Chapter 3.

IEEE Standard 802.1X

The 802.11i standard can be understood as three main components in two specific layers. The lower layer contains the improved encryption algorithms and techniques (TKIP and CCMP), while the layer that resides on top of it contains 802.1X. They work together to provide more layers of protection than the original 802.11 standard.

We covered 802.1X earlier in the chapter, but let's cover it more in depth here. The 802.1X standard is a port-based network access control that ensures a user cannot make a full network connection until he is properly authenticated. This means a user cannot access network resources and no traffic is allowed to pass, other than authentication traffic, from the wireless device to the network until the user is properly authenticated. An analogy is having a chain on your front door that enables you to open the door slightly to identify a person who knocks before you allow him to enter your house.

NOTE 802.1X is not a wireless protocol. It is an access control protocol that can be implemented on both wired and wireless networks.

By incorporating 802.1X, the new standard allows for the user to be authenticated, whereas using only WEP provides *system* authentication. User authentication provides a higher degree of confidence and protection than system authentication.

The 802.1X technology actually provides an authentication framework and a method of dynamically distributing encryption keys. The three main entities in this framework are the supplicant (wireless device), the authenticator (AP), and the authentication server (usually a RADIUS server).

The AP usually does not have much intelligence and acts like a middleman by passing frames between the wireless device and the authentication server. This is usually a good approach, since this does not require a lot of processing overhead for the AP, and the AP can deal with controlling several connections at once instead of having to authenticate each and every user.

The AP controls all communication and allows the wireless device to communicate with the authentication server and wired network only when all authentication steps are completed successfully. This means the wireless device cannot send or receive HTTP, DHCP, SMTP, or any other type of traffic until the user is properly authorized. WEP does not provide this type of strict access control.

Another disadvantage of the original 802.11 standard is that mutual authentication is not possible. When using WEP alone, the wireless device can authenticate to the AP, but the authentication server is not required to authenticate to the wireless device. This means a rogue AP can be set up to capture users' credentials and traffic without the users being aware of this type of attack. 802.11i deals with this issue by using EAP. EAP allows for mutual authentication to take place between the authentication server and wireless device, and provides flexibility in that users can be authenticated by using passwords, tokens, one-time passwords, certificates, smart cards, or Kerberos. This allows wireless users to be authenticated using the current infrastructure's existing authentication technology.

The wireless device and authentication server that are 802.11i-compliant have different authentication modules that plug into 802.1X to allow for these different options. So, 802.1X provides the framework that allows for the different EAP modules to be added by a network administrator. The two entities (supplicant and authenticator) agree upon one of these authentication methods (EAP modules) during their initial handshaking process.

The 802.11i standard does not deal with the full protocol stack, but addresses only what is taking place at the data link layer of the OSI model. Authentication protocols reside at a higher layer than this, so 802.11i does not specify particular authentication protocols. The use of EAP, however, allows different protocols to be used by different vendors. For example, Cisco uses a purely password-based authentication framework called Lightweight Extensible Authentication Protocol (LEAP). Other vendors, including Microsoft, use EAP and Transport Layer Security (EAP-TLS), which carries out authentication through digital certificates. And yet another choice is Protective EAP (PEAP), where only the server uses a digital certificate. EAP-Tunneled Transport Layer Security (EAP-TTLS) is an EAP protocol that extends TLS. EAP-TTLS is designed to provide authentication that is as strong as EAP-TLS, but it does not require that each user be issued a certificate. Instead, only the authentication servers are issued certificates. User authentication is performed by password, but the password credentials are transported in a securely encrypted tunnel established based upon the server certificates.

If EAP-TLS is being used, the authentication server and wireless device exchange digital certificates for authentication purposes. If PEAP is being used instead, the user of the wireless device sends the server a password and the server authenticates to the wireless device with its digital certificate. In both cases, some type of public key infrastructure (PKI) needs to be in place. If a company does not have a PKI currently implemented, it can be an overwhelming and costly task to deploy a PKI just to secure wireless transmissions.

When EAP-TLS is being used, the steps the server takes to authenticate to the wireless device are basically the same as when a TLS connection is being set up between a web server and web browser. Once the wireless device receives and validates the server's digital certificate, it creates a master key, encrypts it with the server's public key, and sends it over to the authentication server. Now the wireless device and authentication server have a master key, which they use to generate individual symmetric session keys. Both entities use these session keys for encryption and decryption purposes, and it is the use of these keys that sets up a secure channel between the two devices.

Companies may choose to use PEAP instead of EAP-TLS because they don't want the hassle of installing and maintaining digital certificates on every wireless device. Before you purchase a WLAN product, you should understand the requirements and complications of each method to ensure you know what you are getting yourself into and if it is the right fit for your environment.

A large concern with current WLANs using just WEP is that if individual wireless devices are stolen, they can easily be authenticated to the wired network. 802.11i has added steps to require the user to authenticate to the network instead of just requiring the wireless device to authenticate. By using EAP, the user must send some type of credential set that is tied to his identity. When using only WEP, the wireless device authenticates itself by proving it has a symmetric key that was manually programmed into it. Since the user does not need to authenticate using WEP, a stolen wireless device can allow an attacker easy access to your precious network resources.

The Answer to All Our Prayers? So does the use of EAP, 802.1X, AES, and TKIP result in secure and highly trusted WLAN implementations? Maybe, but we need to understand what we are dealing with here. TKIP was created as a quick fix to WEP's overwhelming problems. It does not provide an overhaul for the wireless standard itself because WEP and TKIP are still based on the RC4 algorithm, which is not the best fit for this type of technology. The use of AES is closer to an actual overhaul, but it is not backward-compatible with the original 802.11 implementations. In addition, we should understand that using all of these new components and mixing them with the current 802.11 components will add more complexity and steps to the process. Security and complexity do not usually get along. The highest security is usually accomplished with simplistic and elegant solutions to ensure all of the entry points are clearly understood and protected. These new technologies add more flexibility to how vendors can choose to authenticate users and authentication servers, but can also bring us interoperability issues because the vendors will not all choose the same methods. This means that if a company buys an AP from company A, then the wireless cards it buys from companies B and C may not work seamlessly.

So does that mean all of this work has been done for naught? No. 802.11i provides much more protection and security than WEP ever did. The working group has had very knowledgeable people involved and some very large and powerful companies aiding in the development of these new solutions. But the customers who purchase these new products need to understand what will be required of them *after* the purchase order is made out. For example, with the use of EAP-TLS, each wireless device needs its own digital certificate. Are your current wireless devices programmed to handle certificates? How will the certificates be properly deployed to all the wireless devices? How will the certificates be maintained? Will the devices and authentication server verify that certificates have not been revoked by periodically checking a certificate revocation list (CRL)? What if a rogue authentication server or AP was erected with a valid digital certificate? The wireless device would just verify this certificate and trust that this server is the entity it is supposed to be communicating with.

Today, WLAN products are being developed following the stipulations of this 802.11i wireless standard. Many products will straddle the fence by providing TKIP for backward-compatibility with current WLAN implementations and AES for companies that are just now thinking about extending their current wired environments with a wireless component. Before buying wireless products, customers should review the Wi-Fi Alliance's certification findings, which assess systems against the 802.11i proposed standard.

TIP WPA2 is also called Robust Security Network.

We covered the evolution of WLAN security, which is different from the evolution of WLAN transmission speeds and uses. Next we will dive into many of the 802.11 standards that have developed over the last several years.

Wireless Standards

Standards are developed so that many different vendors can create various products that will work together seamlessly. Standards are usually developed on a consensus basis among the different vendors in a specific industry. The IEEE develops standards for a wide range of technologies—wireless being one of them.

The first WLAN standard, 802.11, was developed in 1997 and provided a 1- to 2-Mbps transfer rate. It worked in the 2.4-GHz frequency range. This fell into the available range unlicensed by the FCC, which means that companies and users do not need to pay to use this range.

The 802.11 standard outlines how wireless clients and APs communicate; lays out the specifications of their interfaces; dictates how signal transmission should take place; and describes how authentication, association, and security should be implemented. We already covered IEEE 802.11, 802.11i and 802.11X, so here we focus on the other standards in this family.

Now just because life is unfair, a long list of standards actually fall under the 802.11 main standard. You may have seen this alphabet soup (802.11a, 802.11b, 802.11i, 802.11g, 802.11h, and so on) and not clearly understood the differences among them. IEEE created several task groups to work on specific areas within wireless communications. Each group had its own focus and was required to investigate and develop standards for its specific section. The letter suffixes indicate the order in which they were proposed and accepted.

802.11b

This standard was the first extension to the 802.11 WLAN standard. (Although 802.11a was conceived and approved first, it was not released first because of the technical complexity involved with this proposal.) 802.11b provides a transfer rate of up to 11 Mbps and works in the 2.4-GHz frequency range. It uses DSSS and is backward-compatible with 802.11 implementations.

802.11a

This standard uses a different method of modulating data onto the necessary radio carrier signals. Whereas 802.11b uses DSSS, 802.11a uses OFDM and works in the 5 GHz frequency band. Because of these differences, 802.11a is not backward-compatible with 802.11b or 802.11. Several vendors have developed products that can work with both 802.11a and 802.11b implementations; the devices must be properly configured or may be able to sense the technology already being used and configure themselves appropriately.

OFDM is a modulation scheme that splits a signal over several narrowband channels. The channels are then modulated and sent over specific frequencies. Because the data is divided across these different channels, any interference from the environment will degrade only a small portion of the signal. This allows for greater throughput. Like FHSS and DSSS, OFDM is a physical layer specification. It can be used to transmit high-definition digital audio and video broadcasting as well as WLAN traffic.

This technology offers advantages in two areas: speed and frequency. 802.11a provides up to 54 Mbps, and it does not work in the already very crowded 2.4-GHz spectrum. The 2.4-GHz frequency band is referred to as a "dirty" frequency because several devices already work there—microwaves, cordless phones, baby monitors, and so on. In many situations, this means that contention for access and use of this frequency can cause loss of data or inadequate service. But because 802.11a works at a higher frequency, it does not provide the same range as the 802.11b and 802.11g standards. The maximum speed for 802.11a is attained at short distances from the AP, up to 25 feet.

One downfall of using the 5-GHz frequency range is that other countries have not necessarily allocated this band for use of WLAN transmissions. So 802.11a products may work in the United States, but they may not necessarily work in other countries around the world.

802.11e

This standard has provided QoS and support of multimedia traffic in wireless transmissions. Multimedia and other types of time-sensitive applications have a lower tolerance for delays in data transmission. QoS provides the capability to prioritize traffic and affords guaranteed delivery. This specification and its capabilities have opened the door to allow many different types of data to be transmitted over wireless connections.

802.11f

When a user moves around in a WLAN, her wireless device often needs to communicate with different APs. An AP can cover only a certain distance, and as the user moves out of the range of the first AP, another AP needs to pick up and maintain her signal to ensure she does not lose network connectivity. This is referred to as roaming, and for this to happen seamlessly, the APs need to communicate with each other. If the second AP must take over this user's communication, it will need to be assured that this user has been properly authenticated and must know the necessary settings for this user's connection. This means the first AP would need to be able to convey this information to the second AP. The conveying of this information between the different APs during roaming is what 802.11f deals with. It outlines how this information can be properly shared.

802.11g

We are never happy with what we have; we always need more functions, more room, and more speed. The 802.11g standard provides for higher data transfer rates—up to 54 Mbps. This is basically a speed extension for 802.11b products. If a product meets the specifications of 802.11b, its data transfer rates are up to 11 Mbps, and if a product is based on 802.11g, that new product can be backward-compatible with older equipment but work at a much higher transfer rate.

So do we go with 802.11g or with 802.11a? They both provide higher bandwidth. 802.11g is backward-compatible with 802.11b, so that is a good thing if you already have a current infrastructure. But 802.11g still works in the 2.4-GHz range, which is continually getting more crowded. 802.11a works in the 5-GHz band and may be a better bet if you use other devices in the other, more crowded frequency range. But working at higher frequency means a device's signal cannot cover as wide a range. Your decision will also come down to what standard wins out in the standards war. Most likely, one or the other standard will eventually be ignored by the market, so you will not have to worry about making this decision. Only time will tell which one will be the keeper.

802.11h

As stated earlier, 802.11a works in the 5-GHz range, which is not necessarily available in countries other than the United States for this type of data transmission. The 802.11h standard builds upon the 802.11a specification to meet the requirements of European wireless rules so products working in this range can be properly implemented in European countries.

802.11j

Many countries have been developing their own wireless standards, which inevitably causes massive interoperability issues. This can be frustrating for the customer because he cannot use certain products, and it can be frustrating and expensive for vendors because they have a laundry list of specifications to meet if they want to sell their products in various countries. If vendors are unable to meet these specifications, whole customer bases are unavailable to them. The 802.11j task group has been working on bringing together many of the different standards and streamlining their development to allow for better interoperability across borders.

802.11n

802.11n is designed to be much faster, with throughput at 100 Mbps, and it works at the same frequency range as 802.11a (5 GHz). The intent is to maintain some backward-compatibility with current Wi-Fi standards, while combining a mix of the current technologies. This standard uses a concept called multiple input, multiple output (MIMO) to increase the throughput. This requires the use of two receive and two transmit antennas to broadcast in parallel using a 20-MHz channel.

802.11ac

The IEEE 802.11ac WLAN standard is an extension of 802.11n. It also operates on the 5-GHz band, but increases throughput to 1.3 Gbps. 802.11ac is backward compatible with 802.11a, 802.11b, 802.11g and 802.11n, but if in compatibility mode it slows down to the speed of the slower standard. Another benefit of this newer standard is its support for *beamforming*, which is the shaping of radio signals to improve their performance in specific directions. In simple terms, this means that 802.11ac is better able to maintain high data rates at longer ranges than its predecessors.

Not enough different wireless standards for you? You say you want more? Okay, here you go!

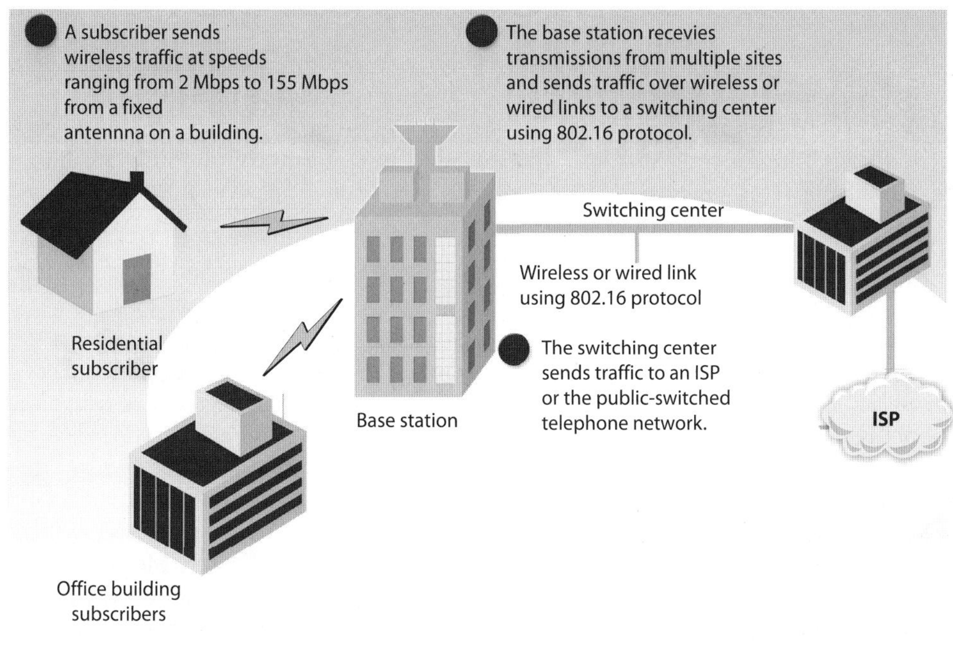

Figure 4-76 Broadband wireless in a MAN

802.16

All the wireless standards covered so far are WLAN-oriented standards. 802.16 is a MAN wireless standard, which allows for wireless traffic to cover a much wider geographical area. This technology is also referred to as *broadband* wireless access. (A commercial technology that is based upon 802.16 is WiMAX.) A common implementation of 802.16 technology is shown in Figure 4-76.

NOTE IEEE 802.16 is a standard for vendors to follow to allow for interoperable broadband wireless connections. IEEE does not test for compliance to this standard. The WiMAX Forum runs a certification program that is intended to guarantee compliance with the standard and interoperability with equipment between vendors.

Optical Wireless

Optical wireless is the combined use of two technologies: radio-frequency (RF) wireless and optical fiber. Long-range links are provided by optical fiber cables, and links from the long-range end-points to end users are accomplished by RF wireless transmitters. The local links can be provided by laser systems, also known as free-space optics (FSO), rather than by RF wireless. FSO is a point-to-point optical

(*Continued*)

connection supporting very high rates in outdoor environments. These types of wireless transmissions are hard to intercept and do not require a license to deploy. While older versions of optical wireless used to be negatively affected by weather conditions, currently all-weather optical wireless systems are continuously becoming available.

802.15.4

This standard deals with a much smaller geographical network, which is referred to as a *wireless personal area network (WPAN)*. This technology allows for connectivity to take place among local devices, such as a computer communicating with a wireless keyboard, a cellular phone communicating with a computer, or a headset communicating with another device. The goal here—as with all wireless technologies—is to allow for data transfer without all of those pesky cables. The IEEE 802.15.4 standard operates in the 2.4-GHz band, which is part of what is known as the Industrial, Scientific and Medical (ISM) band and is unlicensed in many parts of the world. This means that vendors are free to develop products in this band and market them worldwide without having to obtain licenses in multiple countries.

Devices that conform to the IEEE 802.15.4 standard are typically low-cost, low-bandwidth, and ubiquitous. They are very common in industrial settings where machines communicate directly with other machines over relatively short distances (typically no more than 100 meters). For this reason, this standard is emerging as a key enabler of the Internet of Things (IoT) in which everything from your thermostat to your door lock is (relatively) smart and connected.

ZigBee is one of the most popular protocols based on the IEEE 802.15.4 standard. It is intended to be simpler and cheaper than most WPAN protocols and is very popular in the embedded device market. ZigBee links are rated for 250 kbps and support 128 bit symmetric key encryption. You can find ZigBee in a variety of home automation, industrial control, medical, and sensor network applications.

Bluetooth Wireless

The *Bluetooth wireless* technology has a 1- to 3-Mbps transfer rate and works in a range of approximately 1, 10, or 100 meters. If you have a cell phone and a tablet that are both Bluetooth-enabled and both have calendar functionality, you could have them update each other without any need to connect them physically. If you added some information to your cell phone contacts list and task list, for example, you could just place the phone close to your tablet. The tablet would sense that the other device was nearby, and it would then attempt to set up a network connection with it. Once the connection was made, synchronization between the two devices would take place, and the tablet would add the new contacts list and task list data. Bluetooth works in the frequency range of other 802.11 devices (2.4 GHz).

Real security risks exist when transferring unprotected data via Bluetooth in a public area, because any device within a certain range can capture this type of data transfer.

One attack type that Bluetooth is vulnerable to is referred to as *Bluejacking*. In this attack, someone sends an unsolicited message to a device that is Bluetooth-enabled. Bluejackers look for a receiving device (phone, tablet, laptop) and then send a message to it. Often, the Bluejacker is trying to send someone else their business card, which will be added to the victim's contact list in their address book. The countermeasure is to put the Bluetooth-enabled device into nondiscoverable mode so others cannot identify this device in the first place. If you receive some type of message this way, just look around you. Bluetooth only works within a 10-meter distance, so it is coming from someone close by.

NOTE *Bluesnarfing* is the unauthorized access from a wireless device through a Bluetooth connection. This allows access to a calendar, contact list, e-mails, and text messages, and on some phones users can copy pictures and private videos.

Best Practices for Securing WLANs

There is no silver bullet to protect any of our devices or networks. That being said, there are a number of things we can do that will increase the cost of the attack for the adversary. Some of the best practices pertaining to WLAN implementations are as follows:

- Change the default SSID. Each AP comes with a preconfigured default SSID value.
- Implement WPA2 and 802.1X to provide centralized user authentication (e.g., RADIUS, Kerberos). Before users can access the network, require them to authenticate.
- Use separate VLANs for each class of users, just as you would on a wired LAN.
- If you must support unauthenticated users (e.g., visitors), ensure they are connected to an untrusted VLAN that remains outside your network's perimeter.
- Deploy a wireless intrusion detection system (WIDS).
- Physically put the AP at the center of the building. The AP has a specific zone of coverage it can provide.
- Logically put the AP in a DMZ with a firewall between the DMZ and internal network. Allow the firewall to investigate the traffic before it gets to the wired network.
- Implement VPN for wireless devices to use. This adds another layer of protection for data being transmitted.
- Configure the AP to allow only known MAC addresses into the network. Allow only known devices to authenticate. But remember that these MAC addresses are sent in cleartext, so an attacker could capture them and masquerade himself as an authenticated device.
- Carry out penetration tests on the WLAN. Use the tools described in this section to identify APs and attempt to break the current encryption scheme being used.

Satellites

Today, satellites are used to provide wireless connectivity between different locations. For two different locations to communicate via satellite links, they must be within the satellite's line of sight and *footprint* (area covered by the satellite). The sender of information (ground station) modulates the data onto a radio signal that is transmitted to the satellite. A transponder on the satellite receives this signal, amplifies it, and relays it to the receiver. The receiver must have a type of antenna—one of those circular, dish-like things we see on top of buildings. The antenna contains one or more microwave receivers, depending upon how many satellites it is accepting data from.

Satellites provide broadband transmission that is commonly used for television channels and PC Internet access. If a user is receiving TV data, then the transmission is set up as a one-way network. If a user is using this connection for Internet connectivity, then the transmission is set up as a two-way network. The available bandwidth depends upon the antenna and terminal type and the service provided by the service provider. Time-sensitive applications can suffer from the delays experienced as the data goes to and from the satellite. These types of satellites are placed into a low Earth orbit, which means there is not as much distance between the ground stations and the satellites as in other types of satellites. In turn, this means smaller receivers can be used, which makes low-Earth-orbit satellites ideal for two-way paging, international cellular communication, TV stations, and Internet use.

NOTE The two main microwave wireless transmission technologies are satellite (ground to orbiter to ground) and terrestrial (ground to ground).

The size of the footprint depends upon the type of satellite being used. It can be as large as a country or only a few hundred feet in circumference. The footprint covers an area on the Earth for only a few hours or less, so the service provider usually has a large number of satellites dispatched to provide constant coverage at strategic areas.

In most cases, organizations will use a system known as a very small aperture terminal (VSAT), which links a remote office to the Internet through a satellite gateway facility run by a service provider, as shown in Figure 4-77. Alternatively, VSATs can be deployed in stand-alone networks in which the organization also places a VSAT at a central location and has all the remote ones reach into it with no need for a gateway facility. The data rates available can range from a few Kbps to several Mbps. Dropping prices have rendered this technology affordable to many midsized organizations.

Mobile Wireless Communication

Mobile wireless has now exploded into a trillion-dollar industry, with over 7.2 billion subscriptions, fueled by a succession of new technologies and by industry and international standard agreements.

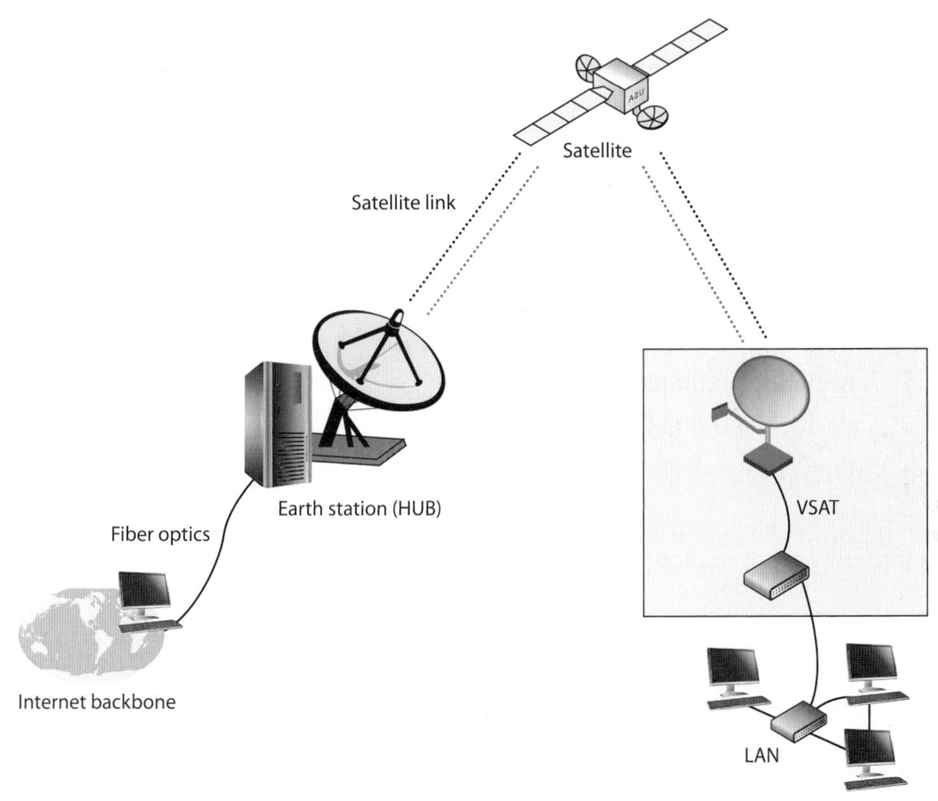

Figure 4-77 Satellite broadband

So what is a mobile phone anyway? It is a device that can send voice and data over wireless radio links. It connects to a cellular network, which is connected to the PSTN. So instead of needing a physical cord and connection that connects your phone and the PSTN, you have a device that allows you to indirectly connect to the PSTN as you move around a wide geographic area.

Radio stations use broadcast networks, which provide one-way transmissions. Mobile wireless communication is also a radio technology, but it works within a cellular network that employs two-way transmissions.

A cellular network distributes radio signals over delineated areas, called cells. Each cell has at least one fixed-location transceiver (base station) and is joined to other cells to provide connections over large geographic areas. So as you are talking on your mobile phone and you move out of range of one cell, the base station in the original cell sends your connection information to the next base station so that your call is not dropped and you can continue your conversation.

We do not have an infinite number of frequencies to work with when it comes to mobile communication. Millions of people around the world are using their cell phones as you read this. How can all of these calls take place if we only have one set of frequencies to use for such activity? A rudimentary depiction of a cellular network is shown in Figure 4-78. Individual cells can use the same frequency range, as long as they are not right next to each other. So the same frequency range can be used in every other cell, which drastically decreased the amount of ranges required to support simultaneous connections.

The industry had to come up with other ways to allow millions of users to be able to use this finite resource (frequency range) in a flexible manner. Over time, mobile wireless has been made up of progressively more complex and more powerful "multiple access" technologies, listed here:

- Frequency division multiple access (FDMA)
- Time division multiple access (TDMA)
- Code division multiple access (CDMA)
- Orthogonal frequency division multiple access (OFDMA)

We quickly go over the characteristics of each of these technologies because they are the foundational constructs of the various cellular network generations.

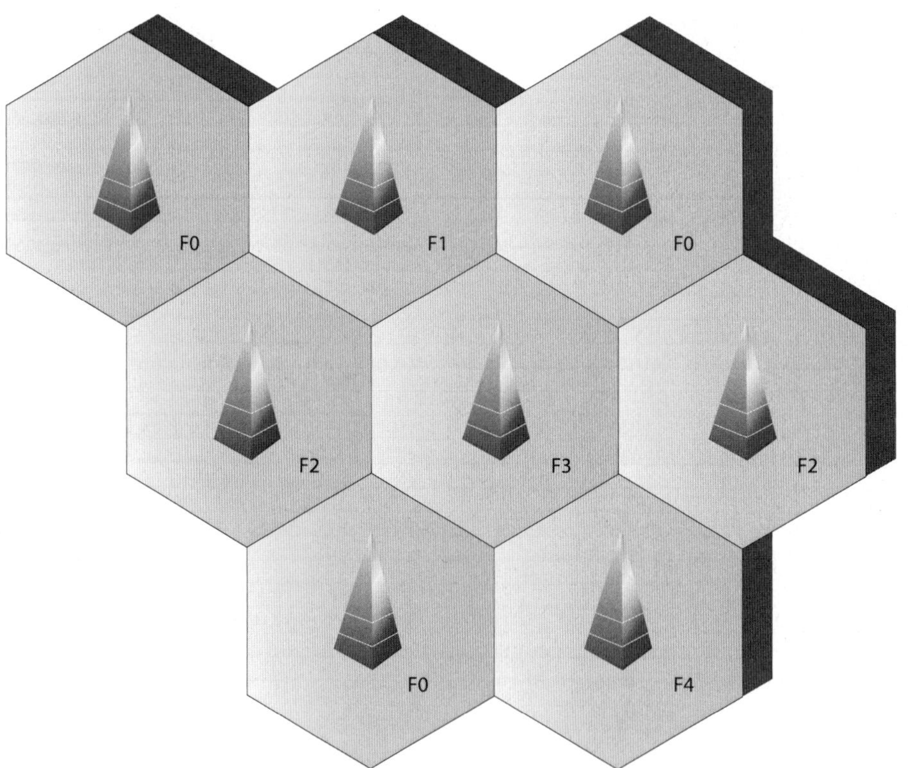

Figure 4-78 Nonadjacent cells can use the same frequency ranges.

Frequency division multiple access (FDMA) was the earliest multiple access technology put into practice. The available frequency range is divided into sub-bands (channels), and one channel is assigned to each subscriber (cell phone). The subscriber has exclusive use of that channel while the call is made, or until the call is terminated or handed off; no other calls or conversations can be made on that channel during that call. Using FDMA in this way, multiple users can share the frequency range without the risk of interference between the simultaneous calls. FDMA was used in the first generation (1G) of cellular networks. 1G mobile had various implementations, such as Advanced Mobile Phone System (AMPS), Total Access Communication System (TACS), and Nordic Mobile Telephone (NMT), used FDMA.

Time division multiple access (TDMA) increases the speed and efficiency of the cellular network by taking the radio-frequency spectrum channels and dividing them into time slots. At various time periods, multiple users can share the same channel; the systems within the cell swap from one user to another user, in effect, reusing the available frequencies. TDMA increased speeds and service quality. A common example of TDMA in action is a conversation. One person talks for a time and then quits, and then a different person talks. In TDMA systems, time is divided into frames. Each frame is divided into slots. TDMA requires that each slot's start and end time are known to both the source and the destination. Mobile communication systems such as Global System for Mobile Communication (GSM), Digital AMPS (D-AMPS), and Personal Digital Cellular (PDC) use TDMA.

Code division multiple access (CDMA) was developed after FDMA, and as the term "code" implies, CDMA assigns a unique code to each voice call or data transmission to uniquely identify it from all other transmissions sent over the cellular network. In a CDMA "spread spectrum" network, calls are spread throughout the entire radio-frequency band. CDMA permits every user of the network to simultaneously use every channel in the network. At the same time, a particular cell can simultaneously interact with multiple other cells. These features make CDMA a very powerful technology. It is the main technology for the mobile cellular networks that presently dominate the wireless space.

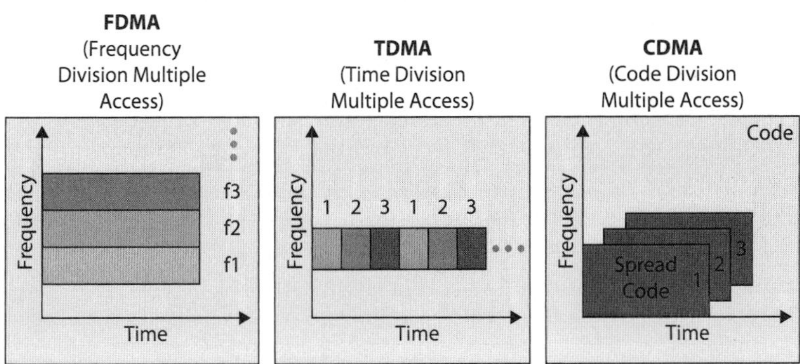

Orthogonal frequency division multiple access (OFDMA) is derived from a combination of FDMA and TDMA. In earlier implementations of FDMA, the different frequencies for each channel were widely spaced to allow analog hardware to separate the different channels. In OFDMA, each of the channels is subdivided into a set of closely spaced orthogonal frequencies with narrow bandwidths (subchannels). Each of the different subchannels can be transmitted and received simultaneously in a multiple input, multiple output (MIMO) manner. The use of orthogonal frequencies and MIMO allows signal processing techniques to reduce the impacts of any interference between different subchannels and to correct for channel impairments, such as noise and selective frequency fading. 4G requires that OFDMA be used.

Mobile wireless technologies have gone through a whirlwind of confusing generations. The first generation (1G) dealt with analog transmissions of voice-only data over circuit-switched networks. This generation provided a throughput of around 19.2 Kbps. The second generation (2G) allows for digitally encoded voice and data to be transmitted between wireless devices, such as cell phones, and content providers. TDMA, CDMA, GSM, and PCS all fall under the umbrella of 2G mobile telephony. This technology can transmit data over circuit-switched networks and supports data encryption, fax transmissions, and short message services (SMSs).

The third-generation (3G) networks became available around the turn of the century. Incorporating FDMA, TDMA, and CDMA, 3G had the flexibility to support a great variety of applications and services. Further, circuit switching was replaced with packet switching. Modular in design to allow ready expandability, backward compatibility with 2G networks, and stressing interoperability among mobile systems, 3G services greatly expanded the applications available to users, such as global roaming (without changing one's cell phone or cell phone number), as well as Internet services and multimedia.

Hacking Mobile Phones

2G networks lack the ability to authenticate towers to phones. In other words, an attacker can easily set up a rogue tower with more power than the nearby legitimate ones and cause the target's mobile phone to connect to it. This type of attack allows attackers to intercept all mobile phone traffic. Though 3G and 4G networks corrected this serious vulnerability, it is still possible to force most 3G and 4G phones to switch down to 2G mode by jamming 3G and 4G towers. In an effort to maintain some form of connectivity, most handsets will then switch down to the vulnerable 2G mode, making the attack possible again.

Devices designed to perform this type of attack are called International Mobile Subscriber Identity (IMSI) catchers. Initially intended for law enforcement and intelligence agency use, IMSI catchers are increasingly available to criminals in the black markets. Moreover, it is possible for anyone to build one of these attack platforms for less than $1,500 as Chris Paget demonstrated at DefCon in 2010. This is yet another example of how backward compatibility can perpetuate vulnerabilities in older protocols.

In addition, reflecting the ever-growing demand from users for greater speed, latency in 3G networks was much reduced as transmission speeds were enhanced. More enhancements to 3G networks, often referred to as 3.5G or as mobile broadband, are taking place under the rubric of the Third Generation Partnership Project (3GPP). 3GPP has a number of new or enhanced technologies. These include Enhanced Data Rates for GSM Evolution (EDGE), High-Speed Downlink Packet Access (HSDPA), CDMA2000, and Worldwide Interoperability for Microwave Access (WiMAX).

There are two competing technologies that fall under the umbrella of 4G, which are Mobile WiMAX and Long-Term Evolution (LTE). A 4G system does not support traditional circuit-switched telephony service as 3G does, but works over a purely packet-based network. 4G devices are IP-based and are based upon OFDMA instead of the previously used multiple carrier access technologies.

Research projects have started on fifth-generation (5G) mobile communication, but standards requirements and implementation are not expected until 2020.

Mobile Technology Generations

Like many technologies, the mobile communication technology has gone through several different generations.

First generation (1G):

- Analog services
- Voice service only

Second generation (2G):

- Primarily voice, some low-speed data (circuit switched)
- Phones were smaller in size
- Added functionality of e-mail, paging, and caller ID

Generation 2½ (2.5G):

- Higher bandwidth than 2G
- "Always on" technology for e-mail and pages

Third generation (3G):

- Integration of voice and data
- Packet-switched technology, instead of circuit-switched

(*Continued*)

Generation 3.5 G (3GPP)

- Higher data rates
- Use of OFDMA technology

Fourth generation (4G)

- Based on an all-IP packet-switched network
- Data exchange at 100 Mbps–1 Gbps

Each of the different mobile communication generations has taken advantage of the improvement of hardware technology and processing power. The increase in hardware has allowed for more complicated data transmission between users and hence the desire for more users to want to use mobile communications.

Table 4-16 illustrates some of the main features of the 1G through 4G networks. It is important to note that this table does not and cannot easily cover all the aspects of each generation. Earlier generations of mobile communication have considerable variability

	1G	2G	3G	4G
Spectrum	900 MHz	1,800 MHz	2 GHz	Various
Multiplexing Type	FDMA	TDMA	CDMA	OFDMA
Voice Support	Basic telephony	Caller ID and voicemail	Conference calls and low-quality video	High-definition video
Messaging Features	None	Text only	Graphics and formatted text	Full unified messaging
Data Support	None	Circuit switched (packet switched in 2.5G)	Packet switched	Native IPv6
Target Data Rate	N/A	115–128 Kbps	2 Mbps (10 Mbps in 3.5G)	100 Mbps (moving) 1 Gbps (stationary)
Interface with Other Devices	Acoustic coupler	RS232 serial cable or IrDA	IEEE 802.11 or Bluetooth	Seamless connection via multiple methods
Timeline	1980–1994	1995–2001	2002–2005	2010 onward

Table 4-16 The Different Characteristics of Mobile Technology

between countries. The variability was due to country-sponsored efforts before agreed-upon international standards were established. Various efforts between the ITU and countries have attempted to minimize the differences.

NOTE While it would be great if the mobile wireless technology generations broke down into clear-cut definitions, they do not. This is because various parts of the world use different foundational technologies, and there are several competing vendors in the space with their own proprietary approaches.

Network Encryption

At this point in our discussion, we have touched on every major technology relevant to modern networks. Along the way, as we paused to consider vulnerabilities and controls, a recurring theme revolves around the use of encryption to protect the confidentiality and integrity of our data. Let us now take a look at three specific applications of encryption to protect our data communications in general and our email and web traffic in particular.

Link Encryption vs. End-to-End Encryption

In each of the networking technologies discussed in this chapter, encryption can be performed at different levels, each with different types of protection and implications. Two general modes of encryption implementation are link encryption and end-to-end encryption. *Link encryption* encrypts all the data along a specific communication path, as in a satellite link, T3 line, or telephone circuit. Not only is the user information encrypted, but the header, trailers, addresses, and routing data that are part of the packets are also encrypted. The only traffic not encrypted in this technology is the data link control messaging information, which includes instructions and parameters that the different link devices use to synchronize communication methods. Link encryption provides protection against packet sniffers and eavesdroppers. In *end-to-end encryption*, the headers, addresses, routing information, and trailer information are not encrypted, enabling attackers to learn more about a captured packet and where it is headed.

Link encryption, which is sometimes called *online encryption*, is usually provided by service providers and is incorporated into network protocols. All of the information is encrypted, and the packets must be decrypted at each hop so the router, or other intermediate device, knows where to send the packet next. The router must decrypt the header portion of the packet, read the routing and address information within the header, and then re-encrypt it and send it on its way.

With end-to-end encryption, the packets do not need to be decrypted and then encrypted again at each hop because the headers and trailers are not encrypted. The devices in between the origin and destination just read the necessary routing information and pass the packets on their way.

End-to-end encryption is usually initiated by the user of the originating computer. It provides more flexibility for the user to be able to determine whether or not certain messages will get encrypted. It is called "end-to-end encryption" because the message stays encrypted from one end of its journey to the other. Link encryption has to decrypt the packets at every device between the two ends.

Encryption at Different Layers

In reality, encryption can happen at different layers of an operating system and network stack. The following are just a few examples:

- End-to-end encryption happens within the applications.
- TLS encryption takes place at the session layer.
- PPTP encryption takes place at the data link layer.
- Link encryption takes place at the data link and physical layers.

Link encryption occurs at the data link and physical layers, as depicted in Figure 4-79. Hardware encryption devices interface with the physical layer and encrypt all data that passes through them. Because no part of the data is available to an attacker, the attacker cannot learn basic information about how data flows through the environment. This is referred to as *traffic-flow security*.

NOTE A *hop* is a device that helps a packet reach its destination. It is usually a router that looks at the packet address to determine where the packet needs to go next. Packets usually go through many hops between the sending and receiving computers.

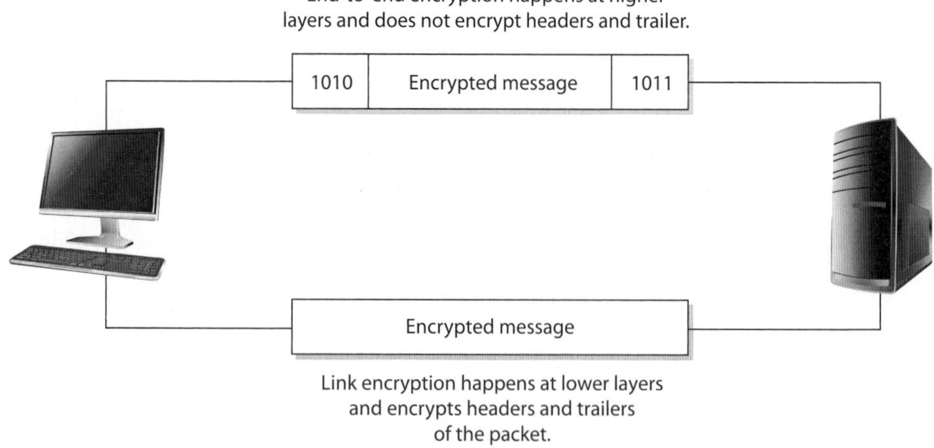

Figure 4-79 Link and end-to-end encryption happen at different OSI layers.

Advantages of end-to-end encryption include the following:

- It provides more flexibility to the user in choosing what gets encrypted and how.
- Higher granularity of functionality is available because each application or user can choose specific configurations.
- Each hop device on the network does not need to have a key to decrypt each packet.

Disadvantages of end-to-end encryption include the following:

- Headers, addresses, and routing information are not encrypted, and therefore not protected.

Hardware vs. Software Cryptography Systems

Encryption can be done through software or hardware, and there are trade-offs with each. Generally, software is less expensive and provides a slower throughput than hardware mechanisms. Software cryptography methods can be more easily modified and disabled compared to hardware systems, but it depends on the application and the hardware product.

If a company needs to perform high-end encryption functions at a higher speed, the company will most likely implement a hardware solution.

Advantages of link encryption include the following:

- All data is encrypted, including headers, addresses, and routing information.
- Users do not need to do anything to initiate it. It works at a lower layer in the OSI model.

Disadvantages of link encryption include the following:

- Key distribution and management are more complex because each hop device must receive a key, and when the keys change, each must be updated.
- Packets are decrypted at each hop; thus, more points of vulnerability exist.

E-mail Encryption Standards

Like other types of technologies, cryptography has industry standards and de facto standards. Standards are necessary because they help ensure interoperability among vendor products. The existence of standards for a certain technology usually means that it has been under heavy scrutiny and has been properly tested and accepted by many similar technology communities. A company still needs to decide what type of standard to follow and what type of technology to implement.

A company needs to evaluate the functionality of the technology and perform a cost-benefit analysis on the competing products within the chosen standards. For a cryptography implementation, the company would need to decide what must be protected by encryption, whether digital signatures are necessary, how key management should take place, what types of resources are available to implement and maintain the technology, and what the overall cost will amount to.

If a company only needs to encrypt some e-mail messages here and there, then Pretty Good Privacy (PGP) may be the best choice. If the company wants all data encrypted as it goes throughout the network and to sister companies, then a link encryption implementation may be the best choice. If a company wants to implement a single sign-on environment where users need to authenticate to use different services and functionality throughout the network, then implementing a PKI or Kerberos might serve it best. To make the most informed decision, the network administrators should understand each type of technology and standard, and should research and test each competing product within the chosen technology before making the final purchase. Cryptography, including how to implement and maintain it, can be a complicated subject. Doing homework versus buying into buzzwords and flashy products might help a company reduce its headaches down the road.

The following sections briefly describe some of the most popular e-mail standards in use.

Multipurpose Internet Mail Extensions

Multipurpose Internet Mail Extensions (MIME) is a technical specification indicating how multimedia data and e-mail binary attachments are to be transferred. The Internet has mail standards that dictate how mail is to be formatted, encapsulated, transmitted, and opened. If a message or document contains a binary attachment, MIME dictates how that portion of the message should be handled.

When an attachment contains an audio clip, graphic, or some other type of multimedia component, the e-mail client will send the file with a header that describes the file type. For example, the header might indicate that the MIME type is Image and that the subtype is JPEG. Although this will be in the header, many times, systems also use the file's extension to identify the MIME type. So, in the preceding example, the file's name might be stuff.jpeg. The user's system will see the extension .jpeg, or will see the data in the header field, and look in its association list to see what program it needs to initialize to open this particular file. If the system has JPEG files associated with the Explorer application, then Explorer will open and present the picture to the user.

Sometimes systems either do not have an association for a specific file type or do not have the helper program necessary to review and use the contents of the file. When a file has an unassociated icon assigned to it, it might require the user to choose the Open With command and choose an application in the list to associate this file with that program. So when the user double-clicks that file, the associated program will initialize and present the file. If the system does not have the necessary program, the website might offer the necessary helper program, like Acrobat or an audio program that plays WAV files.

MIME is a specification that dictates how certain file types should be transmitted and handled. This specification has several types and subtypes, enables different computers to exchange data in varying formats, and provides a standardized way of presenting the data. So if Sean views a funny picture that is in GIF format, he can be sure that when he sends it to Debbie, it will look exactly the same.

Secure MIME (S/MIME) is a standard for encrypting and digitally signing e-mail and for providing secure data transmissions. S/MIME extends the MIME standard by allowing for the encryption of e-mail and attachments. The encryption and hashing algorithms can be specified by the user of the mail application, instead of having it dictated to them. S/MIME follows the Public Key Cryptography Standards (PKCS). S/MIME provides confidentiality through encryption algorithms, integrity through hashing algorithms, authentication through the use of X.509 public key certificates, and nonrepudiation through cryptographically signed message digests.

Pretty Good Privacy

Pretty Good Privacy (PGP) was designed by Phil Zimmerman as a freeware e-mail security program and was released in 1991. It was the first widespread public key encryption program. PGP is a complete cryptosystem that uses cryptographic protection to protect e-mail and files. It can use RSA public key encryption for key management and use the IDEA symmetric cipher for bulk encryption of data, although the user has the option of picking different types of algorithms for these functions. PGP can provide confidentiality by using the IDEA encryption algorithm, integrity by using the MD5 hashing algorithm, authentication by using public key certificates, and nonrepudiation by using cryptographically signed messages. PGP uses its own type of digital certificates rather than what is used in PKI, but they both have similar purposes.

The user's private key is generated and encrypted when the application asks the user to randomly type on her keyboard for a specific amount of time. Instead of using passwords, PGP uses passphrases. The passphrase is used to encrypt the user's private key that is stored on her hard drive.

PGP does not use a hierarchy of CAs, or any type of formal trust certificates, but instead relies on a "web of trust" in its key management approach. Each user generates and distributes his or her public key, and users sign each other's public keys, which creates a community of users who trust each other. This is different from the CA approach, where no one trusts each other; they only trust the CA. For example, if Mark and Joe want to communicate using PGP, Mark can give his public key to Joe. Joe signs Mark's key and keeps a copy for himself. Then, Joe gives a copy of his public key to Mark so they can start communicating securely. Later, Mark would like to communicate with Sally, but Sally does not know Mark and does not know if she can trust him. Mark sends Sally his public key, which has been signed by Joe. Sally has Joe's public key, because they have communicated before, and she trusts Joe. Because Joe signed Mark's public key, Sally now also trusts Mark and sends her public key to him and begins communicating with him.

So, basically, PGP is a system of "I don't know you, but my buddy Joe says you are an all right guy, so I will trust you on Joe's word."

Each user keeps in a file, referred to as a *key ring*, a collection of public keys he has received from other users. Each key in that ring has a parameter that indicates the level of trust assigned to that user and the validity of that particular key. If Steve has known

Liz for many years and trusts her, he might have a higher level of trust indicated on her stored public key than on Tom's, whom he does not trust much at all. There is also a field indicating who can sign other keys within Steve's realm of trust. If Steve receives a key from someone he doesn't know, like Kevin, and the key is signed by Liz, he can look at the field that pertains to whom he trusts to sign other people's keys. If the field indicates that Steve trusts Liz enough to sign another person's key, Steve will accept Kevin's key and communicate with him because Liz is vouching for him. However, if Steve receives a key from Kevin and it is signed by untrustworthy Tom, Steve might choose to not trust Kevin and not communicate with him.

These fields are available for updating and alteration. If one day Steve really gets to know Tom and finds out he is okay after all, he can modify these parameters within PGP and give Tom more trust when it comes to cryptography and secure communication.

Because the web of trust does not have a central leader, such as a CA, certain standardized functionality is harder to accomplish. If Steve were to lose his private key, he would need to notify everyone else trusting his public key that it should no longer be trusted. In a PKI, Steve would only need to notify the CA, and anyone attempting to verify the validity of Steve's public key would be told not to trust it upon looking at the most recently updated CRL. In the PGP world, this is not as centralized and organized. Steve can send out a key revocation certificate, but there is no guarantee it will reach each user's key ring file.

PGP is a public domain software that uses public key cryptography. It has not been endorsed by the NSA, but because it is a great product and free for individuals to use, it has become somewhat of a de facto encryption standard on the Internet.

NOTE PGP is considered a cryptosystem because it has all the necessary components: symmetric key algorithms, asymmetric key algorithms, message digest algorithms, keys, protocols, and the necessary software components.

Internet Security

The Web is not the Internet. The Web runs on top of the Internet, in a sense. The Web is the collection of HTTP servers that holds and processes websites we see. The Internet is the collection of physical devices and communication protocols used to traverse these websites and interact with them. The websites look the way they do because their creators used a language that dictates the look, feel, and functionality of the page. Web browsers enable users to read web pages by enabling them to request and accept web pages via HTTP, and the user's browser converts the language (HTML, DHTML, and XML) into a format that can be viewed on the monitor. The browser is the user's window to the World Wide Web.

Browsers can understand a variety of protocols and have the capability to process many types of commands, but they do not understand them all. For those protocols or commands the user's browser does not know how to process, the user can download and install a viewer or plug-in, a modular component of code that integrates itself into the system or browser. This is a quick and easy way to expand the functionality of the browser. However, this can cause serious security compromises, because the payload of the module can easily carry viruses and malicious software that users don't discover until it's too late.

Start with the Basics

Why do we connect to the Internet? At first, this seems a basic question, but as we dive deeper into the query, complexity creeps in. We connect to download MP3s, check e-mail, order security books, look at websites, communicate with friends, and perform various other tasks. But what are we really doing? We are using services provided by a computer's protocols and software. The services may be file transfers provided by FTP, remote connectivity provided by Telnet, Internet connectivity provided by HTTP, secure connections provided by TLS, and much, much more. Without these protocols, there would be no way to even connect to the Internet.

Management needs to decide what functionality employees should have pertaining to Internet use, and the administrator must implement these decisions by controlling services that can be used inside and outside the network. Services can be restricted in various ways, such as allowing certain services to only run on a particular system and to restrict access to that system; employing a secure version of a service; filtering the use of services; or blocking services altogether. These choices determine how secure the site will be and indicate what type of technology is needed to provide this type of protection.

Let's go through many of the technologies and protocols that make up the World Wide Web.

HTTP TCP/IP is the protocol suite of the Internet, and HTTP is the protocol of the Web. HTTP sits on top of TCP/IP. When a user clicks a link on a web page with her mouse, her browser uses HTTP to send a request to the web server hosting that website. The web server finds the corresponding file to that link and sends it to the user via HTTP. So where is TCP/IP in all of this? TCP controls the handshaking and maintains the connection between the user and the server, and IP makes sure the file is routed properly throughout the Internet to get from the web server to the user. So, IP finds the way to get from A to Z, TCP makes sure the origin and destination are correct and that no packets are lost along the way, and, upon arrival at the destination, HTTP presents the payload, which is a web page.

HTTP is a stateless protocol, which means the client and web server make and break a connection for each operation. When a user requests to view a web page, that web server finds the requested web page, presents it to the user, and then terminates the connection. If the user requests a link within the newly received web page, a new connection must be set up, the request goes to the web server, and the web server sends the requested item and breaks the connection. The web server never "remembers" the users that ask for different web pages, because it would have to commit a lot of resources to the effort.

HTTP Secure *HTTP Secure (HTTPS)* is HTTP running over Secure Sockets Layer (SSL) or Transport Layer Security (TLS). Both of these technologies work to encrypt traffic originating at a higher layer in the OSI model. Though we will discuss SSL next (since it is still in use), you must keep in mind that this technology is now widely regarded as insecure and obsolete. The Internet Engineering Task Force formally deprecated it in June 2015. TLS should be used in its place.

Secure Sockets Layer *Secure Sockets Layer (SSL)* uses public key encryption and provides data encryption, server authentication, message integrity, and optional client authentication. When a client accesses a website, that website may have both secured and public portions. The secured portion would require the user to be authenticated in some fashion. When the client goes from a public page on the website to a secured page, the web server will start the necessary tasks to invoke SSL and protect this type of communication.

The server sends a message back to the client, indicating a secure session should be established, and the client in response sends its security parameters. The server compares those security parameters to its own until it finds a match. This is the handshaking phase. The server authenticates to the client by sending it a digital certificate, and if the client decides to trust the server, the process continues. The server can require the client to send over a digital certificate for mutual authentication, but that is rare.

The client generates a session key and encrypts it with the server's public key. This encrypted key is sent to the web server, and they both use this symmetric key to encrypt the data they send back and forth. This is how the secure channel is established.

SSL keeps the communication path open until one of the parties requests to end the session. The session is usually ended when the client sends the server a FIN packet, which is an indication to close out the channel.

SSL requires an SSL-enabled server and browser. SSL provides security for the connection, but does not offer security for the data once received. This means the data is encrypted while being transmitted, but not after the data is received by a computer. So if a user sends bank account information to a financial institution via a connection protected by SSL, that communication path is protected, but the user must trust the financial institution that receives this information, because at this point, SSL's job is done.

The user can verify that a connection is secure by looking at the URL to see that it includes https://. The user can also check for a padlock or key icon, depending on the browser type, which is shown at the bottom corner of the browser window.

In the protocol stack, SSL lies beneath the application layer and above the network layer. This ensures SSL is not limited to specific application protocols and can still use the communication transport standards of the Internet. Different books and technical resources place SSL at different layers of the OSI model, which may seem confusing at first. But the OSI model is a conceptual construct that attempts to describe the reality of networking. This is like trying to draw nice neat boxes around life—some things don't fit perfectly and hang over the sides. SSL is actually made up of two protocols: one works at the lower end of the session layer, and the other works at the top of the transport layer. This is why one resource will state that SSL works at the session layer and another resource puts it in the transport layer. For the purposes of the CISSP exam, we'll use the latter definition: the SSL protocol works at the transport layer.

Although SSL is almost always used with HTTP, it can also be used with other types of protocols. So if you see a common protocol that is followed by an *S*, that protocol is using SSL to encrypt its data. The final version of SSL was 3.0. SSL is considered insecure today.

Transport Layer Security SSL was developed by Netscape and is not an open-community protocol. This means the technology community cannot easily extend SSL to interoperate and expand in its functionality. If a protocol is proprietary in nature, as SSL is, the technology community cannot directly change its specifications and functionality. If the protocol is an open-community protocol, then its specifications can be modified by individuals within the community to expand what it can do and what technologies it can work with. So the open-community and standardized version of SSL is *Transport Layer Security (TLS).*

Until relatively recently, most people thought that there were very few differences between SSL 3.0 and TLS 1.0 (TLS is currently in version 1.2.). However, the Padding Oracle On Downgraded Legacy Encryption (POODLE) attack in 2014 was the death knell of SSL and demonstrated that TLS was superior security-wise. The key to the attack was to force SSL to downgrade its security, which was allowed for the sake of interoperability. Because TLS implements tighter controls and includes more modern (and more secure) hashing and encryption algorithms, it won the day and is now the standard.

TLS is commonly used when data needs to be encrypted while "in transit," which means as the data is moving from one system to another system. Data must also be encrypted while "at rest," which is when the data is stored. Encryption of data at rest can be accomplished by whole-disk encryption, PGP, or other types of software-based encryption.

Cookies *Cookies* are text files that a browser maintains on a user's hard drive or memory segment. Cookies have different uses, and some are used for demographic and advertising information. As a user travels from site to site on the Internet, the sites could be writing data to the cookies stored on the user's system. The sites can keep track of the user's browsing and spending habits and the user's specific customization for certain sites. For example, if Emily mainly goes to gardening sites on the Internet, those sites will most likely record this information and the types of items in which she shows most interest. Then, when Emily returns to one of the same or similar sites, it will retrieve her cookies, find she has shown interest in gardening books in the past, and present her with its line of gardening books. This increases the likelihood that Emily will purchase a book. This is a way of zeroing in on the right marketing tactics for the right person.

The servers at the website determine how cookies are actually used. When a user adds items to his shopping cart on a site, such data is usually added to a cookie. Then, when the user is ready to check out and pay for his items, all the data in this specific cookie is extracted and the totals are added.

As stated before, HTTP is a stateless protocol, meaning a web server has no memory of any prior connections. This is one reason to use cookies. They retain the memory between HTTP connections by saving prior connection data to the client's computer.

For example, if you carry out your banking activities online, your bank's web server keeps track of your activities through the use of cookies. When you first go to its site and are looking at public information, such as branch locations, hours of operation, and CD rates, no confidential information is being transferred back and forth. Once you make a request to access your bank account, the web server sets up an TLS connection and requires you to send credentials. Once you send your credentials and are authenticated, the server generates a cookie with your authentication and account information in it. The server sends it to your browser, which either saves it to your hard drive or keeps it in memory.

NOTE Some cookies are stored as text files on your hard drive. These files should not contain any sensitive information, such as account numbers and passwords. In most cases, cookies that contain sensitive information stay resident in memory and are not stored on the hard drive.

So, suppose you look at your checking account, do some work there, and then request to view your savings account information. The web server sends a request to see if you have been properly authenticated for this activity by checking your cookie.

Most online banking software also periodically requests your cookie to ensure no man-in-the-middle attacks are going on and that someone else has not hijacked the session.

It is also important to ensure that secure connections time out. This is why cookies have timestamps within them. If you have ever worked on a site that has an TLS connection set up for you and it required you to reauthenticate, the reason is that your session has been idle for a while and, instead of leaving a secure connection open, the web server software closed it out.

A majority of the data within a cookie is meaningless to any entities other than the servers at specific sites, but some cookies can contain usernames and passwords for different accounts on the Internet. The cookies that contain sensitive information should be encrypted by the server at the site that distributes them, but this does not always happen, and a nosy attacker could find this data on the user's hard drive and attempt to use it for mischievous activity. Some people who live on the paranoid side of life do not allow cookies to be downloaded to their systems (which can be configured through browser security settings). Although this provides a high level of protection against different types of cookie abuse, it also reduces their functionality on the Internet. Some sites require cookies because there is specific data within the cookies that the site must utilize correctly in order to provide the user with the services she requested.

TIP Some third-party products can limit the type of cookies downloaded, hide the user's identities as he travels from one site to the next, and mask the user's e-mail addresses and the mail servers he uses if he is concerned about concealing his identity and his tracks.

Secure Shell *Secure Shell (SSH)* functions as a type of tunneling mechanism that provides terminal-like access to remote computers. SSH is a program and a protocol that can be used to log into another computer over a network. For example, the program can

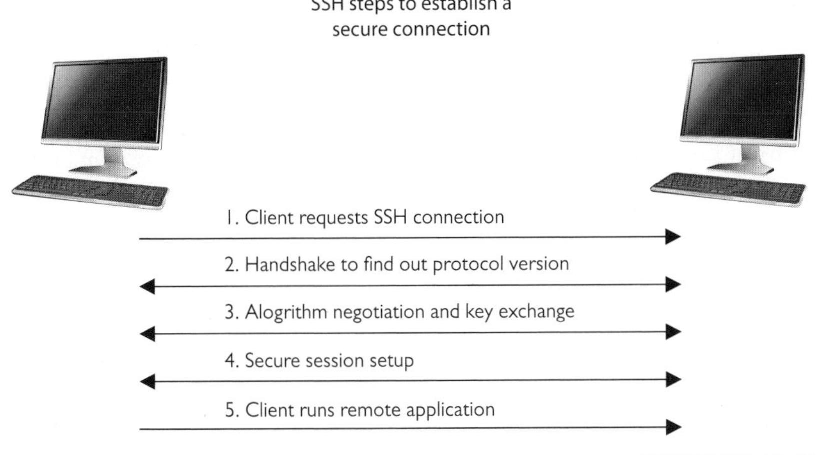
SSH steps to establish a
secure connection
1. Client requests SSH connection
2. Handshake to find out protocol version
3. Alogrithm negotiation and key exchange
4. Secure session setup
5. Client runs remote application

Figure 4-80 SSH is used for remote terminal-like functionality.

let Paul, who is on computer A, access computer B's files, run applications on computer B, and retrieve files from computer B without ever physically touching that computer. SSH provides authentication and secure transmission over vulnerable channels like the Internet.

NOTE SSH can also be used for secure channels for file transfer and port redirection.

SSH should be used instead of Telnet, FTP, rlogin, rexec, or rsh, which provide the same type of functionality SSH offers but in a much less secure manner. SSH is a program and a set of protocols that work together to provide a secure tunnel between two computers. The two computers go through a handshaking process and exchange (via Diffie-Hellman) a session key that will be used during the session to encrypt and protect the data sent. The steps of an SSH connection are outlined in Figure 4-80.

Once the handshake takes place and a secure channel is established, the two computers have a pathway to exchange data with the assurance that the information will be encrypted and its integrity will be protected.

Secure channel

Network Attacks

Our networks continue to be the primary vector for attacks, and there is no reason to believe this will change anytime soon. If you think about it, this makes perfect sense because it allows a cybercriminal across the world to empty out your bank account from the comfort of her own basement, or a foreign nation to steal your personnel files without having to infiltrate a spy into your country. In the sections that follow we will highlight some of the most problematic types of attacks and what we can do about them.

Denial of Service

A *denial-of-service (DoS)* attack can take many forms, but at its essence is a compromise to the availability leg of the AIC triad. A DoS attack results in a service or resource being degraded or made unavailable to legitimate users. By this definition, the theft of a server from our server room would constitute a DoS attack, but for this discussion we will limit ourselves to attacks that take place over a network and involve software.

Malformed Packets

At the birth of the Internet, malformed packets enjoyed a season of notoriety as the tool of choice for disrupting networks. Protocol implementations such as IP and ICMP were in their infancy and there was no shortage of vulnerabilities to be found and exploited. Perhaps the most famous of these (and certainly the one with the most colorful name) was the *Ping of Death*. This attack sent a single ICMP Echo Request to a computer, which resulted in the "death" of its network stack until it was restarted. This attack exploited the fact that many early networking stacks did not enforce the maximum length for an ICMP packet, which is 65,536 bytes. If an attacker sent a ping that was bigger than that, many common operating systems would become unstable and ultimately freeze or crash. While the Ping of Death is a relic from our past, it is illustrative of an entire class of attacks that is with us still.

Defending against this kind of attack is a moving target, because new vulnerabilities are always being discovered in our software systems. The single most important countermeasure here is to keep your systems patched. This will protect you against known vulnerabilities, but what about the rest? Your best bet is to carefully monitor the traffic on your networks and look for oddities (a 66KB ping packet should stand out, right?). This requires a fairly mature security operation and obviously has a high cost. Something else you can do is to subscribe to threat feeds that will give you a heads up whenever anyone else in your provider's network gets hit with a new attack of this type. If you are able to respond promptly, you can reconfigure your firewalls to block the attack before it is effective.

Flooding

Attackers today have another technique that does not require them to figure out an implementation error that results in the opportunity to use a malformed packet to get their work done. This approach is simply to overwhelm the target computer with packets until it is unable to process legitimate user requests. An illustrative example of this technique is called *SYN flooding*, which is an attack that exploits the three-way handshake that TCP uses to establish connections. Recall from earlier in this chapter that TCP connections are established by the client first sending a SYN packet, followed by a SYN/ACK packet from the server, and finally an ACK packet from the client. The server has no way of knowing which connection requests are malicious, so it responds to all of them. All the attacker has to do is send a steady stream of SYN packets, while ignoring the server's responses. The server has a limited amount of buffer space in which to store these half-open connections, so if the attacker can send enough SYN packets, he could fill up this buffer, which results in the server dropping all subsequent connection requests.

Of course, the server will eventually release any half-open connections after a timeout period, and you also have to keep in mind that memory is cheap these days and these buffers tend to be pretty big in practice. Still, all is not lost for the attackers. All they have to do is get enough volume through and they will eventually overwhelm pretty much anyone. How do they get this volume? Why not enlist the help of many tens or hundreds of thousands of hijacked computers? This is the technique we will cover next.

Network-based DoS attacks are fairly rare these days for reasons we will go over in the next section on DDoS. We will therefore defer our discussion of countermeasures until then, since they are the same for both DoS and DDoS.

Distributed Denial of Service

A *distributed denial-of-service (DDoS)* attack is identical to a DoS attack except the volume is much greater. The attacker chooses the flooding technique they want to employ (SYN, ICMP, DNS) and then instruct an army of hijacked or zombie computers to attack at a specific time. Where do these computers come from? Every day, tens of thousands of computers are infected with malware, typically when their users click a link to a malicious website (see the upcoming section "Drive-by Download") or open an attachment on an e-mail message. As part of the infection, and after the cybercriminals extract any useful information like banking information and passwords, the computer is told to execute a program that connects it to a command and control (C&C) network. At this point, the cybercriminals can issue commands, such as "start sending SYN packets as fast as you can to this IP address," to it and to thousands of other similarly infected machines on the same C&C network. Each of these computers is called a *zombie* or a *bot*, and the network they form is called a *botnet*.

Not too long ago, attackers who aspired to launch DDoS attacks had to build their own botnets, which is obviously no small task. We have recently seen the commercialization of botnets. The current model seems to be that a relatively small number of organizations own and rent extremely large botnets numbering in the hundreds of thousands of bots. If you know where to look and have a few hundred dollars to spare, it is not difficult to launch a massive DDoS attack using these resources.

What can you do to defend your network against a barrage of traffic numbering in the gigabits of bandwidth? One of the best, though costliest, approaches is to leverage a content distribution network (CDN), discussed earlier in this chapter. By distributing your Internet points of presence across a very large area using very robust servers, you force the attacker to use an extremely massive botnet. This can be undesirable to the attacker because of the added monetary cost or the risk of exposing one of the few and very precious mega-botnets.

Other countermeasures can be done in house. For instance, if the attack is fairly simple and you can isolate the IP addresses of the malicious traffic, then you can block those addresses at your firewall. Most modern switches and routers have rate-limiting features that can throttle or block the traffic from particularly noisy sources such as these attackers. Finally, if the attack happens to be a SYN flood, you can configure your servers to use a technique known as *delayed binding* in which the half-open connection is not allowed to tie up (or bind to) a socket until the three-way handshake is completed.

Ransomware

There has been an uptick in the use of ransomware for financial profit in recent years. This attack works similarly to the process by which a computer is exploited and made to join a botnet. However, in the case of ransomware, instead of making the computer a bot (or maybe in addition to doing so), the attacker encrypts all user files on the target. The victim receives a message stating that if they want their files back they have to pay a certain amount. When the victim pays, they receive the encryption key together with instructions on how to decrypt their drives and go on with their lives. Interestingly, these cybercriminals appear to be very good at keeping their word here. Their motivation is to have their reliability be spread by word of mouth so that future victims are more willing to pay the ransom.

There is no unique defense against this type of attack, because it is difficult for an attacker to pull off if you are practicing good network hygiene. The following list of standard practices is not all-inclusive, but it is a very solid starting point:

- Keep your software's security patches up to date. Ideally, all your software gets patched automatically.
- Use host-based antimalware software and ensure the signatures are up to date.
- Use spam filters for your e-mail.
- Never open attachments from unknown sources. As a matter of fact, even if you know the source, don't open unexpected attachments without first checking with that person. (It is way too easy to spoof an e-mail's source address.)
- Before clicking a link in an e-mail, float your mouse over it (or right-click the link) to see where it will actually take you. If in doubt (and you trust the site), type the URL in the web browser yourself rather than clicking the link.
- Be very careful about visiting unfamiliar or shady websites.

Sniffing

Network eavesdropping, or *sniffing*, is an attack on the confidentiality of our data. The good news is that it requires a sniffing agent on the inside of our network. That is to say, the attacker must first breach the network and install a sniffer before he is able to carry out the attack. The even better news is that it is possible to detect sniffing because it requires the NIC to be placed in *promiscuous mode*, meaning the NIC's default behavior is overridden and it no longer drops all frames not intended for it. The bad news is that network breaches are all too common and many organizations don't search for interfaces in promiscuous mode.

Sniffing plays an important role in the maintenance and defense of our networks, so it's not all bad. It is very difficult to troubleshoot many network issues without using this technique. The obvious difference is that when the adversary (or at least an unauthorized user) does it, it is quite possible that sensitive information will be compromised.

DNS Hijacking

DNS hijacking is an attack that forces the victim to use a malicious DNS server instead of the legitimate one. The techniques for doing this fairly simple and fall into one of three categories as described next.

- **Host based** Conceptually, this is the simplest hijacking attack in that the adversary just changes the IP settings of the victim's computer to point to the rogue DNS server. Obviously, this requires physical or logical access to the target and typically calls for administrator privileges on it.
- **Network based** In this approach, the adversary is in your network, but not in the client or the DNS server. He could use a technique such as ARP table cache poisoning, described earlier in this chapter, to redirect DNS traffic to his own server.
- **Server based** If the legitimate DNS server is not configured properly, an attacker can tell this server that his own rouge server is the authoritative one for whatever domains he wants to hijack. Thereafter, whenever the legitimate server receives a request for the hijacked domains, it will forward it to the rogue server automatically.

DNS hijacking can be done for a variety of reasons, but is particularly useful for man-in-the-middle attacks. In this scenario, the adversary reroutes all your traffic intended for your bank and hijacks it to his own web server, which presents you with a logon page that is identical to (and probably ripped from) your bank's website. He can then bypass the certificate warnings by giving you a page that is not protected by HTTPS. When you provide your login credentials (in cleartext), he uses them to log into your bank using a separate, encrypted connection. If the bank requires two-factor authentication (e.g., a one-time password), the attacker will pass the request to you and allow you to provide the information, which he then relays to the bank.

Another scenario is one in which the attacker wants to send you to a website of her choosing so that you get infected with malware via a drive-by download, as described in the following section.

There are many other scenarios in which attackers attempt DNS hijacking, but let's pause here and see what we can do to protect ourselves against this threat. As before, we will break this down into three categories depending on the attack vector.

- **Host based** Again, the standard defensive measures we've covered before for end-user computers apply here. The attackers need to compromise your computer first, so if you can keep them out, then this vector is more difficult for them.
- **Network based** Since this attack relies on manipulating network traffic with techniques such as ARP poisoning, watching your network is your best bet. Every popular network intrusion detection system (NIDS) available today has the ability to detect this.
- **Server based** A properly configured DNS server will be a lot more resistant to this sort of attack. If you are unfamiliar with the ins and outs of DNS configuration, find a friend who is or hire a contractor. It will be worth it! Better yet, implement DNSSEC in your organization to drive the risk even lower.

Drive-by Download

A *drive-by download* occurs when a user visits a website that is hosting malicious code and automatically gets infected. This kind of attack exploits vulnerabilities in the user's web browser or, more commonly, in a browser plug-in such as a video player. The website itself could be legitimate, but vulnerable to the attacker. Typically, the user visits the site and is redirected (perhaps invisibly) to wherever the attacker has his malicious code. This code will probe the user's browser for vulnerabilities and, upon finding one, craft an exploit and payload for that user. Once infected, the malware goes to work turning the computer into a zombie, harvesting useful information and uploading it to the malicious site, or encrypting the contents of the hard-drive in the case of a ransomware attack.

Drive-by downloads are one of the most common and dangerous attack vectors, because they require no user interaction besides visiting a website. From there, it takes fractions of a second for the infection to be complete. So what can we do about them? The key is that the most common exploits attack the browser plug-ins. To protect users from this type of attack, ensure that all plug-ins are patched and (here is the important part) disabled by default. If a user visits a website and wants to watch a video, this should require user interaction (e.g., clicking a control that enables the plug-in). Similarly, Java (another common attack vector) should require manual enabling on a case-by-case basis. By taking these steps, the risk of infection from drive-by downloads is reduced significantly.

Admittedly, the users are not going to like this extra step, which is where an awareness campaign comes in handy. If you are able to show your users the risk in an impactful way, they may be more willing to go along with the need for an extra click next time they want to watch a video of a squirrel water-skiing.

Summary

This chapter touched on many of the different technologies within different types of networks, including how they work together to provide an environment in which users can communicate, share resources, and be productive. Each piece of networking is important to security, because almost any piece can introduce unwanted vulnerabilities and weaknesses into the infrastructure. It is important you understand how the various devices, protocols, authentication mechanisms, and services work individually and how they interface and interact with other entities. This may appear to be an overwhelming task because of all the possible technologies involved. However, knowledge and hard work will keep you up to speed and, hopefully, one step ahead of the hackers and attackers.

Quick Tips

- A protocol is a set of rules that dictates how computers communicate over networks.
- The application layer, layer 7, has services and protocols required by the user's applications for networking functionality.
- The presentation layer, layer 6, formats data into a standardized format and deals with the syntax of the data, not the meaning.
- The session layer, layer 5, sets up, maintains, and breaks down the dialog (session) between two applications. It controls the dialog organization and synchronization.
- The transport layer, layer 4, provides end-to-end transmissions.
- The network layer, layer 3, provides routing, addressing, and fragmentation of packets. This layer can determine alternative routes to avoid network congestion.
- Routers work at the network layer, layer 3.
- The data link layer, layer 2, prepares data for the network medium by framing it. This is where the different LAN and WAN technologies work.
- The physical layer, layer 1, provides physical connections for transmission and performs the electrical encoding of data. This layer transforms bits to electrical signals.
- TCP/IP is a suite of protocols that is the de facto standard for transmitting data across the Internet. TCP is a reliable, connection-oriented protocol, while IP is an unreliable, connectionless protocol.
- Data is encapsulated as it travels down the network stack on the source computer, and the process is reversed on the destination computer. During encapsulation, each layer adds its own information so the corresponding layer on the destination computer knows how to process the data.
- Two main protocols at the transport layer are TCP and UDP.
- UDP is a connectionless protocol that does not send or receive acknowledgments when a datagram is received. It does not ensure data arrives at its destination. It provides "best-effort" delivery.
- TCP is a connection-oriented protocol that sends and receives acknowledgments. It ensures data arrives at the destination.

- ARP translates the IP address into a MAC address (physical Ethernet address), while RARP translates a MAC address into an IP address.
- ICMP works at the network layer and informs hosts, routers, and devices of network or computer problems. It is the major component of the ping utility.
- DNS resolves hostnames into IP addresses and has distributed databases all over the Internet to provide name resolution.
- Altering an ARP table so an IP address is mapped to a different MAC address is called ARP poisoning and can redirect traffic to an attacker's computer or an unattended system.
- Packet filtering (screening routers) is accomplished by ACLs and is a first-generation firewall. Traffic can be filtered by addresses, ports, and protocol types.
- Tunneling protocols move frames from one network to another by placing them inside of routable encapsulated frames.
- Packet filtering provides application independence, high performance, and scalability, but it provides low security and no protection above the network layer.
- Dual-homed firewalls can be bypassed if the operating system does not have packet forwarding or routing disabled.
- Firewalls that use proxies transfer an isolated copy of each approved packet from one network to another network.
- An application proxy requires a proxy for each approved service and can understand and make access decisions on the protocols used and the commands within those protocols.
- Circuit-level firewalls also use proxies but at a lower layer. Circuit-level firewalls do not look as deep within the packet as application proxies do.
- A proxy firewall is the middleman in communication. It does not allow anyone to connect directly to a protected host within the internal network. Proxy firewalls are second-generation firewalls.
- Application proxy firewalls provide high security and have full application-layer awareness, but they can have poor performance, limited application support, and poor scalability.
- Stateful inspection keeps track of each communication session. It must maintain a state table that contains data about each connection. It is a third-generation firewall.
- VPN can use PPTP, L2TP, TLS, or IPSec as tunneling protocols.
- PPTP works at the data link layer and can only handle one connection. IPSec works at the network layer and can handle multiple tunnels at the same time.
- Dedicated links are usually the most expensive type of WAN connectivity method because the fee is based on the distance between the two destinations rather than on the amount of bandwidth used. T1 and T3 are examples of dedicated links.

- Frame relay and X.25 are packet-switched WAN technologies that use virtual circuits instead of dedicated ones.
- A switch in star topologies serves as the central meeting place for all cables from computers and devices.
- A switch is a device with combined repeater and bridge technology. It works at the data link layer and understands MAC addresses.
- Routers link two or more network segments, where each segment can function as an independent network. A router works at the network layer, works with IP addresses, and has more network knowledge than bridges, switches, or repeaters.
- A bridge filters by MAC addresses and forwards broadcast traffic. A router filters by IP addresses and does not forward broadcast traffic.
- Layer 3 switching combines switching and routing technology.
- Attenuation is the loss of signal strength when a cable exceeds its maximum length.
- STP and UTP are twisted-pair cabling types that are the most popular, cheapest, and easiest to work with. However, they are the easiest to tap into, have crosstalk issues, and are vulnerable to EMI and RFI.
- Fiber-optic cabling carries data as light waves, is expensive, can transmit data at high speeds, is difficult to tap into, and is resistant to EMI and RFI. If security is extremely important, fiber-optic cabling should be used.
- ATM transfers data in fixed cells, is a WAN technology, and transmits data at very high rates. It supports voice, data, and video applications.
- FDDI is a LAN and MAN technology, usually used for backbones, that uses token-passing technology and has redundant rings in case the primary ring goes down.
- Token Ring, 802.5, is an older LAN implementation that uses a token-passing technology.
- Ethernet uses CSMA/CD, which means all computers compete for the shared network cable, listen to learn when they can transmit data, and are susceptible to data collisions.
- Circuit-switching technologies set up a circuit that will be used during a data transmission session. Packet-switching technologies do not set up circuits—instead, packets can travel along many different routes to arrive at the same destination.
- ISDN has a BRI rate that uses two B channels and one D channel, and a PRI rate that uses up to 23 B channels and one D channel. They support voice, data, and video.
- PPP is an encapsulation protocol for telecommunication connections. It replaced SLIP and is ideal for connecting different types of devices over serial lines.

- PAP sends credentials in cleartext, and CHAP authenticates using a challenge/response mechanism and therefore does not send passwords over the network.
- SOCKS is a proxy-based firewall solution. It is a circuit-based proxy firewall and does not use application-based proxies.
- IPSec tunnel mode protects the payload and header information of a packet, while IPSec transport mode protects only the payload.
- A screened-host firewall lies between the perimeter router and the LAN, and a screened subnet is a DMZ created by two physical firewalls.
- NAT is used when companies do not want systems to know internal hosts' addresses, and it enables companies to use private, nonroutable IP addresses.
- The 802.15 standard outlines wireless personal area network (WPAN) technologies, and 802.16 addresses wireless MAN technologies.
- Environments can be segmented into different WLANs by using different SSIDs.
- The 802.11b standard works in the 2.4-GHz range at 11 Mbps, and 802.11a works in the 5-GHz range at 54 Mbps.
- IPv4 uses 32 bits for its addresses, whereas IPv6 uses 128 bits; thus, IPv6 provides more possible addresses with which to work.
- Subnetting allows large IP ranges to be divided into smaller, logical, and easier-to-maintain network segments.
- SIP (Session Initiation Protocol) is a signaling protocol widely used for VoIP communications sessions.
- Open relay is an SMTP server that is configured in such a way that it can transmit e-mail messages from any source to any destination.
- SNMP uses agents and managers. Agents collect and maintain device-oriented data, which is held in management information bases. Managers poll the agents using community string values for authentication purposes.
- Three main types of multiplexing are statistical time division, frequency division, and wave division.
- Real-time Transport Protocol (RTP) provides a standardized packet format for delivering audio and video over IP networks. It works with RTP Control Protocol, which provides out-of-band statistics and control information to provide feedback on QoS levels.
- 802.1AR provides a unique ID for a device. 802.1AE provides data encryption, integrity, and origin authentication functionality at the data link level. 802.1AF carries out key agreement functions for the session keys used for data encryption. Each of these standards provides specific parameters to work within an 802.1X EAP-TLS framework.

- Lightweight EAP was developed by Cisco and was the first implementation of EAP and 802.1X for wireless networks. It uses preshared keys and MS-CHAP to authenticate client and server to each other.
- In EAP-TLS the client and server authenticate to each other using digital certificates. The client generates a pre-master secret key by encrypting a random number with the server's public key and sends it to the server.
- EAP-TTLS is similar to EAP-TLS, but only the server must use a digital certification for authentication to the client. The client can use any other EAP authentication method or legacy PAP or CHAP methods.
- Network convergence means the combining of server, storage, and network capabilities into a single framework.
- Mobile telephony has gone through different generations and multiple access technologies: 1G (FDMA), 2G (TDMA), 3G (CDMA), and 4G (OFDM).
- Link encryption is limited to two directly connected devices, so the message must be decrypted (and potentially re-encrypted) at each hop.
- The Point-to-Point Tunneling Protocol is an example of a link encryption technology.
- End-to-end encryption involves the source and destination nodes, so the message is not decrypted by intermediate nodes.
- Transport Layer Security (TLS) is an example of an end-to-end encryption technology.
- Multipurpose Internet Mail Extensions (MIME) is a technical specification indicating how multimedia data and e-mail binary attachments are to be transferred.
- Secure MIME (S/MIME) is a standard for encrypting and digitally signing e-mail and for providing secure data transmissions using Public Key Infrastructure (PKI).
- Pretty Good Privacy (PGP) is a freeware email security program that uses PKI based on a web of trust.
- S/MIME and PGP are incompatible because the former uses centralized, hierarchical Certificate Authorities (CAs) while the latter uses a distributed web of trust.
- HTTP Secure (HTTPS) is HTTP running over Secure Sockets Layer (SSL) or Transport Layer Security (TLS).
- SSL was formally deprecated in June of 2015.
- Cookies are text files that a browser maintains on a user's hard drive or memory segment in order to remember the user or maintain the state of a web application.
- Secure Shell (SSH) functions as a type of tunneling mechanism that provides terminal-like access to remote computers.

- A denial-of-service (DoS) attack results in a service or resource being degraded or made unavailable to legitimate users.
- DNS hijacking is an attack that forces the victim to use a malicious DNS server instead of the legitimate one.
- DNS hijacking is an attack that forces the victim to use a malicious DNS server instead of the legitimate one.

Questions

Please remember that these questions are formatted and asked in a certain way for a reason. Keep in mind that the CISSP exam is asking questions at a conceptual level. Questions may not always have the perfect answer, and the candidate is advised against always looking for the perfect answer. Instead, the candidate should look for the best answer in the list.

1. How does TKIP provide more protection for WLAN environments?
   A. It uses the AES algorithm.
   B. It decreases the IV size and uses the AES algorithm.
   C. It adds more keying material.
   D. It uses MAC and IP filtering.
2. Which of the following is not a characteristic of the IEEE 802.11a standard?
   A. It works in the 5-GHz range.
   B. It uses the OFDM spread spectrum technology.
   C. It provides 52 Mbps in bandwidth.
   D. It covers a smaller distance than 802.11b.
3. Why are switched infrastructures safer environments than routed networks?
   A. It is more difficult to sniff traffic since the computers have virtual private connections.
   B. They are just as unsafe as nonswitched environments.
   C. The data link encryption does not permit wiretapping.
   D. Switches are more intelligent than bridges and implement security mechanisms.
4. Which of the following protocols is considered connection-oriented?
   A. IP
   B. ICMP
   C. UDP
   D. TCP

5. Which of the following can take place if an attacker can insert tagging values into network- and switch-based protocols with the goal of manipulating traffic at the data link layer?
    A. Open relay manipulation
    B. VLAN hopping attack
    C. Hypervisor denial-of-service attack
    D. Smurf attack
6. Which of the following proxies cannot make access decisions based upon protocol commands?
    A. Application
    B. Packet filtering
    C. Circuit
    D. Stateful
7. Which of the following is a bridge-mode technology that can monitor individual traffic links between virtual machines or can be integrated within a hypervisor component?
    A. Orthogonal frequency division
    B. Unified threat management modem
    C. Virtual firewall
    D. Internet Security Association and Key Management Protocol
8. Which of the following shows the layer sequence as layers 2, 5, 7, 4, and 3?
    A. Data link, session, application, transport, and network
    B. Data link, transport, application, session, and network
    C. Network, session, application, network, and transport
    D. Network, transport, application, session, and presentation
9. Which of the following technologies integrates previously independent security solutions with the goal of providing simplicity, centralized control, and streamlined processes?
    A. Network convergence
    B. Security as a service
    C. Unified threat management
    D. Integrated convergence management

10. Metro Ethernet is a MAN protocol that can work in network infrastructures made up of access, aggregation, metro, and core layers. Which of the following best describes these network infrastructure layers?

    A. The access layer connects the customer's equipment to a service provider's aggregation network. Aggregation occurs on a core network. The metro layer is the metropolitan area network. The core connects different metro networks.

    B. The access layer connects the customer's equipment to a service provider's core network. Aggregation occurs on a distribution network at the core. The metro layer is the metropolitan area network.

    C. The access layer connects the customer's equipment to a service provider's aggregation network. Aggregation occurs on a distribution network. The metro layer is the metropolitan area network. The core connects different access layers.

    D. The access layer connects the customer's equipment to a service provider's aggregation network. Aggregation occurs on a distribution network. The metro layer is the metropolitan area network. The core connects different metro networks.

11. Which of the following provides an incorrect definition of the specific component or protocol that makes up IPSec?

    A. Authentication Header protocol provides data integrity, data origin authentication, and protection from replay attacks.

    B. Encapsulating Security Payload protocol provides confidentiality, data origin authentication, and data integrity.

    C. Internet Security Association and Key Management Protocol provides a framework for security association creation and key exchange.

    D. Internet Key Exchange provides authenticated keying material for use with encryption algorithms.

12. Systems that are built on the OSI framework are considered open systems. What does this mean?

    A. They do not have authentication mechanisms configured by default.

    B. They have interoperability issues.

    C. They are built with internationally accepted protocols and standards so they can easily communicate with other systems.

    D. They are built with international protocols and standards so they can choose what types of systems they will communicate with.

13. Which of the following protocols work in the following layers: application, data link, network, and transport?
    A. FTP, ARP, TCP, and UDP
    B. FTP, ICMP, IP, and UDP
    C. TFTP, ARP, IP, and UDP
    D. TFTP, RARP, IP, and ICMP
14. What takes place at the data link layer?
    A. End-to-end connection
    B. Dialog control
    C. Framing
    D. Data syntax
15. What takes place at the session layer?
    A. Dialog control
    B. Routing
    C. Packet sequencing
    D. Addressing
16. Which best describes the IP protocol?
    A. A connectionless protocol that deals with dialog establishment, maintenance, and destruction
    B. A connectionless protocol that deals with the addressing and routing of packets
    C. A connection-oriented protocol that deals with the addressing and routing of packets
    D. A connection-oriented protocol that deals with sequencing, error detection, and flow control
17. Which of the following is not a characteristic of the Protected Extensible Authentication Protocol?
    A. Authentication protocol used in wireless networks and point-to-point connections
    B. Designed to provide authentication for 802.11 WLANs
    C. Designed to support 802.1X port access control and Transport Layer Security
    D. Designed to support password-protected connections

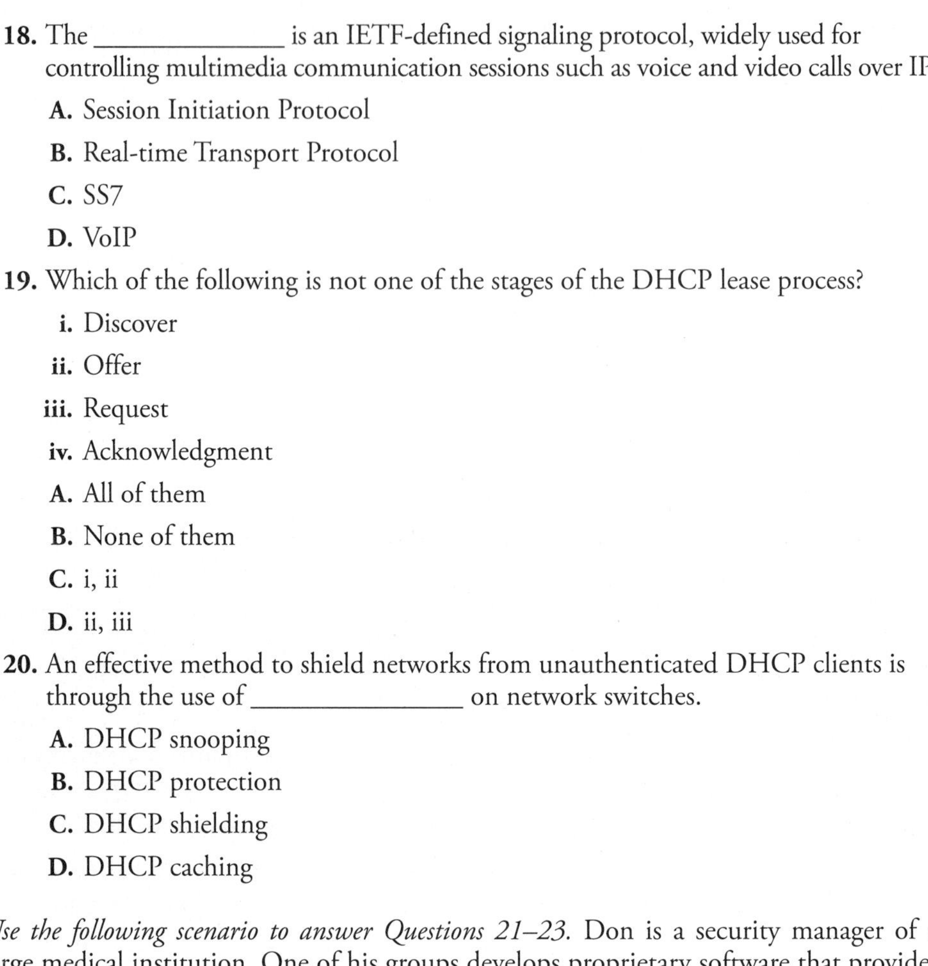

18. The ______________ is an IETF-defined signaling protocol, widely used for controlling multimedia communication sessions such as voice and video calls over IP.
    A. Session Initiation Protocol
    B. Real-time Transport Protocol
    C. SS7
    D. VoIP
19. Which of the following is not one of the stages of the DHCP lease process?
    i. Discover
    ii. Offer
    iii. Request
    iv. Acknowledgment
    A. All of them
    B. None of them
    C. i, ii
    D. ii, iii
20. An effective method to shield networks from unauthenticated DHCP clients is through the use of ______________ on network switches.
    A. DHCP snooping
    B. DHCP protection
    C. DHCP shielding
    D. DHCP caching

Use the following scenario to answer Questions 21–23. Don is a security manager of a large medical institution. One of his groups develops proprietary software that provides distributed computing through a client/server model. He has found out that some of the systems that maintain the proprietary software have been experiencing half-open denial-of-service attacks. Some of the software is antiquated and still uses basic remote procedure calls, which has allowed for masquerading attacks to take place.

21. What type of client ports should Don make sure the institution's software is using when client-to-server communication needs to take place?
    A. Well known
    B. Registered
    C. Dynamic
    D. Free

22. Which of the following is a cost-effective countermeasure that Don's team should implement?
    A. Stateful firewall
    B. Network address translation
    C. SYN proxy
    D. IPv6
23. What should Don's team put into place to stop the masquerading attacks that have been taking place?
    A. Dynamic packet filter firewall
    B. ARP spoofing protection
    C. Disable unnecessary ICMP traffic at edge routers
    D. SRPC

Use the following scenario to answer Questions 24–26. Grace is a security administrator for a medical institution and is responsible for many different teams. One team has reported that when their main FDDI connection failed, three critical systems went offline even though the connection was supposed to provide redundancy. Grace has to also advise her team on the type of fiber that should be implemented for campus building-to-building connectivity. Since this is a training medical facility, many surgeries are video recorded and that data must continuously travel from one building to the next. One other thing that has been reported to Grace is that periodic DoS attacks take place against specific servers within the internal network. The attacker sends excessive ICMP Echo Request packets to all the hosts on a specific subnet, which is aimed at one specific server.

24. Which of the following is most likely the issue that Grace's team experienced when their systems went offline?
    A. Three critical systems were connected to a dual-attached station.
    B. Three critical systems were connected to a single-attached station.
    C. The secondary FDDI ring was overwhelmed with traffic and dropped the three critical systems.
    D. The FDDI ring is shared in a metropolitan environment and only allows each company to have a certain number of systems connected to both rings.
25. Which of the following is the best type of fiber that should be implemented in this scenario?
    A. Single mode
    B. Multimode
    C. Optical carrier
    D. SONET

26. Which of the following is the best and most cost-effective countermeasure for Grace's team to put into place?
    A. Network address translation
    B. Disallowing unnecessary ICMP traffic coming from untrusted networks
    C. Application-based proxy firewall
    D. Screened subnet using two firewalls from two different vendors

Use the following scenario to answer Questions 27–29. John is the manager of the security team within his company. He has learned that attackers have installed sniffers throughout the network without the company's knowledge. Along with this issue his team has also found out that two DNS servers had no record replication restrictions put into place and the servers have been caching suspicious name resolution data.

27. Which of the following is the best countermeasure to put into place to help reduce the threat of network sniffers viewing network management traffic?
    A. SNMP v3
    B. L2TP
    C. CHAP
    D. Dynamic packet filtering firewall
28. Which of the following unauthorized activities have most likely been taking place in this situation?
    A. DNS querying
    B. Phishing
    C. Forwarding
    D. Zone transfer
29. Which of the following is the best countermeasure that John's team should implement to protect from improper caching issues?
    A. PKI
    B. DHCP snooping
    C. ARP protection
    D. DNSSEC

Use the following scenario to answer Questions 30–32. Sean is the new security administrator for a large financial institution. There are several issues that Sean is made aware of the first week he is in his new position. First, spurious packets seem to arrive at critical servers even though each network has tightly configured firewalls at each gateway position to control traffic to and from these servers. One of Sean's team members complains that the current firewall logs are excessively large with useless data. He also tells Sean that the team needs to be using less permissive rules instead of the current "any-any" rule type in place.

Sean has also found out that some team members want to implement tarpits on some of the most commonly attacked systems.

30. Which of the following is most likely taking place to allow spurious packets to gain unauthorized access to critical servers?
    A. TCP sequence hijacking is taking place.
    B. Source routing is not restricted.
    C. Fragment attacks are underway.
    D. Attacker is tunneling communication through PPP.
31. Which of the following best describes the firewall configuration issues Sean's team member is describing?
    A. Clean-up rule, stealth rule
    B. Stealth rule, silent rule
    C. Silent rule, negate rule
    D. Stealth rule, silent rule
32. Which of the following best describes why Sean's team wants to put in the mentioned countermeasure for the most commonly attacked systems?
    A. Prevent production system hijacking
    B. Reduce DoS attack effects
    C. Gather statistics during the process of an attack
    D. Increase forensic capabilities

Use the following scenario to answer Questions 33–35. Tom's company has been experiencing many issues with unauthorized sniffers being installed on the network. One reason is because employees can plug their laptops, smartphones, and other mobile devices into the network, any of which may be infected and have a running sniffer that the owner is not aware of. Implementing VPNs will not work because all of the network devices would need to be configured for specific VPNs, and some devices, as in their switches, do not have this type of functionality available. Another issue Tom's team is dealing with is how to secure internal wireless traffic. While the wireless access points can be configured with digital certificates for authentication, pushing out and maintaining certificates on each wireless user device is cost prohibitive and will cause too much of a burden on the network team. Tom's boss has also told him that the company needs to move from a landline metropolitan area network solution to a wireless solution.

33. What should Tom's team implement to provide source authentication and data encryption at the data link level?
    A. IEEE 802.1AR
    B. IEEE 802.1AE
    C. IEEE 802.1AF
    D. IEEE 802.1X

34. Which of the following solutions is best to meet the company's need to protect wireless traffic?
    A. EAP-TLS
    B. EAP-PEAP
    C. LEAP
    D. EAP-TTLS

35. Which of the following is the best solution to meet the company's need for broadband wireless connectivity?
    A. WiMAX
    B. IEEE 802.12
    C. WPA2
    D. IEEE 802.15

Use the following scenario to answer Questions 36–38. Lance has been brought in as a new security officer for a large medical equipment company. He has been told that many of the firewalls and IDS products have not been configured to filter IPv6 traffic; thus, many attacks have been taking place without the knowledge of the security team. While the network team has attempted to implement an automated tunneling feature to take care of this issue, they have continually run into problems with the network's NAT device. Lance has also found out that caching attacks have been successful against the company's public-facing DNS server. He has also identified that extra authentication is necessary for current LDAP requests, but the current technology only provides password-based authentication options.

36. Based upon the information in the scenario, what should the network team implement as it pertains to IPv6 tunneling?
    A. Teredo should be configured on IPv6-aware hosts that reside behind the NAT device.
    B. 6to4 should be configured on IPv6-aware hosts that reside behind the NAT device.
    C. Intra-Site Automatic Tunnel Addressing Protocol should be configured on IPv6-aware hosts that reside behind the NAT device.
    D. IPv6 should be disabled on all systems.

37. Which of the following is the best countermeasure for the attack type addressed in the scenario?
    A. DNSSEC
    B. IPSec
    C. Split server configurations
    D. Disabling zone transfers

38. Which of the following technologies should Lance's team investigate for increased authentication efforts?
    A. Challenge Handshake Authentication Protocol
    B. Simple Authentication and Security Layer
    C. IEEE 802.2AB
    D. EAP-SSL
39. Wireless LAN technologies have gone through different versions over the years to address some of the inherent security issues within the original IEEE 802.11 standard. Which of the following provides the correct characteristics of Wi-Fi Protected Access 2 (WPA2)?
    A. IEEE 802.1X, WEP, MAC
    B. IEEE 802.1X, EAP, TKIP
    C. IEEE 802.1X, EAP, WEP
    D. IEEE 802.1X, EAP, CCMP
40. Alice wants to send a message to Bob, who is several network hops away from her. What is the best approach to protecting the confidentiality of the message?
    A. PPTP
    B. S/MIME
    C. Link encryption
    D. SSH
41. Charlie uses PGP on his Linux-based email client. His friend Dave uses S/MIME on his Windows-based email. Charlie is unable to send an encrypted email to Dave. What is the likely reason?
    A. PGP and S/MIME are incompatible
    B. Each has a different secret key
    C. Each is using a different CA
    D. There is not enough information to determine the likely reason

Answers

1. **C.** The TKIP protocol actually works with WEP by feeding it keying material, which is data to be used for generating random keystreams. TKIP increases the IV size, ensures it is random for each packet, and adds the sender's MAC address to the keying material.
2. **C.** The IEEE standard 802.11a uses the OFDM spread spectrum technology, works in the 5-GHz frequency band, and provides bandwidth of up to 54 Mbps. The operating range is smaller because it works at a higher frequency.

3. **A.** Switched environments use switches to allow different network segments and/or systems to communicate. When this communication takes place, a virtual connection is set up between the communicating devices. Since it is a dedicated connection, broadcast and collision data are not available to other systems, as in an environment that uses purely bridges and routers.
4. **D.** TCP is the only connection-oriented protocol listed. A connection-oriented protocol provides reliable connectivity and data transmission, while a connectionless protocol provides unreliable connections and does not promise or ensure data transmission.
5. **B.** VLAN hopping attacks allow attackers to gain access to traffic in various VLAN segments. An attacker can have a system act as though it is a switch. The system understands the tagging values being used in the network and the trunking protocols, and can insert itself between other VLAN devices and gain access to the traffic going back and forth. Attackers can also insert tagging values to manipulate the control of traffic at this data link layer.
6. **C.** Application and circuit are the only types of proxy-based firewall solutions listed here. The others do not use proxies. Circuit-based proxy firewalls make decisions based on header information, not the protocol's command structure. Application-based proxies are the only ones that understand this level of granularity about the individual protocols.
7. **C.** Virtual firewalls can be bridge-mode products, which monitor individual traffic links between virtual machines, or they can be integrated within the hypervisor. The hypervisor is the software component that carries out virtual machine management and oversees guest system software execution. If the firewall is embedded within the hypervisor, then it can "see" and monitor all the activities taking place within the one system.
8. **A.** The OSI model is made up of seven layers: application (layer 7), presentation (layer 6), session (layer 5), transport (layer 4), network (layer 3), data link (layer 2), and physical (layer 1).
9. **C.** It has become very challenging to manage the long laundry list of security solutions almost every network needs to have in place. The list includes, but is not limited to, firewalls, antimalware, antispam, IDS\IPS, content filtering, data leak prevention, VPN capabilities, and continuous monitoring and reporting. Unified threat management (UTM) appliance products have been developed that provide all (or many) of these functionalities in a single network appliance. The goals of UTM are simplicity, streamlined installation and maintenance, centralized control, and the ability to understand a network's security from a holistic point of view.
10. **D.** The access layer connects the customer's equipment to a service provider's aggregation network. Aggregation occurs on a distribution network. The metro layer is the metropolitan area network. The core connects different metro networks.

11. **D.** Authentication Header protocol provides data integrity, data origin authentication, and protection from replay attacks. Encapsulating Security Payload protocol provides confidentiality, data origin authentication, and data integrity. Internet Security Association and Key Management Protocol provides a framework for security association creation and key exchange. Internet Key Exchange provides authenticated keying material for use with ISAKMP.
12. **C.** An open system is a system that has been developed based on standardized protocols and interfaces. Following these standards allows the systems to interoperate more effectively with other systems that follow the same standards.
13. **C.** Different protocols have different functionalities. The OSI model is an attempt to describe conceptually where these different functionalities take place in a networking stack. The model attempts to draw boxes around reality to help people better understand the stack. Each layer has a specific functionality and has several different protocols that can live at that layer and carry out that specific functionality. These listed protocols work at these associated layers: TFTP (application), ARP (data link), IP (network), and UDP (transport).
14. **C.** The data link layer, in most cases, is the only layer that understands the environment in which the system is working, whether it be Ethernet, Token Ring, wireless, or a connection to a WAN link. This layer adds the necessary headers and trailers to the frame. Other systems on the same type of network using the same technology understand only the specific header and trailer format used in their data link technology.
15. **A.** The session layer is responsible for controlling how applications communicate, not how computers communicate. Not all applications use protocols that work at the session layer, so this layer is not always used in networking functions. A session layer protocol will set up the connection to the other application logically and control the dialog going back and forth. Session layer protocols allow applications to keep track of the dialog.
16. **B.** The IP protocol is connectionless and works at the network layer. It adds source and destination addresses to a packet as it goes through its data encapsulation process. IP can also make routing decisions based on the destination address.
17. **D.** PEAP is a version of EAP and is an authentication protocol used in wireless networks and point-to-point connections. PEAP is designed to provide authentication for 802.11 WLANs, which support 802.1X port access control and TLS. It is a protocol that encapsulates EAP within a potentially encrypted and authenticated TLS tunnel.
18. **A.** The Session Initiation Protocol (SIP) is an IETF-defined signaling protocol, widely used for controlling multimedia communication sessions such as voice and video calls over IP. The protocol can be used for creating, modifying, and terminating two-party (unicast) or multiparty (multicast) sessions consisting of one or several media streams.

19. **B.** The four-step DHCP lease process is
    1. **DHCPDISCOVER message:** This message is used to request an IP address lease from a DHCP server.
    2. **DHCPOFFER message:** This message is a response to a DHCPDISCOVER message, and is sent by one or numerous DHCP servers.
    3. **DHCPREQUEST message:** The client sends this message to the initial DHCP server that responded to its request.
    4. **DHCPACK message:** This message is sent by the DHCP server to the DHCP client and is the process whereby the DHCP server assigns the IP address lease to the DHCP client.
20. **A.** DHCP snooping ensures that DHCP servers can assign IP addresses to only selected systems, identified by their MAC addresses. Also, advance network switches now have the capability to direct clients toward legitimate DHCP servers to get IP addresses and to restrict rogue systems from becoming DHCP servers on the network.
21. **C.** Well-known ports are mapped to commonly used services (HTTP, FTP, etc.). Registered ports are 1,024 to 49,151, and vendors register specific ports to map to their proprietary software. Dynamic ports (private ports) are available for use by any application.
22. **C.** A half-open attack is a type of DoS that is also referred to as a SYN flood. To thwart this type of attack, Don's team can use SYN proxies, which limit the number of open and abandoned network connections. The SYN proxy is a piece of software that resides between the sender and receiver, and only sends TCP traffic to the receiving system if the TCP handshake process completes successfully.
23. **D.** Basic RPC does not have authentication capabilities, which allows for masquerading attacks to take place. Secure RPC (SRPC) can be implemented, which requires authentication to take place before remote systems can communicate with each other. Authentication can take place using shared secrets, public keys, or Kerberos tickets.
24. **B.** A single-attachment station (SAS) is attached to only one ring (the primary) through a concentrator. If the primary goes down, it is not connected to the backup secondary ring. A dual-attachment station (DAS) has two ports and each port provides a connection for both the primary and the secondary rings.
25. **B.** In single mode, a small glass core is used for high-speed data transmission over long distances. This scenario specifies campus building-to-building connections, which are usually short distances. In multimode, a large glass core is used and is able to carry more data than single-mode fibers, though they are best for shorter distances because of their higher attenuation levels.
26. **B.** The attack description is a smurf attack. In this situation the attacker sends an ICMP Echo Request packet with a spoofed source address to a victim's network

broadcast address. This means that each system on the victim's subnet receives an ICMP Echo Request packet. Each system then replies to that request with an ICMP Echo Response packet to the spoof address provided in the packets—which is the victim's address. All of these response packets go to the victim system and overwhelm it because it is being bombarded with packets it does not necessarily know how to process. Filtering out unnecessary ICMP traffic is the cheapest solution.

27. **A.** SNMP versions 1 and 2 send their community string values in cleartext, but with version 3, cryptographic functionality has been added, which provides encryption, message integrity, and authentication security. So the sniffers that are installed on the network cannot sniff SNMP traffic.

28. **D.** The primary and secondary DNS servers synchronize their information through a zone transfer. After changes take place to the primary DNS server, those changes must be replicated to the secondary DNS server. It is important to configure the DNS server to allow zone transfers to take place only between the specific servers. Attackers can carry out zone transfers to gather very useful network information from victims' DNS servers. Unauthorized zone transfers can take place if the DNS servers are not properly configured to restrict this type of activity.

29. **D.** When a DNS server receives an improper (potentially malicious) name resolution response, it will cache it and provide it to all the hosts it serves unless DNSSEC is implemented. If DNSSEC were enabled on a DNS server, then the server would, upon receiving a response, validate the digital signature on the message before accepting the information to make sure that the response is from an authorized DNS server.

30. **B.** Source routing means the packet decides how to get to its destination, not the routers in between the source and destination computer. Source routing moves a packet throughout a network on a predetermined path. To make sure none of this misrouting happens, many firewalls are configured to check for source routing information within the packet and deny it if it is present.

31. **C.** The following describes the different firewall rule types:
    - **Silent rule** Drops "noisy" traffic without logging it. This reduces log sizes by not responding to packets that are deemed unimportant.
    - **Stealth rule** Disallows access to firewall software from unauthorized systems.
    - **Cleanup rule** The last rule in the rule base, which drops and logs any traffic that does not meet the preceding rules.
    - **Negate rule** Used instead of the broad and permissive "any rules." Negate rules provide tighter permission rights by specifying what system can be accessed and how.

32. **B.** A tarpit is commonly a piece of software configured to emulate a vulnerable, running service. Once the attackers start to send packets to this "service," the connection to the victim system seems to be live and ongoing, but the response

from the victim system is slow and the connection may time out. Most attacks and scanning activities take place through automated tools that require quick responses from their victim systems. If the victim systems do not reply or are very slow to reply, the automated tools may not be successful because the protocol connection times out. This can reduce the effects of a DoS attack.

33. **D.** IEEE 802.1AR provides a unique ID for a device. IEEE 802.1AE provides data encryption, integrity, and origin authentication functionality. IEEE 802.1AF carries out key agreement functions for the session keys used for data encryption. Each of these standards provides specific parameters to work within an IEEE 802.1X EAP-TLS framework. A recent version (802.1X-2010) has integrated IEEE 802.1AE and IEEE 802.1AR to support service identification and optional point-to-point encryption.

34. **D.** EAP-Tunneled Transport Layer Security (EAP-TTLS) is an EAP protocol that extends TLS. EAP-TTLS is designed to provide authentication that is as strong as EAP-TLS, but it does not require that each wireless device be issued a certificate. Instead, only the authentication servers are issued certificates. User authentication is performed by password, but the password credentials are transported in a securely encrypted tunnel established based upon the server certificates.

35. **A.** IEEE 802.16 is a MAN wireless standard that allows for wireless traffic to cover a wide geographical area. This technology is also referred to as broadband wireless access. The commercial name for 802.16 is WiMAX.

36. **A.** Teredo encapsulates IPv6 packets within UDP datagrams with IPv4 addressing. IPv6-aware systems behind the NAT device can be used as Teredo tunnel endpoints even if they do not have a dedicated public IPv4 address.

37. **A.** DNSSEC protects DNS servers from forged DNS information, which is commonly used to carry out DNS cache poisoning attacks. If DNSSEC is implemented, then all responses that the server receives will be verified through digital signatures. This helps ensure that an attacker cannot provide a DNS server with incorrect information, which would point the victim to a malicious website.

38. **B.** Simple Authentication and Security Layer is a protocol-independent authentication framework. This means that any protocol that knows how to interact with SASL can use its various authentication mechanisms without having to actually embed the authentication mechanisms within its code.

39. **D.** Wi-Fi Protected Access 2 requires IEEE 802.1X or preshared keys for access control, EAP or preshared keys for authentication, and AES algorithm in counter mode with CBC-MAC Protocol (CCMP) for encryption.

40. **B.** Secure Multipurpose Internet Email Extensions (S/MIME) is a standard for encrypting and digitally signing e-mail and for providing secure data transmissions using Public Key Infrastructure (PKI).

41. **A.** PGP uses a decentralized web of trust for its PKI, while S/MIME relies on centralized CAs. The two systems are, therefore, incompatible with each other.

CHAPTER 5

Identity and Access Management

This chapter presents the following:

- Identification methods and technologies
- Authentication methods, models, and technologies
- Discretionary, mandatory, and nondiscretionary models
- Accountability, monitoring, and auditing practices
- Registration and proof of identity
- Identity as a service
- Threats to access control practices and technologies

Locks keep out only the honest.

—Proverb

A cornerstone in the foundation of information security is controlling how resources are accessed so they can be protected from unauthorized modification or disclosure. The controls that enforce access control can be technical, physical, or administrative in nature. These control types need to be integrated into policy-based documentation, software and technology, network design, and physical security components.

Access is one of the most exploited aspects of security because it is the gateway that leads to critical assets. Access controls need to be applied in a layered defense-in-depth method, and an understanding of how these controls are exploited is extremely important. In this chapter we will explore access control conceptually and then dig into the technologies the industry puts in place to enforce these concepts. We will also look at the common methods the bad guys use to attack these technologies.

Access Controls Overview

Access controls are security features that control how users and systems communicate and interact with other systems and resources. They protect the systems and resources from unauthorized access and can be components that participate in determining the level of authorization after an authentication procedure has successfully completed. Although we usually think of a user as the entity that requires access to a network resource or information, there are many other types of entities that require access to other network entities and resources that are subject to access control. It is important to understand the definition of a subject and an object when working in the context of access control.

Access is the flow of information between a subject and an object. A *subject* is an active entity that requests access to an object or the data within an object. A subject can be a user, program, or process that accesses an object to accomplish a task. When a program accesses a file, the program is the subject and the file is the object. An *object* is a passive entity that contains information or needed functionality. An object can be a computer, database, file, computer program, directory, or field contained in a table within a database. When you look up information in a database, you are the active subject and the database is the passive object. Figure 5-1 illustrates subjects and objects.

Access control is a broad term that covers several different types of mechanisms that enforce access control features on computer systems, networks, and information. Access control is extremely important because it is one of the first lines of defense in battling unauthorized access to systems and network resources. When a user is prompted for a username and password to use a computer, this is access control. Once the user logs in and later attempts to access a file, that file may have a list of users and groups that have the right to access it. If the user is not on this list, the user is denied. This is another form of access control. The users' permissions and rights may be based on their identity, clearance, and/or group membership. Access controls give organizations the ability to control, restrict, monitor, and protect resource availability, integrity, and confidentiality.

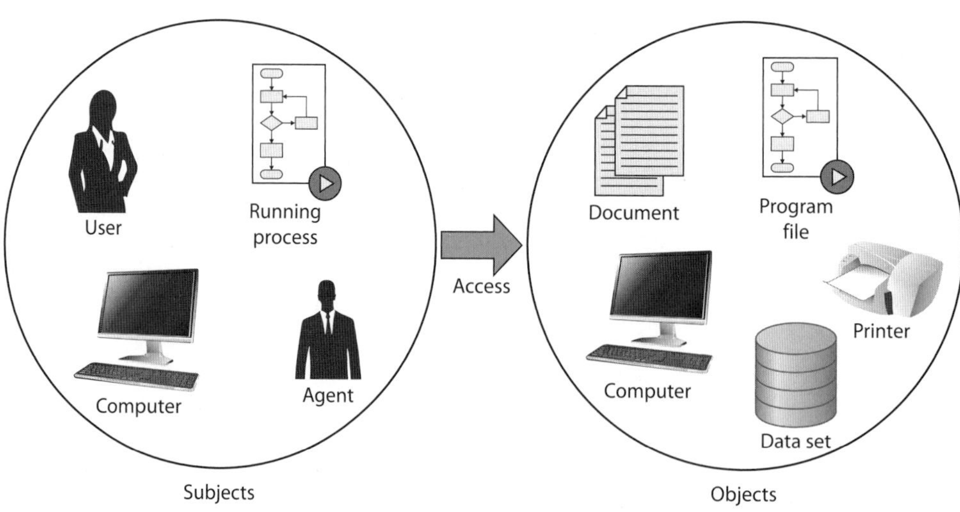

Figure 5-1 Subjects are active entities that access objects, while objects are passive entities.

Security Principles

The three main security principles for any type of security control are

- Availability
- Integrity
- Confidentiality

These principles, which were touched upon in Chapter 1, will be a running theme throughout this book because each core subject of each chapter approaches these principles in a unique way. In Chapter 1, you read that security management procedures include identifying threats that can negatively affect the availability, integrity, and confidentiality of the company's assets and finding cost-effective countermeasures that will protect them. This chapter looks at the ways the three principles can be affected and protected through access control methodologies and technologies.

Every control that is used in computer and information security provides at least one of these security principles. It is critical that security professionals understand all of the possible ways these principles can be provided and circumvented.

Availability

Information, systems, and resources must be available to users in a timely manner so productivity will not be affected. Most information must be accessible and available to users when requested so they can carry out tasks and fulfill their responsibilities. Accessing information does not seem that important until it is inaccessible. Administrators experience this when a file server goes offline or a highly used database is out of service for one reason or another. Fault tolerance and recovery mechanisms are put into place to ensure the continuity of the *availability* of resources. User productivity can be greatly affected if requested data is not readily available.

Information has various attributes, such as accuracy, relevance, timeliness, and privacy. It may be extremely important for a stockbroker to have information that is accurate and timely, so he can buy and sell stocks at the right times at the right prices. The stockbroker may not necessarily care about the privacy of this information, only that it is readily available.

Integrity

Information must be accurate, complete, and protected from unauthorized modification. When a security mechanism provides *integrity*, it protects data, or a resource, from being altered in an unauthorized fashion. If any type of illegitimate modification does occur, the security mechanism must alert the user or administrator in some manner. One example is when a user sends a request to her online bank account to pay her $24.56 water utility bill. The bank needs to be sure the integrity of that transaction was not altered during transmission so the user does not end up paying the utility company $240.56 instead. Integrity of data is very important. What if a confidential e-mail was sent from the secretary of state to the president of the United States and was intercepted and altered without a security mechanism in place that disallows this or alerts the president that this message has been altered? Instead of receiving a message reading, "We would love for you and your wife to stop by for drinks tonight," the message could be altered to say, "We have just bombed Libya." Big difference.

Confidentiality

Confidentiality is the assurance that information is not disclosed to unauthorized individuals, programs, or processes. Some information is more sensitive than other information and requires a higher level of confidentiality. Control mechanisms need to be in place to dictate who can access data and what the subject can do with it once they have accessed it. These activities need to be controlled, audited, and monitored. Examples of information that could be considered confidential are health records, financial account information, criminal records, source code, trade secrets, and military tactical plans. Some security mechanisms that would provide confidentiality are encryption, logical and physical access controls, transmission protocols, database views, and controlled traffic flow.

It is important for a company to identify the data that must be classified so the company can ensure that the top priority of security protects this information and keeps it confidential. If this information is not singled out, too much time and money can be spent on implementing the same level of security for critical and mundane information alike. It may be necessary to configure virtual private networks (VPNs) between organizations and use the IPSec encryption protocol to encrypt all messages passed when communicating about trade secrets, sharing customer information, or making financial transactions. This takes a certain amount of hardware, labor, funds, and overhead. The same security precautions are not necessary when communicating that today's special in the cafeteria is liver and onions with a roll on the side. So, the first step in protecting data's confidentiality is to identify which information is sensitive and to what degree, and then implement security mechanisms to protect it properly.

Different security mechanisms can supply different degrees of availability, integrity, and confidentiality. The environment, the classification of the data that is to be protected, and the security goals must be evaluated to ensure the proper security mechanisms are bought and put into place. Many corporations have wasted a lot of time and money not following these steps and instead buying the new "gee whiz" product that recently hit the market.

Identification, Authentication, Authorization, and Accountability

For a user to be able to access a resource, he first must prove he is who he claims to be, has the necessary credentials, and has been given the necessary rights or privileges to perform the actions he is requesting. Once these steps are completed successfully, the user can access and use network resources; however, it is necessary to track the user's activities and enforce accountability for his actions. *Identification* describes a method by which a subject (user, program, or process) claims to have a specific identity (name, account number, or e-mail address). Identification can be provided with the use of a username or account number. To be properly *authenticated*, the subject is usually required to provide a second piece to the credential set. This piece could be a password, passphrase, cryptographic key, personal identification number (PIN), anatomical attribute, or token. These two credential items are compared to information that has been previously stored for this subject. If these credentials match the stored information, the subject is authenticated. But we are not done yet.

Once the subject provides its credentials and is properly authenticated, the system it is trying to access needs to determine if this subject has been given the necessary rights and privileges to carry out the requested actions. The system will look at some type of access control matrix or compare security labels to verify that this subject may indeed access the requested resource and perform the actions it is attempting. If the system determines that the subject may access the resource, it *authorizes* the subject.

Although identification, authentication, authorization, and accountability have close and complementary definitions, each has distinct functions that fulfill a specific requirement in the process of access control. A user may be properly identified and authenticated to the network, but he may not have the authorization to access the files on the file server. On the other hand, a user may be authorized to access the files on the file server, but until she is properly identified and authenticated, those resources are out of reach. Figure 5-2 illustrates the four steps that must happen for a subject to access an object.

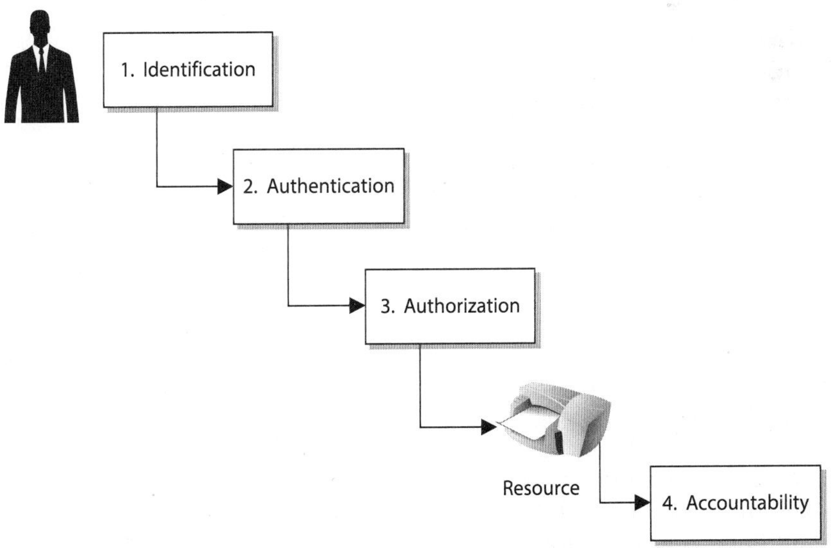

Figure 5-2 Four steps must happen for a subject to access an object: identification, authentication, authorization, and accountability.

The subject needs to be held accountable for the actions taken within a system or domain. The only way to ensure accountability is if the subject is uniquely identified and the subject's actions are recorded.

Race Condition

A *race condition* is when processes carry out their tasks on a shared resource in an incorrect order. A race condition is possible when two or more processes use a shared resource, as in data within a variable. It is important that the processes carry out their functionality in the correct sequence. If process 2 carried out its task on the data before process 1, the result would be much different than if process 1 carried out its tasks on the data before process 2.

In software, when the authentication and authorization steps are split into two functions, there is a possibility an attacker could use a race condition to force the authorization step to be completed *before* the authentication step. This would be a flaw in the software that the attacker has figured out how to exploit. A race condition occurs when two or more processes use the same resource and the sequences of steps within the software can be carried out in an improper order, something that can drastically affect the output. So, an attacker can force the authorization step to take place before the authentication step and gain unauthorized access to a resource.

Logical access controls are technical tools used for identification, authentication, authorization, and accountability. They are software components that enforce access control measures for systems, programs, processes, and information. The logical access controls can be embedded within operating systems, applications, add-on security packages, or database and telecommunication management systems. It can be challenging to synchronize all access controls and ensure all vulnerabilities are covered without producing overlaps of functionality. However, if it were easy, security professionals would not be getting paid the big bucks!

EXAM TIP The words "logical" and "technical" can be used interchangeably in this context. It is conceivable that the CISSP exam would refer to logical and technical controls interchangeably.

An individual's identity must be verified during the authentication process. Authentication usually involves a two-step process: entering public information (a username, employee number, account number, or department ID), and then entering private information (a static password, smart token, cognitive password, one-time password, or PIN). Entering public information is the identification step, while entering private information is the authentication step of the two-step process. Each technique used for identification and authentication has its pros and cons. Each should be properly evaluated to determine the right mechanism for the correct environment.

Identification and Authentication

Once a person has been identified through the user ID or a similar value, she must be authenticated, which means she must prove she is who she says she is. Three general factors can be used for authentication: *something a person knows, something a person has,* and *something a person is.* These factors are also commonly called authentication by knowledge, authentication by ownership, and authentication by characteristic.

One-to-One and One-to-Many

Verification 1:1 is the measurement of an identity against a single claimed identity. The conceptual question is, "Is this person who he claims to be?" So if Bob provides his identity and credential set, this information is compared to the data kept in an authentication database. If they match, we know that it is really Bob. If the identification is 1:N (many), the measurement of a single identity is compared against multiple identities. The conceptual question is, "Who is this person?" An example is if fingerprints were found at a crime scene, the cops would run them through their database to identify the suspect.

Something a person knows (authentication by knowledge) can be, for example, a password, PIN, mother's maiden name, or the combination to a lock. Authenticating a person by something that she knows is usually the least expensive method to implement. The downside to this method is that another person may acquire this knowledge and gain unauthorized access to a resource.

Something a person has (authentication by ownership) can be a key, swipe card, access card, or badge. This method is common for accessing facilities, but could also be used to access sensitive areas or to authenticate systems. A downside to this method is that the item can be lost or stolen, which could result in unauthorized access.

Something specific to a person (authentication by characteristic) becomes a bit more interesting. This is not based on whether the person is a Republican, a Martian, or a moron—it is based on a physical attribute. Authenticating a person's identity based on a unique physical attribute is referred to as biometrics. (For more information, see the upcoming section, "Biometrics.")

Strong authentication contains two or all of these three methods: something a person knows, has, or is. Using a biometric system by itself does not provide strong authentication because it provides only one out of the three methods. Biometrics supplies what a person is, not what a person knows or has. For a strong authentication process to be in place, a biometric system needs to be coupled with a mechanism that checks for one of the other two methods. For example, many times the person has to type a PIN into a keypad before the biometric scan is performed. This satisfies the "what the person knows" category. Conversely, the person could be required to swipe a magnetic card through a reader prior to the biometric scan. This would satisfy the "what the person has" category. Whatever identification system is used, for strong authentication to be in the process, it must include multiple factors.

TIP Strong authentication is also sometimes referred to as *multifactor authentication*, which just means that more than one authentication method is used. *Three-factor authentication* is possible, which includes all authentication approaches.

Identity is a complicated concept with many varied nuances, ranging from the philosophical to the practical. A person can have multiple digital identities. For example, a user could be JPublic in a Windows domain environment, JohnP on a Unix server, JohnPublic on the mainframe, JJP in instant messaging, JohnCPublic in the certification authority, and JohnnyPub on Facebook. If a company would want to centralize all of its access control, these various identity names for the same person may cause the security administrator undue stress.

Creating or issuing secure identities should include three key aspects: uniqueness, nondescriptive, and issuance. The first, *uniqueness*, refers to the identifiers that are specific to an individual, meaning every user must have a unique ID for accountability. Things like fingerprints and retina scans can be considered unique elements in determining identity. *Nondescriptive* means that neither piece of the credential set should indicate the purpose of that account. For example, a user ID should not be "administrator," "backup_operator," or "CEO." The third key aspect in determining identity is *issuance*. These elements are the ones that have been provided by another authority as a means of proving identity. ID cards are a kind of security element that would be considered an issuance form of identification.

NOTE Mutual authentication is when the two communicating entities must authenticate to each other before passing data. For example, an authentication server may be required to authenticate to a user's system before allowing data to flow back and forth.

While most of this chapter deals with user authentication, it is important to realize system-based authentication is possible also. Computers and devices can be identified, authenticated, monitored, and controlled based upon their hardware addresses (media access control) and/or Internet Protocol (IP) addresses. Networks may have network access control (NAC) technology that authenticates systems before they are allowed access to the network. Every network device has a hardware address that is integrated into its network interface card (NIC) and a software-based address (IP) that either is assigned by a DHCP server or locally configured.

Identification Component Requirements

When issuing identification values to users, the following should be in place:

- Each value should be unique, for user accountability.
- A standard naming scheme should be followed.
- The value should be nondescriptive of the user's position or tasks.
- The value should not be shared between users.

CAUTION In technology there are overlapping acronyms. In the CISSP exam you will run into at least three different MAC acronyms. *Media access control* = data link layer functionality and address type within a network protocol stack. *Mandatory access control* = access control model integrated in software used to control subject-to-object access functions through the use of clearance, classifications, and labels. *Message authentication code* = cryptographic function that uses a hashing algorithm and symmetric key for data integrity and system origin functions. The CISSP exam does not use acronyms by themselves, but spells the terms out, so this should not be a problem on the exam.

Access Control Review

The following is a review of the basic concepts in access control:

Identification:

- Subjects supplying identification information
- Username, user ID, account number

Authentication:

- Verifying the identification information
- Passphrase, PIN value, thumbprint, smart card, one-time password

Authorization:

- Using the identity of the subject together with other criteria to make a determination of operations that a subject can carry out on objects
- "I know who you are, now what am I going to allow you to do?"

Accountability:

- Audit logs and monitoring to track subject activities with objects

Identity Management

Identity management is a broad and loaded term that encompasses the use of different products to identify, authenticate, and authorize users through automated means. To many people, the term also includes user account management, access control, password management, single sign-on (SSO) functionality, managing rights and permissions for user accounts, and auditing and monitoring all of these items. The reason that individuals, and companies, have different definitions and perspectives of identity management (IdM) is because it is so large and encompasses so many different technologies and processes. Remember the story of the three blind men who are trying to describe an elephant? One blind man feels the tail and announces, based on his limited experience, that the elephant is like a rope. Another blind man feels the trunk and describes the elephant as a tree branch. Yet another describes it as a pillar after feeling a leg. This is because each man cannot see or comprehend the whole of the large creature—just the piece he is familiar with and knows about. This analogy can be applied to IdM because it is so large and contains so many components that many people may not comprehend the whole—only the component they work with and understand.

It is important for security professionals to understand not only the whole of IdM, but also the technologies that make up a full enterprise IdM solution. IdM requires management of uniquely identified entities, their attributes, credentials, and entitlements. IdM allows organizations to create and manage digital identities' life cycles (create, maintain, terminate) in a timely and automated fashion. The enterprise IdM must meet business needs and scale from internally facing systems to externally facing systems. In this section, we will be covering many of these technologies and how they work together.

Selling identity management products is now a flourishing market that focuses on reducing administrative costs, increasing security, meeting regulatory compliance, and improving upon service levels throughout enterprises. The continual increase in complexity and diversity of networked environments only increases the complexity of keeping track of who can access what and when. Organizations have different types of applications, network operating systems, databases, enterprise resource management (ERM) systems, customer relationship management (CRM) systems, directories, and mainframes—all used for different business purposes. Then the organizations have partners, contractors, consultants, employees, and temporary employees. (Figure 5-3 actually provides a simplistic view of most environments.) Users usually access several different types of systems throughout their daily tasks, which makes controlling access and providing the necessary level of protection on different data types difficult and full of obstacles. This complexity usually results in unforeseen and unidentified holes in asset protection, overlapping and contradictory controls, and policy and regulation noncompliance. It is the goal of identity management technologies to simplify the administration of these tasks and bring order to chaos.

The following are many of the common questions enterprises deal with today in controlling access to assets:

- What should each user have access to?
- Who approves and allows access?
- How do the access decisions map to policies?
- Do former employees still have access?

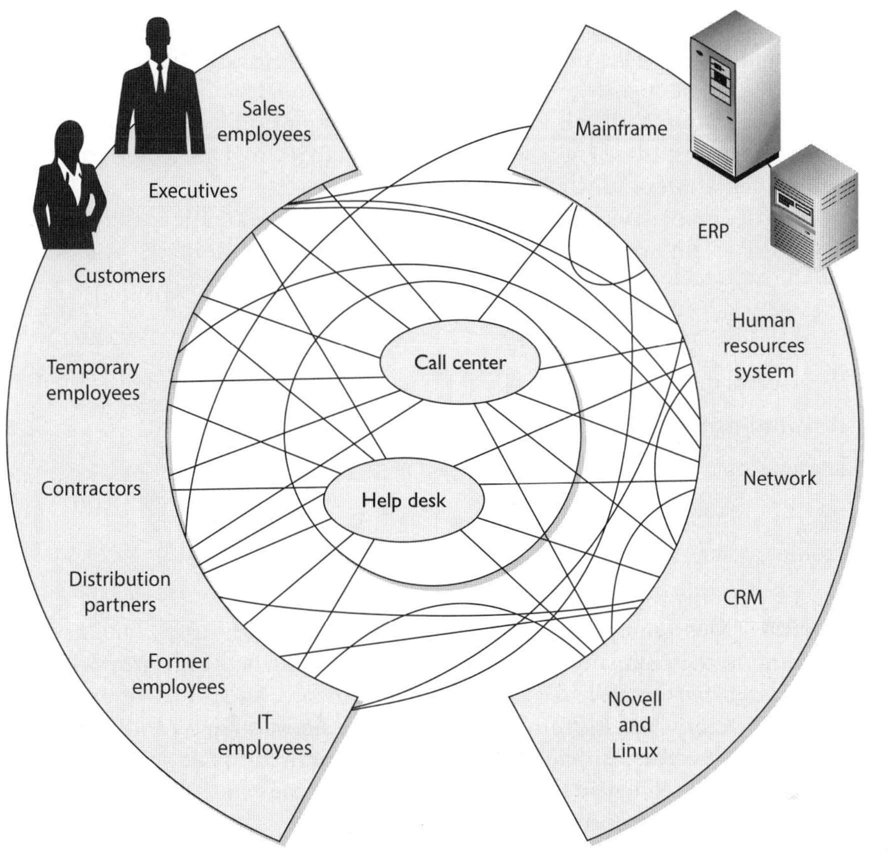

Figure 5-3 Most environments are chaotic in terms of access.

- How do we keep up with our dynamic and ever-changing environment?
- What is the process of revoking access?
- How is access controlled and monitored centrally?
- Why do employees have eight passwords to remember?
- We have five different operating platforms. How do we centralize access when each platform (and application) requires its own type of credential set?
- How do we control access for our employees, customers, and partners?
- How do we make sure we are compliant with the necessary regulations?

The traditional identity management process has been manual, using directory services with permissions, access control lists (ACLs), and profiles. This approach has proven incapable of keeping up with complex demands and thus has been replaced with automated applications rich in functionality that work together to create an IdM infrastructure. The main goals of IdM technologies are to streamline the management of identity, authentication, authorization, and the auditing of subjects on multiple systems throughout the enterprise. The sheer diversity of a heterogeneous enterprise makes proper implementation of IdM a huge undertaking.

Many identity management solutions and products are available in the marketplace. For the CISSP exam, the following are the types of technologies you should be aware of:

- Directories
- Web access management
- Password management
- Legacy single sign-on
- Account management
- Profile update

Directories Most enterprises have some type of directory that contains information pertaining to the company's network resources and users. Most directories follow a hierarchical database format, based on the X.500 standard, and a type of protocol, as in Lightweight Directory Access Protocol (LDAP), that allows subjects and applications to interact with the directory. Applications can request information about a particular user by making an LDAP request to the directory, and users can request information about a specific resource by using a similar request.

The objects within the directory are managed by a directory service. The *directory service* allows an administrator to configure and manage how identification, authentication, authorization, and access control take place within the network and on individual systems. The objects within the directory are labeled and identified with namespaces.

In a Windows environment, when you log in, you are logging in to a domain controller (DC), which has a hierarchical directory in its database. The database is running a directory service (Active Directory), which organizes the network resources and carries out user access control functionality. So once you successfully authenticate to the DC, certain network resources will be available to you (print service, file server, e-mail server, and so on) as dictated by the configuration of AD.

How does the directory service keep all of these entities organized? By using *namespaces*. Each directory service has a way of identifying and naming the objects they will manage. In databases based on the X.500 standard that are accessed by LDAP, the directory service assigns distinguished names (DNs) to each object. Each DN represents a collection of attributes about a specific object and is stored in the directory as an entry.

In the following example, the DN is made up of a common name (cn) and domain components (dc). Since this is a hierarchical directory, .com is the top, LogicalSecurity is one step down from .com, and Shon is at the bottom.

```
dn: cn=Shon Harris,dc=LogicalSecurity,dc=com
cn: Shon Harris
```

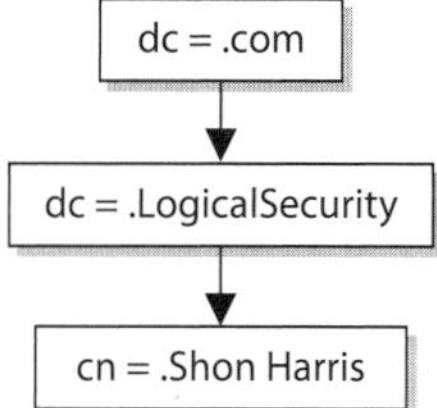

This is a very simplistic example. Companies usually have large trees (directories) containing many levels and objects to represent different departments, roles, users, and resources.

A directory service manages the entries and data in the directory and also enforces the configured security policy by carrying out access control and identity management functions. For example, when you log in to the DC, the directory service (AD) will determine what resources you can and cannot access on the network.

NOTE We touch on directory services again in the "Directory Services" section of this chapter.

So are there any problems with using a directory product for identity management and access control? Yes, there's always something. Many legacy devices and applications cannot be managed by the directory service because they were not built with the necessary client software. The legacy entities must be managed through their inherited management software. This means that most networks have subjects, services, and resources that can be listed in a directory and controlled centrally by an administrator through the use of a directory service. Then there are legacy applications and devices that the administrator must configure and manage individually.

Directories' Role in Identity Management A directory used for IdM is specialized database software that has been optimized for reading and searching operations. It is the main component of an identity management solution. This is because all resource information, users' attributes, authorization profiles, roles, access control policies, and more are stored in this one location. When other IdM software applications need to carry out their functions (authorization, access control, assigning permissions), they now have a centralized location for all of the information they need.

As an analogy, let's say Bob is a store clerk and you enter his store to purchase alcohol. Instead of having to find a picture of you somewhere to validate your identity, go to another place to find your birth certificate to obtain your true birth date, and find proof of which state you are registered in, Bob can look in one place—your driver's license. The directory works in the same way. Some IdM applications may need to know a user's authorization rights, role, employee status, or clearance level, so instead of this application having to make requests to several databases and other applications, it makes its request to this one directory.

A lot of the information stored in an IdM directory is scattered throughout the enterprise. User attribute information (employee status, job description, department, and so on) is usually stored in the HR database, authentication information could be in a Kerberos server, role and group identification information might be in a SQL database, and resource-oriented authentication information may be stored in Active Directory on a domain controller. These are commonly referred to as identity stores and are located in different places on the network. Something nifty that many identity management products do is create meta-directories or virtual directories. A *meta-directory* gathers the necessary information from multiple sources and stores it in one central directory. This provides a unified view of all users' digital identity information throughout the enterprise. The meta-directory synchronizes itself with all of the identity stores periodically to ensure the most up-to-date information is being used by all applications and IdM components within the enterprise.

Organizing All of This Stuff

In a database directory based on the X.500 standard, the following rules are used for object organization:

- The directory has a tree structure to organize the entries using a parent-child configuration.
- Each entry has a unique name made up of attributes of a specific object.
- The attributes used in the directory are dictated by the defined schema.
- The unique identifiers are called distinguished names.

The schema describes the directory structure and what names can be used within the directory, among other things. The following diagram shows how an object

(Kathy Conlon) can have the attributes of ou=General, ou=NCTSW, ou=WNY, ou=locations, ou=Navy, ou=DoD, ou=U.S. Government, and C=US.

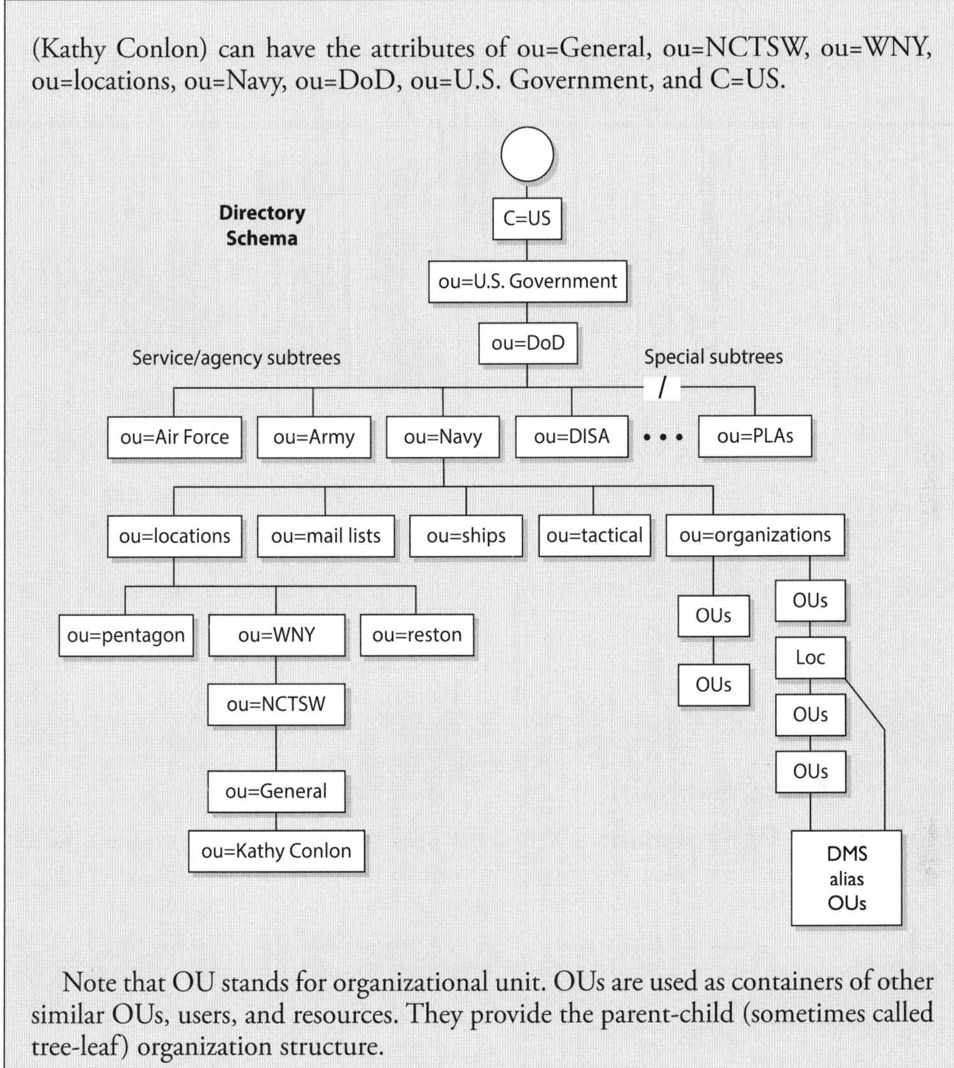

Note that OU stands for organizational unit. OUs are used as containers of other similar OUs, users, and resources. They provide the parent-child (sometimes called tree-leaf) organization structure.

A *virtual directory* plays the same role and can be used instead of a meta-directory. The difference between the two is that the meta-directory physically has the identity data in its directory, whereas a virtual directory does not and points to where the actual data resides. When an IdM component makes a call to a virtual directory to gather identity information on a user, the virtual directory will point to where the information actually lives.

Figure 5-4 illustrates a central LDAP directory that is used by the IdM services: access management, provisioning, and identity management. When one of these services

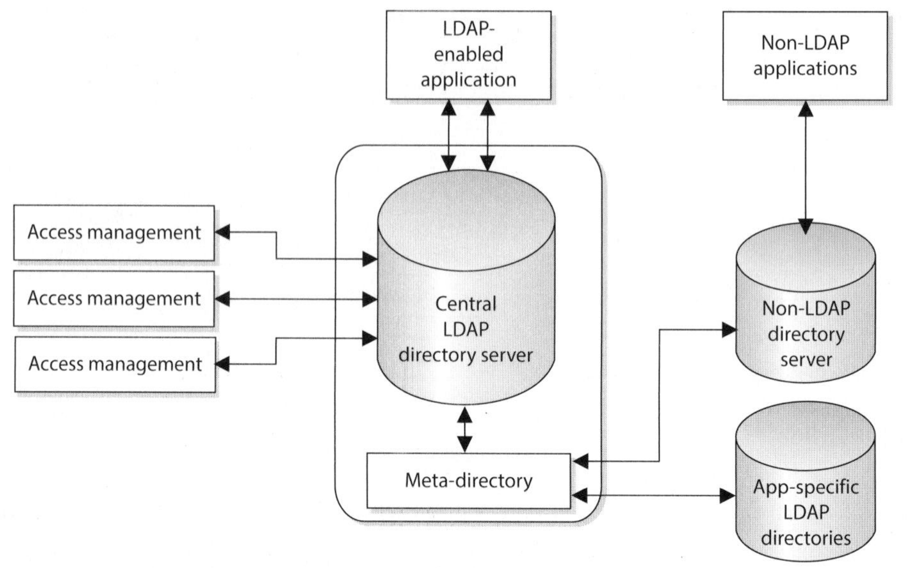

Figure 5-4 Meta-directories pull data from other sources to populate the IdM directory.

accepts a request from a user or application, it pulls the necessary data from the directory to be able to fulfill the request. Since the data needed to properly fulfill these requests is stored in different locations, the metadata directory pulls the data from these other sources and updates the LDAP directory.

Web Access Management *Web access management (WAM)* software controls what users can access when using a web browser to interact with web-based enterprise assets. This type of technology is continually becoming more robust and experiencing increased deployment. This is because of the increased use of e-commerce, online banking, content providing, web services, and more. The Internet only continues to grow, and its importance to businesses and individuals increases as more and more functionality is provided. We just can't seem to get enough of it.

Figure 5-5 shows the basic components and activities in a web access control management process.

1. User sends in credentials to web server.
2. Web server requests the WAM platform to authenticate the user. WAM authenticates against the LDAP directory and retrieves authorizations from the policy database.
3. User requests to access a resource (object).
4. Web server verifies that object access is authorized and allows access to the requested resource.

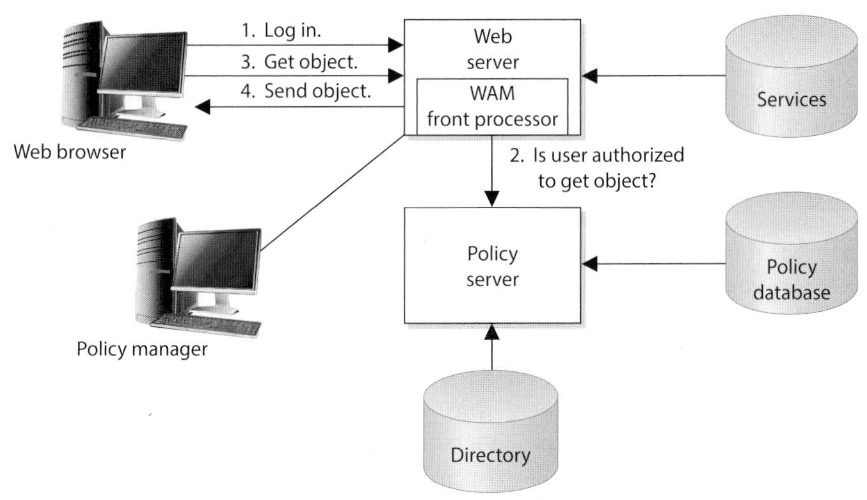

Figure 5-5 A basic example of web access control

This is a simple example. More complexity comes in with all the different ways a user can authenticate (password, digital certificate, token, and others); the resources and services that may be available to the user (transfer funds, purchase product, update profile, and so forth); and the necessary infrastructure components. The infrastructure is usually made up of a web server farm (many servers), a directory that contains the users' accounts and attributes, a database, a couple of firewalls, and some routers, all laid out in a tiered architecture. But let's keep it simple right now.

The WAM software is the main gateway between users and the corporate web-based resources. It is commonly a plug-in for a web server, so it works as a front-end process. When a user makes a request for access, the web server software will query a directory, an authentication server, and potentially a back-end database before serving up the resource the user requested. The WAM console allows the administrator to configure access levels, authentication requirements, and account setup workflow steps and to perform overall maintenance.

WAM tools usually also provide a single sign-on capability so that once a user is authenticated at a website, she can access different web-based applications and resources without having to log in multiple times. When a product provides a single sign-on capability in a web environment, the product must keep track of the user's authentication state and security context as the user moves from one resource to the next.

For example, if Kathy logs on to her online bank website, the communication is taking place over the HTTP protocol. This protocol itself is stateless, which means it will allow a web server to pass a web page to a user without keeping track of the user or the transaction. Many web servers work in a stateless mode because they have so many requests to fulfill and they are just providing users with web pages. Keeping a constant session with each and every user who is requesting to see a web page would sometimes needlessly tie up the web server's resources. When a user has to log on to a website is when "keeping the user's state" is required and a continuous session is needed.

When Kathy first goes to her bank's website, she is viewing publicly available data that does not require her to authenticate before viewing. A constant session is not being kept by the web server, thus it is working in a stateless manner. Once she clicks Access My Account, the web server sets up a secure connection (TLS) with her browser and requests her credentials. After she is authenticated, the web server sends a cookie (small text file) that indicates she has authenticated properly and the type of access she should be allowed. When Kathy requests to move from her savings account to her checking account, the web server will assess the cookie on Kathy's web browser to see if she has the rights to access this new resource. The web server continues to check this cookie during Kathy's session to ensure no one has hijacked the session and that the web server is continually communicating with Kathy's system and not someone else's.

The web server continually asks Kathy's web browser to prove she has been authenticated, which the browser does by providing the cookie information. (The cookie information could include her password, account number, security level, browsing habits, and/or personalization information.) As long as Kathy is authenticated, the web server software will keep track of each of her requests, log her events, and make changes that she requests that can take place in her security context. Security context is the authorization level she is assigned based on her permissions, entitlements, and access rights.

Once Kathy ends the session, the cookie is usually erased from the web browser's memory and the web server no longer keeps this connection open or collects session state information on this user.

NOTE A cookie can be in the format of a text file stored on the user's hard drive (permanent) or it can be only held in memory (session). If the cookie contains any type of sensitive information, then it should only be held in memory and be erased once the session has completed.

As an analogy, let's say Indira is following you in a mall as you are shopping. She is marking down what you purchase, where you go, and the requests you make. Indira knows everything about your actions; she documents them in a log and remembers them as you continue. (Indira is keeping state information on you and your activities.) You can have access to all of these stores if every 15 minutes you show Indira a piece of paper that she gave to you. If you fail to show Indira the piece of paper at the necessary interval, she will push a button and all stores will be locked—you no longer have access to the stores, she no longer collects information about you, and she leaves and forgets all about you. Since you are no longer able to access any sensitive objects (store merchandise), Indira doesn't need to keep track of you and what you are doing.

As long as the web server sends the cookie to the web browser, Kathy does not have to provide credentials as she asks for different resources. This is what single sign-on is. You only have to provide your credentials once, and the continual validation that you have the necessary cookie will allow you to go from one resource to another. If you end your session with the web server and need to interact with it again, you must re-authenticate, a new cookie will be sent to your browser, and it starts all over again.

NOTE We will cover specific single sign-on technologies later in this chapter along with their security issues.

So the WAM product allows an administrator to configure and control access to internal resources. This type of access control is commonly put in place to control external entities requesting access. The product may work on a single web server or a server farm.

Authentication

Let's now take a look at the various methods that are commonly used to verify that users are who they claim to be. This is commonly done these days through the use of passwords, personal identification numbers (PINs), biometrics (e.g., fingerprint scans), and access tokens. Each has specific characteristics that you must understand in order to pass the CISSP exam. Let's start with the most common of all authentication methods: the venerable password.

Password Management

We cover password requirements, security issues, and best practices later in this chapter. At this point, you need to understand how password management can work within an IdM environment.

Help-desk workers and administrators commonly complain about the amount of time they have to spend resetting passwords when users forget them. Another issue is the number of different passwords the users are required to remember for the different platforms within the network. When a password changes, an administrator must connect directly to that management software of the specific platform and change the password value. This may not seem like much of a hassle, but if an organization has 4,000 users, seven different platforms, and 35 different applications, the task of continually making these password modifications could require a full-time person. And who would really want *that* job?

Different types of password management technologies have been developed to get these pesky users off the backs of IT and the help desk by providing a more secure and automated password management system. The most common password management approaches are listed next:

- **Password synchronization** Reduces the complexity of keeping up with different passwords for different systems.
- **Self-service password reset** Reduces help-desk call volumes by allowing users to reset their own passwords.
- **Assisted password reset** Reduces the resolution process for password issues for the help desk. This may include authentication with other types of authentication mechanisms (such as biometrics or tokens).

Password Synchronization If users have too many passwords they need to keep track of, they will write the passwords down on a sticky note and cleverly hide this under their keyboard or just stick it on the side of their monitor. This is certainly easier for the user, but not so great for security.

Password synchronization technologies can allow a user to maintain just one password across multiple systems. The product will synchronize the password to other systems and applications, which happens transparently to the user.

The goal is to require the user to memorize only one password, which enables the organization to enforce more robust and secure password requirements. If a user needs to remember only one password, he is more likely to not have a problem with longer, more complex strings of values. This reduces help-desk call volume and allows the administrator to keep her sanity for just a little bit longer.

One criticism of this approach is that since only one password is used to access different resources, now the hacker only has to figure out one credential set to gain unauthorized access to all resources. But if the password requirements are more demanding (12 characters, no dictionary words, three symbols, uppercase and lowercase letters, and so on) and the password is changed out regularly, the balance between security and usability can be acceptable.

Self-Service Password Reset Some products are implemented to allow users to reset their own passwords. This does not mean that the users have any type of privileged permissions on the systems to allow them to change their own credentials. Instead, during the registration of a user account, the user can be asked to provide several personal questions (school graduated from, favorite teacher, favorite color, and so on) in a question-and-answer form. When the user forgets his password, he may be required to provide another authentication mechanism (smart card, token, etc.) and to answer these previously answered questions to prove his identity.

Products are available that allow users to change their passwords through other means. For example, if you forgot your password, you may be asked to answer some of the questions answered during the registration process of your account. If you do this correctly, an e-mail is sent to you with a link you must click. The password management product has your identity tied to the answers you gave to the questions during your account registration process and to your e-mail address. If you do everything correctly, you are given a screen that allows you to reset your password.

CAUTION The product should not ask for information that is publicly available, as in your mother's maiden name, because anyone can find that out and attempt to identify himself as you.

Assisted Password Reset Some products are created for help-desk employees who need to work with individuals when they forget their password. The help-desk employee should not know or ask the individual for her password. This would be a security risk since only the owner of the password should know the value. The help-desk employee also should not just change a password for someone calling in without authenticating that person first. This can allow social engineering attacks where an attacker calls the help desk and indicates she is someone who she is not. If this took place, then an attacker would have a valid employee password and could gain unauthorized access to the company's jewels.

The products that provide assisted password reset functionality allow the help-desk individual to authenticate the caller before resetting the password. This authentication process is commonly performed through the question-and-answer process described in the previous section. The help-desk individual and the caller must be identified and authenticated through the password management tool before the password can be changed. Once the password is updated, the system that the user is authenticating to should require the user to change her password again. This would ensure that only she (and not she and the help-desk person) knows her password. The goal of an assisted password reset product is to reduce the cost of support calls and ensure all calls are processed in a uniform, consistent, and secure fashion.

Various password management products on the market provide one or all of these functionalities. Since IdM is about streamlining identification, authentication, and access control, one of these products is typically integrated into the enterprise IdM solution.

Legacy Single Sign-On We will cover specific single sign-on technologies later in this chapter, but at this point we want to focus on how SSO products are commonly used as an IdM solution or as part of a larger IdM enterprise-wide solution.

An SSO technology allows a user to authenticate one time and then access resources in the environment without needing to reauthenticate. This may sound the same as password synchronization, but it is not. With password synchronization, a product takes the user's password and updates each user account on each different system and application with that one password. If Tom's password is *tommy2mato*, then this is the value he must type into each and every application and system he must access. In an SSO situation, Tom would send his password to one authentication system. When Tom requests to access a network application, the application will send over a request for credentials, but the SSO software will respond to the application for Tom. So in SSO environments, the SSO software intercepts the login prompts from network systems and applications and fills in the necessary identification and authentication information (that is, the username and password) for the user.

Even though password synchronization and single sign-on are different technologies, they still have the same vulnerability. If an attacker uncovers a user's credential set, she can have access to all the resources that the legitimate user may have access to.

An SSO solution may also provide a bottleneck or single point of failure. If the SSO server goes down, users are unable to access network resources. This is why it's a good idea to have some type of redundancy or fail-over technology in place.

Most environments are not homogeneous in devices and applications, which makes it more difficult to have a true enterprise SSO solution. Legacy systems many times require a different type of authentication process than the SSO software can provide. So potentially 80 percent of the devices and applications may be able to interact with the SSO software and the other 20 percent will require users to authenticate to them directly.

In many of these situations, the IT department may come up with their own homemade solutions, such as using login batch scripts for the legacy systems.

Are there any other downfalls with SSO you should be aware of? Well, it can be expensive to implement, especially in larger environments. Many times companies evaluate purchasing this type of solution and find out it is too cost-prohibitive. The other issue is that it would mean all of the users' credentials for the company's resources are stored in one location. If an attacker was able to break in to this storehouse, she could access whatever she wanted and *do* whatever she wanted with the company's assets.

As always, security, functionality, and cost must be properly weighed to determine the best solution for the company.

Account Management Account management is often not performed efficiently and effectively in companies today. Account management deals with creating user accounts on all systems, modifying the account privileges when necessary, and decommissioning the accounts when they are no longer needed. In most environments, the IT department creates accounts manually on the different systems, users are given excessive rights and permissions, and when an employee leaves the company, many or all of the accounts stay active. This is because a centralized account management technology has not been put into place.

Account management products attempt to attack these issues by allowing an administrator to manage user accounts across multiple systems. When there are multiple directories containing user profiles or access information, the account management software allows for replication between the directories to ensure each contains the same up-to-date information.

Now let's think about how accounts are set up. In many environments, when a new user needs an account, a network administrator will set up the account(s) and provide some type of privileges and permissions. But how would the network administrator know what resources this new user should have access to and what permissions should be assigned to the new account? In most situations, he doesn't—he just wings it. This is how users end up with too much access to too much stuff. What should take place instead is implementation of a workflow process that allows for a request for a new user account. This request is usually approved, by the employee's manager, and the accounts are automatically set up on the systems, or a ticket is generated for the technical staff to set up the account(s). If there is a request for a change to the permissions on the account or if an account needs to be decommissioned, it goes through the same process. The request goes to a manager (or whoever is delegated with this approval task), the manager approves it, and the changes to the various accounts take place.

The automated workflow component is common in account management products that provide IdM solutions. Not only does this reduce the potential errors that can take place in account management, but each step (including account approval) is logged and tracked. This allows for accountability and provides documentation for use in backtracking if something goes wrong. It also helps ensure that only the necessary amount of access is provided to the account and that there are no "orphaned" accounts still active when employees leave the company. In addition, these types of

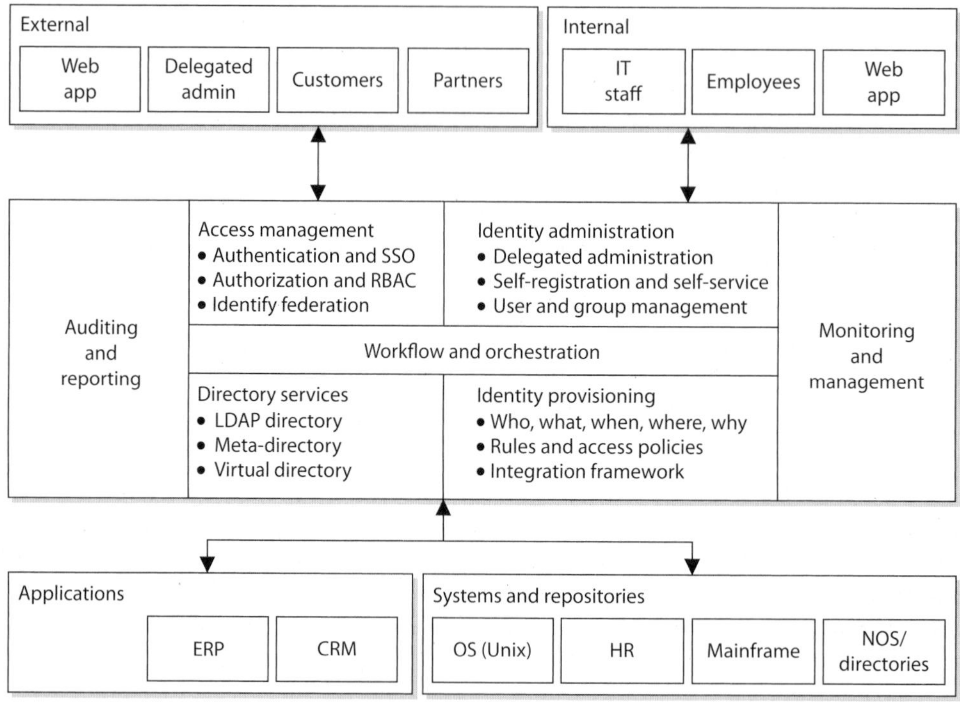

Figure 5-6 Enterprise identity management system components

so on). When this collection of data is associated with the identity of a user, it is called a profile.

The profile should be centrally located for easier management. IdM enterprise solutions have profile update technology that allows an administrator to create, make changes, or delete these profiles in an automated fashion when necessary. Many user profiles contain nonsensitive data that the user can update himself (called *self-service*). So if George moved to a new house, there should be a profile update tool that allows him to go into his profile and change his address information. Now, his profile may also contain sensitive data that should not be available to George—for example, his access rights to resources or information that he is going to get laid off on Friday.

You have interacted with a profile update technology if you have requested to update your personal information on a website, as in Orbitz, Amazon, or Expedia. These companies provide you with the capability to sign in and update the information they allow you to access. This could be your contact information, home address, purchasing preferences, or credit card data. This information is then used to update their CRM system so they know where to send you their junk mail advertisements or spam messages.

Biometrics

Biometrics verifies an individual's identity by analyzing a unique personal attribute or behavior, which is one of the most effective and accurate methods of verifying

identification. Biometrics is a very sophisticated technology; thus, it is much more expensive and complex than the other types of identity verification processes. A biometric system can make authentication decisions based on an individual's behavior, as in signature dynamics, but these can change over time and possibly be forged. Biometric systems that base authentication decisions on physical attributes (such as iris, retina, or fingerprint) provide more accuracy because physical attributes typically don't change, absent some disfiguring injury, and are harder to impersonate.

Biometrics is typically broken up into two different categories. The first is the physiological. These are traits that are physical attributes unique to a specific individual. Fingerprints are a common example of a physiological trait used in biometric systems.

The second category of biometrics is known as behavioral. This is based on a characteristic of an individual to confirm his identity. An example is signature dynamics. Physiological is "what you are" and behavioral is "what you do."

A biometric system scans a person's physiological attribute or behavioral trait and compares it to a record created in an earlier enrollment process. Because this system inspects the grooves of a person's fingerprint, the pattern of someone's retina, or the pitches of someone's voice, it must be extremely sensitive. The system must perform accurate and repeatable measurements of anatomical or behavioral characteristics. This type of sensitivity can easily cause false positives or false negatives. The system must be calibrated so these false positives and false negatives occur infrequently and the results are as accurate as possible.

When a biometric system rejects an authorized individual, it is called a *Type I error* (false rejection rate [FRR]). When the system accepts impostors who should be rejected, it is called a *Type II error* (false acceptance rate [FAR]). The goal is to obtain low numbers for each type of error, but Type II errors are the most dangerous and thus the most important to avoid.

When comparing different biometric systems, many different variables are used, but one of the most important metrics is the *crossover error rate (CER)*. This rating is stated as a percentage and represents the point at which the false rejection rate equals the false acceptance rate. This rating is the most important measurement when determining the system's accuracy. A biometric system that delivers a CER of 3 will be more accurate than a system that delivers a CER of 4.

NOTE Crossover error rate (CER) is also called equal error rate (EER).

What is the purpose of this CER value anyway? Using the CER as an impartial judgment of a biometric system helps create standards by which products from different vendors can be fairly judged and evaluated. If you are going to buy a biometric system, you need a way to compare the accuracy between different systems. You can just go by the different vendors' marketing material (they all say they are the best), or you can compare the different CER values of the products to see which one really is more accurate than

the others. It is also a way to keep the vendors honest. One vendor may tell you, "We have absolutely no Type II errors." This would mean that their product would not allow any imposters to be improperly authenticated. But what if you asked the vendor how many Type I errors their product had and she sheepishly replied, "We average around 90 percent of Type I errors." That would mean that 90 percent of the authentication attempts would be rejected, which would negatively affect your employees' productivity. So you can ask about their CER value, which represents when the Type I and Type II errors are equal, to give you a better understanding of the product's overall accuracy.

Individual environments have specific security level requirements, which will dictate how many Type I and Type II errors are acceptable. For example, a military institution that is very concerned about confidentiality would be prepared to accept a certain rate of Type I errors, but would absolutely not accept any false accepts (Type II errors). Because all biometric systems can be calibrated, if you lower the Type II error rate by adjusting the system's sensitivity, it will result in an increase in Type I errors. The military institution would obviously calibrate the biometric system to lower the Type II errors to zero, but that would mean it would have to accept a higher rate of Type I errors.

Biometrics is the most expensive method of verifying a person's identity, and it faces other barriers to becoming widely accepted. These include user acceptance, enrollment timeframe, and throughput. Many times, people are reluctant to let a machine read the pattern of their retina or scan the geometry of their hand. This lack of enthusiasm has slowed down the widespread use of biometric systems within our society. The enrollment phase requires an action to be performed several times to capture a clear and distinctive reference record. People are not particularly fond of expending this time and energy when they are used to just picking a password and quickly typing it into their console. When a person attempts to be authenticated by a biometric system, sometimes the system will request an action to be completed several times. If the system was unable to get a clear reading of an iris scan or could not capture a full voice verification print, the individual may have to repeat the action. This causes low throughput, stretches the individual's patience, and reduces acceptability.

During enrollment, the user provides the biometric data (e.g., fingerprint, voice print, or retina scan), and the biometric reader converts this data into binary values. Depending on the system, the reader may create a hash value of the biometric data, or it may encrypt the data, or do both. The biometric data then goes from the reader to a back-end authentication database where the user's account has been created. When the user needs to later authenticate to a system, she will provide the necessary biometric data, and the binary format of this information is compared to what is in the authentication database. If they match, then the user is authenticated.

In Figure 5-7, we see that biometric data can be stored on a smart card and used for authentication. Also, you might notice that the match is 95 percent instead of 100 percent. Obtaining a 100 percent match each and every time is very difficult because of the level of sensitivity of the biometric systems. A smudge on the reader, oil on the person's finger, and other small environmental issues can stand in the way of matching 100 percent. If your biometric system was calibrated so it required 100 percent matches, this would mean you would not allow any Type II errors and that users would commonly not be authenticated in a timely manner.

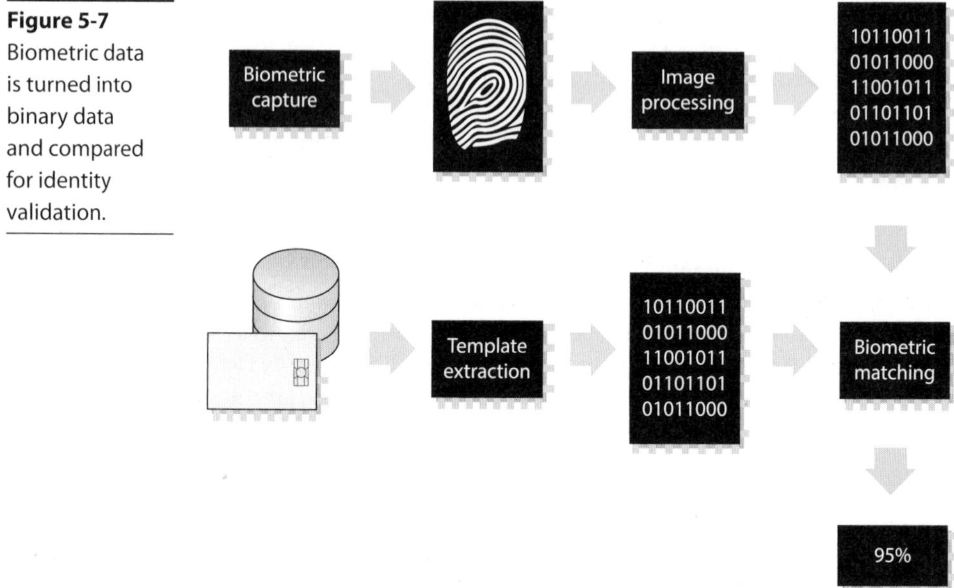

Figure 5-7 Biometric data is turned into binary data and compared for identity validation.

Processing Speed

When reviewing biometric devices for purchase, one component to take into consideration is the length of time it takes to actually authenticate users. From the time a user inserts data until she receives an accept or reject response should take five to ten seconds.

The following is an overview of the different types of biometric systems and the physiological or behavioral characteristics they examine.

Fingerprint Fingerprints are made up of ridge endings and bifurcations exhibited by friction ridges and other detailed characteristics called minutiae. It is the distinctiveness of these minutiae that gives each individual a unique fingerprint. An individual places his finger on a device that reads the details of the fingerprint and compares this to a reference file. If the two match, the individual's identity has been verified.

NOTE Fingerprint systems store the full fingerprint, which is actually a lot of information that takes up hard drive space and resources. The finger-scan technology extracts specific features from the fingerprint and stores just that information, which takes up less hard drive space and allows for quicker database lookups and comparisons.

Palm Scan The palm holds a wealth of information and has many aspects that are used to identify an individual. The palm has creases, ridges, and grooves throughout that are unique to a specific person. The palm scan also includes the fingerprints of each finger. An individual places his hand on the biometric device, which scans and captures this information. This information is compared to a reference file, and the identity is either verified or rejected.

Hand Geometry The shape of a person's hand (the shape, length, and width of the hand and fingers) defines hand geometry. This trait differs significantly between people and is used in some biometric systems to verify identity. A person places her hand on a device that has grooves for each finger. The system compares the geometry of each finger, and the hand as a whole, to the information in a reference file to verify that person's identity.

Retina Scan A system that reads a person's retina scans the blood-vessel pattern of the retina on the backside of the eyeball. This pattern has shown to be extremely unique between different people. A camera is used to project a beam inside the eye and capture the pattern and compare it to a reference file recorded previously.

NOTE Retina scans are extremely invasive and involve a number of privacy issues. Since the information obtained through this scan can be used in the diagnosis of medical conditions, it could very well be considered protected health information (PHI) subject to HIPAA (see Chapter 1).

Iris Scan The iris is the colored portion of the eye that surrounds the pupil. The iris has unique patterns, rifts, colors, rings, coronas, and furrows. The uniqueness of each of these characteristics within the iris is captured by a camera and compared with the information gathered during the enrollment phase. Of the biometric systems, iris scans are the most accurate. The iris remains constant through adulthood, which reduces the type of errors that can happen during the authentication process. Sampling the iris offers more reference coordinates than any other type of biometric. Mathematically, this means it has a higher accuracy potential than any other type of biometric.

NOTE When using an iris pattern biometric system, the optical unit must be positioned so the sun does not shine into the aperture; thus, when implemented, it must have proper placement within the facility.

Signature Dynamics When a person writes a signature, usually they do so in the same manner and speed each time. Writing a signature produces electrical signals that can be captured by a biometric system. The physical motions performed when someone is signing a document create these electrical signals. The signals provide unique characteristics that can be used to distinguish one individual from another. Signature dynamics provides more information than a static signature, so there are more variables to verify when confirming an individual's identity and more assurance that this person is who he claims to be.

Signature dynamics is different from a digitized signature. A digitized signature is just an electronic copy of someone's signature and is not a biometric system that captures the speed of signing, the way the person holds the pen, and the pressure the signer exerts to generate the signature.

Keystroke Dynamics Whereas signature dynamics is a method that captures the electrical signals when a person signs a name, keystroke dynamics captures electrical signals when a person types a certain phrase. As a person types a specified phrase, the biometric system captures the speed and motions of this action. Each individual has a certain style and speed, which translate into unique signals. This type of authentication is more effective than typing in a password, because a password is easily obtainable. It is much harder to repeat a person's typing style than it is to acquire a password.

Voice Print People's speech sounds and patterns have many subtle distinguishing differences. A biometric system that is programmed to capture a voice print and compare it to the information held in a reference file can differentiate one individual from another. During the enrollment process, an individual is asked to say several different words. Later, when this individual needs to be authenticated, the biometric system jumbles these words and presents them to the individual. The individual then repeats the sequence of words given. This technique is used so others cannot attempt to record the session and play it back in hopes of obtaining unauthorized access.

Facial Scan A system that scans a person's face takes many attributes and characteristics into account. People have different bone structures, nose ridges, eye widths, forehead sizes, and chin shapes. These are all captured during a facial scan and compared to an earlier captured scan held within a reference record. If the information is a match, the person is positively identified.

Hand Topography Whereas hand geometry looks at the size and width of an individual's hand and fingers, hand topology looks at the different peaks and valleys of the hand, along with its overall shape and curvature. When an individual wants to be authenticated, she places her hand on the system. Off to one side of the system, a camera snaps a side-view picture of the hand from a different view and angle than that of systems that target hand geometry, and thus captures different data. This attribute is not unique enough to authenticate individuals by itself and is commonly used in conjunction with hand geometry.

Biometric systems are not without their own sets of issues and concerns. Because they depend upon the specific and unique traits of living things, problems can arise. Living things are notorious for not remaining the same, which means they won't present static biometric information for each and every login attempt. Voice recognition can be hampered by a user with a cold. Pregnancy can change the patterns of the retina. Someone could lose a finger. Or all three could happen. You just never know in this crazy world.

Some biometric systems actually check for the pulsation and/or heat of a body part to make sure it is alive. So if you are planning to cut someone's finger off or pluck out someone's eyeball so you can authenticate yourself as a legitimate user, it may not work. Although not specifically stated, this type of activity definitely falls outside the bounds of the CISSP ethics you will be responsible for upholding once you receive your certification.

Passwords

User identification coupled with a reusable password is the most common form of system identification and authorization mechanisms. A *password* is a protected string of characters that is used to authenticate an individual. As stated previously, authentication factors are based on what a person knows, has, or is. A password is something the user knows.

Passwords are one of the most often used authentication mechanisms employed today. It is important to ensure that the passwords are strong and properly managed.

Password Policies Although passwords are the most commonly used authentication mechanism, they are also considered one of the weakest security mechanisms available. Why? Users usually choose passwords that are easily guessed (a spouse's name, a user's birth date, or a dog's name), or tell others their passwords, and many times write the passwords down on a sticky note and hide it under the keyboard. To most users, security is usually not the most important or interesting part of using their computers—except when someone hacks into their computer and steals confidential information, that is. Then security is all the rage.

This is where password policies step in. If passwords are properly generated, updated, and kept secret, they can provide effective security. Password generators can be used to create passwords for users. This ensures that a user will not be using "Bob" or "Spot" for a password, but if the generator spits out "kdjasijew284802h," the user will surely scribble it down on a piece of paper and stick it to the monitor, which defeats the whole purpose. If a password generator is going to be used, the tools should create uncomplicated, pronounceable, nondictionary words to help users remember them so they aren't tempted to write them down.

If the users can choose their own passwords, the operating system should enforce certain password requirements. The operating system can require that a password contain a certain number of characters, unrelated to the user ID, include special characters, include upper- and lowercase letters, and not be easily guessable. The operating system can keep track of the passwords a specific user generates so as to ensure no passwords are reused. The users should also be forced to change their passwords periodically. All of these factors make it harder for an attacker to guess or obtain passwords within the environment.

If an attacker is after a password, she can try a few different techniques:

- **Electronic monitoring** Listening to network traffic to capture information, especially when a user is sending her password to an authentication server. The password can be copied and reused by the attacker at another time, which is called a *replay attack.*
- **Access the password file** Usually done on the authentication server. The password file contains many users' passwords and, if compromised, can be the source of a lot of damage. This file should be protected with access control mechanisms and encryption.

- **Brute-force attacks** Performed with tools that cycle through many possible character, number, and symbol combinations to uncover a password.
- **Dictionary attacks** Files of thousands of words are compared to the user's password until a match is found.
- **Social engineering** An attacker falsely convinces an individual that she has the necessary authorization to access specific resources.
- **Rainbow table** An attacker uses a table that contains all possible passwords already in a hash format.

Certain techniques can be implemented to provide another layer of security for passwords and their use. After each successful logon, a message can be presented to a user indicating the date and time of the last successful logon, the location of this logon, and whether there were any unsuccessful logon attempts. This alerts the user to any suspicious activity and whether anyone has attempted to log on using his credentials. An administrator can set operating parameters that allow a certain number of failed logon attempts to be accepted before a user is locked out; this is a type of *clipping level*. The user can be locked out for five minutes or a full day after the threshold (or clipping level) has been exceeded. It depends on how the administrator configures this mechanism. An audit trail can also be used to track password usage and both successful and unsuccessful logon attempts. This audit information should include the date, time, user ID, and workstation the user logged in from.

NOTE *Clipping level* is an older term that just means threshold. If the number of acceptable failed login attempts is set to three, three is the threshold (clipping level) value.

A password's lifetime should be short but practical. Forcing a user to change a password on a more frequent basis provides more assurance that the password will not be guessed by an intruder. If the lifetime is too short, however, it causes unnecessary management overhead, and users may forget which password is active. A balance between protection and practicality must be decided upon and enforced.

As with many things in life, education is the key. Password requirements, protection, and generation should be addressed in security-awareness programs so users understand what is expected of them, why they should protect their passwords, and how passwords can be stolen. Users should be an extension to a security team, not the opposition.

NOTE Rainbow tables contain passwords already in their hashed format. The attacker just compares a captured hashed password with one that is listed in the table to uncover the plaintext password. This takes much less time than carrying out a dictionary or brute-force attack.

Password Checkers Several organizations test user-chosen passwords using tools that perform dictionary and/or brute-force attacks to detect the weak passwords. This helps make the environment as a whole less susceptible to dictionary and exhaustive attacks used to discover users' passwords. Many times the same tools employed by an attacker to crack a password are used by a network administrator to make sure the password is strong enough. Most security tools have this dual nature. They are used by security professionals and IT staff to test for vulnerabilities within their environment in the hope of uncovering and fixing them before an attacker finds the vulnerabilities. An attacker uses the same tools to uncover vulnerabilities to exploit before the security professional can fix them. It is the never-ending cat-and-mouse game.

If a tool is called a *password checker*, it is used by a security professional to test the strength of a password. If a tool is called a *password cracker*, it is usually used by a hacker; however, most of the time, these tools are one and the same.

You need to obtain management's approval before attempting to test (break) employees' passwords with the intent of identifying weak passwords. Explaining you are trying to help the situation, not hurt it, *after* you have uncovered the CEO's password is not a good situation to be in.

Password Hashing and Encryption In most situations, if an attacker sniffs your password from the network wire, she still has some work to do before she actually knows your password value because most systems hash the password with a hashing algorithm, commonly MD4 or MD5, to ensure passwords are not sent in cleartext.

Although some people think the world is run by Microsoft, other types of operating systems are out there, such as Unix and Linux. These systems do not use registries and SAM databases, but contain their user passwords in a file cleverly called "shadow." This shadow file does not contain passwords in cleartext; instead, your password is run through a hashing algorithm, and the resulting value is stored in this file. Unix-type systems zest things up by using salts in this process. *Salts* are random values added to the encryption process to add more complexity and randomness. The more randomness entered into the encryption process, the harder it is for the bad guy to decrypt and uncover your password. The use of a salt means that the same password can be encrypted into several thousand different hashes. This makes it much more difficult for an adversary to attack the passwords in your system.

Password Aging Many systems enable administrators to set expiration dates for passwords, forcing users to change them at regular intervals. The system may also keep a list of the last five to ten passwords (password history) and not let the users revert to previously used passwords.

Limit Logon Attempts A threshold can be set to allow only a certain number of unsuccessful logon attempts. After the threshold is met, the user's account can be locked for a period of time or indefinitely, which requires an administrator to manually unlock the account. This protects against dictionary and other exhaustive attacks that continually submit credentials until the right combination of username and password is discovered.

Cognitive Password

Cognitive passwords are fact- or opinion-based information used to verify an individual's identity. A user is enrolled by answering several questions based on her life experiences. Passwords can be hard for people to remember, but that same person will not likely forget the first person they kissed, the name of their best friend in 8th grade, or their favorite cartoon character. After the enrollment process, the user can answer the questions asked of her to be authenticated instead of having to remember a password. This authentication process is best for a service the user does not use on a daily basis because it takes longer than other authentication mechanisms. This can work well for help-desk services. The user can be authenticated via cognitive means. This way, the person at the help desk can be sure he is talking to the right person, and the user in need of help does not need to remember a password that may be used once every three months.

EXAM TIP Authentication by knowledge means that a subject is authenticated based upon something she knows. This could be a PIN, password, passphrase, cognitive password, personal history information, or through the use of a CAPTCHA, which is the graphical representation of data. A CAPTCHA is a skewed representation of characteristics a person must enter to prove that the subject is a human and not an automated tool as in a software robot.

One-Time Password

A *one-time password (OTP)* is also called a dynamic password. It is used for authentication purposes and is good only once. After the password is used, it is no longer valid; thus, if a hacker obtained this password, it could not be reused. This type of authentication mechanism is used in environments that require a higher level of security than static passwords provide. One-time password-generating tokens come in two general types: synchronous and asynchronous.

The token device is the most common implementation mechanism for OTP and generates the one-time password for the user to submit to an authentication server. It is commonly implemented in three formats: as a dedicated physical device with a small screen that displays the OTP, as a smartphone application, and as a service that sends an SMS message to your phone. The following sections explain the concepts behind this technology.

The Token Device The token device, or password generator, is usually a handheld device that has an LCD display and possibly a keypad. This hardware is separate from the computer the user is attempting to access. The token device and authentication service must be synchronized in some manner to be able to authenticate a user. The token device presents the user with a list of characters to be entered as a password when logging on to a computer. Only the token device and authentication service know the meaning of these characters. Because the two are synchronized, the token device will present the exact password the authentication service is expecting. This is a one-time password, also called a token, and is no longer valid after initial use.

Synchronous A *synchronous token device* synchronizes with the authentication service by using time or a counter as the core piece of the authentication process. If the synchronization is time-based, the token device and the authentication service must hold the same time within their internal clocks. The time value on the token device and a secret key are used to create the OTP, which is displayed to the user. The user enters this value and a user ID into the computer, which then passes them to the server running the authentication service. The authentication service decrypts this value and compares it to the value it expected. If the two match, the user is authenticated and allowed to use the computer and resources.

If the token device and authentication service use *counter-synchronization*, the user will need to initiate the creation of the OTP by pushing a button on the token device. This causes the token device and the authentication service to advance to the next authentication value. This value and a base secret are hashed and displayed to the user. The user enters this resulting value along with a user ID to be authenticated. In either time- or counter-based synchronization, the token device and authentication service must share the same secret base key used for encryption and decryption.

SecurID

SecurID, from RSA Security, Inc., is a well-known time-based token. One version of the product generates the OTP by using a mathematical function on the time, date, and ID of the token card. Another version of the product requires a PIN to be entered into the token device.

RSA SecureID Time-Synchronous Two-Factor Authentication

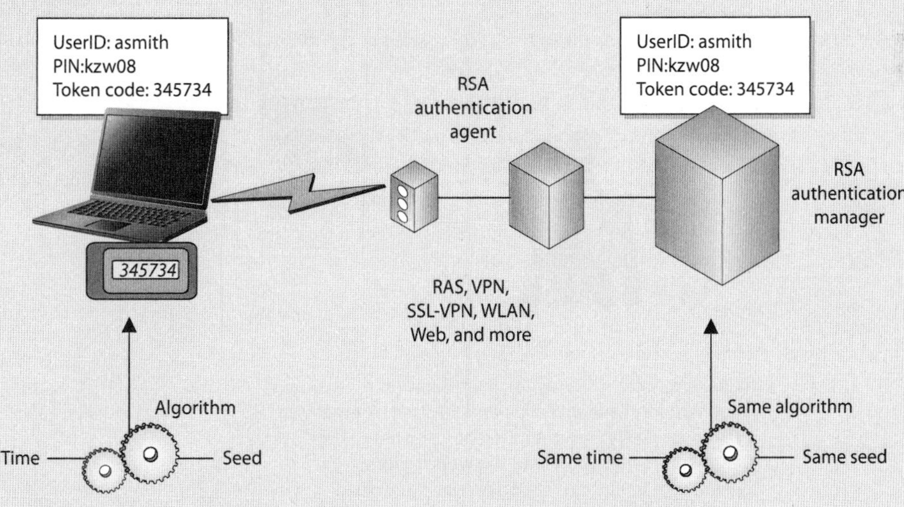

EXAM TIP Synchronous token-based OTP generation can be time-based or counter-based. Another term for counter-based is event-based. Counter-based and event-based are interchangeable terms, and you could see either or both on the CISSP exam.

Asynchronous A token device using an *asynchronous token*–generating method employs a challenge/response scheme to authenticate the user. In this situation, the authentication server sends the user a challenge, a random value, also called a *nonce*. The user enters this random value into the token device, which encrypts it and returns a value the user uses as an OTP. The user sends this value, along with a username, to the authentication server. If the authentication server can decrypt the value and it is the same challenge value sent earlier, the user is authenticated, as shown in Figure 5-8.

EXAM TIP The actual implementation and process that these devices follow can differ between different vendors. What is important to know is that asynchronous is based on challenge/response mechanisms, while synchronous is based on time- or counter-driven mechanisms.

Both token systems can fall prey to masquerading if a user shares his identification information (ID or username) and the token device is shared or stolen. The token device can also have battery failure or other malfunctions that would stand in the way of a

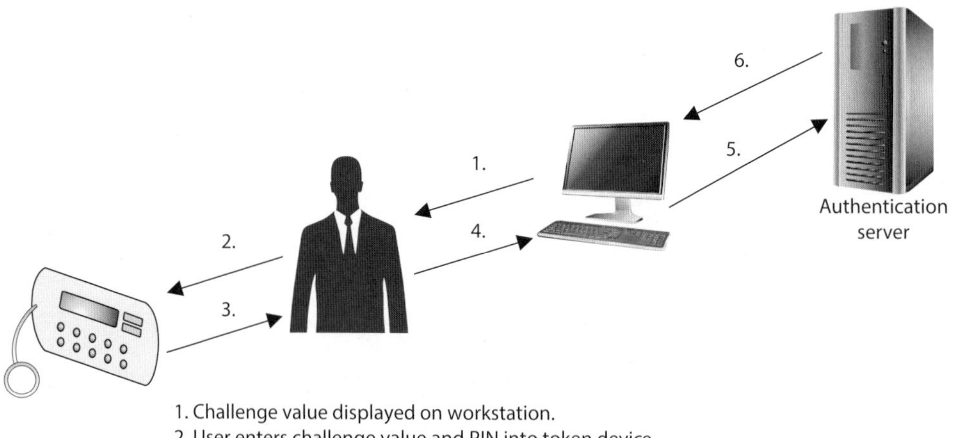
6.
5.
1.
4.
2.
3.
Authentication server
1. Challenge value displayed on workstation.
2. User enters challenge value and PIN into token device.
3. Token device presents a different value to the user.
4. User enters new value into the workstation.
5. Value sent to authentication service on server.
6. AS sends an "allow access" response.

Figure 5-8 Authentication using an asynchronous token device includes a workstation, token device, and authentication service.

successful authentication. However, this type of system is not vulnerable to electronic eavesdropping, sniffing, or password guessing.

If the user has to enter a password or PIN into the token device before it provides an OTP, then strong authentication is in effect because it is using two factors—something the user knows (PIN) and something the user has (the token device).

NOTE One-time passwords can also be generated in software, in which case a piece of hardware such as a token device is not required. These are referred to as *soft tokens* and require that the authentication service and application contain the same base secrets, which are used to generate the OTPs.

Cryptographic Keys

Another way to prove one's identity is to use a private key by generating a digital signature. A digital signature could be used in place of a password. Passwords are the weakest form of authentication and can be easily sniffed as they travel over a network. Digital signatures are forms of authentication used in environments that require higher security protection than what is provided by passwords.

A private key is a secret value that should be in the possession of one person, and one person only. It should never be disclosed to an outside party. A digital signature is a technology that uses a private key to encrypt a hash value (message digest). The act of encrypting this hash value with a private key is called *digitally signing* a message. A digital signature attached to a message proves the message originated from a specific source and that the message itself was not changed while in transit.

A public key can be made available to anyone without compromising the associated private key; this is why it is called a public key. We explore private keys, public keys, digital signatures, and public key infrastructure (PKI) in Chapter 7, but for now, understand that a private key and digital signatures are other mechanisms that can be used to authenticate an individual.

Passphrase

A *passphrase* is a sequence of characters that is longer than a password (thus a "phrase") and, in some cases, takes the place of a password during an authentication process. The user enters this phrase into an application, and the application transforms the value into a *virtual password*, making the passphrase the length and format that is required by the application. (For example, an application may require your virtual password to be 128 bits to be used as a key with the AES algorithm.) If a user wants to authenticate to an application, such as Pretty Good Privacy (PGP), he types in a passphrase, let's say StickWithMeKidAndYouWillWearDiamonds. The application converts this phrase into a virtual password that is used for the actual authentication. The user usually generates the passphrase in the same way a user creates a password the first time he logs on to a computer. A passphrase is more secure than a password because it is longer, and thus harder to obtain by an attacker. In many cases, the user is more likely to remember a passphrase than a password.

Memory Cards

The main difference between memory cards and smart cards is their capacity to process information. A *memory card* holds information but cannot process information. A *smart card* holds information and has the necessary hardware and software to actually process that information. A memory card can hold a user's authentication information so the user only needs to type in a user ID or PIN and present the memory card, and if the data that the user entered matches the data on the memory card, the user is successfully authenticated. If the user presents a PIN value, then this is an example of two-factor authentication—something the user knows and something the user has. A memory card can also hold identification data that is pulled from the memory card by a reader. It travels with the PIN to a back-end authentication server. An example of a memory card is a swipe card that must be used for an individual to be able to enter a building. The user enters a PIN and swipes the memory card through a card reader. If this is the correct combination, the reader flashes green and the individual can open the door and enter the building. Another example is an ATM card. If Buffy wants to withdraw $40 from her checking account, she needs to slide the ATM card (or memory card) through the reader and enter the correct PIN.

Memory cards can be used with computers, but they require a reader to process the information. The reader adds cost to the process, especially when one is needed per computer, and card generation adds cost and effort to the whole authentication process. Using a memory card provides a more secure authentication method than using a password because the attacker would need to obtain the card and know the correct PIN. Administrators and management must weigh the costs and benefits of a memory token–based card implementation to determine if it is the right authentication mechanism for their environment.

Smart Card

A *smart card* has the capability of processing information because it has a microprocessor and integrated circuits incorporated into the card itself. Memory cards do not have this type of hardware and lack this type of functionality. The only function they can perform is simple storage. A smart card, which adds the capability to process information stored on it, can also provide a two-factor authentication method because the user may have to enter a PIN to unlock the smart card. This means the user must provide something she knows (PIN) and something she has (smart card).

Two general categories of smart cards are the contact and the contactless types. The *contact* smart card has a gold seal on the face of the card. When this card is fully inserted into a card reader, electrical fingers wipe against the card in the exact position that the chip contacts are located. This will supply power and data I/O to the chip for authentication purposes. The *contactless* smart card has an antenna wire that surrounds the perimeter of the card. When this card comes within an electromagnetic field of the reader, the antenna within the card generates enough energy to power the internal chip. Now, the results of the smart card processing can be broadcast through the same antenna, and the conversation of authentication can take place. The authentication can be completed by using a one-time password, by employing a challenge/response value, or by providing the user's private key if it is used within a PKI environment.

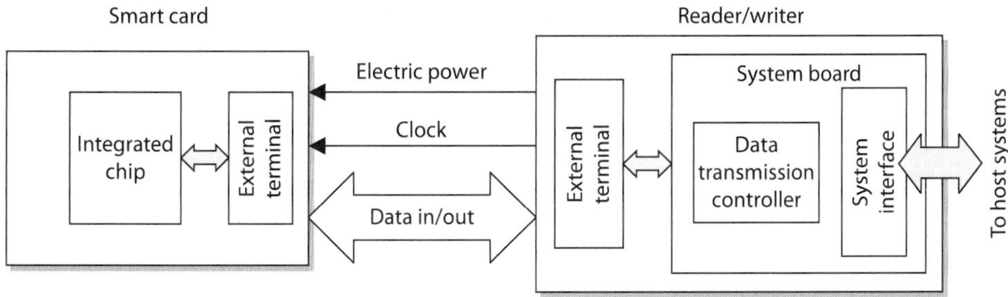

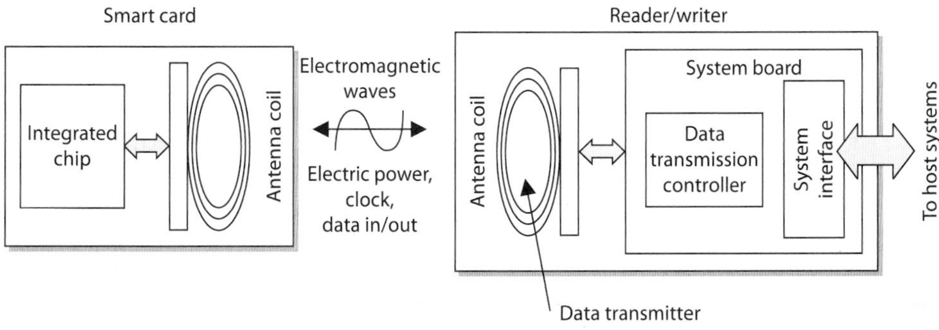

TIP Two types of contactless smart cards are available: hybrid and combi. The hybrid card has two chips, with the capability of utilizing both the contact and contactless formats. A combi card has one microprocessor chip that can communicate to contact or contactless readers.

The information held within the memory of a smart card is not readable until the correct PIN is entered. This fact and the complexity of the smart token make these cards resistant to reverse-engineering and tampering methods. If George loses the smart card he uses to authenticate to the domain at work, the person who finds the card would need to know his PIN to do any real damage. The smart card can also be programmed to store information in an encrypted fashion, as well as detect any tampering with the card itself. In the event that tampering is detected, the information stored on the smart card can be automatically wiped.

The drawbacks to using a smart card are the extra cost of the readers and the overhead of card generation, as with memory cards, although this cost is decreasing. The smart cards themselves are more expensive than memory cards because of the extra integrated circuits and microprocessor. Essentially, a smart card is a kind of computer, and because of that it has many of the operational challenges and risks that can affect a computer.

Smart cards have several different capabilities, and as the technology develops and memory capacities increase for storage, they will gain even more. They can store personal information in a storage manner that is tamper resistant. This also gives them the capability to isolate security-critical computations within themselves. They can be used in encryption systems in order to store keys and have a high level of portability as well as security. The memory and integrated circuit also allow for the capacity to use encryption algorithms on the actual card and use them for secure authorization that can be utilized throughout an entire organization.

Smart Card Attacks Smart cards are more tamperproof than memory cards, but where there is sensitive data, there are individuals who are motivated to circumvent any countermeasure the industry throws at them.

Over the years, criminals have become very inventive in the development of various ways to attack smart cards. For example, attackers have introduced computational errors into smart cards with the goal of uncovering the encryption keys used and stored on the cards. These "errors" are introduced by manipulating some environmental component of the card (changing input voltage, clock rate, temperature fluctuations). The attacker reviews the result of an encryption function after introducing an error to the card, and also reviews the correct result, which the card performs when no errors are introduced. Analysis of these different results may allow an attacker to reverse-engineer the encryption process, with the hope of uncovering the encryption key. This type of attack is referred to as *fault generation*.

Side-channel attacks are nonintrusive and are used to uncover sensitive information about how a component works, without trying to compromise any type of flaw or weakness. As an analogy, suppose you want to figure out what your boss does each day at lunchtime but you feel too uncomfortable to ask her. So you follow her, and you see that she enters a building holding a small black bag and exits exactly 45 minutes later with the same bag and her hair not looking as great as when she went in. You do this day after day for a week and come to the conclusion that she must be exercising.

So a noninvasive attack is one in which the attacker watches how something works and how it reacts in different situations instead of trying to "invade" it with more intrusive measures. Some examples of side-channel attacks that have been carried out on smart cards are *differential power analysis* (examining the power emissions released during processing), *electromagnetic analysis* (examining the frequencies emitted), and *timing* (how long a specific process takes to complete). These types of attacks are used to uncover sensitive information about how a component works without trying to compromise any type of flaw or weakness. They are commonly used for data collection. Attackers monitor and capture the analog characteristics of all supply and interface connections and any other electromagnetic radiation produced by the processor during normal operation. They can also collect the time it takes for the smart card to carry out its function. From the collected data, the attacker can deduce specific information she is after, which could be a private key, sensitive financial data, or an encryption key stored on the card.

Software attacks are also considered noninvasive attacks. A smart card has software just like any other device that does data processing, and anywhere there is software there is the possibility of software flaws that can be exploited. The main goal of this type of attack is to input instructions into the card that will allow the attacker to extract account information, which he can use to make fraudulent purchases. Many of these types of attacks can be disguised by using equipment that looks just like the legitimate reader.

A more intrusive smart card attack is called *microprobing*. Microprobing uses needleless and ultrasonic vibration to remove the outer protective material on the card's circuits. Once this is completed, data can be accessed and manipulated by directly tapping into the card's ROM chips.

Interoperability

In the industry today, lack of interoperability is a big problem. Although vendors claim to be "compliant with ISO/IEC 14443," many have developed technologies and methods in a more proprietary fashion. The lack of true standardization has caused some large problems because smart cards are being used for so many different applications. In the United States, the Department of Defense (DoD) is rolling out smart cards across all of its agencies, and NIST is developing a framework and conformance testing programs specifically for interoperability issues.

An ISO/IEC standard, 14443, outlines the following items for smart card standardization:

- **ISO/IEC 14443-1** Physical characteristics
- **ISO/IEC 14443-3** Initialization and anticollision
- **ISO/IEC 14443-4** Transmission protocol

Radio-Frequency Identification (RFID)

Radio-frequency identification (RFID) is a technology that provides data communication through the use of radio waves. An object contains an electronic tag, which can be identified and communicated with through a reader. The tag has an integrated circuit for storing and processing data, modulating and demodulating a radio-frequency (RF) signal, and other specialized functions. The reader has a built-in antenna for receiving and transmitting the signal. This type of technology can be integrated into smart cards or other mobile transport mechanisms for access control purposes. A common security issue with RFID is that the data can be captured as it moves from the tag to the reader. While encryption can be integrated as a countermeasure, it is not common because RFID is implemented in technology that has low processing capabilities and encryption is very processor-intensive.

Authorization

Although authentication and authorization are quite different, together they comprise a two-step process that determines whether an individual is allowed to access a particular resource. In the first step, authentication, the individual must prove to the system that he is who he claims to be—a permitted system user. After successful authentication, the system must establish whether the user is authorized to access the particular resource and what actions he is permitted to perform on that resource.

Authorization is a core component of every operating system, but applications, security add-on packages, and resources themselves can also provide this functionality. For example, suppose Marge has been authenticated through the authentication server and now wants to view a spreadsheet that resides on a file server. When she finds this spreadsheet and double-clicks the icon, she will see an hourglass instead of a mouse pointer. At this stage, the file server is checking if Marge has the rights and permissions to view the requested spreadsheet. It also checks if Marge can modify, delete, move, or copy the file. Once the file server searches through an access matrix and finds that Marge does indeed have the necessary rights to view this file, the file opens on Marge's desktop. The decision of whether or not to allow Marge to see this file was based on access criteria. Access criteria are the crux of authentication.

Access Criteria

We have gone over the basics of access control. This subject can get very granular in its level of detail when it comes to dictating what a subject can or cannot do to an object or resource. This is a good thing for network administrators and security professionals, because they want to have as much control as possible over the resources they have been put in charge of protecting, and a fine level of detail enables them to give individuals just the precise level of access they need. It would be frustrating if access control permissions were based only on full control or no access. These choices are very limiting, and an administrator would end up giving everyone full control, which would provide no protection. Instead, different ways of limiting access to resources exist, and if they are understood and used properly, they can give just the right level of access desired.

Granting access rights to subjects should be based on the level of trust a company has in a subject and the subject's need to know. Just because a company completely trusts Joyce with its files and resources does not mean she fulfills the need-to-know criteria to access the company's tax returns and profit margins. If Maynard fulfills the need-to-know criteria to access employees' work histories, it does not mean the company trusts him to access all of the company's other files. These issues must be identified and integrated into the access criteria. The different access criteria can be enforced by roles, groups, location, time, and transaction types.

Using *roles* is an efficient way to assign rights to a type of user who performs a certain task. This role is based on a job assignment or function. If there is a position within a company for a person to audit transactions and audit logs, the role this person fills would only need a read function to those types of files. This role would not need full control, modify, or delete privileges.

Using *groups* is another effective way of assigning access control rights. If several users require the same type of access to information and resources, putting them into a group and then assigning rights and permissions to that group is easier to manage than assigning rights and permissions to each and every individual separately. If a specific printer is available only to the accounting group, when a user attempts to print to it, the group membership of the user will be checked to see if she is indeed in the accounting group. This is one way that access control is enforced through a logical access control mechanism.

Physical or logical location can also be used to restrict access to resources. Some files may be available only to users who can log on interactively to a computer. This means the user must be physically at the computer and enter the credentials locally versus logging on remotely from another computer. This restriction is implemented on several server configurations to restrict unauthorized individuals from being able to get in and reconfigure the server remotely.

Logical location restrictions are usually done through network address restrictions. If a network administrator wants to ensure that status requests of an intrusion detection management console are accepted only from certain computers on the network, the network administrator can configure this within the software.

Time of day, or temporal isolation, is another access control mechanism that can be used. If a security professional wants to ensure no one is accessing payroll files between the hours of 8:00 P.M. and 4:00 A.M., she can implement that configuration to ensure access at these times is restricted. If the same security professional wants to ensure no bank account transactions happen during days on which the bank is not open, she can indicate in the logical access control mechanism this type of action is prohibited on Sundays.

Temporal access can also be based on the creation date of a resource. Let's say Russell started working for his company in March 2011. There may be a business need to allow Russell to only access files that have been created after this date and not before.

Transaction-type restrictions can be used to control what data is accessed during certain types of functions and what commands can be carried out on the data. An online banking program may allow a customer to view his account balance, but may not allow the customer to transfer money until he has a certain security level or access right. A bank teller may be able to cash checks of up to $2,000, but would need a supervisor's access code to retrieve more funds for a customer. A database administrator may be able to build a database for the human resources department, but may not be able to read certain confidential files within that database. These are all examples of transaction-type restrictions to control the access to data and resources.

Default to No Access

Access control mechanisms should default to no access so as to provide the necessary level of security and ensure no security holes go unnoticed. A wide range of access levels is available to assign to individuals and groups, depending on the application and/or operating system. A user can have read, change, delete, full control, or no access permissions. The statement that security mechanisms should default to no access means that if nothing has been specifically configured for an individual or the group she belongs to, that user should not be able to access that resource. If access is not explicitly allowed, it should be implicitly denied. Security is all about being safe, and this is the safest approach to practice when dealing with access control methods and mechanisms. In other words, all access controls should be based on the concept of starting with zero access, and building on top of that. Instead of giving access to everything, and then taking away privileges based on need to know, the better approach is to start with nothing and add privileges based on need to know.

Most access control lists (ACLs) that work on routers and packet-filtering firewalls default to no access. Figure 5-9 shows that traffic from Subnet A is allowed to access Subnet B, traffic from Subnet D is not allowed to access Subnet A, and Subnet B is allowed to talk to Subnet A. All other traffic transmission paths not listed here are not allowed by default. Subnet D cannot talk to Subnet B because such access is not explicitly indicated in the router's ACL.

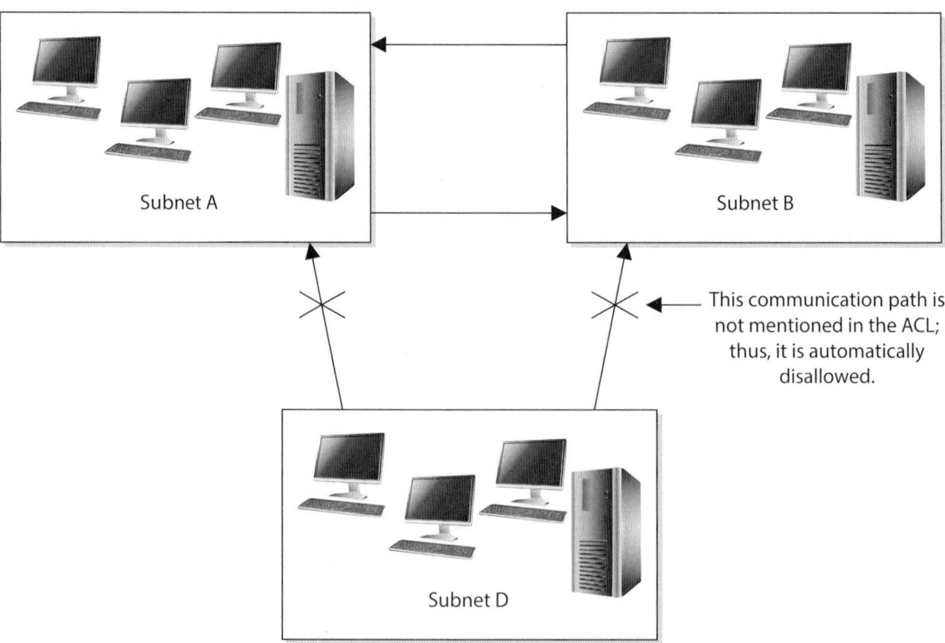

Figure 5-9 What is not explicitly allowed should be implicitly denied.

Need to Know

The *need-to-know* principle is similar to the *least-privilege* principle. It is based on the concept that individuals should be given access only to the information they absolutely require in order to perform their job duties. Giving any more rights to a user just asks for headaches and the possibility of that user abusing the permissions assigned to him. An administrator wants to give a user the least amount of privileges she can, but just enough for that user to be productive when carrying out tasks. Management will decide what a user needs to know, or what access rights are necessary, and the administrator will configure the access control mechanisms to allow this user to have that level of access and no more, and thus the least privilege.

For example, if management has decided that Dan, the copy boy, needs to know where the files he needs to copy are located and needs to be able to print them, this fulfills Dan's need-to-know criteria. Now, an administrator could give Dan full control of all the files he needs to copy, but that would not be practicing the least-privilege principle. The administrator should restrict Dan's rights and permissions to only allow him to read and print the necessary files, and no more. Besides, if Dan accidentally deletes all the files on the whole file server, whom do you think management will hold ultimately responsible? Yep, the administrator.

It is important to understand that it is management's job to determine the security requirements of individuals and how access is authorized. The security administrator configures the security mechanisms to fulfill these requirements, but it is not her job to determine security requirements of users. Those should be left to the owners. If there is a security breach, management will ultimately be held responsible, so it should make these decisions in the first place.

Authorization Creep

As employees work at a company over time and move from one department to another, they often are assigned more and more access rights and permissions. This is commonly referred to as *authorization creep*. It can be a large risk for a company, because too many users have too much privileged access to company assets. In the past, it has usually been easier for network administrators to give more access than less, because then the user would not come back and require more work to be done on her profile. It is also difficult to know the exact access levels different individuals require. This is why user management and user provisioning are becoming more prevalent in identity management products today and why companies are moving more toward role-based access control implementation. Enforcing least privilege on user accounts should be an ongoing job, which means each user's rights are permissions that should be reviewed to ensure the company is not putting itself at risk.

Note that rights and permission reviews have been incorporated into many regulatory-induced processes. As part of the Sarbanes-Oxley (SOX) regulations, managers have to review their employees' permissions to data on an annual basis.

Single Sign-On

Employees typically need to access many different computers, servers, databases, and other resources in the course of a day to complete their tasks. This often requires the employees to remember multiple user IDs and passwords for these different computers. In a utopia, a user would need to enter only one user ID and one password to be able to access all resources in all the networks this user is working in. In the real world, this is hard to accomplish for all system types.

Because of the proliferation of client/server technologies, networks have migrated from centrally controlled networks to heterogeneous, distributed environments. The propagation of open systems and the increased diversity of applications, platforms, and operating systems have caused the end user to have to remember several user IDs and passwords just to be able to access and use the different resources within his own network. Although the different IDs and passwords are supposed to provide a greater level of security, they often end up compromising security (because users write them down) and causing more effort and overhead for the staff that manages and maintains the network.

As any network staff member or administrator can attest to, too much time is devoted to resetting passwords for users who have forgotten them. More than one employee's productivity is affected when forgotten passwords have to be reassigned. The network staff member who has to reset the password could be working on other tasks, and the user who forgot the password cannot complete his task until the network staff member is finished resetting the password. Many help-desk employees report that a majority of their time is spent on users forgetting their passwords. System administrators have to manage multiple user accounts on different platforms, which all need to be coordinated in a manner that maintains the integrity of the security policy. At times the complexity can be overwhelming, which results in poor access control management and the generation of many security vulnerabilities. A lot of time is spent on multiple passwords, and in the end they do not provide us with more security.

The increased cost of managing a diverse environment, security concerns, and user habits, coupled with the users' overwhelming desire to remember one set of credentials, has brought about the idea of *single sign-on (SSO)* capabilities. These capabilities would allow a user to enter credentials one time and be able to access all resources in primary and secondary network domains. This reduces the amount of time users spend authenticating to resources and enables the administrator to streamline user accounts and better control access rights. It improves security by reducing the probability that users will write down passwords and also reduces the administrator's time spent on adding and removing user accounts and modifying access permissions. If an administrator needs to disable or suspend a specific account, she can do it uniformly instead of having to alter configurations on each and every platform.

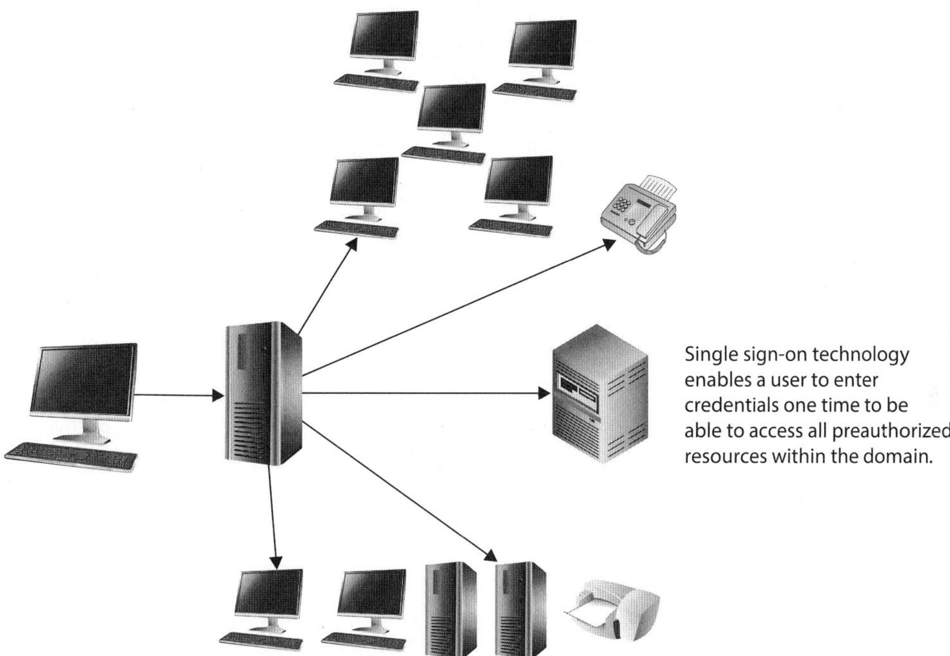

Single sign-on technology enables a user to enter credentials one time to be able to access all preauthorized resources within the domain.

So that is our utopia: log on once and you are good to go. What bursts this bubble? Mainly interoperability issues. For SSO to actually work, every platform, application, and resource needs to accept the same type of credentials, in the same format, and interpret their meanings the same. When Steve logs on to his Windows workstation and gets authenticated by a mixed-mode Windows domain controller, it must authenticate him to the resources he needs to access on the Apple computer, the Unix server running NIS, the mainframe host server, the MICR print server, and the Windows computer in the secondary domain that has the plotter connected to it. A nice idea, until reality hits.

There is also a security issue to consider in an SSO environment. Once an individual is in, he is in. If an attacker was able to uncover one credential set, he would have access to every resource within the environment that the compromised account has access to. This is certainly true, but one of the goals is that if a user only has to remember one password, and not ten, then a more robust password policy can be enforced. If the user has just one password to remember, then it can be more complicated and secure because he does not have nine other ones to remember also.

SSO technologies come in different types. Each has its own advantages and disadvantages, shortcomings, and quality features. It is rare to see a real SSO environment; rather, you will see a cluster of computers and resources that accept the same credentials. Other resources, however, still require more work by the administrator or user side to access the systems. The SSO technologies that may be addressed in the CISSP exam are described in the next sections.

Kerberos *Kerberos* is the name of a three-headed dog that guards the entrance to the underworld in Greek mythology. This is a great name for a security technology that provides authentication functionality, with the purpose of protecting a company's assets. Kerberos is an authentication protocol and was designed in the mid-1980s as part of MIT's Project Athena. It works in a client/server model and is based on symmetric key cryptography. The protocol has been used for years in Unix systems and is currently the default authentication method for Windows 2000 and later operating systems. In addition, Apple OS X, Oracle Solaris, and Red Hat Enterprise Linux all use Kerberos authentication. Commercial products supporting Kerberos are becoming more frequent, so this one might be a keeper.

Kerberos is an example of an SSO system for distributed environments, and is a de facto standard for heterogeneous networks. Kerberos incorporates a wide range of security capabilities, which gives companies much more flexibility and scalability when they need to provide an encompassing security architecture. It has four elements necessary for enterprise access control: scalability, transparency, reliability, and security. However, this open architecture also invites interoperability issues. When vendors have a lot of freedom to customize a protocol, it usually means no two vendors will customize it in the same fashion. This creates interoperability and incompatibility issues.

Kerberos uses symmetric key cryptography and provides end-to-end security. Although it allows the use of passwords for authentication, it was designed specifically to eliminate the need to transmit passwords over the network. Most Kerberos implementations work with shared secret keys.

Main Components in Kerberos The *Key Distribution Center (KDC)* is the most important component within a Kerberos environment. The KDC holds all users' and services' secret keys. It provides an authentication service, as well as key distribution functionality. The clients and services trust the integrity of the KDC, and this trust is the foundation of Kerberos security.

The KDC provides security services to *principals*, which can be users, applications, or network services. The KDC must have an account for, and share a secret key with, each principal. For users, a password is transformed into a secret key value. The secret key can be used to send sensitive data back and forth between the principal and the KDC, and is used for user authentication purposes.

A *ticket* is generated by the *ticket granting service (TGS)* on the KDC and given to a principal when that principal, let's say a user, needs to authenticate to another principal, let's say a print server. The ticket enables one principal to authenticate to another principal. If Emily needs to use the print server, she must prove to the print server she is who she claims to be and that she is authorized to use the printing service. So Emily requests a ticket from the TGS. The TGS gives Emily the ticket, and in turn, Emily passes this ticket on to the print server. If the print server approves this ticket, Emily is allowed to use the print service.

A KDC provides security services for a set of principles. This set is called a *realm* in Kerberos. The KDC is the trusted authentication server for all users, applications, and services within a realm. One KDC can be responsible for one realm or several realms. Realms are used to allow an administrator to logically group resources and users.

So far, we know that principals (users and services) require the KDC's services to authenticate to each other; that the KDC has a database filled with information about each and every principal within its realm; that the KDC holds and delivers cryptographic keys and tickets; and that tickets are used for principals to authenticate to each other. So how does this process work?

The Kerberos Authentication Process The user and the KDC share a secret key, while the service and the KDC share a different secret key. The user and the requested service do not share a symmetric key in the beginning. The user trusts the KDC because they share a secret key. They can encrypt and decrypt data they pass between each other, and thus have a protected communication path. Once the user authenticates to the service, they, too, will share a symmetric key (session key) that is used for authentication purposes.

Here are the exact steps:

1. Emily comes in to work and enters her username and password into her workstation at 8:00 A.M.

   The Kerberos software on Emily's computer sends the username to the authentication service (AS) on the KDC, which in turn sends Emily a ticket granting ticket (TGT) that is encrypted with the TGS's secret key.
2. If Emily has entered her correct password, then this TGT is decrypted and Emily gains access to her local workstation desktop.
3. When Emily needs to send a print job to the print server, her system sends the TGT to the TGS, which runs on the KDC, and a request to access the print server. (The TGT allows Emily to prove she has been authenticated and allows her to request access to the print server.)
4. The TGS creates and sends a second ticket to Emily, which she will use to authenticate to the print server. This second ticket contains two instances of the same session key, one encrypted with Emily's secret key and the other encrypted with the print server's secret key. The second ticket also contains an *authenticator*, which contains identification information on Emily, her system's IP address, sequence number, and a timestamp.
5. Emily's system receives the second ticket, decrypts and extracts the embedded session key, adds a second authenticator set of identification information to the ticket, and sends the ticket on to the print server.
6. The print server receives the ticket, decrypts and extracts the session key, and decrypts and extracts the two authenticators in the ticket. If the print server can decrypt and extract the session key, it knows the KDC created the ticket, because only the KDC has the secret key used to encrypt the session key. If the authenticator information that the KDC and the user put into the ticket matches, then the print server knows it received the ticket from the correct principal.
7. Once this is completed, it means Emily has been properly authenticated to the print server and the server prints her document.

This is an extremely simplistic overview of what is going on in any Kerberos exchange, but it gives you an idea of the dance taking place behind the scenes whenever you interact with any network service in an environment that uses Kerberos. Figure 5-10 provides a simplistic view of this process.

The authentication service is the part of the KDC that authenticates a principal, and the TGS is the part of the KDC that makes the tickets and hands them out to the principals. TGTs are used so the user does not have to enter his password each time he needs to communicate with another principal. After the user enters his password, it is temporarily stored on his system, and any time the user needs to communicate with another principal, he just reuses the TGT.

EXAM TIP Be sure you understand that a session key is different from a secret key. A secret key is shared between the KDC and a principal and is static in nature. A session key is shared between two principals and is generated when needed and destroyed after the session is completed.

If a Kerberos implementation is configured to use an *authenticator*, the user sends to the print server her identification information and a timestamp and sequence number encrypted with the session key they share. The print server decrypts this information and compares it with the identification data the KDC sent to it about this requesting user. If

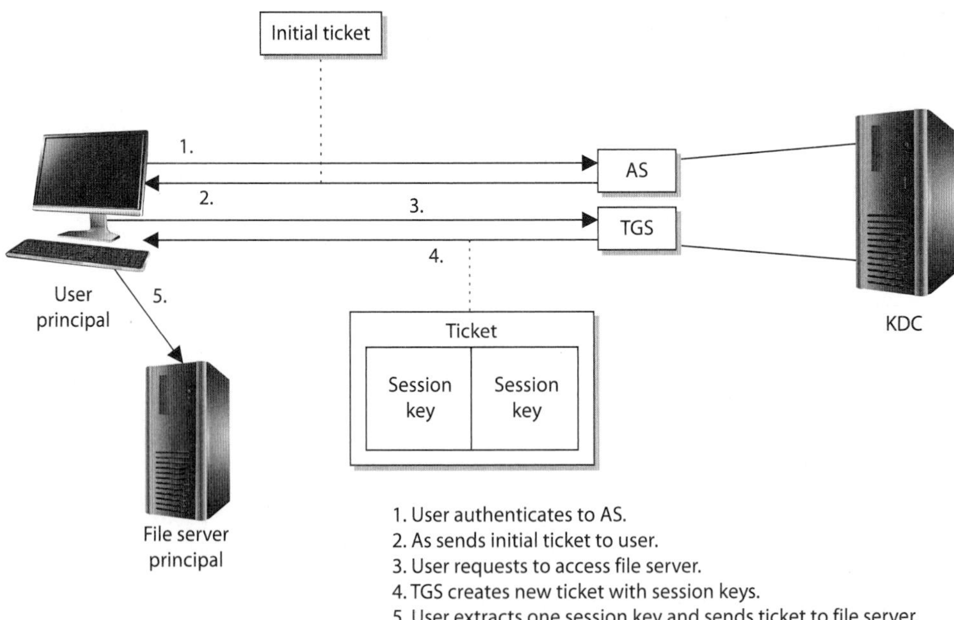
Initial ticket
1.
2.
3.
4.
5.
AS
TGS
KDC
User principal
Ticket
Session key
Session key
File server principal
1. User authenticates to AS.
2. As sends initial ticket to user.
3. User requests to access file server.
4. TGS creates new ticket with session keys.
5. User extracts one session key and sends ticket to file server.

Figure 5-10 The user must receive a ticket from the KDC before being able to use the requested resource.

the data is the same, the print server allows the user to send print jobs. The timestamp is used to help fight against replay attacks. The print server compares the sent timestamp with its own internal time, which helps determine if the ticket has been sniffed and copied by an attacker and then submitted at a later time in hopes of impersonating the legitimate user and gaining unauthorized access. The print server checks the sequence number to make sure that this ticket has not been submitted previously. This is another countermeasure to protect against replay attacks.

NOTE A replay attack is when an attacker captures and resubmits data (commonly a credential) with the goal of gaining unauthorized access to an asset.

The primary reason to use Kerberos is that the principals do not trust each other enough to communicate directly. In our example, the print server will not print anyone's print job without that entity authenticating itself. So none of the principals trust each other directly; they only trust the KDC. The KDC creates tickets to vouch for the individual principals when they need to communicate. Suppose Rodrigo needs to communicate directly with you, but you do not trust him enough to listen and accept what he is saying. If he first gives you a ticket from something you do trust (KDC), this basically says, "Look, the KDC says I am a trustworthy person. The KDC asked me to give this ticket to you to prove it." Once that happens, *then* you will communicate directly with Rodrigo.

The same type of trust model is used in PKI environments. In a PKI environment, users do not trust each other directly, but they all trust the certificate authority (CA). The CA vouches for the individuals' identities by using digital certificates, the same as the KDC vouches for the individuals' identities by using tickets.

So why are we talking about Kerberos? Because it is one example of an SSO technology. The user enters a user ID and password one time and one time only. The tickets have time limits on them that administrators can configure. Many times, the lifetime of a TGT is eight to ten hours, so when the user comes in the next day, he will have to present his credentials again.

NOTE Kerberos is an open protocol, meaning that vendors can manipulate it to work properly within their products and environments. The industry has different "flavors" of Kerberos, since various vendors require different functionality.

Weaknesses of Kerberos The following are some of the potential weaknesses of Kerberos:

- The KDC can be a single point of failure. If the KDC goes down, no one can access needed resources. Redundancy is necessary for the KDC.
- The KDC must be able to handle the number of requests it receives in a timely manner. It must be scalable.

- Secret keys are temporarily stored on the users' workstations, which means it is possible for an intruder to obtain these cryptographic keys.
- Session keys are decrypted and reside on the users' workstations, either in a cache or in a key table. Again, an intruder can capture these keys.
- Kerberos is vulnerable to password guessing. The KDC does not know if a dictionary attack is taking place.
- Network traffic is not protected by Kerberos if encryption is not enabled.
- If the keys are too short, they can be vulnerable to brute-force attacks.
- Kerberos needs all client and server clocks to be synchronized.

Kerberos must be transparent (work in the background without the user needing to understand it), scalable (work in large, heterogeneous environments), reliable (use distributed server architecture to ensure there is no single point of failure), and secure (provide authentication and confidentiality).

Kerberos and Password-Guessing Attacks

Just because an environment uses Kerberos does not mean the systems are vulnerable to password-guessing attacks. The operating system itself will (should) provide the protection of tracking failed login attempts. The Kerberos protocol does not have this type of functionality, so another component must be in place to counter these types of attacks. No need to start ripping Kerberos out of your network environment after reading this section; your operating system provides the protection mechanism for this type of attack.

Security Domains The term "domain" has been around a lot longer than Microsoft, but when people hear this term, they often think of a set of computers and devices on a network segment being controlled by a server that runs Microsoft software, referred to as a domain controller. A domain is really just a set of resources available to a subject. Remember that a subject can be a user, process, or application. Within an operating system, a process has a domain, which is the set of system resources available to the process to carry out its tasks. These resources can be memory segments, hard drive space, operating system services, and other processes. In a network environment, a domain is a set of physical and logical resources that is available, which can include routers, file servers, FTP service, web servers, and so forth.

The term *security domain* just builds upon the definition of domain by adding the fact that resources within this logical structure (domain) are working under the same security policy and managed by the same group. So, a network administrator may put all of the accounting personnel, computers, and network resources in Domain 1 and all of the management personnel, computers, and network resources in Domain 2. These items fall into these individual containers because they not only carry out similar types of business functions, but also, and more importantly, have the same type of trust level. It is this common trust level that allows entities to be managed by one single security policy.

The different domains are separated by logical boundaries, such as firewalls with ACLs, directory services making access decisions, and objects that have their own ACLs indicating which individuals and groups can carry out operations on them. All of these security mechanisms are examples of components that enforce the security policy for each domain.

Domains can be architected in a hierarchical manner that dictates the relationship between the different domains and the ways in which subjects within the different domains can communicate. Subjects can access resources in domains of equal or lower trust levels. Figure 5-11 shows an example of hierarchical network domains. Their communication

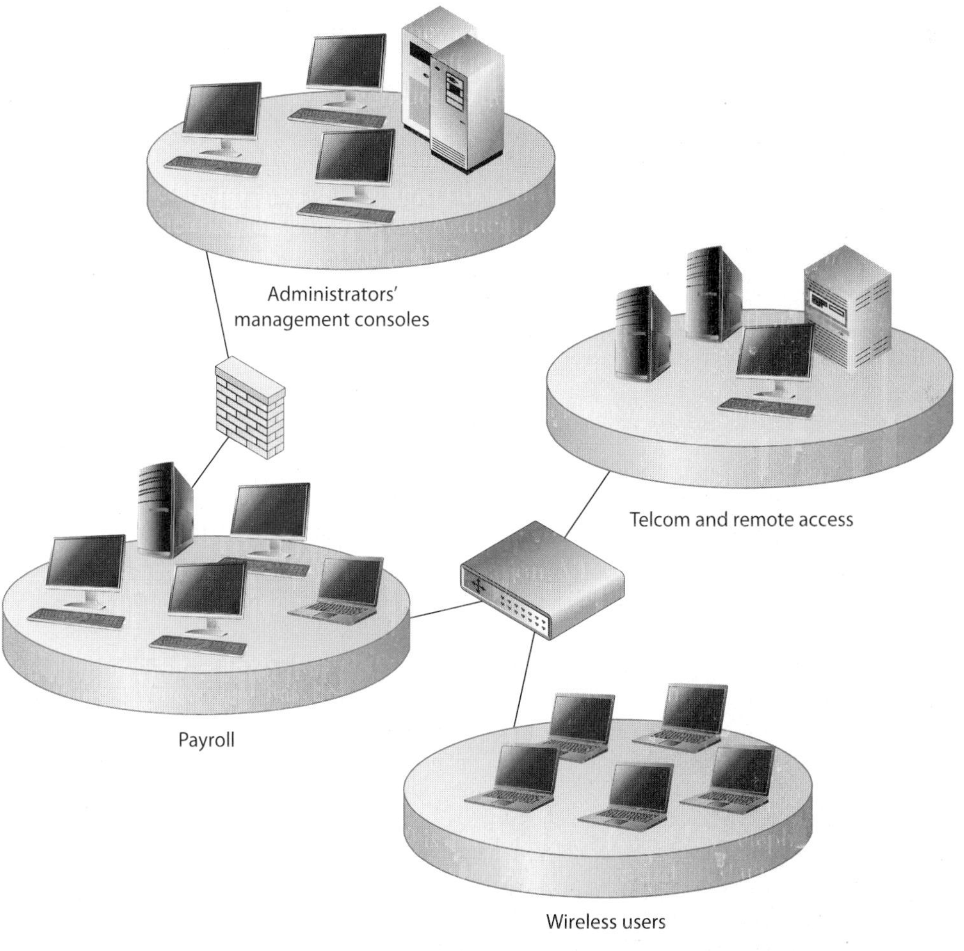

Figure 5-11 Network domains are used to separate different network segments.

channels are controlled by security agents (firewalls, router ACLs, directory services), and the individual domains are isolated by using specific subnet mask addresses.

Remember that a domain does not necessarily pertain only to network devices and segmentations, but can also apply to users and processes. Figure 5-12 shows how users and processes can have more granular domains assigned to them individually based on their trust level. Group 1 has a high trust level and can access both a domain of its own trust level (Domain 1) and a domain of a lower trust level (Domain 2). User 1, who has a lower trust level, can access only the domain at his trust level and nothing higher. The system enforces these domains with access privileges and rights provided by the file system and operating system security kernel.

So why are domains in the "Single Sign-On" section? Because several different types of technologies available today are used to define and enforce these domains and security

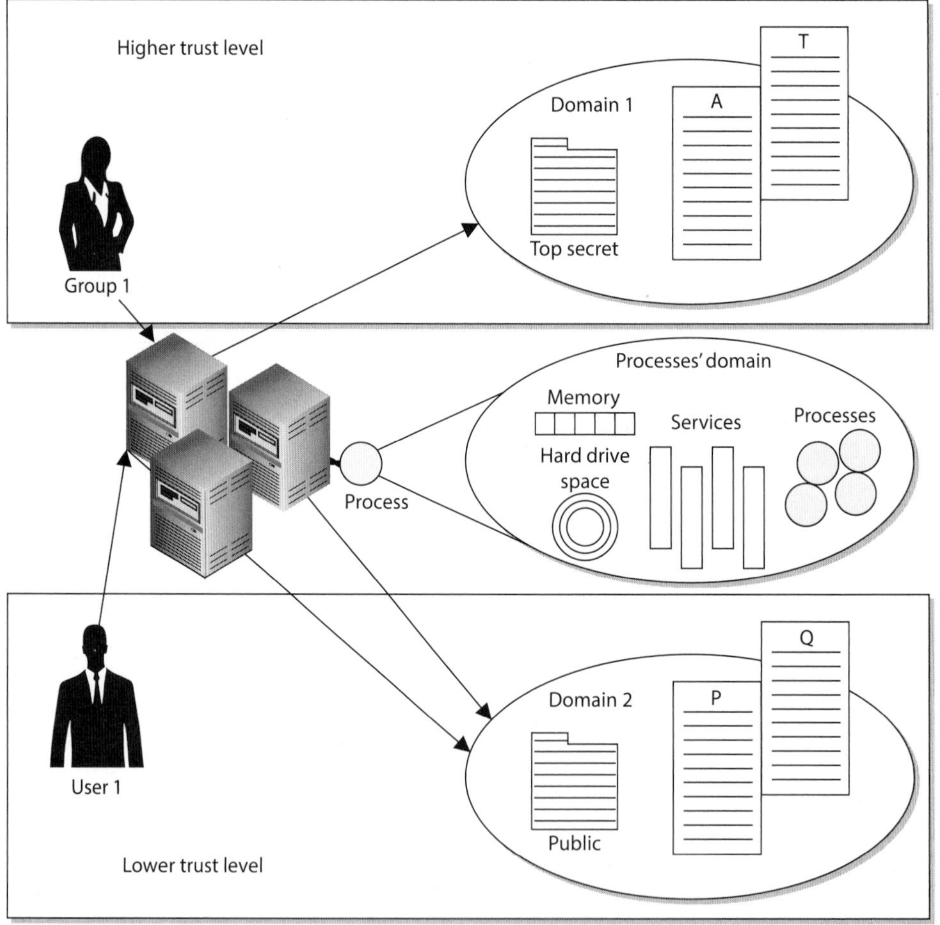

Figure 5-12 Subjects can access specific domains based on their trust levels.

policies mapped to them: domain controllers in a Windows environment, ERM products, Microsoft accounts, and the various products that provide SSO functionality. The goal of each of them is to allow a user (subject) to sign in one time and be able to access the different domains available without having to reenter any other credentials.

Directory Services While we covered directory services in the "Identity Management" section, it is also important for you to realize that it is considered a single sign-on technology in its own right, so we will review the characteristics again within this section.

A network service is a mechanism that identifies resources (printers, file servers, domain controllers, and peripheral devices) on a network. A network directory service contains information about these different resources and the subjects that need to access them and carries out access control activities. If the directory service is working in a database based on the X.500 standard, it works in a hierarchical schema that outlines the resources' attributes, such as name, logical and physical location, subjects that can access them, and the operations that can be carried out on them.

In a database based on the X.500 standard, access requests are made from users and other systems using the LDAP protocol (discussed earlier in the chapter). This type of database provides a hierarchical structure for the organization of objects (subjects and resources). The directory service develops unique distinguished names for each object and appends the corresponding attribute to each object as needed. The directory service enforces a security policy (configured by the administrator) to control how subjects and objects interact.

Network directory services provide users access to network resources transparently, meaning that users don't need to know the exact location of the resources or the steps required to access them. The network directory services handle these issues for the user in the background. Some examples of directory services are LDAP, NetIQ eDirectory, and Microsoft Active Directory (also discussed earlier).

Thin Clients Diskless computers and thin clients cannot store much information because of their lack of onboard storage space and necessary resources. This type of client/server technology forces users to log on to a central server just to use the computer and access network resources. When the user starts the computer, it runs a short list of instructions and then points itself to a server that will actually download the operating system, or interactive operating software, to the terminal. This enforces a strict type of access control, because the computer cannot do anything on its own until it authenticates to a centralized server, and then the server gives the computer its operating system, profile, and functionality. Thin-client technology provides another type of SSO access for users because users authenticate only to the central server or mainframe, which then provides them access to all authorized and necessary resources.

In addition to providing an SSO solution, a thin-client technology offers several other advantages. A company can save money by purchasing thin clients instead of powerful and expensive PCs. The central server handles all application execution, processing, and data storage. The thin client displays the graphical representation and sends mouse clicks and keystroke inputs to the central server. Having all of the software in one location instead of distributed throughout the environment allows for easier administration,

centralized access control, easier updates, and standardized configurations. It is also easier to control malware infestations and the theft of confidential data because the thin clients often do not have optical disc drives or USB ports.

NOTE The technology industry came from a centralized model, with the use of mainframes and dumb terminals, and is in some ways moving back toward this model with the use of terminal services, Citrix, service-oriented architecture, and cloud computing.

Single Sign-On Technologies: A Summary

- **Kerberos** Authentication protocol that uses a KDC and tickets, and is based on symmetric key cryptography
- **Security domains** Resources working under the same security policy and managed by the same group
- **Directory services** Technology that allows resources to be named in a standardized manner and access control to be maintained centrally
- **Thin clients** Terminals that rely upon a central server for access control, processing, and storage

Federation

The world continually gets smaller as technology brings people and companies closer together. Many times, when we are interacting with just one website, we are actually interacting with several different companies—we just don't know it. The reason we don't know it is because these companies are sharing our identity and authentication information behind the scenes. This is not done for nefarious purposes necessarily, but to make our lives easier and to allow merchants to sell their goods without much effort on our part.

Digital Identity

An interesting little fact that not many people are aware of is that a *digital identity* is made up of attributes, entitlements, and traits. Many of us just think of identity as a user ID that is mapped to an individual. The truth is that it is usually more complicated than that.

A user's identity can be a collection of her attributes (department, role in company, shift time, clearance, and others); her entitlements (resources available

to her, authoritative rights in the company, and so on); and her traits (biometric information, height, sex, and so forth).

So if a user requests access to a database that contains sensitive employee information, the IdM solution would need to pull together the necessary identity information and her supplied credentials before she is authorized access. If the user is a senior manager (attribute), with a secret clearance (attribute), and has access to the database (entitlement)—she is granted the permissions read and write to certain records in the database Monday through Friday, 8 A.M. to 5 P.M. (attribute).

Another example is if a soldier requests to be assigned an M-16 firearm. She must be in the 34th division (attribute), have a top secret clearance (attribute), her supervisor must have approved this (entitlement), and her physical features (traits) must match the ID card she presents to the firearm depot clerk.

The directory (or meta-directory) of the IdM system has all of this identity information centralized, which is why it is so important.

Many people think that just logging into a domain controller or a network access server is all that is involved in identity management. But if you peek under the covers, you can find an array of complex processes and technologies working together.

The CISSP exam is not currently getting into this level of detail (entitlement, attribute, traits) pertaining to IdM, but in the real world there are many facets to identification, authentication, authorization, and auditing that make it a complex beast.

For example, a person wants to book an airline flight and a hotel room. If the airline company and hotel company use a federated identity management system, this means they have set up a trust relationship between the two companies and will share customer identification and, potentially, authentication information. So when you book a flight on Southwest, the website asks if you want to also book a hotel room. If you click "Yes," you could then be brought to the Hilton website, which provides information on the closest hotel to the airport you're flying into. Now, to book a room you don't have to log in again. You logged in on the Southwest website, and that website sent your information over to the Hilton website, all of which happened transparently to you.

A *federated identity* is a portable identity, and its associated entitlements, that can be used across business boundaries. It allows a user to be authenticated across multiple IT systems and enterprises. Identity federation is based upon linking a user's otherwise distinct identities at two or more locations without the need to synchronize or consolidate directory information. Federated identity offers businesses and consumers

a more convenient way of accessing distributed resources and is a key component of e-commerce.

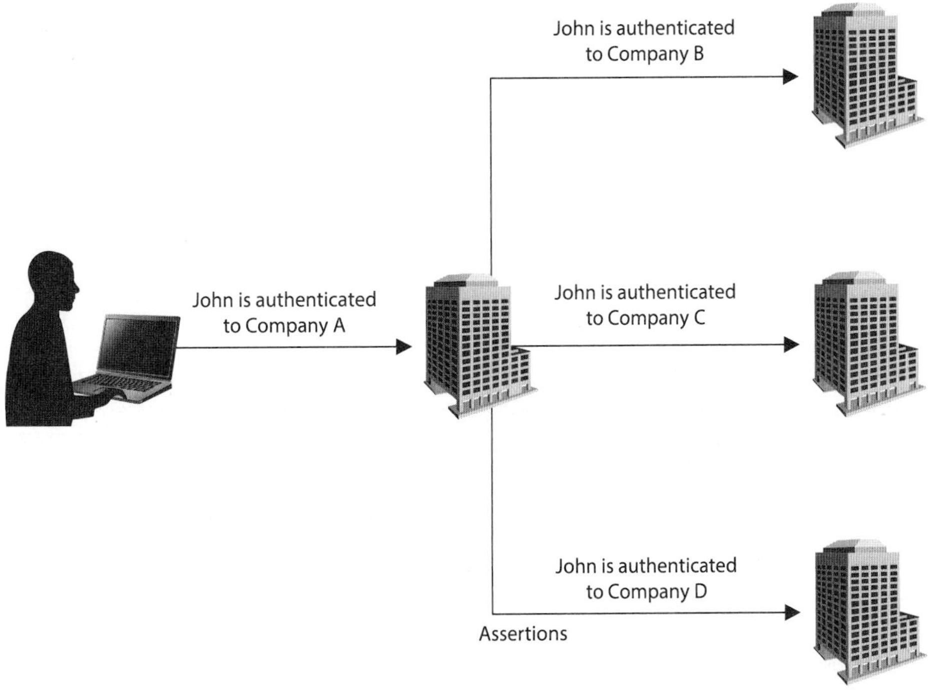
John is authenticated
to Company B
John is authenticated
to Company A
John is authenticated
to Company C
John is authenticated
to Company D
Assertions

Web portal functions are parts of a website that act as a point of access to information. A portal presents information from diverse sources in a unified manner. It can offer various services, as in e-mail, news updates, stock prices, data access, price look-ups, access to databases, and entertainment. Web portals provide a way for organizations to present one consistent interface with one "look and feel" and various functionality types. For example, you log into your company web portal and it provides access to many different systems and their functionalities, but it seems as though you are only interacting with one system because the interface is "clean" and organized. Portals combine web services (web-based functions) from several different entities and present them in one central website.

A web portal is made up of *portlets*, which are pluggable user-interface software components that present information from other systems. A portlet is an interactive application that provides a specific type of web service functionality (e-mail, news feed, weather updates, forums). A portal is made up of individual portlets to provide a plethora of services through one interface. It is a way of centrally providing a set of web services. Users can configure their view to the portal by enabling or disabling these various portlet functions.

Since each of these portlets can be provided by different entities, how user authentication information is handled must be tightly controlled, and there must be a high level of trust

between these different entities. If you worked for a college, for example, there might be one web portal available to students, parents, faculty members, and the public. The public should only be able to view and access a small subset of available portlets and not have access to more powerful web services (e-mails, database access). Students could be able to log in and gain access to their grades, assignments, and a student forum. Faculty members can gain access to all of these web services, including the school's e-mail service and access to the central database, which contains all of the students' information. If there is a software flaw or misconfiguration, it is possible that someone can gain access to something they are not supposed to.

The following sections explain some of the various types of authentication methods commonly used and integrated in many web-based federated identity management processes and products today.

Access Control and Markup Languages

If you can remember when *HyperText Markup Language (HTML)* was *all* we had to make a static web page, you're old. Being old in the technology world is different than in the regular world; HTML came out in the early 1990s. HTML came from Standard Generalized Markup Language (SGML), which came from the Generalized Markup Language (GML). We still use HTML, so it is certainly not dead and gone; the industry has just improved upon the markup languages available for use to meet today's needs.

A markup language is a way to structure text and data sets, and it dictates how these will be viewed and used. When you adjust margins and other formatting capabilities in a word processor, you are marking up the text in the word processor's markup language. If you develop a web page, you are using some type of markup language. You can control how it looks and some of the actual functionality the page provides. The use of a standard markup language also allows for interoperability. If you develop a web page and follow basic markup language standards, the page will basically look and act the same no matter what web server is serving up the web page or what browser the viewer is using to interact with it.

As the Internet grew in size and the World Wide Web (WWW) expanded in functionality, and as more users and organizations came to depend upon websites and web-based communication, the basic and elementary functions provided by HTML were not enough. And instead of every website having its own proprietary markup language to meet its specific functionality requirements, the industry had to have a way for functionality needs to be met and still provide interoperability for all web server and web browser interaction. This is the reason that *Extensible Markup Language (XML)* was developed. XML is a universal and foundational standard that provides a structure for other independent markup languages to be built from and still allow for interoperability. Markup languages with various functionalities were built from XML, and while each language provides its own individual functionality, if they all follow the core rules of XML, then they are interoperable and can be used across different web-based applications and platforms.

As an analogy, let's look at the English language. Samir is a biology scientist, Trudy is an accountant, and Val is a network administrator. They all speak English, so they have a common set of communication rules, which allow them to talk with each other, but each has their own "spin-off" languages that builds upon and uses the English language as its core. Samir uses words like "mitochondrial amino acid genetic strains" and "DNA polymerase." Trudy uses words such as "accrual accounting" and "acquisition indigestion." Val uses terms such as "multiprotocol label switching" and "subkey creation." Each profession has its own "language" to meet its own needs, but each is based off the same core language—English. In the world of the WWW, various websites need to provide different types of functionality through the use of their own language types but still need a way to communicate with each other and their users in a consistent manner, which is why they are based upon the same core language structure (XML).

There are hundreds of markup languages based upon XML, but we are going to focus on the ones that are used for identity management and access control purposes.

The *Service Provisioning Markup Language (SPML)* allows for the exchange of provisioning data between applications, which could reside in one organization or many. SPML allows for the automation of user management (account creation, amendments, revocation) and access entitlement configuration related to electronically published services across multiple provisioning systems. This markup language allows for the integration and interoperation of service provisioning requests across various platforms.

When a new employee is hired at a company, that employee usually needs access to a wide range of systems, servers, and applications. Setting up new accounts on each and every system, properly configuring access rights, and then maintaining those accounts throughout their lifetimes is time-consuming, laborious, and error-prone. What if the company has 20,000 employees and thousands of network resources that each employee needs various access rights to? This opens the door for confusion, mistakes, vulnerabilities, and a lack of standardization.

SPML allows for all these accounts to be set up and managed simultaneously across the various systems and applications. SPML is made up of three main entities: the Requesting Authority (RA), which is the entity that is making the request to set up a new account or make changes to an existing account; the Provisioning Service Provider (PSP), which is the software that responds to the account requests; and the Provisioning Service Target (PST), which is the entity that carries out the provisioning activities on the requested system.

So when a new employee is hired, there is a request to set up the necessary user accounts and access privileges on several different systems and applications across the enterprise. This request originates in a piece of software carrying out the functionality of the RA. The RA creates SPML messages, which provide the requirements of the new account, and sends them to a piece of software that is carrying out the functionality of the PSP. This piece of software reviews the requests and compares them to the organization's approved account creation criteria. If these requests are allowed, the PSP sends new SPML messages to the end systems (PST) that the user actually needs to access. Software on the PST sets up the requested accounts and configures the necessary access rights. If this same employee is fired three months later, the same process is followed and all necessary user accounts are deleted. This allows for consistent account management in complex environments. These steps are illustrated in Figure 5-13.

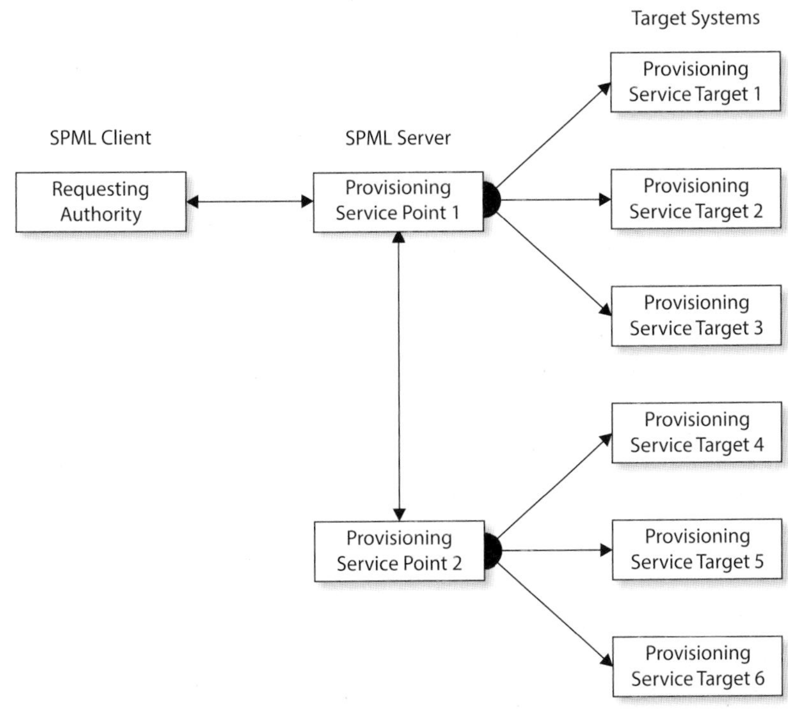

Figure 5-13 SPML provisioning steps

When there is a need to allow a user to log in one time and gain access to different and separate web-based applications, the actual authentication data has to be shared between the systems maintaining those web applications securely and in a standardized manner. This is the role that the *Security Assertion Markup Language (SAML)* plays. It is an XML standard that allows the exchange of authentication and authorization data to be shared between security domains. Suppose your organization, Acme Corp., uses Gmail as its corporate e-mail platform. You would want to ensure that you maintain control over user access credentials so that you could enforce password policies and, for example, prevent access to the e-mail account of an employee who just got fired. You could set up a relationship with Google that would allow you to do just this using SAML. Whenever one of your organization's users attempted to access their corporate Gmail accounts, Gmail would redirect their request to Acme's SSO service, which would authenticate the user and relay (through the user) a SAML response. Figure 5-14 depicts this process, though its multiple steps are largely transparent to the user.

SAML provides the authentication pieces to federated identity management systems to allow business-to-business (B2B) and business-to-consumer (B2C) transactions. In our previous example, the user is considered the *principal*, Acme Corporation is the *identity provider*, and Gmail is the *service provider*.

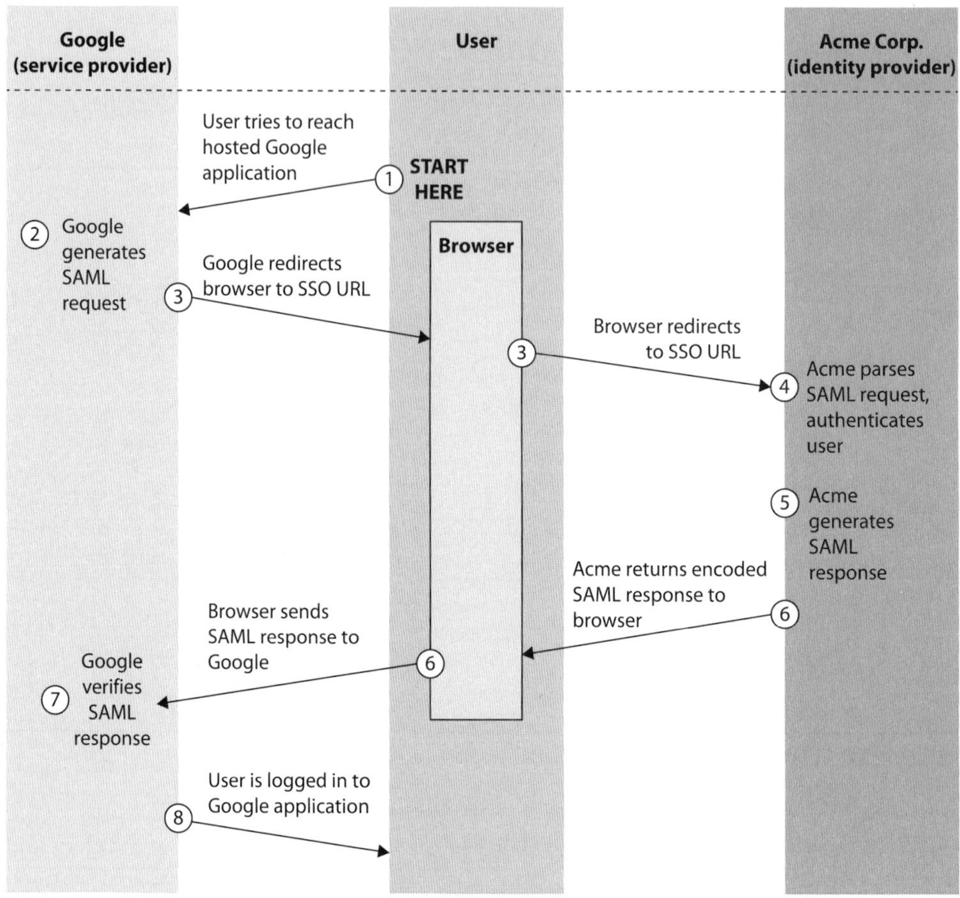

Figure 5-14 SAML authentication

This is not the only way that the SAML language can be used. The digital world has evolved to being able to provide extensive services and functionality to users through web-based machine-to-machine communication standards. *Web services* is a collection of technologies and standards that allow services (weather updates, stock tickers, e-mail, customer resource management, etc.) to be provided on distributed systems and be "served up" in one place.

Transmission of SAML data can take place over different protocol types, but a common one is *Simple Object Access Protocol (SOAP)*. SOAP is a specification that outlines how information pertaining to web services is exchanged in a structured manner. It provides the basic messaging framework, which allows users to request a service and, in exchange, the service is made available to that user. Let's say you need to interact with your company's CRM system, which is hosted and maintained by the vendor—for example, Salesforce.com. You would log into your company's portal and double-click a link for Salesforce. Your company's portal would take this request and your authentication data and package it up in an SAML format and encapsulate that data into a SOAP message. This message would be transmitted over an HTTP connection to the Salesforce vendor site, and once you were authenticated, you would be provided with a screen that shows you the company's customer database. The SAML, SOAP, and HTTP relationship is illustrated in Figure 5-15.

The use of web services in this manner also allows for organizations to provide *service-oriented architecture (SOA)* environments. An SOA is a way to provide independent services residing on different systems in different business domains in one consistent manner. For example, if your company has a web portal that allows you to access the company's CRM, an employee directory, and a help-desk ticketing application, this is most likely being provided through an SOA. The CRM system may be within the marketing department, the employee directory may be within the HR department, and the ticketing system may be within the IT department, but you can interact with all of them through one interface. SAML is a way to send your authentication information to each system, and SOAP allows this type of information to be presented and processed in a unified manner.

The last XML-based standard we will look at is *Extensible Access Control Markup Language (XACML).* XACML is used to express security policies and access rights to assets provided through web services and other enterprise applications. SAML is just a way to send around your authentication information, as in a password, key, or digital certificate, in a standard format. SAML does not tell the receiving system how to interpret

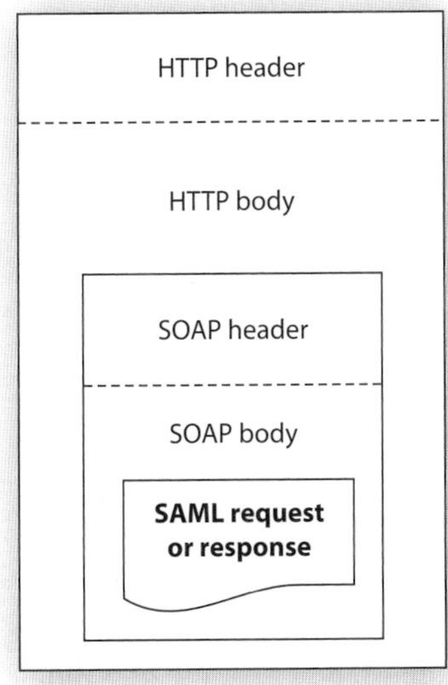

Figure 5-15 SAML material embedded within an HTTP message

and use this authentication data. Two systems have to be configured to use the same type of authentication data. If you log into System A and provide a password and try to access System B, which only uses digital certificates for authentication purposes, your password is not going to give you access to System B's service. So both systems have to be configured to use passwords. But just because your password is sent to System B does not mean you have complete access to all of System B's functionality. System B has access policies that dictate the operations that specific subjects can carry out on its resources. The access policies can be developed in the XACML format and enforced by System B's software. XACML is both an access control policy language and a processing model that allows for policies to be interpreted and enforced in a standard manner. When your password is sent to System B, there is a rules engine on that system that interprets and enforces the XACML access control policies. If the access control policies are created in the XACML format, they can be installed on both System A and System B to allow for consistent security to be enforced and managed.

XACML uses a Subject element (requesting entity), a Resource element (requested entity), and an Action element (types of access). So if you request access to your company's CRM, you are the Subject, the CRM application is the Resource, and your access parameters are outlined in the Action element.

NOTE Who develops and keeps track of all of these standardized languages? The *Organization for the Advancement of Structured Information Standards (OASIS)*. This organization develops and maintains the standards for how various aspects of web-based communication are built and maintained.

Web services, SOA environments, and the implementation of these different XML-based markup languages vary in nature because they allow for extensive flexibility. Because so much of the world's communication takes place through web-based processes, it is becoming increasingly important for security professionals to understand these issues and technologies.

OpenID

OpenID is an open standard for user authentication by third parties. It is a lot like SAML, except that the users' credentials are maintained not by their company but by a third party such as Google, Microsoft, or Yahoo!. Why is this useful? Well, the main draw of it is that it frees up the website developers from the need to implement secure authentication mechanisms (and secure all the credentials) for their sites. Instead, they can leverage one of the big companies that already do this rather well.

OpenID defines three roles:

- **End user** The user who wants to be authenticated in order to use a resource
- **Resource party** The server that owns the resource that the end user is trying to access
- **OpenID provider** The system (e.g., Google) in which the end user already has an account and which will authenticate the user to the resource party

You have probably encountered OpenID if you've ever tried to access a website and were presented with the option to log in using your Google identity. (Oftentimes you see an option for Google and one for Facebook in the same window, but Facebook uses its own protocol called *Facebook Connect.*) The process by which you get authenticated is very similar to that previously shown in Figure 5-15, except that the *service provider* is now called the *resource party* and the *identity provider* is now called the *OpenID provider.*

OAuth

OAuth is an open standard for authorization (not authentication) to third parties. The general idea is that this lets you authorize a website to use something that you control at a different website. For instance, if you have a LinkedIn account, the system might ask you to let it have access to your Google contacts in order to find your friends who already have accounts in LinkedIn. If you agree, you will next see a pop-up from Google asking whether you want to authorize LinkedIn to manage your contacts. If you agree to this, LinkedIn gains access to all your contacts until you rescind this authorization. Figure 5-16 depicts this process.

Identity as a Service

It should not be surprising to consider that cloud service providers are also able to provide identification services. Identity as a Service (IDaaS) is a type of Software as a Service (SaaS) offering that is normally configured to provide SSO, federated IdM, and password management services. Though most IDaaS vendors are focused on cloud- and web-centric systems, it is also possible to leverage their products for IdM on legacy platforms within the enterprise network.

Though IDaaS is a booming sector of the security industry, it is important to note that it is not without potential issues. First and foremost, some regulated industries may

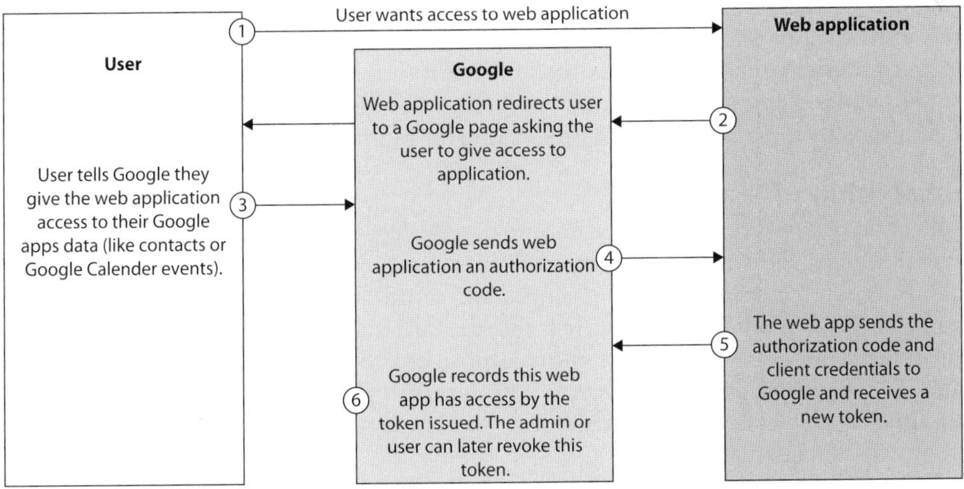

Figure 5-16 OAuth authorization steps

not be able to leverage IDaaS and remain compliant. This is because a critical function (i.e., IdM) is being outsourced and the service provider may not be able to comply with all the regulatory requirements. Another concern is that some of the most critical data in the enterprise is increasingly exposed once it moves out of the enterprise enclaves. Though various cloud service providers will undoubtedly be able to provide equal or better security than the client organization, it is still an important point of discussion before making the decision to go with an IDaaS solution. Finally, there is the issue of integration. Depending on the specific vendor and offering, some legacy applications may not be supported. This too needs to be discussed ahead of signing any contracts.

Integrating Identity Services

Integration of any set of different technologies or products is typically one of the most complex and risky phases of any deployment. In order to mitigate both the complexities and risks, it is necessary to carefully characterize each product or technology as well as the systems and networks into which they will be incorporated. As the old carpentry adage goes, "Measure twice and cut once."

There are two basic approaches to architecting identity services: in-house or outsourced. The first approach, in-house, is simple because all the systems and data are located within the enterprise. In an outsourced model, on the other hand, some or all of the systems or data will be hosted by an external party. In either approach, it is important to ensure that all components play nice with each other. In the following sections we will explore some of the considerations that are common to the successful integration of these services.

Establishing Connectivity

First and foremost, we need to ensure the components are able to communicate with one another in a secure manner. The big difference between the in-house and outsourced models here is that in the former, the chokepoints are all internal to the organization's network, while in the latter, they will also exist in the public Internet. Clearing a path for this traffic will typically mean creating new rules for firewalls and IDS/IPS. These rules must be restrictive enough to allow the IdM traffic, but nothing else, to flow between the various nodes. Depending on the systems being used, ports, protocols, and user accounts may also need to be configured in order to enable bidirectional communication.

Establishing Trust

All traffic between nodes engaged in identity services must be encrypted. (To do otherwise would defeat the whole point of this effort.) From a practical perspective, this almost certainly means that PKI in general and certificate authorities (CAs) in particular will be needed. A potential issue here is that the CAs may not be trusted by default by all the nodes. This is especially true if the enterprise has implemented its own CA internally and is deploying an outsourced service. This is easy to plan ahead of time, but could lead to some big challenges if discovered during the actual roll-out. Trust may also be needed between domains.

Incremental Testing

When dealing with complex systems, it is wise to assume that some important issue will not be covered in the plan. This is why it is important to incrementally test the integration of identity services instead of rolling out the entire system at once. Many organizations choose to roll out new services first to test accounts (i.e., not real users), then to one department or division that is used as the test case, and finally to the entire organization. For critical deployments (and one would assume that identity services would fall in this category), it is best to test as thoroughly as possible in a testbed or sandbox environment. Only then should the integration progress to real systems.

Access Control Models

An *access control model* is a framework that dictates how subjects access objects. It uses access control technologies and security mechanisms to enforce the rules and objectives of the model. There are three main types of access control models: discretionary, mandatory, and role based. Each model type uses different methods to control how subjects access objects, and each has its own merits and limitations. The business and security goals of an organization, along with the culture of the company and the habits of conducting business, will help prescribe what access control model it should use. Some companies use one model exclusively, whereas others combine them to be able to provide the necessary level of protection.

These models are built into the core or the kernel of the different operating systems and possibly their supporting applications. Every operating system has a security kernel that enforces a reference monitor concept, which differs depending upon the type of access control model embedded into the system. For every access attempt, before a subject can communicate with an object, the security kernel reviews the rules of the access control model to determine whether the request is allowed.

The following sections explain these different models, their supporting technologies, and where they should be implemented.

Discretionary Access Control

If a user creates a file, he is the owner of that file. An identifier for this user is placed in the file header and/or in an access control matrix within the operating system. Ownership might also be granted to a specific individual. For example, a manager for a certain department might be made the owner of the files and resources within her department. A system that uses *discretionary access control (DAC)* enables the owner of the resource to specify which subjects can access specific resources. This model is called discretionary because the control of access is based on the discretion of the owner. Many times department managers or business unit managers are the owners of the data within their specific department. Being the owner, they can specify who should have access and who should not.

In a DAC model, access is restricted based on the authorization granted to the users. This means users are allowed to specify what type of access can occur to the objects they own. If an organization is using a DAC model, the network administrator can allow resource owners to control who has access to their files. The most common implementation of DAC is through ACLs, which are dictated and set by the owners and enforced by the operating system. This can make a user's ability to access information dynamic versus the more static role of mandatory access control (MAC).

Most of the operating systems you may be used to dealing with are based on DAC models, such as all Windows, Linux, and OS X systems and most flavors of Unix. When you look at the properties of a file or directory and see the choices that allow you to control which users can have access to this resource and to what degree, you are witnessing an instance of ACLs enforcing a DAC model.

DACs can be applied to both the directory tree structure and the files it contains. The PC world has access permissions of No Access, Read (r), Write (w), Execute (x), Delete (d), Change (c), and Full Control. The Read attribute lets you read the file but not make changes. The Change attribute allows you to read, write, execute, and delete the file but does not let you change the ACLs or the owner of the files. Obviously, the attribute of Full Control lets you make any changes to the file and its permissions and ownership.

Identity-Based Access Control

DAC systems grant or deny access based on the identity of the subject. The identity can be a user identity or a group membership. So, for example, a data owner can choose to allow Bob (user identity) and the Accounting group (group membership identity) to access his file.

While DAC systems provide a lot of flexibility to the user and less administration for IT, it is also the Achilles' heel of operating systems. Malware can install itself and work under the security context of the user. For example, if a user opens an attachment that is infected with a virus, the code can install itself in the background without the user's being aware of this activity. This code basically inherits all the rights and permissions that the user has and can carry out all the activities the user can on the system. It can send copies of itself out to all the contacts listed in the user's e-mail client, install a back door, attack other systems, delete files on the hard drive, and more. The user is actually giving rights to the virus to carry out its dirty deeds, because the user has very powerful discretionary rights and is considered the owner of many objects on the system. And the fact that many users are assigned local administrator or root accounts means that once malware is installed, it can do anything on a system.

As we have said before, there is a constant battle between functionality and security. To allow for the amount of functionality we demand of our operating systems today, they have to work within a DAC model—but because they work in a DAC model, extensive compromises are always possible.

While we may want to give users some freedom to indicate who can access the files that they create and other resources on their systems that they are configured to be "owners" of, we really don't want them dictating all access decisions in environments with assets that need to be protected. We just don't trust them that much, and we shouldn't. In most environments user profiles are created and loaded on user workstations that indicate the level of control the user does and does not have. As a security administrator you might configure user profiles so that users cannot change the system's time, alter system configuration files, access a command prompt, or install unapproved applications. This type of access control is referred to as *nondiscretionary*, meaning that access decisions are not made at the discretion of the user. Nondiscretionary access controls are put into place by an authoritative entity (usually a security administrator) with the goal of protecting the organization's most critical assets.

Mandatory Access Control

In a *mandatory access control (MAC)* model, users do not have the discretion of determining who can access objects as in a DAC model. An operating system that is based upon a MAC model greatly reduces the amount of rights, permissions, and functionality a user has for security purposes. In most systems based upon the MAC model, a user cannot install software, change file permissions, add new users, etc. The system can be used by the user for very focused and specific purposes, and that is it. These systems are usually very specialized and are in place to protected highly classified data. Most people have never interacted with a MAC-based system because they are used by government-oriented agencies that maintain top-secret information.

The MAC model is much more structured and strict than the DAC model and is based on a security label system. Users are given a security clearance (secret, top secret, confidential, and so on), and data is classified in the same way. The clearance and classification data is stored in the security labels, which are bound to the specific subjects and objects. When the system makes a decision about fulfilling a request to access an object, it is based on the clearance of the subject, the classification of the object, and the security policy of the system. The rules for how subjects access objects are made by the organization's security policy, configured by the security administrator, enforced by the operating system, and supported by security technologies.

NOTE Traditional MAC systems are based upon multilevel security policies, which outline how data at different classification levels is to be protected. Multilevel security (MLS) systems allow data at different classification levels to be accessed and interacted with by users with different clearance levels simultaneously.

Security labels are attached to all objects; thus, every file, directory, and device has its own security label with its classification information. A user may have a security clearance of secret, and the data he requests may have a security label with the classification of top secret. In this case, the user will be denied because his clearance is not equivalent or does not dominate (is not equal to or higher than) the classification of the object.

TIP The terms "security labels" and "sensitivity labels" can be used interchangeably.

Each subject and object must have an associated label with attributes at all times, because this is part of the operating system's access-decision criteria. Each subject and object does not require a physically unique label, but can be logically associated. For example, all subjects and objects on Server 1 can share the same label of secret clearance and classification.

This type of model is used in environments where information classification and confidentiality is of utmost importance, such as military institutions, government agencies, and government contract companies. Special types of Unix systems are developed based on the MAC model. A company cannot simply choose to turn on either DAC or MAC. It has to purchase an operating system that has been specifically designed to enforce MAC rules. DAC systems do not understand security labels, classifications, or clearances, and thus cannot be used in institutions that require this type of structure for access control. A publicly released MAC system is SE Linux, developed by the NSA and Secure Computing. Trusted Solaris is a product based on the MAC model that most people are familiar with (relative to other MAC products).

While MAC systems enforce strict access control, they also provide a wide range of security, particularly dealing with malware. Malware is the bane of DAC systems. Viruses, worms, and rootkits can be installed and run as applications on DAC systems. Since users that work within a MAC system cannot install software, the operating system does not allow any type of software, including malware, to be installed while the user is logged in. But while MAC systems might seem an answer to all our security prayers, they have very limited user functionality, require a lot of administrative overhead, are very expensive, and are not user friendly. DAC systems are general-purpose computers, while MAC systems serve a very specific purpose.

EXAM TIP DAC systems are discretionary and MAC systems are considered nondiscretionary because the users cannot make access decisions based upon their own discretion (choice).

Sensitivity Labels

When the MAC model is being used, every subject and object must have a sensitivity label, also called a security label. It contains a classification and different categories. The classification indicates the sensitivity level, and the categories enforce need-to-know rules. Figure 5-17 illustrates a sensitivity label.

The classifications follow a hierarchical structure, with one level being more trusted than another. However, the categories do not follow a hierarchical scheme, because they

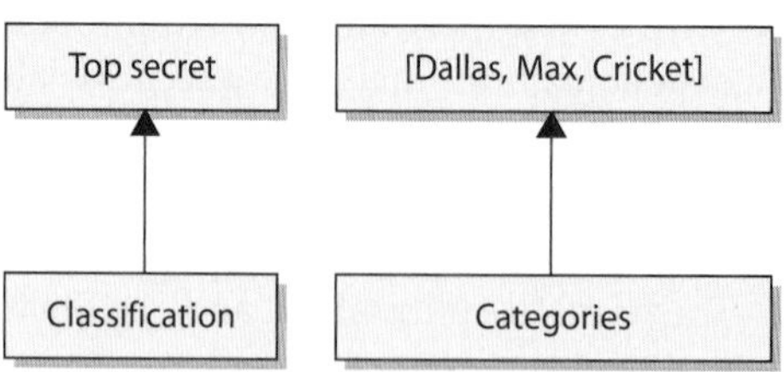

Figure 5-17 A sensitivity label is made up of a classification and categories.

represent compartments of information within a system. The categories can correspond to departments (UN, Information Warfare, Treasury), projects (CRM, AirportSecurity, 2015Budget), or management levels. In a military environment, the classifications could be top secret, secret, confidential, and unclassified. Each classification is more trusted than the one below it. A commercial organization might use confidential, proprietary, corporate, and sensitive. The definition of the classification is up to the organization and should make sense for the environment in which it is used.

The categories portion of the label enforces need-to-know rules. Just because someone has a top-secret clearance does not mean she now has access to all top-secret information. She must also have a need to know. As shown in Figure 5-17, if Cheryl has a top-secret clearance but does not have a need to know that is sufficient to access any of the listed categories (Dallas, Max, Cricket), she cannot look at this object.

EXAM TIP In MAC implementations, the system makes access decisions by comparing the subject's clearance and need-to-know level to the object's security label. In DAC, the system compares the subject's identity to the ACL on the resource.

Software and hardware guards allow the exchange of data between trusted (high assurance) and less trusted (low assurance) systems and environments. For instance, if you were working on a MAC system (working in the dedicated security mode of secret) and you needed it to communicate to a MAC database (working in multilevel security mode, which goes up to top secret), the two systems would provide different levels of protection. If a system with lower assurance can directly communicate with a system of high assurance, then security vulnerabilities and compromises could be introduced. A software guard is really just a front-end product that allows interconnectivity between systems working at different security levels. Different types of guards can be used to carry out filtering, processing requests, data blocking, and data sanitization. A hardware guard can be implemented, which is a system with two NICs connecting the two systems that need to communicate with one another. Guards can be used to connect different MAC systems working in different security modes, and they can be used to connect different networks working at different security levels. In many cases, the less trusted system can send messages to the more trusted system and can only receive acknowledgments back. This is common when e-mail messages need to go from less trusted systems to more trusted classified systems.

Role-Based Access Control

A *role-based access control (RBAC)* model uses a centrally administrated set of controls to determine how subjects and objects interact. The access control levels can be based upon the necessary operations and tasks a user needs to carry out to fulfill her responsibilities without an organization. This type of model lets access to resources be based on the role the user holds within the company. The more traditional access control administration is based on just the DAC model, where access control is specified at the object level with ACLs. This approach is more complex because the administrator must translate an organizational authorization policy into permission when configuring ACLs. As the number of objects and users grows within an environment, users are bound to be granted unnecessary access to some objects, thus violating the least-privilege rule and increasing the risk to the company. The RBAC approach simplifies access control administration by allowing permissions to be managed in terms of user job roles.

In an RBAC model, a role is defined in terms of the operations and tasks the role will carry out, whereas a DAC model outlines which subjects can access what objects based upon the individual user identity.

Let's say we need a research and development analyst role. We develop this role not only to allow an individual to have access to all product and testing data, but also, and more importantly, to outline the tasks and operations that the role can carry out on this data. When the analyst role makes a request to access the new testing results on the file server, in the background the operating system reviews the role's access levels before allowing this operation to take place.

NOTE Introducing roles also introduces the difference between rights being assigned explicitly and implicitly. If rights and permissions are assigned explicitly, they are assigned directly to a specific individual. If they are assigned implicitly, they are assigned to a role or group and the user inherits those attributes.

An RBAC model is the best system for a company that has high employee turnover. If John, who is mapped to the Contractor role, leaves the company, then Chrissy, his replacement, can be easily mapped to this role. That way, the administrator does not need to continually change the ACLs on the individual objects. He only needs to create a role (Contractor), assign permissions to this role, and map the new user to this role.

As discussed in the "Identity Management" section, organizations are moving more toward role-based access models to properly control identity and provisioning activities. The formal RBAC model has several approaches to security that can be used in software and organizations.

Core RBAC

This component will be integrated in every RBAC implementation because it is the foundation of the model. Users, roles, permissions, operations, and sessions are defined and mapped according to the security policy. The core RBAC

- Has a many-to-many relationship among individual users and privileges
- Uses a session as a mapping between a user and a subset of assigned roles
- Accommodates traditional but robust group-based access control

Many users can belong to many groups with various privileges outlined for each group. When the user logs in (this is a session), the various roles and groups this user has been assigned will be available to the user at one time. If you are a member of the Accounting role, RD group, and Administrative role, when you log on, all of the permissions assigned to these various groups are available to you.

This model provides robust options because it can include other components when making access decisions, instead of just basing the decision on a credential set. The RBAC system can be configured to also include time of day, location of role, day of the week, and so on. This means other information, not just the user ID and credential, is used for access decisions.

Hierarchical RBAC

This component allows the administrator to set up an organizational RBAC model that maps to the organizational structures and functional delineations required in a specific environment. This is very useful since businesses are already set up in a personnel hierarchical structure. In most cases, the higher you are in the chain of command, the more access you will most likely have. Hierarchical RBAC

- Uses role relations in defining user membership and privilege inheritance. For example, the Nurse role can access a certain set of files, and the Lab Technician role can access another set of files. The Doctor role inherits the permissions and access rights of these two roles and has more elevated rights already assigned to the Doctor role. So hierarchical RBAC is an accumulation of rights and permissions of other roles.
- Reflects organizational structures and functional delineations.
- Supports two types of hierarchies:
  - **Limited hierarchies** Only one level of hierarchy is allowed (Role 1 inherits from Role 2 and no other role)
  - **General hierarchies** Allows for many levels of hierarchies (Role 1 inherits Role 2's and Role 3's permissions)

Hierarchies are a natural means of structuring roles to reflect an organization's lines of authority and responsibility. Role hierarchies define an inheritance relation among roles. Different separations of duties are provided under this model:

- **Static Separation of Duty (SSD) Relations through RBAC** This would be used to deter fraud by constraining the combination of privileges (such as, the user cannot be a member of both the Cashier and Accounts Receivable groups).
- **Dynamic Separation of Duties (DSD) Relations through RBAC** This would be used to deter fraud by constraining the combination of privileges that can be activated in any session (for instance, the user cannot be in both the Cashier and Cashier Supervisor roles at the same time, but the user can be a member of both). This one is a little more confusing. It means José is a member of both the Cashier and Cashier Supervisor roles. If he logs in as a Cashier, the Supervisor role is unavailable to him during that session. If he logs in as Cashier Supervisor, the Cashier role is unavailable to him during that session.

- Role-based access control can be managed in the following ways:
  - **Non-RBAC** Users are mapped directly to applications and no roles are used.
  - **Limited RBAC** Users are mapped to multiple roles and mapped directly to other types of applications that do not have role-based access functionality.
  - **Hybrid RBAC** Users are mapped to multiapplication roles with only selected rights assigned to those roles.
  - **Full RBAC** Users are mapped to enterprise roles.

NOTE The privacy of many different types of data needs to be protected, which is why many organizations have privacy officers and privacy policies today. The current access control models (MAC, DAC, RBAC) do not lend themselves to protecting data of a given sensitivity level, but instead limit the functions that the users can carry out. For example, managers may be able to access a Privacy folder, but there needs to be more detailed access control that indicates that they can access customers' home addresses but not Social Security numbers. This is referred to as *privacy-aware RBAC*.

RBAC, MAC, and DAC

A lot of confusion exists regarding whether RBAC is a type of DAC model or a type of MAC model. Different sources claim different things, but in fact it is a model in its own right. In the 1960s and 1970s, the U.S. military and NSA did a lot of research on the MAC model. DAC, which also sprang to life in the 1960s and 1970s, has its roots in the academic and commercial research laboratories. The RBAC model, which started gaining popularity in the 1990s, can be used in combination with MAC and DAC systems. For the most up-to-date information on the RBAC model, go to http://csrc.nist.gov/groups/SNS/rbac, which has documents that describe an RBAC standard and independent model, with the goal of clearing up this continual confusion.

In reality, operating systems can be created to use one, two, or all three of these models in some form, but just because they can be used together does not mean that they are not their own individual models with their own strict access control rules.

Rule-Based Access Control

Rule-based access control uses specific rules that indicate what can and cannot happen between a subject and an object. This access control model is built on top of traditional RBAC and is thus commonly called RB-RBAC to disambiguate the otherwise overloaded RBAC acronym. It is based on the simple concept of "if X then Y" programming rules, which can be used to provide finer-grained access control to resources. Before a subject can access an object in a certain circumstance, it must meet a set of predefined rules. This can be simple and straightforward, as in, "If the user's ID matches the unique user ID value in the provided digital certificate, then the user can gain access." Or there could be a set of complex rules that must be met before a subject can access an object. For example, "If the user is accessing the system between Monday and Friday and between 8 A.M. and 5 P.M., and if the user's security clearance equals or dominates the object's classification, and if the user has the necessary need to know, then the user can access the object."

Rule-based access control is not necessarily identity-based. The DAC model is identity-based. For example, an identity-based control would stipulate that Tom Jones can read File1 and modify File2. So when Tom attempts to access one of these files, the operating system will check his identity and compare it to the values within an ACL to see if Tom can carry out the operations he is attempting. In contrast, here is a rule-based example: A company may have a policy that dictates that e-mail attachments can only be 5MB or smaller. This rule affects all users. If rule-based was identity-based, it would mean that Sue can accept attachments of 10MB and smaller, Bob can accept attachments 2MB and smaller, and Don can only accept attachments 1MB and smaller. This would be a mess and too confusing. Rule-based access controls simplify this by setting a rule that will affect all users across the board—no matter what their identity is.

Rule-based access allows a developer to define specific and detailed situations in which a subject can or cannot access an object and what that subject can do once access is granted. Traditionally, rule-based access control has been used in MAC systems as an enforcement mechanism of the complex rules of access that MAC systems provide. Today, rule-based access is used in other types of systems and applications as well. Content filtering uses If-Then programming languages, which is a way to compare data or an activity to a long list of rules. For example, "If an e-mail message contains the word 'Viagra,' then disregard. If an e-mail message contains the words 'sex' and 'free,' then disregard," and so on.

Many routers and firewalls use rules to determine which types of packets are allowed into a network and which are rejected. Rule-based access control is a type of compulsory control, because the administrator sets the rules and the users cannot modify these controls.

Access Control Models

The main characteristics of the four different access control models are important to understand.

- **DAC** Data owners decide who has access to resources, and ACLs are used to enforce these access decisions.
- **MAC** Operating systems enforce the system's security policy through the use of security labels.
- **RBAC** Access decisions are based on each subject's role and/or functional position.
- **RB-RBAC** Adds on to RBAC by imposing rules that further restrict access decisions.

Access Control Techniques and Technologies

Once an organization determines what type of access control model it is going to use, it needs to identify and refine its technologies and techniques to support that model. The following sections describe the different access controls and technologies available to support different access control models.

Constrained User Interfaces

Constrained user interfaces restrict users' access abilities by not allowing them to request certain functions or information, or to have access to specific system resources. Three major types of constrained user interfaces exist: menus and shells, database views, and physically constrained interfaces.

When menu and shell restrictions are used, the options users are given are the commands they can execute. For example, if an administrator wants users to be able to execute only one program, that program would be the only choice available on the menu. This limits the users' functionality. A *shell* is a type of virtual environment within a system. It is the users' interface to the operating system and works as a command interpreter. If restricted shells were used, the shell would contain only the commands the administrator wants the users to be able to execute.

Many times, a database administrator will configure a database so users cannot see fields that require a level of confidentiality. *Database views* are mechanisms used to restrict user access to data contained in databases. If the database administrator wants managers to be able to view their employees' work records but not their salary information, then the salary fields would not be available to these types of users. Similarly, when payroll employees look at the same database, they will be able to view the salary information but not the work history information. This example is illustrated in Figure 5-18.

Harris, D	$45,000	8am-5pm
Torkelson, T	$60,000	6pm-2am
Kowtko, J	$45,000	8am-5pm
Swenson, J	$65,000	6pm-2am

Payroll database view

Harris, D	Work history	8am-5pm
Torkelson, T	Work history	6pm-2am
Kowtko, J	Work history	8am-5pm
Swenson, J	Work history	6pm-2am

Manager database view

Figure 5-18 Different database views of the same tables

User	File1	File2	File3
Diane	Read and execute	Read, write, and execute	No access
Katie	Read and execute	Read	No access
Chrissy	Read, write, and execute	Read and execute	Read
John	Read and execute	No access	Read and write

Table 5-1 Example of an Access Control Matrix

Physically constraining a user interface can be implemented by providing only certain keys on a keypad or certain touch buttons on a screen. You see this when you get money from an ATM machine. This device has a type of operating system that can accept all kinds of commands and configuration changes, but you are physically constrained from being able to carry out these functions. You are presented with buttons that only enable you to withdraw, view your balance, or deposit funds. Period.

Access Control Matrix

An *access control matrix* is a table of subjects and objects indicating what actions individual subjects can take upon individual objects. Matrices are data structures that programmers implement as table lookups that will be used and enforced by the operating system. Table 5-1 provides an example of an access control matrix.

This type of access control is usually an attribute of DAC models. The access rights can be assigned directly to the subjects (capabilities) or to the objects (ACLs).

Capability Table

A *capability table* specifies the access rights a certain subject possesses pertaining to specific objects. A capability table is different from an ACL because the subject is bound to the capability table, whereas the object is bound to the ACL.

The capability corresponds to the subject's row in the access control matrix. In Table 5-1, Diane's capabilities are File1: read and execute; File2: read, write, and execute; File3: no access. This outlines what Diane is capable of doing to each resource. An example of a capability-based system is Kerberos. In this environment, the user is given a ticket, which is his capability table. This ticket is bound to the user and dictates what objects that user can access and to what extent. The access control is based on this ticket, or capability table. Figure 5-19 shows the difference between a capability table and an ACL.

A capability can be in the form of a token, ticket, or key. When a subject presents a capability component, the operating system (or application) will review the access rights and operations outlined in the capability component and allow the subject to carry out just those functions. A capability component is a data structure that contains a unique object identifier and the access rights the subject has to that object. The object may be a file, array, memory segment, or port. Each user, process, and application in a capability system has a list of capabilities.

Access Control Matrix

	Subject	File 1	File 2	File 3	File 4
	Larry	Read	Read, write	Read	Read, write
Capability	Curly	Full control	No access	Full control	Read
	Mo	Read, write	No access	Read	Full control
	Bob	Full control	Full control	Full control	No access
				ACL	

Capability = row in matrix
ACL = column in matrix

Figure 5-19 A capability table is bound to a subject, whereas an ACL is bound to an object.

Access Control Lists

Access control lists (ACLs) are used in several operating systems, applications, and router configurations. They are lists of subjects that are authorized to access a specific object, and they define what level of authorization is granted. Authorization can be specific to an individual, group, or role.

ACLs map values from the access control matrix to the object. Whereas a capability corresponds to a row in the access control matrix, the ACL corresponds to a column of the matrix. The ACL for File1 in Table 5-1 is shown in Table 5-2.

Content-Dependent Access Control

As the name suggests, with *content-dependent access control*, access to objects is determined by the content within the object. The earlier example pertaining to database views showed how content-dependent access control can work. The content of the database fields dictates which users can see specific information within the database tables.

Content-dependent filtering is used when corporations employ e-mail filters that look for specific strings, such as "confidential," "social security number," "top secret," and any other types of words the company deems suspicious. Corporations also have this in place to control web surfing—where filtering is done to look for specific words—to try to figure out whether employees are gambling or looking at pornography.

Table 5-2 The ACL for File1

User	File1
Diane	Read and execute
Katie	Read and execute
Chrissy	Read, write, and execute
John	Read and execute

Context-Dependent Access Control

Context-dependent access control differs from content-dependent access control in that it makes access decisions based on the context of a collection of information rather than on the sensitivity of the data. A system that is using context-dependent access control "reviews the situation" and then makes a decision. For example, firewalls make context-based access decisions when they collect state information on a packet before allowing it into the network. A stateful firewall understands the necessary steps of communication for specific protocols. For example, in a TCP connection, the sender sends a SYN packet, the receiver sends a SYN/ACK, and then the sender acknowledges that packet with an ACK packet. A stateful firewall understands these different steps and will not allow packets to go through that do not follow this sequence. So, if a stateful firewall receives a SYN/ACK and there was not a previous SYN packet that correlates with this connection, the firewall understands this is not right and disregards the packet. This is what stateful means—something that understands the necessary steps of a dialog session. And this is an example of context-dependent access control, where the firewall understands the *context* of what is going on and includes that as part of its access decision.

Some software can track a user's access requests in sequence and make decisions based upon the previous access requests. For example, let's say that we have a database that contains information about our military's mission and efforts. A user might have a secret clearance and thus can access data with this level of classification. But if he accesses a data set that indicates a specific military troop location, then accesses a different data set that indicates the new location this military troop will be deployed to, and then accesses another data set that specifies the types of weapons that are being shipped to the new troop location, he might be able to figure out information that is classified as top secret, which is above his classification level. While it is okay that he knows that there is a military troop located in Kuwait, it is not okay that he knows that this troop is being deployed to Libya with fully armed drones. This is top-secret information that is outside his clearance level.

To ensure that a user cannot piece these different data sets together and figure out a secret we don't want him to know, but still allow him access to specific data sets so he can carry out his job, we would need to implement software that can track his access requests. Each access request he makes is based upon his previous requests. So while he could access data set A, then data set B, he cannot access data sets A, B, and C.

Access Control Administration

Once an organization develops a security policy supporting procedures, standards, and guidelines, it must choose the type of access control model: DAC, MAC, or RBAC. After choosing a model, the organization must select and implement different access control technologies and techniques. Access control matrices; restricted interfaces; and content-dependent, context-dependent, and rule-based controls are just a few of the choices.

If the environment does not require a high level of security, the organization will choose discretionary and/or role-based. The DAC model enables data owners to allow other users to access their resources, so an organization should choose the DAC model only if it is fully aware of what it entails. If an organization has a high turnover rate and/or requires a more centralized access control method, the role-based model is more appropriate. If the environment requires a higher security level and only the administrator should be able to grant access to resources, then a MAC model is the best choice.

What is left to work out is how the organization will administer the access control model. Access control administration comes in two basic flavors: centralized and decentralized. The decision makers should understand both approaches so they choose and implement the proper one to achieve the level of protection required.

Access Control Techniques

Access control techniques are used to support the access control models.

- **Access control matrix** Table of subjects and objects that outlines their access relationships
- **Access control list** Bound to an object and indicates what subjects can access it and what operations they can carry out
- **Capability table** Bound to a subject and indicates what objects that subject can access and what operations it can carry out
- **Content-based access** Bases access decisions on the sensitivity of the data, not solely on subject identity
- **Context-based access** Bases access decisions on the state of the situation, not solely on identity or content sensitivity
- **Restricted interface** Limits the user's environment within the system, thus limiting access to objects

Centralized Access Control Administration

A *centralized access control administration* method is basically what it sounds like: one entity (department or individual) is responsible for overseeing access to all corporate resources. This entity configures the mechanisms that enforce access control, processes any changes that are needed to a user's access control profile, disables access when necessary, and completely removes these rights when a user is terminated, leaves the company, or moves to a different position. This type of administration provides a consistent and uniform method of controlling users' access rights. It supplies strict control over data because only one entity has the necessary rights to change access control profiles and permissions. Although this provides for a more consistent and reliable environment, it can be a slow one, because all changes must be processed by one entity.

The following sections present some examples of centralized remote access control technologies. Each of these authentication protocols is referred to as an AAA protocol, which stands for authentication, authorization, and auditing. (Some resources have the last A stand for accounting, but it is the same functionality—just a different name.)

Depending upon the protocol, there are different ways to authenticate a user in this client/server architecture. The traditional authentication protocols are Password Authentication Protocol (PAP), Challenge Handshake Authentication Protocol (CHAP), and a newer method referred to as Extensible Authentication Protocol (EAP). Each of these authentication protocols is discussed at length in Chapter 6.

RADIUS

Remote Authentication Dial-In User Service (RADIUS) is a network protocol that provides client/server authentication and authorization, and audits remote users. A network may have access servers, a modem pool, DSL, ISDN, or a T1 line dedicated for remote users to communicate through. The access server requests the remote user's logon credentials and passes them back to a RADIUS server, which houses the usernames and password values. The remote user is a client to the access server, and the access server is a client to the RADIUS server.

Most ISPs today use RADIUS to authenticate customers before they are allowed access to the Internet. The access server and customer's software negotiate through a handshake procedure and agree upon an authentication protocol (PAP, CHAP, or EAP). The customer provides to the access server a username and password. This communication takes place over a Point-to-Point Protocol (PPP) connection. The access server and RADIUS server communicate over the RADIUS protocol. Once the authentication is completed properly, the customer's system is given an IP address and connection parameters, and is allowed access to the Internet. The access server notifies the RADIUS server when the session starts and stops for billing purposes.

RADIUS is also used within corporate environments to provide road warriors and home users access to network resources. RADIUS allows companies to maintain user profiles in a central database. When a user dials in and is properly authenticated, a preconfigured profile is assigned to him to control what resources he can and cannot access. This technology allows companies to have a single administered entry point, which provides standardization in security and a simplistic way to track usage and network statistics.

RADIUS was developed by Livingston Enterprises for its network access server product series, but was then published as a set of standards (RFC 2865 and RFC 2866). This means it is an open protocol that any vendor can use and manipulate so it will work within its individual products. Because RADIUS is an open protocol, it can be used in different types of implementations. The format of configurations and user credentials can be held in LDAP servers, various databases, or text files. Figure 5-20 shows some examples of possible RADIUS implementations.

TACACS

Terminal Access Controller Access Control System (TACACS) has a very funny name. Not funny ha-ha, but funny "huh?" TACACS has been through three generations: TACACS, Extended TACACS (XTACACS), and TACACS+. TACACS combines its authentication

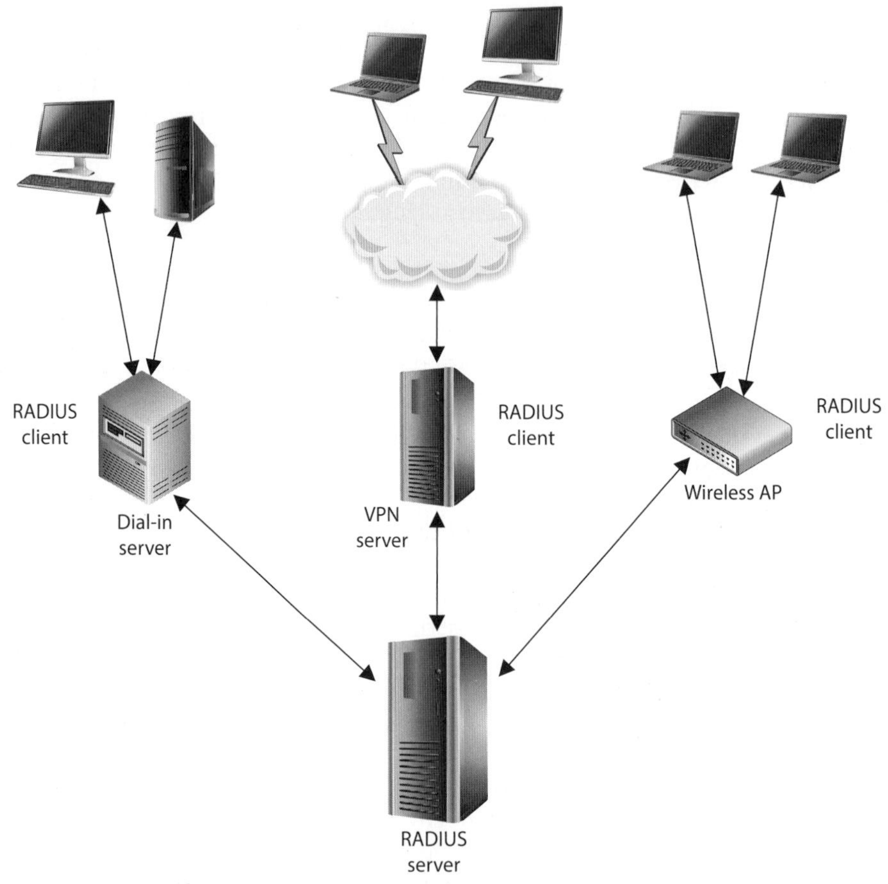

Figure 5-20 Environments can implement different RADIUS infrastructures.

and authorization processes; XTACACS separates authentication, authorization, and auditing processes; and TACACS+ is XTACACS with extended two-factor user authentication. TACACS uses fixed passwords for authentication, while TACACS+ allows users to employ dynamic (one-time) passwords, which provides more protection.

NOTE TACACS+ is really not a new generation of TACACS and XTACACS; it is a distinct protocol that provides similar functionality and shares the same naming scheme. Because it is a totally different protocol, it is not backward-compatible with TACACS or XTACACS.

TACACS+ provides basically the same functionality as RADIUS with a few differences in some of its characteristics. First, TACACS+ uses TCP as its transport protocol, while RADIUS uses UDP. "So what?" you may be thinking. Well, any software that is developed to use UDP as its transport protocol has to be "fatter" with intelligent code that will look out for the items that UDP will not catch. Since UDP is a connectionless protocol, it will not detect or correct transmission errors. So RADIUS must have the necessary code to detect packet corruption, long timeouts, or dropped packets. Since the developers of TACACS+ chose to use TCP, the TACACS+ software does not need to have the extra code to look for and deal with these transmission problems. TCP is a connection-oriented protocol, and that is its job and responsibility.

RADIUS encrypts the user's password only as it is being transmitted from the RADIUS client to the RADIUS server. Other information, as in the username, accounting, and authorized services, is passed in cleartext. This is an open invitation for attackers to capture session information for replay attacks. Vendors who integrate RADIUS into their products need to understand these weaknesses and integrate other security mechanisms to protect against these types of attacks. TACACS+ encrypts all of this data between the client and server and thus does not have the vulnerabilities inherent in the RADIUS protocol.

The RADIUS protocol combines the authentication and authorization functionality. TACACS+ uses a true authentication, authorization, and accounting/audit (AAA) architecture, which separates the authentication, authorization, and accounting functionalities. This gives a network administrator more flexibility in how remote users are authenticated. For example, if Tomika is a network administrator and has been assigned the task of setting up remote access for users, she must decide between RADIUS and TACACS+. If the current environment already authenticates all of the local users through a domain controller using Kerberos, then Tomika can configure the remote users to be authenticated in this same manner, as shown in Figure 5-21. Instead of having to maintain a remote access server database of remote user credentials and a database within Active Directory for local users, Tomika can just configure and maintain one database. The separation of authentication, authorization, and accounting functionality provides this capability. TACACS+ also enables the network administrator to define more granular user profiles, which can control the actual commands users can carry out.

Remember that RADIUS and TACACS+ are both protocols, and protocols are just agreed-upon ways of communication. When a RADIUS client communicates with a RADIUS server, it does so through the RADIUS protocol, which is really just a set of defined fields that will accept certain values. These fields are referred to as attribute-value pairs (AVPs). As an analogy, suppose Ivan sends you a piece of paper that has several different boxes drawn on it. Each box has a headline associated with it: first name, last name, hair color, shoe size. You fill in these boxes with your values and send it back to her. This is basically how protocols work; the sending system just fills in the boxes (fields) with the necessary information for the receiving system to extract and process.

Since TACACS+ allows for more granular control on what users can and cannot do, TACACS+ has more AVPs, which allows the network administrator to define ACLs, filters, user privileges, and much more. Table 5-3 points out the differences between RADIUS and TACACS+.

So, RADIUS is the appropriate protocol when simplistic username/password authentication can take place and users only need an Accept or Deny for obtaining access,

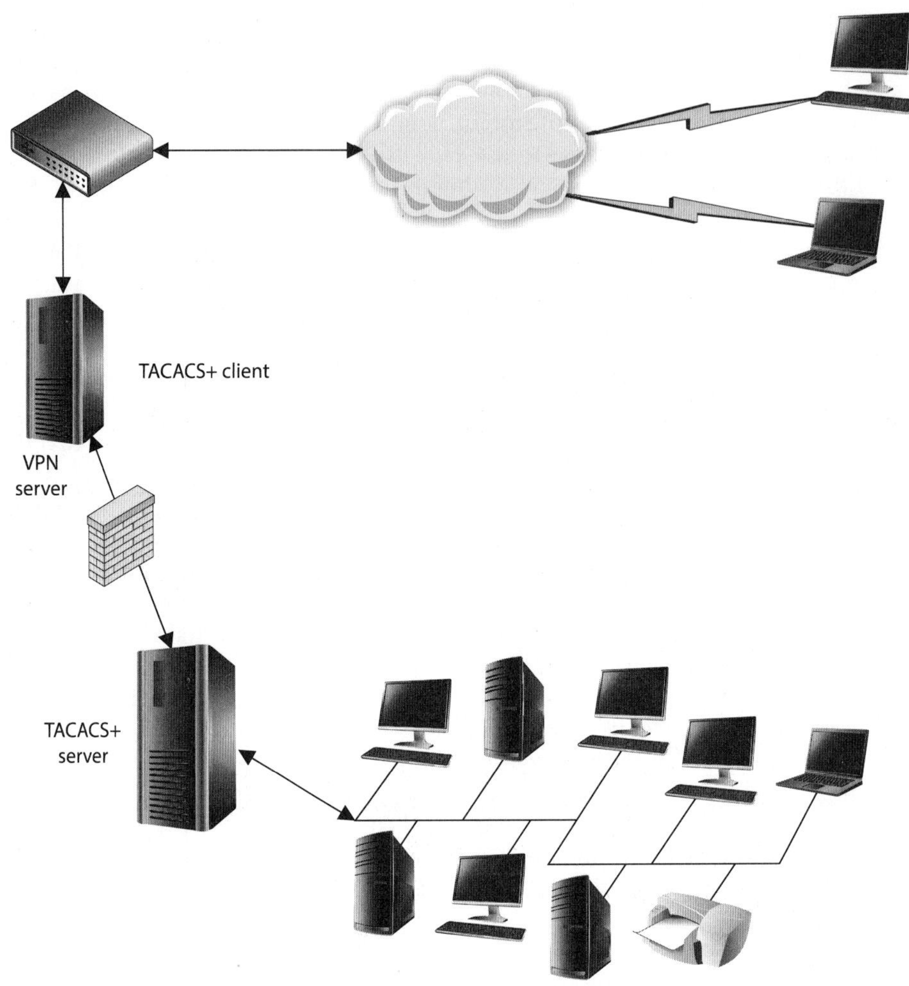

Figure 5-21 TACACS+ works in a client/server model.

	RADIUS	TACACS+
Packet delivery	UDP	TCP
Packet encryption	Encrypts only the password from the RADIUS client to the server.	Encrypts all traffic between the client and server.
AAA support	Combines authentication and authorization services.	Uses the AAA architecture, separating authentication, authorization, and auditing.
Multiprotocol support	Works over PPP connections.	Supports other protocols, such as AppleTalk, NetBIOS, and IPX.
Responses	Uses single-challenge response when authenticating a user, which is used for all AAA activities.	Uses multiple-challenge response for each of the AAA processes. Each AAA activity must be authenticated.

Table 5-3 Specific Differences Between These Two AAA Protocols

as in ISPs. TACACS+ is the better choice for environments that require more sophisticated authentication steps and tighter control over more complex authorization activities, as in corporate networks.

Diameter

Diameter is a protocol that has been developed to build upon the functionality of RADIUS and overcome many of its limitations. The creators of this protocol decided to call it Diameter as a play on the term RADIUS—as in *the diameter is twice the radius.*

Diameter is another AAA protocol that provides the same type of functionality as RADIUS and TACACS+ but also provides more flexibility and capabilities to meet the new demands of today's complex and diverse networks. At one time, all remote communication took place over PPP and Serial Line Internet Protocol (SLIP) connections, and users authenticated themselves through PAP or CHAP. Those were simpler, happier times when our parents had to walk uphill both ways to school wearing no shoes. As with life, technology has become much more complicated, and there are more devices and protocols to choose from than ever before. Today, we want our wireless devices and smartphones to be able to authenticate themselves to our networks, and we use roaming protocols, Mobile IP, Ethernet over PPP, Voice over IP (VoIP), and other crazy stuff that the traditional AAA protocols cannot keep up with. So the smart people came up with a new AAA protocol, Diameter, that can deal with these issues and many more.

Mobile IP

This technology allows a user to move from one network to another and still use the same IP address. It is an improvement upon the IP protocol because it allows a user to have a *home IP address*, associated with his home network, and a *care-of address*. The care-of address changes as he moves from one network to the other. All traffic that is addressed to his home IP address is forwarded to his care-of address.

Diameter protocol consists of two portions. The first is the base protocol, which provides the secure communication among Diameter entities, feature discovery, and version negotiation. The second is the extensions, which are built on top of the base protocol to allow various technologies to use Diameter for authentication.

Up until the conception of Diameter, IETF had individual working groups who defined how VoIP, Fax over IP (FoIP), Mobile IP, and remote authentication protocols work. Defining and implementing them individually in any network can easily result in too much confusion and interoperability. It requires customers to roll out and configure several different policy servers and increases the cost with each new added service. Diameter provides a base protocol, which defines header formats, security options, commands, and AVPs. This base protocol allows for extensions to tie in other services, such as VoIP, FoIP, Mobile IP, wireless, and cell phone authentication. So Diameter can be used as an AAA protocol for all of these different uses.

As an analogy, consider a scenario in which ten people all need to get to the same hospital, which is where they all work. They all have different jobs (doctor, lab technician, nurse, janitor, and so on), but they all need to end up at the same location. So, they can either all take their own cars and their own routes to the hospital, which takes up more hospital parking space and requires the gate guard to authenticate each and every car, or they can take a bus. The bus is the common element (base protocol) to get the individuals (different services) to the same location (networked environment). Diameter provides the common AAA and security framework that different services can work within.

RADIUS and TACACS+ are client/server protocols, which means the server portion cannot send unsolicited commands to the client portion. The server portion can only speak when spoken to. Diameter is a peer-based protocol that allows either end to initiate communication. This functionality allows the Diameter server to send a message to the access server to request the user to provide another authentication credential if she is attempting to access a secure resource.

Diameter is not directly backward-compatible with RADIUS but provides an upgrade path. Diameter uses TCP and AVPs, and provides proxy server support. It has better error detection and correction functionality than RADIUS, as well as better failover properties, and thus provides better network resilience.

Diameter has the functionality and ability to provide the AAA functionality for other protocols and services because it has a large AVP set. RADIUS has 2^8 (256) AVPs, while Diameter has 2^{32} (a whole bunch). Recall from earlier in the chapter that AVPs are like boxes drawn on a piece of paper that outline how two entities can communicate back and forth. So, having more AVPs allows for more functionality and services to exist and communicate between systems.

Diameter provides the following AAA functionality:

Authentication:

- PAP, CHAP, EAP
- End-to-end protection of authentication information
- Replay attack protection

Authorization:

- Redirects, secure proxies, relays, and brokers
- State reconciliation
- Unsolicited disconnect
- Reauthorization on demand

Accounting:

- Reporting, roaming operations (ROAMOPS) accounting, event monitoring

You may not be familiar with Diameter because it is relatively new. It probably won't be taking over the world tomorrow, but it will be used by environments that need to provide the type of services being demanded of them, and then slowly seep down into corporate networks as more products are available. RADIUS has been around for a long time and has served its purpose well, so don't expect it to exit the stage any time soon.

Decentralized Access Control Administration

A *decentralized access control administration* method gives control of access to the people closer to the resources—the people who may better understand who should and should not have access to certain files, data, and resources. In this approach, it is often the functional manager who assigns access control rights to employees. An organization may choose to use a decentralized model if its managers have better judgment regarding which users should be able to access different resources, and there is no business requirement that dictates strict control through a centralized body is necessary.

Changes can happen faster through this type of administration because not just one entity is making changes for the whole organization. However, there is a possibility that conflicts of interest could arise that may not benefit the organization. Because no single entity controls access as a whole, different managers and departments can practice security and access control in different ways. This does not provide uniformity and fairness across the organization. One manager could be too busy with daily tasks and decide it is easier to let everyone have full control over all the systems in the department. Another department may practice a stricter and detail-oriented method of control by giving employees only the level of permissions needed to fulfill their tasks.

Also, certain controls can overlap, in which case actions may not be properly proscribed or restricted. If Mike is part of the accounting group and recently has been under suspicion for altering personnel account information, the accounting manager may restrict his access to these files to read-only access. However, the accounting manager does not realize that Mike still has full-control access under the network group he is also a member of. This type of administration does not provide methods for consistent control as a centralized method would. Another issue that comes up with decentralized administration is lack of proper consistency pertaining to the company's protection. For example, when Sean is fired for looking at pornography on his computer, some of the groups Sean is a member of may not disable his account. So, Sean may still have access after he is terminated, which could cause the company heartache if Sean is vindictive.

Access Control Methods

Access controls can be implemented at various layers of a network and individual systems. Some controls are core components of operating systems or embedded into applications and devices, and some security controls require third-party add-on packages. Although different controls provide different functionality, they should all work together to keep the bad guys out and the good guys in, and to provide the necessary quality of protection.

Companies do not want people to be able to walk into their building arbitrarily, sit down at an employee's computer, and access network resources. Companies also don't want every employee to be able to access all information within the company, as in human resource records, payroll information, and trade secrets. Companies want some assurance that employees who can access confidential information will have some restrictions put upon them, making sure, say, a disgruntled employee does not have the ability to delete financial statements, tax information, and top-secret data that would put the company at risk. Several types of access controls prevent these things from happening, as discussed in the sections that follow.

Access Control Layers

Access control consists of three broad categories: administrative, technical, and physical. Each category has different access control mechanisms that can be carried out manually or automatically. All of these access control mechanisms should work in concert with each other to protect an infrastructure and its data.

Each category of access control has several components that fall within it, as shown next:

Administrative controls:

- Policy and procedures
- Personnel controls
- Supervisory structure
- Security-awareness training
- Testing

Physical controls:

- Network segregation
- Perimeter security
- Computer controls
- Work area separation
- Data backups
- Cabling
- Control zone

Technical controls:

- System access
- Network architecture
- Network access
- Encryption and protocols
- Auditing

The following sections explain each of these categories and components and how they relate to access control.

Administrative Controls

Senior management must decide what role security will play in the organization, including the security goals and objectives. These directives will dictate how all the supporting mechanisms will fall into place. Basically, senior management provides the skeleton of a security infrastructure and then appoints the proper entities to fill in the rest.

The first piece to building a security foundation within an organization is a security policy. It is management's responsibility to construct a security policy and delegate the development of the supporting procedures, standards, and guidelines; indicate which personnel controls should be used; and specify how testing should be carried out to ensure all pieces fulfill the company's security goals. These items are *administrative controls* and work at the top layer of a hierarchical access control model. (Administrative controls are examined in detail in Chapter 1, but are mentioned here briefly to show the relationship to logical and physical controls pertaining to access control.)

Personnel Controls

Personnel controls indicate how employees are expected to interact with security mechanisms and address noncompliance issues pertaining to these expectations. These controls indicate what security actions should be taken when an employee is hired, terminated, suspended, moved into another department, or promoted. Specific procedures must be developed for each situation, and many times the human resources and legal departments are involved with making these decisions.

Supervisory Structure

Management must construct a supervisory structure in which each employee has a superior to report to, and that superior is responsible for that employee's actions. This forces management members to be responsible for employees and take a vested interest in their activities. If an employee is caught hacking into a server that holds customer credit card information, that employee *and* her supervisor will face the consequences. This is an administrative control that aids in fighting fraud and enforcing proper control.

Security-Awareness Training

In many organizations, management has a hard time spending money and allocating resources for items that do not seem to affect the bottom line: profitability. This is why training traditionally has been given low priority, but as computer security becomes more and more of an issue to companies, they are starting to recognize the value of security-awareness training.

A company's security depends upon technology and people, and people are usually the weakest link and cause the most security breaches and compromises. If users understand how to properly access resources, why access controls are in place, and the ramifications for not using the access controls properly, a company can reduce many types of security incidents.

Testing

All security controls, mechanisms, and procedures must be tested on a periodic basis to ensure they properly support the security policy, goals, and objectives set for them. This testing can be a drill to test reactions to a physical attack or disruption of the network, a penetration test of the firewalls and perimeter network to uncover vulnerabilities, a query to employees to gauge their knowledge, or a review of the procedures and standards to make sure they still align with implemented business or technology changes. Because change is constant and environments continually evolve, security procedures and practices should be continually tested to ensure they align with management's expectations and stay up-to-date with each addition to the infrastructure. It is management's responsibility to make sure these tests take place.

Physical Controls

We discussed physical security in Chapter 3, but it is important to understand that certain physical controls must support and work with administrative and technical (logical) controls to supply the right degree of access control. Examples of physical controls include having a security guard verify individuals' identities prior to allowing them to enter a facility, erecting fences around the exterior of the facility, making sure server rooms and wiring closets are locked and protected from environmental elements (humidity, heat, and cold), and allowing only certain individuals to access work areas that contain confidential information.

Network Segregation

Network segregation can be carried out through physical and logical means. A network might be physically designed to have all computers and databases in a certain area. This area may have doors with security swipe cards that allow only individuals who have a specific clearance to access this section and these computers. Another section of the network may contain web servers, routers, and switches, and yet another network portion may have employee workstations. Each area would have the necessary physical controls to ensure that only the permitted individuals have access into and out of those sections.

Perimeter Security

How perimeter security is implemented depends upon the company and the security requirements of that environment. One environment may require employees to be authorized by a security guard by showing a security badge that contains a picture identification before being allowed to enter a section. Another environment may require no authentication process and let anyone and everyone into different sections. Perimeter security can also encompass closed-circuit TVs that scan the parking lots and waiting areas, fences surrounding a building, the lighting of walkways and parking areas, motion detectors, sensors, alarms, and the location and visual appearance of a building. These are examples of perimeter security mechanisms that provide physical access control by providing protection for individuals, facilities, and the components within facilities.

Computer Controls

Each computer can have physical controls installed and configured, such as locks on the cover so the internal parts cannot be stolen, the removal of the USB and optical drives to prevent copying of confidential information, or implementation of a protection device that reduces the electrical emissions to thwart attempts to gather information through airwaves.

Work Area Separation

Some environments might dictate that only particular individuals can access certain areas of the facility. For example, research companies might not want office personnel to be able to enter laboratories, so that they can't disrupt or taint experiments or access test data. Most network administrators allow only network staff in the server rooms and wiring closets to reduce the possibilities of errors or sabotage attempts. In financial institutions, only certain employees can enter the vaults or other restricted areas. These examples of work area separation are physical controls used to support access control and the overall security policy of the company.

Cabling

Different types of cabling can be used to carry information throughout a network. Some cable types have sheaths that protect the data from being affected by the electrical interference of other devices that emit electrical signals. Some types of cable have protection material around each individual wire to ensure there is no crosstalk between the different wires. All cables need to be routed throughout the facility so they are not in the way of employees or exposed to any dangers like being cut, burnt, crimped, or eavesdropped upon.

Control Zone

The company facility should be split up into zones depending upon the sensitivity of the activity that takes place per zone. The front lobby could be considered a public area, the product development area could be considered top secret, and the executive offices could be considered secret. It does not matter what classifications are used, but it should be understood that some areas are more sensitive than others, which will require different access controls based on the needed protection level. The same is true of the company network. It should be segmented, and access controls should be chosen for each zone based on the criticality of devices and the sensitivity of data being processed.

Technical Controls

Technical controls are the software tools used to restrict subjects' access to objects. They are core components of operating systems, add-on security packages, applications, network hardware devices, protocols, encryption mechanisms, and access control matrices. These controls work at different layers within a network or system and need to maintain a synergistic relationship to ensure there is no unauthorized access to resources and that the resources' availability, integrity, and confidentiality are guaranteed. Technical controls protect the integrity and availability of resources by limiting the number of subjects that can access them and protecting the confidentiality of resources by preventing disclosure to unauthorized subjects. The following sections explain how some technical controls work and where they are implemented within an environment.

System Access

Different types of controls and security mechanisms control how a computer is accessed. If an organization is using a MAC architecture, the clearance of a user is identified and compared to the resource's classification level to verify that this user can access the requested object. If an organization is using a DAC architecture, the operating system checks to see if a user has been granted permission to access this resource. The sensitivity of data, clearance level of users, and users' rights and permissions are used as logical controls to control access to a resource.

Many types of technical controls enable a user to access a system and the resources within that system. A technical control may be a username and password combination, a Kerberos implementation, biometrics, public key infrastructure (PKI), RADIUS, TACACS+, or authentication using a smart card through a reader connected to a system. These technologies verify the user is who he says he is by using different types of authentication methods. Once a user is properly authenticated, he can be authorized and allowed access to network resources. These technologies are addressed in further detail in future chapters, but for now understand that system access is a type of technical control that can enforce access control objectives.

Network Architecture

The architecture of a network can be constructed and enforced through several logical controls to provide segregation and protection of an environment. Whereas a network can be segregated physically by walls and location, it can also be segregated logically through IP address ranges and subnets and by controlling the communication flow between the segments. Often, it is important to control how one segment of a network communicates with another segment.

Figure 5-22 shows an example of how an organization may segregate its network and determine how network segments can communicate. This example shows that the organization does not want the internal network and the demilitarized zone (DMZ) to have open and unrestricted communication paths. There is usually no reason for internal users to have direct access to the systems in the DMZ, and cutting off this type of communication reduces the possibilities of internal attacks on those systems. Also, if an attack comes from the Internet and successfully compromises a system on the DMZ, the attacker must not be able to easily access the internal network, which this type of logical segregation protects against.

This example also shows how the management segment can communicate with all other network segments, but those segments cannot communicate in return. The segmentation is implemented because the management consoles that control the firewalls and IDSs reside in the management segment, and there is no reason for users, other than the administrator, to have access to these computers.

A network can be segregated physically and logically. This type of segregation and restriction is accomplished through logical controls.

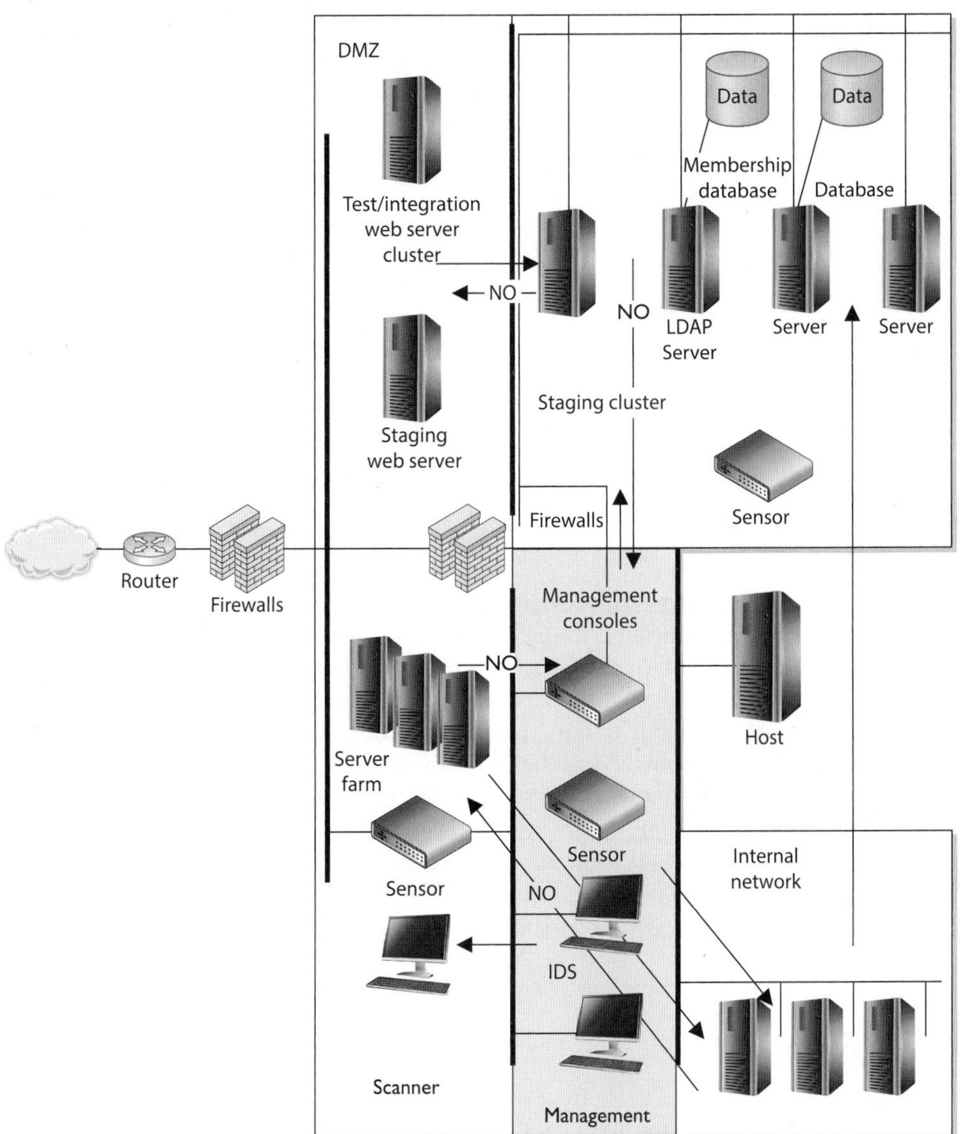

Figure 5-22 Technical network segmentation controls how different network segments communicate.

Network Access

Systems have logical controls that dictate who can and cannot access them and what those individuals can do once they are authenticated. This is also true for networks. Routers, switches, firewalls, and gateways all work as technical controls to enforce access restriction into and out of a network and access to the different segments within the network. If an attacker from the Internet wants to gain access to a specific computer, chances are she will have to hack through a firewall, router, and a switch just to be able to start an attack on a specific computer that resides within the internal network. Each device has its own logical controls that make decisions about what entities can access them and what type of actions they can carry out.

Access to different network segments should be granular in nature. Routers and firewalls can be used to ensure that only certain types of traffic get through to each segment.

Encryption and Protocols

Encryption and protocols work as technical controls to protect information as it passes throughout a network and resides on computers. They ensure that the information is received by the correct entity and that it is not modified during transmission. These logical controls can preserve the confidentiality and integrity of data and enforce specific paths for communication to take place. (Chapter 3 discusses cryptography and encryption mechanisms.)

Auditing

Auditing tools are technical controls that track activity within a network, on a network device, or on a specific computer. Even though auditing is not an activity that will deny an entity access to a network or computer, it will track activities so a network administrator can understand the types of access that took place, identify a security breach, or warn the administrator of suspicious activity. This information can be used to point out weaknesses of other technical controls and help the administrator understand where changes must be made to preserve the necessary security level within the environment.

NOTE What is important to understand is that there are administrative, technical, and physical controls that work toward providing access control, and you should know several examples of each for the exam.

Accountability

Auditing capabilities ensure users are accountable for their actions, verify that the security policies are enforced, and can be used as investigation tools. There are several reasons why network administrators and security professionals want to make sure accountability mechanisms are in place and configured properly: to be able to track bad deeds back to individuals, detect intrusions, reconstruct events and system conditions, provide legal recourse material, and produce problem reports. Audit documentation and log files hold a mountain of information—the trick is usually deciphering it and presenting it in a useful and understandable format.

Accountability is tracked by recording user, system, and application activities. This recording is done through auditing functions and mechanisms within an operating system or application. Audit trails contain information about operating system activities,

application events, and user actions. Audit trails can be used to verify the health of a system by checking performance information or certain types of errors and conditions. After a system crashes, a network administrator often will review audit logs to try and piece together the status of the system and attempt to understand what events could be attributed to the disruption.

Audit trails can also be used to provide alerts about any suspicious activities that can be investigated at a later time. In addition, they can be valuable in determining exactly how far an attack has gone and the extent of the damage that may have been caused. It is important to make sure a proper chain of custody is maintained to ensure any data collected can later be properly and accurately represented in case it needs to be used for later events such as criminal proceedings or investigations.

It is a good idea to keep the following in mind when dealing with auditing:

- Store the audits securely.
- The right audit tools will keep the size of the logs under control.
- The logs must be protected from any unauthorized changes in order to safeguard data.
- Train the right people to review the data in the right manner.
- Make sure the ability to delete logs is only available to administrators.
- Logs should contain activities of all high-privileged accounts (root, administrator).

An administrator configures what actions and events are to be audited and logged. In a high-security environment, the administrator would configure more activities to be captured and set the threshold of those activities to be more sensitive. The events can be reviewed to identify where breaches of security occurred and if the security policy has been violated. If the environment does not require such levels of security, the events analyzed would be fewer, with less demanding thresholds.

Items and actions to be audited can become an endless list. A security professional should be able to assess an environment and its security goals, know what actions should be audited, and know what is to be done with that information after it is captured—without wasting too much disk space, CPU power, and staff time. The following gives a broad overview of the items and actions that can be audited and logged:

System-level events:

- System performance
- Logon attempts (successful and unsuccessful)
- Logon ID
- Date and time of each logon attempt
- Lockouts of users and terminals

- Use of administration utilities
- Devices used
- Functions performed
- Requests to alter configuration files

Application-level events:

- Error messages
- Files opened and closed
- Modifications of files
- Security violations within applications

User-level events:

- Identification and authentication attempts
- Files, services, and resources used
- Commands initiated
- Security violations

The threshold (clipping level) and parameters for each of these items must be configured. For example, an administrator can audit each logon attempt or just each failed logon attempt. System performance can look at the amount of memory used within an eight-hour period or the memory, CPU, and hard drive space used within an hour.

Intrusion detection systems (IDSs) continually scan audit logs for suspicious activity. If an intrusion or harmful event takes place, audit logs are usually kept to be used later to prove guilt and prosecute if necessary. If severe security events take place, many times the IDS will alert the administrator or staff member so they can take proper actions to end the destructive activity. If a dangerous virus is identified, administrators may take the mail server offline. If an attacker is accessing confidential information within the database, this computer may be temporarily disconnected from the network or Internet. If an attack is in progress, the administrator may want to watch the actions taking place so she can track down the intruder. IDSs can watch for this type of activity during real time and/or scan audit logs and watch for specific patterns or behaviors.

Review of Audit Information

Audit trails can be reviewed manually or through automated means—either way, they must be reviewed and interpreted. If an organization reviews audit trails manually, it needs to establish a system of how, when, and why they are viewed. Usually audit logs are very popular items right after a security breach, unexplained system action, or system disruption. An administrator or staff member rapidly tries to piece together the

activities that led up to the event. This type of audit review is event-oriented. Audit trails can also be viewed periodically to watch for unusual behavior of users or systems and to help understand the baseline and health of a system. Then there is a real-time, or near real-time, audit analysis that can use an automated tool to review audit information as it is created. Administrators should have a scheduled task of reviewing audit data. The audit material usually needs to be parsed and saved to another location for a certain time period. This retention information should be stated in the company's security policy and procedures.

Reviewing audit information manually can be overwhelming. There are applications and audit trail analysis tools that reduce the volume of audit logs to review and improve the efficiency of manual review procedures. A majority of the time, audit logs contain information that is unnecessary, so these tools parse out specific events and present them in a useful format.

An *audit-reduction tool* does just what its name suggests—reduces the amount of information within an audit log. This tool discards mundane task information and records system performance, security, and user functionality information that can be useful to a security professional or administrator.

Today, more organizations are implementing *security event management (SEM)* systems, also called *security information and event management (SIEM)* systems. These products gather logs from various devices (servers, firewalls, routers, etc.) and attempt to correlate the log data and provide analysis capabilities. Reviewing logs manually looking for suspicious activity on a continuous manner is not only mind-numbing, it is close to impossible to be successful. So many packets and network communication data sets are passing along a network, humans cannot collect all the data in real or near real time, analyze it, identify current attacks, and react—it is just too overwhelming. We also have different *types* of systems on a network (routers, firewalls, IDS, IPS, servers, gateways, proxies) collecting logs in various proprietary formats, which requires centralization, standardization, and normalization. Log formats are different per product type and vendor. The format of logs created by Juniper network device systems is different from the format of logs created by Cisco systems, which in turn is different from the format created by Palo Alto and Barracuda firewalls. It is important to gather logs from various different systems within an environment so that some type of situational awareness can take place. Once the logs are gathered, intelligence routines need to be processed on them so that data mining can take place to identify patterns. The goal is to piece together seemingly unrelated event data so that the security team can fully understand what is taking place within the network and react properly.

NOTE Situational awareness means that you understand the current environment even though it is complex, dynamic, and made up of seemingly unrelated data points. You need to be able to understand each data point in its own context within the surrounding environment so that you can make the best possible decisions.

Protecting Audit Data and Log Information

If an intruder breaks into your house, he will do his best to cover his tracks by not leaving fingerprints or any other clues that can be used to tie him to the criminal activity. The same is true in computer fraud and illegal activity. The intruder will work to cover his tracks. Attackers often delete audit logs that hold this incriminating information. (Deleting specific incriminating data within audit logs is called *scrubbing*.) Deleting this information can cause the administrator to not be alerted or aware of the security breach and can destroy valuable data. Therefore, audit logs should be protected by strict access control and stored on a remote host.

Only certain individuals (the administrator and security personnel) should be able to view, modify, and delete audit trail information. No other individuals should be able to view this data, much less modify or delete it. The integrity of the data can be ensured with the use of digital signatures, hashing tools, and strong access controls. Its confidentiality can be protected with encryption and access controls, if necessary, and it can be stored on *write-once media* (CD-ROMs) to prevent loss or modification of the data. Unauthorized access attempts to audit logs should be captured and reported.

Audit logs may be used in a trial to prove an individual's guilt, demonstrate how an attack was carried out, or corroborate a story. The integrity and confidentiality of these logs will be under scrutiny. Proper steps need to be taken to ensure that the confidentiality and integrity of the audit information is not compromised in any way.

Keystroke Monitoring

Keystroke monitoring is a type of monitoring that can review and record keystrokes entered by a user during an active session. The person using this type of monitoring can have the characters written to an audit log to be reviewed at a later time. This type of auditing is usually done only for special cases and only for a specific length of time, because the amount of information captured can be overwhelming and much of that information may be unimportant. If a security professional or administrator is suspicious of an individual and his activities, she may invoke this type of monitoring. In some authorized investigative stages, a keyboard dongle (hardware key logger) may be unobtrusively inserted between the keyboard and the computer to capture all the keystrokes entered, including power-on passwords.

A hacker can also use this type of monitoring. If an attacker can successfully install a Trojan horse on a computer, the Trojan horse can install an application that captures data as it is typed into the keyboard. Typically, these programs are most interested in user credentials and can alert the attacker when credentials have been successfully captured.

Privacy issues are involved with this type of monitoring, and administrators could be subject to criminal and civil liabilities if it is done without proper notification to the employees and authorization from management. If a company wants to use this type of auditing, it should state so in the security policy, address the issue in security-awareness training, and present a banner notice to users warning that the activities at that computer may be monitored in this fashion. These steps should be taken to protect the company from violating an individual's privacy and to inform users where their privacy boundaries start and stop pertaining to computer use.

Access Control Practices

We have gone over how users are identified, authenticated, and authorized and how their actions are audited. These are necessary parts of a healthy and safe network environment. You also want to take steps to ensure there are no unnecessary open doors and that the environment stays at the same security level you have worked so hard to achieve. This means you need to implement good access control practices. Not keeping up with daily or monthly tasks usually causes the most vulnerabilities in an environment. It is hard to put out all the network fires, fight the political battles, fulfill all the users' needs, and still keep up with small maintenance tasks. However, many companies have found that not doing these small tasks caused them the greatest heartache of all.

The following is a list of tasks that must be done on a regular basis to ensure security stays at a satisfactory level:

- Deny access to systems to undefined users or anonymous accounts.
- Limit and monitor the usage of administrator and other powerful accounts.
- Suspend or delay access capability after a specific number of unsuccessful logon attempts.
- Remove obsolete user accounts as soon as the user leaves the company.
- Suspend inactive accounts after 30 to 60 days.
- Enforce strict access criteria.
- Enforce the need-to-know and least-privilege practices.
- Disable unneeded system features, services, and ports.
- Replace default password settings on accounts.
- Limit and monitor global access rules.
- Remove redundant resource rules from accounts and group memberships.
- Remove redundant user IDs, accounts, and role-based accounts from resource access lists.
- Enforce password rotation.
- Enforce password requirements (length, contents, lifetime, distribution, storage, and transmission).
- Audit system and user events and actions, and review reports periodically.
- Protect audit logs.

Even if all of these countermeasures are in place and properly monitored, data can still be lost in an unauthorized manner in other ways. The next section looks at these issues and their corresponding countermeasures.

Unauthorized Disclosure of Information

Several things can make information available to others for whom it is not intended, which can bring about unfavorable results. Sometimes this is done intentionally; other

times, unintentionally. Information can be disclosed unintentionally when one falls prey to attacks that specialize in causing this disclosure. These attacks include social engineering, covert channels, malicious code, and electrical airwave sniffing. Information can be disclosed accidentally through object reuse methods, which are explained next.

Object Reuse

Object reuse issues pertain to reassigning to a subject media that previously contained one or more objects. Huh? This means before someone uses a hard drive, USB drive, or tape, it should be cleared of any residual information still on it. This concept also applies to objects reused by computer processes, such as memory locations, variables, and registers. Any sensitive information that may be left by a process should be securely cleared before allowing another process the opportunity to access the object. This ensures that information not intended for this individual or any other subject is not disclosed. Many times, USB drives are exchanged casually in a work environment. What if a supervisor lent a USB drive to an employee without erasing it and it contained confidential employee performance reports and salary raises forecasted for the next year? This could prove to be a bad decision and may turn into a morale issue if the information was passed around. Formatting a disk or deleting files only removes the pointers to the files; it does not remove the actual files. This information will still be on the disk and available until the operating system needs that space and overwrites those files. So, for media that holds confidential information, more extreme methods should be taken to ensure the files are actually gone, not just their pointers.

Sensitive data should be classified (secret, top secret, confidential, unclassified, and so on) by the data owners. How the data is stored and accessed should also be strictly controlled and audited by software controls. However, the task does not end there. Before allowing someone to use previously used media, it should be erased or degaussed. (This responsibility usually falls on the operations department.) If media holds sensitive information and cannot be purged, steps should be created describing how to properly destroy it so no one else can obtain this information.

TIP Sometimes hackers actually configure a sector on a hard drive so it is marked as bad and unusable to an operating system but that is actually fine and may hold malicious data. The operating system will not write information to this sector because it thinks it is corrupted. This is a form of data hiding. Some boot-sector virus routines are capable of putting the main part of their code (payload) into a specific sector of the hard drive, overwriting any data that may have been there, and then protecting it as a bad block.

Emanation Security

All electronic devices emit electrical signals. These signals can hold important information, and if an attacker buys the right equipment and positions himself in the right place, he could capture this information from the airwaves and access data transmissions as if he had a tap directly on the network wire.

Several incidents have occurred in which intruders have purchased inexpensive equipment and used it to intercept electrical emissions as they radiated from a computer. This equipment can reproduce data streams and display the data on the intruder's monitor, enabling the intruder to learn of covert operations, find out military strategies, and uncover and exploit confidential information. This is not just stuff found in spy novels. It really happens. So, the proper countermeasures have been devised.

TEMPEST *TEMPEST* started out as a study carried out by the DoD and then turned into a standard that outlines how to develop countermeasures that control spurious electrical signals emitted by electrical equipment. Special shielding is used on equipment to suppress the signals as they are radiated from devices. TEMPEST equipment is implemented to prevent intruders from picking up information through the airwaves with listening devices. This type of equipment must meet specific standards to be rated as providing TEMPEST shielding protection. TEMPEST refers to standardized technology that suppresses signal emanations with shielding material. Vendors who manufacture this type of equipment must be certified to this standard.

The devices (monitors, computers, printers, and so on) have an outer metal coating, referred to as a *Faraday cage*. This is made of metal with the necessary depth to ensure only a certain amount of radiation is released. In devices that are TEMPEST rated, other components are also modified, especially the power supply, to help reduce the amount of electricity used.

Even allowable limits of emission levels can radiate and still be considered safe. The approved products must ensure only this level of emissions is allowed to escape the devices. This type of protection is usually needed only in military institutions, although other highly secured environments do utilize this kind of safeguard.

Many military organizations are concerned with stray radio frequencies emitted by computers and other electronic equipment because an attacker may be able to pick them up, reconstruct them, and give away secrets meant to stay secret.

TEMPEST technology is complex, cumbersome, and expensive, and therefore only used in highly sensitive areas that really need this high level of protection.

Two alternatives to TEMPEST exist: use white noise or use a control zone concept, both of which are explained next.

NOTE TEMPEST is the name of a program, and now a standard, that was developed in the late 1950s by the U.S. and British governments to deal with electrical and electromagnetic radiation emitted from electrical equipment, mainly computers. This type of equipment is usually used by intelligence, military, government, and law enforcement agencies, and the selling of such items is under constant scrutiny.

White Noise A countermeasure used to keep intruders from extracting information from electrical transmissions is *white noise*, a uniform spectrum of random electrical signals. It is distributed over the full spectrum so the bandwidth is constant and an intruder is not able to decipher real information from random noise or random information.

Control Zone Another alternative to using TEMPEST equipment is to use the zone concept, which was addressed earlier in this chapter. Some facilities use material in their walls to contain electrical signals, which acts like a large Faraday cage. This prevents intruders from being able to access information emitted via electrical signals from network devices. This control zone creates a type of security perimeter and is constructed to protect against unauthorized access to data or the compromise of sensitive information.

Access Control Monitoring

Access control monitoring is a method of keeping track of who attempts to access specific company resources. It is an important detective mechanism, and different technologies exist that can fill this need. It is not enough to invest in antivirus and firewall solutions. Companies are finding that monitoring their own internal network has become a way of life.

Intrusion Detection Systems

Intrusion detection systems (IDSs) are different from traditional firewall products because they are designed to detect a security breach. *Intrusion detection* is the process of detecting an unauthorized use of, or attack upon, a computer, network, or telecommunications infrastructure. IDSs are designed to aid in mitigating the damage that can be caused by hacking or by breaking into sensitive computer and network systems. The basic intent of the IDS tool is to spot something suspicious happening on the network and sound an alarm by flashing a message on a network manager's screen, or possibly sending an e-mail or even reconfiguring a firewall's ACL setting. The IDS tools can look for sequences of data bits that might indicate a questionable action or event, or monitor system log and activity recording files. The event does not need to be an intrusion to sound the alarm—any kind of "non-normal" behavior may do the trick.

Although different types of IDS products are available, they all have three common components: sensors, analyzers, and administrator interfaces. The sensors collect traffic and user activity data and send it to an analyzer, which looks for suspicious activity. If the analyzer detects an activity it is programmed to deem as fishy, it sends an alert to the administrator's interface.

IDSs come in two main types: *network-based*, which monitor network communications, and *host-based*, which can analyze the activity within a particular computer system.

IDSs can be configured to watch for attacks, parse audit logs, terminate a connection, alert an administrator as attacks are happening, expose a hacker's techniques, illustrate which vulnerabilities need to be addressed, and possibly help track down individual hackers.

Network-Based IDSs

A *network-based IDS (NIDS)* uses sensors, which are either host computers with the necessary software installed or dedicated appliances—each with its network interface card (NIC) in promiscuous mode. Normally, NICs watch for traffic that has the address of its host system, broadcasts, and sometimes multicast traffic. The NIC driver copies the data from the transmission medium and sends it up the network protocol stack for processing. When a NIC is put into promiscuous mode, the NIC driver captures all traffic, makes a copy of all packets, and then passes one copy to the TCP stack and one copy to an analyzer to look for specific types of patterns.

A NIDS monitors network traffic and cannot "see" the activity going on inside a computer itself. To monitor the activities within a computer system, a company would need to implement a host-based IDS.

Host-Based IDSs

A *host-based IDS (HIDS)* can be installed on individual workstations and/or servers to watch for inappropriate or anomalous activity. HIDSs are usually used to make sure users do not delete system files, reconfigure important settings, or put the system at risk in any other way. So, whereas the NIDS understands and monitors the network traffic, a HIDS's universe is limited to the computer itself. A HIDS does not understand or review network traffic, and a NIDS does not "look in" and monitor a system's activity. Each has its own job and stays out of the other's way.

In most environments, HIDS products are installed only on critical servers, not on every system on the network, because of the resource overhead and the administration nightmare that such an installation would cause.

Just to make life a little more confusing, HIDS and NIDS can be one of the following types:

Signature-based:

- Pattern matching
- Stateful matching

Anomaly-based:

- Statistical anomaly–based
- Protocol anomaly–based
- Traffic anomaly–based
- Rule- or heuristic-based

Knowledge- or Signature-Based Intrusion Detection

Knowledge is accumulated by the IDS vendors about specific attacks and how they are carried out. Models of how the attacks are carried out are developed and called *signatures*. Each identified attack has a signature, which is used to detect an attack in progress or determine if one has occurred within the network. Any action that is not recognized as an attack is considered acceptable.

NOTE Signature-based is also known as pattern matching.

An example of a signature is a packet that has the same source IP address and destination IP address. All packets should have different source and destination IP addresses, and if they have the same address, this means a Land attack is under way. In a Land attack, a hacker modifies the packet header so that when a receiving system responds to the sender, it is responding to its own address. Now that seems as though it should be benign enough, but vulnerable systems just do not have the programming code to know what to do in this situation, so they freeze or reboot. Once this type of attack was discovered, the signature-based IDS vendors wrote a signature that looks specifically for packets that contain the same source and destination address.

Signature-based IDSs are the most popular IDS products today, and their effectiveness depends upon regularly updating the software with new signatures, as with antivirus software. This type of IDS is weak against new types of attacks because it can recognize only the ones that have been previously identified and have had signatures written for them. Attacks or viruses discovered in production environments are referred to as being "in the wild."

State-Based IDSs

Before delving too deep into how a state-based IDS works, you need to understand what the state of a system or application actually is. Every change that an operating system experiences (user logs on, user opens application, application communicates to another application, user inputs data, and so on) is considered a state transition. In a very technical sense, all operating systems and applications are just lines and lines of instructions written to carry out functions on data. The instructions have empty variables, which is where the data is held. So when you use the calculator program and type in 5, an empty variable is instantly populated with this value. By entering that value, you change the state of the application. When applications communicate with each other, they populate empty variables provided in each application's instruction set. So, a state transition is when a variable's value changes, which usually happens continuously within every system.

Specific state changes (activities) take place with specific types of attacks. If an attacker will carry out a remote buffer overflow, then the following state changes will occur:

1. The remote user connects to the system.
2. The remote user sends data to an application (the data exceeds the allocated buffer for this empty variable).
3. The data is executed and overwrites the buffer and possibly other memory segments.
4. A malicious code executes.

So, *state* is a snapshot of an operating system's values in volatile, semipermanent, and permanent memory locations. In a state-based IDS, the initial state is the state prior to the execution of an attack, and the compromised state is the state after successful penetration. The IDS has rules that outline which state transition sequences should sound an alarm. The activity that takes place between the initial and compromised state is what the state-based IDS looks for, and it sends an alert if any of the state-transition sequences match its preconfigured rules.

This type of IDS scans for attack signatures in the context of a stream of activity instead of just looking at individual packets. It can only identify known attacks and requires frequent updates of its signatures.

Statistical Anomaly–Based IDS

A *statistical anomaly–based IDS* is a behavioral-based system. Behavioral-based IDS products do not use predefined signatures, but rather are put in a learning mode to build a profile of an environment's "normal" activities. This profile is built by continually sampling the environment's activities. The longer the IDS is put in a learning mode, in most instances, the more accurate a profile it will build and the better protection it will provide. After this profile is built, all future traffic and activities are compared to it. The same type of sampling that was used to build the profile takes place, so the same type of data is being compared. Anything that does not match the profile is seen as an attack, in response to which the IDS sends an alert. With the use of complex statistical algorithms, the IDS looks for anomalies in the network traffic or user activity. Each packet is given an anomaly score, which indicates its degree of irregularity. If the score is higher than the established threshold of "normal" behavior, then the preconfigured action will take place.

The benefit of using a statistical anomaly–based IDS is that it can react to new attacks. It can detect "zero-day" attacks, which means an attack is new to the world and no signature or fix has been developed yet. These products are also capable of detecting the "low and slow" attacks, in which the attacker is trying to stay under the radar by sending packets little by little over a long period of time. The IDS should be able to detect these types of attacks because they are different enough from the contrasted profile.

Now for the bad news. Since the only thing that is "normal" about a network is that it is constantly changing, developing the correct profile that will not provide an overwhelming number of false positives can be difficult. Many IT staff members know all too well this dance of chasing down alerts that end up being benign traffic or activity. In fact, some environments end up turning off their IDS because of the amount of time these activities take up. (Proper education on tuning and configuration will reduce the number of false positives.)

If an attacker detects there is an IDS on a network, she will then try to detect the type of IDS it is so she can properly circumvent it. With a behavioral-based IDS, the attacker could attempt to integrate her activities into the behavior pattern of the network traffic. That way, her activities are seen as "normal" by the IDS and thus go undetected. It is a good idea to ensure no attack activity is under way when the IDS is in learning mode. If this takes place, the IDS will never alert you of this type of attack in the future because it sees this traffic as typical of the environment.

If a corporation decides to use a statistical anomaly–based IDS, it must ensure that the staff members who are implementing and maintaining it understand protocols and packet analysis. Because this type of an IDS sends generic alerts, compared to other types of IDSs, it is up to the network engineer to figure out what the actual issue is. For example, a signature-based IDS reports the type of attack that has been identified, while a rule-based IDS identifies the actual rule the packet does not comply with. In a statistical anomaly–based IDS, all the product really understands is that something "abnormal" has happened, which just means the event does not match the profile.

NOTE IDS and some antimalware products are said to have "heuristic" capabilities. The term heuristic means to create new information from different data sources. The IDS gathers different "clues" from the network or system and calculates the probability an attack is taking place. If the probability hits a set threshold, then the alarm sounds.

Attack Techniques

It is common for hackers to first identify whether an IDS is present on the network they are preparing to attack. If one is present, that attacker may implement a denial-of-service attack to bring it offline. Another tactic is to send the IDS incorrect data, which will make the IDS send specific alerts indicating a certain attack is under way, when in truth it is not. The goal of these activities is either to disable the IDS or to distract the network and security individuals so they will be busy chasing the wrong packets while the real attack takes place.

Determining the proper thresholds for statistically significant deviations is really the key for the successful use of a behavioral-based IDS. If the threshold is set too low, nonintrusive activities are considered attacks (false positives). If the threshold is set too high, some malicious activities won't be identified (false negatives).

Once an IDS discovers an attack, several things can happen, depending upon the capabilities of the IDS and the policy assigned to it. The IDS can send an alert to a console to tell the right individuals an attack is being carried out, send an e-mail or text to the individual assigned to respond to such activities, kill the connection of the detected attack, or reconfigure a router or firewall to try to stop any further similar attacks. A modifiable response condition might include anything from blocking a specific IP address to redirecting or blocking a certain type of activity.

Protocol Anomaly–Based IDS

A statistical anomaly–based IDS can use *protocol anomaly–based filters*. These types of IDSs have specific knowledge of each protocol they will monitor. A protocol anomaly pertains to the format and behavior of a protocol. The IDS builds a model (or profile) of each protocol's "normal" usage. Keep in mind, however, that protocols have *theoretical* usage, as outlined in their corresponding RFCs, and *real-world* usage, which refers to the fact that vendors seem to always "color outside the boxes" and don't strictly follow the RFCs in their protocol development and implementation. So, most profiles of individual protocols are a mix between the official and real-world versions of the protocol and its usage. When the IDS is activated, it looks for anomalies that do not match the profiles built for the individual protocols.

Although several vulnerabilities within operating systems and applications are available to be exploited, many more successful attacks take place by exploiting vulnerabilities in the protocols themselves. At the OSI data link layer, the Address Resolution Protocol (ARP) does not have any protection against ARP attacks where bogus data is inserted into its table. At the network layer, the Internet Control Message Protocol (ICMP) can be used in a Loki attack to move data from one place to another, when this protocol was designed to only be used to send status information—not user data. IP headers can be easily modified for spoofed attacks. At the transport layer, TCP packets can be injected into the connection between two systems for a session hijacking attack.

NOTE When an attacker compromises a computer and loads a back door on the system, he will need to have a way to communicate to this computer through this back door and stay "under the radar" of the network firewall and IDS. Hackers have figured out that a small amount of code can be inserted into an ICMP packet, which is then interpreted by the back-door software loaded on a compromised system. Security devices are usually not configured to monitor this type of traffic because ICMP is a protocol that is supposed to be used just to send status information—not commands to a compromised system.

Because every packet formation and delivery involves many protocols, and because more attack vectors exist in the protocols than in the software itself, it is a good idea to integrate protocol anomaly–based filters in any network behavioral-based IDS.

Traffic Anomaly–Based IDS

Most behavioral-based IDSs have *traffic anomaly–based filters*, which detect changes in traffic patterns, as in DoS attacks or a new service that appears on the network. Once a profile is built that captures the baselines of an environment's ordinary traffic, all future traffic patterns are compared to that profile. As with all filters, the thresholds are tunable to adjust the sensitivity and to reduce the number of false positives and false negatives. Since this is a type of statistical anomaly–based IDS, it can detect unknown attacks.

Rule-Based IDS

A *rule-based IDS* takes a different approach than a signature-based or statistical anomaly–based system. A signature-based IDS is very straightforward. For example, if a signature-based IDS detects a packet that has all of its TCP header flags with the bit value of 1, it knows that an Xmas attack is under way—so it sends an alert. A statistical anomaly–based IDS is also straightforward. For example, if Bob has logged on to his computer at 6 A.M. and the profile indicates this is abnormal, the IDS sends an alert, because this is seen as an activity that needs to be investigated. Rule-based intrusion detection gets a little trickier, depending upon the complexity of the rules used.

Rule-based intrusion detection is commonly associated with the use of an expert system. An expert system is made up of a knowledge base, inference engine, and rule-based programming. Knowledge is represented as rules, and the data to be analyzed is referred to as facts. The knowledge of the system is written in rule-based programming (IF *situation* THEN *action*). These rules are applied to the facts, the data that comes in from a sensor, or a system that is being monitored. For example, in scenario 1 the IDS pulls data from a system's audit log and stores it temporarily in its fact database, as illustrated in Figure 5-23. Then, the preconfigured rules are applied to this data to indicate whether anything suspicious is taking place. In our scenario, the rule states "IF *a root user creates File1* AND *creates File2* SUCH THAT *they are in the same directory* THEN *there is a call to Administrative Tool1* TRIGGER *send alert.*" This rule has been defined such that if a root user creates two files in the same directory and then makes a call to a specific administrative tool, an alert should be sent.

It is the inference engine that provides some artificial intelligence into this process. An inference engine can infer new information from provided data by using inference rules. To understand what inferring means in the first place, let's look at the following:

Socrates is a man.
All men are mortals.

Thus, we can infer that Socrates is mortal. If you are asking, "What does this have to do with a hill of beans?" just hold on to your hat—here we go.

Regular programming languages deal with the "black and white" of life. The answer is either yes or no, not maybe this or maybe that. Although computers can carry out complex computations at a much faster rate than humans, they have a harder time guessing, or inferring, answers because they are very structured. The fifth-generation

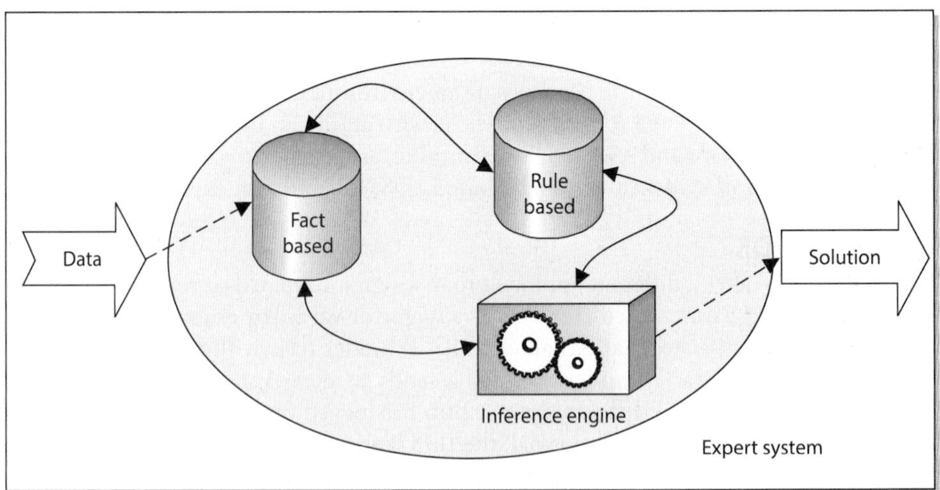

Figure 5-23 Rule-based IDS and expert system components

programming languages (artificial intelligence languages) are capable of dealing with the grayer areas of life and can attempt to infer the right solution from the provided data.

So, in a rule-based IDS founded on an expert system, the IDS gathers data from a sensor or log, and the inference engine uses its preprogrammed rules on it. If the characteristics of the rules are met, an alert or solution is provided.

IDS Types

It is important to understand the characteristics that make the different types of IDS technologies distinct. The following is a summary:

Signature-based:

- Pattern matching, similar to antivirus software
- Signatures must be continuously updated
- Cannot identify new attacks
- Two types:
  - **Pattern matching** Compares packets to signatures
  - **Stateful matching** Compares patterns to several activities at once

Anomaly-based:

- Behavioral-based system that learns the "normal" activities of an environment
- Can detect new attacks
- Also called behavior- or heuristic-based
- Three types:
  - **Statistical anomaly–based** Creates a profile of "normal" and compares activities to this profile
  - **Protocol anomaly–based** Identifies protocols used outside of their common bounds
  - **Traffic anomaly–based** Identifies unusual activity in network traffic

Rule-based:

- Use of IF/THEN rule-based programming within expert systems
- Use of an expert system allows for artificial intelligence characteristics
- The more complex the rules, the more demands on software and hardware processing requirements
- Cannot detect new attacks

Application-based IDS

There are specialized IDS products that can monitor specific applications for malicious activities. Since their scopes are very focused (only one application), they can gather fine-grained and detailed activities. They can be used to capture very specific application attack types, but it is important to realize that these product types will miss more general operating system–based attacks because this is not what they are programmed to detect.

It might be important to implement this type of IDS if a critical application is carrying out encryption functions that would obfuscate its communication channels and activities from other types of IDS (host, network).

IDS Sensors

Network-based IDSs use sensors for monitoring purposes. A sensor, which works as an analysis engine, is placed on the network segment the IDS is responsible for monitoring. The sensor receives raw data from an event generator, as shown in Figure 5-24, and compares it to a signature database, profile, or model, depending upon the type of IDS. If there is some type of a match, which indicates suspicious activity, the sensor works with the response module to determine what type of activity must take place (alerting through instant messaging, paging, or by e-mail; carrying out firewall reconfiguration; and so on). The sensor's role is to filter received data, discard irrelevant information, and detect suspicious activity.

A monitoring console monitors all sensors and supplies the network staff with an overview of the activities of all the sensors in the network. These are the components that enable network-based intrusion detection to actually work. Sensor placement is a critical part of configuring an effective IDS. An organization can place a sensor outside of the firewall to detect attacks and place a sensor inside the firewall (in the perimeter network) to detect actual intrusions. Sensors should also be placed in highly sensitive areas, DMZs, and on extranets. Figure 5-25 shows the sensors reporting their findings to the central console.

The IDS can be centralized, as firewall products that have IDS functionality integrated within them, or distributed, with multiple sensors throughout the network.

Network Traffic

If the network traffic volume exceeds the IDS system's threshold, attacks may go unnoticed. Each vendor's IDS product has its own threshold, and you should know and understand that threshold before you purchase and implement the IDS.

In very high-traffic environments, multiple sensors should be in place to ensure all packets are investigated. If necessary to optimize network bandwidth and speed, different sensors can be set up to analyze each packet for different signatures. That way, the analysis load can be broken up over different points.

Intrusion Prevention Systems

In the industry, there is constant frustration with the inability of existing products to stop the bad guys from accessing and manipulating corporate assets. This has created a market

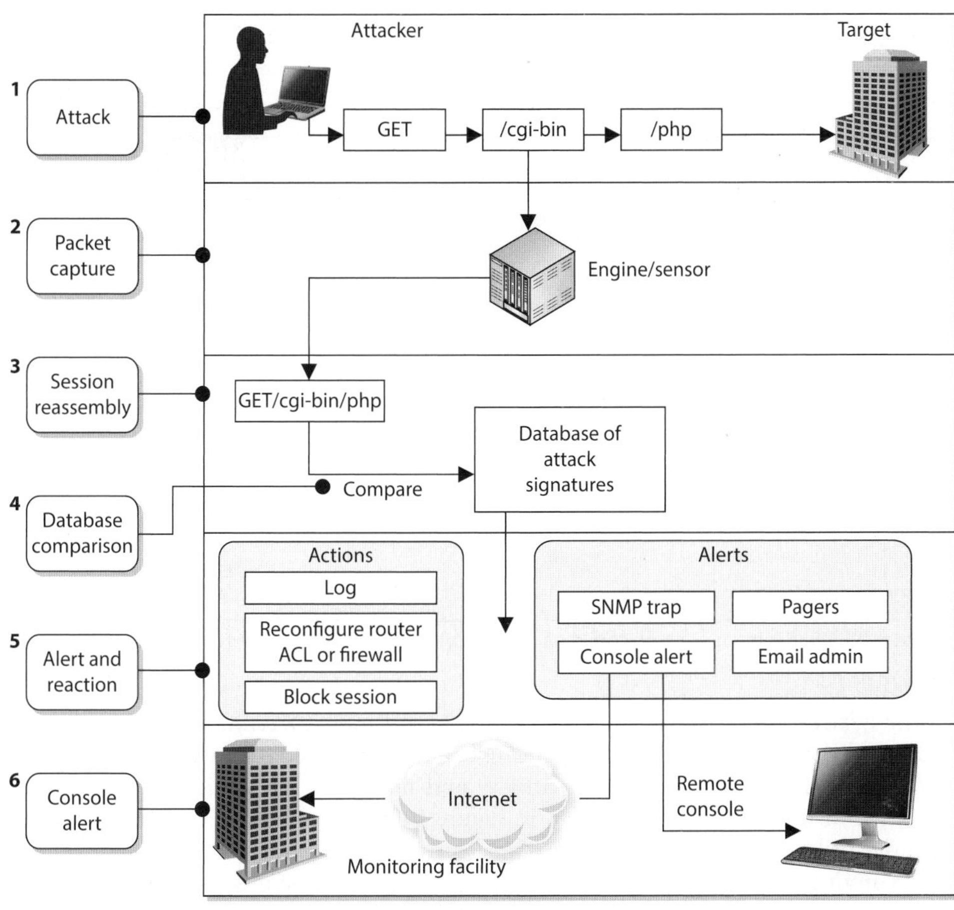

Figure 5-24 The basic architecture of a NIDS

demand for vendors to get creative and come up with new, innovative technologies and new products for companies to purchase, implement, and still be frustrated with.

Switched Environments

NIDSs have a harder time working on a switched network, compared to traditional nonswitched environments, because data is transferred through independent virtual circuits and not broadcasted, as in nonswitched environments. The IDS sensor acts as a sniffer and does not have access to all the traffic in these individual circuits. So, we have to take all the data on each individual virtual private connection, make a copy of it, and put the copies on one port (spanning port) where the sensor is located. This allows the sensor to have access to all the data going back and forth on a switched network.

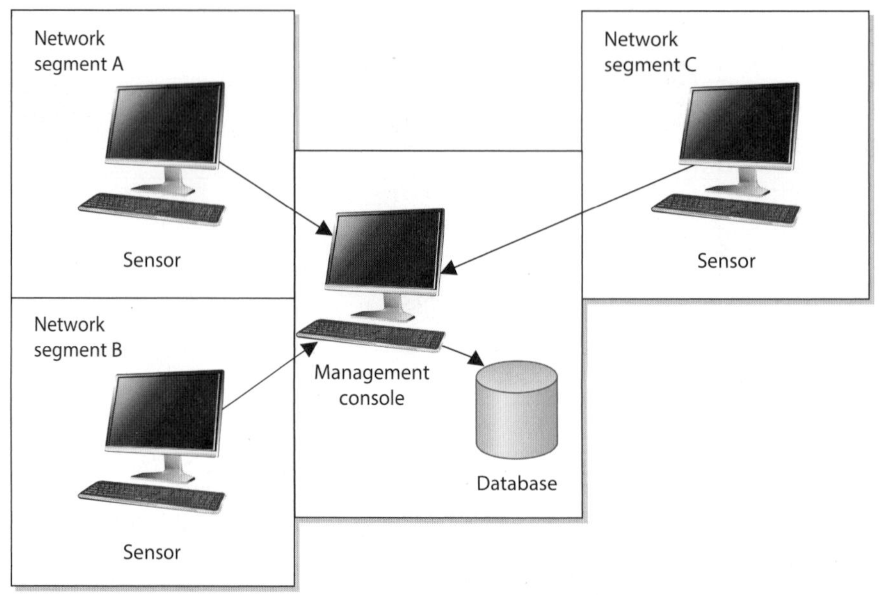

Figure 5-25 Sensors must be placed in each network segment to be monitored by the IDS.

The next evolution in the IDS arena was the *intrusion prevention system (IPS)*. The traditional IDS only detects that something bad may be taking place and sends an alert. The goal of an IPS is to detect this activity and not allow the traffic to gain access to the target in the first place, as shown in Figure 5-26. So, an IPS is a preventative and proactive technology, whereas an IDS is a detective and after-the-fact technology.

IPS products can be host-based or network-based, just as IDS products. IPS technology can be "content-based," meaning that it makes decisions pertaining to what is malicious and what is not based upon protocol analysis or signature matching capabilities. An IPS technology can also use a rate-based metric, which focuses on the volume of traffic. The volume of network traffic increases in case of a flood attack (denial of service) or when excessive system scans take place. IPS rate-based metrics can also be set to identify traffic flow anomalies, which could detect the "slow and low" stealth attack types that attempt to "stay under the radar."

Honeypot

A *honeypot* is a computer set up as a sacrificial lamb on the network. The system is not locked down and has open ports and services enabled. This is to entice a would-be attacker to this computer instead of attacking authentic production systems on a network. The honeypot contains no real company information, and thus will not be at risk if and when it is attacked.

This enables the administrator to know when certain types of attacks are happening so he can fortify the environment and perhaps track down the attacker. The longer the hacker stays at the honeypot, the more information will be disclosed about her techniques.

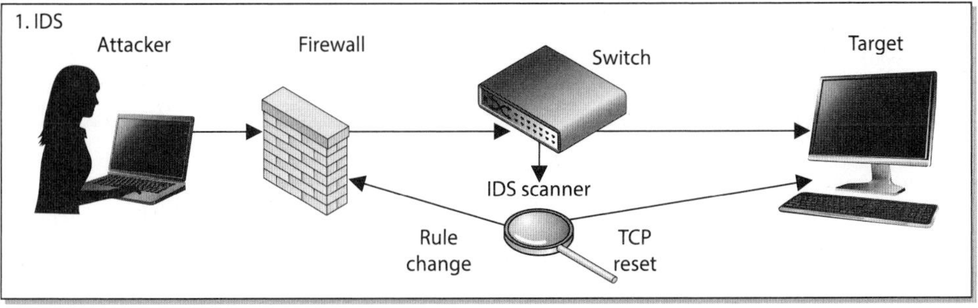

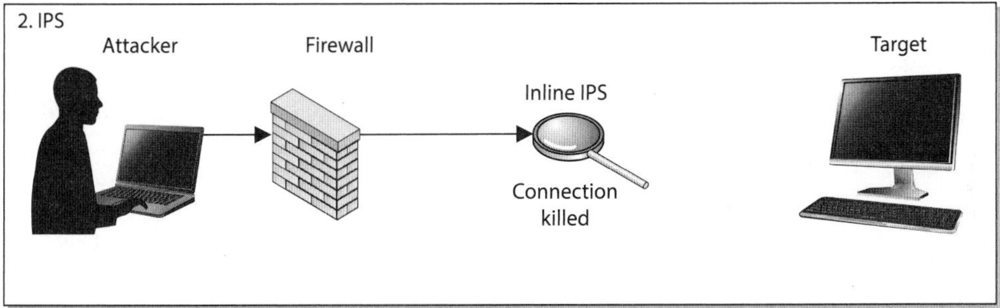

Figure 5-26 IDS vs. IPS architecture

It is important to draw a line between *enticement* and *entrapment* when implementing a honeypot system. Legal and liability issues surround each. If the system only has open ports and services that an attacker might want to take advantage of, this would be an example of enticement. If the system has a web page indicating the user can download files, and once the user does this the administrator charges this user with trespassing, it would be entrapment. Entrapment is where the intruder is induced or tricked into committing a crime. Entrapment is illegal and cannot be used when charging an individual with hacking or unauthorized activity.

NOTE You should always check with your legal counsel before setting up a honeypot, as there may be liability issues that could pose risk to you or your organization.

Intrusion Responses

Most IDSs and IPSs are capable of several types of responses to a triggered event. An IDS can send out a special signal to drop or kill the packet connections at both the source and destinations. This effectively disconnects the communication and does not allow traffic to be transmitted. An IDS might block a user from accessing a resource on a host system if the threshold is set to trigger this response. An IDS can send alerts of an event trigger to other hosts, IDS monitors, and administrators.

Network Sniffers

A packet or network *sniffer* is a general term for programs or devices able to examine traffic on a LAN segment. Traffic that is being transferred over a network medium is transmitted as electrical signals encoded in binary representation. The sniffer has to have a protocol-analysis capability to recognize the different protocol values to properly interpret their meaning.

The sniffer has to have access to a network adapter that works in promiscuous mode and a driver that captures the data. This data can be overwhelming, so it must be properly filtered. The filtered data is stored in a buffer, and this information is displayed to a user and/or captured in logs. Some utilities have sniffer and packet-modification capabilities, which is how some types of spoofing and man-in-the-middle attacks are carried out.

CAUTION Sniffers are dangerous and very hard to detect, and their activities are difficult to audit.

Network sniffers are used by the people in the white hats (administrators and security professionals) usually to try and track down a recent problem with the network. But the guys in the black hats (attackers and crackers) can use them to learn about what type of data is passed over a specific network segment and to modify data in an unauthorized manner. Black hats usually use sniffers to obtain credentials as they pass over the network medium.

EXAM TIP A sniffer is just a tool that can capture network traffic. If it has the capability of understanding and interpreting individual protocols and their associated data, this type of tool is referred to as a protocol analyzer.

Threats to Access Control

As a majority of security professionals know, there is more risk and a higher probability of an attacker causing mayhem from within an organization than from outside it. However, many people within organizations do not know this fact because they only hear stories about the outside attackers who defaced a web server or circumvented a firewall to access confidential information.

An attacker from the outside can enter through remote access entry points, enter through firewalls and web servers, physically break in, carry out social engineering attacks, or exploit a partner communication path (extranet, vendor connection, and so on). An insider has legitimate reasons for using the systems and resources, but can misuse his privileges and launch an actual attack also. The danger of insiders is that they have already been given a wide range of access that a hacker would have to work hard to obtain; they probably have intimate knowledge of the environment; and, generally, they are trusted. We have discussed many different types of access control mechanisms that work to keep the outsiders outside and restrict insiders' abilities to a minimum and audit their actions. Now we will look at some specific attacks commonly carried out in environments today by insiders or outsiders.

Dictionary Attack

Several programs can enable an attacker (or proactive administrator) to identify user credentials. This type of program is fed lists (dictionaries) of commonly used words or combinations of characters, and then compares these values to capture passwords. In other words, the program hashes the dictionary words and compares the resulting message digest with the system password file that also stores its passwords in a one-way hashed format. If the hashed values match, it means a password has just been uncovered. Once the right combination of characters is identified, the attacker can use this password to authenticate herself as a legitimate user. Because many systems have a threshold that dictates how many failed logon attempts are acceptable, the same type of activity can happen to a captured password file. The dictionary-attack program hashes the combination of characters and compares it to the hashed entries in the password file. If a match is found, the program has uncovered a password.

The dictionaries come with the password-cracking programs, and extra dictionaries can be found on several sites on the Internet.

CAUTION Passwords should never be transmitted or stored in cleartext. Most operating systems and applications put the passwords through hashing algorithms, which result in hash values, also referred to as message digest values.

Countermeasures

To properly protect an environment against dictionary and other password attacks, the following practices should be followed:

- Do not allow passwords to be sent in cleartext.
- Encrypt the passwords with encryption algorithms or hashing functions.
- Employ one-time password tokens.
- Use hard-to-guess passwords.
- Rotate passwords frequently.
- Employ an IDS to detect suspicious behavior.
- Use dictionary-cracking tools to find weak passwords chosen by users.
- Use special characters, numbers, and upper- and lowercase letters within the password.
- Protect password files.

Brute-Force Attacks

Several types of *brute-force attacks* can be implemented, but each continually tries different inputs to achieve a predefined goal. Brute force is defined as "trying every possible combination until the correct one is identified." So in a brute-force password attack, the software tool will see if the first letter is an "a" and continue through the alphabet until that single value is uncovered. Then the tool moves on to the second value, and so on.

The most effective way to uncover passwords is through a hybrid attack, which combines a dictionary attack and a brute-force attack. If a dictionary tool has found that a user's password starts with Dallas, then the brute-force tool will try Dallas1, Dallas01, Dallasa1, and so on until a successful logon credential is uncovered. (A brute-force attack is also known as an exhaustive attack.)

These attacks are also used in *war dialing* efforts, in which the war dialer inserts a long list of phone numbers into a war-dialing program in hopes of finding a modem that can be exploited to gain unauthorized access. A program is used to dial many phone numbers and weed out the numbers used for voice calls and fax machine services. The attacker usually ends up with a handful of numbers he can now try to exploit to gain access into a system or network.

So, a brute-force attack perpetuates a specific activity with different input parameters until the goal is achieved.

Countermeasures

For phone brute-force attacks, auditing and monitoring of this type of activity should be in place to uncover patterns that could indicate a war-dialing attack:

- Perform brute-force attacks to find weaknesses and hanging modems.
- Make sure only necessary phone numbers are made public.
- Provide stringent access control methods that would make brute-force attacks less successful.
- Monitor and audit for such activity.
- Employ an IDS to watch for suspicious activity.
- Set lockout thresholds.

Spoofing at Logon

An attacker can use a program that presents to the user a fake logon screen, which often tricks the user into attempting to log on. The user is asked for a username and password, which are stored for the attacker to access at a later time. The user does not know this is not his usual logon screen because they look exactly the same. A fake error message can appear, indicating that the user mistyped his credentials. At this point, the fake logon program exits and hands control over to the operating system, which prompts the user for a username and password. The user assumes he mistyped his information and doesn't give it a second thought, but an attacker now knows the user's credentials.

Phishing and Pharming

Phishing is a type of social engineering with the goal of obtaining personal information, credentials, credit card number, or financial data. The attackers lure, or fish, for sensitive data through various different methods.

The term *phishing* was coined in 1996 when hackers started stealing America Online (AOL) passwords. The hackers would pose as AOL staff members and send messages to victims asking them for their passwords in order to verify correct billing information or verify information about the AOL accounts. Once the password was provided, the hacker authenticated as that victim and used his e-mail account for criminal purposes, as in spamming, pornography, and so on.

Although phishing has been around since the 1990s, many people did not fully become aware of it until mid-2003 when these types of attacks spiked. Phishers created convincing e-mails requesting potential victims to click a link to update their bank account information.

Victims click these links and are presented with a form requesting bank account numbers, Social Security numbers, credentials, and other types of data that can be used in identity theft crimes. These types of phishing e-mail scams have increased dramatically in recent years with some phishers masquerading as large banking companies, PayPal, eBay, Amazon.com, and other well-known Internet entities.

Phishers also create websites that look very similar to legitimate sites and lure victims to them through e-mail messages and other websites to gain the same type of information. Some sites require the victims to provide their Social Security numbers, date of birth, and mother's maiden name for authentication purposes before they can update their account information.

The nefarious websites not only have the look and feel of the legitimate website, but attackers would provide URLs with domain names that look very similar to the legitimate site's address. For example, www.amazon.com might become www.amzaon.com. Or use a specially placed @ symbol. For example, www.msn.com@notmsn.com would actually take the victim to the website notmsn.com and provide the username of www.msn.com to this website. The username www.msn.com would not be a valid username for notmsn .com, so the victim would just be shown the home page of notmsn.com. Now, notmsn .com is a nefarious site and created to look and feel just like www.msn.com. The victim feels comfortable he is at a legitimate site and logs on with his credentials.

Some JavaScript commands are even designed to show the victim an incorrect web address. So let's say Bob is a suspicious and vigilant kind of a guy. Before he inputs his username and password to authenticate and gain access to his online bank account, he always checks the URL values in the address bar of his browser. Even though he closely inspects it to make sure he is not getting duped, there could be a JavaScript replacing the URL www.evilandwilltakeallyourmoney.com with www.citibank.com so he thinks things are safe and life is good.

NOTE There have been fixes to the previously mentioned attack dealing with URLs, but it is important to know that attackers will continually come up with new ways of carrying out these attacks. Just knowing about phishing doesn't mean you can properly detect or prevent it. As a security professional, you must keep up with the new and tricky strategies deployed by attackers.

Some attacks use pop-up forms when a victim is at a legitimate site. So if you were at your bank's actual website and a pop-up window appeared asking you for some sensitive information, this probably wouldn't worry you since you were communicating with your actual bank's website. You may believe the window came from your bank's web server, so you fill it out as instructed. Unfortunately, this pop-up window could be from another source entirely, and your data could be placed right in the attacker's hands, not your bank's.

With this personal information, phishers can create new accounts in the victim's name, gain authorized access to bank accounts, and make illegal credit card purchases or obtain cash advances.

As more people have become aware of these types of attacks and grown wary of clicking embedded links in e-mail messages, phishers have varied their attack methods. For instance, they began sending e-mails that indicate to the user that they have won a prize or that there is a problem with a financial account. The e-mail instructs the person to call a number, which has an automated voice asking the victim to type in their credit card number or Social Security number for authentication purposes.

As phishing attacks increase and more people have become victims of fraud, financial institutions have been implementing two-factor authentication for online transactions. To meet this need, some banks provided their customers with token devices that created one-time passwords. Countering, phishers set up fake websites that looked like the financial institution, duping victims into typing their one-time passwords. The websites would then send these credentials to the actual bank website, authenticate as this user, and gain access to their account.

Spear-phishing

When a phishing attack is crafted to trick a specific target and not a large generic group of people, this is referred to as a *spear-phishing attack*. If someone knows about your specific likes, political motives, shopping habits, etc., the attacker can craft an attack that is directed only at you. For example, if an attacker sends you a spoofed e-mail that seems to have come from your mother with the subject line of "Emily's Birthday Pictures" and an e-mail attachment, you will most likely think it came from your mother and open the file, which will then infect your system. These specialized attacks take more time for the hacker to craft because unique information has to be gathered about the target, but they are more successful because they are more convincing.

A similar type of attack is called *pharming*, which redirects a victim to a seemingly legitimate, yet fake, website. In this type of attack, the attacker carries out something called *DNS poisoning*, in which a DNS server resolves a hostname into an incorrect IP address. When you type www.logicalsecurity.com into the address bar of your web browser, your computer really has no idea what this data is. So an internal request is made to review your TCP/IP network setting, which contains the IP address of the DNS server your computer is supposed to use. Your system then sends a request to this DNS server basically asking, "Do you have the IP address for www.logicalsecurity.com?" The DNS server reviews its resource records and, if it has one with this information in it, sends the IP address for the server that is hosting www.logicalsecurity.com to your computer. Your browser then shows the home page of this website you requested.

Now, what if an attacker poisoned this DNS server so the resource record has the wrong information? When you type in www.logicalsecurity.com and your system sends a request to the DNS server, the DNS server will send your system the IP address that it has recorded, not knowing it is incorrect. So instead of going to www.logicalsecurity.com, you are sent to www.weownyou.com.

So, let's say the victim types in a web address of www.nicebank.com, as illustrated in Figure 5-27. The victim's system sends a request to a poisoned DNS server, which points the victim to a different website. This different website looks and feels just like the requested website, so the user enters his username and password and may even be presented with web pages that look legitimate.

The benefit of a pharming attack to the attacker is that it can affect a large number of victims without the need to send out e-mails, and the victims usually fall for this more easily since they are requesting to go to a website themselves.

Countermeasures to phishing attacks include the following:

- Be skeptical of e-mails indicating you must make changes to your accounts, or warnings stating an account will be terminated if you don't perform some online activity.
- Call the legitimate company to find out if this is a fraudulent message.

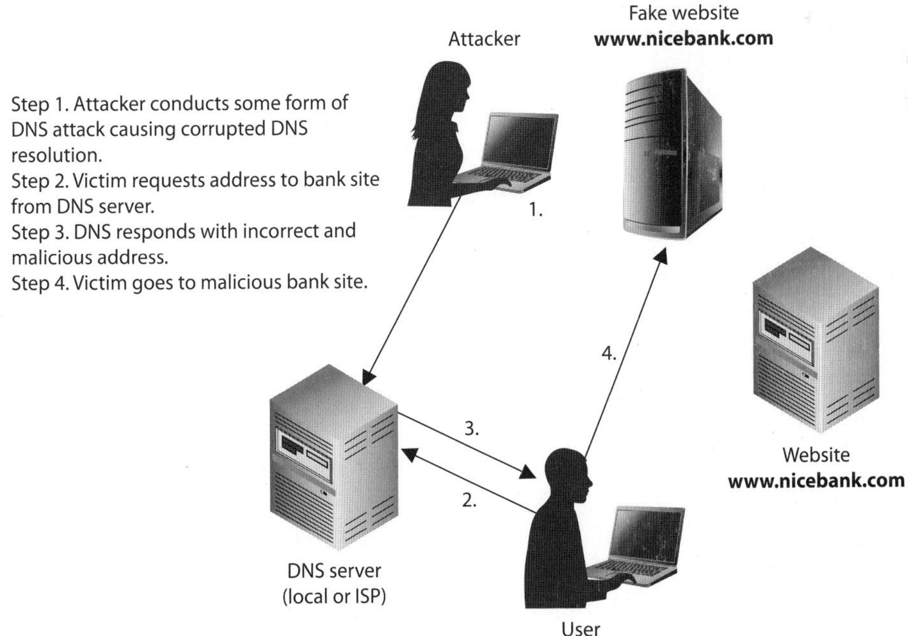

Figure 5-27 Pharming has been a common attack over the last couple of years.

- Review the address bar to see if the domain name is correct.
- When submitting any type of financial information or credential data, a TLS connection should be set up, which may be indicated in the address bar (https://) or as a closed-padlock icon in the browser.
- Do not click an HTML link within an e-mail. Type the URL out manually instead.
- Do not accept e-mail in HTML format.

Summary

Access controls are security features that are usually considered the first line of defense in asset protection. They are used to dictate how subjects access objects, and their main goal is to protect the objects from unauthorized access. These controls can be administrative, physical, or technical in nature and should be applied in a layered approach, ensuring that an intruder would have to compromise more than one countermeasure to access critical assets.

Access control defines how users should be identified, authenticated, and authorized. These issues are carried out differently in different access control models and technologies, and it is up to the organization to determine which best fits its business and security needs.

Access control needs to be integrated into the core of operating systems through the use of DAC, MAC, and RBAC models. It needs to be embedded into applications, network devices, and protocols and enforced in the physical world through the use of security zones, network segmentation, locked doors, and security guards. Security is all about keeping the bad guys out, and unfortunately there are many different types of "doorways" they can exploit to get access to our most critical assets.

Quick Tips

- Access is a flow of information between a subject and an object.
- A subject is an active entity that requests access to an object, which is a passive entity.
- A subject can be a user, program, or process.
- Some security mechanisms that provide confidentiality are encryption, logical and physical access control, transmission protocols, database views, and controlled traffic flow.
- Identity management (IdM) solutions include directories, web access management, password management, legacy single sign-on, account management, and profile update.
- Password synchronization reduces the complexity of keeping up with different passwords for different systems.

- Self-service password reset reduces help-desk call volumes by allowing users to reset their own passwords.
- Assisted password reset reduces the resolution process for password issues for the help-desk department.
- IdM directories contain all resource information, users' attributes, authorization profiles, roles, and possibly access control policies so other IdM applications have one centralized resource from which to gather this information.
- An automated workflow component is common in account management products that provide IdM solutions.
- User provisioning refers to the creation, maintenance, and deactivation of user objects and attributes as they exist in one or more systems, directories, or applications.
- The HR database is usually considered the authoritative source for user identities because that is where each user's identity is first developed and properly maintained.
- There are three main access control models: discretionary, mandatory, and role-based.
- Discretionary access control (DAC) enables data owners to dictate what subjects have access to the files and resources they own.
- The mandatory access control (MAC) model uses a security label system. Users have clearances, and resources have security labels that contain data classifications. MAC systems compare these two attributes to determine access control capabilities.
- Role-based access control (RBAC) is based on the user's role and responsibilities (tasks) within the company.
- Rule-based RBAC (RB-RBAC) builds on RBAC by adding Boolean logic in the form of rules or policies that further restrict access.
- Three main types of restricted interface measurements exist: menus and shells, database views, and physically constrained interfaces.
- Access control lists are bound to objects and indicate what subjects can use them.
- A capability table is bound to a subject and lists what objects it can access.
- Access control can be administered in two main ways: centralized and decentralized.
- Some examples of centralized administration access control technologies are RADIUS, TACACS+, and Diameter.
- A decentralized administration example is a peer-to-peer working group.
- Examples of administrative controls are a security policy, personnel controls, supervisory structure, security-awareness training, and testing.

- Examples of physical controls are network segregation, perimeter security, computer controls, work area separation, and cable.
- Examples of technical controls are system access, network architecture, network access, encryption and protocols, and auditing.
- For a subject to be able to access a resource, it must be identified, authenticated, and authorized, and should be held accountable for its actions.
- Authentication can be accomplished by biometrics, a password, a passphrase, a cognitive password, a one-time password, or a token.
- A Type I error in biometrics means the system rejected an authorized individual, and a Type II error means an imposter was authenticated.
- A memory card cannot process information, but a smart card can through the use of integrated circuits and processors.
- Least-privilege and need-to-know principles limit users' rights to only what is needed to perform tasks of their job.
- Single sign-on capabilities can be accomplished through Kerberos, domains, and thin clients.
- The Kerberos user receives a ticket granting ticket (TGT), which allows him to request access to resources through the ticket granting service (TGS). The TGS generates a new ticket with the session keys.
- Types of access control attacks include denial of service, spoofing, dictionary, brute force, and war dialing.
- Keystroke monitoring is a type of auditing that tracks each keystroke made by a user.
- Object reuse can unintentionally disclose information by assigning media to a subject before it is properly erased.
- Just removing pointers to files (deleting file, formatting hard drive) is not always enough protection for proper object reuse.
- Information can be obtained via electrical signals in airwaves. The ways to combat this type of intrusion are TEMPEST, white noise, and control zones.
- User authentication is accomplished by what someone knows, is, or has.
- One-time password-generating token devices can use synchronous (time, event) or asynchronous (challenge-based) methods.
- Strong authentication requires two of the three user authentication attributes (what someone knows, is, or has).
- The following are weaknesses of Kerberos: the KDC is a single point of failure; it is susceptible to password guessing; session and secret keys are locally stored; KDC needs to always be available; and there must be management of secret keys.

- Phishing is a type of social engineering with the goal of obtaining personal information, credentials, credit card numbers, or financial data.
- A race condition is possible when two or more processes use a shared resource and the access steps could take place out of sequence.
- Mutual authentication is when two entities must authenticate to each other before sending data back and forth. Also referred to as two-way authentication.
- A directory service is a software component that stores, organizes, and provides access to resources, which are listed in a directory (listing) of resources. Individual resources are assigned names within a namespace.
- A cookie is data that is held permanently on a hard drive in the format of a text file or held temporarily in memory. It can be used to store browsing habits, authentication data, or protocol state information.
- A federated identity is a portable identity, and its associated entitlements, that can be used across business boundaries without the need to synchronize or consolidate directory information.
- Extensible Markup Language (XML) is a set of rules for encoding documents in machine-readable form to allow for interoperability between various web-based technologies.
- Service Provisioning Markup Language (SPML) is an XML-based framework being developed by OASIS for exchanging user, resource, and service provisioning information between cooperating organizations.
- Extensible Access Control Markup Language (XACML), which is both a declarative access control policy language implemented in XML and a processing model, describes how to interpret security policies.
- Replay attack is a form of network attack in which a valid data transmission is maliciously or fraudulently repeated with the goal of obtaining unauthorized access.
- Clipping level is a threshold value. Once a threshold value is passed, the activity is considered to be an event that is logged, investigated, or both.
- A rainbow table is a set of precomputed hash values that represents password combinations. Rainbow tables are used in password attack processes and usually produce results more quickly than dictionary or brute-force attacks.
- Cognitive passwords are fact- or opinion-based information used to verify an individual's identity.
- Smart cards can require physical interaction with a reader (contact) or no physical interaction with the reader (contactless architectures). Two contactless architectures are combi (one chip) and hybrid (two chips).

- A side channel attack is carried out by gathering data pertaining to how something works and using that data to attack it or crack it, as in differential power analysis or electromagnetic analysis.
- Authorization creep takes place when a user gains too much access rights and permissions over time.
- Security information and event management implements data mining and analysis functionality to be carried out on centralized logs for situational awareness capabilities.
- Intrusion detection systems are either host or network based and provide behavioral (statistical) or signature (knowledge) types of functionality.
- Phishing is a type of social engineering attack. If it is crafted for a specific individual, it is called spear-phishing. If a DNS server is poisoned and points users to a malicious website, this is referred to as pharming.
- A web portal is commonly made up of portlets, which are pluggable user interface software components that present information and services from other systems.
- The Service Provisioning Markup Language (SPML) allows for the automation of user management (account creation, amendments, revocation) and access entitlement configuration related to electronically published services across multiple provisioning systems.
- The Security Assertion Markup Language (SAML) allows for the exchange of authentication and authorization data to be shared between security domains.
- OpenID is an open standard and protocol that allows third-party authentication of a user.
- OAuth is an open standard that allows a user to grant authority to some web resource, like a contacts database, to a third party.
- The Simple Object Access Protocol (SOAP) is a protocol specification for exchanging structured information in the implementation of web services and networked environments.
- Service-oriented architecture (SOA) environments allow for a suite of interoperable services to be used within multiple, separate systems from several business domains.
- Radio-frequency identification (RFID) is a technology that provides data communication through the use of radio waves.

Questions

Please remember that these questions are formatted and asked in a certain way for a reason. Keep in mind that the CISSP exam is asking questions at a conceptual level. Questions may not always have the perfect answer, and the candidate is advised against always looking for the perfect answer. Instead, the candidate should look for the best answer in the list.

1. Which of the following statements correctly describes biometric methods?
   A. They are the least expensive and provide the most protection.
   B. They are the most expensive and provide the least protection.
   C. They are the least expensive and provide the least protection.
   D. They are the most expensive and provide the most protection.
2. Which of the following statements correctly describes passwords?
   A. They are the least expensive and most secure.
   B. They are the most expensive and least secure.
   C. They are the least expensive and least secure.
   D. They are the most expensive and most secure.
3. How is a challenge/response protocol utilized with token device implementations?
   A. This protocol is not used; cryptography is used.
   B. An authentication service generates a challenge, and the smart token generates a response based on the challenge.
   C. The token challenges the user for a username and password.
   D. The token challenges the user's password against a database of stored credentials.
4. Which access control method is considered user-directed?
   A. Nondiscretionary
   B. Mandatory
   C. Identity-based
   D. Discretionary
5. Which item is not part of a Kerberos authentication implementation?
   A. Message authentication code
   B. Ticket granting service
   C. Authentication service
   D. Users, programs, and services

6. If a company has a high turnover rate, which access control structure is best?
   A. Role-based
   B. Decentralized
   C. Rule-based
   D. Discretionary
7. The process of mutual authentication involves _______________.
   A. a user authenticating to a system and the system authenticating to the user
   B. a user authenticating to two systems at the same time
   C. a user authenticating to a server and then to a process
   D. a user authenticating, receiving a ticket, and then authenticating to a service
8. In discretionary access control security, who has delegation authority to grant access to data?
   A. User
   B. Security officer
   C. Security policy
   D. Owner
9. Which could be considered a single point of failure within a single sign-on implementation?
   A. Authentication server
   B. User's workstation
   C. Logon credentials
   D. RADIUS
10. What role does biometrics play in access control?
    A. Authorization
    B. Authenticity
    C. Authentication
    D. Accountability
11. Who or what determines if an organization is going to operate under a discretionary, mandatory, or nondiscretionary access control model?
    A. Administrator
    B. Security policy
    C. Culture
    D. Security levels

12. Which of the following best describes what role-based access control offers companies in reducing administrative burdens?

A. It allows entities closer to the resources to make decisions about who can and cannot access resources.

B. It provides a centralized approach for access control, which frees up department managers.

C. User membership in roles can be easily revoked and new ones established as job assignments dictate.

D. It enforces enterprise-wide security policies, standards, and guidelines.

13. Which of the following is the best description of directories that are used in identity management technology?

A. Most are hierarchical and follow the X.500 standard.

B. Most have a flat architecture and follow the X.400 standard.

C. Most have moved away from LDAP.

D. Many use LDAP.

14. Which of the following is not part of user provisioning?

A. Creation and deactivation of user accounts

B. Business process implementation

C. Maintenance and deactivation of user objects and attributes

D. Delegating user administration

15. What is the technology that allows a user to remember just one password?

A. Password generation

B. Password dictionaries

C. Password rainbow tables

D. Password synchronization

16. Which of the following is not considered an anomaly-based intrusion protection system?

A. Statistical anomaly–based

B. Protocol anomaly–based

C. Temporal anomaly–based

D. Traffic anomaly–based

17. This graphic covers which of the following?

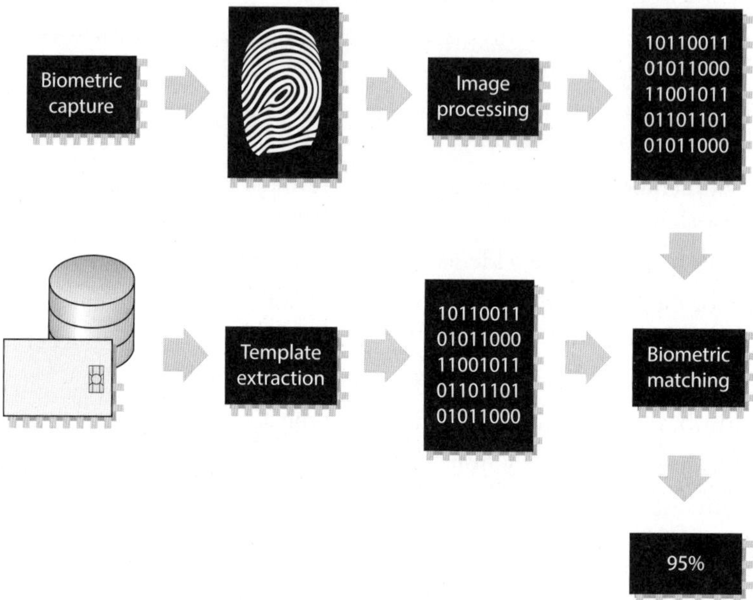

A. Crossover error rate
B. Identity verification
C. Authorization rates
D. Authentication error rates

18. The diagram shown here explains which of the following concepts?

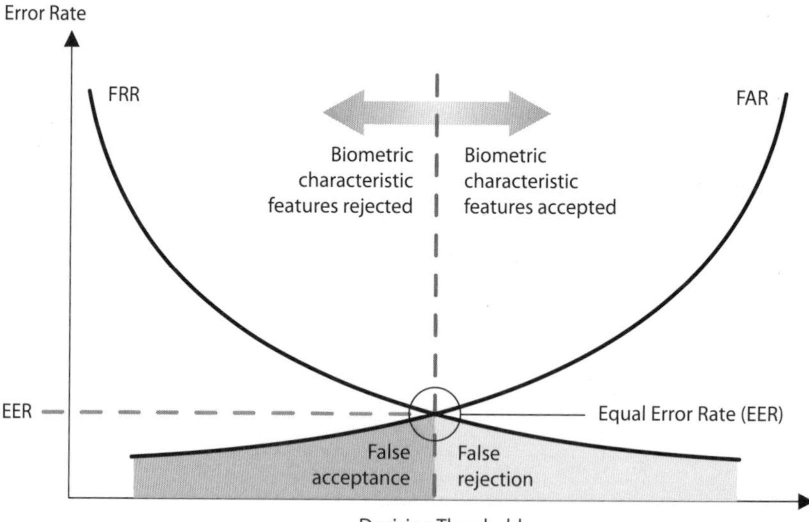

A. Crossover error rate.
B. Type III errors.
C. FAR equals FRR in systems that have a high crossover error rate.
D. Biometrics is a high acceptance technology.

19. The graphic shown here illustrates how which of the following works?

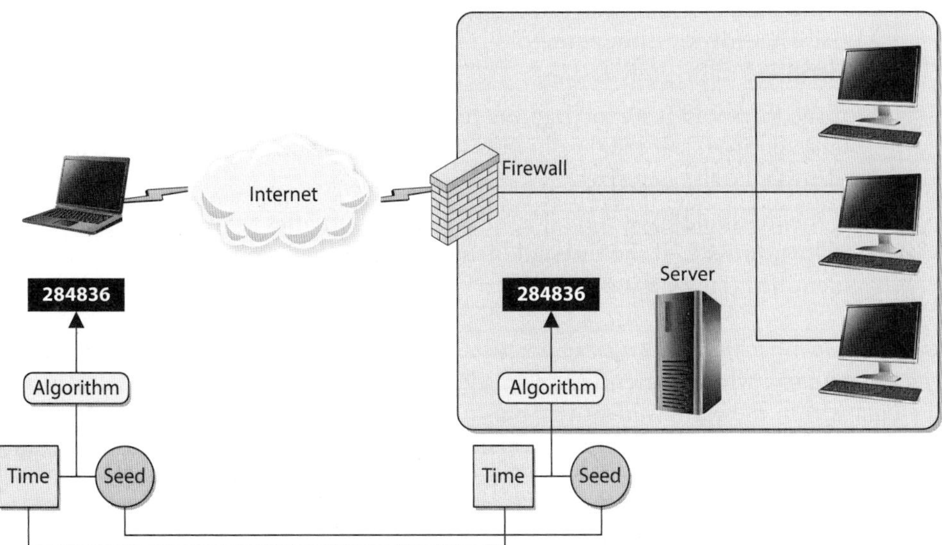

A. Rainbow tables
B. Dictionary attack
C. One-time password
D. Strong authentication

20. Which of the following has the correct term-to-definition mapping?

i. **Brute-force attacks:** Performed with tools that cycle through many possible character, number, and symbol combinations to uncover a password.

ii. **Dictionary attacks:** Files of thousands of words are compared to the user's password until a match is found.

iii. **Social engineering:** An attacker falsely convinces an individual that she has the necessary authorization to access specific resources.

iv. **Rainbow table:** An attacker uses a table that contains all possible passwords already in a hash format.

A. i, ii
B. i, ii, iv
C. i, ii, iii, iv
D. i, ii, iii

21. George is responsible for setting and tuning the thresholds for his company's behavior-based IDS. Which of the following outlines the possibilities of not doing this activity properly?
    A. If the threshold is set too low, nonintrusive activities are considered attacks (false positives). If the threshold is set too high, malicious activities are not identified (false negatives).
    B. If the threshold is set too low, nonintrusive activities are considered attacks (false negatives). If the threshold is set too high, malicious activities are not identified (false positives).
    C. If the threshold is set too high, nonintrusive activities are considered attacks (false positives). If the threshold is set too low, malicious activities are not identified (false negatives).
    D. If the threshold is set too high, nonintrusive activities are considered attacks (false positives). If the threshold is set too high, malicious activities are not identified (false negatives).

Use the following scenario to answer Questions 22–24. Tom is a new security manager for a retail company, which currently has an identity management system (IdM) in place. The data within the various identity stores updates more quickly than the current IdM software can keep up with, so some access decisions are made based upon obsolete information. While the IdM currently provides centralized access control of internal network assets, it is not tied into the web-based access control components that are embedded within the company's partner portals. Tom also notices that help-desk technicians are spending too much time resetting passwords for internal employees.

22. Which of the following changes would be best for Tom's team to implement?
    A. Move from namespaces to distinguished names.
    B. Move from meta-directories to virtual directories.
    C. Move from RADIUS to TACACS+.
    D. Move from a centralized to a decentralized control model.
23. Which of the following components should Tom make sure his team puts into place?
    A. Single sign-on module
    B. LDAP directory service synchronization
    C. Web access management
    D. X.500 database
24. Tom has been told that he has to reduce staff from the help-desk team. Which of the following technologies can help with the company's help-desk budgetary issues?
    A. Self-service password support
    B. RADIUS implementation
    C. Reduction of authoritative IdM sources
    D. Implement a role-based access control model

Use the following scenario to answer Questions 25–27. Lenny is a new security manager for a retail company that is expanding its functionality to its partners and customers. The company's CEO wants to allow its partners' customers to be able to purchase items through the company's web stores as easily as possible. The CEO also wants the company's partners to be able to manage inventory across companies more easily. The CEO wants to be able to understand the network traffic and activities in a holistic manner, and he wants to know from Lenny what type of technology should be put into place to allow for a more proactive approach to stopping malicious traffic if it enters the network. The company is a high-profile entity constantly dealing with zero-day attacks.

25. Which of the following is the best identity management technology that Lenny should consider implementing to accomplish some of the company's needs?

A. LDAP directories for authoritative sources

B. Digital identity provisioning

C. Active Directory

D. Federated identity

26. Lenny has a meeting with the internal software developers who are responsible for implementing the necessary functionality within the web-based system. Which of the following best describes the two items that Lenny needs to be prepared to discuss with this team?

A. Service Provisioning Markup Language and the Extensible Access Control Markup Language

B. Standard Generalized Markup Language and the Generalized Markup Language

C. Extensible Markup Language and the HyperText Markup Language

D. Service Provisioning Markup Language and the Generalized Markup Language

27. Pertaining to the CEO's security concerns, what should Lenny suggest the company put into place?

A. Security event management software, an intrusion prevention system, and behavior-based intrusion detection

B. Security information and event management software, an intrusion detection system, and signature-based protection

C. An intrusion prevention system, security event management software, and malware protection

D. An intrusion prevention system, security event management software, and war-dialing protection

Use the following scenario to answer Questions 28–29. Robbie is the security administrator of a company that needs to extend its remote access functionality. Employees travel around the world, but still need to be able to gain access to corporate assets such as databases, servers, and network-based devices. Also, while the company has had a VoIP telephony solution in place for two years, it has not been integrated into a centralized access control solution. Currently the network administrators have to maintain access control separately for internal resources, external entities, and VoIP end systems. Robbie has also been asked to look into some suspicious e-mails that the CIO's secretary has been receiving, and her boss has asked her to remove some old modems that are no longer being used for remote dial-in purposes.

28. Which of the following is the best remote access technology for this situation?

A. RADIUS

B. TACACS+

C. Diameter

D. Kerberos

29. What are the two main security concerns Robbie is most likely being asked to identify and mitigate?

A. Social engineering and spear-phishing

B. War dialing and pharming

C. Spear-phishing and war dialing

D. Pharming and spear-phishing

Use the following scenario to answer Questions 30–32. Tanya is working with the company's internal software development team. Before a user of an application can access files located on the company's centralized server, the user must present a valid one-time password, which is generated through a challenge/response mechanism. The company needs to tighten access control for these files and reduce the number of users who can access each and every file. The company is looking to Tanya and her team for solutions to better protect the data that has been classified and deemed critical to the company's missions. Tanya has also been asked to implement a single sign-on technology for all internal users, but she does not have the budget to implement a public key infrastructure.

30. Which of the following best describes what is currently in place?

A. Capability-based access system

B. Synchronous tokens that generate one-time passwords

C. RADIUS

D. Kerberos

31. Which of the following is one of the easiest and best solutions Tanya can consider for proper data protection?
    - A. Implementation of mandatory access control
    - B. Implementation of access control lists
    - C. Implementation of digital signatures
    - D. Implementation of multilevel security
32. Which of the following is the best single sign-on technology for this situation?
    - A. PKI
    - B. Kerberos
    - C. RADIUS
    - D. TACACS+

Use the following scenario to answer Questions 33–35. Harry is overseeing a team that has to integrate various business services provided by different company departments into one web portal for both internal employees and external partners. His company has a diverse and heterogeneous environment with different types of systems providing customer relationship management, inventory control, e-mail, and help-desk ticketing capabilities. His team needs to allow different users access to these different services in a secure manner.

33. Which of the following best describes the type of environment Harry's team needs to set up?
    - A. RADIUS
    - B. Service-oriented architecture
    - C. Public key infrastructure
    - D. Web services
34. Which of the following best describes the types of languages and/or protocols that Harry needs to ensure are implemented?
    - A. Security Assertion Markup Language, Extensible Access Control Markup Language, Service Provisioning Markup Language
    - B. Service Provisioning Markup Language, Simple Object Access Protocol, Extensible Access Control Markup Language
    - C. Extensible Access Control Markup Language, Security Assertion Markup Language, Simple Object Access Protocol
    - D. Service Provisioning Markup Language, Security Association Markup Language

35. The company's partners need to integrate compatible authentication functionality into their web portals to allow for interoperability across the different company boundaries. Which of the following will deal with this issue?

    A. Service Provisioning Markup Language

    B. Simple Object Access Protocol

    C. Extensible Access Control Markup Language

    D. Security Assertion Markup Language

Answers

1. **D.** Compared with the other available authentication mechanisms, biometric methods provide the highest level of protection and are the most expensive.
2. **C.** Passwords provide the least amount of protection, but are the cheapest because they do not require extra readers (as with smart cards and memory cards), do not require devices (as do biometrics), and do not require a lot of overhead in processing (as in cryptography). Passwords are the most common type of authentication method used today.
3. **B.** An asynchronous token device is based on challenge/response mechanisms. The authentication service sends the user a challenge value, which the user enters into the token. The token encrypts or hashes this value, and the user uses this as her one-time password.
4. **D.** The DAC model allows users, or data owners, the discretion of letting other users access their resources. DAC is implemented by ACLs, which the data owner can configure.
5. **A.** Message authentication code (MAC) is a cryptographic function and is not a key component of Kerberos. Kerberos is made up of a KDC, a realm of principals (users, services, applications, and devices), an authentication service, tickets, and a ticket granting service.
6. **A.** A role-based structure is easier on the administrator because she only has to create one role, assign all of the necessary rights and permissions to that role, and plug a user into that role when needed. Otherwise, she would need to assign and extract permissions and rights on all systems as each individual came and left the company.
7. **A.** Mutual authentication means it is happening in both directions. Instead of just the user having to authenticate to the server, the server also must authenticate to the user.
8. **D.** This question may seem a little confusing if you were stuck between user and owner. Only the data owner can decide who can access the resources she owns. She may or may not be a user. A user is not necessarily the owner of the resource. Only the actual owner of the resource can dictate what subjects can actually access the resource.

9. **A.** In a single sign-on technology, all users are authenticating to one source. If that source goes down, authentication requests cannot be processed.
10. **C.** Biometrics is a technology that validates an individual's identity by reading a physical attribute. In some cases, biometrics can be used for identification, but that was not listed as an answer choice.
11. **B.** The security policy sets the tone for the whole security program. It dictates the level of risk that management and the company are willing to accept. This in turn dictates the type of controls and mechanisms to put in place to ensure this level of risk is not exceeded.
12. **C.** An administrator does not need to revoke and reassign permissions to individual users as they change jobs. Instead, the administrator assigns permissions and rights to a role, and users are plugged into those roles.
13. **A.** Most enterprises have some type of directory that contains information pertaining to the company's network resources and users. Most directories follow a hierarchical database format, based on the X.500 standard, and a type of protocol, as in Lightweight Directory Access Protocol (LDAP), that allows subjects and applications to interact with the directory. Applications can request information about a particular user by making an LDAP request to the directory, and users can request information about a specific resource by using a similar request.
14. **B.** User provisioning refers to the creation, maintenance, and deactivation of user objects and attributes as they exist in one or more systems, directories, or applications, in response to business processes. User provisioning software may include one or more of the following components: change propagation, self-service workflow, consolidated user administration, delegated user administration, and federated change control. User objects may represent employees, contractors, vendors, partners, customers, or other recipients of a service. Services may include electronic mail, access to a database, access to a file server or mainframe, and so on.
15. **D.** Password synchronization technologies can allow a user to maintain just one password across multiple systems. The product will synchronize the password to other systems and applications, which happens transparently to the user.
16. **C.** An anomaly-based IPS is a behavioral-based system that learns the "normal" activities of an environment. The three types are listed next:
    - **Statistical anomaly–based** Creates a profile of "normal" and compares activities to this profile
    - **Protocol anomaly–based** Identifies protocols used outside of their common bounds
    - **Traffic anomaly–based** Identifies unusual activity in network traffic

17. **B.** These steps are taken to convert the biometric input for identity verification:
    i. A software application identifies specific points of data as match points.
    ii. An algorithm is used to process the match points and translate that information into a numeric value.
    iii. Authentication is approved or denied when the database value is compared with the end user input entered into the scanner.
18. **A.** This rating is stated as a percentage and represents the point at which the false rejection rate equals the false acceptance rate. This rating is the most important measurement when determining a biometric system's accuracy.
    - **Type I error** Rejects authorized individual
        - False rejection rate (FRR)
    - **Type II error** Accepts impostor
        - False acceptance rate (FAR)
19. **C.** Different types of one-time passwords are used for authentication. This graphic illustrates a synchronous token device, which synchronizes with the authentication service by using time or a counter as the core piece of the authentication process.
20. **C.** The list has all the correct term-to-definition mappings.
21. **C.** If the threshold is set too high, nonintrusive activities are considered attacks (false positives). If the threshold is set too low, malicious activities are not identified (false negatives).
22. **B.** A meta-directory within an IdM physically contains the identity information within an identity store. It allows identity information to be pulled from various locations and be stored in one local system (identity store). The data within the identity store is updated through a replication process, which may take place weekly, daily, or hourly depending upon configuration. Virtual directories use pointers to where the identity data resides on the original system; thus, no replication processes are necessary. Virtual directories usually provide the most up-to-date identity information since they point to the original source of the data.
23. **C.** Web access management (WAM) is a component of most IdM products that allows for identity management of web-based activities to be integrated and managed centrally.
24. **A.** If help-desk staff is spending too much time with password resetting, then a technology should be implemented to reduce the amount of time paid staff is spending on this task. The more tasks that can be automated through technology, the less of the budget that has to be spent on staff. The following are password management functionalities that are included in most IdM products:
    - **Password synchronization** Reduces the complexity of keeping up with different passwords for different systems.

- **Self-service password reset** Reduces help-desk call volumes by allowing users to reset their own passwords.
- **Assisted password reset** Reduces the resolution process for password issues for the help desk. This may include authentication with other types of authentication mechanisms (biometrics, tokens).

25. **D.** Federation identification allows for the company and its partners to share customer authentication information. When a customer authenticates to a partner website, that authentication information can be passed to the retail company, so when the customer visits the retail company's website, the user has to submit less user profile information and the authentication steps the user has to go through during the purchase process could potentially be reduced. If the companies have a set trust model and share the same or similar federated identity management software and settings, this type of structure and functionality is possible.
26. **A.** The Service Provisioning Markup Language (SPML) allows company interfaces to pass service requests, and the receiving company provisions (allows) access to these services. Both the sending and receiving companies need to be following the XML standard, which will allow this type of interoperability to take place. When using the Extensible Access Control Markup Language (XACML), application security policies can be shared with other applications to ensure that both are following the same security rules. The developers need to integrate both of these language types to allow for their partner employees to interact with their inventory systems without having to conduct a second authentication step. The use of the languages can reduce the complexity of inventory control between the different companies.
27. **A.** Security event management software allows for network traffic to be viewed holistically by gathering log data centrally and analyzing it. The intrusion prevention system allows for proactive measures to be put into place to help in stopping malicious traffic from entering the network. Behavior-based intrusion detection can identify new types of attacks (zero day) compared to signature-based intrusion detection.
28. **C.** The Diameter protocol extends the RADIUS protocol to allow for various types of authentication to take place with a variety of different technologies (PPP, VoIP, Ethernet, etc.). It has extensive flexibility and allows for the centralized administration of access control.
29. **C.** Spear-phishing is a targeted social engineering attack, which is what the CIO's secretary is most likely experiencing. War dialing is a brute-force attack against devices that use phone numbers, as in modems. If the modems can be removed, the risk of war-dialing attacks decreases.
30. **A.** A capability-based access control system means that the subject (user) has to present something, which outlines what it can access. The item can be a ticket, token, or key. A capability is tied to the subject for access control purposes. A synchronous token is not being used, because the scenario specifically states that a challenge\ response mechanism is being used, which indicates an asynchronous token.

31. **B.** Systems that provide mandatory access control (MAC) and multilevel security are very specialized, require extensive administration, are expensive, and reduce user functionality. Implementing these types of systems is not the easiest approach out of the list. Since there is no budget for a PKI, digital signatures cannot be used because they require a PKI. In most environments access control lists (ACLs) are in place and can be modified to provide tighter access control. ACLs are bound to objects and outline what operations specific subjects can carry out on them.
32. **B.** The scenario specifies that PKI cannot be used, so the first option is not correct. Kerberos is based upon symmetric cryptography; thus, it does not need a PKI. RADIUS and TACACS+ are remote centralized access control protocols.
33. **B.** A service-oriented architecture (SOA) will allow Harry's team to create a centralized web portal and offer the various services needed by internal and external entities.
34. **C.** The most appropriate languages and protocols for the purpose laid out in the scenario are Extensible Access Control Markup Language, Security Assertion Markup Language, and Simple Object Access Protocol. Harry's group is not necessarily overseeing account provisioning, so the Service Provisioning Markup Language is not necessary, and there is no language called "Security Association Markup Language."
35. **D.** Security Assertion Markup Language allows the exchange of authentication and authorization data to be shared between security domains. It is one of the most commonly used approaches to allow for single sign-on capabilities within a web-based environment.

CHAPTER 6

Security Assessment and Testing

This chapter presents the following:

- Internal and third-party audits
- Vulnerability testing
- Penetration testing
- Log reviews
- Synthetic transactions
- Code reviews
- Misuse case testing
- Interface testing
- Account management
- Backup data verification
- Disaster recovery and business continuity testing
- Security training and security awareness
- Key performance and risk indicators
- Reporting
- Management review

Trust, but verify.

—Russian proverb

You can hire the best people, develop sound policies and procedures, and deploy world-class technology in an effort to secure your information systems, but if you do not regularly assess the effectiveness of these measures, your organization will not be secure for long. Unfortunately, thousands of well-intentioned organizations have learned the truth of this statement the hard way, realizing only after a security breach has occurred that the state-of-the-art controls they put into place initially have become less effective over time. So unless your organization is continuously assessing and improving its security posture, that posture will become ineffective over time.

This chapter covers some of the most important elements of security assessments and testing. It is divided into four sections. We start by discussing audit strategies, particularly the pros and cons of using our own internal auditors or bringing in external contractors. We then move on to approaches to testing our technical security controls. The third major section deals with testing our administrative controls, which are mostly implemented through polices. Finally, after we have enough empirical data to assess our posture, we discuss how to report our findings and how those findings play into the executive decision making within the organization.

Audit Strategies

An *audit* is simply a systematic assessment. In the context of the CISSP exam, we can narrow that down to mean a systematic assessment of the security controls of an information system. Drilling down a bit more, an *information system* is broadly accepted to mean a specific set of people, computers, processes, and information. Putting it all together, we see that an information system's security audit is a systematic assessment of the security controls on a specific set of people, computers, processes, and information. Why should we spend any time whatsoever splitting hairs like this with a definition? Because it is critically important to consider *all* the elements of an information system when we devise our audit strategies.

All too often, a security audit is equated with a vulnerability assessment or a penetration test (pen test), or both, against a given computing platform. While vulnerability assessments and pen tests often are helpful techniques, they are not sufficient to truly assess our security posture. To do it right, we have to take a holistic look at the information system and then ask ourselves, what are our goals for the audit?

As simple as it sounds, establishing a clear set of goals is probably the most important step of planning a security audit. Since we usually can't test everything, we have to focus our efforts on whatever it is that we are most concerned about. An audit could be driven by regulatory or compliance requirements, by a significant change to the architecture of the information system, or by new developments in the threat facing the organization. There are many other possible scenarios, but these examples are illustrative of the vastly different objectives for our assessments.

Once our goals are established, we need to define the scope of the assessment:

- Which subnets and systems are we going to test?
- Are we going to look at user artifacts, such as passwords, files, and log entries, or at user behaviors, such as their response to social engineering attempts?
- Which information will we assess for confidentiality, integrity, and availability?
- What are the privacy implications of our audit?
- How will we evaluate our processes, and to what extent?

If our goals are clearly laid out, answering these questions should be a lot easier.

The scope of the audit should be determined in coordination with business unit managers. All too often security professionals focus on IT and forget about the business cases.

In fact, business managers should be included early in the audit planning process and should remain engaged throughout the exercise. Not only will this help bridge the gap between the two camps, but it will also help identify potential areas of risk to the organization brought on by the audit itself. Just imagine what would happen if your assessment interfered with a critical but nonobvious business process and ended up costing the organization a huge amount of money. (We call that an RGE, or résumé-generating event.)

A key decision is whether the audit will be performed by an internal team or by a third party. If you don't have the in-house expertise, then this decision may very well already have been made for you. But even if your team has this expertise, you may still choose to bring in external auditors for any of a variety of reasons. For example, there may be a regulatory requirement that an external party test your systems; or you may want to benchmark your own internal assets against an external team; or perhaps your own team of testers is not large enough to cover all the auditing requirements and thus you want to bring in outside help. In any case, there are important considerations, which we will discuss in the following sections.

Information System Security Audit Process

1. **Determine the goals**, because everything else hinges on this.
2. **Involve the right business unit leaders** to ensure the needs of the business are identified and addressed.
3. **Determine the scope**, because not everything can be tested.
4. **Choose the audit team**, which may consist of internal or external personnel, depending on the goals, scope, budget, and available expertise.
5. **Plan the audit** to ensure all goals are met on time and on budget.
6. **Conduct the audit** while sticking to the plan and documenting any deviations therefrom.
7. **Document the results**, because the wealth of information generated is both valuable and volatile.
8. **Communicate the results** to the right leaders in order to achieve and sustain a strong security posture.

Having decided who will actually conduct our audit, we are now in a position to plan the event. The plan is important for a variety of reasons:

- We must ensure that we are able to address whatever risks we may be introducing into the business processes. Without a plan, these risks are unknown and not easily mitigated.
- Documenting the plan ensures that we meet each of our audit goals. Audit teams sometimes attempt to follow their own scripted plan, which may or may not address all of the organization's goals for a specific audit.

- Documenting the plan will help us remember the items that were *not* in the scope of the assessment. Recall that we already acknowledged that we can't possibly test everything, so this specifies the things we did not test.
- The plan ensures that the audit process is repeatable. Like any good science experiment, we should be able to reproduce the results by repeating the process. This is particularly important because we may encounter unexpected results worth further investigation.

Having developed a detailed plan for the audit, we are finally in a position to get to the fun stuff. No matter how much time and effort we put into planning, inevitably we will find tasks we have to add, delete, change, or modify. Though we clearly want to minimize the number of these changes, they are really a part of the process that we just have to accept. The catch is that we must consciously decide to accept them, and then we absolutely must document them.

NOTE In certain cases, such as regulatory compliance, the parameters of the audit may be dictated and performed by an external team of auditors. This means that the role of the organization is limited to preparing for the audit by ensuring all required resources are available to the audit team.

The documentation we start during the planning process must continue all the way through to the results. In all but the most trivial assessments, we are likely to generate reams of data and information. This information is invaluable in that it captures a snapshot in time of our security posture. If nothing else, it will serve to benchmark the effectiveness of our controls so that we can compare audits and determine trends. Typically, however, this detailed documentation allows the security staff to drill into unexpected or unexplainable results and do some root cause analysis. If you capture all the information, it will be easier to produce reports for target audiences without concern that you may have deleted (or failed to document) any important data points.

Ultimately, the desired end state of any audit is to effectively communicate the results to the target audiences. The manner in which we communicate results to executives will be very different from the manner in which we communicate results to the IT team members. This gets back to the point made earlier about capturing and documenting both the plan and the details and products of its execution. It is always easier to distill information from a large data set than to justify a conclusion when the facts live only in our brains. Many a security audit has been ultimately unsuccessful because the team has not been able to communicate effectively with the key stakeholders.

Internal Audits

In a perfect world, every organization would have an internal team capable of performing whatever audits were needed. Alas, we live in a far-from-perfect world in which even some of the best-resourced organizations lack this capability. But if your organization does have such a team on hand, its ability to implement continuous improvement of your organization's security posture offers some tremendous advantages.

One of the benefits of using your own personnel to do an audit is that they are familiar with the inner workings of your organization. This familiarity allows them to get right to work and not have to spend too much time getting oriented to the cyber terrain. Some may say that this insider knowledge gives them an unrealistic advantage because few adversaries could know as much about the systems as those who operate and defend them. It is probably more accurate to state that advanced adversaries can often approach the level of knowledge about an organization that an internal audit team would have. In any case, if the purpose of the audit is to leave no stone unturned and test the weakest, most obscure parts of an information system, then an internal team will likely get closer to that goal than any other.

Using internal assets also allows the organization to be more agile in its assessment efforts. Since the team is always available, all that the leadership would need to do is to reprioritize their tests to adapt to changing needs. For example, suppose a business unit is scheduled to be audited yearly, but the latest assessment's results from a month ago were abysmal and represent increased risk to the organization. The security management could easily reschedule other tests to conduct a follow-up audit three months later. This agility comes at no additional cost to the organization, which typically would not be true if engaging a third-party team.

The downsides of using an internal team include the fact that they likely have limited exposure to other approaches to both securing and exploiting information systems. Unless the team has some recent hires with prior experience, the team will probably have a lot of depth in the techniques they know, but not a lot of breadth, since they will have developed mostly the skills needed to test only their own organization.

A less obvious disadvantage of using internal auditors is the potential for conflicts of interest to exist. If the auditors believe that their bosses or coworkers may be adversely affected by a negative report or even by the documented presence of flaws, the auditors may be reluctant to accurately report their findings. The culture of the organization is probably the most influential factor in this potential conflict. If the climate is one of openness and trust, then the auditors are less likely to perceive any risk to their higher-ups or coworkers regardless of their findings. Conversely, in very rigid bureaucratic organizations with low tolerance for failures, the potential for conflicts of interest will likely be higher.

Another aspect of the conflict of interest issue is that the team members or their bosses may have an agenda to pursue with the audit. If they are intent on securing better funding, they may be tempted to overstate or even fabricate security flaws. Similarly, if they believe that another department needs to be taught a lesson (perhaps in order to get them to improve their willingness to "play nice" with the security team), the results could deliberately or subconsciously be less than objective. Politics and team dynamics clearly should be considered when deciding whether to use internal audit teams.

Third-Party Audits

Bringing in external auditors has advantages over using an internal team. For starters, the external auditors probably have seen and tested many information systems in different organizations. This means that they will almost certainly bring to your organization knowledge that it wouldn't otherwise be able to acquire. Even if you have some internal auditors with prior experience, they are unlikely to approach the breadth of experience that contractors who regularly test a variety of organizations will bring to the table.

Another advantage of third-party auditors is that they are unaware of the internal dynamics and politics of the target organization. This means that they have no favorites or agendas other than the challenge of finding flaws. This objectivity may give them an edge in testing, particularly if the alternative would've been to use internal personnel who played a role in implementing the controls in the first place and thus may overlook or subconsciously impede the search for defects in those controls.

The obvious disadvantage of hiring an external team is cost. Price tags in the tens of thousands of dollars are not uncommon, even on the low end of the scale. If nothing else, this probably means that you won't be able to use external auditors frequently (if at all). Even at the high end of the pay scale, it is not uncommon to find testers who rely almost exclusively on high-end scanners that do all the work (and thinking) for them. It is truly unfortunate when an organization spends a significant amount of money only to find out the tester simply plugs his laptop into the network, runs a scanner, and prints a report.

Even if you find an affordable and competent team to test your information systems, you still have to deal with the added resources required to orient them to the organization and supervise their work. Even with signed nondisclosure agreements (NDAs), most companies don't give free rein to their external auditors without some level of supervision. In addition, the lack of knowledge of the inner workings of the organization typically translates into the auditors taking a longer time to get oriented and be able to perform the test.

NOTE Signing a nondisclosure agreement is almost always a prerequisite before a third-party team is permitted to audit an organization's systems.

While there is no clear winner between using internal auditors and third-party auditors, sometimes the latter is the only choice where regulatory requirements such as the Sarbanes-Oxley Act force an organization to outsource the test. These are called *compliance audits* and must be performed by external parties.

Service Organization Controls

When companies come together to work in an integrated manner, special care must be taken to ensure that each party promises to provide the necessary level of protection, liability, and responsibility, which should be clearly defined in the contracts each party signs. *Service organizations* are organizations that provide outsourcing services that can directly impact the control environment of a company's customers. Examples of service organizations are insurance and medical claims processors, trust companies, hosted data centers, application service providers (ASPs), managed security providers, credit processing organizations, and clearinghouses.

Auditing and testing should be performed to ensure that each party is indeed holding up its side of the bargain. Perhaps the most notable early attempt at accomplishing this aim was developed by the American Institute of Certified Public Accountants (AICPA). Their *Statement on Auditing Standards No. 70: Service Organizations (SAS 70)* defined audits carried out by third parties to assess the internal controls of a service organization. Having an SAS 70 audit carried out was a way to ensure that a company you work with and depend upon was really protecting your company's assets as they claimed to be.

The original focus of SAS 70 was on financial issues, but the industry stretched the use of the SAS 70 beyond its original intended purpose. Organizations needed to make sure that their service providers were providing the necessary protection of their digital assets, but the industry did not have a specific standard for this type of evaluation, so everyone used SAS 70, which was really just for financial control evaluation.

Other evaluation types have existed, as in WebTrust (e-commerce controls) and SysTrust (operational controls), but these three evaluation standard sets did not meet the needs of ensuring that outsourced services were secure and trustworthy in a holistic fashion. So new evaluation standards were developed to better meet the needs of companies today.

In 2011, the AICPA released a new framework of auditing standards on Service Organization Controls (SOC), which are defined in the American Statement on Standards for Attestation Engagements (SSAE) 16 and the International Computing Centre's (ACC) International Standard on Assurance Engagements (ISAE) No. 3402. There are three kinds of SOC reports:

- **SOC 1** Pertains to financial controls
- **SOC 2** Pertains to trust services (Security, Availability, Confidentiality, Process Integrity, and Privacy)
- **SOC 3** Also pertains to trust services (Security, Availability, Confidentiality, Process Integrity, and Privacy)

The difference between SOC 2 and 3 is that the resulting SOC 2 report provides very detailed data pertaining to the controls that provide the listed trust services, which is not for the general public. SOC 3 results in a report that has less detail and can be used for general purposes.

An SOC 2 report includes a description of the tests performed by the auditor and the results of those tests and the auditor's opinion of the effectiveness of the individual controls and systems. SOC 3 does not contain test information and details on the controls in place, but just reports whether the systems meet the requirements of the criteria for the specific trust service. SOC 3 is commonly used as a "seal of approval" and placed on service providers' websites and marketing collateral.

Auditing Technical Controls

A *technical control* is a security control implemented through the use of an IT asset. This asset is usually, but not always, some sort of software that is configured in a particular way. When we audit our technical controls, we are testing their ability to mitigate the risks that we identified in our risk management process (see Chapter 1 for a detailed discussion). This linkage between controls and the risks they are meant to mitigate is important because we need to understand the context in which specific controls were implemented.

Once we understand what a technical control was intended to accomplish, we are able to select the proper means of testing whether it is being effective. We may be better off testing third-party software for vulnerabilities than attempting a code review. As security professionals, we must be familiar, and ideally experienced, with the most common approaches to auditing technical controls so that we are able to select the right one for the job at hand.

Vulnerability Testing

Vulnerability testing, whether manual, automated, or—preferably—a combination of both, requires staff and/or consultants with a deep security background and the highest level of trustworthiness. Even the best automated vulnerability scanning tool will produce output that can be misinterpreted as crying wolf (false positive) when there is only a small puppy in the room, or alert you to something that is indeed a vulnerability but that either does not matter to your environment or is adequately compensated elsewhere. There may also be two individual vulnerabilities that exist, which by themselves are not very important but when put them together are critical. And, of course, false negatives will also crop up, such as an obscure element of a single vulnerability that matters greatly to your environment but is not called out by the tool.

NOTE Before carrying out vulnerability testing, a written agreement from management is required! This protects the tester against prosecution for doing his job and ensures there are no misunderstandings by providing in writing what the tester should—and should not—do.

The goals of the assessment are to

- Evaluate the true security posture of an environment (don't cry wolf, as discussed earlier).
- Identify as many vulnerabilities as possible, with honest evaluations and prioritizations of each.
- Test how systems react to certain circumstances and attacks, to learn not only what the known vulnerabilities are (such as this version of the database, that version of the operating system, or a user ID with no password set), but also how the unique elements of the environment might be abused (SQL injection attacks, buffer overflows, and process design flaws that facilitate social engineering).
- Before the scope of the test is decided and agreed upon, the tester must explain the testing ramifications. Vulnerable systems could be knocked offline by some of the tests, and production could be negatively affected by the loads the tests place on the systems.

Management must understand that results from the test are just a "snapshot in time." As the environment changes, new vulnerabilities can arise. Management should also understand that various types of assessments are possible, each one able to expose different kinds of vulnerabilities in the environment, and each one limited in the completeness of results it can offer:

- **Personnel testing** includes reviewing employee tasks and thus identifying vulnerabilities in the standard practices and procedures that employees are instructed to follow, demonstrating social engineering attacks and the value of training users to detect and resist such attacks, and reviewing employee policies and procedures to ensure those security risks that cannot be reduced through physical and logical controls are met with the final control category: administrative.
- **Physical testing** includes reviewing facility and perimeter protection mechanisms. For instance, do the doors actually close automatically, and does an alarm sound if a door is held open too long? Are the interior protection mechanisms of server rooms, wiring closets, sensitive systems, and assets appropriate? (For example, is the badge reader working, and does it really limit access to only authorized personnel?) Is dumpster diving a threat? (In other words, is sensitive information being discarded without proper destruction?) And what about protection mechanisms for manmade, natural, or technical threats? Is there a fire suppression system? Does it work, and is it safe for the people and the equipment in the building? Are sensitive electronics kept above raised floors so they survive a minor flood? And so on.
- **System and network testing** are perhaps what most people think of when discussing information security vulnerability testing. For efficiency, an automated scanning product identifies known system vulnerabilities, and some may (if management has signed off on the performance impact and the risk of disruption) attempt to exploit vulnerabilities.

Because a security assessment is a point-in-time snapshot of the state of an environment, assessments should be performed regularly. Lower-priority, better-protected, and less-at-risk parts of the environment may be scanned once or twice a year. High-priority, more vulnerable targets, such as e-commerce web server complexes and the middleware just behind them, should be scanned nearly continuously.

To the degree automated tools are used, more than one tool—or a different tool on consecutive tests—should be used. No single tool knows or finds every known vulnerability. The vendors of different scanning tools update their tools' vulnerability databases at different rates, and may add particular vulnerabilities in different orders. Always update the vulnerability database of each tool just before the tool is used. Similarly, from time to time different experts should run the test and/or interpret the results. No single expert always sees everything there is to be seen in the results.

Most networks consist of many heterogeneous devices, each of which will likely have its own set of potential vulnerabilities, as shown in Figure 6-1. The potential issues we would seek in, say, the perimeter router ("1." in Figure 6-1) are very different than those in a wireless access point (WAP) ("7." in Figure 6-1) or a back-end database management server (DBMS) ("11." in Figure 6-1). Vulnerabilities in each of these devices, in turn, will

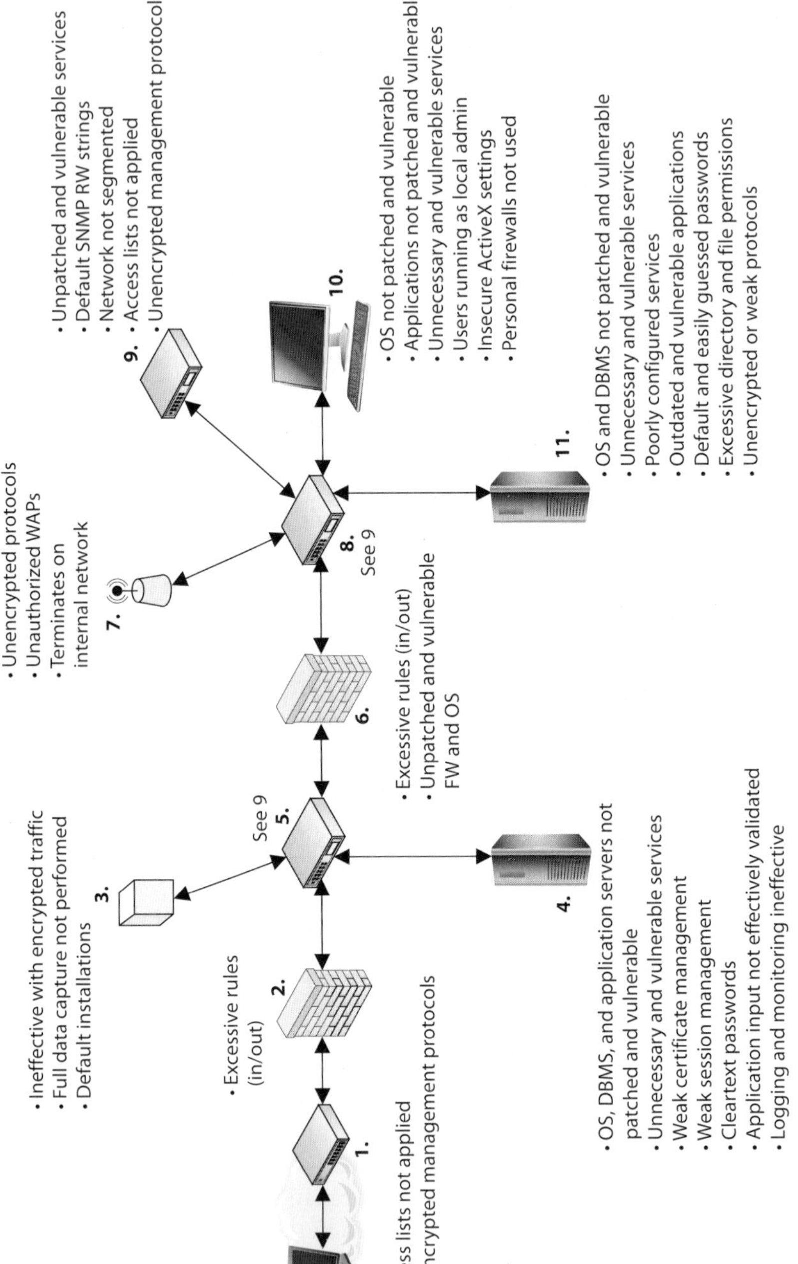

Figure 6-1 Vulnerabilities in heterogeneous networks

depend on the specific hardware, software, and configurations in use. Even if you were able to find an individual or tool who had expert knowledge on the myriad of devices and device-specific security issues, that person or tool would come with its own inherent biases. It is best to leverage team/tool heterogeneity in order to improve the odds of covering blind spots.

Vulnerability and Penetration Testing: What Color Is Your Box?

Vulnerability testing and penetration testing come in boxes of at least three colors: black, white, and gray. The color, of course, is metaphorical, but security professionals need to be aware of the three types. None is clearly superior to the others in all situations, so it is up to us to choose the right approach for our purposes.

- **Black box testing** treats the system being tested as completely opaque. This means that the tester has no *a priori* knowledge of the internal design or features of the system. All knowledge will come to the tester only through the assessment itself. This approach simulates an external attacker best and may yield insights into information leaks that can give an adversary better information on attack vectors. The disadvantage of black box testing is that it will probably not cover all of the internal controls since some of them are unlikely to be discovered in the course of the audit. Another issue is that, with no knowledge of the innards of the system, the test team may inadvertently target a subsystem that is critical to daily operations.
- **White box testing** affords the auditor complete knowledge of the inner workings of the system even before the first scan is performed. This approach allows the test team to target specific internal controls and features and should yield a more complete assessment of the system. The downside is that white box testing may not be representative of the behaviors of an external attacker, though it may be a more accurate depiction of an insider threat.
- **Gray box testing** meets somewhere between the other two approaches. Some, but not all, information on the internal workings is provided to the test team. This helps guide their tactics toward areas we want to have thoroughly tested, while also allowing for a degree of realism in terms of discovering other features of the system. This approach mitigates the issues with both white and black box testing.

Penetration Testing

Penetration testing is the process of simulating attacks on a network and its systems at the request of the owner, senior management. Penetration testing uses a set of procedures and tools designed to test and possibly bypass the security controls of a system. Its goal is to measure an organization's level of resistance to an attack and to uncover any weaknesses within the environment. Organizations need to determine the effectiveness of their security measures and not just trust the promises of the security vendors. Good computer security is based on reality, not on some lofty goals of how things are supposed to work.

A penetration test emulates the same methods attackers would use. Attackers can be clever, creative, and resourceful in their techniques, so penetration attacks should align with the newest hacking techniques along with strong foundational testing methods. The test should look at each and every computer in the environment, as shown in Figure 6-2, because an attacker will not necessarily scan one or two computers only and call it a day.

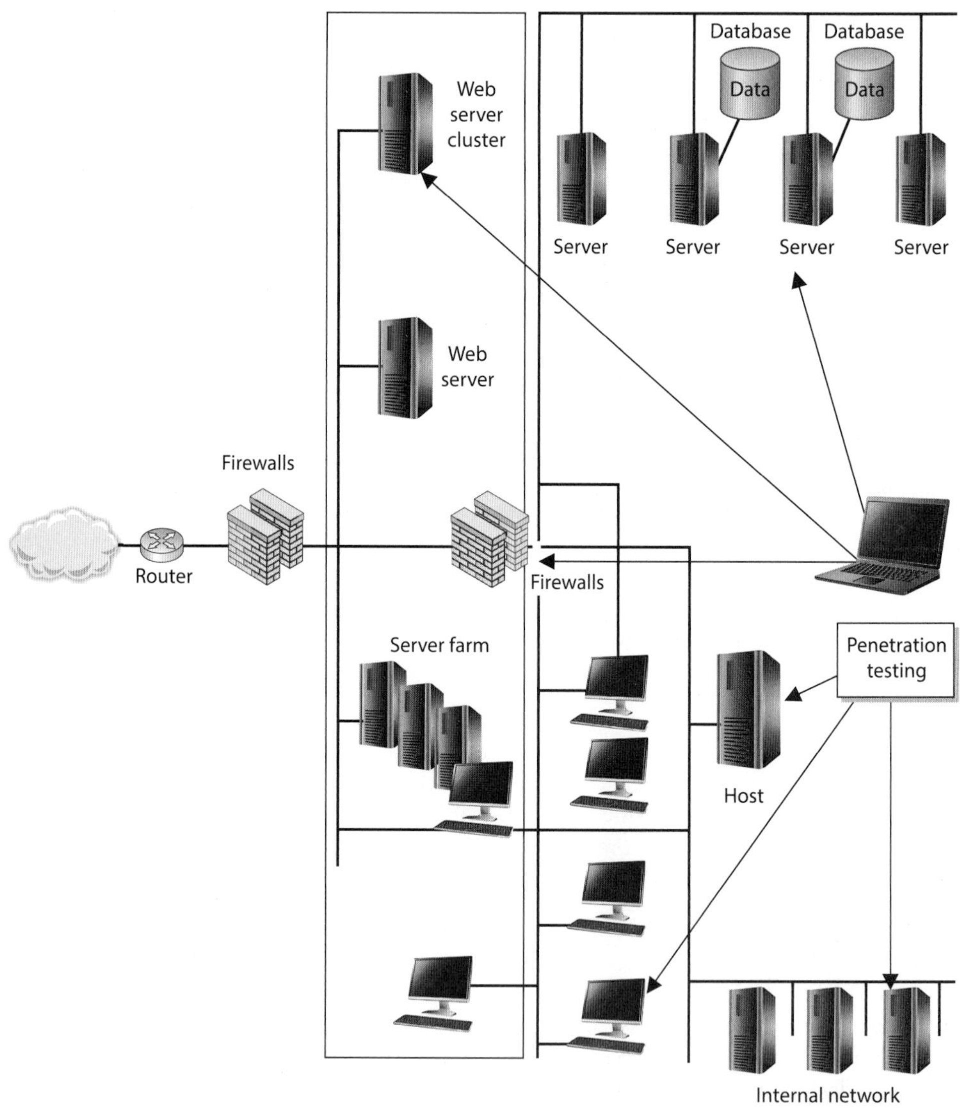

Figure 6-2 Penetration testing is used to prove an attacker can actually compromise systems.

The type of penetration test that should be used depends on the organization, its security objectives, and the management's goals. Some corporations perform periodic penetration tests on themselves using different types of tools, or they use scanning devices that continually examine the environment for new vulnerabilities in an automated fashion. Other corporations ask a third party to perform the vulnerability and penetration tests to provide a more objective view.

Penetration tests can evaluate web servers, Domain Name System (DNS) servers, router configurations, workstation vulnerabilities, access to sensitive information, remote dial-in access, open ports, and available services' properties that a real attacker might use to compromise the company's overall security. Some tests can be quite intrusive and disruptive. The timeframe for the tests should be agreed upon so productivity is not affected and personnel can bring systems back online if necessary.

NOTE Penetration tests are not necessarily restricted to information technology, but may include physical security as well as personnel security. Ultimately, the purpose is to compromise one or more controls, which could be technical, physical, or administrative.

Vulnerability Scanning Recap

Vulnerability scanners provide the following capabilities:

- The identification of active hosts on the network
- The identification of active and vulnerable services (ports) on hosts
- The identification of applications and banner grabbing
- The identification of operating systems
- The identification of vulnerabilities associated with discovered operating systems and applications
- The identification of misconfigured settings
- Test for compliance with host applications' usage/security policies
- The establishment of a foundation for penetration testing

The result of a penetration test is a report given to management that describes the vulnerabilities identified and the severity of those vulnerabilities, along with suggestions on how to deal with them properly. From there, it is up to management to determine how the vulnerabilities are actually dealt with and what countermeasures are implemented.

It is critical that senior management be aware of any risks involved in performing a penetration test before it gives the authorization for one. In rare instances, a system or application may be taken down inadvertently using the tools and techniques employed during the test. As expected, the goal of penetration testing is to identify vulnerabilities, estimate the true protection the security mechanisms within the environment are providing, and see how suspicious activity is reported—but accidents can and do happen.

Security professionals should obtain an authorization letter that includes the extent of the testing authorized, and this letter or memo should be available to members of the team during the testing activity. This type of letter is commonly referred to as a "Get Out of Jail Free Card." Contact information for key personnel should also be available, along with a call tree in the event something does not go as planned and a system must be recovered.

NOTE A "Get Out of Jail Free Card" is a document you can present to someone who thinks you are up to something malicious, when in fact you are carrying out an approved test. There have been many situations in which an individual (or a team) was carrying out a penetration test and was approached by a security guard or someone who thought this person was in the wrong place at the wrong time.

When performing a penetration test, the team goes through a five-step process:

1. **Discovery** Footprinting and gathering information about the target
2. **Enumeration** Performing port scans and resource identification methods
3. **Vulnerability mapping** Identifying vulnerabilities in identified systems and resources
4. **Exploitation** Attempting to gain unauthorized access by exploiting vulnerabilities
5. **Report to management** Delivering to management documentation of test findings along with suggested countermeasures

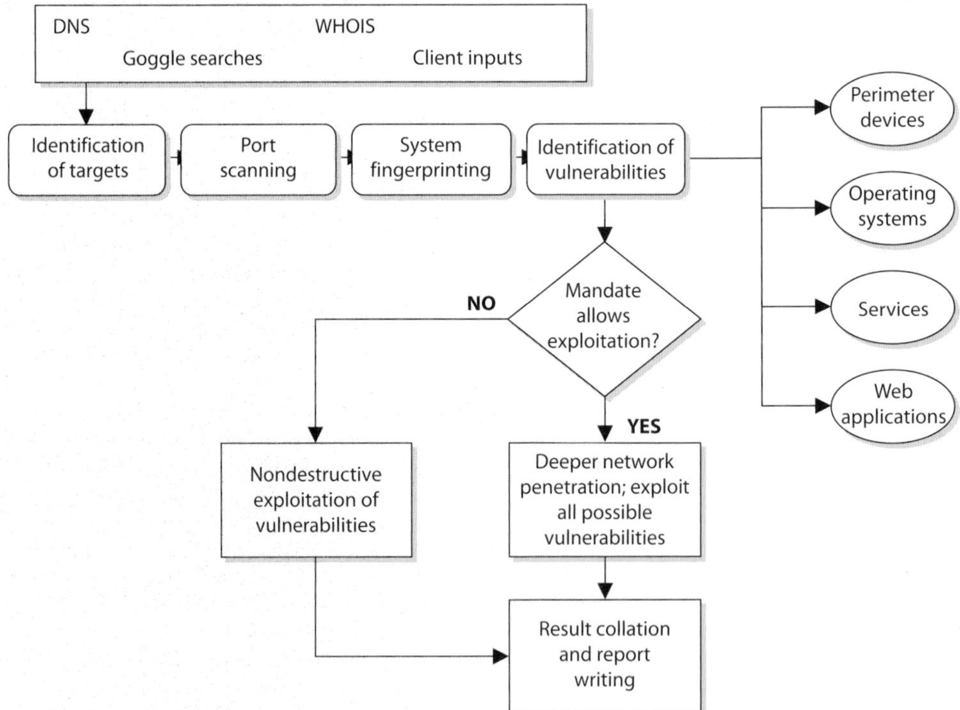

The penetration testing team can have varying degrees of knowledge about the penetration target before the tests are actually carried out:

- **Zero knowledge** The team does not have any knowledge of the target and must start from ground zero.
- **Partial knowledge** The team has some information about the target.
- **Full knowledge** The team has intimate knowledge of the target.

Security testing of an environment may take several forms, in the sense of the degree of knowledge the tester is permitted to have up front about the environment, and also the degree of knowledge the environment is permitted to have up front about the tester.

Tests should be conducted externally (from a remote location) or internally (meaning the tester is within the network). Both should be carried out to understand threats from either domain (internal and external).

Tests may be blind, double-blind, or targeted. A *blind test* is one in which the assessors only have publicly available data to work with. The network security staff is aware that this type of test will take place.

A *double-blind test* (stealth assessment) is also a blind test to the assessors, as mentioned previously, but in this case the network security staff is not notified. This enables the test to evaluate the network's security level and the staff's responses, log monitoring, and escalation processes, and is a more realistic demonstration of the likely success or failure of an attack.

Vulnerability Test vs. Penetration Test

A vulnerability assessment identifies a wide range of vulnerabilities in the environment. This is commonly carried out through a scanning tool. The idea is to identify any vulnerabilities that *potentially* could be used to compromise the security of our systems. By contrast, in a penetration test, the security professional exploits one or more vulnerabilities to prove to the customer (or your boss) that a hacker can *actually* gain access to company resources.

Targeted tests can involve external consultants and internal staff carrying out focused tests on specific areas of interest. For example, before a new application is rolled out, the team might test it for vulnerabilities before installing it into production. Another example is to focus specifically on systems that carry out e-commerce transactions and not the other daily activities of the company.

It is important that the team start off with only basic user-level access to properly simulate different attacks. The team needs to utilize a variety of different tools and attack methods and look at all possible vulnerabilities because this is how actual attackers will function.

The following sections cover common activities carried out in a penetration test.

War Dialing

War dialing allows attackers and administrators to dial large blocks of phone numbers in search of available modems. In today's era of almost ubiquitous broadband connectivity, it may seem a little antiquated to worry about dial-up modem connections. The reality of it is that many organizations still employ small numbers of modems, primarily for certain control systems and for backup communications. The fact that they are fairly obscure and not well known may mean that their security controls are not as carefully planned and managed as others. This could present a wonderful opportunity for an adversary.

NOTE Many facsimile (FAX) machines are remotely exploitable and could allow attackers to get copies of faxes transmitted or received by that device. Many financial institutions still do a fair amount of business over FAX.

Several free and commercial tools are available to dial all of the telephone numbers in a phone exchange (for example, all numbers from 212-555-0000 through 212-555-9999) and make note of those numbers answered by a modem. War dialers can be configured to call only those specific exchanges and their subsets that are known to belong to a company. They can be smart, calling only at night when most telephones are not monitored, to reduce the likelihood of several people noticing the odd hang-up phone calls and thus raising the alarm. War dialers can call in random order so nobody notices the phones are ringing at one desk after another after another, and thus raise an alarm. War dialing is a mature science, and can be accomplished quickly with low-cost equipment. War dialers can go so far as to fingerprint the hosts that answer, similar to a network vulnerability scanner, and attempt a limited amount of automated penetration testing, returning a ready-made compromise of the environment to the attacker. Finally, some private branch exchanges (PBXs) (phone systems) or telephony diagnostic tools may be able to identify modem lines and report on them.

Testing Oneself

Some of the same tactics an attacker may use when war dialing may be useful to the system administrator, such as war dialing at night to reduce disruption to the business. Be aware when performing war dialing proactively that dialing at night may also miss some unauthorized modems that are attached to systems that are turned off by their users at the end of the day. War dialers can be configured to avoid certain numbers or blocks of numbers, so the system administrator can avoid dialing numbers known to be voice-only, such as help desks. This can also be done on more advanced PBXs, with any number assigned to a digital voice device that is configured to not support a modem.

Any unauthorized modems identified by war dialing should be investigated and either brought into compliance or removed, and staff who installed the unauthorized modems should be retrained or disciplined.

Other Vulnerability Types

As noted earlier, vulnerability scans find the potential vulnerabilities. Penetration testing is required to identify those vulnerabilities that can actually be exploited in the environment and cause damage.

Commonly exploited vulnerabilities include the following:

- **Kernel flaws** These are problems that occur below the level of the user interface, deep inside the operating system. Any flaw in the kernel that can be reached by an attacker, if exploitable, gives the attacker the most powerful level of control over the system.

  Countermeasure: Ensure that security patches to operating systems—after sufficient testing—are promptly deployed in the environment to keep the window of vulnerability as small as possible.

- **Buffer overflows** Poor programming practices, or sometimes bugs in libraries, allow more input than the program has allocated space to store it. This overwrites data or program memory after the end of the allocated buffer, and sometimes allows the attacker to inject program code and then cause the processor to execute it. This gives the attacker the same level of access as that held by the program that was attacked. If the program was run as an administrative user or by the system itself, this can mean complete access to the system.

  Countermeasure: Good programming practices and developer education, automated source code scanners, enhanced programming libraries, and strongly typed languages that disallow buffer overflows are all ways of reducing this extremely common vulnerability.

- **Symbolic links** Though the attacker may be properly blocked from seeing or changing the content of sensitive system files and data, if a program follows a symbolic link (a stub file that redirects the access to another place) and the attacker can compromise the symbolic link, then the attacker may be able to gain unauthorized access. (Symbolic links are used in Unix and Linux type systems.) This may allow the attacker to damage important data and/or gain privileged access to the system. A historical example of this was to use a symbolic link to cause a program to delete a password database, or replace a line in the password database with characters that, in essence, created a password less root-equivalent account.

  Countermeasure: Programs, and especially scripts, must be written to ensure that the full path to the file cannot be circumvented.

- **File descriptor attacks** File descriptors are numbers many operating systems use to represent open files in a process. Certain file descriptor numbers are universal, meaning the same thing to all programs. If a program makes unsafe use of a file descriptor, an attacker may be able to cause unexpected input to be provided to the program, or cause output to go to an unexpected place with the privileges of the executing program.

  Countermeasure: Good programming practices and developer education, automated source code scanners, and application security testing are all ways of reducing this type of vulnerability.

- **Race conditions** Race conditions exist when the design of a program puts it in a vulnerable condition before ensuring that those vulnerable conditions are mitigated. Examples include opening temporary files without first ensuring the files cannot be read or written to by unauthorized users or processes, and running in privileged mode or instantiating dynamic load library functions without first verifying that the dynamic load library path is secure. Either of these may allow an attacker to cause the program (with its elevated privileges) to read or write unexpected data or to perform unauthorized commands. An example of a race condition is a time-of-check/time-of-use attack, discussed in Chapter 3.

  Countermeasure: Good programming practices and developer education, automated source code scanners, and application security testing are all ways of reducing this type of vulnerability.

- **File and directory permissions** Many of the previously described attacks rely on inappropriate file or directory permissions—that is, an error in the access control of some part of the system, on which a more secure part of the system depends. Also, if a system administrator makes a mistake that results in decreasing the security of the permissions on a critical file, such as making a password database accessible to regular users, an attacker can take advantage of this to add an unauthorized user to the password database or an untrusted directory to the dynamic load library search path.

  Countermeasure: File integrity checkers, which should also check expected file and directory permissions, can detect such problems in a timely fashion, hopefully before an attacker notices and exploits them.

Many, many types of vulnerabilities exist, and we have covered some, but certainly not all, here in this book. The previous list includes only a few specific vulnerabilities you should be aware of for exam purposes.

Postmortem

Once the tests are over and the interpretation and prioritization are done, management will have in its hands a compilation of many of the ways the company could be successfully attacked. This is the input to the next cycle in the remediation strategy. Every company has only so much money, time, and personnel to commit to defending its network, and thus can mitigate only so much of the total risk. After balancing the risks and risk appetite of the company and the costs of possible mitigations and the value gained from each, management must direct the system and security administrators as to where to spend those limited resources. An oversight program is required to ensure that the mitigations work as expected and that the estimated cost of each mitigation action is closely tracked by the actual cost of implementation. Any time the cost rises significantly or the value is found to be far below what was expected, the process should be briefly paused and reevaluated. It may be that a risk-versus-cost option initially considered less desirable will now make more sense than continuing with the chosen path.

Finally, when all is well and the mitigations are underway, everyone can breathe easier…except the security engineer who has the task of monitoring vulnerability announcements and discussion mailing lists, as well as the early warning services offered by some vendors. To put it another way, the risk environment keeps changing. Between tests, monitoring may make the company aware of newly discovered vulnerabilities that would be found the next time the test is run but that are too high risk to allow to wait that long. And so another, smaller cycle of mitigation decisions and actions must be taken, and then it is time to run the tests again.

Table 6-1 provides an example of a testing schedule that each operations and security department should develop and carry out.

Test Type	Frequency	Benefits
Network scanning	Continuously to quarterly	• Enumerates the network structure and determines the set of active hosts and associated software • Identifies unauthorized hosts connected to a network • Identifies open ports • Identifies unauthorized services
War dialing	Annually	• Detects unauthorized modems and prevents unauthorized access to a protected network
War driving	Continuously to weekly	• Detects unauthorized wireless access points and prevents unauthorized access to a protected network
Virus detectors	Weekly or as required	• Detects and deletes viruses before successful installation on the system
Log reviews	Daily for critical systems	• Validates that the system is operating according to policy
Password cracking	Continuously to same frequency as expiration policy	• Verifies the policy is effective in producing passwords that are difficult to break • Verifies that users select passwords compliant with the organization's security policy
Vulnerability scanning	Quarterly or bimonthly (more often for high-risk systems), or whenever the vulnerability database is updated	• Enumerates the network structure and determines the set of active hosts and associated software • Identifies a target set of computers to focus vulnerability analysis • Identifies potential vulnerabilities on the target set • Validates operating systems and major applications are up-to-date with security patches and software versions
Penetration testing	Annually	• Determines how vulnerable an organization's network is to penetration and the level of damage that can be incurred • Tests the IT staff's response to perceived security incidents and their knowledge and implementation of the organization's security policy and the system's security requirements
Integrity checkers	Monthly and in case of a suspicious event	• Detects unauthorized file modifications

Table 6-1 Example Testing Schedules for Each Operations and Security Department

Log Reviews

A *log review* is the examination of system log files to detect security events or to verify the effectiveness of security controls. Log reviews actually start way before the first event is examined by a security specialist. In order for event logs to provide meaningful information, they must capture a very specific but potentially large amount of information that is grounded on both industry best practices and the organization's risk management process. There is no one-size-fits-all set of event types that will help you assess your security posture. Instead, you need to constantly tune your systems in response to the ever-changing threat landscape.

Another critical element when setting up effective log reviews for an organization is to ensure that time is standardized across all networked devices. If an incident affects three devices and their internal clocks are off by even a few seconds, then it will be significantly more difficult to determine the sequence of events and understand the overall flow of the attack. Although it is possible to normalize differing timestamps, it is an extra step that adds complexity to an already challenging process of understanding an adversary's behavior on our networks. Standardizing and synchronizing time is not a difficult thing to do. The Network Time Protocol (NTP) version 4, described in RFC 5905, is the industry standard for synchronizing computer clocks between networked devices.

Network Time Protocol

The Network Time Protocol (NTP) is one of the oldest protocols used on the Internet and is still in widespread use today. It was originally developed in the 1980s in part to solve the problem of synchronizing trans-Atlantic network communications. Its current version, 4, still leverages statistical analysis of round-trip delays between a client and one or more time servers. The time itself is sent in a UDP datagram that carries a 64-bit timestamp on port 123.

Despite its client/server architecture, NTP employs a hierarchy of time sources organized into strata, with stratum 0 being the most authoritative. A network device on a lower stratum acts as a client to a server on a higher stratum, but could itself be a server to a node further downstream from it. Furthermore, nodes on the same stratum can and often do communicate with each other to improve the accuracy of their times.

Stratum 0 consists of highly accurate time sources such as atomic clocks, global positioning system (GPS) clocks, or radio clocks. Stratum 1 consists of primary time sources, typically network appliances with highly accurate internal clocks that are connected directly to a stratum 0 source. Stratum 2 is where you would normally see your network servers, such as your local NTP servers and your domain controllers. Stratum 3 can be thought of as other servers and the client computers on your network, although the NTP standard does not define this stratum as such.

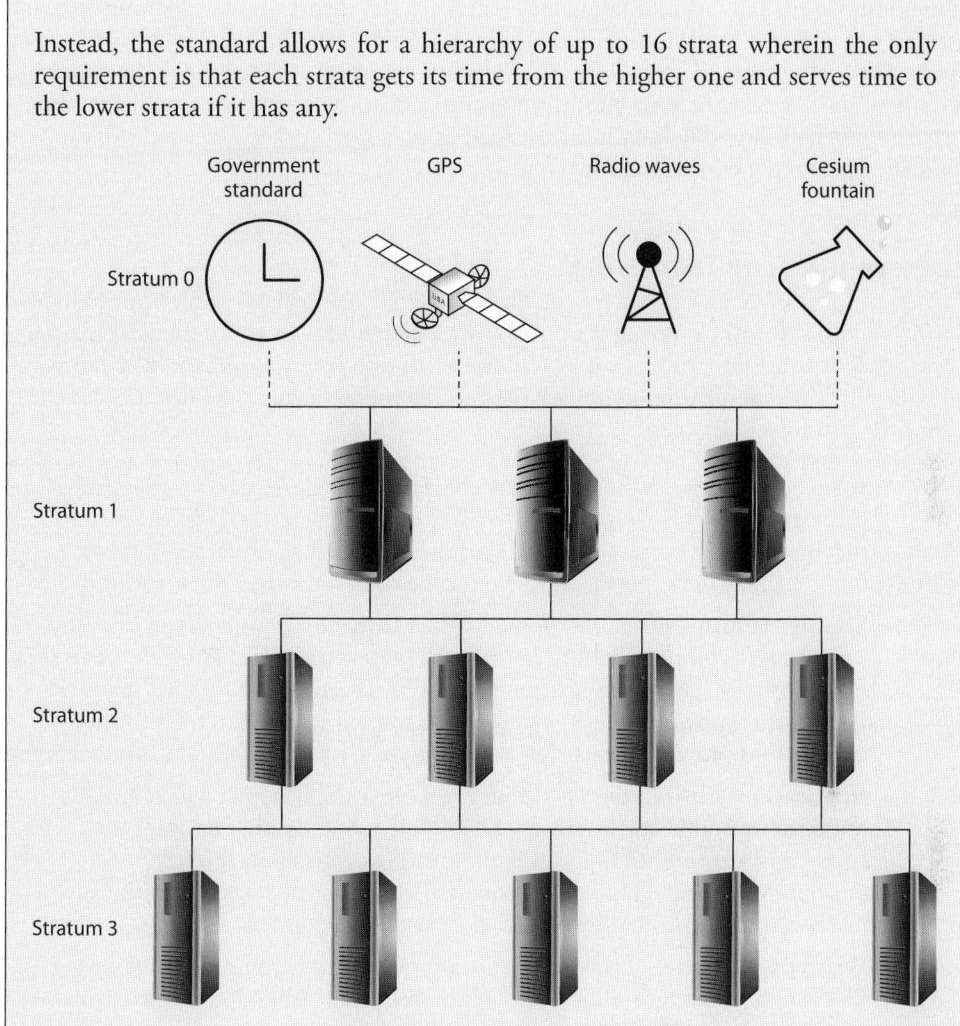
Instead, the standard allows for a hierarchy of up to 16 strata wherein the only requirement is that each strata gets its time from the higher one and serves time to the lower strata if it has any.
Government standard
GPS
Radio waves
Cesium fountain
Stratum 0
Stratum 1
Stratum 2
Stratum 3

Now that you have carefully defined the events you want to track and ensured all timestamps are synchronized across your network, you still need to determine where the events will be stored. By default, most log files are stored locally on the corresponding device. The challenge with this approach is that it makes it more difficult to correlate events across devices to a given incident. Additionally, it makes it easier for attackers to alter the log files of whatever devices they compromise. By centralizing the location of all log files across the organization, we address both issues and also make it easier to archive the logs for long-term retention.

Efficient archiving is important because the size of these logs will likely be significant. In fact, unless your organization is extremely small, you will likely have to deal with thousands (or perhaps even millions) of events each day. Most of these are mundane and probably irrelevant, but we usually don't know which events are important and which aren't until we've done some analysis. In many investigations, the seemingly unimportant events of days, weeks, or even months ago turn out to be the keys to understanding a security incident. So while retaining as much as possible is necessary, we need a way to quickly separate the wheat from the chaff.

Preventing Log Tampering

Log files are often among the first artifacts that attackers will use to attempt to hide their actions. Knowing this, it is up to us as security professionals to do what we can to make it infeasible, or at least very difficult, for attackers to successfully tamper with our log files. The following are the top five steps we can take to raise the bar for the bad folks:

- **Remote logging** When attackers compromise a device, they often gain sufficient privileges to modify or erase the log files on that device. Putting the log files on a separate box will require the attackers to target that box too, which at the very least buys you some time to notice the intrusion.
- **Simplex communication** Some high-security environments use one-way (or simplex) communications between the reporting devices and the central log repository. This is easily accomplished by severing the "receive" pairs on an Ethernet cable. The term *data diode* is sometimes used to refer to this approach to physically ensuring a one-way path.
- **Replication** It is never a good idea to keep a single copy of such an important resource as the consolidated log entries. By making multiple copies and keeping them in different locations, you make it harder for attackers to alter the log files, particularly if at least one of the locations is not accessible from the network (e.g., a removable device).
- **Write-once media** If one of the locations to which you back up your log files can be written to only once, you make it impossible for attackers to tamper with that copy of the data. Of course, they can still try to physically steal the media, but now you force them to move into the physical domain, which many attackers (particularly ones overseas) will not do.
- **Cryptographic hash chaining** A powerful technique for ensuring events that are modified or deleted are easily noticed is to use cryptographic hash chaining. In this technique, each event is appended the cryptographic hash (e.g., SHA-256) of the preceding event. This creates a chain that can attest to the completeness and the integrity of every event in it.

Fortunately, many solutions, both commercial and free, now exist for analyzing and managing log files and other important event artifacts. *Security information and event managers (SIEMs)* are systems that enable the centralization, correlation, analysis, and retention of event data in order to generate automated alerts. Typically, an SIEM provides a dashboard interface that highlights possible security incidents. It is then up to the security specialists to investigate each alert and determine if further action is required. The challenge, of course, is ensuring that the number of false positives is kept fairly low and that the number of false negatives is kept even lower.

Synthetic Transactions

Many of our information systems operate on the basis of transactions. A user (typically a person) initiates a transaction that could be anything from a request for a given web page to a wire transfer of half a million dollars to an account in Switzerland. This transaction is processed by any number of other servers and results in whatever action the requestor wanted. This is considered a real transaction. Now suppose that a transaction is not generated by a person but by a script. This is considered a *synthetic transaction.*

The usefulness of synthetic transactions is that they allow us to systematically test the behavior and performance of critical services. Perhaps the simplest example is a scenario in which you want to ensure that your home page is up and running. Rather than waiting for an angry customer to send you an e-mail saying that your home page is unreachable, or spending a good chunk of your day visiting the page on your browser, you could write a script that periodically visits your home page and ensures that a certain string is returned. This script could then alert you as soon as the page is down or unreachable, allowing you to investigate before you would've otherwise noticed it. This could be an early indicator that your web server was hacked or that you are under a distributed denial of service (DDoS) attack.

Synthetic transactions can do more than simply tell you whether a service is up or down. They can measure performance parameters such as response time, which could alert you to network congestion or server overutilization. They can also help you test new services by mimicking typical end-user behaviors to ensure the system works as it ought to. Finally, these transactions can be written to behave as malicious users by, for example, attempting a cross-site scripting (XSS) attack and ensuring your controls are effective. This is an effective way of testing software from the outside.

Real User Monitoring vs. Synthetic Transactions

Real user monitoring (RUM) is a passive way to monitor the interactions of real users with a web application or system. It uses agents to capture metrics such as delay, jitter, and errors from the user's perspective. RUM differs from synthetic transactions in that it uses real people instead of scripted commands. While RUM more accurately captures the actual user experience, it tends to produce noisy data (e.g., incomplete transactions due to users changing their minds or losing mobile connectivity) and thus may require more back-end analysis. It also lacks the

(*Continued*)

elements of predictability and regularity, which could mean that a problem won't be detected during low utilization periods.

Synthetic transactions, on the other hand, are very predictable and can be very regular, because their behaviors are scripted. They can also detect rare occurrences more reliably than waiting for a user to actually trigger that behavior. Synthetic transactions also have the advantage of not having to wait for a user to become dissatisfied or encounter a problem, which makes them a more proactive approach.

It is important to note that RUM and synthetic transactions are different ways of achieving the same goal. Neither approach is the better one in all cases, so it is common to see both employed contemporaneously.

Misuse Case Testing

Use cases are structured scenarios that are commonly used to describe required functionality in an information system. Think of them as stories in which an external actor (e.g., a user) wants to accomplish a given goal on the system. The use case describes the sequence of interactions between the actor and the system that result in the desired outcome. Use cases are textual, but are often summarized and graphically depicted using a Unified Modeling Language (UML) use case diagram such as the one shown in Figure 6-3. This figure illustrates a very simple view of a system in which a customer places online orders. According to the UML, actors such as our user are depicted using stick figures, and the actors' use cases are depicted as verb phrases inside ovals. Use cases can be related to one another in a variety of ways, which we call *associations*. The most common ways in which use cases are associated are by including another use case (that is, the included use case is always executed when the preceding one is) or by extending a use case (meaning that the second use case may or may not be executed depending on a decision point in the main

Figure 6-3 UML use case diagram

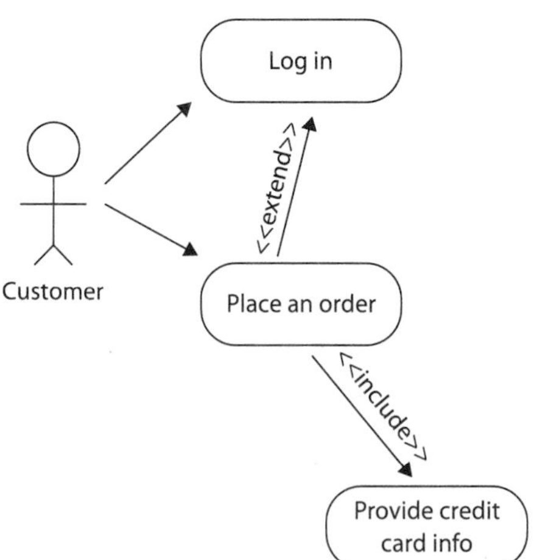

use case). In Figure 6-3, our customer attempts to place an order and may be prompted to log in if she hasn't already done so, but she will always be asked to provide her credit card information.

While use cases are very helpful in analyzing requirements for the normal or expected behavior of a system, they are not particularly useful for assessing its security. That is what misuse cases do for us. A *misuse case* is a use case that includes threat actors and the tasks they want to perform on the system. Threat actors are normally depicted as stick figures with shaded heads and their actions (or misuse cases) are depicted as shaded ovals, as shown in Figure 6-4. As you can see, the attacker in this scenario is interested in guessing passwords and stealing credit card information.

Misuse cases introduce new associations to our UML diagram. The threat actor's misuse cases are meant to threaten a specific portion or legitimate use case of our system. You will typically see shaded ovals connected to unshaded ones with an arrow labeled <<threaten>> to denote this relationship. On the other hand, system developers and security personnel can implement controls that mitigate these misuses. These create new unshaded ovals connected to shaded ones with arrows labeled <<mitigate>>.

The idea behind misuse case testing is to ensure we have effectively addressed each of the risks we identified and decided to mitigate during our risk management process and that are applicable to the system under consideration. This doesn't mean that misuse case testing needs to include all the possible threats to our system, but it should include the ones we decided to address. This process forces system developers and integrators to incorporate the products of our risk management process into the early stages of any system development effort. It also makes it easier to quickly step through a complex system and ensure that effective security controls are in the right places without having to get deep into the source code, which is what we describe next.

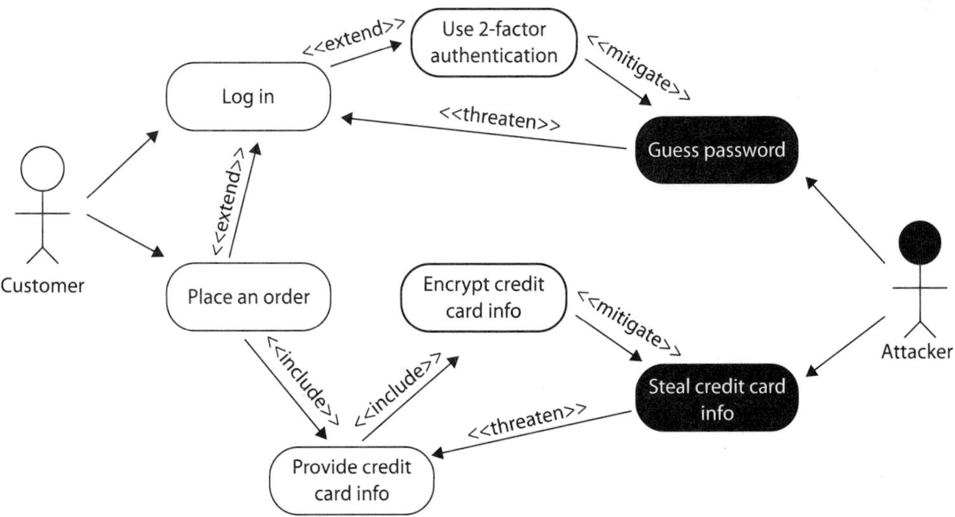

Figure 6-4 UML misuse case diagram

Code Reviews

So far, all the security testing we have discussed looks at the system as a black box. This means that we are only assessing the externally visible features without visibility into the inner workings of the system. If you want to test your own software system from the inside, you could use a *code review*, a systematic examination of the instructions that comprise a piece of software, performed by someone other than the author of that code. This approach is a hallmark of mature software development processes. In fact, in many organizations, developers are not allowed to push out their software modules until someone else has signed off on them after doing a code review. Think of this as proofreading an important document before you send it to an important person. If you try to proofread it yourself, you will probably not catch all those embarrassing typos and grammatical errors as easily as someone else could who is checking it for you.

Code reviews go way beyond checking for typos, though that is certainly one element of it. It all starts with a set of coding standards developed by the organization that wrote the software. This could be an internal team, an outsourced developer, or a commercial vendor. Obviously, code reviews of off-the-shelf commercial software are extremely rare unless the software is open source or you happen to be a major government agency. Still, each development shop will have a style guide or a set of documented coding standards that covers everything from how to indent the code to when and how to use existing code libraries. So a preliminary step to the code review is to ensure the author followed the team's style guide or standards. In addition to helping the maintainability of the software, this step gives the code reviewer a preview of the magnitude of the work ahead; a sloppy coder will probably have a lot of other, harder-to-find defects in his code.

After checking the structure and format of the code, the reviewer looks for uncalled or unneeded functions or procedures. These lead to "code bloat," which makes it harder to maintain and secure the application. For this same reason, the reviewer looks for modules that are excessively complex and should be restructured or split into multiple routines. Finally, in terms of reducing complexity, the reviewer looks for blocks of repeated code that could be refactored. Even better, these could be pulled out and turned into external reusable components such as library functions.

An extreme example of unnecessary (and dangerous) procedures are the code stubs and test routines that developers often include in their developmental software. There have been too many cases in which developers left test code (sometimes including hard-coded credentials) in final versions of software. Once adversaries discover this condition, exploiting the software and bypassing security controls is trivial. This problem is insidious, because developers sometimes comment out the code for final testing, just in case the tests fail and they have to come back and rework it. They may make a mental note to revisit the file and delete this dangerous code, but then forget to do so. While commented code is unavailable to an attacker after a program is compiled (unless they have access to the source code), the same is not true of the scripts that are often found in distributed applications.

Defensive programming is a best practice that all software development operations should adopt. In a nutshell, it means that as you develop or review the code, you are

A Code Review Process

1. Identify the code to be reviewed (usually a specific function or file).
2. The team leader organizes the inspection and makes sure everyone has access to the correct version of the source code, along with all supporting artifacts.
3. Everyone prepares for inspection by reading through the code and making notes.
4. All the obvious errors are collated offline (not in a meeting) so they don't have to be discussed during the inspection meeting (which would be a waste of time).
5. If everyone agrees the code is ready for inspection, then the meeting goes ahead.
6. The team leader displays the code (with line numbers) via an overhead projector so everyone can read through it. Everyone discusses bugs, design issues, and anything else that comes up about the code. A scribe (not the author of the code) writes everything down.
7. At the end of the meeting, everyone agrees on a "disposition" for the code:
   - Passed: Code is good to go
   - Passed with rework: Code is good so long as small changes are fixed
   - Reinspect: Fix problems and have another inspection
8. After the meeting, the author fixes any mistakes and checks in the new version.
9. If the disposition of the code in step 7 was passed with rework, the team leader checks off the bugs that the scribe wrote down and makes sure they're all fixed.
10. If the disposition of the code in step 7 was reinspect, the team leader goes back to step 2 and starts over again.

constantly looking for opportunities for things to go badly. Perhaps the best example of defensive programming is the practice of treating all inputs, whether they come from a keyboard, a file, or the network, as untrusted until proven otherwise. This user input validation can be a bit trickier than it sounds, because you must understand the context surrounding the input. Are you expecting a numerical value? If so, what is the acceptable range for that value? Can this range change over time? These and many other questions need to be answered before we can decide whether the inputs are valid. Keep in mind that many of the oft-exploited vulnerabilities we see have a lack of input validation as their root cause.

Interface Testing

When we think of interfaces, we usually envision a graphical user interface (GUI) for an application. While GUIs are one kind of interface, there are others that are potentially more important. At its essence, an interface is an exchange point for data between systems and/or users. You can see this in your computer's network interface card (NIC), which is the exchange point for data between your computer (a system) and the local area network (another system). Another example of an interface is an application programming interface (API), a set of points at which a software system (e.g., the application) exchanges information with another software system (e.g., the libraries).

Interface testing is the systematic evaluation of a given set of these exchange points. This assessment should include both known good exchanges and known bad exchanges in order to ensure the system behaves correctly at both ends of the spectrum. The real rub is in finding test cases that are somewhere in between. In software testing, these are called *boundary conditions* because they lie at the boundary that separates the good from the bad. For example, if a given packet should contain a payload of no more than 1024 bytes, how would the system behave when presented with 1024 bytes plus one bit (or byte) of data? What about exactly 1024 bytes? What about 1024 bytes minus one bit (or byte) of data? As you can see, the idea is to flirt with the line that separates the good from the bad and see what happens when we get really close to it.

There are many other test cases we could consider, but the most important lesson here is that the primary task of interface testing is to dream up all the test cases ahead of time, document them, and then insert them into a repeatable and (hopefully) automated test engine. This way you can ensure that as the system evolves, a specific interface is always tested against the right set of test cases. We will talk more about software testing in Chapter 8, but for now you should remember that interface testing is a special case of something called *integration testing*, which is the assessment of how different parts of a system interact with each other.

Auditing Administrative Controls

So far in this chapter, we have only discussed the auditing of technical controls. Just as important, or maybe even more so, is the testing of administrative controls. Recall that an administrative control is typically one that is implemented primarily through policies or procedures. In this section, we discuss some key ways in which to test administrative controls.

Account Management

A preferred technique of attackers is to become "normal" privileged users of the systems they compromise as soon as possible. They can accomplish this in at least three ways: compromise an existing privileged account, create a new privileged account, or elevate the privileges of a regular user account. The first approach can be mitigated through the use of strong authentication (e.g., strong passwords or, better yet, two-factor authentication) and by having administrators use privileged accounts only for specific tasks.

The second and third approaches can be mitigated by paying close attention to the creation, modification, or misuse of user accounts. These controls all fall in the category of account management.

Adding Accounts

When new employees arrive, they should be led through a well-defined process that is aimed at ensuring not only that they understand their duties and responsibilities, but also that they are assigned the required company assets and that these are properly configured, protected, and accounted for. While the specifics of how this is accomplished will vary from organization to organization, there are some specific administrative controls that should be universal.

First, all new users should be required to read through and acknowledge they understand (typically by signing) all policies that apply to them. At a minimum, every organization should have (and every user should sign) an acceptable use policy (AUP) that specifies what the organization considers acceptable use of the information systems that are made available to the employee. Using a workplace computer to view pornography, send hate e-mail, or hack other computers is almost always forbidden. On the other hand, many organizations allow their employees limited personal use, such as checking personal e-mail or surfing the Web during breaks. The AUP is a useful first line of defense, because it documents when each user was made aware of what is and is not acceptable use of computers (and other resources) at work. This makes it more difficult for a user to claim ignorance if they subsequently violate the AUP.

Testing that all employees are aware of the AUP and other applicable policies can be the first step in auditing user accounts. Since every user should have a signed AUP, for instance, all we need is to get a list of all users in the organization and then compare it to the files containing the signed documents. In many cases, all the documents a new employee signs are maintained by human resources (HR) and the computer accounts are maintained by IT. Cross-checking AUPs and user accounts can also verify that these two departments are communicating effectively.

The policies also should dictate the default expiration date of accounts, the password policy, and the information to which a user should have access. This last part becomes difficult because the information needs of individual users typically vary over time.

Modifying Accounts

Suppose a newly hired IT technician is initially assigned the task of managing backups for a set of servers. Over time, you realize this individual is best suited for internal user support, including adding new accounts, resetting passwords, and so forth. The privileges needed in each role are clearly different, so how should you handle this? Many organizations, unfortunately, resort to giving all privileges that a user may need. We have all been in, seen, or heard of organizations where every user is a local admin on his or her computer and every member of the IT department is a domain admin. This is an exceptionally dangerous practice, especially if they all use these elevated credentials by default. This is often referred to as *privilege accumulation*.

Adding, removing, or modifying the permissions that a user has should be a carefully controlled and documented process. When are the new permissions effective? Why are they needed? Who authorized the change? Organizations that are mature in their security processes will have a change control process in place to address user privileges. While many auditors will focus on who has administrative privileges in the organization, there are many custom sets of permissions that approach the level of an admin account. It is important, then, to have and test processes by which elevated privileges are issued.

The Problem with Running as Root

It is undoubtedly easier to do all your work from one user account, especially if that account has all the privileges you could ever need. The catch, as you may well know, is that if your account is compromised, the malicious processes will run with whatever privileges the account has. If you run as root (or admin) all the time, you can be certain that if an attacker compromises your box, he will instantly have the privileges to do whatever he needs or wants to do.

A better approach is to do as much of your daily work as you can using a restricted account and elevate to a privileged account only when you must. The way in which you do this varies by operating system:

- Windows operating systems allow you to right-click any program and select Run As to elevate your privileges. From the command prompt, you can use the command `runas /user:<AccountName>` to accomplish the same goal.
- In Linux operating systems, you can simply type `sudo <SomeCommand>` at the command line to run a program as the super (or root) user. If the program is a GUI one, you need to start it from the command line using the command `gksudo` (or `kdesudo` for Kubuntu). Linux has no way to run a program with elevated privileges directly from the GUI; you must start from the command line.
- In Mac OS X, you use `sudo` from the Terminal app just like you would do from a Linux terminal. However, if you want to run a GUI app with elevated privileges, you need to use `sudo open -a <AppName>` since there is no `gksudo` or `kdesudo` command.

Suspending Accounts

Another important practice in account management is to suspend accounts that are no longer needed. Every large organization eventually stumbles across one or more accounts that belong to users who are no longer part of the organization. In extreme cases, an organization discovers that a user who left several months ago still has privileged accounts. The unfettered presence of these accounts on our networks gives adversaries a powerful means to become seemingly legitimate users, which makes our job of detecting and repulsing them that much more difficult.

Accounts may become unneeded, and thus require suspension, for a variety of reasons, but perhaps the most common one would be that the user of the account was terminated or otherwise left the organization. Other reasons for suspension include reaching the account's default expiration date, and temporary, but extended, absences of employees (e.g., maternity leave, military deployment). Whatever the reason, we must ensure that the account of someone who is not present to use it is suspended until that person returns or the term of our retention policy is met.

Testing the administrative controls on suspended accounts follows the same pattern already laid out in the preceding two sections: look at each account (or take a representative sample of all of them) and compare it with the status of its owner according to our HR records. Alternatively, we can get a list of employees who are temporarily or permanently away from the organization and check the status of those accounts. It is important that accounts are deleted only in strict accordance with the data retention policy. Many investigations into terminated employees have been thwarted because administrators have prematurely deleted user accounts and/or files.

Backup Verification

Modern organizations deal with vast amounts of data, which must be protected for a variety of reasons, including disaster recovery (DR). We have all been in at least one situation in which we have lost data and needed to get it back. Some of us have had a rude awakening upon discovering that the data was lost permanently. The specific nature of the backup media is not as important as the fact that the data must be available when we need it most.

Magnetic tapes are now able to hold over 180 terabytes of data, which makes this seemingly antiquated technology the best in terms of total cost of ownership. That being said, many organizations prefer other technologies for daily operations, and relegate tapes to the role of backup to the backup. In other words, it is not uncommon for an organization to back up their user and enterprise data to a storage area network (SAN) on a daily basis, and back up these backups to tape on a weekly basis. Obviously, the frequency of each backup (hourly, daily, weekly) is driven by the risk management process discussed in Chapter 1.

Whatever the approach to backing up our organizational data, we need to periodically test it to ensure that the backups will work as promised when we need them. There are some organizations that have faced an event or disaster that required them to restore some or all data from backups, only to discover that the backups were missing, corrupted, or outdated. This section discusses some approaches to assess whether the data will be there when we need it.

CAUTION Never back up your data to the same device on which the original data exists.

Types of Data

Not all data is created equal, and different types may have unique requirements when it comes to backups. The following sections discuss some of the major categories of data that most of us deal with and some considerations when planning to preserve that data. Keep in mind, however, that there are many other types of data that we will not discuss here for the sake of brevity.

User Data Files This is the type of data with which most of us are familiar. These are the documents, presentations, and spreadsheets that we create or use on a daily basis. Though backing up these files may seem simple, challenges arise when users put "backup" copies in multiple locations for safekeeping. Users, if left to their own devices, may very well end up with inconsistently preserved files and may even violate retention requirements. The challenge with this type of data is ensuring that it is consistently backed up in accordance with all applicable policies, regulations, and laws.

Databases Databases are different from regular files in that they typically store the entire database in a special file that has its own file system within it. In order to make sense of this embedded file system, your database software uses metadata that lives in other files within your system. This architecture can create complex interdependencies among files on the database server. Fortunately, all major database management systems (DBMSs) include one or more means to back up their databases. The challenge is in ensuring that the backup will be sufficient to reconstitute the databases if necessary. To verify the backups, many organizations use a test database server that is periodically used to verify that the databases can be recovered from backup and that the queries will execute properly from the restored data.

Mailbox Data By some estimates, as much as 75 percent of an average organization's data lives in its mailboxes. Depending on the mail system you are running, the backup process may be very different. Still, some commonalities exist across all platforms, such as the critical need to document in excruciating detail every aspect of the configuration of the mail servers. Most medium-sized to large organizations will have multiple mail servers (perhaps backing each other up), so it is a good idea not to back them up at the same time. Finally, whatever backup mechanism you have in place for your mail servers should facilitate compliance with e-discovery.

Virtualization as a Backup and Security Strategy

Many organizations have virtualized their server infrastructure for performance and maintenance reasons. Some are also virtualizing their client systems and turning their workstations into thin clients to a virtualization infrastructure. The next step in this evolution is the use of virtual machine (VM) snapshots as a backup strategy. The main advantage to this approach is that restoration is almost instantaneous. All you typically have to do is click a button or issue a scripted command and the VM will revert to the designated state. Another key advantage is that this approach lends itself to automation and integration with other security systems so that if, for example, a workstation is compromised because the user clicked on a link and an intrusion detection system (IDS) detected this incident, then the VM can be instantly quarantined for later analysis while the user is dropped into the most recent snapshot automatically with very little impact to productivity.

Verification

Having data backups is not particularly helpful unless we are able to use them to recover from mistakes, accidents, attacks, or disasters. Central to verifying this capability is understanding the sorts of things that can go wrong and which of them would require backups. Recall from our discussion on threat modeling in Chapter 1 that an important step in understanding risk is to consider what can happen or be done to our systems that would destroy, degrade, or disrupt our ability to operate. It is helpful to capture these possibilities in scenarios that can then inform how we go about ensuring that we are prepared for the likely threats to our information systems. It is also helpful to automate as much of the testing as possible, particularly in large organizations. This will ensure that we cover the likely contingencies in a very methodical and predictable manner.

Some tests may cause disruptions to our business processes. It is difficult to imagine how a user's backups can be fully tested without involving that user in the process to some extent. If, for instance, our users store files locally and we want to test Mary's workstation backup, an approach could be to restore her backup to a new computer and have Mary log into and use the new computer as if it were the original. She would be in a better position than anyone else to determine whether everything works as expected. This kind of thorough testing is expensive and disruptive, but it ensures that we have in place what we need. Obviously, we have to be very selective about when and how we impact our business processes, so it becomes a trade-off.

However you decide to implement your backup verification, you must ensure that you are able to assert that all critical data is backed up and that you will be able to restore it in time of need. This means that you will probably have to develop an inventory of data and a schedule for testing it as part of your plan. This inventory will be a living document, so you must have a means to track and document changes to it. Fortunately, major items such as mail and database servers don't change very frequently. The challenge will be in verifying the backups of user data.

This brings us back to our policies. We already discussed the importance of the organization's data retention policy, but an equally important one is the policy that dictates how user data is backed up. Many organizations require their staff to maintain their files on file shares on network servers, but we all know that users don't necessarily always do this. It is not uncommon for users to keep a local folder with the data that is most important to them. If the local files are not being backed up, then we risk losing the most critical files, particularly if backups can be disabled by the user. The point of this is that policies need to be carefully thought out and aggressively enforced if we are to be ready for the day when things go badly for us.

Testing Data Backups

- **Develop scenarios** that capture specific sets of events that are representative of the threats facing the organization.
- **Develop a plan** that tests all the mission-critical data backups in each of the scenarios.
- **Leverage automation** to minimize the effort required by the auditors and ensure tests happen periodically.
- **Minimize impact on business** processes of the data backup test plan so that it can be executed regularly.
- **Ensure coverage** so that every system is tested, though not necessarily in the same test.
- **Document the results** so you know what is working and what needs to be worked on.
- **Fix or improve** any issues you documented.

Disaster Recovery and Business Continuity

Most organizations cannot afford to be incapable of performing their business processes for very long. Depending on the specific organization, the acceptable downtime can be measured in minutes, hours, or, in some noncritical sectors, maybe days. Consequently, we all need to have a plan for ensuring we can go on working regardless of what happens around or to us. As introduced in Chapter 1, *business continuity* is the term used to describe the processes enacted by an organization to ensure that its vital business processes remain unaffected or can be quickly restored following a serious incident. Business continuity looks holistically at the entire organization. A subset of this effort, called *disaster recovery*, focuses on restoring the information systems after a disastrous event. Like any other business process, these processes must be periodically assessed to ensure they are still effective.

Testing and Revising the Business Continuity Plan

The business continuity plan (BCP), which should incorporate a disaster recovery plan (DRP), should be tested regularly because environments continually change. Interestingly, many organizations are moving away from the concept of "testing," because a test naturally leads to a pass or fail score, and in the end, that type of score is not very productive. Instead, many organizations are adopting the concept of exercises, which appear to be less stressful, better focused, and ultimately more productive. Each time the BCP is exercised or tested, improvements and efficiencies are generally uncovered, yielding better and better results over time. The responsibility of establishing periodic exercises and the maintenance of the plan should be assigned to a specific person or persons who will have overall ownership responsibilities for the business continuity initiatives within the organization.

The maintenance of the BCP should be incorporated into change management procedures. That way, any changes in the environment are reflected in the plan itself. Plan maintenance is discussed in the next section, "Maintaining the Plan."

Tests and disaster recovery drills and exercises should be performed at least once a year. A company should have no real confidence in a developed plan until it has actually been tested. The tests and drills prepare personnel for what they may face and provide a controlled environment to learn the tasks expected of them. These tests and drills also point out issues to the planning team and management that may not have been previously thought about and addressed as part of the planning process. The exercises, in the end, demonstrate whether a company can actually recover after a disaster.

The exercise should have a predetermined scenario that the company may indeed be faced with one day. Specific parameters and a scope of the exercise must be worked out before sounding the alarms. The team of testers must agree upon what exactly is getting tested and how to properly determine success or failure. The team must agree upon the timing and duration of the exercise, who will participate in the exercise, who will receive which assignments, and what steps should be taken. Also, the team needs to determine whether hardware, software, personnel, procedures, and communications lines are going to be tested and whether it is all or a subset of these resources that will be included in the event. If the test will include moving some equipment to an alternate site, then transportation, extra equipment, and alternate site readiness must be addressed and assessed.

Most companies cannot afford to have these exercises interrupt production or productivity, so the exercises may need to take place in sections or at specific times, which will require logistical planning. Written exercise plans should be developed that will test for specific weaknesses in the overall BCP. The first exercises should not include all employees, but rather a small representative sample of the organization. This allows both the planners and the participants to refine the plan. It also allows each part of the organization to learn its roles and responsibilities. Then, larger drills can take place so overall operations will not be negatively affected.

The people conducting these drills should expect to encounter problems and mistakes. After all, identifying potential problems and mistakes is why they are conducting the drills in the first place. A company would rather have employees make mistakes during a drill so they can learn from them and perform their tasks more effectively during a real disaster.

NOTE After a disaster, telephone service may not be available. For communications purposes, alternatives should be in place, such as mobile phones or walkie-talkies.

A few different types of drills and tests can be used, each with its own pros and cons. The following sections explain the different types of drills.

Checklist Test In this type of test, copies of the DRP or BCP are distributed to the different departments and functional areas for review. This enables each functional manager to review the plan and indicate if anything has been left out or if some approaches should be modified or deleted. This method ensures that nothing is taken for granted or omitted, as might be the case in a single-department review. Once the departments have reviewed their copies and made suggestions, the planning team then integrates those changes into the master plan.

EXAM TIP The checklist test is also called the desk check test.

Structured Walk-Through Test In this test, representatives from each department or functional area come together and go over the plan to ensure its accuracy. The group reviews the objectives of the plan; discusses the scope and assumptions of the plan; reviews the organization and reporting structure; and evaluates the testing, maintenance, and training requirements described. This gives the people responsible for making sure a disaster recovery happens effectively and efficiently a chance to review what has been decided upon and what is expected of them.

The group walks through different scenarios of the plan from beginning to end to make sure nothing was left out. This also raises the awareness of team members about the recovery procedures.

Simulation Test This type of test takes a lot more planning and people. In this situation, all employees who participate in operational and support functions, or their representatives, come together to practice executing the disaster recovery plan based on a specific scenario. The scenario is used to test the reaction of each operational and support representative. Again, this is done to ensure specific steps were not left out and that certain threats were not overlooked. It raises the awareness of the people involved.

The drill includes only those materials that will be available in an actual disaster to portray a more realistic environment. The simulation test continues up to the point of actual relocation to an offsite facility and actual shipment of replacement equipment.

Parallel Test In a parallel test, some systems are moved to the alternate site and processing takes place. The results are compared with the regular processing that is done at the original site. This ensures that the specific systems can actually perform adequately at the alternate offsite facility, and points out any tweaking or reconfiguring that is necessary.

Full-Interruption Test This type of test is the most intrusive to regular operations and business productivity. The original site is actually shut down, and processing takes place at the alternate site. The recovery team fulfills its obligations in preparing the systems and environment for the alternate site. All processing is done only on devices at the alternate offsite facility.

This is a full-blown drill that takes a lot of planning and coordination, but it can reveal many holes in the plan that need to be fixed before an actual disaster hits. Full-interruption tests should be performed only after all other types of tests have been successful. They are the most risky and can impact the business in very serious and devastating ways if not managed properly; therefore, senior management approval needs to be obtained prior to performing full-interruption tests.

The type of organization and its goals will dictate what approach to the training exercise is most effective. Each organization may have a different approach and unique aspects. If detailed planning methods and processes are going to be taught, then specific training may be required rather than general training that provides an overview. Higher-quality training will result in an increase in employee interest and commitment.

During and after each type of test, a record of the significant events should be documented and reported to management so it is aware of all outcomes of the test.

Other Types of Training Other types of training employees need in addition to disaster recovery training include first aid and cardiac pulmonary resuscitation (CPR), how to properly use a fire extinguisher, evacuation routes and crowd control methods, emergency communications procedures, and how to properly shut down equipment in different types of disasters.

The more technical employees may need training on how to redistribute network resources and how to use different telecommunications lines if the main one goes down. They may need to know about redundant power supplies and be trained and tested on the procedures for moving critical systems from one power supply to the next.

Emergency Response Often, the initial response to an emergency affects the ultimate outcome. Emergency response procedures are the prepared actions that are developed to help people in a crisis situation better cope with the disruption. These procedures are the first line of defense when dealing with a crisis situation.

People who are up-to-date on their knowledge of disaster recovery will perform the best, which is why training and drills are very important. Emergencies are unpredictable, and no one knows when they will be called upon to perform their disaster recovery duties.

Protection of life is of the utmost importance and should be dealt with first before attempting to save material objects. Training and drills should show the people in charge how to evacuate personnel safely (see Table 6-2). All personnel should know their designated emergency exits and destinations. Emergency gathering spots should take into consideration the effects of seasonal weather. One person in each designated group is often responsible for making sure all people are accounted for. One person in particular should be responsible for notifying the appropriate authorities: the police department, security guards, fire department, emergency rescue, and management. With proper training, employees will be better equipped to handle emergencies and avoid the reflex to just run to the exit.

Procedure: Personnel Evacuation Description	Location	Names of Staff Trained to Carry Out Procedure	Date Last Carried Out
Each floor within the building must have two individuals who will ensure that all personnel have been evacuated from the building after a disaster. These individuals are responsible for performing employee head count, communicating with the BCP coordinator, and assessing emergency response needs for their employees.	West wing parking lot	David Miller Mike Lester	Drills were carried out on May 4, 2015.
Comments: These individuals are responsible for maintaining an up-to-date listing of employees on their specific floor. These individuals must have a company-issued walkie-talkie and proper training for this function.			

Table 6-2 Sample Emergency Response Procedure

If the situation is not life threatening, systems should be shut down in an orderly fashion, and critical data files or resources should be removed during evacuation for safekeeping. There is a reason for the order of activities. As with all processes, there are dependencies with everything we do. Deciding to skip steps or add steps could in fact cause more harm than good.

Once things have approached a reasonable plateau of activity, one or more people will most likely be required to interface with external entities, such as the press, customers, shareholders, and civic officials. One or more people should be prepped in their reaction and response to the recent disaster so a uniform and reasonable response is given to explain the circumstances, how the company is dealing with the disaster, and what customers and others should now expect from the company. The company should quickly present this information instead of allowing others to come to their own conclusions and start false rumors. At least one person should be available to the press to ensure proper messages are being reported and sent out.

Another unfortunate issue needs to be addressed prior to an emergency: potential looting, vandalism, and fraud opportunities from both a physical perspective and a logical perspective. After a company is hit with a large disturbance or disaster, it is usually at its most vulnerable, and others may take advantage of this vulnerability. Careful thought and planning, such as provision of sufficient security personnel on site, enable the organization to deal with these issues properly and provide the necessary and expected level of protection at all times.

Maintaining the Plan

Unfortunately, the various plans that have been covered in this chapter can become quickly out of date. An out-of-date BCP may provide a company with a false sense of security, which could be devastating if and when a disaster actually takes place.

The main reasons plans become outdated include the following:

- The business continuity process is not integrated into the change management process.
- Changes occur to the infrastructure and environment.
- Reorganization of the company, layoffs, or mergers occur.
- Changes in hardware, software, and applications occur.
- After the plan is constructed, people feel their job is done.
- Personnel turnover.
- Large plans take a lot of work to maintain.
- Plans do not have a direct line to profitability.

Organizations can keep the plan updated by taking the following actions:

- Make business continuity a part of every business decision.
- Insert the maintenance responsibilities into job descriptions.
- Include maintenance in personnel evaluations.
- Perform internal audits that include disaster recovery and continuity documentation and procedures.
- Perform regular drills that use the plan.
- Integrate the BCP into the current change management process.
- Incorporate lessons learned from actual incidents into the plan.

One of the simplest and most cost-effective and process-efficient ways to keep a plan up-to-date is to incorporate it within the change management process of the organization. When you think about it, this approach makes a lot of sense. Where do you document new applications, equipment, or services? Where do you document updates and patches? Your change management process should be updated to incorporate fields and triggers that alert the BCP team when a significant change will occur and should provide a means to update the recovery documentation. What's the point of removing the dust bunnies off a plan if it has your configurations from three years ago? There is nothing worse than that feeling at the pit of your stomach when you realize the one thing you thought was going to save you will in fact only serve to keep a fire stoked with combustible material.

Moreover, you should incorporate lessons learned from any actual incidents and actual responses. The team should perform a "postmortem" on the response and have necessary changes made to plans, contracts, personnel, processes, and procedures.

BCP Life Cycle

Remember that most organizations aren't static, but change, often rapidly, as do the conditions under which organizations must operate. Thus, the BCP should be considered a life cycle in order to deal with the constant and inevitable change that will affect it. Understanding and maintaining each step of the life cycle is critical if the BCP is to be useful to the organization. The BCP life cycle is outlined in Figure 6-5.

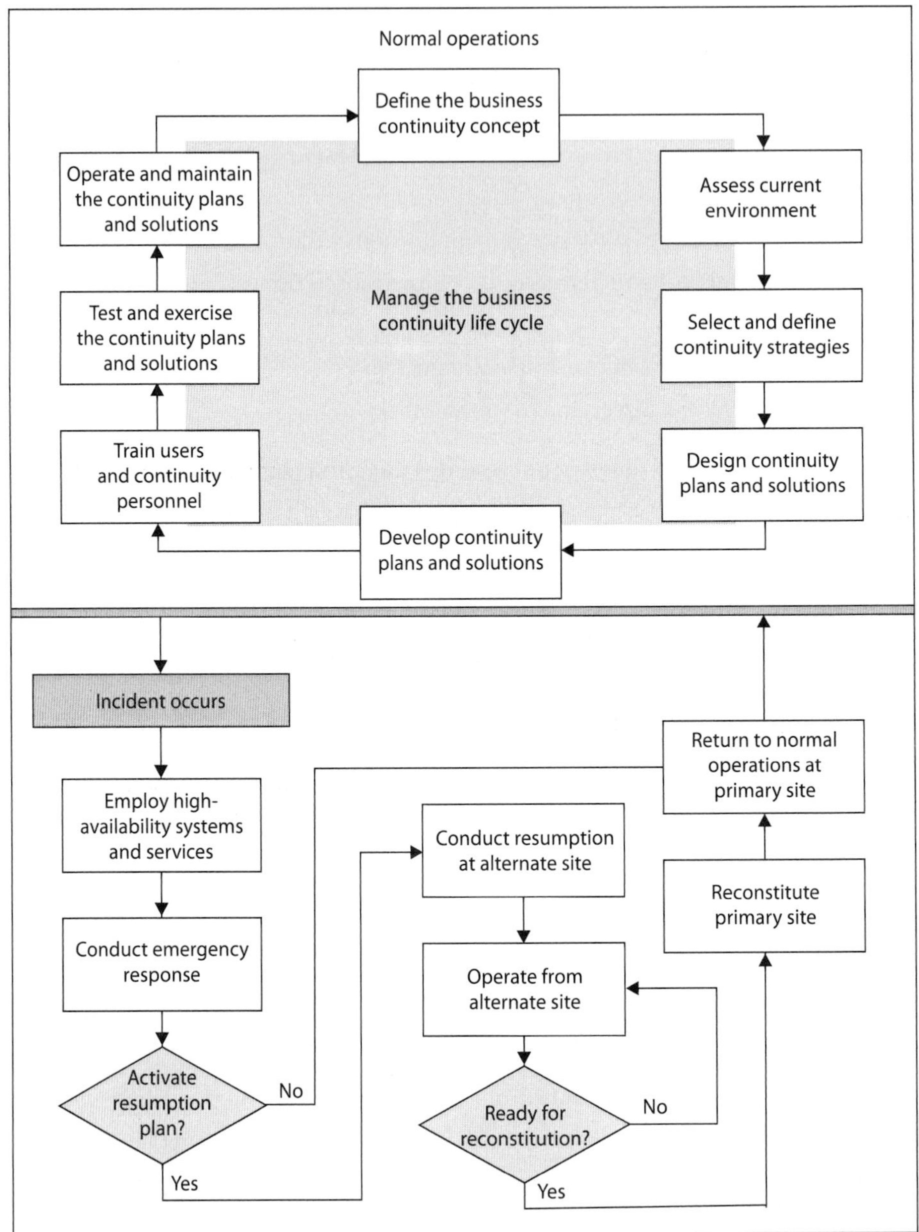

Figure 6-5 BCP life cycle

Security Training and Security Awareness Training

As should be clear from the preceding discussions, having a staff that is well trained in security issues is crucial to the security of our organizations. The terms training and awareness are often used interchangeably, but they have subtly different meanings. *Security training* is the process of teaching a skill or set of skills that will allow people to perform specific functions better. *Security awareness training*, on the other hand, is the process of exposing people to security issues so that they may be able to recognize them and better respond to them. Security training is typically provided to security personnel, while security awareness training should be provided to every member of the organization.

Assessing the effectiveness of our security training programs is fairly straightforward because the training is tied to specific security functions. Therefore, in order to test the effectiveness of a training program, all we have to do is test the performance of an individual on those functions before and after the training. If the performance improves, then the training was probably effective. Keep in mind that skills atrophy over time, so the effectiveness of the training should be measured immediately after it concludes. Otherwise, we are assessing the long-term retention of the functional skills.

We now turn our attention to the somewhat more difficult issue of assessing the effectiveness of a security awareness training program. As we broach this subject, keep in mind that the end state is to better equip our teammates to recognize and deal with security issues. This implies that a key measure of the effectiveness of the security awareness program is the degree to which people change their behaviors when presented with certain situations. If this change is toward a better security posture, then we can infer that the program was effective. In the following sections, we take a look at specific components of a security awareness training program that are common to many organizations.

Social Engineering

Social engineering, in the context of information security, is the process of manipulating individuals so that they perform actions that violate security protocols. Whether the action is divulging a password, letting someone into the building, or simply clicking a link, it has been carefully designed by the adversaries to help them exploit our information systems. A common misconception is that social engineering is an art of improvisation. While improvising may help the attacker better respond to challenges, the fact of the matter is that most effective social engineering is painstakingly designed against a particular target, usually a specific individual.

Perhaps the most popular form of social engineering is *phishing*, which is social engineering conducted through a digital communication. Figure 6-6 depicts the flow of a typical e-mail phishing attack. (While e-mail phishing receives a lot of attention, text messages can also be used to similar effect.) Like casting a baited fishing line into a pond full of fish, phishing relies on the odds that if enough people receive an enticing or believable message, at least one of them will click an embedded link within it.

Some adversaries target specific individuals or groups, which is referred to as *spear phishing*. In some cases, the targets are senior executives, in which case it is called *whaling*. In whatever variety it comes, the desired result of phishing is almost always to have the

Figure 6-6 Typical phishing attack

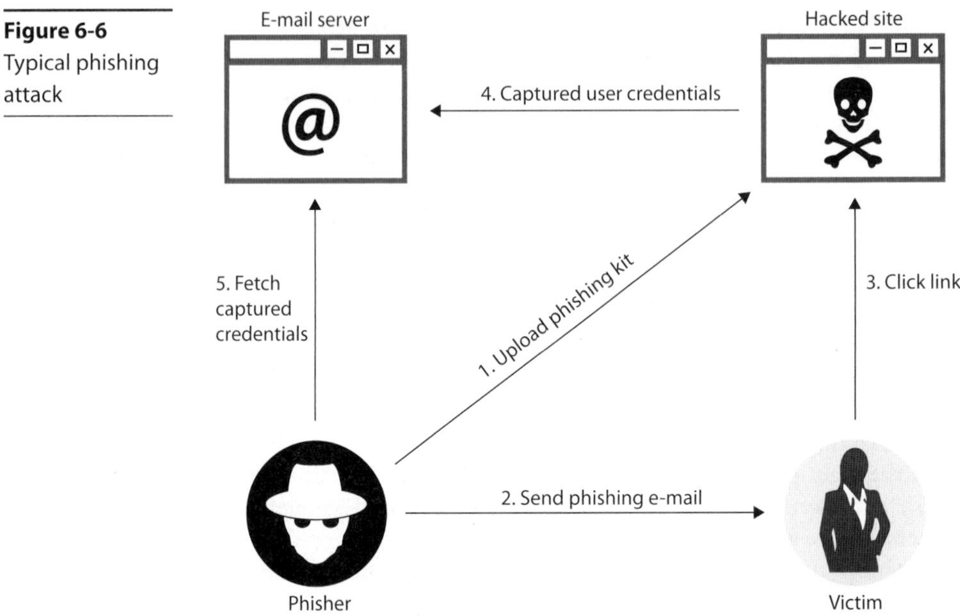

target click a link that will take them to a website under the control of the attacker. Sometimes the website will look like the legitimate logon page of a trusted site, such as that of the user's bank. Other times, the website is a legitimate one that has been compromised by the attacker to redirect users somewhere else. In the case of a *drive-by download*, the site will invisibly redirect the user to a malware distribution server, as shown in Figure 6-7.

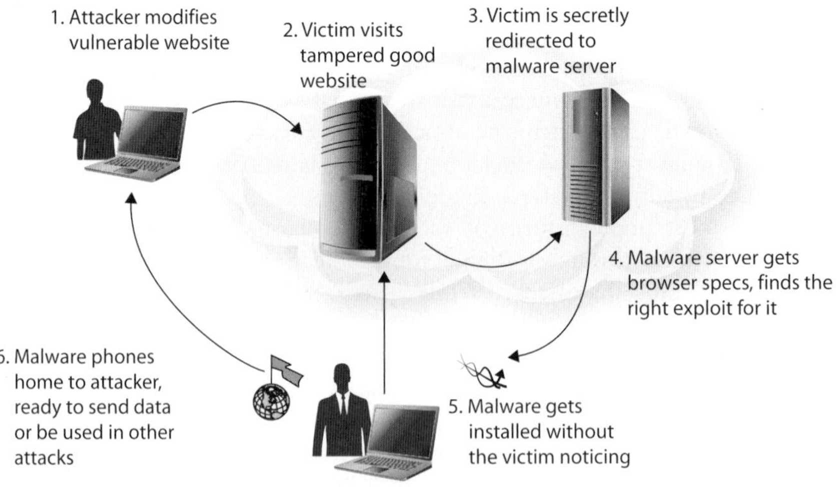

Figure 6-7 Drive-by downloads

Pretexting is a form of social engineering, typically practiced in person or over the phone, in which the attacker invents a believable scenario in an effort to persuade the target to violate a security policy. A common example is a call received from (allegedly) customer service or fraud prevention at a bank in which the attacker tries to get the target to reveal account numbers, personal identification numbers (PINs), passwords, or similarly valuable information. Remarkably, pretexting was legal in the United States until 2007, as long as it was not used to obtain financial records. In 2006, Hewlett-Packard became embroiled in a scandal dealing with its use of pretexting in an effort to identify the sources of leaks on its board of directors. Congress responded by passing the Telephone Records and Privacy Protection Act of 2006, which imposes stiff criminal penalties on anyone who uses pretexting to obtain confidential information.

So how does one go about assessing security awareness programs aimed at countering social engineering in all its forms? One way is to keep track of the number of times users fall victim to these attacks before and after the awareness training effort. The challenge with this approach is that victims may not spontaneously confess to falling for these tricks, and our security systems will certainly not detect all instances of successful attacks. Another approach is to have auditors (internal or external) conduct benign social engineering campaigns against our users. When users click a link inserted by the auditors, they are warned that they did something wrong and perhaps are redirected to a web page or short video explaining how to avoid such mistakes in the future. All the while, our automated systems are keeping tabs on which users are most susceptible and how often these attacks are successful. Anecdotal evidence suggests that there is a group of users who will not respond to remedial training, so the leadership should decide what to do with individuals who repeatedly make the wrong choices.

Online Safety

Oftentimes users don't have to be tricked into doing something wrong, but willingly go down that path. This is often the result of ignorance of the risks, and the remediation of this ignorance is the whole point of the security awareness campaign. An effective security awareness program should include issues associated with unsafe online behavior that could represent risk for the organization.

Perhaps one of the most important elements of safe online behavior is the proper use of social media. A good starting point is the proper use of privacy settings, particularly considering that all major social media sites have means to restrict what information is shared with whom. The default settings are not always privacy-focused, so it is important for users to be aware of their options. This becomes particularly important when users post information concerning their workplace. Part of the security awareness program should be to educate users about the risks they can pose to their employers if their posts reveal sensitive information. Once posted, the information cannot be recalled; it is forevermore out there.

Sometimes it is not what goes out to the Internet, but what comes in from it that should concern users. Simply surfing to the wrong website, particularly from a workplace computer, may be all it takes to bring down the whole company. A *drive-by download* is an automatic attack that is triggered simply by visiting a malicious website. While the mechanisms vary, the effect can be the execution of malware on the client computer, with or without additional user interaction. While web filters can mitigate some of the risk of surfing to inappropriate sites, malicious websites sometimes are legitimate ones that have been compromised, which means that the filters may not be effective.

While some downloads happen without user knowledge or interaction, others are intentional. It is not unusual for naïve users to attempt to download and install unauthorized and potentially risky applications on their computers. Unfortunately, many organizations do not use software whitelisting and even allow their users to have administrative privileges on their computers, which allows them to install any application they desire. Even benign applications can be problematic for the security of our systems, but when you consider that the software may come from an untrusted and potentially malicious source, the problem is compounded.

Assessing the effectiveness of an awareness campaign that promotes users' online safety is not easy and typically requires a multipronged approach. Social media posts may be detected using something as simple as Google Alerts, which trigger whenever Google's robots find a term of interest online. A simple script can then filter out the alerts by source in order to separate, say, a news outlet report on our organization from an ill-advised social media post. The software download problem (whether intentional or not) can be assessed by a well-tuned IDS. Over time, with an effective awareness campaign, we should see the number of incidents go down, which will allow us to focus our attention on repeat offenders.

Data Protection

We already covered data protection in Chapter 2, but for the purposes of assessing a security awareness program, it bears repeating that sensitive data must always be encrypted whether at rest or in transit. It is possible for users to circumvent controls and leave this data unprotected, so awareness is a key to preventing this type of behavior. Unencrypted data is vulnerable to leaks if it is stored in unauthorized online resources or intentionally (but perhaps not maliciously) shared with others. Another topic we covered in Chapter 2 is the proper destruction of sensitive data when it is no longer needed and falls out of the mandatory retention period.

Testing the degree to which our users are aware of data protection requirements and best practices can best be done by using tags in our files' metadata. The information classification labels we discussed in Chapter 2 become an effective means of tracking where our data is. Similarly, data loss prevention (DLP) solutions can help stop leaks and identify individuals who are maliciously or inadvertently exposing our sensitive information. This allows us to target those users either with additional awareness training or with disciplinary actions.

Culture

At the end of the day, the best way to test the security awareness of an organization may be by assessing its security culture. Do we have the kind of environment in which users feel safe self-reporting? Are they well incentivized to do so? Do they actively seek information and guidance when encountering a strange or suspicious situation? Self-reports and requests for information by users provide a good indicator of whether the organizational culture is helping or hindering us in securing our systems.

Key Performance and Risk Indicators

How can you tell whether you are moving toward or away from your destination? In the physical world, we use all sorts of environmental cues such as road signs and landmarks. Oftentimes, we can also use visual cues to assess the likely risk in our travels. For instance, if a sign on a hiking trail is loose and can pivot around its pole, then we know that there is a chance that the direction in which it points is not the right one. If a landmark is a river crossing and the waters are much higher than normal, we know we run the risk of being swept downstream. But when it comes to our security posture, how can we tell whether we're making progress and whether we're taking risks?

There is no shortage of security metrics in the industry, but here we focus on two of the most important categories of metrics: key performance indicators (KPIs) and key risk indicators (KRIs). KPIs measure how well things are going now, while KRIs measure how badly things could go in the future.

Key Performance Indicators

Attempting to run an information security management system (ISMS) without adequate metrics is perhaps more dangerous than not managing security at all. The reason is that, like following misplaced trail signs, using the wrong metrics can lead the organization down the wrong path and result in worse outcomes than would be seen if all is left to chance. Fortunately, the International Organization for Standardization (ISO) has published an industry standard for developing and using metrics that measure the effectiveness of a security program. ISO 27004, titled Information Security Metrics Implementation, outlines a process by which to measure the performance of security controls and processes. Keep in mind that a key purpose of this standard is to support continuous improvement in an organization's security posture.

At this point, it will be helpful to define a handful of terms:

- **Factor** An attribute of the ISMS that can be described as a value that can change over time. Examples of factors are the number of alerts generated by an IDS or the number of events investigated by incident response (IR) teams.
- **Measurement** The value of a factor at a particular point in time. In other words, this is raw data. Two examples of measurements would be 356 IDS alerts in the last 24 hours and 42 verified events investigated by IR teams in the month of January.
- **Baseline** An arbitrary value for a factor that provides a point of reference or denotes that some condition is met by achieving some threshold value. For example, a baseline could be the historic trend in the number of IDS alerts over the past 12 months (a reference line) or a goal that IR teams will investigate 100 events or less in any given month (a threshold value).

- **Metric** A derived value that is generated by comparing multiple measurements against each other or against a baseline. Metrics are, by their very nature, comparative. Building upon the previous examples, an effective metric could be the ratio of verified incidents to IDS alerts during a 30-day period.
- **Indicator** An interpretation of one or more metrics that describes an element of the effectiveness of the ISMS. In other words, indicators are meaningful to management. If one of management's goals is to tune the organization's sensors so as to reduce the error rate (and hence utilize its IR team more effectively), then an indicator could be a green traffic light showing that a threshold ratio of no more than 30 percent false or undetected (by IDS) events has been met for a reporting period.

It follows from the foregoing definitions that a *key performance indicator* is an indicator that is particularly significant in showing the performance of an ISMS. KPIs are carefully chosen from among a larger pool of indicators to show at a high level whether our ISMS is keeping pace with the threats to our organization or showing decreased effectiveness. KPIs should be easily understood by business and technical personnel alike and should be aligned with one or (better yet) multiple organizational goals.

The process by which we choose KPIs is really driven by organizational goals. In an ideal case, the senior leadership sets (or perhaps approves) goals for the security of the organization. The ISMS team then gets to work on how to show whether we are moving toward or away from those goals. The process can be summarized as follows.

1. Choose the factors that can show the state of our security. In doing this, we want to strike a balance between the number of data sources and the resources required to capture all their data.
2. Define baselines for some or all of the factors under consideration. As we do this, it is helpful to consider which measurements will be compared to each other and which to some baseline. Keep in mind that a given baseline may apply to multiple factors' measurements.
3. Develop a plan for periodically capturing the values of these factors, and fix the sampling period. Ideally, we use automated means of gathering this data so as to ensure the periodicity and consistency of the process.
4. Analyze and interpret the data. While some analysis can (and probably should) be automated, there will be situations that require human involvement. In some cases, we'll be able to take the data at face value, while in others we will have to dig into it and get more information before reaching a conclusion about it.
5. Communicate the indicators to all stakeholders. In the end, we need to package the findings in a way that is understandable by a broad range of stakeholders. A common approach is to start with a nontechnical summary that is supported by increasingly detailed layers of supporting technical information. On the summary side of this continuum is where we select and put our KPIs.

The preceding process and definitions are not universal, but represent some best practices in the business. At the end of the day, the KPIs are the product of distilling a large amount of information with the goal of answering one specific question: Are we managing our information security well enough? There is no such thing as perfect security, so what we are really trying to do is find the sweet spot where the performance of the ISMS is adequate and sustainable using an acceptable amount of resources. Clearly, this spot is a moving target given the ever-changing threat and risk landscape.

Key Risk Indicators

While KPIs tell us where we are today with regard to our goals, key risk indicators (KRIs) tell us where we are today in relation to our risk appetite. They measure how risky an activity is so that the leadership can make informed decisions about that activity, all the while taking into account potential resource losses. Like KPIs, KRIs are selected for their impact on the decisions of the senior leaders in the organization. This means that KRIs often are not specific to one department or business function, but rather affect multiple aspects of the organization. KRIs have, by definition, a very high business impact.

When considering KRIs, it is useful to relate them to single loss expectancy (SLE) equations. Recall from Chapter 1 that the SLE is the organization's potential monetary loss if a specific threat were to be realized. It is the product of the loss and the likelihood that the threat will occur. In other words, if we have a proprietary process for building widgets valued at $500,000 and we estimate a 5 percent chance of an attacker stealing and monetizing that process, then our SLE would be $25,000. Now, clearly, that 5 percent figure is affected by a variety of activities within the organization, such as IDS tuning, IR team proficiency, and end-user security awareness.

Over time, the likelihood of the threat being realized will change based on multiple activities going on within the organization. As this value changes, the risk changes too. A KRI would capture this and allow us to notice when we have crossed a threshold that makes our current activities too risky for our stated risk appetite. This trigger condition enables the organization to change its behavior to compensate for excessive risk. For instance, it could trigger an organizational stand-down for security awareness training.

In the end, the important thing to remember about KRIs is that they are designed to work much as mine canaries: they alert us when something bad is likely to happen so that we can change our behavior and defeat the threat.

Reporting

Report writing is perhaps one of the least favorite tasks for security professionals, and yet it is often one of the most critical tasks. While we all thrive on putting hands on keyboards and patch panels when it comes to securing our networks, we often cringe at the thought of putting in writing what it is that we've done and what it means to the organization. This is probably the task that best distinguishes the true security professional from the security practitioner: the professional understands the role of information systems security within the broader context of the business and is able to communicate it to technical and nontechnical audiences alike.

It seems that many of us have no difficulty (though perhaps a bit of reluctance) describing the technical details of a plan we are proposing, a control we have implemented, or an audit we have conducted. It may be a bit tedious, but we've all done this at some point in our careers. The problem with these technical reports, important though they are, is that they are written by and for technical personnel. If your CEO is a technical person running a technical company, this may work fine. However, sooner or later most of us will work in organizations that are not inherently technical. The decision makers therein will probably not be as excited about the details of an obscure vulnerability you just discovered as they will be about its impact on the business. If your report is to have a business impact, it must be both technically sound and written in the language of the business.

Technical Reporting

A technical report should be much more than the output of an automated scanning tool or a generic checklist with yes and no boxes. There are way too many so-called auditors that simply push the start button on a scanning tool, wait for it to do its job, and then print a report with absolutely no customization or analysis. A technical report should be the application of a standard methodology to the specific context of the system under study (SUS). In other words, the report must show that this was a tailored audit. It must document the methodology that was used, the manner in which it was tailored to the SUS, the findings, and the recommended controls or changes. The raw data and automated reports should be provided in an appendix. Above all else, the report should speak to the organization's risk posture.

The following are key elements of a good technical audit report:

- **The threats** The risk management process (RMP), discussed in Chapter 1, details the manner in which an organization determines threats to it. The report should consider those threats in order to remain aligned with the RMP.
- **The vulnerabilities** These are tied to the threats in that a vulnerability that is not exploitable by any of the threats we are tracking is probably less important than one that is exploitable. The context of the vulnerability is what matters most, not its existence.
- **The probability of exploitation** A vulnerability that is regularly being exploited elsewhere by the threats we are tracking is likely to affect our organization too if we don't do anything about it. Determining likelihood is important in order to prioritize efforts and better assess the impact of a successful exploit.
- **The impact of exploitation** This is often expressed in monetary terms so that it is better aligned with our RMP.
- **Recommended actions** These are the steps that should be taken to address the vulnerabilities in order to reduce the probability and/or impact of an exploitation.

Always be wary of reports that look auto-generated since they usually point to an ineffective auditing team. Also be careful about reports that, having failed to find any significant vulnerabilities, overemphasize the importance of less important flaws. If the security posture of the organization is good, then the auditors should not shy away from saying so.

Executive Summaries

Getting into the technical weeds with an audit report is wonderful for techies, but it doesn't do the business folks any good. The next step in writing impactful reports is to translate the key findings and recommendations into language that is approachable and meaningful to the senior leadership of your organization. After all, it is their support that will allow you to implement the necessary changes. They will provide both the authority and resources that you will need.

Typically, technical reports (among others) include an executive summary of no more than a page or two, which highlights what senior leaders need to know from the report. The goal is to get their attention and effect the desired change. One way to get a business leader's attention is to explain the audit findings in terms of risk exposure. Security is almost always perceived as a cost center for the business. A good way to show return on investment (ROI) for a department that doesn't generate profits is by quantifying how much money a recommended change could potentially save the company.

One way to quantify risk is to express it in monetary terms. We could say that the risk (in dollars) is the value of an asset multiplied by the probability of the loss of that asset. In other words, if our customer's data is worth $1 million and there is a 10 percent chance that this data will be breached, then our risk for this data breach would be $100,000. How can we come up with these values? There are different ways in which accountants valuate other assets, but the most common are the following.

- The *cost approach* simply looks at the cost of acquiring or replacing the asset. This is the approach we oftentimes take to valuating our IT assets (minus information, of course). How might it be applied to information? Well, if an information asset is a file containing a threat intelligence report that cost the organization $10,000, then the cost approach would attach that value to this asset.
- The *income approach* considers the expected contribution of the asset to the firm's revenue stream. The general formula is value equals expected (or potential) income divided by capitalization rate. The capitalization rate is the actual net income divided by the value of the asset. So, for instance, if that $10,000 threat intelligence report brought in $1,000 in net income last year (so the capitalization rate is 0.10) and our projections are that it will bring in $2,000 this year, then its present value would be $2,000 ÷ 0.10 or $20,000. As you should be able to see, the advantage of this approach is that it takes into account the past and expected business conditions.

- The *market approach* is based on determining how much other firms are paying for a similar asset in the marketplace. It requires a fair amount of transparency in terms of what other organizations are doing. For instance, if we have no way of knowing how much others paid for that threat intelligence report, then we couldn't use a market approach to valuating it. If, on the other hand, we were able to find out that the going rate for the report is actually $12,000, then we can use that value for our report (asset) and celebrate that we got a really good deal.

So, as long as the life-cycle costs of implementing our proposed controls (say, $180,000) are less than the risks they mitigate (say, $1,000,000), it should be obvious that we should implement the control, right? Not quite. The controls, after all, are not perfect. They will not be able to eliminate the risk altogether, and will sometimes fail. This means that we need to know the likelihood that the control will be effective at thwarting an attack. Let's say that we are considering a solution that has been shown to be effective about 80 percent of the time and costs $180,000. We know that we have a 10 percent chance of being attacked and, if we are, that we have a 20 percent chance of our control failing to protect us. This means that the residual risk is 2 percent of $1,000,000, or $20,000. This is then added to the cost of our control ($180,000) to give us the total effective cost of $200,000.

This is the sort of content that is impactful when dealing with senior leaders. They want to know the answers to questions such as these: How likely is this to work? How much will it save us? How much will it cost? The technical details are directly important to the ISMS team and only indirectly important to the business leaders. Keep that in mind the next time you package an audit report for executive-level consumption.

Management Review

A management review is a formal meeting of senior organizational leaders to determine whether the management systems are effectively accomplishing their goals. In the context of the CISSP, we are particularly interested in the performance of the ISMS. While we restrict our discussion here to the ISMS, you should be aware that the management review is typically much broader in scope.

While management reviews have been around for a very long time, the modern use of the term is perhaps best grounded in quality standards such as the ISO 9000 series. These standards define a Plan-Do-Check-Act loop, depicted in Figure 6-8. This cycle

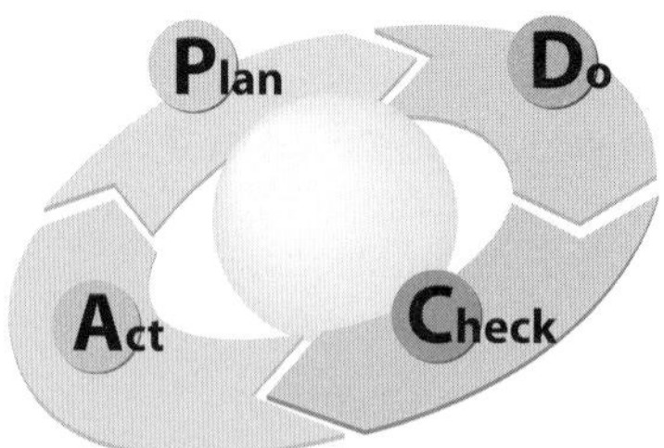

Figure 6-8 The Plan-Do-Check-Act loop

of continuous improvement elegantly captures the essence of most topics we cover in this book. The Plan phase mostly maps to the material in Chapter 1. This phase is the foundation of everything else we do in an ISMS, because it determines our goals and drives our policies. The Do phase of the loop is covered in a variety of places, but is the focal point of Chapter 7. The Check phase is the main topic of most of this chapter. Lastly, the Act phase is what we formally do in the management review. We take all the information derived from the preceding stages and decide whether we need to adjust our goals, standards, or policies in order to continuously improve our posture.

The management review, unsurprisingly, looks at the big picture in order to help set the strategy moving forward. For this reason, a well-run review will not be drawn into detailed discussions on very specific technical topics. Instead, it will take a holistic view of the organization and make strategic decisions, which is the primary reason why the management review must include all the key decision makers in the organization. This top-level involvement is what gives our ISMS legitimacy and power.

When communicating with senior executives, it is important to speak the language of the business and to do so in a succinct manner. We already discussed this style of communication when we covered reports in the previous section, but it bears repeating here. If we are not able to clearly and quickly get the point across to senior leaders on the first try, we may not get another chance to do so.

Before the Management Review

The management review should happen periodically. The more immature the management system and/or the organization, the more frequent these reviews should take place. Obviously, the availability of the key leaders will be a limiting factor during scheduling. This periodicity helps ensure that the entire organization is able to develop an operational rhythm that feeds the senior-level decision-making process. Absent this regularity, the reviews risk becoming reactive rather than proactive.

The frequency of the meetings should also be synchronized with the length of time required to implement the decisions of the preceding review. If, for instance, the leaders decided to implement sweeping changes that will take a year to develop, integrate, and measure, then having a review before the year is up may not be particularly effective. This is not to say that enough time must lapse to allow every single change to yield measurable results, but if these reviews are conducted too frequently, management won't be able to make decisions that are informed by the results of the previous set of actions.

Reviewing Inputs

The inputs to the management review come from a variety of sources. A key input is the results of relevant audits, both external and internal. These are, in part, the reports described earlier in the chapter. In addition to making the audit reports available for review, it is also necessary to produce executive summaries that describe the key findings, the impact to the organization, and the recommended changes (if any). Remember to write these summaries in business language.

Another important input to the review is the list of open issues and action items from the previous management review. Ideally, all these issues have been addressed and all actions have been completed and verified. If that is not the case, it is important to highlight whatever issues (e.g., resources, regulations, changes in the landscape) prevented them from being closed. Senior leaders normally don't like surprises (particularly unpleasant ones), so it might be wise to warn them of any unfinished business before the review is formally convened.

In addition to the feedback from auditors and action officers, customer feedback is an important input to the management review. Virtually every organization has customers, and they are normally the reason for the organization to exist in the first place. Their satisfaction, or lack thereof, is crucial to the organization's success. This chapter already mentioned real user monitoring (RUM) as one way of measuring their interactions with our information systems. Organizations are also increasingly relying on social media analysis to measure customer sentiments with regard to the organization in general and specific issues. Finally, we can use questionnaires or surveys, although these tend to have a number of challenges, including very low response rates and negative bias among respondents.

The final inputs to the management review are the recommendations for improvement based on all the other inputs. This is really the crux of the review. (While it is technically possible for a review to include no substantive change recommendations, it would be extremely unusual since it would mean that the ISMS team cannot think of any way to improve the organizational posture.) The ISMS team will present proposed high-level changes that require the approval and/or support of the senior leaders. This is not the place to discuss low-level tactical changes; we can take care of those ourselves. Instead, we would want to ask for changes to key policies or additional resources. These recommendations must logically follow from the other inputs that have been presented to the review panel.

In setting the stage for the senior leaders' decision-making process, it is often useful to present them with a range of options. Many security professionals typically offer three to five choices, depending on the complexity of the issues. For instance, one option could be "do nothing," which describes what happens if no changes are made. At the other end of the spectrum, we could state an option that amounts to the solid-gold approach in which we pull out all the stops and make bold and perhaps costly changes that are all but guaranteed to take care of the problems. In between, we would offer one to three other choices with various levels of risk, resource requirements, and business appeal.

When we present the options, we should also present objective evaluative criteria for management to consider. A criterion that is almost always required in the presentation is the monetary cost of the change. This factor should be the life-cycle cost of the option, not just the cost of implementation. It is a common mistake to overlook the maintenance costs over the life of the system/process, disregarding the fact that these costs are often much greater than the acquisition price tag. Other factors you may want to consider presenting are risk, impact on existing systems or processes, training requirements, and complexity. But whatever evaluative factors you choose, you should apply them to each of the options in order to assess which is the best one.

Management Actions

The senior leadership considers all the inputs; typically asks some pretty pointed questions; and then decides to approve, reject, or defer the recommendations. The amount of debate or discussion at this point is typically an indicator of how effective the ISMS team was at presenting sound arguments for changes that are well nested within (and supportive of) the business processes. Obviously, the leadership's decisions are the ultimate testament to how convincing the ISMS team's arguments were.

Typically, senior management will decide to either accept the recommendation in its entirety, accept it with specific changes, reject the recommendation, or send the ISMS team back to either get more supporting data or redesign the options. Regardless of the outcome, there will likely be a list of deliverables for the next management review that will have to be addressed. It is a good idea to conclude the management review with a review of open and action items, who will address them, and when they are each due. These all become inputs to the next management review in a cycle that continues indefinitely.

Summary

Evaluating our security posture is an iterative and continuous process. In this chapter, we discussed a variety of techniques that are helpful in determining how well we are mitigating risks with our technical and administrative controls. Whether you are doing your own audits or validating the audit plans provided by a third party, you should now know what to look for and how to evaluate proposals.

Along the way, we also covered some specific threats and opportunities that should play a role in your assessment plan. It is important to keep in mind that everything we covered in this chapter is grounded in the risk management discussed in Chapter 1. If we do not keep in mind the specific threats and risks with which our organization is concerned, then it is very difficult to properly address them. Equally important is our ability to communicate our results and recommendations to our senior leaders in order to gain their support in implementing whatever changes are needed to continuously improve our security posture.

Quick Tips

- An audit is a systematic assessment of the security controls of an information system.
- Setting a clear set of goals is probably the most important step of planning a security audit.
- Internal audits benefit from the auditors' familiarity with the systems, but may be hindered by a lack of exposure to how others attack and defend systems.
- External audits typically bring a much broader background of experience that can provide fresh insights, but can be expensive.

- Service organizations are those that provide outsourcing services that can directly impact the control environment of a company's customers.
- An SAS 70 audit is carried out by a third party to assess the internal controls of a service organization.
- Service Organization Controls (SOC) are auditing standards for service organizations.
- SOC 1 pertains to financial controls.
- SOC 2 is a very detailed report that pertains to trust services (Security, Availability, Confidentiality, Process Integrity, and Privacy) and is intended for management and regulators.
- SOC 3 also pertains to trust services (Security, Availability, Confidentiality, Process Integrity, and Privacy), but is a less detailed report that is intended for publication for the general public.
- A vulnerability test is an examination of a system for the purpose of identifying, defining, and ranking its vulnerabilities.
- Black box testing treats the system being tested as completely opaque.
- White box testing affords the auditor complete knowledge of the inner workings of the system even before the first scan is performed.
- Gray box testing gives the auditor some, but not all, information about the internal workings of the system.
- Penetration testing is the process of simulating attacks on a network and its systems at the request of the owner.
- A blind test is one in which the assessors only have publicly available data to work with and the network security staff is aware that the testing will occur.
- A double-blind test (stealth assessment) is a blind test in which the network security staff is not notified that testing will occur.
- War dialing allows attackers and administrators to dial large blocks of phone numbers in search of available modems.
- A log review is the examination of system log files to detect security events or to verify the effectiveness of security controls.
- Synthetic transactions are scripted events that mimic the behaviors of real users and allow security professionals to systematically test the performance of critical services.
- A misuse case is a use case that includes threat actors and the tasks they want to perform on the system.
- A code review is a systematic examination of the instructions that comprise a piece of software, performed by someone other than the author of that code.

- Interface testing is the systematic evaluation of a given set of exchange points for data between systems and/or users.
- Administrative controls are implemented primarily through policies or procedures.
- Privileged user accounts pose significant risk to the organization and should be carefully managed and controlled.
- User accounts should be promptly suspended whenever the user departs the organization permanently or for an extended period.
- Data backups should not be considered reliable unless they have been verified to be usable to restore data.
- A business continuity plan (BCP) ensures that the critical business processes of an organization remain uninterrupted or are quickly restored after a serious event.
- A disaster recovery plan (DRP) ensures that the information systems supporting critical business processes remain operational or are quickly restored in the event of a disaster.
- The BCP and DRP both need to be evaluated regularly to ensure they remain effective in the face of environmental changes in and around the organization.
- Security training is the process of teaching a skill or set of skills that will allow people to better perform specific functions.
- Security awareness training is the process of exposing people to security issues so that they may be able to recognize them and better respond to them.
- Social engineering, in the context of information security, is the process of manipulating individuals so that they perform actions that violate security protocols.
- Phishing is social engineering conducted through a digital communication.
- A drive-by download is an automatic attack that is triggered simply by visiting a malicious website.
- Key performance indicators (KPIs) measure the effectiveness of an organization in performing a given task at a given point in time.
- Key risk indicators (KRIs) measure the risk inherent in performing a given action or set of actions.
- Reports must be written with a specific audience in mind if they are to be effective.
- A management review is a formal meeting in which senior organizational leaders determine whether the information security management systems are effectively accomplishing their goals.

Questions

Please remember that these questions are formatted and asked in a certain way for a reason. Keep in mind that the CISSP exam is asking questions at a conceptual level. Questions may not always have the perfect answer, and the candidate is advised against always looking for the perfect answer. Instead, the candidate should look for the best answer in the list.

1. Internal audits are the preferred approach when which of the following is true?
   - **A.** The organization lacks the organic expertise to conduct them.
   - **B.** Regulatory requirements dictate the use of a third-party auditor.
   - **C.** The budget for security testing is limited or nonexistent.
   - **D.** There is concern over the spillage of proprietary or confidential information.
2. All of the following are steps in the security audit process *except* which one?
   - **A.** Document the results.
   - **B.** Convene a management review.
   - **C.** Involve the right business unit leaders.
   - **D.** Determine the scope.
3. Which of the following is an advantage of using third-party auditors?
   - **A.** They may have knowledge that an organization wouldn't otherwise be able to leverage.
   - **B.** Their cost.
   - **C.** The requirement for NDAs and supervision.
   - **D.** Their use of automated scanners and reports.
4. Choose the term that describes an audit report that covers the information security controls of a service organization and is intended for public release.
   - **A.** SOC 1
   - **B.** SOC 2
   - **C.** SOC 3
   - **D.** Both B and C.
5. Which of the following is true of a vulnerability assessment?
   - **A.** The aim is to identify as many vulnerabilities as possible.
   - **B.** It is not concerned with the effects of the assessment on other systems.
   - **C.** It is a predictive test aimed at assessing the future performance of a system.
   - **D.** Ideally the assessment is fully automated with no human involvement.

6. An assessment whose goal is to assess the susceptibility of an organization to social engineering attacks is best classified as
   A. Physical testing
   B. Personnel testing
   C. Vulnerability testing
   D. Network testing
7. Which of the following is an assessment that affords the auditor detailed knowledge of the system's architecture before conducting the test?
   A. White box testing
   B. Gray box testing
   C. Black box testing
   D. Zero knowledge testing
8. Vulnerability scans normally involve all of the following *except* which one?
   A. The identification of active hosts on the network
   B. The identification of malware on all hosts
   C. The identification of misconfigured settings
   D. The identification of operating systems
9. Security event logs can best be protected from tampering by which one of the following?
   A. Encrypting the contents using asymmetric key encryption
   B. Ensuring every user has administrative rights on their own workstations
   C. Using remote logging over simplex communications media
   D. Storing the event logs on DVD-RW
10. Synthetic transactions are best described as
   A. Real user monitoring (RUM)
   B. Transactions that fall outside the normal purpose of a system
   C. Transactions that are synthesized from multiple users' interactions with the system
   D. A way to test the behavior and performance of critical services

11. Suppose you want to study the actions an adversary may attempt against your system and test the effectiveness of the controls you have emplaced to mitigate the associated risks. Which of the following approaches would best allow you to accomplish this goal?
    - **A.** Misuse case testing
    - **B.** Use case testing
    - **C.** Real user monitoring (RUM)
    - **D.** Fuzzing
12. Code reviews include all the following *except* which one?
    - **A.** Ensuring the code conforms to applicable coding standards
    - **B.** Discussing bugs, design issues, and anything else that comes up about the code
    - **C.** Agreeing on a "disposition" for the code
    - **D.** Fuzzing the code
13. Interface testing could involve which of the following?
    - **A.** The application programming interface (API)
    - **B.** The graphical user interface (GUI)
    - **C.** Both of the above
    - **D.** None of the above
14. One of the actions that attackers typically attempt after compromising a system is to acquire the ability to mimic a normal privileged user. What is one way in which they may accomplish this?
    - **A.** Rebooting the compromised host
    - **B.** Exporting the password hash table
    - **C.** Pivoting from the compromised host to another target
    - **D.** Adding a privileged user account
15. Which of the following is not normally an element of user accounts management audits?
    - **A.** Password hashing
    - **B.** Signed AUPs
    - **C.** Privileged accounts
    - **D.** Suspended accounts

16. How might one test adherence to the user accounts policy?
    A. User self-reporting
    B. Penetration testing
    C. Management review
    D. User records auditing
17. Which operating systems allows users to temporarily elevate their privileges in order to launch an application at a higher privilege level?
    A. All major desktop operating systems
    B. Recent versions of Windows
    C. Linux and Windows
    D. Recent versions of Mac OS X
18. All of the following are normally legitimate reasons to suspend rather than delete user accounts *except* which one?
    A. Regulatory compliance
    B. Protection of the user's privacy
    C. Investigation of a subsequently discovered event
    D. Data retention policy
19. Data backup verification efforts should
    A. Have the smallest scope possible
    B. Be based on the threats to the organization
    C. Maximize impact on business
    D. Focus on user data
20. Why would an organization need to periodically test disaster recovery and business continuity plans if they've already been shown to work?
    A. Environmental changes may render them ineffective over time.
    B. It has low confidence in the abilities of the testers.
    C. To appease senior leadership.
    D. Resources may not be available in the future to test again.
21. All of the following are types of tests for disaster recovery and business continuity plans *except* which one?
    A. Structured walk-through test
    B. Simulation test
    C. Null hypothesis test
    D. Full-interruption test

22. What is the difference between security training and security awareness training?
    A. Security training is focused on skills, while security awareness training is focused on recognizing and responding to issues.
    B. Security training must be performed, while security awareness training is an aspirational goal.
    C. Security awareness training is focused on security personnel, while security training is geared toward all users.
    D. There is no difference. These terms refer to the same process.
23. Which of the following is *not* a form of social engineering?
    A. Pretexting
    B. Fishing
    C. Whaling
    D. Blackmailing
24. What is a key performance indicator (KPI)?
    A. Any attribute of the ISMS that can be described as a value
    B. The value of a factor at a particular point in time
    C. A derived value that is generated by comparing multiple measurements against each other or against a baseline
    D. An interpretation of one or more metrics that describes the effectiveness of the ISMS
25. Which of the following is true about key risk indicators (KRIs)?
    A. They tell managers where an organization stands with regard to its goals.
    B. They are inputs to the calculation of single loss expectancy (SLE).
    C. They tell managers where an organization stands with regard to its risk appetite.
    D. An interpretation of one or more metrics that describes the effectiveness of the ISMS.
26. Which of the following is true of management reviews?
    A. They happen periodically and include results of audits as a key input.
    B. They happen in an ad hoc manner as the needs of the organization dictate.
    C. They are normally conducted by mid-level managers, but their reports are presented to the key business leaders.
    D. They are focused on assessing the management of the information systems.

Answers

1. **C.** Third-party auditors are almost always fairly expensive, so if the organization's budget does not support their use, it may be necessary to use internal assets to conduct the audit.
2. **B.** The management review is not a part of any audit. Instead, this review typically uses the results of one or more audits in order to make strategic decisions.
3. **A.** Because they perform audits in multiple other organizations, and since their knowledge is constantly refreshed, third-party auditors almost always have knowledge and insights that would otherwise be unavailable to the organization.
4. **C.** The SOC 2 and SOC 3 reports are similar in scope, but the SOC 3 report is more general and intended for wider distribution than the SOC 2, which is more detailed.
5. **A.** One of the principal goals of a vulnerability assessment is to identify as many security flaws as possible within a given system, while being careful not to disrupt other systems.
6. **B.** Social engineering is focused on people, so personnel testing is the best answer.
7. **A.** White box testing gives the tester detailed information about the internal workings of the system under study. Gray box testing provides *some* information, so it is not the best answer to this question.
8. **B.** Vulnerability testing does not normally include scanning hosts for malware. Instead, it focuses on finding flaws that malware could potentially exploit.
9. **C.** Using a remote logging host raises the bar for attackers because if they are able to compromise one host, they would have to compromise the remote logger in order to tamper with the logs. The use of a simplex channel further hinders the attackers.
10. **D.** Synthetic transactions are those that simulate the behavior of real users, but are not the result of real user interactions with the system. They allow an organization to ensure that services are behaving properly without having to rely on user complaints to detect problems.
11. **A.** Misuse case testing allows us to document both an adversary's desired actions on a system and the controls that are meant to thwart that adversary. It is similar to developing use cases, but with a malicious user's actions in mind instead of those of legitimate users.
12. **D.** Fuzzing is a technique for detecting flaws in the code by bombarding it with massive amounts of random data. This is not part of a code review, which focuses on analyzing the source code, not its response to random data.

13. **C.** Interface testing covers the exchange points within different components of the system. The API is the exchange point between the system and the libraries it leverages, while the GUI is the exchange point between the system and the users. Testing either of these would constitute an interface test.
14. **D.** After compromising a host, attackers may attempt a number of actions, but will typically attempt to blend in by acquiring administrative privileges. They can do this by either compromising a privileged account, adding a privileged account, or elevating the privileges of the account they compromised.
15. **A.** Password hashing (covered in Chapter 5) is a very common approach to protecting user account passwords, but varies from one platform to the next. It is almost always controlled by the system itself and would normally not be part of the user accounts management audit.
16. **D.** A records audit can verify that users have acknowledged acceptance of the policy, that accounts of departed users have been suspended, that users have the appropriate access to information, and many other aspects of the policy.
17. **A.** All major operating systems allow for the temporary elevation of user privileges, but Mac OS X and some versions of Linux require the user to do so from a terminal window.
18. **B.** If the organization was intentionally attempting to protect the privacy of its users, suspension of the account would be a poor privacy measure compared to outright deletion.
19. **B.** The verification of data backups should focus on assessing the organization's ability to respond to the threats identified during the threat modeling and risk management processes. If the organization can't respond to these threats, then its backups may be useless.
20. **A.** The best reason to periodically test DRPs and BCPs is to assess the effects of internal or external environment changes on them. Changes to these plans are inevitable and often frequently required, which puts an organization at risk of unacceptably long system outages if it doesn't periodically test its DRPs/BCPs.
21. **C.** The null hypothesis test is used in statistical analysis. Though it could conceivably be used to analyze the results of a DRP/BCP test, it would not be in and of itself a feasible way to test these plans.
22. **A.** Security training is the process of teaching a skill or set of skills that will allow people to better perform specific functions. Security awareness training, on the other hand, is the process of exposing people to security issues so that they may be able to recognize them and better respond to them. Security training is typically provided to security personnel, while security awareness training should be provided to every member of the organization.
23. **B.** The correct term for social engineering conducted over digital communications means is phishing, not fishing.

24. **D.** Key performance indicators (KPIs) are used by managers to assess the effectiveness of any critical business function. In the context of security, KPIs are based on metrics and are meant to answer the following question: Are we managing our information security well enough?
25. **C.** Key risk indicators (KRIs) allow managers to understand when specific activities of the organization are moving it toward a higher level of risk. They are useful to understanding changes and managing the overall risk.
26. **A.** Management reviews work best when they are regularly scheduled events involving the key organizational leaders, because this allows the subordinate leaders to plan and conduct the assessments, such as audits that provide inputs to the review.

CHAPTER 7

Security Operations

This chapter presents the following:

- Operations department responsibilities
- Administrative management responsibilities
- Assurance levels
- Configuration management
- Physical security
- Secure resource provisioning
- Network and resource availability
- Preventative measures
- Patch management
- Incident management
- Recovery strategies
- Disaster recovery
- Business continuity planning and exercises
- Liability
- Investigations
- Personal safety concerns

There are two types of companies in the world: those that know they've been hacked, and those that don't.

–Misha Glenny

Security operations pertains to everything that takes place to keep networks, computer systems, applications, and environments up and running in a secure and protected manner. It consists of ensuring that people, applications, and servers have the proper access privileges to only the resources to which they are entitled and that oversight is implemented via monitoring, auditing, and reporting controls. Operations take place after the network is developed and implemented. This includes the continual maintenance of an environment and the activities that should take place on a day-to-day or week-to-week basis. These activities are routine in nature and enable the network and individual computer systems to continue running correctly and securely.

Networks and computing environments are evolving entities; just because they are secure one week does not mean they are still secure three weeks later. Many companies pay security consultants to come in and advise them on how to improve their infrastructure, policies, and procedures. A company can then spend thousands or even hundreds of thousands of dollars to implement the consultant's suggestions and install properly configured firewalls, intrusion detection systems (IDSs), antivirus software, and patch management systems. However, if the IDS and antivirus software do not continually have updated signatures, if the systems are not continually patched and monitored, if firewalls and devices are not tested for vulnerabilities, or if new software is added to the network and not added to the operations plan, then the company can easily slip back into an insecure and dangerous place. This can happen if the company does not keep its operational security tasks up-to-date.

Even if you take great care to ensure you are watching your perimeters (both virtual and physical) and ensuring that you provision new services and retire unneeded ones in a secure manner, odds are that some threat source will be able to compromise your information systems. What then? Security operations also involves the detection, containment, eradication, and recovery that is required to ensure the continuity of business operations. It may also require addressing liability and compliance issues. In short, security operations encompasses all the activities required to ensure the security of information systems. It is the culmination of most of what we've discussed in the book thus far.

Most of the necessary operational security issues have been addressed in earlier chapters. They were integrated with related topics and not necessarily pointed out as actual operational security issues. So instead of repeating what has already been stated, this chapter reviews and points out the operational security topics that are important for organizations and CISSP candidates.

The Role of the Operations Department

The continual effort to make sure the correct policies, procedures, standards, and guidelines are in place and being followed is an important piece of the *due care* and *due diligence* efforts that companies need to perform. Due care and due diligence are comparable to the "prudent person" concept. A prudent person is seen as responsible, careful, cautious, and practical, and a company practicing due care and due diligence is seen in the same light. The right steps need to be taken to achieve the necessary level of security, while balancing ease of use, compliance with regulatory requirements, and cost constraints. It takes continued effort and discipline to retain the proper level of security. Security operations is all about ensuring that people, applications, equipment, and the overall environment are properly and adequately secured.

Although operational security is the practice of continual maintenance to keep an environment running at a necessary security level, liability and legal responsibilities also exist when performing these tasks. Companies, and senior executives at those companies, often have legal obligations to ensure that resources are protected, safety measures are in place, and security mechanisms are tested to guarantee they are actually providing the

necessary level of protection. If these operational security responsibilities are not fulfilled, the company may have more than attackers to be concerned about.

An organization must consider many threats, including disclosure of confidential data, theft of assets, corruption of data, interruption of services, and destruction of the physical or logical environment. It is important to identify systems and operations that are sensitive (meaning they need to be protected from disclosure) and critical (meaning they must remain available at all times). These issues exist within a context of legal, regulatory, and ethical responsibilities of companies when it comes to security.

It is also important to note that while organizations have a significant portion of their operations activities tied to computing resources, they may also rely on physical resources to make things work, including paper documents and data stored on microfilm, tapes, and other removable media. A large part of operational security includes ensuring that the physical and environmental concerns are adequately addressed, such as temperature and humidity controls, media reuse, disposal, and destruction of media containing sensitive information.

Overall, operational security is about configuration, performance, fault tolerance, security, and accounting and verification management to ensure that proper standards of operations and compliance requirements are met.

Administrative Management

Administrative management is a very important piece of operational security. One aspect of administrative management is dealing with personnel issues. This includes separation of duties and job rotation. The objective of *separation of duties* is to ensure that one person acting alone cannot compromise the company's security in any way. High-risk activities should be broken up into different parts and distributed to different individuals or departments. That way, the company does not need to put a dangerously high level of trust in certain individuals. For fraud to take place, collusion would need to be committed, meaning more than one person would have to be involved in the fraudulent activity. Separation of duties, therefore, is a preventive measure that requires collusion to occur in order for someone to commit an act that is against policy.

Table 7-1 shows many of the common roles within organizations and their corresponding job definitions. Each role needs to have a completed and well-defined job description. Security personnel should use these job descriptions when assigning access rights and permissions in order to ensure that individuals have access only to those resources needed to carry out their tasks.

Table 7-1 contains just a few roles with a few tasks per role. Organizations should create a *complete* list of roles used within their environment, with each role's associated tasks and responsibilities. This should then be used by data owners and security personnel when determining who should have access to specific resources and the type of access.

Separation of duties helps prevent mistakes and minimize conflicts of interest that can take place if one person is performing a task from beginning to end. For instance, a programmer should not be the only one to test her own code. Another person with a different job and agenda should perform functionality and integrity testing on the

Organizational Role	Core Responsibilities
Control Group	Obtains and validates information obtained from analysts, administrators, and users and passes it on to various user groups.
Systems Analyst	Designs data flow of systems based on operational and user requirements.
Application Programmer	Develops and maintains production software.
Help Desk/Support	Resolves end-user and system technical or operations problems.
IT Engineer	Performs the day-to-day operational duties on systems and applications.
Database Administrator	Creates new database tables and manages the database.
Network Administrator	Installs and maintains the local area network/wide area network (LAN/WAN) environment.
Security Administrator	Defines, configures, and maintains the security mechanisms protecting the organization.
Tape Librarian	Receives, records, releases, and protects system and application files backed up on media such as tapes or disks.
Quality Assurance	Can consist of both Quality Assurance (QA) and Quality Control (QC). QA ensures that activities meet the prescribed standards regarding supporting documentation and nomenclature. QC ensures that the activities, services, equipment, and personnel operate within the accepted standards.

Table 7-1 Roles and Associated Tasks

programmer's code, because the programmer may have a focused view of what the program is supposed to accomplish and thus may test only certain functions and input values, and only in certain environments.

Another example of separation of duties is the difference between the functions of a computer user and the functions of a security administrator. There must be clear-cut lines drawn between system administrator duties and computer user duties. These will vary from environment to environment and will depend on the level of security required within the environment. System and security administrators usually have the responsibility of performing backups and recovery procedures, setting permissions, adding and removing users, and developing user profiles. The computer user, on the other hand, may be allowed to install software, set an initial password, alter desktop configurations, and modify certain system parameters. The user should not be able to modify her own security profile, add and remove users globally, or make critical access decisions pertaining to network resources. This would breach the concept of separation of duties.

Job rotation means that, over time, more than one person fulfills the tasks of one position within the company. This enables the company to have more than one person who understands the tasks and responsibilities of a specific job title, which provides backup and redundancy if a person leaves the company or is absent. Job rotation also helps identify fraudulent activities, and therefore can be considered a detective type of control.

If Keith has performed David's position, Keith knows the regular tasks and routines that must be completed to fulfill the responsibilities of that job. Thus, Keith is better able to identify whether David does something out of the ordinary and suspicious.

Least privilege and need to know are also administrative-type controls that should be implemented in an operations environment. *Least privilege* means an individual should have just enough permissions and rights to fulfill his role in the company and no more. If an individual has excessive permissions and rights, it could open the door to abuse of access and put the company at more risk than is necessary. For example, if Dusty is a technical writer for a company, he does not necessarily need to have access to the company's source code. So, the mechanisms that control Dusty's access to resources should not let him access source code. This would properly fulfill operational security controls that are in place to protect resources.

Least privilege and need to know have a symbiotic relationship. Each user should have a need to know about the resources that she is allowed to access. If Mikela does not have a need to know how much the company paid last year in taxes, then her system rights should not include access to these files, which would be an example of exercising least privilege. The use of new identity management software that combines traditional directories; access control systems; and user provisioning within servers, applications, and systems is becoming the norm within organizations. This software provides the capabilities to ensure that only specific access privileges are granted to specific users, and it often includes advanced audit functions that can be used to verify compliance with legal and regulatory directives.

A user's access rights may be a combination of the least-privilege attribute, the user's security clearance, the user's need to know, the sensitivity level of the resource, and the mode in which the computer operates. A system can operate in different modes depending on the sensitivity of the data being processed, the clearance level of the users, and what those users are authorized to do. The security modes of operation describe the conditions under which the system actually functions. These are clearly defined in Chapter 5.

Mandatory vacations are another type of administrative control, though the name may sound a bit odd at first. Chapter 1 touched on reasons to make sure employees take their vacations. Reasons include being able to identify fraudulent activities and enabling job rotation to take place. If an accounting employee has been performing a salami attack by shaving off pennies from multiple accounts and putting the money into his own account, a company would have a better chance of figuring this out if that employee is required to take a vacation for a week or longer. When the employee is on vacation, another employee has to fill in. She might uncover questionable documents and clues of previous activities, or the company may see a change in certain patterns once the employee who is committing fraud is gone for a week or two.

It is best for auditing purposes if the employee takes two contiguous weeks off from work to allow more time for fraudulent evidence to appear. Again, the idea behind mandatory vacations is that, traditionally, those employees who have committed fraud are usually the ones who have resisted going on vacation because of their fear of being found out while away.

Security and Network Personnel

The security administrator should not report to the network administrator because their responsibilities have different focuses. The network administrator is under pressure to ensure high availability and performance of the network and resources and to provide the users with the functionality they request. But many times this focus on performance and user functionality is at the cost of security. Security mechanisms commonly decrease performance in either processing or network transmission because there is more involved: content filtering, virus scanning, intrusion detection prevention, anomaly detection, and so on. Since these are not the areas of focus and responsibility of many network administrators, a conflict of interest could arise. The security administrator should be within a different chain of command from that of the network personnel to ensure that security is not ignored or assigned a lower priority.

The following list lays out tasks that should be carried out by the security administrator, not the network administrator:

- **Implements and maintains security devices and software** Despite some security vendors' claims that their products will provide effective security with "set it and forget it" deployments, security products require monitoring and maintenance in order to provide their full value. Version updates and upgrades may be required when new capabilities become available to combat new threats, and when vulnerabilities are discovered in the security products themselves.
- **Carries out security assessments** As a service to the business that the security administrator is working to secure, a security assessment leverages the knowledge and experience of the security administrator to identify vulnerabilities in the systems, networks, software, and in-house developed products used by a business. These security assessments enable the business to understand the risks it faces and to make sensible business decisions about products and services it considers purchasing, and risk mitigation strategies it chooses to fund versus risks it chooses to accept, transfer (by buying insurance), or avoid (by not taking an action that isn't worth the risk or risk mitigation cost).
- **Creates and maintains user profiles and implements and maintains access control mechanisms** The security administrator puts into practice the security policies of least privilege and oversees accounts that exist, along with the permissions and rights they are assigned.
- **Configures and maintains security labels in mandatory access control (MAC) environments** MAC environments, mostly found in government and military agencies, have security labels set on data objects and subjects. Access decisions are based on comparing the object's classification and the subject's clearance, as covered extensively in Chapter 3. It is the responsibility of the security administrator to oversee the implementation and maintenance of these access controls.
- **Manages password policies** New accounts must be protected from attackers who might know patterns used for passwords, or might find accounts that have been newly created without any passwords, and take over those accounts before

the authorized user accesses the account and changes the password. The security administrator operates automated new-password generators or manually sets new passwords, and then distributes them to the authorized user so attackers cannot guess the initial or default passwords on new accounts, and so new accounts are never left unprotected. Security administrators also ensure strong passwords are implemented and used throughout the organization's information systems, periodically audit those passwords using password crackers or rainbow tables, ensure the passwords are changed periodically in accordance with the password policy, and handle user requests for password resets.

- **Reviews audit logs** While some of the strongest security protections come from preventive controls (such as firewalls that block unauthorized network activity), detective controls such as reviewing audit logs are also required. Suppose the firewall blocked 100,000 unauthorized access attempts yesterday. The only way to know if that's a good thing or an indication of a bad thing is for the security administrator (or automated technology under his control) to review those firewall logs to look for patterns. If those 100,000 blocked attempts were the usual low-level random noise of the Internet, then things are (probably) normal; but if those attempts were advanced and came from a concentrated selection of addresses on the Internet, a more deliberate (and more possibly successful) attack may be underway. The security administrator's review of audit logs detects bad things as they occur and, hopefully, before they cause real damage.

Accountability

Users' access to resources must be limited and properly controlled to ensure that excessive privileges do not provide the opportunity to cause damage to a company and its resources. Users' access attempts and activities while using a resource need to be properly monitored, audited, and logged. The individual user ID needs to be included in the audit logs to enforce individual responsibility. Each user should understand his responsibility when using company resources and be accountable for his actions.

Capturing and monitoring audit logs helps determine if a violation has actually occurred or if system and software reconfiguration is needed to better capture only the activities that fall outside of established boundaries. If user activities were not captured and reviewed, it would be very hard to determine if users have excessive privileges or if there has been unauthorized access.

Auditing needs to take place in a routine manner. Also, someone needs to review audit and log events. If no one routinely looks at the output, there really is no reason to create logs. Audit and function logs often contain too much cryptic or mundane information to be interpreted manually. This is why products and services are available that parse logs for companies and report important findings. Logs should be monitored and reviewed, through either manual or automatic methods, to uncover suspicious activity and to identify an environment that is shifting away from its original baselines. This is how administrators can be warned of many problems before they become too big and out of control.

When monitoring, administrators need to ask certain questions that pertain to the users, their actions, and the current level of security and access:

- *Are users accessing information and performing tasks that are not necessary for their job description?* The answer would indicate whether users' rights and permissions need to be reevaluated and possibly modified.
- *Are repetitive mistakes being made?* The answer would indicate whether users need to have further training.
- *Do too many users have rights and privileges to sensitive or restricted data or resources?* The answer would indicate whether access rights to the data and resources need to be reevaluated, whether the number of individuals accessing them needs to be reduced, and/or whether the extent of their access rights should be modified.

Clipping Levels

Companies can set predefined thresholds for the number of certain types of errors that will be allowed before the activity is considered suspicious. The threshold is a baseline for violation activities that may be normal for a user to commit before alarms are raised. This baseline is referred to as a *clipping level.* Once this clipping level has been exceeded, further violations are recorded for review. The goal of using clipping levels, auditing, and monitoring is to discover problems before major damage occurs and, at times, to be alerted if a possible attack is underway within the network.

Most of the time, IDS software is used to track these activities and behavior patterns, because it would be too overwhelming for an individual to continually monitor stacks of audit logs and properly identify certain activity patterns. Once the clipping level is exceeded, the IDS can notify security personnel or just add this information to the logs, depending on how the IDS software is configured.

NOTE The security controls and mechanisms that are in place must have a degree of inconspicuousness. This enables the user to perform tasks and duties without having to go through extra steps because of the presence of the security controls. Inconspicuousness also prevents the users from knowing too much about the controls, which helps prevent them from figuring out how to circumvent security. If the controls are too obvious, an attacker can figure out how to compromise them more easily.

Assurance Levels

When products are evaluated for the level of trust and assurance they provide, many times operational assurance and life-cycle assurance are part of the evaluation process. *Operational assurance* concentrates on the product's architecture, embedded features, and functionality that enable a customer to continually obtain the necessary level of protection when using the product. Examples of operational assurances examined in the evaluation process are access control mechanisms, the separation of privileged and user program code, auditing and monitoring capabilities, covert channel analysis, and trusted recovery when the product experiences unexpected circumstances.

Life-cycle assurance pertains to how the product was developed and maintained. Each stage of the product's life cycle has standards and expectations it must fulfill before it can be deemed a highly trusted product. Examples of life-cycle assurance standards are design specifications, clipping-level configurations, unit and integration testing, configuration management, and trusted distribution. Vendors looking to achieve one of the higher security ratings for their products will have each of these issues evaluated and tested.

The following sections address several of these types of operational assurance and life-cycle assurance issues, not only as they pertain to evaluation, but also as they pertain to a company's responsibilities once the product is implemented. A product is just a tool for a company to use for functionality and security. It is up to the company to ensure that this functionality and security are continually available through responsible and proactive steps.

Operational Responsibilities

Operational security encompasses safeguards and countermeasures to protect resources, information, and the hardware on which the resources and information reside. The goal of operational security is to reduce the possibility of damage that could result from unauthorized access or disclosure by limiting the opportunities of misuse.

Some organizations may have an actual operations department that is responsible for activities and procedures required to keep the network running smoothly and to keep productivity at a certain level. Other organizations may have a few individuals who are responsible for these things, but no structured department dedicated just to operations. Either way, the people who hold these responsibilities are accountable for certain activities and procedures and must monitor and control specific issues.

Operations within a computing environment may pertain to software, personnel, and hardware, but an operations department often focuses on the hardware and software aspects. Management is responsible for employees' behavior and responsibilities. The people within the operations department are responsible for ensuring that systems are protected and continue to run in a predictable manner.

The operations department usually has the objectives of preventing recurring problems, reducing hardware and software failures to an acceptable level, and reducing the impact of incidents or disruption. This group should investigate any unusual or unexplained occurrences, unscheduled initial program loads, deviations from standards, or other odd or abnormal conditions that take place on the network.

Unusual or Unexplained Occurrences

Networks, and the hardware and software within them, can be complex and dynamic. At times, conditions occur that are at first confusing and possibly unexplainable. It is up to the operations department to investigate these issues, diagnose the problem, and come up with a logical solution.

One example could be a network that has hosts that are continually kicked off the network for no apparent reason. The operations team should conduct controlled troubleshooting to make sure it does not overlook any possible source for the disruption and that it investigates different types of problems. The team may look at connectivity issues between the hosts and the wiring closet, the hubs and switches that control their connectivity, and any possible cabling defects. The team should work methodically until it finds a specific problem. Central monitoring systems and event management solutions can help pinpoint the root cause of problems and save much time and effort in diagnosing problems.

NOTE Event management means that a product is being used to collect various logs throughout the network. The product identifies patterns and potentially malicious activities that a human would most likely miss because of the amount of data in the various logs.

Deviations from Standards

In this instance, "standards" pertains to computing service levels and how they are measured. Each device can have certain standards applied to it: the hours of time to be online, the number of requests that can be processed within a defined period of time, bandwidth usage, performance counters, and more. These standards provide a baseline that is used to determine whether there is a problem with the device. For example, if a device usually accepts approximately 300 requests per minute, but suddenly it is only able to accept 3 per minute, the operations team would need to investigate the deviation from the standard that is usually provided by this device. The device may be failing or under a denial-of-service (DoS) attack, or be subject to legitimate business-use cases that had not been foreseen when the device was first implemented.

Sometimes the standard needs to be recalibrated so it portrays a realistic view of the service level the device can provide. If a server was upgraded from 4 to 16 cores, the memory was quadrupled, the swap file was increased, and three extra hard drives were added, the service level of this server should be reevaluated.

Unscheduled Initial Program Loads (aka Rebooting)

Initial program load (IPL) is a mainframe term for loading the operating system's kernel into the computer's main memory. On a personal computer, booting into the operating system is the equivalent to IPLing. This activity takes place to prepare the computer for user operation. IPLs on workstations are fairly normal at the start or end of a business day (depending on the organization), but should be pretty rare during the workday itself. On servers and appliances, IPLs should almost certainly be scheduled or, at least, intentionally triggered by an authorized person or process.

The operations team should investigate computers that reboot for no reason. In the best case, these are unscheduled reboots caused by well-intentioned personnel who simply failed to coordinate their actions with the operations team. The event could also be the result of faulty configurations, software, or hardware on that system, which should be addressed before it leads to serious damage. Finally, and most troublesome, is the possibility that the reboot was triggered by a successful attacker who may have gained a foothold in that system. As you can see from this short list of causes, these events may start off being investigated by the network operations team and then be handed over to the security operations team if the source appears to be a violation of the system's security.

Configuration Management

Configuration management is the process of establishing and maintaining effective system controls, which is also part of operational security. Within the operating system itself, certain controls must be in place to ensure that instructions are being executed in the correct security context. The system has mechanisms that restrict the execution of certain types of instructions so they can take place only when the operating system is in a privileged or supervisor state. This protects the overall security and state of the system and helps ensure it runs in a stable and predictable manner.

Operational procedures need to be developed that indicate what constitutes the proper operation of a system or resource. This would include a system startup and shutdown sequence, error handling, and restoration from a known good source.

An operating system does not provide direct access to hardware by processes of lower privilege, which are usually processes used by user applications. If a program needs to send instructions to hardware devices, the request is passed off to a process of higher privilege. To execute privileged hardware instructions, a process must be running in a restrictive and protective state. This is an integral part of the operating system's architecture, and the determination of which processes can submit what type of instructions is made based on the operating system's control tables.

Many input/output (I/O) instructions are defined as privileged and can be executed only by the operating system kernel processes. When a user program needs to interact with any I/O activities, it must notify the system's core privileged processes that work at the inner rings of the system. Either these processes (called system services) authorize the user program processes to perform these actions and temporarily increase their privileged state, or the system's processes are used to complete the request on behalf of the user program. The following sections cover important aspects of configuration management dealing specifically with system controls.

Trusted Recovery

When an operating system or application crashes or freezes, it should not put the system in any type of insecure state. The usual reason for a system crash in the first place is that it encountered something it perceived as insecure or did not understand and decided it was safer to freeze, shut down, or reboot than to perform the current activity.

An operating system's response to a type of failure can be classified as one of the following:

- System reboot
- Emergency system restart
- System cold start

A *system reboot* takes place after the system shuts itself down in a controlled manner in response to a kernel failure. If the system finds inconsistent data structures or if there is not enough space in some critical tables, a system reboot may take place. This releases resources and returns the system to a more stable and safe state.

An *emergency system restart* takes place after a system failure happens in an uncontrolled manner. This could be a kernel or media failure caused by lower-privileged user processes attempting to access memory segments that are restricted. The system sees this as an insecure activity that it cannot properly recover from without rebooting. The kernel and user objects could be in an inconsistent state, and data could be lost or corrupted. The system thus goes into a maintenance mode and recovers from the actions taken. Then it is brought back up in a consistent and stable state.

A *system cold start* takes place when an unexpected kernel or media failure happens and the regular recovery procedure cannot recover the system to a more consistent state. The system, kernel, and user objects may remain in an inconsistent state while the system attempts to recover itself, and intervention may be required by the user or administrator to restore the system.

It is important to ensure that the system does not enter an insecure state when it is affected by any of these types of problems, and that it shuts down and recovers properly to a secure and stable state.

After a System Crash

When systems go down (and they will), it is important that the operations personnel know how to troubleshoot and fix the problem. The following are some steps that could be taken:

1. *Enter into single user or safe mode.* When a system cold start takes place, due to the system's inability to automatically recover itself to a secure state, the administrator must be involved. The system either will automatically boot up only so far as a "single user mode" or must be manually booted to a "recovery console." These are modes wherein the systems do not start services for users or the network, file systems typically remain unmounted, and only the local console is accessible. As a result, the administrator must either physically be at the console or have deployed external technology such as secured dial-in/dial-back modems attached to serial console ports or remote KVM (keyboard, video, mouse) switches attached to graphic consoles.
2. *Fix issue and recover files.* In single user mode, the administrator salvages file systems from damage that may have occurred as a result of the unclean, sudden shutdown of the system and then attempts to identify the cause of the shutdown to prevent it from recurring. Sometimes the administrator will also have to roll back or roll forward databases or other applications in single user mode. Other times, these will occur automatically when the administrator brings the system out of single user mode, or will be performed manually by the system administrator before applications and services return to their normal state.

3. *Validate critical files and operations.* If the investigation into the cause of the sudden shutdown suggests corruption has occurred (for example, through software or hardware failure, or user/administrator reconfiguration, or some kind of attack), then the administrator must validate the contents of configuration files and ensure system files (operating system program files, shared library files, possibly application program files, and so on) are consistent with their expected state. Cryptographic checksums of these files, verified by programs such as Tripwire, can perform validations of system files. The administrator must verify the contents of system configuration files against the system documentation.

Security Concerns

When an operating system moves into any type of unstable state, there are always concerns that the system is vulnerable in some fashion. The system needs to be able to protect itself and the sensitive data that it maintains. The following lists just a few of the security issues that should be addressed properly in a trusted recovery process.

- **Protect the bootup sequence (C:, A:, D:)** To ensure that systems recover to a secure state, the design of the system must prevent an attacker from changing the bootup sequence of the system. For example, on a Windows workstation or server, only authorized users should have access to BIOS settings to allow the user to change the order in which bootable devices are checked by the hardware. If the approved boot order is C: (the main hard drive) only, with no other hard drives and no removable devices (for example CD/DVD, or USB) allowed, then the hardware settings must prohibit the user (and the attacker) from changing those device selections and the order in which they are used. If the user or attacker can change the bootable device selections or order and can cause the system to reboot (which is always possible with physical access to a system), they can boot their own media and attack the software and/or data on the system.
- **Do not allow bypassing of writing actions to system logs** Through separation of duties and access controls, system logs and system state files must be preserved against attempts by users/attackers to hide their actions or change the state to which the system will next restart. If any system configuration file can be changed by an unauthorized user, and then the user can find a way to cause the system to restart, the new—possibly insecure—configuration will take effect.
- **Do not allow system forced shutdowns** To reduce the possibility of an unauthorized configuration change taking effect, and to reduce the possibility of denial of service through an inappropriate shutdown, only administrators should have the ability to instruct critical systems to shut down. Obviously, this will not stop attackers who have exploited privileged accounts or escalated their privileges, but it does raise the bar for a significant class of attacks.
- **Do not allow outputs to be rerouted** Diagnostic output from a system can contain sensitive information. The diagnostic log files, including console output, must be protected by access controls from being read by anyone other than authorized administrators. Unauthorized users must not be able to redirect the destination of diagnostic logs and console output.

Input and Output Controls

What is input into an application has a direct correlation to what that application outputs. Thus, input needs to be monitored for errors and suspicious activity. If a checker at a grocery store continually puts in the amount of $1.20 for each prime rib steak customers buy, the store could eventually lose a good amount of money. This activity could be done either by accident, which would require proper retraining, or on purpose, which would require disciplinary actions.

The applications themselves also need to be programmed to only accept certain types of values input into them and to do some type of logic checking about the received input values. If an application requests the user to input a mortgage value of a property and the user enters 25 cents, the application should ask the user for the value again so that wasted time and processing is not done on an erroneous input value. Also, if an application has a field that holds only monetary values, a user should not be able to enter "bob" in the field without the application barking.

All the controls mentioned in the previous sections must be in place and must continue to function in a predictable and secure fashion to ensure that the systems, applications, and the environment as a whole continue to be operational. Let's look at a few more I/O issues that can cause problems if not dealt with properly:

- Data entered into a system should be in the correct format and validated to ensure that it is not malicious.
- Transactions should be *atomic*, meaning that they cannot be interrupted between the input being provided and the generation of the output. (Atomicity protects against a class of attacks called time-of-check/time-of-use, or TOCTOU.)
- Transactions must be timestamped and logged.
- Safeguards should be implemented to ensure output reaches the proper destinations securely:
  - Cryptographic hashes or, better yet, message authentication codes (which are digitally signed hashes) should be used to ensure the integrity of critical files.
  - The output should be clearly labeled to indicate the sensitivity or classification of the data.
  - Once output is created, it must have the proper access controls implemented, no matter what its format (paper, digital, tape).
  - If a report has no information (nothing to report), it should contain "no output."

Some people get confused by the last bullet item. The logical question would be, "If there is nothing to report, why generate a report with no information." Let's say each Friday you send your boss a report outlining that week's security incidents and mitigation steps. One Friday, she receives no report from you. Instead of forcing others to chase you down or, worse yet, assume there was no report (when in fact there was, but it was intercepted or compromised), stating "no output" will assure the recipients that the task was indeed carried out.

Another type of input to a system could be ActiveX components, plug-ins, updated configuration files, or device drivers. It is best if these are cryptographically signed by the trusted authority before distribution. This allows the administrator manually, and/or the system automatically, to validate that the files are from the trusted authority (manufacturer, vendor, supplier) before the files are put into production on a system. All current versions of Apple, Linux, and Microsoft operating systems support code signing, whereby the operating system warns the user if a device driver or other software has not been signed by an entity with a certificate from a trusted certificate authority. Note that the fact that an application installer or device driver is signed does not mean it is safe or reliable—it only means the user has a high degree of assurance of the origin of the software or driver. If the user does not trust the entity (the company or developer) that signed the software or driver, or the software or driver is not signed at all, this should be a red flag that stops the user from using the software or driver until its security and reliability can be confirmed by some other channel.

NOTE Many users routinely disregard warnings concerning unsigned code. Whenever possible, such code should be prohibited by using system policies that cannot be overridden by the users.

System Hardening

A recurring theme in security is that controls may be generally described as being physical, administrative, or technical. It has been said that if unauthorized physical access can be gained to a security-sensitive item, then the security of the item is virtually impossible to ensure. (This is why all data on portable devices should be encrypted.) In other words, "If I can put my hands on the computer, I can own it." Obviously, the data center itself must be physically secured. This could include guards, gates, fences, barbed wire, lights, locked doors, and so on. This creates a strong physical security perimeter around the facilities where valuable information is stored.

Across the street from that data center may be an office building in which hundreds or thousands of employees sit day after day, accessing the valuable information from their desktop PCs, laptops, and handheld devices over a variety of networks. Convergence of data and voice means devices such as telephones may be plugged into this same network infrastructure. In an ideal world, the applications and methods by which the information is accessed would secure the information against any network attack; however, the world is not ideal, and it is the security professional's responsibility to secure valuable information in the real world. Therefore, the physical components that make up those networks through which the valuable information flows also must be secured:

- Wiring closets should be locked.
- Network switches and hubs, when it is not practical to place them in locked wiring closets, should be inside locked cabinets.
- Network ports in public places (for example, kiosk computers and even telephones) should be made physically inaccessible.

Laptops, "thumb drives" (USB removable storage devices), portable hard drives, mobile devices, and even camera memory cards all can contain large amounts of information, some of it sensitive and valuable. Users must know where these devices are at all times, and store them securely when not actively in use. Laptops disappear from airport security checkpoints; thumb drives are tiny and get left behind and forgotten; and mobile devices are stolen every day. So if physical security is in place, do we really still need technical security? Yes.

A best practice for managing and securing workstations is to develop a standard hardened image, sometimes called a Gold Master (GM). To build a GM, you start by determining which applications and services are needed by all users of that system image. You then develop secure configurations for all software, and ensure that they still provide all required user functionality and interoperability with the rest of the network. Next, you subject the image to thorough vulnerability scanning and, ideally, penetration testing. Finally, you roll out the image by cloning it onto the hard drives of all your users' workstations. As changes to this baseline are subsequently required (for instance, because a new application is needed in the organization), you go back to step one and start building a new version of the GM all over again.

An application that is not installed, or a system service that is not enabled, cannot be attacked. Even a disabled system service may include vulnerable components that an advanced attack could leverage, so it is better for unnecessary components to not exist at all in the environment. Those components that cannot be left off of a system at installation time, and that cannot be practically removed due to the degree of integration into a system, should be disabled so as to make them impractical to re-enable by anyone except an authorized system administrator. Every installed application, and especially every operating service, must be part of the overall configuration management database so vulnerabilities in these components may be tracked.

Components that can be neither left off nor disabled must be configured to the most conservative practical setting that still allows the system to operate efficiently for those business purposes that require the component's presence in the system. Database engines, for example, should run as an unprivileged user, rather than as root or SYSTEM. If a system will run multiple application services, each one should run under its own least-privileged user ID so a compromise to one service on the system does not grant access to the other services on the system. Just as totally unnecessary services should be left off of a system, unnecessary parts of a single service should be left uninstalled if possible, and disabled otherwise.

TIP Locked-down systems are referred to as bastion hosts.

Licensing Issues

Companies have the ethical obligation to use only legitimately purchased software applications. Software makers and their industry representation groups such as the Business Software Alliance (BSA) use aggressive tactics to target companies that use pirated (illegal) copies of software.

Companies are responsible for ensuring that software in the corporate environment is not pirated, and that the licenses (that is, license counts) are being abided by. An operations or configuration management department is often where this capability is located in a company. Automated asset management systems, or more general system management systems, may be able to report on the software installed throughout an environment, including a count of installations of each. These counts should be compared regularly (perhaps quarterly) against the inventory of licensed applications and counts of licenses purchased for each application. Applications that are found in the environment and for which no license is known to have been purchased by the company, or applications found in excess of the number of licenses known to have been purchased, should be investigated. When applications are found in the environment for which the authorized change control and supply chain processes were not followed, they need to be brought under control, and the business area that acquired the application outside of the approved processes must be educated as to the legal and information security risks their actions may pose to the company. Many times, the business unit manager would need to sign a document indicating he understands this risk and is personally accepting it.

Applications for which no valid business need can be found should be removed, and the person who installed them should be educated and warned that future such actions may result in more severe consequences—like termination. This may sound extreme, but installing pirated software is not only an ethical violation, but also both a liability risk and a potential vector for introducing malware. Organizations that use or tolerate unlicensed products are sometimes turned in by disgruntled employees as an act of revenge.

Companies should have an acceptable use policy (AUP), which indicates what software users can install and informs users that the environment will be surveyed from time to time to verify compliance. Technical controls should be emplaced to prevent unauthorized users from being able to install unauthorized software in the environment.

Remote Access Security

Remote access is a major component of normal operations, and a great enabler of organizational resilience in the face of certain types of disasters. If a regional disaster makes it impractical for large numbers of employees to commute to their usual work site, but the data center—or a remote backup data center—remains operational, remote access to computer resources can allow many functions of a company to continue almost as usual. Remote access can also be a way to reduce normal operational costs by reducing the amount of office space that must be owned or rented, furnished, cleaned, cooled and heated, and provided with parking, since employees will instead be working from home. Remote access may also be the only way to enable a mobile workforce, such as traveling salespeople, who need access to company information while in several different cities each week to meet with current and potential customers.

As with all things that enable business and bring value, remote access also brings risks. Is the person logging in remotely who he claims to be? Is someone physically or electronically looking over his shoulder, or tapping the communication line? Is the client device from which he is performing the remote access in a secure configuration, or has it been compromised by spyware, Trojan horses, and other malicious code?

This has been a thorn in the side of security groups and operation departments for basically every company. It is dangerous to allow computers to be able to directly connect to the corporate network without knowing if they are properly patched, if the virus signatures are updated, if they are infected with malware, and so on. This has been a direct channel used by many attackers to get to the heart of an organization's environment. Because of this needed protection, vendors have been developing technology to quarantine systems and ensure they are properly secured before allowing them access to corporate assets.

Remote Systems Administration

To gain the benefits of remote access without taking on unacceptable risks, remote administration needs to take place securely. The following are just a few of the guidelines to use:

- For best security, require a virtual private network (VPN) connection protected by two-factor authentication for any internal system access from an external (e.g., Internet) host.
- Commands and data should not take place in cleartext (that is, they should be encrypted), even if using a VPN to remotely connect to the network. For example, Secure Shell (SSH) should be used.
- Strong authentication should be in place for any administration activities.
- Truly critical systems should be administered locally instead of remotely.
- Only a small number of administrators should be able to carry out this remote functionality.

Physical Security

Just as important as remote access is local access, for which the first line of defense is perimeter control at the site location to prevent unauthorized access to the facility. As any other defensive technique, physical security should be implemented by using a layered approach. For example, before an intruder can get to the written recipe for your company's secret barbeque sauce, she will need to climb or cut a fence, slip by a security guard, pick a door lock, circumvent a biometric access control reader that protects access to an internal room, and then break into the safe that holds the recipe. The idea is that if an attacker breaks through one control layer, there will be others in her way before she can obtain the company's crown jewels.

NOTE It is also important to have a diversity of controls. For example, if one key works on four different door locks, the intruder has to obtain only one key. Each entry should have its own individual key or authentication combination.

This defense model should work in two main modes: one mode during normal facility operations and another mode during the time the facility is closed. When the facility is closed, all doors should be locked with monitoring mechanisms in strategic positions to alert security personnel of suspicious activity. When the facility is in operation, security gets more complicated because authorized individuals need to be distinguished from unauthorized individuals. Perimeter security deals with facility and personnel access controls, external boundary protection mechanisms, intrusion detection, and corrective actions. The following sections describe the elements that make up these categories.

Facility Access Control

Access control needs to be enforced through physical and technical components when it comes to physical security. Physical access controls use mechanisms to identify individuals who are attempting to enter a facility or area. They make sure the right individuals get in and the wrong individuals stay out, and provide an audit trail of these actions. Having personnel within sensitive areas is one of the best security controls because they can personally detect suspicious behavior. However, they need to be trained on what activity is considered suspicious and how to report such activity.

Before a company can put into place the proper protection mechanisms, it needs to conduct a detailed review to identify which individuals should be allowed into what areas. Access control points can be identified and classified as external, main, and secondary entrances. Personnel should enter and exit through a specific entry, deliveries should be made to a different entry, and sensitive areas should be restricted. Figure 7-1 illustrates the different types of access control points into a facility. After a company has identified and classified the access control points, the next step is to determine how to protect them.

Locks

Locks are inexpensive access control mechanisms that are widely accepted and used. They are considered *delaying* devices to intruders. The longer it takes to break or pick a lock, the longer a security guard or police officer has to arrive on the scene if the intruder has been detected. Almost any type of a door can be equipped with a lock, but keys can be easily lost and duplicated, and locks can be picked or broken. If a company depends solely on a lock-and-key mechanism for protection, an individual who has the key can come and go as he likes without control and can remove items from the premises without detection. Locks should be used as part of the protection scheme, but should not be the sole protection scheme.

Locks vary in functionality. Padlocks can be used on chained fences, preset locks are usually used on doors, and programmable locks (requiring a combination to unlock) are used on doors or vaults. Locks come in all types and sizes. It is important to have the right type of lock so it provides the correct level of protection.

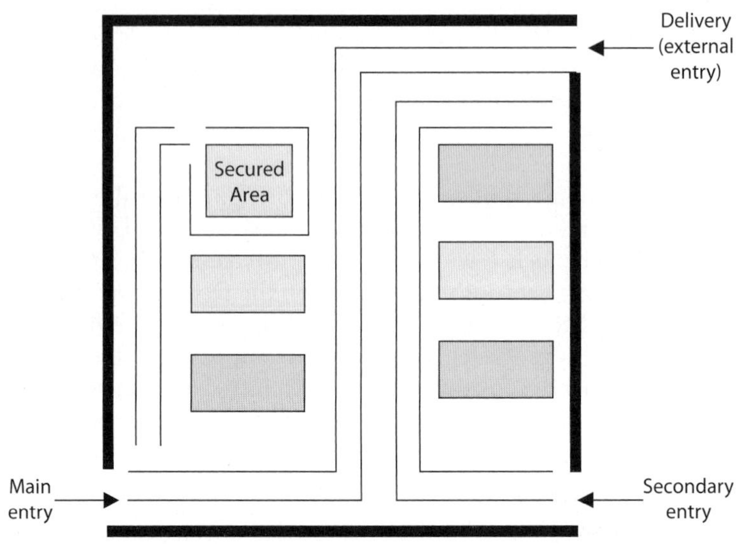

Figure 7-1 Access control points should be identified, marked, and monitored properly.

To the curious mind or a determined thief, a lock can be considered a little puzzle to solve, not a deterrent. In other words, locks may be merely a challenge, not necessarily something to stand in the way of malicious activities. Thus, you need to make the challenge difficult, through the complexity, strength, and quality of the locking mechanisms.

NOTE The delay time provided by the lock should match the penetration resistance of the surrounding components (door, door frame, hinges). A smart thief takes the path of least resistance, which may be to pick the lock, remove the pins from the hinges, or just kick down the door.

Mechanical Locks Two main types of mechanical locks are available: the warded lock and the tumbler lock. The *warded lock* is the basic padlock, as shown in Figure 7-2. It has a spring-loaded bolt with a notch cut in it. The key fits into this notch and slides the bolt from the locked to the unlocked position. The lock has wards in it, which are metal projections around the keyhole, as shown in Figure 7-3. The correct key for a specific warded lock has notches in it that fit in these projections and a notch to slide the bolt back and forth. These are the cheapest locks, because of their lack of any real sophistication, and are also the easiest to pick.

The *tumbler lock* has more pieces and parts than a ward lock. As shown in Figure 7-4, the key fits into a cylinder, which raises the lock metal pieces to the correct height so the bolt can slide to the locked or unlocked position. Once all of the metal pieces are at the correct level, the internal bolt can be turned. The proper key has the required size and sequences of notches to move these metal pieces into their correct position.

Figure 7-2
A warded lock

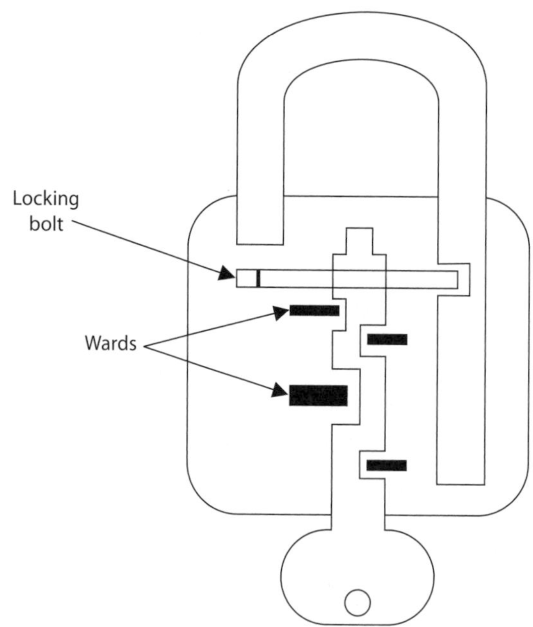

Figure 7-3
A key fits into a notch to turn the bolt to unlock the lock.

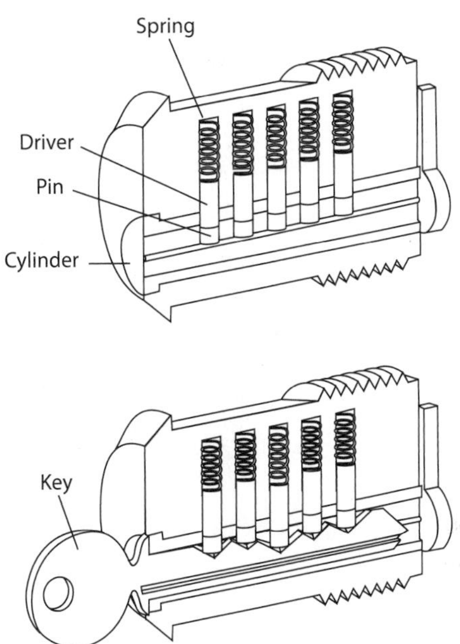

Figure 7-4 Tumbler lock

The three types of tumbler locks are the pin tumbler, wafer tumbler, and lever tumbler. The *pin tumbler* lock, shown in Figure 7-4, is the most commonly used tumbler lock. The key has to have just the right grooves to put all the spring-loaded pins in the right position so the lock can be locked or unlocked.

Wafer tumbler locks (also called disc tumbler locks) are the small, round locks you usually see on file cabinets. They use flat discs (wafers) instead of pins inside the locks. They often are used as car and desk locks. This type of lock does not provide much protection because it can be easily circumvented.

NOTE Some locks have interchangeable cores, which allow for the core of the lock to be taken out. You would use this type of lock if you wanted one key to open several locks. You would just replace all locks with the same core.

Combination locks, of course, require the correct combination of numbers to unlock them. These locks have internal wheels that have to line up properly before being unlocked. A user spins the lock interface left and right by so many clicks, which lines up the internal wheels. Once the correct turns have taken place, all the wheels are in the right position for the lock to release and open the door. The more wheels within the locks, the more protection provided. Electronic combination locks do not use internal wheels, but rather have a keypad that allows a person to type in the combination instead of turning a knob with a combination faceplate. An example of an electronic combination lock is shown in Figure 7-5.

Figure 7-5 An electronic combination lock

Cipher locks, also known as programmable locks, are keyless and use keypads to control access into an area or facility. The lock requires a specific combination to be entered into the keypad and possibly a swipe card. Cipher locks cost more than traditional locks, but their combinations can be changed, specific combination sequence values can be locked out, and personnel who are in trouble or under duress can enter a specific code that will open the door and initiate a remote alarm at the same time. Thus, compared to traditional locks, cipher locks can provide a much higher level of security and control over who can access a facility.

The following are some functionalities commonly available on many cipher combination locks that improve the performance of access control and provide for increased security levels:

- **Door delay** If a door is held open for a given time, an alarm will trigger to alert personnel of suspicious activity.
- **Key override** A specific combination can be programmed for use in emergency situations to override normal procedures or for supervisory overrides.
- **Master keying** Supervisory personnel can change access codes and other features of the cipher lock.
- **Hostage alarm** If an individual is under duress and/or held hostage, a combination he enters can communicate this situation to the guard station and/or police station.

If a door is accompanied by a cipher lock, it should have a corresponding visibility shield so a bystander cannot see the combination as it is keyed in. Automated cipher locks must have a backup battery system and be set to unlock during a power failure so personnel are not trapped inside during an emergency.

CAUTION It is important to change the combination of locks and to use random combination sequences. Often, people do not change their combinations or clean the keypads, which allows an intruder to know what key values are used in the combination, because they are the dirty and worn keys. The intruder then just needs to figure out the right combination of these values.

Some cipher locks require all users to know and use the same combination, which does not allow for any individual accountability. Some of the more sophisticated cipher locks permit specific codes to be assigned to unique individuals. This provides more accountability, because each individual is responsible for keeping his access code secret, and entry and exit activities can be logged and tracked. These are usually referred to as *smart locks*, because they are designed to allow only authorized individuals access at certain doors at certain times.

NOTE Hotel key cards are also known as smart cards. The access code on the card can allow access to a hotel room, workout area, business area, and better yet—the mini bar.

Device Locks Unfortunately, hardware has a tendency to "walk away" from facilities; thus, device locks are necessary to thwart these attempts. Cable locks consist of a vinyl-coated steel cable that can secure a computer or peripheral to a desk or other stationary components, as shown in Figure 7-6.

Figure 7-6 FMJ/PAD.LOCK's notebook security cable kit secures a notebook by enabling the user to attach the device to a stationary component within an area.

The following are some of the device locks available and their capabilities:

- **Switch controls** Cover on/off power switches
- **Slot locks** Secure the system to a stationary component by the use of steel cable that is connected to a bracket mounted in a spare expansion slot
- **Port controls** Block access to disk drives or unused serial or parallel ports
- **Peripheral switch controls** Secure a keyboard by inserting an on/off switch between the system unit and the keyboard input slot
- **Cable traps** Prevent the removal of input/output devices by passing their cables through a lockable unit

Administrative Responsibilities It is important for a company not only to choose the right type of lock for the right purpose, but also to follow proper maintenance and procedures. Keys should be assigned by facility management, and this assignment should be documented. Procedures should be written out detailing how keys are to be assigned, inventoried, and destroyed when necessary, and what should happen if and when keys are lost. Someone on the company's facility management team should be assigned the responsibility of overseeing key and combination maintenance.

Most organizations have master keys and submaster keys for the facility management staff. A master key opens all the locks within the facility, and the submaster keys open one or more locks. Each lock has its own individual unique keys as well. So if a facility has 100 offices, the occupant of each office can have his or her own key. A master key allows access to all offices for security personnel and for emergencies. If one security guard is responsible for monitoring half the facility, the guard can be assigned one of the submaster keys for just those offices.

Since these master and submaster keys are powerful, they must be properly guarded and not widely shared. A security policy should outline what portions of the facility and which device types need to be locked. As a security professional, you should understand what type of lock is most appropriate for each situation, the level of protection provided by various types of locks, and how these locks can be circumvented.

Circumventing Locks Each lock type has corresponding tools that can be used to pick it (open it without the key). A *tension wrench* is a tool shaped like an L and is used to apply tension to the internal cylinder of a lock. The lock picker uses a lock pick to manipulate the individual pins to their proper placement. Once certain pins are "picked" (put in their correct place), the tension wrench holds these down while the lock picker figures out the correct settings for the other pins. After the intruder determines the proper pin placement, the wrench is used to then open the lock.

Intruders may carry out another technique, referred to as *raking*. To circumvent a pin tumbler lock, a lock pick is pushed to the back of the lock and quickly slid out while providing upward pressure. This movement makes many of the pins fall into place.

A tension wrench is also put in to hold the pins that pop into the right place. If all the pins do not slide to the necessary height for the lock to open, the intruder holds the tension wrench and uses a thinner pick to move the rest of the pins into place.

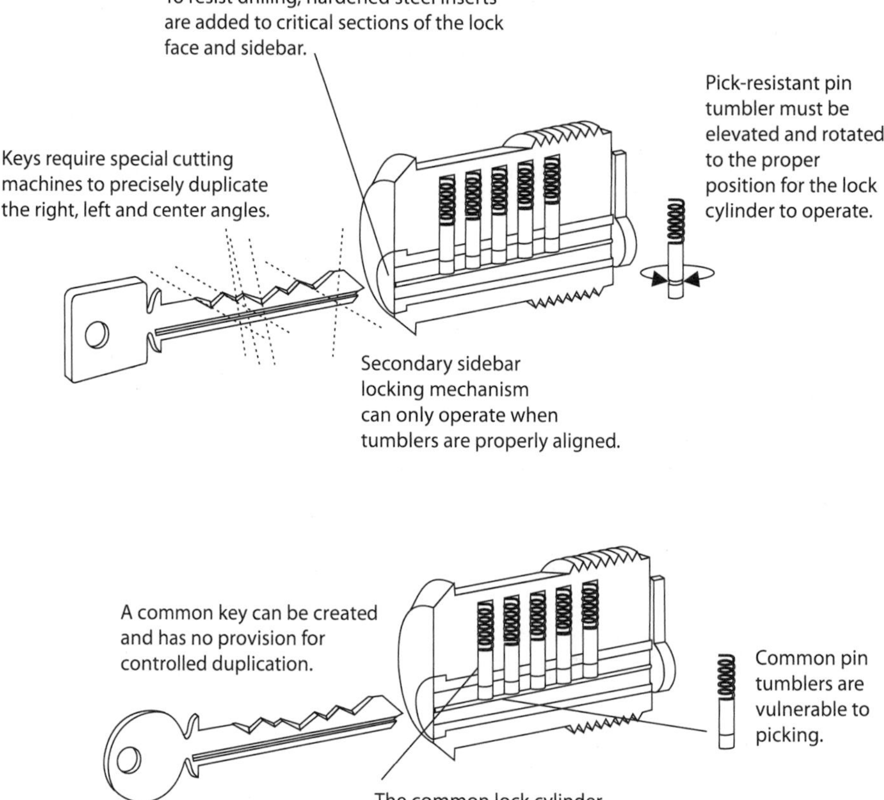
To resist drilling, hardened steel inserts are added to critical sections of the lock face and sidebar.
Pick-resistant pin tumbler must be elevated and rotated to the proper position for the lock cylinder to operate.
Keys require special cutting machines to precisely duplicate the right, left and center angles.
Secondary sidebar locking mechanism can only operate when tumblers are properly aligned.
A common key can be created and has no provision for controlled duplication.
Common pin tumblers are vulnerable to picking.
The common lock cylinder, with no hardened steel inserts, offers little protection against drilling.

Lock Strengths

Basically, three grades of locks are available:

- **Grade 1** Commercial and industrial use
- **Grade 2** Heavy-duty residential/light-duty commercial
- **Grade 3** Residential/consumer

The cylinders within the locks fall into three main categories:

- **Low security** No pick or drill resistance provided (can fall within any of the three grades of locks)
- **Medium security** A degree of pick resistance protection provided (uses tighter and more complex keyways [notch combination]; can fall within any of the three grades of locks)
- **High security** Pick resistance protection through many different mechanisms (only used in grade 1 and 2 locks)

Lock bumping is a tactic that intruders can use to force the pins in a tumbler lock to their open position by using a special key called a *bump key*. The stronger the material that makes up the lock, the smaller the chance that this type of lock attack would be successful.

Now, if this is all too much trouble for the intruder, she can just drill the lock, use bolt cutters, attempt to break through the door or the doorframe, or remove the hinges. There are just so many choices for the bad guys.

Personnel Access Controls

Proper identification verifies whether the person attempting to access a facility or area should actually be allowed in. Identification and authentication can be verified by matching an anatomical attribute (biometric system), using smart or memory cards (swipe cards), presenting a photo ID to a security guard, using a key, or providing a card and entering a password or PIN.

A common problem with controlling authorized access into a facility or area is called *piggybacking*. This occurs when an individual gains unauthorized access by using someone else's legitimate credentials or access rights. Usually an individual just follows another person closely through a door without providing any credentials. The best preventive measures against piggybacking are to have security guards at access points and to educate employees about good security practices.

If a company wants to use a card badge reader, it has several types of systems to choose from. Individuals usually have cards that have embedded magnetic strips that contain access information. The reader can just look for simple access information within the magnetic strip, or it can be connected to a more sophisticated system that scans the information, makes more complex access decisions, and logs badge IDs and access times.

If the card is a memory card, then the reader just pulls information from it and makes an access decision. If the card is a smart card, the individual may be required to enter a PIN or password, which the reader compares against the information held within the card or in an authentication server.

These access cards can be used with *user-activated readers*, which just means the user actually has to do something—swipe the card or enter a PIN. *System sensing access control readers*, also called *transponders*, recognize the presence of an approaching object within a specific area. This type of system does not require the user to swipe the card through the reader. The reader sends out interrogating signals and obtains the access code from the card without the user having to do anything.

EXAM TIP *Electronic access control (EAC) tokens* is a generic term used to describe proximity authentication devices, such as proximity readers, programmable locks, or biometric systems, which identify and authenticate users before allowing them entrance into physically controlled areas.

External Boundary Protection Mechanisms

Proximity protection components are usually put into place to provide one or more of the following services:

- Control pedestrian and vehicle traffic flows
- Various levels of protection for different security zones
- Buffers and delaying mechanisms to protect against forced entry attempts
- Limit and control entry points

These services can be provided by using the following control types:

- **Access control mechanisms** Locks and keys, an electronic card access system, personnel awareness
- **Physical barriers** Fences, gates, walls, doors, windows, protected vents, vehicular barriers
- **Intrusion detection** Perimeter sensors, interior sensors, annunciation mechanisms
- **Assessment** Guards, CCTV cameras
- **Response** Guards, local law enforcement agencies
- **Deterrents** Signs, lighting, environmental design

Several types of perimeter protection mechanisms and controls can be put into place to protect a company's facility, assets, and personnel. They can deter would-be intruders, detect intruders and unusual activities, and provide ways of dealing with these issues when they arise. Perimeter security controls can be natural (hills, rivers) or manmade (fencing, lighting, gates). Landscaping is a mix of the two. In Chapter 3, we explored Crime Prevention Through Environmental Design (CPTED) and how this approach is used to reduce the likelihood of crime. Landscaping is a tool employed in the CPTED method. Sidewalks, bushes, and created paths can point people to the correct entry points, and trees and spiky bushes can be used as natural barriers. These bushes and trees should be placed such that they cannot be used as ladders or accessories to gain unauthorized access to unapproved entry points. Also, there should not be an overwhelming number of trees and bushes, which could provide intruders with places to hide. In the following sections, we look at the manmade components that can work within the landscaping design.

Fencing

Fencing can be quite an effective physical barrier. Although the presence of a fence may only delay dedicated intruders in their access attempts, it can work as a psychological deterrent by telling the world that your company is serious about protecting itself.

Fencing can provide crowd control and helps control access to entrances and facilities. However, fencing can be costly and unsightly. Many companies plant bushes or trees in front of the fencing that surrounds their buildings for aesthetics and to make the building less noticeable. But this type of vegetation can damage the fencing over time or negatively affect its integrity. The fencing needs to be properly maintained, because if a company has a sagging, rusted, pathetic fence, it is equivalent to telling the world that the company is not truly serious and disciplined about protection. But a nice, shiny, intimidating fence can send a different message—especially if the fencing is topped with three rungs of barbed wire.

When deciding upon the type of fencing, several factors should be considered. The gauge of the metal should correlate to the types of physical threats the company would most likely face. After carrying out the risk analysis (covered in Chapter 1), the physical security team should understand the probability of enemies attempting to cut the fencing, drive through it, or climb over or crawl under it. Understanding these threats will help the team determine the necessary gauge and mesh sizing of the fence wiring.

The risk analysis results will also help indicate what height of fencing the organization should implement. Fences come in varying heights, and each height provides a different level of security:

- Fences *three to four feet high* only deter casual trespassers.
- Fences *six to seven feet high* are considered too high to climb easily.
- Fences *eight feet high* (possibly with strands of barbed or razor wire at the top) means you are serious about protecting your property. They often deter the more determined intruder.

The barbed wire on top of fences can be tilted in or out, which also provides extra protection. If the organization is a prison, it would have the barbed wire on top of the fencing pointed in, which makes it harder for prisoners to climb and escape. If the organization is a military base, the barbed wire would be tilted out, making it harder for someone to climb over the fence and gain access to the premises.

Critical areas should have fences at least eight feet high to provide the proper level of protection. The fencing should not sag in any areas and must be taut and securely connected to the posts. The fencing should not be easily circumvented by pulling up its posts. The posts should be buried sufficiently deep in the ground and should be secured with concrete to ensure they cannot be dug up or tied to vehicles and extracted. If the ground is soft or uneven, this might provide ways for intruders to slip or dig under the fence. In these situations, the fencing should actually extend into the dirt to thwart these types of attacks.

Fences work as "first line of defense" mechanisms. A few other controls can be used also. Strong and secure gates need to be implemented. It does no good to install a highly fortified and expensive fence and then have an unlocked or weenie gate that allows easy access.

Fencing: Gauges, Mesh Sizes, and Security

The gauge of fence wiring is the thickness of the wires used within the fence mesh. The lower the gauge number, the larger the wire diameter:

- **11 gauge** = 0.0907-inch diameter
- **9 gauge** = 0.1144-inch diameter
- **6 gauge** = 0.162-inch diameter

The mesh sizing is the minimum clear distance between the wires. Common mesh sizes are 2 inches, 1 inch, and 3/8 inch. It is more difficult to climb or cut fencing with smaller mesh sizes, and the heavier-gauged wiring is harder to cut. The following list indicates the strength levels of the most common gauge and mesh sizes used in chain-link fencing today:

- **Extremely high security** 3/8-inch mesh, 11 gauge
- **Very high security** 1-inch mesh, 9 gauge
- **High security** 1-inch mesh, 11 gauge
- **Greater security** 2-inch mesh, 6 gauge
- **Normal industrial security** 2-inch mesh, 9 gauge

PIDAS Fencing

Perimeter Intrusion Detection and Assessment System (PIDAS) is a type of fencing that has sensors located on the wire mesh and at the base of the fence. It is used to detect if someone attempts to cut or climb the fence. It has a passive cable vibration sensor that sets off an alarm if an intrusion is detected. PIDAS is very sensitive and can cause many false alarms.

Gates basically have four distinct classifications:

- **Class I** Residential usage
- **Class II** Commercial usage, where general public access is expected; examples include a public parking lot entrance, a gated community, or a self-storage facility

- **Class III** Industrial usage, where limited access is expected; an example is a warehouse property entrance not intended to serve the general public
- **Class IV** Restricted access; this includes a prison entrance that is monitored either in person or via closed circuitry

Each gate classification has its own long list of implementation and maintenance guidelines in order to ensure the necessary level of protection. These classifications and guidelines are developed by Underwriters Laboratory (UL), a nonprofit organization that tests, inspects, and classifies electronic devices, fire protection equipment, and specific construction materials. This is the group that certifies these different items to ensure they are in compliance with national building codes. A specific UL code, UL-325, deals with garage doors, drapery, gates, and louver and window operators and systems.

So, whereas in the information security world we look to NIST for our best practices and industry standards, in the physical security world, we look to UL for the same type of direction.

Bollards

Bollards usually look like small concrete pillars outside a building. Sometimes companies try to dress them up by putting flowers or lights in them to soften the look of a protected environment. They are placed by the sides of buildings that have the most immediate threat of someone driving a vehicle through the exterior wall. They are usually placed between the facility and a parking lot and/or between the facility and a road that runs close to an exterior wall. Within the United States after September 11, 2001, many military and government institutions that did not have bollards hauled in huge boulders to surround and protect sensitive buildings. They provided the same type of protection that bollards would provide. These were not overly attractive, but provided the sense that the government was serious about protecting those facilities.

Lighting

Many of the items mentioned in this chapter are things people take for granted day in and day out during our usual busy lives. Lighting is certainly one of those items you probably wouldn't give much thought to, unless it wasn't there. Unlit (or improperly lit) parking lots and parking garages have invited many attackers to carry out criminal activity that they may not have engaged in otherwise with proper lighting. Breaking into cars, stealing cars, and attacking employees as they leave the office are the more common types of attacks that take place in such situations. A security professional should understand that the right illumination needs to be in place, that no dead spots (unlit areas) should exist between the lights, and that all areas where individuals may walk should be properly lit. A security professional should also understand the various types of lighting available and where they should be used.

Wherever an array of lights is used, each light covers its own zone or area. The zone each light covers depends upon the illumination of light produced, which usually has a direct relationship to the wattage capacity of the bulbs. In most cases, the higher the lamp's wattage, the more illumination it produces. It is important that the zones of illumination coverage overlap. For example, if a company has an open parking lot, then light poles must be positioned within the correct distance of each other to eliminate any dead spots. If the lamps that will be used provide a 30-foot radius of illumination, then the light poles should be erected less than 30 feet apart so there is an overlap between the areas of illumination.

NOTE Critical areas need to have illumination that reaches at least eight feet with the illumination of two foot-candles. Foot-candle is a unit of measure of the intensity of light.

If an organization does not implement the right types of lights and ensure they provide proper coverage, the probability of criminal activity, accidents, and lawsuits increases.

Exterior lights that provide protection usually require less illumination intensity than interior working lighting, except for areas that require security personnel to inspect identification credentials for authorization. It is also important to have the correct lighting when using various types of surveillance equipment. The correct contrast between a potential intruder and background items needs to be provided, which only happens with the correct illumination and placement of lights. If the light is going to bounce off of dark, dirty, or darkly painted surfaces, then more illumination is required for the necessary contrast between people and the environment. If the area has clean concrete and light-colored painted surfaces, then not as much illumination is required. This is because when the same amount of light falls on an object and the surrounding background, an observer must depend on the contrast to tell them apart.

When lighting is installed, it should be directed toward areas where potential intruders would most likely be coming from and directed away from the security force posts. For example, lighting should be pointed at gates or exterior access points, and the guard locations should be more in the shadows, or under a lower amount of illumination. This is referred to as *glare protection* for the security force. If you are familiar with military operations, you might know that when you are approaching a military entry point, there is a fortified guard building with lights pointing toward the oncoming cars. A large sign instructs you to turn off your headlights, so the guards are not temporarily blinded by your lights and have a clear view of anything coming their way.

Lights used within the organization's security perimeter should be directed outward, which keeps the security personnel in relative darkness and allows them to easily view intruders beyond the company's perimeter.

An array of lights that provides an even amount of illumination across an area is usually referred to as *continuous lighting*. Examples are the evenly spaced light poles in a parking lot, light fixtures that run across the outside of a building, or series of fluorescent lights used in parking garages. If the company building is relatively close to another company's property, a railway, an airport, or a highway, the owner may need to ensure the lighting does not "bleed over" property lines in an obtrusive manner. Thus, the illumination needs to be *controlled*, which just means an organization should erect lights and use illumination in such a way that it does not blind its neighbors or any passing cars, trains, or planes.

You probably are familiar with the special home lighting gadgets that turn certain lights on and off at predetermined times, giving the illusion to potential burglars that a house is occupied even when the residents are away. Companies can use a similar technology, which is referred to as *standby lighting*. The security personnel can configure the times that different lights turn on and off, so potential intruders think different areas of the facility are populated.

NOTE Redundant or backup lights should be available in case of power failures or emergencies. Special care must be given to understand what type of lighting is needed in different parts of the facility in these types of situations. This lighting may run on generators or battery packs.

Responsive area illumination takes place when an IDS detects suspicious activities and turns on the lights within a specific area. When this type of technology is plugged into automated IDS products, there is a high likelihood of false alarms. Instead of continually having to dispatch a security guard to check out these issues, a CCTV camera can be installed to scan the area for intruders.

If intruders want to disrupt the security personnel or decrease the probability of being seen while attempting to enter a company's premises or building, they could attempt to turn off the lights or cut power to them. This is why lighting controls and switches should be in protected, locked, and centralized areas.

Surveillance Devices

Usually, installing fences and lights does not provide the necessary level of protection a company needs to protect its facility, equipment, and employees. Areas need to be under surveillance so improper actions are noticed and taken care of before damage occurs. Surveillance can happen through visual detection or through devices that use sophisticated means of detecting abnormal behavior or unwanted conditions. It is important that every organization have a proper mix of lighting, security personnel, IDSs, and surveillance technologies and techniques.

Visual Recording Devices

Because surveillance is based on sensory perception, surveillance devices usually work in conjunction with guards and other monitoring mechanisms to extend their capabilities and range of perception. A *closed-circuit TV (CCTV)* system is a commonly used monitoring device in most organizations, but before purchasing and implementing a CCTV system, you need to consider several items:

- **The purpose of CCTV** To detect, assess, and/or identify intruders
- **The type of environment the CCTV camera will work in** Internal or external areas
- **The field of view required** Large or small area to be monitored
- **Amount of illumination of the environment** Lit areas, unlit areas, areas affected by sunlight
- **Integration with other security controls** Guards, IDSs, alarm systems

The reason you need to consider these items before you purchase a CCTV product is that there are so many different types of cameras, lenses, and monitors that make up the different CCTV products. You must understand what is expected of this physical security control, so that you purchase and implement the right type.

CCTVs are made up of cameras, transmitters, receivers, a recording system, and a monitor. The camera captures the data and transmits it to a receiver, which allows the data to be displayed on a monitor. The data is recorded so that it can be reviewed at a later time if needed. Figure 7-7 shows how multiple cameras can be connected to one multiplexer, which allows several different areas to be monitored at one time. The multiplexer accepts video feed from all the cameras and interleaves these transmissions over one line to the central monitor. This is more effective and efficient than the older systems that require the security guard to physically flip a switch from one environment to the next. In these older systems, the guard can view only one environment at a time, which, of course, makes it more likely that suspicious activities will be missed.

A CCTV sends the captured data from the camera's transmitter to the monitor's receiver, usually through a coaxial cable, instead of broadcasting the signals over a public network. This is where the term "closed-circuit" comes in. This circuit should be tamperproof, which means an intruder cannot manipulate the video feed that the security guard is monitoring. The most common type of attack is to replay previous recordings without the security personnel knowing it. For example, if an attacker is able to compromise a

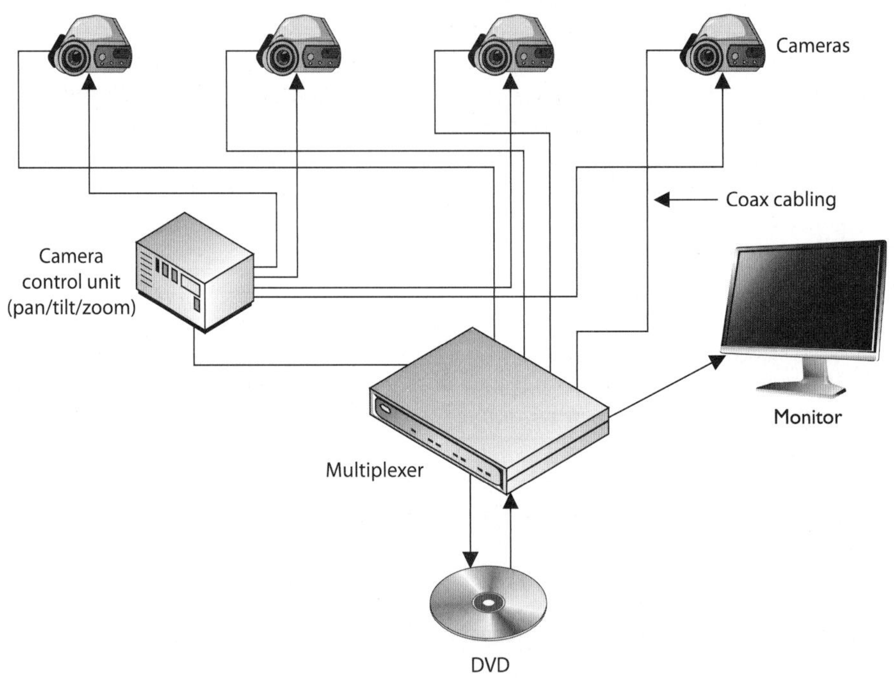

Figure 7-7 Several cameras can be connected to a multiplexer.

company's CCTV and play the recording from the day before, the security guard would not know an intruder is in the facility carrying out some type of crime. This is one reason why CCTVs should be used in conjunction with intruder detection controls, which we address in the next section.

NOTE CCTVs should have some type of recording system. Digital recorders save images to hard drives and allow advanced search techniques that are not possible with videotape recorders. Digital recorders use advanced compression techniques, which drastically reduce the storage media requirements.

Most of the CCTV cameras in use today employ light-sensitive chips called *charged-coupled devices (CCDs)*. The CCD is an electrical circuit that receives input light from the lens and converts it into an electronic signal, which is then displayed on the monitor. Images are focused through a lens onto the CCD chip surface, which forms the electrical representation of the optical image. It is this technology that allows for the capture of extraordinary detail of objects and precise representation, because it has sensors that work in the infrared range, which extends beyond human perception. The CCD sensor picks up this extra "data" and integrates it into the images shown on the monitor to allow for better granularity and quality in the video.

Two main types of lenses are used in CCTV: fixed focal length and zoom (varifocal). The *focal length* of a lens defines its effectiveness in viewing objects from a horizontal and vertical view. The focal length value relates to the angle of view that can be achieved. Short focal length lenses provide wider-angle views, while long focal length lenses provide a narrower view. The size of the images shown on a monitor, along with the area covered by one camera, is defined by the focal length. For example, if a company implements a CCTV camera in a warehouse, the focal length lens values should be between 2.8 and 4.3 millimeters (mm) so the whole area can be captured. If the company implements another CCTV camera that monitors an entrance, that lens value should be around 8mm, which allows a smaller area to be monitored.

NOTE Fixed focal length lenses are available in various fields of views: wide, medium, and narrow. A lens that provides a "normal" focal length creates a picture that approximates the field of view of the human eye. A wide-angle lens has a short focal length, and a telephoto lens has a long focal length. When a company selects a fixed focal length lens for a particular view of an environment, it should understand that if the field of view needs to be changed (wide to narrow), the lens must be changed.

So, if we need to monitor a large area, we use a lens with a smaller focal length value. Great, but what if a security guard hears a noise or thinks he sees something suspicious? A fixed focal length lens does not allow the user to optically change the area that fills the monitor. Though digital systems exist that allow this change to happen in logic, the resulting image quality is decreased as the area being studied becomes smaller. This is because the logic circuits are, in effect, cropping the broader image without increasing the number of pixels in it. This is called *digital zoom* (as opposed to optical zoom) and is a common feature in many cameras. The *optical zoom* lenses provide flexibility by allowing the viewer to change the field of view while maintaining the same number of pixels in the resulting image, which makes it much more detailed. The security personnel usually have a remote-control component integrated within the centralized CCTV monitoring area that allows them to move the cameras and zoom in and out on objects as needed. When both wide scenes and close-up captures are needed, an optical zoom lens is best.

To understand the next characteristic, depth of field, think about pictures you might take while on vacation with your family. For example, if you want to take a picture of your spouse with the Grand Canyon in the background, the main object of the picture is your spouse. Your camera is going to zoom in and use a *shallow depth of focus*. This provides a softer backdrop, which will lead the viewers of the photograph to the foreground, which is your spouse. Now, let's say you get tired of taking pictures of your spouse and want to get a scenic picture of just the Grand Canyon itself. The camera would use a *greater depth of focus*, so there is not such a distinction between objects in the foreground and background.

The depth of field is necessary to understand when choosing the correct lenses and configurations for your company's CCTV. The *depth of field* refers to the portion of the environment that is in focus when shown on the monitor. The depth of field varies depending upon the size of the lens opening, the distance of the object being focused on, and the focal length of the lens. The depth of field increases as the size of the lens opening decreases, the subject distance increases, or the focal length of the lens decreases. So, if you want to cover a large area and not focus on specific items, it is best to use a wide-angle lens and a small lens opening.

CCTV lenses have *irises*, which control the amount of light that enters the lens. *Manual iris lenses* have a ring around the CCTV lens that can be manually turned and controlled. A lens with a manual iris would be used in areas that have fixed lighting, since the iris cannot self-adjust to changes of light. An *auto iris lens* should be used in environments where the light changes, as in an outdoor setting. As the environment brightens, this is sensed by the iris, which automatically adjusts itself. Security personnel will configure the CCTV to have a specific fixed exposure value, which the iris is responsible for maintaining. On a sunny day, the iris lens closes to reduce the amount of light entering the camera, while at night, the iris opens to capture more light—just like our eyes.

When choosing the right CCTV for the right environment, you must determine the amount of light present in the environment. Different CCTV camera and lens products have specific illumination requirements to ensure the best quality images possible. The illumination requirements are usually represented in the *lux* value, which is a metric used to represent illumination strengths. The illumination can be measured by using a light meter. The intensity of light (illumination) is measured and represented in measurement units of lux or foot-candles. (The conversion between the two is one foot-candle = 10.76 lux.) The illumination measurement is not something that can be accurately provided by the vendor of a light bulb, because the environment can directly affect the illumination. This is why illumination strengths are most effectively measured where the light source is implemented.

Next, you need to consider the mounting requirements of the CCTV cameras. The cameras can be implemented in a *fixed mounting* or in a mounting that allows the cameras to move when necessary. A fixed camera cannot move in response to security personnel commands, whereas cameras that provide *PTZ capabilities* can pan, tilt, or zoom (PTZ) as necessary.

So, buying and implementing a CCTV system may not be as straightforward as it seems. As a security professional, you would need to understand the intended use of the CCTV, the environment that will be monitored, and the functionalities that will be required by the security staff that will use the CCTV on a daily basis. The different components that can make up a CCTV product are shown in Figure 7-8.

Great—your assessment team has done all of its research and bought and implemented the correct CCTV system. Now it would be nice if someone actually watched the monitors for suspicious activities. Realizing that monitor watching is a mentally deadening activity may lead your team to implement a type of *annunciator system*.

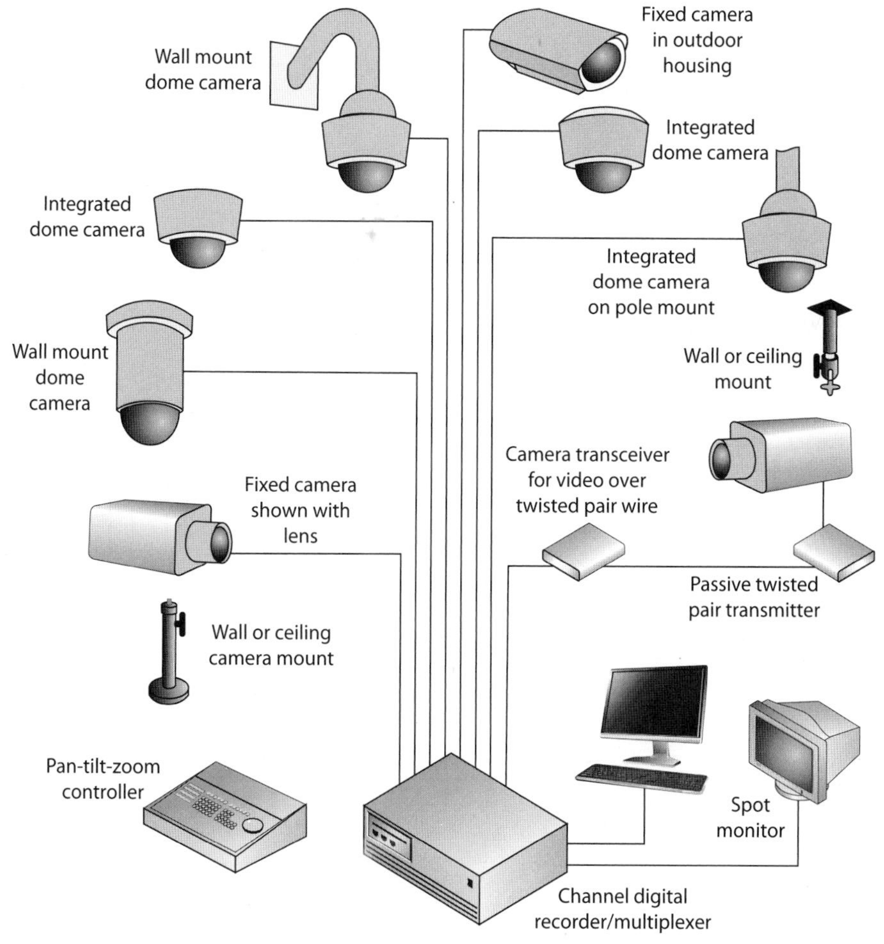

Figure 7-8 A CCTV product can comprise several components.

Different types of annunciator products are available that can either "listen" for noise and activate electrical devices, such as lights, sirens, or CCTV cameras, or detect movement. Instead of expecting a security guard to stare at a CCTV monitor for eight hours straight, the guard can carry out other activities and be alerted by an annunciator if movement is detected on a screen.

Intrusion Detection Systems

Surveillance techniques are used to watch an area, whereas intrusion detection devices are used to sense changes that take place in an environment. Both are monitoring methods, but they use different devices and approaches. This section addresses the types of technologies that can be used to detect the presence of an intruder. One such technology, a perimeter scanning device, is shown in Figure 7-9.

IDSs are used to detect unauthorized entries and to alert a responsible entity to respond. These systems can monitor entries, doors, windows, devices, or removable coverings of equipment. Many work with magnetic contacts or vibration-detection devices that are sensitive to certain types of changes in the environment. When a change is detected, the IDS device sounds an alarm either in the local area or in both the local area and a remote police or guard station.

IDSs can be used to detect changes in the following:

- Beams of light
- Sounds and vibrations
- Motion
- Different types of fields (microwave, ultrasonic, electrostatic)
- Electrical circuit

Figure 7-9 Different perimeter scanning devices work by covering a specific area.

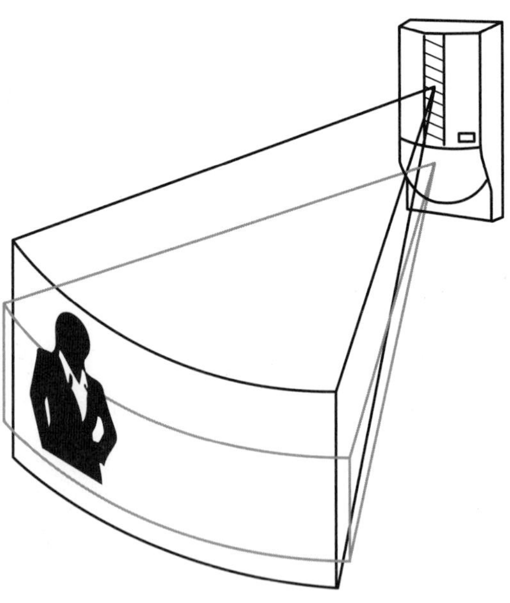

IDSs can be used to detect intruders by employing electromechanical systems (magnetic switches, metallic foil in windows, pressure mats) or volumetric systems. Volumetric systems are more sensitive because they detect changes in subtle environmental characteristics, such as vibration, microwaves, ultrasonic frequencies, infrared values, and photoelectric changes.

Electromechanical systems work by detecting a change or break in a circuit. The electrical circuits can be strips of foil embedded in or connected to windows. If the window breaks, the foil strip breaks, which sounds an alarm. Vibration detectors can detect movement on walls, screens, ceilings, and floors when the fine wires embedded within the structure are broken. Magnetic contact switches can be installed on windows and doors. If the contacts are separated because the window or door is opened, an alarm will sound. Another type of electromechanical detector is a pressure pad. This is placed underneath a rug or portion of the carpet and is activated after hours. If someone steps on the pad, an alarm can be triggered.

A *photoelectric system*, or *photometric system*, detects the change in a light beam and thus can be used only in windowless rooms. These systems work like photoelectric smoke detectors, which emit a beam that hits the receiver. If this beam of light is interrupted, an alarm sounds. The beams emitted by the photoelectric cell can be cross-sectional and can be invisible or visible beams. *Cross-sectional* means that one area can have several different light beams extending across it, which is usually carried out by using hidden mirrors to bounce the beam from one place to another until it hits the light receiver. These are the most commonly used systems in the movies. You have probably seen James Bond and other noteworthy movie spies or criminals use night-vision goggles to see the invisible beams and then step over them.

A *passive infrared (PIR) system* identifies the changes of heat waves in an area it is configured to monitor. If the particles' temperature within the air rises, it could be an indication of the presence of an intruder, so an alarm is sounded.

An *acoustical detection system* uses microphones installed on floors, walls, or ceilings. The goal is to detect any sound made during a forced entry. Although these systems are easily installed, they are very sensitive and cannot be used in areas open to sounds of storms or traffic. *Vibration sensors* are similar and are also implemented to detect forced entry. Financial institutions may choose to implement these types of sensors on exterior walls, where bank robbers may attempt to drive a vehicle through. They are also commonly used around the ceiling and flooring of vaults to detect someone trying to make an unauthorized bank withdrawal.

Wave-pattern motion detectors differ in the frequency of the waves they monitor. The different frequencies are microwave, ultrasonic, and low frequency. All of these devices generate a wave pattern that is sent over a sensitive area and reflected back to a receiver. If the pattern is returned undisturbed, the device does nothing. If the pattern returns altered because something in the room is moving, an alarm sounds.

A *proximity detector*, or *capacitance detector*, emits a measurable magnetic field. The detector monitors this magnetic field, and an alarm sounds if the field is disrupted. These devices are usually used to protect specific objects (artwork, cabinets, or a safe) versus protecting a whole room or area. Capacitance change in an electrostatic field can be used to catch a bad guy, but first you need to understand what capacitance change means.

An electrostatic IDS creates an electrostatic magnetic field, which is just an electric field associated with static electric charges. Most objects have a measurable static electric charge. They are all made up of many subatomic particles, and when everything is stable and static, these particles constitute one holistic electric charge. This means there is a balance between the electric capacitance and inductance. Now, if an intruder enters the area, his subatomic particles will mess up this lovely balance in the electrostatic field, causing a capacitance change, and an alarm will sound. So if you want to rob a company that uses these types of detectors, leave the subatomic particles that make up your body at home.

The type of motion detector that a company chooses to implement, its power capacity, and its configurations dictate the number of detectors needed to cover a sensitive area. Also, the size and shape of the room and the items within the room may cause barriers, in which case more detectors would be needed to provide the necessary level of coverage.

IDSs are support mechanisms intended to detect and announce an attempted intrusion. They will not prevent or apprehend intruders, so they should be seen as an aid to the organization's security forces.

Intrusion Detection Systems Characteristics

IDSs are very valuable controls to use in every physical security program, but several issues need to be understood before implementing them:

- They are expensive and require human intervention to respond to the alarms.
- They require a redundant power supply and emergency backup power.
- They can be linked to a centralized security system.
- They should have a fail-safe configuration, which defaults to "activated."
- They should detect, and be resistant to, tampering.

Patrol Force and Guards

One of the best security mechanisms is a security guard and/or a patrol force to monitor a facility's grounds. This type of security control is more flexible than other security mechanisms, provides good response to suspicious activities, and works as a great deterrent. However, it can be a costly endeavor because it requires a salary, benefits, and time off. People sometimes are unreliable. Screening and bonding is an important part of selecting a security guard, but this only provides a certain level of assurance. One issue is if the security guard decides to make exceptions for people who do not follow the organization's approved policies. Because basic human nature is to trust and help people, a seemingly innocent favor can put an organization at risk.

IDSs and physical protection measures ultimately require human intervention. Security guards can be at a fixed post or can patrol specific areas. Different organizations will have different needs from security guards. They may be required to check individual credentials and enforce filling out a sign-in log. They may be responsible for monitoring IDSs and expected to respond to alarms. They may need to issue and recover visitor badges, respond to fire alarms, enforce rules established by the company within the building, and control what materials can come into or go out of the environment. The guard may need to verify that doors, windows, safes, and vaults are secured; report identified safety hazards; enforce restrictions of sensitive areas; and escort individuals throughout facilities.

The security guard should have clear and decisive tasks that she is expected to fulfill. The guard should be fully trained on the activities she is expected to perform and on the responses expected from her in different situations. She should also have a central control point to check in to, two-way radios to ensure proper communication, and the necessary access into areas she is responsible for protecting.

The best security has a combination of security mechanisms and does not depend on just one component of security. Thus, a security guard should be accompanied by other surveillance and detection mechanisms.

Dogs

Dogs have proven to be highly useful in detecting intruders and other unwanted conditions. Their senses of smell and hearing outperform those of humans, and their intelligence and loyalty can be used for protection. The best security dogs go through intensive training to respond to a wide range of commands and to perform many tasks. Dogs can be trained to hold an intruder at bay until security personnel arrive or to chase an intruder and attack. Some dogs are trained to smell smoke so they can alert personnel to a fire.

Of course, dogs cannot always know the difference between an authorized person and an unauthorized person, so if an employee goes into work after hours, he can have more on his hands than expected. Dogs can provide a good supplementary security mechanism.

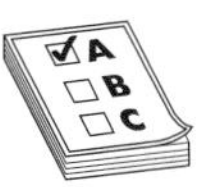

EXAM TIP Because the use of guard dogs introduces significant risks to personal safety, which is paramount for CISSPs, exam answers that include dogs are likelier to be incorrect. Be on the lookout for these.

Auditing Physical Access

Physical access control systems can use software and auditing features to produce audit trails or access logs pertaining to access attempts. The following information should be logged and reviewed:

- The date and time of the access attempt
- The entry point at which access was attempted
- The user ID employed when access was attempted
- Any unsuccessful access attempts, especially if during unauthorized hours

As with audit logs produced by computers, access logs are useless unless someone actually reviews them. A security guard may be required to review these logs, but a security professional or a facility manager should also review these logs periodically. Management needs to know where entry points into the facility exist and who attempts to use them.

Audit and access logs are detective, not preventive. They are used to piece together a situation after the fact instead of attempting to prevent an access attempt in the first place.

Secure Resource Provisioning

The term "provisioning" is overloaded in the technology world, which is to say that it means different actions to different people. To a telecommunications service provider, it could mean the process of running wires, installing customer premises equipment, configuring services, and setting up accounts to provide a given service (e.g., DSL). To an IT department, it could mean the acquisition, configuration, and deployment of an information system (e.g., a new server) within a broader enterprise environment. Finally, to a cloud services provider, provisioning could mean automatically spinning up a new instance of that physical server that the IT department delivered to us.

For the purpose of the CISSP exam, *provisioning* is the set of all activities required to provide one or more new information services to a user or group of users ("new" meaning previously not available to that user or group). Though this definition is admittedly broad, it does subsume all that the overloaded term means. As you will see in the following sections, the specific actions included in various types of provisioning vary significantly, while remaining squarely within our given definition.

At the heart of provisioning is the imperative to provide these services in a secure manner. In other words, we must ensure the services themselves are secure. We also must ensure that the users or systems that can avail themselves of these services are accessing them in a secure manner and in accordance with their own authorizations and the application of the principle of least privilege.

Asset Inventory

Perhaps the most essential aspect of securing our information systems is knowing what it is that we are defending. Though the approaches to tracking hardware and software vary, they are both widely recognized as critical controls. At the very least, it is very difficult to defend an asset that you don't know you have. As obvious as this sounds, many organizations lack an accurate and timely inventory of their hardware and software.

Tracking Hardware

Seemingly, maintaining awareness of which devices are in your organization should be an easier task than tracking your software. A hardware device can be seen, touched, and bar-scanned. It can also be sensed electronically once it is connected to the network. If you have the right tools and processes available, tracking hardware should not be all that difficult, right? Not so fast. It turns out that the set of problems ranges from supply chain security to insider threats and everything in between.

Let's start with the basics. How do you ensure that a new device you've ordered is the right one and free of back doors or piracy issues? There have been multiple reports in the news media recently of confirmed or suspected back doors installed in hardware assets by either manufacturers (e.g., pirated hardware) or by third parties (e.g., government spy agencies) before they get to the organization that acquired them. In response to these and other threats, the International Organization for Standardization published ISO/PAS 28000:2007 as a means for organizations to use a consistent approach to securing their supply chains. In essence, we want to ensure we purchase from trusted sources, use a trusted transportation network, and have effective inspection processes to mitigate the risk of pirated, tampered, or stolen hardware.

But even if we can assure ourselves that all the hardware we acquire is legitimate, how would we know if someone else were to add devices to our networks? Asset monitoring includes not only tracking our known devices, but also identifying unknown ones that may occasionally pop up in our enclaves. Examples that come to mind from personal experience include rogue wireless access points, personal mobile devices, and even telephone modems. Each introduces unknown (and thus unmitigated) risks. The solution is to have a comprehensive monitoring process that actively searches for these devices and ensures compliance with your organization's security policies.

In many cases, monitoring devices on the premises can be as simple as having a member of the security or IT team randomly walk through every space in the organization looking for things that are out of place. This becomes even more effective if this person does this after work hours and also looks for wireless networks as part of these walks. Alternatively, much of this can be done using device management platforms and a variety of sensors.

Tracking Software

Obviously, we can't just walk around and inventory our software. Still, the risks introduced by software are every bit as significant as those introduced by hardware (and perhaps more so). Fundamentally, these risks can be grouped into those that raise liability issues and those that raise security issues.

Unlicensed or pirated software not only is unethical, but also exposes an organization to financial liability from the legitimate product vendors. This liability can manifest in a number of ways, including having the organization reported to the vendor by a disgruntled employee. It could also come up when certain software packages "phone home" to the vendors' servers or when downloading software patches and updates. Depending on the number and types of licenses, this could end up costing significant amounts of money in retroactive licensing fees.

Pirated software is even more problematic because many forms of it include backdoors installed by the pirates or are Trojan horses. Even if this were not the case, it would almost certainly be impossible to update or patch this software, which makes it inherently more insecure. Since no IT staff in their right mind would seriously consider using pirated software as an organizational policy, its presence on a network would suggest that at least some users have privileges that are being abused and to which they may not be entitled.

The solution to the software asset inventory problem is multifaceted. It starts with an assessment of the legitimate application requirements of the organization. Perhaps some users need an expensive photo editing software suite, but it's provisioning should be carefully controlled and only available to that set of users in order to minimize the licensing costs. Once the requirements are known and broken down by class of user, there are several ways to keep a handle on what software exists on which systems. Here are some of the most widely accepted best practices:

- **Application whitelisting** A whitelist is a list of software that is allowed to execute on a device or set of devices. Implementing this approach not only prevents unlicensed or unauthorized software from being installed, but also protects against many classes of malware.
- **Using Gold Masters** As introduced earlier in the chapter, a Gold Master is a standard image workstation or server that includes properly configured and authorized software. Organizations may have multiple images representing different sets of users. The use of Gold Masters simplifies new device provisioning and configuration, particularly if the users are not allowed to modify them.
- **Enforcing the principle of least privilege** If the typical users are not able to install any software on their devices, then it becomes a lot harder for rogue applications to show up in our networks. Furthermore, if we apply this approach, we mitigate risks from a very large set of attacks.
- **Automated scanning** Every device on your network should be periodically scanned to ensure it is running only approved software with proper configurations. Deviations from this policy should be logged and investigated by the IT or security team.

Controlling the existing hardware and software on our networks should be a precondition to provisioning new services and capabilities. To do otherwise risks making an already untenable position even worse.

Configuration Management

Once we have a good handle on what hardware and software we have in our organization, we need to also ensure that we get (and keep) a handle on how these assets are configured. Sadly, most default configurations are woefully insecure. This means that if we do not configure security when we provision new hardware or software, we are virtually guaranteeing successful attacks on our systems. *Configuration management (CM)* is the process of establishing and maintaining consistent baselines on all of our systems.

Every company should have a policy indicating how changes take place within a facility, who can make the changes, how the changes are approved, and how the changes are documented and communicated to other employees. Without these policies in place, people can make changes that others do not know about and that have not been approved, which can result in a confusing mess at the lowest end of the impact scale, and a complete breakdown of operations at the high end. Heavily regulated industries such as finance, pharmaceuticals, and energy have very strict guidelines regarding what specifically can be done and at exactly what time and under which conditions. These guidelines are intended to avoid problems that could impact large segments of the population or downstream partners. Without strict controls and guidelines, vulnerabilities can be introduced into an environment. Tracking down and reversing the changes after everything is done can be a very complicated and nearly impossible task.

The changes can happen to network configurations, system parameters, applications, and settings when adding new technologies, application configurations, or devices, or when modifying the facility's environmental systems. Change control is important not only for an environment, but also for a product during its development and life cycle. Changes must be effective and orderly, because time and money can be wasted by continually making changes that do not meet an ultimate goal.

Some changes can cause a serious network disruption and affect systems' availability. This means changes must be thought through, approved, and carried out in a structured fashion. Backup plans may be necessary in case the change causes unforeseen negative effects. For example, if a server is going to be replaced with a different server type, interoperability issues could prevent users from accessing specific resources, so a backup or redundant server should be in place to ensure availability and continued productivity.

Change Control Process

A well-structured change control process should be put into place to aid staff members through many different types of changes to the environment. This process should be laid out in the change control policy. Although the types of changes vary, a standard list of procedures can help keep the process under control and ensure it is carried out in a predictable manner. The following steps are examples of the types of procedures that should be part of any change control policy:

1. **Request for a change to take place** Requests should be presented to an individual or group that is responsible for approving changes and overseeing the activities of changes that take place within an environment.
2. **Approval of the change** The individual requesting the change must justify the reasons and clearly show the benefits and possible pitfalls of (that is, risk introduced by) the change. Sometimes the requester is asked to conduct more research and provide more information before the change is approved.
3. **Documentation of the change** Once the change is approved, it should be entered into a change log. The log should be updated as the process continues toward completion. Denied requests must also be documented, so that there is a record of the rationale for not making the change.
4. **Tested and presented** The change must be fully tested to uncover any unforeseen results. Regardless of how well we test, there is always a chance that the change will cause an unacceptable loss or outage, so every change request should also have a rollback plan that restores the system to the last known-good configuration. Depending on the severity of the change and the company's organization, the change and implementation may need to be presented to a change control committee. This helps show different sides to the purpose and outcome of the change and the possible ramifications.

5. **Implementation** Once the change is fully tested and approved, a schedule should be developed that outlines the projected phases of the change being implemented and the necessary milestones. These steps should be fully documented and progress should be monitored.
6. **Report change to management** A full report summarizing the change should be submitted to management. This report can be submitted on a periodic basis to keep management up-to-date and ensure continual support.

These steps, of course, usually apply to large changes that take place within an organization. These types of changes are typically expensive and can have lasting effects on a company. However, smaller changes should also go through some type of change control process. If a server needs to have a patch applied, it is not good practice to have an engineer just apply it without properly testing it on a nonproduction server, without having the approval of the IT department manager or network administrator, and without having backup and backout plans in place in case the patch causes some negative effect on the production server. Of course, these changes need to be documented.

As stated previously, it is critical that the operations department create approved backout plans before implementing changes to systems or the network. It is very common for changes to cause problems that were not properly identified before the implementation process began. Many network engineers have experienced the headaches of applying poorly developed "fixes" or patches that end up breaking something else in the system. To ensure productivity is not negatively affected by these issues, a backout plan should be developed. This plan describes how the team will restore the system to its original state before the change was implemented.

Change Control Documentation

Failing to document changes to systems and networks is only asking for trouble, because no one will remember, for example, what was done to that one server in the demilitarized zone (DMZ) six months ago or how the main router was fixed when it was acting up last year. Changes to software configurations and network devices take place pretty often in most environments, and keeping all of these details properly organized is impossible, unless someone maintains a log of this type of activity.

Numerous changes can take place in a company, some of which are as follows:

- New computers installed
- New applications installed
- Different configurations implemented
- Patches and updates installed
- New technologies integrated
- Policies, procedures, and standards updated
- New regulations and requirements implemented
- Network or system problems identified and fixes implemented

- Different network configuration implemented
- New networking devices integrated into the network
- Company acquired by, or merged with, another company

The list could go on and on and could be general or detailed. Many companies have experienced some major problem that affects the network and employee productivity. The IT department may run around trying to figure out the issue and go through hours or days of trial-and-error exercises to find and apply the necessary fix. If no one properly documents the incident and what was done to fix the issue, the company may be doomed to repeat the same scramble six months to a year down the road.

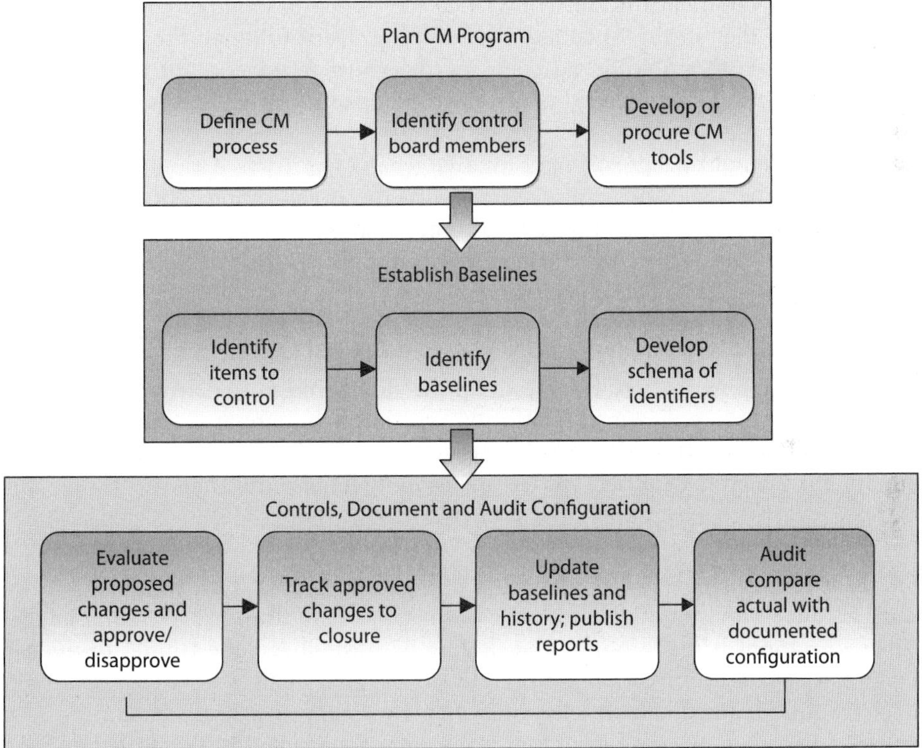

Provisioning Cloud Assets

Generally, cloud provisioning is the set of all activities required to provide one or more new cloud assets to a user or group of users. So what exactly are these cloud assets? As described in Chapter 3, cloud computing is generally divided into three types of service: Infrastructure as a Service (IaaS), Platform as a Service (PaaS), and Software as a Service (SaaS). The provisioning of each type of service presents its own set of issues.

When we are dealing with provisioning IaaS assets, our user population is limited to the IT department. To see why this is true, we need only consider a noncloud (that is, physical) equivalent: provisioning a new server or router. Because these assets typically impact a large number of users in the organization, we must be very careful in planning and testing their provisioning. Accordingly, these provisioning actions often require the approval of the senior leadership or of the change control committee. Only a very small group of IT personnel should be able to perform such provisioning.

PaaS is similar to IaaS in terms of organizational impact, but oftentimes has a more limited scope. Recall that a platform, in this context, is typically a service such as a web or database management service. Though the IT team typically handles the provisioning, in some cases someone else in the organization may handle it. Consider, for example, the case of a development (intranet-only) web service that is being provisioned to test a web application that a team of coders is developing. Depending on the scope, context, and accessibility, this provisioning could be delegated to any one of the developers, though someone in IT would first constrain the platform to ensure it is accessible only to that team.

Finally, SaaS could be provisioned by a larger pool of users within the constraints established by the IT team in accordance with the organizational policy. If a given group of users is authorized to use the customer relations manager (CRM), then those users should be able to log into their accounts and self-provision that and any other applications to which they are authorized.

As you can see, the provisioning of cloud assets should be increasingly more controlled depending on the organizational impact and the risk profile of the specific asset. The key to secure provisioning is carefully setting up the cloud computing environment so that properly configured applications, platforms, and infrastructure are rapidly available to authorized users when and where they need them. After all, one of the benefits of cloud computing is the promise of self-service provisioning in near real time.

Network and Resource Availability

Secure resource provisioning is only part of the story here. Another key component of security operations is planning for and dealing with the inevitable failures of the component parts of our information systems. In the triad of security services, *availability* is one of the foundational components (the other two being *confidentiality* and *integrity*). Network and resource availability often is not fully appreciated until it is gone. That is why administrators and engineers need to implement effective backup and redundant systems to make sure that when something happens (and something will happen), users' productivity will not be drastically affected.

The network needs to be properly maintained to make sure the network and its resources will always be available when they're needed. For example, the cables need to be the correct type for the environment and technology used, and cable runs should not exceed the recommended lengths. Older cables should be replaced with newer ones, and periodic checks should be made for possible cable cuts and malfunctions.

Device backup and other availability solutions are chosen to balance the value of having information available against the cost of keeping that information available:

- *Redundant hardware* ready for "hot swapping" keeps information highly available by having multiple copies of information (mirroring) or enough extra information available to reconstruct information in case of partial loss (parity, error correction). Hot swapping allows the administrator to replace the failed component while the system continues to run and information remains available; usually degraded performance results, but unplanned downtime is avoided.
- *Fault-tolerant technologies* keep information available against not only individual storage device faults but even against whole system failures. Fault tolerance is among the most expensive possible solutions, and is justified only for the most mission-critical information. All technology will eventually experience a failure of some form. A company that would suffer irreparable harm from any unplanned downtime, or that would accumulate millions of dollars in losses for even a very brief unplanned downtime, can justify paying the high cost for fault-tolerant systems.
- *Service level agreements (SLAs)* help service providers, whether they are an internal IT operation or an outsourcer, decide what type of availability technology is appropriate. From this determination, the price of a service or the budget of the IT operation can be set. The process of developing an SLA with a business is also beneficial to the business. While some businesses have performed this type of introspection on their own, many have not, and being forced to go through the exercise as part of budgeting for their internal IT operations or external sourcing helps the business understand the real value of its information.
- *Solid operational procedures* are also required to maintain availability. The most reliable hardware with the highest redundancy or fault tolerance, designed for the fastest mean time to repair, will mostly be a waste of money if operational procedures, training, and continuous improvement are not part of the operational environment: one slip of the finger by an IT administrator can halt the most reliable system.

We need to understand when system failures are most likely to happen....

Mean Time Between Failures

Mean time between failures (MTBF) is a measure of how long we expect a piece of equipment to operate reliably. MTBF is normally calculated by staking the average of the time between failures of a system. For example, suppose you buy a lot of 100 hard disk drives, install them, and start using them on the same day. You subsequently note that one of them fails after 10 days, a second fails after 500 days, and a third fails after 600 days.

At that point, you could calculate your MTBF for the lot to be 370 days (1110 days / 3 failures). Normally, however, we rely on the vendor of the equipment or a third party to calculate this value, since they have access to information on many more devices than we do. The reason for using MTBF is to know approximately when a particular device will need to be repaired or replaced. It is used as a benchmark for reliability.

EXAM TIP MTBF implies that the device or component is repairable. If it isn't, then we use the term mean time to failure (MTTF).

Organizations trending MTBF over time for the devices they use may be able to identify types of devices that are failing above the averages promised by the devices' manufacturers and take action. For example, if the devices are still under warranty, an organization may proactively contact the manufacturer to seek replacement; if not under warranty, the organization may decide to replace the devices preemptively before larger-scale failures and operational disruptions occur.

Mean Time to Repair

Mean time to repair (MTTR) is the expected amount of time it will take to get a device fixed and back into production after its failure. For a hard drive in a redundant array, the MTTR is the amount of time between the actual failure and the time when, after noticing the failure, someone has replaced the failed drive and the redundant array has completed rewriting the information on the new drive. This is likely to be measured in hours. For a nonredundant hard drive in a desktop PC, the MTTR is the amount of time between when the user emits a loud curse and calls the help desk, and the point at which the replaced hard drive has been reloaded with the operating system, software, and any backed-up data belonging to the user. This is likely to be measured in days. For an unplanned reboot, the MTTR is the amount of time between the failure of the system and the point in time when it has rebooted its operating system, checked the state of its disks (hopefully finding nothing that its file systems cannot handle), and restarted its applications, and its applications have checked the consistency of their data (hopefully finding nothing that their journals cannot handle) and once again begun processing transactions. For well-built hardware running high-quality, well-managed operating systems and software, this may be only minutes. For commodity equipment without high-performance journaling file systems and databases, this may be hours, or, worse, days if automated recovery/rollback does not work and a restore of data from tape is required:

- The MTTR may pertain to fixing a component of the device, or replacing the device, or perhaps refers to a vendor's SLA.
- If the MTTR is too high for a critical device, then redundancy should be used.

The MTBF and MTTR numbers provided by manufacturers are useful in choosing how much to spend on new systems. Systems that can be down for brief periods of time without significant impact may be built from inexpensive components with lower MTBF expectations and modest MTTR. Higher MTBF numbers are often accompanied by higher prices, but can be justified for mission-critical systems. Systems that cannot be allowed to be down at all need redundant components with high MTBF values.

Single Points of Failure

A *single point of failure* poses a lot of potential risk to a network, because if the device fails, a segment or even the entire network is negatively affected. Devices that could represent single points of failure are firewalls, routers, network access servers, T1 lines, switches, bridges, hubs, and authentication servers—to name a few. The best defenses against being vulnerable to these single points of failure are proper maintenance, regular backups, redundancy, and fault tolerance.

More Components Can Mean Less Reliability

MTBF can be misleading. Putting aside questions of whether manufacturer-predicted MTBFs are believable, consider a desktop PC with a single hard drive installed, where the hard drive has an MTBF estimate by the manufacturer of 30,000 hours. Thus, 30,000 hours / 8,760 hours/year = an MTBF of a little over three years. This suggests that this model of hard drive, on average, will last over three years before it fails. Put aside the notions of whether the office environment in which that PC is located is temperature-, humidity-, shock-, and coffee spill–controlled, and install a second identical hard drive in that PC. The possibility of failure may have now doubled, giving two chances in that three-year period of suffering a failure of a hard drive in the PC. Extrapolate this to a data center with thousands of these hard drives in it, and it becomes clear that a hard drive replacement budget is required each year, along with redundancy for important data.

Multiple paths should exist between routers in case one router goes down, and dynamic routing protocols should be used so each router will be informed when a change to the network takes place. For WAN connections, a failover option should be configured to enable an Integrated Services Digital Network (ISDN) connection to be available if the WAN router fails. Figure 7-10 illustrates a common e-commerce environment that contains redundant devices.

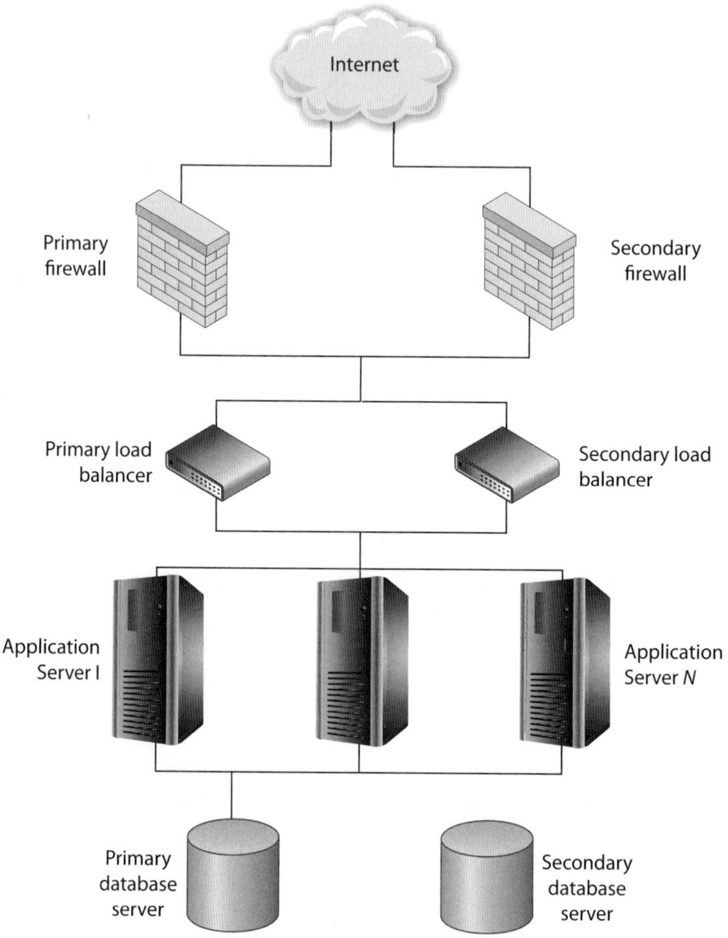

Figure 7-10 Each critical device may require a redundant partner to ensure availability.

The following sections address technologies that can be used to help prevent productivity disruption because of single points of failure.

RAID

Redundant array of independent disks (RAID) is a technology used for redundancy and/or performance improvement that combines several physical disks and aggregates them into logical arrays. Redundancy and speed are provided by breaking up the data and writing it across several disks so different disk heads can work simultaneously to retrieve the requested information. Control data is also spread across each disk—this is called *parity*—so that if one disk fails, the other disks can work together and restore its data. A RAID appears as a single drive to applications and other devices.

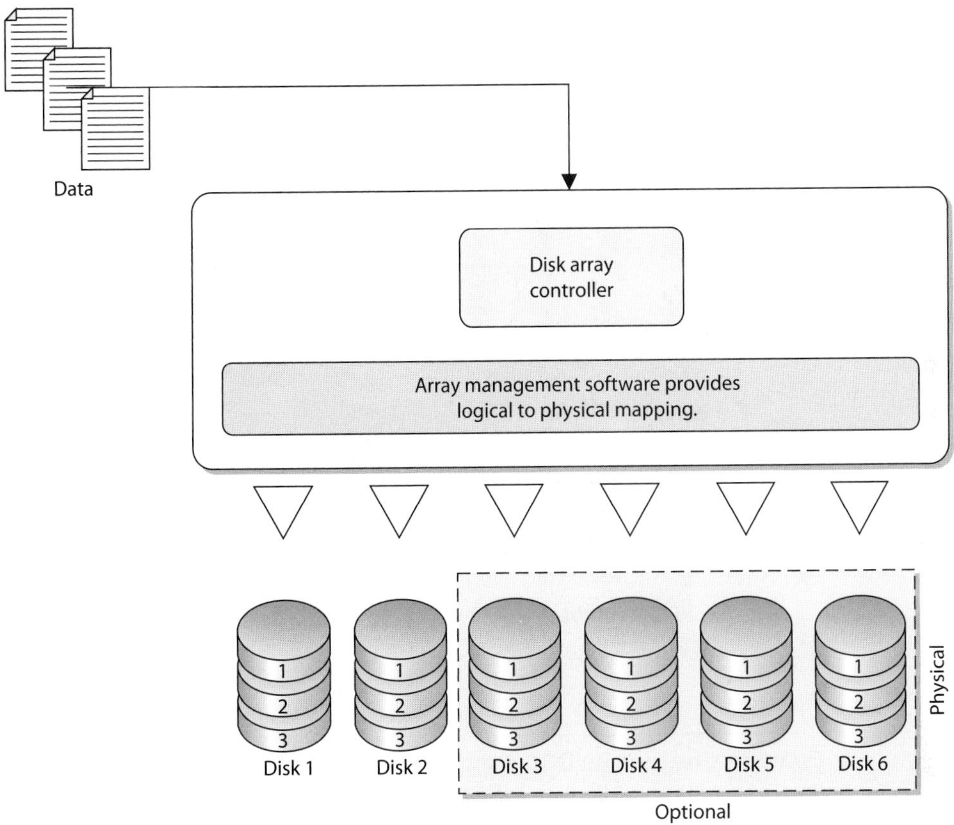

When data is written across all drives, the technique of *striping* is used. This activity divides and writes the data over several drives. The write performance is not affected, but the read performance is increased dramatically because more than one head is retrieving data at the same time. It might take the RAID system six seconds to write a block of data to the drives and only two seconds or less to read the same data from the disks.

Various levels of RAID dictate the type of activity that will take place within the RAID system. Some levels deal only with performance issues, while other levels deal with performance and fault tolerance. If fault tolerance is one of the services a RAID level provides, parity is involved. If a drive fails, the parity is basically instructions that tell the RAID system how to rebuild the lost data on the new hard drive. Parity is used to rebuild a new drive so all the information is restored. Most RAID systems have *hot-swapping* disks, which means they can replace drives while the system is running.

When a drive is swapped out, or added, the parity data is used to rebuild the data on the new disk that was just added.

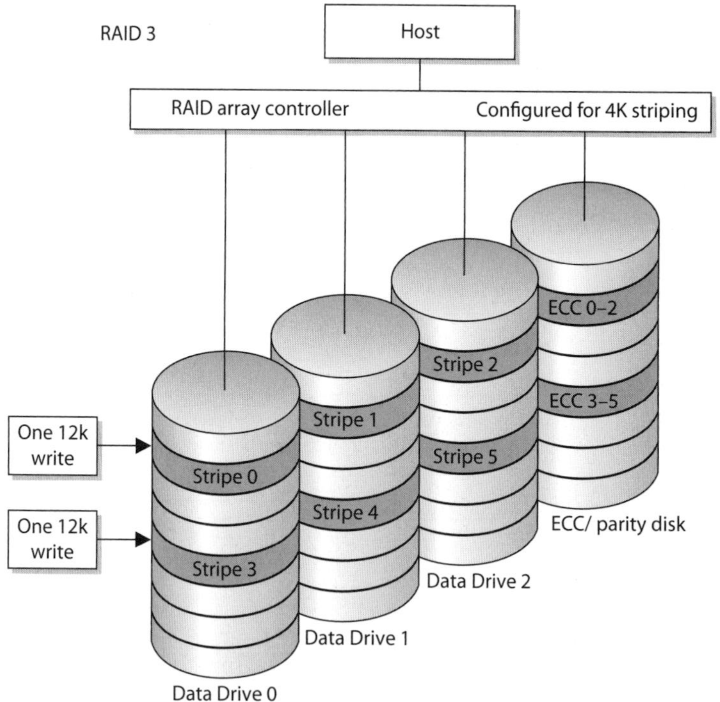

EXAM TIP The term RAID 10 is sometimes used to refer to a combination of levels 1 and 0. The CBK may refer to this as either RAID 0+1 or RAID 1+0.

The most common RAID level used today is level 5. Table 7-2 describes each of the possible RAID levels.

NOTE RAID level 5 is the most commonly used mode.

Direct Access Storage Device

Direct access storage device (DASD) is a general term for magnetic disk storage devices, which historically have been used in mainframe and minicomputer (mid-range computer) environments. RAID is a type of DASD. The key distinction between DASDs and sequential access storage devices (SASDs) is that any point on a DASD may be

RAID Level	Activity	Name
0	Data striped over several drives. No redundancy or parity is involved. If one volume fails, the entire volume can be unusable. It is used for performance only.	Striping
1	Mirroring of drives. Data is written to two drives at once. If one drive fails, the other drive has the exact same data available.	Mirroring
2	Data striping over all drives at the bit level. Parity data is created with a hamming code, which identifies any errors. This level specifies that up to 39 disks can be used: 32 for storage and 7 for error recovery data. This is not used in production today.	Hamming code parity
3	Data striping over all drives and parity data held on one drive. If a drive fails, it can be reconstructed from the parity drive.	Byte-level parity
4	Same as level 3, except parity is created at the block level instead of the byte level.	Block-level parity
5	Data is written in disk sector units to all drives. Parity is written to all drives also, which ensures there is no single point of failure.	Interleave parity
6	Similar to level 5 but with added fault tolerance, which is a second set of parity data written to all drives.	Second parity data (or double parity)
10	Data is simultaneously mirrored and striped across several drives and can support multiple drive failures.	Striping and mirroring

Table 7-2 Different RAID Levels

promptly reached, whereas every point in between the current position and the desired position of a SASD must be traversed in order to reach the desired position. Tape drives are SASDs. Some tape drives have minimal amounts of direct access intelligence built in. These include multitrack tape devices that store at specific points on the tape and cache in the tape drive information about where major sections of data on the tape begin, allowing the tape drive to more quickly reach a track and a point on the track from which to begin the now much shorter traversal of data from that indexed point to the desired point. While this makes such tape drives noticeably faster than their purely sequential peers, the difference in performance between SASDs and DASDs is orders of magnitude.

Massive Array of Inactive Disks

A relatively recent entrant into the medium-scale storage arena (in the hundreds of terabytes) is *massive array of inactive disks (MAID)*. MAID has a particular (possibly large) niche, where up to several hundred terabytes of data storage are needed, but it carries out mostly write operations. Smaller storage requirements generally do not justify the increased acquisition cost and operational complexity of a MAID. Medium-to-large storage requirements where much of the data is regularly active would not accomplish a true benefit from MAID since the performance of a MAID in such a use case declines rapidly as more drives are needed to be active than the MAID is intended to offer. At the very highest end of storage, with a typical write-mostly use case, tape drives remain the most economical solution due to the lower per-unit cost of tape storage and the decreasing percent of the total media needed to be online at any given time.

In a MAID, rack-mounted disk arrays have all inactive disks powered down, with only the disk controller alive. When an application asks for data, the controller powers up the appropriate disk drive(s), transfers the data, and then powers the drive(s) down again. By powering down infrequently accessed drives, energy consumption is significantly reduced, and the service life of the disk drives may be increased.

Redundant Array of Independent Tapes

Redundant array of independent tapes (RAIT) is similar to RAID, but uses tape drives instead of disk drives. Tape storage is the lowest-cost option for very large amounts of data, but is very slow compared to disk storage. For very large write-mostly storage applications where MAID is not economical and where a higher performance than typical tape storage is desired, or where tape storage provides appropriate performance and higher reliability is required, RAIT may fit.

As in RAID 1 striping, in RAIT, data is striped in parallel to multiple tape drives, with or without a redundant parity drive. This provides the high capacity at low cost typical of tape storage, with higher-than-usual tape data transfer rates and optional data integrity.

Storage Area Networks

Drawing from the local area network (LAN), wide area network (WAN), and metropolitan area network (MAN) nomenclature, a *storage area network (SAN)* consists of numerous storage devices linked together by a high-speed private network and storage-specific switches. This creates a "fabric" that allows users to attach to and interact in a transparent mode. When a user makes a request for a file, he does not need to know which server or tape drive to go to—the SAN software finds it and provides it to the user.

Many infrastructures have data spewed all over the network, and tracking down the necessary information can be frustrating, but backing up all of the necessary data can also prove challenging in this setup.

SANs provide redundancy, fault tolerance, reliability, and backups, and allow the users and administrators to interact with the SAN as one virtual entity. Because the network that carries the data in the SAN is separate from a company's regular data network, all of this performance, reliability, and flexibility comes without impact to the data networking capabilities of the systems on the network.

SANs are not commonly used in small or midsized companies. They are for companies that have to keep track of terabytes of data and have the funds for this type of technology. The storage vendors are currently having a heyday, not only because everything we do business-wise is digital and must be stored, but because government regulations are requiring companies to keep certain types of data for a specific retention period. Imagine storing all of your company's e-mail traffic for seven years…that's just one type of data that must be retained.

NOTE Tape drives, optical jukeboxes, and disk arrays may also be attached to, and referenced through, a SAN.

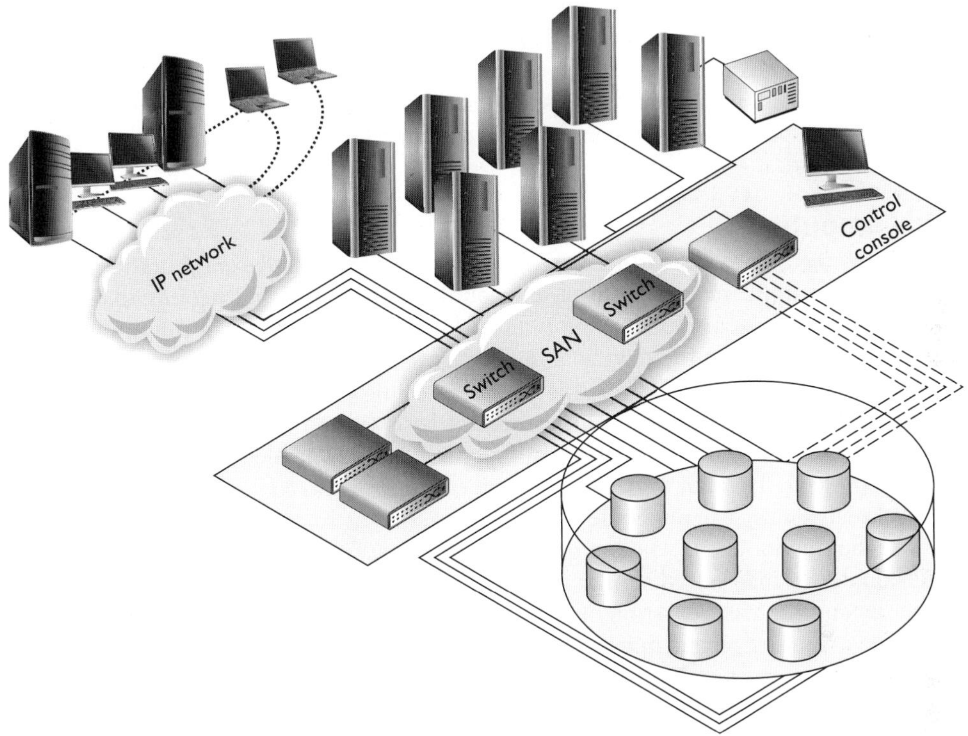

Clustering

Clustering is a fault-tolerant server technology that is similar to redundant servers, except each server takes part in processing services that are requested. A *server cluster* is a group of servers that are viewed logically as one server to users and can be managed as a single logical system. Clustering provides for availability and scalability. It groups physically different systems and combines them logically, which provides immunity to faults and improves performance. Clusters work as an intelligent unit to balance traffic, and users who access the cluster do not know they may be accessing different systems at different times. To the users, all servers within the cluster are seen as one unit. Clusters may also be referred to as server farms.

If one of the systems within the cluster fails, processing continues because the rest pick up the load, although degradation in performance could occur. This is more attractive, however, than having a secondary (redundant) server that waits in the wings in case a primary server fails, because this secondary server may just sit idle for a long period of time, which is wasteful. When clustering is used, all systems are used to process requests and none sit in the background waiting for something to fail. Clustering is a logical outgrowth of redundant servers. Consider a single server that requires high availability, and so has a hot standby redundant server allocated. For each such single server requiring high availability, an additional redundant server must be purchased. Since failure of multiple primary servers at once is unlikely, it would be economically efficient to have a small number of extra servers, any of which could take up the load of any single failed primary server. Thus was born the cluster.

Clustering offers a lot more than just availability. It also provides load balancing (each system takes a part of the processing load), redundancy, and failover (other systems continue to work if one fails).

Grid Computing

Grid computing is another load-balanced parallel means of massive computation, similar to clusters but implemented with loosely coupled systems that may join and leave the grid randomly. Most computers have extra CPU processing power that is not being used many times throughout the day. So some smart people thought that was wasteful and came up with a way to use all of this extra processing power. Just like the power grid provides electricity to entities on an as-needed basis (if you pay your bill), computers can volunteer to allow their extra processing power to be available to different groups for different projects. The first project to use grid computing was SETI (Search for Extraterrestrial Intelligence), where people allowed their systems to participate in scanning the universe looking for aliens who are trying to talk to us.

Although this may sound similar to clustering, where in a cluster a central controller has master control over allocation of resources and users to cluster nodes and the nodes in the cluster are under central management (in the same trust domain), in grid computing the nodes do not trust each other and have no central control.

Applications that may be technically suitable to run in a grid and that would enjoy the economic advantage of a grid's cheap massive computing power, but which require secrecy, may not be good candidates for a grid computer since the secrecy of the content of a workload unit allocated to a grid member cannot be guaranteed by the grid against the owner of the individual grid member. Additionally, because the grid members are of variable capacity and availability and do not trust each other, grid computing is not appropriate for applications that require tight interactions and coordinated scheduling among multiple workload units. This means sensitive data should not be processed over a grid, and this is not the proper technology for time-sensitive applications.

A more appropriate use of grid computing is projects like financial modeling, weather modeling, and earthquake simulation. Each of these has an incredible amount of variables and input that need to be continually computed. This approach has also been used to try and crack algorithms and was used to generate rainbow tables.

NOTE Rainbow tables consist of all possible passwords in hashed formats. This allows attackers to uncover passwords much more quickly than carrying out a dictionary or brute-force attack.

Backups

Backing up software and having backup hardware devices are two large parts of network availability. You need to be able to restore data if a hard drive fails, a disaster takes place, or some type of software corruption occurs.

A policy should be developed that indicates what gets backed up, how often it gets backed up, and how these processes should occur. If users have important information on their workstations, the operations department needs to develop a method that indicates that backups include certain directories on users' workstations or that users move their critical data to a server share at the end of each day to ensure it gets backed up. Backups may occur once or twice a week, every day, or every three hours. It is up to the company to determine this interval. The more frequent the backups, the more resources will be dedicated to it, so there needs to be a balance between backup costs and the actual risk of potentially losing data.

A company may find that conducting automatic backups through specialized software is more economical and effective than spending IT work-hours on the task. The integrity of these backups needs to be checked to ensure they are happening as expected—rather than finding out right after two major servers blow up that the automatic backups were saving only temporary files. (Review Chapter 6 for more information on backup issues.)

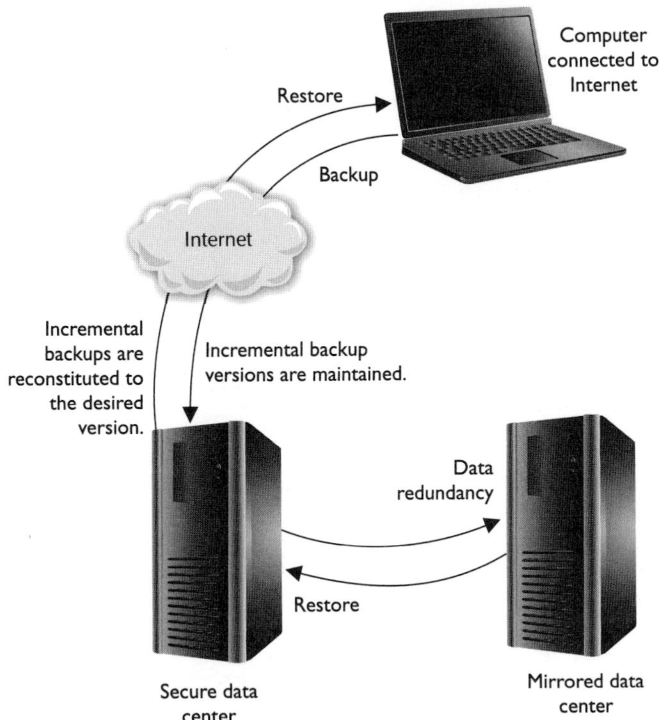

Hierarchical Storage Management

Hierarchical storage management (HSM) provides continuous online backup functionality. It combines hard disk technology with the cheaper and slower optical or tape jukeboxes. The HSM system dynamically manages the storage and recovery of files, which are copied to storage media devices that vary in speed and cost. The faster media holds the files that are accessed more often, and the seldom-used files are stored on the slower devices, or *near-line* devices, as shown in Figure 7-11. The storage media could include optical discs, magnetic disks, and tapes. This functionality happens in the background without the knowledge of the user or any need for user intervention.

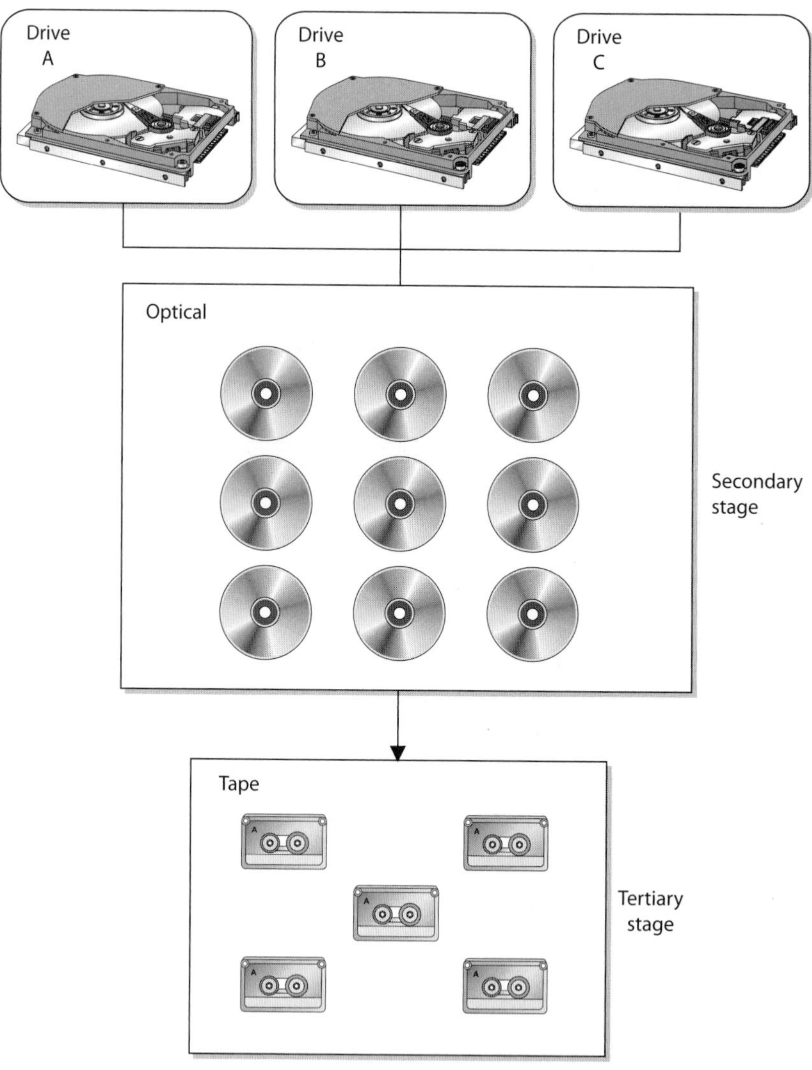

Figure 7-11 HSM provides an economical and efficient way of storing data.

HSM works, according to tuning based on the trade-off between the cost of storage and the availability of information, by migrating the actual content of less used files to lower-speed, lower-cost storage, while leaving behind a "stub," which looks to the user like it contains the full data of the migrated file. When the user or an application accesses the stub, the HSM uses the information in the stub to find the real location of the information and then retrieve it transparently for the user.

This type of technology was created to save money and time. If all data was stored on hard drives, that would be expensive. If a lot of the data was stored on tapes, it would take too long to retrieve the data when needed. So HSM provides a terrific approach by providing you with the data you need, when you need it, without having to bother the administrator to track down some tape or optical disc.

Backups should include the underlying operating system and applications, as well as the configuration files for both. Systems are attached to networks, and network devices can experience failures and data losses as well. Data loss of a network device usually means the configuration of the network device is lost completely (and the device will not even boot up), or that the configuration of the network device reverts to defaults (which, though it will boot up, does your network little good). Therefore, the configurations of network and other nonsystem devices (for example, the phone system) in the environment are also necessary.

CAUTION Trivial File Transfer Protocol (TFTP) servers are commonly used to save the configuration settings from network devices. However, TFTP is an insecure protocol, some network settings are sensitive and should be kept confidential, and a coordinated attack is possible against network devices that load their configurations using TFTP by first causing the network device to fail and then attacking the TFTP download of the configuration to cause a malicious configuration to be loaded. Alternatives to TFTP should be sought.

Contingency Planning

When an incident strikes, more is required than simply knowing how to restore data from backups. Also necessary are the detailed procedures that outline the activities to keep the critical systems available and ensure that operations and processing are not interrupted. Contingency management defines what should take place during and after an incident. Actions that are required to take place for emergency response, continuity of operations, and dealing with major outages must be documented and readily available to the operations staff. There should be at least three instances of these documents: the original that is on site; a copy that is also on site but in a protective, fireproof safe; and a copy that is at an offsite location.

Contingency plans should not be trusted until they have been tested. Organizations should carry out exercises to ensure that the staff fully understands their responsibilities and how to carry them out. Another issue to consider is how to keep these plans up-to-date. As our dynamic, networked environments change, so must our plans on how to rescue them when necessary.

Although in the security industry "contingency planning" and "business continuity planning (BCP)" are commonly used interchangeably, it is important that you understand the actual difference for the CISSP exam. BCP addresses how to keep the organization in business after a disaster takes place. It is about the survivability of the organization and making sure that critical functions can still take place even after a disaster. Contingency plans address how to deal with small incidents that do not qualify as disasters, as in power outages, server failures, a down communication link to the Internet, or the corruption of software. It is important that organizations be ready to deal with large and small issues that they may run into one day.

Summary of Technologies That Improve Resource Availability

The following are the items you will most likely run into when taking the CISSP exam:

- Redundant servers
- RAID, MAID, RAIT
- Direct access storage device
- Storage area networks
- Clustering
- Grid computing
- Backups

Preventative Measures

A good way to reduce the likelihood of contingencies and disasters is to ensure your defensive architectures include the right set of tools. These technical controls need to be carefully considered in the context of your own conditions to decide which are useful and which aren't. Regardless of the tools you employ, there is an underlying process that drives their operation in a live environment. The steps of this generalized process are described here:

1. **Understand the risk.** Chapter 1 presented the risk management process that organizations should use. The premise of this process is that you can't ever eliminate all risks and should therefore devote your scarce resources to mitigating the most dangerous risks to a point where their likelihood is acceptable to the senior leaders. If you don't focus on that set of risks, you will likely squander your resources countering threats that are not the ones your CEO is really concerned about.

2. **Use the right controls.** Once you are focused on the right set of risks, you can more easily identify the controls that will appropriately mitigate them. The relationship between risks and controls is many to many, since a given risk can have multiple controls assigned to it and a given control can be used to mitigate multiple risks. In fact, the number of risks mitigated by one control should give you an indicator of the value of that control to the organization. On the other hand, having multiple controls mitigating a risk may be less efficient, but may provide resiliency.
3. **Use the controls correctly.** Selecting the right tools is only part of the battle. You also need to ensure they are emplaced and configured correctly. The network architectures covered in Chapter 4 place some very significant limitations on the effectiveness of tools based on where they are plugged in. If an IDS is deployed on the wrong subnet, it may not be able to monitor all the traffic from the threat sources against which it is supposed to defend. Similarly, that same IDS with the wrong configuration or rule set could well become an expensive ornament on the network.
4. **Manage your configuration.** One of the certainties in life is that, left alone, every configuration is guaranteed to become obsolete at some point in the future. Even if it is not left alone, making unauthorized or undocumented changes will introduce risk at best and at worst quietly render your network vulnerable to an immediate threat. Properly done, configuration management will ensure you have ground truth about your network so that you can better answer the questions that are typically asked when doing security operations.
5. **Assess your operation.** You should constantly (or at least periodically) be looking at your defensive plan, comparing it with your latest threat and risk assessments, and asking yourself: are we still properly mitigating the risks? You should test your controls using cases derived from your risk assessment. This verifies that you are correctly mitigating those risks. However, you should also occasionally test your controls against an unconstrained set of threats in order to validate that you are mitigating the correct risks. A good penetration test (pen test) can both verify and validate the controls.

This process can yield a huge amount of possible preventative controls. There are some controls, however, that are so pervasive that every information security professional should be able to incorporate them into a defensive architecture. In the following sections, we describe the most important ones.

Firewalls

Among all preventative measures, perhaps none is more popular than the firewall. Back in Chapter 4, we discussed firewalls as network devices. We now revisit them as a common tool in many security toolkits. We should stress that this is just one tool and that it is not universal. In fact, stand-alone firewalls have been replaced in many cases by security appliances or software solutions that subsume the traditional firewall functionality and add significant other capabilities.

As always, you should start with the threat and how it creates specific risks to your organization. From there, you should clearly define the subset of risks that is appropriately mitigated by firewalls. Once you have this control-risk pairing done, you can look at your network and decide where are the best places to locate firewalls to mitigate those risks. Do you have the right number (and kind) of firewalls? Are they in the right places? In some cases, the answer to one or the other question is "no," which will allow you to reposition or requisition your assets to better defend yourself.

Obviously, the placement of firewalls is not the only concern. Firewalls operate by enforcing rules, and those rules are mostly static. The operational challenge is to both accurately track the current sets of rules and have a process to identify rules that must be added, modified, or deleted. We already touched on this idea when we discussed configuration management earlier in this chapter, and the concept is particularly applicable to firewalls. It is difficult to overstate the number of firewalls with obsolete and ineffective rules that are operating on live networks. While the use of a next-generation firewall (NGFW) simplifies this process by using connections to external data sources (like policy servers and Active Directory), even they need a formal process to ensure that the right rules get to the right places at the right time.

Finally, you need a plan to routinely assess the effectiveness of your firewall defenses. To this end you simply go back to the first step in this process and look again at your threats and risks. These will drive what should be a fairly obvious set of test cases with which you will be able to answer the question we should always be asking ourselves: are we still properly mitigating the risk?

Intrusion Detection and Prevention Systems

We already covered intrusion detection systems in the context of facility security earlier in this chapter. We also covered IDSs and intrusion prevention systems (IPSs) in detail within the context of access control monitoring in Chapter 5. Let's now turn our attention to how we might employ IDSs and IPSs in the context of network security operations.

As a refresher, the main difference between an IDS and an IPS is that an IDS will only detect and report suspected intrusions, while an IPS will detect, report, and stop suspected intrusions. The types of intrusions given the highest priority should be those that have the potential to realize the risks we identified in our risk management plan. Accordingly, we must ensure that we address those threats first before we open our aperture to include others. Some organizations incorrectly assume that deploying the latest IDS/IPS technology will keep them safe, but this really depends on what exactly it is that they want to be safe from.

Once we are clear on the risk we are trying to mitigate, we can start deciding which intrusion detection and prevention controls offer the best return on investment. The options include host-based intrusion detection systems (HIDSs), network intrusion detection systems (NIDSs), and wireless intrusion detection systems (WIDSs). Each may operate in detection or prevention mode depending on the specific product and how it is employed. Finally, each may be rule or anomaly based, or, in some cases, a hybrid of both.

NOTE Any inline network security device (e.g., firewall, IDS, IPS) will have a maximum rated throughput. It is imperative to match that throughput with the load on the network segment on which the device is deployed. Doing otherwise risks creating a bottleneck and/or dropping packets.

Of course, the placement of network sensors is critical with IDSs/IPSs just as it is with firewalls. In principle, we want to start as close to the edge routers as we can while staying inside the perimeter. As resources and needs dictate, we can then place additional IDSs and IPSs in and/or between subnets. In most cases, we will want protection from the edge all the way to the end point (i.e., the workstation or server).

NOTE The term "perimeter" has lost some of its importance of late. While it remains an important concept in terms of security architecting, it can mislead some into imagining a wall separating us from the bad guys. A best practice is to assume the adversaries are already "inside the wire," which downplays the importance of a perimeter in security operations.

As with any other detection system, it is important to take steps to make the IDS or IPS less error-prone. *False positives*—that is, detecting intrusions when none happened—can lead to fatigue and desensitizing the personnel who need to examine each of these alerts. Conversely, *false negatives* are events that the system incorrectly classifies as benign, delaying the response until the intrusion is detected through some other means. Obviously, both are bad outcomes.

Perhaps the most important step toward reducing errors is to baseline the system. *Baselining* is the process of establishing the normal patterns of behavior for a given network or system. Most of us think of baselining only in terms of anomaly-based IDSs because these typically have to go through a period of learning before they can determine what is anomalous. However, even rule-based IDSs should be configured in accordance with whatever is normal for an organization. There is no such thing as a one-size-fits-all *set* of IDS/IPS rules, though some *individual* rules may very well be applicable to all (e.g., detecting a known specimen of malware).

Even after the initial configuration of the systems in the context of their specific networks or systems, we need to have a process in place for tuning our IDS/IPS to reduce false positives. Like any other change away from an established baseline, this should be part of our broader configuration management plan. This is particularly important for IDSs/IPSs, because of their dependence on whitelists and blacklists. A *whitelist* is a set of known-good resources such as IP addresses, domain names, or applications. Conversely, a *blacklist* is a set of known-bad resources. The operation of an IDS/IPS benefits tremendously from using these lists, partly because a whitelist will likely reduce the number of false positives. Another way in which we improve the performance of these systems is by maintaining accurate asset inventories. It is very useful for an IDS to know that a specific device is authorized (or not) to run a specific application.

Antimalware

Antimalware (commonly called antivirus) software is designed to detect and neutralize malicious software, including viruses, worms, and Trojan horses. The vast majority of commercially available antimalware software is rule based, with new malware definition files automatically downloaded from the vendor on a weekly (or shorter) basis. The way this software works is by identifying a distinctive attribute of the malware, extracting that as its signature, and then updating all software systems with it. Antimalware software works by identifying malware that is already known to the vendor, which means that it may not detect new malware (or "old" malware that has been modified).

There are at least a dozen major antimalware products in the market at the time of this writing. While none offers 100 percent protection against malicious software, all fall in the range of 90 to 99.9 percent effectiveness rate against *known* malware according to independent testing. Combine this with a relatively low price compared to other security solutions, and antimalware products offer very cost-effective protection. Still, it is not difficult to develop malware that is specifically designed to be invisible to any one product. This means that if a sophisticated adversary knows which antimalware product you use, they will not have much difficulty bypassing it.

Patch Management

According to NIST Special Publication 800-40, Revision 3, "Guide to Enterprise Patch Management Technologies," patch management is "the process for identifying, acquiring, installing, and verifying patches for products and systems." *Patches* are software updates intended to remove a vulnerability or defect in the software, or to provide new features or functionality for it. Patch management is, at least in a basic way, an established part of organizations' IT or security operations already.

Unmanaged Patching

One approach to patch management is to use a decentralized or unmanaged model in which each software package on each device periodically checks for updates and, if any are available, automatically applies them. While this approach may seem like a simple solution to the problem, it does have significant issues that could render it unacceptably risky for an organization. Among these risks are the following:

- **Credentials** Installing patches typically requires users to have admin credentials, which violates the principle of least privilege.
- **Configuration management** It may be difficult (or impossible) to attest to the status of every application in the organization, which makes configuration management much more difficult.
- **Bandwidth utilization** Having each application or service independently download the patches will lead to network congestion, particularly if there is no way to control when this will happen.

- **Service availability** Servers are almost never configured to automatically update themselves because this could lead to unscheduled outages that have a negative effect on the organization.

There is almost no advantage to decentralized patch management, except that it is better than doing nothing. The effort saved by not having management overhead is more than balanced by the additional effort you'll have to put into responding to incidents and solving configuration and interoperability problems. Still, there may be situations in which it is not possible to actively manage some devices. For instance, if you have a highly mobile workforce or if your users are allowed to work from home using personal devices, then it would be difficult to implement the centralized approach we discuss next. In such situations, the decentralized model may be the best to take, provided you also have a way to periodically (say, each time users do connect back to the mother ship) check the status of their updates.

Centralized Patch Management

Centralized patch management is considered a best practice for security operations. There are multiple approaches to implementing it, however, so you must carefully consider the pluses and minuses of each. The most common approaches are

- **Agent based** In this approach, an update agent is installed on each device. This agent communicates with one or more update servers and compares available patches with software and versions on the local host, updating as needed.
- **Agentless** Another way to manage patches is to have one or more hosts that remotely connect to each device on the network using admin credentials and check the remote device for needed updates. A spin on this is the use of Active Directory objects in a domain controller to manage patch levels.
- **Passive** Depending on the fidelity that an organization requires, it may be possible to passively monitor network traffic to infer the patch levels on each networked application or service. While minimally intrusive to the end devices, this approach is also the least effective since it may not always be possible to uniquely identify software versions through their network traffic artifacts.

Regardless of the approach you take, you want to apply the patches as quickly as possible. After all, every day you delay is an extra day that your adversaries have to exploit your vulnerabilities. The truth is that you can't (or at least shouldn't) always roll out the patch as soon as it comes out. There is no shortage of reports of major outages caused by rolling out patches. Sometimes the fault lies with the vendor, who, perhaps in its haste to remove a vulnerability, failed to properly test that the patch wouldn't break any other functionality of the product. Other times the patch may be rock solid and yet have a detrimental second or third order effect on other systems on your hosts or networks. This is why testing the patch before rolling it out is a good idea.

Virtualization technologies make it easier to set up a patch test lab. At a minimum, you want to replicate your critical infrastructure (e.g., domain controller and production servers) in this virtual test environment. Most organizations will also create at least one virtual machine (VM) that mimics each deployed operating system, with representative services and applications.

NOTE It is often possible to mitigate the risk created by a software vulnerability using other controls, such as rules for your firewalls, IDS, or IPS. This can buy time for you to test the patches. It also acts as a secondary control.

Whether or not you are able to test the patches before pushing them out (and you really should), it is also a good idea to patch your subnets incrementally. It may take longer to get to all systems, but if something goes wrong, it will only affect a subset of your users and services. This gradual approach to patching also serves to reduce network congestion that could result from all systems attempting to download patches at the same time. Obviously, the benefits of gradual patching need to be weighed against the additional exposure that the inherent delays will cause.

Reverse Engineering Patches

Zero-day exploits are able to successfully attack vulnerabilities that are not known to the software vendor or users of its software. For that reason, they are able to bypass the vast majority of controls such as firewalls, antimalware, and IDS/IPS. Though zero-day exploits are very powerful, they are also exceptionally hard to develop and very expensive to buy in the underground markets.

There is an easier and cheaper way for attackers to exploit recent vulnerabilities, and that is by reverse engineering the software patches that vendors push out. This approach takes advantage of the delay between a patch being available and it getting pushed to all the vulnerable computers in the organization. If the attacker can reverse engineer the patch faster than the defenders use it to update all computers, then the attacker wins. Some vendors are mitigating this threat by using *code obfuscation*, which, in an ironic turn of events, is a technique developed by attackers almost 30 years ago in an effort to thwart the then simple pattern-matching approach of antimalware solutions.

Even with code obfuscation, it is just a matter of time before the bad guys figure out what the vulnerability is. This puts pressure on the defenders to roll out the patches across the entire organization as quickly as possible. In this haste, organizations sometimes overlook problem indicators. Add to this a healthy application of Murphy's law and you will see why it is imperative to have a way to deal with these unknowns. A *rollback plan* describes the steps by which a change is reversed in order to restore functionality or integrity.

Sandboxing

A *sandbox* is an application execution environment that isolates the executing code from the operating system to prevent security violations. To the code, the sandbox looks just like the environment in which it would expect to run. For instance, when we sandbox an application, it behaves as if it were communicating directly with the OS. In reality, it is interacting with another piece of software whose purpose is to ensure compliance with security policies. Another instance is that of software (such as helper objects) running in a web browser. The software acts as if it were communicating directly with the browser, but those interactions are mediated by a policy enforcer of some sort. The power of sandboxes is that they offer an additional layer of protection when running code that we are not certain is safe to execute.

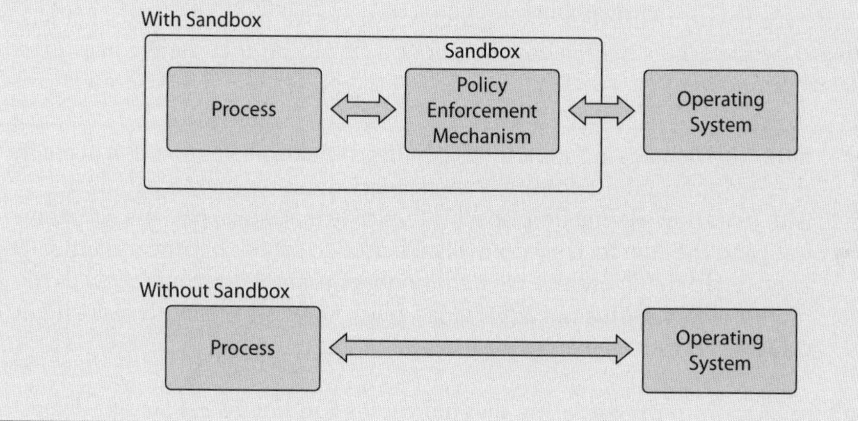

Honeypots

We introduced honeypots in Chapter 4. As a refresher, a *honeypot* is a device that is developed in order to deceive attackers into believing it is a real production system, entice and allow these adversaries to compromise it, and then monitor their activities on the compromised honeypot to observe and learn their behaviors. Wow! That was a mouthful! Think of honeypots as marketing devices; they are designed to attract a segment of the market, get them to buy something, and keep them coming back. Meanwhile, friendly threat analysts are keeping tabs on their adversaries' tactics, techniques, and procedures. Let's now look at how we can leverage this concept in other related ways.

A *honeynet* is an entire network that is meant to be compromised. While it may be tempting to describe honeynets as networks of honeypots, that description might be a bit misleading. Some honeynets are simply two or more honeypots used together. However, others are designed to ascertain a specific attacker's intent and dynamically spawn honeypots that are designed to be appealing to that particular attacker. As you can see, these very sophisticated honeynets are not networks of preexisting honeypots, but rather adaptive networks that interact with the adversaries in order to keep them engaged (and thus under observation) for as long as possible.

Wrapping up the honey collection, *honeyclients* are synthetic applications meant to allow an attacker to conduct a client-side attack while also allowing the friendly analysts an opportunity to observe the techniques being used by their adversaries. Honeyclients are particularly important in the honey family, because most of the successful attacks happen on the client side, and honeypots are not particularly well suited to track client-side attacks. Suppose you have a suspected phishing or spearphishing attack that you'd like to investigate. You could use a honeyclient to visit the link in the e-mail and pretend it is a real user. Instead of getting infected, however, the honeyclient safely catches all the attacks thrown at it and reports them to you. Since it is not really the web browser it is claiming to be, it will be impervious to the attack and will provide you with information about the actual tools the attacker is throwing at you. Honeyclients come in different flavors, with some being highly interactive (meaning a human has to operate them), while others involve low interaction (meaning their behavior is mostly or completely automated).

NOTE Black holes are sometimes confused with honeynets, when in reality they are almost the opposite of them. Black holes typically are routers with rules that silently drop specific (typically malicious) packets without notifying the source. They normally are used to render botnet and other known-bad traffic useless. Whereas honeypots and honeynets allow us to more closely observe our adversaries, black holes are meant to make them go away for us.

It should be clear from the foregoing that honeypots and honeynets are not defensive controls like firewalls and IDSs, but rather help us collect threat intelligence. In order to be effective, they must be closely monitored by a competent threat analyst. By themselves, honeypots and honeynets will not improve your security posture. However, they can give your threat intelligence team invaluable insights into your adversaries' methods and capabilities.

Of course, honeynets and honeypots are only useful insofar as they convince the attackers that they are real production systems and not sting operations. The first key to success is to ensure that the typical probing used by attackers to determine whether or not they are being watched is thwarted. This is a game of leapfrog wherein one side makes an advance and then the other learns how to exploit it. Still, the harder you make it for attackers to notice they are in a honeypot, the more time you have to observe them.

Another key to honeypot success is to provide the right kind of bait. When someone attacks your organization, what is it that they are after? Is it credit card information, patient files, intellectual property? Your honeypots should look like systems that would allow them to access the assets for which they are searching. Once compromised, the directories and files containing this information must appear to be credible. It should also take a long time to extract the information, so that we maximize the contact time with our "guests."

The Incident Management Process

There are many incident management models, but all share some basic characteristics. They all require that we identify the event, analyze it to determine the appropriate counteractions, correct the problem(s), and, finally, keep the event from happening again. $(ISC)^2$ has broken out these four basic actions and prescribes seven phases in the incident management process: detect, respond, mitigate, report, recover, remediate, and learn. Your own organization will have a unique approach, but it is helpful to baseline it off the industry standard.

Although we commonly use the terms "event" and "incident" interchangeably, there are subtle differences between the two. An *event* is any occurrence that can be observed, verified, and documented, whereas an *incident* is one or more related events that negatively affect the company and/or impact its security posture. This is why we call reacting to these issues "incident response" (or "incident handling"), because something is negatively affecting the company and causing a security breach.

Many types of incidents (viruses, insider attacks, terrorist attacks, and so on) exist, and sometimes an incident is just human error. Indeed, many incident response individuals have received a frantic call in the middle of the night because a system is acting "weird." The reasons could be that a deployed patch broke something, someone misconfigured a device, or the administrator just learned a new scripting language and rolled out some code that caused mayhem and confusion.

When a company is victimized by a computer crime, it should leave the environment and evidence unaltered and contact whomever has been delegated to investigate these types of situations. Someone who is unfamiliar with the proper process of collecting data and evidence from a crime scene could instead destroy that evidence, and in doing so destroy all hope of prosecuting individuals and achieving a conviction. Companies should have procedures in place for many issues in computer security, such as enforcement procedures, disaster recovery and continuity procedures, and backup procedures. It is also necessary to have a procedure for dealing with computer incidents, because they have become an increasingly important issue for today's information security departments to address. This is a direct result of the ever-increasing number of attacks against networks and information systems. Although specific numbers aren't available due to a lack of universal reporting and reporting in general, it is clear that the volume of attacks is increasing. Just think about all the spam, phishing scams, malware, distributed denial-of-service, and other attacks you see on your own network and hear about in the news.

Unfortunately, many companies are at a loss as to who to call or what to do right after they have been the victim of a cybercrime. Therefore, all companies should have an incident response policy that indicates who has the authority to initiate an incident response, with supporting procedures set up before an incident takes place. This policy should be managed by the legal department and security department. They need to work together to make sure the technical security issues are covered and the legal issues that surround criminal activities are properly dealt with.

The incident response policy should be clear and concise. For example, it should indicate whether systems can be taken offline to try to save evidence or must continue functioning at the risk of destroying evidence. Each system and functionality should have a priority assigned to it. For instance, if the file server is infected, it should be removed from the network, but not shut down. However, if the mail server is infected, it should not be removed from the network or shut down because of the priority the company attributes to the mail server over the file server. Tradeoffs and decisions will have to be made, but it is better to think through these issues before the situation occurs, because better logic is usually possible before a crisis, when there's less emotion and chaos.

All organizations should develop an *incident response team*, as mandated by the incident response policy, to respond to the large array of possible security incidents. The purpose of having an incident response team is to ensure that there is a group of people who are properly skilled, who follow a standard set of procedures, and who are singled out and called upon when this type of event takes place. The team should have proper reporting procedures established, be prompt in their reaction, work in coordination with law enforcement, and be an important element of the overall security program. The team should consist of representatives from various business units, such as the legal department, HR, executive management, the communications department, physical/corporate security, IS security, and information technology.

Incident Management

Incident management includes proactive and reactive processes. Proactive measures need to be put into place so that incidents can actually be detected in a controllable manner, and reactive measures need to be put into place so those incidents are then dealt with properly.

Most organizations have only incident response processes, which walk through how an incident should be handled. A more holistic approach is an incident management program, which ensures that triggers are monitored to make sure all incidents are actually uncovered. This commonly involves log aggregation, a security information and event management system (SIEM), and user education. Having clear ways of dealing with incidents is not necessarily useful if you don't have a way to find out if incidents are indeed taking place.

There are three different types of incident response teams that an organization can choose to put into place. A *virtual* team is made up of experts who have other duties and assignments within the organization. This type of team introduces a slower response time, and members must neglect their regular duties should an incident occur. However, a *permanent* team of folks who are dedicated strictly to incident response can be cost prohibitive to smaller organizations. The third type of incident response team is a *hybrid* of the virtual and permanent models. Certain core members are permanently assigned to the team, whereas others are called in as needed.

The incident response team should have the following basic items available:

- A list of outside agencies and resources to contact or report to.
- An outline of roles and responsibilities.

- A call tree to contact these roles and outside entities.
- A list of computer or forensic experts to contact.
- A list of steps to take to secure and preserve evidence.
- A list of items that should be included in a report for management and potentially the courts.
- A description of how the different systems should be treated in this type of situation. (For example, the systems should be removed from both the Internet and the network and powered down.)

When a suspected crime is reported, the incident response team should follow a set of predetermined steps to ensure uniformity in their approach and make sure no steps are skipped. First, the incident response team should investigate the report and determine that an actual crime has been committed. If the team determines that a crime has been carried out, senior management should be informed immediately. If the suspect is an employee, a human resources representative must be called right away. The sooner the documenting of events begins, the better. If someone is able to document the starting time of the crime, along with the company employees and resources involved, that provides a good foundation for evidence. At this point, the company must decide if it wants to conduct its own forensic investigation or call in experts. If experts are going to be called in, the system that was attacked should be left alone in order to try and preserve as much evidence of the attack as possible. If the company decides to conduct its own forensic investigation, it must deal with many issues and address tricky elements. (Forensics will be discussed later in this chapter.)

Computer networks and business processes face many types of threats, each requiring a specialized type of recovery. However, an incident response team should draft and enforce a basic outline of how *all* incidents are to be handled. This is a much better approach than the way many companies deal with these threats, which is usually in an ad hoc, reactive, and confusing manner. A clearly defined incident-handling process is more cost effective, enables recovery to happen more quickly, and provides a uniform approach with certain expectation of its results.

Incident handling should be closely related to disaster recovery planning and should be part of the company's disaster recovery plan, usually as an appendix. Both are intended to react to some type of incident that requires a quick response so the company can return to normal operations. Incident handling is a recovery plan that responds to malicious technical threats. The primary goal of incident handling is to contain and mitigate any damage caused by an incident and to prevent any further damage. This is commonly done by detecting a problem, determining its cause, resolving the problem, and documenting the entire process.

Without an effective incident-handling program, individuals who have the best intentions can sometimes make the situation worse by damaging evidence, damaging systems, or spreading malicious code. Many times, the attacker booby-traps the compromised system to erase specific critical files if a user does something as simple as list the files in a directory. A compromised system can no longer be trusted because the internal commands listed in the path could be altered to perform unexpected activities.

The system could now have a back door for the attacker to enter when he wants, or could have a logic bomb silently waiting for a user to start snooping around only to destroy any and all evidence.

Incident handling should also be closely linked to the company's security training and awareness program to ensure that these types of mishaps do not take place. Past issues that the incident recovery team encountered can be used in future training sessions to help others learn what the company is faced with and how to improve response processes.

Employees need to know how to report an incident. Therefore, the incident response policy should detail an escalation process so that employees understand when evidence of a crime should be reported to higher management, outside agencies, or law enforcement. The process must be centralized, easy to accomplish (or the employees won't bother), convenient, and welcomed. Some employees feel reluctant to report incidents because they are afraid they will get pulled into something they do not want to be involved with or accused of something they did not do. There is nothing like trying to do the right thing and getting hit with a big stick. Employees should feel comfortable about the process, and not feel intimidated by reporting suspicious activities.

The incident response policy should also dictate how employees should interact with external entities, such as the media, government, and law enforcement. This, in particular, is a complicated issue influenced by jurisdiction, the status and nature of the crime, and the nature of the evidence. Jurisdiction alone, for example, depends on the country, state, or federal agency that has control. Given the sensitive nature of public disclosure, communications should be handled by communications, human resources, or other appropriately trained individuals who are authorized to publicly discuss incidents. Public disclosure of an event can lead to two possible outcomes. If not handled correctly, it can compound the negative impact of an incident. For example, given today's information-driven society, denial and "no comment" may result in a backlash. On the other hand, if public disclosure is handled well, it can provide the organization with an opportunity to win back public trust. Some countries and jurisdictions either already have or are contemplating breach disclosure laws that require organizations to notify the public if a security breach involving personally identifiable information is even suspected. So it's to your benefit to make sure you are open and forthright with third parties.

A sound incident-handling program works with outside agencies and counterparts. The members of the team should be on the mailing list of the Computer Emergency Response Team (CERT) so they can keep up-to-date about new issues and can spot malicious events, hopefully before they get out of hand. CERT is an organization that is responsible for monitoring and advising users and companies about security preparation and security breaches.

NOTE Resources for CERT can be found at https://www.cert.org/incident-management/.

The Cyber Kill Chain

Even as we think about how best to manage incidents, it is helpful to consider a model for the attacker's behaviors. In their seminal 2011 paper titled "Intelligence-Driven Computer Network Defense Informed by Analysis of Adversary Campaigns and Intrusion Kill Chains," Hutchins, Cloppert, and Amin describe a seven-stage intrusion model that has become an industry standard. Their seven stages are described here:

1. **Reconnaissance** The adversary has developed an interest in your organization as a target and begins a deliberate information-gathering effort to find vulnerabilities.
2. **Weaponization** Armed with detailed-enough information, the adversary determines the best way into your systems and begins preparing and testing the weapons to be used against you.
3. **Delivery** In this phase, the cyber weapon is delivered into your system. In over 95 percent of the published cases, this delivery happens via e-mail and usually in the form of a link to a malicious website.
4. **Exploitation** The malicious software is executing on a CPU within your network. This may have launched when the target user clicked a link, opened an attachment, visited a website, or plugged in a USB thumb drive. It could also (in somewhat rare cases) be the result of a remote exploit. One way or another, the attacker's software is now running in your systems.
5. **Installation** Most malicious software is delivered in stages. First, there is the exploit that compromised the system in the prior step. Then, some other software is installed in the target system to ensure persistence, ideally with a good measure of stealth.
6. **Command and Control (C&C)** Once the first two stages of the software (exploit and persistence) have been executed, most malware will "phone home" to the attackers to let them know the attack was successful and to request updates and instructions.
7. **Actions on the Objective** Finally, the malware is ready to do whatever it is it was designed to do. Perhaps the intent is to steal intellectual property and send it to an overseas server. Or perhaps this particular effort is an early phase in a grander attack, so the malware will pivot off the compromised system. Whatever the case, the attacker has won at this point.

As you can probably imagine, the earlier in the kill chain we identify the attack, the greater our odds are of preventing the adversaries from achieving their objectives.

(*Continued*)

This is a critical concept in this model: if you can thwart the attack before stage four (exploitation), you stand a better chance of winning. Early detection, then, is the key to success.

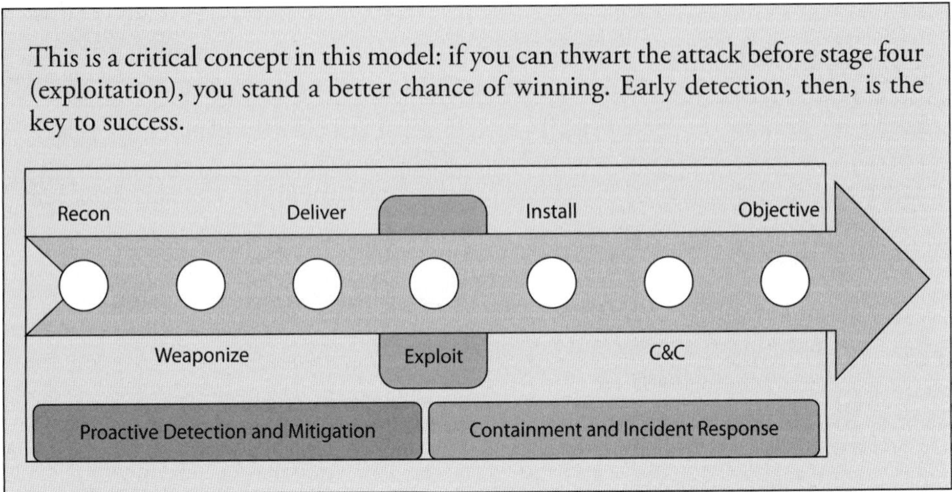

Detection

The first and most important step in responding to an incident is to realize that you have a problem in the first place. Despite an abundance of sensors, this can be harder than it sounds for a variety of reasons. First, sophisticated adversaries may use tools and techniques that you are unable to detect (at least at first). Even if the tools or techniques are known to you, they may very well be hiding under a mound of false positives in your SIEMs. In some (improperly tuned) systems, the ratio of false positives to true positives can be ten to one (or higher). This underscores the importance of tuning your sensors and analysis platforms to reduce the rate of false positive as much as possible.

Response

Having detected the incident, the next step is to determine what the appropriate response might be. Though the instinctive reaction may be to clean up the infected workstation or add rules to your firewalls, IDS, and IPS, this well-intentioned response could lead you on an endless game of whack-a-mole or, worse yet, blind you to the adversary's real objective. What do you know about the adversary? Who is it? What are they after? Is this tool and its use consistent with what you have already seen? Part of the early stages of a response is to figure out what information you need in order to restore security.

This is the substage of analysis, where more data is gathered (audit logs, video captures, human accounts of activities, system activities) to try and figure out the root cause of the incident. The goals are to figure out who did this, how they did it, when they did it, and why. Management must be continually kept abreast of these activities because they will be making the big decisions on how this situation is to be handled.

The group of individuals who make up the response team must have a variety of skills. They must also have a solid understanding of the systems affected by the incident, the system and application vulnerabilities, and the network and system configurations.

Although formal education is important, real-world applied experience combined with proper training is key for these folks.

One of the biggest challenges the response team faces is the dynamic nature of logs. Many systems are configured to purge or overwrite their logs in a short timeframe, and time is lost the moment the incident occurs. Several hours may pass before an incident is reported or detected. Some countries are considering legislation that would require longer log file retention. However, such laws pose privacy and storage challenges.

Once you have a hypothesis about the adversary's goals and plans, you can test it. If this particular actor is usually interested in PII on your high-net-worth clients but the incident you detected was on a (seemingly unrelated) host in the warehouse, was that an initial entry or pivot point? If so, then you may have caught them before they worked their way further along the kill chain. But what if you got your attribution wrong? How could you test for that? This chain of questions, combined with quantifiable answers from your systems, forms the basis for an effective response. To quote the famous hockey player Wayne Gretzky, we should all "skate to where the puck is going to be, not where it has been."

NOTE It really takes a fairly mature threat intelligence capability to determine who is behind an attack (attribution), what are their typical tools, techniques, and procedures, and what might be their ultimate objective. If you do not have this capability, you may have no choice but to respond only to what you're detecting, without regard for what they may actually be trying to do.

Mitigation

By this point in the incident response process, you should know what happened as well as what you think is likely to happen next. The next step is to *mitigate* or contain the damage that has been or is about to be done to your most critical assets, followed by mitigation of less important assets. Returning to the earlier PII example, a naïve response could be to take the infected system (in the warehouse) offline and preserve evidence. The problem is that if that system was simply an entry or pivot point, you may very well already be behind your adversary. Unless you look for other indicators, how would you know whether they already compromised the next system in the chain? Why bother quarantining a host that has already served its purpose (to your adversaries) when you haven't yet taken a look at the (presumed) ultimate target?

The goal of mitigation is to prevent or reduce any further damage from this incident so that you can begin to recover and remediate. A proper mitigation strategy buys the incident response team time for a proper investigation and determination of the incident's root cause. The mitigation strategy should be based on the category of the attack (that is, whether it was internal or external), the assets affected by the incident, and the criticality of those assets. So what kind of mitigation strategy is best? Well, it depends. Mitigation strategies can be proactive or reactive. Which is best depends on the environment and the category of the attack. In some cases, the best action might be to disconnect the affected system from the network. However, this reactive approach could cause a denial of service or limit functionality of critical systems.

When complete isolation or containment is not a viable solution, you may opt to use network segmentation to virtually isolate a system or systems. Boundary devices can also be used to stop one system from infecting another. Another reactive strategy involves reviewing and revising firewall/filtering router rule configuration. Access control lists can also be applied to minimize exposure. These mitigation strategies indicate to the attacker that his attack has been noticed and countermeasures are being implemented. But what if, in order to perform a root cause analysis, you need to keep the affected system online and not let on that you've noticed the attack? In this situation, you might consider installing a honeynet or honeypot to provide an area that will contain the attacker but pose minimal risk to the organization. This decision should involve legal counsel and upper management because honeynets and honeypots can introduce liability issues. Once the incident has been contained, you need to figure out what just happened by putting the available pieces together.

Reporting

Though we discuss reporting here in order to remain consistent with (ISC)², incident reporting and documentation occurs at various stages in the response process. In many cases involving sophisticated attackers, the response team first learns of the incident because someone else reports it. Whether it is an internal user, an external client or partner, or even a three-letter government entity, this initial report becomes the start point of the entire process. In more mundane cases, we become aware that something is amiss thanks to a vigilant member of the security staff or one of the sensors deployed to detect attacks. However we learn of the incident, this first report starts what should be a continuous process of documentation.

According to NIST Special Publication 800-61, Revision 2, "Computer Security Incident Handling Guide," the following information should be reported for each incident:

- Summary of the incident
- Indicators
- Related incidents
- Actions taken
- Chain of custody for all evidence (if applicable)
- Impact assessment
- Identity and comments of incident handlers
- Next steps to be taken

Recovery

Once the incident is mitigated, you must turn your attention to the recovery phase, in which you return all systems and information to a known-good state. It is important to gather evidence before you recover systems and information. The reason is that in many cases you won't know that you will need legally admissible evidence until days, weeks, or even months after an incident. It pays, then, to treat each incident as if it will eventually end up in a court of justice.

Once all relevant evidence is captured, you can begin to fix all that was broken. The aim is to restore full, trustworthy functionality to the organization. For hosts that were compromised, the best practice is to simply reinstall the system from a gold master image and then restore data from the most recent backup that occurred prior to the attack. You may also have to roll back transactions and restore databases from backup systems. Once you are done, it is as if the incident never happened. Well, almost.

CAUTION An attacked or infected system should never be trusted, because you do not necessarily know all the changes that have taken place and the true extent of the damage. Some malicious code could still be hiding somewhere. Systems should be rebuilt to ensure that all of the potential bad mojo has been released by carrying out a proper exorcism.

Remediation

It is not enough to put the pieces of Humpty Dumpty back together again. You also need to ensure that the attack is never again successful. During the mitigation phase, you identified quick fixes to neutralize or reduce the effectiveness of the incident. Now, in the remediation phase, you decide which of those measures (e.g., firewall or IDS/IPS rules) need to be made permanent and which additional controls may be needed.

Another aspect of remediation is the identification of your indicators of attack (IOA) that can be used in the future to detect this attack in real time (i.e., as it is happening) as well as indicators of compromise (IOC), which tell you when an attack has been successful and your security has been compromised. Typical indicators of both attack and compromise include the following.

- Outbound traffic to a particular IP address or domain name
- Abnormal DNS query patterns
- Unusually large HTTP requests and/or responses
- DDoS traffic
- New Registry entries (in Windows systems)

At the conclusion of the remediation phase, you have a high degree of confidence that this particular attack will never again be successful against your organization. Ideally, you should share your lessons learned in the form of IOAs and IOCs with the community so that no other organization can be exploited in this manner. This kind of collaboration with partners (and even competitors) makes the adversary have to work harder.

Learning as Part of the Incident Response Process

Closure of an incident is determined by the nature or category of the incident, the desired incident response outcome (for example, business resumption or system restoration), and the team's success in determining the incident's source and root cause. Once it is determined that the incident is closed, it is a good idea to have a team briefing that includes all groups affected by the incident to answer the following questions:

- What happened?
- What did we learn?
- How can we do it better next time?

The team should review the incident and how it was handled and carry out a postmortem analysis. The information that comes out of this meeting should indicate what needs to go into the incident response process and documentation, with the goal of continual improvement. Instituting a formal process for the briefing will provide the team with the ability to start collecting data that can be used to track its performance metrics.

Disaster Recovery

So far we have discussed preventing and responding to security incidents as part of standard security operations. These are things we do day in and day out. But what happens on those rare occasions when an incident has disastrous effects? This is a great point at which to circle back to a discussion we started in Chapter 1 on business continuity planning. Recall that we discussed the role of maximum tolerable downtime (MTD) values. In reality, basic MTD values are a good start, but are not granular enough for a company to figure out what it needs to put into place to be able to absorb the impact of a disaster. MTD values are usually "broad strokes" that do not provide enough detail to help pinpoint the actual recovery solutions that need to be purchased and implemented. For example, if the BCP team determines that the MTD value for the customer service department is 48 hours, this is not enough information to fully understand what redundant solutions or backup technology should be put into place. MTD in this example does provide a basic deadline that means if customer service is not up within 48 hours, the company may not be able to recover and everyone should start looking for new jobs.

As shown in Figure 7-12, more than just MTD metrics are needed to get production back to normal operations after a disruptive event. We will walk through each of these metric types and see how they are best used together.

The *recovery time objective (RTO)* is the maximum time period within which a business process must be restored to a designated service level after a disaster to avoid unacceptable

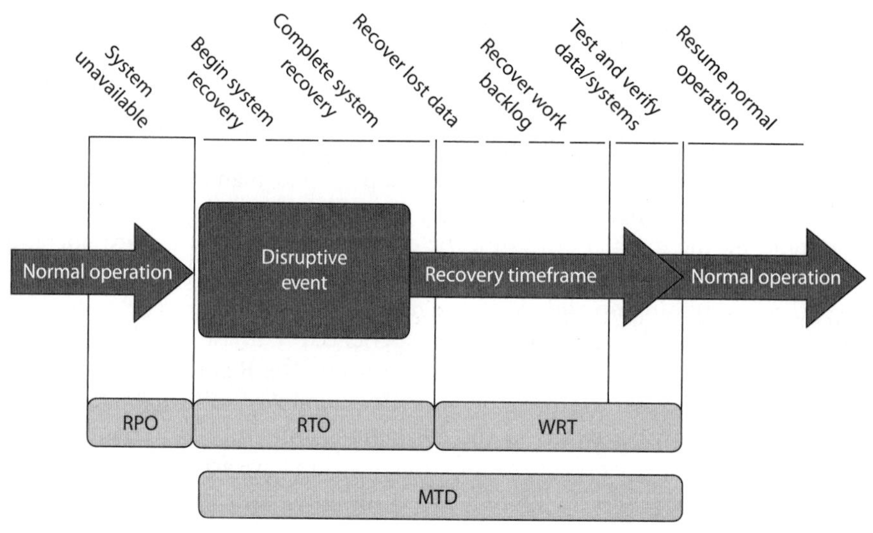

Figure 7-12 Metrics used for disaster recovery

consequences associated with a break in business continuity. The RTO value is smaller than the MTD value, because the MTD value represents the time after which an inability to recover significant operations will mean severe and perhaps irreparable damage to the organization's reputation or bottom line. The RTO assumes that there is a period of acceptable downtime. This means that a company can be out of production for a certain period of time (RTO) and still get back on its feet. But if the company cannot get production up and running within the MTD window, the company is sinking too fast to properly recover.

The *work recovery time (WRT)* is the remainder of the overall MTD value after the RTO has passed. RTO usually deals with getting the infrastructure and systems back up and running, and WRT deals with restoring data, testing processes, and then making everything "live" for production purposes.

The *recovery point objective (RPO)* is the acceptable amount of data loss measured in time. This value represents the earliest point in time at which data must be recovered. The higher the value of data, the more funds or other resources that can be put into place to ensure a smaller amount of data is lost in the event of a disaster. Figure 7-13 illustrates the relationship and differences between the use of RPO and RTO values.

Figure 7-13 RPO and RTO metrics in use

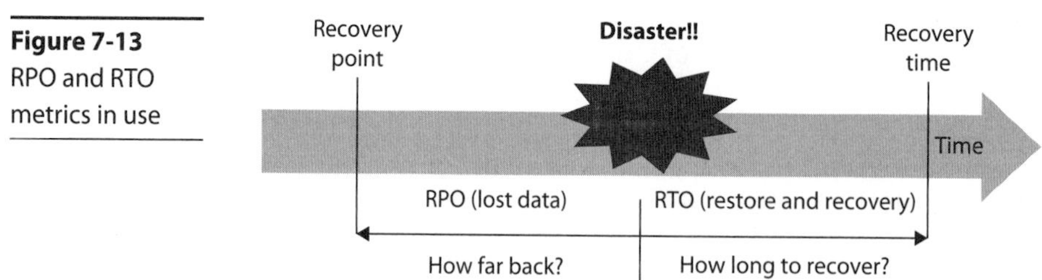

The RTO, RPO, and WRT values are critical to understand because they will be the basic foundational metrics used when determining the type of recovery solutions a company must put into place, so let's dig a bit deeper into them. As an example of RTO, let's say a company has determined that if it is unable to process product order requests for 12 hours, the financial hit will be too large for it to survive. So the company develops methods to ensure that orders can be processed manually if their automated technological solutions become unavailable. But if it takes the company 24 hours to actually stand up the manual processes, the company could be in a place operationally and financially where it can never fully recover. So RTO deals with "how much time do we have to get everything up and working again?"

Now let's say that the same company experienced a disaster and got its manual processes up and running within two hours, so it met the RTO requirement. But just because business processes are back in place, the company still might have a critical problem. The company has to restore the data it lost during the disaster. It does no good to restore data that is a week old. The employees need to have access to the data that was being processed right before the disaster hit. If the company can only restore data that is a week old, then all the orders that were in some stage of being fulfilled over the last seven days could be lost. If the company makes an average of $25,000 per day in orders and all the order data was lost for the last seven days, this can result in a loss of $175,000 and a lot of unhappy customers. So just getting things up and running (RTO) is part of the picture. Getting the necessary data in place so that business processes are up-to-date and relevant (RPO) is just as critical.

To take things one step further, let's say the company stood up its manual order-filling processes in two hours. It also had real-time data backup systems in place, so all of the necessary up-to-date data is restored. But no one actually tested these manual processes, everyone is confused, and orders still cannot be processed and revenue cannot be collected. This means the company met its RTO requirement and its RPO requirement, but failed its WRT requirement, and thus failed the MTD requirement. Proper business recovery means *all* of the individual things have to happen correctly for the overall goal to be successful.

EXAM TIP An RTO is the amount of time it takes to recover from a disaster, and an RPO is the amount of acceptable data, measured in time, that can be lost from that same event.

The actual MTD, RTO, and RPO values are derived during the business impact analysis (BIA), the purpose of which is to be able to apply criticality values to specific business functions, resources, and data types. A simplistic example is shown in Table 7-3. The company must have data restoration capabilities in place to ensure that mission-critical data is never older than one minute. The company cannot rely on something as slow as backup tape restoration, but must have a high-availability data replication solution in place. The RTO value for mission-critical data processing is two minutes or less. This means that the technology that carries out the processing functionality for

Data Type	RPO	RTO
Mission Critical	Continuous to 1 Minute	Instantaneous to 2 Minutes
Business Critical	5 Minutes	10 Minutes
Business	3 Hours	8 Hours

Table 7-3 RPO and RTO Value Relationships

this type of data cannot be down for more than two minutes. The company may choose to have a cluster technology in place that will shift the load once it notices that a server goes offline.

In this same scenario, data that is classified as "Business" can be up to three hours old when the production environment comes back online, so a slower data replication process is acceptable. Since the RTO for business data is eight hours, the company can choose to have hot-swappable hard drives available instead of having to pay for the more complicated and expensive clustering technology.

The BCP team has to figure out what the company needs to do to actually recover the processes and services it has identified as being so important to the organization overall. In its business continuity and recovery strategy, the team closely examines the critical, agreed-upon business functions, and then evaluates the numerous recovery and backup alternatives that might be used to recover critical business operations. It is important to choose the right tactics and technologies for the recovery of each critical business process and service in order to assure that the set MTD values are met.

So what does the BCP team need to accomplish? The team needs to actually define the recovery processes, which are sets of predefined activities that will be implemented and carried out in response to a disaster. More importantly, these processes must be constantly re-evaluated and updated as necessary to ensure that the organization meets or exceeds the MTDs.

What Is the Difference Between Preventive Measures and Recovery Strategies?

Preventive mechanisms are put into place not only to try to reduce the possibility that the company will experience a disaster, but also, if a disaster does hit, to lessen the amount of damage that will take place. Although the company cannot stop a tornado from coming, for example, it could choose to move its facility from Tornado Alley to an area less prone to tornados. As another example, the company cannot stop a car from plowing into and taking out a transformer that it relies on for power, but it can have a separate power feed from a different transformer in case this happens.

Recovery strategies are processes on how to rescue the company after a disaster takes place. These processes will integrate mechanisms such as establishing alternate sites for facilities, implementing emergency response procedures, and possibly activating the preventive mechanisms that have already been implemented.

Business Process Recovery

A business process is a set of interrelated steps linked through specific decision activities to accomplish a specific task. Business processes have starting and ending points and are repeatable. The processes should encapsulate the knowledge about services, resources, and operations provided by a company. For example, when a customer requests to buy a book via an organization's e-commerce site, a set of steps must be followed, such as these:

1. Validate that the book is available.
2. Validate where the book is located and how long it would take to ship it to the destination.
3. Provide the customer with the price and delivery date.
4. Verify the customer's credit card information.
5. Validate and process the credit card order.
6. Send a receipt and tracking number to the customer.
7. Send the order to the book inventory location.
8. Restock inventory.
9. Send the order to accounting.

The BCP team needs to understand these different steps of the company's most critical processes. The data is usually presented as a workflow document that contains the roles and resources needed for each process. The BCP team must understand the following about critical business processes:

- Required roles
- Required resources
- Input and output mechanisms
- Workflow steps
- Required time for completion
- Interfaces with other processes

This will allow the BCP team to identify threats and the controls to ensure the least amount of process interruption.

Facility Recovery

Disruptions, in BCP terms, are of three main types: nondisasters, disasters, and catastrophes. A *nondisaster* is a disruption in service that has significant but limited impact on the conduct of business processes at a facility. The solution could include hardware, software, or file restoration. A *disaster* is an event that causes the entire facility to be unusable for a day or longer. This usually requires the use of an alternate processing facility and restoration of software and data from offsite copies. The alternate site must

be available to the company until its main facility is repaired and usable. A *catastrophe* is a major disruption that destroys the facility altogether. This requires both a short-term solution, which would be an offsite facility, and a long-term solution, which may require rebuilding the original facility. Disasters and catastrophes are rare compared to nondisasters, thank goodness.

An organization has various recovery alternatives to choose from, such as a redundant site, outsourcing, a rented offsite installation, or a reciprocal agreement with another organization. The organization has three basic options: select a dedicated site that the organization operates itself; lease a commercial facility, such as a "hot site" that contains all the equipment and data needed to quickly restore operations; or enter into a formal agreement with another facility, such as a service bureau, to restore its operations.

In all these cases, the organization estimates the alternative's ability to support its operations, to do it quickly, and to do it at a fair cost. It should closely query the alternative facility about such things as: How long will it take to recover from a certain incident to a certain level of operations? Will it give priority to restoring the operations of one organization over another after a disaster? What are its costs for performing various functions? What are its specifications for IT and security functions? Is the workspace big enough for the required number of employees?

An important consideration with third parties is their reliability, both in normal times and during an emergency. Their reliability can depend on considerations such as their track record, the extent and location of their supply inventory, and their access to supply and communication channels.

For larger disasters that affect the primary facility, an offsite backup facility must be accessible. Generally, contracts are established with third-party vendors to provide such services. The client pays a monthly fee to retain the right to use the facility in a time of need, and then incurs an activation fee when the facility actually has to be used. In addition, there would be a daily or hourly fee imposed for the duration of the stay. This is why subscription services for backup facilities should be considered a short-term solution, not a long-term solution.

It is important to note that most recovery site contracts do not promise to house the company in need at a specific location, but rather promise to provide what has been contracted for somewhere within the company's locale. On, and subsequent to, September 11, 2001, many organizations with Manhattan offices were surprised when they were redirected by their backup site vendor not to sites located in New Jersey (which were already full), but rather to sites located in Boston, Chicago, or Atlanta. This adds yet another level of complexity to the recovery process, specifically the logistics of transporting people and equipment to unplanned locations.

Companies can choose from three main types of leased or rented offsite facilities:

- **Hot site** A facility that is leased or rented and is fully configured and ready to operate within a few hours. The only missing resources from a hot site are usually the data, which will be retrieved from a backup site, and the people who will be processing the data. The equipment and system software must absolutely be compatible with the data being restored from the main site and must not cause any negative interoperability issues. Some facilities, for a fee, store data backups close to the hot site. These sites are a good choice for a company that needs to ensure a site will be available for it as soon as possible. Most hot-site facilities support annual tests that can be done by the company to ensure the site is functioning in the necessary state of readiness.

This is the most expensive of the three types of offsite facilities. It can pose problems if a company requires proprietary or unusual hardware or software.

NOTE To attract the largest customer base, the vendor of a hot site will provide the most commonly used hardware and software products. This most likely will not include the specific customer's proprietary or unusual hardware or software products.

- **Warm site** A leased or rented facility that is usually partially configured with some equipment, such as HVAC, and foundational infrastructure components, but not the actual computers. In other words, a warm site is usually a hot site without the expensive equipment such as communication equipment and servers. Staging a facility with duplicate hardware and computers configured for immediate operation is extremely expensive, so a warm site provides an alternate facility with some peripheral devices.

  This is the most widely used model. It is less expensive than a hot site, and can be up and running within a reasonably acceptable time period. It may be a better choice for companies that depend upon proprietary and unusual hardware and software, because they will bring their own hardware and software with them to the site after the disaster hits. Drawbacks, however, are that much of the equipment has to be procured, delivered to, and configured at the warm site after the fact, and the annual testing available with hot-site contracts is not usually available with warm-site contracts. Thus, a company cannot be certain that it will in fact be able to return to an operating state within hours.
- **Cold site** A leased or rented facility that supplies the basic environment, electrical wiring, air conditioning, plumbing, and flooring, but none of the equipment or additional services. A cold site is essentially an empty data center. It may take weeks to get the site activated and ready for work. The cold site could have equipment racks and dark fiber (fiber that does not have the circuit engaged) and maybe even desks. However, it would require the receipt of equipment from the client, since it does not provide any.

  The cold site is the least expensive option, but takes the most time and effort to actually get up and functioning right after a disaster, as the systems and software must be delivered, set up, and configured. Cold sites are often used as backups for call centers, manufacturing plants, and other services that can be moved lock, stock, and barrel in one shot.

After a catastrophic loss of the primary facility, some places will start their recovery in a hot or warm site, and transfer some operations over to a cold site after the latter has had time to set up.

It is important to understand that the different site types listed here are provided by service bureaus. A *service bureau* is a company that has additional space and capacity to provide applications and services such as call centers. A company pays a monthly subscription fee to a service bureau for this space and service. The fee can be paid for contingencies such as disasters and emergencies. You should evaluate the ability of a service bureau to provide services as you would divisions within your own organization, particularly on matters such as its ability to alter or scale its software and hardware configurations or to expand its operations to meet the needs of a contingency.

NOTE Related to a service bureau is a *contingency company*; its purpose is to supply services and materials temporarily to an organization that is experiencing an emergency. For example, a contingent supplier might provide raw materials such as heating fuel or backup telecommunication services. In considering contingent suppliers, the BCP team should think through considerations such as the level of services and materials a supplier can provide, how quickly a supplier can ramp up to supply them, and whether the supplier shares similar communication paths and supply chains as the affected organization.

Most companies use *warm sites*, which have some devices such as disk drives, tape drives, and controllers, but very little else. These companies usually cannot afford a hot site, and the extra downtime would not be considered detrimental. A warm site can provide a longer-term solution than a hot site. Companies that decide to go with a *cold site* must be able to be out of operation for a week or two. The cold site usually includes power, raised flooring, climate control, and wiring.

The following provides a quick overview of the differences between offsite facilities:

Hot Site Advantages

- Ready within hours for operation
- Highly available
- Usually used for short-term solutions, but available for longer stays
- Annual testing available

Hot Site Disadvantages

- Very expensive
- Limited on hardware and software choices

Warm and Cold Site Advantages

- Less expensive
- Available for longer timeframes because of the reduced costs
- Practical for proprietary hardware or software use

Warm and Cold Site Disadvantages

- Operational testing not usually available
- Resources for operations not immediately available

Tertiary Sites

The BCP team may recognize the danger of the primary backup facility not being available when needed, which could require a tertiary site. This is a secondary backup site, just in case the primary backup site is unavailable. The secondary backup site is sometimes referred to as a "backup to the backup." This is basically plan B if plan A does not work out.

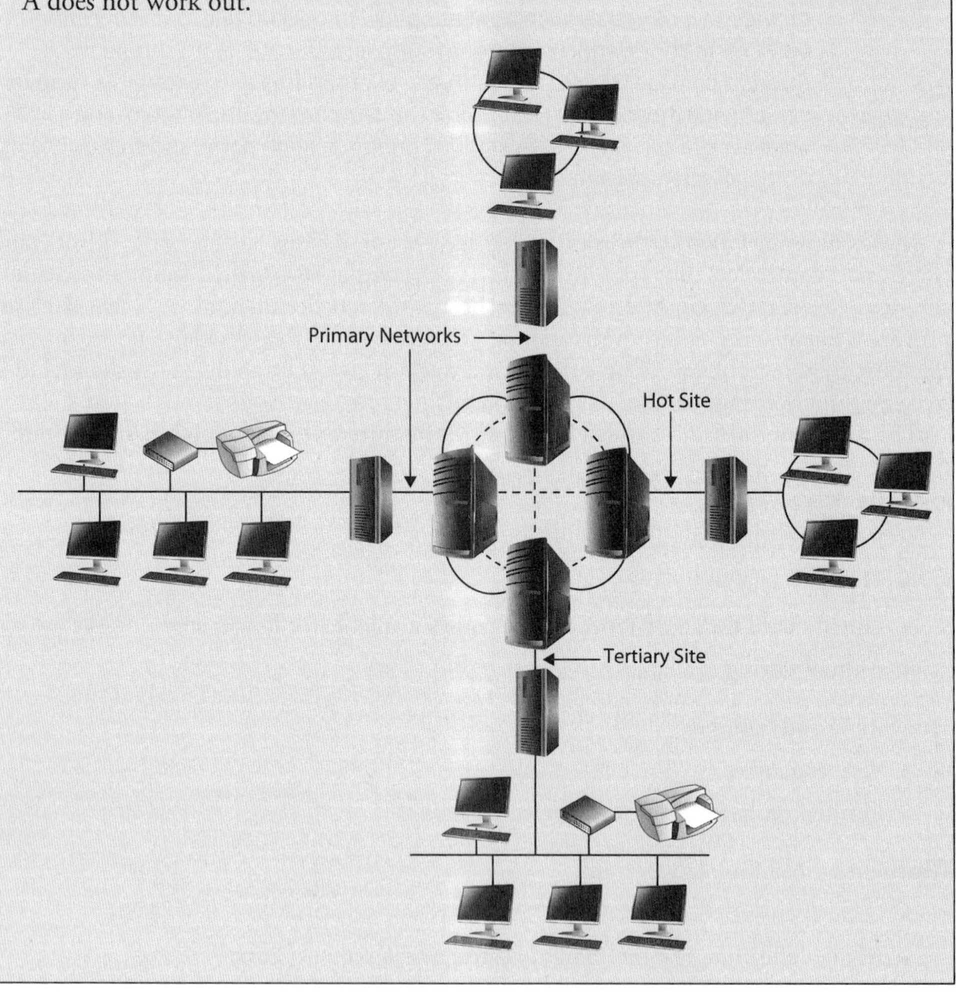

Backup tapes or other media should be tested periodically on the equipment kept at the hot site to make sure the media is readable by those systems. If a warm site is used, the tapes should be brought to the *original* site and tested on those systems. The reason for the difference is that when a company uses a hot site, it depends on the systems located at the hot site; therefore, the media needs to be readable by those systems. If a company depends on a warm site, it will most likely bring its original equipment with it, so the media needs to be readable by the company's systems.

Reciprocal Agreements

Another approach to alternate offsite facilities is to establish a *reciprocal agreement* with another company, usually one in a similar field or that has similar technological infrastructure. This means that company A agrees to allow company B to use its facilities if company B is hit by a disaster, and vice versa. This is a cheaper way to go than the other offsite choices, but it is not always the best choice. Most environments are maxed out pertaining to the use of facility space, resources, and computing capability. To allow another company to come in and work out of the same shop could prove to be detrimental to both companies. Whether it can assist the other company while tending effectively to its own business is an open question. The stress of two companies working in the same environment could cause tremendous levels of tension. If it did work out, it would only provide a short-term solution. Configuration management could be a nightmare. Does the other company upgrade to new technology and retire old systems and software? If not, one company's systems may become incompatible with that of the other company

If you allow another company to move into your facility and work from there, you may have a solid feeling about your friend, the CEO, but what about all of her employees, whom you do not know? The mixing of operations could introduce many security issues. Now you have a new subset of people who may need to have privileged and direct access to your resources in the shared environment. This other company could be your competitor in the business world, so many of the employees may see you and your company more as a threat than one that is offering a helping hand in need. Close attention needs to be paid when assigning these other people access rights and permissions to your critical assets and resources, if they need access at all. Careful testing is recommended to see if one company or the other can handle the extra loads.

Offsite Location

When choosing a backup facility, it should be far enough away from the original site so that one disaster does not take out both locations. In other words, it is not logical to have the backup site only a few miles away if the company is concerned about tornado damage, because the backup site could also be affected or destroyed. There is a rule of thumb that suggests that alternate facilities should be, at a bare minimum, at least 5 miles away from the primary site, while 15 miles is recommended for most low-to-medium critical environments, and 50 to 200 miles is recommended for critical operations to give maximum protection in cases of regional disasters.

Reciprocal agreements have been known to work well in specific businesses, such as newspaper printing. These businesses require very specific technology and equipment that will not be available through any subscription service. These agreements follow a "you scratch my back and I'll scratch yours" mentality. For most other organizations, reciprocal agreements are generally, at best, a secondary option for disaster protection. The other issue to consider is that these agreements are not enforceable. This means that although company A said company B could use its facility when needed, when the need arises, company A legally does not have to fulfill this promise. However, there are still many companies who do opt for this solution either because of the appeal of low cost or, as noted earlier, because it may be the only viable solution in some cases.

Important issues need to be addressed before a disaster hits if a company decides to participate in a reciprocal agreement with another company:

- How long will the facility be available to the company in need?
- How much assistance will the staff supply in integrating the two environments and ongoing support?
- How quickly can the company in need move into the facility?
- What are the issues pertaining to interoperability?
- How many of the resources will be available to the company in need?
- How will differences and conflicts be addressed?
- How does change control and configuration management take place?
- How often can drills and testing take place?
- How can critical assets of both companies be properly protected?

A variation on a reciprocal agreement is a consortium, or *mutual aid agreement*. In this case, more than two organizations agree to help one another in case of an emergency. Adding multiple organizations to the mix, as you might imagine, can make things even more complicated. The same concerns that apply with reciprocal agreements apply here, but even more so. Organizations entering into such agreements need to formally and legally write out their mutual responsibilities in advance. Interested parties, including the legal and IT departments, should carefully scrutinize such accords before the organization signs onto them.

Redundant Sites

Some companies choose to have *redundant sites*, or mirrored sites, meaning one site is equipped and configured exactly like the primary site, which serves as a redundant environment. The business-processing capabilities between the two sites can be completely synchronized. These sites are owned by the company and are mirrors of the original production environment. A redundant site has clear advantages: it has full availability, is ready to go at a moment's notice, and is under the organization's complete control. This is, however, one of the most expensive backup facility options, because a full environment must be maintained even though it usually is not used for regular production activities until after a disaster takes place that triggers the relocation of services to the redundant site. But "expensive" is relative here. If the company would lose a million dollars if it were out of business for just a few hours, the loss potential would override the cost of this option. Many organizations are subjected to regulations that dictate they must have redundant sites in place, so expense is not a matter of choice in these situations.

EXAM TIP A *hot* site is a subscription service. A *redundant* site, in contrast, is a site owned and maintained by the company, meaning the company does not pay anyone else for the site. A redundant site might be "hot" in nature, meaning it is ready for production quickly. However, the CISSP exam differentiates between a hot site (a subscription service) and a redundant site (owned by the company).

Another type of facility-backup option is a *rolling hot site*, or mobile hot site, where the back of a large truck or a trailer is turned into a data processing or working area. This is a portable, self-contained data facility. The trailer has the necessary power, telecommunications, and systems to do some or all of the processing right away. The trailer can be brought to the company's parking lot or another location. Obviously, the trailer has to be driven over to the new site, the data has to be retrieved, and the necessary personnel have to be put into place.

Another, similar solution is a prefabricated building that can be easily and quickly put together. Military organizations and large insurance companies typically have rolling hot sites or trucks preloaded with equipment because they often need the flexibility to quickly relocate some or all of their processing facilities to different locations around the world depending on where the need arises.

Another option for organizations is to have *multiple processing centers*. An organization may have ten different facilities throughout the world, which are connected with specific technologies that could move all data processing from one facility to another in a matter of seconds when an interruption is detected. This technology can be implemented within the organization or from one facility to a third-party facility. Certain service providers provide this type of functionality to their customers. So if a company's data processing is interrupted, all or some of the processing can be moved to the service provider's servers.

It is best if a company is aware of all available options for hardware and facility backups to ensure it makes the best decision for its specific business and critical needs.

Supply and Technology Recovery

The BCP should also include backup solutions for the following:

- Network and computer equipment
- Voice and data communications resources
- Human resources
- Transportation of equipment and personnel

- Environment issues (HVAC)
- Data and personnel security issues
- Supplies (paper, forms, cabling, and so on)
- Documentation

Outsourcing

Part of the planned response to a disaster may be to outsource some of the affected activities to another organization. Organizations do outsource things—help desk services, manufacturing, legal advice—all the time, so why not important functions affected by a disaster? Some companies specialize in disaster response and continuity planning, and can act as expert consultants.

That is all well and good. However, be aware that your organization is still ultimately responsible for the continuity of a product or service that is outsourced. Clients and customers will expect the organization to ensure continuity of its products and services, either by itself or by having chosen the right outside vendors to do the outsourcing. If outside vendors are brought in, the active participation of key in-house managers in their work is still essential. They still need to supervise the work of the outside vendors.

This same concern applies to normal, third-party suppliers of goods and services to the organization. Any BCP should take them into account as well. Note that the process for evaluating an outsourced company for BCP is like that for evaluating the organization itself. The organization must make sure that the outsourced company is financially viable and has a solid record in BCP.

The organization can take the following steps to better ensure the continuity of its outsourcing:

- Make the ability of such companies to reliably assure continuity of products and services part of any work proposals.
- Make sure that business continuity planning is included in contracts with such companies, and that their responsibilities and levels of service are clearly spelled out.
- Draw up realistic and reasonable service levels that the outsourced firm will meet during an incident.
- If possible, have the outsourcing companies take part in BCP awareness programs, training, and testing.

The goal is to make the supply of goods and services from outsources as resilient as possible in the wake of a disaster.

The organization's current technical environment must be understood. This means the planners have to know the intimate details of the network, communications technologies, computers, network equipment, and software requirements that are necessary to get the critical functions up and running. What is surprising to some people is that many organizations do not *totally* understand how their network is configured and how it actually works, because the network may have been established 10 to 15 years ago and has kept growing and changing under different administrators and personnel. New devices are added, new computers are added, new software packages are added, Voice over Internet Protocol (VoIP) may have been integrated, and the DMZ may have been split up into three DMZs, with an extranet for the company's partners. Maybe the company bought and merged with another company and network. Over ten years, a number of technology refreshes most likely have taken place, and the individuals who are maintaining the environment now likely are not the same people who built it ten years ago. Many IT departments experience extensive employee turnover every five years. And most organizational network schematics are notoriously out of date because everyone is busy with their current tasks (or will come up with new tasks just to get out of having to update the schematic).

So the BCP team has to make sure that if the networked environment is partially or totally destroyed, the recovery team has the knowledge and skill to properly rebuild it.

NOTE Many organizations have moved to VoIP, which means that if the network goes down, network and voice capability are unavailable. The team should address the possible need of redundant voice systems.

The BCP team needs to take into account several things that are commonly overlooked, such as hardware replacements, software products, documentation, environmental needs, and human resources.

Hardware Backups

The BCP needs to identify the equipment required to keep the critical functions up and running. This may include servers, user workstations, routers, switches, tape backup devices, and more. The needed inventory may seem simple enough, but as they say, the devil is in the details. If the recovery team is planning to use images to rebuild newly purchased servers and workstations because the original ones were destroyed, for example, will the images work on the new computers? Using images instead of building systems from scratch can be a time-saving task, unless the team finds out that the replacement equipment is a newer version and thus the images cannot be used. The BCP should plan for the recovery team to use the company's current images, but also have a manual process of how to build each critical system from scratch with the necessary configurations.

The BCP also needs to be based on accurate estimates of how long it will take for new equipment to arrive. For example, if the organization has identified Dell as its equipment replacement supplier, how long will it take this vendor to send 20 servers and 30 workstations to the offsite facility? After a disaster hits, the company could be in its offsite facility only to find that its equipment will take three weeks to be delivered. So, the SLA for the identified vendors needs to be investigated to make sure the company is not further damaged by delays. Once the parameters of the SLA are understood, the team must make a decision between depending upon the vendor and purchasing redundant systems and storing them as backups in case the primary equipment is destroyed.

As described earlier, when potential company risks are identified, it is better to take preventive steps to reduce the potential damage. After the calculation of the MTD values, the team will know how long the company can be without a specific device. This data should be used to make the decision on whether the company should depend on the vendor's SLA or make readily available a hot-swappable redundant system. If the company will lose $50,000 per hour if a particular server goes down, then the team should elect to implement redundant systems and technology.

If an organization is using any legacy computers and hardware and a disaster hits tomorrow, where would it find replacements for this legacy equipment? The team should identify legacy devices and understand the risk the organization is facing if replacements are unavailable. This finding has caused many companies to move from legacy systems to commercial off-the-shelf (COTS) products to ensure that replacement is possible.

NOTE Different types of backup tape technologies can be used (digital linear tape, digital audio tape, advanced intelligent tape). The team needs to make sure it knows the type of technology that is used by the company and identify the necessary vendor in case the tape-reading device needs to be replaced.

Software Backups

Most companies' IT departments have their array of software disks and licensing information here or there—or possibly in one centralized location. If the facility were destroyed and the IT department's current environment had to be rebuilt, how would it gain access to these software packages? The BCP team should make sure to have an inventory of the necessary software required for mission-critical functions and have backup copies at an offsite facility. Hardware is usually not worth much to a company without the software required to run on it. The software that needs to be backed up can be in the form of applications, utilities, databases, and operating systems. The continuity plan must have provisions to back up and protect these items along with hardware and data.

The BCP team should make sure there are at least two copies of the company's operating system software and critical applications. One copy should be stored onsite and the other copy should be stored at a secure offsite location. These copies should be tested periodically and re-created when new versions are rolled out.

It is common for organizations to work with software developers to create customized software programs. For example, in the banking world, individual financial institutions need software that will allow their bank tellers to interact with accounts, hold account information in databases and mainframes, provide online banking, carry out data replication, and perform a thousand other types of bank-like functionalities. This specialized type of software is developed and available through a handful of software vendors that specialize in this market. When bank A purchases this type of software for all of its branches, the software has to be specially customized for its environment and needs. Once this banking software is installed, the whole organization depends upon it for its minute-by-minute activities.

When bank A receives the specialized and customized banking software from the software vendor, bank A does not receive the source code. Instead, the software vendor provides bank A with a compiled version. Now, what if this software vendor goes out of business because of a disaster or bankruptcy? Then bank A will require a new vendor to maintain and update this banking software; thus, the new vendor will need access to the source code.

The protection mechanism that bank A should implement is called *software escrow*, in which a third party holds the source code, backups of the compiled code, manuals, and other supporting materials. A contract between the software vendor, customer, and third party outlines who can do what, and when, with the source code. This contract usually states that the customer can have access to the source code only if and when the vendor goes out of business, is unable to carry out stated responsibilities, or is in breach of the original contract. If any of these activities takes place, then the customer is protected because it can still gain access to the source code and other materials through the third-party escrow agent.

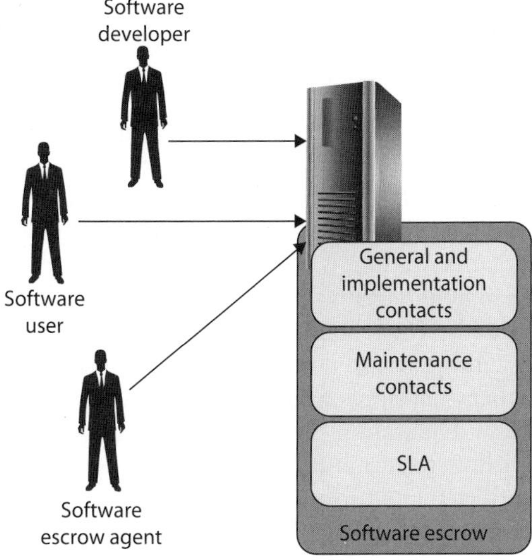

Many companies have been crippled by not implementing software escrow. Such a company would have paid a software vendor to develop specialized software, and when the software vendor went belly up, the customer did not have access to the code that its whole company ran on.

Choosing a Software Backup Facility

A company needs to address several issues and ask specific questions when it is deciding upon a storage facility for its backup materials. The following provides a list of just some of the issues that need to be thought through before committing to a specific vendor for this service:

- Can the media be accessed in the necessary timeframe?
- Is the facility closed on weekends and holidays, and does it only operate during specific hours of the day?
- Are the access control mechanisms tied to an alarm and/or the police station?
- Does the facility have the capability to protect the media from a variety of threats?
- What is the availability of a bonded transport service?
- Are there any geographical environmental hazards such as floods, earthquakes, tornadoes, and so on that might affect the facility?
- Does the facility have a fire detection and suppression system?
- Does the facility provide temperature and humidity monitoring and control?
- What type of physical, administrative, and logical access controls are used?

The questions and issues that need to be addressed will vary depending on the type of company, its needs, and the requirements of a backup facility.

Documentation

Documentation seems to be a dreaded task to most people, who will find many other tasks to take on to ensure they are not the ones stuck with documenting processes and procedures. However, a company does a great and responsible job by backing up hardware and software to an offsite facility, maintaining it, and keeping everything up-to-date and current; without documentation, when a disaster hits, no one will know how to put Humpty Dumpty back together again.

Restoration of files can be challenging, but restoring a whole environment that was swept away in a flood can be overwhelming, if not impossible. Procedures need to be documented because when they are actually needed, it will most likely be a chaotic and frantic atmosphere with a demanding time schedule. The documentation may need to include information on how to install images, configure operating systems and servers, and properly install utilities and proprietary software. Other documentation could include a calling tree, which outlines who should be contacted, in what order, and who is responsible for doing the calling. The documentation must also contain contact information for specific vendors, emergency agencies, offsite facilities, and any other entity that may need to be contacted in a time of need.

Most network environments evolve over time. Software has been installed on top of other software, configurations have been altered over the years to properly work in a unique environment, and service packs and patches have been installed to fix this problem or that issue. To expect one person or a group of people to go through all of these steps during a crisis and end up with an environment that looks and behaves exactly like the original environment and in which all components work together seamlessly may be a lofty dream.

So, the dreaded task of documentation may be the saving grace one day. It is an essential piece of business, and therefore an essential piece in disaster recovery and business continuity.

It is important to make one or more roles responsible for proper documentation. As with all the items addressed in this chapter, simply saying "All documentation will be kept up to date and properly protected" is the easy part—saying and doing are two different things. Once the BCP team identifies tasks that must be done, the tasks must be assigned to individuals, and those individuals have to be accountable. If these steps are not taken, the BCP team could have wasted a lot of time and resources defining these tasks, and the company could be in grave danger if a disaster occurs.

NOTE An organization may need to solidify communications channels and relationships with government officials and emergency response groups. The goal of this activity is to solidify proper protocol in case of a city- or region-wide disaster. During the BIA phase, local authorities should be contacted so the team understands the risks of its geographical location and how to access emergency zones. If the company has to initiate its BCP, it will need to contact many of these emergency response groups during the recovery stage.

Human Resources

One of the resources commonly left out of the equation is people. A company may restore its networks and critical systems and get business functions up and running, only to realize it doesn't know the answer to the question, "Who will take it from here?" The area of human resources is a critical component to any recovery and continuity process, and it needs to be fully thought out and integrated into the plan.

What happens if we have to move to an offsite facility that is 250 miles away? We cannot expect people to drive back and forth from home to work. Should we pay for temporary housing for the necessary employees? Do we have to pay their moving costs? Do we need to hire new employees in the area of the offsite facility? If so, what skill set do we need from them? The BCP team should go through a long succession of these types of questions.

Storing Business Continuity and Disaster Recovery Plans

Once the business continuity and disaster recovery plans are completed, where should they be stored? Should the company have only one copy and keep it safely in a file cabinet next to Bob so that he feels safe? Nope. There should be two or three copies of these plans. One copy may be at the primary location, but the other copies should be at other locations in case the primary facility is destroyed. This reduces the risk of not having access to the plans when needed.

These plans should not be stored in a file cabinet, but rather in a fire-resistant safe. When they are stored offsite, they need to be stored in a way that provides just as much protection as the primary site would provide.

The BCP project expands job responsibilities, descriptions, hours, and even workplaces. The project has to identify the critical personnel and subordinates who will develop the plan and execute key duties during an incident. Among the key players may be heads of BCP coordination, IT systems, data and voice communications, business units, transport, logistics, security, safety, facilities, finance, auditing, legal, and public relations.

Multiple people should be trained in executing the duties and procedures spelled out in the plan so that one person can fill another's shoes in an emergency. Clear documentation is vital in such cross-training. The HR department normally manages the availability of personnel for the continuity process.

If a large disaster takes place that affects not only the company's facility but also surrounding areas, including housing, employees will be more worried about their families than their company. Some companies assume that employees will be ready and available to help them get back into production, when in fact they may need to be at home because they have responsibilities to their families.

Regrettably, some employees may be killed or severely injured in the disaster, and the team should have plans in place to replace employees quickly through a temporary employment agency or a job recruiter. This is an extremely unfortunate scenario to contemplate, but it is part of reality. The team that considers all threats and is responsible for identifying practical solutions needs to think through all of these issues.

Organizations should already have *executive succession planning* in place. This means that if someone in a senior executive position retires, leaves the company, or is killed, the organization has predetermined steps to carry out to protect the company. The loss of a senior executive could tear a hole in the company's fabric, creating a leadership vacuum that must be filled quickly with the right individual. The line-of-succession plan defines who would step in and assume responsibility for this role. Many organizations have "deputy" roles. For example, an organization may have a deputy CIO, deputy CFO, and deputy CEO ready to take over the necessary tasks if the CIO, CFO, or CEO becomes unavailable.

Often, larger organizations also have a policy indicating that two or more of the senior staff cannot be exposed to a particular risk at the same time. For example, the CEO and president cannot travel on the same plane. If the plane were to crash and both individuals were killed, then the company could be in danger. This is why you don't see the president of the United States and the vice president together too often. It is not because they don't like each other and thus keep their distance from each other. It is because there is a policy indicating that to protect the United States, its top leaders cannot be under the same risk at the same time.

End-User Environment

Because the end users are usually the worker bees of a company, they must be provided a functioning environment as soon as possible after a disaster hits. This means that the BCP team must understand the current operational and technical functioning environment and examine critical pieces so they can replicate them.

The first issue pertaining to users is how they will be notified of the disaster and who will tell them where to go and when. A tree structure of managers can be developed so that once a disaster hits, the person at the top of the tree calls two managers, and they in turn call three managers, and so on until all managers are notified. Each manager would be responsible for notifying the people he is responsible for until everyone is on the same page. Then, one or two people must be in charge of coordinating the issues pertaining to users. This could mean directing them to a new facility, making sure they have the necessary resources to complete their tasks, restoring data, and being a liaison between the different groups.

In most situations, after a disaster, only a skeleton crew is put back to work. The BCP committee identified the most critical functions of the company during the analysis stage, and the employees who carry out those functions must be put back to work first. So the recovery process for the user environment should be laid out in different stages. The first stage is to get the most critical departments back online, the next stage is to get the second most important back online, and so on.

The BCP team needs to identify user requirements, such as whether users can work on stand-alone PCs or need to be connected in a network to fulfill specific tasks. For example, in a financial institution, users who work on stand-alone PCs might be able to accomplish some small tasks like filling out account forms, word processing, and accounting tasks, but they might need to be connected to a host system to update customer profiles and to interact with the database.

The BCP team also needs to identify how current automated tasks can be carried out manually if that becomes necessary. If the network is going to be down for 12 hours, could the necessary tasks be carried out through traditional pen-and-paper methods? If the Internet connection is going to be down for five hours, could the necessary communications take place through phone calls? Instead of transmitting data through the internal mail system, could couriers be used to run information back and forth? Today, we are extremely dependent upon technology, but we often take for granted that it will always be there for us to use. It is up to the BCP team to realize that technology may be unavailable for a period of time and to come up with solutions for those situations.

Data Backup Alternatives

As we have discussed so far, backup alternatives are needed for hardware, software, personnel, and offsite facilities. It is up to each company and its continuity team to decide if all of these components are necessary for its survival and the specifics for each type of backup needed.

Data has become one of the most critical assets to nearly all organizations. It may include financial spreadsheets, blueprints on new products, customer information, product inventory, trade secrets, and more. In Chapter 1, we stepped through risk analysis procedures and, in Chapter 2, data classification. The BCP team should not be responsible for setting up and maintaining the company's data classification procedures, but the team should recognize that the company is at risk if it does not have these procedures in place. This should be seen as a vulnerability that is reported to management. Management would need to establish another group of individuals who would identify the company's data, define a loss criterion, and establish the classification structure and processes.

The BCP team's responsibility is to provide solutions to protect this data and identify ways to restore it after a disaster. In this section, we look at different ways data can be protected and restored when needed.

Data usually changes more often than hardware and software, so these backup or archival procedures must happen on a continual basis. The data backup process must make sense and be reasonable and effective. If data in the files changes several times a day, backup procedures should happen a few times a day or nightly to ensure all the changes are captured and kept. If data is changed once a month, backing up data every night is a waste of time and resources. Backing up a file and its corresponding changes is usually more desirable than having multiple copies of that one file. Online backup technologies usually record the changes to a file in a transaction log, which is separate from the original file.

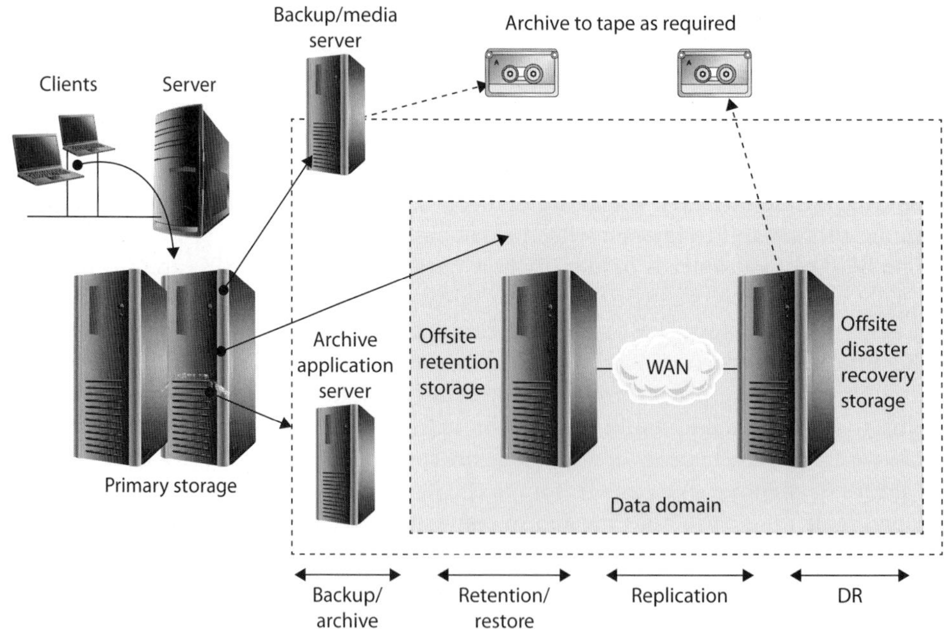

The operations team is responsible for defining which data gets backed up and how often. These backups can be full, differential, or incremental, and are usually used in some type of combination with each other. Most files are not altered every day, so, to save time and resources, it is best to devise a backup plan that does not continually back up data that has not been modified. So, how do we know which data has changed and needs to be backed up without having to look at every file's modification date? This is accomplished by an *archive bit*. Operating systems' file systems keep track of what files have been modified by setting an archive bit. If a file is modified or created, the file system sets the archive bit to 1. Backup software has been created to review this bit setting when making its determination on what gets backed up and what does not.

The first step is to do a *full backup*, which is just what it sounds like—all data is backed up and saved to some type of storage media. During a full backup, the archive bit is cleared, which means that it is set to 0. A company can choose to do full backups only, in which case the restoration process is just one step, but the backup and restore processes could take a long time.

Most companies choose to combine a full backup with a differential or incremental backup. A *differential process* backs up the files that have been modified since the *last full backup*. When the data needs to be restored, the full backup is laid down first, and then the most recent differential backup is put down on top of it. The differential process does not change the archive bit value.

An *incremental process* backs up all the files that have changed since the *last full or incremental backup* and sets the archive bit to 0. When the data needs to be restored, the full backup data is laid down, and then each incremental backup is laid down on top of it in the proper order (see Figure 7-14). If a company experienced a disaster and it used the incremental process, it would first need to restore the full backup on its hard drives and lay down every incremental backup that was carried out before the disaster took place (and after the last full backup). So, if the full backup was done six months ago and the operations department carried out an incremental backup each month, the restoration team would restore the full backup and start with the older incremental backups taken since the full backup and restore each one of them until they were all restored.

Which backup process is best? If a company wants the backup and restoration processes to be simplistic and straightforward, it can carry out just full backups—but this may require a lot of hard drive space and time. Although using differential and incremental backup processes is more complex, it requires fewer resources and less time. A differential backup takes more time in the backing-up phase than an incremental backup, but it also takes less time to restore than an incremental backup because carrying out restoration of a differential backup happens in two steps, whereas in an incremental backup, every incremental backup must be restored in the correct sequence.

Whatever the organization chooses, it is important to not mix differential and incremental backups. This overlap could cause files to be missed, since the incremental backup changes the archive bit and the differential backup does not.

Critical data should be backed up and stored at an onsite area *and* an offsite area. The onsite backup copies should be easily accessible in case of nondisasters and should provide a quick restore process so operations can return to normal. However, onsite backup copies are not enough to provide real protection. The data should also be held in

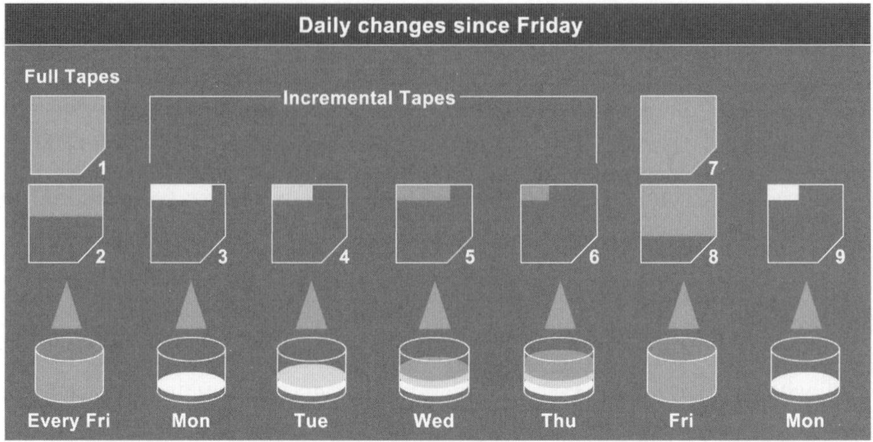

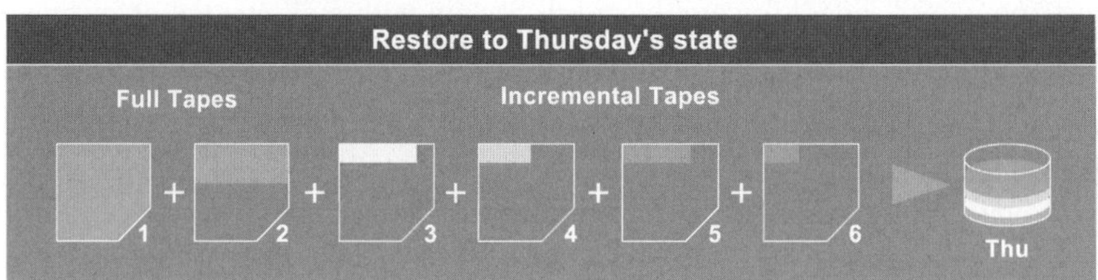

Figure 7-14 Backup software steps

an offsite facility in case of actual disasters or catastrophes. One decision that needs to be made is where the offsite location should be in reference to the main facility. The closer the offsite backup storage site is, the easier it is to access, but this can put the backup copies in danger if a large-scale disaster manages to take out the company's main facility and the backup facility. It may be wiser to choose a backup facility farther away, which makes accessibility harder but reduces the risk. Some companies choose to have more than one backup facility: one that is close and one that is farther away.

The onsite backup information should be stored in a fire-resistant, heat-resistant, and waterproof safe. The procedures for backing up and restoring data should be easily accessible and comprehensible even to operators or administrators who are not intimately familiar with a specific system. In an emergency situation, the same guy who always does the backing up and restoring may not be around, or outsourced consultants may need to be temporarily hired in order to meet the restoration time constraints.

A backup strategy must take into account that failure can take place at any step of the process, so if there is a problem during the backup or restoration process that could corrupt the data, there should be a graceful way of backing out or reconstructing the data from the beginning.

Can we actually restore data? Backing up data is a wonderful thing in life, but making sure it can be properly restored is even better. Many organizations have developed a false sense of security based on the fact that they have a very organized and effective process of backing up their data. That sense of security can disappear in seconds when a company realizes in a time of crisis that its restore processes do not work. For example, one company had paid an offsite backup facility to use a courier to collect its weekly backup tapes and transport them to the offsite facility for safekeeping. What the company did not realize was that this courier used the subway and many times set the tapes on the ground while waiting for the subway train. A subway has many large engines that create their own magnetic field. This can have the same effect on media as large magnets, meaning that the data can be erased or corrupted. The company never tested its restore processes and eventually experienced a disaster. Much to its surprise, it found out that three years of data were corrupted and unusable.

Many other stories and experiences like this are out there. Don't let your organization end up as an anecdote in someone else's book because it failed to verify that its backups could be restored.

Electronic Backup Solutions

Manually backing up systems and data can be time-consuming, error-prone, and costly. Several technologies serve as automated backup alternatives. Although these technologies are usually more expensive, they are quicker and more accurate, which may be necessary for online information that changes often.

Among the many technologies and ways to back up data electronically is disk shadowing, which is very similar to data mirroring.

NOTE *Disk duplexing* means there is more than one disk controller. If one disk controller fails, the other is ready and available.

Disk shadowing is used to ensure the availability of data and to provide a fault-tolerant solution by duplicating hardware and maintaining more than one copy of the information. The data is dynamically created and maintained on two or more identical disks. If only *disk mirroring* is used, then each disk would have a corresponding mirrored disk that contains the exact same information. If shadow sets are used, the data can be stored as images on two or more disks.

Systems that need to interact with this data are connected to all the drives at the same time. All of these drives "look" like just one drive to the user. This provides transparency to the user so that when she needs to retrieve a file, she does not have to worry about which drive to go to for this process. When a user writes data to be stored on this media, the data is written to all disks in the shadow set.

Disk shadowing provides online backup storage, which can either reduce or replace the need for periodic offline manual backup operations. Another benefit to this solution is that it can boost read operation performance. Multiple paths are provided to duplicate data, and a shadow set can carry out multiple read requests in parallel.

Disk shadowing is commonly seen as an expensive solution because two or more hard drives are used to hold the exact same data. If a company has data that will fill up 100 hard drives, it must purchase and maintain at least 200 hard drives. A company would choose this solution if fault tolerance were required.

If a disk drive fails, at least one shadow set is still available. A new disk can be assigned to this set through proper configurations, and the data can be copied from the shadow set. The copying can take place offline, but this means the data is unavailable for a period of time. Most products that provide disk-shadowing functionality allow for online copying, where disks are hot swapped into the set, and can carry out the necessary copy functions without having to bring the drives offline.

Electronic vaulting and remote journaling are other solutions that companies should be aware of. *Electronic vaulting* makes copies of files as they are modified and periodically transmits them to an offsite backup site. The transmission does not happen in real time, but is carried out in batches. So, a company can choose to have all files that have been changed sent to the backup facility every hour, day, week, or month. The information can be stored in an offsite facility and retrieved from that facility in a short time.

This form of backup takes place in many financial institutions, so when a bank teller accepts a deposit or withdrawal, the change to the customer's account is made locally to that branch's database and to the remote site that maintains the backup copies of all customer records.

Electronic vaulting is a method of transferring bulk information to offsite facilities for backup purposes. *Remote journaling* is another method of transmitting data offsite, but this usually only includes moving the journal or transaction logs to the offsite facility, not the actual files. These logs contain the deltas (changes) that have taken place to the individual files. If and when data is corrupted and needs to be restored, the bank can retrieve these logs, which are used to rebuild the lost data. Journaling is efficient for database recovery, where only the reapplication of a series of changes to individual records is required to resynchronize the database.

EXAM TIP Remote journaling takes place in real time and transmits only the file deltas. Electronic vaulting takes place in batches and moves the entire file that has been updated.

It may be necessary to keep different versions of software and files, especially in a software development environment. The object and source code should be backed up along with libraries, patches, and fixes. The offsite facility should mirror the onsite facility, meaning it does not make sense to keep all of this data at the onsite facility and only the source code at the offsite facility. Each site should have a full set of the most current and updated information and files.

Another software backup technology we will discuss is referred to as *tape vaulting*. Many businesses back up their data to tapes that are then manually transferred to an offsite facility by a courier or an employee. With automatic tape vaulting, the data is sent over a serial line to a backup tape system at the offsite facility. The company that maintains the offsite facility maintains the systems and changes out tapes when necessary. Data can be quickly backed up and retrieved when necessary. This technology reduces the manual steps in the traditional tape backup procedures.

Basic vaulting of tape data sends backup tapes to an offsite location, but a manual process can be error-prone. Electronic tape vaulting transmits data over a network to tape devices located at an alternate data center. Electronic tape vaulting improves recovery speed and reduces errors, and backups can be run more frequently.

Data repositories commonly have replication capabilities, so that when changes take place to one repository (i.e., database) they are replicated to all of the other repositories within the organization. The replication can take place over telecommunication links, which allow offsite repositories to be continuously updated. If the primary repository goes down or is corrupted, the replication flow can be reversed, and the offsite repository updates and restores the primary repository. Replication can be asynchronous or synchronous. *Asynchronous replication* means the primary and secondary data volumes are out of sync. Synchronization may take place in seconds, hours, or days, depending upon the technology in place. With *synchronous replication*, the primary and secondary repositories are always in sync, which provides true real-time duplication. Figure 7-15 shows how offsite replication can take place.

The BCP team must balance the cost to recover against the cost of the disruption. The balancing point becomes the recovery time objective. Figure 7-16 illustrates the relationship between the cost of various recovery technologies and the provided recovery times.

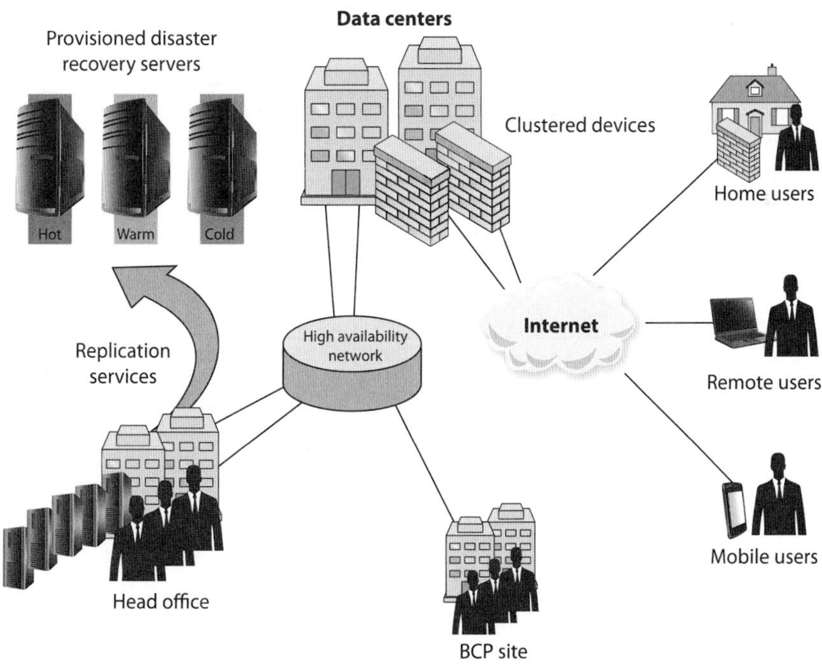

Figure 7-15 Offsite data replication for data recovery purposes

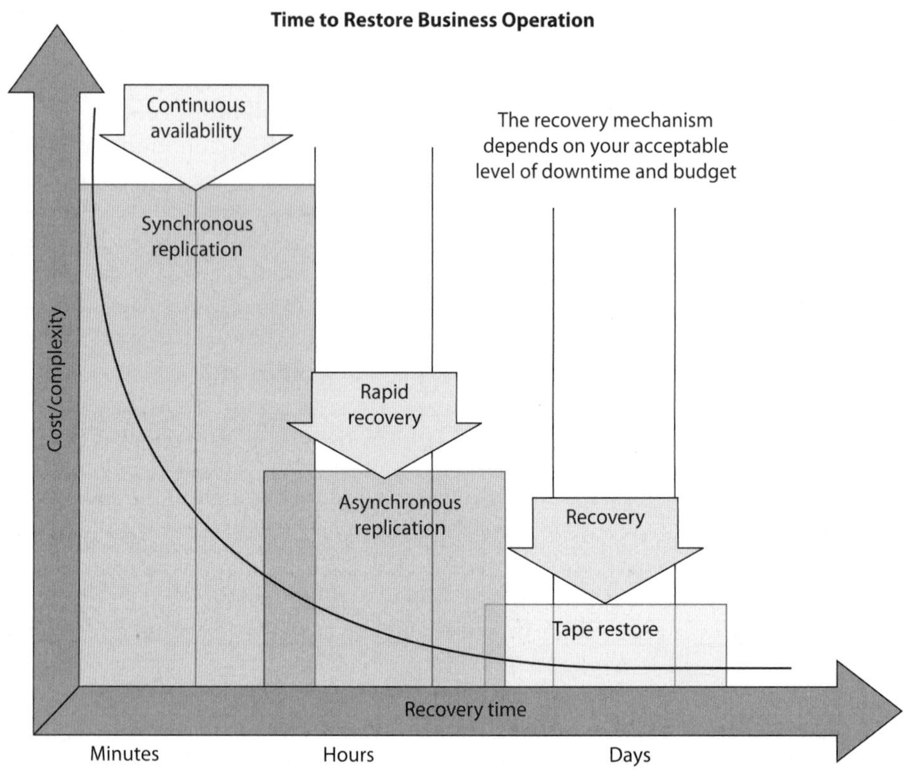

Figure 7-16 The criticality of data recovery will dictate the recovery solution.

High Availability

High availability (HA) is a combination of technologies and processes that work together to ensure that some specific thing is always up and running. The specific thing can be a database, a network, an application, a power supply, etc. Service providers have SLAs with their customers, which outline the amount of uptime they promise to provide and a turnaround time to get the item fixed if it does go down. For example, a hosting company can promise to provide 98 percent uptime for Internet connectivity. This means they are guaranteeing that at least 98 percent of the time, the Internet connection you purchase from them will be up and running. The hosting company knows that some things may take place to interrupt this service, but within your SLA with them, it promises an eight-hour turnaround time. This means if your Internet connection does go down, they will either fix it or provide you with a different connection within eight hours.

To provide this level of high availability, the hosting company has to have a long list of technologies and processes that provide redundancy, fault tolerance, and failover capabilities. *Redundancy* is commonly built into the network at a routing protocol level. The routing protocols are configured so if one link goes down or gets congested, then traffic is routed over a different network link. Redundant hardware can also be available so if a primary device goes down, the backup component can be swapped out and activated.

Fault tolerance is the capability of a technology to continue to operate as expected even if something unexpected takes place (a fault). If a database experiences an unexpected glitch, it can roll back to a known-good state and continue functioning as though nothing bad happened. If a packet gets lost or corrupted during a TCP session, the TCP protocol will resend the packet so that system-to-system communication is not affected. If a disk within a RAID system gets corrupted, the system uses its parity data to rebuild the corrupted data so that operations are not affected.

If a technology has a *failover* capability, this means that if there is a failure that cannot be handled through normal means, then processing is "switched over" to a working system. For example, two servers can be configured to send each other heartbeat signals every 30 seconds. If server A does not receive a heartbeat signal from server B after 40 seconds, then all processes are moved to server A so that there is no lag in operations. Also, when servers are *clustered*, this means that there is an overarching piece of software monitoring each server and carrying out load balancing. If one server within the cluster goes down, the clustering software stops sending it data to process so that there are no delays in processing activities.

Redundancy, fault tolerance, and failover capabilities increase the reliability of a system or network, where *reliability* is the probability that a system performs the necessary function for a specified period under defined conditions. High reliability allows for high availability, which is a measure of its readiness. If the probability of a system performing as expected under defined conditions is low, then the availability for this system cannot be high. For a system to have the characteristic of high availability, then high reliability must be in place. Figure 7-17 illustrates where load balancing, clustering, failover devices, and replication commonly take place in a network architecture.

Remember that data restoration (RPO) requirements can be different from processing restoration (RTO) requirements. Data can be restored through backup tapes, electronic vaulting, synchronous or asynchronous replication, or RAID. Processing capabilities can be restored through clustering, load balancing, mirroring, redundancy, and failover technologies. If the results of the BCP team's BIA indicate that the RPO value is two days, then the company can use tape backups. If the RPO value is one minute, then synchronous replication needs to be in place. If the BIA indicates that the RTO value is three days, then redundant hardware can be used. If the RTO value is one minute, then clustering and load balancing should be used.

HA and disaster recovery (DR) are not the same, but they have a relationship. HA technologies and processes are commonly put into place so that if a disaster does take place, either the critical functions are likelier to remain available or the delay of getting them back online and running is low.

In the industry, HA is usually thought about only in technology terms, but remember that there are many things that an organization needs to keep functioning. Availability of each of the following items must be thought through and planned:

- Facility (cold, warm, hot, redundant, rolling, reciprocal sites)
- Infrastructure (redundancy, fault tolerance)
- Storage (RAID, SAN, mirroring, disk shadowing, cloud)
- Server (clustering, load balancing)

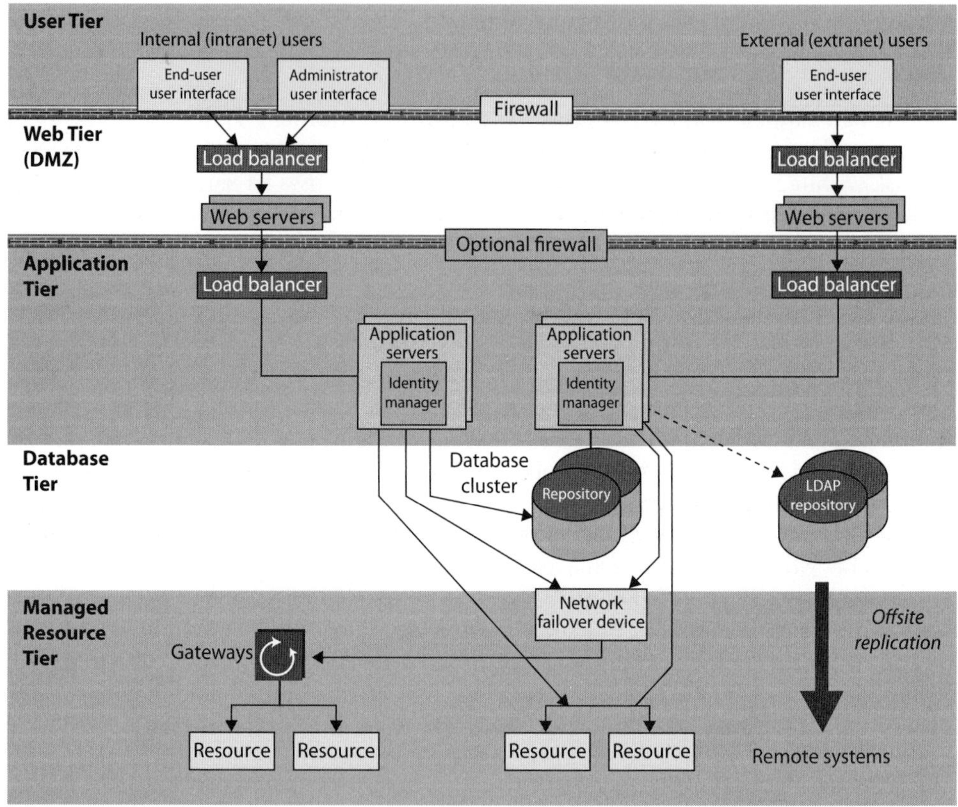

Figure 7-17 High-availability technologies

- Data (tapes, backups, vaulting, online replication)
- Business processes
- People

NOTE Virtualization and cloud computing are covered in Chapter 3. We will not go over those technologies again in this chapter, but know that the use of these technologies has drastically increased in the realm of BCP and DRP recovery solutions.

Insurance

During the business impact analysis (BIA), discussed in Chapter 1, the team most likely uncovered several threats that the organization could not prevent. Taking on the full risk of these threats often is dangerous, which is why insurance exists. The decision of whether or not to obtain insurance for a particular threat, and how much coverage to obtain when choosing to insure, should be based on the probability of the threat becoming real and the loss potential, which was identified during the BIA. The BCP team should work with management to understand what the current coverage is, the various insurance options, and the limits of each option. The goal here is to make sure the insurance coverage fills in the gap of what the current preventive countermeasures cannot protect against. We can eat healthy, work out, and take our vitamins—but these things cannot always prevent serious health issues. We purchase medical insurance to help cover the costs of any unexpected health conditions. Organizations also need insurance to protect them from unexpected events.

Just as people are given different premiums on health and life insurance, companies are given different premiums on the type of insurance they purchase. Different types of insurance policies can be purchased by companies, cyber insurance being one of them. *Cyber insurance* is a new type of coverage that insures losses caused by denial-of-service attacks, malware damages, hackers, electronic theft, privacy-related lawsuits, and more. Whereas a person is asked how old he is, which previous health issues he's had, if he smokes, and so on, to determine his health insurance premium, companies are asked questions about their security program, such as whether they have an IDS, antivirus software, firewalls, and other security measures.

A company could also choose to purchase a *business interruption insurance* policy. With this type of policy, if the company is out of business for a certain length of time, the insurance company will pay for specified expenses and lost earnings. Another policy that can be bought insures accounts receivable. If a company cannot collect on its accounts receivable for one reason or another, this type of coverage covers part or all of the losses and costs.

The company's insurance should be reviewed annually because threat levels may change and the company may expand into new ventures that need to be properly covered. Purchasing insurance should not lull a company into a false sense of security, though. Insurance coverage has its limitations, and if the company does not practice due care, the insurance company may not be legally obligated to pay if a disaster hits. It is important to read and understand the fine print when it comes to insurance and to make sure you know what is expected of your company—not just what is expected from the insurance organization.

Recovery and Restoration

The BCP coordinator needs to define several different teams that should be properly trained and available if a disaster hits. The types of teams an organization needs depends upon the organization. The following are some examples of teams that a company may need to construct:

- Damage assessment team
- Legal team
- Media relations team
- Recovery team
- Relocation team

- Restoration team
- Salvage team
- Security team

The BCP coordinator should have an understanding of the needs of the company and the types of teams that need to be developed and trained. Employees should be assigned to the specific teams based on their knowledge and skill set. Each team needs to have a designated leader, who will direct the members and their activities. These team leaders will be responsible not only for ensuring that their team's objectives are met, but also for communicating with each other to make sure each team is working in parallel phases.

The *restoration team* should be responsible for getting the alternate site into a working and functioning environment, and the *salvage team* should be responsible for starting the recovery of the original site. Both teams must know how to do many tasks, such as install operating systems, configure workstations and servers, string wire and cabling, set up the network and configure networking services, and install equipment and applications. Both teams must also know how to restore data from backup facilities. They also must know how to do so in a secure manner, one that ensures the confidentiality, integrity, and availability of the system and data.

The BCP must outline the specific teams, their responsibilities, and notification procedures. The plan must indicate the methods that should be used to contact team leaders during business hours and after business hours.

A role, or a team, needs to be created to carry out a *damage assessment* once a disaster has taken place. The assessment procedures should be properly documented and include the following steps:

- Determine the cause of the disaster.
- Determine the potential for further damage.
- Identify the affected business functions and areas.
- Identify the level of functionality for the critical resources.
- Identify the resources that must be replaced immediately.
- Estimate how long it will take to bring critical functions back online.
- If it will take longer than the previously estimated MTD values to restore operations, then a disaster should be declared and the BCP should be put into action.

After this information is collected and assessed, it will indicate which teams need to be called to action and whether the BCP actually needs to be activated. The BCP coordinator and team must develop activation criteria. After the damage assessment, if one or more of the situations outlined in the criteria have taken place, then the team is moved into recovery mode.

Different organizations have different criteria because the business drivers and critical functions will vary from organization to organization. The criteria may comprise some or all of the following elements:

- Danger to human life
- Danger to state or national security
- Damage to facility
- Damage to critical systems
- Estimated value of downtime that will be experienced

Once the damage assessment is completed and the plan is activated, various teams must be deployed, which signals the company's entry into the *recovery phase*. Each team has its own tasks—for example, the restoration team prepares the offsite facility (if needed), the network team rebuilds the network and systems, and the relocation team starts organizing the staff to move into a new facility.

The recovery process needs to be well organized to get the company up and running as soon as possible. This is much easier to state in a book than to carry out in reality. This is why written procedures are critical. During the BIA, the critical functions and their resources were identified. These are the things that the teams need to work together on getting up and running first.

Templates should have been developed during the plan development stage. These templates are used by the different teams to step them through the necessary phases and to document their findings. For example, if one step could not be completed until new systems were purchased, this should be indicated on the template. If a step is partially completed, this should be documented so the team does not forget to go back and finish that step when the necessary part arrives. These templates keep the teams on task and also quickly tell the team leaders about the progress, obstacles, and potential recovery time.

TIP Examples of possible templates can be found in NIST Special Publication 800-34, Revision 1, "Contingency Planning Guide for Federal Information Systems," which is available online at http://csrc.nist.gov/publications/nistpubs/800-34-rev1/sp800-34-rev1_errata-Nov11-2010.pdf.

When it is time for the company to move back into its original site or a new site, the company enters the *reconstitution phase*. A company is not out of an emergency state until it is back in operation at the original primary site or a new site that was constructed to replace the primary site, because the company is always vulnerable while operating in a backup facility. Many logistical issues need to be considered as to when a company must return from the alternate site to the original site. The following lists a few of these issues:

- Ensuring the safety of employees
- Ensuring an adequate environment is provided (power, facility infrastructure, water, HVAC)
- Ensuring that the necessary equipment and supplies are present and in working order
- Ensuring proper communications and connectivity methods are working
- Properly testing the new environment

Once the coordinator, management, and salvage team sign off on the readiness of the facility, the salvage team should carry out the following steps:

- Back up data from the alternate site and restore it within the new facility.
- Carefully terminate contingency operations.
- Securely transport equipment and personnel to the new facility.

The least critical functions should be moved back first, so if there are issues in network configurations or connectivity, or important steps were not carried out, the critical operations of the company are not negatively affected. Why go through the trouble of moving the most critical systems and operations to a safe and stable site, only to return them to a main site that is untested? Let the less critical departments act as the canary in the coal mine. If they survive, then move the more critical components of the company to the main site.

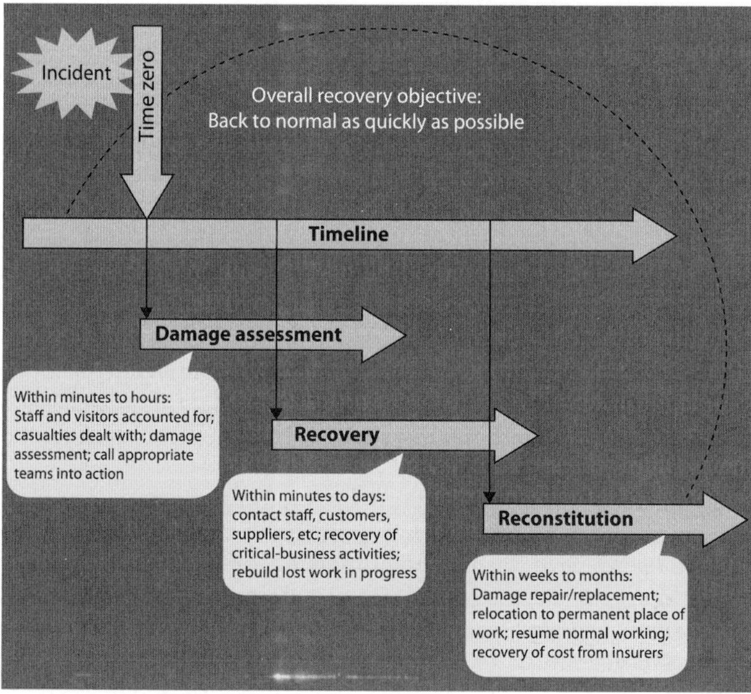

Developing Goals for the Plans

If you do not have established goals, how do you know when you are done and whether your efforts were actually successful? Goals are established so everyone knows the ultimate objectives. Establishing goals is important for any task, but especially for business continuity and recovery plans. The definition of the goals helps direct the proper allocation of resources and tasks, develops necessary strategies, and assists in economical justification of the plans and program overall. Once the goals are set, they provide a guide to the development of the actual plans themselves. Anyone who has been involved in large projects that entail many small, complex details knows that at times it is easy to get off track and not actually accomplish the major goals of the project. Goals are established to keep everyone on track and to ensure that the efforts pay off in the end.

BCP Development Products

Since there is so much work in collecting, analyzing, and maintaining DRP and BCP data, using a product that automates these tasks can prove to be extremely helpful.

"Automated" plan development can help you create

- Customizable questionnaires through the use of expert-system templates
- Timetables for disaster recovery procedures
- What-if scenario modeling
- Reports on financial and operational impact analysis
- Graphic representations of the analysis results
- Sample questionnaires, forms, and templates
- Permission-based plan maintenance
- Central version control and integration
- Regulatory compliance

Great—we have established that goals are important. But the goal could be, "Keep the company in business if an earthquake hits." Good goal, but not overly useful without more clarity and direction. To be useful, a goal must contain certain key information, such as the following:

- **Responsibility** Each individual involved with recovery and continuity should have their responsibilities spelled out in writing to ensure a clear understanding in a chaotic situation. Each task should be assigned to the individual most logically situated to handle it. These individuals must know what is expected of them, which is done through training, drills, communication, and documentation. So, for example, instead of just running out of the building screaming, an individual must know that he is responsible for shutting down the servers before he can run out of the building screaming.
- **Authority** In times of crisis, it is important to know who is in charge. Teamwork is important in these situations, and almost every team does much better with an established and trusted leader. Such leaders must know that they are expected to step up to the plate in a time of crisis and understand what type of direction they should provide to the rest of the employees. Clear-cut authority will aid in reducing confusion and increasing cooperation.

- **Priorities** It is extremely important to know what is critical versus what is merely nice to have. Different departments provide different functionality for an organization. The critical departments must be singled out from the departments that provide functionality that the company can live without for a week or two. It is necessary to know which department must come online first, which second, and so on. That way, the efforts are made in the most useful, effective, and focused manner. Along with the priorities of departments, the priorities of systems, information, and programs must be established. It may be necessary to ensure that the database is up and running before working to bring the web servers online. The general priorities must be set by management with the help of the different departments and IT staff.
- **Implementation and testing** It is great to write down very profound ideas and develop plans, but unless they are actually carried out and tested, they may not add up to a hill of beans. Once a continuity plan is developed, it actually has to be put into action. It needs to be documented and put in places that are easily accessible in times of crisis. The people who are assigned specific tasks need to be taught and informed how to fulfill those tasks, and dry runs must be done to walk people through different situations. The drills should take place at least once a year, and the entire program should be continually updated and improved.

Studies have shown that 65 percent of businesses that lose computing capabilities for over one week are never able to recover and subsequently go out of business. Not being able to bounce back quickly or effectively by setting up shop somewhere else can make a company lose business and, more importantly, its reputation. In such a competitive world, customers have a lot of options. If one company is not prepared to bounce back after a disruption or disaster, customers may go to another vendor and stay there.

The biggest effect of an incident, especially one that is poorly managed or that was preventable, is on an organization's reputation or brand. This can result in a considerable and even irreparable loss of trust by customers and clients. On the other hand, handling an incident well, or preventing great damage through smart, preemptive measures, can enhance the reputation of, or trust in, an organization.

Implementing Strategies

As stated previously, copies of the plan need to be kept in one or more locations other than the primary site, so that if the primary site is destroyed or negatively affected, the continuity plan is still available to the teams. It is also critical that different formats of the plan be available to the team, including both electronic and paper versions. An electronic version of the plan is not very useful if you don't have any electricity to run a computer. In addition to having copies of the recovery documents located at their offices and homes, key individuals should have easily accessible versions of critical procedures and call tree information.

One simple way to accomplish this is to publish the call tree data on cards that can be affixed to personnel badges or kept in a wallet. In an emergency situation, valuable minutes are better spent responding to an incident than looking for a document or having to wait for a laptop to power up.

The plan should address in detail all of the topics we have covered so far. The actual format of the plan will depend on the environment, the goals of the plan, priorities, and identified threats. After each of those items is examined and documented, the topics of the plan can be divided into the necessary categories.

A commonly accepted structure for a BCP is illustrated in Figure 7-18. Each organization's BCP looks different, but these core topics should be covered in some fashion. The role of the plan is to provide preplanned and sequenced structure to these different processes. The plan also needs to integrate a degree of flexibility, because no one knows exactly what type of disaster will take place, nor its effects. Although procedures need to be documented for the different phases of the plan, a balance between detail and flexibility must be achieved so the company is ready for any type of disaster.

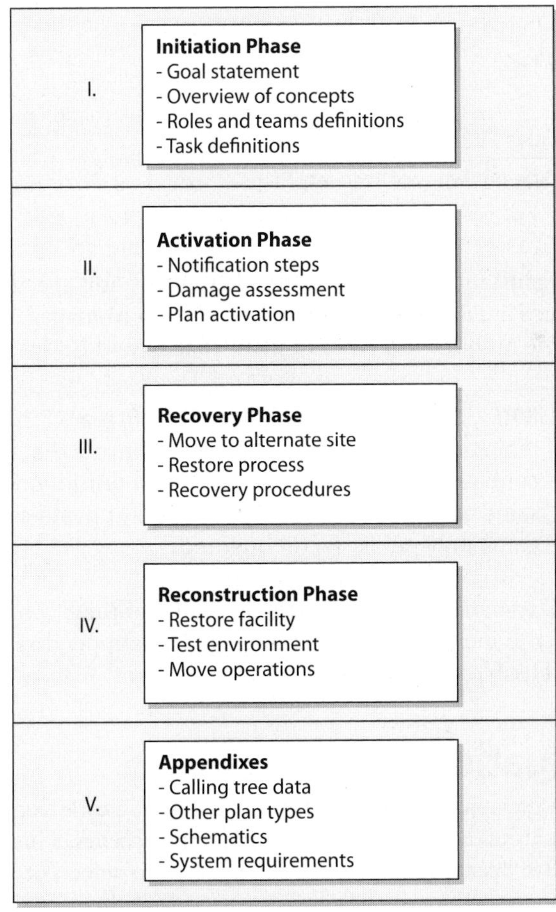

I.
Initiation Phase
- Goal statement
- Overview of concepts
- Roles and teams definitions
- Task definitions
II.
Activation Phase
- Notification steps
- Damage assessment
- Plan activation
III.
Recovery Phase
- Move to alternate site
- Restore process
- Recovery procedures
IV.
Reconstruction Phase
- Restore facility
- Test environment
- Move operations
V.
Appendixes
- Calling tree data
- Other plan types
- Schematics
- System requirements

Figure 7-18 The general structure of a business continuity plan

Plan Type	Description
Business resumption plan	Focuses on how to re-create the necessary business processes that need to be reestablished instead of focusing on IT components (i.e., process-oriented instead of procedural-oriented).
Continuity of operations (COOP) plan	Establishes senior management and a headquarters after a disaster. Outlines roles and authorities, orders of succession, and individual role tasks. COOP is the term commonly used by the U.S. government for BCP.
IT contingency plan	Plan for systems, networks, and major applications recovery procedures after disruptions. A contingency plan should be developed for each major system and application.
Crisis communications plan	Includes internal and external communications structure and roles. Identifies specific individuals who will communicate with external entities. Contains previously developed statements that are to be released.
Cyber incident response plan	Focuses on malware, hackers, intrusions, attacks, and other security issues. Outlines procedures for incident response.
Disaster recovery plan	Focuses on how to recover various IT mechanisms after a disaster. Whereas a contingency plan is usually for nondisasters, a DRP is for disasters that require IT processing to take place at another facility.
Occupant emergency plan	Establishes personnel safety and evacuation procedures.

Table 7-4 Different Types of Recovery Plans

Some organizations develop individual plans for specific tasks and goals. These different plans are described in Table 7-4. It is up to management and the BCP team to determine the number and types of plans that should be developed and implemented.

NOTE Continuity of operations (COOP) is a U.S. government initiative, required by presidential directive, to ensure that agencies are able to continue operations after a disaster or disruption. BCP and COOP have the same basic goals, but BCP is commonly private-sector oriented and COOP is commonly public-sector oriented.

The BCP team can choose to integrate many of these components into the BCP. It is usually better to include these stand-alone plans as appendixes so each document is clear, concise, and usable.

Investigations

Whether an incident is a nondisaster, a disaster, or a catastrophe, we should treat the systems and facilities that it affects as potential crime scenes. This is because what may at first appear to have been a hardware failure, a software defect, or an accidental fire may have in fact been caused by a malicious actor targeting the organization. Even acts of nature like storms or earthquakes may provide opportunities for adversaries to victimize us.

Because we are never (initially) quite sure whether an incident may have a criminal element, we should treat all incidents as if they do (until proven otherwise).

Since computer crimes are only increasing and will never really go away, it is important that all security professionals understand how computer investigations should be carried out. This includes understanding legal requirements for specific situations, the "chain of custody" for evidence, what type of evidence is admissible in court, incident response procedures, and escalation processes.

When a potential computer crime takes place, it is critical that the investigation steps are carried out properly to ensure that the evidence will be admissible to the court if things go that far and that it can stand up under the cross-examination and scrutiny that will take place. As a security professional, you should understand that an investigation is not just about potential evidence on a disk drive. The whole environment will be part of an investigation, including the people, network, connected internal and external systems, federal and state laws, management's stance on how the investigation is to be carried out, and the skill set of whomever is carrying out the investigation. Messing up on just one of these components could make your case inadmissible or at least damage it if it is brought to court.

Cops or No Cops?

Management needs to make the decision as to whether law enforcement should be called in to handle the security breach. The following are some of the issues to understand if law enforcement is brought in:

- Law enforcement agencies bring significant investigative capability.
- The company may lose control over where the investigation leads once law enforcement is involved.
- Secrecy of compromise is not promised; it could become part of public record.
- Effects on reputation need to be considered (the ramifications of this information reaching customers, shareholders, and so on).
- Evidence will be collected and may not be available for a long period of time. It may take a year or so to get into court.

Computer Forensics and Proper Collection of Evidence

Forensics is a science and an art that requires specialized techniques for the recovery, authentication, and analysis of electronic data for the purposes of a digital criminal investigation. It is the coming together of computer science, information technology, and engineering with law. When discussing computer forensics with others, you might hear the terms computer forensics, network forensics, electronic data discovery, cyberforensics, and forensic computing. $(ISC)^2$ uses *digital forensics* as a synonym for all of these other terms, so that's what you'll see on the CISSP exam. Computer forensics encompasses all domains

in which evidence is in a digital or electronic form, either in storage or on the wire. At one time computer forensic results were differentiated from network and code analysis, but now this entire area is referred to as *digital evidence.*

The people conducting the forensic investigation must be properly skilled in this trade and know what to look for. If someone reboots the attacked system or inspects various files, this could corrupt viable evidence, change timestamps on key files, and erase footprints the criminal may have left. Most digital evidence has a short lifespan and must be collected quickly in order of volatility. In other words, the most volatile or fragile evidence should be collected first. In some situations, it is best to remove the system from the network, dump the contents of the memory, power down the system, and make a sound image of the attacked system and perform forensic analysis on this copy. Working on the copy instead of the original drive will ensure that the evidence stays unharmed on the original system in case some steps in the investigation actually corrupt or destroy data. Dumping the memory contents to a file before doing any work on the system or powering it down is a crucial step because of the information that could be stored there. This is another method of capturing fragile information. However, this creates a sticky situation: capturing RAM or conducting live analysis can introduce changes to the crime scene because various state changes and operations take place. Whatever method the forensic investigator chooses to use to collect digital evidence, that method must be documented. This is the most important aspect of evidence handling.

NOTE The forensics team needs specialized tools, an evidence collection notebook, containers, a camera, and evidence identification tags. The notebook should not be a spiral notebook but rather a notebook that is bound in a way that one can tell if pages have been removed.

Digital evidence must be handled in a careful fashion so it can be used in different courts, no matter what jurisdiction is prosecuting a suspect. Within the United States, there is the *Scientific Working Group on Digital Evidence (SWGDE)*, which aims to ensure consistency across the forensic community. The principles developed by the SWGDE for the standardized recovery of computer-based evidence are governed by the following attributes:

- Consistency with all legal systems
- Allowance for the use of a common language
- Durability
- Ability to cross international and state boundaries
- Ability to instill confidence in the integrity of evidence
- Applicability to all forensic evidence
- Applicability at every level, including that of individual, agency, and country

The SWGDE principles are listed next:

1. When dealing with digital evidence, all of the general forensic and procedural principles must be applied.
2. Upon the seizing of digital evidence, actions taken should not change that evidence.
3. When it is necessary for a person to access original digital evidence, that person should be trained for the purpose.
4. All activity relating to the seizure, access, storage, or transfer of digital evidence must be fully documented, preserved, and available for review.
5. An individual is responsible for all actions taken with respect to digital evidence while the digital evidence is in their possession.
6. Any agency that is responsible for seizing, accessing, storing, or transferring digital evidence is responsible for compliance with these principles.

NOTE The Digital Forensic Research Workshop (DFRWS) brings together academic researchers and forensic investigators to also address a standardized process for collecting evidence, to research practitioner requirements, and to incorporate a scientific method as a tenant of digital forensic science. Learn more at www.dfrws.org/index.shtml.

Motive, Opportunity, and Means

Today's computer criminals are similar to their traditional counterparts. To understand the "whys" in crime, it is necessary to understand the motive, opportunity, and means—or MOM. This is the same strategy used to determine the suspects in a traditional, non-computer crime.

Motive is the "who" and "why" of a crime. The motive may be induced by either internal or external conditions. A person may be driven by the excitement, challenge, and adrenaline rush of committing a crime, which would be an internal condition. Examples of external conditions might include financial trouble, a sick family member, or other dire straits. Understanding the motive for a crime is an important piece in figuring out who would engage in such an activity. For example, in the past many hackers attacked big-name sites because when the sites went down, it was splashed all over the news. However, once technology advanced to the point where attacks could not bring down these sites, or once these activities were no longer so highly publicized, many individuals eventually moved on to other types of attacks.

Opportunity is the "where" and "when" of a crime. Opportunities usually arise when certain vulnerabilities or weaknesses are present. If a company does not have a firewall, hackers and attackers have all types of opportunities within that network. If a company does not perform access control, auditing, and supervision, employees may have many opportunities to embezzle funds and defraud the company. Once a crime fighter finds out why a person would want to commit a crime (motive), she will look at what could allow the criminal to be successful (opportunity).

Means pertains to the abilities a criminal would need to be successful. Suppose a crime fighter was asked to investigate a complex embezzlement that took place within a financial institution. If the suspects were three people who knew how to use a mouse, keyboard, and a word processing application, but only one of them was a programmer and system analyst, the crime fighter would realize that this person may have the means to commit this crime much more successfully than the other two individuals.

Computer Criminal Behavior

Like traditional criminals, computer criminals have a specific modus operandi (MO, pronounced "em-oh"). In other words, criminals use a distinct method of operation to carry out their crime that can be used to help identify them. The difference with computer crimes is that the investigator, obviously, must have knowledge of technology. For example, an MO for computer criminals may include the use of specific hacking tools, or targeting specific systems or networks. The method usually involves repetitive signature behaviors, such as sending e-mail messages or programming syntax. Knowledge of the criminal's MO and signature behaviors can be useful throughout the investigative process. Law enforcement can use the information to identify other offenses by the same criminal, for example. The MO and signature behaviors can also provide information that is useful during the interview process and potentially a trial.

Psychological crime scene analysis (profiling) can also be conducted using the criminal's MO and signature behaviors. Profiling provides insight into the thought processes of the attacker and can be used to identify the attacker or, at the very least, the tool he used to conduct the crime.

NOTE *Locard's exchange principle* also applies to profiling. The principle states that a criminal leaves something behind at the crime scene and takes something with them. This principle is the foundation of criminalistics. Even in an entirely digital crime scene, Locard's exchange principle can shed light on who the perpetrator(s) may be.

Incident Investigators

Incident investigators are a breed of their own. The good ones must be aware of suspicious or abnormal activities that others might normally ignore. This is because, due to their training and experience, they may know what is potentially going on behind some abnormal system activity, while another employee would just respond, "Oh, that just happens sometimes. We don't know why."

The investigator could identify suspicious activities, such as port scans, attempted SQL injections, or evidence in a log that describes a dangerous activity that took place. Identifying abnormal activities is a bit more difficult, because it is more subtle. These activities could be increased network traffic, an employee's staying late every night, unusual requests to specific ports on a network server, and so on. On top of being observant, the investigator must understand forensic procedures, evidence collection

issues, and how to analyze a situation to determine what is going on and know how to pick out the clues in system logs.

Different Types of Assessments an Investigator Can Perform

There are four general types of assessments performed by investigators.

Network analysis

- Traffic analysis
- Log analysis
- Path tracing

Media analysis

- Disk imaging
- Timeline analysis (modify, access, create times)
- Registry analysis
- Slack space analysis
- Shadow volume analysis

Software analysis

- Reverse engineering
- Malicious code review
- Exploit review

Hardware/embedded device analysis

- Dedicated appliance attack points
- Firmware and dedicated memory inspections
- Embedded operating systems, virtualized software, and hypervisor analysis

The Forensic Investigation Process

To ensure that forensic activities are carried out in a standardized manner and the evidence collected is admissible, it is necessary for the team to follow specific laid-out steps so that nothing is missed. Figure 7-19 illustrates the phases through a common investigation process. Each team or company may commonly come up with their own steps, but all should be essentially accomplishing the same things:

- Identification
- Preservation
- Collection

Identification	Preservation	Collection	Examination	Analysis	Presentation
Event/crime detection	Case management	Preservation	Preservation	Preservation	Documentation
Resolve signature	Imaging technologies	Approved methods	Traceability	Traceability	Expert testimony
Profile detection	Chain of custody	Approved software	Validation techniques	Statistical	Clarification
Anomalous detection	Time synchronization	Approved hardware	Filtering techniques	Protocols	Mission impact statement
Complaints		Legal authority	Pattern matching	Data mining	Recommended countermeasure
System monitoring		Lossless compression	Hidden data discovery	Timeline	Statistical interpretation
Audit analysis		Sampling	Hidden data extraction	Link	
Etc.		Data reducation		Spatial	
		Recovery techniques			

Figure 7-19 Characteristics of the different phases through an investigation process

- Examination
- Analysis
- Presentation
- Decision

NOTE The principles of criminalistics are included in the forensic investigation process. They are identification of the crime scene, protection of the environment against contamination and loss of evidence, identification of evidence and potential sources of evidence, and the collection of evidence. In regard to minimizing the degree of contamination, it is important to understand that it is impossible not to change a crime scene—be it physical or digital. The key is to minimize changes and document what you did and why, and how the crime scene was affected.

During the examination and analysis process of a forensic investigation, it is critical that the investigator works from an image that contains *all* of the data from the original disk. It must be a bit-level copy, sector by sector, to capture deleted files, slack spaces, and unallocated clusters. These types of images can be created through the use of a specialized tool such as Forensic Toolkit (FTK), EnCase Forensic, or the dd Unix utility. A file copy tool does not recover all data areas of the device necessary for examination. Figure 7-20 illustrates a commonly used tool in the forensic world for evidence collection.

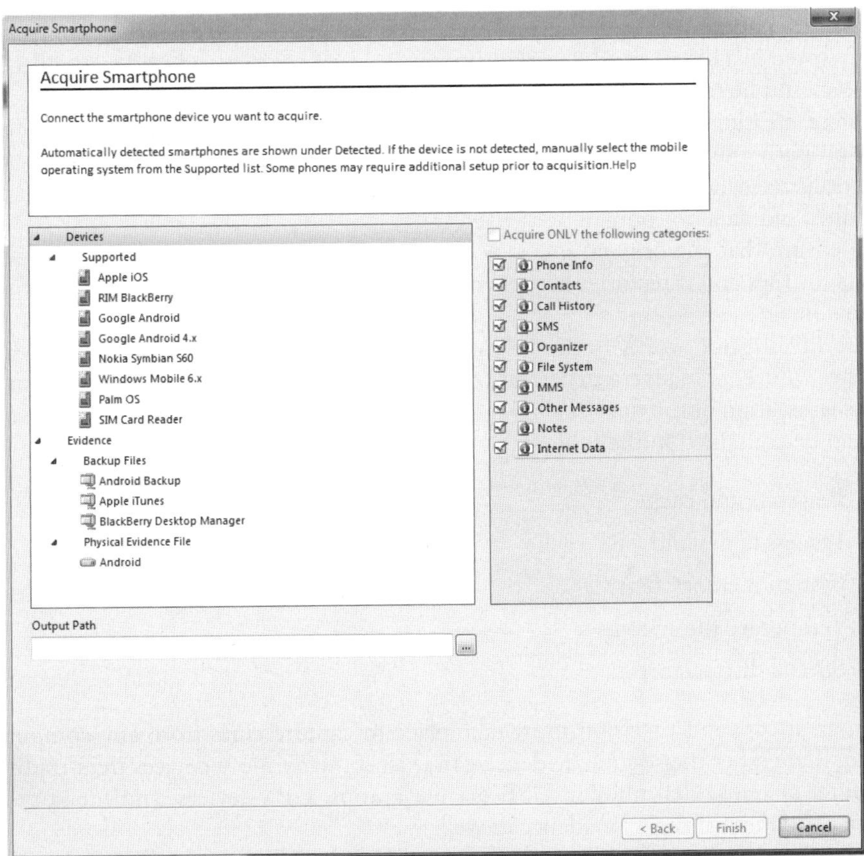

Figure 7-20 EnCase Forensic can be used to collect digital forensic data.

Controlling the Crime Scene

Whether the crime scene is physical or digital, it is important to control who comes in contact with the evidence of the crime to ensure its integrity. The following are just some of the steps that should take place to protect the crime scene:

- Only allow authorized individuals access to the scene. These individuals should have knowledge of basic crime scene analysis.
- Document who is at the crime scene. In court, the integrity of the evidence may be in question if there are too many people milling around.
- Document who were the last individuals to interact with the systems.
- If the crime scene does become contaminated, document it. The contamination may not negate the derived evidence, but it will make investigating the crime more challenging.

The original media should have two copies created: a *primary image* (a control copy that is stored in a library) and a *working image* (used for analysis and evidence collection). These should be timestamped to show when the evidence was collected.

Before creating these images, the investigator must make sure the new media has been properly purged, meaning it does not contain any residual data. Some incidents have occurred where drives that were new and right out of the box (shrink-wrapped) contained old data not purged by the vendor.

To ensure that the original image is not modified, it is important to create message digests for files and directories before and after the analysis to prove the integrity of the original image.

The investigator works from the duplicate image because it preserves the original evidence, prevents inadvertent alteration of original evidence during examination, and allows re-creation of the duplicate image if necessary. Much of the needed data is volatile and can be contained in the following:

- Registers and cache
- Process tables and ARP cache
- System memory (RAM)
- Temporary file systems
- Special disk sectors

So, great care and precision must take place to capture clues from any computer or device. Remember that digital evidence can exist in many more devices than traditional computer systems. Cell phones, USB drives, laptops, GPS devices, and memory cards can be containers of digital evidence as well.

Acquiring evidence on live systems and those using network storage further complicates matters because you cannot turn off the system in order to make a copy of the hard drive. Imagine the reaction you'd receive if you were to tell an IT manager that you need to shut down a primary database or e-mail system. It wouldn't be favorable. So these systems and others, such as those using on-the-fly encryption, must be imaged while they are running.

Forensics Field Kits

When forensics teams are deployed, they should be properly equipped with all of the tools and supplies needed. The following are some of the common items in the forensics field kits:

- **Documentation tools** Tags, labels, and time-lined forms
- **Disassembly and removal tools** Antistatic bands, pliers, tweezers, screwdrivers, wire cutters, and so on

- **Package and transport supplies** Antistatic bags, evidence bags and tape, cable ties, and others

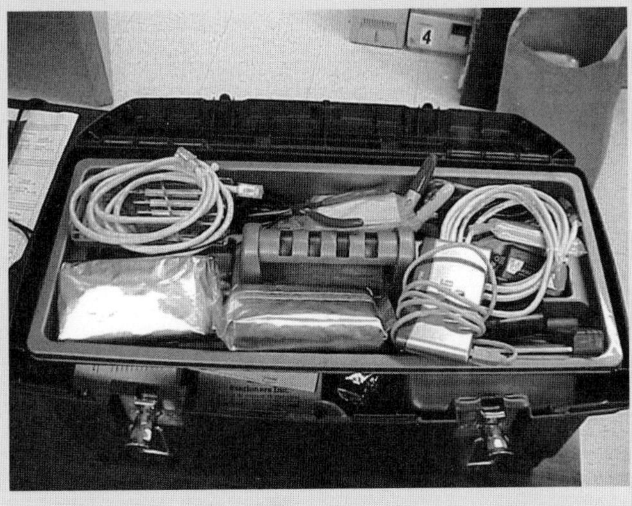

The next crucial piece is to keep a proper *chain of custody* of the evidence. Because evidence from these types of crimes can be very volatile and easily dismissed from court because of improper handling, it is important to follow very strict and organized procedures when collecting and tagging evidence in every single case—no exceptions! Furthermore, the chain of custody should follow evidence through its entire life cycle, beginning with identification and ending with its destruction, permanent archiving, or return to owner.

NOTE A chain of custody is a history that shows how evidence was collected, analyzed, transported, and preserved in order to be presented in court. Because electronic evidence can be easily modified, a clearly defined chain of custody demonstrates that the evidence is trustworthy.

When copies of data need to be made, this process must meet certain standards to ensure quality and reliability. Specialized software for this purpose can be used. The copies must be able to be independently verified and must be tamperproof.

Each piece of evidence should be marked in some way with the date, time, initials of the collector, and a case number if one has been assigned. Magnetic disk surfaces should not be marked on. The piece of evidence should then be sealed in a container, which should be marked with the same information. The container should be sealed with evidence tape, and if possible, the writing should be on the tape so a broken seal can be detected. An example of the data that should be collected and displayed on each evidence container is shown in Figure 7-21.

EVIDENCE

Station/Section/Unit/Dept__________

Case number__________ Item#__________

Type of offense__________

Description of evidence__________

____

____

Suspect__________

Victim__________

Date and time of recovery__________

Location of recovery__________

Recovered by__________

CHAIN OF CUSTODY

Received from__________ By__________

Date__________ Time__________ A.M./P.M.

Received from__________ By__________

Date__________ Time__________ A.M./P.M.

Received from__________ By__________

Date__________ Time__________ A.M./P.M.

Received from__________ By__________

Date__________ Time__________ A.M./P.M.

WARNING: THIS IS A TAMPER EVIDENT SECURITY PACKAGE. ONCE SEALED, ANY ATTEMPT TO OPEN WILL RESULT IN OBVIOUS SIGNS OF TAMPERING.

Figure 7-21 Evidence container data

NOTE The chain of custody of evidence dictates that all evidence be labeled with information indicating who secured and validated it.

Wires and cables should be labeled, and a photograph of the labeled system should be taken before it is actually disassembled. Media should be write-protected if possible. Storage of media evidence should be dust free and kept at room temperature without much humidity, and, of course, the media should not be stored close to any strong magnets or magnetic fields.

If possible, the crime scene should be photographed, including behind the computer if the crime involved some type of physical break-in. Documents, papers, and devices should be handled with cloth gloves and placed into containers and sealed. All storage media should be contained, even if it has been erased, because data still may be obtainable.

Because this type of evidence can be easily erased or destroyed and is complex in nature, identification, recording, collection, preservation, transportation, and interpretation are all important. After everything is properly labeled, a chain of custody log should be made of each container and an overall log should be made capturing all events.

For a crime to be successfully prosecuted, solid evidence is required. Computer forensics is the art of retrieving this evidence and preserving it in the proper ways to make it admissible in court. Without proper computer forensics, hardly any computer crimes could ever be properly and successfully presented in court.

The most common reasons for improper evidence collection are lack of an established incident response team, lack of an established incident response procedures, poorly written policy, or a broken chain of custody.

The next step is the analysis of the evidence. Forensic investigators use a scientific method that involves

- Determining the characteristics of the evidence, such as whether it's admissible as primary or secondary evidence, as well as its source, reliability, and permanence
- Comparing evidence from different sources to determine a chronology of events
- Event reconstruction, including the recovery of deleted files and other activity on the system

This can take place in a controlled lab environment or, thanks to hardware write-blockers and forensic software, in the field. When investigators analyze evidence in a lab, they are dealing with dead forensics; that is, they are working only with static data. Live forensics, which takes place in the field, includes volatile data. If evidence is lacking, then an experienced investigator should be called in to help complete the picture.

Finally, the interpretation of the analysis should be presented to the appropriate party. This could be a judge, lawyer, CEO, or board of directors. Therefore, it is important to present the findings in a format that will be understood by a nontechnical audience. As a CISSP, you should be able to explain these findings in layman's terms using metaphors and analogies. Of course, the findings, which are top secret or company confidential, should be disclosed only to authorized parties. This may include the legal department or any outside counsel that assisted with the investigation.

What Is Admissible in Court?

Computer logs are important in many aspects of the IT world. They are generally used to troubleshoot an issue or to try to understand the events that took place at a specific moment in time. When computer logs are to be used as evidence in court, they must be collected in the regular course of business. Most of the time, computer-related documents are considered *hearsay*, meaning the evidence is secondhand evidence. Hearsay evidence is not normally admissible in court unless it has firsthand evidence that can be used to prove the evidence's accuracy, trustworthiness, and reliability, such as the testimony of a businessperson who generated the computer logs and collected them. This person must generate and collect logs as a normal part of his business activities and not just this one time for court. The value of evidence depends upon the genuineness and competence of the source.

> **Business Records Exception**
>
> A legal exception to the U.S. hearsay rule of the Federal Rules of Evidence (FRE) is called the business records exception rule or business entry rule.
>
> Under this rule, a party could admit any records of a business (1) that were made in the regular course of business; (2) that the business has a regular practice to make such records; (3) that were made at or near the time of the recorded event; and (4) that contain information transmitted by a person with knowledge of the information within the document.

It is important to show that the logs, and all evidence, have not been tampered with in any way, which is the reason for the chain of custody of evidence. Several tools are available that run checksums or hashing functions on the logs, which will allow the team to be alerted if something has been modified.

When evidence is being collected, one issue that can come up is the user's expectation of privacy. If an employee is suspected of, and charged with, a computer crime, he might claim that his files on the computer he uses are personal and not available to law enforcement and the courts. This is why it is important for companies to conduct security-awareness training, have employees sign documentation pertaining to the acceptable use of the company's computers and equipment, and have legal banners pop up on every employee's computer when they log on. These are key elements in establishing that a user has no right to privacy when he is using company equipment. The following banner is suggested by CERT Advisory:

> *This system is for the use of authorized users only. Individuals using this computer system without authority, or in excess of their authority, are subject to having all of their activities on this system monitored and recorded by system personnel.*
>
> *In the course of monitoring an individual improperly using this system, or in the course of system maintenance, the activities of authorized users may also be monitored.*
>
> *Anyone using this system expressly consents to such monitoring and is advised that if such monitoring reveals possible evidence of criminal activity, system personnel may provide the evidence of such monitoring to law enforcement officials.*

This explicit warning strengthens a legal case that can be brought against an employee or intruder, because the continued use of the system after viewing this type of warning implies that the person acknowledges the security policy and gives permission to be monitored.

Evidence has its own life cycle, and it is important that the individuals involved with the investigation understand the phases of the life cycle and properly follow them.

The life cycle of evidence includes

- Collection and identification
- Storage, preservation, and transportation

- Presentation in court
- Return of the evidence to the victim or owner

Several types of evidence can be used in a trial, such as written, oral, computer generated, and visual or audio. Oral evidence is testimony of a witness. Visual or audio is usually a captured event during the crime or right after it.

It is important that evidence be relevant, complete, sufficient, and reliable to the case at hand. These four characteristics of evidence provide a foundation for a case and help ensure that the evidence is legally permissible.

For evidence to be *relevant*, it must have a reasonable and sensible relationship to the findings. If a judge rules that a person's past traffic tickets cannot be brought up in a murder trial, this means the judge has ruled that the traffic tickets are not relevant to the case at hand. Therefore, the prosecuting lawyer cannot even mention them in court.

For evidence to be *complete*, it must present the whole truth of an issue. For the evidence to be *sufficient*, or believable, it must be persuasive enough to convince a reasonable person of the validity of the evidence. This means the evidence cannot be subject to personal interpretation. Sufficient evidence also means it cannot be easily doubted.

For evidence to be *reliable*, or accurate, it must be consistent with the facts. Evidence cannot be reliable if it is based on someone's opinion or copies of an original document, because there is too much room for error. Reliable evidence means it is factual and not circumstantial.

NOTE Don't dismiss the possibility that as an information security professional you will be responsible for entering evidence into court. Most tribunals, commissions, and other quasi-legal proceedings have admissibility requirements. Because these requirements can change between jurisdictions, you should seek legal counsel to better understand the specific rules for your jurisdiction.

Surveillance, Search, and Seizure

Two main types of surveillance are used when it comes to identifying computer crimes: physical surveillance and computer surveillance. *Physical surveillance* pertains to security cameras, security guards, and closed-circuit TV (CCTV), which may capture evidence. Physical surveillance can also be used by an undercover agent to learn about the suspect's spending activities, family and friends, and personal habits in the hope of gathering more clues for the case.

Computer surveillance pertains to auditing events, which passively monitors events by using network sniffers, keyboard monitors, wiretaps, and line monitoring. In most jurisdictions, active monitoring may require a search warrant. In most workplace environments, to legally monitor an individual, the person must be warned ahead of time that her activities may be subject to this type of monitoring.

Search and seizure activities can get tricky depending on what is being searched for and where. For example, American citizens are protected by the Fourth Amendment against unlawful search and seizure, so law enforcement agencies must have probable cause and request a search warrant from a judge or court before conducting such a search. The actual search can take place only in the areas outlined by the warrant. The Fourth Amendment does not apply to actions by private citizens unless they are acting as police agents. So, for example, if Kristy's boss warned all employees that the management could remove files from their computers at any time, and her boss was not a police officer or acting as a police agent, she could not successfully claim that her Fourth Amendment rights were violated. Kristy's boss may have violated some specific privacy laws, but he did not violate Kristy's Fourth Amendment rights.

In some circumstances, a law enforcement agent may seize evidence that is not included in the warrant, such as if the suspect tries to destroy the evidence. In other words, if there is an impending possibility that evidence might be destroyed, law enforcement may quickly seize the evidence to prevent its destruction. This is referred to as *exigent circumstances*, and a judge will later decide whether the seizure was proper and legal before allowing the evidence to be admitted. For example, if a police officer had a search warrant that allowed him to search a suspect's living room but no other rooms and then he saw the suspect dumping cocaine down the toilet, the police officer could seize the cocaine even though it was in a room not covered under his search warrant.

After evidence is gathered, the chain of custody needs to be enacted and enforced to make sure the evidence's integrity is not compromised.

A thin line exists between enticement and entrapment when it comes to capturing a suspect's actions. *Enticement* is legal and ethical, whereas *entrapment* is neither legal nor ethical. In the world of computer crimes, a honeypot is always a good example to explain the difference between enticement and entrapment. Companies put systems in their screened subnets that either emulate services that attackers usually like to take advantage of or actually have the services enabled. The hope is that if an attacker breaks into the company's network, she will go right to the honeypot instead of the systems that are actual production machines. The attacker will be *enticed* to go to the honeypot system because it has many open ports and services running and exhibits vulnerabilities that the attacker would want to exploit. The company can log the attacker's actions and later attempt to prosecute.

The action in the preceding example is legal unless the company crosses the line to entrapment. For example, suppose a web page has a link that indicates that if an individual clicks it, she could then download thousands of MP3 files for free. However, when she clicks that link, she is taken to the honeypot system instead, and the company records all of her actions and attempts to prosecute. Entrapment does not prove that the suspect had the intent to commit a crime; it only proves she was successfully tricked.

Interviewing Suspects

Once surveillance and search and seizure activities have been performed, it is very likely that suspects must be interviewed. However, interviewing is both an art and a science, and the interview should be conducted by a properly trained professional. Even then, the interview may only be conducted after consultation with legal counsel. This doesn't, however, completely relieve you as an information security professional from responsibility during the interviewing process. You may be asked to provide input or observe an interview in order to clarify technical information that comes up in the course of questioning. When this is needed, there should be one person in charge of the interview, with one or two others present. Both the topics of discussion and the questions should be prepared beforehand and asked in a systematic and calm fashion, because the interview could yield evidence for a trial.

The employee interviewer should be in a position that is senior to the employee suspect. A vice president is not going to be very intimidated or willing to spill his guts to the mailroom clerk. The interview should be held in a private place, in an environment conducive to making the suspect relatively comfortable and at ease. If exhibits are going to be shown to the suspect, they should be shown one at a time, and otherwise kept in a folder. It is not necessary to read a person their rights before questioning unless law enforcement officers do the interrogation.

What the interviewers do not want to happen during an interview is to be deceived by the suspect, to relinquish important information pertaining to the investigation, or to have the suspect flee before a trial date is set.

Liability and Its Ramifications

As legislatures, courts, and law enforcement develop and refine their respective approaches to computer crimes, so too must corporations. Corporations should develop not only their preventive, detective, and corrective approaches, but also their liability and responsibility approaches. As these crimes increase in frequency and sophistication, so do their destruction and lasting effects. In most cases, the attackers are not caught, but there is plenty of blame to be passed around, so a corporation needs to take many steps to ensure that the blame and liability do not land clearly at its doorstep.

The same is true for other types of threats that corporations have to deal with today. If a company has a facility that burns to the ground, the arsonist is only one small piece of this tragedy. The company is responsible for providing fire detection and suppression systems, fire-resistant construction material in certain areas, alarms, exits, fire extinguishers, and backups of all the important information that could be affected by a fire. If a fire burns a company's building to the ground and consumes all the records (customer data, inventory records, and similar information that is necessary to rebuild the business), then the company did not exercise due care (acting responsibly) to ensure it was protected from such loss (by backing up to an offsite location, for example). In this case, the employees, shareholders, customers, and everyone affected could successfully sue the company. However, if the company did everything expected of it in the previously listed respects, it could not be successfully sued for failure to practice due care.

In the context of security, *due care* means that a company did all it could have reasonably done, under the circumstances, to prevent security breaches, and also took reasonable steps to ensure that if a security breach did take place, proper controls or countermeasures were in place to mitigate the damages. In short, due care means that a company practiced common sense and prudent management and acted responsibly. *Due diligence* means that the company properly investigated all of its possible weaknesses and vulnerabilities.

Before you can figure out how to properly protect yourself, you need to find out what it is you are protecting yourself against. This is what due diligence is all about—researching and assessing the current level of vulnerabilities so the true risk level is understood. Only after these steps and assessments take place can effective controls and safeguards be identified and implemented.

Due Care vs. Due Diligence

Due diligence is the act of gathering the necessary information so the best decision-making activities can take place. Before a company purchases another company, it should carry out due diligence activities so that the purchasing company does not have any "surprises" down the road. The purchasing company should investigate all relevant aspects of the past, present, and predictable future of the business of the target company. If this does not take place and the purchase of the new company hurts the original company financially or legally, the decision makers could be found liable (responsible) and negligent by the shareholders.

In information security, similar data gathering should take place so that there are no "surprises" down the road and the risks are fully understood before they are accepted. If a financial company is going to provide online banking functionality to its customers, the company needs to fully understand all the risks this service entails for the company. Website hacking will increase, account fraud will increase, database attacks will increase, social engineering attacks will increase, etc. While this company is offering its customers a new service, it is also making itself a juicier target for attackers and lawyers. The company needs to carry out due diligence to understand all these risks before offering this new service so that the company can make the best business decisions. If it doesn't implement proper countermeasures, the company opens itself up to potential criminal charges, civil suits, regulatory fines, loss of market share, and more.

Due care pertains to acting responsibly and "doing the right thing." It is a legal term that defines the standards of performance that can be expected, either by contract or by implication, in the execution of a particular task. Due care ensures that a minimal level of protection is in place in accordance with the best practice in the industry.

If a company does not have sufficient security policies, necessary countermeasures, and proper security awareness training in place, it is not practicing due care and can be found negligent. If a financial institution that offers online banking does not implement TLS for account transactions, for example, it is not practicing due care.

Many times due diligence (data gathering) has to be performed so that proper due care (prudent actions) can take place.

The same type of responsibility is starting to be expected of corporations pertaining to computer crime and resource protection. Security is developed and implemented to protect an organization's valuable resources; thus, appropriate safeguards need to be in place to protect the company's mission by protecting its tangible and intangible resources, reputation, employees, customers, shareholders, and legal position. Security is a means to an end and not an end within itself. It is not practiced just for the sake of doing it. It should be practiced in such a way as to accomplish fully understood, planned, and attainable goals.

Senior management has an obligation to protect the company from a long list of activities that can negatively affect it, including protection from malicious code, natural disasters, privacy violation, infractions of the law, and more.

The costs and benefits of security should be evaluated in monetary and nonmonetary terms to ensure that the cost of security does not outweigh the expected benefits. Security should be proportional to potential loss estimates pertaining to the severity, likelihood, and extent of potential damage.

As the following illustration shows, there are many costs to consider when it comes to security breaches: loss of business, response activities, customer and partner notification, and detection and escalation measures. These types of costs need to be understood through due diligence exercises so that the company can practice proper due care by implementing the necessary controls to reduce the risks and these costs. Security mechanisms should be employed to reduce the frequency and severity of security-related losses. A sound security program is a smart business practice.

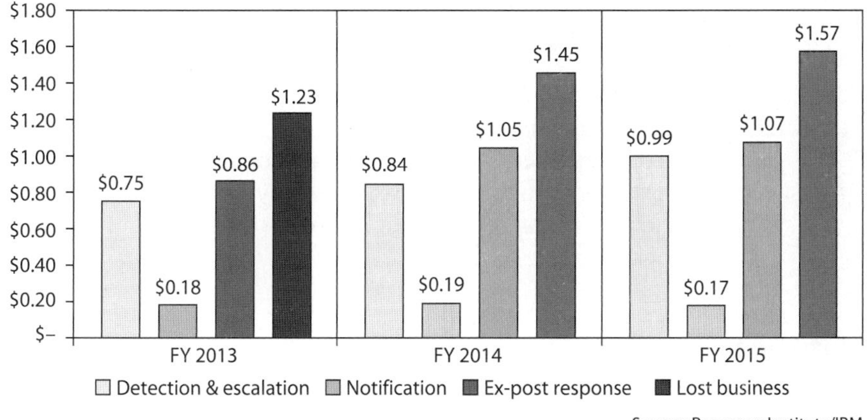

Source: Ponemon Institute/IBM

Senior management needs to decide upon the amount of risk it is willing to take pertaining to computer and information security, and implement security in an economical and responsible manner. (These issues are discussed in great detail in Chapter 1.) These risks do not always stop at the boundaries of the organization. Many companies work with third parties, with whom they must share sensitive data. The main company is still liable for the protection of this sensitive data that it owns, even if the data is on another company's network. This is why more and more regulations are requiring companies to evaluate their third-party security measures.

If one of the companies does not provide the necessary level of protection and its negligence affects a partner it is working with, the affected company can sue the upstream company. For example, let's say company A and company B have constructed an extranet. Company A does not put in controls to detect and deal with viruses. Company A gets infected with a destructive virus and it is spread to company B through the extranet. The virus corrupts critical data and causes a massive disruption to company B's production. Therefore, company B can sue company A for being negligent. Both companies need to make sure they are doing their part to ensure that their activities, or the lack of them, will not negatively affect another company, which is referred to as *downstream liability*.

EXAM TIP *Responsibility* generally refers to the obligations and expected actions and behaviors of a particular party. An obligation may have a defined set of specific actions that are required, or a more general and open approach, which enables the party to decide how it will fulfill the particular obligation. *Accountability* refers to the ability to hold a party responsible for certain actions or inaction.

Each company has different requirements when it comes to its list of due care responsibilities. If these steps are not taken, the company may be charged with negligence if damage arises out of its failure to follow these steps. To prove negligence in court, the plaintiff must establish that the defendant had a *legally recognized obligation*, or duty, to protect the plaintiff from unreasonable risks and that the defendant's failure to protect the plaintiff from an unreasonable risk (breach of duty) was the *proximate cause* of the plaintiff's damages. Penalties for negligence can be either civil or criminal, ranging from actions resulting in compensation for the plaintiff to jail time for violation of the law.

EXAM TIP *Proximate cause* is an act or omission that naturally and directly produces a consequence. It is the superficial or obvious cause for an occurrence. It refers to a cause that leads directly, or in an unbroken sequence, to a particular result. It can be seen as an element of negligence in a court of law.

Liability Scenarios

The following are some sample scenarios in which a company could be held liable for negligence in its actions and responsibilities.

Personal Information

In this scenario, a company that holds medical information, Medical Information, Inc., does not have strict procedures on how patient information is disseminated or shared. A person pretending to be a physician calls Medical Information, Inc., and requests medical information on the patient Don Hammy. The receptionist does not question the caller and explains that Don Hammy has a brain tumor. A week later, Don Hammy does not receive the job he interviewed for and finds out that the employer called Medical Information, Inc., for his medical information.

So what was improper about this activity and how would liability be determined? If and when this case went to court, the following items would be introduced and addressed:

- **Legally recognized obligation**
  - Medical Information, Inc., does not have policies and procedures in place to protect patient information.
  - The employer does not have the right to make this kind of call and is not able to use medical information against potential employees.
- **Failure to conform to the required standard**
  - Sensitive information was released to an unauthorized person by a Medical Information, Inc., employee.
  - The employer requested information it did not have a right to.
- **Proximate causation and resulting injury or damage**
  - The information provided by Medical Information, Inc., caused Don Hammy great emotional distress and prevented him from obtaining a specific job.
  - The employer made its decision based on information it did not have a right to inquire about in the first place. The employer's illegal acquisition and review of Don's private medical information caused it to not hire him.

The outcome was a long legal battle, but Don Hammy ended up successfully suing both companies, recovered from his brain tumor, bought an island, and has never had to work again.

Hacker Intrusion

Suppose that a financial institution, Cheapo, Inc., buys the necessary middleware to enable it to offer online bank account transactions for its customers. It does not add any of the necessary security safeguards required for this type of transaction to take place securely over the Internet. Within the first two weeks of offering this service, 22 customers have their checking and savings accounts hacked into, with a combined loss of $439,344.09.

What was improper about this activity and how would liability be determined? If and when this case went to court, the following items would be introduced and addressed:

- **Legally recognized obligation**
  - Cheapo, Inc., did not implement a firewall or IDS, harden the database holding the customer account information, or use encryption for customer transactions.
  - Cheapo, Inc., did not effectively protect its customers' assets.
- **Failure to conform to the required standard**
  - By not erecting the proper security policy and program and implementing the necessary security controls, Cheapo, Inc., broke 12 federal regulations used to govern financial institutions.
- **Proximate causation and resulting injury or damage**
  - The financial institution's failure to practice due care and implement the basic requirements of online banking directly caused 22 clients to lose $439,344.09.

Eventually, a class action suit was brought against Cheapo, Inc., a majority of the customers got most of their money back, and the facility Cheapo, Inc., was using as a financial institution is now used to sell tacos.

These scenarios are simplistic and described in a light-hearted manner, but failure to implement computer and information security properly can expose a company and its board of directors to litigation and legal punishment. In cases of serious misconduct, executives are not able to hide behind the legal concept of the corporation and are held accountable individually and personally. The board of directors can shirk its responsibilities to the stockholders, customers, and employees by not ensuring that due care is practiced and that the company is not being negligent in any way.

Third-Party Risk

Most organizations outsource more business functions than they realize, and that trend is only increasing. Through the use of cloud computing, Software as a Service (SaaS) in particular, organizations are increasingly turning to third-party service providers to maintain, manage, transmit, or store company-owned information resources to improve delivery of services, gain efficiencies, and reduce cost. Information security issues should be defined and assessed before engaging a third-party service provider to host or provide a service on behalf of the organization. To ensure that adequate security controls are in place prior to finalizing any contract agreement, the organization should conduct a third-party risk assessment for all services (applications, hosting, systems, etc.) that would involve the collection, processing, transmission, or storage of sensitive data or provide critical business functionality processing.

Contractual Agreements

While often overlooked, it is critical that information security issues are addressed in many of the contracts organizations use or enter into during regular business activities. Security considerations should be taken for at least the following contracts types:

- Outsourcing agreements
- Hardware supply
- System maintenance and support
- System leasing agreements
- Consultancy service agreements
- Website development and support
- Nondisclosure and confidentiality agreements
- Information security management agreements
- Software development agreements
- Software licensing

The organization must understand its regulatory and legal requirements pertaining to the items the previous contract list involves, and security requirements must be integrated properly in the contractual clauses. Contractual agreements not only need to be created in a manner that covers regulatory, legal, and security requirements, but also must be reviewed periodically to ensure that they are still relevant and provide the necessary level of protection.

Procurement and Vendor Processes

Before purchasing any product or service, the organization's security requirements need to be fully understood so that they can be expressed and integrated into the *procurement process*. Procurement is not just purchasing something, but includes the activities and processes involved with defining requirements, evaluating vendors, contract negotiation, purchasing, and receiving the needed solution.

The acquisition of a solution (system, application, or service) often includes a *Request for Proposals (RFP)*, which is usually designed to get vendors to provide solutions to a business problem or requirement, bring structure to the procurement decision, and allow the risks and benefits of a solution to be identified clearly up-front. It is important that the RFP conveys the necessary security requirements and elicits meaningful and specific responses that describe how the vendor will meet those requirements. Federal and state legal requirements, regulation, and business contractual obligations must be thought through when constructing the requirements laid out in the RFPs.

The initial security requirements can be used to formulate questions for the RFP. The answers to the RFP can be used to evaluate vendors and refine the security requirements. The evaluation and risk assessment of vendor finalists refine the security requirements that will, in turn, be added as language to the contract or statement of work.

While procurement is an activity an organization carries out to properly identify, solicit, and select vendors for products and services, *vendor management* is an activity that involves developing and monitoring vendor relationships after the contracts are in place. Since organizations are extremely dependent upon their vendors and outsourcing providers, if something slips up, operations will be affected, which always drains the bottom line (profit margin) and could put the company at risk. For example, suppose your cloud computing provider downgrades its data encryption strength (from AES-256 to 3DES with a 56-bit key) so that it can meet a wider range of client requirements, but fails to inform you about the change. Next time your organization goes through a PCI-DSS audit, it can be found out of compliance and your company could be fined. If your company pays a software development company to develop a specialized application, do you have a way to test the code to make sure it is providing the level of protection the developer is claiming? Or what if you set up a contract with a vendor to scan your external websites each week and you get busy with a million other things and six months down the line, the contractor just stops scanning and you are not informed. You assume it is being taken care of, but you do not have governing processes in place to make sure this is true.

A *vendor management governing* process needs to be set up, which includes performance metrics, SLAs, scheduled meetings, a reporting structure, and someone who is directly responsible. Your company is always responsible for its own risk. Just because it farms out some piece of its operations does not resolve it of this responsibility. The company needs to have a holistic program that defines procurement, contracting, vendor assessment, and monitoring to make sure things are continually healthy and secure.

Compliance

While it is important to know *what* laws and regulations your company needs to be compliant with, it is also important to know *how* to ensure that compliance is being met and how to properly convey that to the necessary stakeholders. A compliance program should be developed, which outlines what needs to be put into place to be compliant with the necessary internal and external drivers. Then, an audit team will assess how well the organization is meeting the identified requirements.

The first step is to understand what laws and regulations your organization needs to be compliant with (SOX, HIPAA, PCI DSS, GLBA, FISMA, etc.). This will help determine the type of security framework that should be set up within the organization (ISO\IEC 27001, COSO, Zachman). Then a risk methodology needs to be decided upon (ISO\IEC 27005, NIST 800-30, OCTAVE, AS/NZS 4360). The regulatory and legal requirements will help determine which control objective standard to follow (COBIT, NIST 800-53). Once these pieces are established and put into place, the auditors have stuff to audit. If the organization must be compliant with SOX and HIPAA, does it meet all the requirements of these regulations? If the organization set up its security program based upon the ISO\IEC 27001 standard, are all the pieces in place or are a third of them missing? If the organization chose to use the NIST 800-30 risk management standard, is it actually carrying it out properly? If the organization must comply with the NIST 800-53 standard by implementing all the controls listed within the standard, are the controls in place and working properly?

NOTE Most of these items were covered in Chapter 1. The role of auditors and an audit committee were covered in Chapter 6.

Auditors can be internal or external to the organization. The auditors will have long checklists of items that correspond with the legal, regulatory, and policy requirements the organization must meet. Figure 7-22 shows a small portion of the audit checklists auditors follow when determining if an organization is compliant with the specifics of the PCI-DSS regulation.

It is common for organizations to develop *governance, risk, and compliance (GRC)* programs, which allow for the integration and alignment of the activities that take place in each one of these silos of a security program. If the same *key performance indicators (KPIs)* are used in the GRC auditing activities, then the resulting reports can effectively

PCI DSS Requirements	Testing Procedures	In Place	Not in Place	Target Date/ Comments
1.1 Establish and implement firewall and router configuration standards that include the following:	**1.1** Inspect the firewall and router configuration standards and other documentation specified below and verify that standards are complete and implemented as follows:			
1.1.1 A formal process for approving and testing all network connections and changes to the firewall and router configurations	**1.1.1.a** Examine documented procedures to verify there is a formal process for testing and approval of all: • Network connections and • Changes to firewall and router configurations			
	1.1.1.b For a sample of network connections, interview responsible personnel and examine records to verify that network connections were approved and tested.			
	1.1.1.c Identify a sample of actual changes made to firewall and router configurations, compare to the change records, and interview responsible personnel to verify the changes were approved and tested.			
1.1.2 Current network diagram that identifies all connections between the cardholder data environment and other networks, including any wireless networks	**1.1.2.a** Examine diagram(s) and observe network configurations to verify that a current network diagram exists and that it documents all connections to cardholder data, including any wireless networks.			
	1.1.2.b Interview responsible personnel to verify that the diagram is kept current.			
1.1.3 Current diagram that shows all cardholder data flows across systems and networks	**1.1.3** Examine data-flow diagram and interview personnel to verify the diagram • Shows all cardholder data flows across systems and networks • Is kept current and updated as needed upon changes to the environment			
1.1.4 Requirements for a firewall at each Internet connection and between any demilitarized zone (DMZ) and the internal network zone	**1.1.4.a** Examine the firewall configuration standards and verify that they include requirements for a firewall at each Internet connection and between any DMZ and the internal network zone.			
	1.1.4.b Verify that the current network diagram is consistent with the firewall configuration standards.			

Figure 7-22 Checklist component of PCI DSS used by auditors (*continued*)

	1.1.4.c Observe network configurations to verify that a firewall is in place at each Internet connection and between any demilitarized zone (DMZ) and the internal network zone, per the documented configuration standards and network diagrams.			
1.1.5 Description of groups, roles, and responsibilities for management of network components	**1.1.5.a** Verify that firewall and router configuration standards include a description of groups, roles, and responsibilities for management of network components.			
	1.1.5.b Interview personnel responsible for management of network components to confirm that roles and responsibilities are assigned as documented.			
1.1.6 Documentation and business justification for use of all services, protocols, and ports allowed, including documentation of security features implemented for those protocols considered to be insecure. Examples of insecure services, protocols, or ports include but are not limited to FTP, Telnet, POP3, IMAP, and SNMP v1 and v2.	**1.1.6.a** Verify that firewall and router configuration standards include a documented list of all services, protocols and ports, including business justification for each—for example, Hypertext Transfer Protocol (HTTP) and Secure Sockets Layer (SSL), Secure Shell (SSH), and Virtual Private Network (VPN) protocols.			
	1.1.6.b Identify insecure services, protocols, and ports allowed; and verify that security features are documented for each service.			
	1.1.6.c Examine firewall and router configurations to verify that the documented security features are implemented for each insecure service, protocol, and port.			
1.1.7 Requirement to review firewall and router rule sets at least every six months	**1.1.7.a** Verify that firewall and router configuration standards require review of firewall and router rule sets at least every six months.			
	1.1.7.b Examine documentation relating to rule set reviews and interview responsible personnel to verify that the rule sets are reviewed at least every six months.			

Figure 7-22 Checklist component of PCI DSS used by auditors

illustrate the overlap and integration of these different concepts. For example, if an organization is not compliant with various HIPAA requirements, this is a type of risk that management must be aware of so that the right activities and controls can be put into place. Also, how does executive management carry out security governance if it does not understand the risks the company is facing and the outstanding compliance issues? It is important for all of these things to be understood by the decision makers

in a holistic manner so that they can make the best decisions pertaining to protecting the organization as a whole. The agreed-upon KPI values are commonly provided to executive management in dashboards or scorecard formats, which allow them to quickly understand the health of the organization from a GRC point of view.

Personal Safety Concerns

The single most valuable asset for an organization, and the one that involves the highest moral and ethical standards, is its people. Our safety focus in security operations will be on our own employees, but we also need to take proper steps to ensure the safety of visitors, clients, and anyone who enters into our physical or virtual spaces. While the scope of safety is broader than information systems security, there are important contributions that we as security professionals make to this effort.

EXAMP TIP Human safety almost always trumps all other concerns. If an exam question has a possible answer that focuses on safety, it is likelier to be the right one.

A common tool for ensuring the safety of personnel during emergencies is the occupant emergency plan (OEP). The OEP describes the actions that facility occupants should take in order to ensure their safety during an emergency situation. This plan should address the range of emergencies from individual to facility-wide, and it should be integrated into the security operations of the organization.

Perhaps the best example of the intersection of safety and security occurs in the area of physical access control. A well-designed system of physical access controls will constrain the movement of specific individuals in and out of certain spaces. For instance, we only want authorized persons to enter the server room. But what if the server room offers the best escape route for people who would normally not be allowed in it? While we would not design a facility in which this would be the case, we sometimes end up occupying less than ideal facilities. If this were the case, what process would we implement to ensure we can get people out of the building quickly and not force them to take a circuitous route that could put them in danger, but keeps them out of the sensitive area?

Another example involves access for emergency responders. If a fire alarm is triggered in the building, how do we ensure we can evacuate all personnel while giving fire fighters access to all spaces (without requiring them to break down doors)? In this context, how do we simultaneously ensure the safety of our personnel while maintaining security of our information systems?

Lastly, many modern physical access controls require electricity. If an electronic lock does not have a battery backup, will it automatically unlock in the absence of power or will it remain in the locked state? A *fail-safe device* is one that will automatically move to the state that ensures safety in the event of a failure such as loss of power. Fail-safe controls, while critical to human safety, must be carefully considered because they introduce risks to the security of our information systems.

Summary

Security operations involve keeping up with implemented solutions, keeping track of changes, properly maintaining systems, continually enforcing necessary standards, and following through with security practices and tasks. It does not do much good for a company to develop a strong password policy if, after a few months, enforcement gets lax and users can use whatever passwords they want. It is similar to working out and staying physically fit. Just because someone lifts weights and jogs for a week does not mean he can spend the rest of the year eating jelly donuts and expect to stay physically fit. Security requires discipline day in and day out, sticking to a regimen, and practicing due care.

Quick Tips

- Facilities that house systems that process sensitive information should have physical access controls to limit access to authorized personnel only.
- Clipping levels should be implemented to establish a baseline of user activity and acceptable errors.
- Separation of responsibilities and duties should be in place so that if fraud takes place, it requires collusion.
- Access to resources should be limited to authorized personnel, applications, and services and should be audited for compliance to stated policies.
- Change control and configuration management should be put in place so changes are approved, documented, tested, and properly implemented.
- Activities that involve change management include requesting a change, approving a change, documenting a change, testing a change, implementing a change, and reporting to management.
- Proper fault-tolerant mechanisms should be put in place to counter equipment failure.
- Antivirus and IDS signatures should be updated on a continual basis.
- The key aspects of operational security include resource protection, change control, hardware and software controls, trusted system recovery, separation of duties, and least privilege.
- Least privilege ensures that users, administrators, and others accessing a system have access only to the objects they absolutely require to complete their job.
- The operations department is responsible for any unusual or unexplained occurrences, unscheduled initial program loads, and deviations from standards.
- Standards need to be established that indicate the proper startup and shutdown sequence, error handling, and restoration procedures.
- Some physical security controls may conflict with the safety of people. These issues need to be addressed; human life is always more important than protecting a facility or the assets it contains.

- Proximity identification devices can be user-activated (action needs to be taken by a user) or system sensing (no action needs to be taken by the user).
- A transponder is a proximity identification device that does not require action by the user. The reader transmits signals to the device, and the device responds with an access code.
- Exterior fencing can be costly and unsightly, but can provide crowd control and help control access to the facility.
- If interior partitions do not go all the way up to the true ceiling, an intruder can remove a ceiling tile and climb over the partition into a critical portion of the facility.
- Intrusion detection devices include motion detectors, CCTVs, vibration sensors, and electromechanical devices.
- Intrusion detection devices can be penetrated, are expensive to install and monitor, require human response, and are subject to false alarms.
- CCTV enables one person to monitor a large area, but should be coupled with alerting functions to ensure proper response.
- Security guards are expensive but provide flexibility in response to security breaches and can deter intruders from attempting an attack.
- A whitelist is a set of known-good resources such as IP addresses, domain names, or applications.
- Patch management is the process for identifying, acquiring, installing, and verifying patches for products and systems.
- Offsite backup locations can supply hot, warm, or cold sites.
- A reciprocal agreement is one in which a company promises another company it can move in and share space if it experiences a disaster, and vice versa. Reciprocal agreements are very tricky to implement and may be unenforceable. However, they offer a relatively cheap offsite option and are sometimes the only choice.
- A hot site is fully configured with hardware, software, and environmental needs. It can usually be up and running in a matter of hours. It is the most expensive option, but some companies cannot be out of business longer than a day without very detrimental results.
- A warm site does not have computers, but it does have some peripheral devices, such as disk drives, controllers, and tape drives. This option is less expensive than a hot site, but takes more effort and time to become operational.
- A cold site is just a building with power, raised floors, and utilities. No devices are available. This is the cheapest of the three options, but can take weeks to get up and operational.
- Recovery time objective (RTO) is the maximum time period within which a business process must be restored to a designated service level after a disaster to avoid unacceptable consequences.

- Recovery point objective (RPO) is the acceptable amount of data loss measured in time.
- Mean time between failures (MTBF) is the predicted amount of time between inherent failures of a system during operation.
- Mean time to repair (MTTR) is the estimated amount of time it will take to get a device fixed and back into production after its failure.
- High availability refers to a system, component, or environment that is continuously operational.
- High availability for disaster-recovery needs is often a combination of technologies and processes that include backups, redundancy, fault tolerance, clustering, and load balancing.
- Data recovery and restoration are often carried out through vaulting, backups, and replication technologies.
- When returning to the original site after a disaster, the least critical organizational units should go back first.
- COOP focuses on restoring an organization's (usually a headquarters element) essential functions at an alternate site and performing those functions for up to 30 days before returning to normal operations. This term is commonly used by the U.S. government to denote BCP.
- An important part of the business continuity plan is to communicate its requirements and procedures to all employees.
- Business interruption insurance covers the loss of income that an organization suffers after a disaster while it is in its recovery stage.
- If a company does not practice due care in its efforts to protect itself from computer crime, it can be found to be negligent and legally liable for damages.
- Elements of negligence include not fulfilling a legally recognized obligation, failure to conform to a standard of care that results in injury or damage, and proximate causation.
- The primary reason for the chain of custody of evidence is to ensure that it will be admissible in court by showing it was properly controlled and handled before being presented in court.
- To be admissible in court, business records have to be made and collected in the normal course of business, not specially generated for a case in court. Business records can easily be hearsay if there is no firsthand proof of their accuracy and reliability.
- The life cycle of evidence includes the identification and collection of the evidence, and its storage, preservation, transportation, presentation in court, and return to the owner.

- Collection of computer evidence is a very complex and detail-oriented task. Only skilled people should attempt it; otherwise, evidence can be ruined forever.
- When looking for suspects, it is important to consider the motive, opportunity, and means (MOM).
- For evidence to be admissible in court, it needs to be relevant, complete, sufficient, and reliable to the case at hand.
- Evidence must be legally permissible, meaning it was seized legally and the chain of custody was not broken.

Questions

Please remember that these questions are formatted and asked in a certain way for a reason. Keep in mind that the CISSP exam is asking questions at a conceptual level. Questions may not always have the perfect answer, and the candidate is advised against always looking for the perfect answer. Instead, the candidate should look for the best answer in the list.

1. What is the difference between due care and due diligence?
   A. Due care is the continual effort to ensure that the right thing takes place, and due diligence is the continual effort to stay compliant with regulations.
   B. Due care is based on the prudent person concept, whereas due diligence is not.
   C. They mean the same thing.
   D. Due diligence involves investigating the risks, whereas due care involves carrying out the necessary steps to mitigate these risks.
2. Why should employers make sure employees take their vacations?
   A. They have a legal obligation.
   B. It is part of due diligence.
   C. It is a way for fraud to be uncovered.
   D. To ensure the employee does not get burnt out.
3. Which of the following best describes separation of duties and job rotation?
   A. Separation of duties ensures that more than one employee knows how to perform the tasks of a position, and job rotation ensures that one person cannot perform a high-risk task alone.
   B. Separation of duties ensures that one person cannot perform a high-risk task alone, and job rotation can uncover fraud and ensure that more than one person knows the tasks of a position.
   C. They are the same thing, but with different titles.
   D. They are administrative controls that enforce access control and protect the company's resources.

4. If a programmer is restricted from updating and modifying production code, what is this an example of?
   A. Rotation of duties
   B. Due diligence
   C. Separation of duties
   D. Controlling input values
5. Why is it important to control and audit input and output values?
   A. Incorrect values can cause mistakes in data processing and be evidence of fraud.
   B. Incorrect values can be the fault of the programmer and do not comply with the due care clause.
   C. Incorrect values can be caused by brute-force attacks.
   D. Incorrect values are not security issues.
6. What is the difference between least privilege and need to know?
   A. A user should have least privilege that restricts her need to know.
   B. A user should have a security clearance to access resources, a need to know about those resources, and least privilege to give her full control of all resources.
   C. A user should have a need to know to access particular resources, and least privilege should be implemented to ensure she only accesses the resources she has a need to know.
   D. They are two different terms for the same issue.
7. Which of the following would not require updated documentation?
   A. An antivirus signature update
   B. Reconfiguration of a server
   C. A change in security policy
   D. The installation of a patch to a production server
8. A company needs to implement a CCTV system that will monitor a large area outside the facility. Which of the following is the correct lens combination for this?
   A. A wide-angle lens and a small lens opening
   B. A wide-angle lens and a large lens opening
   C. A wide-angle lens and a large lens opening with a small focal length
   D. A wide-angle lens and a large lens opening with a large focal length

9. Which of the following is not a true statement about CCTV lenses?
   A. Lenses that have a manual iris should be used in outside monitoring.
   B. Zoom lenses will carry out focus functionality automatically.
   C. Depth of field increases as the size of the lens opening decreases.
   D. Depth of field increases as the focal length of the lens decreases.
10. What is true about a transponder?
   A. It is a card that can be read without sliding it through a card reader.
   B. It is a biometric proximity device.
   C. It is a card that a user swipes through a card reader to gain access to a facility.
   D. It exchanges tokens with an authentication server.
11. When is a security guard the best choice for a physical access control mechanism?
   A. When discriminating judgment is required
   B. When intrusion detection is required
   C. When the security budget is low
   D. When access controls are in place
12. Which of the following is not a characteristic of an electrostatic intrusion detection system?
   A. It creates an electrostatic field and monitors for a capacitance change.
   B. It can be used as an intrusion detection system for large areas.
   C. It produces a balance between the electric capacitance and inductance of an object.
   D. It can detect if an intruder comes within a certain range of an object.
13. What is a common problem with vibration-detection devices used for perimeter security?
   A. They can be defeated by emitting the right electrical signals in the protected area.
   B. The power source is easily disabled.
   C. They cause false alarms.
   D. They interfere with computing devices.
14. Which of the following is not considered a delaying mechanism?
   A. Locks
   B. Defense-in-depth measures
   C. Warning signs
   D. Access controls

15. What are the two general types of proximity identification devices?
    A. Biometric devices and access control devices
    B. Swipe card devices and passive devices
    C. Preset code devices and wireless devices
    D. User-activated devices and system sensing devices
16. Which is not a drawback to installing intrusion detection and monitoring systems?
    A. It's expensive to install.
    B. It cannot be penetrated.
    C. It requires human response.
    D. It's subject to false alarms.
17. What is a cipher lock?
    A. A lock that uses cryptographic keys
    B. A lock that uses a type of key that cannot be reproduced
    C. A lock that uses a token and perimeter reader
    D. A lock that uses a keypad
18. If a cipher lock has a door delay option, what does that mean?
    A. After a door is open for a specific period, the alarm goes off.
    B. It can only be opened during emergency situations.
    C. It has a hostage alarm capability.
    D. It has supervisory override capability.
19. Which of the following best describes the difference between a warded lock and a tumbler lock?
    A. A tumbler lock is more simplistic and easier to circumvent than a warded lock.
    B. A tumbler lock uses an internal bolt, and a warded lock uses internal cylinders.
    C. A tumbler lock has more components than a warded lock.
    D. A warded lock is mainly used externally, and a tumbler lock is used internally.
20. All of the following are best practices for controlling the software that is installed and authorized to run in our systems *except* which?
    A. Application whitelisting
    B. Code reviews
    C. Gold Masters
    D. Least privilege

21. You come across an advanced piece of polymorphic malware that uses a custom communications protocol for network traffic. This protocol has a distinctive signature in its header. Which tool is best suited to mitigate this malware by preventing the packets from traversing the network?
    - **A.** Antimalware
    - **B.** Stateful firewall
    - **C.** Intrusion detection system (IDS)
    - **D.** Intrusion prevention system (IPS)
22. Which best describes a hot-site facility versus a warm- or cold-site facility?
    - **A.** A site that has disk drives, controllers, and tape drives
    - **B.** A site that has all necessary PCs, servers, and telecommunications
    - **C.** A site that has wiring, central air-conditioning, and raised flooring
    - **D.** A mobile site that can be brought to the company's parking lot
23. Which is the best description of remote journaling?
    - **A.** Backing up bulk data to an offsite facility
    - **B.** Backing up transaction logs to an offsite facility
    - **C.** Capturing and saving transactions to two mirrored servers in-house
    - **D.** Capturing and saving transactions to different media types
24. Which of the following is something that should be required of an offsite backup facility that stores backed-up media for companies?
    - **A.** The facility should be within 10 to 15 minutes of the original facility to ensure easy access.
    - **B.** The facility should contain all necessary PCs and servers and should have raised flooring.
    - **C.** The facility should be protected by an armed guard.
    - **D.** The facility should protect against unauthorized access and entry.
25. Which of the following does not describe a reciprocal agreement?
    - **A.** The agreement is enforceable.
    - **B.** It is a cheap solution.
    - **C.** It may be able to be implemented right after a disaster.
    - **D.** It could overwhelm a current data processing site.
26. Which of the following describes a cold site?
    - **A.** Fully equipped and operational in a few hours
    - **B.** Partially equipped with data processing equipment
    - **C.** Expensive and fully configured
    - **D.** Provides environmental measures but no equipment

27. After a computer forensic investigator seizes a computer during a crime investigation, what is the next step?
    A. Label and put it into a container, and then label the container
    B. Dust the evidence for fingerprints
    C. Make an image copy of the disks
    D. Lock the evidence in the safe
28. Which of the following is a necessary characteristic of evidence for it to be admissible?
    A. It must be real.
    B. It must be noteworthy.
    C. It must be reliable.
    D. It must be important.
29. If a company deliberately planted a flaw in one of its systems in the hope of detecting an attempted penetration and exploitation of this flaw, what would this be called?
    A. Incident recovery response
    B. Entrapment
    C. Illegal
    D. Enticement

Answers

1. **D.** Due care and due diligence are legal terms that do not just pertain to security. Due diligence involves going through the necessary steps to know what a company's or individual's actual risks are, whereas due care involves carrying out responsible actions to reduce those risks. These concepts correspond with the "prudent person" concept.
2. **C.** Many times, employees who are carrying out fraudulent activities do not take the vacation they have earned because they do not want anyone to find out what they have been doing. Forcing employees to take vacations means that someone else has to do that person's job and can possibly uncover any misdeeds.
3. **B.** Rotation of duties enables a company to have more than one person trained in a position and can uncover fraudulent activities. Separation of duties is put into place to ensure that one entity cannot carry out a critical task alone.
4. **C.** This is just one of several examples of separation of duties. A system must be set up for proper code maintenance to take place when necessary, instead of allowing a programmer to make changes arbitrarily. These types of changes should go through a change control process and should have more entities involved than just one programmer.

5. **A.** There should be controls in place to make sure the data input into a system and the results generated are in the proper format and have expected values. Improper data being put into an application or system could cause bad output and security issues, such as buffer overflows.
6. **C.** Users should be able to access only the resources they need to fulfill the duties of their positions. They also should only have the level of permissions and rights for those resources that are required to carry out the exact operations they need for their jobs, and no more. This second concept is more granular than the first, but they have a symbiotic relationship.
7. **A.** Documentation is very important for data processing and networked environments. This task often gets pushed to the back burner or is totally ignored. If things are not properly documented, employees will forget what actually took place with each device. If the environment needs to be rebuilt, for example, it may be done incorrectly if the procedure was poorly or improperly documented. When new changes need to be implemented, the current infrastructure may not be totally understood. Continually documenting when virus signatures are updated would be overkill. The other answers contain events that certainly require documentation.
8. **A.** The depth of field refers to the portion of the environment that is in focus when shown on the monitor. The depth of field varies depending upon the size of the lens opening, the distance of the object being focused on, and the focal length of the lens. The depth of field increases as the size of the lens opening decreases, the subject distance increases, or the focal length of the lens decreases. So if you want to cover a large area and not focus on specific items, it is best to use a wide-angle lens and a small lens opening.
9. **A.** Manual iris lenses have a ring around the CCTV lens that can be manually turned and controlled. A lens that has a manual iris would be used in an area that has fixed lighting, since the iris cannot self-adjust to changes of light. An auto iris lens should be used in environments where the light changes, such as an outdoor setting. As the environment brightens, this is sensed by the iris, which automatically adjusts itself. Security personnel will configure the CCTV to have a specific fixed exposure value, which the iris is responsible for maintaining. The other answers are true.
10. **A.** A transponder is a type of physical access control device that does not require the user to slide a card through a reader. The reader and card communicate directly. The card and reader have a receiver, transmitter, and battery. The reader sends signals to the card to request information. The card sends the reader an access code.
11. **A.** Although many effective physical security mechanisms are on the market today, none can look at a situation, make a judgment about it, and decide what the next step should be. A security guard is employed when a company needs to have a countermeasure that can think and make decisions in different scenarios.

12. **B.** An electrostatic IDS creates an electrostatic field, which is just an electric field associated with static electric charges. The IDS creates a balanced electrostatic field between itself and the object being monitored. If an intruder comes within a certain range of the monitored object, there is capacitance change. The IDS can detect this change and sound an alarm.
13. **C.** This type of system is sensitive to sounds and vibrations and detects the changes in the noise level of an area it is placed within. This level of sensitivity can cause many false alarms. These devices do not emit any waves; they only listen for sounds within an area and are considered passive devices.
14. **C.** Every physical security program should have delaying mechanisms, which have the purpose of slowing down an intruder so security personnel can be alerted and arrive at the scene. A warning sign is a deterrence control, not a delaying control.
15. **D.** A user-activated device requires the user to do something: swipe the card through the reader and/or enter a code. A system sensing device recognizes the presence of the card and communicates with it without the user needing to carry out any activity.
16. **B.** Monitoring and intrusion detection systems are expensive, require someone to respond when they set off an alarm, and, because of their level of sensitivity, can cause several false alarms. Like any other type of technology or device, they have their own vulnerabilities that can be exploited and penetrated.
17. **D.** Cipher locks, also known as programmable locks, use keypads to control access into an area or facility. The lock can require a swipe card and a specific combination that's entered into the keypad.
18. **A.** A security guard would want to be alerted when a door has been open for an extended period. It may be an indication that something is taking place other than a person entering or exiting the door. A security system can have a threshold set so that if the door is open past the defined time period, an alarm sounds.
19. **C.** The tumbler lock has more pieces and parts than a warded lock. The key fits into a cylinder, which raises the lock metal pieces to the correct height so the bolt can slide to the locked or unlocked position. A warded lock is easier to circumvent than a tumbler lock.
20. **B.** Code reviews are focused on finding and fixing defects in software that is undergoing development. It is not helpful in controlling which applications run on our computers.
21. **D.** The intrusion prevention system is the best answer because these systems can stop packets containing specific signatures. Although some antimalware software might be able to this also, this functionality is not a universal feature in this sort of solution.
22. **B.** A hot site is a facility that is fully equipped and properly configured so that it can be up and running within hours to get a company back into production. Answer B gives the best definition of a fully functional environment.

23. **B.** Remote journaling is a technology used to transmit data to an offsite facility, but this usually only includes moving the journal or transaction logs to the offsite facility, not the actual files.

24. **D.** This question addresses a facility that is used to store backed-up data; it is not talking about an offsite facility used for disaster recovery purposes. The facility should not be only 10 to 15 minutes away, because some types of disasters could destroy both the company's main facility and this facility if they are that close together, in which case the company would lose all of its information. The facility should have the same security standards as the company's security, including protection against unauthorized access.

25. **A.** A reciprocal agreement is not enforceable, meaning that the company that agreed to let the damaged company work out of its facility can decide not to allow this to take place. A reciprocal agreement is a better secondary backup option if the original plan falls through.

26. **D.** A cold site only provides environmental measures—wiring, air conditioning, raised floors—basically a shell of a building and no more.

27. **C.** Several steps need to be followed when gathering and extracting evidence from a scene. Once a computer has been confiscated, the first thing the computer forensics team should do is make an image of the hard drive. The team will work from this image instead of the original hard drive so that the original stays in a pristine state and the evidence on the drive is not accidentally corrupted or modified.

28. **C.** For evidence to be admissible, it must be relevant, complete, sufficient, and reliable to the case. For evidence to be reliable, it must be consistent with fact and must not be based on opinion or be circumstantial.

29. **D.** Companies need to be very careful about the items they use to entice intruders and attackers, because this may be seen as entrapment by the court. It is best to get the legal department involved before implementing these items. Putting a honeypot in place is usually seen as the use of enticement tools.

CHAPTER 8

Software Development Security

This chapter presents the following:

- Common software development issues
- Software development life cycles
- Secure software development approaches
- Development/operations integration (DevOps)
- Change control and configuration management
- Security of code repositories
- Programming language types
- Database concepts and security issues
- Malware types and attacks

A good programmer is someone who always looks both ways before crossing a one-way street.

—Doug Linder

Software is usually developed with a strong focus on functionality, not security. In many cases, security controls are bolted on as an afterthought (if at all). To get the best of both worlds, security and functionality would have to be designed and integrated at each phase of the development life cycle. Security should be interwoven into the core of a product and provide protection at the necessary layers. This is a better approach than trying to develop a front end or wrapper that may reduce the overall functionality and leave security holes when the software has to be integrated into a production environment.

In this chapter we will cover the complex world of secure software development and the bad things that can happen when security is not interwoven into products properly.

Building Good Code

Quality can be defined as fitness for purpose. In other words, quality refers to how good or bad something is for its intended purpose. A high-quality car is good for transportation. We don't have to worry about it breaking down, failing to protect its occupants in a crash, or being easy for a thief to steal. When we need to go somewhere, we can count on a high-quality car to get us to wherever we need to go. Similarly, we don't have to worry about high-quality software crashing, corrupting our data under unforeseen circumstances, or being easy for someone to subvert. Sadly, many developers still think of functionality first (or only) when thinking about quality. When we look at it holistically, we see that quality is the most important concept in developing secure software.

Code reviews and interface testing, discussed in Chapter 6, are key elements in ensuring software quality. We also discussed misuse case testing, the goal of which is to identify the ways in which adversaries might try to subvert our code and then allow us to identify controls that would prevent them from doing so. So, while controls are critical to our systems' security, they need to be considered in the context of overall software quality.

Software controls come in various flavors and have many different goals. They can control input, encryption, logic processing, number-crunching methods, interprocess communication, access, output, and interfacing with other software. Software controls should be developed with potential risks in mind, and many types of threat models and risk analyses should be invoked at different stages of development. The goals are to reduce vulnerabilities and the possibility of system compromise. The controls can be preventive, detective, or corrective. While security controls can be administrative and physical in nature, the controls used within software are usually more technical in nature.

Which specific software controls should be used depends on the software itself, its objectives, the security goals of its associated security policy, the type of data it will process, the functionality it is to carry out, and the environment in which it will be placed. If an application is purely proprietary and will run only in closed, trusted environments, fewer security controls may be needed than those required for applications that will connect businesses over the Internet and provide financial transactions. The trick is to understand the security needs of a piece of software, implement the right controls and mechanisms, thoroughly test the mechanisms and how they integrate into the application, follow structured development methodologies, and provide secure and reliable distribution methods.

Though this may all sound overwhelming, software can be developed securely. In fact, despite some catastrophic failures that occasionally show up in the news media, programmers and vendors are steadily getting better at secure development. We will walk through many of the requirements necessary to create secure software throughout this chapter.

Where Do We Place Security?

Today, many security efforts look to solve security problems through controls such as firewalls, intrusion detection systems (IDSs), content filtering, antimalware software, vulnerability scanners, and much more. This reliance on a long laundry list of security technologies occurs mainly because our software contains many vulnerabilities. Our environments are commonly referred to as hard and crunchy on the outside and soft and chewy on the inside. This means our perimeter security is fortified and solid, but our internal environment and software are easy to exploit once access has been obtained.

In reality, the flaws within the software cause a majority of the vulnerabilities in the first place. Several reasons explain why perimeter devices are more often considered than dealing with the insecurities within the software:

- In the past, it was not considered crucial to implement security during the software development stages; thus, many programmers today do not practice these procedures.
- Most security professionals are not software developers, and thus do not have complete insight to software vulnerability issues.
- Most software developers are not security professionals and do not have security as a main focus. Functionality is usually considered more important than security.
- Software vendors are trying to get their products to market in the quickest possible time and may not take the time for proper security architecture, design, and testing steps.
- The computing community has gotten used to receiving software with flaws and then applying patches. This has become a common and seemingly acceptable practice.
- Customers cannot control the flaws in the software they purchase, so they must depend upon perimeter protection.

Finger-pointing and quick judgments are neither useful nor necessarily fair at this stage of our computing evolution. Twenty years ago, mainframes did not require much security because only a handful of people knew how to run them, users worked on computers (dumb terminals) that could not introduce malicious code to the mainframe, and environments were closed. The core protocols and computing framework were developed at a time when threats and attacks were not prevalent. Such stringent security wasn't needed. Then, computer and software evolution took off, and the possibilities splintered into a thousand different directions. The high demand for computer technology and different types of software increased the demand for programmers, system designers, administrators, and engineers. This demand brought in a wave of people who had little experience pertaining to security. The lack of experience, the high change rate of technology, the focus on functionality, and the race to market vendors experience just to stay competitive have added problems to security measures that are not always clearly understood.

Although it is easy to blame the big software vendors for producing flawed or buggy software, this is driven by customer demand. Since at least the turn of the century, we have been demanding more and more functionality from software vendors. The software vendors have done a wonderful job in providing these perceived necessities. Only recently have customers (especially corporate ones) started to also demand security. Meeting this demand is difficult for several reasons: programmers traditionally have not been properly educated in secure coding; operating systems and applications were not built on secure architectures from the beginning; software development procedures have not been security oriented; and integrating security as an afterthought makes the process clumsier

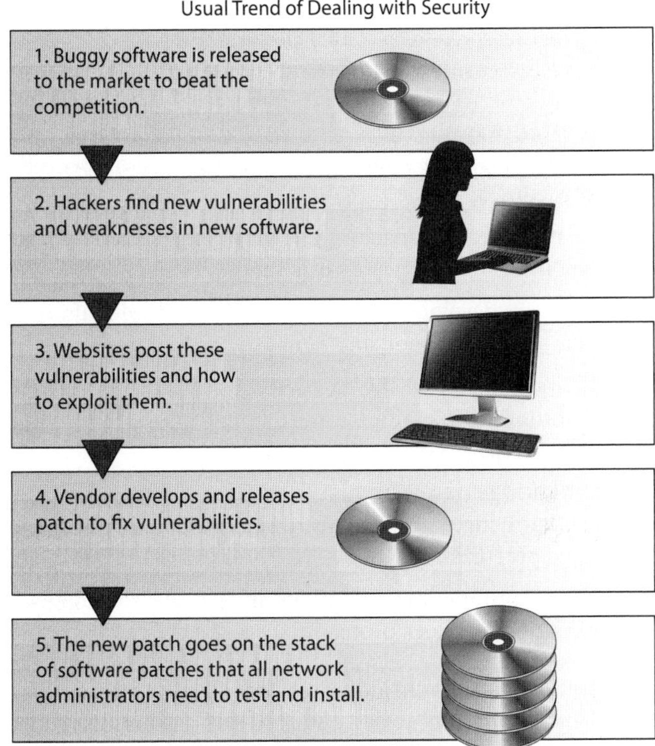

Usual Trend of Dealing with Security
1. Buggy software is released to the market to beat the competition.
2. Hackers find new vulnerabilities and weaknesses in new software.
3. Websites post these vulnerabilities and how to exploit them.
4. Vendor develops and releases patch to fix vulnerabilities.
5. The new patch goes on the stack of software patches that all network administrators need to test and install.

Figure 8-1 The usual trend of software being released to the market and how security is dealt with

and costlier. So although software vendors should be doing a better job by providing us with more secure products, we should also understand that this is a relatively new requirement and there is much more complexity when you peek under the covers than most consumers can even comprehend.

This chapter is an attempt to show how to address security at its source, which is at the software development level. This requires a shift from *reactive* to *proactive* actions toward security problems to ensure they do not happen in the first place, or at least happen to a smaller extent. Figure 8-1 illustrates our current way of dealing with security issues.

Different Environments Demand Different Security

Today, network and security administrators are in an overwhelming position of having to integrate different applications and computer systems to keep up with their company's demand for expandable functionality and the new gee-whiz components that executives buy into and demand quick implementation of. This integration is further frustrated by the company's race to provide a well-known presence on the Internet by implementing websites with the capabilities of taking online orders, storing credit card information, and setting up extranets with partners. This can quickly turn into a confusing ball of protocols, devices, interfaces, incompatibility issues, routing and switching techniques,

telecommunications routines, and management procedures—all in all, a big enough headache to make an administrator buy some land in Montana and go raise goats instead.

On top of this, security is expected, required, and depended upon. When security compromises creep in, the finger-pointing starts, liability issues are tossed like hot potatoes, and people might even lose their jobs. An understanding of the environment, what is currently in it, and how it works is required so these new technologies can be implemented in a more controlled and comprehensible fashion.

The days of developing a simple web page and posting it on the Internet to illustrate your products and services are long gone. Today, the customer front end, complex middleware, and multitiered architectures must be integrated seamlessly. Networks are commonly becoming "borderless" since everything from smartphones and iPads to other mobile devices are being plugged in, and remote users are becoming more of the norm instead of the exception. As the complexity of these types of environments grows, tracking down errors and security compromises becomes an awesome task.

Environment vs. Application

Software controls can be implemented by the operating system or by the application—and usually a combination of both is used. Each approach has its strengths and weaknesses, but if they are all understood and programmed to work in a concerted manner, then many different undesirable scenarios and types of compromises can be thwarted. One downside to relying mainly on operating system controls is that although they can control a subject's access to different objects and restrict the actions of that subject within the system, they do not necessarily restrict the subject's actions within an application. If an application has a security vulnerability within its own programmed code, it is not always possible for the operating system to predict and control this vulnerability. An operating system is a broad environment for many applications to work within. It is unrealistic to expect the operating system to understand all the nuances of different programs and their internal mechanisms.

On the other hand, application controls and database management controls are very specific to their needs and in the security compromises they understand. Although an application might be able to protect data by allowing only certain types of input and not permitting certain users to view data kept in sensitive database fields, it cannot prevent the user from inserting bogus data into the Address Resolution Protocol (ARP) table—this is the responsibility of the operating system and its network stack. Operating system and application controls have their place and limitations. The trick is to find out where one type of control stops so the next type of control can be configured to kick into action.

Security has been mainly provided by security products and perimeter devices rather than controls built into applications. The security products can cover a wide range of applications, can be controlled by a centralized management console, and are further away from application control. However, this approach does not always provide the necessary level of granularity and does not approach compromises that can take place because of problematic coding and programming routines. Firewalls and access control mechanisms can provide a level of protection by preventing attackers from gaining access

to be able to exploit known vulnerabilities, but the best protection happens at the core of the problem—proper software development and coding practices must be in place.

Functionality vs. Security

Programming code is complex—the code itself, routine interaction, global and local variables, input received from other programs, output fed to different applications, attempts to envision future user inputs, calculations, and restrictions form a long list of possible negative security consequences. Many times, trying to account for all the "what-ifs" and programming on the side of caution can reduce the overall functionality of the application. As you limit the functionality and scope of an application, the market share and potential profitability of that program could be reduced. A balancing act always exists between functionality and security, and in the development world, functionality is usually deemed the most important.

So, programmers and application architects need to find a happy medium between the necessary functionality of the program, the security requirements, and the mechanisms that should be implemented to provide this security. This can add more complexity to an already complex task.

More than one road may lead to enlightenment, but as these roads increase in number, it is hard to know if a path will eventually lead you to bliss or to fiery doom in the underworld. Many programs accept data from different parts of the program, other programs, the system itself, and user input. Each of these paths must be followed in a methodical way, and each possible scenario and input must be thought through and tested to provide a deep level of assurance. It is important that each module be capable of being tested individually and in concert with other modules. This level of understanding and testing will make the product more secure by catching flaws that could be exploited.

Implementation and Default Issues

As many people in the technology field know, out-of-the-box implementations are usually far from secure. Most security has to be configured and turned on after installation—not being aware of this can be dangerous for the inexperienced security person. The Windows operating system has received its share of criticism for lack of security, but the platform can be secured in many ways. It just comes out of the box in an insecure state because settings have to be configured to properly integrate it into different environments, and this is a friendlier way of installing the product for users. For example, if Mike is installing a new software package that continually throws messages of "Access Denied" when he is attempting to configure it to interoperate with other applications and systems, his patience might wear thin, and he might decide to hate that vendor for years to come because of the stress and confusion inflicted upon him.

Yet again, we are at a hard place for developers and architects. When a security application or device is installed, it should default to "No Access." This means that when Laurel installs a packet-filter firewall, it should not allow any packets to pass into the network that were not specifically granted access. However, this requires Laurel to know how to configure the firewall for it to ever be useful. A fine balance exists between

security, functionality, and user friendliness. If an application is extremely user friendly, it is probably not as secure. For an application to be user friendly, it usually requires a lot of extra coding for potential user errors, dialog boxes, wizards, and step-by-step instructions. This extra coding can result in bloated code that can create unforeseeable compromises. So vendors have a hard time winning, but they usually keep making money while trying.

NOTE Later versions of Windows have services turned off and require the user to turn them on as needed. This is a step closer to "default with no access," but we still have a ways to go.

Implementation errors and misconfigurations are common items that cause many of the security issues in networked environments. Most people do not realize that various services are enabled when a system is installed. These services can provide adversaries with information and vectors that can be used during an attack. Many services provide an actual way into the environment itself. For example, NetBIOS services, which have few, if any, security controls, can be enabled to permit sharing resources in Windows environments. Other services, such as File Transfer Protocol (FTP), Trivial File Transfer Protocol (TFTP), and older versions of the Simple Network Management Protocol (SNMP), have no real safety measures in place. Some of these services (as well as others) are enabled by default, so when an administrator installs an operating system and does not check these services to properly restrict or disable them, they are available for attackers to uncover and use.

Because vendors have user friendliness and user functionality in mind, the product will usually be installed with defaults that provide no, or very little, security protection. It would be very hard for vendors to know the security levels required in all the environments the product will be installed in, so they usually do not attempt it. It is up to the person installing the product to learn how to properly configure the settings to achieve the necessary level of protection.

Another problem in implementation and security is the number of unpatched systems. Once security issues are identified, vendors develop patches or updates to address and fix these security holes. However, these often do not get installed on the systems that are vulnerable in a timely manner. The reasons for this vary: administrators may not keep up to date on the recent security vulnerabilities and necessary patches, they may not fully understand the importance of these patches, or they may be afraid the patches will cause other problems. All of these reasons are quite common, but they all have the same result—insecure systems. Many vulnerabilities that are exploited today have had patches developed and released months or years ago.

It is unfortunate that adding security (or service) patches can adversely affect other mechanisms within the system. The patches should be tested for these types of activities before they are applied to production servers and workstations to help prevent service disruptions that can affect network and employee productivity. Of course, the best way to reduce the need for patching is by developing the software properly in the first place, which is the issue to which we turn our attention next.

Software Development Life Cycle

The life cycle of software development deals with putting repeatable and predictable processes in place that help ensure functionality, cost, quality, and delivery schedule requirements are met. So instead of winging it and just starting to develop code for a project, how can we make sure we build the best software product possible?

There have been several *software development life cycle (SDLC)* models developed over the years, which we will cover later in this section, but the crux of each model deals with the following phases:

- **Requirements gathering** Determine *why* to create this software, *what* the software will do, and *for whom* the software will be created
- **Design** Deals with *how* the software will accomplish the goals identified, which are encapsulated into a functional design
- **Development** Programming software code to meet specifications laid out in the design phase and integrating that code with existing systems and/or libraries
- **Testing/validation** Verifying and validating software to ensure that the software works as planned and that goals are met
- **Release/maintenance** Deploying the software and then ensuring that it is properly configured, patched, and monitored

In the following sections we will cover the different phases that make up a software development life-cycle model and some specific items about each phase that are important to understand. Keep in mind that the discussion that follows covers phases that may happen repeatedly and in limited scope depending on the development methodology being used.

Project Management

Before we get into the phases of the SDLC, let's first introduce the glue that holds them together: project management. Many developers know that good project management keeps the project moving in the right direction, allocates the necessary resources, provides the necessary leadership, and plans for the worst yet hopes for the best. Project management processes should be put into place to make sure the software development project executes each life-cycle phase properly. Project management is an important part of product development, and security management is an important part of project management.

A security plan should be drawn up at the beginning of a development project and integrated into the functional plan to ensure that security is not overlooked. The first plan is broad, covers a wide base, and refers to documented references for more detailed information. The references could include computer standards (RFCs, IEEE standards, and best practices), documents developed in previous projects, security policies, accreditation statements, incident-handling plans, and national or international guidelines. This helps ensure that the plan stays on target.

The security plan should have a lifetime of its own. It will need to be added to, subtracted from, and explained in more detail as the project continues. It is important to keep it up to date for future reference. It is always easy to lose track of actions, activities, and decisions once a large and complex project gets underway.

The security plan and project management activities may likely be audited so security-related decisions can be understood. When assurance in the product needs to be guaranteed, indicating that security was fully considered in each phase of the life cycle, the procedures, development, decisions, and activities that took place during the project will be reviewed. The documentation must accurately reflect how the product was built and how it is supposed to operate once implemented into an environment.

If a software product is being developed for a specific customer, it is common for a *Statement of Work (SOW)* to be developed, which describes the product and customer requirements. A detail-oriented SOW will help ensure that these requirements are properly understood and assumptions are not made.

Sticking to what is outlined in the SOW is important so that *scope creep* does not take place. If the scope of a project continually extends in an uncontrollable manner (creeps), the project may never end, not meet its goals, run out of funding, or all of the above. If the customer wants to modify its requirements, it is important that the SOW is updated and funding is properly reviewed.

A *work breakdown structure (WBS)* is a project management tool used to define and group a project's individual work elements in an organized manner. It is a deliberate decomposition of the project into tasks and subtasks that result in clearly defined deliverables. The SDLC should be illustrated in a WBS format, so that each phase is properly addressed.

Requirements Gathering Phase

This is the phase when everyone involved attempts to understand why the project is needed and what the scope of the project entails. Either a specific customer needs a new application or a demand for the product exists in the market. During this phase, the team examines the software's requirements and proposed functionality, engages in brainstorming sessions, and reviews obvious restrictions.

A conceptual definition of the project should be initiated and developed to ensure everyone is on the right page and that this is a proper product to develop. This phase could include evaluating products currently on the market and identifying any demands not being met by current vendors. It could also be a direct request for a specific product from a current or future customer.

As it pertains to security, the following items should be accomplished in this phase:

- Security requirements
- Security risk assessment
- Privacy risk assessment
- Risk-level acceptance

The security requirements of the product should be defined in the categories of availability, integrity, and confidentiality. What type of security is required for the software product and to what degree?

An initial security risk assessment should be carried out to identify the potential threats and their associated consequences. This process usually involves asking many, many questions to draw up the laundry list of vulnerabilities and threats, the probability of these vulnerabilities being exploited, and the outcome if one of these threats actually becomes real and a compromise takes place. The questions vary from product to product—such as its intended purpose, the expected environment it will be implemented in, the personnel involved, and the types of businesses that would purchase and use the product.

The sensitivity level of the data the software will be maintaining and processing has only increased in importance over the years. After a *privacy risk assessment*, a *Privacy Impact Rating* can be assigned, which indicates the sensitivity level of the data that will be processed or accessible. Some software vendors incorporate the following Privacy Impact Ratings in their software development assessment processes:

- **P1, High Privacy Risk** The feature, product, or service stores or transfers personally identifiable information (PII), monitors the user with an ongoing transfer of anonymous data, changes settings or file type associations, or installs software.
- **P2, Moderate Privacy Risk** The sole behavior that affects privacy in the feature, product, or service is a one-time, user-initiated anonymous data transfer (e.g., the user clicks on a link and goes out to a website).
- **P3, Low Privacy Risk** No behaviors exist within the feature, product, or services that affect privacy. No anonymous or personal data is transferred, no PII is stored on the machine, no settings are changed on the user's behalf, and no software is installed.

The software vendor can develop its own Privacy Impact Ratings and their associated definitions. As of this writing there is no standardized approach to defining these rating types, but as privacy increases in importance, we might see more standardization in these ratings and associated metrics.

A clear risk-level acceptance criteria needs to be developed to make sure that mitigation efforts are prioritized. The acceptable risks will depend upon the results of the security and privacy risk assessments. The evaluated threats and vulnerabilities are used to estimate the cost/benefit ratios of the different security countermeasures. The level of each security attribute should be focused upon so a clear direction on security controls can begin to take shape and can be integrated into the design and development phases.

Design Phase

This is the phase that starts to map theory to reality. The theory encompasses all of the requirements that were identified in previous phases, and the design outlines how the product is actually going to accomplish these requirements.

The software design phase is a process used to describe the requirements and the internal behavior of the software product. It then maps the two elements to show how the internal behavior actually accomplishes the defined requirements.

Some companies skip the functional design phase, which can cause major delays down the road and redevelopment efforts because a broad vision of the product needs to be understood before looking strictly at the details.

Software requirements commonly come from three models:

- **Informational model** Dictates the type of information to be processed and how it will be processed
- **Functional model** Outlines the tasks and functions the application needs to carry out
- **Behavioral model** Explains the states the application will be in during and after specific transitions take place

For example, an antimalware software application may have an informational model that dictates what information is to be processed by the program, such as virus signatures, modified system files, checksums on critical files, and virus activity. It would also have a functional model that dictates that the application should be able to scan a hard drive, check e-mail for known virus signatures, monitor critical system files, and update itself. The behavioral model would indicate that when the system starts up, the antimalware software application will scan the hard drive and memory segments. The computer coming online would be the event that changes the state of the application. If a virus were found, the application would change state and deal with the virus appropriately. Each state must be accounted for to ensure that the product does not go into an insecure state and act in an unpredictable way.

The informational, functional, and behavioral model data go into the software design as requirements. What comes out of the design is the data, architectural, and procedural design, as shown in Figure 8-2.

From a security point of view, the following items should also be accomplished in this phase:

- Attack surface analysis
- Threat modeling

An *attack surface* is what is available to be used by an attacker against the product itself. As an analogy, if you were wearing a suit of armor and it covered only half of your body, the other half would be your vulnerable attack surface. Before you went into battle, you would want to reduce this attack surface by covering your body with as much protective armor as possible. The same can be said about software. The development team should reduce the attack surface as much as possible because the greater the attack surface of software, the more avenues for the attacker; and hence, the greater the likelihood of a successful compromise.

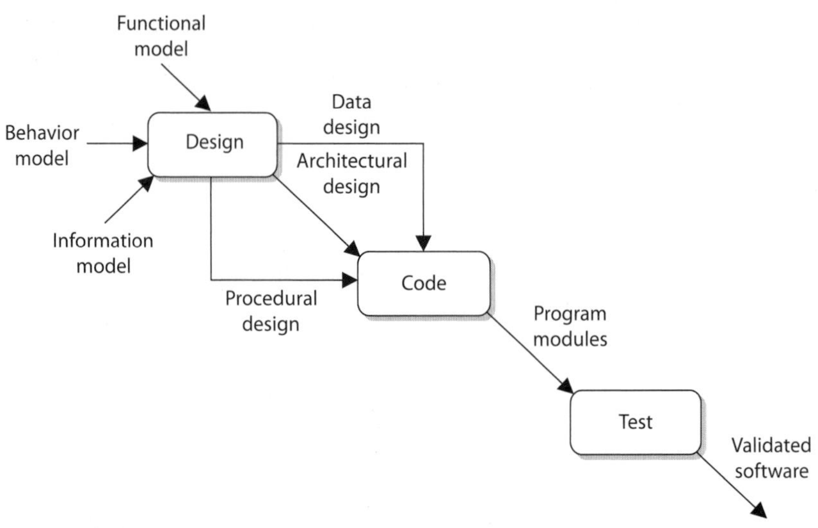

Figure 8-2 Information from three models can go into the design.

The aim of an *attack surface analysis* is to identify and reduce the amount of code and functionality accessible to untrusted users. The basic strategies of attack surface reduction are to reduce the amount of code running, reduce entry points available to untrusted users, reduce privilege levels as much as possible, and eliminate unnecessary services. Attack surface analysis is generally carried out through specialized tools to enumerate different parts of a product and aggregate their findings into a numeral value. Attack surface analyzers scrutinize files, Registry keys, memory data, session information, processes, and services details. A sample attack surface report is shown in Figure 8-3.

Threat modeling, which we covered in detail in Chapter 1 in the context of risk management, is a systematic approach used to understand how different threats could be realized and how a successful compromise could take place. As a hypothetical example, if you were responsible for ensuring that the government building in which you work is safe from terrorist attacks, you would run through scenarios that terrorists would most likely carry out so that you fully understand how to protect the facility and the people within it. You could think through how someone could bring a bomb into the building, and then you would better understand the screening activities that need to take place at each entry point. A scenario of someone running a car into the building would bring up the idea of implementing bollards around the sensitive portions of the facility. The scenario of terrorists entering sensitive locations in the facility (data center, CEO office) would help illustrate the layers of physical access controls that should be implemented. These same scenario-based exercises should take place during the design phase of software development. Just as you would think about how potential terrorists could enter and exit a facility, the design team should think through how potentially malicious activities can happen at different input and output points of the software and the types of compromises that can take place within the guts of the software itself.

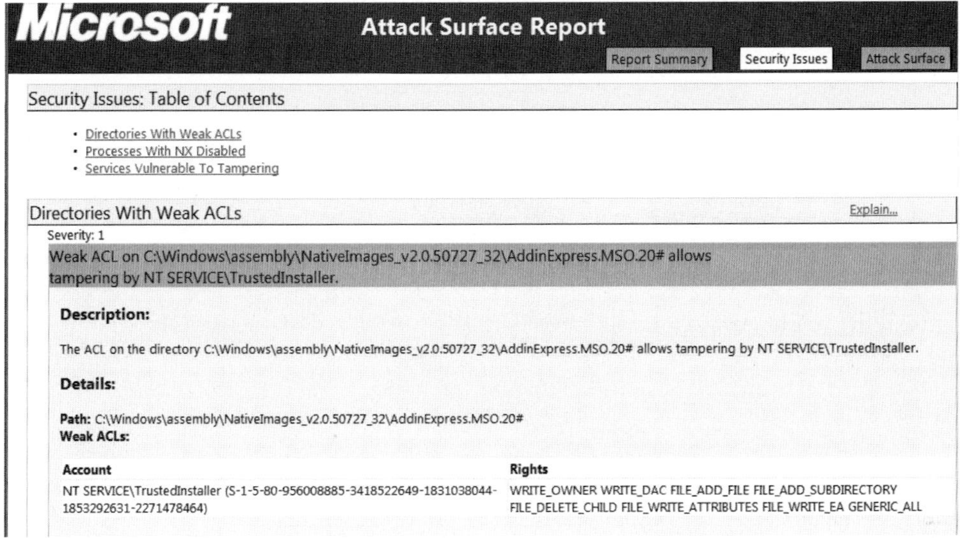

Figure 8-3 Attack surface analysis result

It is common for software development teams to develop threat trees, as shown in Figure 8-4. The tree is a tool that allows the development team to understand all the ways specific threats can be realized; thus, it helps them understand what type of security controls should be implemented to mitigate the risks associated with each threat type.

There are many automated tools in the industry that software development teams can use to ensure that various threat types are addressed during their design stage. Figure 8-5 shows the interface to one of these types of tools. The tool describes how specific vulnerabilities could be exploited and suggests countermeasures and coding practices that should be followed to address the vulnerabilities.

The decisions made during the design phase are pivotal steps to the development phase. Software design serves as a foundation and greatly affects software quality. If good product design is not put into place in the beginning of the project, the following phases will be much more challenging.

Development Phase

This is the phase where the programmers become deeply involved. The software design that was created in the previous phase is broken down into defined deliverables, and programmers develop code to meet the deliverable requirements.

There are many *computer-aided software engineering (CASE)* tools that programmers can use to generate code, test software, and carry out debugging activities. When these types of activities are carried out through automated tools, development usually takes place more quickly with fewer errors.

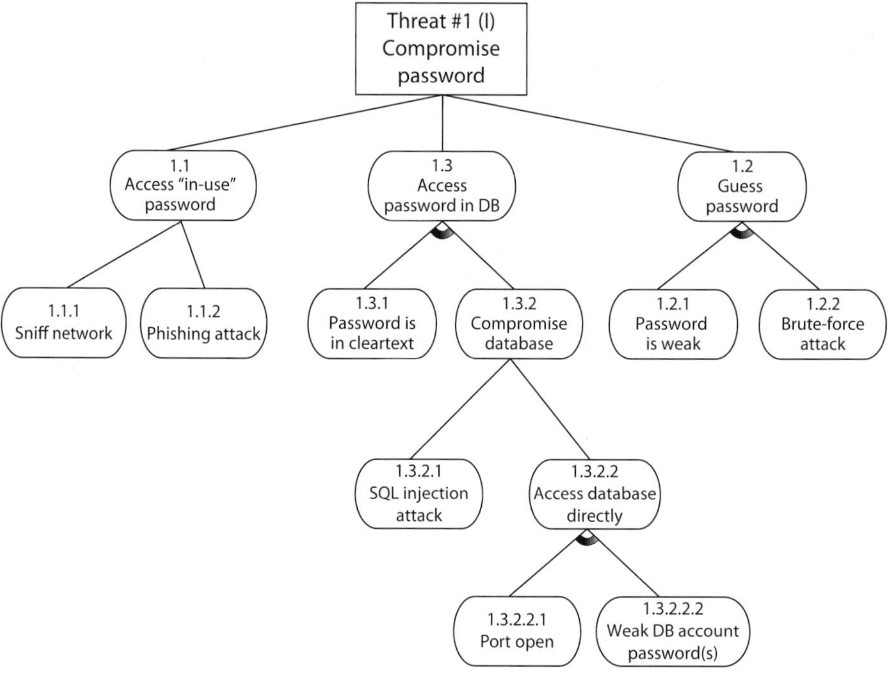

Figure 8-4 Threat tree used in threat modeling

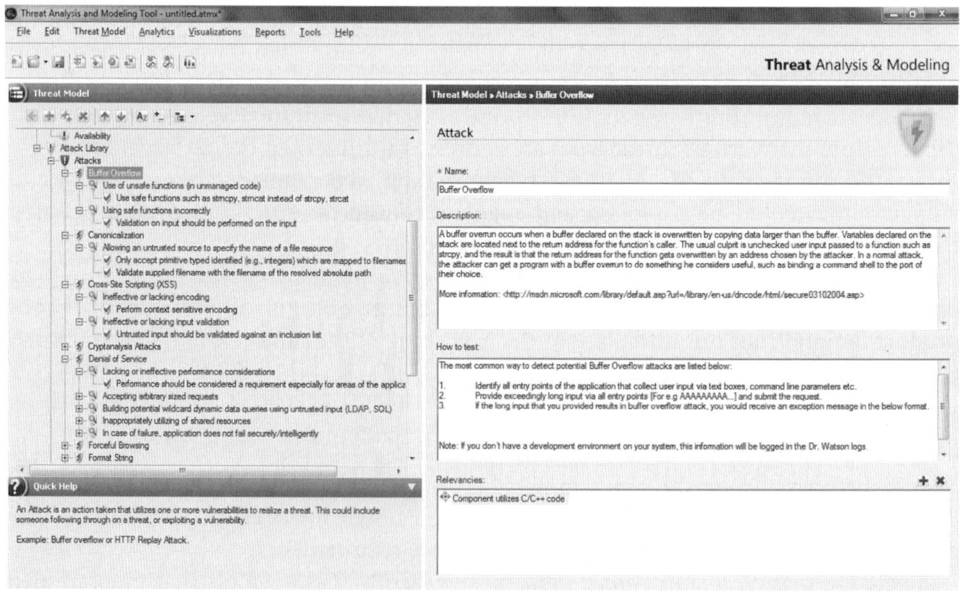

Figure 8-5 Threat modeling tool

CASE refers to any type of software tool that allows for the automated development of software, which can come in the form of program editors, debuggers, code analyzers, version-control mechanisms, and more. These tools aid in keeping detailed records of requirements, design steps, programming activities, and testing. A CASE tool is aimed at supporting one or more software engineering tasks in the process of developing software. Many vendors can get their products to the market faster because they are "computer aided."

In later sections we will cover different software development models and the programming languages that can be used to create software. At this point let's take a quick peek into the abyss of "secure coding." As stated previously, most vulnerabilities that corporations, organizations, and individuals have to worry about reside within the programming code itself. When programmers do not follow strict and secure methods of creating programming code, the effects can be widespread and the results can be devastating. But programming securely is not an easy task. The list of errors that can lead to serious vulnerabilities in software is long. To illustrate, the MITRE organization's Common Weakness Enumeration (CWE) initiative, which it describes as "A Community-Developed Dictionary of Software Weakness Types," collaborates with the SANS Institute to maintain a list of the top most dangerous software errors. Figure 8-6 shows the most recent CWE/SANS Top 25 Most Dangerous Software Errors

Rank	Score	ID	Name
1	93.8	CWE-89	Improper Neutralization of Special Elements used in an SQL Command ("SQL Injection")
2	83.3	CWE-78	Improper Neutralization of Special Elements used in an OS Command ("OS Command Injection")
3	79.0	CWE-120	Buffer Copy without Checking Size of Input ("Classic Buffer Overflow")
4	77.7	CWE-79	Improper Neutralization of Input During Web Page Generation ("Cross-site Scripting")
5	76.9	CWE-306	Missing Authentication for Critical Function
6	76.8	CWE-862	Missing Authorization
7	75.0	CWE-798	Use of Hard-coded Credentials
8	75.0	CWE-311	Missing Encryption of Sensitive Data
9	74.0	CWE-434	Unrestricted Upload of File with Dangerous Type
10	73.8	CWE-807	Reliance on Untrusted Inputs in a Security Decision
11	73.1	CWE-250	Execution with Unnecessary Privileges
12	70.1	CWE-352	Cross-Site Request Forgery (CSRF)
13	69.3	CWE-22	Improper Limitation of a Pathname to a Restricted Directory ("Path Traversal")
14	68.5	CWE-494	Download of Code Without Integrity Check
15	67.8	CWE-863	Incorrect Authorization
16	66.0	CWE-829	Inclusion of Functionality from Untrusted Control Sphere
17	65.5	CWE-732	Incorrect Permission Assignment for Critical Resource
18	64.6	CWE-676	Use of Potentially Dangerous Function
19	64.1	CWE-327	Use of a Broken or Risky Cryptographic Algorithm
20	62.4	CWE-131	Incorrect Calculation of Buffer Size
21	61.5	CWE-307	Improper Restriction of Excessive Authentication Attempts
22	61.1	CWE-601	URL Redirection to Untrusted Site ("Open Redirect")
23	61.0	CWE-134	Uncontrolled Format String
24	60.3	CWE-190	Integer Overflow or Wraparound
25	59.9	CWE-759	Use of a One-Way Hash without a Salt

Figure 8-6 2011 CWE/SANS Top 25 Most Dangerous Software Errors list

list, which can be found at http://cwe.mitre.org/top25/#Listing. Although this was last updated in 2011, sadly, it is as relevant today as it was back then.

Many of these software issues are directly related to improper or faulty programming practices. Among other issues to address, the programmers need to check input lengths so buffer overflows cannot take place, inspect code to prevent the presence of covert channels, check for proper data types, make sure checkpoints cannot be bypassed by users, verify syntax, and verify checksums. Different attack scenarios should be played out to see how the code could be attacked or modified in an unauthorized fashion. Code reviews and debugging should be carried out by peer developers, and everything should be clearly documented.

A particularly important area of scrutiny is input validation. Though we discuss it in detail later in this chapter, it is worthwhile pointing out that improper validation of inputs leads to serious vulnerabilities. A buffer overflow is a classic example of a technique that can be used to exploit improper input validation. A *buffer overflow* (which is described in detail in Chapter 3) takes place when too much data is accepted as input to a specific process. The process' memory buffer can be overflowed by shoving arbitrary data into various memory segments and inserting a carefully crafted set of malicious instructions at a specific memory address.

Buffer overflows can also lead to illicit escalation of privileges. *Privilege escalation* is the process of exploiting a process or configuration setting in order to gain access to resources that would normally not be available to the process or its user. For example, an attacker can compromise a regular user account and escalate its privileges in order to gain administrator or even system privileges on that computer. This type of attack usually exploits the complex interactions of user processes with device drivers and the underlying operating system. A combination of input validation and configuring the system to run with least privilege can help mitigate the threat of escalation of privileges.

Some of the most common errors (buffer overflow, injection, parameter validation) are covered later in this chapter along with organizations that provide secure software development guidelines (OWASP, DHS, MITRE). At this point we are still marching through the software development life-cycle phases, so we want to keep our focus. What is important to understand is that secure coding practices need to be integrated into the development phase of SDLC. Security has to be addressed at each phase of SDLC, with this phase being one of the most critical.

Static Analysis

Static analysis is a technique meant to help identify software defects or security policy violations and is carried out by examining the code without executing the program, and therefore is carried out before the program is compiled. The term static analysis is generally reserved for automated tools that assist analysts and developers, whereas manual inspection by humans is generally referred to as code review.

Static analysis allows developers to quickly scavenge their source code for programming flaws and vulnerabilities. Additionally, static analysis provides a scalable method of security code review and ensures that secure coding policies are being followed. There are numerous manifestations of static analysis tools, ranging from tools that simply consider the behavior of single statements to tools that analyze the entire source code at once. However, it must be remembered that static code analysis can never reveal logical errors and design flaws, and therefore must be used in conjunction with manual code review to ensure thorough evaluation.

Testing/Validation Phase

Formal and informal testing should begin as soon as possible. *Unit testing* is concerned with ensuring the quality of individual code modules or classes. Mature developers will develop the unit tests for their modules before they even start coding, or at least in parallel with the coding. This approach is known as *test-driven development* and tends to result in much higher-quality code with significantly fewer vulnerabilities.

Unit tests are meant to simulate a range of inputs to which the code may be exposed. These inputs range from the mundanely expected, to the accidentally unfortunate, to the intentionally malicious. The idea is to ensure the code always behaves in an expected and secure manner. Once a module and its unit tests are finished, the unit tests are run (usually in an automated framework) on that code. The goal of this type of testing is to isolate each part of the software and show that the individual parts are correct.

Unit testing usually continues throughout the development phase. A totally different group of people should carry out the formal testing. This is an example of separation of duties. A programmer should not develop, test, and release software. The more eyes that see the code, the greater the chance that flaws will be found before the product is released.

No cookie-cutter recipe exists for security testing because the applications and products can be so diverse in functionality and security objectives. It is important to map security risks to test cases and code. Linear thinking can be followed by identifying a vulnerability, providing the necessary test scenario, performing the test, and reviewing the code for how it deals with such a vulnerability. At this phase, tests are conducted in an environment that should mirror the production environment to ensure the code does not work only in the labs.

Security attacks and penetration tests usually take place during this phase to identify any missed vulnerabilities. Functionality, performance, and penetration resistance are evaluated. All the necessary functionality required of the product should be in a checklist to ensure each function is accounted for.

Security tests should be run to test against the vulnerabilities identified earlier within the project. Buffer overflows should be attempted, interfaces should be hit with unexpected inputs, denial of service (DoS) situations should be tested, unusual user activity should take place, and if a system crashes, the product should react by reverting to a secure state. The product should be tested in various environments with different applications, configurations, and hardware platforms. A product may respond fine when installed on a clean Windows 10 installation on a stand-alone PC, but it may throw unexpected errors when installed on a laptop that is remotely connected to a network and has a virtual private network (VPN) client installed.

Separation of Duties

Different environmental types (development, testing, and production) should be properly separated, and functionality and operations should not overlap. Developers should not have access to modify code used in production. The code should be tested, submitted to a library, and then sent to the production environment.

Testing Types

There are different types of tests the software should go through because there are different potential flaws the team should be looking for. The following are some of the most common testing approaches:

- **Unit testing** Testing individual components in a controlled environment where programmers validate data structure, logic, and boundary conditions
- **Integration testing** Verifying that components work together as outlined in design specifications
- **Acceptance testing** Ensuring that the code meets customer requirements
- **Regression testing** After a change to a system takes place, retesting to ensure functionality, performance, and protection

A well-rounded security test encompasses both manual and automatic tests. Automated tests help locate a wide range of flaws generally associated with careless or erroneous code implementations. Some automated testing environments run specific inputs in a scripted and repeatable manner. While these tests are the bread and butter of software testing, we sometimes want to simulate random and unpredictable inputs to supplement the scripted tests. A commonly used approach is to use programs known as fuzzers.

Fuzzers use complex input to impair program execution. *Fuzzing* is a technique used to discover flaws and vulnerabilities in software by sending large amounts of malformed, unexpected, or random data to the target program in order to trigger failures. Attackers can then manipulate these errors and flaws to inject their own code into the system and compromise its security and stability. Fuzzing tools are commonly successful at identifying buffer overflows, DoS vulnerabilities, injection weaknesses, validation flaws, and other activities that can cause software to freeze, crash, or throw unexpected errors.

A manual test is used to analyze aspects of the program that require human intuition and can usually be judged using computing techniques. Testers also try to locate design flaws. These include logical errors, where attackers may manipulate program flow by using shrewdly crafted program sequences to access greater privileges or bypass authentication mechanisms. Manual testing involves code auditing by security-centric programmers who try to modify the logical program structure using rogue inputs and reverse-engineering techniques. Manual tests simulate the live scenarios involved in real-world attacks. Some manual testing also involves the use of social engineering to analyze the human weakness that may lead to system compromise.

Dynamic analysis refers to the evaluation of a program in real time, when it is running. Dynamic analysis is commonly carried out once a program has cleared the static analysis stage and basic programming flaws have been rectified offline. It enables developers to trace subtle logical errors in the software that are likely to cause security mayhem later on. The primary advantage of this technique is that it eliminates the need to create artificial error-inducing scenarios. Dynamic analysis is also effective for compatibility testing, detecting memory leakages, and identifying dependencies, and for analyzing software without having to access the software's actual source code.

At this stage, issues found in testing procedures are relayed to the development team in problem reports. The problems are fixed and programs retested. This is a continual process until everyone is satisfied that the product is ready for production. If there is a specific customer, the customer would run through a range of tests before formally accepting the product; if it is a generic product, beta testing can be carried out by various potential customers and agencies. Then the product is formally released to the market or customer.

NOTE Sometimes developers enter lines of code in a product that will allow them to do a few keystrokes and get right into the application. This allows them to bypass any security and access controls so they can quickly access the application's core components. This is referred to as a "back door" or "maintenance hook" and must be removed before the code goes into production.

Release/Maintenance Phase

Once the software code is developed and properly tested, it is released so that it can be implemented within the intended production environment. The software development team's role is not finished at this point. Newly discovered problems and vulnerabilities are commonly identified. For example, if a company developed a customized application for a specific customer, the customer could run into unforeseen issues when rolling out the product within their various networked environments. Interoperability issues might come to the surface, or some configurations may break critical functionality. The developers would need to make the necessary changes to the code, retest the code, and re-release the code.

Verification vs. Validation

Verification determines if the product accurately represents and meets the specifications. After all, a product can be developed that does not match the original specifications, so this step ensures the specifications are being properly met. It answers the question: Did we build the product right?

Validation determines if the product provides the necessary solution for the intended real-world problem. In large projects, it is easy to lose sight of the overall goal. This exercise ensures that the main goal of the project is met. It answers the question: Did we build the right product?

From a security point of view, new vulnerabilities are discovered almost daily. While the developers may have carried out extensive security testing, it is close to impossible to identify all the security issues at one point and time. Zero-day vulnerabilities may be identified, coding errors may be uncovered, or the integration of the software with another piece of software may uncover security issues that have to be addressed. The development team must develop patches, hotfixes, and new releases to address these items.

NOTE *Zero-day vulnerabilities* are vulnerabilities that do not currently have a resolution. If a vulnerability is identified and there is not a pre-established fix (patch, configuration, update), it is considered a zero day.

SDLC and Security

The main phases of a software development life cycle are shown here with some specific security tasks.

Requirements gathering:

- Security risk assessment
- Privacy risk assessment
- Risk-level acceptance
- Informational, functional, and behavioral requirements

Design:

- Attack surface analysis
- Threat modeling

Development:

- Automated CASE tools
- Static analysis

Testing/validation:

- Dynamic analysis
- Fuzzing
- Manual testing
- Unit, integration, acceptance, and regression testing

Release/maintenance:

- Final security review

Secure Software Development Best Practices

The *Open Web Application Security Project (OWASP)* is an organization that deals specifically with web security issues. Along with a long list of tools, articles, and resources that developers can exploit to create secure software, OWASP also has individual member meetings (chapters) throughout the world. The group provides development guidelines, testing procedures, and code review steps, but is probably best known for its OWASP Top 10 list of web application security risks that it maintains. The following is the most recent Top 10 list as of this writing, from 2013:

- A1: Injection
- A2: Broken Authentication and Session Management
- A3: Cross-Site Scripting (XSS)
- A4: Insecure Direct Object References
- A5: Security Misconfiguration
- A6: Sensitive Data Exposure
- A7: Missing Function Level Access Controls
- A8: Cross-Site Request Forgery (CSRF)
- A9: Using Components with Known Vulnerabilities
- A10: Unvalidated Redirects and Forwards

This list represents the most common vulnerabilities that reside in web-based software and are exploited most often. You can find out more information pertaining to these vulnerabilities at https://www.owasp.org/index.php/Top_10_2013-Top_10.

The U.S. Department of Homeland Security (DHS) also provides best practices, tools, guidelines, rules, principles, and other resources that software developers, architects, and security practitioners can use to build security into software in every phase of its development. This DHS initiative is called *Build Security In (BSI)*, and as with the other mentioned organizations, it is a collaborative effort that allows many entities across the industry to participate and provide useful material. DHS has a Software Assurance Program that maintains BSI. This program's mission statement is as follows:

> *The Department of Homeland Security's Software Assurance Program seeks to reduce software vulnerabilities, minimize exploitation, and address ways to improve the routine development and deployment of trustworthy software products. Together, these activities will enable more secure and reliable software that supports mission requirements across enterprises and the critical infrastructure. Because software is essential to the operation of the Nation's critical infrastructure and it is estimated that 90 percent of reported security incidents result from exploits against defects in the design or code of software, ensuring the integrity of software is key to protecting the infrastructure from threats and vulnerabilities, and reducing overall risk to cyber attacks.*

BSI provides a process-agnostic approach that deals with requirements, architecture and design, code, test, system, management, and fundamentals. This effort is tightly coupled with The MITRE organization's CWE initiative, introduced earlier in the "Development Phase" section.

As always seems to be the case in the technology world, we exist without standards and best practices for many years and just develop technology as the needs and desires arise. We create things in an ad hoc manner with no great overall vision of how they will integrate or interoperate. Once we create a whole bunch of things in this crazy manner, the industry has a collective thought of, "Hey, we should carry out these activities in a structured and controlled manner." Then we have several organizations that come up with very similar standards and best practices to meet this void. Then we have too many standards and guidelines, and as the years march by the best ones usually prove their worth and the others fade in existence.

So along with the other organizations who have created software development standards, we also have the ISO/IEC, which was covered in Chapter 1. The *ISO/IEC 27034* standard covers the following areas: application security overview and concepts, organization normative framework, application security management process, protocols and application security control data structure, case studies, and application security assurance prediction. It is part of the ISO/IEC 27000 series, which facilitates aligning the secure software development processes with ISO/IEC's information security management system (ISMS) model.

Software Development Models

Several software development models have been emerged over the past 20 or so years. Each model has its own characteristics, pros, cons, SDLC phases, and best use-case scenarios. While some models include security issues in certain phases, these are not considered "security-centric development models." These are classical approaches to building and developing software. A brief discussion of some of the models that have been used over the years is presented next.

EXAM TIP It is exceptionally rare to see a development methodology used in its pure form in the real world. Instead, organizations will start with a base methodology and modify it to suit their own unique environment. For purposes of the CISSP exam, however, you should focus on what differentiates each development approach.

Build and Fix Model

Basically, no architecture design is carried out in the *Build and Fix model*; instead, development takes place immediately with little or no planning involved. Problems are dealt with as they occur, which is usually after the software product is released to the customer.

This is not really a formal SDLC model, since SDLC is hardly involved, but it has been a common approach by many vendors over the years. There are no formal feedback mechanisms to allow for development improvements; instead, bug fixes, service packs, and upgrades are developed as soon as possible and released to the customer for "damage control."

This is not a proactive method of ensuring quality, but a reactive way of dealing with problems as they come up. There is no way to properly assess progress, quality, or risks, and many times identified issues require a major design overhaul since things were not properly thought through and planned in the beginning. While this approach gets the software product out of the door as soon as possible, the costs involved with addressing issues after the product is released will, in all likelihood, continue to increase.

Waterfall Model

The *Waterfall model* uses a linear-sequential life-cycle approach, illustrated in Figure 8-7. Each phase must be completed in its entirety before the next phase can begin. At the end of each phase, a review takes place to make sure the project is on the correct path and should continue.

In this model all requirements are gathered in the initial phase and there is no formal way to integrate changes as more information becomes available or requirements change. It is hard to know everything at the beginning of a project, so waiting until the whole project is complete to integrate necessary changes can be ineffective and time consuming. As an analogy, let's say that you are planning to landscape your backyard that is one acre in size. In this scenario, you can only go to the gardening store one time to get all of your supplies. If you identify that you need more topsoil, rocks, or pipe for the sprinkler system, you have to wait and complete the whole yard before you can return to the store for extra or more suitable supplies.

This is a very rigid approach that could be useful for smaller projects that have all of the requirements fully understood, but it is a dangerous model for complex projects, which commonly contain many variables that affect the scope as the project continues.

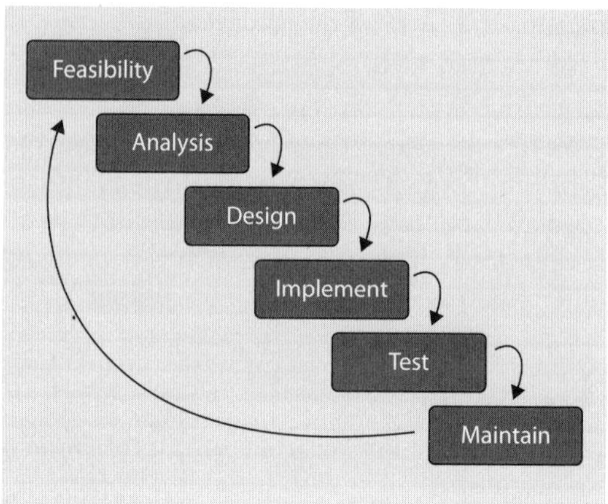

Figure 8-7 Waterfall model used for software development

V-Shaped Model (V-Model)

The *V-model* was developed after the Waterfall model. Instead of following a flat linear approach in the software development processes, it follows steps that are laid out in a V format, as shown in Figure 8-8. This model emphasizes the verification and validation of the product at each phase and provides a formal method of developing testing plans as each coding phase is executed.

Just like the Waterfall model, the V-shaped model lays out a sequential path of execution processes. Each phase must be completed before the next phase begins. But because the V-shaped model requires testing throughout the development phases and not just waiting until the end of the project, it has a higher chance of success compared to the Waterfall model.

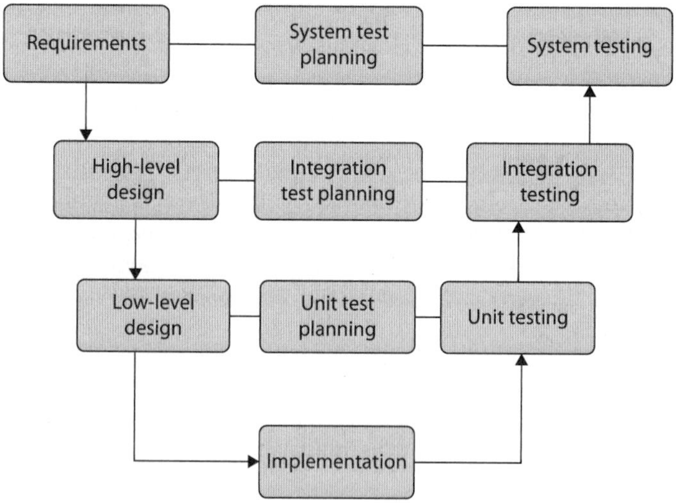

Figure 8-8 V-shaped model

The V-shaped model is still very rigid, as is the Waterfall model. This level of rigidness does not allow for much flexibility; thus, adapting to changes is more difficult and expensive. This model does not allow for the handling of events concurrently, it does not integrate iterations of phases, and it does not contain risk analysis activities as later models do. This model is best used when all requirements can be understood up front and potential scope changes are small.

Prototyping

A *prototype* is a sample of software code or a model that can be developed to explore a specific approach to a problem before investing expensive time and resources. A team can identify the usability and design problems while working with a prototype and adjust their approach as necessary. Within the software development industry three main prototype models have been invented and used. These are the rapid prototype, evolutionary prototype, and operational prototype.

Rapid prototyping is an approach that allows the development team to quickly create a prototype (sample) to test the validity of the current understanding of the project requirements. In a software development project, the team could quickly develop a prototype to see if their ideas are feasible and if they should move forward with their current solution. The rapid prototype approach (also called throwaway) is a "quick and dirty" method of creating a piece of code and seeing if everyone is on the right path or if another solution should be developed. The rapid prototype is not developed to be built upon, but to be discarded after serving its purposes.

When *evolutionary prototypes* are developed, they are built with the goal of incremental improvement. Instead of being discarded after being developed, as in the rapid prototype approach, the prototype in this model is continually improved upon until it reaches the final product stage. Feedback that is gained through each development phase is used to improve the prototype and get closer to accomplishing the customer's needs.

The *operational prototypes* are an extension of the evolutionary prototype method. Both models (operational and evolutionary) improve the quality of the prototype as more data is gathered, but the operational prototype is designed to be implemented within a production environment as it is being tweaked. The operational prototype is updated as customer feedback is gathered, and the changes to the software happen within the working site.

So the rapid prototype is developed to give a quick understanding of the suggested solution, the evolutionary prototype is created and improved upon within a lab environment, and an operational prototype is developed and improved upon within a production environment.

Incremental Model

If a development team follows the *Incremental model*, this allows them to carry out multiple development cycles on a piece of software throughout its development stages. This would be similar to "multi-Waterfall" cycles taking place on one piece of software as it matures through the development stages. A version of the software is created in the first

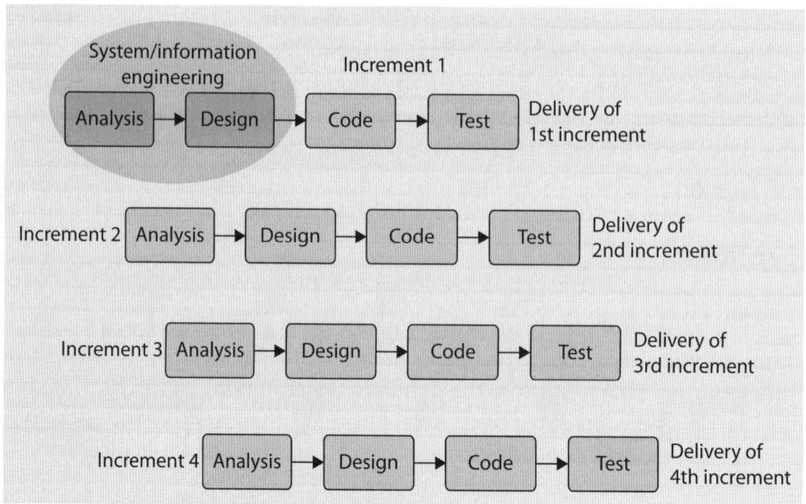

Figure 8-9 Incremental development model

iteration and then it passes through each phase (requirements analysis, design, coding, testing, implementation) of the next iteration process. The software continues through the iteration of phases until a satisfactory product is produced. This model is illustrated in Figure 8-9.

When using the Incremental model, each incremental phase results in a deliverable that is an operational product. This means that a working version of the software is produced after the first iteration and that version is improved upon in each of the subsequent iterations. Some benefits to this model are that a working piece of software is available in early stages of development, the flexibility of the model allows for changes to take place, testing uncovers issues more quickly than the Waterfall model since testing takes place after each iteration, and each iteration is an easily manageable milestone.

Since each release delivers an operational product, the customer can respond to each build and help the development team in its improvement processes. Since the initial product is delivered more quickly compared to other models, the initial product delivery costs are lower, the customer gets its functionality earlier, and the risks of critical changes being introduced are lower.

This model is best used when issues pertaining to risk, program complexity, funding, and functionality requirements need to be understood early in the product development cycle. If a vendor needs to get the customer some basic functionality quickly as it works on the development of the product, this can be a good model to follow.

Spiral Model

The *Spiral model* uses an iterative approach to software development and places emphasis on risk analysis. The model is made up of four main phases: determine objectives, risk analysis, development and test, and plan the next iteration. The development team starts with the initial requirements and goes through each of these phases, as shown in Figure 8-10. Think about starting a software development project at the center of this graphic. You have your initial understanding and requirements of the project, develop specifications that map to these requirements, carry out a risk analysis, build prototype specifications, test your specifications, build a development plan, integrate newly discovered information, use the new information to carry out a new risk analysis, create a prototype, test the prototype, integrate resulting data into the process, etc. As you gather more information about the project, you integrate it into the risk analysis process, improve your prototype, test the prototype, and add more granularity to each step until you have a completed product.

The iterative approach provided by the Spiral model allows new requirements to be addressed as they are uncovered. Each prototype allows for testing to take place early in the development project, and feedback based upon these tests is integrated into the following iteration of steps. The risk analysis ensures that all issues are actively reviewed and analyzed so that things do not "slip through the cracks" and the project stays on track.

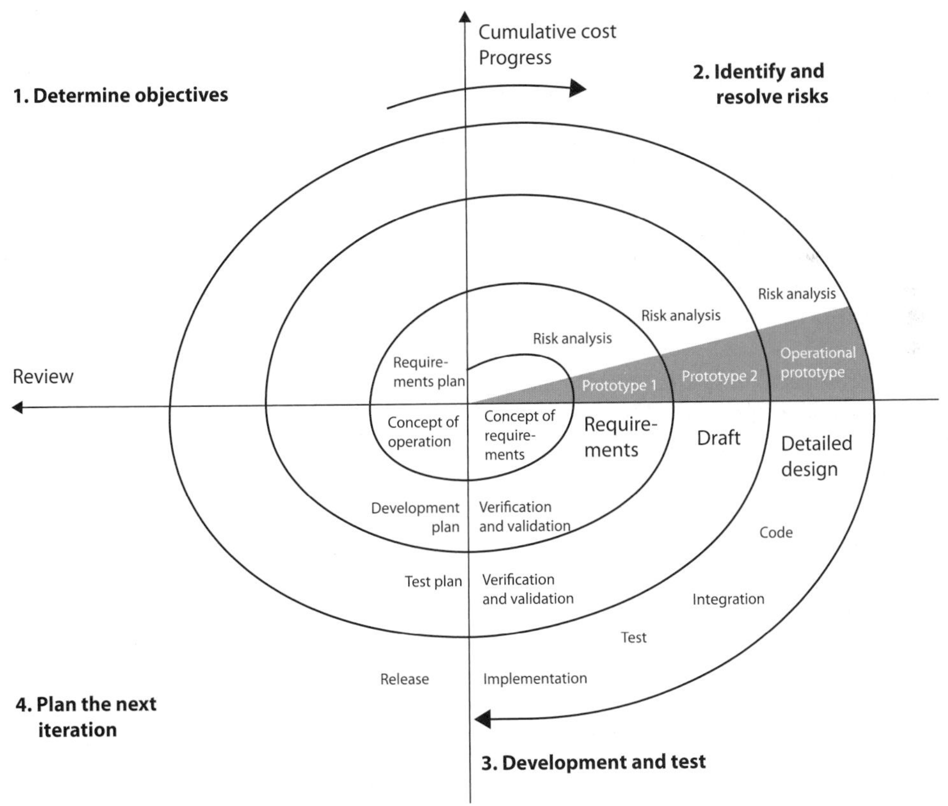

Figure 8-10 Spiral model for software development

In the Spiral model the last phase allows the customer to evaluate the product in its current state and provide feedback, which is an input value for the next spiral of activity. This is a good model for complex projects that have fluid requirements.

NOTE Within this model the angular aspect represents progress and the radius of the spirals represents cost.

Rapid Application Development

The *Rapid Application Development (RAD)* model relies more on the use of rapid prototyping than on extensive upfront planning. In this model, the planning of how to improve the software is interleaved with the processes of developing the software, which allows for software to be developed quickly. The delivery of a workable piece of software can take place in less than half the time compared to the Waterfall model. The RAD model combines the use of prototyping and iterative development procedures with the goal of accelerating the software development process. The development process begins with creating data models and business process models to help define what the end-result software needs to accomplish. Through the use of prototyping, these data and process models are refined. These models provide input to allow for the improvement of the prototype, and the testing and evaluation of the prototype allow for the improvement of the data and process models. The goal of these steps is to combine business requirements and technical design statements, which provide the direction in the software development project.

Figure 8-11 illustrates the basic differences between traditional software development approaches and RAD. As an analogy, let's say that the development team needs you to tell them what it is you want so that they can build it for you. You tell them that the thing you want has four wheels and an engine. They draw a picture of a two-seat convertible on a piece of paper and ask, "Is this what you want?" You say no, so they throw away that piece of paper (prototype). They ask for more information from you, and you tell them the thing must be able to seat four adults. They draw a picture of a four-seat convertible and show it to you and you tell them they are getting closer, but are still wrong. They throw away that piece of paper, and you tell them the thing must have four doors. They draw a picture of a sedan, and you nod your head in agreement. That back and forth is what is taking place in the circle portion of Figure 8-11.

The main reason that the RAD model was developed was that by the time software was completely developed following other models, the requirements changed and the developers had to "go back to the drawing board." If a customer needs you to develop a software product and it takes you a year to do so, by the end of that year the customer's needs for the software have probably advanced and changed. The RAD model allows for the customer to be involved during the development phases so that the end result maps to their needs in a more realistic manner.

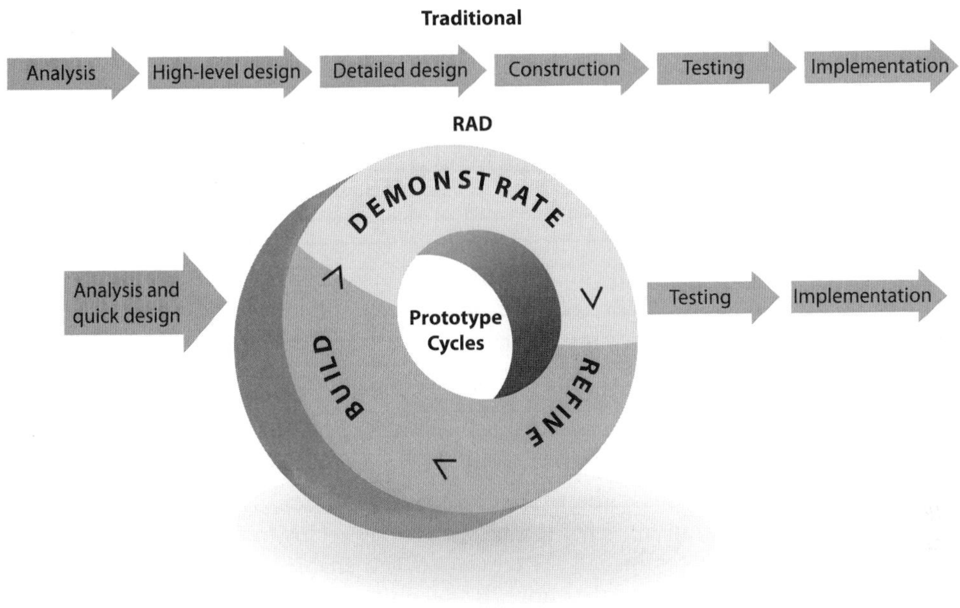

Figure 8-11 Rapid Application Development model

Agile Models

The industry seems to be full of software development models, each trying to improve upon the deficiencies of the ones before it. Before the Agile approach to development was created, teams were following rigid process-oriented models. These approaches focused more on following procedures and steps instead of potentially carrying out tasks in a more efficient manner. As an analogy, if you have ever worked within or interacted with a large government agency, you may have come across silly processes that took too long and involved too many steps. If you are a government employee and need to purchase a new chair, you might have to fill out four sets of documents that need to be approved by three other departments. You probably have to identify three different chair vendors, who have to submit a quote, which goes through the contracting office. It might take you a few months to get your new chair. The focus is to follow a protocol and rules instead of efficiency.

Many of the classical software development approaches, as in Waterfall, provide rigid processes to follow that do not allow for much flexibility and adaptability. Commonly, the software development projects that follow these approaches end up failing by not meeting schedule time release, running over budget, and/or not meeting the needs of the customer. Sometimes you need the freedom to modify steps to best meet the situation's needs.

The *Agile model* is an umbrella term for several development methodologies. It focuses not on rigid, linear, stepwise processes, but instead on incremental and iterative development methods that promote cross-functional teamwork and continuous feedback mechanisms. This model is considered "lightweight" compared to the traditional methods that are "heavyweight," which just means this model is not confined to a tunneled vision and overly structured approach. It is nimble and flexible enough to adapt to each project's needs. The industry found out that even an exhaustive library of defined processes cannot handle every situation that could arise during a development project. So instead of investing time and resources into big upfront design analysis, this model focuses on small increments of functional code that are created based upon business need.

The model focuses on individual interaction instead of processes and tools. It emphasizes developing the right software product over comprehensive and laborious documentation. It promotes customer collaboration instead of contract negotiation, and abilities to respond to change instead of strictly following a plan.

A notable element of many Agile methodologies is their focus on user stories. A *user story* is a sentence that describes what a user wants to do and why. For instance, a user story could be "As a customer, I want to search for products so that I can buy some." Notice the structure of the story is: As a <user role>, I want to <accomplish some goal> so that <reason for accomplishing the goal>. This method of documenting user requirements is very familiar to the customers and enables their close collaboration with the development team. Furthermore, by keeping this user focus, validation of the features is simpler because the "right system" is described up front by the users in their own words.

EXAM TIP The Agile models do not use prototypes to represent the full product, but break the product down into individual features that are constantly being delivered.

Another important characteristic of the Agile model is that the development team can take pieces and parts of all of the available SDLC methods and combine them in a manner that best meets the specific project needs. These various combinations have resulted in many methodologies that fall under the Agile model.

Scrum

Scrum is one of the most widely adopted agile methodologies in use today. It lends itself to projects of any size and complexity and is very lean and customer focused. Scrum is a methodology that acknowledges the fact that customer needs cannot be completely understood and will change over time. It focuses on team collaboration, customer involvement, and continuous delivery.

The term *scrum* originates from the sport of rugby. Whenever something interrupts play (e.g., a penalty or the ball goes out of bounds) and the game needs to be restarted, all players come together in an organized mob that is resolved when one team or the other gains possession of the ball, allowing the game to continue. Extending this analogy, the Scrum methodology allows the project to be reset by allowing product features to be added, changed, or removed at clearly defined points. Since the customer is intimately involved in the development process, there should be no surprises, cost overruns, or

schedule delays. This allows a product to be iteratively developed and changed even as it is being built.

The change points happen at the conclusion of each *sprint*, a fixed-duration development interval that is usually (but not always) two weeks in length and promises delivery of a very specific set of features. These features are chosen by the team, but with a lot of input from the customer. There is a process for adding features at any time by inserting them in the feature backlog. However, these features can be considered for actual work only at the beginning of a new sprint. This shields the development team from changes during a sprint, but allows for them in between sprints.

Extreme Programming

If you take away the regularity of Scrum's sprints and backlogs and add a lot of code reviewing, you get our next agile model. Extreme Programming (XP) is a development methodology that takes code reviews (discussed in Chapter 6) to the extreme (hence the name) by having them take place continuously. These continuous reviews are accomplished using an approach called *pair programming*, in which one programmer dictates the code to her partner, who then types it. While this may seem inefficient, it allows two pairs of eyes to constantly examine the code as it is being typed. It turns out that this approach significantly reduces the incidence of errors and improves the overall quality of the code.

Another characteristic of XP is its reliance on test-driven development, in which the unit tests are written before the code. The programmer first writes a new unit test case, which of course fails because there is no code to satisfy it. The next step is to add just enough code to get the test to pass. Once this is done, the next test is written, which fails, and so on. The consequence is that only the minimal amount of code needed to pass the tests is developed. This extremely minimal approach reduces the incidence of errors because it weeds out complexity.

Kanban

Kanban is a production scheduling system developed by Toyota to more efficiently support just-in-time delivery. Over time, it was adopted by IT and software systems developers. In this context, the *Kanban* development methodology is one that stresses visual tracking of all tasks so that the team knows what to prioritize at what point in time in order to deliver the right features right on time. Kanban projects used to be very noticeable because entire walls in conference rooms would be covered in sticky notes representing the various tasks that the team was tracking. Nowadays, many Kanban teams opt for virtual walls on online systems.

The Kanban wall is usually divided vertically by production phase. Typical columns are labeled Planned, In Progress, and Done. Each sticky note can represent a user story as it moves through the development process, but more importantly, the sticky note can also be some other work that needs to be accomplished. For instance, suppose that one of the user stories is the search feature described earlier in this section. While it is being developed, the team realizes that the searches are very slow. This could result in a task being added to change the underlying data or network architecture or to upgrade hardware. This sticky note then gets added to the Planned column and starts being prioritized

and tracked together with the rest of the remaining tasks. This process highlights how Kanban allows the project team to react to changing or unknown requirements, which is a common feature among all Agile models.

Review of Development Methodologies

A quick review of the various models we have covered up to this point is provided here:

- **Break and Fix** No real planning up front. Flaws are reactively dealt with after release with the creation of patches and updates.
- **Waterfall** Very rigid, sequential approach that requires each phase to complete before the next one can begin. Difficult to integrate changes. Inflexible model.
- **V-model** Emphasizes verification and validation at each phase and testing to take place throughout the project, not just at the end.
- **Prototyping** Creating a sample or model of the code for proof-of-concept purposes.
- **Incremental** Multiple development cycles are carried out on a piece of software throughout its development stages. Each phase provides a usable version of software.
- **Spiral** Iterative approach that emphasizes risk analysis per iteration. Allows for customer feedback to be integrated through a flexible evolutionary approach.
- **Rapid Application Development** Combines prototyping and iterative development procedures with the goal of accelerating the software development process.
- **Agile** Iterative and incremental development processes that encourage team-based collaboration. Flexibility and adaptability are used instead of a strict process structure.

Other Models

There seems to be no shortage of SDLC and software development models in the industry. The following is a quick summary of a few others that can also be used:

- **Exploratory model** A method that is used in instances where clearly defined project objectives have not been presented. Instead of focusing on explicit tasks, the exploratory model relies on covering a set of specifications likely to affect the final product's functionality. Testing is an important part of exploratory development, as it ascertains that the current phase of the project is compliant with likely implementation scenarios.

- **Joint Application Development (JAD)** A method that uses a team approach in application development in a workshop-oriented environment. This model is distinguished by its inclusion of members other than coders in the team. It is common to find executive sponsors, subject matter experts, and end users spending hours or days in collaborative development workshops.
- **Reuse model** A model that approaches software development by using progressively developed models. Reusable programs are evolved by gradually modifying pre-existing prototypes to customer specifications. Since the reuse model does not require programs to be built from scratch, it drastically reduces both development cost and time.
- **Cleanroom** An approach that attempts to prevent errors or mistakes by following structured and formal methods of developing and testing. This approach is used for high-quality and mission-critical applications that will be put through a strict certification process.

We only covered the most commonly used models in this section, but there are many more that exist. New models have evolved as technology and research have advanced and various weaknesses of older models have been addressed. Most of the models exist to meet a specific software development need, and choosing the wrong model for a certain project could be devastating to its overall success.

Integrated Product Team

An *integrated product team (IPT)* is a multidisciplinary development team with representatives from many or all the stakeholder populations. The idea makes a lot of sense when you think about it. Why should programmers learn or guess the manner in which the accounting folks handle accounts payable? Why should testers and quality control personnel wait until a product is finished before examining it? Why should the marketing team wait until the project (or at least the prototype) is finished before determining how best to sell it? A comprehensive IPT includes business executives and end users and everyone in between.

The Joint Application Development (JAD) methodology, in which users join developers during extensive workshops, works well with the IPT approach. IPTs extend this concept by ensuring that the right stakeholders are represented in every phase of the development as formal team members. In addition, whereas JAD is focused on involving the user community, IPT is typically more inward facing and focuses on bringing in the business stakeholders.

An IPT is not a development methodology. Instead, it is a management technique. When project managers decide to use IPTs, they still have to select a methodology. These days, IPTs are often associated with Agile methodologies.

DevOps

Traditionally, the software development team and the IT team are two separate (and sometimes antagonistic) groups within an organization. Many problems stem from poor

collaboration between these two teams during the development process. It is not rare to have the IT team berating the developers because a feature push causes the IT team to have to stay late or work on a weekend or simply drop everything they were doing in order to "fix" something that the developers "broke." This friction makes a lot of sense when you consider that each team is incentivized by different outcomes. Developers want to push out finished code, usually under strict schedules. The IT staff, on the other hand, wants to keep the IT infrastructure operating effectively. Many project managers who have managed software development efforts will attest to having received complaints from developers that the IT team was being unreasonable and uncooperative, while the IT team was simultaneously complaining about buggy code being tossed over the fence at them at the worst possible times and causing problems on the rest of the network.

A good way to solve this friction is to have both developers and members of the operations staff (hence the term DevOps) on the software development team. *DevOps* is the practice of incorporating development, IT, and quality assurance (QA) staff into software development projects to align their incentives and enable frequent, efficient, and reliable releases of software products. This relationship is illustrated in Figure 8-12.

Ultimately, DevOps is about changing the culture of an organization. It has a huge positive impact on security, because in addition to QA, the IT teammates will be involved at every step of the process. Multifunctional integration allows the team to identify potential defects, vulnerabilities, and friction points early enough to resolve them proactively. This is one of the biggest selling points for DevOps. According to multiple surveys, there are a few other, perhaps more powerful benefits: DevOps increases trust within an organization and increases job satisfaction among developers, IT staff, and QA personnel. Unsurprisingly, it also improves the morale of project managers.

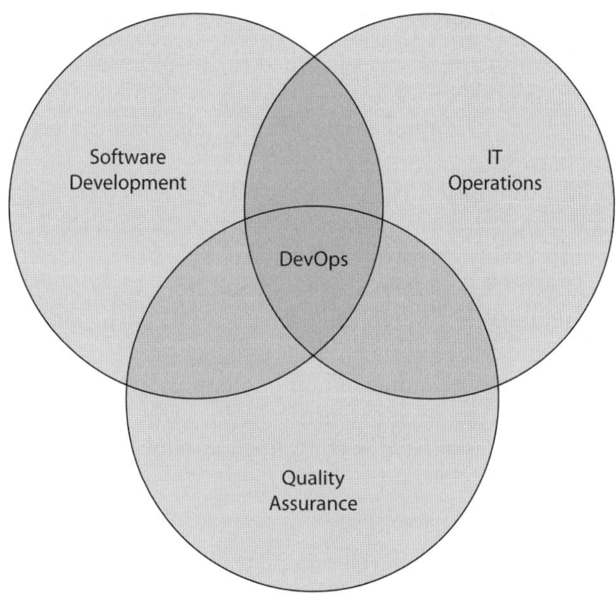

Figure 8-12 DevOps exists at the intersection of software development, IT, and QA.

Capability Maturity Model Integration

Capability Maturity Model Integration (CMMI) is a comprehensive, integrated set of guidelines for developing products and software. It addresses the different phases of a software development life cycle, including concept definition, requirements analysis, design, development, integration, installation, operations, and maintenance, and what should happen in each phase. It can be used to evaluate security engineering practices and identify ways to improve them. It can also be used by customers in the evaluation process of a software vendor. Ideally, software vendors would use the model to help improve their processes, and customers would use the model to assess the vendors' practices.

CMMI describes procedures, principles, and practices that underlie software development process maturity. This model was developed to help software vendors improve their development processes by providing an evolutionary path from an ad hoc "fly by the seat of your pants" approach to a more disciplined and repeatable method that improves software quality, reduces the life cycle of development, provides better project management capabilities, allows for milestones to be created and met in a timely manner, and takes a more proactive approach than the less effective reactive approach. It provides best practices to allow an organization to develop a standardized approach to software development that can be used across many different groups. The goal is to continue to review and improve upon the processes to optimize output, increase capabilities, and provide higher-quality software at a lower cost through the implementation of continuous improvement steps.

If the company Stuff-R-Us wants a software development company, Software-R-Us, to develop an application for it, it can choose to buy into the sales hype about how wonderful Software-R-Us is, or it can ask Software-R-Us whether it has been evaluated against the CMMI model. Third-party companies evaluate software development companies to certify their product development processes. Many software companies have this evaluation done so they can use this as a selling point to attract new customers and provide confidence for their current customers.

The five maturity levels of the CMMI model are

1. **Initial** Development process is ad hoc or even chaotic. The company does not use effective management procedures and plans. There is no assurance of consistency, and quality is unpredictable. Success is usually the result of individual heroics.
2. **Repeatable** A formal management structure, change control, and quality assurance are in place. The company can properly repeat processes throughout each project. The company does not have formal process models defined.
3. **Defined** Formal procedures are in place that outline and define processes carried out in each project. The organization has a way to allow for quantitative process improvement.
4. **Managed** The company has formal processes in place to collect and analyze quantitative data, and metrics are defined and fed into the process-improvement program.

5. **Optimizing** The company has budgeted and integrated plans for continuous process improvement.

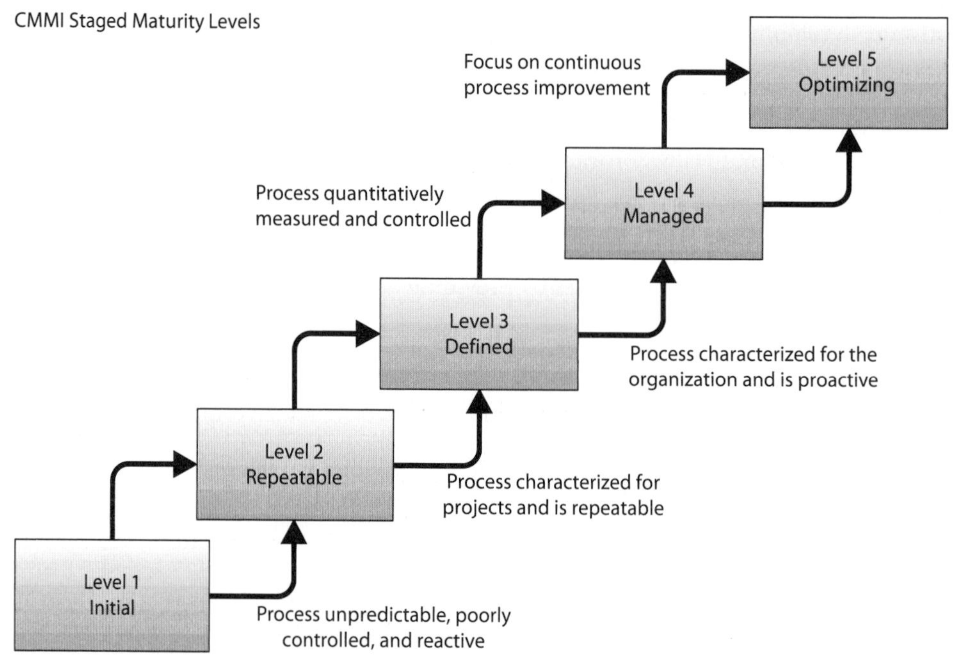

Each level builds upon the previous one. For example, a company that accomplishes a Level 5 CMMI rating must meet all the requirements outlined in Levels 1–4 along with the requirements of Level 5.

If a software development vendor is using the Build and Fix model that was discussed earlier in this chapter, the vendor would most likely only achieve a CMMI Level 1, because their practices are ad hoc, not consistent, and the level of the quality that their software products contain is questionable. If this company practiced a strict Agile SDLC model consistently and carried out development, testing, and documentation precisely, they would have a higher chance of obtaining a higher CMMI level.

Capability maturity models (CMMs) are used for many different purposes, software development processes being one of them. They are general models that allow for maturity-level identification and maturity improvement steps. We showed how CMM integration can be used for organizational security program improvement processes in Chapter 1.

The software industry ended up with several different CMMs, which led to confusion. CMMI was developed to bring many of these different maturity models together and allow them to be used in one framework. CMMI was developed by industry experts, government entities, and the Software Engineering Institute at Carnegie Mellon University. So CMMI has replaced CMM in the software engineering world, but you may still see CMM referred to within the industry and even on the CISSP exam. Their ultimate goals are the same, which is process improvement.

NOTE The CMMI is continually being updated and improved upon. The latest copy can be viewed at https://resources.sei.cmu.edu/library/asset-view.cfm?assetID=9661.

Change Control

One of the key processes on which to focus for improvement is change control. Changes during a product's life cycle can cause a lot of havoc if not done properly and in a controlled manner. Changes could take place for several reasons. During the development phases, a customer may alter requirements and ask that certain functionalities be added, removed, or modified. In production, changes may need to happen because of other changes in the environment, new requirements of a software product or system, or newly released patches or upgrades. These changes should be controlled to make sure they are approved, incorporated properly, and do not affect any original functionality in an adverse way. *Change control* is the process of controlling the changes that take place during the life cycle of a system and documenting the necessary change control activities.

A process for dealing with changes needs to be in place at the beginning of a project so everyone knows how changes are dealt with and what is expected of each entity when a change request is made. Some projects have been doomed from the start because proper change control was not put into place and enforced. Many times in development, the customer and vendor agree on the design of the product, the requirements, and the specifications. The customer is then required to sign a contract confirming this is the agreement and that if they want any further modifications, they will have to pay the vendor for that extra work. If this is not put into place, then the customer can continually request changes, which requires the development team to put in the extra hours to provide these changes, the result of which is that the vendor loses money, the product does not meet its completion deadline, and scope creep occurs.

Other reasons exist to have change control in place. These reasons deal with organization, standard procedures, and expected results. If a product is in the last phase of development and a change request comes in, the team should know how to deal with it. Usually, the team leader must tell the project manager how much extra time will be required to complete the project if this change is incorporated and what steps need to be taken to ensure this change does not affect other components within the product. If these processes are not controlled, one part of a development team could implement the change without another part of the team being aware of it. This could break some of the other development team's software pieces. When the pieces of the product are integrated and it is found that some pieces are incompatible, some jobs may be in jeopardy, because management never approved the change in the first place.

The change must be approved, documented, and tested. Some tests may need to be rerun to ensure the change does not affect the product's capabilities. When a programmer makes a change to source code, it should be done on the test version of the code. Under no conditions should a programmer change the code that is already in production. The changes to the code should be made and tested, and then the new code should go to the librarian. Production code should come only from the librarian and not from a programmer or directly from a test environment.

Change control processes should be evaluated during system audits. It is possible to overlook a problem that a change has caused in testing, so the procedures for how change control is implemented and enforced should be examined during a system audit.

The following are some necessary steps for a change control process:

1. Make a formal request for a change.
2. Analyze the request.
   a. Develop the implementation strategy.
   b. Calculate the costs of this implementation.
   c. Review security implications.
3. Record the change request.
4. Submit the change request for approval.
5. Develop the change.
   a. Recode segments of the product and add or subtract functionality.
   b. Link these changes in the code to the formal change control request.
   c. Submit software for testing and quality control.
   d. Repeat until quality is adequate.
   e. Make version changes.
6. Report results to management.

The changes to systems may require another round of certification and accreditation. If the changes to a system are significant, then the functionality and level of protection may need to be reevaluated (certified), and management would have to approve the overall system, including the new changes (accreditation).

Software Configuration Management

When changes take place to a software product during its development life cycle, a configuration management system can be put into place that allows for change control processes to take place through automation. A product that provides *software configuration management (SCM)* identifies the attributes of software at various points in time, and performs a methodical control of changes for the purpose of maintaining software integrity and traceability throughout the software development life cycle. It defines the need to track changes and provides the ability to verify that the final delivered software has all of the approved changes that are supposed to be included in the release.

During a software development project, the centralized code repositories are often kept in systems that can carry out SCM functionality, which manage and track revisions made by multiple people against a single master set. These SCM systems should provide concurrency management, versioning, and synchronization. Concurrency management deals with the issues that arise when multiple people extract the same file from a central repository and make their own individual changes. If they submit their updated files in an uncontrolled manner, the files would just write over each other and changes would be lost. Many SCM systems use algorithms to version, fork, and merge the changes as files are checked back into the repository.

Versioning deals with keeping track of file revisions, which makes it possible to "roll back" to a previous version of the file. An archive copy of every file can be made when it is checked into the repository, or every change made to a file can be saved to a transaction log. Versioning systems should also create log reports of who made changes, when they were made, and what the changes were.

Some SCM systems allow individuals to check out complete or partial copies of the repositories and work on the files as needed. They can then commit their changes back to the master repository as needed, and update their own personal copies to stay up to date with changes other people have made. This process is called *synchronization*.

Software Escrow

If a company pays another company to develop software for it, it should have some type of *software escrow* in place for protection. We covered this topic in Chapter 7 from a business continuity perspective, but since it directly deals with software development, we will mention it here also.

In a software escrow framework, a third party keeps a copy of the source code, and possibly other materials, which it will release to the customer only if specific circumstances arise, mainly if the vendor who developed the code goes out of business or for some reason is not meeting its obligations and responsibilities. This procedure protects the customer, because the customer pays the vendor to develop software code for it, and if the vendor goes out of business, the customer otherwise would no longer have access to the actual code. This means the customer code could never be updated or maintained properly.

A logical question would be, "Why doesn't the vendor just hand over the source code to the customer, since the customer paid for it to be developed in the first place?" It does not always work that way. The code may be the vendor's intellectual property. The vendor employs and pays people with the necessary skills to develop that code, and if the vendor were to just hand it over to the customer, it could be giving away its intellectual property, its secrets. The customer oftentimes gets compiled code instead of source code. *Compiled code* is code that has been put through a compiler and is unreadable to humans. Most software profits are based on licensing, which outlines what customers can do with the compiled code. For an added fee, of course, most custom software developers will also provide the source, which could be useful in sensitive applications.

Security of Code Repositories

The code repository, which is typically a version control system, is the vault containing the crown jewels of any organization involved in software development. If we put on our adversarial hats for a few minutes, we could come up with all kinds of nefarious scenarios involving these repositories. Perhaps the simplest is that someone could steal our source code, which embodies not only many staff hours of work, but more significantly, our intellectual property. An adversary could also use our source code to look for vulnerabilities to exploit later, once the code is in production. Finally, adversaries could deliberately insert vulnerabilities into our software, perhaps after it has undergone all testing and is trusted, so that it can be exploited later at a time of their choosing. Clearly, securing our source code is critical.

Perhaps the most secure way of managing security for your code repositories is to implement them on an isolated (or "air-gaped") network that includes the development, test, and QA environments. The development team would have to be on this network to do their work, and the code, once verified, could be exported to the production servers using removable storage media. The challenge with this approach is that it severely limits the manner in which the development team can connect to the code. It also makes it difficult to collaborate with external parties, and for developers to work from remote or mobile locations.

A pretty good alternative would be to host the repository on the intranet, which would require developers to either be on the local network or connect to it using a VPN connection. As an added layer of security, the repositories can be configured to require the use of Secure Shell (SSH), which would ensure all traffic is encrypted even inside the intranet to mitigate the risk of sniffing. Finally, SSH can be configured to use public key infrastructure (PKI), which allows us to implement not only confidentiality and integrity, but also nonrepudiation. If you have to allow remote access to your repository, this would be a good way to go about it.

Finally, if you are operating on a limited budget or have limited security expertise in this area, you can choose one of the many web-based repository service providers and let them take care of the security for you. While this may mitigate the basic risks for small organizations, it is probably not an acceptable course of action for projects with significant investments of intellectual property.

Programming Languages and Concepts

All software is written in some type of programming language. Programming languages have gone through several generations over time, each generation building on the next, providing richer functionality and giving the programmers more powerful tools as they evolve.

The main categories of languages are machine language, assembly language, and high-level languages. *Machine language* is in a format that the computer's processor can understand and work with directly. Every processor family has its own machine code instruction set, as we covered in Chapter 3. Machine code is represented in a binary format (1 and 0) and is considered to be the most primitive form of programming language and the first generation of programming languages. Machine languages were used as the sole method of programming in the early 1950s. Early computers used only basic binary instructions because compilers and interpreters were nonexistent at the time. Programmers had to manually calculate and allot memory addresses and instructions had to be sequentially fed, as there was no concept of abstraction. Not only was programming in binary extremely time consuming, it was also highly prone to errors. (If you think about writing out thousands of 1's and 0's to represent what you want a computer to do, this puts this approach into perspective.) This forced programmers to keep a tight rein on their program lengths, resulting in programs that were very rudimentary.

An *assembly language* is considered a low-level programming language and is the symbolic representation of machine-level instructions. It is "one step above" machine language. It uses symbols (called mnemonics) to represent complicated binary codes. Programmers using assembly language could use commands like ADD, PUSH, POP, etc., instead of the binary codes (1001011010, etc.). Assembly languages use programs called *assemblers*, which automatically convert these assembly codes into the necessary machine-compatible binary language. To their credit, assembly languages drastically reduced programming and debugging times, introduced the concept of variables, and freed programmers from manually calculating memory addresses. But like machine code, programming in an assembly language requires extensive knowledge of a computer's architecture. It is easier than programming in binary format, but more challenging compared to the high-level languages most programmers use today.

Programs written in assembly language are also hardware specific, so a program written for an ARM-based processor would be incompatible with Intel-based systems; thus, these types of languages are not portable.

NOTE Assembly language allows for direct control of very basic activities within a computer system, as in pushing data on a memory stack and popping data off a stack. Attackers commonly use these languages to tightly control how malicious instructions are carried out on victim systems.

The third generation of programming languages started to emerge in the early 1960s. Third-generation programming languages are known as *high-level languages* due to their refined programming structures. High-level languages use abstract statements. Abstraction naturalized multiple assembly language instructions into a single high-level statement, e.g., the IF – THEN – ELSE. This allowed programmers to leave low-level (system architecture) intricacies to the programming language and focus on their programming objectives. In addition, high-level languages are easier to work with compared to machine and assembly languages, as their syntax is similar to human languages. The use of mathematical operators also simplified arithmetic and logical operations. This drastically reduced program development time and allowed for more simplified debugging. This means the programs are easier to write and mistakes (bugs) are easier to identify. High-level languages are processor independent. Code written in a high-level language can be converted to machine language for different processor architectures using compilers and interpreters. When code is independent of a specific processor type, the programs are portable and can be used on many different system types.

Fourth-generation languages (*very high-level languages*) were designed to further enhance the natural language approach instigated within the third-generation language. Fourth-generation languages are meant to take natural language–based statements one step further. Fourth-generation programming languages focus on highly abstract algorithms that allow straightforward programming implementation in specific environments. The most remarkable aspect of fourth-generation languages is that the amount of manual coding required to perform a specific task may be ten times less than for the same task on a third-generation language. This is especially important as these languages have been developed to be used by inexpert users and not just professional programmers.

As an analogy, let's say that you need to pass a calculus exam. You need to be very focused on memorizing the necessary formulas and applying the formulas to the correct word problems on the test. Your focus is on how calculus works, not on how the calculator you use as a tool works. If you had to understand how your calculator is moving data from one transistor to the other, how the circuitry works, and how the calculator stores and carries out its processing activities just to use it for your test, this would be overwhelming. The same is true for computer programmers. If they had to worry about how the operating system carries out memory management functions, input/output activities, and how processor-based registers are being used, it would be difficult for them to also focus on real-world problems they are trying to solve with their software. High-level languages hide all of this background complexity and take care of it for the programmer.

The early 1990s saw the conception of the fifth generation of programming languages (*natural languages*). These languages approach programming from a completely different perspective. Program creation does not happen through defining algorithms and function statements, but rather by defining the constraints for achieving a specified result. The goal is to create software that can solve problems by itself instead of a programmer having to develop code to deal with individual and specific problems. The applications work more like a black box—a problem goes in and a solution comes out. Just as the introduction of assembly language eliminated the need for binary-based programming, the full impact of fifth-generation programming techniques may bring to an end the traditional programming approach. The ultimate target of fifth-generation languages is to eliminate the need for programming expertise and instead use advanced knowledge-based processing and artificial intelligence.

The industry has not been able to fully achieve all the goals set out for these fifth-generation languages. The human insight of programmers is still necessary to figure out the problems that need to be solved, and the restrictions of the structure of a current computer system do not allow software to "think for itself" yet. We are getting closer to achieving artificial intelligence within our software, but we still have a long way to go.

The following lists the basic software programming language generations:

- **Generation one** Machine language
- **Generation two** Assembly language
- **Generation three** High-level language
- **Generation four** Very high-level language
- **Generation five** Natural language

Language Levels

The "higher" the language, the more abstraction that is involved. *Abstraction* means that the details of something are far away and/or hidden. A programming language that provides a high level of abstraction means that the programmer does not need to worry about the intricate details of the computer system itself, as in registers, memory addresses, complex Boolean expressions, thread management, etc. The programmer can use simple statements such as "print" and does not need to worry about how the computer will actually get the data over to the printer. Instead, the programmer can focus on the core functionality that the application is supposed to provide and not be bothered with the complex things taking place in the belly of the operating system and motherboard components.

As an analogy, you do not need to understand how your engine or brakes work in your car—there is a level of abstraction. You just turn the steering wheel and step on the pedal when necessary, and you can focus on getting to your destination.

There are so many different programming languages today, it is hard to fit them neatly in the five generations described in this chapter. These generations are the classical way of describing the differences in software programming approaches and what you will see on the CISSP exam.

Assemblers, Compilers, Interpreters

No matter what type or generation of programming language is used, all of the instructions and data have to end up in a binary format for the processor to understand and work with. Just like our food has to be broken down into molecules for our body to be able to process it, all code must end up in a format that is consumable for specific systems. Each programming language type goes through this transformation through the use of assemblers, compilers, or interpreters.

Assemblers are tools that convert assembly language source code into machine code. Assembly language consists of mnemonics, which are incomprehensible to processors and therefore need to be translated into operation instructions.

Compilers are tools that convert high-level language statements into the necessary machine-level format (.exe, .dll, etc.) for specific processors to understand. The compiler transforms instructions from a source language (high-level) to a target language (machine), which allows the code to be executable. A programmer may develop an application in the C++ language, but when you purchase this application you do not receive the source code, but you will receive the executable code that will run on your type of computer. The source code was put through a compiler, which resulted in an executable file that can run on your specific processor type.

Compilers allow developers to create software code that can be developed once in a high-level language and compiled for various platforms. So you could develop one piece of software, which is then compiled by five different compilers to allow it to be able to run on five different systems.

If a programming language is considered "interpreted," then a tool called an *interpreter* does the last step of transforming high-level code to machine-level code. For example, applications that are developed to work in a .NET environment are translated into an intermediate, platform-independent format. The applications are deployed, and upon runtime the applications' code is interpreted into processor-specific code. The goal is to improve portability. The same is true for the Java programming language. Programs written in Java have their source code compiled into an intermediate code, called bytecode. When the instructions of the application need to run, they are executed in a Java Virtual Machine (JVM). The JVM has an interpreter specific for the platform it is installed on, as illustrated in Figure 8-13. The interpreter converts the bytecode into a machine-level format for execution.

The greatest advantage of executing a program in an interpreted environment is that the platform independence and memory management functions are part of an interpreter. The major disadvantage with this approach is that the program cannot run as a stand-alone application, but requires the interpreter to be installed on the local machine.

From a security point of view, it is important to understand vulnerabilities that are inherent in specific programming languages. For example, programs written in the C language could be vulnerable to buffer overrun and format string errors. The issue is that some of the C standard software libraries do not check the length of the strings of data they manipulate by default. Consequently, if a string is obtained from an untrusted source (i.e., the Internet) and is passed to one of these library routines, parts of memory

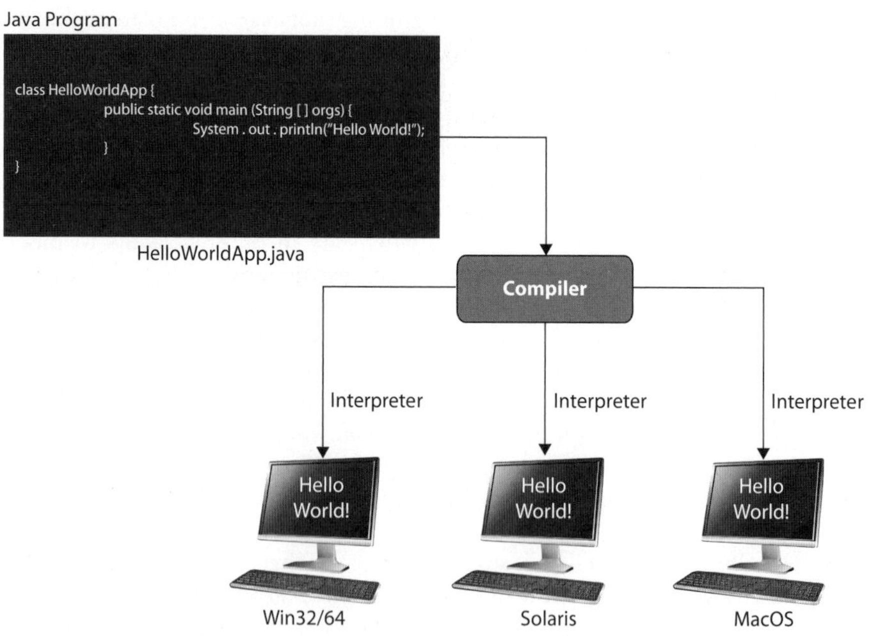

Figure 8-13 Java bytecode is converted by interpreters.

may be unintentionally overwritten with untrustworthy data—this vulnerability can potentially be used to execute arbitrary and malicious software. Some programming languages, such as Java, perform automatic garbage collection; others, such as C, require the developer to perform it manually, thus leaving opportunity for error.

Garbage collection is an automated way for software to carry out part of its memory management tasks. A *garbage collector* identifies blocks of memory that were once allocated but are no longer in use and deallocates the blocks and marks them as free. It also gathers scattered blocks of free memory and combines them into larger blocks. It helps provide a more stable environment and does not waste precious memory. If garbage collection does not take place properly, not only can memory be used in an inefficient manner, an attacker could carry out a denial-of-service attack specifically to artificially commit all of a system's memory rendering it unable to function.

CAUTION Nothing in technology seems to be getting any simpler, which makes learning this stuff much harder as the years go by. Ten years ago assembly, compiled, and interpreted languages were more clear-cut and their definitions straightforward. For the most part, only scripting languages required interpreters, but as languages have evolved they have become extremely flexible to allow for greater functionality, efficiency, and portability. Many languages can have their source code compiled or interpreted depending upon the environment and user requirements.

Object-Oriented Concepts

Software development used to be done by classic input-processing-output methods. This development used an information flow model from hierarchical information structures. Data was input into a program, and the program passed the data from the beginning to end, performed logical procedures, and returned a result.

Object-oriented programming (OOP) methods perform the same functionality, but with different techniques that work in a more efficient manner. First, you need to understand the basic concepts of OOP.

OOP works with classes and objects. A real-world object, such as a table, is a member (or an instance) of a larger class of objects called "furniture." The furniture class will have a set of attributes associated with it, and when an object is generated, it inherits these attributes. The attributes may be color, dimensions, weight, style, and cost. These attributes apply if a chair, table, or loveseat object is generated, also referred to as *instantiated*. Because the table is a member of the class furniture, the table inherits all attributes defined for the class (see Figure 8-14).

The programmer develops the class and all of its characteristics and attributes. The programmer does not develop each and every object, which is the beauty of this approach. As an analogy, let's say you developed an advanced coffee maker with the goal of putting Starbucks out of business. A customer punches the available buttons on your coffee maker interface, ordering a large latte, with skim milk, vanilla and raspberry flavoring, and an extra shot of espresso, where the coffee is served at 250 degrees. Your coffee maker

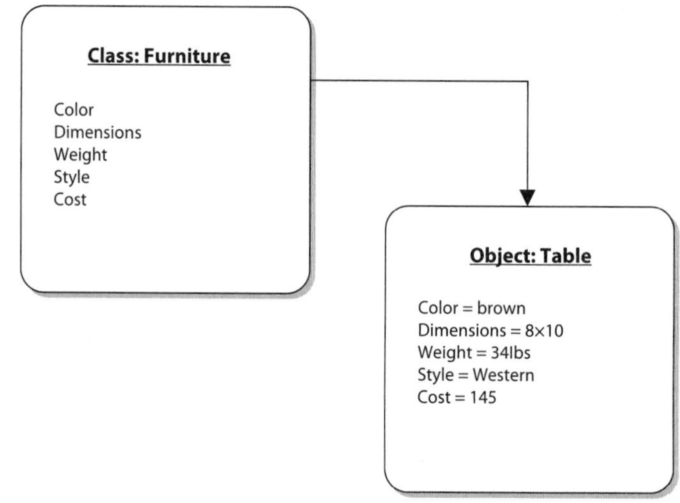

Figure 8-14 In object-oriented inheritance, each object belongs to a class and takes on the attributes of that class

does all of this through automation and provides the customer with a lovely cup of coffee exactly to her liking. The next customer wants a mocha frappuccino, with whole milk, and extra foam. So the goal is to make something once (coffee maker, class), allow it to accept requests through an interface, and create various results (cups of coffee, objects) depending upon the requests submitted.

But how does the class create objects based on requests? A piece of software that is written in OOP will have a request sent to it, usually from another object. The requesting object wants a new object to carry out some type of functionality. Let's say that object A wants object B to carry out subtraction on the numbers sent from A to B. When this request comes in, an object is built (instantiated) with all of the necessary programming code. Object B carries out the subtraction task and sends the result back to object A. It does not matter what programming language the two objects are written in; what matters is if they know how to communicate with each other. One object can communicate with another object if it knows the application programming interface (API) communication requirements. An API is the mechanism that allows objects to talk to each other. Let's say you want to talk to Jorge, but can only do so by speaking French and can only use three phrases or less, because that is all Jorge understands. As long as you follow these rules, you can talk to Jorge. If you don't follow these rules, you can't talk to Jorge.

TIP An object is an instance of a class.

So what's so great about OOP? If you look at Figure 8-15, you can see the difference between OOP and non-OOP techniques. Non-OOP applications are written as monolithic entities. This means an application is just one big pile of code (sometimes

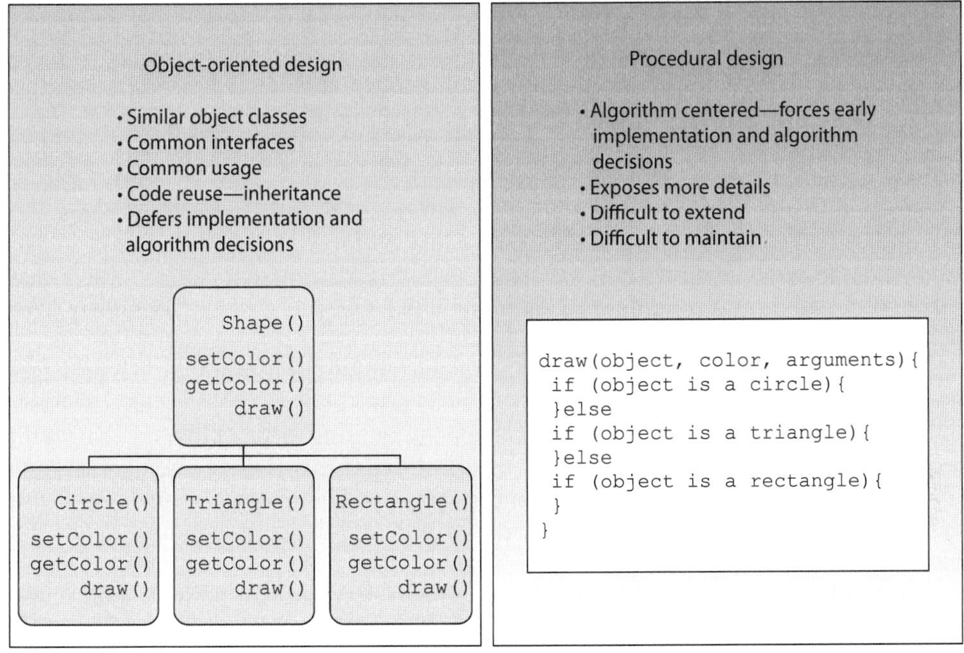

Figure 8-15 Procedural vs. object-oriented programming

called spaghetti code). If you need to change something in this pile, you would need to go through the whole program's logic functions to figure out what your one change is going to break. If the program contains hundreds or thousands of lines of code, this is not an easy or enjoyable task. Now, if you choose to write your program in an object-oriented language, you don't have one monolithic application, but an application that is made up of smaller components (objects). If you need to make changes or updates to some functionality in your application, you can just change the code within the class that creates the object carrying out that functionality and not worry about everything else the program actually carries out. The following breaks down the benefits of OOP:

- **Modularity** The building blocks of software are autonomous objects, cooperating through the exchange of messages.
- **Deferred commitment** The internal components of an object can be redefined without changing other parts of the system.
- **Reusability** Classes are reused by other programs, though they may be refined through inheritance.
- **Naturalness** Object-oriented analysis, design, and modeling map to business needs and solutions.

Most applications have some type of functionality in common. Instead of developing the same code to carry out the same functionality for ten different applications, using OOP allows you to just create the object only once and let it be reused in other applications. This reduces development time and saves money.

Now that we've covered the concepts of OOP, let's clarify the terminology used. A *method* is the functionality or procedure an object can carry out. An object may be constructed to accept data from a user and to reformat the request so a back-end server can understand and process it. Another object may perform a method that extracts data from a database and populates a web page with this information. Or an object may carry out a withdrawal procedure to allow the user of an ATM to extract money from her account.

The objects *encapsulate* the attribute values, which means this information is packaged under one name and can be reused as one entity by other objects. Objects need to be able to communicate with each other, and this happens by using *messages* that are sent to the receiving object's API. If object A needs to tell object B that a user's checking account must be reduced by $40, it sends object B a message. The message is made up of the destination, the method that needs to be performed, and the corresponding arguments. Figure 8-16 shows this example.

Messaging can happen in several ways. A given object can have a single connection (one-to-one) or multiple connections (one-to-many). It is important to map these communication paths to identify if information can flow in a way that is not intended. This will help ensure that sensitive data cannot be passed to objects of a lower security level.

An object can have a shared portion and a private portion. The *shared* portion is the interface (API) that enables it to interact with other components. Messages enter through the interface to specify the requested operation, or method, to be performed. The *private* portion of an object is how it actually works and performs the requested operations. Other components need not know how each object works internally—only that it does the job requested of it. This is how *data hiding* is possible. The details of the processing are hidden from all other program elements outside the object. Objects communicate through well-defined interfaces; therefore, they do not need to know how each other works internally.

NOTE Data hiding is provided by encapsulation, which protects an object's private data from outside access. No object should be allowed to, or have the need to, access another object's internal data or processes.

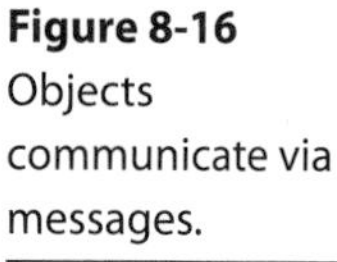

Figure 8-16 Objects communicate via messages.

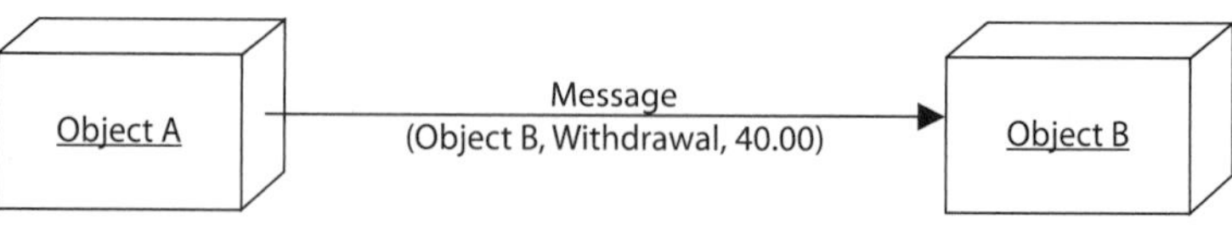

These objects can grow to great numbers, so the complexity of understanding, tracking, and analyzing can get a bit overwhelming. Many times, the objects are shown in connection to a reference or pointer in documentation. Figure 8-17 shows how related objects are represented as a specific piece, or reference, in a bank ATM system. This enables analysts and developers to look at a higher level of operation and procedures without having to view each individual object and its code. Thus, this modularity provides for a more easily understood model.

Abstraction, as discussed earlier, is the capability to suppress unnecessary details so the important, inherent properties can be examined and reviewed. It enables the separation of conceptual aspects of a system. For example, if a software architect needs to understand how data flows through the program, she would want to understand the big pieces of the program and trace the steps the data takes from first being input into the program all the way until it exits the program as output. It would be difficult to understand this concept if the small details of every piece of the program were presented. Instead, through abstraction, all the details are suppressed so the software architect can understand a crucial part of the product. It is like being able to see a forest without having to look at each and every tree.

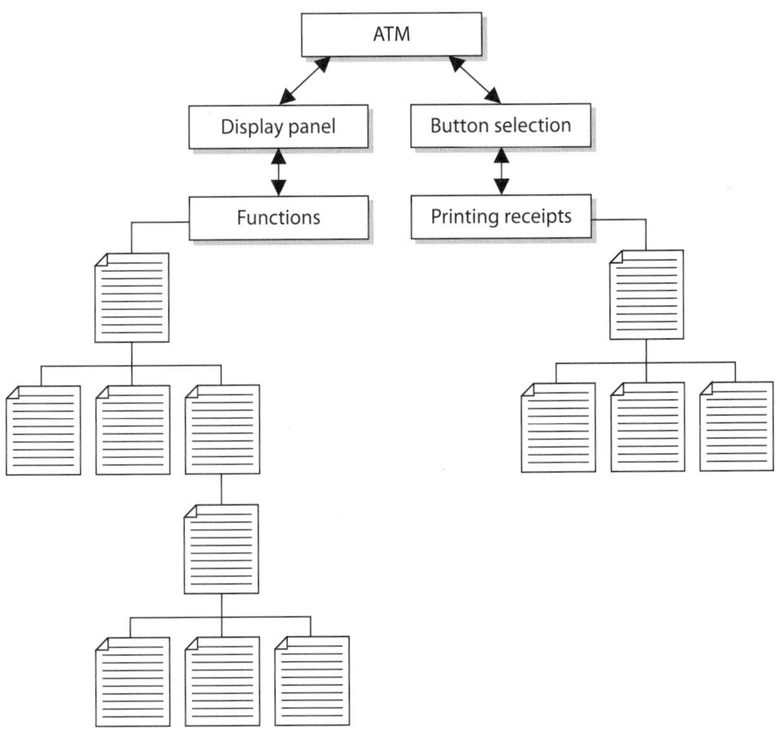

Figure 8-17 Object relationships within a program

Each object should have specifications it adheres to. This discipline provides cleaner programming and reduces programming errors and omissions. The following list is an example of what should be developed for each object:

- Object name
- Attribute descriptions
- Attribute name
- Attribute content
- Attribute data type
- External input to object
- External output from object
- Operation descriptions
- Operation name
- Operation interface description
- Operation processing description
- Performance issues
- Restrictions and limitations
- Instance connections
- Message connections

The developer creates a class that outlines these specifications. When objects are instantiated, they inherit these attributes.

Each object can be reused as stated previously, which is the beauty of OOP. This enables a more efficient use of resources and the programmer's time. Different applications can use the same objects, which reduces redundant work, and as an application grows in functionality, objects can be easily added and integrated into the original structure.

The objects can be catalogued in a library, which provides an economical way for more than one application to call upon the objects (see Figure 8-18). The library provides an index and pointers to where the objects actually live within the system or on another system.

When applications are developed in a modular approach, like object-oriented methods, components can be reused, complexity is reduced, and parallel development can be done. These characteristics allow for fewer mistakes, easier modification, resource efficiency, and more timely coding than the classic programming languages. OOP also provides functional independence, which means each module addresses a specific subfunction of requirements and has an interface that is easily understood by other parts of the application.

An object is *encapsulated*, meaning the data structure (the operation's functionality) and the acceptable ways of accessing it are grouped into one entity. Other objects, subjects, and applications can use this object and its functionality by accessing it through controlled and standardized interfaces and sending it messages (see Figure 8-19).

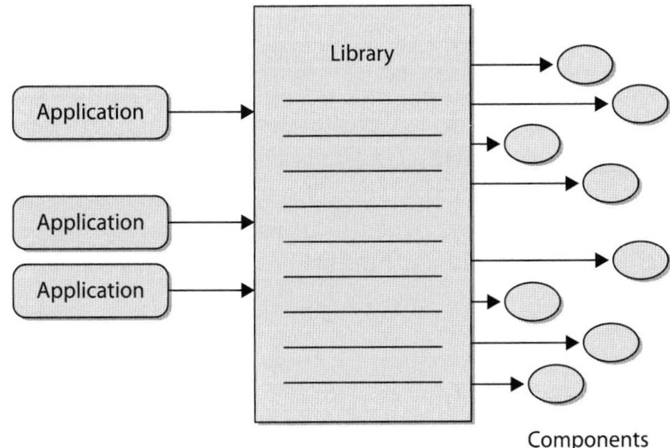

Figure 8-18 Applications locate the necessary objects through a library index.

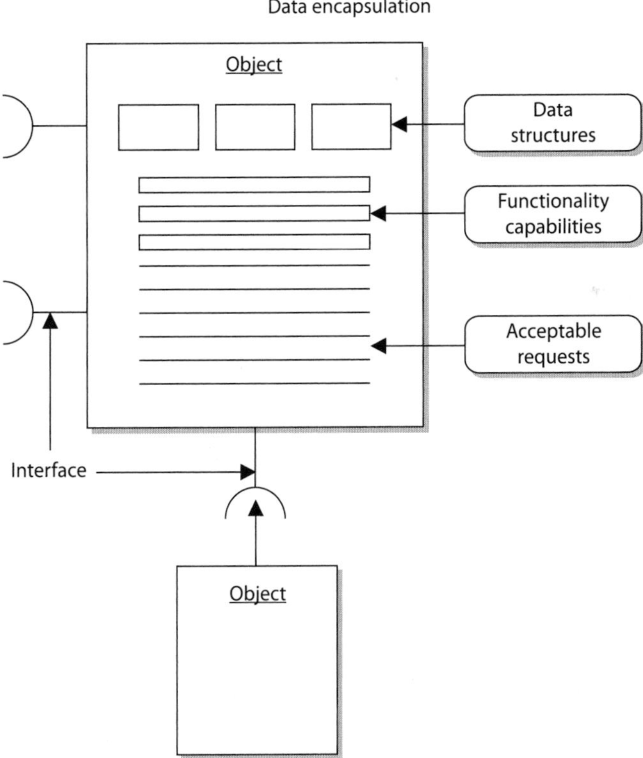

Figure 8-19 The different components of an object and the way it works are hidden from other objects.

Polymorphism

Polymorphism comes from the Greek, meaning "having multiple forms." This concept usually confuses people, so let's jump right into an example. If you develop a program in an OOP language, you can create a variable that can be used in different forms. The application will determine what form to use at the time of execution (run time). So if your variable is named USERID and you develop the object so the variable can accept either an integer or letters, this provides flexibility. This means the user ID can be accepted as a number (account number) or name (characters). If application A uses this object, it can choose to use integers for the user IDs, while application B can choose to use characters.

What confuses people about the term polymorphism is that the International Information Systems Security Certification Consortium, known as $(ISC)^2$, commonly uses the following definition or description: "Two objects can receive the same input and have different outputs." Clear as mud.

As a simplistic example of polymorphism, suppose three different objects receive the input "Bob." Object A would process this input and produce the output "43-year-old white male." Object B would receive the input "Bob" and produce the output "Husband of Sally." Object C would produce the output "Member of User group." Each object received the same input, but responded with a different output.

Polymorphism can also take place in the following example: Object A and Object B are created from the same parent class, but Object B is also under a subclass. Object B would have some different characteristics from Object A because of this inheritance from the parent class *and* the subclass. When Object A and Object B receive the same input, they would result in different outputs because only one of them inherited characteristics from the subclass.

EXAM TIP Polymorphism takes place when different objects respond to the same command, input, or message in different ways.

OOA vs. OOD

Object-oriented analysis (OOA) is the process of classifying objects that will be appropriate for a solution. A problem is analyzed to determine the classes of objects to be used in the application.

Object-oriented design (OOD) creates a representation of a real-world problem and maps it to a software solution using OOP. The result of an OOD is a design that modularizes data and procedures. The design interconnects data objects and processing operations.

Other Software Development Concepts

Regardless of the approach to software development, there are some concepts that are universal in this field. Data modeling, data structures, and the concepts of cohesion and coupling are important when developing quality software. Quality is focused on minimizing the number of errors, which in turn means the software will have fewer vulnerabilities and be more secure.

Data Modeling

Data modeling considers data independently of both the way the data is processed and the components that process the data. A data model follows an input value from beginning to end and verifies that the output is correct. OOA is an example of a structured analysis approach. If an analyst is reviewing the OOA of an application, she will make sure all relationships are set up correctly, that the inheritance flows in a predictable and usable manner, that the instances of objects are practical and provide the necessary functionality, and that the attributes of each class cover all the necessary values used by the application. When another analyst does a data model review of the same application, he will follow the data and the returned values after processing takes place. An application can have a perfect OOA structure, but when 1 + 1 is entered and it returns –3, something is wrong. This is one aspect that data modeling looks at.

Another example of data modeling deals with databases. Data modeling can be used to provide insight into the data and the relationships that govern it. A data item in one file structure, or data store, might be a pointer to another file structure or to a different data store. These pointers must actually point to the right place. Data modeling would verify this, not OOA structure analysis.

Data Structures

A *data structure* is a representation of the logical relationship between elements of data. It dictates the degree of association among elements, methods of access, processing alternatives, and the organization of data elements.

The structure can be simple in nature, like the scalar item, which represents a single element that can be addressed by an identifier and accessed by a single address in storage. The scalar items can be grouped in arrays, which provide access by indexes. Other data structures include hierarchical structures by using multilinked lists that contain scalar items, vectors, and possibly arrays. The hierarchical structure provides categorization and association. If a user can make a request of an application to find all computer books written on security, and that application returns a list, then this application is using a hierarchical data structure of some kind. Figure 8-20 shows simple and complex data structures.

So from a security perspective, not only do you need to understand the vulnerabilities related to a poorly architected and designed piece of software, but you need to understand the complexity issues of how the software components communicate with each other and the type of data format that is used.

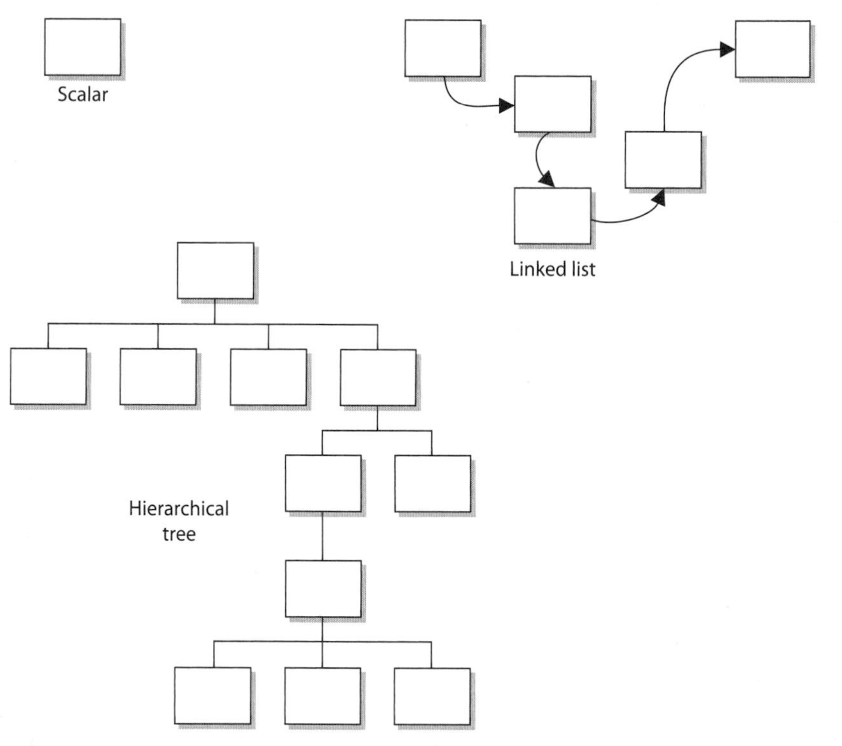

Figure 8-20 Data structures range from very simple to very complex in nature and design.

Cohesion and Coupling

Cohesion reflects how many different types of tasks a module can carry out. If a module carries out only one task (i.e., subtraction) or tasks that are very similar (i.e., subtract, add, multiply), it is described as having high cohesion, which is a good thing. The higher the cohesion, the easier it is to update or modify and not affect other modules that interact with it. This also means the module is easier to reuse and maintain because it is more straightforward when compared to a module with low cohesion. An object with low cohesion carries out multiple *different* tasks and increases the complexity of the module, which makes it harder to maintain and reuse. So you want your objects focused, manageable, and understandable. Each object should carry out a single function or similar functions. One object should not carry out mathematical operations, graphic rendering, and cryptographic functions—these are separate functionality types and it would be confusing to keep track of this level of complexity. If you do this, you are trying to shove too much into one object. Objects should carry out modular, simplistic functions—that is the whole point of OOP.

Coupling is a measurement that indicates how much interaction one module requires to carry out its tasks. If a module has low (loose) coupling, this means the module does not need to communicate with many other modules to carry out its job. High (tight) coupling means a module depends upon many other modules to carry out its tasks. Low coupling is more desirable because the modules are easier to understand and easier to reuse, and changes can take place and not affect many modules around it. Low coupling indicates that the programmer created a well-structured module. As an analogy, a company would want its employees to be able to carry out their individual jobs with the least amount of dependencies on other workers. If Joe has to talk with five other people just to get one task done, too much complexity exists, it's too time-consuming, and more places are created where errors can take place.

If modules are tightly coupled, the ripple effect of changing just one module can drastically affect the other modules. If they are loosely coupled, this level of complexity reduces.

An example of *low coupling* would be one module passing a variable value to another module. As an example of *high coupling*, Module A would pass a value to Module B, another value to Module C, and yet another value to Module D. Module A could not complete its tasks until Modules B, C, and D completed their tasks and returned results back to Module A.

EXAM TIP Objects should be self-contained and perform a single logical function, which is high cohesion. Objects should not drastically affect each other, which is low coupling.

The level of complexity involved with coupling and cohesion can have a direct relationship on the security level of a program. The more complex something is, the harder it is to secure. Developing "tight code" not only allows for efficiencies and effectiveness, but also reduces the software's attack surface. Decreasing complexity where possible reduces the number of potential holes a bad guy can sneak through. As an analogy, if you were responsible for protecting a facility, it would be easier if the facility had a small number of doors, windows, and people coming in and out of it. The smaller number of variables and moving pieces would help you keep track of things and secure them.

Application Programming Interfaces

When we discussed some of the attributes of object-oriented development, we spent a bit of time on the concept of abstraction. Essentially, it is all about defining *what* a class or object does with no regard to *how* that is accomplished internally. An *application programming interface (API)* specifies the manner in which a software component interacts with other software components. Not only does this encourage software reuse, but it also makes the software more maintainable by localizing the changes that need to be made while eliminating (or at least reducing) cascading effects of fixes or changes.

APIs are perhaps most familiar to us in the context of software libraries. A software library is a collection of components that do specific things that are useful to many other components. For example, there are software libraries for various encryption algorithms, managing network connections, and displaying graphics. These allow software developers to work on whatever makes their program unique, while leveraging known-good code for the things that similar programs routinely do. All the programmer needs to do is understand the API for the libraries she intends to use. This reduces the amount of new code that needs to be developed, which in turn makes it easier to secure and maintain.

Besides the advantages of reduced effort and improved maintainability, APIs are oftentimes required in order to employ the underlying operating system's functionality. Apple Mac OS X and iOS, Google Android, and Microsoft Windows all require developers to use standard APIs for access to operating system functionality such as opening and closing files and network connections, among many others. This is also true of many disturbed computing frameworks, which is a topic we discuss next.

Distributed Computing

Many of our applications work in a client/server model, which means the smaller part (client) of the application can run on different systems and the larger piece (server) of the application runs on a single, and commonly more powerful, back-end system. The server portion carries out more functionality and has more horsepower compared to the clients. The clients will send the server requests, and the server will respond with results. Simple enough, but how do the client and server pieces actually carry out communication with each other?

A distributed object computing model needs to *register* the client and server components, which means to find out where they live on the network, what their names or IDs are, and what type of functionality the different components carry out. So the first step is basically, "Where are all the pieces, how do I call upon them when I need them, and what do they do?" This organization must be put in place because the coordination between the components should be controlled and monitored, and requests and results must be able to pass back and forth between the correct components.

Life might be easier if we had just one intercomponent communication architecture for developers to follow, but what fun would that be? The various architectures work a little differently from each other and are necessary to work in specific production environments. Nevertheless, they all perform the basic function of allowing components on the client and server sides to communicate with each other.

Distributed Computing Environment

Distributed Computing Environment (DCE) is a standard developed by the Open Software Foundation (OSF), also called Open Group. It is a client/server framework that is available to many vendors to use within their products. This framework illustrates how various capabilities can be integrated and shared between heterogeneous systems. DCE provides a Remote Procedure Call (RPC) service, security service, directory service, time service, and distributed file support. It was one of the first attempts at distributed computing in the industry.

DCE is a set of management services with a communications layer based on RPC. It is a layer of software that sits on the top of the network layer and provides services to the applications above it. DCE and Distributed Component Object Model (DCOM) offer much of the same functionality. DCOM, however, was developed by Microsoft and is more proprietary in nature.

DCE's time service provides host clock synchronization and enables applications to determine sequencing and to schedule events based on this clock synchronization. This time synchronization is for applications. Users cannot access this functionality directly. The directory service enables users, servers, and resources to be contacted anywhere on the network. When the directory service is given the name, it returns the network address of the resource along with other necessary information. DCOM uses a *globally unique identifier (GUID)*, while DCE uses a *universal unique identifier (UUID)*. They are both used to uniquely identify users, resources, and components within an environment. DCE is illustrated in Figure 8-21.

The RPC function collects the arguments and commands from the sending program and prepares them for transmission over the network. RPC determines the network transport protocol to be used and finds the receiving host's address in the directory service. The thread service provides real-time priority scheduling in a multithreading environment. The security services support authentication and authorization services.

DCE was the first attempt at standardizing heterogeneous system communication through a client/server model. Though one would be hard-pressed to find it running as such on any production system, it provided many of the foundational concepts for distributed computing technologies that followed it, as in CORBA, DCOM, and J2EE, which we will cover next. Microsoft DCOM, in particular, relies extensively on DCE and RPC.

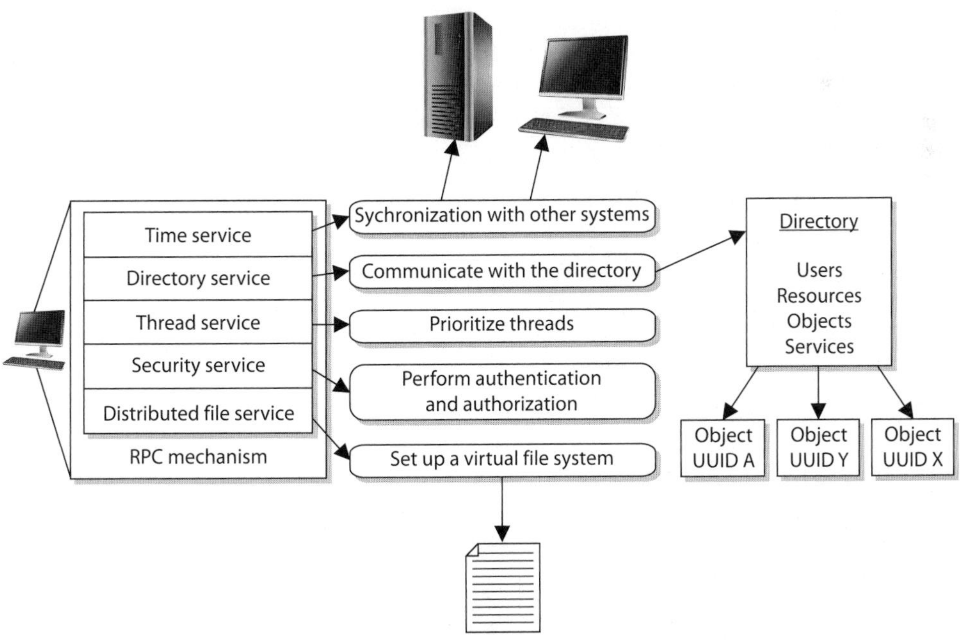

Figure 8-21 DCE provides many services, which are all wrapped into one technology.

CORBA and ORBs

If we want software components to be able to communicate with each other, this means standardized interfaces and communication methods must be used. This is the only way interoperability can take place.

Common Object Request Broker Architecture (CORBA) is an open object-oriented standard architecture developed by the Object Management Group (OMG). It provides interoperability among the vast array of software, platforms, and hardware in environments today. CORBA enables applications to communicate with one another no matter where the applications are located or who developed them.

This standard defines the APIs, communication protocol, and client/server communication methods to allow heterogeneous applications written in different programming languages and run on various platforms to work together. The model defines object semantics so the external visible characteristics are standard and are viewed the same by all other objects in the environment. This standardization enables many different developers to write hundreds or thousands of components that can interact with other components in an environment without having to know how the components actually work. The developers know how to communicate with the components because the interfaces are uniform and follow the rules of the model.

In this model, clients request services from objects. The client passes the object a message that contains the name of the object, the requested operation, and any necessary parameters.

The CORBA model provides standards to build a complete distributed environment. It contains two main parts: system-oriented components (*object request brokers [ORBs]* and object services) and application-oriented components (application objects and common facilities). The ORB manages all communications between components and enables them to interact in a heterogeneous and distributed environment, as shown in Figure 8-22. The ORB works independently of the platforms where the objects reside, which provides greater interoperability.

Figure 8-22 The ORB enables different components throughout a network to communicate and work with each other.

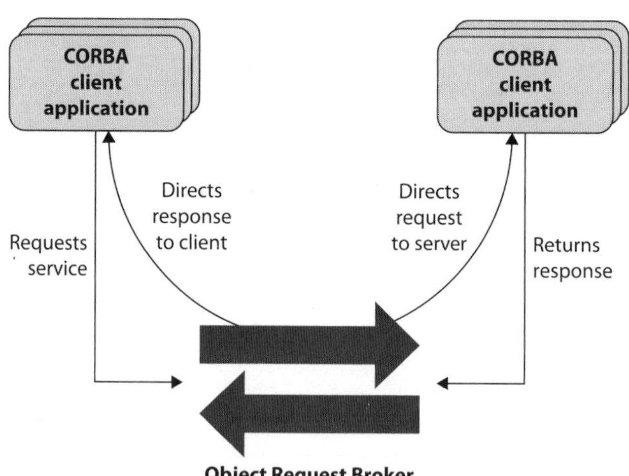

ORB is the middleware that allows the client/server communication to take place between objects residing on different systems. When a client needs some type of functionality to be carried out, the ORB receives the request and is responsible for locating the necessary object for that specific task. Once the object is found, the ORB invokes a method (or operation), passes the parameters, and returns the result to the client. The client software does not need to know where the object resides or go through the trouble of finding it. That is the ORB's job. As an analogy, when you call someone on your mobile phone, you do not have to worry about physically locating that person so your data can be passed back and forth. The mobile phones and the telecommunications network take care of that for you.

Software that works within the CORBA model can use objects that are written in different programming languages and that reside on different operating systems and platforms, as long as the software follows all the rules to allow for such interoperability (see Figure 8-23).

ORBs provide communications between distributed objects. If an object on a workstation must have an object on a server process data, it can make a request through the ORB, which will track down the needed object and facilitate the communication path between these two objects until the process is complete.

ORBs are mechanisms that enable objects to communicate locally or remotely. They enable objects to make requests to objects and receive responses. This happens transparently to the client and provides a type of pipeline between all corresponding objects. Using CORBA enables an application to be usable with many different types of ORBs. It provides portability for applications and tackles many of the interoperability

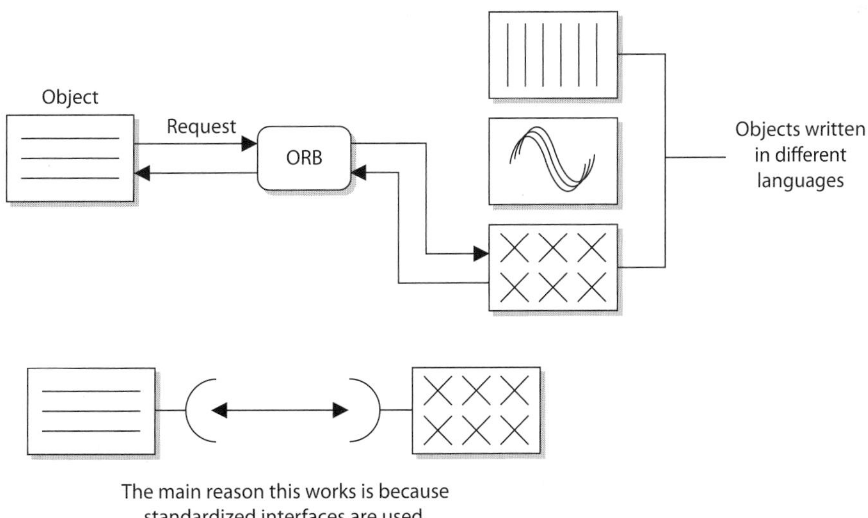

Figure 8-23 CORBA provides standard interface definitions, which offer greater interoperability in heterogeneous environments.

issues that many vendors and developers run into when their products are implemented into different environments.

COM and DCOM

The *Component Object Model (COM)* allows for interprocess communication within one application or between applications on the same computer system. The model was created by Microsoft and outlines standardized APIs, component naming schemes, and communication standards. So if you are a developer and you want your application to be able to interact with the Windows operating system and the different applications developed for this platform, you will follow the COM outlined standards.

The *Distributed Component Object Model (DCOM)* supports the same model for component interaction, and also supports *distributed* interprocess communication (IPC). COM enables applications to use components on the same systems, while DCOM enables applications to access objects that reside in different parts of a network. So this is how the client/server-based activities are carried out by COM-based operating systems and/or applications.

Without DCOM, programmers would have to write much more complicated code to find necessary objects, set up network sockets, and incorporate the services necessary to allow communication. DCOM takes care of these issues (and more), and enables the programmer to focus on his tasks of developing the necessary functionality within his application. DCOM has a library that takes care of session handling, synchronization, buffering, fault identification and handling, and data format translation.

DCOM works as the middleware that enables distributed processing and provides developers with services that support process-to-process communications across networks (see Figure 8-24).

Other types of distributed interprocessing technologies provide similar functionality: ORB, message-oriented middleware (MOM), Open Database Connectivity (ODBC), and so on. DCOM provides ORB-like services, data connectivity services, distributed

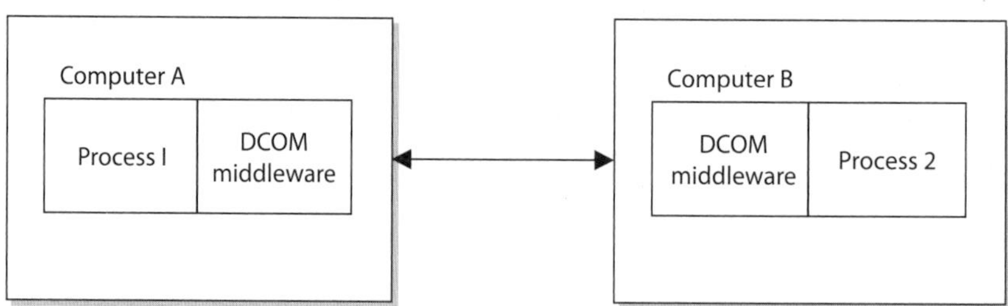

Figure 8-24 DCOM provides communication mechanisms in a distributed environment and works in the COM architecture.

messaging services, and distributed transaction services layered over its RPC mechanism. DCOM integrates all of these functionalities into one technology that uses the same interface as COM.

Although DCOM is still in use on many systems, it has been largely replaced with the *.NET framework*, which is mainly used for applications that run in Windows environments. The framework has a large library that different applications can call upon. The libraries provide functions as in data access, database connectivity, network communication, etc. Programs that are written to work in this framework execute in application virtual machines, which provide memory management, exception handling, and many types of security services. A program that is written to work in this type of environment is compiled to an intermediate code type (Common Language Runtime), and then when the code is executed at run time, this happens within the application virtual machine, as illustrated in Figure 8-25.

Object Linking and Embedding

Object Linking and Embedding (OLE) provides a way for objects to be shared on a local personal computer and to use COM as their foundation. OLE enables objects—such as graphics, clipart, and spreadsheets—to be embedded into documents. The capability for

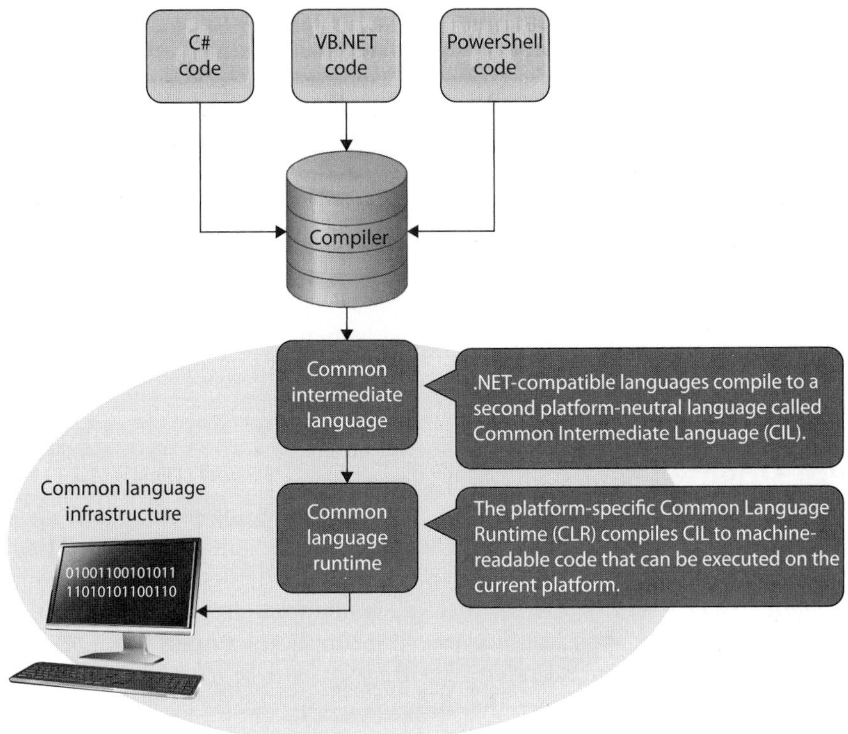

Figure 8-25 .NET Framework components

one program to call another program is called *linking*. The capability to place a piece of data inside a foreign program or document is called *embedding*.

OLE also allows for linking different objects and documents. For example, when Chrissy creates a document that contains a Uniform Resource Locator (URL), that URL turns blue and is underlined, indicating a user can just double-click it to be taken to the appropriate website. This is an example of linking capabilities. If Chrissy inserts a spreadsheet into her document, this is also an instance of embedding. If she needs to edit the spreadsheet, she can double-click the spreadsheet, and the operating system will open the correct environment (which might be Excel) to let her make her changes.

This technology was evolved to work on the World Wide Web and is called ActiveX, which we cover later in this chapter. The components are meant to be portable. ActiveX components can run on any platform that supports DCOM (using the COM model) or that communicates using DCOM services.

Java Platform, Enterprise Edition

Another distributed computing model is based upon the Java programming language, which is the *Java Platform, Enterprise Edition (Java EE)*. Just as the COM and CORBA models were created to allow a modular approach to programming code with the goal of interoperability, Java EE defines a client/server model that is object oriented and platform independent.

Java EE is an enterprise Java computing platform. This means it is a framework that is used to develop enterprise software written mainly in the Java programming language. It provides APIs for networking services, fault tolerance, security, and web services for large-scale, multitiered network applications. It takes advantage of the "Write Once, Run Anywhere" capability of Java; it provides a Java-based, database-access API; and its interprocess communications are based upon CORBA. The main goal is to have a standardized method of implementing back-end code that carries out business logic for enterprise-wide applications.

The Java EE application server can handle scalability, concurrency, transactions, and various security services for the client. The goal is to allow the developers to be able to concentrate on the business logic functionality instead of the "plumbing" that is under the covers.

Service-Oriented Architecture

While many of the previously described distributed computing technologies are still in use, the industry has moved toward and integrated another approach in providing commonly needed application functionality and procedures across various environments. A *service-oriented architecture (SOA)* provides standardized access to the most needed services to many different applications at one time. Application functionality is separated into distinct units (services) and offered up through well-defined interfaces and data-sharing standardization. This means that individual applications do not need to possess the same redundant code and functionality. The functionality can be offered by an individual entity and then all other applications can just call upon and use the one instance.

This is really the crux of all distributed computing technologies and approaches—SOA is just a more web-based approach.

As an analogy, every home does not have its own electrical power grid. A geographical area has a power grid, and all homes and offices tap into that one resource. There is a standardized method of each home accessing the power grid and obtaining the energy it needs. The same concept applies with SOA: applications access one centralized place that provides the functionality they require. A simple interface abstracts (hides) the underlying complexity, which allows for applications to call upon the services without needing to understand the service provider's programming language or its platform implementation. For services to be able to be used (and reused) in an interoperable manner, they must be modular in nature, autonomous, loosely coupled, follow standardized service identification and categorization, and provide provisioning and delivery.

The entity that will provide a service in an SOA environment sends a service-description document to a service broker. The *service broker* is basically a map of all the services available within a specific environment. When an application needs a specific service, it makes a call to the broker, which points the application to the necessary service provider, as shown in Figure 8-26.

Services within an SOA are usually provided through web services. A *web service* allows for web-based communication to happen seamlessly using web-based standards, as in Simple Object Access Protocol (SOAP), HTTP, Web Services Description Language (WSDL), Universal Description, Discovery and Integration (UDDI), and Extensible Markup Language (XML). WSDL provides a machine-readable description of the specific operations provided by the service. UDDI is an XML-based registry that lists available services. It provides a method for services to be registered by service providers and located by service consumers. UDDI provides the mechanisms to allow businesses around the world to publish their services and others to discover and use these services. When a service consumer needs to know what service is available and where it is located, it sends a message to the service broker. Through its UDDI approach, the broker can provide access to the WSDL document that describes the requirements for interacting with the requested service. The service consumer now knows how to locate the service provider and how to communicate with it. The consumer then requests and accesses the

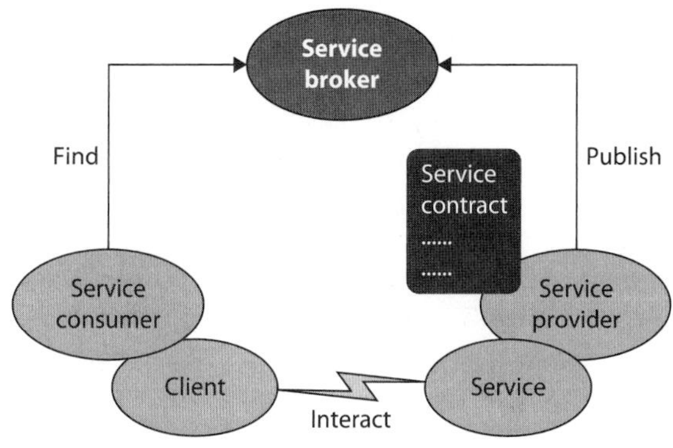

Figure 8-26 Services are located through brokers in an SOA.

service using SOAP, which is an XML-based protocol that is used to exchange messages between a requester and provider of a web service. Figure 8-27 illustrates how these different components work together.

Web services commonly provide the functional building blocks for an SOA. New services are represented in this format using these standards, and/or existing applications are wrapped within a web service structure to allow for legacy systems to participate in SOA environments also.

There has been controversy and confusion on the distinction and similarities among SOA, mashups, Web 2.0, Software as a Service (SaaS), and cloud computing. The evolution of Web 1.0 to *Web 2.0* pertains to the move from static websites that provide content and some functionality to an Internet where everyone can basically be a content provider and consumer. Through the use of Facebook, YouTube, Twitter, Flickr, and other sites, normal users can provide content to the digital world without having to understand HTML, JavaScript, web server software, and other technologies. Websites provide intricate functionality instead of just static content. The extensive manner in which information sharing, collaboration, and interaction can happen through social networking sites, blogs, wikis, hosted services, mashups, and video sharing really embodies the essence of the concept of Web 2.0. This makes for a more exciting Internet, but increased complexity for security professionals, who are responsible for understanding and securing software that maintains sensitive information.

A *mashup* is the combination of functionality, data, and presentation capabilities of two or more sources to provide some type of new service or functionality. Open APIs and data sources are commonly aggregated and combined to provide a more useful and powerful resource. For example, the site http://popurls.com combines the functionality of APIs provided by sites like Digg, Del.icio.us, Flickr, and YouTube to provide integrated social news.

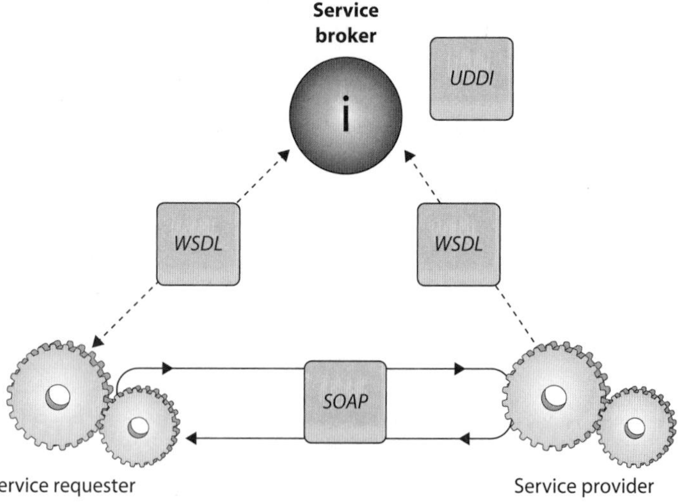

Figure 8-27 Web services are posted and used via standard approaches.

SOAP

What if we need applications running on different operating systems, which were written in different programming languages, to communicate over web-based communication methods? We would use *Simple Object Access Protocol (SOAP)*. SOAP is an XML-based protocol that encodes messages in a web service environment. It actually defines an XML schema of how communication is going to take place. The SOAP XML schema defines how objects communicate directly.

So SOAP is a component that helps provide distributed computing through the use of web applications. A request for an application comes from one computer (client) and is transmitted over a web-based environment (i.e., Internet) to another computer (server). While there are various distributed computing technologies, SOAP makes it easy by using XML and HTTP, which are already standard web formats.

One advantage of SOAP is that the program calls will most likely get through firewalls because HTTP communication is commonly allowed. This helps ensure that the client/server model is not broken by getting denied by a firewall in between the communicating entities.

Cloud computing is a method of providing computing as a service rather than as a physical product. It provides processing computation capabilities, storage, and software without the end user needing to know or worry about the physical location and/or configuration of the devices and software that provide this functionality. Cloud computing extends technical capabilities through a subscription-based or pay-per-use service structure. Scalable resources are consolidated and commonly used in a virtualized manner. This technology is covered more in depth in Chapter 3, but it is being presented here to illustrate the differences and similarities pertaining to the outgrowth of Internet capabilities and the use of distributed computing technologies.

Software as a Service (SaaS) is a cloud computing model that allows applications and data to be centrally hosted and accessed by thin clients, commonly web browsers. It is similar to the old centralized mainframe model, but commonly takes place over the Internet. SaaS delivers many business applications providing functionality, as in customer relationship management (CRM), enterprise resource planning (ERP), human resource management (HRM), content management (CM), and more. Most people are familiar with Salesforce.com, which was one of the first SaaS products to become available.

So DCE was the first attempt at providing client/server distributed computing capabilities and worked mainly in Unix-based environments. CORBA is a model that allows for interoperability and distributed computing for mostly non-Microsoft applications. Software that needed to work in a distributed computing environment of mostly Microsoft products first followed the DCOM model, which evolved into the .NET framework. Large enterprise-wide applications that are based upon Java can carry out distributed computing by following the Java EE model. And web-based distributed computing happens through web services and SOA frameworks. Each of these has the same basic goal, which is to allow a client application component on one computer to be able to communicate with a server application on another computer. The biggest difference between these models pertains to the environment the applications will be working within: Unix, Windows, heterogeneous, or web-based.

While distributed computing technologies allow for various systems and applications to communicate and share functionality, this can add layers of complexity when it comes to security. The client and server portions need to carry out mutual authentication to ensure that hackers do not introduce rogue applications and carry out man-in-the-middle attacks. Each communicating component needs to share similar cryptographic functionality so that the necessary encryption can take place. The integrity of the data and messages that are passed between communicating components needs to be protected. End-to-end secure transmission channels might be necessary to protect communication data. The list of security requirements can go on and on, but the point is that just getting software components to be able to communicate in a heterogeneous environment can be challenging—but securing these complex communication methods can prove to be maddening.

As a security professional, you really need to understand how software talks to other software under the covers. You can patch systems, implement access control lists (ACLs), harden operating systems, and more but still have unprotected RPC traffic taking place between applications that are totally insecure. Security has to be integrated at *every* level, including interprocess communication channels.

Mobile Code

Code that can be transmitted across a network, to be executed by a system or device on the other end, is called *mobile code*. There are many legitimate reasons to use mobile code—for example, web browser applets that may execute in the background to download additional content for the web page, such as plug-ins that allow you to view a video.

The cautions arise when a website downloads code intended to do malicious or compromising actions, especially when the recipient is unaware that the compromising activity is taking place. If a website is compromised, it can be used as a platform from which to launch attacks against anyone visiting the site and just browsing. Some of the common types of mobile code are covered in the next sections.

CAUTION Mobile code has been a regular vector for attacks for years. Except in carefully controlled environments, it should be considered risky.

Java Applets

Java is an object-oriented, platform-independent programming language. It is employed as a full-fledged programming language and is used to write complete programs and small components, called *applets*, which commonly run in a user's web browser.

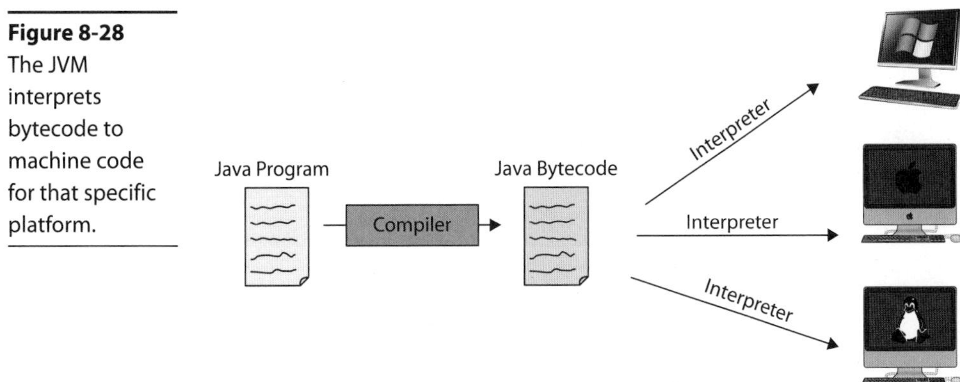

Figure 8-28 The JVM interprets bytecode to machine code for that specific platform.

Other languages are compiled to object code for a specific operating system and processor. This is why a particular application may run on Windows but not on Mac OS. An Intel processor does not necessarily understand machine code compiled for an ARM processor, and vice versa. Java is platform independent because it creates intermediate code, *bytecode*, which is not processor-specific. The *Java Virtual Machine (JVM)* converts the bytecode to the machine code that the processor on that particular system can understand (see Figure 8-28). Let's quickly walk through these steps:

1. A programmer creates a Java applet and runs it through a compiler.
2. The Java compiler converts the source code into bytecode (non-processor-specific).
3. The user downloads the Java applet.
4. The JVM converts the bytecode into machine-level code (processor-specific).
5. The applet runs when called upon.

When an applet is executed, the JVM will create a virtual machine, which provides an environment called a *sandbox*. This virtual machine is an enclosed environment in which the applet carries out its activities. Applets are commonly sent over within a requested web page, which means the applet executes as soon as it arrives. It can carry out malicious activity on purpose or accidentally if the developer of the applet did not do his part correctly. So the sandbox strictly limits the applet's access to any system resources. The JVM mediates access to system resources to ensure the applet code behaves and stays within its own sandbox. These components are illustrated in Figure 8-29.

NOTE The Java language itself provides protection mechanisms, such as garbage collection, memory management, validating address usage, and a component that verifies adherence to predetermined rules.

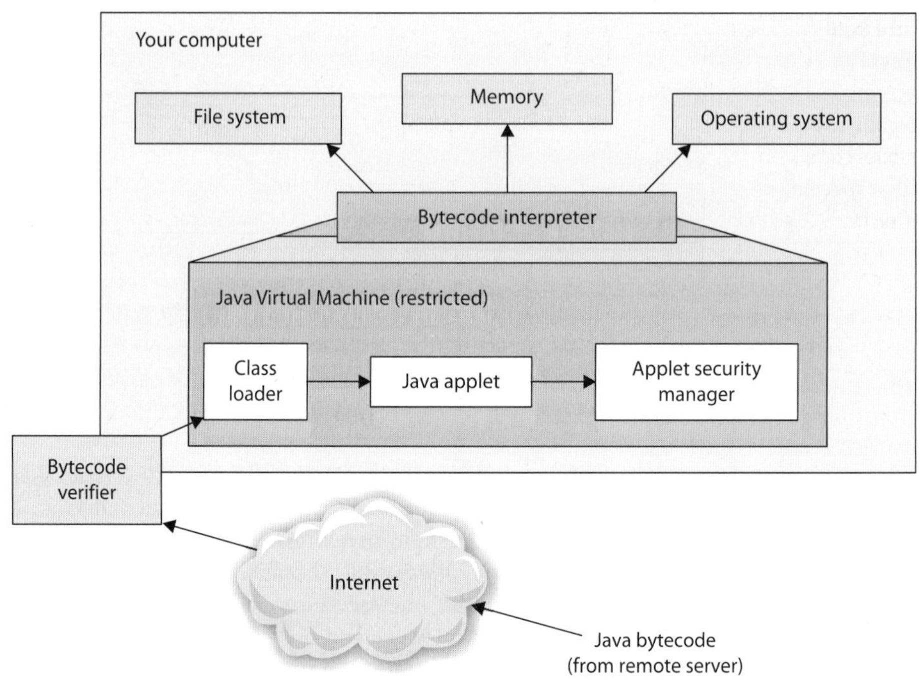

Figure 8-29 Java's security model

However, as with many other things in the computing world, the bad guys have figured out how to escape the confines and restrictions of the sandbox. Programmers have figured out how to write applets that enable the code to access hard drives and resources that are supposed to be protected by the Java security scheme. This code can be malicious in nature and cause destruction and mayhem to the user and her system.

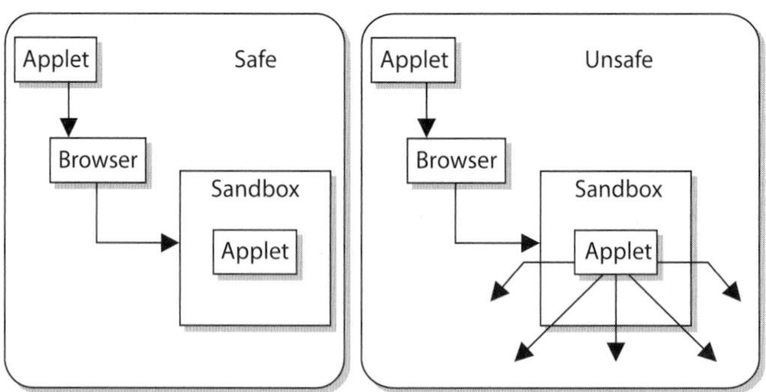

ActiveX Controls

ActiveX is a Microsoft technology composed of a set of OOP technologies and tools based on COM and DCOM. A programmer uses these tools to create *ActiveX controls*, which are self-sufficient programs (similar to Java applets) that can be executed in the Windows environment. ActiveX controls can be reused by many applications within one system or different systems within an environment. These controls can be downloaded from websites to add extra functionality (as in providing animations for web pages), but they are also components of Windows operating systems themselves (dynamic link libraries [DLLs]) and carry out common operating system tasks.

ActiveX allow web browsers to execute other software applications within the browser that can play media files, open Portable Document Files (PDF) documents, etc. An ActiveX control can be automatically downloaded and executed by a web browser. Once downloaded, an ActiveX control in effect becomes part of the operating system. Initially ActiveX controls were intended to work on individual systems only, and hence there weren't many security issues. Security issues started emerging only after OLE began to be used to embed ActiveX controls in web pages. The problem lay in the fact that ActiveX controls shared the privilege levels of the current user on a system, and since these controls could be built by anyone, a malicious ActiveX control would have sufficient privilege to compromise the system security and other systems connected through it. This was worsened by the fact that ActiveX controls were able to download further ActiveX components without user authentication, creating a very favorable environment for worm propagation.

ActiveX comes with a *component container* feature that allows multiple applications and networked computers to reuse active components. This drastically reduced the program development time. This feature too has been exploited by attackers to gain access to critical files on networked systems. Numerous patches have been released to counter reported ActiveX exploits.

ActiveX technology provides security levels and authentication settings, letting users control the security of the ActiveX components they download. Unlike Java applets, ActiveX components are downloaded to a user's hard drive when he chooses to add the functionality the component provides. This means the ActiveX component has far greater access to the user's system compared to Java applets.

The security-level setting of the user's browser dictates whether an ActiveX component is downloaded automatically or whether the user is first prompted with a warning. The security level is configurable by the user via his browser controls. As the security level increases, so, too, does the browser's sensitivity level to digitally signed and unsigned components and controls, and to the initialization of ActiveX scripts.

The main security difference between Java applets and ActiveX controls is that Java sets up a sandbox for the applet code to execute in, and this restricts the code's access to resources within the user's computer. ActiveX uses Authenticode technology, which relies on digital certificates and trusting certificate authorities. Although both are extremely important and highly used technologies, they have inherent flaws. Java has not been able to ensure that all code stays within the sandbox, which has caused several types of security compromises. Authenticode doesn't necessarily provide security—in fact, it often presents annoying dialog boxes to users. Since most users do not understand this technology, they continually click OK because they don't understand the risks involved.

NOTE Microsoft now longer supports ActiveX in its Edge web browser.

Web Security

When it comes to the Internet and web-based applications, many security situations are unique to this area. Companies use the Internet to expose products or services to the widest possible audience; thus, they need to allow an uncontrollable number of entities on the Internet to access their web servers. In most situations companies must open up the ports related to the web-based traffic (80 and 443) on their firewalls, which are commonly used avenues for a long list of attacks.

The web-based applications themselves are somewhat mysterious to the purveyors of the Internet as well. If you want to sell your homemade pies via the Internet, you'll typically need to display them in graphic form and allow some form of communication for questions (via e-mail or online chat). You'll need some sort of shopping cart if you want to actually collect money for your pies, and typically you'll have to deal with interfacing with shipping and payment processing channels. If you are a master baker, you probably *aren't* a webmaster, so now you'll have to rely on someone else to set up your website and load the appropriate applications on it. Should you develop your own PHP- or Java-based application, the benefits could be wonderful, having a customized application that would further automate your business, but the risks of developing an in-house application (especially if it's your first time) are great if you haven't developed the methodology, development process, quality assurance, and change control, as well as identified the risks and vulnerabilities.

The alternative to developing your own web application is using an off-the-shelf variety instead. Many commercial and free options are available for nearly every e-commerce need. These are written in a variety of languages, by a variety of entities, so now the issue is, "Whom should we trust?" Do these developers have the same processes in place that you would have used yourself? Have these applications been developed and tested with the appropriate security in mind? Will these applications introduce any vulnerabilities along with the functionality they provide? Does your webmaster understand the security implications associated with the web application he suggests you use on your site for certain functionality? These are the problems that plague not only those wanting to sell homemade pies on the Internet, but also financial institutions, auction sites, and everyone who is involved in e-commerce. With these issues in mind, let's try to define the most glaring threats associated with web-based applications and transactions.

Specific Threats for Web Environments

The most common types of vulnerabilities, threats, and complexities are covered in the following sections, which we will explore one at a time:

- Administrative interfaces
- Authentication and access control

- Input validation
- Parameter validation
- Session management

Administrative Interfaces

Everyone wants to work from the coffee shop or at home in their pajamas. Webmasters and web developers are particularly fond of this concept. Although some systems mandate that administration be carried out from a local terminal, in most cases, there is an interface to administer the systems remotely, even over the Web. While this may be convenient to the webmaster, it also provides an entry point into the system for an unauthorized user.

Since we are talking about the Web, using a web-based administrative interface is, in most opinions, a bad idea. If we are willing to accept the risk, the administrative interface should be at least as secure as (if not more than) the web application or service we are hosting.

A bad habit that's found even in high-security environments is hard-coding authentication credentials into the links to the management interfaces, or enabling the "remember password" option. This does make it easier on the administrator but offers up too much access to someone who stumbles across the link, regardless of their intentions.

Most commercial software and web application servers install some type of administrative console by default. Knowing this and being cognizant of the information-gathering techniques previously covered should be enough for organizations to take this threat seriously. If the management interface is not needed, it should be disabled. When custom applications are developed, the existence of management interfaces is less known, so consideration should be given to this in policy and procedures.

The simple countermeasure for this threat requires that the management interfaces be removed, but this may upset your administrators. Using a stronger authentication mechanism would be better than the standard username/password scenario. Controlling which systems are allowed to connect and administer the system is another good technique. Many systems allow specific IP addresses or network IDs to be defined that only allow administrative access from these stations.

Ultimately, the most secure management interface for a system would be one that is *out-of-band*, meaning a separate channel of communication is used to avoid any vulnerabilities that may exist in the environment that the system operates in. An example of out-of-band would be using a modem connected to a web server to dial in directly and configure it using a local interface, as opposed to connecting via the Internet and using a web interface. This should only be done through an encrypted channel, as in Secure Shell (SSH).

Authentication and Access Control

If you've used the Internet for banking, shopping, registering for classes, or working from home, you most likely logged in through a web-based application. From the consumer side or the provider side, the topic of authentication and access control is an obvious issue. Consumers want an access control mechanism that provides the security and privacy they would expect from a trusted entity, but they also don't want to be too burdened by the process. From the service providers' perspective, they want to provide the highest amount of security to the consumer that performance, compliance, and cost will allow. So, from both of these perspectives, typically usernames and passwords are still used to control access to most web applications.

Passwords do not provide much confidence when it comes to truly proving the identity of an entity. They are used because they are cheap, already built into existing software, and users are comfortable with using them. But passwords don't prove conclusively that the user "jsmith" is *really* John Smith; they just prove that the person using the account jsmith has typed in the correct password. Systems that hold sensitive information (medical, financial, and so on) are commonly identified as targets for attackers. Mining usernames via search engines or simply using common usernames (like jsmith) and attempting to log in to these sites is very common. If you've ever signed up at a website for access to download a "free" document or file, what username did you use? Is it the same one you use for other sites? Maybe even the same password? Crafty attackers might be mining information via other websites that seem rather friendly, offering to evaluate your IQ and send you the results, or enter you into a sweepstakes. Remember that untrained, unaware users are an organization's biggest threat.

Many financial organizations that provide online banking functionality have implemented multifactor authentication requirements. A user may need to provide a username, password, and then a one-time password value that was sent to their cell phone or e-mail during the authentication process.

Finally, a best practice is to exchange all authentication information (and all authenticated content) via a secure mechanism. This will typically mean to encrypt the credential and the channel of communication through Transport Layer Security (TLS). Some sites, however, still don't use encrypted authentication mechanisms and have exposed themselves to the threat of attackers sniffing usernames and passwords.

Input Validation

Web servers are just like any other software applications; they can only carry out the functionality their instructions dictate. They are designed to process requests via a certain protocol. When a person searches on Google for the term "cissp," the browser sends a request of the form *https://www.google.com/?q=cissp* using a protocol called Hypertext Transfer Protocol (HTTP). It passes the parameter "q=cissp" to the web application on the host called www in the domain google.com. A request in this form is called a Uniform Resource Locator (URL). Like many situations in our digital world, there is more than one way to request something because computers speak several different "languages"—such as binary, hexadecimal, and many encoding mechanisms—each of which is interpreted and processed by the system as valid commands. Validating that these requests are allowed is part of *input validation* and is usually tied to coded validation rules within the web server software. Attackers have figured out how to bypass some of these coded validation rules.

Some input validation attack examples follow:

- **Path or directory traversal** This attack is also known as the "dot dot slash" because it is perpetrated by inserting the characters "../" several times into a URL to back up or traverse into directories that weren't supposed to be accessible from the Web. The command "../" at the command prompt tells the system to back up to the previous directory (i.e., "cd ../"). If a web server's default directory is c:\inetpub\www, a URL requesting http://www.website.com/scripts/../../../../../windows/system32/cmd.exe?/c+dir+c:\ would issue the command to back up several directories to ensure it has gone all the way to the root of the drive and then make the request to change to the operating system directory (windows\system32) and run the cmd.exe listing the contents of the C: drive. Access to the command shell allows extensive access for the attacker.
- **Unicode encoding** Unicode is an industry-standard mechanism developed to represent the entire range of over 100,000 textual characters in the world as a standard coding format. Web servers support Unicode to support different character sets (for different languages), and, at one time, many web server software applications supported it by default. So, even if we told our systems to not allow the "../" directory traversal request previously mentioned, an attacker using Unicode could effectively make the same directory traversal request without using "/" but with any of the Unicode representations of that character (three exist: %c1%1c, %c0%9v, and %c0%af). That request may slip through unnoticed and be processed.
- **URL encoding** Ever notice a "space" that appears as "%20" in a URL in a web browser? The "%20" represents the space because spaces aren't allowed characters in a URL. Much like the attacks using Unicode characters, attackers found that they could bypass filtering techniques and make requests by representing characters differently.

Almost every web application is going to have to accept some input. When you use the Web, you are constantly asked to input information such as usernames, passwords, and credit card information. To a web application, this input is just data that is to be processed like the rest of the code in the application. Usually, this input is used as a variable and fed into some code that will process it based on its logic instructions, such as IF [username input field]=X AND [password input field]=Y THEN Authenticate. This will function well assuming there is always correct information put into the input fields. But what if the wrong information is input? Developers have to cover all the angles. They have to assume that sometimes the wrong input will be given, and they have to handle that situation appropriately. To deal with this, a routine is usually coded in that will tell the system what to do if the input isn't what was expected.

Client-side validation is when the input validation is done at the client before it is even sent back to the server to process. If you've missed a field in a web form and before clicking Submit, you immediately receive a message informing you that you've forgotten to fill in one of the fields, you've experienced client-side validation. Client-side validation is a good idea because it avoids incomplete requests being sent to the server and the server having to send back an error message to the user. The problem arises when the client-side validation is the *only* validation that takes place. In this situation, the server trusts that the client has done its job correctly and processes the input as if it is valid. In normal situations, accepting this input would be fine, but when an attacker can intercept the traffic between the client and server and modify it or just directly make illegitimate requests to the server without using a client, a compromise is more likely.

In an environment where input validation is weak, an attacker will try to input specific operating system commands into the input fields instead of what the system is expecting (such as the username and password) in an effort to trick the system into running the rogue commands. Remember that software can only do what it's programmed to do, and if an attacker can get it to run a command, the software will execute the command just as it would if the command came from a legitimate application. If the web application is written to access a database, as most are, there is the threat of *SQL injection*, where instead of valid input, the attacker puts actual database commands into the input fields, which are then parsed and run by the application. SQL (Structured Query Language) statements can be used by attackers to bypass authentication and reveal all records in a database.

Remember that different layers of a system (see Figure 8-30) all have their own vulnerabilities that must be identified and fixed.

A similar type of attack is *cross-site scripting (XSS)*, in which an attacker discovers and exploits a vulnerability on a website to inject malicious code into a web application. XSS attacks enable an attacker to inject their malicious code (in client-side scripting languages, such as JavaScript) into vulnerable web pages. When an unsuspecting user visits the infected page, the malicious code executes on the victim's browser and may lead to stolen cookies, hijacked sessions, malware execution, or bypassed access control, or aid in exploiting browser vulnerabilities. There are three different XSS vulnerabilities:

- *Nonpersistent XSS* vulnerabilities, or reflected vulnerabilities, occur when an attacker tricks the victim into processing a URL programmed with a rogue script to steal the victim's sensitive information (cookie, session ID, etc.). The principle behind this attack lies in exploiting the lack of proper input or output validation on dynamic websites.
- *Persistent XSS* vulnerabilities, also known as stored or second-order vulnerabilities, are generally targeted at websites that allow users to input data that is stored in a database or any other such location, e.g., forums, message boards, guest books, etc. The attacker posts some text that contains some malicious JavaScript, and when other users later view the posts, their browsers render the page and execute the attacker's JavaScript.
- *DOM (Document Object Model)*–based XSS vulnerabilities are also referred to as local cross-site scripting. DOM is the standard structure layout to represent HTML and XML documents in the browser. In such attacks the document components such as form fields and cookies can be referenced through JavaScript. The attacker uses the DOM environment to modify the original client-side JavaScript. This causes the victim's browser to execute the resulting abusive JavaScript code.

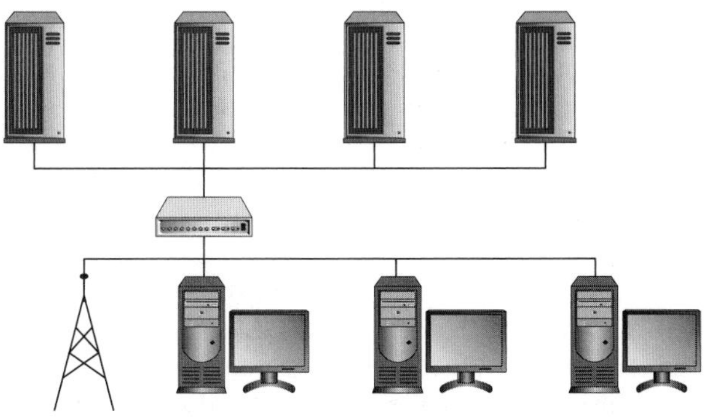

Security policies	Password policy audit policy, system access policy, user rights...
Web applications	Apache, Internet Explorer, Firefox, Microsoft IIS, FTP, Tomcat, WebLogic, ColdFusion, SSH, Telnet...
Third-party applications	IBM Notes, Microsoft Exchange, Adobe Acrobat, Windows Media, Sendmail...
Databases	Oracle, Microsoft SQL Server, MySQL, IBM DB2, Sybase, IBM Domino...
Operating systems	Microsoft Windows, Linux, Unix Solaris, Mac OS, BSD, AIX, Novell NetWare......
Networks	IPSec, PPTP, Network File System, DHCP, DNS, LDAP, SNMP...
Hardware	Routers, switches, hubs, wireless access points, hardware firewalls...

Figure 8-30 Attacks can take place at many levels.

A number of applications are vulnerable to XSS attacks. The most common ones include online forums, message boards, search boxes, social networking websites, links embedded in e-mails, etc. Although cross-site attacks are primarily web application vulnerabilities, they may be used to exploit vulnerabilities in the victim's web browser. Once the system is successfully compromised by the attackers, they may further penetrate into other systems on the network or execute scripts that may spread through the internal network.

The attacks in this section have the related issues of assuming that you can think of all the possible input values that will reach your web application, the effects that specially encoded data has on an application, and believing the input that is received is always valid. The countermeasures to many of these attacks would be to filter out all "known" malicious requests, never trust information coming from the client without first validating it, and implement a strong policy to include appropriate parameter checking in all applications.

Parameter Validation

The issue of parameter validation is akin to the issue of input validation mentioned earlier. *Parameter validation* is where the values that are being received by the application are validated to be within defined limits before the server application processes them within the system. The main difference between parameter validation and input validation would have to be whether the application was expecting the user to input a value as opposed to an environment variable that is defined by the application. Attacks in this area deal with manipulating values that the system would assume are beyond the client being able to configure, mainly because there isn't a mechanism provided in the interface to do so.

In an effort to provide a rich end-user experience, web application designers have to employ mechanisms to keep track of the thousands of different web browsers that could be connected at any given time. The HTTP protocol by itself doesn't facilitate managing the state of a user's connection; it just connects to a server, gets whatever objects (the .htm file, graphics, and so forth) are requested in the HTML code, and then disconnects. If the browser disconnects or times out, how does the server know how to recognize this? Would you be irritated if you had to re-enter *all* of your information *again* because you spent too long looking at possible flights while booking a flight online? Since most people would, web developers employ the technique of passing a cookie to the client to help the server remember things about the state of the connection. A cookie isn't a program, but rather just data passed and stored in memory (called a *session cookie*), or locally as a file (called a *persistent cookie*), to pass state information back to the server. An example of how cookies are employed would be a shopping cart application used on a commercial website. As you put items into your cart, they are maintained by updating a session cookie on your system. You may have noticed the "Cookies must be enabled" message that some websites issue as you enter their site.

Since accessing a session cookie in memory is usually beyond the reach of most users, most web developers didn't think about this as a serious threat when designing their systems. It is not uncommon for web developers to enable account lockout after a certain number of unsuccessful login attempts have occurred. If a developer is using a session cookie to keep track of how many times a client has attempted to log in, there may be a vulnerability here. If an application didn't want to allow more than three unsuccessful logins before locking a client out, the server might pass a session cookie to the client, setting a value such as "number of allowed logins = 3." After each unsuccessful attempt, the server would tell the client to decrement the "number of allowed logins" value. When the value reaches 0, the client would be directed to a "Your account has been locked out" page.

A *web proxy* is a piece of software installed on a system that is designed to intercept all traffic between the local web browser and the web server. Using freely available web proxy software (such as Paros Proxy or Burp Suite), an attacker could monitor and modify any information as it travels in either direction. In the preceding example, when the server tells the client via a session cookie that the "number of allowed logins = 3," if that information is intercepted by an attacker using one of these proxies and he changes the value to "number of allowed logins = 50000," this would effectively allow a brute-force attack on the system if it has no other validation mechanism in place.

Using a web proxy can also exploit the use of hidden fields in web pages. As its name indicates, a hidden field is not shown in the user interface, but contains a value that is passed to the server when the web form is submitted. The exploit of using hidden values can occur when a web developer codes the prices of items on a web page as hidden values instead of referencing the items and their prices on the server. The attacker uses the web proxy to intercept the submitted information from the client and changes the value (the price) before it gets to the server. This is surprisingly easy to do and, assuming no other checks are in place, would allow the perpetrator to see the new values specified in the e-commerce shopping cart.

The countermeasure that would lessen the risk associated with these threats would be *adequate parameter validation*, which may include pre-validation and post-validation controls. In a client/server environment, pre-validation controls may be placed on the client side prior to submitting requests to the server. Even when these are employed, the server should perform parallel pre-validation of input prior to application submission because a client will have fewer controls than a server, and may have been compromised or bypassed.

- **Pre-validation** Input controls verifying data is in appropriate format and compliant with application specifications prior to submission to the application. An example of this would be form field validation, where web forms do not allow letters in a field that is expecting to receive a number (currency) value.
- **Post-validation** Ensuring an application's output is consistent with expectations (that is, within predetermined constraints of reasonableness).

Session Management

As highlighted earlier, managing several thousand different clients connecting to a web-based application is a challenge. The aspect of *session management* requires consideration before delivering applications via the Web. The most commonly used method of managing client sessions is to assign unique session IDs to every connection. A *session ID* is a value sent by the client to the server with every request that uniquely identifies the client to the server or application. In the event that an attacker were able to acquire or even guess an authenticated client's session ID and render it to the server as its own session ID, the server would be fooled and the attacker would have access to the session.

The old "never send anything in cleartext" rule certainly applies here. HTTP traffic is unencrypted by default and does nothing to combat an attacker sniffing session IDs off the wire. Because session IDs are usually passed in, and maintained, via HTTP, they should be protected in some way.

An attacker being able to predict or guess the session IDs would also be a threat in this type of environment. Using sequential session IDs for clients would be a mistake.

Random session IDs of an appropriate length would counter session ID prediction. Building in some sort of timestamp or time-based validation will combat *replay attacks*, a simple attack in which an attacker captures the traffic from a legitimate session and replays it to authenticate his session. Finally, any cookies that are used to keep state on the connection should also be encrypted.

Web Application Security Principles

Considering their exposed nature, websites are primary targets during an attack. It is, therefore, essential for web developers to abide by the time-honored and time-tested principles to provide the maximum level of deterrence to attackers. Web application security principles are meant to govern programming practices to regulate programming styles and strategically reduce the chances of repeating known software bugs and logical flaws.

A good number of websites are exploited on the basis of vulnerabilities arising from reckless programming. With the forever growing number of websites out there, the possibility of exploiting the exploitable code is vast.

The first pillar of implementing security principles is analyzing the website architecture. The clearer and simpler a website is, the easier it is to analyze its various security aspects. Once a website has been strategically analyzed, the user-generated input fed into the website also needs to be critically scrutinized. As a rule, all input must be considered unsafe, or rogue, and ought to be sanitized before being processed. Likewise, all output generated by the system should also be filtered to ensure private or sensitive data is not being disclosed.

In addition, using encryption helps secure the input/output operations of a web application. Though encrypted data may be intercepted by malicious users, it should only be readable, or modifiable, by those with the secret key used to encrypt it.

In the event of an error, websites ought to be designed to behave in a predictable and noncompromising manner. This is also generally referred to as *failing securely*. Systems that fail securely display friendly error messages without revealing internal system details.

An important element in designing security functionality is keeping in perspective the human element. Though programmers may be tempted to prompt users for passwords on every mouse click, to keep security effective, web developers must maintain a state of equilibrium between functionality and security. Tedious authentication techniques usually do not stay in practice for too long. Experience has shown that the best security measures are those that are simple, intuitive, and psychologically acceptable.

A common but ineffective approach to security implementation is the use of "security through obscurity." Security through obscurity assumes that creating overly complex or perplexing programs can reduce the chances of interventions in the software. Though obscure programs may take a tad longer to dissect, this does not guarantee protection from resolute and determined attackers. Protective measures, hence, cannot consist solely of obfuscation.

At the end, it is important to realize that the implementation of even the most beefy security techniques, without tactical considerations, will cause a website to remain as weak as its weakest link. That link could very well allow adversaries to reach the crown jewels of most organizations: their data.

Database Management

Databases have a long history of storing important intellectual property and items that are considered valuable and proprietary to companies. Because of this, they usually live in an environment of mystery to all but the database and network administrators. The less anyone knows about the databases, the better. Users generally access databases indirectly through a client interface, and their actions are restricted to ensure the confidentiality, integrity, and availability of the data held within the database and the structure of the database itself.

The risks are increasing as companies run to connect their networks to the Internet, allow remote user access, and provide more and more access to external entities. A large risk to understand is that these activities can allow indirect access to a back-end database. In the past, employees accessed customer information held in databases instead of allowing customers to access it themselves. Today, many companies allow their customers to access data in their databases through a browser. The browser makes a connection to the company's middleware, which then connects them to the back-end database. This adds levels of complexity, and the database is accessed in new and unprecedented ways.

One example is in the banking world, where online banking is all the rage. Many financial institutions want to keep up with the times and add the services they think their customers will want. But online banking is not just another service like being able to order checks. Most banks work in closed (or semiclosed) environments, and opening their environments to the Internet is a huge undertaking. The perimeter network needs to be secured, middleware software has to be developed or purchased, and the database should be behind one or, preferably, multiple firewalls. Many times, components in the business application tier are used to extract data from the databases and process the customer requests.

Access control can be restricted by only allowing roles to interact with the database. The database administrator can define specific roles that are allowed to access the database. Each role has assigned rights and permissions, and customers and employees are then ported into these roles. Any user who is not within one of these roles is denied access. This means that if an attacker compromises the firewall and other perimeter network protection mechanisms, and then is able to make requests to the database, if he is not in one of the predefined roles, the database is still safe. This process streamlines access control and ensures that no users or evildoers can access the database directly, but must access it indirectly through a role account. Figure 8-31 illustrates these concepts.

Database Management Software

A *database* is a collection of data stored in a meaningful way that enables multiple users and applications to access, view, and modify that data as needed. Databases are managed with software that provides these types of capabilities. It also enforces access control restrictions, provides data integrity and redundancy, and sets up different procedures for data manipulation. This software is referred to as a *database management system (DBMS)* and is usually controlled by database administrators. Databases not only store data, but may also process data and represent it in a more usable and logical form. DBMSs

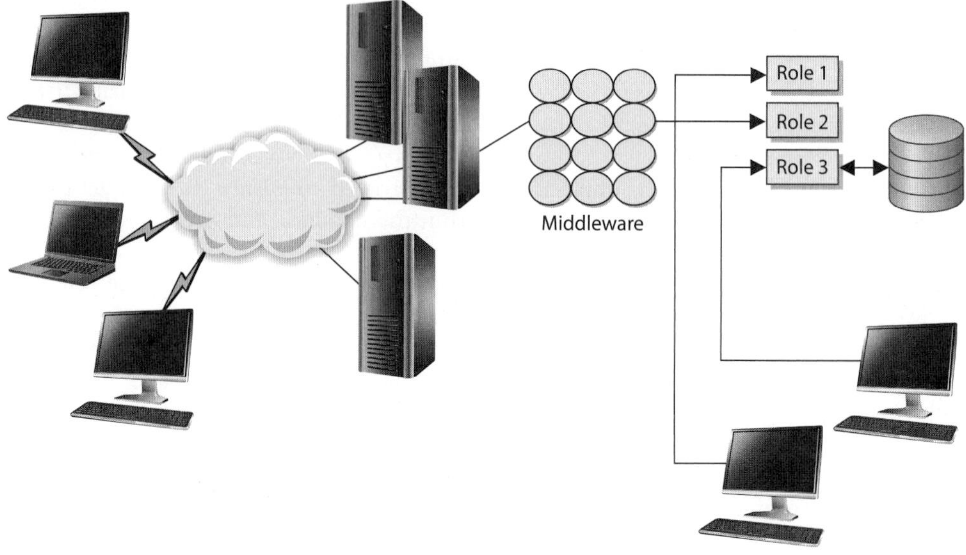

Figure 8-31 One type of database security is to employ roles.

interface with programs, users, and data within the database. They help us store, organize, and retrieve information effectively and efficiently.

NOTE A database management system (DBMS) is a suite of programs used to manage large sets of structured data with ad hoc query capabilities for many types of users. A DBMS can also control the security parameters of the database.

A database is the mechanism that provides structure for the data collected. The actual specifications of the structure may be different per database implementation, because different organizations or departments work with different types of data and need to perform diverse functions upon that information. There may be different workloads, relationships between the data, platforms, performance requirements, and security goals. Any type of database should have the following characteristics:

- It ensures consistency among the data held on several different servers throughout the network.
- It allows for easier backup procedures.
- It provides transaction persistence.
- It provides recovery and fault tolerance.
- It allows the sharing of data with multiple users.
- It provides security controls that implement integrity checking, access control, and the necessary level of confidentiality.

NOTE *Transaction persistence* means the database procedures carrying out transactions are durable and reliable. The state of the database's security should be the same after a transaction has occurred, and the integrity of the transaction needs to be ensured.

Because the needs and requirements for databases vary, different data models can be implemented that align with different business and organizational needs.

Database Models

The database model defines the relationships between different data elements; dictates how data can be accessed; and defines acceptable operations, the type of integrity offered, and how the data is organized. A model provides a formal method of representing data in a conceptual form and provides the necessary means of manipulating the data held within the database. Databases come in several types of models, as listed next:

- Relational
- Hierarchical
- Network
- Object-oriented
- Object-relational

A *relational database model* uses attributes (columns) and tuples (rows) to contain and organize information (see Figure 8-32). The relational database model is the most widely used model today. It presents information in the form of tables. A relational database is composed of two-dimensional tables, and each table contains unique rows, columns, and cells (the intersection of a row and a column). Each cell contains only one data value that represents a specific attribute value within a given tuple. These data entities are linked by relationships. The relationships between the data entities provide the framework for organizing data. A *primary key* is a field that links all the data within a record to a unique value. For example, in the table in Figure 8-32, the primary keys are Product G345 and

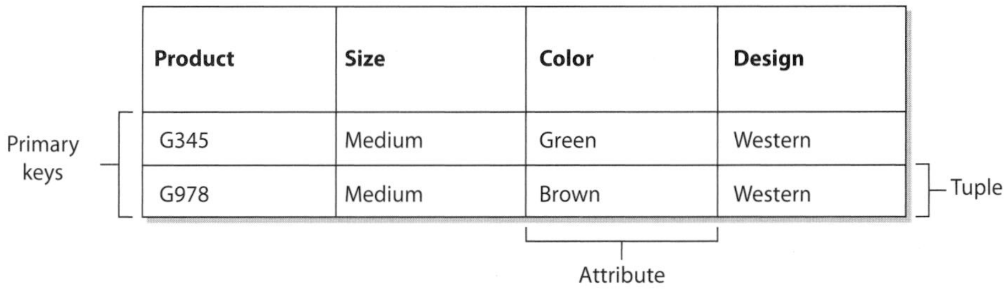

Product	Size	Color	Design
G345	Medium	Green	Western
G978	Medium	Brown	Western

Figure 8-32 Relational databases hold data in table structures.

Product G978. When an application or another record refers to this primary key, it is actually referring to all the data within that given row.

A *hierarchical data model* (see Figure 8-33) combines records and fields that are related in a logical tree structure. The structure and relationship between the data elements are different from those in a relational database. In the hierarchical database the parents can have one child, many children, or no children. The tree structure contains branches, and each branch has a number of leaves, or data fields. These databases have well-defined, prespecified access paths, but are not as flexible in creating relationships between data elements as a relational database. Hierarchical databases are useful for mapping one-to-many relationships.

The hierarchical structured database is one of the first types of database model created, but is not as common as relational databases. To be able to access a certain data entity within a hierarchical database requires the knowledge of which branch to start with and which route to take through each layer until the data is reached. Unlike relational databases, it does not use indexes to search procedures, and links (relationships) cannot be created between different branches and leaves on different layers.

NOTE The hierarchical model is almost always employed when building indexes for relational databases. An index can be built on any attribute and allows for very fast searches of the data over that attribute.

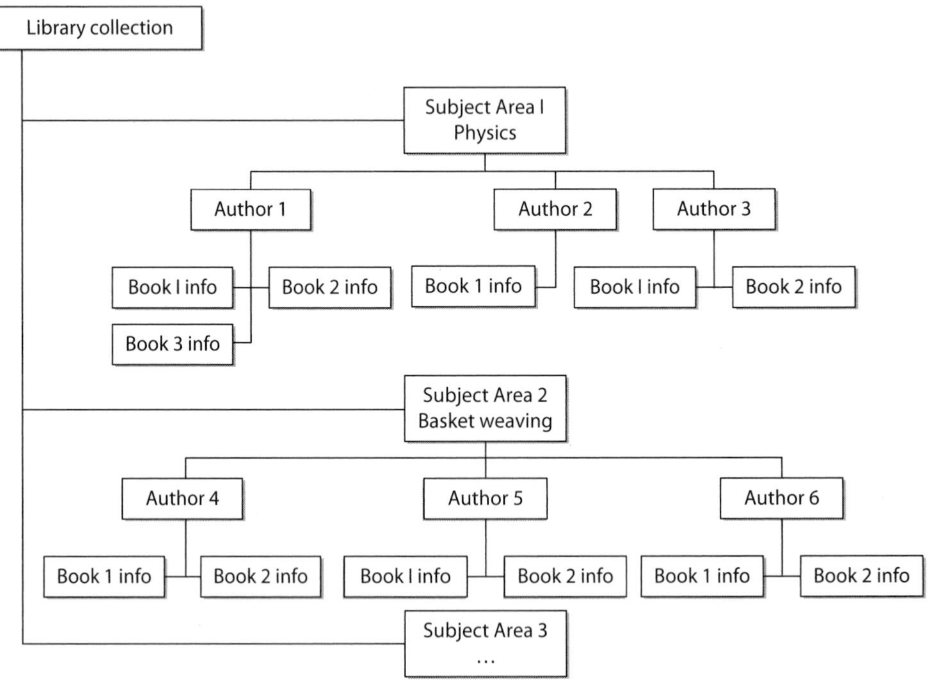

Figure 8-33 A hierarchical data model uses a tree structure and a parent/child relationship.

The most commonly used implementation of the hierarchical model is in the Lightweight Directory Access Protocol (LDAP) model. This model is used in the Windows Registry structure and different file systems, but it is not commonly used in newer database products.

The *network database model* is built upon the hierarchical data model. Instead of being constrained by having to know how to go from one branch to another and then from one parent to a child to find a data element, the network database model allows each data element to have multiple parent and child records. This forms a redundant network-like structure instead of a strict tree structure. (The name does not indicate it is on or distributed throughout a network; it just describes the data element relationships.) Figure 8-34 shows how a network database model sets up a structure that is similar to a mesh network topology for the sake of redundancy and allows for quick retrieval of data compared to the hierarchical model.

The network database model uses the constructs of records and sets. A record contains fields, which may lay out in a hierarchical structure. Sets define the one-to-many relationships between the different records. One record can be the "owner" of any number of sets, and the same "owner" can be a member of different sets. This means that one record can be the "top dog" and have many data elements underneath it, or

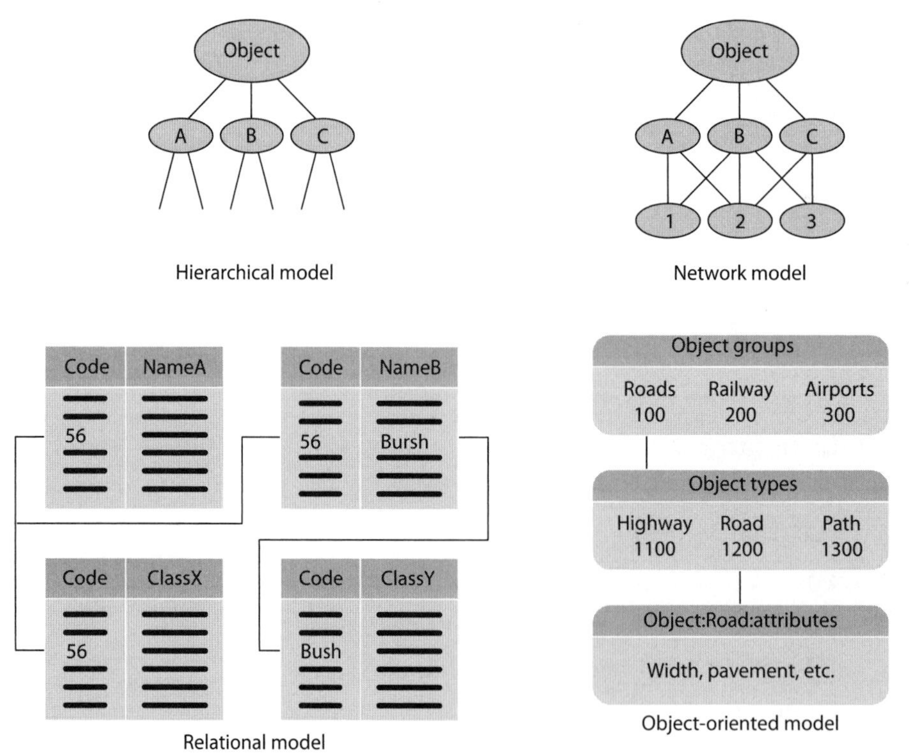

Figure 8-34 Various database models

that record can be lower on the totem pole and be beneath a different field that is *its* "top dog." This allows for a lot of flexibility in the development of relationships between data elements.

An *object-oriented database* is designed to handle a variety of data types (images, audio, documents, video). An object-oriented database management system (ODBMS) is more dynamic in nature than a relational database, because objects can be created when needed and the data *and* procedure (called method) go with the object when it is requested. In a relational database, the application has to use its own procedures to obtain data from the database and then process the data for its needs. The relational database does not actually provide procedures, as object-oriented databases do. The object-oriented database has classes to define the attributes and procedures of its objects.

As an analogy, let's say two different companies provide the same data to their customer bases. If you go to Company A (relational), the person behind the counter will just give you a piece of paper that contains information. Now you have to figure out what to do with that information and how to properly use it for your needs. If you go to Company B (object-oriented), the person behind the counter will give you a box. Within this box is a piece of paper with information on it, but you will also be given a couple of tools to process the data for your needs instead of you having to do it yourself. So in object-oriented databases, when your application queries for some data, what is returned is not only the data, but also the code to carry out procedures on this data.

The goal of creating this type of model was to address the limitations that relational databases encountered when large amounts of data must be stored and processed. An object-oriented database also does not depend upon SQL for interactions, so applications that are not SQL clients can work with these types of databases.

NOTE Structured Query Language (SQL) is a standard programming language used to allow clients to interact with a database. Many database products support SQL. It allows clients to carry out operations such as inserting, updating, searching, and committing data. When a client interacts with a database, it is most likely using SQL to carry out requests.

Database Jargon

The following are some key database terms:

- **Record** A collection of related data items.
- **File** A collection of records of the same type.
- **Database** A cross-referenced collection of data.
- **DBMS** Manages and controls the database.
- **Tuple** A row in a two-dimensional database.
- **Attribute** A column in a two-dimensional database.

- **Primary key** Columns that make each row unique. (Every row of a table must include a primary key.)
- **View** A virtual relation defined by the database administrator in order to keep subjects from viewing certain data.
- **Foreign key** An attribute of one table that is related to the primary key of another table.
- **Cell** An intersection of a row and a column.
- **Schema** Defines the structure of the database.
- **Data dictionary** Central repository of data elements and their relationships.

An *object-relational database (ORD)* or object-relational database management system (ORDBMS) is a relational database with a software front end that is written in an object-oriented programming language. Why would we create such a silly combination? Well, a relational database just holds data in static two-dimensional tables. When the data is accessed, some type of processing needs to be carried out on it—otherwise, there is really no reason to obtain the data. If we have a front end that provides the procedures (methods) that can be carried out on the data, then each and every application that accesses this database does not need to have the necessary procedures. This means that each and every application does not need to contain the procedures necessary to gain what it really wants from this database.

Different companies will have different business logic that needs to be carried out on the stored data. Allowing programmers to develop this front-end software piece allows the business logic procedures to be used by requesting applications and the data within the database. For example, if we had a relational database that contains inventory data for our company, we might want to be able to use this data for different business purposes. One application can access that database and just check the quantity of widget A products we have in stock. So a front-end object that can carry out that procedure will be created, the data will be grabbed from the database by this object, and the answer will be provided to the requesting application. We also have a need to carry out a trend analysis, which will indicate which products were moved the most from inventory to production. A different object that can carry out this type of calculation will gather the necessary data and present it to our requesting application. We have many different ways we need to view the data in that database: how many products were damaged during transportation, how fast did each vendor fulfill our supply requests, how much does it cost to ship the different products based on their weights, and so on. The data objects in Figure 8-35 contain these different business logic instructions.

Database Programming Interfaces

Data is useless if you can't access it and use it. Applications need to be able to obtain and interact with the information stored in databases. They also need some type of interface

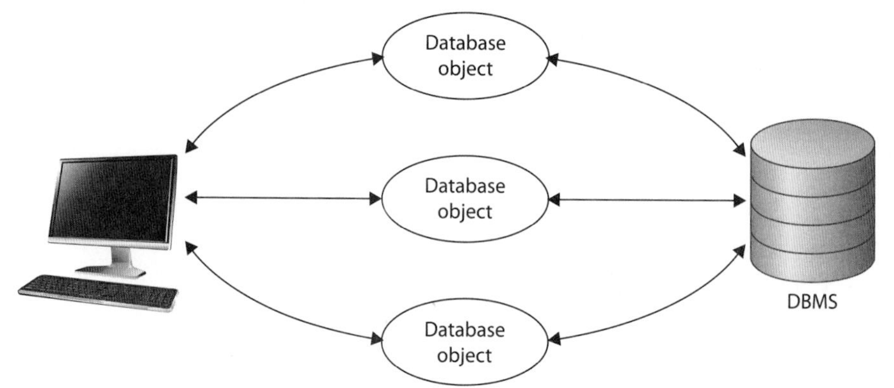

Figure 8-35 The object-relational model allows objects to contain business logic and functions.

and communication mechanism. The following sections address some of these interface languages.

Open Database Connectivity (ODBC) An API that allows an application to communicate with a database, either locally or remotely. The application sends requests to the ODBC API. ODBC tracks down the necessary database-specific driver for the database to carry out the translation, which in turn translates the requests into the database commands that a specific database will understand.

Object Linking and Embedding Database (OLE DB) Separates data into components that run as middleware on a client or server. It provides a low-level interface to link information across different databases and provides access to data no matter where it is located or how it is formatted.

The following are some characteristics of an OLE DB:

- It's a replacement for ODBC, extending its feature set to support a wider variety of nonrelational databases, such as object databases and spreadsheets that do not necessarily implement SQL.
- A set of COM-based interfaces provides applications with uniform access to data stored in diverse data sources (see Figure 8-36).
- Because it is COM-based, OLE DB is limited to being used by Microsoft Windows–based client tools.
- A developer accesses OLE DB services through ActiveX Data Objects (ADO).
- It allows different applications to access different types and sources of data.

ActiveX Data Objects (ADO) An API that allows applications to access back-end database systems. It is a set of ODBC interfaces that exposes the functionality of data sources through accessible objects. ADO uses the OLE DB interface to connect with the

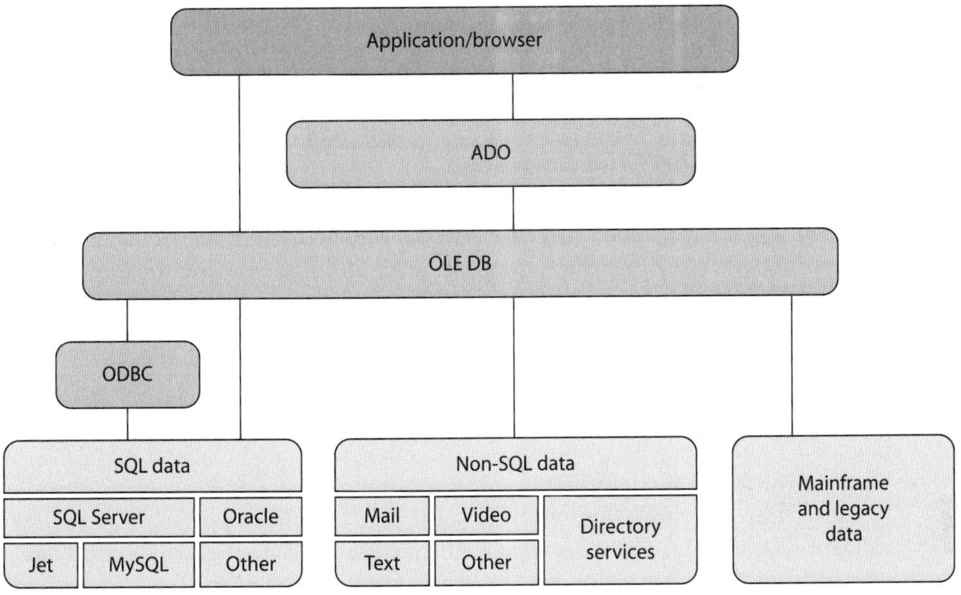

Figure 8-36 OLE DB provides an interface to allow applications to communicate with different data sources.

database, and can be developed with many different scripting languages. It is commonly used in web applications and other client/server applications. The following are some characteristics of ADO:

- It's a high-level data access programming interface to an underlying data access technology (such as OLE DB).
- It's a set of COM objects for accessing data sources, not just database access.
- It allows a developer to write programs that access data without knowing how the database is implemented.
- SQL commands are not required to access a database when using ADO.

Java Database Connectivity (JDBC) An API that allows a Java application to communicate with a database. The application can bridge through ODBC or directly to the database. The following are some characteristics of JDBC:

- It is an API that provides the same functionality as ODBC but is specifically designed for use by Java database applications.

- It has database-independent connectivity between the Java platform and a wide range of databases.
- It is a Java API that enables Java programs to execute SQL statements.

Relational Database Components

Like all software, databases are built with programming languages. Most database languages include a *data definition language (DDL)*, which defines the schema; a *data manipulation language (DML)*, which examines data and defines how the data can be manipulated within the database; a *data control language (DCL)*, which defines the internal organization of the database; and an *ad hoc query language (QL)*, which defines queries that enable users to access the data within the database.

Each type of database model may have many other differences, which vary from vendor to vendor. Most, however, contain the following basic core functionalities:

- **Data definition language (DDL)** Defines the structure and schema of the database. The *structure* could mean the table size, key placement, views, and data element relationship. The *schema* describes the type of data that will be held and manipulated, and their properties. It defines the structure of the database, access operations, and integrity procedures.
- **Data manipulation language (DML)** Contains all the commands that enable a user to view, manipulate, and use the database (view, add, modify, sort, and delete commands).
- **Query language (QL)** Enables users to make requests of the database.
- **Report generator** Produces printouts of data in a user-defined manner.

Data Dictionary

A *data dictionary* is a central collection of data element definitions, schema objects, and reference keys. The schema objects can contain tables, views, indexes, procedures, functions, and triggers. A data dictionary can contain the default values for columns, integrity information, the names of users, the privileges and roles for users, and auditing information. It is a tool used to centrally manage parts of a database by controlling data about the data (referred to as *metadata*) within the database. It provides a cross-reference between groups of data elements and the databases.

The database management software creates and reads the data dictionary to ascertain what schema objects exist and checks to see if specific users have the proper access rights to view them (see Figure 8-37). When users look at the database, they can be restricted by specific views. The different view settings for each user are held within the data dictionary. When new tables, new rows, or new schemas are added, the data dictionary is updated to reflect this.

Primary vs. Foreign Key

The *primary key* is an identifier of a row and is used for indexing in relational databases. Each row must have a unique primary key to properly represent the row as one entity.

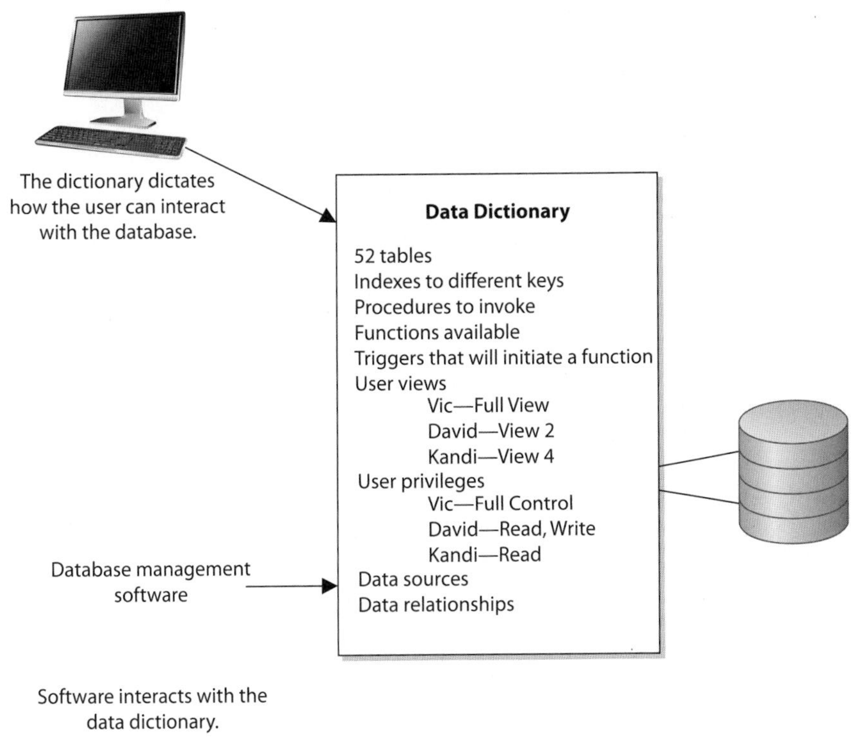

Figure 8-37 The data dictionary is a centralized program that contains information about a database.

When a user makes a request to view a record, the database tracks this record by its unique primary key. If the primary key were not unique, the database would not know which record to present to the user. In the following illustration, the primary keys for Table A are the dogs' names. Each row (tuple) provides characteristics for each dog (primary key). So when a user searches for Cricket, the characteristics of the type, weight, owner, and color will be provided.

Attribute

Table A

Dog	Type	Weight	Owner	Color
Dallas	Lab	85 lb	David	Black
Cricket	Terrier	9 lb	George	White
Max	Lab	80 lb	Diane	Yellow
Shannon	Shepherd	72 lb	Marge	Brown

Primary keys

Tuple

A primary key is different from a foreign key, although they are closely related. If an attribute in one table has a value matching the primary key in another table and there is a relationship set up between the two of them, this attribute is considered a *foreign key*. This foreign key is not necessarily the primary key in its current table. It only has to contain the same information that is held in another table's primary key and be mapped to the primary key in this other table. In the following illustration, a primary key for Table A is Dallas. Because Table B has an attribute that contains the same data as this primary key and there is a relationship set up between these two keys, it is referred to as a foreign key. This is another way for the database to track relationships between the data that it houses.

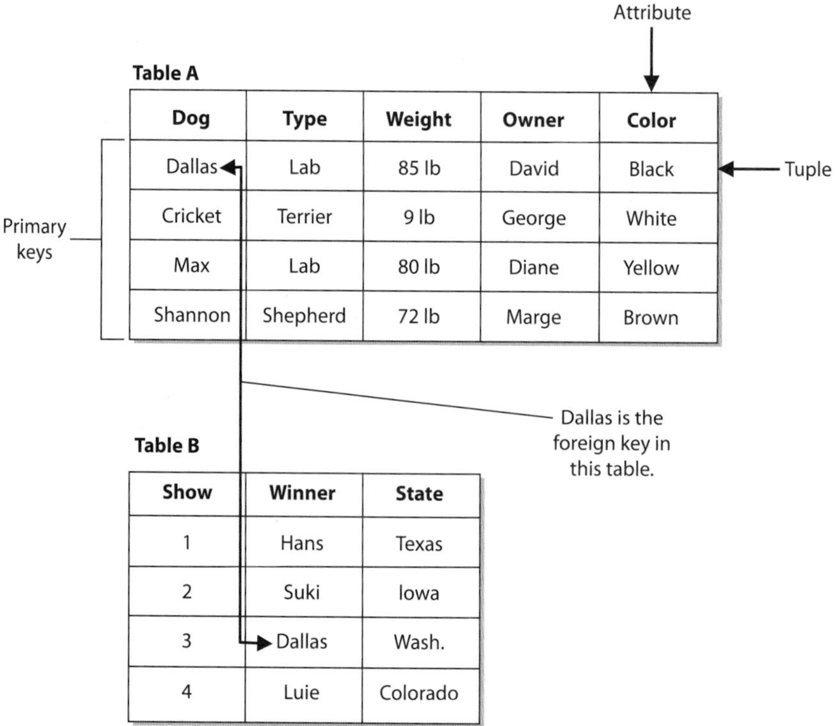

We can think of being presented with a web page that contains the data on Table B. If we want to know more about this dog named Dallas, we double-click that value and the browser presents the characteristics about Dallas that are in Table A.

This allows us to set up our databases with the relationship between the different data elements as we see fit.

Integrity

Like other resources within a network, a database can run into *concurrency* problems. Concurrency issues come up when there is data that will be accessed and modified at the same time by different users and/or applications. As an example of a concurrency problem, suppose that two groups use one price sheet to know how much stock to order for the next week and also to calculate the expected profit. If Dan and Elizabeth copy this price sheet from the file server to their workstations, they each have a copy of the original file. Suppose that Dan changes the stock level of computer books from 120 to 5 because his group sold 115 book in the last three days. He also uses the current prices listed in the price sheet to estimate his group's expected profits for the next week. Elizabeth reduces the price on several computer books on her copy of the price sheet and sees that the stock level of computer books is still over 100, so she chooses not to order any more for next week for her group. Dan and Elizabeth do not communicate this different information to each other, but instead upload their copies of the price sheet to the server for everyone to view and use.

Dan copies his changes back to the file server, and then 30 seconds later Elizabeth copies her changes over Dan's changes. So, the file only reflects Elizabeth's changes. Because they did not synchronize their changes, they are both now using incorrect data. Dan's profit estimates are off because he does not know that Elizabeth reduced the prices, and next week Elizabeth will have no computer books because she did not know that the stock level had dropped to five.

The same thing happens in databases. If controls are not in place, two users can access and modify the same data at the same time, which can be detrimental to a dynamic environment. To ensure that concurrency issues do not cause problems, processes can *lock* tables within a database, make changes, and then release the software lock. The next process that accesses the table will then have the updated information. Locking ensures that two processes do not access the same table at the same time. Pages, tables, rows, and fields can be locked to ensure that updates to data happen one at a time, which enables each process and subject to work with correct and accurate information.

Database software performs three main types of integrity services:

- A *semantic integrity* mechanism makes sure structural and semantic rules are enforced. These rules pertain to data types, logical values, uniqueness constraints, and operations that could adversely affect the structure of the database.
- A database has *referential integrity* if all foreign keys reference existing primary keys. There should be a mechanism in place that ensures no foreign key contains a reference to a primary key of a nonexistent record, or a null value.
- *Entity integrity* guarantees that the tuples are uniquely identified by primary key values. In the previous illustration, the primary keys are the names of the dogs, in which case, no two dogs could have the same name. For the sake of entity integrity, every tuple must contain one primary key. If it does not have a primary key, it cannot be referenced by the database.

The database must not contain unmatched foreign key values. Every foreign key refers to an existing primary key. In the example presented in the previous section, if the foreign key in Table B is Dallas, then Table A must contain a record for a dog named Dallas.

If these values do not match, then their relationship is broken, and again the database cannot reference the information properly.

Other configurable operations are available to help protect the integrity of the data within a database. These operations are rollbacks, commits, savepoints, checkpoints, and two-phase commits.

The *rollback* is an operation that ends a current transaction and cancels the current changes to the database. These changes could have taken place to the data held within the database or a change to the schema. When a rollback operation is executed, the changes are cancelled and the database returns to its previous state. A rollback can take place if the database has some type of unexpected glitch or if outside entities disrupt its processing sequence. Instead of transmitting and posting partial or corrupt information, the database will roll back to its original state and log these errors and actions so they can be reviewed later.

The *commit* operation completes a transaction and executes all changes just made by the user. As its name indicates, once the commit command is executed, the changes are committed and reflected in the database. These changes can be made to data or schema information. Because these changes are committed, they are then available to all other applications and users. If a user attempts to commit a change and it cannot complete correctly, a rollback is performed. This ensures that partial changes do not take place and that data is not corrupted.

Savepoints are used to make sure that if a system failure occurs, or if an error is detected, the database can attempt to return to a point before the system crashed or hiccupped. For a conceptual example, say Dave typed, "Jeremiah was a bullfrog. He was <savepoint> a good friend of mine." (The system inserted a savepoint.) Then a freak storm came through and rebooted the system. When Dave got back into the database client application, he might see "Jeremiah was a bullfrog. He was," but the rest was lost. Therefore, the savepoint saved some of his work. Databases and other applications will use this technique to attempt to restore the user's work and the state of the database after a glitch, but some glitches are just too large and invasive to overcome.

Savepoints are easy to implement within databases and applications, but a balance must be struck between too many and not enough savepoints. Having too many savepoints can degrade the performance, whereas not having enough savepoints runs the risk of losing data and decreasing user productivity because the lost data would have to be reentered. Savepoints can be initiated by a time interval, a specific action by the user, or the number of transactions or changes made to the database. For example, a database can set a savepoint for every 15 minutes, every 20 transactions completed, each time a user gets to the end of a record, or every 12 changes made to the databases.

So a savepoint restores data by enabling the user to go back in time before the system crashed or hiccupped. This can reduce frustration and help us all live in harmony.

Checkpoints are very similar to savepoints. When the database software fills up a certain amount of memory, a checkpoint is initiated, which saves the data from the memory segment to a temporary file. If a glitch is experienced, the software will try to use this information to restore the user's working environment to its previous state.

A *two-phase commit* mechanism is yet another control that is used in databases to ensure the integrity of the data held within the database. Databases commonly carry out transaction processes, which means the user and the database interact at the same time. The opposite is *batch processing*, which means that requests for database changes are put into a queue and activated all at once—not at the exact time the user makes the request. In transactional processes, many times a transaction will require that more than one database be updated during the process. The databases need to make sure each database is properly modified, or no modification takes place at all. When a database change is submitted by the user, the different databases initially store these changes temporarily. A transaction monitor will then send out a "pre-commit" command to each database. If all the right databases respond with an acknowledgment, then the monitor sends out a "commit" command to each database. This ensures that all of the necessary information is stored in all the right places at the right time.

Database Security Issues

The two main database security issues this section addresses are aggregation and inference. *Aggregation* happens when a user does not have the clearance or permission to access specific information, but she does have the permission to access components of this information. She can then figure out the rest and obtain restricted information. She can learn of information from different sources and combine it to learn something she does not have the clearance to know.

EXAM TIP Aggregation is the act of combining information from separate sources. The combination of the data forms new information, which the subject does not have the necessary rights to access. The combined information has a sensitivity that is greater than that of the individual parts.

The following is a silly conceptual example. Let's say a database administrator does not want anyone in the Users group to be able to figure out a specific sentence, so he segregates the sentence into components and restricts the Users group from accessing it, as represented in Figure 8-38. Emily, through each of three different roles she has, can access components A, C, and F. Because she is particularly bright (a *Wheel of Fortune* whiz), she figures out the sentence and now knows the restricted secret.

To prevent aggregation, the subject, and any application or process acting on the subject's behalf, needs to be prevented from gaining access to the whole collection, including the independent components. The objects can be placed into containers, which are classified at a higher level to prevent access from subjects with lower-level permissions or clearances. A subject's queries can also be tracked, and context-dependent access control can be enforced. This would keep a history of the objects that a subject has accessed and restrict an access attempt if there is an indication that an aggregation attack is under way.

The other security issue is *inference*, which is the intended result of aggregation. The inference problem happens when a subject deduces the full story from the pieces

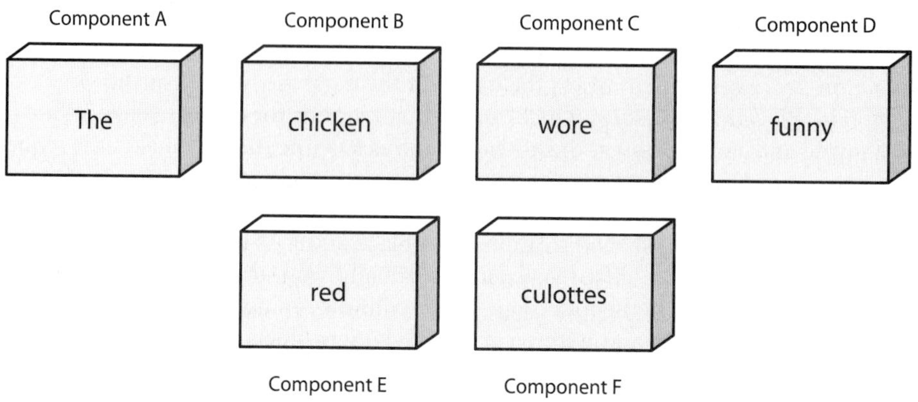

Figure 8-38 Because Emily has access to components A, C, and F, she can figure out the secret sentence through aggregation.

he learned of through aggregation. This is an issue when data at a lower security level indirectly portrays data at a higher level.

EXAM TIP Inference is the ability to derive information not explicitly available.

For example, if a clerk were restricted from knowing the planned movements of troops based in a specific country, but did have access to food shipment requirements forms and tent allocation documents, he could figure out that the troops were moving to a specific place because that is where the food and tents are being shipped. The food shipment and tent allocation documents were classified as confidential, and the troop movement was classified as top secret. Because of the varying classifications, the clerk could access and ascertain top-secret information he was not supposed to know.

The trick is to prevent the subject, or any application or process acting on behalf of that subject, from indirectly gaining access to the inferable information. This problem is usually dealt with in the development of the database by implementing content- and context-dependent access control rules. *Content-dependent access control* is based on the sensitivity of the data. The more sensitive the data, the smaller the subset of individuals who can gain access to the data.

Context-dependent access control means that the software "understands" what actions should be allowed based upon the state and sequence of the request. So what does that mean? It means the software must keep track of previous access attempts by the user and understand what sequences of access steps are allowed. Content-dependent access control can go like this: "Does Julio have access to File A?" The system reviews the ACL on File A and returns with a response of "Yes, Julio can access the file, but can only read it." In a context-dependent access control situation, it would be more like this: "Does Julio have access to File A?" The system then reviews several pieces of data: What other access attempts has Julio made? Is this request out of sequence of how a safe series of requests takes place? Does this request fall within the allowed time period of system access (8 A.M. to 5 P.M.)? If the answers to all of these questions are within a set of preconfigured parameters, Julio can access the file. If not, he is denied access.

If context-dependent access control is being used to protect against inference attacks, the database software would need to keep track of what the user is requesting. So Julio makes a request to see field 1, then field 5, then field 20, which the system allows, but once he asks to see field 15, the database does not allow this access attempt. The software must be preprogrammed (usually through a rule-based engine) as to what sequence and how much data Julio is allowed to view. If he is allowed to view more information, he may have enough data to infer something we don't want him to know.

Obviously, content-dependent access control is not as complex as context-dependent access control because of the amount of items that needs to be processed by the system.

Some other common attempts to prevent inference attacks are cell suppression, partitioning the database, and noise and perturbation. *Cell suppression* is a technique used to hide specific cells that contain information that could be used in inference attacks. *Partitioning* a database involves dividing the database into different parts, which makes it much harder for an unauthorized individual to find connecting pieces of data that can be brought together and other information that can be deduced or uncovered. *Noise and perturbation* is a technique of inserting bogus information in the hopes of misdirecting an attacker or confusing the matter enough that the actual attack will not be fruitful.

Often, security is not integrated into the planning and development of a database. Security is an afterthought, and a trusted front end is developed to be used with the database instead. This approach is limited in the granularity of security and in the types of security functions that can take place.

As previously mentioned in this chapter, a common theme in security is a balance between effective security and functionality. In many cases, the more you secure something, the less functionality you have. Although this could be the desired result, it is important not to impede user productivity when security is being introduced.

Database Views

Databases can permit one group, or a specific user, to see certain information while restricting another group from viewing it altogether. This functionality happens through the use of *database views*, illustrated in Figure 8-39. If a database administrator wants to allow middle management members to see their departments' profits and expenses but not show them the whole company's profits, the DBA can implement views. Senior management would be given all views, which contain all the departments' and the company's profit and expense values, whereas each individual manager would only be able to view his or her department values.

Like operating systems, databases can employ discretionary access control (DAC) and mandatory access control (MAC), which are explained in Chapter 5. Views can be displayed according to group membership, user rights, or security labels. If a DAC system is employed, then groups and users can be granted access through views based on their identity, authentication, and authorization. If a MAC system in place, then

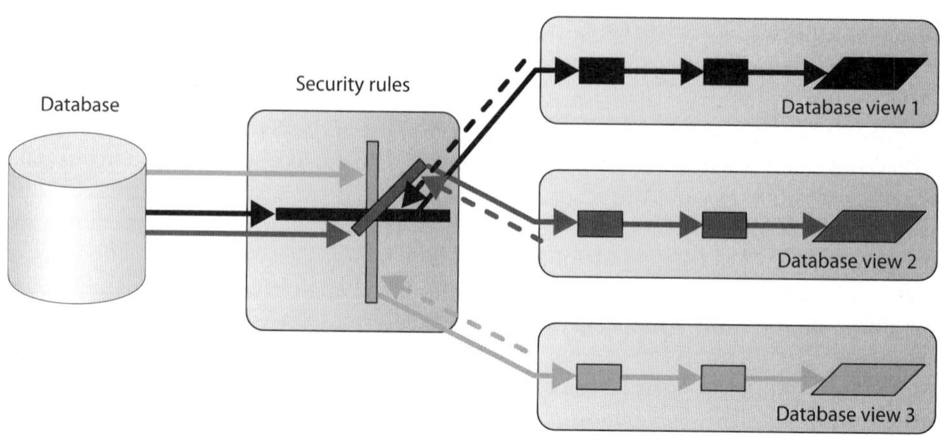

Figure 8-39 Database views are a logical type of access control.

groups and users can be granted access based on their security clearance and the data's classification level.

Polyinstantiation

Sometimes a company does not want users at one level to access and modify data at a higher level. This type of situation can be handled in different ways. One approach denies access when a lower-level user attempts to access a higher-level object. However, this gives away information indirectly by telling the lower-level entity that something sensitive lives inside that object at that level.

Another way of dealing with this issue is *polyinstantiation*. This enables a table that contains multiple tuples with the same primary keys, with each instance distinguished by a security level. When this information is inserted into a database, lower-level subjects must be restricted from it. Instead of just restricting access, another set of data is created to fool the lower-level subjects into thinking the information actually means something else. For example, if a naval base has a cargo shipment of weapons going from Delaware to Ukraine via the ship *Oklahoma*, this type of information could be classified as top secret. Only the subjects with the security clearance of top secret and above should know this information, so a dummy file is created that states the *Oklahoma* is carrying a shipment from Delaware to Africa containing food, and it is given a security clearance of unclassified, as shown in Table 8-1. It will be obvious that the *Oklahoma* is gone, but individuals at lower security levels will think the ship is on its way to Africa, instead of Ukraine. This also makes sure no one at a lower level tries to commit the *Oklahoma* for

Level	Ship	Cargo	Origin	Destination
Top Secret	Oklahoma	Weapons	Delaware	Ukraine
Unclassified	Oklahoma	Food	Delaware	Africa

Table 8-1 Example of Polyinstantiation to Provide a Cover Story to Subjects at Lower Security Levels

any other missions. The lower-level subjects know that the *Oklahoma* is not available, and they will assign other ships for cargo shipments.

EXAM TIP Polyinstantiation is a process of interactively producing more detailed versions of objects by populating variables with different values or other variables. It is often used to prevent inference attacks.

In this example, polyinstantiation is used to create two versions of the same object so that lower-level subjects do not know the true information, thus stopping them from attempting to use or change that data in any way. It is a way of providing a cover story for the entities that do not have the necessary security level to know the truth. This is just one example of how polyinstantiation can be used. It is not strictly related to security, however, even though that is a common use. Whenever a copy of an object is created and populated with different data, meaning two instances of the same object have different attributes, polyinstantiation is in place.

Online Transaction Processing

Online transaction processing (OLTP) is generally used when databases are clustered to provide fault tolerance and higher performance. OLTP provides mechanisms that watch for problems and deal with them appropriately when they do occur. For example, if a process stops functioning, the monitor mechanisms within OLTP can detect this and attempt to restart the process. If the process cannot be restarted, then the transaction taking place will be rolled back to ensure no data is corrupted or that only part of a transaction happens. Any erroneous or invalid transactions detected should be written to a transaction log. The transaction log also collects the activities of successful transactions. Data is written to the log before and after a transaction is carried out so a record of events exists.

The main goal of OLTP is to ensure that transactions either happen properly or don't happen at all. Transaction processing usually means that individual indivisible operations are taking place independently. If one of the operations fails, the rest of the operations needs to be rolled back to ensure that only accurate data is entered into the database.

The set of systems involved in carrying out transactions is managed and monitored with a software OLTP product to make sure everything takes place smoothly and correctly.

OLTP can load-balance incoming requests if necessary. This means that if requests to update databases increase and the performance of one system decreases because of the large volume, OLTP can move some of these requests to other systems. This makes sure all requests are handled and that the user, or whoever is making the requests, does not have to wait a long time for the transaction to complete.

When there is more than one database, it is important they all contain the same information. Consider this scenario: Katie goes to the bank and withdraws $6,500 from her $10,000 checking account. Database A receives the request and records a new checking account balance of $3,500, but database B does not get updated. It still shows a balance of $10,000. Then, Katie makes a request to check the balance on her checking account, but that request gets sent to database B, which returns inaccurate information because the withdrawal transaction was never carried over to this database. OLTP makes sure a transaction is not complete until all databases receive and reflect this change.

OLTP records transactions as they occur (in real time), which usually updates more than one database in a distributed environment. This type of complexity can introduce many integrity threats, so the database software should implement the characteristics of what's known as the ACID test:

- **Atomicity** Divides transactions into units of work and ensures that all modifications take effect or none takes effect. Either the changes are committed or the database is rolled back.
- **Consistency** A transaction must follow the integrity policy developed for that particular database and ensure all data is consistent in the different databases.
- **Isolation** Transactions execute in isolation until completed, without interacting with other transactions. The results of the modification are not available until the transaction is completed.
- **Durability** Once the transaction is verified as accurate on all systems, it is committed and the databases cannot be rolled back.

Data Warehousing and Data Mining

Data warehousing combines data from multiple databases or data sources into a large database for the purpose of providing more extensive information retrieval and data analysis. Data from different databases is extracted and transferred to a central data storage device called a warehouse. The data is normalized, which means redundant information is stripped out and data is formatted in the way the data warehouse expects it. This enables users to query one entity rather than accessing and querying different databases.

The data sources the warehouse is built from are used for operational purposes. A data warehouse is developed to carry out analysis. The analysis can be carried out to make business forecasting decisions and identify marketing effectiveness, business trends, and even fraudulent activities.

Data warehousing is not simply a process of mirroring data from different databases and presenting the data in one place. It provides a base of data that is then processed and presented in a more useful and understandable way. Related pieces of data are summarized and correlated before being presented to the user. Instead of having every piece of data presented, the user is given data in a more abridged form that best fits her needs.

Although this provides easier access and control, because the data warehouse is in one place, it also requires more stringent security. If an intruder were able to get into the data warehouse, he could access all of the company's information at once.

Data mining is the process of massaging the data held in the data warehouse into more useful information. Data-mining tools are used to find an association and correlation in data to produce *metadata*. Metadata can show previously unseen relationships between individual subsets of information. Metadata can reveal abnormal patterns not previously apparent. A simplistic example in which data mining could be useful is in detecting insurance fraud. Suppose the information, claims, and specific habits of millions of customers are kept in a database warehouse, and a mining tool is used to look for certain patterns in claims. It might find that each time John Smith moved, he had an insurance claim two to three months following the move. He moved in 2006 and two months later had a suspicious fire, then moved in 2010 and had a motorcycle stolen three months after that, and then moved again in 2013 and had a burglar break in two months afterward. This pattern might be hard for people to manually catch because he had different insurance agents over the years, the files were just updated and not reviewed, or the files were not kept in a centralized place for agents to review.

Data mining can look at complex data and simplify it by using fuzzy logic (a set theory) and expert systems (that is, systems that use artificial intelligence) to perform the mathematical functions and look for patterns in data that are not so apparent. In many ways, the metadata is more valuable than the data it is derived from; thus, metadata must be highly protected.

The goal of data warehouses and data mining is to be able to extract information to gain knowledge about the activities and trends within the organization, as shown in Figure 8-40. With this knowledge, people can detect deficiencies or ways to optimize operations. For example, if we operate a retail store company, we want consumers to spend gobs of money at the stores. We can more successfully get their business if we understand customers' purchasing habits. For example, if our data mining reveals that placing candy and other small items at the checkout stand increases purchases of those items 65 percent compared to placing them somewhere else in the store, we will place them at the checkout stand. If one store is in a more affluent neighborhood and we see a constant (or increasing) pattern of customers purchasing expensive wines there, that is

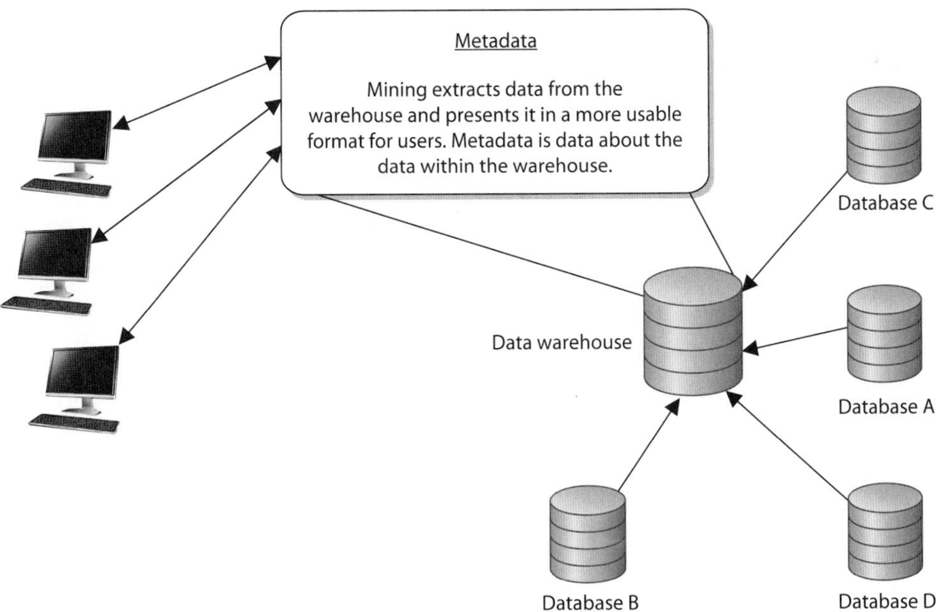

Figure 8-40 Mining tools are used to identify patterns and relationships in data warehouses.

where we would also sell our expensive cheeses and gourmet items. We would not place our gourmet items at another store that hardly ever sells expensive wines, and in fact we would probably stop selling expensive wines at that store.

NOTE Data mining is the process of analyzing a data warehouse using tools that look for trends, correlations, relationships, and anomalies without knowing the meaning of the data. Metadata is the result of storing data within a data warehouse and mining the data with tools. Data goes into a data warehouse and metadata comes out of that data warehouse.

So we would carry out these activities if we wanted to harness organization-wide data for comparative decision making, workflow automation, and/or competitive advantage. It is not just information aggregation; management's goals in understanding different aspects of the company are to enhance business value and help employees work more productively.

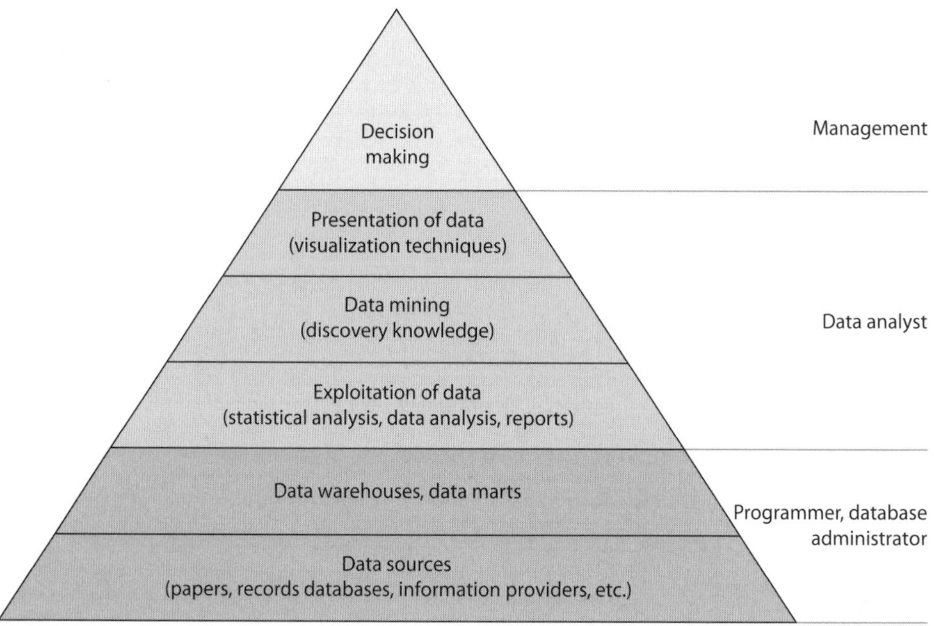

Data mining is also known as *knowledge discovery in database (KDD)*, and is a combination of techniques to identify valid and useful patterns. Different types of data can have various interrelationships, and the method used depends on the type of data and the patterns sought. The following are three approaches used in KDD systems to uncover these patterns:

- **Classification** Groups together data according to shared similarities
- **Probabilistic** Identifies data interdependencies and applies probabilities to their relationships
- **Statistical** Identifies relationships between data elements and uses rule discovery

It is important to keep an eye on the output from the KDD and look for anything suspicious that would indicate some type of internal logic problem. For example, if you wanted a report that outlines the net and gross revenues for each retail store, and instead get a report that states "Bob," there may be an issue you need to look into.

Table 8-2 outlines the different types of systems used, depending on the requirements of the resulting data.

Big data is a term that is related to, but distinct from, data warehousing and data mining. *Big data* is broadly defined as very large data sets with characteristics that make them unsuitable for traditional analysis techniques. These traits are widely agreed to include heterogeneity, complexity, variability, lack of reliability, and sheer volume. Heterogeneity speaks to the diversity of both sources and structure of the data, which means that some data could be images while other data could be free text. Big data is also complex, particularly in terms of interrelationships such as the one between images that are trending on social media and news articles describing current events. By variability, we mean that some sources produce nearly constant data while other sources produce data much more sporadically or rarely. Related to this challenge is the fact that some sources of big data may be unreliable or of unknown reliability. Finally, and as if these were not enough challenges, the basic characteristic of big data is its sheer volume: enough to overwhelm most if not all of the traditional DBMSs.

EXAM TIP *Big data* is stored in specialized systems like *data warehouses* and is exploited using approaches such as *data mining*. These three terms are related but distinct.

	Data-Based System	Rules-Based System	Knowledge-Based System
Can Process	Data	Data rules	Data rules knowledge
Can Output	Information	• Information decisions • Real-time decisions	• Information decisions • Answers • Expert advice • Recommendations
Commonly Used for	Hard-coded rules	Enterprise rules	Departmental rules
Ideal for	IT/system rules	Simplistic business rules	Complex business rules
Best for These Types of Applications	Traditional information systems	Decisioning compliance	• Advising product selection • Recommending • Troubleshooting
Domain Scope	—	Broad logic	Deep logic

Table 8-2 Various Types of Systems Based on Capabilities

Malicious Software (Malware)

Several types of malicious code, or malware, exist, such as viruses, worms, Trojan horses, and logic bombs. They usually are dormant until activated by an event the user or system initiates. They can be spread by e-mail, sharing media, sharing documents and programs, or downloading things from the Internet, or they can be purposely inserted by an attacker.

Adhering to the usual rules of not opening an e-mail attachment or clicking on a link that comes from an unknown source is one of the best ways to combat malicious code. However, recent viruses and worms have infected personal e-mail address books, so this precaution is not a sure thing to protect systems from malicious code. If an address book is infected and used during an attack, the victim gets an e-mail message that seems to have come from a person he knows. Because he knows this person, he will proceed to open the e-mail message and double-click the attachment or click on the link. And Bam! His computer is now infected and uses the e-mail client's address book to spread the virus to all his friends and acquaintances.

There are many infection channels other than through e-mail, but it is a common one since so many people use and trust these types of messages coming into and out of their systems on a daily basis. In fact, by many estimates, upward of 95 percent of all compromises use e-mail as the principal attack vector.

Manual attacks on systems do not happen as much as they did in the past. Today hackers automate their attacks by creating a piece of malicious software (malware) that can compromise thousands of systems at one time with more precision. While malware can be designed to carry out a wide range of malicious activities, most malware is created to obtain sensitive information (credit card data, Social Security numbers, credentials, etc.), gain unauthorized access to systems, and/or carry out a profit-oriented scheme.

The proliferation of malware has a direct relationship to the large amount of profit individuals can make without much threat of being caught. The most commonly used schemes for making money through malware are as follows:

- Systems are compromised with bots and are later used in distributed denial-of-service (DDoS) attacks, spam distribution, or as part of a botnet's command and control system.
- Ransomware encrypts some or all of the users' files with keys that are only given to the users after they pay a ransom, typically using cryptocurrencies.
- Spyware collects personal data for the malware developer to resell to others.
- Malware redirects web traffic so that people are pointed toward a specific product for purchase.
- Malware installs key loggers, which collect sensitive financial information for the malware author to use.
- Malware is used to carry out phishing attacks, fraudulent activities, identity theft steps, and information warfare activities.

The sophistication level of malware continues to increase at a rapid pace. Years ago you just needed an antimalware product that looked for obvious signs of an infection (new files, configuration changes, system file changes, etc.), but today's malware can bypass these simplistic detection methods.

Some malware is stored in RAM and not saved to a hard drive, which makes it harder to detect. The RAM is flushed when the system reboots, so there is hardly any evidence that it was there in the first place. Malware can be installed in a "drive-by-download" process, which means that the victim is tricked into clicking something malicious (web link, system message, pop-up window), which in turn infects his computer.

As discussed earlier, there are many web browser and web server vulnerabilities that are available through exploitation. Many websites are infected with malware, and the website owners do not know this because the malware encrypts itself, encodes itself, and carries out activities in a random fashion so that its malicious activities are not easily replicated and studied.

We will cover the main categories of malware in the following sections, but the main reasons that they are all increasing in numbers and potency are as follows:

- Many environments are homogeneous, meaning that one piece of malware will work on many or most devices.
- Everything is becoming a computer (phones, TVs, game consoles, power grids, medical devices, etc.), and thus all are capable of being compromised.
- More people and companies are storing all of their data in some digital format.
- More people and devices are connecting through various interfaces (phone apps, Facebook, websites, e-mail, texting, e-commerce, etc.).
- Many accounts are configured with too much privilege (administrative or root access).
- More people who do not understand technology are using it for sensitive purposes (online banking, e-commerce, etc.).

The digital world has provided many ways to carry out various criminal activities with a low risk of being caught.

Viruses

A *virus* is a small application, or string of code, that infects software. The main function of a virus is to reproduce and deliver its payload, and it requires a host application to do this. In other words, viruses cannot replicate on their own. A virus infects a file by inserting or attaching a copy of itself to the file. The virus is just the "delivery mechanism." It can have any type of payload (deleting system files, displaying specific messages, reconfiguring systems, stealing sensitive data, installing a sniffer or back door).

A virus is a subcategory of the overall umbrella category "malware." What makes a software component an actual virus is the fact that it can self-replicate. There are several other malware types that infect our systems and cause mayhem, but if they cannot self-replicate they do not fall into the subcategory of "virus."

Several viruses have been released that achieved self-perpetuation by mailing themselves to every entry in a victim's personal address book. The virus masqueraded as coming from a trusted source. The ILOVEYOU, Melissa, and Naked Wife viruses are older viruses that used the programs Outlook and Outlook Express as their host applications and were replicated when the victim chose to open the message. Several types of viruses have been developed and deployed, which we will cover next.

Macros are programs written in Visual Basic or VBScript and are generally used with Microsoft Office products. Macros automate tasks that users would otherwise have to carry out themselves. Users can define a series of activities and common tasks for the application to perform when a button is clicked, instead of doing each of those tasks individually. A *macro virus* is a virus written in one of these macro languages and is platform independent. Macro viruses infect and replicate in templates and within documents. They are common because they are extremely easy to write and are used extensively in commonly used products (i.e., Microsoft Office).

Some viruses infect the boot sector (*boot sector viruses*) of a computer and either move data within the boot sector or overwrite the sector with new information. Some boot sector viruses have part of their code in the boot sector, which can initiate the viruses when a system boots up, and the rest of their code in sectors on the hard drive that the virus has marked off as bad. Because the sectors are marked as bad, the operating system and applications will not attempt to use those sectors; thus, they will not get overwritten.

A *stealth virus* hides the modifications it has made to files or boot records. This can be accomplished by monitoring system functions used to read files or sectors and forging the results. This means that when an antimalware program attempts to read an infected file or sector, the original uninfected form will be presented instead of the actual infected form. The virus can hide itself by masking the size of the file it is hidden in or actually move itself temporarily to another location while an antimalware program is carrying out its scanning process.

So a stealth virus is a virus that hides its tracks after infecting a system. Once the system is infected, the virus can make modifications to make the computer appear the same as before. The virus can show the original file size of a file it infected instead of the new, larger size to try to trick the antimalware software into thinking no changes have been made.

A *polymorphic virus* produces varied but operational copies of itself. This is done in the hopes of outwitting a virus scanner. Even if one or two copies are found and disabled, other copies may still remain active within the system.

The polymorphic virus can use different encryption schemes requiring different decryption routines. This would require an antimalware scan for several scan strings, one for each possible decryption method, in order to identify all copies of this type of virus.

These viruses can also vary the sequence of their instructions by including *noise*, or bogus instructions, with other useful instructions. They can also use a mutation engine and a random-number generator to change the sequence of their instructions in the hopes of not being detected. A polymorphic virus has the capability to change its own code, enabling the virus to have hundreds or thousands of variants. These activities can cause the virus scanner to not properly recognize the virus and to leave it alone.

A *multipart virus* (also called multipartite virus) has several components to it and can be distributed to different parts of the system. For example, a multipart virus might infect both the boot sector of a hard drive and executable files. By using multiple vectors it can spread more quickly than a virus using only one vector.

Meme viruses are not actual computer viruses, but types of e-mail messages that are continually forwarded around the Internet. They can be chain letters, e-mail hoax virus alerts, religious messages, or pyramid selling schemes. They are replicated by humans, not software, and can waste bandwidth and spread fear. Several e-mails have been passed around describing dangerous viruses even though the viruses weren't real. People believed the e-mails and felt as though they were doing the right thing by passing them along to tell friends about this supposedly dangerous malware, when really the people were duped and were themselves spreading a meme virus.

Script viruses have been quite popular and damaging over the last several years. Scripts are files that are executed by an interpreter—for example, Microsoft Windows Script Host, which interprets different types of scripting languages. Websites have become more dynamic and interactive through the use of script files written in Visual Basic (VBScript) and Java (JScript) as well as other scripting languages that are embedded in HTML. When a web page that has these scripts embedded is requested by a web browser, these embedded scripts are executed, and if they are malicious, then everything just blows up. Okay, this is a tad overdramatic. The virus will carry out the payload (instructions) that the virus writer has integrated into the script, whether it is sending out copies of itself to everyone in your contact list or deleting critical files. Scripts are just another infection vector used by malware writers to carry out their evil ways.

Another type of virus, called the *tunneling virus*, attempts to install itself "under" the antimalware program. When the antimalware goes around doing its health check on critical files, file sizes, modification dates, and so on, it makes a request to the operating system to gather this information. Now, if the virus can put itself between the antimalware and the operating system, when the antimalware sends out a command (system call) for this type of information, the tunneling virus can intercept this call. Instead of the operating system responding to the request, the tunneling virus responds with information that indicates that everything is fine and healthy and that there is no indication of any type of infection.

So what is the difference between a stealth virus and a tunneling virus? A stealth virus is just a general term for a virus that somehow attempts to hide its actions. A stealth virus can use tunneling tactics or other tactics to hide its footprint and activities.

People in the information security industry used to know all the popular viruses and other malware types by name. For example, security professionals knew what someone was referring to when discussing the Melissa virus, ILOVEYOU virus, Code Red, SQL Slammer, Blaster, or Sasser worm. Today there are thousands of new malware variants created each day and no one can keep up. PandaLabs reported that in the third quarter of 2015, there was a daily average of 230,000 new samples of malware.

Malware Components

It is common for malware to have six main elements, although it is not necessary for them *all* to be in place:

- **Insertion** Installs itself on the victim's system
- **Avoidance** Uses methods to avoid being detected
- **Eradication** Removes itself after the payload has been executed
- **Replication** Makes copies of itself and spreads to other victims
- **Trigger** Uses an event to initiate its payload execution
- **Payload** Carries out its function (that is, deletes files, installs a back door, exploits a vulnerability, and so on)

Worms

Worms are different from viruses in that they can reproduce on their own without a host application, and are self-contained programs. As an analogy, medical viruses (e.g., the common cold) spread through human hosts. The virus can make our noses run or cause us to sneeze, which are just the virus's way of reproducing and spreading itself. The virus is a collection of particles (DNA, RNA, proteins, lipids) and can only replicate within living cells. A virus cannot fall on the floor and just wait for someone to pass by and infect—it requires host-to-host transmission. A computer virus also requires a host, because it is not a full and self-sufficient program. A computer virus cannot make our computer sneeze, but it could make our applications share infected files, which is similar in nature.

In the nondigital world, worms are not viruses. They are invertebrate animals that can function on their own. They reproduce through some type of sexual or asexual replication process, but do not require a "host environment" of a living cell to carry out these activities. In the digital world, worms are just little programs, and like viruses they are used to transport and deliver malicious payloads. One of the most famous computer worms is Stuxnet, which targeted Siemens supervisory control and data acquisition (SCADA) software and equipment. It has a highly specialized payload that was used against Iran's uranium enrichment infrastructures with the goal of damaging the country's nuclear program.

Rootkit

When a system is successfully compromised, an attacker may attempt to elevate his privileges to obtain administrator- or root user–level access. Once the level of access is achieved, the attacker can upload a bundle of tools, collectively called a *rootkit*. The first thing that is usually installed is a back-door program, which allows the attacker to enter the system at any time without having to go through any authentication steps. The other common tools in a rootkit allow for credential capturing, sniffing, attacking other systems, and covering the attacker's tracks.

The rootkit is just a set of tools that is placed on the compromised system for future use. Once the rootkit is loaded, the attacker can use these tools against the system or other systems it is connected to whenever he wants to.

The attacker usually replaces default system tools with new compromised tools, which share the same name. They are referred to as "Trojaned programs" because they carry out the intended functionality but do some malicious activity in the background. This is done to help ensure that the rootkit is not detected.

Most rootkits have Trojaned programs that replace these tools, because the root user could run `ps` or `top` and see there is a back-door service running, and thus detect the presence of a compromise. But when this user runs one of these Trojaned programs, the compromised tool lists all other services except the back-door process. Most rootkits also contain sniffers, so the data can be captured and reviewed by the attacker. For a sniffer to work, the system's network interface card (NIC) must be put into promiscuous mode, which just means it can "hear" all the traffic on the network link. The default ipconfig utility allows the root user to employ a specific parameter to see whether or not the NIC is running in promiscuous mode. So, the rootkit also contains a Trojaned ipconfig program, which hides the fact that the NIC is in promiscuous mode.

Rootkits commonly include "log scrubbers," which remove traces of the attacker's activities from the system logs. They can also contain Trojaned programs that replace `find` and `ls` Unix utilities, so that when a user does a listing of what is in a specific directory, the rootkit will not be listed.

Some of the more powerful rootkits actually update the kernel of the system instead of just replacing individual utilities. Modifying the kernel's code gives the attacker much more control over a system. It is also very difficult to detect kernel updates, compared to replaced utilities, because most host IDS (HIDS) products look at changes to file sizes and modification dates, which would apply to utilities and programs but not necessarily to the kernel of the operating system.

Rootkit detection can be difficult because the rootkit may be able to subvert the software that is intended to find it. Detection methods include behavioral-based methods, signature-based scanning, and memory dump analysis. Removal can be complicated, especially in cases where the rootkit resides in the kernel; reinstallation of the operating system may be the only available solution to the problem.

Rootkits and their payloads have many functions, including concealing other malware, as in password-stealing key loggers and computer viruses. A rootkit might also install software that allows the compromised system to become a zombie for specific botnets.

Rootkits can reside at the user level of an operating system, at the kernel level, in a system's firmware, or in a hypervisor of a system using virtualization. A user-level rootkit does not have as much access or privilege compared to a kernel-level rootkit, and thus cannot carry out as much damage.

If a rootkit resides in the hypervisor of a system, it can exploit hardware virtualization features and target host operating systems. This allows the rootkit to intercept hardware calls made by the original operating system. This is not a very common type of rootkit that is deployed and used in the industry, but it is something that will probably become more popular because of the expansive use of virtualization.

Rootkits that reside in firmware are difficult to detect because software integrity checking does not usually extend down to the firmware level. If a rootkit is installed on a system's firmware, that can allow it to load into memory before the full operating system and protection tools are loaded on the system.

Spyware and Adware

Spyware is a type of malware that is covertly installed on a target computer to gather sensitive information about a victim. The gathered data may be used for malicious activities, such as identity theft, spamming fraud, etc. Spyware can also gather information about a victim's online browsing habits, which is then often used by spammers to send targeted advertisements. Spyware can also be used by an attacker to direct a victim's computer to perform tasks such as installing software, changing system settings, transferring browsing history, logging keystrokes, taking screenshots, etc.

Adware is software that automatically generates (renders) advertisements. The ads can be provided through pop-ups, user interface components, or screens presented during the installation of updates of other products. The goal of adware is to generate sales revenue, not carry out malicious activities, but some adware uses invasive measures, which can cause security and privacy issues.

Botnets

A "bot" is short for "robot" and is a piece of code that carries out functionality for its master, who could be the author of this code. Bots allow for simple tasks to be carried out in an automated manner in a web-based environment. While bot software can be used for legitimate purposes (e.g., web crawling), we are going to focus on how it can be used in a malicious manner.

Bots are a type of malware and are being installed on thousands of computers even now as you're reading this sentence. They are installed on vulnerable victim systems through infected e-mail messages, drive-by downloads, Trojan horses, and the use of shared media. Once the bot is loaded on a victim system, it usually lies dormant (zombie code) and waits for command instructions for activation purposes.

The bot can send a message to the hacker indicating that a specific system has been compromised and the system is now available to be used by the attacker as she wishes. When a hacker has a collection of these compromised systems, it is referred to as a *botnet* (network of bots). The hacker can use all of these systems to carry out powerful DDoS attacks or even rent these systems to spammers.

The owner of this botnet (commonly referred to as the *bot herder*) controls the systems remotely, usually through the Internet Relay Chat (IRC) protocol.

The common steps of the development and use of a botnet are listed next:

1. A hacker sends out malicious code that has the bot software as its payload.
2. Once installed, the bot logs into an IRC or web server that it is coded to contact. The server then acts as the controlling server of the botnet.
3. A spammer pays the hacker to use these systems and sends instructions to the controller server, which causes all of the infected systems to send out spam messages to mail servers.

Spammers use this method so their messages have a higher likelihood of getting through mail server spam filters since the sending IP addresses are those of the victims' systems. Thus, the source IP addresses change constantly. This is how you are constantly updated on the new male enhancement solutions and ways to purchase Viagra.

Figure 8-41 illustrates the life cycle of a botnet. The botnet herder works with, or pays, hackers to develop and spread malware to infect systems that will become part of the botnet. Whoever wants to tell you about a new product they just released, carry out identity theft, conduct attacks, and so on can pay the herder to use the botnet for their purposes.

Botnets can be used for spamming, brute-force and DDoS attacks, click fraud, fast flux techniques, and the spread of illegal material. The traffic can pass over IRC or HTTP and even be tunneled through Twitter, instant messaging, and other common traffic types. The servers that send the bots instructions and manage the botnets are commonly referred to as *command-and-control (C&C)* servers, and they can maintain thousands or millions of computers at one time.

NOTE *Fast flux* is an evasion technique. Botnets can use fast flux functionality to hide the phishing and malware delivery sites they are using. One common method is to rapidly update DNS information to disguise the hosting location of the malicious websites.

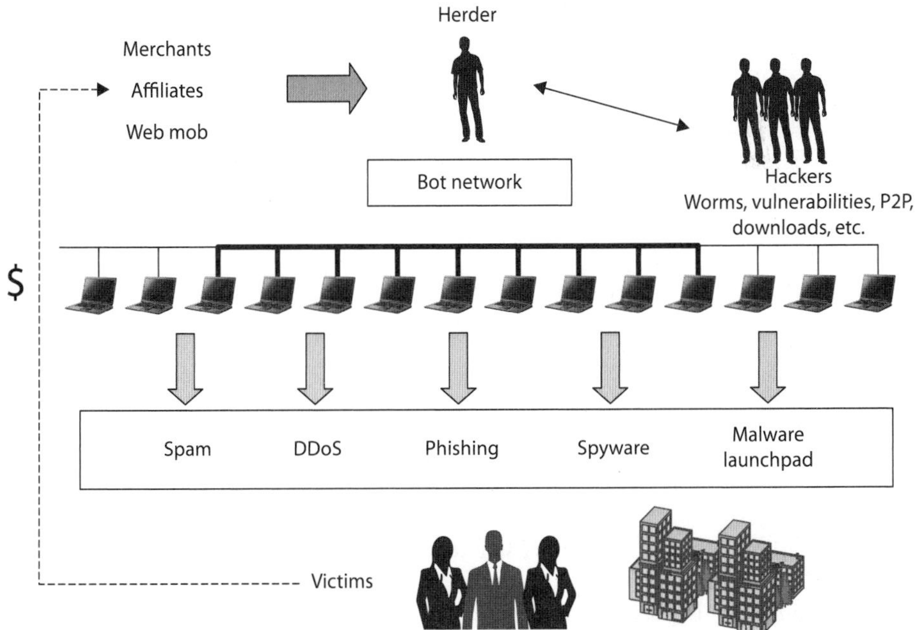

Figure 8-41 The cycle of how botnets are created, maintained, and used

Logic Bombs

A *logic bomb* executes a program, or string of code, when a certain set of conditions is met. For example, a network administrator may install and configure a logic bomb that is programmed to delete the company's whole database if he is terminated.

The logic bomb software can have many types of triggers that activate its payload execution, as in time and date or after a user carries out a specific action. For example, many times compromised systems have logic bombs installed so that if forensics activities are carried out the logic bomb initiates and deletes all of the digital evidence. This thwarts the investigation team's success and helps hide the attacker's identity and methods.

Trojan Horses

A *Trojan horse* is a program that is disguised as another program. For example, a Trojan horse can be named Notepad.exe and have the same icon as the regular Notepad program. However, when a user executes Notepad.exe, the program can delete system files. Trojan horses perform a useful functionality in addition to the malicious functionality in the background. So the Trojan horse named Notepad.exe may still run the Notepad program for the user, but in the background it will manipulate files or cause other malicious acts.

Trojan horses are one of the fastest growing malware types in the world. In fact, PandaLabs reported that over 69 percent of malware samples observed during 2015 were Trojans. Users are commonly tricked into downloading some type of software from a website that is actually malicious. The Trojan horse can then set up a back door, install keystroke loggers, implement rootkits, upload files from the victim's system, install bot software, and perform many other types of malicious acts. Trojan horses are commonly used to carry out various types of online banking fraud and identity theft activities.

Remote access Trojans (RATs) are malicious programs that run on systems and allow intruders to access and use a system remotely. They mimic the functionality of legitimate remote control programs used for remote administration, but are used for sinister purposes instead of helpful activities. They are developed to allow for stealth installation and operation, and are usually hidden in some type of mobile code, such as Java applets or ActiveX controls, that are downloaded from websites.

Several RAT programs are available to the hacker (Sakula, KjW0rm, Havex, Dark Comet, and others). Once the RAT is loaded on the victim's system, the attacker can download or upload files, send commands, monitor user behaviors, install zombie software, activate the webcam, take screenshots, alter files, and use the compromised system as he pleases.

Crimeware Toolkits

Creating and spreading malware used to require programming knowledge, but today people can purchase crimeware toolkits that allow them to create their own tailored malware through GUI-based tools. These toolkits provide predeveloped malicious code that can be easily customized, deployed, and automated. The kits

are sold in the online underground black market and allow people with little to no technical skill to carry out cybercrime activities. These "out-of-the-box" solutions have lowered the entry barrier for cybercriminals by making sophisticated attacks easy to carry out.

The following shows the administrative interface provided by a commonly used crimeware toolkit, Spy Eye, that attackers can use to maintain and control their compromised systems.

Antimalware Software

Traditional antimalware software uses signatures to detect malicious code. Signatures, sometimes referred to as fingerprints, are created by antimalware vendors. An individual signature is a sequence of code that an antimalware vendor has extracted from the virus itself. Just like our bodies have antibodies that identify and go after a specific type of foreign material, an antimalware software package has an engine that uses these signatures to identify malware. The antimalware software scans files, e-mail messages, and other data passing through specific protocols, and then compares them to its database of signatures. When there is a match, the antimalware software carries out whatever activities it is configured to do, which can be to quarantine the file, attempt to clean the file (remove the virus), provide a warning message dialog box to the user, and/or log the event.

Signature-based detection (also called *fingerprint detection*) is a reasonably effective way to detect conventional malware, but there is a delayed response time to new threats. Once a virus is detected, the antimalware vendor must study it, develop and test a new signature, release the signature, and all customers must download it. If the malicious code is just sending out silly pictures to all of your friends, this delay is not so critical. If the malicious software is similar to the Slammer worm, this amount of delay can be devastating.

Since new malware is released daily, it is hard for antimalware software to keep up. The technique of using signatures means this software can only detect viruses that have been identified and where a signature is created. Since virus writers are prolific and busy beasts, and because viruses can morph, it is important that the antimalware software have other tricks up its sleeve to detect malicious code.

Another technique that almost all antimalware software products use is referred to as *heuristic detection*. This approach analyzes the overall structure of the malicious code, evaluates the coded instructions and logic functions, and looks at the type of data within the virus or worm. So, it collects a bunch of information about this piece of code and assesses the likelihood of it being malicious in nature. It has a type of "suspiciousness counter," which is incremented as the program finds more potentially malicious attributes. Once a predefined threshold is met, the code is officially considered dangerous and the antimalware software jumps into action to protect the system. This allows antimalware software to detect unknown malware, instead of just relying on signatures.

As an analogy, let's say Barney is the town cop who is employed to root out the bad guys and lock them up (quarantine). If Barney was going to use a signature method, he would compare a stack of photographs to each person he sees on the street. When he sees a match, he quickly throws the bad guy into his patrol car and drives off. If he was going to use the heuristic method, he would be watching for suspicious activity. So if someone with a ski mask was standing outside a bank, Barney would assess the likelihood of this being a bank robber against it just being a cold guy in need of some cash.

CAUTION Diskless workstations are still vulnerable to viruses, even though they do not have a hard disk and a full operating system. They can still get viruses that load and reside in memory. These systems can be rebooted remotely (remote booting) to bring the memory back to a clean state, which means the virus is "flushed" out of the system.

Some antimalware products create a simulated environment, called a virtual machine or sandbox, and allow some of the logic within the suspected code to execute in the protected environment. This allows the antimalware software to see the code in question in action, which gives it more information as to whether or not it is malicious.

NOTE The virtual machine or sandbox is also sometimes referred to as an *emulation buffer*. They are all the same thing—a piece of memory that is segmented and protected so that if the code is malicious, the system is protected.

Reviewing information about a piece of code is called *static analysis*, while allowing a portion of the code to run in a virtual machine is called *dynamic analysis*. They are both considered heuristic detection methods.

Now, even though all of these approaches are sophisticated and effective, they are not 100-percent effective because malware writers are crafty. It is a continual cat-and-mouse game that is carried out each and every day. The antimalware industry comes out with a

new way of detecting malware, and the very next week the malware writers have a way to get around this approach. This means that antimalware vendors have to continually increase the intelligence of their products and you have to buy a new version every year.

The next phase in the antimalware software evolution is referred to as behavior blockers. Antimalware software that carries out *behavior blocking* actually allows the suspicious code to execute within the operating system unprotected and watches its interactions with the operating system, looking for suspicious activities. The antimalware software would be watching for the following types of actions:

- Writing to startup files or the Run keys in the Registry
- Opening, deleting, or modifying files
- Scripting e-mail messages to send executable code
- Connecting to network shares or resources
- Modifying an executable logic
- Creating or modifying macros and scripts
- Formatting a hard drive or writing to the boot sector

Immunizers

Another approach some antimalware software uses is called *immunization*. Products with this type of functionality would make it look as though a file, program, or disk was already infected. An *immunizer* attaches code to the file or application, which would fool a virus into "thinking" it was already infected. This would cause the virus to not infect this file (or application) and move onto the next file.

Immunizers are usually virus specific, since a specific virus is going to make a distinct call to a file to uncover if it has been infected. The challenge is that as the number of viruses (and other malware types) increases so do the number of files that need to be immunized. Because of this challenge, immunizers are not normally part of common antimalware solutions. They are still, however, a topic of research and show promise as we look at intelligent, adaptive systems that can respond to attacks at machine speed.

If the antimalware program detects some of these potentially malicious activities, it can terminate the software and provide a message to the user. The newer generation behavior blockers actually analyze sequences of these types of operations before determining the system is infected. (The first-generation behavior blockers only looked for individual actions, which resulted in a large number of false positives.) The newer generation software can intercept a dangerous piece of code and not allow it to interact with other running processes. They can also detect rootkits. In addition, some of these antimalware programs can allow the system to roll back to a state before an infection took place so the damages inflicted can be "erased."

While it sounds like behavior blockers might bring us our well-deserved bliss and utopia, one drawback is that the malicious code must actually execute in real time; otherwise, our systems can be damaged. This type of constant monitoring also requires a high level of system resources. We just can't seem to win.

EXAM TIP Heuristic detection and behavior blocking is considered proactive and can detect new malware, sometimes called "zero day" attacks. Signature-based detection cannot detect new malware.

Most antimalware vendors use a blend of all of these technologies to provide as much protection as possible. The individual antimalware attack solutions are shown in Figure 8-42.

NOTE Another antimalware technique is referred to as "reputation-based protection." An antimalware vendor collects data from many (or all) of its customers' systems and mines that data to search for patterns to help identify good and bad files. Each file type is assigned a reputation metric value, indicating the probability of it being "good" or "bad." These values are used by the antimalware software to help it identify "bad" (suspicious) files.

Spam Detection

We are all pretty tired of receiving e-mails that try to sell us things we don't need. A great job working from home, a master's degree that requires no studying, and a great sex life are all just a click away (and only $19.99!)—as promised by this continual stream of messages. These e-mails have been given the label *spam*, which is unsolicited junk e-mail. Along with being a nuisance, spam eats up a lot of network bandwidth and can be the source of spreading malware. Many organizations have spam filters on their mail servers, and users can configure spam rules within their e-mail clients, but just as virus writers always come up with ways to circumvent antimalware software, spammers come up with clever ways of getting around spam filters.

Detecting spam properly has become a science in itself. One technique used is called *Bayesian filtering*. Many moons ago, a gentleman named Thomas Bayes (a mathematician) developed a way to actually guess the probability of something being true by using math. Now what is fascinating about this is that in mathematics things are either true or they are not. This is the same in software. Software deals with 1's and 0's, on and off, true and false. Software does not deal with the grays (probabilities) of life too well.

Bayesian logic reviews prior events to predict future events, which is basically quantifying uncertainty. Conceptually, this is not too hard to understand. If you run into a brick wall three times and fall down, you should conclude that your future attempts will result in the same painful outcomes. What is more interesting is when this logic is performed on activities that contain many more variables. For example, how does a spam filter ensure you do not receive e-mails trying to sell you Viagra, but does

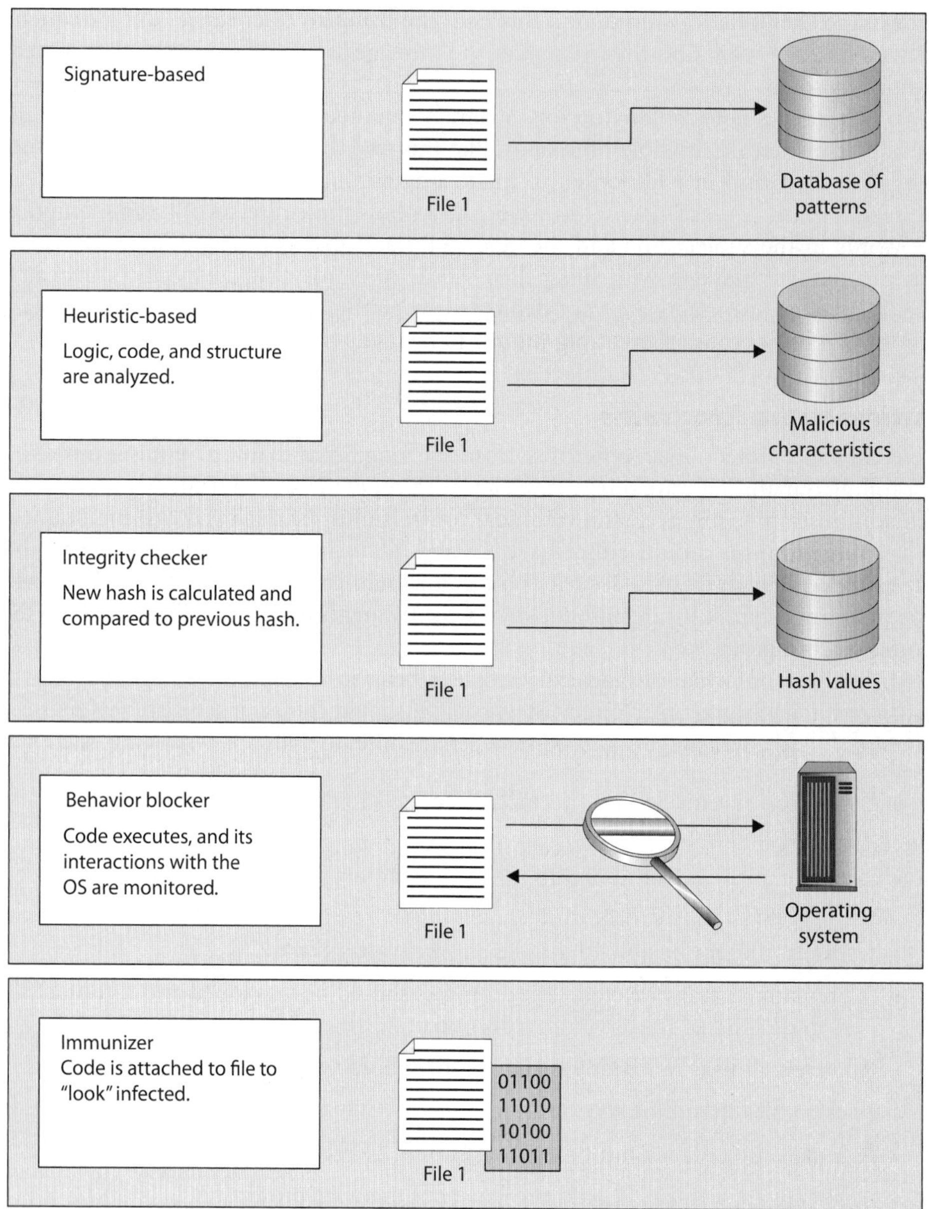

Figure 8-42 Antimalware vendors use various types of malware detection.

allow the e-mails from your friend who is obsessed with Viagra and wants to continue e-mailing you about this drug's effects and attributes? A Bayesian filter applies statistical modeling to the words that make up an e-mail message. This means the words that make up the message have mathematical formulas performed on them to be able to fully

understand their relationship to one another. The Bayesian filter carries out a frequency analysis on each word and then evaluates the message as a whole to determine whether or not it is spam.

So this filter is not just looking for "Viagra," "manhood," "sex," and other words that cannot be printed in a wholesome book like this one. It is looking at how often these words are used, and in what order, to make a determination as to whether or not this message is spam. Unfortunately, spammers know how these filters work and manipulate the words in the subject line and message to try and fool the spam filter. This is why you can receive messages with misspelled words or words that use symbols instead of characters. The spammers are very dedicated to getting messages promising utopia to your e-mail box because there is big money to be made that way.

Antimalware Programs

Detecting and protecting an enterprise from the long list of malware requires more than just rolling out antimalware software. Just as with other pieces of a security program, certain administrative, physical, and technical controls must be deployed and maintained.

The organization should either have a stand-alone antimalware policy or have one incorporated into an existing security policy. It should include standards outlining what type of antimalware software and antispyware software should be installed and how they should be configured.

Antimalware information and expected user behaviors should be integrated into the security-awareness program, along with who a user should contact if she discovers a virus. A standard should cover the do's and don'ts when it comes to malware, which are listed next:

- Every workstation, server, and mobile device should have antimalware software installed.
- An automated way of updating malware signatures should be deployed on each device.
- Users should not be able to disable antimalware software.
- A preplanned malware eradication process should be developed and a contact person designated in case of an infection.
- All external disks (USB drives and so on) should be scanned automatically.
- Backup files should be scanned.
- Antimalware policies and procedures should be reviewed annually.
- Antimalware software should provide boot malware protection.
- Antimalware scanning should happen at a gateway and on each device.
- Virus scans should be automated and scheduled. Do not rely on manual scans.
- Critical systems should be physically protected so malicious software cannot be installed locally.

NOTE Antimalware files that contain updates (new signatures) are called DAT files. It is just a data file with the file extension of .dat.

Since malware has cost organizations millions of dollars in operational costs and productivity hits, many have implemented antimalware solutions at network entry points. The scanning software can be integrated into a mail server, proxy server, or firewall. (They solutions are sometimes referred to as *virus walls.*) This software scans incoming traffic, looking for malware so it can be detected and stopped before entering the network. These products can scan Simple Mail Transport Protocol (SMTP), HTTP, FTP, and possibly other protocol types, but what is important to realize is that the product is only looking at one or two protocols and not *all* of the incoming traffic. This is the reason each server and workstation should also have antimalware software installed.

Assessing the Security of Acquired Software

Most organizations do not have the in-house capability to develop their own software systems. Their only feasible options are either to acquire standard software or to have a vendor customize a standard software system to their particular environment. In either case, software from an external source will be allowed to execute in a trusted environment. Depending on how trustworthy the source and the code are, this could have some profound implications to the security posture of the organization's systems. As always, we need to ground our response on our risk management process.

In terms of managing the risk associated with acquired software, the essential question to ask is: How is the organization affected if this software behaves improperly? Improper behavior could be the consequence of either defects or misconfiguration. The defects can manifest themselves as computing errors (e.g., wrong results) or vulnerability to intentional attack. A related question is: What is it that we are protecting and this software could compromise? Is it PII, intellectual property, or national security information? The answers to these and other questions will dictate the required thoroughness of our approach.

In many cases, our approach to mitigating the risks of acquired software will begin with an assessment of the vendor. Characteristics that correlate to a lower risk from a given vendor's software include the reputation of the vendor and the regularity of its patch pushes. Conversely, vendors may be riskier if they are small or new companies, if they have immature or undocumented development processes, or if their products have broad marketplace presence (meaning they are more lucrative targets to exploit developers).

A key element in assessing the security of acquired software is, rather obviously, its performance on an internal assessment. Ideally, we are able to obtain the source code from the vendor so that we can do our own code reviews, vulnerability assessments, and penetration tests. In many cases, however, this will not be possible. Our only possible assessment may be a penetration test. The catch is that we may not have the in-house

capability to perform such a test. In such cases, and depending on the potential risk posed by this software, we may be well advised to hire an external party to perform an independent penetration test for us. This is likely a costly affair that would only be justifiable in cases where a successful attack against the software system would likely lead to significant losses for the organization.

Even in the most constrained case, we are still able to mitigate the risk of acquisition. If we don't have the means to do code reviews, vulnerability assessments, or penetration tests, we can still mitigate the risk by deploying the software only in specific subnetworks, with hardened configurations, and with restrictive IDS/IPS rules monitoring its behavior. Though this approach may initially lead to constrained functionality and excessive false positives on our intrusion detection/prevention systems, we can always gradually loosen the controls as we gain assurances that the software is trustworthy. That is, after all, the bottom line for this entire chapter.

Summary

Although functionality is the first concern when developing software, adding security into the mix before the project starts and then integrating it into every step of the development process is highly beneficial. Although many companies do not view this as the most beneficial approach to software development, they are becoming convinced of it over time as more security patches and fixes must be developed and released, and as their customers continually demand more secure products.

Software development is a complex task, especially as technology changes at the speed of light, environments evolve, and more expectations are placed upon vendors who wish to be the "king of the mountain" within the software market. This complexity also makes implementing effective security more challenging. Years ago, programmers and developers did not need to consider security issues within their code, but this has not been true for a very long time. Education, experience, awareness, enforcement, and the demands of the consumers are all necessary pieces to bring more secure practices and technologies to the program code we all use.

Quick Tips

- Security should be addressed in each phase of system development. It should not be addressed only at the end of development because of the added cost, time, and effort and the lack of functionality.
- The attack surface is the collection of possible entry points for an attacker. The reduction of this surface reduces the possible ways that an attacker can exploit a system.
- Threat modeling is a systematic approach used to understand how different threats could be realized and how a successful compromise could take place.

- Computer-aided software engineering refers to any type of software that allows for the automated development of software, which can come in the form of program editors, debuggers, code analyzers, version-control mechanisms, and more. The goals are to increase development speed and productivity and reduce errors.
- Various levels of testing should be carried out during development: unit (testing individual components), integration (verifying components work together in the production environment), acceptance (ensuring code meets customer requirements), regression (testing after changes take place), static analysis (reviewing programming code), and dynamic analysis (reviewing code during execution).
- Fuzzing is the act of sending random data to the target program in order to trigger failures.
- Zero-day vulnerabilities are vulnerabilities that do not currently have a resolution or solution.
- The ISO/IEC 27034 standard covers the following items: application security overview and concepts, organization normative framework, application security management process, protocols and application security control data structure, case studies, and application security assurance prediction.
- The Open Web Application Security Project (OWASP) is an organization dedicated to helping the industry develop more secure software.
- An integrated product team (IPT) is a multidisciplinary development team with representatives from many or all the stakeholder populations.
- The CMMI model uses five maturity levels designated by the numbers 1 through 5. Each level represents the maturity level of the process quality and optimization. The levels are organized as follows: 1 = Initial, 2 = Repeatable, 3 = Defined, 4 = Managed, 5 = Optimizing.
- CMMI (Capability Maturity Model Integration) is a process improvement approach that provides organizations with the essential elements of effective processes, which will improve their performance.
- Change control needs to be put in place at the beginning of a project and must be enforced through each phase. Changes must be authorized, tested, and recorded. The changes must not affect the security level of the system or its capability to enforce the security policy.
- There are several SDLC models: Waterfall (sequential approach that requires each phase to complete before the next one can begin), V-model (emphasizes verification and validation at each phase), Prototyping (creating a sample of the code for proof-of-concept purposes), Incremental (multiple development cycles are carried out on a piece of software throughout its development stages), Spiral (iterative approach that emphases risk analysis per iteration), Rapid Application Development (combines prototyping and iterative development procedures with

the goal of accelerating the software development process), and Agile (iterative and incremental development processes that encourage team-based collaboration, and flexibility and adaptability are used instead of a strict process structure).

- Software configuration management (SCM) is the task of tracking and controlling changes in the software through the use of authentication, revision control, the establishment of baselines, and auditing. It has the purpose of maintaining software integrity and traceability throughout the software development life cycle.
- Programming languages have gone through evolutionary processes. Generation one is machine language (binary format). Generation two is assembly language (which is translated by an assembler into machine code). Generation three is high-level language (which provides a level of abstraction). Generation four is a very high-level language (which provides more programming abstraction). Generation five is natural language (which is used for artificial intelligence purposes).
- Data modeling is a process used to define and analyze data requirements needed to support the business processes within the scope of corresponding systems and software applications.
- Object-oriented programming provides modularity, reusability, and more granular control within the programs themselves compared to classical programming languages.
- Objects are members, or instances, of classes. The classes dictate the objects' data types, structure, and acceptable actions.
- In OOP, objects communicate with each other through messages, and a method is functionality that an object can carry out. Objects can communicate properly because they use standard interfaces.
- Polymorphism is when different objects are given the same input and react differently.
- Data and operations internal to objects are hidden from other objects, which is referred to as data hiding. Each object encapsulates its data and processes.
- Object-oriented design represents a real-world problem and modularizes the problem into cooperating objects that work together to solve the problem.
- If an object does not require much interaction with other modules, it has low coupling.
- The best programming design enables objects to be as independent and as modular as possible; therefore, the higher the cohesion and the lower the coupling, the better.
- An object request broker (ORB) manages communications between objects and enables them to interact in a heterogeneous and distributed environment.
- Common Object Request Broker Architecture (CORBA) provides a standardized way for objects within different applications, platforms, and environments to communicate. It accomplishes this by providing standards for interfaces between objects.

- Component Object Model (COM) provides an architecture for components to interact on a local system. Distributed COM (DCOM) uses the same interfaces as COM, but enables components to interact over a distributed, or networked, environment.
- Open Database Connectivity (ODBC) enables several different applications to communicate with several different types of databases by calling the required driver and passing data through that driver.
- Object linking and embedding (OLE) enables a program to call another program (linking) and permits a piece of data to be inserted inside another program or document (embedding).
- Service-oriented architecture (SOA) provides standardized access to the most needed services to many different applications at one time. Service interactions are self-contained and loosely coupled so that each interaction is independent of any other interaction.
- Java security employs a sandbox so the applet is restricted from accessing the user's hard drive or system resources. Programmers have figured out how to write applets that escape the sandbox.
- SOAP allows programs created with different programming languages and running on different operating systems to interact without compatibility issues.
- There are three main types of cross-site scripting (XSS) attacks: nonpersistent XSS (exploiting the lack of proper input or output validation on dynamic websites), persistent XSS (attacker loads malicious code on a server that attacks visiting browsers), and DOM (attacker uses the DOM environment to modify the original client-side JavaScript).
- A database management system (DBMS) is the software that controls the access restrictions, data integrity, redundancy, and the different types of manipulation available for a database.
- A database primary key is how a specific row is located from other parts of the database in a relational database.
- A view is an access control mechanism used in databases to ensure that only authorized subjects can access sensitive information.
- A relational database uses two-dimensional tables with rows (tuples) and columns (attributes).
- A hierarchical database uses a tree-like structure to define relationships between data elements, using a parent/child relationship.
- Most databases have a data definition language (DDL), a data manipulation language (DML), a query language (QL), and a report generator.
- A data dictionary is a central repository that describes the data elements within a database and their relationships.

- Database integrity is provided by concurrency mechanisms. One concurrency control is locking, which prevents users from accessing and modifying data being used by someone else.
- Entity integrity makes sure that a row, or tuple, is uniquely identified by a primary key, and referential integrity ensures that every foreign key refers to an existing primary key.
- A rollback cancels changes and returns the database to its previous state. This takes place if there is a problem during a transaction.
- A commit statement saves all changes to the database.
- A checkpoint is used if there is a system failure or problem during a transaction. The user is then returned to the state of the last checkpoint.
- Aggregation can happen if a user does not have access to a group of elements, but has access to some of the individual elements within the group. Aggregation happens if the user combines the information of these individual elements and figures out the information of the group of data elements, which is at a higher sensitivity level.
- Inference is the capability to derive information that is not explicitly available.
- Common attempts to prevent inference attacks are partitioning the database, cell suppression, and adding noise to the database.
- Polyinstantiation is the process of allowing a table to have multiple rows with the same primary key. The different instances can be distinguished by their security levels or classifications.
- Data warehousing combines data from multiple databases and data sources.
- Data mining is the process of searching, filtering, and associating data held within a data warehouse to provide more useful information to users.
- Data-mining tools produce metadata, which can contain previously unseen relationships and patterns.
- A virus is an application that requires a host application for replication.
- Macro viruses are common because the languages used to develop macros are easy to use and they infect Microsoft Office products, which are everywhere.
- A polymorphic virus tries to escape detection by making copies of itself and modifying the code and attributes of those copies.
- A worm does not require a host application to replicate.
- A logic bomb executes a program when a predefined event takes place, or a date and time are met.
- A Trojan horse is a program that performs useful functionality apparent to the user and malicious functionally without the user knowing it.
- Botnets are networks of bots that are controlled by C&C servers and bot herders.

- Antimalware software is most effective when it is installed in every entry and end point and covered by a policy that delineates user training as well as software configuration and updating.
- Assessing the security of acquired software, in addition to internal or third-party tests, requires that we assess the reliability and maturity of the vendor.

Questions

Please remember that these questions are formatted and asked in a certain way for a reason. Keep in mind that the CISSP exam is asking questions at a conceptual level. Questions may not always have the perfect answer, and the candidate is advised against always looking for the perfect answer. Instead, the candidate should look for the best answer in the list.

1. An application is downloaded from the Internet to perform disk cleanup and to delete unnecessary temporary files. The application is also recording network login data and sending it to another party. This application is best described as which of the following?
   A. A virus
   B. A Trojan horse
   C. A worm
   D. A logic bomb
2. Which of the following best describes the term DevOps?
   A. The practice of incorporating development, IT, and quality assurance (QA) staff into software development projects.
   B. A multidisciplinary development team with representatives from many or all the stakeholder populations.
   C. The operationalization of software development activities to support just-in-time delivery.
   D. A software development methodology that relies more on the use of operational prototypes than on extensive upfront planning.
3. A system has been patched many times and has recently become infected with a dangerous virus. If antimalware software indicates that disinfecting a file may damage it, what is the correct action?
   A. Disinfect the file and contact the vendor
   B. Back up the data and disinfect the file
   C. Replace the file with the file saved the day before
   D. Restore an uninfected version of the patched file from backup media

4. What is the purpose of polyinstantiation?
   A. To restrict lower-level subjects from accessing low-level information
   B. To make a copy of an object and modify the attributes of the second copy
   C. To create different objects that will react in different ways to the same input
   D. To create different objects that will take on inheritance attributes from their class
5. Database views provide what type of security control?
   A. Detective
   B. Corrective
   C. Preventive
   D. Administrative
6. Which of the following techniques or set of techniques is used to deter database inference attacks?
   A. Partitioning, cell suppression, and noise and perturbation
   B. Controlling access to the data dictionary
   C. Partitioning, cell suppression, and small query sets
   D. Partitioning, noise and perturbation, and small query sets
7. When should security first be addressed in a project?
   A. During requirements development
   B. During integration testing
   C. During design specifications
   D. During implementation
8. An online transaction processing (OLTP) system that detects an invalid transaction should do which of the following?
   A. Roll back and rewrite over original data
   B. Terminate all transactions until properly addressed
   C. Write a report to be reviewed
   D. Checkpoint each data entry

9. Which of the following are rows and columns within relational databases?
    A. Rows and tuples
    B. Attributes and rows
    C. Keys and views
    D. Tuples and attributes
10. Databases can record transactions in real time, which usually updates more than one database in a distributed environment. This type of complexity can introduce many integrity threats, so the database software should implement the characteristics of what's known as the ACID test. Which of the following are incorrect characteristics of the ACID test?
    i. **Atomicity** Divides transactions into units of work and ensures that all modifications take effect or none takes effect.
    ii. **Consistency** A transaction must follow the integrity policy developed for that particular database and ensure all data is consistent in the different databases.
    iii. **Isolation** Transactions execute in isolation until completed, without interacting with other transactions.
    iv. **Durability** Once the transaction is verified as inaccurate on all systems, it is committed and the databases cannot be rolled back.
    A. i, ii
    B. ii. iii
    C. ii, iv
    D. iv
11. The software development life cycle has several phases. Which of the following lists these phases in the correct order?
    A. Requirements gathering, design, development, maintenance, testing, release
    B. Requirements gathering, design, development, testing, release
    C. Prototyping, build and fix, increment, test, maintenance
    D. Prototyping, testing, requirements gathering, integration, testing

12. John is a manager of the application development department within his company. He needs to make sure his team is carrying out all of the correct testing types and at the right times of the development stages. Which of the following accurately describe types of software testing that should be carried out?
    i. **Unit testing** Testing individual components in a controlled environment where programmers validate data structure, logic, and boundary conditions.
    ii. **Integration testing** Verifying that components work together as outlined in design specifications.
    iii. **Acceptance testing** Ensuring that the code meets customer requirements.
    iv. **Regression testing** After a change to a system takes place, retesting to ensure functionality, performance, and protection.
    A. i, ii
    B. ii, iii
    C. i, ii, iv
    D. i, ii, iii, iv
13. Tim is a software developer for a financial institution. He develops middleware software code that carries out his company's business logic functions. One of the applications he works with is written in the C programming language and seems to be taking up too much memory as it runs over time. Which of the following best describes what Tim should implement to rid this software of this type of problem?
    A. Bounds checking
    B. Garbage collector
    C. Parameter checking
    D. Compiling
14. Marge has to choose a software development model that her team should follow. The application that her team is responsible for developing is a critical application that can have few to no errors. Which of the following best describes the type of model her team should follow?
    A. Cleanroom
    B. Joint Analysis Development (JAD)
    C. Rapid Application Development (RAD)
    D. Reuse model
15. __________ is a software testing technique that provides invalid, unexpected, or random data to the input interfaces of a program.
    A. Agile testing
    B. Structured testing
    C. Fuzzing
    D. EICAR

16. Which of the following is the second level of the Capability Maturity Model Integration?
    A. Repeatable
    B. Defined
    C. Managed
    D. Optimizing
17. One of the characteristics of object-oriented programming is deferred commitment. Which of the following is the best description for this characteristic?
    A. The building blocks of software are autonomous objects, cooperating through the exchange of messages.
    B. The internal components of an object can be redefined without changing other parts of the system.
    C. Classes are reused by other programs, though they may be refined through inheritance.
    D. Object-oriented analysis, design, and modeling map to business needs and solutions.
18. Which of the following attack types best describes what commonly takes place when you insert specially crafted and excessively long data into an input field?
    A. Traversal attack
    B. Unicode encoding attack
    C. URL encoding attack
    D. Buffer overflow attack
19. Which of the following has an incorrect attack to definition mapping?
    A. **EBJ XSS attack** Content processing stages performed by the client, typically in client-side Java.
    B. **Nonpersistent XSS attack** Improper sanitation of response from a web client.
    C. **Persistent XSS attack** Data provided by attackers is saved on the server.
    D. **DOM-based XSS attack** Content processing stages performed by the client, typically in client-side JavaScript.
20. John is reviewing database products. He needs a product that can manipulate a standard set of data for his company's business logic needs. Which of the following should the necessary product implement?
    A. Relational database
    B. Object-relational database
    C. Network database
    D. Dynamic-static

21. ActiveX Data Objects (ADO) is an API that allows applications to access back-end database systems. It is a set of ODBC interfaces that exposes the functionality of data sources through accessible objects. Which of the following are incorrect characteristics of ADO?
    i. It's a low-level data access programming interface to an underlying data access technology (such as OLE DB).
    ii. It's a set of COM objects for accessing data sources, not just database access.
    iii. It allows a developer to write programs that access data without knowing how the database is implemented.
    iv. SQL commands are required to access a database when using ADO.
    A. i, iv
    B. ii, iii
    C. i, ii, iii
    D. i, ii, iii, iv
22. Database software performs three main types of integrity services: semantic, referential, and entity. Which of the following correctly describes one of these services?
    i. A semantic integrity mechanism makes sure structural and semantic rules are enforced.
    ii. A database has referential integrity if all foreign keys reference existing primary keys.
    iii. Entity integrity guarantees that the tuples are uniquely identified by primary key values.
    A. ii
    B. ii, iii
    C. i, ii, iii
    D. i, ii
23. Which of the following is not very useful in assessing the security of acquired software?
    A. The reliability and maturity of the vendor
    B. The NIST's National Software Reference Library
    C. Third-party vulnerability assessments
    D. In-house code reviews

Use the following scenario to answer Questions 24–26. Sandy has just started as the manager of software development at a new company. As she interviews her new team members, she is finding out a few things that may need to be approached differently. Programmers currently develop software code and upload it to a centralized server for backup purposes. The server software does not have versioning control capability, so sometimes the end software product contains outdated code elements. She has also discovered that many in-house business software packages follow the Common Object Request Broker Architecture, which does not necessarily allow for easy reuse of distributed web services available throughout the network. One of the team members has combined several open API functionalities within a business-oriented software package.

24. Which of the following is the best technology for Sandy's team to implement as it pertains to the previous scenario?

A. Computer-aided software engineering tools

B. Software configuration management

C. Software development life-cycle management

D. Software engineering best practices

25. Which is the best software architecture that Sandy should introduce her team to for effective business application use?

A. Distributed component object architecture

B. Simple Object Access Protocol architecture

C. Enterprise JavaBeans architecture

D. Service-oriented architecture

26. Which best describes the approach Sandy's team member took when creating the business-oriented software package mentioned within the scenario?

A. Software as a Service

B. Cloud computing

C. Web services

D. Mashup

27. Karen wants her team to develop software that allows her company to take advantage of and use many of the web services currently available by other companies. Which of the following best describes the components that need to be in place and what their roles are?

   A. Web service provides the application functionality. Universal Description, Discovery, and Integration describes the web service's specifications. The Web Services Description Language provides the mechanisms for web services to be posted and discovered. The Simple Object Access Protocol allows for the exchange of messages between a requester and provider of a web service.

   B. Web service provides the application functionality. The Web Services Description Language describes the web service's specifications. Universal Description, Discovery, and Integration provides the mechanisms for web services to be posted and discovered. The Simple Object Access Protocol allows for the exchange of messages between a requester and provider of a web service.

   C. Web service provides the application functionality. The Web Services Description Language describes the web service's specifications. The Simple Object Access Protocol provides the mechanisms for web services to be posted and discovered. Universal Description, Discovery, and Integration allows for the exchange of messages between a requester and provider of a web service.

   D. Web service provides the application functionality. The Simple Object Access Protocol describes the web service's specifications. Universal Description, Discovery, and Integration provides the mechanisms for web services to be posted and discovered. The Web Services Description Language allows for the exchange of messages between a requester and provider of a web service.

Use the following scenario to answer Questions 28–30. Brad is a new security administrator within a retail company. He is discovering several issues that his security team needs to address to better secure their organization overall. When reviewing different web server logs, he finds several HTTP server requests with the following characters "%20" and "../". The web server software ensures that users input the correct information within the forms that are presented to them via their web browsers. Brad identifies that the organization has a two-tier network architecture in place, which allows the web servers to directly interact with the back-end database.

28. Which of the following best describes attacks that could be taking place against this organization?

   A. Cross-site scripting and certification stealing

   B. URL encoding and directory traversal attacks

   C. Parameter validation manipulation and session management attacks

   D. Replay and password brute-force attacks

29. Which of the following functions is the web server software currently carrying out, and what is an associated security concern Brad should address?
    A. **Client-side validation** The web server should carry out a secondary set of input validation rules on the presented data before processing it.
    B. **Server-side includes validation** The web server should carry out a secondary set of input validation rules on the presented data before processing it.
    C. **Data Source Name logical naming access** The web server should be carrying out a second set of reference integrity rules.
    D. **Data Source Name logical naming access** The web server should carry out a secondary set of input validation rules on the presented data before processing it.
30. Pertaining to the network architecture described in the previous scenario, which of the following attack types should Brad be concerned with?
    A. Parameter validation attack
    B. Injection attack
    C. Cross-site scripting
    D. Database connector attack

Answers

1. **B.** A Trojan horse looks like an innocent and helpful program, but in the background it is carrying out some type of malicious activity unknown to the user. The Trojan horse could be corrupting files, sending the user's password to an attacker, or attacking another computer.
2. **A.** DevOps is a type of integrated product team (IPT) that focuses on three communities: software development, IT operations, and quality assurance. The idea is to reduce the friction that oftentimes exists between the developers and IT staff in order to improve quality and velocity.
3. **D.** Some files cannot be properly sanitized by the antivirus software without destroying them or affecting their functionality. So, the administrator must replace such a file with a known uninfected file. Plus, the administrator needs to make sure he has the patched version of the file, or else he could be introducing other problems. Answer C is not the *best* answer because the administrator may not know the file was clean yesterday, so just restoring yesterday's file may put him right back in the same boat.
4. **B.** Instantiation is what happens when an object is created from a class. Polyinstantiation is when more than one object is made and the other copy is modified to have different attributes. This can be done for several reasons. The example given in the chapter was a way to use polyinstantiation for security purposes to ensure that a lower-level subject could not access an object at a higher level.

5. **C.** A database view is put into place to prevent certain users from viewing specific data. This is a preventive measure, because the administrator is preventing the users from seeing data not meant for them. This is one control to prevent inference attacks.
6. **A.** Partitioning means to logically split the database into parts. Views then dictate which users can view specific parts. Cell suppression means that specific cells are not viewable by certain users. And noise and perturbation is when bogus information is inserted into the database to try to give potential attackers incorrect information.
7. **A.** The trick to this question, and any one like it, is that security should be implemented at the first possible phase of a project. Requirements are gathered and developed at the beginning of a project, which is project initiation. The other answers are steps that follow this phase, and security should be integrated right from the beginning instead of in the middle or at the end.
8. **C.** This can seem like a tricky question. It states that the system has detected an invalid transaction, which is most likely a user error. This error should be logged so it can be reviewed. After the review, the supervisor, or whoever makes this type of decision, will decide whether or not it was a mistake and, if so, investigate it as needed. If the system had a glitch, power fluctuation, hang-up, or any other software- or hardware-related error, it would not be an invalid transaction, and in that case the system would carry out a rollback function.
9. **D.** In a relational database, a row is referred to as a tuple, whereas a column is referred to as an attribute.
10. **D.** The following are correct characteristics of the ACID test:
    - **Atomicity** Divides transactions into units of work and ensures that all modifications take effect or none take effect. Either the changes are committed or the database is rolled back.
    - **Consistency** A transaction must follow the integrity policy developed for that particular database and ensure all data is consistent in the different databases.
    - **Isolation** Transactions execute in isolation until completed, without interacting with other transactions. The results of the modification are not available until the transaction is completed.
    - **Durability** Once the transaction is verified as *accurate* on all systems, it is committed and the databases cannot be rolled back.
11. **B.** The following outlines the common phases of the software development life cycle:

    i. Requirements gathering

    ii. Design

    iii. Development

iv. Testing/Validation

v. Release/Maintenance

12. **D.** There are different types of tests the software should go through because there are different potential flaws we will be looking for. The following are some of the most common testing approaches:
    - **Unit testing** Testing individual components in a controlled environment where programmers validate data structure, logic, and boundary conditions.
    - **Integration testing** Verifying that components work together as outlined in design specifications.
    - **Acceptance testing** Ensuring that the code meets customer requirements.
    - **Regression testing** After a change to a system takes place, retesting to ensure functionality, performance, and protection.
13. **B.** Garbage collection is an automated way for software to carry out part of its memory management tasks. A garbage collector identifies blocks of memory that were once allocated but are no longer in use and deallocates the blocks and marks them as free. It also gathers scattered blocks of free memory and combines them into larger blocks. It helps provide a more stable environment and does not waste precious memory. Some programming languages, such as Java, perform automatic garbage collection; others, such as C, require the developer to perform it manually, thus leaving opportunity for error.
14. **A.** The listed software development models and their definitions are as follows:
    - **Joint Analysis Development (JAD)** A method that uses a team approach in application development in a workshop-oriented environment.
    - **Rapid Application Development (RAD)** A method that combines the use of prototyping and iterative development procedures with the goal of accelerating the software development process.
    - **Reuse model** A model that approaches software development by using progressively developed models. Reusable programs are evolved by gradually modifying pre-existing prototypes to customer specifications. Since the reuse model does not require programs to be built from scratch, it drastically reduces both development cost and time.
    - **Cleanroom** An approach that attempts to prevent errors or mistakes by following structured and formal methods of developing and testing. This approach is used for high-quality and critical applications that will be put through a strict certification process.
15. **C.** Fuzz testing or fuzzing is a software testing technique that provides invalid, unexpected, or random data to the input interfaces of a program. If the program fails (for example, by crashing or failing built-in code assertions), the defects can be noted.

16. **A.** The five levels of the Capability Maturity Integration Model are
    - **Initial** Development process is ad hoc or even chaotic. The company does not use effective management procedures and plans. There is no assurance of consistency, and quality is unpredictable. Success is usually the result of individual heroics.
    - **Repeatable** A formal management structure, change control, and quality assurance are in place. The company can properly repeat processes throughout each project. The company does not have formal process models defined.
    - **Defined** Formal procedures are in place that outline and define processes carried out in each project. The organization has a way to allow for quantitative process improvement.
    - **Managed** The company has formal processes in place to collect and analyze quantitative data, and metrics are defined and fed into the process-improvement program.
    - **Optimizing** The company has budgeted and integrated plans for continuous process improvement.
17. **B.** The characteristics and their associated definitions are listed as follows:
    - **Modularity** Autonomous objects, cooperation through exchanges of messages.
    - **Deferred commitment** The internal components of an object can be redefined without changing other parts of the system.
    - **Reusability** Refining classes through inheritance. Other programs using the same objects.
    - **Naturalness** Object-oriented analysis, design, and modeling map to business needs and solutions.
18. **D.** The buffer overflow is probably the most notorious of input validation mistakes. A buffer is an area reserved by an application to store something in it, such as some user input. After the application receives the input, an instruction pointer points the application to do something with the input that's been put in the buffer. A buffer overflow occurs when an application erroneously allows an invalid amount of input to be written into the buffer area, overwriting the instruction pointer in the code that tells the program what to do with the input. Once the instruction pointer is overwritten, whatever code has been placed in the buffer can then be executed, all under the security context of the application.
19. **A.** The nonpersistent cross-site scripting vulnerability is when the data provided by a web client, most commonly in HTTP query parameters or in HTML form submissions, is used immediately by server-side scripts to generate a page of results for that user without properly sanitizing the response. The persistent XSS vulnerability occurs when the data provided by the attacker is saved by the server and then permanently displayed on "normal" pages returned to other users in

the course of regular browsing without proper HTML escaping. DOM-based vulnerabilities occur in the content processing stages performed by the client, typically in client-side JavaScript.

20. **B.** An object-relational database (ORD) or object-relational database management system (ORDBMS) is a relational database with a software front end that is written in an object-oriented programming language. Different companies will have different business logic that needs to be carried out on the stored data. Allowing programmers to develop this front-end software piece allows the business logic procedures to be used by requesting applications and the data within the database.

21. **A.** The following are correct characteristics of ADO:
    - It's a high-level data access programming interface to an underlying data access technology (such as OLE DB).
    - It's a set of COM objects for accessing data sources, not just database access.
    - It allows a developer to write programs that access data without knowing how the database is implemented.
    - SQL commands are not required to access a database when using ADO.

22. **C.** A *semantic integrity* mechanism makes sure structural and semantic rules are enforced. These rules pertain to data types, logical values, uniqueness constraints, and operations that could adversely affect the structure of the database. A database has *referential integrity* if all foreign keys reference existing primary keys. There should be a mechanism in place that ensures no foreign key contains a reference to a primary key of a nonexistent record, or a null value. *Entity integrity* guarantees that the tuples are uniquely identified by primary key values. For the sake of entity integrity, every tuple must contain one primary key. If it does not have a primary key, it cannot be referenced by the database.

23. **B.** The National Software Reference Library (NSRL) is the only term that was not addressed in this chapter. It comprises a collection of digital signatures of known, traceable software applications intended to assist in the investigation of crimes involving computers. All other three answers are part of a rigorous assessment of the security of acquired software.

24. **B.** Software configuration management (SCM) identifies the attributes of software at various points in time, and performs a methodical control of changes for the purpose of maintaining software integrity and traceability throughout the software development life cycle. It defines the need to track changes and provides the ability to verify that the final delivered software has all of the approved changes that are supposed to be included in the release.

25. **D.** A service-oriented architecture (SOA) provides standardized access to the most needed services to many different applications at one time. This approach allows for different business applications to access the current web services available within the environment.

26. **D.** A mashup is the combination of functionality, data, and presentation capabilities of two or more sources to provide some type of new service or functionality. Open APIs and data sources are commonly aggregated and combined to provide a more useful and powerful resource.
27. **B.** Web service provides the application functionality. WSDL describes the web service's specifications. UDDI provides the mechanisms for web services to be posted and discovered. SOAP allows for the exchange of messages between a requester and provider of a web service.
28. **B.** The characters "%20" are encoding values that attackers commonly use in URL encoding attacks. These encoding values can be used to bypass web server filtering rules and can result in the attacker being able to gain unauthorized access to components of the web server. The characters "../" can be used by attackers in similar web server requests, which instruct the web server software to traverse directories that should be inaccessible. This is commonly referred to as a path or directory traversal attack.
29. **A.** Client-side validation is being carried out. This procedure ensures that the data that is inserted into the form contains valid values before being sent to the web server for processing. The web server should not just rely upon client-side validation, but should also carry out a second set of procedures to ensure that the input values are not illegal and potentially malicious.
30. **B.** The current architecture allows for web server software to directly communicate with a back-end database. Brad should ensure that proper database access authentication is taking place so that SQL injection attacks cannot be carried out. In a SQL injection attack the attacker sends over input values that the database carries out as commands and can allow authentication to be successfully bypassed.

APPENDIX A

Comprehensive Questions

Use the following scenario to answer Questions 1–3. Josh has discovered that an organized hacking ring in China has been targeting his company's research and development department. If these hackers have been able to uncover his company's research finding, this means they probably have access to his company's intellectual property. Josh thinks that an e-mail server in his company's DMZ may have been successfully compromised and a rootkit loaded.

1. Based upon this scenario, what is most likely the biggest risk Josh's company needs to be concerned with?
   A. Market share drop if the attackers are able to bring the specific product to market more quickly than Josh's company.
   B. Confidentiality of e-mail messages. Attackers may post all captured e-mail messages to the Internet.
   C. Impact on reputation if the customer base finds out about the attack.
   D. Depth of infiltration of attackers. If attackers have compromised other systems, more confidential data could be at risk.
2. The attackers in this situation would be seen as which of the following?
   A. Vulnerability
   B. Threat
   C. Risk
   D. Threat agent
3. If Josh is correct in his assumptions, which of the following best describes the vulnerability, threat, and exposure, respectively?
   A. E-mail server is hardened, an entity could exploit programming code flaw, server is compromised and leaking data.
   B. E-mail server is not patched, an entity could exploit a vulnerability, server is hardened.
   C. E-mail server misconfiguration, an entity could exploit misconfiguration, server is compromised and leaking data.
   D. DMZ firewall misconfiguration, an entity could exploit misconfiguration, internal e-mail server is compromised.

4. Aaron is a security manager who needs to develop a solution to allow his company's mobile devices to be authenticated in a standardized and centralized manner using digital certificates. The applications these mobile clients use require a TCP connection. Which of the following is the best solution for Aaron to implement?
   - **A.** SESAME using PKI
   - **B.** RADIUS using EAP
   - **C.** Diameter using EAP
   - **D.** RADIUS using TTLS
5. Terry is a security manager for a credit card processing company. His company uses internal DNS servers, which are placed within the LAN, and external DNS servers, which are placed in the DMZ. The company also relies upon DNS servers provided by its service provider. Terry has found out that attackers have been able to manipulate several DNS server caches to point employee traffic to malicious websites. Which of the following best describes the solution this company should implement?
   - **A.** IPSec
   - **B.** PKI
   - **C.** DNSSEC
   - **D.** MAC-based security
6. It is important to deal with the issue of "reasonable expectation of privacy" (REP) when it comes to employee monitoring. In the U.S. legal system the expectation of privacy is used when defining the scope of the privacy protections provided by the ______________.
   - **A.** Federal Privacy Act
   - **B.** PATRIOT Act
   - **C.** Fourth Amendment of the Constitution
   - **D.** Bill of Rights
7. Jane is suspicious that an employee is sending sensitive data to one of the company's competitors. The employee has to use this data for daily activities, thus it is difficult to properly restrict the employee's access rights. In this scenario, which best describes the company's vulnerability, threat, risk, and necessary control?
   - **A.** Vulnerability is employee access rights, threat is internal entities misusing privileged access, risk is the business impact of data loss, and the necessary control is detailed network traffic monitoring.
   - **B.** Vulnerability is lenient access rights, threat is internal entities misusing privileged access, risk is the business impact of data loss, and the necessary control is detailed user monitoring.
   - **C.** Vulnerability is employee access rights, threat is internal employees misusing privileged access, risk is the business impact of confidentiality, and the necessary control is multifactor authentication.

D. Vulnerability is employee access rights, threat is internal users misusing privileged access, risk is the business impact of confidentiality, and the necessary control is CCTV.

8. Which of the following best describes what role-based access control offers companies in reducing administrative burdens?
   A. It allows entities closer to the resources to make decisions about who can and cannot access resources.
   B. It provides a centralized approach for access control, which frees up department managers.
   C. User membership in roles can be easily revoked and new ones established as job assignments dictate.
   D. It enforces an enterprise-wide security policy, standards, and guidelines.
9. Mark works for a large corporation operating in multiple countries worldwide. He is reviewing his company's policies and procedures dealing with data breaches. Which of the following is an issue that he must take into consideration?
   A. Each country may or may not have unique notification requirements.
   B. All breaches must be announced to affected parties within 24 hours.
   C. Breach notification is a "best effort" process and not a guaranteed process.
   D. Breach notifications are avoidable if all PII is removed from data stores.
10. A software development company released a product that committed several errors that were not expected once deployed in their customers' environments. All of the software code went through a long list of tests before being released. The team manager found out that after a small change was made to the code, the program was not tested before it was released. Which of the following tests was most likely not conducted?
   A. Unit
   B. Compiled
   C. Integration
   D. Regression
11. It is important to choose the right risk analysis methodology to meet the goals of the organization's needs. Which of the following best describes when the risk management standard AS/NZS 4360 should be used?
   A. When there is a need to assess items of an organization that are directly related to information security
   B. When there is a need to assess items of an organization that are not just restricted to information security
   C. When a qualitative method is needed to prove the compliance levels as they pertain to regulations
   D. When a qualitative method is needed to prove the compliance levels as they pertain to laws

12. Companies should follow certain steps in selecting and implementing a new computer product. Which of the following sequences is ordered correctly?
   A. Evaluation, accreditation, certification
   B. Evaluation, certification, accreditation
   C. Certification, evaluation, accreditation
   D. Certification, accreditation, evaluation

Use the following scenario to answer Questions 13–15. Jack has just been hired as the security officer for a large hospital. The organization develops some of its own proprietary applications. The organization does not have as many layers of controls when it comes to the data processed by these applications, since it is assumed that external entities will not understand the internal logic of the applications. One of the first things that Jack wants to carry out is a risk assessment to determine the organization's current risk profile. He also tells his boss that the hospital should become ISO certified to bolster its customers' and partners' confidence.

13. Which of the following approaches has been implemented in this scenario?
   A. Defense-in-depth
   B. Security through obscurity
   C. Information security management system
   D. BS 17799
14. Which ISO/IEC standard would be best for Jack to follow to meet his goals?
   A. ISO/IEC 27002
   B. ISO/IEC 27004
   C. ISO/IEC 27005
   D. ISO/IEC 27006
15. Which standard should Jack suggest to his boss for compliance?
   A. BS 17799
   B. ISO/IEC 27004
   C. ISO/IEC 27799
   D. BS 7799:2011

16. An operating system maintains several processes in memory at the same time. The processes can only interact with the CPU during their assigned time slices since there is only one CPU and many processes. Each process is assigned an interrupt value to allow for this type of time slicing to take place. Which of the following best describes the difference between maskable and nonmaskable interrupts?
   A. A maskable interrupt is assigned to a critical process, and a nonmaskable interrupt is assigned to a noncritical process.
   B. A maskable interrupt is assigned to a process in ring 0, and a nonmaskable interrupt is assigned to a process in ring 3.
   C. A maskable interrupt is assigned to a process in ring 3, and a nonmaskable interrupt is assigned to a process in ring 4.
   D. A maskable interrupt is assigned to a noncritical process, and a nonmaskable interrupt is assigned to a critical process.

17. The confidentiality of sensitive data is protected in different ways depending on the state of the data. Which of the following is the best approach to protecting data in transit?
   A. SSL
   B. VPN
   C. IEEE 802.1x
   D. Whole-disk encryption

18. There are different categories for evidence depending upon what form it is in and possibly how it was collected. Which of the following is considered supporting evidence?
   A. Best evidence
   B. Corroborative evidence
   C. Conclusive evidence
   D. Direct evidence

19. A(n)_______________ is the graphical representation of data commonly used on websites. It is a skewed representation of characteristics a person must enter to prove that the subject is a human and not an automated tool, as in a software robot.
   A. Anti-spoofing symbol
   B. CAPTCHA
   C. Spam anti-spoofing symbol
   D. CAPCHAT

20. Mark has been asked to interview individuals to fulfill a new position in his company, chief privacy officer (CPO). What is the function of this type of position?

    A. Ensuring that company financial information is correct and secure
    B. Ensuring that customer, company, and employee data is protected
    C. Ensuring that security policies are defined and enforced
    D. Ensuring that partner information is kept safe

21. A risk management program must be developed properly and in the right sequence. Which of the following provides the correct sequence for the steps listed?

    1) Develop a risk management team
    2) Calculate the value of each asset
    3) Identify the vulnerabilities and threats that can affect the identified assets
    4) Identify company assets to be assessed

    A. 1, 3, 2, 4
    B. 2, 1, 4, 3
    C. 3, 1, 4, 2
    D. 1, 4, 2, 3

22. Jack needs to assess the performance of a critical web application that his company recently upgraded. Some of the new features are very profitable, but not frequently used. He wants to ensure that the user experience is positive, but doesn't want to wait for the users to report problems. Which of the following techniques should Jack use?

    A. Real user monitoring
    B. Synthetic transactions
    C. Log reviews
    D. Management review

23. Which of the following best describes a technical control for dealing with the risks presented by data remanence?

    A. Encryption
    B. Data retention policies
    C. File deletion
    D. Using solid-state drives (SSD)

24. George is the security manager of a large bank, which provides online banking and other online services to its customers. George has recently found out that some of the bank's customers have complained about changes to their bank accounts that they did not make. George worked with the security team and found out that all changes took place after proper authentication steps were completed. Which of the following describes what most likely took place in this situation?

A. Web servers were compromised through cross-scripting attacks.

B. TLS connections were decrypted through a man-in-the-middle attack.

C. Personal computers were compromised with Trojan horses that installed keyloggers.

D. Web servers were compromised and masquerading attacks were carried out.

25. Internet Protocol Security (IPSec) is actually a suite of protocols. Each protocol within the suite provides different functionality. Which of the following is not a function or characteristic of IPSec?

A. Encryption

B. Link layer protection

C. Authentication

D. Protection of packet payloads and the headers

26. In what order would a typical PKI infrastructure perform the following transactions?

1) Receiver decrypts and obtains session key.

2) Sender requests receiver's public key.

3) Public key is sent from a public directory.

4) Sender sends a session key encrypted with receiver's public key.

A. 4, 3, 2, 1

B. 2, 1, 3, 4

C. 2, 3, 4, 1

D. 2, 4, 3, 1

Use the following scenario to answer Questions 27–28. Tim is the CISO for a large distributed financial investment organization. The company's network is made up of different network devices and software applications, which generate their own proprietary logs and audit data. Tim and his security team have become overwhelmed with trying to review all of the log files when attempting to identify if anything suspicious is taking place within the network. Another issue Tim's team needs to deal with is that many of the network devices have automated IPv6-to-IPv4 tunneling enabled by default.

27. Which of the following is the best solution for this company to implement as it pertains to the first issue addressed in the scenario?

A. Event correlation tools

B. Intrusion detection systems

C. Security information and event management

D. Security event correlation management tools

28. Which of the following best describes why Tim should be concerned about the second issue addressed in the scenario?
    A. Software and devices that are scanning traffic for suspicious activity may only be configured to evaluate one system type.
    B. Software and devices that are monitoring traffic for illegal activity may only be configured to evaluate one service type.
    C. Software and devices that are monitoring traffic for illegal activity may only be configured to evaluate two protocol types.
    D. Software and devices that are monitoring traffic for suspicious activity may only be configured to evaluate one traffic type.
29. Which of the following is not a concern of a security professional considering adoption of Internet of Things (IoT) devices?
    A. Weak or nonexistent authentication mechanisms
    B. Vulnerability of data at rest and data in motion
    C. Difficulty of deploying patches and updates
    D. High costs associated with connectivity
30. What type of rating system is used within the Common Criteria structure?
    A. PP
    B. EPL
    C. EAL
    D. A–D
31. ______________, a declarative access control policy language implemented in XML and a processing model, describes how to interpret security policies. ______________ is an XML-based framework being developed by OASIS for exchanging user, resource, and service provisioning information between cooperating organizations.
    A. Service Provisioning Markup Language (SPML), Extensible Access Control Markup Language (XACML)
    B. Extensible Access Control Markup Language (XACML), Service Provisioning Markup Language (SPML)
    C. Extensible Access Control Markup Language (XACML), Security Assertion Markup Language (SAML)
    D. Security Assertion Markup Language (SAML), Service Provisioning Markup Language (SPML)
32. Doors configured in fail-safe mode assume what position in the event of a power failure?
    A. Open and locked
    B. Closed and locked

C. Closed and unlocked

D. Open

33. Next-generation firewalls combine the best attributes of other types of firewalls. Which of the following is not a common characteristic of these firewall types?

A. Integrated intrusion prevention system

B. Sharing signatures with cloud-based aggregators

C. Automated incident response

D. High cost

34. The purpose of security awareness training is to expose personnel to security issues so that they may be able to recognize them and better respond to them. Which of the following is not normally a topic covered in security awareness training?

A. Social engineering

B. Phishing

C. Whaling

D. Trolling

Use the following scenario to answer Questions 35–36. Zack is a security consultant who has been hired to help an accounting company improve some of their current e-mail security practices. The company wants to ensure that when their clients send the company accounting files and data, the clients cannot later deny sending these messages. The company also wants to integrate a more granular and secure authentication method for their current mail server and clients.

35. Which of the following best describes how client messages can be dealt with and addresses the first issue outlined in the scenario?

A. The company needs to integrate a public key infrastructure and the Diameter protocol.

B. Clients must encrypt messages with their public key before sending them to the accounting company.

C. The company needs to have all clients sign a formal document outlining nonrepudiation requirements.

D. Clients must digitally sign messages that contain financial information.

36. Which of the following would be the best solution to integrate to meet the authentication requirements outlined in the scenario?

A. TLS

B. IPSec

C. 802.1x

D. SASL

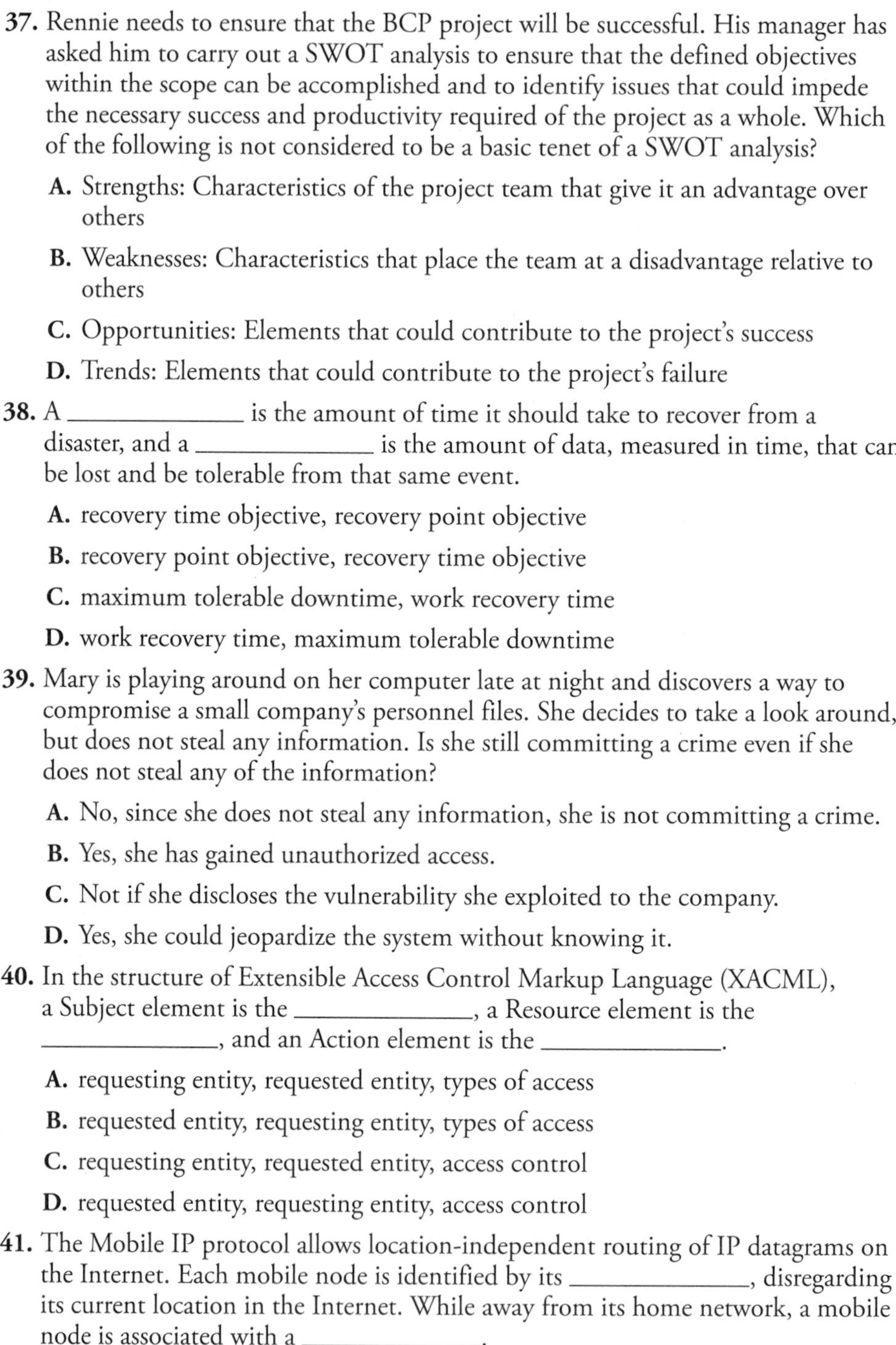

37. Rennie needs to ensure that the BCP project will be successful. His manager has asked him to carry out a SWOT analysis to ensure that the defined objectives within the scope can be accomplished and to identify issues that could impede the necessary success and productivity required of the project as a whole. Which of the following is not considered to be a basic tenet of a SWOT analysis?

    A. Strengths: Characteristics of the project team that give it an advantage over others

    B. Weaknesses: Characteristics that place the team at a disadvantage relative to others

    C. Opportunities: Elements that could contribute to the project's success

    D. Trends: Elements that could contribute to the project's failure

38. A ____________ is the amount of time it should take to recover from a disaster, and a ____________ is the amount of data, measured in time, that can be lost and be tolerable from that same event.

    A. recovery time objective, recovery point objective

    B. recovery point objective, recovery time objective

    C. maximum tolerable downtime, work recovery time

    D. work recovery time, maximum tolerable downtime

39. Mary is playing around on her computer late at night and discovers a way to compromise a small company's personnel files. She decides to take a look around, but does not steal any information. Is she still committing a crime even if she does not steal any of the information?

    A. No, since she does not steal any information, she is not committing a crime.

    B. Yes, she has gained unauthorized access.

    C. Not if she discloses the vulnerability she exploited to the company.

    D. Yes, she could jeopardize the system without knowing it.

40. In the structure of Extensible Access Control Markup Language (XACML), a Subject element is the ____________, a Resource element is the ____________, and an Action element is the ____________.

    A. requesting entity, requested entity, types of access

    B. requested entity, requesting entity, types of access

    C. requesting entity, requested entity, access control

    D. requested entity, requesting entity, access control

41. The Mobile IP protocol allows location-independent routing of IP datagrams on the Internet. Each mobile node is identified by its ____________, disregarding its current location in the Internet. While away from its home network, a mobile node is associated with a ____________.

A. prime address, care-of address

B. home address, care-of address

C. home address, secondary address

D. prime address, secondary address

42. Instead of managing and maintaining many different types of security products and solutions, Joan wants to purchase a product that combines many technologies into one appliance. She would like to have centralized control, streamlined maintenance, and a reduction in stove pipe security solutions. Which of the following would best fit Joan's needs?

A. Dedicated appliance

B. Centralized hybrid firewall applications

C. Hybrid IDS\IPS integration

D. Unified threat management

43. Why is it important to have a clearly defined incident-handling process in place?

A. To avoid dealing with a computer and network threat in an ad hoc, reactive, and confusing manner

B. To provide a quick reaction to a threat so that a company can return to normal operations as soon as possible

C. To provide a uniform approach with certain expectations of the results

D. All of the above

44. Which of the following is an international organization that helps different governments come together and tackle the economic, social, and governance challenges of a globalized economy and provides guidelines on the protection of privacy and transborder flows of personal data rules?

A. Council of Global Convention on Cybercrime

B. Council of Europe Convention on Cybercrime

C. Organisation for Economic Co-operation and Development

D. Organisation for Cybercrime Co-operation and Development

45. System ports allow different computers to communicate with each other's services and protocols. Internet Corporation for Assigned Names and Numbers has assigned registered ports to be ____________ and dynamic ports to be ____________.

A. 0–1024, 49152–65535

B. 1024–49151, 49152–65535

C. 1024–49152, 49153–65535

D. 0–1024, 1025–49151

46. When conducting a quantitative risk analysis, items are gathered and assigned numeric values so that cost/benefit analysis can be carried out. Which of the following provides the correct formula to understand the value of a safeguard?
   A. (ALE before implementing safeguard) – (ALE after implementing safeguard) – (annual cost of safeguard) = value of safeguard to the company
   B. (ALE before implementing safeguard) – (ALE during implementing safeguard) – (annual cost of safeguard) = value of safeguard to the company
   C. (ALE before implementing safeguard) – (ALE while implementing safeguard) – (annual cost of safeguard) = value of safeguard to the company
   D. (ALE before implementing safeguard) – (ALE after implementing safeguard) – (annual cost of asset) = value of safeguard to the company
47. Patty is giving a presentation next week to the executive staff of her company. She wants to illustrate the benefits of the company using specific cloud computing solutions. Which of the following does not properly describe one of these benefits or advantages?
   A. Organizations have more flexibility and agility in IT growth and functionality.
   B. Cost of computing can be increased since it is a shared delivery model.
   C. Location independence can be achieved because the computing is not centralized and tied to a physical data center.
   D. Scalability and elasticity of resources can be accomplished in near real-time through automation.

Use the following scenario to answer Questions 48–49. Frank is the new manager of the in-house software designers and programmers. He has been telling his team that before design and programming on a new product begins, a formal architecture needs to be developed. He also needs this team to understand security issues as they pertain to software design. Frank has shown the team how to follow a systematic approach that allows them to understand how different compromises could take place with the software products they develop.

48. Which of the following best describes what an architecture is in the context of this scenario?
   A. Tool used to conceptually understand the structure and behavior of a complex entity through different views
   B. Formal description and representation of a system and the components that make it up

C. Framework used to create individual architectures with specific views

D. Framework that is necessary to identify needs and meet all of the stakeholder requirements

49. Which of the following best describes the approach Frank has shown his team as outlined in the scenario?

A. Attack surface analysis

B. Threat modeling

C. Penetration testing

D. Double-blind penetration testing

50. Barry was told that the IDS product that is being used on the network has heuristic capabilities. Which of the following best describes this functionality?

A. Gathers packets and reassembles the fragments before assigning anomaly values

B. Gathers data to calculate the probability of an attack taking place

C. Gathers packets and compares their payload values to a signature engine

D. Gathers packet headers to determine if something suspicious is taking place within the network traffic

51. Bringing in external auditors has advantages over using an internal team. Which of the following is not true about using external auditors?

A. They are required by certain governmental regulations.

B. They bring experience gained by working in many other organizations.

C. They know the organization's processes and technology better than anyone else.

D. They are less influenced by internal culture and politics.

52. Don is a senior manager of an architectural firm. He has just found out that a key contract was renewed, allowing the company to continue developing an operating system that was idle for several months. Excited to get started, Don begins work on the operating system privately, but cannot tell his staff until the news is announced publicly in a few days. However, as Don begins making changes in the software, various staff members notice changes in their connected systems, even though they work in a lower security level. What kind of model could be used to ensure this does not happen?

A. Biba

B. Bell-LaPadula

C. Noninterference

D. Clark-Wilson

53. Betty has received several e-mail messages from unknown sources that try and entice her to click a specific link using a "Click Here" approach. Which of the following best describes what is most likely taking place in this situation?
    - A. DNS pharming attack
    - B. Embedded hyperlink is obfuscated
    - C. Malware back-door installation
    - D. Bidirectional injection attack

54. Rebecca is an internal auditor for a large retail company. The company has a number of web applications that run critical business processes with customers and partners around the world. Her company would like to ensure the security of technical controls on these processes. Which of the following would not be a good approach to auditing these technical controls?
    - A. Log reviews
    - B. Code reviews
    - C. Personnel background checks
    - D. Misuse case testing

55. Which of the following multiplexing technologies analyzes statistics related to the typical workload of each input device and makes real-time decisions on how much time each device should be allocated for data transmission?
    - A. Time-division multiplexing
    - B. Wave-division multiplexing
    - C. Frequency-division multiplexing
    - D. Statistical time-division multiplexing

56. In a VoIP environment, the Real-time Transport Protocol (RTP) and RTP Control Protocol (RTCP) are commonly used. Which of the following best describes the difference between these two protocols?
    - A. RTCP provides a standardized packet format for delivering audio and video over IP networks. RTP provides out-of-band statistics and control information to provide feedback on QoS levels.
    - B. RTP provides a standardized packet format for delivering data over IP networks. RTCP provides control information to provide feedback on QoS levels.
    - C. RTP provides a standardized packet format for delivering audio and video over MPLS networks. RTCP provides control information to provide feedback on QoS levels.
    - D. RTP provides a standardized packet format for delivering audio and video over IP networks. RTCP provides out-of-band statistics and control information to provide feedback on QoS levels.

57. ISO/IEC 27031:2011 is an international standard for business continuity that organizations can follow. Which of the following is a correct characteristic of this standard?
    - **A.** Guidelines for information and communications technology readiness for business continuity
    - **B.** ISO/IEC standard that is a component of the overall BS 7999 series
    - **C.** Standard that was developed by NIST and evolved to be an international standard
    - **D.** Component of the Safe Harbor requirements
58. A preferred technique of attackers is to become "normal" privileged users of the systems they compromise as soon as possible. This can normally be accomplished in all the following ways except which one?
    - **A.** Compromising an existing privileged account
    - **B.** Creating a new privileged account
    - **C.** Deleting the /etc/passwd file
    - **D.** Elevating the privileges of an existing account
59. IPSec's main protocols are AH and ESP. Which of the following services does AH provide?
    - **A.** Confidentiality and authentication
    - **B.** Confidentiality and availability
    - **C.** Integrity and accessibility
    - **D.** Integrity and authentication
60. When multiple databases exchange transactions, each database is updated. This can happen many times and in many different ways. To protect the integrity of the data, databases should incorporate a concept known as an ACID test. What does this acronym stand for?
    - **A.** Availability, confidentiality, integrity, durability
    - **B.** Availability, consistency, integrity, durability
    - **C.** Atomicity, confidentiality, isolation, durability
    - **D.** Atomicity, consistency, isolation, durability

Use the following scenario to answer Questions 61–62. Jim works for a large energy company. His senior management just conducted a meeting with Jim's team with the purpose of reducing IT costs without degrading their security posture. The senior management decided to move all administrative systems to a cloud provider. These systems are proprietary applications currently running on Linux servers.

61. Which of the following services would allow Jim to transition all administrative custom applications to the cloud while leveraging the service provider for security and patching of the cloud platforms?
    - A. IaaS
    - B. PaaS
    - C. SaaS
    - D. IDaaS

62. Which of the following would *not* be an issue that Jim would have to consider in transitioning administrative services to the cloud?
    - A. Privacy and data breach laws in the country where the cloud servers are located
    - B. Loss of efficiencies, performance, reliability, scalability, and security
    - C. Security provisions in the terms of service
    - D. Total cost of ownership compared to the current systems

63. Henry is the team leader of a group of software designers. They are at a stage in their software development project where they need to reduce the amount of code running, reduce entry points available to untrusted users, reduce privilege levels as much as possible, and eliminate unnecessary services. Which of the following best describes the first step the team needs to carry out to accomplish these tasks?
    - A. Attack surface analysis
    - B. Software development life cycle
    - C. Risk assessment
    - D. Unit testing

64. Jenny needs to engage a new software development company to create her company's internal banking software. It will need to be created specifically for her company's environment, so it must be proprietary in nature. Which of the following would be useful for Jenny to use as a gauge to determine how advanced and mature the various software development companies are in their processes?
    - A. SaS 70
    - B. Capability Maturity Model Integration level
    - C. Auditing results
    - D. Key performance metrics

65. Which of the following is a representation of the logical relationship between elements of data and dictates the degree of association among elements, methods of access, processing alternatives, and the organization of data elements?

A. Data element

B. Array

C. Secular component

D. Data structure

66. Kerberos is a commonly used access control and authentication technology. It is important to understand what the technology can and cannot do and its potential downfalls. Which of the following is not a potential security issue that must be addressed when using Kerberos?

i. The KDC can be a single point of failure.

ii. The KDC must be scalable.

iii. Secret keys are temporarily stored on the users' workstations.

iv. Kerberos is vulnerable to password guessing.

A. i, iv

B. iii

C. All of them

D. None of them

67. If the ALE for a specific asset is $100,000, and after implementation of the control the new ALE is $45,000 and the annual cost of the control is $30,000, should the company implement this control?

A. Yes

B. No

C. Not enough information

D. It depends on the ARO

68. ISO/IEC 27000 is a growing family of ISO/IEC information security management system (ISMS) standards. It comprises information security standards published jointly by the International Organization for Standardization (ISO) and the International Electrotechnical Commission (IEC). Which of the following provides an incorrect mapping of the individual standards that make up this family of standards?

A. ISO/IEC 27002: Code of practice for information security management

B. ISO/IEC 27003: Guideline for ISMS implementation

C. ISO/IEC 27004: Guideline for information security management measurement and metrics framework

D. ISO/IEC 27005: Guideline for bodies providing audit and certification of information security management systems

69. When a CPU is passed an instruction set and data to be processed and the program status word (PSW) register contains a value indicating that execution should take place in privileged mode, which of the following would be considered true?

    A. Operating system is executing in supervisory mode
    B. Request came from a trusted process
    C. Functionality that is available in user mode is not available
    D. An untrusted process submitted the execution request

70. Encryption and decryption can take place at different layers of an operating system, application, and network stack. End-to-end encryption happens within the ______________. IPSec encryption takes place at the ______________ layer. PPTP encryption takes place at the ______________ layer. Link encryption takes place at the ______________ and ______________ layers.

    A. applications, transport, data link, data link, physical
    B. applications, transport, network, data link, physical
    C. applications, network, data link, data link, physical
    D. network, transport, data link, data link, physical

71. Which of the following best describes the difference between hierarchical storage management (HSM) and storage area network (SAN) technologies?

    A. HSM uses optical or tape jukeboxes, and SAN is a network of connected storage systems.
    B. SAN uses optical or tape jukeboxes, and HSM is a network of connected storage systems.
    C. HSM and SAN are one and the same. The difference is in the implementation.
    D. HSM uses optical or tape jukeboxes, and SAN is a standard of how to develop and implement this technology.

72. Which legal system is characterized by its reliance on previous interpretations of the law?

    A. Tort
    B. Customary
    C. Common
    D. Civil (code)

73. In order to be admissible in court, evidence should normally be which of the following?

    A. Subpoenaed
    B. Relevant

C. Motioned

D. Adjudicated

74. A fraud analyst with a national insurance company uses database tools every day to help identify violations and identify relationships between the captured data through the uses of rule discovery. These tools help identify relationships among a wide variety of information types. What kind of knowledge discovery in database (KDD) is this considered?

A. Probability

B. Statistical

C. Classification

D. Behavioral

75. Which of the following is an XML-based protocol that defines the schema of how web service communication takes place over HTTP transmissions?

A. Service-Oriented Protocol

B. Active X Protocol

C. Simple Object Access Protocol

D. JVEE

76. Which of the following has an incorrect definition mapping?

i. **Operationally Critical Threat, Asset, and Vulnerability Evaluation (OCTAVE)** Team-oriented approach that assesses organizational and IT risks through facilitated workshops

ii. **AS/NZS 4360** Australia and New Zealand business risk management assessment approach

iii. **ISO/IEC 27005** International standard for the implementation of a risk management program that integrates into an information security management system (ISMS)

iv. **Failure Modes and Effect Analysis (FMEA)** Approach that dissects a component into its basic functions to identify flaws and those flaws' effects

v. **Fault tree analysis** Approach to map specific flaws to root causes in complex systems

A. None of them

B. ii

C. iii, iv

D. v

77. For an enterprise security architecture to be successful in its development and implementation, which of the following items must be understood and followed?
   i. Strategic alignment
   ii. Process enhancement
   iii. Business enablement
   iv. Security effectiveness
   A. i, ii
   B. ii, iii
   C. i, ii, iii, iv
   D. iii, iv
78. Which of the following best describes the purpose of the Organisation for Economic Co-operation and Development (OECD)?
   A. An international organization that helps different governments come together and tackle the economic, social, and governance challenges of a globalized economy
   B. A national organization that helps different governments come together and tackle the economic, social, and governance challenges of a globalized economy
   C. An international organization that helps different organizations come together and tackle the economic, social, and governance challenges of a globalized economy
   D. A national organization that helps different organizations come together and tackle the economic, social, and governance challenges of a globalized economy
79. There are many enterprise architecture models that have been developed over the years for specific purposes. Some of them can be used to provide structure for information security processes and technology to be integrated throughout an organization. Which of the following provides an incorrect mapping between the architect type and the associated definition?
   A. **Zachman Framework** Model and methodology for the development of information security enterprise architectures
   B. **TOGAF** Model and methodology for the development of enterprise architectures developed by The Open Group
   C. **DoDAF** U.S. Department of Defense architecture framework that ensures interoperability of systems to meet military mission goals
   D. **MODAF** Architecture framework used mainly in military support missions developed by the British Ministry of Defence
80. Which of the following best describes the difference between the role of the ISO/IEC 27000 series and COBIT?
   A. COBIT provides a high-level overview of security program requirements, while the ISO/IEC 27000 series provides the objectives of the individual security controls.

B. The ISO/IEC 27000 series provides a high-level overview of security program requirements, while COBIT provides the objectives of the individual security controls.

C. COBIT is process oriented, and the ISO/IEC 27000 series is solution oriented.

D. The ISO/IEC 27000 series is process oriented, and COBIT is solution oriented.

81. The Capability Maturity Model Integration (CMMI) approach is being used more frequently in security program and enterprise development. Which of the following provides an incorrect characteristic of this model?

A. It provides a pathway for how incremental improvement can take place.

B. It provides structured steps that can be followed so an organization can evolve from one level to the next and constantly improve its processes.

C. It was created for process improvement and developed by Carnegie Mellon.

D. It was built upon the SABSA model.

82. If Joe wanted to use a risk assessment methodology that allows the various business owners to identify risks and know how to deal with them, what methodology would he use?

A. Qualitative

B. COSO

C. FRAP

D. OCTAVE

83. Information security is a field that is maturing and becoming more organized and standardized. Organizational security models should be based upon a formal architecture framework. Which of the following best describes what a formal architecture framework is and why it would be used?

A. Mathematical model that defines the secure states that various software components can enter and still provide the necessary protection

B. Conceptual model that is organized into multiple views addressing each of the stakeholder's concerns

C. Business enterprise framework that is broken down into six conceptual levels to ensure security is deployed and managed in a controllable manner

D. Enterprise framework that allows for proper security governance

84. Which of the following provides a true characteristic of a fault tree analysis?

A. Fault trees are assigned qualitative values to faults that can take place over a series of business processes.

B. Fault trees are assigned failure mode values.

C. Fault trees are labeled with actual numbers pertaining to failure probabilities.

D. Fault trees are used in a stepwise approach to software debugging.

85. Several models and frameworks have been developed by different organizations over the years to help businesses carry out processes in a more efficient and effective manner. Which of the following provides the correct definition mapping of one of these items?
    i. **COSO** A framework and methodology for enterprise security architecture and service management
    ii. **ITIL** Processes to allow for IT service management developed by the United Kingdom's Office of Government Commerce
    iii. **Six Sigma** Business management strategy that can be used to carry out process improvement
    iv. **Capability Maturity Model Integration (CMMI)** Organizational development for process improvement developed by Carnegie Mellon

    A. i

    B. i, iii

    C. ii, iv

    D. ii, iii, iv

86. It is important that organizations ensure that their security efforts are effective and measurable. Which of the following is not a common method used to track the effectiveness of security efforts?

    A. Service level agreement

    B. Return on investment

    C. Balanced scorecard system

    D. Provisioning system

87. Capability Maturity Model Integration (CMMI) is a process improvement approach that is used to help organizations improve their performance. The CMMI model may also be used as a framework for appraising the process maturity of the organization. Which of the following is an incorrect mapping of the levels that may be assigned to an organization based upon this model?
    i. Maturity Level 2 – Managed or Repeatable
    ii. Maturity Level 3 – Defined
    iii. Maturity Level 4 – Quantitatively Managed
    iv. Maturity Level 5 – Optimizing

    A. i

    B. i, ii

    C. All of them

    D. None of them

88. An organization's information system risk management (ISRM) policy should address many items to provide clear direction and structure. Which of the following is not a core item that should be covered in this type of policy?

   i. The objectives of the IRM team
   ii. The level of risk the organization will accept and what is considered an acceptable level of risk
   iii. Formal processes of risk identification
   iv. The connection between the IRM policy and the organization's strategic planning processes
   v. Responsibilities that fall under IRM and the roles to fulfill them
   vi. The mapping of risk to specific physical controls
   vii. The approach toward changing staff behaviors and resource allocation in response to risk analysis
   viii. The mapping of risks to performance targets and budgets
   ix. Key indicators to monitor the effectiveness of controls

   A. ii, v, ix
   B. vi
   C. v
   D. vii, ix

89. More organizations are outsourcing business functions to allow them to focus on their core business functions. Companies use hosting companies to maintain websites and e-mail servers, service providers for various telecommunication connections, disaster recovery companies for co-location capabilities, cloud computing providers for infrastructure or application services, developers for software creation, and security companies to carry out vulnerability management. Which of the following items should be included during the analysis of an outsourced partner or vendor?

   i. Conduct onsite inspection and interviews
   ii. Review contracts to ensure security and protection levels are agreed upon
   iii. Ensure service level agreements are in place
   iv. Review internal and external audit reports and third-party reviews
   v. Review references and communicate with former and existing customers
   vi. Review Better Business Bureau reports

   A. ii, iii, iv
   B. iv, v, vi
   C. All of them
   D. i, ii, iii

90. Which of the following is normally not an element of e-Discovery?
    A. Identification
    B. Preservation
    C. Production
    D. Remanence

91. A financial institution has developed its internal security program based upon the ISO/IEC 27000 series. The security officer has been told that metrics need to be developed and integrated into this program so that effectiveness can be gauged. Which of the following standards should be followed to provide this type of guidance and functionality?
    A. ISO/IEC 27002
    B. ISO/IEC 27003
    C. ISO/IEC 27004
    D. ISO/IEC 27005

92. Which of the following is not an advantage of using content distribution networks?
    A. Improved responsiveness to regional users
    B. Resistance to ARP spoofing attacks
    C. Customization of content for regional users
    D. Resistance to DDoS attacks

93. Sue has been asked to install a web access management (WAM) product for her company's environment. What is the best description for what WAMs are commonly used for?
    A. Control external entities requesting access to internal objects
    B. Control internal entities requesting access to external objects
    C. Control external entities requesting access through X.500 databases
    D. Control internal entities requesting access through X.500 databases

94. A user's digital identity is commonly made up of more than just a username. Which of the following is not a common item that makes up a user's identity?
    A. Entitlements
    B. Traits
    C. Figures
    D. Attributes

95. Which of the following is a true statement pertaining to markup languages?

A. HyperText Markup Language (HTML) came from Generalized Markup Language (GML), which came from the Standard Generalized Markup Language (SGML).

B. HyperText Markup Language (HTML) came from Standard Generalized Markup Language (SGML), which came from the Generalized Markup Language (GML).

C. Standard Generalized Markup Language (SGML) came from the HyperText Markup Language (HTML), which came from the Generalized Markup Language (GML).

D. Standard Generalized Markup Language (SGML) came from the Generalized Markup Language (GML), which came from the HyperText Markup Language (HTML).

96. What is Extensible Markup Language (XML), and why was it created?

A. A specification that is used to create various types of markup languages for specific industry requirements

B. A specification that is used to create static and dynamic websites

C. A specification that outlines a detailed markup language dictating all formats of all companies that use it

D. A specification that does not allow for interoperability for the sake of security

97. Which access control policy is enforced in an environment that uses containers and implicit permission inheritance using a nondiscretionary model?

A. Rule-based

B. Role-based

C. Identity-based

D. Mandatory

98. Which of the following centralized access control protocols would a security professional choose if her network consisted of multiple protocols, including Mobile IP, and had users connecting via wireless and wired transmissions?

A. RADIUS

B. TACACS+

C. Diameter

D. Kerberos

99. Jay is the security administrator at a credit card processing company. The company has many identity stores, which are not properly synchronized. Jay is going to oversee the process of centralizing and synchronizing the identity data within the company. He has determined that the data in the HR database will be considered the most up-to-date data, which cannot be overwritten by the software in other identity stores during their synchronization processes. Which of the following best describes the role of this database in the identity management structure of the company?

    A. Authoritative system of record

    B. Infrastructure source server

    C. Primary identity store

    D. Hierarchical database primary

100. Proper access control requires a structured user provisioning process. Which of the following best describes user provisioning?

    A. The creation, maintenance, and deactivation of user objects and attributes as they exist in one or more systems, directories, or applications, in response to business processes

    B. The creation, maintenance, activation, and delegation of user objects and attributes as they exist in one or more systems, directories, or applications, in response to compliance processes

    C. The maintenance of user objects and attributes as they exist in one or more systems, directories, or applications, in response to business processes

    D. The creation and deactivation of user objects and attributes as they exist in one or more systems, directories, or applications, in response to business processes

101. A user's identity can be a collection of her _____________ (department, role in company, shift time, clearance); her _____________ (resources available to her, authoritative rights in the company); and her _____________ (biometric information, height, sex,).

    A. attributes, access, traits

    B. attributes, entitlements, access

    C. attributes, characteristics, traits

    D. attributes, entitlements, traits

102. John needs to ensure that his company's application can accept provisioning data from the company's partner's application in a standardized method. Which of the following best describes the technology that John should implement?

    A. Service Provisioning Markup Language

    B. Extensible Provisioning Markup Language

C. Security Assertion Markup Language

D. Security Provisioning Markup Language

103. Lynn logs into a website and purchases an airline ticket for her upcoming trip. The website also offers her pricing and package deals for hotel rooms and rental cars while she is completing her purchase. The airline, hotel, and rental companies are all separate and individual companies. Lynn decides to purchase her hotel room through the same website at the same time. The website is using Security Assertion Markup Language to allow for this type of federated identity management functionality. In this example which entity is the principal, which entity is the identity provider, and which entity is the service provider?

A. Portal, Lynn, hotel company

B. Lynn, airline company, hotel company

C. Lynn, hotel company, airline company

D. Portal, Lynn, airline company

104. John is the new director of software development within his company. Several proprietary applications offer individual services to the employees, but the employees have to log into each and every application independently to gain access to these discrete services. John would like to provide a way that allows each of the services provided by the various applications to be centrally accessed and controlled. Which of the following best describes the architecture that John should deploy?

A. Service-oriented architecture

B. Web services architecture

C. Single sign-on architecture

D. Hierarchical service architecture

105. Which security model enforces the principle that the security levels of an object should never change and is known as the "strong tranquility" property?

A. Biba

B. Bell-LaPadula

C. Brewer-Nash

D. Noninterference

106. Khadijah is leading a software development team for her company. She knows the importance of conducting an attack surface analysis and developing a threat model. During which phase of the software development life cycle should she perform these actions?

A. Requirements gathering

B. Testing and validation

C. Release and maintenance

D. Design

107. There is a specific terminology taxonomy used in the discipline of formal architecture framework development and implementation. Which of the following terms has an incorrect definition?

i. **Architecture** Fundamental organization of a system embodied in its components, their relationships to each other and to the environment, and the principles guiding its design and evolution.

ii. **Architectural description (AD)** Representation of a whole system from the perspective of a related set of concerns.

iii. **Stakeholder** Individual, team, or organization (or classes thereof) with interests in, or concerns relative to, a system.

iv. **View** Collection of document types to convey an architecture in a formal manner.

v. **Viewpoint** A specification of the conventions for constructing and using a view. A template from which to develop individual views by establishing the purposes and audience for a view and the techniques for its creation and analysis.

A. i, iii

B. ii, iv

C. iv, v

D. ii

108. Operating systems may not work on systems with specific processors. Which of the following best describes why one operating system may work on an Intel processor but not on an AMD processor?

A. The operating system was not developed to work within the architecture of a specific processor and cannot use that specific processor instruction set.

B. The operating system was developed before the new processor architecture was released, and thus is not backward compatible.

C. The operating system is programmed to use a different instruction set.

D. The operating system is platform dependent, and thus can work only on one specific processor family.

109. Which of the following best describes how an address bus and a data bus are used for instruction execution?

A. The CPU sends a "fetch" request on the data bus, and the data residing at the requested address is returned on the address bus.

B. The CPU sends a "get" request on the address bus, and the data residing at the requested address is returned on the data bus.

C. The CPU sends a "fetch" request on the address bus, and the data residing at the requested address is returned on the data bus.

D. The CPU sends a "get" request on the data bus, and the data residing at the requested address is returned on the address bus.

110. An operating system has many different constructs to keep all of the different execution components in the necessary synchronization. One construct the operating system maintains is a process table. Which of the following best describes the role of a process table within an operating system?

A. The table contains information about each process that the CPU uses during the execution of the individual processes' instructions.

B. The table contains memory boundary addresses to ensure that processes do not corrupt each other's data.

C. The table contains condition bits that the CPU uses during state transitions.

D. The table contains I/O and memory addresses.

111. Hanna is a security manager of a company that relies heavily on one specific operating system. The operating system is used in the employee workstations and is embedded within devices that support the automated production line software. She has uncovered that the operating system has a vulnerability that could allow an attacker to force applications to not release memory segments after execution. Which of the following best describes the type of threat this vulnerability introduces?

A. Injection attacks

B. Memory corruption

C. Denial of service

D. Software locking

112. Which of the following architecture frameworks has a focus on command, control, communications, computers, intelligence, surveillance, and reconnaissance systems and processes?

A. DoDAF

B. TOGAF

C. CMMI

D. MODAF

113. Many operating systems implement address space layout randomization (ASLR). Which of the following best describes this type of technology?

A. Randomly arranging memory address values

B. Restricting the types of processes that can execute instructions in privileged mode

C. Running privileged instructions in virtual machines

D. Randomizing return pointer values

114. A company needs to implement a CCTV system that will monitor a large area of the facility. Which of the following is the correct lens combination for this?

A. A wide-angle lens and a small lens opening

B. A wide-angle lens and a large lens opening

C. A wide-angle lens and a large lens opening with a small focal length

D. A wide-angle lens and a large lens opening with a large focal length

115. What is the name of a water sprinkler system that keeps pipes empty and doesn't release water until a certain temperature is met and a "delay mechanism" is instituted?

A. Wet

B. Preaction

C. Delayed

D. Dry

116. There are different types of fire suppression systems. Which of the following answers best describes the difference between a deluge and a preaction system?

A. A deluge system provides a delaying mechanism that allows someone to deactivate the system in case of a false alarm or if the fire can be extinguished by other means. A preaction system provides similar functionality but has wide open sprinkler heads that allow a lot of water to be dispersed quickly.

B. A preaction system provides a delaying mechanism that allows someone to deactivate the system in case of a false alarm or if the fire can be extinguished by other means. A deluge system has wide open sprinkler heads that allow a lot of water to be dispersed quickly.

C. A dry pipe system provides a delaying mechanism that allows someone to deactivate the system in case of a false alarm or if the fire can be extinguished by other means. A deluge system has wide open sprinkler heads that allow a lot of water to be dispersed quickly.

D. A preaction system provides a delaying mechanism that allows someone to deactivate the system in case of a false alarm or if the fire can be extinguished by other means. A deluge system provides similar functionality but has wide open sprinkler heads that allow a lot of water to be dispersed quickly.

117. Which of the following best describes why Crime Prevention Through Environmental Design (CPTED) would integrate block parties and civic meetings?

A. These activities are designed to get people to work together to increase the overall crime and criminal behavior in the area.

B. These activities are designed to get corporations to work together to increase the overall awareness of acceptable and unacceptable activities in the area.

C. These activities are designed to get people to work together to increase the three strategies of this design model.

D. These activities are designed to get people to work together to increase the overall awareness of acceptable and unacceptable activities in the area.

118. Which of the following frameworks is a two-dimensional model that uses six basic communication interrogatives intersecting with different viewpoints to give a holistic understanding of the enterprise?

A. SABSA

B. TOGAF

C. CMMI

D. Zachman

119. Not every data transmission incorporates the session layer. Which of the following best describes the functionality of the session layer?

A. End-to-end data transmission

B. Application client/server communication mechanism in a distributed environment

C. Application-to-computer physical communication

D. Provides application with the proper syntax for transmission

120. What is the purpose of the Logical Link Control (LLC) layer in the OSI model?

A. Provides a standard interface for the network layer protocol

B. Provides the framing functionality of the data link layer

C. Provides addressing of the packet during encapsulation

D. Provides the functionality of converting bits into electrical signals

121. Which of the following best describes why classless interdomain routing (CIDR) was created?

A. To allow IPv6 traffic to tunnel through IPv4 networks

B. To allow IPSec to be integrated into IPv4 traffic

C. To allow an address class size to meet an organization's need

D. To allow IPv6 to tunnel IPSec traffic

122. John is a security engineer at a company that develops highly confidential products for various government agencies. While his company has VPNs set up to protect traffic that travels over the Internet and other nontrusted networks, he knows that internal traffic should also be protected. Which of the following is the best type of approach John's company should take?

A. Implement a data link technology that provides 802.1AE security functionality.

B. Implement a network-level technology that provides 802.1AE security functionality.

C. Implement TLS over L2TP.

D. Implement IPSec over L2TP.

123. IEEE ______________ provides a unique ID for a device. IEEE ______________ provides data encryption, integrity, and origin authentication functionality. IEEE ______________ carries out key agreement functions for the session keys used for data encryption. Each of these standards provides specific parameters to work within an IEEE ______________ framework.

A. 802.1AF, 802.1AE, 802.1AR, 802.1X EAP-TLS

B. 802.1AT, 802.1AE, 802.1AM, 802.1X EAP-SSL

C. 802.1AR, 802.1AE, 802.1AF, 802.1X EAP-SSL

D. 802.1AR, 802.1AE, 802.1AF, 802.1X EAP-TLS

124. Bob has noticed that one of the network switches has been acting strangely over the last week. Bob installed a network protocol analyzer to monitor the traffic going to the specific switch. He has identified UDP traffic coming from an outside source using the destination port 161. Which of the following best describes what is most likely taking place?

A. An attacker is modifying the switch SNMP MIB.

B. An attacker is carrying out a selective DoS attack.

C. An attacker is manipulating the ARP cache.

D. An attacker is carrying out an injection attack.

125. Larry is a seasoned security professional and knows the potential dangers associated with using an ISP's DNS server for Internet connectivity. When Larry stays at a hotel or uses his laptop in any type of environment he does not fully trust, he updates values in his HOSTS file. Which of the following best describes why Larry carries out this type of task?

A. Reduces the risk of an attacker sending his system a corrupt ARP address that points his system to a malicious website.

B. Ensures his host-based IDS is properly updated.

C. Reduces the risk of an attacker sending his system an incorrect IP address-to-host mapping that points his system to a malicious website.

D. Ensures his network-based IDS is properly synchronized with his host-based IDS.

126. John has uncovered a rogue system on the company network that emulates a switch. The software on this system is being used by an attacker to modify frame tag values. Which of the following best describes the type of attack that has most likely been taking place?

A. DHCP snooping

B. VLAN hopping

C. Network traffic shaping

D. Network traffic hopping

127. Frank is a new security manager for a large financial institution. He has been told that the organization needs to reduce the total cost of ownership for many components of the network and infrastructure. The organization currently maintains many distributed networks, software packages, and applications. Which of the following best describes the cloud services that are most likely provided by service providers for Frank to choose from?

   A. Infrastructure as a Service provides an environment similar to an operating system, Platform as a Service provides operating systems and other major processing platforms, and Software as a Service provides specific application-based functionality.

   B. Infrastructure as a Service provides an environment similar to a data center, Platform as a Service provides operating systems and other major processing platforms, and Software as a Service provides specific application-based functionality.

   C. Infrastructure as a Service provides an environment similar to a data center, Platform as a Service provides application-based functionality, and Software as a Service provides specific operating system functionality.

   D. Infrastructure as a Service provides an environment similar to a database, Platform as a Service provides operating systems and other major processing platforms, and Software as a Service provides specific application-based functionality.

128. Terry is told by his boss that he needs to implement a networked-switched infrastructure that allows several systems to be connected to any storage device. What does Terry need to roll out?

   A. Electronic vaulting

   B. Hierarchical storage management

   C. Storage area network

   D. Remote journaling

129. On a Tuesday morning, Jami is summoned to the office of the security director, where she finds six of her peers from other departments. The security director gives them instructions about an event that will be taking place in two weeks. Each of the individuals will be responsible for removing specific systems from the facility, bringing them to the offsite facility, and implementing them. Each individual will need to test the installed systems and ensure the configurations are correct for production activities. What event is Jami about to take part in?

   A. Parallel test

   B. Full-interruption test

   C. Simulation test

   D. Structured walk-through test

130. While DRP and BCP are directed at the development of "plans," ______________ is the holistic management process that should cover both of them. It provides a framework for integrating resilience with the capability for effective responses that protects the interests of the organization's key stakeholders.

   A. continuity of operations
   B. business continuity management
   C. risk management
   D. enterprise management architecture

131. The "Safe Harbor" privacy framework was created to:

   A. Ensure that personal information should be collected only for a stated purpose by lawful and fair means and with the knowledge or consent of the subject
   B. Provide a streamlined means for U.S. organizations to comply with European privacy laws
   C. Require the federal government to release to citizens the procedures for how records are collected, maintained, used, and distributed
   D. None of the above

132. The European Union's Directive on Data Protection forbids the transfer of individually identifiable information to a country outside the EU, unless:

   A. The receiving country grants individuals adequate privacy protection.
   B. The receiving country pays a fee to the EU.
   C. There are no exceptions; no information is ever transferred.
   D. The receiving country is a member of the Fair Trade Organization.

133. The main goal of the Wassenaar Arrangement is to prevent the buildup of military capabilities that could threaten regional and international security and stability. How does this relate to technology?

   A. Cryptography is a dual-use tool.
   B. Technology is used in weaponry systems.
   C. Military actions directly relate to critical infrastructure systems.
   D. Critical infrastructure systems can be at risk under this agreement.

134. Which world legal system of law is used in continental European countries, such as France and Spain, and is rule-based law, not precedence based?

   A. Civil (code) law system
   B. Common law system

C. Customary law system

D. Mixed law system

135. Which of the following is not a correct characteristic of the Failure Modes and Effect Analysis (FMEA) method?

A. Determining functions and identifying functional failures

B. Assessing the causes of failure and their failure effects through a structured process

C. Structured process carried out by an identified team to address high-level security compromises

D. Identifying where something is most likely going to break and either fixing the flaws that could cause this issue or implementing controls to reduce the impact of the break

136. A risk analysis can be carried out through qualitative or quantitative means. It is important to choose the right approach to meet the organization's goals. In a quantitative analysis, which of the following items would not be assigned a numeric value?

i. Asset value

ii. Threat frequency

iii. Severity of vulnerability

iv. Impact damage

v. Safeguard costs

vi. Safeguard effectiveness

vii. Probability

A. All of them

B. None of them

C. ii

D. vii

137. Uncovering restricted information by using permissible data is referred to as ________________.

A. inference

B. data mining

C. perturbation

D. cell suppression

138. Tim recently started working at an organization with no defined security processes. One of the areas he'd like to improve is software patching. Consistent with the organizational culture, he is considering a decentralized or unmanaged model for patching. Which of the following is not one of the risks his organization would face with such a model?

A. This model typically requires users to have admin credentials, which violates the principle of least privilege.

B. It will be easier to ensure that all software is updated, since they will be configured to do so automatically.

C. It may be difficult (or impossible) to attest to the status of every application in the organization.

D. Having each application or service independently download the patches will lead to network congestion.

139. An attacker can modify the client-side JavaScript that provides structured layout and HTML representation. This commonly takes place through form fields within compromised web servers. Which of the following best describes this type of attack?

A. Injection attack

B. DOM-based XSS

C. Persistent XSS

D. Session hijacking

140. COBIT and COSO can be used together, but have different goals and focuses. Which of the following is incorrect as it pertains to these two models?

i. COSO is a model for corporate governance, and COBIT is a model for IT governance.

ii. COSO deals more at the strategic level, while COBIT focuses more at the operational level.

iii. COBIT is a way to meet many of the COSO objectives, but only from the IT perspective.

iv. COSO deals with non-IT items also, as in company culture, financial accounting principles, board of director responsibility, and internal communication structures.

A. None

B. All

C. i, ii

D. ii, iii

Use the following scenario to answer Questions 141–142. Ron is in charge of updating his company's business continuity and disaster recovery plans and processes. After conducting a business impact analysis, his team has told him that if the company's e-commerce payment gateway was unable to process payments for 24 hours or more, this could drastically affect the survivability of the company. The analysis indicates that after an outage, the payment gateway and payment processing should be restored within 13 hours. Ron's team needs to integrate solutions that provide redundancy, fault tolerance, and failover capability.

141. In the scenario, what does the 24-hour time period represent and what does the 13-hour time period represent?

A. Maximum tolerable downtime, recovery time objective

B. Recovery time objective, maximum tolerable downtime

C. Maximum tolerable downtime, recovery data period

D. Recovery time objective, data recovery period

142. Which of the following best describes the type of solution Ron's team needs to implement?

A. RAID and clustering

B. Storage area networks

C. High availability

D. Grid computing and clustering

Answers

1. **A.** While they are all issues to be concerned with, risk is a combination of probability and business impact. The largest business impact out of this list and in this situation is the fact that intellectual property for product development has been lost. If a competitor can produce the product and bring it to market quickly, this can have a long-lasting financial impact on the company.
2. **D.** The attackers are the entities that have exploited a vulnerability; thus, they are the threat agent.
3. **C.** In this situation the e-mail server most likely is misconfigured or has a programming flaw that can be exploited. Either of these would be considered a vulnerability. The threat is that someone would find out about this vulnerability and exploit it. In this scenario since the server is compromised, it is the item that is providing exposure to the company. This exposure is allowing sensitive data to be accessed in an unauthorized manner.
4. **C.** Diameter is a protocol that has been developed to build upon the functionality of RADIUS and to overcome many of its limitations. Diameter is an AAA protocol that provides the same type of functionality as RADIUS and TACACS+ but also provides more flexibility and capabilities, including working with EAP. RADIUS uses UDP, and cannot effectively deal well with remote access, IP mobility, and policy control.

5. **C.** DNSSEC (DNS security, which is part of the many current implementations of DNS server software) works within a PKI and uses digital signatures, which allows DNS servers to validate the origin of a message to ensure that it is not spoofed and potentially malicious. If DNSSEC were enabled on server A, then server A would, upon receiving a response, validate the digital signature on the message before accepting the information to make sure that the response is from an authorized DNS server. So even if an attacker sent a message to a DNS server, the DNS server would discard it because the message would not contain a valid digital signature. DNSSEC allows DNS servers to send and receive only authenticated and authorized messages between themselves and thwarts the attacker's goal of poisoning a DNS cache table.
6. **C.** It is important to deal with the issue of "reasonable expectation of privacy" (REP) when it comes to employee monitoring. In the U.S. legal system the expectation of privacy is used when defining the scope of the privacy protections provided by the Fourth Amendment of the Constitution. If it is not specifically explained to an employee that monitoring is possible and/or probable, when the monitoring takes place he could claim that his privacy rights have been violated and launch a civil suit against a company.
7. **B.** A vulnerability is a lack or weakness of a control. In this situation the access control may be weak in nature, thus exploitable. The vulnerability is that the user, who must be given access to the sensitive data, is not properly monitored to deter and detect a willful breach of security. The threat is that any internal entity might misuse given access. The risk is the business impact of losing sensitive data. One control that could be put into place is monitoring so that access activities can be closely watched.
8. **C.** An administrator does not need to revoke and reassign permissions to individual users as they change jobs. Instead, the administrator assigns permissions and rights to a role, and users are plugged into those roles.
9. **A.** Many (but not all) countries have data breach notification requirements, and these vary greatly in their specifics. While some countries have very strict requirements, others have more lax requirement, or lack them altogether. This requires the security professional to ensure compliance in the appropriate territory. Applying the most stringent rules universally (e.g., 24-hour notification) is usually not a good idea from a business perspective. The term "best effort" is not acceptable in countries with strict rules, nor is the notion that personally identifiable information (PII) is the only type of data that would trigger a mandatory notification.
10. **D.** Regression testing should take place after a change to a system takes place, retesting to ensure functionality, performance, and protection.

11. **B.** AS/NZS 4360 takes a much broader approach to risk management than just information security. This Australian and New Zealand methodology can be used to understand a company's financial, capital, human safety, and business decisions risks. Although it can be used to analyze security risks, it was not created specifically for this purpose. This risk management standard is more focused on the health of a company from a business point of view, not security.
12. **B.** The first step is evaluation. Evaluation involves reviewing the product's protection functionality and assurance ratings. The next phase is certification. Certification involves testing the newly purchased product within the company's environment. The final stage is accreditation, which is management's formal approval.
13. **B.** Security through obscurity is depending upon complexity or secrecy as a protection method. Some organizations feel that since their proprietary code is not standards based, outsiders will not know how to compromise its components. This is an insecure approach. Defense-in-depth is a better approach with the assumption that anyone can figure out how something works.
14. **C.** ISO/IEC 27005 is the international standard for risk assessments and analysis.
15. **C.** The ISO/IEC 27799 is a guideline for information security management in health organizations. It deals with how organizations that store and process sensitive medical information should protect it.
16. **D.** A maskable interrupt is assigned to an event that may not be overly important, and the programmer can indicate that if that interrupt calls, the program does not stop what it is doing. This means the interrupt is ignored. Nonmaskable interrupts can never be overridden by an application because the event that has this type of interrupt assigned to it is critical.
17. **B.** A virtual private network (VPN) provides confidentiality for data being exchanged between two endpoints. While the use of VPNs may not be sufficient in every case, it is the only answer among those provided that addresses the question. The use of Secure Sockets Layer (SSL) is not considered secure. IEEE 802.1x is an authentication protocol that does not protect data in transit. Finally, whole-disk encryption may be a good approach to protecting sensitive data, but only while it is at rest.
18. **B.** Corroborative evidence cannot stand alone, but instead is used as supporting information in a trial. It is often testimony indirectly related to the case but offers enough correlation to supplement the lawyer's argument. The other choices are all types of evidence that can stand alone.
19. **B.** A CAPTCHA is a skewed representation of characteristics a person must enter to prove that the subject is a human and not an automated tool, as in a software robot. It is the graphical representation of data.
20. **B.** The CPO is a newer position, created mainly because of the increasing demands on organizations to protect a long laundry list of different types of data. This role is responsible for ensuring that customer, company, and employee data is secure and kept secret, which keeps the company out of criminal and civil courts and hopefully out of the headlines.

21. **D.** The correct steps for setting up a risk management program are as follows:
    1) Develop a risk management team
    2) Identify company assets to be assessed
    3) Calculate the value of each asset
    4) Identify the vulnerabilities and threats that can affect the identified assets
22. **B.** Synthetic transactions are scripted events that mimic the behaviors of real users and allow security professionals to systematically test the performance of critical services. They are the best approach, because they can detect problems before users notice them. Real user monitoring would rely on users encountering the problem, whereupon the system would automatically report it.
23. **A.** Data remanence refers to the persistence of data on storage media after it has been deleted. Encrypting this data is the best of the listed choices because the recoverable data will be meaningless to an adversary. Retention policies are important, but are considered administrative controls that don't deal with remanence directly. Simply deleting the file will not normally render the data unrecoverable, nor will the use of SSDs even though these devices will sometimes (though not always) make it difficult to recover the deleted data.
24. **C.** While all of these situations could have taken place, the most likely attack type in this scenario is the use of a keylogger. Attackers commonly compromise personal computers by tricking the users into installing Trojan horses that have the capability to install keystroke loggers. The keystroke logger can capture authentication data that the attacker can use to authenticate as a legitimate user and carry out malicious activities.
25. **B.** IPSec is a protocol used to provide VPNs that use strong encryption and authentication functionality. It can work in two different modes: tunnel mode (payload and headers are protected) or transport mode (payload protection only). IPSec works at the network layer, not the data link layer.
26. **C.** The sender would need to first obtain the receiver's public key, which could be from the receiver or a public directory. The sender needs to protect the symmetric session key as it is being sent, so she encrypts it with the receiver's public key. The receiver decrypts the session key with his private key.
27. **C.** Today, more organizations are implementing security event management (SEM) systems, also called security information and event management (SIEM) systems. These products gather logs from various devices (servers, firewalls, routers, etc.) and attempt to correlate the log data and provide analysis capabilities. We also have different types of systems on a network (routers, firewalls, IDS, IPS, servers, gateways, proxies) collecting logs in various proprietary formats, which requires centralization, standardization, and normalization. Log formats are different per product type and vendor.
28. **D.** While many of these automatic tunneling techniques reduce administration overhead because network administrators do not have to configure each and every system and network device with two different IP addresses, there are security

risks that need to be understood. Many times users and network administrators do not know that automatic tunneling capabilities are enabled, thus they do not ensure that these different tunnels are secured and/or are being monitored. If you are an administrator of a network and have IDS, IPS, and firewalls that are only configured to monitor and restrict IPv4 traffic, then all IPv6 traffic could be traversing your network insecurely. Attackers use these protocol tunnels and misconfigurations to get past these types of security devices so that malicious activities can take place unnoticed. Products and software may need to be updated to address both traffic types, proxies may need to be deployed to manage traffic communication securely, IPv6 should be disabled if not needed, and security appliances need to be configured to monitor all traffic types.

29. **D.** IoT devices run the gamut of cost, from the very cheap to the very expensive. Cost, among the listed options, is the least likely to be a direct concern for a security professional. Lack of authentication, encryption, and update mechanisms are much more likely to be significant issues in any IoT adoption plan.

30. **C.** The Common Criteria uses a different assurance rating system than the previously used criteria. It has packages of specifications that must be met for a product to obtain the corresponding rating. These ratings and packages are called Evaluation Assurance Levels (EALs).

31. **B.** Extensible Access Control Markup Language (XACML), a declarative access control policy language implemented in XML and a processing model, describes how to interpret security policies. Service Provisioning Markup Language (SPML) is an XML-based framework being developed by OASIS for exchanging user, resource, and service provisioning information between cooperating organizations.

32. **C.** A company must decide how to handle physical access control in the event of a power failure. In fail-safe mode, doorways are automatically unlocked. This is usually dictated by fire codes to ensure that people do not get stuck inside of a burning building. Fail-secure means that the door will default to lock.

33. **C.** Incident response typically requires humans in the loop. Next-generation firewalls (NGFWs) do not completely automate the process of responding to security incidents. NGFWs typically involve integrated IPS and signature sharing capabilities with cloud-based aggregators, but are also significantly more expensive than other firewall types.

34. **D.** Trolling is the term used to describe people who sow discord on various social platforms on the Internet by starting arguments or making inflammatory statements aimed at upsetting others. This is not a topic normally covered in security awareness training. Social engineering, phishing, and whaling are important topics to include in any security awareness program.

35. **D.** When clients digitally sign messages, this ensures nonrepudiation. Since the client should be the only person who has his private key, and only his public key can decrypt it, the e-mail must have been sent from the client. Digital signatures provide nonrepudiation protection, which is what this company needs.

36. **D.** Simple Authentication and Security Layer (SASL) is a protocol-independent authentication framework. It is a framework for authentication and data security in Internet protocols. It decouples authentication mechanisms from application protocols, with the goal of allowing any authentication mechanism supported by SASL to be used in any application protocol that uses SASL. SASL's design is intended to allow new protocols to reuse existing mechanisms without requiring redesign of the mechanisms, and allows existing protocols to make use of new mechanisms without redesign of protocols.

37. **D.** The individual objectives of a project must be analyzed to ensure that each is actually attainable. A part of scope analysis that may prove useful is SWOT analysis. SWOT stands for Strengths/Weaknesses/Opportunities/Threats, and its basic tenets are as follows:
    - Strengths: Characteristics of the project team that give it an advantage over others
    - Weaknesses: Characteristics that place the team at a disadvantage relative to others
    - Opportunities: Elements that could contribute to the project's success
    - Threats: Elements that could contribute to the project's failure

38. **A.** A recovery time objective (RTO) is the amount of time it takes to recover from a disaster, and a recovery point objective (RPO) is the amount of data, measured in time, that can be lost and be tolerable from that same event. The RPO is the acceptable amount of data loss measured in time. This value represents the earliest point in time by which data must be recovered. The higher the value of data, the more funds or other resources that can be put into place to ensure a smaller amount of data is lost in the event of a disaster. RTO is the maximum time period within which a business process must be restored to a designated service level after a disaster to avoid unacceptable consequences associated with a break in business continuity.

39. **B.** Computer crime can broadly be defined as criminal activity involving an information technology infrastructure, including illegal access, illegal interception, data interference, systems interference, misuse of devices, forgery, and electronic fraud.

40. **A.** XACML uses a Subject element (requesting entity), a Resource element (requested entity), and an Action element (types of access). XACML defines a declarative access control policy language implemented in XML.

41. **B.** The Mobile IP protocol allows location-independent routing of IP packets on web-based environments. Each mobile device is identified by its home address. While away from its home network, a mobile node is associated with a care-of address, which identifies its current location, and its home address is associated with the local endpoint of a tunnel to its home agent. Mobile IP specifies how a mobile device registers with its home agent and how the home agent routes packets to the mobile device.

42. **D.** The list of security solutions most companies need includes, but is not limited to, firewalls, antimalware, antispam, IDS\IPS, content filtering, data leak prevention, VPN capabilities, continuous monitoring, and reporting. Unified threat management (UTM) appliance products have been developed that provide all (or many) of these functionalities into a single network appliance. The goals of UTM are simplicity, streamlined installation and maintenance, centralized control, and the ability to understand a network's security from a holistic point of view.
43. **D.** A clearly defined incident-handling process can be more cost effective, enable recovery to happen more quickly, and provide a uniform approach with certain expectations of the results. Incident handling should be closely related to disaster recovery planning and should be part of the company's disaster recovery plan.
44. **C.** Global organizations that move data across other country boundaries must be aware of and follow the Organisation for Economic Co-operation and Development (OECD) *Guidelines on the Protection of Privacy and Transborder Flows of Personal Data.* Since most countries have a different set of laws pertaining to the definition of private data and how it should be protected, international trade and business get more convoluted and can negatively affect the economy of nations. The OECD is an international organization that helps different governments come together and tackle the economic, social, and governance challenges of a globalized economy. Because of this, the OECD came up with guidelines for the various countries to follow so that data is properly protected and everyone follows the same type of rules.
45. **B.** Registered ports are 1024–49151, which can be registered with the Internet Corporation for Assigned Names and Numbers (ICANN) for a particular use. Vendors register specific ports to map to their proprietary software. Dynamic ports are 49152–65535 and are available to be used by any application on an "as needed" basis.
46. **A.** The correct formula for cost/benefit analysis is (ALE before implementing safeguard) – (ALE after implementing safeguard) – (annual cost of safeguard) = value of safeguard to the company.
47. **B.** Each of the listed items are correct benefits or characteristics of cloud computing except "Cost of computing can be increased since it is a shared delivery model." The correct answer would be "Cost of computing can be *decreased* since it is a shared delivery model."
48. **A.** An architecture is a tool used to conceptually understand the structure and behavior of a complex entity through different views. An architecture provides different views of the system, based upon the needs of the stakeholders of that system.
49. **B.** Threat modeling is a systematic approach used to understand how different threats could be realized and how a successful compromise could take place. A threat model is a description of a set of security aspects that can help define a threat and a set of possible attacks to consider. It may be useful to define different

threat models for one software product. Each model defines a narrow set of possible attacks to focus on. A threat model can help to assess the probability, the potential harm, and the priority of attacks, and thus help to minimize or eradicate the threats.

50. **B.** IDS and some antimalware products are said to have "heuristic" capabilities. The term heuristic means to create new information from different data sources. The IDS gathers different "clues" from the network or system and calculates the probability an attack is taking place. If the probability hits a set threshold, then the alarm sounds.

51. **C.** External auditors have certain advantages over in-house teams, but they will almost certainly not be as knowledgeable of internal processes and technology as the folks who deal with them on a daily basis.

52. **C.** In this example, lower-ranked staffers could have deduced that the contract had been renewed by paying attention to the changes in their systems. The noninterference model addresses this specifically by dictating that no action or state in higher levels can impact or be visible to lower levels. In this example, the staff could learn something indirectly or infer something that they do not have a right to know yet.

53. **B.** HTML documents and e-mails allow users to attach or embed hyperlinks in any given text, such as the "Click Here" links you commonly see in e-mail messages or web pages. Attackers misuse hyperlinks to deceive unsuspecting users into clicking rogue links. The most common approach is known as URL hiding.

54. **C.** Personnel background checks are a common administrative (not technical) control. This type of audit would have nothing to do with the web applications themselves. The other three options (log reviews, code reviews, misuse case testing) are typical ways in which we verify the effectiveness of our technical controls.

55. **D.** Statistical time-division multiplexing (STDM) transmits several types of data simultaneously across a single transmission line. STDM technologies analyze statistics related to the typical workload of each input device and make real-time decisions on how much time each device should be allocated for data transmission.

56. **D.** The actual voice stream is carried on media protocols such as the Real-time Transport Protocol (RTP). RTP provides a standardized packet format for delivering audio and video over IP networks. RTP is a session layer protocol that carries data in media stream format, as in audio and video, and is used extensively in VoIP, telephony, video conferencing, and other multimedia streaming technologies. It provides end-to-end delivery services and is commonly run over the transport layer protocol UDP. RTP Control Protocol (RTCP) is used in conjunction with RTP and is also considered a session layer protocol. It provides out-of-band statistics and control information to provide feedback on QoS levels of individual streaming multimedia sessions.

57. **A.** ISO/IEC 27031:2011 is a set of guidelines for information and communications technology readiness for business continuity. This ISO/IEC standard is a component of the overall ISO/IEC 27000 series.

58. **C.** The /etc/passwd file contains user account information on Linux systems. Though it might be possible to download its contents and thus attack the passwords of privileged accounts, deleting the file (even if it was possible) would simply deprive the system of the ability to authenticate users.

59. **D.** IPSec is made up of two main protocols, Authentication Header (AH) and Encapsulating Security Payload (ESP). AH provides system authentication and integrity, but not confidentiality or availability. ESP provides system authentication, integrity, and confidentiality, but not availability. Nothing within IPSec can ensure the availability of the system it is residing on.

60. **D.** The ACID test concept should be incorporated into the software of a database. ACID stands for:
    - **Atomicity** Divides transactions into units of work and ensures that either all modifications take effect or none take effect. Either the changes are committed or the database is rolled back.
    - **Consistency** A transaction must follow the integrity policy developed for that particular database and ensure that all data is consistent in the different databases.
    - **Isolation** Transactions execute in isolation until completed, without interacting with other transactions. The results of the modification are not available until the transaction is completed.
    - **Durability** Once the transaction is verified as accurate on all systems, it is committed and the databases cannot be rolled back.

61. **B.** In a Platform as a Service (PaaS) contract, the service provider normally takes care of all configuration, patches, and updates for the virtual platform. Jim would only have to worry about porting the applications and running them.

62. **B.** The biggest advantages of cloud computing are enhanced efficiency, performance, reliability, scalability, and security. Still, cloud computing is not a panacea. We must still carefully consider legal, contractual, and cost issues since they could potentially place an organization in a difficult position.

63. **A.** The aim of an attack surface analysis is to identify and reduce the amount of code accessible to untrusted users. The basic strategies of attack surface reduction are to reduce the amount of code running, reduce entry points available to untrusted users, reduce privilege levels as much as possible, and eliminate unnecessary services. Attack surface analysis is generally carried out through specialized tools to enumerate different parts of a product and aggregate their findings into a numerical value. Attack surface analyzers scrutinize files, registry keys, memory data, session information, processes, and services details.

64. B. The Capability Maturity Model Integration (CMMI) model outlines the necessary characteristics of an organization's security engineering process. It addresses the different phases of a secure software development life cycle, including concept definition, requirements analysis, design, development, integration, installation, operations, and maintenance, and what should happen in each phase. It can be used to evaluate security engineering practices and identify ways to improve them. It can also be used by customers in the evaluation process of a software vendor. In the best of both worlds, software vendors would use the model to help improve their processes and customers would use the model to assess the vendor's practices.

65. D. A data structure is a representation of the logical relationship between elements of data. It dictates the degree of association among elements, methods of access, processing alternatives, and the organization of data elements. The structure can be simple in nature, like the scalar item, which represents a single element that can be addressed by an identifier and accessed by a single address in storage. The scalar items can be grouped in arrays, which provide access by indexes. Other data structures include hierarchical structures by using multilinked lists that contain scalar items, vectors, and possibly arrays. The hierarchical structure provides categorization and association.

66. D. These are all issues that are directly related to Kerberos. These items are as follows:

- The KDC can be a single point of failure. If the KDC goes down, no one can access needed resources. Redundancy is necessary for the KDC.
- The KDC must be able to handle the number of requests it receives in a timely manner. It must be scalable.
- Secret keys are temporarily stored on the users' workstations, which means it is possible for an intruder to obtain these cryptographic keys.
- Session keys are decrypted and reside on the users' workstations, either in a cache or in a key table. Again, an intruder can capture these keys.
- Kerberos is vulnerable to password guessing. The KDC does not know if a dictionary attack is taking place.

67. A. Yes, the company should implement the control, as the value would be $25,000.

68. D. The correct mappings for the individual standards are as follows:

- ISO/IEC 27002: Code of practice for information security management
- ISO/IEC 27003: Guideline for ISMS implementation
- ISO/IEC 27004: Guideline for information security management measurement and metrics framework
- ISO/IEC 27005: Guideline for information security risk management
- ISO/IEC 27006: Guideline for bodies providing audit and certification of information security management systems

69. **B.** If the PSW has a bit value that indicates the instructions to be executed should be carried out in privileged mode, this means a trusted process (e.g., an operating system process) made the request and can have access to the functionality that is not available in user mode.

70. **C.** End-to-end encryption happens within the applications. IPSec encryption takes place at the network layer. PPTP encryption takes place at the data link layer. Link encryption takes place at the data link and physical layers.

71. **A.** Hierarchical storage management (HSM) provides continuous online backup functionality. It combines hard disk technology with the cheaper and slower optical or tape jukeboxes. Storage area network (SAN) is made up of several storage systems that are connected together to form a single backup network.

72. **C.** The common law system is the only one that is based on previous interpretations of the law. This means that the system consists of both laws and court decisions in specific cases. Torts can be (and usually are) part of a common law system, but that would be an incomplete answer to this question.

73. **B.** It is important that evidence be relevant, complete, sufficient, and reliable to the case at hand. These four characteristics of evidence provide a foundation for a case and help ensure that the evidence is legally permissible.

74. **B.** Data mining is also known as knowledge discovery in database (KDD), which is a combination of techniques used to identify valid and useful patterns. Different types of data can have various interrelationships, and the method used depends on the type of data and patterns that are sought. The following are three approaches used in KDD systems to uncover these patterns:
    - **Classification** Groups together data according to shared similarities
    - **Probabilistic** Identifies data interdependencies and applies probabilities to their relationships
    - **Statistical** Identifies relationships between data elements and uses rule discovery.

75. **C.** Simple Object Access Protocol (SOAP) enables programs running on different operating systems and written in different programming languages to communicate over web-based communication methods. SOAP is an XML-based protocol that encodes messages in a web service environment. SOAP actually defines an XML schema or a structure of how communication is going to take place. The SOAP XML schema defines how objects communicate directly.

76. **A.** Each answer lists the correct definition mapping.

77. **C.** For an enterprise security architecture to be successful in its development and implementation, the following items must be understood and followed: strategic alignment, process enhancement, business enablement, and security effectiveness.

78. **A.** The OECD is an international organization that helps different governments come together and tackle the economic, social, and governance challenges of a globalized economy. Thus, the OECD came up with guidelines for the various countries to follow so data is properly protected and everyone follows the same type of rules.

79. **A.** The Zachman Framework is for business enterprise architectures, not security enterprises. The proper definition mappings are as follows:
    - **Zachman Framework** Model for the development of enterprise architectures developed by John Zachman
    - **TOGAF** Model and methodology for the development of enterprise architectures developed by The Open Group
    - **DoDAF** U.S. Department of Defense architecture framework that ensures interoperability of systems to meet military mission goals
    - **MODAF** Architecture framework used mainly in military support missions developed by the British Ministry of Defence
    - **SABSA model** Model and methodology for the development of information security enterprise architectures
80. **B.** The ISO/IEC 27000 series provides a high-level overview of security program requirements, while COBIT provides the objectives of the individual security controls. COBIT provides the objectives that the real-world implementations (controls) you chose to put into place need to meet.
81. **D.** This model was not built upon the SABSA model. All other characteristics are true.
82. **D.** Operationally Critical Threat, Asset, and Vulnerability Evaluation (OCTAVE) is a methodology that is intended to be used in situations where people manage and direct the risk evaluation for information security within their company. This places the people who work inside the organization in the position of being able to make decisions regarding the best approach for evaluating the security of their organization.
83. **B.** A formal architecture framework is a conceptual model in which an architecture description is organized into multiple architecture views, where each view addresses specific concerns originating with the specific stakeholders. Individual stakeholders have a variety of system concerns, which the architecture must address. To express these concerns, each view applies the conventions of its architecture viewpoint.
84. **C.** Fault tree analysis follows this general process. First, an undesired effect is taken as the root, or top, event of a tree of logic. Then, each situation that has the potential to cause that effect is added to the tree as a series of logic expressions. Fault trees are then labeled with actual numbers pertaining to failure probabilities.
85. **D.** Each of the listed answers in ii, iii, and iv has the correct definition mapping. Answer i is incorrect. COSO is an organization that provides leadership in the areas of organizational governance, internal control, enterprise risk management, fraud, business ethics, and financial reporting. The incorrect description for COSO in answer i maps to SABSA.

86. **D.** Security effectiveness deals with metrics, meeting service level agreement (SLA) requirements, achieving return on investment (ROI), meeting set baselines, and providing management with a dashboard or balanced scorecard system. These are ways to determine how useful the current security solutions and architecture as a whole are performing.
87. **D.** Each answer provides the correct definition of the four levels that can be assigned to an organization during its evaluation against the CMMI model. This model can be used to determine how well the organization's processes compare to CMMI best practices, and to identify areas where improvement can be made. Maturity Level 1 is Initial.
88. **B.** The information risk management (IRM) policy should map to all of the items listed except specific physical controls. Policies should not specify any type of controls, whether they are administrative, physical, or technical.
89. **C.** Each of these items should be considered before committing to an outsource partner or vendor.
90. **D.** The steps normally involved in the discovery of electronically stored information, or e-Discovery, are identifying, preserving, collecting, processing, reviewing, analyzing, and producing the data in compliance of the court order. Data remanence is not part of e-Discovery, though it could influence the process.
91. **C.** ISO/IEC 27004:2009, which is used to assess the effectiveness of an ISMS and the controls that make up the security program as outlined in ISO/IEC 27001. ISO/IEC 27004 is the guideline for information security management measurement and metrics framework.
92. **B.** Content distribution networks (CDNs) work by replicating content across geographically dispersed nodes. This means that regional users (those closest to a given node) will see improved responsiveness and could have tailored content delivered to them. It also means that it is much more difficult to mount a successful DDoS attack. An ARP spoofing attack, however, takes place on the local area network and is therefore unrelated to the advantages of CDNs.
93. **A.** A WAM product allows an administrator to configure and control access to internal resources. This type of access control is commonly put in place to control external entities requesting access. The product may work on a single web server or a server farm.
94. **C.** A user's identity is commonly a collection of her attributes (department, role in company, shift time, clearance, and others), her entitlements (resources available to her, authoritative rights in the company, and so on), and her traits (biometric information, height, sex, and so forth).
95. **B.** HTML came from Standard Generalized Markup Language (SGML), which came from the Generalized Markup Language (GML). A markup language is a way to structure text and how it will be presented. You can control how the text looks and some of the actual functionality the page provides.

96. **A.** Extensible Markup Language (XML) was created as a specification to create various markup languages. From this specification, more specific markup language standards were created to be able to provide individual industries with the functions they required. Individual industries use markup languages to meet different needs, but there is an interoperability issue in that the industries still need to be able to communicate with each other.

97. **B.** Roles work as containers for users. The administrator or security professional creates the roles and assigns rights to them and then assigns users to the container. The users then inherit the permissions and rights from the containers (roles), which is how implicit permissions are obtained.

98. **C.** Diameter is a more diverse centralized access control administration technique than RADIUS and TACACS+ because it supports a wide range of protocols that often accompany wireless technologies. RADIUS supports PPP, SLIP, and traditional network connections. TACACS+ is a RADIUS-like protocol that is Cisco-proprietary. Kerberos is a single sign-on technology, not a centralized access control administration protocol that supports all stated technologies.

99. **A.** An authoritative system of record (ASOR) is a hierarchical tree-like structure system that tracks subjects and their authorization chains. The authoritative source is the "system of record," or the location where identity information originates and is maintained. It should have the most up-to-date and reliable identity information.

100. **A.** User provisioning refers to the creation, maintenance, and deactivation of user objects and attributes as they exist in one or more systems, directories, or applications in response to business processes.

101. **D.** A user's identity can be a collection of her attributes (department, role in company, shift time, clearance, and others), her entitlements (resources available to her, authoritative rights in the company, and so on), and her traits (biometric information, height, sex, and so forth).

102. **A.** The Service Provisioning Markup Language (SPML) allows for the exchange of provisioning data between applications, which could reside in one organization or many. SPML allows for the automation of user management (account creation, amendments, revocation) and access entitlement configuration related to electronically published services across multiple provisioning systems. This markup language allows for the integration and interoperation of service provisioning requests across various platforms.

103. **B.** In this scenario, Lynn is considered the principal, the airline company is considered the identity provider, and the hotel company that receives the user's authentication information from the airline company web server is considered the service provider. Security Assertion Markup Language (SAML) provides the authentication pieces to federated identity management systems to allow business-to-business (B2B) and business-to-consumer (B2C) transactions.

104. A. The use of web services in this manner also allows for organizations to provide service-oriented architecture (SOA) environments. SOA is way to provide independent services residing on different systems in different business domains in one consistent manner. This architecture is a set of principles and methodologies for designing and developing software in the form of interoperable services.

105. B. Bell-LaPadula models have rigid security policies that are built to ensure confidentiality. The "strong tranquility" property is an inflexible mechanism that enforces the consistent security classification of an object.

106. D. In the system design phase we gather system requirement specifications and determine how the system will accomplish design goals, such as required functionality, compatibility, fault tolerance, extensibility, security, usability, and maintainability. The attack surface analysis, together with the threat model, inform the developers' decisions because they can look at proposed architectures and competing designs from the perspective of an attacker. This allows them to develop a more defensible system. Though it is possible to start the threat model during the earlier phase of requirements gathering, this modeling effort is normally not done that early. Furthermore, the attack surface cannot be properly studied until there is a proposed architecture to analyze. Performing this activity later in the SDLC is less effective and usually results in security being "bolted-on" instead of "baked-in."

107. B. Formal enterprise architecture frameworks use the following terms:

- **Architecture** Fundamental organization of a system embodied in its components, their relationships to each other and to the environment, and the principles guiding its design and evolution.
- **Architectural description (AD)** Collection of document types to convey an architecture in a formal manner.
- **Stakeholder** Individual, team, or organization (or classes thereof) with interests in, or concerns relative to, a system.
- **View** Representation of a whole system from the perspective of a related set of concerns.
- **Viewpoint** A specification of the conventions for constructing and using a view. A template from which to develop individual views by establishing the purposes and audience for a view and the techniques for its creation and analysis.

108. A. Each CPU type has a specific architecture and set of instructions that it can carry out. The operating system must be designed to work within this CPU architecture. This is why one operating system may work on an Intel processor but not on an AMD processor.

109. C. If the CPU needs to access some data, either from memory or from an I/O device, it sends a "fetch" request on the address bus. The fetch request contains the address of where the needed data is located. The circuitry associated with the memory or I/O device recognizes the address the CPU sent down the address bus and instructs the memory or device to read the requested data and put it on the data bus. So the address bus is used by the CPU to indicate the location of the needed information, and the memory or I/O device responds by sending the information that resides at that memory location through the data bus.

110. A. The operating system keeps a process table, which has one entry per process. The table contains each individual process's state, stack pointer, memory allocation, program counter, and status of open files in use. The reason the operating system documents all of this status information is that the CPU needs all of it loaded into its registers when it needs to interact with, for example, process 1. The CPU uses this information during the execution activities for specific processes.

111. C. Attackers have identified programming errors in operating systems that allow them to "starve" the system of its own memory. This means the attackers exploit a software vulnerability that ensures that processes do not properly release their memory resources. Memory is continually committed and not released, and the system is depleted of this resource until it can no longer function. This is an example of a denial-of-service attack.

112. A. The Department of Defense Architecture Framework (DoDAF) has a focus on command, control, communications, computers, intelligence, surveillance, and reconnaissance systems and processes. When the U.S. DoD purchases technology products and weapon systems, enterprise architecture documents must be created based upon DoDAF standards to illustrate how they will properly integrate into the current infrastructures.

113. A. Address space layout randomization (ASLR) is a control that involves randomly arranging processes' address space and other memory segments. ASLR makes it more difficult for an attacker to predict target addresses for specific memory attacks.

114. A. The depth of field refers to the portion of the environment that is in focus when shown on the monitor. The depth of field varies, depending upon the size of the lens opening, the distance of the object being focused on, and the focal length of the lens. The depth of field increases as the size of the lens opening decreases, the subject distance increases, or the focal length of the lens decreases. So if you want to cover a large area and not focus on specific items, it is best to use a wide-angle lens and a small lens opening.

115. B. A link must melt before the water will pass through the sprinkler heads, which creates the delay in water release. This type of suppression system is best in data-processing environments because it allows time to deactivate the system if there is a false alarm.

116. B. A preaction system has a link that must be burned through before water is released. This is the mechanism that provides the delay in water release. A deluge system has wide open sprinkler heads that allow a lot of water to be released quickly. It does not have a delaying component.

117. D. CPTED encourages activity support, which is planned activities for the areas to be protected. These activities are designed to get people to work together to increase the overall awareness of acceptable and unacceptable activities in the area. The activities could be neighborhood watch groups, company barbeques, block parties, or civic meetings. This strategy is sometimes the reason for particular placement of basketball courts, soccer fields, or baseball fields in open parks. The increased activity will hopefully keep the bad guys from milling around doing things the community does not welcome.

118. D. The Zachman Framework is a two-dimensional model that uses six basic communication interrogatives (What, How, Where, Who, When, and Why) intersecting with different viewpoints (Planner, Owner, Designer, Builder, Implementer, and User) to give a holistic understanding of the enterprise. This framework was developed in the 1980s and is based on the principles of classical business architecture that contain rules that govern an ordered set of relationships.

119. B. The communication between two pieces of the same software product that reside on different computers needs to be controlled, which is why session layer protocols even exist. Session layer protocols take on the functionality of middleware, enabling software on two different computers to communicate.

120. A. The data link layer has two sublayers: the Logical Link Control (LLC) and Media Access Control (MAC) layers. The LLC provides a standard interface for whatever network protocol is being used. This provides an abstraction layer so that the network protocol does not need to be programmed to communicate with all of the possible MAC level protocols (Ethernet, Token Ring, WLAN, FDDI, etc.).

121. C. A Class B address range is usually too large for most companies, and a Class C address range is too small, so CIDR provides the flexibility to increase or decrease the class sizes as necessary. CIDR is the method to specify more flexible IP address classes.

122. A. 802.1AE is the IEEE MAC Security standard (MACSec), which defines a security infrastructure to provide data confidentiality, data integrity, and data origin authentication. Where a VPN connection provides protection at the higher networking layers, MACSec provides hop-by-hop protection at layer 2.

123. D. 802.1AR provides a unique ID for a device. 802.1AE provides data encryption, integrity, and origin authentication functionality. 802.1AF carries out key agreement functions for the session keys used for data encryption. Each of these standards provides specific parameters to work within an 802.1X EAP-TLS framework.

124. A. If an attacker can uncover the read-write string, she could change values held within the MIB, which could reconfigure the device. The usual default read-only community string is "public" and the read-write string is "private." Many companies do not change these, so anyone who can connect to port 161 can read the status information of a device and potentially reconfigure it. The SNMP ports (161 and 162) should not be open to untrusted networks, like the Internet, and if needed they should be filtered to ensure only authorized individuals can connect to them.

125. **C.** The HOSTS file resides on the local computer and can contain static hostname-to-IP mapping information. If you do not want your system to query a DNS server, you can add the necessary data in the HOSTS file, and your system will first check its contents before reaching out to a DNS server. Some people use these files to reduce the risk of an attacker sending their system a bogus IP address that points them to a malicious website.

126. **B.** An attacker can have a system act as though it is a switch. The system understands the tagging values being used in the network and the trunking protocols, and can insert itself between other VLAN devices and gain access to the traffic going back and forth. Attackers can also insert tagging values to manipulate the control of traffic at the data link layer.

127. **B.** The most common cloud service models are

    - **Infrastructure as a Service (IaaS)** Cloud providers offer the infrastructure environment of a traditional data center in an on-demand delivery method.
    - **Platform as a Service (PaaS)** Cloud providers deliver a computing platform, which can include an operating system, database, and web server as a holistic execution environment.
    - **Software as a Service (SaaS)** Provider gives users access to specific application software (CRM, e-mail, games).

128. **C.** A storage area network (SAN) is made up of several storage systems that are connected together to form a single storage network. A SAN is a networked infrastructure that allows several systems to be connected to any storage device. This is usually provided by using switches to create a switching fabric. The switching fabric allows for several devices to communicate with back-end storage devices and provides redundancy and fault tolerance by not depending upon one specific line or connection.

129. **A.** Parallel tests are similar to simulation tests, except that parallel tests include moving some of the systems to the offsite facility. Simulation tests stop just short of the move. Parallel tests are effective because they ensure that specific systems work at the new location, but the test itself does not interfere with business operations at the main facility.

130. **B.** While DRP and BCP are directed at the development of "plans," business continuity management (BCM) is the holistic management process that should cover both of them. BCM provides a framework for integrating resilience with the capability for effective responses in a manner that protects the interests of the organization's key stakeholders. The main objective of BCM is to allow the organization to continue to perform business operations under various conditions. BCM is the overarching approach to managing all aspects of BCP and DRP.

131. **B.** The U.S. approach to privacy protection relies on industry-specific legislation, regulation, and self-regulation, whereas the European Union relies

on comprehensive privacy regulation. In order to bridge these different privacy approaches, the U.S. Department of Commerce and the European Commission developed a "Safe Harbor" framework. In late 2015, the EU Court of Justice ruled that the Safe Harbor pact did not comply with EU privacy laws. As of this writing, it is being replaced with the EU-US Privacy Shield.

132. A. The European Union has restrictions on "transborder data flows" that would allow private data to flow to countries whose laws would not protect that data. In order for organizations outside the EU to be able to store and process protected data on EU persons, they must first show that they apply equivalent protections for that data. This happens within the framework of an international pact such as the now-defunct Safe Harbor pact and its successor, the EU-US Privacy Shield.

133. A. The Wassenaar Arrangement implements export controls for "Conventional Arms and Dual-Use Goods and Technologies." The main goal of this arrangement is to prevent the buildup of military capabilities that could threaten regional and international security and stability. So everyone is keeping an eye on each other to make sure no one country's weapons can take everyone else out. One item the agreement deals with is cryptography, which is seen as a dual-use good. It can be used for military and civilian uses. It is seen to be dangerous to export products with cryptographic functionality to countries that are in the "offensive" column, meaning that they are thought to have friendly ties with terrorist organizations and/or want to take over the world through the use of weapons of mass destruction.

134. A. The civil (code) law system is used in continental European countries such as France and Spain. It is a different legal system from the common law system used in the United Kingdom and United States. A civil law system is rule-based law, not precedence based. For the most part, a civil law system is focused on codified law—or written laws.

135. C. Failure Modes and Effect Analysis (FMEA) is a method for determining functions, identifying functional failures, and assessing the causes of failure and their failure effects through a structured process. It is commonly used in product development and operational environments. The goal is to identify where something is most likely going to break and either fix the flaws that could cause this issue or implement controls to reduce the impact of the break.

136. B. Each of these items would be assigned a numeric value in a quantitative risk analysis. Each element is quantified and entered into equations to determine total and residual risks. It is more of a scientific or mathematical approach to risk analysis compared to qualitative.

137. A. Aggregation and inference go hand in hand. For example, a user who uses data from a public database in order to figure out classified information is exercising aggregation (the collection of data) and can then infer the relationship between that data and the data he does not have access to. This is called an inference attack.

138. B. This option is not a risk, but a (probably unrealistic) benefit so it cannot be the right answer. The other three options are all risks associated with an unmanaged patching model.

139. B. DOM (Document Object Model)–based XSS vulnerabilities are also referred to as local cross-site scripting. DOM is the standard structure layout to represent HTML and XML documents in the browser. In such attacks the document components such as form fields and cookies can be referenced through JavaScript. The attacker uses the DOM environment to modify the original client-side JavaScript. This causes the victim's browser to execute the resulting abusive JavaScript code.

140. A. They are all correct.

141. A. RTO is an allowable amount of downtime, and the MTD is a time period that represents the inability to recover. The RTO value is smaller than the MTD value because the MTD value represents the time after which an inability to recover significant operations will mean severe and perhaps irreparable damage to the organization's reputation or bottom line. The RTO assumes that there is a period of acceptable downtime. This means that a company can be out of production for a certain period of time (RTO) and still get back on its feet. But if the company cannot get production up and running within the MTD window, the company is sinking too fast to properly recover.

142. C. High availability (HA) is a combination of technologies and processes that work together to ensure that critical functions are always up and running at the necessary level. To provide this level of high availability, a company has to have a long list of technologies and processes that provide redundancy, fault tolerance, and failover capabilities.

About the CD-ROM

The CD-ROM that comes with this book includes

- **Practice questions** Total Seminars' Total Tester Premium Practice Exam Software, with over 1,400 practice questions covering all eight CISSP domains.
- **Hotspot and Drag-and-Drop Questions** In 2014, $(ISC)^2$ added interactive hotspot and drag-and-drop questions to the exam. These question types attempt to test an examinee's knowledge from a different perspective as compared to a more traditional text-based, multiple-choice question format.
- **Electronic copy of the book** in secure PDF format

System Requirements

The software requires Windows Vista or higher and 30MB of hard disk space for full installation, in addition to a current or prior major release of Chrome, Firefox, Internet Explorer, or Safari. To run, the screen resolution must be set to 1024 × 768 or higher. The PDF copy of the book requires Adobe Acrobat, Adobe Reader, or Adobe Digital Editions.

Total Tester Premium Practice Exam Software

Total Tester provides you with a simulation of the CISSP exam.

The multiple-choice exams can be taken in either Practice Mode or Exam Mode. Practice Mode provides an assistance window with hints, references to the book, explanations of the correct and incorrect answers, and the option to check your answer as you take the test. Exam Mode provides a simulation of the actual exam. The number of questions, the types of questions, and the time allowed are intended to be an accurate representation of the exam environment. Both Practice Mode and Exam Mode provide an overall grade and a grade broken down by certification objectives.

You can also use Custom Mode to create custom exams from selected certification domains or chapters. You can further customize the number of questions and time allowed.

To take a test, launch the program and select the exam suite from the Installed Question Packs list. You can then select Practice Mode, Exam Mode, or Custom Mode. After making your selection, click Start Exam to begin.

Installing and Running Total Tester Premium Practice Exam Software

From the main screen you may install the Total Tester by clicking the Total Tester Premium Practice Exams button. This will begin the installation process and place an icon on your desktop and in your Start menu. To run Total Tester, navigate to Start | (All) Programs | Total Seminars, or double-click the icon on your desktop.

To uninstall the Total Tester software, go to Start | Control Panel | Programs And Features, and then select the Total Tester program. Select Remove, and Windows will completely uninstall the software.

Hotspot and Drag-and-Drop Questions

In addition to the multiple-choice practice exam questions featured in the Total Tester Premium Practice Exam Software, simulated hotspot and drag-and-drop questions are included on the CD-ROM to allow you practice with these question types. You can access the hotspot and drag-and-drop questions by clicking the Launch Hotspot and Drag-and-Drop Practice Exam Questions button on the CD-ROM's main launch page.

Hotspot questions are graphical in nature and require the test taker to understand the concepts of the question from a practical and graphical aspect. You will have to point to the correct component within the graphic to properly answer the exam question. For example, you might be required to point to a specific point in a network diagram, point to a location in a network stack graphic, or choose the right location of a component within a graphic illustrating e-commerce–based authentication. It is not as easy to memorize answers for these types of questions, and they in turn make passing the exam more difficult.

The drag-and-drop questions are not as drastically different in format as compared to the hotspot questions. These questions just require the test taker to choose the correct answer and drag it to the right location. This question type is similar to the traditional multiple-choice (A, B, C, D) questions on the exam. You will be asked to choose one right answer out of a set of provided answers.

PDF Copy of the Book

The entire contents of the book are provided in PDF on the CD-ROM. This file is viewable on your computer and many portable devices.

- **To view the PDF on a computer**, Adobe Acrobat, Adobe Reader, or Adobe Digital Editions is required. A link to Adobe's website, where you can download and install Adobe Reader, has been included on the CD-ROM.

NOTE For more information on Adobe Reader and to check for the most recent version of the software, visit Adobe's website at www.adobe.com and search for the free Adobe Reader, or look for Adobe Reader on the product page. Adobe Digital Editions can also be downloaded from the Adobe website.

- **To view the PDF on a portable device**, copy the PDF file to your computer from the CD-ROM, and then copy the file to your portable device using a USB or other connection. Adobe offers a mobile version of Adobe Reader, the Adobe Reader mobile app, which currently supports iOS and Android. For customers using Adobe Digital Editions and an iPad, you may have to download and install a separate reader program on your device. The Adobe website has a list of recommended applications, and McGraw-Hill Education recommends the Bluefire Reader.

Technical Support

Technical Support information is provided in the following sections by feature.

Total Seminars Technical Support

For questions regarding the Total Tester software or operation of the CD-ROM, visit **www.totalsem.com** or e-mail **support@totalsem.com**.

McGraw-Hill Education Content Support

For questions regarding the PDF copy of the book, visit **http://mhp.softwareassist.com** or e-mail **techsolutions@mhedu.com**.

For questions regarding book content, e-mail **customer.service@mheducation.com**. For customers outside the United States, e-mail **international_cs@mheducation.com**.

access A subject's ability to view, modify, or communicate with an object. Access enables the flow of information between the subject and the object.

access control Mechanisms, controls, and methods of limiting access to resources to authorized subjects only.

access control list (ACL) A list of subjects that are authorized to access a particular object. Typically, the types of access are read, write, execute, append, modify, delete, and create.

access control mechanism Administrative, physical, or technical control that is designed to detect and prevent unauthorized access to a resource or environment.

accountability A security principle indicating that individuals must be identifiable and must be held responsible for their actions.

accredited A computer system or network that has received official authorization and approval to process sensitive data in a specific operational environment. There must be a security evaluation of the system's hardware, software, configurations, and controls by technical personnel.

add-on security Security protection mechanisms that are hardware or software retrofitted to a system to increase that system's protection level.

administrative controls Security mechanisms that are management's responsibility and referred to as "soft" controls. These controls include the development and publication of policies, standards, procedures, and guidelines; the screening of personnel; security-awareness training; the monitoring of system activity; and change control procedures.

aggregation The act of combining information from separate sources of a lower classification level that results in the creation of information of a higher classification level, which the subject does not have the necessary rights to access.

AIC triad The three security principles: availability, integrity, and confidentiality.

annualized loss expectancy (ALE) A dollar amount that estimates the loss potential from a risk in a span of a year.

single loss expectancy (SLE) × annualized rate of occurrence (ARO) = ALE

antimalware Software whose principal functions include the identification and mitigation of malware; also known as antivirus, although this term could be specific to only one type of malware.

annualized rate of occurrence (ARO) The value that represents the estimated possibility of a specific threat taking place within a one-year timeframe.

assurance A measurement of confidence in the level of protection that a specific security control delivers and the degree to which it enforces the security policy.

attack An attempt to bypass security controls in a system with the mission of using that system or compromising it. An attack is usually accomplished by exploiting a current vulnerability.

audit trail A chronological set of logs and records used to provide evidence of a system's performance or activity that took place on the system. These logs and records can be used to attempt to reconstruct past events and track the activities that took place, and possibly detect and identify intruders.

authenticate To verify the identity of a subject requesting the use of a system and/or access to network resources. The steps to giving a subject access to an object should be identification, authentication, and authorization.

authorization Granting access to an object after the subject has been properly identified and authenticated.

availability The reliability and accessibility of data and resources to authorized individuals in a timely manner.

back door An undocumented way of gaining access to a computer system. After a system is compromised, an attacker may load a program that listens on a port (back door) so that the attacker can enter the system at any time. A back door is also referred to as a trapdoor.

back up Copy and move data to a medium so that it may be restored if the original data is corrupted or destroyed. A full backup copies all the data from the system to the backup medium. An incremental backup copies only the files that have been modified since the previous backup. A differential backup backs up all files since the last full backup.

baseline The minimum level of security necessary to support and enforce a security policy.

Bell-LaPadula model The model uses a formal state transition model that describes its access controls and how they should perform. When the system must transition from one state to another, the security of the system should never be lowered or compromised. See also multilevel security, simple security property, and star property (*-property).

Biba model A formal state transition system of computer security policy that describes a set of access control rules designed to ensure data integrity.

biometrics When used within computer security, identifies individuals by physiological characteristics, such as a fingerprint, hand geometry, or pattern in the iris.

blacklist A set of known bad resources such as IP addresses, domain names, or applications.

browsing Searching through storage media looking for specific information without necessarily knowing what format the information is in. A browsing attack is one in which the attacker looks around a computer system either to see what looks interesting or to find specific information.

brute-force attack An attack that continually tries different inputs to achieve a predefined goal, which can be used to obtain credentials for unauthorized access.

business impact analysis (BIA) A functional analysis in which a team collects data, documents business functions, develops a hierarchy of business functions, and applies a classification scheme to indicate each individual function's criticality level.

callback A procedure for identifying a system that accessed an environment remotely. In a callback, the host system disconnects the caller and then dials the authorized telephone number of the remote terminal in order to reestablish the connection. Synonymous with dialback.

capability A capability outlines the objects a subject can access and the operations the subject can carry out on the different objects. It indicates the access rights for a specific subject; many times, the capability is in the form of a ticket.

capability maturity model integration (CMMI) A process model that captures the organization's maturity and fosters continuous improvement.

certification The technical evaluation of the security components and their compliance for the purpose of accreditation. A certification process can use safeguard evaluation, risk analysis, verification, testing, and auditing techniques to assess the appropriateness of a specific system processing a certain level of information within a particular environment. The certification is the testing of the security component or system, and the accreditation is the approval from management of the security component or system.

challenge/response method A method used to verify the identity of a subject by sending the subject an unpredictable or random value. If the subject responds with the expected value in return, the subject is authenticated.

ciphertext Data that has been encrypted and is unreadable until it has been converted into plaintext.

Clark-Wilson model An integrity model that addresses all three integrity goals: prevent unauthorized users from making modifications, prevent authorized users from making improper modifications, and maintain internal and external consistency through auditing.

classification A systematic arrangement of objects into groups or categories according to a set of established criteria. Data and resources can be assigned a level of sensitivity as they are being created, amended, enhanced, stored, or transmitted. The classification level then determines the extent to which the resource needs to be controlled and secured, and is indicative of its value in terms of information assets.

cleartext In data communications, cleartext is the form of a message or data, which is transferred or stored without cryptographic protection.

cloud computing The use of shared remote computing devices for the purpose of providing improved efficiencies, performance, reliability, scalability, and security.

collusion Two or more people working together to carry out a fraudulent activity. More than one person would need to work together to cause some type of destruction or fraud; this drastically reduces its probability.

communications security Controls in place to protect information as it is being transmitted, especially by telecommunications mechanisms.

compartment A class of information that has need-to-know access controls beyond those normally provided for access to confidential, secret, or top-secret information. A compartment is the same thing as a category within a security label. Just because a subject has the proper classification, that does not mean it has a need to know. The category, or compartment, of the security label enforces the subject's need to know.

compensating controls Controls that are alternative procedures designed to reduce the risk. They are used to "counterbalance" the effects of an internal control weakness.

compromise A violation of the security policy of a system or an organization such that unauthorized disclosure or modification of sensitive information occurs.

computer fraud Computer-related crimes involving deliberate misrepresentation, modification, or disclosure of data in order to compromise a system or obtain something of value.

confidentiality A security principle that works to ensure that information is not disclosed to unauthorized subjects.

configuration management The identification, control, accounting, and documentation of all changes that take place to system hardware, software, firmware, supporting documentation, and test results throughout the lifespan of the system.

confinement Controlling information in a manner that prevents sensitive data from being leaked from a program to another program, subject, or object in an unauthorized manner.

contingency plan A plan put in place before any potential emergencies, with the mission of dealing with possible future emergencies. It pertains to training personnel, performing backups, preparing critical facilities, and recovering from an emergency or disaster so that business operations can continue.

control zone The space within a facility that is used to protect sensitive processing equipment. Controls are in place to protect equipment from physical or technical unauthorized entry or compromise. The zone can also be used to prevent electrical waves carrying sensitive data from leaving the area.

copyright A legal right that protects the expression of ideas.

cost/benefit analysis An assessment that is performed to ensure that the cost of a safeguard does not outweigh the benefit of the safeguard. Spending more to protect an asset than the asset is actually worth does not make good business sense. All possible safeguards must be evaluated to ensure that the most security-effective and cost-effective choice is made.

countermeasure A control, method, technique, or procedure that is put into place to prevent a threat agent from exploiting a vulnerability. A countermeasure is put into place to mitigate risk. Also called a safeguard or control.

covert channel A communications path that enables a process to transmit information in a way that violates the system's security policy.

covert storage channel A covert channel that involves writing to a storage location by one process and the direct or indirect reading of the storage location by another process. Covert storage channels typically involve a resource (for example, sectors on a disk) that is shared by two subjects at different security levels.

covert timing channel A covert channel in which one process modulates its system resource (for example, CPU cycles), which is interpreted by a second process as some type of communication.

cryptanalysis The practice of breaking cryptosystems and algorithms used in encryption and decryption processes.

cryptography The science of secret writing that enables storage and transmission of data in a form that is available only to the intended individuals.

cryptology The study of cryptography and cryptanalysis.

cryptosystem The hardware or software implementation of cryptography.

data at rest Data that resides in external or auxiliary storage devices such as hard disk drives, solid-state drives, or DVDs.

data classification Assignments to data that indicate the level of availability, integrity, and confidentiality that is required for each type of information.

data custodian An individual who is responsible for the maintenance and protection of the data. This role is usually filled by the IT department (usually the network administrator). The duties include performing regular backups of the data; implementing security mechanisms; periodically validating the integrity of the data; restoring data from backup media; and fulfilling the requirements specified in the company's security policy, standards, and guidelines that pertain to information security and data protection.

Data Encryption Standard (DES) Symmetric key encryption algorithm that was adopted by the government as a federal standard for protecting sensitive unclassified information. DES was later replaced with Advanced Encryption Standard (AES).

data in transit (or data in motion) Data that is moving between computing nodes over a data network such as the Internet.

data in use Data that temporarily resides in primary storage such as registers, caches, or RAM while the CPU is using it.

data leak prevention (DLP) The actions that organizations take to prevent unauthorized external parties from gaining access to sensitive data.

data mining The analysis of the data held in data warehouses in order to produce new and useful information.

data remanence A measure of the magnetic flux density remaining after removal of the applied magnetic force, which is used to erase data. Refers to any data remaining on magnetic storage media.

data warehousing The process of combining data from multiple databases or data sources into a large data store for the purpose of providing more extensive information retrieval and data analysis.

database shadowing A mirroring technology used in databases, in which information is written to at least two hard drives for the purpose of redundancy.

declassification An administrative decision or procedure to remove or reduce the security classification information.

dedicated security mode The mode in which a system operates if all users have the clearance or authorization to access, and the need to know about, all data processed within the system. All users have been given formal access approval for all information on the system and have signed nondisclosure agreements pertaining to this information.

degauss Process that demagnetizes magnetic media so that a very low residue of magnetic induction is left on the media. Used to effectively erase data from media.

Delphi technique A group decision method used to ensure that each member of a group gives an honest and anonymous opinion pertaining to the company's risks.

denial of service (DoS) Any action, or series of actions, that prevents a system, or its resources, from functioning in accordance with its intended purpose.

DevOps The practice of incorporating developers and members of operations and quality assurance (QA) staff into software development projects to align their incentives and enable frequent, efficient, and reliable releases of software products.

dial-up The service whereby a computer terminal can use telephone lines, usually via a modem, to initiate and continue communication with another computer system.

dictionary attack A form of attack in which an attacker uses a large set of likely combinations to guess a secret, usually a password.

digital signature An electronic signature based upon cryptographic methods of originator authentication, computed by using a set of rules and a set of parameters such that the identity of the signer and the integrity of the data can be verified.

disaster recovery plan A plan developed to help a company recover from a disaster. It provides procedures for emergency response, extended backup operations, and post-disaster recovery when an organization suffers a loss of computer processing capability or resources and physical facilities.

discretionary access control (DAC) An access control model and policy that restricts access to objects based on the identity of the subjects and the groups to which those subjects belong. The data owner has the discretion of allowing or denying others access to the resources it owns.

Distributed Network Protocol 3 (DNP3) A communications protocol designed for use in SCADA systems, particularly those within the power sector, that does not include routing functionality.

domain The set of objects that a subject is allowed to access. Within this domain, all subjects and objects share a common security policy, procedures, and rules, and they are managed by the same management system.

due care Steps taken to show that a company has taken responsibility for the activities that occur within the corporation and has taken the necessary steps to help protect the company, its resources, and employees.

due diligence The process of systematically evaluating information to identify vulnerabilities, threats, and issues relating to an organization's overall risk.

electronic discovery (e-discovery) The process of producing for a court or external attorney all electronically stored information pertinent to a legal proceeding.

electronic vaulting The transfer of backup data to an offsite location. This process is primarily a batch process of transmitting data through communications lines to a server at an alternative location.

emanations Electrical and electromagnetic signals emitted from electrical equipment that can transmit through the airwaves. These signals carry information that can be captured and deciphered, which can cause a security breach. These are also called emissions.

encryption The transformation of plaintext into unreadable ciphertext.

end-to-end encryption A technology that encrypts the data payload of a packet.

exposure An instance of being exposed to losses from a threat. A weakness or vulnerability can cause an organization to be exposed to possible damages.

exposure factor The percentage of loss a realized threat could have on a certain asset.

failover A backup operation that automatically switches to a standby system if the primary system fails or is taken offline. It is an important fault-tolerant function that provides system availability.

fail-safe A functionality that ensures that when software or a system fails for any reason, it does not end up in a vulnerable state. After a failure, software might default to no access instead of allowing full control, which would be an example of a fail-safe measure.

Fibre Channel over Ethernet (FCoE) A converged protocol that allows Fibre Channel frames to ride over Ethernet networks.

firmware Software instructions that have been written into read-only memory (ROM) or a programmable ROM (PROM) chip.

formal security policy model A mathematical statement of a security policy. When an operating system is created, it can be built upon a predeveloped model that lays out how all activities will take place in each and every situation. This model can be expressed mathematically, which is then translated into a programming language.

formal verification Validating and testing of highly trusted systems. The tests are designed to show design verification, consistency between the formal specifications and the formal security policy model, implementation verification, consistency between the formal specifications, and the actual implementation of the product.

gateway A system or device that connects two unlike environments or systems. The gateway is usually required to translate between different types of applications or protocols.

guidelines Recommended actions and operational guides for users, IT staff, operations staff, and others when a specific standard does not apply.

handshaking procedure A dialog between two entities for the purpose of identifying and authenticating the entities to one another. The dialog can take place between two computers or two applications residing on different computers. It is an activity that usually takes place within a protocol.

honeynet A network connecting two or more honeypots that is created for the sole purpose of luring an attacker in order to compromise it.

honeypot A computer set up as a sacrificial lamb on the network in the hope that attackers will attack this system instead of actual production systems.

identification A subject provides some type of data to an authentication service. Identification is the first step in the authentication process.

inference The ability to derive information not explicitly available.

information owner The person who has final corporate responsibility of data protection and would be the one held liable for any negligence when it comes to protecting the company's information assets. The person who holds this role—usually a senior executive within the management group of the company—is responsible for assigning a classification to the information and dictating how the information should be protected.

Integrated Product Team (IPT) A multidisciplinary software development team with representatives from many or all the stakeholder populations.

integrity A security principle that makes sure that information and systems are not modified maliciously or accidentally.

Internet Small Computer System Interface (iSCSI) A converged protocol that encapsulates SCSI data in TCP segments in order to allow peripherals to be connected to computers across networks.

intrusion detection system (IDS) Software employed to monitor and detect possible attacks and behaviors that vary from the normal and expected activity. The IDS can be network based, which monitors network traffic, or host based, which monitors activities of a specific system and protects system files and control mechanisms.

isolation The containment of processes in a system in such a way that they are separated from one another to ensure integrity and confidentiality.

kernel The core of an operating system, a kernel manages the machine's hardware resources (including the processor and the memory) and provides and controls the way any other software component accesses these resources.

key A discrete data set that controls the operation of a cryptography algorithm. In encryption, a key specifies the particular transformation of plaintext into ciphertext, or vice versa, during decryption. Keys are also used in other cryptographic algorithms, such as digital signature schemes and keyed-hash functions (also known as HMACs), which are often used for authentication and integrity.

keystroke monitoring A type of auditing that can review or record keystrokes entered by a user during an active session.

lattice-based access control model A mathematical model that allows a system to easily represent the different security levels and control access attempts based on those levels. Every pair of elements has a highest lower bound and a lowest upper bound of access rights. The classes stemmed from military designations.

least privilege The security principle that requires each subject to be granted the most restrictive set of privileges needed for the performance of authorized tasks. The application of this principle limits the damage that can result from accident, error, or unauthorized use.

life-cycle assurance Confidence that a trusted system is designed, developed, and maintained with formal designs and controls. This includes design specification and verification, implementation, testing, configuration management, and distribution.

Lightweight Directory Access Protocol (LDAP) A directory service based on a subset of the X.500 standard that allows users and applications to interact with a directory.

link encryption A type of encryption technology that encrypts packets' headers, trailers, and the data payload. Each network communications node, or hop, must decrypt the packets to read its address and routing information and then re-encrypt the packets. This is different from **end-to-end encryption**.

logic bomb A malicious program that is triggered by a specific event or condition.

loss potential The potential losses that can be accrued if a threat agent actually exploits a vulnerability.

maintenance hook Instructions within a program's code that enable the developer or maintainer to enter the program without having to go through the usual access control and authentication processes. Maintenance hooks should be removed from the code before it is released to production; otherwise, they can cause serious security risks. Also called trapdoor or back door.

malware Malicious software. Code written to perform activities that circumvent the security policy of a system. Examples are viruses, malicious applets, Trojan horses, logical bombs, and worms.

mandatory access control (MAC) An access policy that restricts subjects' access to objects based on the security clearance of the subject and the classification of the object. The system enforces the security policy, and users cannot share their files with other users.

masquerading Impersonating another user, usually with the intention of gaining unauthorized access to a system.

message authentication code (MAC) In cryptography, a message authentication code (MAC) is a generated value used to authenticate a message. A MAC can be generated by HMAC or CBC-MAC methods. The MAC protects both a message's integrity (by ensuring that a different MAC will be produced if the message has changed) and its authenticity, because only someone who knows the secret key could have modified the message.

multilevel security A class of systems containing information with different classifications. Access decisions are based on the subject's security clearances, need to know, and formal approval.

Multiprotocol Label Switching (MPLS) A converged data communications protocol designed to improve the routing speed of high-performance networks.

need to know A security principle stating that users should have access only to the information and resources necessary to complete their tasks that fulfill their roles within an organization. Need to know is commonly used in access control criteria by operating systems and applications.

node A system that is connected to a network.

nonrepudiation A service that ensures the sender cannot later falsely deny sending a message.

object A passive entity that contains or receives information. Access to an object potentially implies access to the information that it contains. Examples of objects include records, pages, memory segments, files, directories, directory trees, and programs.

object reuse Reassigning to a subject media that previously contained information. Object reuse is a security concern because if insufficient measures were taken to erase the information on the media, the information may be disclosed to unauthorized personnel.

one-time pad A method of encryption in which the plaintext is combined with a random "pad," which should be the same length as the plaintext. This encryption process uses a nonrepeating set of random bits that are combined bitwise (XOR) with the message to produce ciphertext. A one-time pad is a perfect encryption scheme because it is unbreakable and each pad is used exactly once, but it is impractical because of all of the required overhead.

operational assurance A level of confidence of a trusted system's architecture and implementation that enforces the system's security policy. This can include system architecture, covert channel analysis, system integrity, and trusted recovery.

operational goals Daily goals to be accomplished to ensure the proper operation of an environment.

operator An individual who supports the operations of computer systems—usually a mainframe. The individual may monitor the execution of the system, control the flow of jobs, and develop and schedule batch jobs.

overt channel A path within a computer system or network that is designed for the authorized transfer of data.

password A sequence of characters used to prove one's identity. It is used during a logon process and should be highly protected.

payment card industry data security standard (PCI DSS) An information security standard for organizations that are involved in payment card transactions.

penetration A successful attempt at circumventing security controls and gaining access to a system.

penetration testing Penetration testing is a method of evaluating the security of a computer system or network by simulating an attack that a malicious hacker would carry out. This is done so that vulnerabilities and weaknesses can be uncovered.

permissions The type of authorized interactions that a subject can have with an object. Examples include read, write, execute, add, modify, and delete.

personnel security The procedures that are established to ensure that all personnel who have access to sensitive information have the required authority as well as appropriate clearances. Procedures confirm a person's background and provide assurance of necessary trustworthiness.

physical controls Controls that pertain to controlling individual access into the facility and different departments, locking systems and removing unnecessary floppy or CD-ROM drives, protecting the perimeter of the facility, monitoring for intrusion, and checking environmental controls.

physical security Controls and procedures put into place to prevent intruders from physically accessing a system or facility. The controls enforce access control and authorized access.

piggyback Unauthorized access to a system by using another user's legitimate credentials.

plaintext In cryptography, the original readable text before it is encrypted.

playback attack Capturing data and resending the data at a later time in the hope of tricking the receiving system. This is usually carried out to obtain unauthorized access to specific resources.

privacy A security principle that protects an individual's information and employs controls to ensure that this information is not disseminated or accessed in an unauthorized manner.

procedure Detailed step-by-step instructions to achieve a certain task, which are used by users, IT staff, operations staff, security members, and others.

protection ring An architecture that provides hierarchies of privileged operation modes of a system, which gives certain access rights to processes that are authorized to operate in that mode. Supports the integrity and confidentiality requirements of multitasking operating systems and enables the operating system to protect itself from user programs and rogue processes.

protocol A set of rules and formats that enables the standardized exchange of information between different systems.

pseudo-flaw An apparent loophole deliberately implanted in an operating system or program as a trap for intruders.

public key encryption A type of encryption that uses two mathematically related keys to encrypt and decrypt messages. The private key is known only to the owner, and the public key is available to anyone.

public key infrastructure (PKI) A framework of programs, procedures, communication protocols, and public key cryptography that enables a diverse group of individuals to communicate securely.

purge The removal of sensitive data from a system, storage device, or peripheral device with storage capacity at the end of a processing period. This action is performed in such a way that there is assurance proportional to the sensitivity of the data that the data cannot be reconstructed.

qualitative risk analysis A risk analysis method that uses intuition and experience to judge an organization's exposure to risks. It uses scenarios and ratings systems. Compare to quantitative risk analysis.

quantitative risk analysis A risk analysis method that attempts to use percentages in damage estimations and assigns real numbers to the costs of countermeasures for particular risks and the amount of damage that could result from the risk. Compare to qualitative risk analysis.

RADIUS (Remote Authentication Dial-in User Service) A security service that authenticates and authorizes dial-up users and is a centralized access control mechanism.

read An operation that results in the flow of information from an object to a subject and does not give the subject the ability to modify the object or the data within the object.

recovery planning The advance planning and preparations that are necessary to minimize loss and to ensure the availability of the critical information systems of an organization after a disruption in service or a disaster.

recovery point objective The acceptable amount of data loss measured in time.

recovery time objective The maximum time period within which a business process must be restored to a designated service level after a disaster to avoid unacceptable consequences.

reference monitor concept An access control concept that refers to an abstract machine that mediates all accesses to objects by subjects. The security kernel enforces the reference monitor concept.

reliability The assurance of a given system, or individual component, performing its mission adequately for a specified period of time under the expected operating conditions.

remote journaling A method of transmitting changes to data to an offsite facility. This takes place as parallel processing of transactions, meaning that changes to the data are saved locally and to an off-site facility. These activities take place in real time and provide redundancy and fault tolerance.

repudiation When the sender of a message denies sending the message. The countermeasure to this is to implement digital signatures.

residual risk The remaining risk after the security controls have been applied. The conceptual formulas that explain the difference between total and residual risk are

threats × vulnerability × asset value = total risk
(threats × vulnerability × asset value) × controls gap = residual risk

risk The likelihood of a threat agent taking advantage of a vulnerability and the resulting business impact. A risk is the loss potential, or probability, that a threat will exploit a vulnerability.

risk analysis A method of identifying risks and assessing the possible damage that could be caused in order to justify security safeguards.

risk management The process of identifying, assessing, and reducing the risk to an acceptable level and implementing the right mechanisms to maintain that level of risk.

role-based access control (RBAC) Type of model that provides access to resources based on the role the user holds within the company or the tasks that the user has been assigned.

safeguard A software configuration, hardware, or procedure that eliminates a vulnerability or reduces the risk of a threat agent from being able to exploit a vulnerability. Also called a countermeasure or control.

sandboxing A type of control that isolates processes from the operating system to prevent security violations.

secure configuration management Implementing the set of appropriate procedures to control the life cycle of an application, document the necessary change control activities, and ensure that the changes will not violate the security policy.

Security Assertion Markup Language (SAML) An XML standard that allows the exchange of authentication and authorization data to be shared between security domains.

security evaluation Assesses the degree of trust and assurance that can be placed in systems for the secure handling of sensitive information.

security kernel The hardware, firmware, and software elements of a trusted computing base (TCB) that implement the reference monitor concept. The kernel must mediate all access between subjects and objects, be protected from modification, and be verifiable as correct.

security label An identifier that represents the security level of an object.

security perimeter An imaginary boundary between the components within the trusted computing base (TCB) and mechanisms that do not fall within the TCB. It is the distinction between trusted and untrusted processes.

security policy Documentation that describes senior management's directives toward the role that security plays within the organization. It provides a framework within which an organization establishes needed levels of information security to achieve the desired confidentiality, availability, and integrity goals. A policy is a statement of information values, protection responsibilities, and organization commitment managing risks.

security testing Testing all security mechanisms and features within a system to determine the level of protection they provide. Security testing can include penetration testing, formal design and implementation verification, and functional testing.

sensitive information Information that would cause a negative effect on the company if it were lost or compromised.

sensitivity label A piece of information that represents the security level of an object. Sensitivity labels are used by the TCB as the basis for mandatory access control (MAC) decisions.

separation of duties A security principle that splits up a critical task among two or more individuals to ensure that one person cannot complete a risky task by himself.

shoulder surfing When a person looks over another person's shoulder and watches keystrokes or watches data as it appears on the screen in order to uncover information in an unauthorized manner.

simple security property A Bell-LaPadula security model rule that stipulates that a subject cannot read data at a higher security level.

single loss expectancy (SLE) A dollar amount that is assigned to a single event that represents the company's potential loss amount if a specific threat were to take place.

asset value × exposure factor = SLE

single sign-on (SSO) A technology that allows a user to authenticate one time and then access resources in the environment without needing to reauthenticate.

social engineering The act of tricking another person into providing confidential information by posing as an individual who is authorized to receive that information.

software-defined networking (SDN) An approach to networking that relies on distributed software to provide improved agility and efficiency by centralizing the configuration and control of networking devices.

spoofing Presenting false information, usually within packets, to trick other systems and hide the origin of the message. This is usually done by hackers so that their identity cannot be successfully uncovered.

standards Rules indicating how hardware and software should be implemented, used, and maintained. Standards provide a means to ensure that specific technologies, applications, parameters, and procedures are carried out in a uniform way across the organization. They are compulsory.

star property (*-property) A Bell-LaPadula security model rule that stipulates that a subject cannot write data to an object at a lower security level.

strategic goals Long-term goals that are broad, general statements of intent. Operational and tactical goals support strategic goals and all are a part of a planning horizon.

subject An active entity, generally in the form of a person, process, or device, that causes information to flow among objects or that changes the system state.

supervisor state One of several states in which an operating system may operate, and the only one in which privileged instructions may be executed by the CPU.

supervisory control and data acquisition (SCADA) A system for remotely monitoring and controlling physical systems such as power and manufacturing plants.

synthetic transaction A transaction that is executed in real time by a software agent to test or monitor the performance of a distributed system.

TACACS (Terminal Access Controller Access Control System) A client/server authentication protocol that provides the same type of functionality as RADIUS and is used as a central access control mechanism mainly for remote users.

tactical goals Midterm goals to accomplish. These may be milestones to accomplish within a project or specific projects to accomplish in a year. Strategic, tactical, and operational goals make up a planning horizon.

technical controls These controls, also called logical access control mechanisms, work in software to provide confidentiality, integrity, or availability protection. Some examples are passwords, identification and authentication methods, security devices, auditing, and the configuration of the network.

Tempest The study and control of spurious electronic signals emitted by electrical equipment. Tempest equipment is implemented to prevent intruders from picking up information through the airwaves with listening devices.

threat Any potential danger that a vulnerability will be exploited by a threat agent.

top-down approach An approach in which the initiation, support, and direction for a project come from top management and work their way down through middle management and then to staff members.

topology The physical construction of how nodes are connected to form a network.

total risk When a safeguard is not implemented, an organization is faced with the total risk of that particular vulnerability.

trademark A legal right that protects a word, name, product shape, symbol, color, or a combination of these used to identify a product or a company.

Trojan horse A computer program that has an apparently or actually useful function, but that also contains hidden malicious capabilities to exploit a vulnerability and/or provide unauthorized access into a system.

trusted computer system A system that has the necessary controls to ensure that the security policy will not be compromised and that can process a range of sensitive or classified information simultaneously.

trusted computing base (TCB) All of the protection mechanisms within a computer system (software, hardware, and firmware) that are responsible for enforcing a security policy.

trusted path A mechanism within the system that enables the user to communicate directly with the TCB. This mechanism can be activated only by the user or the TCB and not by an untrusted mechanism or process.

trusted recovery A set of procedures that restores a system and its data in a trusted manner after the system has been disrupted or a system failure has occurred.

user A person or process that is accessing a computer system.

user ID A unique set of characters or code that is used to identify a specific user to a system.

validation The act of performing tests and evaluations to test a system's security level to see if it complies with security specifications and requirements.

virus A small application, or string of code, that infects applications. The main function of a virus is to reproduce, and it requires a host application to do this. It can damage data directly or degrade system performance.

vulnerability The absence or weakness of a safeguard that could be exploited.

war dialing An attack in which a long list of phone numbers is inserted into a war-dialing program in the hope of finding a modem that can be exploited to gain unauthorized access.

whitelist A set of known good resources such as IP addresses, domain names, or applications.

work factor The estimated time and effort required for an attacker to overcome a security control.

worm An independent program that can reproduce by copying itself from one system to another. It may damage data directly or degrade system performance by tying up resources.

write An operation that results in the flow of information from a subject to an object.

INDEX

Numbers

1G mobile wireless, 683, 684
2G mobile wireless, 683, 684
2.5G mobile wireless, 683
3DES (Triple-DES), 370, 377–378
3G mobile wireless, 683, 684
3.5G mobile wireless, 684
4G mobile wireless, 684
5G mobile wireless, 683
6to4 tunneling, 508
10Base-T, 532
10GBase-T, 533–534
32-bit addressing, 259
32-bit operating system, 298
64-bit addressing, 259
64-bit operating system, 298
100Base-TX, 532
802.1AE standard, 509, 510
802.1AF standard, 510
802.1AR standard, 508, 510
802.1X standard, 669–671
802.1X technology, 667
802.11 standard, 665–667, 672
802.11a standard, 672–673
802.11ac standard, 674
802.11b standard, 672
802.11e standard, 673
802.11f standard, 673
802.11g standard, 673–674
802.11h standard, 674
802.11i standard, 667–668, 669, 671
802.11j standard, 674
802.11n standard, 674
802.15.4 standard, 676
802.16 standard, 675
1000Base-T, 532–533

A

AAA (authentication, authorization, and accounting/audit) protocols, 800–806
ABR (available bit rate), 631
absolute addresses, 263, 264
abstraction, 280–281, 1117, 1119, 1125
academic software, 68
acceptable use policy (AUP), 887, 939
access
  default settings and, 1082–1083
  described, 722
  local, 940–941
  remote, 644–645, 803, 939–940
access control
  access control matrix, 797
  access criteria, 762–763
  administration, 222, 799–807
  considerations, 194, 730–732, 807–808
  constrained user interfaces, 796–797
  content-dependent, 325, 798, 1170–1171
  context-dependent, 325, 799, 1170–1171
  DAC model, 787–789, 790, 794, 795
  databases, 1155, 1156
  defaulting to no access, 763–764
  facility, 941–949, 1063
  identity based, 787–789
  information disclosure, 819–820
  layers, 808–809
  MAC model, 789–791, 794, 795
  markup languages and, 779–784
  media, 222
  methods, 807–814
  monitoring, 822–834
  need-to-know principle, 765
  networks, 813–814
  nondiscretionary, 789
  overview, 721–722, 729
  personnel, 949–950
  physical, 222, 422–424, 941–949
  practices, 819–822
  RBAC model, 791–794, 795
  RB-RBAC model, 794–795
  reference monitor and, 304–305
  regular tasks, 819
  resources, 929–930
  single sign-on, 766–776

access control (*Cont.*)
  system access, 812
  technical, 222
  techniques, 800
  threats, 834–840
  web environment, 1147–1148
access control lists (ACLs), 594, 764, 798
access control matrix, 797
access control models, 787–795
access points (APs), 664–665, 666, 673
account management, 742–743, 886–889
accountability, 814–818, 929–930, 1056
accreditation, 318–320
ACID test, 1174
ACK packets, 500, 586–587, 697
ACLs (access control lists), 594, 764, 798
acquisition phase, 190–191
active attacks, 408
ActiveX controls, 1144–1146
ActiveX Data Objects (ADO), 1162–1163
ActiveX technology, 1138
AD (architecture description), 248, 250
ad hoc WLANs, 664
address buses, 255, 256–257
Address Resolution Protocol (ARP), 539–540
address space layout randomization (ASLR), 269–270
ADM (Architecture Development Method), 24–25
administration
  access control, 222, 799–807
  of locks, 947
  network, 610–611, 926
  remote systems, 939–940, 1186
administrative access controls, 222
administrative controls, 886–905
  account management, 886–889
  backup verification, 889–892
  components, 808, 809–810
  described, 8, 11
  disaster recovery/business continuity, 892–898
  functionality, 12
administrative interfaces, 822, 1147
administrative management, 925–930
administrative/regulatory law, 60, 62
administrators
  administrative interfaces, 822, 1157
  audit data and, 814, 815–818
  considerations, 1183
  database, 796, 926, 1155
  monitoring and, 930
  network, 14, 803, 926, 928–930
  roles/tasks, 926
  running as root, 888
  security, 205, 789, 926–930, 1080, 1081
  security vs. network administrators, 928–930
  separation of duties and, 926
ADO (ActiveX Data Objects), 1162–1163
ADO API, 1162–1163
ADSL (Asymmetric DSL), 648
Advanced Encryption Standard. *See* AES
advanced persistent threat (APT), 51–52
advisory policies, 90
adware, 1184
AES (Advanced Encryption Standard), 93, 371, 378
AES algorithm, 668
aggregation, 324–325, 1169–1170
agile models, 1105–1108
AH (Authentication Header), 653
AIC (availability, integrity, and confidentiality), 3
AIC triad, 3–6
AIK (Attestation Identity Key), 408
air quality, 446
ALE (annual loss expectancy), 114, 115, 120
alerts
  audit trails, 815
  Google Alerts, 902
  IDS, 121, 825, 826, 833, 903–904
algebraic attacks, 413
algorithm/key relationship, 352
algorithms. *See also* ciphers
  asymmetric. *See* asymmetric algorithms
  broken, 371
  considerations, 343–344, 348
  hashing, 393–396
  overview, 340–342
  patents and, 66
  public vs. secret, 411
  symmetric. *See* symmetric algorithms
ALU (arithmetic logic unit), 253–256
America Online (AOL), 837
American National Standards Institute (ANSI), 534
American Society for Testing and Materials (ASTM), 450
amplitude, 660
analog transmission, 512–514
analysis, functional, 146
analytic attacks, 413
annual loss expectancy (ALE), 114, 115, 120
annualized rate of occurrence (ARO), 114
anomaly-based IDS, 827, 829

ANSI (American National Standards Institute), 534
answers, 1249–1268
antimalware, 1187–1190
immunizers, 1189
keeping up to date, 7
overview, 988, 1187
policies/procedures, 1192–1193
tunneling virus and, 1181
viruses and, 1180
antivirus software, 924, 988. *See also* antimalware
anycast address, 506
AOL (America Online), 837
APIs (application programming interfaces)
ADO, 1162–1163
described, 484, 1122
JDBC, 1163–1164
ODBC, 1162
OLE DB, 1162, 1163
overview, 289–290, 1131–1132
SDN approach and, 612
applets, 1142–1144
appliances, 595
application controls, 1081–1082
application error, 94
application layer, 480, 483–484, 492
application programmers, 926
application programming interfaces. *See* APIs
application-based IDS, 830
application-level events, 816
application-level proxy firewalls, 590–593, 596
applications. *See also* software
classifications, 197
communications between, 486
connections between, 488
crashes/freezes, 933–935
default settings and, 1082–1083
I/O issues, 936–937
legacy, 299
licensing issues, 938–939, 965
maintenance hooks, 333
multi-threaded, 276
pirated, 68–69, 939, 965
unnecessary, 938, 939
user friendliness, 1083
web. *See* web applications
whitelisting, 966
APs (access points), 664–665, 666, 673
APT (advanced persistent threat), 51–52
architecture
computer. *See* computer architecture
defined, 250
described, 248
operating system, 291–300
system, 248–252
system security, 301–307
architecture description (AD), 248, 250
Architecture Development Method (ADM), 24–25
architecture frameworks, 20
architecture views, 251
archival phase, 190, 191–192
archive bit, 1023
arithmetic logic unit (ALU), 253–256
ARO (annualized rate of occurrence), 114
ARP (Address Resolution Protocol), 539–540
ARP poisoning attack, 540
ASLR (address space layout randomization), 269–270
AS/NZS 4360, 108, 112
ASOR (authoritative system of record), 744
ASs (autonomous systems), 562–563
assemblers, 1117, 1119
assembly language, 1117
assessment plans, 129
asset inventory, 964–966
asset protection, 215–224
data at rest, 216–217
data in motion, 217–218
data in use, 218–219
data security controls, 216–219
location of data, 217
media controls, 219–224
mobile devices, 234–235
overview, 215, 439
paper records, 235–236
real loss, 215
safes, 236
assets
assigning values to, 149–152
cloud, 969–970
costs associated with, 105
data leakage, 225–234
defined, 189
electronic, 49–50
loss of, 106–107
protecting. *See* asset protection
security, 189–236
tangible vs. intangible, 105
types of, 189
value of, 104–105, 907–908
associations, 882
assurance evaluation, 313
assurance levels, 930–931
assurance rating, 315

ASTM (American Society for Testing and Materials), 450
asymmetric algorithms, 380–388
  Diffie-Hellman algorithm, 380–383
  El Gamal algorithm, 386
  elliptic curve cryptosystem, 386–387
  knapsack algorithms, 387
  one-way functions, 385–386
  overview, 356–358, 380
  PKI and, 399
  pros/cons, 358
  RSA algorithm, 383–386
  vs. symmetric algorithms, 353, 357, 358
  using with symmetric algorithms, 364–366
  zero knowledge proof, 387–388
Asymmetric DSL (ADSL), 648
asymmetric keys, 353, 356, 358, 364–366, 398
asymmetric mode, 257, 258
asynchronous attacks, 334
asynchronous token device, 756–757
Asynchronous Transfer Mode. *See* ATM
asynchronous transmission, 514–515
ATM (Asynchronous Transfer Mode), 618–619, 629–631, 643
ATM packets, 618
atomic transactions, 936
atomicity, 936, 1174
atoms, 221
attachments, email, 688, 698
attack chain, 101
attack surface, 1087–1089
attack trees, 101–102
attackers, 2, 14, 48–54, 106. *See also* hackers
attacks, 100–101. *See also specific attacks*
  active, 408
  algebraic, 413
  analytic, 413
  asynchronous, 334
  birthday, 396
  brute-force, 371, 752, 835–836
  ciphertext, 410–411
  cryptography, 409–414
  DDoS, 603, 649, 697–698
  dictionary, 752, 835
  from different countries, 53, 54–58
  at different layers, 483
  double tagging, 575
  electromagnetic analysis, 760
  e-mail spoofing, 559–560
  evolution of, 50–53
  fault generation, 760
  file descriptor, 875
  flooding, 696–697, 698
  fragmentation, 603
  honeypots and, 607
  ICMP, 543–545
  "in the wild," 824
  inference, 1171, 1173
  input validation, 1149–1152
  "low and slow," 825
  man-in-the-middle, 217–218
  meet-in-the-middle, 414
  network. *See* network attacks
  passive, 408
  password-guessing, 772
  phishing, 559–560, 836–840, 1178
  plaintext, 410
  POODLE, 693
  replay, 413, 751, 771, 1154
  routing protocol, 566
  side-channel, 412
  sniffing, 698–699
  social engineering. *See* social engineering
  spoofing, 559–560, 575, 603
  statistical, 413
  teardrop, 603
  techniques for, 826
  timing, 760
  TOC/TOU, 333–335
  VLAN hopping, 575
  on websites, 1154
  wormhold, 566
  XSS, 1150–1151
  zero-day, 825, 990
attenuation, 521
Attestation Identity Key (AIK), 408
attributes, 1160
audit logging, 221
audit logs, 814–818, 878–881, 929
audit process, 861
audit team, 861, 862–864
audit trails, 814–818
auditing
  access control and, 814
  considerations, 194, 815, 929
  log reviews, 878–881
  physical access, 963–964
  strategies, 860–865
  technical controls, 865–866
  war dialing, 874
auditors, 206, 1060
audit-reduction tools, 817
audits. *See also* testing
  communicating results of, 862
  compliance, 864
  described, 860

documenting, 861–862
goals of, 860
internal, 863–864
password usage, 752
planning for, 861–862
postmortem, 876–877
protecting audit/log data, 818
reviewing, 814–818
scope of, 860–861
service organization controls, 864–865
third-party, 863–865
AUP (acceptable use policy), 887, 939
authentication, 739–761
biometrics, 727, 744–751
CHAP, 657–658
considerations, 727–728
cryptographic keys, 757
cryptosystems, 344
data origin, 391
EAP, 658–659
EAP-TLS, 510, 511
memory cards, 758
multifactor, 728
mutual, 728
PAP, 657, 658
passphrase, 757
passwords. *See* passwords
remote connections, 657–659
RPC, 487
SASL, 557
smart cards, 758–761
SMTP-AUTH, 559
strong, 727–728
system, 391
system-based, 728
three-factor, 728
web environment, 1147–1148
authentication, authorization, and accounting/audit (AAA) protocols, 800–806
authentication by characteristic, 727
authentication by knowledge, 727, 754
authentication by ownership, 727
Authentication Header (AH), 653
authenticators, 770
Authenticode technology, 1145
authoritative source, 743
authoritative system of record (ASOR), 744
authorization, 762–776
access criteria, 762–763
cryptosystems, 344
defaulting to no access, 763–764
e-mail, 557
Kerberos and, 768–776
need-to-know principle, 765
overview, 762
single sign-on, 766–776
authorization creep, 765
automated risk analysis methods, 113
automatic tunneling, 508
automation, 405, 610–611, 780, 1114
autonomous systems (ASs), 562–563
availability
business continuity planning and, 131, 132
considerations, 970
networks, 970–984
overview, 3–4, 723
resources, 3–4, 723, 970–984
availability controls, 5–6
availability, integrity, and confidentiality. *See* AIC
available bit rate (ABR), 631
avalanche effect, 360

B

back doors, 827
background checks, 156–157
backup facilities, 1010, 1011, 1018–1021
backup software, 1023, 1024
backups
alternatives, 1021–1025
automatic, 981
clearance level, 196
considerations, 192
data leakage and, 228
differential, 1023
documenting procedures, 1024
electronic solutions, 1025–1028
full, 1023
hardware, 1015–1016
HSM system, 982–983
incremental, 1023
integrity of, 981
offsite storage, 1010, 1011, 1023–1025
onsite copies, 1023–1024
overview, 981
policies, 981
software, 1016–1018
tape media, 1016
testing, 892
tracking, 222
verifying, 891–892, 1011
versions, 222, 1026
virtualization and, 890–891
badge reader, 949
bandwidth, 514, 517
base register, 282

baseband transmission, 516–517
baselines
described, 91, 93
evaluating security via, 417–419, 903–904
implementation, 93–94
overview, 91–92
verifying security effectiveness, 31
baselining, 987
Basic Rate Interface (BRI) ISDN, 646, 647
Basic Service Set (BSS), 665
bastion hosts, 596–597, 938
batch processing, 1169
Bayesian filtering, 1190–1192
BCM (business continuity management), 131, 134–139, 140
BCP (business continuity plan), 134–148. *See also* DRP; risk management
advantages of, 133
assigning values to assets, 149–152
automated/manual tasks, 131
availability and, 131, 132
vs. BCM, 131, 140
business impact analysis, 146–152
considerations, 131–132
vs. contingency plan, 984
vs. COOP, 1038
cost considerations, 138–139, 141, 143, 150
critical functions, 133, 134, 138, 146–152
data backup options, 1021–1025
definition of terms, 144
described, 130–131
vs. disaster recovery, 130–131
drills, 893–896
due diligence/due care, 145
end-user environment and, 1021
enterprise-wide, 142
establishing, 138
general structure of, 1037
goal setting, 1034–1036
goals of, 137–138, 141, 153
hardware backups, 1015–1016
human resources and, 1019–1021
identifying priorities, 138, 140, 146
initiation process for, 140
insurance options, 1030–1031
integration of, 137
interdependencies, 153–154
life cycle of, 897–898
loss criteria, 150
maintenance of, 138–139, 892–893, 896–897
management support, 138–139, 145–146, 154
maximum tolerable downtime, 150–151
personnel, 153
planning requirements, 145–146
policy for, 142
progress reviews, 140
project components, 139–154
project management, 143–144
project plan, 144
recovery/restoration, 1031–1038
resources, 147, 149–152
risk assessment, 143, 147–149
scope, 141–144
senior management and, 137, 138–141, 145, 154
software backups, 1016–1018
software tools, 154
standards/best practices, 133–136
storing plans for, 1020
SWOT analysis, 143–144
team members, 139–140, 141, 142, 154
testing/revising plans, 892–895
BCP committee, 139
BCP coordinator, 139, 140, 144
BCP development procedures, 1035
BCP team, 139–142, 154, 1005, 1006
beamforming, 674
BEDO DRAM (burst EDO DRAM), 259
behavior blocking, 1189–1190
behavioral model, 1087
behavioral-based IDS, 825–826
Bell-LaPadula model, 307–308, 309, 312
best practices, 91, 133–136
best-effort service, QoS, 631
BGP (Border Gateway Protocol), 565–566
BIA (business impact analysis), 146–152, 1030–1031
Biba model, 308–309, 313
big data, 1177
biometrics, 727, 744–751
birthday attack, 395–396
BISDN (Broadband ISDN), 646
bits, 341, 359–363, 374–375, 514
BitTorrent protocol, 64
black box testing, 869
black holes, 563, 992
blacklists, 987
blind test, 873
block ciphers, 359–360, 363
blocked state, 272, 273
Blowfish algorithm, 379
Bluesnarfing, 677
Bluetooth technology, 676–677
bollards, 422, 953

BOOTP (Bootstrap Protocol), 543
BOOTP servers, 543
boot-sector viruses, 820
Bootstrap Protocol (BOOTP), 543
bootup sequence, 935
Border Gateway Protocol (BGP), 565–566
border routers, 569
botnets, 48, 697, 1184–1185
bots, 48, 697, 1178, 1184
boundary conditions, 886
bounds checking, 267
Brewer and Nash model, 311, 313
BRI (Basic Rate Interface) ISDN, 646, 647
bridges, 567–569, 571, 578
British Standard 7799 (BS7799), 16–18
Broadband ISDN (BISDN), 646
broadband transmission, 516–517
broadband wireless access, 675
broadcast domains, 530
broadcast storms, 568
broadcast transmission, 536, 537
browsers
  accessing data via, 1155
  ActiveX and, 1145
  certificate authorities, 738
  cookies and, 693–694
  drive-by downloads, 699, 700, 900, 901–902
  security and, 690–691
  web access management, 738
brute-force attacks, 371, 752, 835–836
BS7799 (British Standard 7799), 16–18
BSA (Business Software Alliance), 68–69
BSA Global Software Survey, 68–69
BSI (Build Security In), 1098
BSS (Basic Service Set), 665
buffer overflows, 265–269, 875, 1092
buffers, 265
bugs, 219, 300, 332, 875, 885
Build and Fix model, 1099
Build Security In (BSI), 1098
building codes, 429
bulletproof material, 433
bump key, 949
burst EDO DRAM (BEDO DRAM), 259
bus topology, 524, 525
business continuity, 137, 153, 892. *See also* *BCP/BCM entries*
business continuity coordinator, 139, 140, 144
Business Continuity Institute, 135
business continuity management. *See* BCM
business continuity plan. *See* BCP
business enablement, 30–31
business functions, outsourcing, 126
business impact analysis (BIA), 146–152, 1030–1031
business process recovery, 1006
Business Software Alliance (BSA), 68–69
businesses. *See* organizations
bytecode, 1143

C

C&A (certification and accreditation), 320
cable locks, 946, 947
cable modems, 648–649
cabling, 517–522
  attenuation, 521
  bandwidth values, 517
  coaxial, 517–518, 648
  considerations, 811
  copper, 519
  crosstalk, 521–522
  fiber-optic, 519–520, 648
  fire ratings, 522
  noise, 520–521
  plenum space and, 522
  problems with, 520–522
  twisted-pair, 518–519
cache memory, 261
Caesar cipher, 336–337, 351
call-processing manager, 636
CAN bus (Controller Area Network bus) protocol, 496–497
Capability Maturity Model Integration. *See* CMMI
capability maturity models (CMMs), 1112–1113
capability tables, 797–798
CAPTCHA, 754
card badge reader, 949
care-of address, 805
carrier, 527
carrier sense multiple access (CSMA), 527–528
carrier sense multiple access with collision avoidance (CSMA/CA), 527, 528, 660
carrier sense multiple access with collision detection (CSMA/CD), 527–528, 660
carrier signal, 512
carrier-sensing access methods, 528
CAs (certificate authorities), 399–404, 689, 690
CASE (computer-aided software engineering) tools, 1089–1091
catastrophes, 1007
CBC (Cipher Block Chaining) mode, 373–374

CBC-MAC (Cipher Block Chaining Message Authentication Code), 391–392, 393
CBK (Common Body of Knowledge), xxx, xxxiv, 137
CBK domains, xxxi–xxxii
CBR (constant bit rate), 630
C&C (command-and-control) servers, 1185
CCDs (charged-coupled devices), 957
CCTV (closed-circuit TV) system, 955–960
CDDI (Copper Distributed Data Interface), 536
CDMA (code division multiple access), 681–682, 683
CDN (content distribution network), 608–609, 697–698
CDs, 223
ceiling panels, 435
cell phones. *See* mobile devices
cell suppression, 325–326, 1171
cells, 1161
cellular networks, 679–681
Central Computing & Telecommunications Agency Risk Analysis & Management Method (CRAMM), 111
central processing unit. *See* CPU
CEO (chief executive officer), 199–200
CEO role, 199–200
CER (crossover error rate), 746–747
CERT (Computer Emergency Response Team), 996
certificate authorities (CAs), 399–404, 689, 690
certificate revocation list (CRL), 401–402
certificates, 399–404
certification, 318–320
certification and accreditation (C&A), 320
Certified Information Systems Security Professional. *See* CISSP
CFB (Cipher Feedback) mode, 374–375
CFO (chief financial officer), 200–201
CFO role, 200–201
chain of custody, 1047–1049
Challenge Handshake Authentication Protocol (CHAP), 657–658
change control, 1113–1116
change control analyst role, 205
change control documentation, 968–969
change control process, 967–968
channel service unit/data service unit (CSU/DSU), 624–625
channels, 664
CHAP (Challenge Handshake Authentication Protocol), 657–658
charged-coupled devices (CCDs), 957
checklist test, 894
checkpoints, 1168
checksums, 935
chief executive officer (CEO), 199–200
chief financial officer (CFO), 200–201
chief information officer (CIO), 201–202
chief information security officer (CISO), 161, 164, 203
chief privacy officer (CPO), 202
chief security officer (CSO), 202–203
Chinese Wall model, 311
chipping code, 662
chips, 662
CIA (confidentiality, integrity, and availability), 3
CIDR (classless interdomain routing), 505
CIO (chief information officer), 201–202
CIO role, 201–202
Cipher Block Chaining. *See* CBC
Cipher Feedback (CFB) mode, 374–375
cipher locks, 945–946
Cipher-Based Message Authentication Code (CMAC), 391–392, 393
ciphers, 345–353. *See also* algorithms; cryptography
  block ciphers, 359–360, 363
  Caesar cipher, 336–337, 351
  concealment ciphers, 347–348, 350
  described, 335, 340
  null ciphers, 348
  one-time pad, 345–347, 362
  overview, 350–351
  RC4/RC5/RC6 ciphers, 379–380
  ROT13 cipher, 337
  running, 347–348
  scytale cipher, 336
  stream ciphers, 359, 360–362, 363
  substitution ciphers, 335, 337, 350–353
  transposition ciphers, 351–353
  Vernam cipher, 345
  Vigenère cipher, 337
ciphertext, 337, 340
ciphertext attacks, 410–411
CIR (committed information rate), 627, 628
circuit switching, 625–627
circuit-level proxy firewalls, 590–593, 596
CIS (computer information system), 99
CISO (chief information security officer), 161, 164, 203
CISSP (Certified Information Systems Security Professional), xxix–xxxiv
CISSP certification, xxix
CISSP exam, xxx–xxxiv, 2

civil law, 62
civil law system, 58
civil legal systems, 58
civil/tort law, 59–60
Clark-Wilson model, 309–310, 313
classes, 503
classification. *See* information classification
classification controls, 197–198
classless interdomain routing (CIDR), 505
classless IP addresses, 505
cleanroom approach, 1109
cleartext, 1153
cleartext passwords, 835
clients
  honeyclients, 992
  network, 542
  proxy servers and, 605–606
  session IDs, 1153
  SQL, 1160
  thin, 775–776
  web-based, 612
client/server model, 1132, 1133, 1135, 1141
client-side validation, 1149–1150
climate issues, 446–447
Clinger-Cohen Act, 22
clipping levels, 752, 930
closed systems, 320–321
closed-circuit TV (CCTV) system, 955–960
cloud assets, 969–970
cloud computing, 322, 969–970, 1141
cloud network, 628
clustered servers, 1029
clustering, 979–980
CM. *See* configuration management
CMAC (Cipher-Based Message Authentication Code), 391–392, 393
CMMI (Capability Maturity Model Integration), 16, 39–40, 1111–1113
CMMI model, 1111–1113
CMMs (capability maturity models), 1112–1113
coaxial cables, 517–518, 648
COBIT (Control Objectives for Information and related Technology), 33–34
COBIT 5 framework, 15
COBIT framework, 33–34
code, 1122–1123. *See also* programming
  bugs, 219, 300, 332, 875, 885
  compiled, 1115
  debugging, 300, 1089, 1092, 1117
  exploiting security holes, 70
  high-quality, 1077–1078
  malicious, 700, 1001
  mobile, 1142–1146
  open-source, 13
  sandboxes, 991
  testing/validating, 1084, 1093–1095, 1097
  "tight code," 1131
  unsigned, 937
  versions, 1115, 1116
"code bloat," 884
code division multiple access (CDMA), 681–682, 683
code obfuscation, 990
Code of Ethics, 165
code repositories, 1116
code reviews, 884–886
code signing, 937
code stubs, 884
CoE (Council of Europe), 54–55
cognitive passwords, 754
cohesion, 1130, 1131
cold sites, 1008–1011
cold starts, 934
collections, 271
collision domains, 529–530
collisions, 395, 528–530, 660
collusion, 155, 416
COM (Component Object Model), 1136–1137
command-and-control (C&C) servers, 1185
commercial off-the-shelf (COTS) products, 1016
commercial software, 68
commit operation, 1168
committed information rate (CIR), 627, 628
Committee of Sponsoring Organizations. *See* COSO
Common Body of Knowledge. *See* CBK
common controls, 128–129
Common Criteria, 92, 313–318
common law system, 59–60
Common Object Request Broker Architecture (CORBA), 1134–1136
Common Weakness Enumeration (CWE), 1091–1092
communications
  analog/digital, 512–514
  broadband/baseband, 516–517
  synchronous/asynchronous, 514–515
communities, 546–547
community strings, 546–547
companies. *See* organizations
compensating controls, 10, 11–13
compiled code, 1115

compilers, 1119
compliance audits, 864
compliance programs, 1060–1063
Component Object Model (COM), 1136–1137
components, trusted, 262, 288, 304
compression, 363, 485, 514, 515, 957
computer architecture, 252–270. *See also* architecture
  central processing unit, 252–257
  memory types, 258–270
  multiprocessing, 257–258
computer controls, 811
computer crime. *See also* cybercrime
  criminal behavior, 1042
  forensics. *See* computer forensics
  incident investigators, 1042–1043
  interviewing suspects, 1052–1053
  investigating. *See* investigations
  motive/opportunity/means, 1041–1042
  surveillance. *See* surveillance
computer crime laws (cyberlaw), 45–47
computer criminal behavior, 1042
Computer Emergency Response Team (CERT), 996
Computer Ethics Institute, 166
computer forensics, 1039–1041
  forensic software, 1044–1045
  forensics field kits, 1046–1047
  forensics team, 1040, 1043
  investigation process, 1043–1049
  overview, 1039–1040
  SWGDE attributes/principles, 1040–1041
computer information system (CIS), 99
computer is incidental crime, 46
computer systems. *See* systems
computer-aided software engineering (CASE) tools, 1089–1091
computer-assisted crimes, 45, 46
computer/equipment rooms, 435–439
computers
  disposal/destruction of, 220–221
  laptop. *See* laptop computers
  mainframes, 522
  malicious uses for, 50, 51
  microcomputers, 522
  obsolete, 220
computer-targeted crime, 45–46
concealment ciphers, 347, 348, 350
concentrators, 567
concurrency problems, 1166–1167
Confidential data classification, 195, 196
confidentiality
  Bell-LaPadula model, 307–308
  business continuity planning and, 131, 132
  cryptosystems, 344
  overview, 5, 724
confidentiality controls, 6
confidentiality, integrity, and availability (CIA), 3
configuration management (CM), 933–940
  change control documentation, 968–969
  change control process, 967–968
  considerations, 966–967, 985
  input/output controls, 936–937
  overview, 933–935, 966
  remote access security, 939–940
  remote systems administration, 939–940
  resource provisioning and, 966–970
  security concerns, 935
  system hardening, 937–939
  trusted recovery, 933–935
confusion, 359–360
connectionless protocols, 488, 497, 498
connection-oriented protocols, 488, 497, 498
connections
  dial-up, 644–645
  full-duplex, 486, 502
  half-duplex, 486
  remote. *See* remote connectivity
  between systems, 488
connectivity, 786
consistency, 1174
consortium, 1012
constant bit rate (CBR), 630
constrained user interfaces, 796–797
content distribution network (CDN), 608–609, 697–698
content-dependent access control, 325, 798, 1170–1171
contention-based environments, 529
context-dependent access control, 325, 799, 1170–1171
contingencies, 984–992
contingency companies, 1009
contingency planning, 983–984
continuity, business. *See BCP/BCM entries*
continuity of operations (COOP), 1038
continuity planning. *See* BCP
contractors, 106
contractual agreements, 1058–1059
control group, 926
Control Objectives for Information and related Technology. *See* COBIT

control plane, 610
control unit, 254
control zones, 811, 822
Controller Area Network bus (CAN bus) protocol, 496–497
controls, 102. *See also* security controls
  administrative. *See* administrative controls
  application, 1081–1082
  availability, 5–6
  categorization of, 35
  common, 128–129
  computer controls, 811
  considerations, 985
  described, 7, 102
  diversity of, 941
  hybrid, 129
  input/output, 936–937
  physical, 9, 808, 810–811
  risk and, 865, 985
  security. *See* security controls
  service organization, 864–865
  system-specific, 129
  technical, 8–12, 811–814, 865–866
Convention on Cybercrime, 54–55
convergence, 203
cookies, 693–694, 738, 1152, 1154
COOP (continuity of operations), 1038
Copper Distributed Data Interface (CDDI), 536
Copyright Directive, 70
copyright law, 64–65
CORBA (Common Object Request Broker Architecture), 1134–1136
Core RBAC, 792–793
corporate ethics, 168
corrective controls, 10, 11
COSO (Committee of Sponsoring Organizations), 15, 36–37
COSO frameworks, 36–37, 127
cost/benefit analysis, 102, 120
COTS (commercial off-the-shelf) products, 1016
Council of Europe (CoE), 54–55
Counter (CTR) mode, 376–377
countermeasures, 7, 102, 121–122. *See also* safeguards; security controls
counter-synchronization, 755
coupling, 1130–1131
covert channels, 310–311
CPO (chief privacy officer), 202
CPO role, 202
CPTED (Crime Prevention Through Environmental Design), 420–426
CPU (central processing unit)
  architecture integration, 287–291
  memory and, 261–265
  multiple cores, 279
  operation modes, 290
  overview, 252–257
CPU registers, 218, 219
CPU time, 271–272
CRAMM (Central Computing & Telecommunications Agency Risk Analysis & Management Method), 111
credit card fraud, 79–80
Crime Prevention Through Environmental Design (CPTED), 420–426
crimes. *See* computer crime; cybercrime
crimeware toolkits, 1186–1187
criminal law, 59, 62
CRL (certificate revocation list), 401–402
CRM (customer relationship management), 128, 783, 784
cross-certification, 401
crossover error rate (CER), 746–747
cross-site scripting. *See* XSS
crosstalk, 521–522
cryptanalysis, 339–340, 411, 412
cryptographic algorithms, 14
cryptographic checksums, 935
cryptographic hash chaining, 880
cryptographic keys, 757
cryptography, 335–350. *See also* cryptosystems; encryption
  asymmetric. *See* asymmetric algorithms
  attacks on, 409–414
  ciphers. *See* ciphers
  ciphertext, 337, 340
  considerations, 404
  definitions/concepts, 340–350
  digital signatures, 396–399
  hardware vs. software, 687
  history of, 335–340
  key management, 404–407
  message integrity and, 388–399
  overview, 335
  PKI, 383, 399–404
  plaintext, 337, 340
  public key, 383
  steganography, 348–350
  symmetric. *See* symmetric algorithms
  transformation techniques, 363
  Trusted Platform Module, 407–409
  zero knowledge proof, 387–388
cryptography notation, 380
cryptography systems, 687

cryptosystems. *See also* ciphers; cryptography
asymmetric, 356
cybertext/plaintext attacks, 410–411
described, 340, 342
Kerckhoffs' principle, 342–343
key in, 341, 342, 343
services, 344–345
strength of, 343–344
symmetric, 355
synchronous vs. asynchronous, 377
CSMA (carrier sense multiple access), 527–528
CSMA/CA (carrier sense multiple access with collision avoidance), 527, 528, 660
CSMA/CD (carrier sense multiple access with collision detection), 527–528, 660
CSO (chief security officer), 202–203
CSO role, 202–203
CSU/DSU (channel service unit/data service unit), 624–625
CTR (Counter) mode, 376–377
culture, 902–903
customer data, 215
customer relationship management (CRM), 128, 783, 784
customary law system, 60
CWE (Common Weakness Enumeration), 1091–1092
cyber kill chains, 997–998
cyber squatting, 554–555
cybercrime, 48–62. *See also* computer crime
common Internet schemes, 53
complexities in, 48–62
computer-assisted crimes, 45, 46
computer-targeted crimes, 45–46
electronic assets, 49–50
import/export legal issues, 57–58
inside jobs, 54
international issues, 54–58
overview, 48–49
perpetrators, 50–54
cyberlaw, 45–47
cyber-physical systems, 328–330

D

DAC (discretionary access control), 787–790, 794, 795, 1171
DAC (dual-attached concentrator), 536
damage assessment, 1032
DAS (data acquisition servers), 331
DAS (dual-attachment station), 536
DASDs (direct access storage devices), 976–977
data. *See also* information
backing up. *See* backups
big data, 1177
biometric, 747–748
changing format, 222
classification. *See* information classification
confidentiality, 307–308
customer, 215
database, 890
described, 21–22
destruction of. *See* data disposal/destruction
employee, 215
encapsulation, 279, 481–482, 502, 1124–1127
high-value, 227
integrity, 4, 308–309, 723–724, 1166–1169
location of, 217
locking, 1167
loss of, 94
mailbox, 890
malicious, 820
metadata. *See* metadata
misuse of, 94
ownership, 228
private, 215
replication of, 1027
at rest, 693
retaining. *See* data retention
sensitive, 820
states of, 216–219
in transit, 693
transmission. *See* data transmission
types of, 890
user, 890
data access, 194
data acquisition servers (DAS), 331
data analyst roles, 205
data archive, 192
data at rest, 99, 216–217
data breaches, 84–86, 225
data buses, 256–257
data centers, 436–439, 445
data circuit-terminating equipment (DCE) device, 625, 627–628
data control language (DCL), 1164
data custodian role, 204
data definition language (DDL), 1164
data dictionaries, 1161, 1164, 1165
data diode, 880
data disposal/destruction
considerations, 190
data remanence and, 211–214

degaussing, 214, 221
destroying physical media, 214, 223
encryption, 214
overview, 192–193
overwriting data, 214
Data Encryption Algorithm (DEA), 370, 378
Data Encryption Standard. *See* DES
data execution prevention (DEP), 270
data files, 890
data flows, 228
data frames, 526
data hiding, 279, 293, 1124
data in motion, 99, 217–218
data in use, 99, 218–219
data inventories, 227–228
data leak prevention (DLP), 226–234
data leakage, 225–234
data life cycle, 229
data link layer, 490–491, 493, 509–511
data link protocols, 515, 633–634
data loss, 226, 902
data loss prevention (DLP), 902
data manipulation language (DML), 1164
data modeling, 1129
data origin authentication, 391
data owner role, 203–204
data owners
described, 203–204
privacy issues and, 210–211
data ownership, 203–204
data parallelism, 323
data processors, 211
data protection, 228–229, 902
data protection strategy, 228–229
data remanence, 211–214
data retention. *See also* archival
classification and, 208
considerations, 191–192
e-discovery, 209–210
indexing and, 208
normalization and, 208
period of retention, 208–209
policies, 206–210
taxonomies, 208
type of data retained, 209
data security controls, 216–219
data storage, 206
data structures, 502–503, 1129–1130
data throughput, 514, 517
data transmission
analog/digital, 512–514
asynchronous/synchronous, 514–515
broadband/baseband, 516–517
methods, 536–538
types of, 512–517
data warehousing, 1174–1177
database administrator, 796, 926, 1155
database management, 1155–1177
data warehousing/mining, 1174–1177
database models, 1157–1161
DBMS, 1155–1157, 1160
integrity, 1166–1169
overview, 1155
programming interfaces, 1161–1164
relational databases, 1164–1166
security issues, 324–326, 1169–1174
database management system (DBMS), 1155–1157, 1160
database models, 1157–1161
database programming interfaces, 1161–1164
database security, 1169–1174
aggregation, 324–325, 1169–1170
considerations, 1171
database views, 1171–1172
inference attacks, 325, 1171
OLTP, 1173–1174
overview, 1169–1171
polyinstantiation, 1172–1173
roles, 1155, 1156
database views, 796, 1171–1172
databases
access control, 1155, 1156
aggregation, 324–325
batch processing, 1169
characteristics, 1156
checkpoints, 1168
commits, 1168
described, 1160
hierarchical, 1158–1159
integrity, 1166–1169
interference, 325
locking data, 1167
network, 1159–1160
object-oriented, 1159, 1160
object-relational, 1161, 1162
partitioning, 326, 1171
relational, 1157–1158, 1159
risk, 1155
rollbacks, 1168
savepoints, 1168
security issues. *See* database security
terminology, 1160–1161
two-phase commits, 1169
types of data, 890
using browser to access, 1155

datagrams, 502
data-mining, 1174–1177
Data-Over-Cable Service Interface Specifications (DOCSIS), 649
DBMS (database management system), 1155–1157, 1160
DCE (Distributed Computing Environment), 1132–1133
DCE (data circuit-terminating equipment) device, 625, 627–628
DCL (data control language), 1164
DCOM (Distributed Component Object Model), 1132–1133, 1136–1137
DCS (distributed control system), 331
DDL (data definition language), 1164
DDoS attacks, 603, 649, 697–698
DDR (dial-on-demand routing), 647
DDR SDRAM (double data rate SDRAM), 260
DEA (Data Encryption Algorithm), 370, 378
debugging, 300, 1089, 1092, 1117
dedicated links, 620–624
defense-in-depth, 9–10
degaussing, 214, 221
delayed binding, 698
delayed loss, 106–107
Delphi technique, 118
demilitarized zone. *See* DMZ
DEP (data execution prevention), 270
Department of Defense Architecture Framework (DoDAF), 25–26
Department of Veterans Affairs Information Security Protection Act, 77
DES (Data Encryption Standard), 339, 370–377
DES (Triple-DES), 370, 377–378
DES modes, 372–377
design phase, 249, 1084, 1086–1089, 1096
desk check test, 894
detective controls, 10, 11
deterrent controls, 10
development, defined, 249
development phase, 1084, 1089–1093, 1097
devices. *See also* hardware
  automated scanning of, 966
  fail-safe, 1063
  input/output, 285–287
  mean time between failures, 971–972, 973
  mean time to repair, 972–973
  mobile. *See* mobile devices
  near-line, 982
  networking. *See* networking devices
  potable, 937–938
  RAID, 974–976
  redundant, 971, 973
  single points of failure, 973–980
  storage. *See* storage devices
  surveillance, 955–960
DevOps, 1109–1110
DFRWS (Digital Forensic Research Workshop), 1041
DHCP (Dynamic Host Configuration Protocol), 540–543
DHCP clients, 541–542
DHCP servers, 541–542, 549
DHCP snooping, 542
DHS (U.S. Department of Homeland Security), 1098
diagnostic logs, 935
dialog management, 486
dial-on-demand routing (DDR), 647
dial-up connections, 644–645
Diameter protocol, 805–807
dictionary attacks, 752, 835
differential backups, 1023
differential cryptanalysis, 411
differential power analysis attacks, 760
differentiated service, QoS, 631
Diffie-Hellman algorithm, 380–383
diffusion, 359, 360
digital certificates, 399–404
digital envelopes, 367
digital evidence, 1040. *See also* evidence
Digital Forensic Research Workshop (DFRWS), 1041
digital forensics, 1039. *See also* computer forensics
digital identities, 776–777
Digital Millennium Copyright Act (DMCA), 70
Digital Signature Algorithm (DSA), 399
Digital Signature Standard (DSS), 395, 398–399
digital signatures, 396–399, 757
digital subscriber line (DSL), 647–648, 649
digital transmission, 512–514
direct access storage devices (DASDs), 976–977
direct memory access (DMA), 286
direct sequence spread spectrum (DSSS), 661, 662–663
directives, 73–74, 86, 91, 93
directories
  IdM, 733–734
  LDAP, 735–736
  meta-directories, 734–735, 736
  overview, 732–736

permissions, 876
structure, 734–735
directory services, 732–733, 775, 776
directory traversal, 1149
disaster recovery, 130–154. *See also* DRP; *recovery entries*
catastrophes, 1007
vs. continuity planning, 130–131
described, 892
goal of, 130
management support, 145–146
disaster recovery plan. *See* DRP
disasters
actions taken after, 138
damage assessment, 1032
defined, 1006
natural, 100
vs. nondisasters, 1006
planning for. *See* DRP
discretionary access control (DAC), 787–790, 794, 795, 1171
disk duplexing, 1025
disk shadowing, 1025
diskless workstations, 542–543
disks
DASDs, 976–977
HSM system, 982–983
MAID, 977–978
mirroring, 1025
RAID, 974–976, 977
SASDs, 976–977
disposal phase, 190, 192–193
distance-vector routing protocols, 564, 565
distinguished names (DNs), 732
Distributed Component Object Model (DCOM), 1132–1133, 1136–1137
distributed computing, 1132–1142
COM/DCOM, 1136–1137
considerations, 1142
CORBA/ORBs, 1134–1136
DCE, 1132–1133
Java EE, 1138
OLE, 1137–1138
overview, 1132
SOA, 1138–1142
Distributed Computing Environment (DCE), 1132–1133
distributed control system (DCS), 331
Distributed Network Protocol 3 (DNP3), 496
distributed system security, 321–332
cloud computing, 322
cyber-physical systems, 328–330
databases, 324–326
industrial control systems, 330–332
mobile devices, 327–328
parallel computing, 323
web applications, 326–327
distributed systems, 321
DLL (dynamic link library), 282
DLP (data leak prevention), 226–234
DLP (data loss prevention), 902
DLP resiliency, 231
DLP solutions, 227, 228, 230, 231
DMA (direct memory access), 286
DMCA (Digital Millennium Copyright Act), 70
DML (data manipulation language), 1164
DMZ (demilitarized zone)
considerations, 812, 1061–1062
firewalls and, 581–582, 597–599, 600
illustrated, 813
WLANs and, 677
DNP3 (Distributed Network Protocol 3), 496
DNs (distinguished names), 732
DNS (Domain Name Service), 547–555
naming hierarchy, 549–550
overview, 547–548
threats, 552–554
DNS hijacking, 699–700
DNS namespaces, 548
DNS poisoning, 838–839
DNS proxy servers, 606
DNS resolver, 551
DNS security (DNSSEC), 552–553
DNS servers, 548–555, 699, 838–839
DNS splitting, 553
DNSSEC (DNS security), 552–553
DoAF framework, 15
DOCSIS (Data-Over-Cable Service Interface Specifications), 649
documentation
audits, 861–862
backups, 1024
for business continuity, 1018–1019
change control, 968–969
for disaster recovery, 1018–1019
restoring data, 1024
security programs, 87
templates, 1033
DoDAF (Department of Defense Architecture Framework), 25–26
dogs, guard, 963
domain grabbing, 554–555
Domain Name Service. *See* DNS
domain names, 554–555
domain registration, 554–555

domains
CBK, xxxi–xxxii
described, 291
Internet, 549–552
security, xxxi–xxxii, 772–775, 776
single sign-on and, 772–775, 776
DOM-based XSS vulnerabilities, 1150
DoS attacks, 566, 588, 603, 696–698
"dot dot slash" attack, 1149
double data rate SDRAM (DDR SDRAM), 260
double tagging attacks, 575
double-blind test, 873
DRAM (dynamic RAM), 258–259
DRI International Institute, 135
drive-by downloads, 699, 700, 900, 901–902
drives
floppy, 272
hard, 408, 975
tape, 978
USB, 820
DRP (disaster recovery plan), 1002–1030. *See also* business continuity; disasters; recovery process
availability and, 131, 132
backup facility options, 1010, 1011, 1018–1021
business continuity plan. *See BCP entries*
business process recovery, 1006
communications, 132
damage assessment, 1032
data backup options, 1021–1025
described, 1038
disasters vs. nondisasters, 1006
documentation and, 1018–1019
end-user environment and, 1021
facility recovery, 1006–1013
goal setting, 1034–1036
hardware backups, 1015–1016
high availability and, 1028–1030
human resources and, 1019–1021
implementing strategies for, 1036–1038
insurance options, 1030–1031
maximum tolerable downtime, 1002–1005
Occupant Emergency Plan, 1063–1064
outsourcing and, 1014
overview, 1002–1005
preventive measures, 984–992
preventive vs. recovery strategies, 1005
purpose of, 130
reconstitution phase, 1033–1034
recovery activation criteria, 1032–1033
recovery time objective, 1002–1005
recovery/restoration, 1031–1038
redundant sites, 1012–1013
software backups, 1016–1018
storing plans for, 1020
supply/technology recovery, 1013–1015
vulnerabilities after disaster, 132
DSA (Digital Signature Algorithm), 399
DSL (digital subscriber line), 647–648, 649
DSS (Digital Signature Standard), 395, 398–399
DSSS (direct sequence spread spectrum), 661, 662–663
DTE, 627, 628
dual control, 155
dual-attached concentrator (DAC), 536
dual-attachment station (DAS), 536
dual-homed firewalls, 597–598, 600
due care, 145, 924, 1053, 1054
due diligence, 145, 924, 1053, 1054
dumpster diving, 221, 223
durability, 1174
dust, 222
DVDs, 223
dynamic analysis, 1095, 1188
Dynamic Host Configuration Protocol. *See* DHCP
dynamic link library (DLL), 282
dynamic mapping, 561
dynamic packet-filtering firewalls, 593–594, 596
dynamic passwords, 754
dynamic ports, 500
dynamic RAM (DRAM), 258–259
dynamic routing protocols, 563

E

EAC (electronic access control) tokens, 950
EAL (Evaluation Assurance Level), 92, 314
EAP (Extensible Authentication Protocol), 658–659, 669–670
EAP-TLS (Extensible Authentication Protocol-Transport Layer Security), 510, 511, 670
EAP-TTLS (EAP-Tunneled Transport Layer Security), 670
EAP-Tunneled Transport Layer Security (EAP-TTLS), 670
e-carriers, 621–622
ECB (Electronic Code Book) mode, 372–373
ECC (elliptic curve cryptosystem), 386–387
Economic Espionage Act of 1996, 85
EDI (electronic data interchange), 613, 614
e-discovery, 209–210
EDLP (endpoint DLP), 232–233
EDO DRAM (extended data out DRAM), 259

EDRM (Electronic Discovery Reference Model), 209–210
EEPROM (electrically erasable programmable read-only memory), 260–261
EER (equal error rate), 746
EF (exposure factor), 114
EGPs (exterior gateway protocols), 565–566
egress filtering, 584
EIGRP (Enhanced Interior Gateway Routing Protocol), 565
EK (Endorsement Key), 408
El Gamal algorithm, 386
electric power, 441–446
  best practices, 446
  fluctuations in, 444–445
  generators, 443
  in-rush current, 445
  interference, 443–444
  power failure, 441, 442–443, 945
  power grid, 441–442
  power losses, 440–441
  power protection, 442–443
  smart grid, 441–442
  UPS devices, 438, 442–443
electrically erasable programmable read-only memory (EEPROM), 260–261
electricity, 430, 441
electromagnetic analysis attacks, 760
electromagnetic interference (EMI), 443–444, 517–518
electronic access control (EAC) tokens, 950
electronic assets, 49–50
Electronic Code Book (ECB) mode, 372–373
electronic data interchange (EDI), 613, 614
Electronic Discovery Reference Model (EDRM), 209–210
electronic vaulting, 1026–1027
electronically stored information (ESI), 209–210
electrostatic IDS, 962
e-mail, 555–560
  attachments, 688, 698, 1178
  authorization, 557
  encryption, 687–690
  IMAP, 556–557
  monitoring of, 81–83
  overview, 555–556
  PGP, 689–690
  phishing, 837, 838
  POP, 556
  relaying, 557–559
  SMTP, 555–556, 559
  spam, 557–559, 642, 1190–1192
  viruses/worms in, 1178
e-mail clients, 484
e-mail gateways, 577
e-mail policy, 89
e-mail spoofing attacks, 559–560
emanation security, 820–822
embedded systems, 329
embedding, 1138
emergencies, 138
emergency responders, 1063
emergency response procedures, 895–896
emergency system restart, 934
EMI (electromagnetic interference), 443–444, 517–518
employees. *See* personnel
emulation buffer, 1188
encapsulated processes, 279
Encapsulating Security Payload (ESP), 653
encapsulation, 279, 481–482, 502, 1124–1127
encryption. *See also* cryptography
  asymmetric. *See* asymmetric algorithms
  considerations, 814
  digital signatures, 396–399
  e-mail, 687–690
  hybrid methods, 364–369
  importance of, 937
  key, 341, 342, 343
  methods of, 353–369
  networks. *See* network encryption
  passwords, 753
  presentation layer and, 485
  rendering data unrecoverable, 214
  RSA public key, 689
  session keys, 367–369
  steganography, 348–350
  storage devices, 216–217
  swap space and, 285
  symmetric. *See* symmetric algorithms
  symmetric vs. asymmetric, 353–359
  websites, 1154
End User License Agreement (EULA), 68
Endorsement Key (EK), 408
endpoint DLP (EDLP), 232–233
end-to-end encryption, 685–687
end-user environment, 1021
Enhanced Interior Gateway Routing Protocol (EIGRP), 565
Enhanced Performance Architecture (EPA), 496
Enigma machine, 338–339
enterprise architecture development, 19–32
  enterprise security architecture, 26–32
  enterprise vs. system architectures, 32
  frameworks, 21–26

enterprise architecture development (*Cont.*)
  military-oriented frameworks, 25–26
  overview, 19–21
  TOGAF, 24–25
  Zachman Framework, 15, 22–24
enterprise architecture frameworks, 21–22
enterprise security architecture, 26–32
enticement, 833, 1052
entity integrity, 1167
entrapment, 833, 1052
environmental conditions, 222
environmental controls/issues
  CPTED concepts, 420–426
  electric power, 441–446
  fire suppression, 448–449, 452–453
  overview, 446–448
Environmental Protection Agency (EPA), 427
EPA (Enhanced Performance Architecture), 496
EPA (Environmental Protection Agency), 427
EPROM (erasable programmable read-only memory), 260
equal error rate (EER), 746
equipment. *See also* devices; hardware
  damage to, 439
  malfunction, 94
  obsolete, 220
  stolen, 439
equipment rooms, 435–439
erasable programmable read-only memory (EPROM), 260
errors, software, 1091–1092
ESI (electronically stored information), 209–210
ESP (Encapsulating Security Payload), 653
Ethernet networks, 490, 531–534
Ethernet technology
  characteristics, 537
  Metro Ethernet, 615–617
ethical fallacies, 165–166
ethics, 165–168
EU (European Union), 56–57
EU laws, 85–86
EULA (End User License Agreement), 68
European Union. *See* EU
Evaluation Assurance Level (EAL), 92, 314
event logs, 878–881, 929
event management, 932
events
  application-level, 816
  described, 993
  vs. incidents, 993
  system-level, 815–816
  user-level, 816
evidence
  admissibility of, 1049–1051
  analysis, 1049
  chain of custody, 1047–1049
  collection of, 1040–1041, 1047–1049
  considerations, 1039–1041, 1049
  life cycle, 1050–1051
  search and seizure, 1051–1052
exclusive-OR (XOR), 345
execution domain, 303
executive management
  abuse of roles, 200–201
  business continuity plan, 137, 138–141, 145, 154
  CEO, 199–200
  CFO, 200–201
  CIO, 201–202
  CISO, 161, 164, 203
  CPO, 202
  CSO, 202–203
  layers of responsibility, 199–203
  liability issues and, 1055
  roles, 199–203
  security and, 87
  succession planning, 1020–1021
executive summaries, 907–908
exigent circumstances, 1052
exploratory model, 1108
exposure, defined, 7
exposure factor (EF), 114
extended data out DRAM (EDO DRAM), 259
Extended TACACS (XTACACS), 802
Extensible Access Control Markup Language (XACML), 783–784
Extensible Authentication Protocol (EAP), 658–659, 669–670
Extensible Authentication Protocol-Transport Layer Security (EAP-TLS), 510, 511, 670
Extensible Markup Language. *See* XML
exterior gateway protocols (EGPs), 565–566
extranets, 612–614
Extreme Programming (XP), 1107

F

facial scans, 750
Facilitated Risk Analysis Process (FRAP), 108
facilities
  access controls, 941–949, 1063
  building codes, 429
  cold sites, 1008–1011
  construction materials, 429–432
  data center, 436–437
  doors, 429, 430, 433–434, 436, 439

electric power, 441–446
entry points, 432–433
environmental planning, 446–448
hot sites, 1007–1009, 1011, 1013
load, 429
location, 428–429
locks, 941–949
moving back after disaster, 1033–1034
Occupant Emergency Plan, 1063–1064
reciprocal agreements, 1011
recovery operations, 1006–1013
redundant sites, 1012–1013
reinforcement, 432
restricted areas, 436
security. *See* facility security
structure, 429
temperature control, 446, 448
types of disruptions, 1006–1007
warm sites, 1008–1011
windows, 324, 429, 431, 434
facility safety officer, 427
facility security, 414–439. *See also* physical security
assessing protection level of, 426–428
computer/equipment rooms, 435–439
considerations, 428–429
construction issues, 429–432
doors, 429, 430, 433–434, 436, 439
entry points, 429–432
internal compartments, 435
internal support systems, 440–454
overview, 414–415
protecting assets, 439–440
site planning process, 415–439
threats, 414
windows, 434
factors, 903
failing securely, 326, 1154
failover capability, 1029
fail-safe devices, 1063
fail-safe setting, 434
fail-secure setting, 434
failure modes, 109
Failure Modes and Effect Analysis (FMEA), 109–110
false positives/negatives, 987, 998
Faraday cage, 821
FAST (Federation Against Software Theft), 69
Fast Ethernet, 532
fast flux, 1185
FAT (File Allocation Table) file system, 211–214
fault generation attacks, 760
fault tolerance, 971, 1029
fault tree analysis, 110
fault trees, 110–111
fax machines, 874
FCC (Federal Communications Commission), 479
FCoE (Fibre Channel over Ethernet), 511
FCS (frame check sequence) numbers, 626
FDDI rings, 534, 535, 536, 537, 614
FDDI (Fiber Distributed Data Interface) technology, 534–536
FDDI-2, 536
FDM (frequency-division multiplexing), 623
FDMA (frequency division multiple access), 681
Federal Communications Commission (FCC), 479
Federal Information Security Management Act (FISMA), 75–76
Federal Privacy Act of 1974, 75
federated identities, 776–785
federation, 776–785
Federation Against Software Theft (FAST), 69
fencing, 951–953
fetch request, 255–256
FHSS (frequency hopping spread spectrum), 661–662, 663
fiber cables, 648
Fiber Distributed Data Interface. *See* FDDI
fiber-optic cables, 519–520
Fibre Channel over Ethernet (FCoE), 511
File Allocation Table (FAT) file system, 211–214
file descriptor attacks, 875
file descriptors, 875
file integrity checkers, 876
File Transfer Protocol (FTP), 586–587
files
database, 1160
log. *See* log files
password, 751, 835
permissions, 876
recovering, 934
shadow, 753
FILO (first in, last out), 266
financial institutions, 79
financial privacy rule, 79
fingerprint detection, 1187
fingerprint systems, 748
fingerprints, 1187
fire, 106
fire detection, 448, 449–451, 453
fire extinguishers, 448, 449–450, 454, 895
fire prevention, 448

fire resistance ratings, 450
fire suppression, 448–449, 452–453
fire-resistant materials, 432
firewalls, 581–605
  appliances, 595
  architecture, 596–599
  best practices/rules, 603–605
  considerations, 13, 14, 605, 986
  DMZ and, 581–582, 597–599, 600
  dual-homed, 597–598, 600
  dynamic packet-filtering, 593–594, 596
  issues, 604
  kernel proxy, 594, 596
  multihomed, 597, 598–599
  NGFW, 595–596, 986
  overview, 581–582, 985–986
  packet-filtering, 582–585, 596
  proxy, 589–593
  screened host, 598, 601
  screened-subnet, 598–599, 601
  SOCKS, 592
  software-based, 595
  stateful, 584, 585–588, 596
  stateless, 584
  types of, 582
  virtual, 599–603
  WAFs, 327
first in, last out (FILO), 266
FISMA (Federal Information Security Management Act), 75–76
flooding attacks, 696–697, 698
floppy drives, 272
FMEA (Failure Modes and Effect Analysis), 109–110
footprint, satellite, 678
foreign keys
  considerations, 1167–1168
  described, 1161, 1166
  vs. primary key, 1164–1166
  unmatched values, 1167–1168
forensics. *See* computer forensics
forensics field kits, 1046–1047
forensics team, 1040, 1043
forwarding plane, 610
forwarding proxies, 604–605
forwarding tables, 568–569
fragmentation attacks, 603
frame check sequence (FCS) numbers, 626
frame relay, 627–628, 643
frames, 491, 502, 526, 539
frameworks
  described, 126
  enterprise architecture, 20
  risk management, 126–130
  security governance, 159–165
framing, 491
FRAP (Facilitated Risk Analysis Process), 108
free-space optics (FSO), 675–676
freeware, 68
frequency, 660
frequency analysis, 352–353
frequency division multiple access (FDMA), 681
frequency hopping spread spectrum (FHSS), 661–662, 663
frequency-division multiplexing (FDM), 623
FSO (free-space optics), 675–676
FTP (File Transfer Protocol), 586–587
full backups, 1023
full-duplex communication option, 486, 502
full-interruption test, 894–895
fully mapped I/O, 287
function logs, 929
functional analysis, 146
functional model, 1087
functional policies, 88–89
functionality vs. security, 45
fuzzing, 1094

G

garbage collectors, 270, 1121
gas lines, 446, 447
gateways, 576–577, 578, 636–638
Generalized Markup Language (GML), 779
generators, 443
Generic Routing Encapsulation (GRE), 650
Gigabit Ethernet, 532–533
glare protection, 954
GLBA (Gramm-Leach-Bliley Act), 78–79, 85
Global Positioning System (GPS), 515
globalization, 72, 74
globally unique identifier (GUID), 1133
GM (Gold Master), 938, 966
GML (Generalized Markup Language), 779
Gold Master (GM), 938, 966
Good Practice Guidelines (GPG), 135
Google Alerts, 902
governance, risk, and compliance (GRC) programs, 1060–1063
GPG (Good Practice Guidelines), 135
GPS (Global Positioning System), 515
Graham-Denning model, 311–312, 313
Gramm-Leach-Bliley Act (GLBA), 78–79, 85
graphical user interface (GUI), 886
gray box testing, 869
GRC (governance, risk, and compliance) programs, 1060–1063

GRE (Generic Routing Encapsulation), 650
grep process, 272–273
grid computing, 980
ground, 430
ground connector, 430
groups, access control, 763
guaranteed service, QoS, 631
guard dogs, 963
guards, security, 962–963
GUI (graphical user interface), 886
GUID (globally unique identifier), 1133
guidelines, 92–94

H

H.323 gateways, 636–638
HA (high availability), 1028–1030
hackers, 50–54. *See also* attackers
  advanced persistent threat, 51–52
  considerations, 48
  evolution of, 50–51
  international, 54–56
  liability scenario, 1057–1058
  mobile phones, 682
  risks, 106, 116–117, 132
  script kiddies, 50
  shotgun approach, 50
  as threat agent, 106
hacktivists/hacktivism, 46
HAIPE (High Assurance Internet Protocol Encryptor), 654
half-duplex communication option, 486
halon gas, 453
hand geometry, 749
hand topology, 750–751
hard drives, 408, 975
hardware. *See also* devices; equipment
  architecture. *See* computer architecture
  backing up for disaster recovery, 1015–1016
  hot swapping, 971, 975–976
  redundant, 971, 973
  segmentation, 260
  tracking, 964–965
hardware backups, 1015–1016
hardware cryptography methods, 687
Harris, Shon, xxi–xxii
Harrison-Ruzzo-Ullman (HRU) model, 312, 313
Hash Message Authentication Code (HMAC), 389–391, 393
hashes/hashing
  birthday attacks, 396
  compared, 398
  considerations, 388
  cryptographic, 936
  digital signatures, 396–399
  HMAC, 389–391, 393
  MD4, 394
  MD5, 394–395
  one-way hash functions, 388–389, 395–396
  overview, 393–394
  passwords, 752, 753
  SHA, 395
hashing algorithms, 393–396
HDLC (High-level Data Link Control), 629, 632, 633–634
HDSL (High-Bit-Rate DSL), 648
Health Information Technology for Economic and Clinical Health (HITECH), 77–78, 84–85
Health Insurance Portability & Accountability Act (HIPAA), 72, 77, 84
heartbeat messages, 219
Heartbleed security bug, 219
heat-activated detectors, 450
help desk, 926
heuristic capabilities, 826
heuristic detection, 1188
HIDS (host-based IDS), 822, 823, 986
hierarchical databases, 1158–1159
hierarchical RBAC, 793–794
hierarchical storage management (HSM), 982–983
hierarchies, 793–794
High Assurance Internet Protocol Encryptor (HAIPE), 654
high availability (HA), 1028–1030
High-Bit-Rate DSL (HDSL), 648
High-level Data Link Control (HDLC), 629, 632, 633–634
high-level languages, 1117–1118
High-Speed Serial Interface (HSSI), 634–635, 644
HIPAA (Health Insurance Portability and Accountability Act), 72, 77, 84
hiring practices, 155–157
HITECH (Health Information Technology for Economic and Clinical Health), 77–78, 84–85
HMAC (Hash Message Authentication Code), 389–391, 393
HMI (human-machine interface), 331
holistic risk management, 95
home IP address, 805
honeyclients, 992
honeynets, 991–992
honeypots, 607, 832–833, 991–992

hop sequence, 661
hops, 686
host address, 504
hostage alarm, 945
host-based IDS (HIDS), 822, 823, 986
hostnames, 505, 548
HOSTS files, 553–554
hot sites, 1007–1009, 1011, 1013
hot swap capability, 971, 975–976
HRU (Harrison-Ruzzo-Ullman) model, 312, 313
HSM (hierarchical storage management), 982–983
HSSI (High-Speed Serial Interface), 634–635, 644
HTML (HyperText Markup Language), 779
HTML code, 1152
HTML documents, 554
HTTP (Hypertext Transfer Protocol), 593, 691–692, 1148
HTTP communication, 1141
HTTP protocol, 1152
HTTP Secure (HTTPS), 691–692
HTTPS (HTTP Secure), 691–692
hubs, 567
human interaction, 94
human resources, 1019–1021
human-machine interface (HMI), 331
humidity, 222, 447
HVAC system, 438, 453
hybrid controls, 129
hybrid DLP, 233–234
hybrid microkernel OS model, 295, 296, 297
hygrometers, 448
hyperlinks, 554
HyperText Markup Language. *See* HTML
Hypertext Transfer Protocol. *See* HTTP
hypervisors, 298, 299, 602–603

I

IaaS (Infrastructure as a Service), 322, 969–970
IAB (Internet Architecture Board), 166–168
ICANN (Internet Corporation for Assigned Names and Numbers), 500
ICMP (Internet Control Message Protocol), 543–545, 586–587
ICMP attacks, 543–545
ICMP Echo Requests, 696
ICMP messages, 543–545
ICMP packets, 696
ICMP tunneling, 543–545
ICS (industrial control systems), 330–332
ICVs (integrity check values), 509–510, 666–667
IDaaS (Identity as a Service), 785–786
IDEA (International Data Encryption Algorithm), 378–379, 689
identification, 727–739
  considerations, 728
  digital identities, 776–777
  federated identities, 776–785
  key aspects, 728
  requirements, 728
  verification of, 727, 746, 747
Identity as a Service (IDaaS), 785–786
identity federation, 776–785
identity management (IdM), 729–739
identity repository, 743
identity services, 786–795
identity theft, 1178
iDevID (initial secure device identity), 510
IdM (identity management), 729–739
IDS sensors, 830
IDS/IPS rules, 987
IDSs (intrusion detection systems), 822–830
  alerts, 825, 826, 833, 903–904
  anomaly-based, 827, 829
  application-based, 830
  baselining, 987
  behavioral-based, 825–826
  characteristics, 962
  considerations, 7
  costs associated with, 120–121
  false positives/negatives, 987, 998
  HIDS, 986
  host-based, 822, 823
  vs. IPSs, 986
  knowledge-based, 823–824
  network security, 986–987
  network traffic volume and, 830
  network-based, 822–823
  NIDS, 986
  overview, 822, 960–962
  protocol anomaly–based, 826–827
  rule-based, 827–829
  signature-based, 823–824, 829
  state-based, 824–825
  statistical anomaly–based, 825–826
  traffic anomaly–based, 827, 829
  types of, 829
  WIDS, 986
IEC (International Electrotechnical Commission), 16–17
IEEE 802.1AR standard, 510
IEEE 802.3 standard, 531

IEEE standards. *See numerical entries*
IETF (Internet Engineering Task Force), 166, 502
IGMP (Internet Group Management Protocol), 538
IGP (Interior Gateway Protocol), 562
IGRP (Interior Gateway Routing Protocol), 565
IKE (Internet Key Exchange), 653
IMAP (Internet Message Access Protocol), 556–557
immunization, 1189
immunizers, 1189
implementation, 93–94
import/export issues, 57–58
IMSI (International Mobile Subscriber Identity) catchers, 682
incident handling, 995–998
incident intrusion stages, 997–998
incident investigators, 1042–1043
incident management, 993–1002
incident response, 164, 994, 995–996. *See also* incidents
incident response teams, 994–995, 996, 998–999
incidents
  considerations, 993–994
  contingency plans, 983–984
  cyber kill chains, 997–998
  described, 993
  detecting, 998
  vs. events, 993
  learning from, 1002
  mitigating, 999–1000
  overview, 993
  public disclosure, 996
  recovery, 1001
  remediation, 1001–1002
  reporting, 996, 1000
  responding to. *See* incident response
  types of, 993
incremental backups, 1023
incremental model, 1101–1102
indexing, described, 208
indicators, 904
indicators of attack (IOA), 1001
indicators of compromise (IOC), 1001
industrial control systems (ICS), 330–332
inference, 1169–1170, 1171, 1173
inference attacks, 1171, 1173
information. *See also* data
  accessing. *See* data access
  acquisition of, 190–191
  archiving, 190, 191–192
  availability of, 3–4, 723
  classification. *See* information classification
  confidentiality, 5, 724
  copying, 190
  criticality of, 193
  destruction of. *See* data disposal/destruction
  indexing, 190
  layers of responsibility, 199–206
  retaining, 192
  sensitivity of, 193–198
  unauthorized disclosure of, 819–820
  using, 190, 191
  value of, 104–105
  vulnerabilities, 99
information assets, 16, 189, 193, 217. *See also* assets
information classification, 193–198
  applications, 197
  considerations, 208, 820
  levels of, 194–197
  military, 194, 195–196
  overview, 193–194
  procedures, 198
  systems, 197
information life cycle, 190–193
information security management system. *See* ISMS
information systems, 128, 130, 860
Information Systems Audit and Control Association. *See* ISACA
information systems risk management. *See* ISRM
information technology. *See* IT
Information Technology Infrastructure Library (ITIL), 16, 37–38
informational model, 1087
informative policies, 90
Infrastructure as a Service (IaaS), 322, 969–970
infrastructure WLANs, 664
ingress filtering, 584
initial program load (IPL), 932–933
initial secure device identity (iDevID), 510
initialization vectors (IVs), 362–363, 666
input validation, 1092, 1148–1152
input validation attacks, 1149–1152
input/output. *See* I/O
instantiation, 1121–1122, 1126
instruction set, 252, 255, 287
insurance options, 1030–1031
integrated product team (IPT), 1109–1110

Integrated Services Digital Network (ISDN), 645–647
integration testing, 886
integrity
  backups, 981
  business continuity planning and, 131, 132
  cryptosystems, 344
  data, 4, 308–309, 723–724, 1166–1169
  database, 1166–1169
  entity, 1167
  media, 223
  message, 388–399
  overview, 4, 723–724
  referential, 1167
  resources, 4, 723–724
  semantic, 1167
integrity check values (ICVs), 509–510, 666–667
integrity controls, 6
intellectual property (IP)
  data breaches and, 84
  espionage and, 85
  internal protection of, 67–68
  patent law, 65–67
  software piracy, 68–70
intellectual property laws, 62–70
  copyright law, 64–65
  overview, 62–63
  patent law, 65–67
  trade secret law, 63–64
  trademark law, 65
interface testing, 886
interference, 325, 443–444, 514, 661–662
Interior Gateway Protocol (IGP), 562
Interior Gateway Routing Protocol (IGRP), 565
Intermediate System to Intermediate System (IS-IS), 565
international cybercrime, 54–58
International Data Encryption Algorithm (IDEA), 378–379, 689
International Electrotechnical Commission (IEC), 16–17
International Information Systems Security Certification Consortium (ISC), xxx
international issues, 54–57
international laws
  data breaches, 85–86
  import/export legal requirements, 57–58
  Safe Harbor pact, 56–57
  Wassenaar Arrangement, 57–58
International Mobile Subscriber Identity (IMSI) catchers, 682
International Organization for Standardization. *See* ISO
International Telecommunication Union (ITU), 479
Internet. *See also* websites
  data in motion, 217–218
  markup languages and, 779–784
  naming hierarchy, 549–550
  online safety, 901–902
Internet Architecture Board (IAB), 166–168
Internet Control Message Protocol. *See* ICMP
Internet Corporation for Assigned Names and Numbers (ICANN), 500
Internet Engineering Task Force (IETF), 166, 502
Internet Group Management Protocol (IGMP), 538
Internet Key Exchange (IKE), 653
Internet Message Access Protocol (IMAP), 556–557
Internet of Things (IoT), 329–330, 495
Internet Protocol. *See* IP
Internet Protocol Security. *See* IPSec
Internet Relay Chat (IRC), 52
Internet security, 690–695
  browsers and, 690–691
  cookies, 693–694
  HTTP, 691
  HTTPS, 691–692
  overview, 690–691
  SSH, 694–695
  SSL, 691, 692–693
  TLS, 691–692, 693
Internet Security Association and Key Management Protocol (ISAKMP), 653
Internet service providers (ISPs), 548
Internet services, 691
Internet Small Computer System Interface (iSCSI), 512
internetworks, 569
interoperability, 230, 761
interpreters, 1120
interrupt vector, 285
interrupt-driven I/O, 286
interrupts, 273, 274–275, 285–287
intranets, 612–614
intraorganizational configuration, 638
Intra-Site Automatic Tunnel Addressing Protocol (ISATAP), 508
intruders, 106
intrusion detection, 822
intrusion detection systems. *See* IDSs
intrusion prevention systems. *See* IPSs

inventories
  assets, 964–966
  data, 227–228
investigations, 1038–1053. *See also* computer crime
  chain of custody, 1047–1049
  computer criminal behavior, 1042
  computer forensics, 1039–1041
  controlling crime scene, 1045
  evidence. *See* evidence
  forensic software, 1044–1045
  forensics field kits, 1046–1047
  forensics investigation process, 1043–1049
  incident investigators, 1042–1043
  interviewing suspects, 1052–1053
  law enforcement agencies, 1039
  motive/opportunity/means, 1041–1042
  overview, 1038–1039
  photographing crime scene, 1048
  profiling and, 1042
  surveillance. *See* surveillance
I/O (input/output)
  fully mapped, 287
  interrupt-driven, 286
  premapped, 286–287
  programmable, 286
  using DMA, 286
I/O controls, 936–937
I/O device management, 285–287
I/O devices, 285–287
IOA (indicators of attack), 1001
IOC (indicators of compromise), 1001
IoT (Internet of Things), 329–330, 495
IP. *See* intellectual property
IP (Internet Protocol), 497, 691, 805
IP addresses
  ARP and, 539
  classless, 505
  considerations, 560, 562
  DHCP and, 540–543
  NAT and, 560–562
  private, 560–562
  public, 561
IP addressing, 503–506
IP convergence, 512
IP fragmentation, 603
IP next generation (IPng), 506–509
IP telephony, 637, 641–643
IP telephony device, 636
IP version 4. *See* IPv4
IP version 6. *See* IPv6
IPL (initial program load), 932–933
IPng (IP next generation), 506–509
IPSec (Internet Protocol Security), 653–654
  configuration options, 655
  data in motion and, 217
  features, 656, 657
IPSs (intrusion prevention systems), 830–834
  honeypots, 832–833
  vs. IDSs, 986
  network security, 986–987
  overview, 830–832
IPT (integrated product team), 1109–1110
IPv4 (IP version 4), 503, 507, 538
  addresses, 506
  traffic, 509
  tunneling, 508
IPv6 (IP version 6), 503, 538
  addressing, 506–509
  specification, 506–507
  traffic, 509
  tunneling, 508
IRC (Internet Relay Chat), 52
iris scans, 749
ISACA (Information Systems Audit and Control Association), 33
ISACA Risk IT framework, 127
ISAKMP (Internet Security Association and Key Management Protocol), 653
ISATAP (Intra-Site Automatic Tunnel Addressing Protocol), 508
ISC (International Information Systems Security Certification Consortium), xxx
iSCSI (Internet Small Computer System Interface), 512
ISDN (Integrated Services Digital Network), 645–647
IS-IS (Intermediate System to Intermediate System), 565
ISMS (information security management system), 16, 17, 30, 108–109, 903–905
ISMS team, 910
ISO (International Organization for Standardization), 16, 17, 313, 479
ISO 22301:2012 standard, 134
ISO 31000:2009 standard, 127
ISO/IEC 14443 standard, 761
ISO/IEC 27000 series, 15, 16–19, 30
ISO/IEC 27001 standard, 163
ISO/IEC 27004 standard, 163
ISO/IEC 27004:2009 standard, 163
ISO/IEC 27005, 108–109, 112
ISO/IEC 27031:2011 standard, 134
ISO/IEC 27034 standard, 1098
ISO/IEC standards, 17–18, 163, 250, 317, 761, 1098

isolation, 1174
ISPs (Internet service providers), 548
ISRM (information systems risk management) policy, 95–96
ISRM team, 96–97
IT engineer, 926
IT Governance Institute (ITGI), 33
IT team, 1109–1110
ITGI (IT Governance Institute), 33
ITIL (Information Technology Infrastructure Library), 16, 37–38
ITU (International Telecommunication Union), 479
IVs (initialization vectors), 362–363, 666

J

JAD (Joint Application Development), 1109
Java Applets, 1142–1144
Java Database Connectivity. *See* JDBC
Java EE (Java Platform, Enterprise Edition), 1138
Java language, 1138, 1142–1144
Java Platform, Enterprise Edition (Java EE), 1138
Java programming language, 1120
Java Virtual Machine (JVM), 1120, 1143
JavaScript, 1150
JDBC (Java Database Connectivity), 1163–1164
JDBC API, 1163–1164
jitter, 635–636
job rotation, 926–927
Joint Application Development (JAD), 1109
jumbograms, 507
JVM (Java Virtual Machine), 1120, 1143

K

Kanban methodology, 1107–1108
KDC (Key Distribution Center), 405, 768–772
KDD (knowledge discovery in database), 1176–1177
KDFs (Key Derivation Functions), 353
Kerberos protocol, 405, 768–776
Kerckhoffs' principle, 342–343
kernel flaws, 875
kernel proxy firewalls, 594, 596
key agreement, 381
key, bump, 949
Key Derivation Functions (KDFs), 353
Key Distribution Center (KDC), 405, 768–772
key escrow, 407
key exchange, 381
key exchange protocol, 383
key input, 909
key loggers, 1178
key management, 404–407
key performance indicators (KPIs), 903–905, 1060–1063
key recovery, 407
key ring, 689–690
key risk indicators (KRIs), 903, 905
key/algorithm relationship, 352
keys
    asymmetric, 353, 356, 358, 364–366, 398
    in encryption, 341, 342, 343
    foreign. *See* foreign keys
    primary. *See* primary keys
    private, 353, 356, 757
    public, 353, 356, 689–690, 757
    rules for, 407
    secret, 353, 354, 369
    session, 770
    storage, 408
    symmetric, 354–355, 364–368, 398, 666
keys, master (locks), 947
keyspaces, 341
keystream generators, 360, 361, 362
keystroke dynamics, 750
keystroke monitoring, 818
kill chains, 101, 997–998
knapsack algorithms, 387
knowledge discovery in database (KDD), 1176–1177
knowledge-based IDS, 823–824
KPIs (key performance indicators), 903–905, 1060–1063
KRIs (key risk indicators), 903, 905

L

L2TP (Layer 2 Tunneling Protocol), 651–653, 656, 657
LAN technologies, 617, 619
Land attack, 824
landscaping, 950–951
LANs (local area networks), 490, 526, 531, 569
laptop computers
    data at rest, 216–217
    protecting from access/loss, 439–440
    tracking software for, 440
last in, first out (LIFO), 275
law enforcement agencies, 1039
laws. *See also legal entries*
    common law system, 59–60
    computer crime laws, 45–47

copyright law, 64–65
customary law system, 60
vs. ethics, 165–166
Federal Information Security Management Act, 75–76
intellectual property, 62–70
mixed law system, 61–62
overview, 73–75
privacy. *See* privacy laws
religious law system, 60–61
trade secret law, 63–64
trademark law, 65
lawyers, 74
Layer 2 Tunneling Protocol (L2TP), 651–653, 656, 657
layered OS architecture, 292–293, 296
LDAP (Lightweight Directory Access Protocol), 732, 1159
LDAP directory, 735–736
LEAP (Lightweight Extensible Authentication Protocol), 670
leased lines, 620–624
leashes, 566
least privilege, 927, 966
least significant bit (LSB), 349
legacy applications, 299
legal department, 74
legal systems, 58–62. *See also law entries*
civil law system, 58
common law system, 59–60
customary law system, 60
mixed law system, 61–62
physical security and, 420, 427
religious law system, 60–61
liability issues, 62, 1053–1060
liability scenarios, 1056–1058
licensing issues, 938–939, 965
life cycle, data, 229
life safety, 414–415
life-cycle assurance standards, 931
life-cycle models, 190–193
life-cycle security components, 41–42
LIFO (last in, first out), 275
lighting, exterior, 953–955
Lightweight Directory Access Protocol. *See* LDAP
Lightweight Extensible Authentication Protocol (LEAP), 670
limit register, 282
Linder, Doug, 1077
line conditioners, 445
linear cryptanalysis, 412
linear topology, 524
Link Control Protocol (LCP), 633
link encryption, 685–687
linking, 1137–1138
link-state routing protocols, 564, 565
Linux operating systems, 888
LLC (Logical Link Control), 490
load, 429
local access, 940–941
local area networks. *See* LANs
local bridge, 568
Locard's exchange principle, 1042
lock bumping, 949
locking data, 1167
locks, 941–949
administrative responsibilities, 947
automatic, 434
cable locks, 946, 947
cipher, 945–946
circumventing, 947–948
device locks, 946–947
mechanical, 942–946
overview, 941–942
raking, 947–948
strengths, 948–949
log events, 929
log files
access logs, 964
audit logs, 814–818, 878–881, 929
diagnostic, 935
event logs, 878–881, 929
function logs, 929
monitoring, 932
protecting, 818, 880–881
system logs, 878–881, 935
transaction logs, 1173
log reviews, 878–881
log scrubbers, 1183
logic bombs, 1186
logical addresses, 263, 264
logical controls, 8–9
Logical Link Control (LLC), 490
logical partitions, 504
logon screen, fake, 836
"low and slow" attacks, 825
LSB (least significant bit), 349
Lucifer project, 339

M

MAC (mandatory access control), 729, 789–795, 928, 1171
MAC (Media Access Control), 490, 729
MAC (message authentication code), 389–393, 668, 729, 936

MAC addresses, 539
Mac OS X, 888
MAC Security standard (MACSec), 509–510
machine languages, 1116–1117
MACSec (MAC Security standard), 509–510
magnetic fields, 222
MAID (massive array of inactive disks), 977–978
mail server, 556. *See also* e-mail
mailbox data, 890
mainframe computers, 522
maintenance hooks, 333
maintenance/release phase, 1084, 1095–1096, 1097
malformed packets, 696
malicious code, 700, 1001
malicious data, 820
malware, 1178–1194
  adware, 1184
  antimalware software, 1187–1190
  botnets, 1184–1185
  crimeware toolkits, 1186–1187
  in e-mail, 1178
  increase in, 1178, 1179
  logic bombs, 1186
  main elements, 1182
  money-making schemes, 1178–1179
  overview, 1178–1179
  rootkits, 1182–1184
  signatures, 1187
  spyware, 1184
  as threat agent, 106
  trojan horses, 1186
  viruses, 1179–1181
  vulnerabilities, 106
  worms, 1182
MAN wireless standard, 675
management
  BCP support, 154
  executive. *See* executive management
  layers of responsibility, 199–203
  roles, 199–203
  security and, 87
  security-awareness training, 158
  support for BCP, 138–139, 145–146
management actions, 911
Management Information Base (MIB), 545–547
management review, 908–911
mandatory access control (MAC), 729, 789–795, 928, 1171
mandatory vacations, 155, 927
man-in-the-middle (MitM) attacks, 217–218
MANs (metropolitan area networks), 534, 536, 614–617, 660
mantraps, 434
manual testing, 1094–1095
markup languages, 779–784
mashups, 1140
masquerading, 603
massive array of inactive disks (MAID), 977–978
master keys, 947
master security policies, 87–89
matrices, 797
MAU (Multistation Access Unit), 534
maximum period time of disruption (MPTD), 150–151
maximum tolerable downtime (MTD), 150–151, 1002–1005
maximum transmission unit (MTU), 507, 526
MD4 hash function, 394
MD5 hash function, 394–395
mean time between failures (MTBF), 971–972, 973
mean time to repair (MTTR), 972–973
measurements, 903
media
  access controls, 222
  clearing/purging, 220–221
  disposal of, 214, 223
  documenting changes, 222
  environmental conditions, 222
  environmental issues, 219
  erasing, 220–221
  examples of, 219
  integrity, 223
  inventorying, 223
  labeling, 223
  lifespan, 223
  overwriting, 212–214, 219–221
  physical destruction of, 220
  sanitized, 221
  tracking, 221
Media Access Control (MAC), 490, 729
media access technologies, 526–536
media controls, 219–224
media gateway, 636
media libraries, 219–220, 222
media management, 221–224
media sharing, 527
meet-in-the-middle attacks, 414
memory
  BEDO DRAM, 259
  buffer overflows, 265–269, 875, 1092
  cache, 261

DDR SDRAM, 260
DRAM, 258–259
EDO DRAM, 259
EEPROM, 260–261
EPROM, 260
hierarchy, 281
management, 280–285
mapping, 261–265, 280
NVRAM, 408
persistent, 408–409
PROM, 260
RAM, 258–260, 284
ROM, 260–261
SDRAM, 259
SRAM, 259
static, 408–409
types of, 258–270
versatile, 408–409
virtual, 283–285
volatile, 218
memory caches, 218
memory cards, 758
memory leaks, 270
memory management, 280–285
memory manager, 281–282
memory protection, 269–270, 283
memory stacks, 266, 275
Menezes-Qu-Vanstone (MQV), 383
mesh topology, 525
message authentication code (MAC), 389–393, 668, 729, 936
message integrity, 388–399
CBC-MAC function, 391–392, 393
CMAC, 391–392, 393
overview, 388
message-oriented middleware (MOM), 1136
messages, 502, 1124
metadata
business process, 190
classification levels, 193–198
in data dictionary, 1164, 1165
data mining/data warehousing, 1174–1176
system, 190
meta-directories, 734–735, 736
methods, 1124, 1160
metrics, 160–165, 418, 904
Metro Ethernet, 615–617
metropolitan area networks. *See* MANs
MIB (Management Information Base), 545–547
MIC values, 668
microarchitecture, 287
microcomputers, 522
microdot, 350
microkernel OS model, 293–294, 296, 297
microprobing, 761
Microsoft Point-to-Point Encryption (MPPE), 650–651
military data classifications, 194, 195–196
military-oriented frameworks, 25–26
MIME (Multipurpose Internet Mail Extensions), 688–689
MIMO (multiple input, multiple output), 674, 682
Ministry of Defence Architecture Framework (MODAF), 25–26
misuse case testing, 882–883
misuse cases, 230, 231
mitigation strategies, 999–1000
MitM (man-in-the-middle) attacks, 217–218
mixed law system, 61–62
mobile code, 1142–1146
ActiveX controls, 1144–1146
Java applets, 1142–1146
overview, 1142
risks, 1142
mobile devices
loss of, 439–440
protecting, 234–235, 439–440
security issues, 327–328
theft of, 234–235
tracking software for, 440
mobile IP, 805
mobile wireless, 678–685
cellular networks, 679–681
characteristics, 684
frequency range, 680–682
generations, 683–684
hacking mobile phones, 682
overview, 678–680
MODAF framework, 15
mode transitions, 294
modems
cable, 648–649
described, 644
dial-up connections, 644–645
war dialing and, 874
mold/mildew, 437
MOM (message-oriented middleware), 1136
monitoring
access control, 822–834
e-mail, 81–83
employees, 81–83
keystrokes, 818
risk, 97
security controls, 130

monolithic OS architecture, 291–292, 296, 297
motherboards, 261
motion detectors, 962
MPLS (Multiprotocol Label Switching), 511, 573, 574, 615–616
MPPE (Microsoft Point-to-Point Encryption), 650–651
MPTD (maximum period time of disruption), 150–151
MQV (Menezes-Qu-Vanstone), 383
MTBF (mean time between failures), 971–972, 973
MTD (maximum tolerable downtime), 150–151, 1002–1005
MTTR (mean time to repair), 972–973
MTU (maximum transmission unit), 507, 526
multicast routing, 506
multicast transmission, 536, 537–538
multihomed devices, 597
multiple input, multiple output (MIMO), 674, 682
multiplexing, 279–280, 617, 620
multiprocessing, 257–258
multiprogramming, 271
Multiprotocol Label Switching (MPLS), 511, 573, 574, 615–616
Multipurpose Internet Mail Extensions (MIME), 688–689
multiservice access technologies, 635–636
Multistation Access Unit (MAU), 534
multitasking, 271, 279–280
multi-threaded applications, 276

N

namespaces, 732–733
naming distinctions, 280
NAT (network address translation), 506, 560–562
NAT servers, 561
National Institute of Standards and Technology. *See* NIST
National Security Agency (NSA), 370, 411
natural access control, 422–424
natural disasters, 100
natural surveillance, 424–425
natural territorial reinforcement, 425–426
natural threats, 148
NCPs (Network Control Protocols), 633
NDAs (nondisclosure agreements), 63, 155–156, 864
NDLP (network DLP), 231–232
near-line devices, 982
need-to-know principle, 765
negligence, 1056
.NET framework, 1137
network address, 504
network address translation. *See* NAT
network administrator, 14, 803, 926, 928–930
network attacks, 696–700
  DDoS, 603, 649, 697–698
  at different layers, 483
  DNS hijacking, 699–700
  DoS, 566, 588, 603, 696–698
  drive-by downloads, 699, 700
  flooding attacks, 696–697, 698
  malformed packets, 696
  overview, 696
  ransomware, 698
  sniffing attacks, 698–699
network cards, 491
Network Control Protocols (NCPs), 633
network database model, 1159–1160
network DLP (NDLP), 231–232
network eavesdropping. *See* sniffing
network encryption, 685–695
  at different layers, 686
  e-mail, 687–690
  end-to-end encryption, 685–687
  hardware vs. software cryptography, 687
  link encryption, 685–687
  MIME, 688–689
network interface card (NIC), 1183
network layer, 489, 493
network personnel, 928–929
network protocols/services
  ARP, 539–540
  CAN bus, 496–497
  converged, 511–512
  described, 480
  DHCP, 540–543
  DNP3, 496
  DNS. *See* DNS
  ICMP, 543–545
  IP, 497
  multi-layer, 495–497
  OSI. *See OSI entries*
  overview, 480–483, 538
  services, 538
  SNMP, 545–547
  TCP, 498–500
  TCP/IP. *See TCP/IP entries*
network segregation, 810
network sniffers, 834
network stack, 19

network testing, 867
Network Time Protocol (NTP), 878–879
network topologies, 523–525
network-based IDS (NIDS), 822–823, 986
networking, 522–566
  considerations, 523
  emerging technologies, 477–478
  evolution of, 522–523
  extranets, 612–614
  infrastructure, 523
  intranets, 612–614
  media access technologies, 526–536
  overview, 477–478
  protocols. *See* network protocols/services
  remote connectivity, 644–659
networking devices, 567–612
  bridges, 567–569
  comparison of, 577, 578
  gateways, 576–577
  PBXs, 577–581
  repeaters, 567, 571
  routers. *See* routers
  switches. *See* switches
networks
  access to, 813–814
  administration, 610–611, 926
  architecture, 481, 812–813
  attacks on. *See* network attacks
  automation and, 926
  availability, 970–984
  cellular, 679–681
  cloud, 628
  data in motion, 217–218
  diagramming, 579–581
  encryption. *See* network encryption
  Ethernet, 490, 531–534
  extranets, 612–614
  internetworks, 569
  intranets, 612–614
  LANs, 490, 526, 531, 569
  MANs, 534, 536, 614–617, 660
  partitioned, 504
  private, 628
  SANs, 978–979
  satellite, 660, 678, 679
  SDLC, 631–632, 644
  single points of failure, 973–980
  social, 99
  SONET, 614–615, 619
  subnetting, 504–505
  VANs, 613–614
  VLANs, 574–576, 615
  VoIP, 635, 641–643
  VPNs. *See* VPNs
  WANs. *See* WANs
  wired, 660
  wireless. *See* wireless networks
  WLANs. *See* WLANs
  WPANs, 660, 676
next-generation firewall (NGFW), 595–596, 986
NGFW (next-generation firewall), 595–596, 986
NIC (network interface card), 1183
NIDS (network-based IDS), 822–823, 986
NIST (National Institute of Standards and Technology), 20, 21, 34, 370
NIST RMF (SP 800-37rl), 127–128
NIST SP 800-30, 107–108, 112
NIST SP 800-39, 95
NIST SP 800-53, 15, 34–35, 76
NIST SP 800-55 standard, 163, 164
noise and perturbation, 326, 1171
noise, cables, 520–521
nondisasters, 1006
nondisclosure agreements (NDAs), 63, 155–156, 864
noninterference model, 310, 313
nonpracticing entities (NPEs), 66–67
nonrepudiation, 344
nonvolatile RAM (NVRAM), 408
normalization, 208
NPEs (nonpracticing entities), 66–67
NSA (National Security Agency), 370, 411
NTP (Network Time Protocol), 878–879
null ciphers, 348
number generator, 346
NVRAM (nonvolatile RAM), 408

O

OASIS (Organization for the Advancement of Structured Information Standards), 784
OAuth standard, 785
Object Linking and Embedding (OLE), 1137–1138
Object Linking and Embedding Database (OLE DB), 1162, 1163
Object Management Group (OMG), 1134
object request brokers (ORBs), 1134–1136
object reuse issues, 820
object-oriented analysis (OOA), 1128, 1129
object-oriented databases, 1159, 1160
object-oriented design (OOD), 1128
object-oriented programming. *See* OOP
object-relational database (ORD), 1161, 1162

objects
  access control and, 722
  described, 722
  encapsulated, 1124–1127
  instantiated, 1121–1122
  polyinstantiation, 1172–1173
  specifications, 1126
  versions of, 1172–1173
OC (optical carrier), 619, 622
Occupant Emergency Plan (OEP), 1063–1064
Occupational Safety and Health Administration (OSHA), 427
OCSP (Online Certificate Status Protocol), 401–402
OCTAVE (Operationally Critical Threat, Asset, and Vulnerability Evaluation), 108, 112
ODBC (Open Database Connectivity), 1136, 1162
ODBC API, 1162
OECD (Organisation for Economic Co-operation and Development), 55–56
OEP (Occupant Emergency Plan), 1063–1064
OFB (Output Feedback) mode, 375–376
OFDM (orthogonal frequency-division multiplexing), 663, 672–673
Office of Government Commerce (OGC), 37
OGC (Office of Government Commerce), 37
OLE (Object Linking and Embedding), 1137–1138
OLE DB (Object Linking and Embedding Database), 1162, 1163
OLE DB API, 1162, 1163
OLTP (online transaction processing), 1173–1174
OMG (Object Management Group), 1134
one-time pads, 345–347, 362
one-time password (OTP), 754–757
one-way functions, 385–386
one-way hash, 388–389, 395–396
Online Certificate Status Protocol (OCSP), 401–402
online encryption, 685–687
online safety, 901–902
online transaction processing (OLTP), 1173–1174
OOA (object-oriented analysis), 1128, 1129
OOD (object-oriented design), 1128
OOP (object-oriented programming), 1121–1128
  benefits of, 1122–1123
  cohesion and coupling, 1130–1131
  data modeling, 1129
  data structures, 1129–1130
  encapsulation, 1124–1127
  object specifications, 1126
  overview, 1121–1123
  polymorphism, 1128
Open Database Connectivity (ODBC), 1136, 1162
open message format, 357
open network architecture, 481
open proxies, 604–605
Open Shortest Path First (OSPF), 564
open system authentication (OSA), 665–666
open systems, 320–321, 482–483
Open Systems Interconnection. *See* OSI
Open Web Application Security Project (OWASP), 1097
OpenFlow, 611
OpenID standard, 784–785
open-source code, 13
operating systems, 271–300
  architectures, 291–300
  CPU architecture integration, 287–291
  described, 271
  input/output device management, 285–287
  memory management, 280–285
  process management, 271–280
  protection mechanisms, 288–290
  running multiple, 300
  virtual machines, 298–300
operational assurances, 930–931
operational responsibilities, 931–933
Operationally Critical Threat, Asset, and Vulnerability Evaluation (OCTAVE), 108, 112
operations department role, 924–925
optical carrier (OC), 619, 622
optical fiber, 675
optical wireless, 675–676
ORBs (object request brokers), 1134–1136
ORD (object-relational database), 1161, 1162
ORDBMS, 1161
Organisation for Economic Co-operation and Development (OECD), 55–56
Organization for the Advancement of Structured Information Standards (OASIS), 784
organizational changes, 229
organizational security policy, 87–89
organizations
  changes in, 968–969
  culture, 902–903
  liability issues, 1053–1060
  nonprofit, 138
  priorities, 138

revenues and, 138
types of, 138
understanding, 136
orthogonal frequency-division multiplexing (OFDM), 663, 672–673
OSA (open system authentication), 665–666
OSHA (Occupational Safety and Health Administration), 427
OSI (Open Systems Interconnection) model, 479–497
application layer, 480, 483–484, 492
data link layer, 490–491, 493
device types and, 494–495
network layer, 489, 493
networking languages and, 516–517
overview, 479–480
physical layer, 491, 493–494
presentation layer, 484–485, 492
protocols/functions, 480–483, 492–494
session layer, 485–487, 492
vs. TCP/IP, 480
transport layer, 480, 487–488, 493
OSPF (Open Shortest Path First), 564
OTP (one-time password), 754–757
out-of-band interface, 1147
Output Feedback (OFB) mode, 375–376
outsourcing, 126, 206, 1014
overlapping fragment attacks, 603
overlays, 612
overwriting data, 214
overwriting media, 212–214, 219–221
OWASP (Open Web Application Security Project), 1097

P

PaaS (Platform as a Service), 322, 969–970
packet filtering, 584
packet switching, 625, 626–627
packet-filtering firewalls, 582–585, 596
packets
ACK, 500, 586–587, 697
communication, 499
encapsulation, 482
flooding, 696–697
ICMP, 696
malformed, 696
SYN, 500, 502, 586–587, 697
SYN/ACK, 500, 586–587, 697
transmission of, 536–538
Padding Oracle On Downgraded Legacy Encryption (POODLE) attack, 693
pages, 283–284
pair programming, 1107
palm scans, 749
PAP (Password Authentication Protocol), 657, 658
paper records, 235–236
parallel computing, 323
parallel test, 894
parallelism, 323
parameter validation, 1152–1153
partitioning, 326, 1171
partitions, 504
passive attacks, 408
passive infrared (PIR) system, 961
passphrase, 757
password aging, 753
Password Authentication Protocol (PAP), 657, 658
password checkers, 753
password cracking, 753, 835
password file, 751, 835
password generators, 751, 754–757
password hashing, 752, 753
password management, 739–745
password-guessing attacks, 772
passwords, 751–761
attacks on, 751–752
changes to, 739, 740–741
cleartext, 835
cognitive, 754
community strings, 546–547
cracking, 753
dynamic, 754
encrypted, 753
expired, 753
forgotten, 739, 740–741
guessing, 772
lifetime of, 752
limiting logon attempts, 753
one-time, 754–757
plaintext, 752
policies, 751–752, 928–929
resetting, 739, 740–741
SSO, 741–742
synchronization, 739, 740, 741
vulnerabilities, 99
weak, 753
web applications, 1148
PAT (port address translation), 561
patch management, 988–991
patches
described, 988
managing, 988, 989–990
reverse engineering, 990
security issues, 1083

patches (*Cont.*)
subnets, 990
unmanaged, 988–989
patent law, 65–67
patent trolls, 66–67
patents, 65–67
path traversal, 1149
Patriot Act, 78
pattern matching, 823
Payment Card Industry Data Security Standard. *See* PCI DSS
PBXs (private branch exchanges), 577–581, 874
PCI DSS (Payment Card Industry Data Security Standard), 80–81
PCI-DSS regulation, 1060
PCR (Platform Configuration Registers), 408
PEAP (Protective EAP), 670
penetration testing, 860, 869–873, 877
penetration tests, 873, 1193–1194
perimeter, defined, 987
Perimeter Intrusion Detection and Assessment System (PIDAS), 952
perimeter protection, 304, 810, 941, 950–960
permanent virtual circuits (PVCs), 629
permissions. *See also* privileges
authorization creep and, 765
directories, 876
files, 876
groups, 763
MAC and, 789
managing, 742
modifying, 888
need-to-know principle, 765
RBAC and, 792–793
persistent cookie, 1152
persistent memory, 408–409
personal information, 1056–1057
Personal Information Protection and Electronic Documents Act (PIPEDA), 72, 79
personal privacy protection, 83
personally identifiable information (PII), 70, 71, 84, 85, 191, 202
personnel. *See also* users
accountability, 814–818, 929–930
background checks, 156–157
business continuity plans and, 153
clearance level, 196
collusion, 155
data leakage and, 225–226
degrees vs. certification, 159
disgruntled, 54, 100–101, 149, 157
education, 159
employee data, 215
executives. *See* executive management
hiring practices, 155–157
improper termination, 83
job rotation, 926–927
layers of responsibility, 199–206
least privilege and, 927, 966
mandatory vacations, 155, 927
monitoring, 81–83
need to know and, 927
network, 928–929
nondisclosure agreements, 155–156
outsourcing, 1014
prescreening, 82
privacy issues, 81–83
reference checking, 156
risks, 154
roles. *See* roles
rotation of duties, 155
security precautions, 154–159, 928–929
security training, 157–159, 809, 899
separation of duties, 154–155, 925–926, 1094
supervisory structure, 809
tasks, 925–926
terminations, 157
testing/evaluating skills, 155
threats, 106
personnel access controls, 949–950
personnel controls, 809
personnel security, 154–159, 928–929
personnel testing, 867
PGP (Pretty Good Privacy), 689–690
pharming, 838
PHI (protected health information), 84
phishing, 559–560, 899–900
phishing attacks, 836–840, 1178
phone hackers (phreakers), 579
photoelectric device, 450, 451
phreakers (phone hackers), 579
physical access controls, 222, 1063
physical controls, 9, 808, 810–811
physical damage, 94
physical layer, 491, 493–494
physical media, 214
physical security, 940–964
auditing physical access, 963–964
bollards, 953
CCTV systems, 955–960
considerations, 11–13, 229
CPTED approach, 419–426
described, 414, 416
external boundary protections, 950–960
facility. *See* facility security

fencing, 951–953
fire suppression, 448–449, 452–453
guard dogs, 963
importance of, 937
intrusion detection systems, 960–962
landscaping and, 950–951
lighting options, 953–955
locks, 941–949
modes, 941
natural access control, 422–424
natural surveillance, 424–425
natural territorial reinforcement, 425–426
perimeter protection, 304, 810, 941, 950–960
personnel access controls, 949–950
risk analysis, 418–419, 432
safes, 440
security guards, 962–963
security zones, 423
target hardening, 421
threats, 414
physical security program
CPTED and, 420–426
designing, 426–439
facility/site. *See* facility security
goals, 416–417
legal issues, 420, 427
performance metrics, 417–418
planning for, 419–420
physical testing, 867
PID (process identification), 280
PIDAS (Perimeter Intrusion Detection and Assessment System), 952
piggybacking, 434, 949
PII (personally identifiable information), 70, 71, 84, 85, 191, 202
Ping of Death, 696
PIPEDA (Personal Information Protection and Electronic Documents Act), 72, 79
PIR (passive infrared) system, 961
pirated software, 68–70, 939, 965
PKCS (Public Key Cryptography Standards), 689
PKI (public key infrastructure), 383, 399–404, 670, 1116
plaintext, 337, 340
plaintext attacks, 410
Platform as a Service (PaaS), 322, 969–970
Platform Configuration Registers (PCR), 408
PLCs (programmable logic controllers), 330–331
plenum areas, 453
plenum space, 522
point-to-point links, 620–624
Point-to-Point Protocol (PPP), 633–634, 644
Point-To-Point Tunneling Protocol (PPTP), 649–651, 652, 656, 657
policies
advisory, 90
antimalware, 1192
backups, 981
BCP, 142
data retention, 206–210
e-mail usage, 89
guidelines, 92
incident response, 996
informative, 90
passwords, 751–752, 928–929
regulatory, 90
routing, 566
security. *See* security policies
types of, 90
policy engines, 230
polling, 530
polyalphabetic algorithms, 337, 338
polyinstantiation, 1172–1173
polymorphism, 1128
polyvinyl chloride (PVC), 522
POODLE (Padding Oracle On Downgraded Legacy Encryption) attack, 693
POP (Post Office Protocol), 556
pop-ups, 838
port address translation (PAT), 561
port types, 500
portals, 778–779
portlets, 778–779
ports
dynamic, 500
HTTP, 593
mapped to protocols, 500
registered, 500
SNMP, 547
TCP, 498–500
UDP, 498–500
well-known, 500, 593
positive drains, 446
Post Office Protocol (POP), 556
postmortem, 876–877
portable devices, 937–938
power failure, 441, 442–443, 945
power grid, 441–442
power losses, 440–441
power protection, 442–443
PPP (Point-to-Point Protocol), 633–634, 644, 650–653

PPTP (Point-To-Point Tunneling Protocol), 649–651, 652, 656, 657
premapped I/O, 286–287
presentation layer, 484–485, 492
pretexting, 79, 901
Pretty Good Privacy (PGP), 689–690
preventive controls, 10, 11
preventive measures, 984–992
  antimalware, 988
  firewalls. *See* firewalls
  honeypots, 991–992
  intrusion detection. *See IDS entries*
  intrusion prevention. *See IPS entries*
  overview, 984–985
  patch management, 988–991
  preventive vs. recovery strategies, 1005
  vs. recovery strategies, 1005
  sandboxing and, 991
PRI (Primary Rate Interface) ISDN, 646, 647
primary image, media, 1046
primary keys
  described, 1161, 1164
  vs. foreign key, 1164–1166
  relational databases, 1157–1158, 1159
Primary Rate Interface (PRI) ISDN, 646, 647
privacy, 70–83
  considerations, 229
  data owners and, 210–211
  data processors and, 211
  data remanence, 211–214
  described, 72, 202
  limiting collection of, 214–215
  personally identifiable information, 70, 71
  personnel, 81–83
  protecting, 210–215
  vs. security, 72, 202
  users, 83
Privacy Act of 1974, 75
Privacy Impact Ratings, 1086
privacy laws
  considerations, 81
  need for, 72–73
  Privacy Act of 1974, 75
  types of, 83
privacy risk assessment, 1086
private algorithms, 411
private branch exchanges (PBXs), 577–581, 874
Private data classification, 195
private keys, 353, 356, 757
privilege accumulation, 887
privilege escalation, 1092
privileged mode, 255
privileges. *See also* permissions
  accountability and, 929
  buffer overflows and, 1092
  considerations, 887–888
  excessive, 929, 930
  least, 927, 966
  least privilege, 927, 966
  modifying, 888
  running as root, 888
procedures, 93–94
process activity, 278–280
process domains, 291
process enhancement, 31
process identification (PID), 280
process isolation, 278–279
process management, 271–280
process management development, 37–45
  CMMI, 16, 39–40
  ITIL, 16, 37–38
  Six Sigma, 16, 38–39
process reengineering, 31
process table, 273, 274
processes
  described, 271
  encapsulated, 279
  scheduling, 277–278
  states, 272–273
  trusted, 255, 277, 288–290
  vulnerabilities, 99
procurement processes, 1059
profile updates, 744–745
profiling, 1042
program status word (PSW), 255
programmable I/O, 286
programmable logic controllers (PLCs), 330–331
programmable read-only memory (PROM), 260
programmers, 926
programming. *See also* code
  bugs, 219, 300, 332, 875, 885
  code reviews, 884–885
  defensive, 884–885
  development phase, 1084, 1089–1093, 1097
  improper/faulty practices, 1092
  maintenance hooks, 333
  object-oriented. *See* OOP
  procedural vs. object-oriented, 1122–1123
  "secure coding," 1091
  testing/validating, 1084, 1093–1095, 1097
programming languages, 1116–1132
  assemblers, 1117, 1119
  assembly languages, 1117

compilers, 1119
high-level languages, 1117–1118
interpreters, 1120
Java, 1138, 1142–1144
language levels, 1118, 1119
machine languages, 1116–1117
natural languages, 1118
OOP. *See* OOP
overview, 1116–1118
very high-level languages, 1118
vulnerabilities in, 1120–1121
programs. *See* applications; software
project management
BCP, 143–144
in SDLC, 1084–1085
project sizing, 103
PROM (programmable read-only memory), 260
promiscuous mode, 699, 1183
protected health information (PHI), 84
protection mechanisms, 119–122, 343–344
protection profiles, 314–315, 316
Protective EAP (PEAP), 670
protocol anomaly–based IDS, 826–827
protocols
considerations, 814
converged, 511–512
described, 21
ports mapped to, 500
routing protocols, 562–566
stateless, 691, 693
streaming, 641
prototype model, 1101
prototypes, 1101
provisioning
cloud assets, 969–970
considerations, 744
overview, 743
resources, 964–970
user, 744
proximate cause, 1056
proxy firewalls, 589–593
proxy servers, 605–606, 640
PSTN (public-switched telephone network), 479, 635
PSW (program status word), 255
public algorithms, 411
Public data classification, 195
public key cryptography, 364, 383
Public Key Cryptography Standards (PKCS), 689
public key infrastructure (PKI), 383, 399–404, 670, 1116
public keys, 353, 356, 689–690, 757
public-switched telephone network (PSTN), 479, 635
PVC (polyvinyl chloride), 522
PVCs (permanent virtual circuits), 629

Q

QA (quality assurance), 926
QA teams, 228
QC (quality control), 926
QL (query language), 1164
QoS (Quality of Service), 506, 630–631, 673
qualitative risk analysis, 112, 113, 116–119, 149
quality assurance. *See* QA
quality control (QC), 926
quality, of code, 1077–1078
Quality of Service (QoS), 506, 630–631, 673
quantitative risk analysis, 112–119
queries, DNS servers, 551–552
query language (QL), 1164
questions, comprehensive, 1213–1249

R

race conditions, 334, 726, 876
RAD (Rapid Application Development) model, 1104–1105
radio frequency interference (RFI), 443–444
radio-frequency identification (RFID), 761
radio-frequency (RF) wireless, 675
RADIUS (Remote Authentication Dial-in User Service), 801–807
RADSL (Rate-Adaptive Digital Subscriber Line), 648
RAID (redundant array of independent disks), 974–976
RAID levels, 975–976, 977
rainbow tables, 752, 980
RAIT (redundant array of independent tapes), 978
raking, 947–948
RAM (random access memory), 258–260, 284
random access memory (RAM), 258–260, 284
ransomware, 698, 1178
Rapid Application Development (RAD) model, 1104–1105
RARP (Reverse Address Resolution Protocol) frames, 542–543
RARP servers, 543
RAs (registration authorities), 400, 402
Rate-Adaptive Digital Subscriber Line (RADSL), 648
RATs (remote access Trojans), 1186

RBAC (role-based access control), 791–794, 795
RB-RBAC (rule-based access control), 794–795
RC4 algorithm, 379, 666
RC5 cipher, 379
RC6 cipher, 379
R&D (research and development), 207
read-only memory (ROM), 260–261
ready state, 272, 273
real loss, 439
real user monitoring (RUM), 881–882, 910
realms, 768–769
Real-time Transport Protocol (RTP), 639
reasonable expectation of privacy (REP), 82
reboots, system, 932–933, 934
reciprocal agreements, 1011
reconstitution phase, 1033–1034
records
  defined, 75
  described, 1160
  paper, 235–236
recovery activation criteria, 1032–1033
recovery controls, 10
recovery plans, 1038
recovery point objective (RPO), 1003–1005, 1029
recovery process. *See also* disaster recovery; DRP
  activation of, 1032–1033
  after system crashes, 934–935
  business process recovery, 1006
  considerations, 1033
  data leakage and, 228
  facility recovery, 1006
  files, 934
  goal setting, 1034–1036
  incidents, 1001
  vs. preventive measures, 1005
  security concerns, 935
  supply/technology recovery, 1013–1015
  trusted, 933–935
recovery teams, 1031–1038
recovery time objective (RTO), 1002–1005, 1029
redirect servers, 640
reduction analysis, 101–102
redundancy, 1029
redundant array of independent disks. *See* RAID
redundant array of independent tapes (RAIT), 978
reference monitor, 304–305, 306
referential integrity, 1167
registers, 253, 255, 282
registrar server, 640
registration authorities (RAs), 400, 402
regulations, 73–76, 81, 86, 87
regulatory law, 60, 62
regulatory policies, 90
relational database components, 1164–1166
relational databases, 1157–1158, 1159
relative addresses, 263
relay agent, 557–559
release/maintenance phase, 1084, 1095–1096, 1097
reliability, 1029
religious law system, 60–61
remediation, 1001–1002
remote access, 644–645, 803, 939–940
remote access Trojans (RATs), 1186
Remote Authentication Dial-in User Service (RADIUS), 801–807
remote bridge, 568
remote connectivity, 644–659
  authentication, 657–659
  cable modems, 648–649
  dial-up connections, 644–645
  DSL, 647–648, 649
  ISDN, 645–647
  overview, 644
  tunneling protocols, 649–657
  VPNs. *See* VPNs
remote journaling, 1026
remote logging, 880
Remote Procedure Call (RPC), 487, 1132, 1133
remote systems, 657, 939–940, 1186
remote systems administration, 939–940
remote terminal units (RTUs), 331, 496
REP (reasonable expectation of privacy), 82
repeaters, 567, 571, 578
replay attacks, 413, 751, 771, 1154
replication, 880, 1027
report generator, 1164
reports/reporting, 905–908
  executive summaries, 907–908
  incidents, 996, 1000
  "no input," 936
  overview, 905–906
  technical report, 906–907
Request for Proposals (RFP), 1059
requirements gathering phase, 1084, 1085–1086, 1096
research and development (R&D), 207
residual risk, 123–124
resiliency, 231

resource provisioning, 964–970
resource records, 548
resources
  access to, 929–930
  availability, 3–4, 723, 970–984
  integrity, 4, 723–724
  releasing, 278
  requests for, 277–278
responsibility, 1056
restarting system, 934
restoration teams, 1031–1038
restoring data, 1024–1025
restricted areas, 436
retina scans, 749
return pointer (RP), 266, 268, 275
reuse model, 1109
Reverse Address Resolution Protocol (RARP) frames, 542–543
reverse proxy, 606
RF (radio-frequency) wireless, 675
RFC 1087, 168
RFC 2460, 506–507
RFC 4987, 502
RFI (radio frequency interference), 443–444
RFID (radio-frequency identification), 761
RFP (Request for Proposals), 1059
Rijndael algorithm, 371, 378
ring topology, 523–524, 525, 536
ring wrap, 534
RIP (Routing Information Protocol), 564
risk
  acceptance of, 124–125
  acquired software, 1193–1194
  backups, 228
  categories, 94–95
  considerations, 21, 984
  controls and, 865, 985
  data in motion, 217–218
  data in use, 218–219
  defined, 106
  described, 7, 94
  framing, 97
  hackers, 106, 116–117, 132
  handling, 124–125
  laptops, 216–217
  loss potential, 106
  mitigating, 124, 125
  monitoring, 97
  preventive measures, 984–992
  privacy, 1086
  questions to ask, 104
  recovery, 228
  remote access, 940
  response to, 97
  storage devices, 216–217
  third-party, 1058
  total vs. residual, 123–124
  transferring, 124, 125
risk analysis, 102–103
  approaches to, 112–113
  automated methods, 113
  considerations, 146
  performing, 123
  physical security, 418–419, 432
  process, 147
  qualitative, 112, 113, 116–119, 149
  quantitative, 112–119
  risk/effectiveness of countermeasures, 121–122
  uncertainty, 115
risk analysis team, 103–104
risk assessment, 102–126
  BCP, 143, 147–149
  considerations, 103, 985
  described, 112
  evaluation/process, 148–149
  goals of, 148
  main components, 148
  methodologies for, 107–112
  overview, 102–103
  scenarios, 149
  threats, 148–149
  vs. vulnerability assessments, 113
risk avoidance, 124, 125
risk framing, 97
risk management, 94–98
  holistic, 95
  ISRM policy, 95–96
  process for, 97–98
  tiers, 95
risk management frameworks (RMFs), 126–130
risk management process (RMP), 906
risk management program, 125
risk management team, 96–97
Rivest-Shamir-Adleman. *See* RSA
RMFs (risk management frameworks), 126–130
RMP (risk management process), 906
Robust Security Network. *See* WPA2
role-based access control (RBAC), 791–794, 795
roles, 199–206
  associated tasks, 926
  auditor, 206
  CEO, 199–200
  CFO, 200–201

roles (*Cont.*)
  change control analyst, 205
  CIO, 201–202
  considerations, 206, 762
  CPO, 202
  CSO, 202–203
  data analyst, 205
  data custodian, 204
  data owner, 203–204
  database security and, 1155, 1156
  hierarchies, 793–794
  listed, 925, 926
  overview, 925
  security administrator, 205
  supervisor, 205
  system owner, 204
  user, 206
  user manager, 205
rollback operations, 1168
rollback plans, 990
rolling hot sites, 1013
ROM (read-only memory), 260–261
root user, 888
rootkits, 1182–1184
ROT13 cipher, 337
rotor cipher machine, 337–338
route flapping, 563
routers
  attacks on, 566
  border, 569
  vs. bridges, 568, 569, 571
  functionality, 578
  multiple paths between, 973
  overview, 569–571
  protocols, 562–566
Routing Information Protocol (RIP), 564
routing policy, 566
routing protocol attacks, 566
routing protocols, 489, 562–566
routing tables, 489
RP (return pointer), 266, 268, 275
RPC (Remote Procedure Call), 487, 1132, 1133
RPO (recovery point objective), 1003–1005, 1029
RSA (Rivest-Shamir-Adleman) algorithm, 383–386, 399
RSA public key encryption, 689
RTCP (RTP Control Protocol), 641
RTO (recovery time objective), 1002–1005, 1029
RTP (Real-time Transport Protocol), 639
RTP Control Protocol (RTCP), 641
RTUs (remote terminal units), 331, 496
rule-based access control (RB-RBAC), 794–795
rule-based IDS, 827–829
rules, 90
RUM (real user monitoring), 881–882, 910
running key ciphers, 347–348
running state, 272, 273

S

SaaS (Software as a Service), 322, 969–970, 1141
SABSA (Sherwood Applied Business Security Architecture), 15, 27–29
SAC (single-attached concentrator), 536
Safe Harbor Privacy Principles, 56–57
safe mode, 934
safeguards
  control selection and, 120–123
  described, 7
  features, 121–122
  guidelines, 55
  risk analysis, 116, 117
safeguards rule, 79
safes, 236, 440
salts, 753
salvage team, 1032
SAML (Security Assertion Markup Language), 781–784
sandboxes, 300, 1143, 1188
SANs (storage area networks), 978–979
Sarbanes–Oxley Act (SOX), 37, 201–202
SAs (security associations), 653–654
SAS (single-attachment station), 536
SAS (Statement on Auditing Standards), 865
SAS 70, 126
SASDs (sequential access storage devices), 976–977
SASL (Simple Authentication and Security Layer), 557
satellite networks, 660, 678, 679
savepoints, 1168
S-boxes, 360
SBU (sensitive but unclassified), 195, 196
SCADA (supervisory control and data acquisition) systems, 331–332, 496
schemas, 1161
Scientific Working Group on Digital Evidence (SWGDE), 1040–1041
SCM (software configuration management), 1114–1115
scope
  audits, 860–861
  BCP, 141–144
  project, 102–103

scope creep, 1085
screened host firewalls, 598, 601
screened-subnet architecture, 598–599, 601
script kiddies, 50
scripts, 1181
Scrum methodology, 1106–1107
SCSI technology, 512
scytale cipher, 336
SDLC (Synchronous Data Link Control), 631–632, 644, 1084–1097
SDN (software-defined networking), 609–612
SDRAM (synchronous DRAM), 259
SDSL (Symmetric DSL), 648
Search for Extraterrestrial Intelligence (SETI), 980
SEC (Securities and Exchange Commission), 37, 201–202
secondary storage, 283–284
Secret data classification, 195, 196
secret keys, 353, 354, 369
Secure Hash Algorithm (SHA), 395
secure message format, 357
Secure MIME (S/MIME), 689
Secure RCP (SRPC), 487
Secure RP (SRPC), 487
Secure Shell (SSH), 694–695, 1116
Secure Sockets Layer (SSL), 691, 692–693
Securities and Exchange Commission (SEC), 37, 201–202
security
- assets. *See* asset protection
- balanced, 5–6
- clipping levels, 930
- databases. *See* database security
- defined, 202
- deviations from standards, 932
- distributed system. *See* distributed system security
- facility. *See* facility security
- firewalls. *See* firewalls
- vs. functionality, 45
- fundamental principles of, 3–6, 723–724
- goals of, 3–6
- industrial control systems, 330–332
- Internet. *See* Internet security
- investigations. *See* investigations
- layer 2 protection, 509–511
- layered approach, 9–10
- mobile devices, 327–328
- overview, 1–3
- perimeter, 304, 810, 941, 950–960
- personnel, 154–159, 928–929
- physical. *See* physical security
- preventative. *See* preventive measures
- vs. privacy, 72, 202
- relationships, 7–8
- remote access, 939–940
- software. *see* software development security
- terminology, 6–8
- testing, 810
- traffic-flow, 686
- trusted computing base, 302–304
- unusual/unexplained occurrences, 931–932
- VoIP, 642–643
- vulnerabilities, 98
- web. *See* web security
- web applications, 326–327
- websites and, 326, 690
- WLANs, 665–672, 677

security administrator, 205, 789, 926–930, 1080, 1081
Security Assertion Markup Language (SAML), 781–784
security assessments, 860–863, 928
security associations (SAs), 653–654
security audits. *See* auditing; audits
security breaches, 48–49
security controls
- administrative controls, 8, 11, 12
- assessing, 129
- availability controls, 5–6
- classification controls, 197–198
- compensating controls, 10, 11–13
- confidentiality controls, 6
- considerations, 1078
- control definition, 7
- corrective controls, 10, 11
- cost/benefit analysis, 120
- countermeasure definition, 7
- data states and, 216–219
- detective controls, 10, 11
- deterrent controls, 10
- development, 33–37
- functionalities, 10, 11–12
- implementing, 129
- integrity controls, 6
- logical controls, 8–9
- media controls, 219–224
- monitoring, 130
- physical controls, 9, 11, 12
- preventive controls, 10, 11
- principles of, 3–6, 723–724
- for protecting assets, 215–224
- recovery controls, 10
- selection of, 120–122, 128–129
- soft controls, 8

security controls (*Cont.*)
vs. software controls, 1078
types of, 5–6, 8–13
security controls development, 33–37
COBIT, 33–34
components, 15
COSO, 36–37
NIST SP 800-53, 34–35
security culture, 229, 902–903
security definitions, 6–8
security domains, xxxi–xxxii, 772–775, 776
security effectiveness, 31
security enterprise architecture, 30
security event management (SEM), 817
security frameworks, 13–45
security governance, 159–165
metrics, 160–165
overview, 159–160
security guards, 962–963
security information and event managers (SIEMs), 817, 880–881
security kernel, 305–307
security mechanisms, 119
security models, 307–313
security operations, 923–1075
administrative management, 925–930
assurance levels, 930–931
compliance programs, 1060–1063
configuration management, 933–940
considerations, 924
disaster recovery. *See* DRP
incident management, 993–1002
insurance, 1030–1031
investigations. *See* investigations
liability issues, 1053–1060
operational responsibilities, 931–933
overview, 923–924
physical security. *See* physical security
preventive measures, 984–992
recovery/restoration, 1031–1038
resource provisioning, 964–970
role of, 924–925
system hardening, 937–939
security plan, 1084–1085
security policies. *See also* policies
common hierarchy of, 89
defined, 87
implementation, 93–94
issue-specific, 88–89
locks/keys, 947
master, 87–89
multilevel, 306
organizational, 87–89
overview, 87–90, 301–302
system-specific, 89–90
security principles, 723–724
security program development, 15
security programs
considerations, 2
control mechanisms, 11–12
documentation, 87
enforcing. *See* security governance
metrics, 160–165
policies for. *See* security policies
security risk assessment, 1086
security through obscurity, 13–14, 327, 1154
security training, 157–159, 809, 899
security zones, 423
security/sensitivity labels, 789, 790–791
segments, 502–503
SEM (security event management), 817
semantic integrity, 1167
Sender Policy Framework (SPF), 559
sensitive but unclassified (SBU), 195, 196
sensitive data, 820
sensitive data awareness, 229
Sensitive data classification, 195
separation of duties, 154–155, 925–926, 1094
September 11 attacks, 210
sequential access storage devices (SASDs), 976–977
server clusters, 979–980
servers
BOOTP, 543
C&C, 1185
clustered, 1029
DHCP, 541–542, 549
DNS, 548–555, 699, 838–839
NAT, 561
POP, 556
proxy, 605–606, 640
RARP, 543
redirect, 640
registrar, 640
SMTP, 556
TFTP, 983
voicemail, 642
web, 691, 1148–1152
service broker, 1139, 1140
service bureaus, 1009
service level agreements (SLAs), 151, 971
Service Organization Controls (SOC), 864–865
service organizations, 864
Service Provisioning Markup Language (SPML), 780–781
Service Set IDs (SSIDs), 665

service-oriented architecture (SOA), 783, 1138–1142
services, unnecessary, 938, 939
session cookie, 1152
session IDs, 1153–1154
Session Initiation Protocol (SIP), 635
session keys, 367–369, 770
session layer, 485–487, 492
session management, 1153–1154
SETI (Search for Extraterrestrial Intelligence), 980
SGML (Standard Generalized Markup Language), 779
SHA (Secure Hash Algorithm), 395
SHA-1 algorithm, 395
shadow files, 753
shared key authentication (SKA), 665–666
shareware, 68
shell, 272, 796
Sherwood Applied Business Security Architecture (SABSA), 15, 27–29
shielded twisted pair (STP) cables, 518, 522
shoulder surfing, 5
shutdown, forced, 935
side channels, 218, 412
side-channel attacks, 412, 760
SIEMs (security information and event managers), 817, 880–881
Signaling System 7 (SS7) protocol, 635
signals, 512–514
signature dynamics, 749–750
signature-based detection, 1187
signature-based IDS, 823–824, 829
signatures, 823–824, 1187
Simple Authentication and Security Layer (SASL), 557
Simple Mail Transfer Protocol. *See* SMTP
Simple Network Management Protocol (SNMP), 545–547
Simple Object Access Protocol (SOAP), 782–783, 1139–1140, 1141
simplex communication, 486, 880
simulation test, 894
single keys, 369
single loss expectancy (SLE), 114, 115, 905
single points of failure, 973–980
single sign-on (SSO), 741–742, 766–776
single-attached concentrator (SAC), 536
single-attachment station (SAS), 536
SIP (Session Initiation Protocol), 635, 638–641
site planning process, 415–439
SITT (Spectrum, Information Technologies and Telecommunications) standard, 479
situational awareness, 817
Six Sigma, 16, 38–39
SKA (shared key authentication), 665–666
Skype, 641
SLAs (service level agreements), 151, 971
SLE (single loss expectancy), 114, 115, 905
smart cards, 758–761
smart grid, 441–442
smartphones, protecting, 234–235
S/MIME (Secure MIME), 689
smoke detectors, 437, 449, 450, 451
SMTP (Simple Mail Transfer Protocol), 399, 484, 555–556
SMTP authentication (SMTP-AUTH), 559
SMTP servers, 556
SMTP-AUTH (SMTP authentication), 559
sniffers, 530, 698–699, 834
sniffing attacks, 698–699
SNMP (Simple Network Management Protocol), 545–547
SNMP ports, 547
Snowden, Edward, 210
SOA (service-oriented architecture), 783, 1138–1142
SOAP (Simple Object Access Protocol), 782–783, 1139–1140, 1141
SOC (Service Organization Controls), 864–865
social engineering
  described, 5, 99
  obtaining passwords via, 752
  overview, 899–901
  phishing attacks. *See* phishing
  piggybacking, 434, 949
  pretexting, 79, 901
social engineering attacks, 413
social media, 901, 902
social networks, 99
sockets, 499
SOCKS proxy firewalls, 592
soft controls, 8
software. *See also* applications
  academic, 68
  assessing security of, 1193–1194
  backing up, 1016–1018
  bulk licenses, 68
  commercial, 68
  licensing issues, 938–939, 965
  maintenance hooks, 333
  most dangerous errors, 1091–1092
  pirated, 68–69, 939, 965
  ransomware, 698
  threats, 332–335
  tracking, 965–966

Software as a Service (SaaS), 322, 969–970, 1141
Software Assurance Program, 1098
software attacks, 761
software backup facilities, 1018–1021
software configuration management (SCM), 1114–1115
software controls, 1078, 1081
software cryptography methods, 687
software deadlock, 278
software development, 1077, 1111–1116
software development models, 1098–1109
  agile model, 1105–1108
  Build and Fix model, 1099
  cleanroom approach, 1109
  exploratory model, 1108
  incremental model, 1101–1102
  JAD model, 1109
  prototype model, 1101
  RAD model, 1104–1105
  reuse model, 1109
  spiral model, 1102–1104
  V-shaped model, 1100–1101
  Waterfall model, 1099–1100
software development security, 1077–1212
  access issues, 1082–1083
  basics, 1078–1083
  best practices, 1097–1098
  building good code, 1077–1078
  current methodology for, 1080
  default settings and, 1082–1083
  vs. functionality, 1082
  implementation issues, 1082–1083
  for multiple environments, 1080–1081
  overview, 1077–1080
software escrow, 1017, 1115
software libraries, 1131–1132
software piracy, 68–70
software requirements, 1087
software-defined networking (SDN), 609–612
SONET (Synchronous Optical Network), 614–615, 618, 619
SONET rings, 614–616, 618
source routing, 569
SOW (Statement of Work), 1085
SOX (Sarbanes–Oxley Act), 37, 201–202
Spafford, Eugene H., 1
spaghetti code, 1122–1123
spam, 557–559, 642, 1185
spam detection, 1190–1192
Spam over Internet Technology (SPIT), 642
Spanning Tree Algorithm (STA), 569
spawning, 272
spear phishing, 560, 838, 899
Spectrum, Information Technologies and Telecommunications (SITT) standard, 479
SPF (Sender Policy Framework), 559
Spiral model, 1102–1104
SPIT (Spam over Internet Technology), 642
split DNS, 553
split knowledge, 155
SPML (Service Provisioning Markup Language), 780–781
spoofing, at logon, 836
spoofing attacks, 559–560, 575, 603
spread spectrum, 661–663
sprinkler systems, 449, 453–454
sprints, 1107
spyware, 1178, 1184
SQL (Structured Query Language), 1150, 1160
SQL injection, 1150
SRAM (static RAM), 259
SRK (Storage Root Key), 408
SRPC (Secure RCP), 487
SS7 (Signaling System 7) protocol, 635
SSH (Secure Shell), 694–695, 1116
SSIDs (Service Set IDs), 665
SSL (Secure Sockets Layer), 80, 691, 692–693
SSO (single sign-on), 741–742, 766–776
STA (Spanning Tree Algorithm), 569
stack pointer, 275
stakeholders, 20, 200, 250, 251
Standard Generalized Markup Language (SGML), 779
standards, 90–94
star topology, 524, 525
state table, 585
state-based IDS, 824–825
stateful firewalls, 584, 585–588, 596
stateless firewalls, 584
stateless inspection, 584
stateless protocols, 691, 693
Statement of Work (SOW), 1085
Statement on Auditing Standards (SAS), 865
states, 824–825
static analysis, 1092–1093, 1188
static electricity, 447
static mapping, 561
static RAM (SRAM), 259
static routing protocols, 563
statistical attacks, 413
statistical anomaly–based IDS, 825–826
statistical time-division multiplexing (STDM), 623

STDM (statistical time-division multiplexing), 623
stealth assessment, 873
steam lines, 446, 447
steganography, 228, 348–350
storage area networks (SANs), 978–979
storage devices
  data at rest, 216–217
  data in use, 218–219
  encryption, 216–217
  risks, 216–217
storage keys, 408
Storage Root Key (SRK), 408
STP (shielded twisted pair) cables, 518, 522
strategic alignment, 29
stream ciphers, 359, 360–362, 363
streaming protocols, 641
striping, 975
Structured Query Language. *See* SQL
structured walk-through test, 894
stub, 983
Stuxnet worm, 478–479
subjects, 722
subkeys, 353
subnet mask, 503
subnets, 503–505
subnetting, 504–505
substitution ciphers, 335, 337, 350–353
supervisor role, 205
supervisory control and data acquisition (SCADA) systems, 331–332, 496
supervisory structure, 809
supply/technology recovery, 1013–1015
support role, 926
surveillance
  computer, 1051
  intrusion detection systems, 960–962
  during investigations, 1051
  natural, 424–425
  physical, 1051
surveillance devices, 955–960
SVCs (switched virtual circuits), 629
swap space, 283–285
SWGDE (Scientific Working Group on Digital Evidence), 1040–1041
switch spoofing attacks, 575
switched environments, 831
switched virtual circuits (SVCs), 629
switches, 571–576, 578
switching, 625–627
SWOT (Strengths, Weaknesses, Opportunities, Threats), 143–144
symbolic links, 875
symmetric algorithms, 369–380
  vs. asymmetric algorithms, 353, 357, 358
  Blowfish algorithm, 379
  DES, 370–377
  EAS, 378
  IDEA, 378–379, 689
  overview, 354–355, 369
  pros/cons, 355
  RC4/RC5/RC6, 379–380
  RSA and, 383–384
  Triple-DES, 370, 377–378
  using with asymmetric algorithms, 364–366
Symmetric DSL (SDSL), 648
symmetric keys, 354–355, 364–368, 398, 666
symmetric mode, 257–258
SYN caches, 502
SYN flooding, 502, 696–697, 698
SYN packets, 500, 502, 586–587, 697
SYN/ACK packets, 500, 586–587, 697
synchronization, 514, 1115
Synchronous Data Link Control. *See* SDLC
Synchronous Digital Hierarchy (SDH), 619
synchronous DRAM (SDRAM), 259
Synchronous Optical Network. *See* SONET
synchronous token device, 755–756
synchronous transmission, 514–515
synthetic transactions, 881–882
system access, 812
system administrators, 934–935
system architecture, 32, 248–252
system authentication, 391
system failure, 934–935
system logs, 878–881, 935
system metadata, 190
system owner role, 204
system reboot, 934
system restart, 934
system security architecture, 301–307
system sensing access control readers, 949–950
system services, 933
system-level events, 815–816
systems
  availability of, 3–4, 723
  bastion host, 596–597
  classifications, 197
  cold start, 934
  connections between, 488
  crashes/freezes, 933–935
  cyber-physical, 328–330
  defined, 249
  distributed, 321
  embedded, 329
  forced shutdowns, 935

systems (*Cont.*)
goals, 251
hardening, 937–939
Internet of Things, 329–330
locked-down, 938
open vs. closed, 320–321
sealing, 408
testing, 867
trusted recovery, 933–935
systems analyst, 926
systems evaluation, 313–318

T

tables
capability, 797–798
forwarding, 568–569
rainbow, 752, 980
routing, 489
TACACS (Terminal Access Controller Access Control System), 801–805
TACACS+, 802–805
tactics, techniques, and procedures (TTPs), 100, 130
tape backups, 1016
tape drives, 978
tape librarian, 926
tape vaulting, 1026–1027
target hardening, 421
targeted tests, 873
tarpits, 607
taxonomy, 208
t-carriers, 620–621
TCB (trusted computing base), 302–304
TCG (Trusted Computing Group), 407
TCP (Transmission Control Protocol), 498–500
data structures, 502–503
described, 497
IP addressing, 503–506
overview, 498
stateful firewalls and, 586–587
vs. UDP, 488, 500, 501
TCP handshake, 500–502
TCP ports, 498–500
TCP sequence numbers, 502
TCP session hijacking, 502
TCP/IP (Transmission Control Protocol/Internet Protocol), 497–512
as Internet protocol, 691
IPv6 addressing, 506–509
vs. OSI, 480
overview, 497
VoIP integration with, 641–643
TDM (time-division multiplexing), 620
TDMA (time division multiple access), 681
teardrop attacks, 603
technical access controls, 222
technical controls, 8–12, 811–814, 865–866
technical reporting, 906–907
telecommunications, 479, 617–620
temperature, 222
temperature control, 446, 448
TEMPEST (Transient Electromagnetic Pulse Emanation Standard), 821
templates, 1033
temporal isolation, 763
Temporal Key Integrity Protocol (TKIP), 667, 668
Teredo tunneling, 508
Terminal Access Controller Access Control System. *See* TACACS
termination, employee, 157
territorial reinforcement, 425–426
terrorist attacks, 210
tertiary sites, 1010
test-driven development, 1093
testing schedules, 877
testing/validation phase, 1084, 1093–1095, 1097
tests/testing. *See also* audits
acceptance testing, 1094
black box, 869
blind tests, 873
business continuity plan, 892–895
code reviews, 884–886
data backups, 892
gray box, 869
identity services and, 787
integration testing, 1094
interface testing, 886
misuse case, 882–883
network vulnerabilities, 867
penetration testing, 860, 869–873, 877, 1193
personnel vulnerabilities, 867
physical protection, 867
postmortem, 876–877
regression testing, 1094
security mechanisms, 810
synthetic transactions and, 881–882
system vulnerabilities, 867
targeted tests, 873
types of, 1094–1095
on virtual machines, 300
vulnerability, 860, 866–869
white box, 869

TFTP (Trivial File Transfer Protocol), 983
TGS (ticket granting service), 405, 768–769
The Open Group Architecture Framework. *See* TOGAF
theft, 439
thin clients, 775–776
thread management, 275–277
threat agents, 6–7
threat modeling, 98–102, 1088–1089, 1090
threat trees, 1089, 1090
threats. *See also specific threats*
  to access control, 834–840
  collusion, 375, 416
  defined, 6
  described, 416
  external, 416
  facility/site, 414
  identifying, 106–107
  internal, 416
  maintenance hooks, 333
  manmade, 148–149
  natural, 148
  overview, 100
  physical security, 414
  software, 332–335
  technical, 148–149
  TOC/TOU attacks, 333–335
  types of, 148–149
  vulnerabilities and, 106–107
thunking, 298
ticket granting service (TGS), 405, 768–769
time division multiple access (TDMA), 681
time multiplexing, 279–280
Time to Live (TTL) values, 506
time-division multiplexing (TDM), 620
time-of-check/time-of-use (TOC/TOU) attacks, 333–335
timing attacks, 760
TKIP (Temporal Key Integrity Protocol), 667, 668
TLS (Transport Layer Security), 80, 217, 654–657, 691–693
TOC/TOU (time-of-check/time-of-use) attacks, 333–335
TOGAF (The Open Group Architecture Framework), 24–25
TOGAF model, 15
token devices, 754–757
token passing, 527
Token Ring network, 534, 535
Token Ring technology, 534, 537
token-passing access methods, 528
token-passing technology, 534
tokens, 527, 534
Top Secret data classification, 195, 196
topology, 523
tort law, 62
ToS (Type of Service) capability, 506
total risk, 123–124
TPM (Trusted Platform Module), 407–409
Traceroute tool, 545
tracking, 221, 222
trade secret law, 63–64
trade secrets, 63–64
trademark law, 65
trademarks, 65
traffic anomaly–based IDS, 827
traffic shaping, 631
traffic-flow security, 686
training, security, 157–159, 809, 899
transaction logs, 1173
transaction persistence, 1157
transaction processing, 1173–1174
transactions
  atomic, 936
  synthetic, 881–882
  well-formed, 309
Transient Electromagnetic Pulse Emanation Standard (TEMPEST), 821
translation bridge, 568
Transmission Control Protocol. *See* TCP
Transmission Control Protocol/Internet Protocol. *See* TCP/IP
transparent bridging, 568–569
transponders, 949–950
transport adjacency, 655
transport layer, 480, 487–488, 493, 498
Transport Layer Security (TLS), 80, 217, 654–657, 691–693
transposition ciphers, 350–353
trapdoor function, 385
tree topology, 524, 525
trialware, 68
Triple-DES (3DES), 370, 377–378
Trivial File Transfer Protocol (TFTP), 983
Trojan horse, 530, 1186
Trojaned programs, 1183
trust, identity services and, 786
trusted components, 262, 288, 304
trusted computing base (TCB), 302–304
Trusted Computing Group (TCG), 407
trusted path, 303
Trusted Platform Module (TPM), 407–409
trusted processes, 255, 277, 288–290
trusted recovery, 933–935
trusted shell, 303

TTL (Time to Live) values, 506
TTPs (tactics, techniques, and procedures), 100, 130
tunneling, 507–509, 543–545
tunneling protocols
IPSec, 653–654
L2TP, 651–653, 656, 657
PPTP, 649–651, 652, 656, 657
tuples, 1160
twisted-pair cables, 518–519
two-phase commits, 1169
Type of Service (ToS) capability, 506

U

UAC (User Agent Client), 638
UBR (unspecified bit rate), 631
UDDI (Universal Description, Discovery and Integration), 1139
UDP (User Datagram Protocol)
described, 497
how it works, 498–500
RTP and, 641
stateful firewalls and, 586–587
vs. TCP, 488, 500, 501
UDP port, 498–500
UL (Underwriters Laboratory), 953
UML (Unified Modeling Language), 882–883
uncertainty, in risk analysis, 115
Unclassified data classification, 195, 196
Underwriters Laboratory (UL), 953
unicast transmission, 536, 537
Unicode encoding, 1149
Unified Modeling Language (UML), 882–883
unified threat management (UTM), 607–608
Uniform Resource Locator. *See* URL
uninterruptible power supply (UPS), 438, 442–443
unit testing, 1093, 1094
Universal Description, Discovery and Integration (UDDI), 1139
universal unique identifier (UUID), 1133
unshielded twisted pair (UTP) cables, 518–519, 522
unspecified bit rate (UBR), 631
UPS (uninterruptible power supply), 438, 442–443
URL (Uniform Resource Locator), 548, 837, 1138, 1148
URL encoding, 1149
URL hiding, 554
U.S. Department of Homeland Security (DHS), 1098
USA PATRIOT Act, 78
USB drives, 820
use cases, 230, 882–883
use phase, 190, 191
user accounts
adding, 887
managing, 742–743, 886–889
modifying, 887–888
profile updates, 744–745
provisioning, 743–744
suspending, 888–889
User Agent Client (UAC), 638
User Agent Server (UAS), 638
user data files, 890
User Datagram Protocol. *See* UDP
user manager role, 205
user mode, 255
user profiles, 928
user provisioning, 744
user role, 206
user stories, 1106
user-activated readers, 949–950
user-level events, 816
usernames, 1148
users. *See also* personnel
accountability, 814–818, 929–930
data integrity and, 4
described, 206
disclosing sensitive information, 4
errors, 106
keystroke monitoring, 818
privacy, 83
shoulder surfing, 5
social engineering and. *See* social engineering
as threat agent, 106
UTM (unified threat management), 607–608
UTP (unshielded twisted pair) cables, 518–519, 522
UUID (universal unique identifier), 1133

V

vacations, mandatory, 155, 927
validation
client-side, 1149–1150
described, 1096
input, 1148–1152
parameter, 1152–1153
post-validation, 1153
pre-validation, 1153
vs. verification, 1096

validation/testing phase, 1084, 1093–1095, 1097
value-added networks (VANs), 613–614
VANs (value-added networks), 613–614
variable bit rate (VBR), 631
VBR (variable bit rate), 631
VDSL (Very High-Data-Rate Digital Subscriber Line), 648
vender processes, 1059–1060
vendor management, 1059
verification
  backups, 891–892, 1011
  described, 1096
  of identity, 727, 746, 747
  vs. validation, 1096
Vernam cipher, 345
versatile memory, 408–409
versioning, 1115, 1116
Very High-Data-Rate Digital Subscriber Line (VDSL), 648
very small aperture terminal (VSAT), 678
viewpoint, defined, 250
views, 20, 250, 796, 1161
Vigenère cipher, 337
virtual address memory mapping, 280
virtual circuits, 629
virtual directories, 735
virtual firewalls, 599–603
virtual LANs. *See* VLANs
virtual machine (VM) snapshots, 890–891
virtual machines, 298–300, 1188
virtual memory, 283–285
virtual private LAN service (VPLS), 617
virtual private networks. *See* VPNs
Virtual Router Redundancy Protocol (VRRP), 565
virtual swap space, 284
virtualization, 298, 890–891
virus walls, 1193
viruses, 53, 820, 1178–1181
visual recording devices, 955–960
VLAN hopping attacks, 575
VLANs (virtual LANs), 574–576, 615
VM (virtual machine) snapshots, 890–891
voice gateway, 636
Voice over IP. *See* VoIP
voice print, 750
voicemail servers, 642
voicemail system, 636
VoIP (Voice over IP)
  considerations, 511, 1015
  vs. IP telephony, 637
  multiservice access technologies, 635–636
  security, 642–643
VoIP networks, 635, 641–643
volatile memory, 218
voltage regulators, 445
VPLS (virtual private LAN service), 617
VPNs (virtual private networks), 649–657
  IPSec, 653–654
  overview, 649
  remote administration and, 940
  tunneling protocols, 649–657
  uses for, 218
VRRP (Virtual Router Redundancy Protocol), 565
VSAT (very small aperture terminal), 678
V-shaped model, 1100–1101
vulnerabilities, 98–99
  attacks, 100–101
  common, 875–876
  considerations, 332
  described, 6, 416
  examples of, 52–53
  identifying, 106–107
  information, 99
  overview, 98
  people, 99
  processes, 99
  programming languages, 1120–1121
  reduction analysis, 101–102
  testing, 860, 866–869
  threats, 100
  threats and, 106–107
  web environments, 1146–1154
  websites, 1154
  XSS, 1150
vulnerability assessments, 113
vulnerability scanners, 864, 871, 875, 876
vulnerability tests, 873

W

WAFs (web application firewalls), 327
WAM (web access management) software, 736–739
WAN technologies, 624–644
  ATM, 618–619, 629–631
  CSU/DSU, 624–625
  frame relay, 627–628, 643
  H.323 gateways, 636–638
  HSSI, 634–635, 644
  vs. LAN technologies, 617, 619
  multiservice access technologies, 635–636
  overview, 617–618
  PPP, 633–634, 644

WAN technologies (*Cont.*)
SDLC, 631–632, 644
SIP, 638–641
summary, 643–644
switching, 625–627
virtual circuits, 629
X-25 protocol, 629
WANs (wide area networks), 617–644
considerations, 490, 531
dedicated links, 620–624
vs. LANs, 526
wireless, 614, 660, 663
war dialing, 836, 874
warez sites, 64–65
warm sites, 1008–1011
Wassenaar Arrangement, 57–58
watchdog timer, 275
water damage, 437, 438
water detectors, 438
water lines, 446, 447
water sprinkler systems, 449, 453–454
Waterfall model, 1099–1100
wave-division multiplexing (WDM), 624
WBS (work breakdown structure), 1085
WDM (wave-division multiplexing), 624
Web. *See* Internet; World Wide Web
Web 1.0, 1140
Web 2.0, 1140
web access management (WAM) software, 736–739
web application firewalls (WAFs), 327
web applications. *See also* applications
input validation, 1149–1152
passwords, 1148
security issues, 326–327
security principles, 1154
usernames, 1148
web browsers. *See* browsers
web pages, 691
web portals, 778–779
web proxy, 1152–1153
web proxy servers, 606
web security, 1146–1154
administrative interfaces, 1147
applications, 1154
authentication/access control, 1147–1148
input validation, 1148–1152
overview, 1146
parameter validation, 1152–1153
session management, 1153–1154
threats/vulnerabilities, 1146–1154
web servers, 691, 1148–1152
web services, 1139, 1140
Web Services Description Language (WSDL), 1139
web-based clients, 612
websites. *See also* Internet
drive-by downloads, 900, 901–902
malicious code, 700
phishing scams. *See phishing entries*
script viruses, 1181
security and, 326, 690
vulnerabilities, 1154
well-known ports, 593
WEP (Wired Equivalent Privacy), 665–667
whaling attack, 560, 899
white box testing, 869
white noise, 821
whitelisting, 966, 987
wide area networks. *See* WANs
WIDS (wireless IDS), 677, 986
Wi-Fi Protected Access (WPA), 667
Wi-Fi Protected Access II (WPA2), 667–668
windows, 324, 429, 431, 434
Windows operating systems, 888
WIPO (World Intellectual Property Organization), 65
Wired Equivalent Privacy (WEP), 665–667
wired networks, 660
wireless communications techniques, 660–664
wireless IDS (WIDS), 986
wireless intrusion detection system (WIDS), 677
wireless LANs. *See* WLANs
wireless networks, 659–685
Bluetooth, 676–677
LANS. *See* WLANs
MANs, 660
WPANs, 660, 676
wireless personal area networks (WPANs), 660, 676
wireless technologies, 659–685
Bluetooth, 676–677
DSSS approach, 661, 662–663
FHSS approach, 661–662, 663
mobile wireless. *See* mobile wireless
OFDM, 663
optical wireless, 675–676
overview, 659
satellites, 678, 679
security, 665–672, 677
spread spectrum, 661–663

wireless standards, 672–677
WLANs. *See* WLANs
wireless WANs, 614, 660, 663
WLANs (wireless LANs)
ad hoc, 664
Bluetooth, 676–677
collisions and, 660
components, 664–665
illustrated, 660
infrastructure, 664
security, 665–672, 677
wireless standards, 672–677
work breakdown structure (WBS), 1085
work factor, 343, 385–386
work recovery time (WRT), 1003–1004
working image, media, 1046
World Intellectual Property Organization (WIPO), 65
World Wide Web (WWW), 690, 779, 780, 1140
wormhold attack, 566
worms, 478–479, 1178, 1182
WPA (Wi-Fi Protected Access), 667
WPA2 (Wi-Fi Protected Access II), 667–668
WPANs (wireless personal area networks), 660, 676
write-once media, 880
WRT (work recovery time), 1003–1004
WSDL (Web Services Description Language), 1139
WWW (World Wide Web), 690, 779, 780, 1140

X

X.25 protocol, 629, 643
X.500 standard, 775
X.509 standard, 402
XACML (Extensible Access Control Markup Language), 783–784
xDSL, 648
XML (Extensible Markup Language), 779, 780
XML schemas, 1141
XOR (exclusive-OR), 345
XP (Extreme Programming), 1107
XSS (cross-site scripting), 1150
XSS attacks, 1150–1151
XSS vulnerabilities, 1150
XTACACS (Extended TACACS), 802

Z

Zachman Framework, 15, 22–24, 136
zero knowledge proof, 387–388
zero-day attacks, 825, 990
zero-day vulnerabilities, 1096
Zigbee protocol, 676
zombies, 48, 603, 697
zone transfers, 549
zones
control, 11, 822
demilitarized. *See* DMZ
DNS, 548–549, 551
security, 811
trust, 580

LICENSE AGREEMENT

THIS PRODUCT (THE "PRODUCT") CONTAINS PROPRIETARY SOFTWARE, DATA AND INFORMATION (INCLUDING DOCUMENTATION) OWNED BY McGRAW-HILL EDUCATION AND ITS LICENSORS. YOUR RIGHT TO USE THE PRODUCT IS GOVERNED BY THE TERMS AND CONDITIONS OF THIS AGREEMENT.

LICENSE: Throughout this License Agreement, "you" shall mean either the individual or the entity whose agent opens this package. You are granted a non-exclusive and non-transferable license to use the Product subject to the following terms:
(i) If you have licensed a single user version of the Product, the Product may only be used on a single computer (i.e., a single CPU). If you licensed and paid the fee applicable to a local area network or wide area network version of the Product, you are subject to the terms of the following subparagraph (ii).
(ii) If you have licensed a local area network version, you may use the Product on unlimited workstations located in one single building selected by you that is served by such local area network. If you have licensed a wide area network version, you may use the Product on unlimited workstations located in multiple buildings on the same site selected by you that is served by such wide area network; provided, however, that any building will not be considered located in the same site if it is more than five (5) miles away from any building included in such site. In addition, you may only use a local area or wide area network version of the Product on one single server. If you wish to use the Product on more than one server, you must obtain written authorization from McGraw-Hill Education and pay additional fees.
(iii) You may make one copy of the Product for back-up purposes only and you must maintain an accurate record as to the location of the back-up at all times.

COPYRIGHT; RESTRICTIONS ON USE AND TRANSFER: All rights (including copyright) in and to the Product are owned by McGraw-Hill Education and its licensors. You are the owner of the enclosed disc on which the Product is recorded. You may not use, copy, decompile, disassemble, reverse engineer, modify, reproduce, create derivative works, transmit, distribute, sublicense, store in a database or retrieval system of any kind, rent or transfer the Product, or any portion thereof, in any form or by any means (including electronically or otherwise) except as expressly provided for in this License Agreement. You must reproduce the copyright notices, trademark notices, legends and logos of McGraw-Hill Education and its licensors that appear on the Product on the back-up copy of the Product which you are permitted to make hereunder. All rights in the Product not expressly granted herein are reserved by McGraw-Hill Education and its licensors.

TERM: This License Agreement is effective until terminated. It will terminate if you fail to comply with any term or condition of this License Agreement. Upon termination, you are obligated to return to McGraw-Hill Education the Product together with all copies thereof and to purge all copies of the Product included in any and all servers and computer facilities.

DISCLAIMER OF WARRANTY: THE PRODUCT AND THE BACK-UP COPY ARE LICENSED "AS IS." McGRAW-HILL EDUCATION, ITS LICENSORS AND THE AUTHORS MAKE NO WARRANTIES, EXPRESS OR IMPLIED, AS TO THE RESULTS TO BE OBTAINED BY ANY PERSON OR ENTITY FROM USE OF THE PRODUCT, ANY INFORMATION OR DATA INCLUDED THEREIN AND/OR ANY TECHNICAL SUPPORT SERVICES PROVIDED HEREUNDER, IF ANY ("TECHNICAL SUPPORT SERVICES"). McGRAW-HILL EDUCATION, ITS LICENSORS AND THE AUTHORS MAKE NO EXPRESS OR IMPLIED WARRANTIES OF MERCHANTABILITY OR FITNESS FOR A PARTICULAR PURPOSE OR USE WITH RESPECT TO THE PRODUCT. McGRAW-HILL EDUCATION, ITS LICENSORS, AND THE AUTHORS MAKE NO GUARANTEE THAT YOU WILL PASS ANY CERTIFICATION EXAM WHATSOEVER BY USING THIS PRODUCT. NEITHER McGRAW-HILL EDUCATION, ANY OF ITS LICENSORS NOR THE AUTHORS WARRANT THAT THE FUNCTIONS CONTAINED IN THE PRODUCT WILL MEET YOUR REQUIREMENTS OR THAT THE OPERATION OF THE PRODUCT WILL BE UNINTERRUPTED OR ERROR FREE. YOU ASSUME THE ENTIRE RISK WITH RESPECT TO THE QUALITY AND PERFORMANCE OF THE PRODUCT.

LIMITED WARRANTY FOR DISC: To the original licensee only, McGraw-Hill Education warrants that the enclosed disc on which the Product is recorded is free from defects in materials and workmanship under normal use and service for a period of ninety (90) days from the date of purchase. In the event of a defect in the disc covered by the foregoing warranty, McGraw-Hill Education will replace the disc.

LIMITATION OF LIABILITY: NEITHER McGRAW-HILL EDUCATION, ITS LICENSORS NOR THE AUTHORS SHALL BE LIABLE FOR ANY INDIRECT, SPECIAL OR CONSEQUENTIAL DAMAGES, SUCH AS BUT NOT LIMITED TO, LOSS OF ANTICIPATED PROFITS OR BENEFITS, RESULTING FROM THE USE OR INABILITY TO USE THE PRODUCT EVEN IF ANY OF THEM HAS BEEN ADVISED OF THE POSSIBILITY OF SUCH DAMAGES. THIS LIMITATION OF LIABILITY SHALL APPLY TO ANY CLAIM OR CAUSE WHATSOEVER WHETHER SUCH CLAIM OR CAUSE ARISES IN CONTRACT, TORT, OR OTHERWISE. Some states do not allow the exclusion or limitation of indirect, special or consequential damages, so the above limitation may not apply to you.

U.S. GOVERNMENT RESTRICTED RIGHTS: Any software included in the Product is provided with restricted rights subject to subparagraphs (c), (1) and (2) of the Commercial Computer Software-Restricted Rights clause at 48 C.F.R. 52.227-19. The terms of this Agreement applicable to the use of the data in the Product are those under which the data are generally made available to the general public by McGraw-Hill Education. Except as provided herein, no reproduction, use, or disclosure rights are granted with respect to the data included in the Product and no right to modify or create derivative works from any such data is hereby granted.

GENERAL: This License Agreement constitutes the entire agreement between the parties relating to the Product. The terms of any Purchase Order shall have no effect on the terms of this License Agreement. Failure of McGraw-Hill Education to insist at any time on strict compliance with this License Agreement shall not constitute a waiver of any rights under this License Agreement. This License Agreement shall be construed and governed in accordance with the laws of the State of New York. If any provision of this License Agreement is held to be contrary to law, that provision will be enforced to the maximum extent permissible and the remaining provisions will remain in full force and effect.